ON PIANO PLAYING

On Piano Playing

Motion, Sound and Expression

Gyorgy Sandor

SCHIRMER BOOKS
An Imprint of Simon & Schuster Macmillan
NEW YORK

Prentice Hall International
LONDON · MEXICO CITY · NEW DELHI · SINGAPORE · SYDNEY · TORONTO

Schirmer Books
An Imprint of Simon & Schuster Macmillan
1633 Broadway, New York, NY 10019-6785

Library of Congress Catalog Card Number: 80–5442

Printed in the United States of America

PRINTING: 12 13 14 15 16   YEAR: 7 8 9 00

Library of Congress Cataloging in Publication Data

Sandor, Gyorgy
  On Piano Playing

    1. Piano--Instruction and study. I. Title.
MT220.S19   786.3'041   80-5442
ISBN 0-02-872280-9   AACR2

Contents

Preface

Since the introduction of the modern piano (approx. 1709), innumerable books have been written on piano technique; indeed, there are also quite a few books to be found on the keyboard technique of the piano's predecessors, the clavichord and the harpsichord. The purpose of my book is not to list and describe the content of these works or to give a bibliography on the subject. Rather, its aim is to clarify concepts of piano playing, describe and organize fundamental elements of technique, and indicate how to apply these elements in performance. In a broad sense, technique is the sum total of organized motions executed by the performer. These motions produce sounds that recreate the moods of the composer in the performer's own interpretation.

Many intangibles are obviously involved in this process. Mood, interpretation, improvisation, inspiration, and creativity are terms that are hard to define. They are subject to discussion and to varying opinions and tastes. Technique, however, is a skill—a well-coordinated system of motions conditioned by the anatomy of the human body and the nature of the piano. Even the most complex technical activities can and should be comprehended by anyone who wishes to master them. They can be reduced to their components: motions executed by the fingers, hand, wrist, arm, and body—in fact, by the entire human anatomy. The coordination of this human mechanism is based on simple common-sense principles of physiology and the force of gravity. When you dance or when you play golf, ping-pong, tennis, the violin, or the piano, you are subject to these same conditions whether you know it or not. You might as well be aware of them!

It is not that awareness of these factors is essential to an artistic and inspired performance; in fact, quite the opposite is the case—creative processes are hardly conscious. But the preparation—the innumerable hours spent practicing—must be purposeful, not automatic and mechanical, and it must be consciously controlled by the mind.

While we are practicing we must know what we are doing; otherwise we will waste most of our time. Some of us enjoy practicing for its own sake and are hardly aware of the enormous amounts of time consumed in the process. For the majority of us, it is reassuring to realize that our practice time can be drastically reduced by the conscious application of correct principles and that this kind of practicing produces the best results.

Sustained muscular tension: the cause of fatigue, ailments, and poor tone production

The spectacularly high incidence of ailments among pianists (fatigue, muscle pain, tendonitis, bursitis, and other temporary and chronic afflictions) is primarily the result of faulty practice habits, of excessive tensions, and of muscle-building exercises. These undesirable and troublesome symptoms result from the continuous abuse of our muscular system; they can and must be avoided. I must disagree with the many pianists who believe that muscular fatigue is inevitable when playing the Chopin *Etude*, opus 10 no. 1 or 2, the extended and rapid octave passages of such pieces as Chopin's *Polonaise in A Flat*, opus 53, or Liszt's "Les Funérailles." They attribute their fatigue to the weakness of their muscles, which, they contend, must be built up. Nothing can be further from the truth! The finer, smaller muscles of our forearms move our fingers and are responsible for precision work. When the stronger upper-arm, shoulder, and body muscles are properly activated, they assist the weaker muscles and prevent all causes of fatigue. Our task is to know how to coordinate and activate the stronger muscles within the entire apparatus and to acquire the habit of doing so whenever we play the piano. The purpose of practice is to establish the right habits, not to spend unnecessary hours with mechanical warming-up exercises. Technique must be based not on the strength and endurance of our muscles but rather on their optimal coordination.

All pianistic problems solved by a limited number of motion patterns and their combinations.

Most books on piano playing have certain merits. Some of them, such as Rudolf Breithaupt's book *Die Grundlage der natürliche Klaviertechnik* (1925), were quite a revelation in their day. Others present valid observations on technique, interpretation, and performance practice. Still others are filled with impressive biological, chemical, and anatomical statistics and resemble nothing so much as scientific textbooks. Obviously all of these aspects must be considered in examining piano technique. But I believe that it is the totality of piano playing that must be understood and described and not just some of its components. In fact, a strict correlation exists between the visual patterns of the score and the technical formulas that we use to interpret them. We may go a step further and state that motion patterns produce and correspond to sonorities that reflect the varying moods of the music. It is these moods that we aim to evoke in the listener through our own interpretation. Therefore interpretation and technique are indivisible.

Fundamentals explained in their respective chapters.

This categorical statement and many other principles set down in this book run the risk of seeming either simplistic and arbitrary or not quite clear. I hope you will have the patience to read the respective chapters in which they are explored and save your evaluation until you have read these descriptions. I assure you that I not only formulate principles and rules, but I also describe, explain, and justify them. When the technique of piano playing is reduced to its fundamentals, it turns out to be a skill that is rather uncomplicated and unproblematical, but it is nonetheless a composite one; that is, the individual motions of the fingers, hand, arm, and shoulder are very simple in scope and in function, but they all must be coordinated and synchronized. If any element fails to function, or if it does too much or too little, the entire apparatus is affected. If the playing mechanism malfunctions, tone, touch, phrasing, breathing, the shaping of the music, and the interpretation as a whole are adversely affected. Thus musicianship and technique are inseparable!

Technique: the mastery of motions. Motion and emotion to correspond.

This book deals with the technique and art of piano playing. Technique precedes art, and therefore it must be discussed first. In our examination of technique we will be concerned with the human anatomy, sources of energy (muscles and the force of gravity), and the characteristics of the piano. While innumerable motions are involved in piano playing, we can identify them as variants of a very limited number of fundamental motions. These fundamental motion patterns will be properly defined, described, and differentiated; they will then be integrated into the composite activities that comprise piano playing. It will then be necessary for them to be related unequivocally to their counterparts in the score.

In music, as in any kinetic art (such as dancing, acting, or conducting), emotions are expressed by motions; although we are not suggesting that these motions be executed with even a hint of uniformity, we recognize certain fundamental ways in which the motions correspond to and reflect the emotions that generate them. To illustrate this point in a rather obvious way, a delicate, dreamy, and subtle passage in a Chopin nocturne or in a Debussy prelude should not be performed with angular or abrupt motions.

Visual and motion patterns interrelated.

There is one respect in which this book may transcend similar books on piano playing. Here technique will be reduced to a handful of fundamental motions and patterns, the combinations and variants of which form the entire scope of technique. What is of greater importance, however, is that the reader will discover that the types of motion

The art of
technique

patterns to be used are indicated by the written score and will have to be identified by him. As we will see, visual features of the music (for example, phrasing, intervallic patterns, dynamics, and the location of notes on the keyboard) have their equivalents in the appropriate motion patterns.

These motion patterns by no means limit the freedom a performer seeks in his interpretations; instead they serve as guidelines in the choice of technical solutions. The art of piano technique begins at the point where technical problems have already been resolved and where a sophisticated technique serves the creative purposes of the interpreter.

PART ONE

The Determining Factors
in Piano Technique

1   Music, Motions and Emotions

Music begins with modification of pitch, volume, timbre, and duration of sound.

The human ear responds to sounds and noises within a limited range of pitch and volume. We cannot hear sounds above or below certain pitches—namely, above 25,000 and below 20 vibrations per second, approximately. Nor can the ear distinguish extremely soft or loud sounds. As to music, I would not attempt to formulate a precise definition, but I'd be satisfied to live with the assumption that sound alone, without variation in pitch, timbre, or intensity is not music. Not unless we have a certain modification in any or all of these characteristics will sound turn into music. The sound of a foghorn, of a stationary beep, or even of any one note played on the organ with unchanging volume and color does not impress one as music; what transforms sound into music is its alteration. The expressiveness of music depends on the degree and quality of change of pitch, color and volume. When a musical instrument produces variances in pitch, dynamics, or color, then we may have music. Although I will not elaborate further on this topic now, I would like to submit that it is the motions used to alter the sound that determine how sound changes, how music develops, and what it expresses. The manner in which a pianist attacks the keyboard, the way the violinist uses his bow arm and fingers, and the way singers and wind-instrument players control their breath determine the quality of the tone they produce. Their music is the result of the motions they employ. In other words, the subtleties of their sound production arise from the motions that created them.

Sound modifications reflect motions; motions reflect emotions.

That is why technique cannot be separated from music and why faulty technique results in faulty music. One must achieve a well-coordinated correct technique in order to produce a beautiful varied sound expressive of all the infinite shadings of human emotions. Yet the sound we produce does not always have to be beautiful—if we choose it not to be. We are dealing with the entire range of human emotions, and beautiful sensations and experiences are not the only feelings we wish to express.

Just as motions and sounds are interrelated, so are motions and emotions. Sounds are the result of motions, and motions must correspond to emotions. Although emotional responses to music are individual, they should always manifest themselves in a manner that corresponds in degree and quality to the feelings of the composer. Obviously the mood that inspired Chopin to write some of his gentle, lovely nocturnes is not evoked by spastic, sudden, angular, or overtense motions. Nor should one respond to the tempestuous vehemence and ecstasy of a Scriabin etude with dreamy, subtle gestures. Whether repressed or not, the degree and intensity of a pianist's feelings are expressed by the motions of his physical organism; these motions are transmitted through the piano and generate the same responses in the listener.

Composer, performer, listener

The chain of events is therefore established: we go from emotions to motions (technique) and from motions to sounds (music). The complete cycle in the creation of music is rather simple too: the emotions that prompt the composer to create his music are expressed by his music. When this music is notated, it becomes visible (musical score). The performer's role is to recreate the music (and the emotions that inspired its creator) in a manner that generates similar moods in the listener. The important link in this chain is technique—the motions employed by the performer to recreate the music. Under ideal circumstances, the listener's emotions are evoked by music played by the performer, whose mood and emotions reflect those of the composer. The performer's competence hinges on whether or not he interprets the written text according to the composer's indications and whether his technique (motions) corresponds to the emotional content of these indications.

This explanation may seem repetitious to some; to others it may seem like an oversimplification of a rather complex and subtle procedure. What I am trying to describe is the sequence of the composer's, performer's, and listener's roles in creating, recreating, and responding to music. I do so to call attention to a fundamentally important factor: the written image of music (the notes) indicates with unequivocal clarity the type of motions (technique) to be employed in the process of performing the music. The notated score establishes an absolutely clear connection between emotions and motions. One will find in the visible image of the music the corresponding motion patterns that provide the technical solution for any particular passage.

Limited number of fundamental motion patterns

One must simply organize the innumerable movements of the human body into a few clearly defined fundamental motion patterns, which form the essence of technique, and identify these with the visual patterns of the music itself. It is easy to do so because the human anatomy is basically the same all over the world and has been so from time immemorial, certainly so since the invention of the piano. Given this uniformity, it is possible for us to establish human motion patterns that are basic to piano playing. Yet there is a welcome and limitless variety within this uniformity: the size, weight, and proportions of the components within the body are different for each individual. This variety in body types provides an unlimited variety of movements within these fundamental motion patterns. Thus every individual can produce his own distinctive sound—his own tonal palette of touch and color—when playing the piano.

Practicing: the establishment of habits through conscious repetition

The descriptions and groupings of these basic motion patterns are provided in the appropriate chapters. In order to develop a good technique the student and performer must learn and master these motion patterns—that is, he must make them an innate part of his physical movements. After he determines the specific motion pattern required from the score, he then applies it to the music. The practicing of technique is nothing other than the process of assimilating motion patterns through repetition. If these motions are executed correctly and consciously, relatively few repetitions will suffice. Practice methods will be discussed more fully in chapter fourteen; for now I'd like to suggest that once our motion habits have been correctly and firmly acquired, a need to practice technique no longer exists. All we need to do then is to apply these motion patterns to our repertory. Our technique continues to improve, and it becomes an obedient tool in our search for musical interpretation.

Coordination

Let us assume that most people who study music and are practicing musicians were born with a certain degree of coordination. The innate coordination of the human body enables us to survive, to function in our daily life, to move about, and to respond to challenges. If our coordination is properly developed, it may enable us to achieve peak accomplishments. Breaking world records in swimming, running, or pole vaulting and developing an exceptionally brilliant and expressive technique as a pianist or violinist are matters of coordination of the highest order. Besides training their coordination skills athletes must also build endurance and muscular strength, but musicians only need to develop coordination. We do not build strong muscles; instead we learn to activate the ones that are already strong and to use them in collaboration with the weaker ones in order to help them. Using the strong muscles to help the weaker ones is the essence of coordination, and this kind of skill is what we must put in the service of art. Tempting as it may be for some, music and practicing need not be regarded as athletic activity.

Don't build muscles; coordinate them.

There are many ways to practice this coordination—this interdependence of the entire body. Practicing to develop independence of the fingers from one another has its merits too, but we should be careful in its application. As a rule these exercises abuse the forearm muscles by fixing and forcing them; they are based on the erroneous idea that our forearm muscles become tired because they are weak and therefore have to be strengthened by exercises. In fact, they become tired because they are being abused! What we may possibly gain in independence of the fingers, we will lose by disrupting the interdependence of the entire apparatus. Actually, nothing is gained, as I will explain in chapter eleven. Now I will simply say that finger exercises are useful only if they serve to create interdependence. By consistently placing the arm in the correct position for each and every finger, we relieve strain and avoid the overall fixed position that causes strain. The aim is not to strengthen muscles but to learn to synchronize them in the most effortless way. Any strain you feel in the arm is a sure warning that the muscles have been abused and are calling for help. We have mentioned some of the ailments (tendonitis, ganglia, bursitis) that result from faulty practice habits, continuous abuse of the muscles, forcing and fixing the joints, and extended pressure on the keys.

Our main concern now is not the unsuccessful performances that result from these wrongs, but all the damage caused during the countless hours, weeks, and years spent practicing. How much discomfort and suffering we must put up with! They can and must be avoided, especially since pianists have an enormous repertoire to cope with, larger than any other instrumentalist, and cannot afford to waste time and energy on wrong practice habits. With all the frustrations of strenuous practicing, many pianists become either discouraged or obsessive about proving themselves and will make a virtue of punishing themselves in the name of Art. It is for this reason that many people measure the quality, depth, and value of art by the amount of suffering poured into it. My apologies for sounding glib, but I wish merely to make the point that the mechanics of piano playing ought to be completely painless, enjoyable, and gratifying whether one practices or concertizes.

Our observations about the correct functioning of the human anatomy must be related to the characteristics of the piano itself. As we know, the sound of the piano is produced by hammers striking strings. The volume of the sound depends exclusively on the speed with which the hammer hits the string. It is important to realize this mechanical fact, since many confusing things have been said about weight, mass, force, strength, pressure, and, last but not least, about relaxation. The old school of piano playing emphasized "finger" strength. While this kind of technique sufficed for the harpsichord, clavichord, and organ, it became completely unsatisfactory for the modern concert grand piano. The strain on the muscles was such that a new approach had to be developed, and that new approach was

Inter-dependence vs. independence

Practicing, not performing, is our present concern.

Volume of sound contingent upon speed of hammer

Relaxation?

called weight technique. By using weight instead of force, considerable relief was felt in the abused muscles: thus appeared the school of relaxation. Unfortunately, although this method became very popular, it wasn't satisfactory either. Use of weight in itself merely achieved a relatively comfortable sensation in the arm and body, compared to the tenseness inherent in the old technique. However, the "relaxed" muscles now tended to play sloppily, unevenly, and inaccurately, and they could not be controlled like the tense muscles. It should be obvious that there is no such thing as complete relaxation during piano playing: some of the muscles work some of the time, others relax, and one must identify those that are to be activated.

Sources of energy: force of gravity and the muscles

I have mentioned before that volume of sound is contingent on hammer speed. In order to mobilize the playing apparatus and generate the desired speed in the hammers, there are no other but two sources of energy available: the force of gravity, which pulls everything down toward the center of the earth, and muscular energy, or the force of our own muscles, which pulls the finger and the arm toward the affixed portion of the contracting muscles. These forces, and their combinations, provide all the sources of energy available to activate the entire playing equipment. The force of gravity helps immeasurably if the mass of the playing equipment is exposed to it judiciously. Most of the time, it is the participation of both energy sources that provides the optimal solution. Our aim is to achieve the greatest results with the least expenditure of energy. It will be up to us to determine when to utilize the force of gravity exclusively, when to use muscular energy exclusively, and when and how to combine both. Total relaxation is nonexistent in piano playing. Even when we rely purely on the force of gravity, we must use the necessary muscular equipment to lift and place the arm and hand in their proper positions. Most motions are executed by antagonistic sets of muscles: while one group (for example, the flexors) works, the other group (extensors) relaxes. Partial relaxation alternates with muscular activity at all times; complete relaxation exists only if we lie down and rest.

Position of equipment when activated

Our task is to determine what the position of the various components of the playing apparatus should be at activation, what groups of muscles should be activated, and how these muscles should function in order to achieve optimum results both technically and musically. What we seek is the maximum expression with the least expenditure of physical energy. One should not mistakenly equate inner intensity with continuous muscular tension, nor cultivate inner tension by stimulation of muscular activities (pressing the keys).

Pressure?

We must remember that once the piano's hammer strikes, we cannot alter the sound by any subsequent activity. Pressure and extended leaning on the keys (a futile throwback to the *Bebung* of the clavichord) may create the illusion that the sound is altered, but its effect is only visual; all this pressure will only hinder the attack on the following note. The string player's technique includes pressure, the pianist's does not. If pressure is used on the piano, it must be used only instantaneously, at the moment of impact, never extendedly!

Weight: of value only when set into motion

Weight alone is also of little use, unless it is set in motion. Even if a ton of weight is applied to the key, it does not produce a sound unless it moves downward with a certain speed. It is speed that generates sound, not weight; therefore let us use as little weight as possible when generating speed. Muscular force is of use only in generating speed in the hammers, not as energy spent statically. The simultaneous and extended activation of an antagonistic set of muscles (for example, the flexors and extensors of the forearm or the biceps and triceps of the upper arm) is unproductive, and in spite of a vigorous feeling of energy and tension in the arm, it is totally superfluous and therefore should be avoided. All it causes is immobility and stiffness, which ultimately result in a poor sound. The inescapable conclusion is that technique must concern itself with setting the hammers in motion, using the force of gravity, and expending a minimal and efficient amount of our own muscular energy. A maximum fortissimo as well as the lightest pianissimo can be produced by these procedures in a completely effortless manner.

Stress alters respiration and phrasing.

One cannot emphasize too strongly the fact that music and technique are indivisible. The human organism is affected by and responds to stress and soothing: one's breathing, pulse, metabolism will also accelerate or decrease according to emotions and musical experiences. This is inevitable, even desirable. And, if the human organism is under stress for purely physical reasons (overtense muscles, a depressed diaphragm or off-balance sitting), forced and unsatisfactory breathing results. This altered respiration affects musical phrasing and the shaping of melodic lines, not only while playing under stress in public, but at all times. A malfunctioning apparatus affects phrasing, tone production, dynamics, rubatos, accents, tempo changes, and expression—almost everything that is vital to music. Rapid and short breathing generates a hectic mood, and, in general, melodic and rhythmic distortions are caused by excessive muscular contractions in and around the respiratory system. Stiff muscles and joints cause a hard sound, while excessively soft ones produce a pale, anemic sound.

Tone quality: essential in performance

Although the piano is far less responsive and sensitive than string instruments (not to mention the human voice), it does nevertheless respond to one's technique, and it produces sounds accordingly. In the last analysis, it is tone quality—the sound—that is the most essential artistic ingredient in the world of music. Every artist has a touch

and timbre that we can recognize as his own. Certainly one can identify the sound of Horowitz or Rostropovich in a live performance, and
this sound may even be evident on a recording, in spite of the ultra-
homogenizing effects of electronic reproduction. It is unfortunate that
the piano (especially the lower-quality instruments) has a rather pre-
fabricated sound. But if we succeed in cultivating tone quality through
a well-coordinated and natural technique, we will realize that we are
the fortunate possessors of a miraculously expressive and complete
instrument, one that is capable of every shading. Pianists are doubly
blessed because they have the possibility of using this technique in
the service of a fabulous repertoire.

2 The Piano

The piano: the most complete instrument

As a solo instrument, the modern piano is second to none. Even if its expressive qualities don't match those of some of the string instruments or of the human voice, its range of pitch, dynamics, and coloring makes it the most complete instrument. Because of its harmonic capabilities and its range, all other solo instruments enlist its services most of the time. Seldom do composers write for any other instrument alone, without the accompaniment of the piano. Its repertoire is enormous, composed for it during the past two hundred years or so. Not all of this music is of the best quality, of course, but many of the greatest composers overwhelmingly favored the piano to other solo instruments.

Its forerunners: harpsichord and clavichord

Of the piano's predecessors, the clavichord is the closest to it. The clavichord produces a sound that can vary in dynamic level and color according to the player's touch. The volume of the clavichord, however, is minimal and unsuitable for most concert halls today. The piano has maintained and developed the first two characteristics of the clavichord (its ability to vary dynamics and color), but in addition its volume has grown considerably. The harpsichord cannot produce gradations of volume and color by touch, only by mechanical manipulation, but it has much more volume than the clavichord and can double, triple, and quadruple its notes by using added sets of 'strings, thereby producing a wider variety of sound. The piano has all the expressiveness of the clavichord and can be louder than the harpsichord, but it lacks the mechanical couplings of the latter instrument. However, with its great pitch span and its ability to vary dynamics and tone color, the piano is unsurpassed.*

* There is one instrument that surpasses the piano. It is the Moór-Duplex piano, a double-keyboard piano that was invented by Emanuel Moór during the first quarter of this century. Unfortunately it has been totally ignored since World War II. It has the same sound and coloring possibilities as the ordinary piano, but it also has an upper octave-coupling device (middle pedal). Its upper keyboard sounds an octave higher and by the simultaneous use of both keyboards by the same hands, the reach of the hands is twice that of the normal piano! Also, a chromatic glissando can be played on the lower keyboard (in octaves, too, when the coupling

Compositional devices: arpeggios, tremolos, and others

With all its wealth of sound, the piano still has certain limiting characteristics; for example, its sound fades rapidly. Composers have compensated for this deficiency by developing styles that are typically pianistic, or rather "keyboardistic," since the harpsichord and clavichord also suffer from the same limitation. Since the duration of any one note is extremely short on these keyboard instruments, the continuity in the sound has to be supplemented by trills, tremolos, repeated notes, arpeggios, filling notes, passage-work, and pedaling. These devices are used both in sustained melodies and in accompanying passages in practically all periods and styles.

Ornaments

Another device, the ornament, was thoroughly explored and utilized on instruments like the harpsichord and the organ. Since these instruments cannot emphasize individual notes within any one given tone color and register, the only way to accent an important note is to add a dissonance to it. Grace notes, mordents, and trills contain dissonant neighboring notes. These widely used instruments made the ornaments very popular during the Baroque period, and their indiscriminate use spread to other keyboard instruments, especially to the clavichord and the piano. These instruments are fully capable of accentuating, coloring, and emphasizing any note. Therefore it is not necessary to resort to certain ornaments on them.

Transcriptions

When Bach wrote for the violin or for voice, he seldom used mordents or prallers. However, when he transcribed string music for the keyboard (as in the first movement of the *Sonata for Unaccompanied Violin in C Major* or the entire *Partita for Unaccompanied Violin in A Minor*), he added a number of these ornaments for emphasis. (It is

Example 1. Bach, *Sonata in C for Solo Violin*, first movement

Example 2. Bach, *Sonata in C for Solo Violin*, transcribed, in G, for keyboard

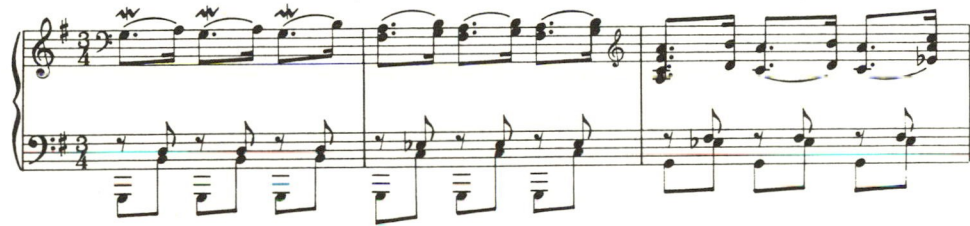

pedal is activated), since the white keys are elevated to the level of the black ones where adjacent to the upper keyboard. The technique of the Moór piano is essentially the same as of the normal piano, but can be expanded spectacularly. For composers it has unlimited possibilities. One can only hope that the Moór piano is merely dormant and not extinct!

interesting that he used the key of G major for his keyboard version of a C major composition on the violin, and D minor for the A minor Partita.) It is also noteworthy that Baroque composers very seldom specified whether their keyboard music was for the clavichord, the harpsichord, or the organ. For example, two of the best known "organ" compositions by Bach, the *Passacaglia in C Minor* and the *Fantasy and Fugue in G Minor,* were originally conceived for the two-keyboard and pedal harpsichord; only later were they adopted by organists. The practice of interchanging instruments was always very common in the past.

Ornamentation varies with the instrument.

Since the choice of instruments was mostly a matter of opportunity and convenience and since all of these instruments were strikingly different in terms of their tone quality and technique, it is evident that devices like ornamentation should be used according to the needs and characteristics of each instrument. Common sense dictates much less ornamentation on the piano and on the clavichord than on the harpsichord and the organ. Also the type of ornament should be selected according to the instrument. When a melody begins at the same time as its accompaniment on the harpsichord or the organ, one simply cannot hear the melody because it is one of the overtones of the bass note and it is impossible to play it louder or differently. Therefore a mordent or grace note is used in order to call attention to it. In the case of the clavichord or the piano, the melody can be played louder— simply by playing it louder! Therefore the mordent is often not necessary. Furthermore, the ground rule that we know so well about trills and ornaments to start on the upper note in the Baroque and early Classical periods needs reconsideration. This rule was necessitated by the condition mentioned above—that of the inaudibility of the main note when it was played at the same time as the bass. In the first place, there is no need for the mordent on the piano, because you can emphasize the desired note; then if you still wish to affix the ornament, it doesn't make any difference whether you start it on the upper note or the main note. You might as well emphasize the main note by an accent or by a difference in shading, since the piano can do this easily. The validity of all the treatises and articles written about ornamentation is highly debatable when they are applied to the piano. To support the above argument, examine the beginnings of melodies by Bach for strings, winds, and voice to see whether they start with a mordent or with the main note. No matter how slow the piece is, you will not find a single work that begins with an ornament. On the other hand, look at the first notes of the melodies of the second movement of the *Italian Concerto,* the Adagio of the *Organ Toccata in C Major,* and the *Toccata and Fugue in D Minor*: all of them begin with some kind of ornament, because they were written for Baroque keyboard instruments. When these pieces are played on the harpsichord or organ, ornamentation should be applied, but it is not absolutely necessary when the piano or clavichord is used.

The span of the hand: a limiting factor

Another limiting factor on use of the piano, in addition to the rapid decay of its sound, is the limited span of the human hand. Since its reach usually includes nine or ten notes at the most, most broad orchestral chords must be arpeggiated. This condition helped to develop compositional styles that turned this disadvantage into an asset. Just think of the Chopin *Etude,* opus 10 no. 1, or his arpeggio etude in E flat, opus 25 no. 12, or the opening of the second movement of the Schumann *Fantasy,* opus 17. Innumerable works are based on runs and passage-work that present and enhance broad harmonic progressions. The limitations of the hand also created another condition. Composers were obliged to choose only from the notes that were reachable. Instead of selecting notes within the overtone series, as they did for works for orchestra and string quartet, they usually selected four notes for the top and four for the bottom register.

Example 3. Chord for piano and orchestra

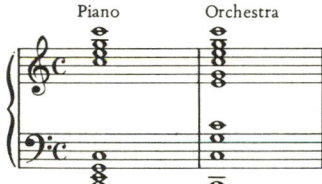

Of course, the piano chord doesn't sound as good as the orchestral chord: the four notes in the bass are too thick, there is nothing in the middle register, and the top notes are too shrill or thin. We have become used to these sonorities by now (we have no choice), but if we wanted a fuller, rounder, and more beautiful sonority, we would need either a third hand or another instrument like the Moór-Duplex piano. Beethoven and other composers often employed pedal effects and shifts of register to compensate for this limitation. And again, this condition gave rise to a number of compositional problems in piano writing.

Black keys, white keys: shifting arm positions

When we examine certain aspects of piano playing, we find that many difficulties can be overcome if we are aware of the obvious fact that the black keys are about two inches farther away from us and about half an inch higher than the white keys. In order for the hand to play on black keys with the same ease as on white keys, the upper arm, the wrist, and even the body must be shifted slightly. When one plays on black keys, the upper arm (elbow) should move slightly forward and up in order to create a wrist position that is exactly the same as it is when one plays on white keys. (For a more detailed discussion of the white and black keys, see chapter five.)

Piano sound: volume and tone quality

The sound of the piano is produced when the hammer strikes the strings and thereby brings them into vibration; thus the substance, quality, hardness or softness, elasticity, and the state of humidity of the surface of the hammer (which is covered with felt) influence the tone quality. If these conditions are satisfactory, we are able to modify the dynamic level and tone quality by altering the speed with which the hammer strikes the strings. All our concern with matters of weight, mass, force, strength, tension, relaxation, fixed positions, muscles, nerves, joints, bones, shoulders, arms, hands, and fingers is related to the skill and technique required to set these hammers in motion with the proper speed in order to produce the desired piano sound.

While everyone agrees about the piano's capability to vary dynamics from triple piano to triple forte, its ability to vary tone color is a topic that is quite controversial. It has been "proven" by some "experts" that it is only the volume of the sound that can be altered and that altering tone quality is purely a matter of imagination. This may be true in playing one single note, but a series of sounds in sequence is quite another matter: touch and tone quality are most personal things, and they are clearly recognizable. Even if they are hard to define, the difference in tone qualities among certain artists undoubtedly exists and is not imagined. Perhaps it is caused by the rate of acceleration of the speed of the hammers; perhaps it is the way the damper stops the sound when it descends on the strings; perhaps it is the spacing of notes, the agogic qualities of the playing, or the flexibility of metric units—these and many other factors may influence tone quality. But differences do exist! There can be no argument that the piano sounds different when Horowitz, Richter, Michelangeli, or Argerich play it. Also of great importance is the way the particular instrument we are playing responds to touch. There are many pianos that have a rather pleasant but "ready-made" sound. They respond only to quantitative changes of dynamics and not to different shadings of touch, to the reflexes of the performer. It would be most beneficial if all pianists could do all their practicing, not just performing, on instruments that were sensitive enough to respond to shadings of color as well as to dynamics.

Limits to the response of the piano

Speaking of dynamics, we must realize that the piano, like any other musical instrument, is limited in the amount of sound it can produce and in the responsiveness of its mechanism. It might not be as sensitive as the human voice, which simply cracks when forced. But if the piano is hit hard—if it is beaten by a stiff, rigid equipment—its volume and carrying power will be impaired and its sound will become hard and hollow. Forcing only spoils the sound. Under no circumstances must one exert oneself when playing fortissimo! Although the piano can produce a tremendous volume, its maximum sonorities will come about not when the maximum amount of energy is used, but when the limits of elasticity in its mechanism are arrived at but not surpassed. If one reaches the limit of elasticity in the felt, wood, and metal, and employs the minimum effort to achieve this limit, one gets the crashing fortissimos that may be the real climactic moments of a performance.

Spirituality not found in excessive muscular tension.

The lowest level of sonority, the pianissimo, must also be totally effortless in its production. It is really amazing how many pianists cultivate extreme strain and tension when they play softly. Gritting their teeth and breathing heavily, they expend enough energy to lift the piano, even though they are playing a gentle, soft little melody. Maybe they have the idea that control can be best achieved by tensing up various sets of antagonistic muscles simultaneously. Instead of using soft equipment and minimum muscular activity, they tighten up. Worst of all, this extreme state of muscular tension is supposed to represent a state of sublime "spiritual" exaltation, when in reality we are witnessing the consequences of excessive discharges of the thyroid and adrenal glands. Mind you, there is nothing wrong with glandular responses to the stimuli of music, but the question is when, where, and how much? In any case, if we are going to produce soft sounds, our joints and muscles must be resilient, and they must contract and fixate gently. We'll discuss this further in chapter thirteen.

Let us not equate inner intensity with stiff muscles. It is quite fashionable nowadays to overproject and overintensify musical performances. This is understandable when one considers the enormous size of concert halls, the vast open-air spaces where outdoor concerts are given, and the huge size of concert audiences, who may not be familiar with the repertoire. There are many pressures on pianists to impress audiences instantaneously. However most music suffers by overselling. Music should be narrated, sung, and sometimes even whispered and hummed; seldom should it be shouted or screamed.

CHAPTER

3   The Human Performing Mechanism

Characteristics
of the human
equipment

Before we confront the many challenges of artistic problems—the matters of interpretative, creative, and improvisatory elements in music—we must investigate a much more tangible and equally essential area. I refer to the playing mechanism—the individual components and the totality of the human body that participate in creating musical sounds. In order to establish the technical formulas that serve to make music, we must examine the mechanism itself—the individual parts, characteristics, and actions of the human apparatus. We need not make a complete anatomic survey of every particle of the human body, but we do need an elementary knowledge of the equipment we constantly use. While art is a matter of unpredictables (inspiration, instinct, and improvisation), technique is a skill that one must develop intelligently, effectively, and without abusing the participating mechanism. Our muscles, joints, nervous system, and breathing mechanism function at their best when we know how to put them to good use. The same is true of any mechanism—your bicycle, typewriter, or car. It is true that you don't need to know much about them when they work satisfactorily—you simply use them. But if they get out of order, or if you want them to function beyond their obvious capabilities, you'd better know them quite thoroughly. We all reach a certain level of playing by just "doing what comes naturally." But when you reach the limit of a purely instinctive activity (the limit may be extremely low or high; it depends on your talents), if all you do is practice mechanically, you won't make much progress. You must know how to practice intelligently.

Coordination,
not muscle
building; small
muscles for
precision, larger
muscles for
assisting

As I mentioned before, piano playing is not a matter of muscular strength and endurance. We have a rather complex set of muscles at our command. Some of these muscles are small and weak, made for precision work, others are strong and powerful. If we can activate these larger muscles properly, we do not need to strengthen the weaker ones. We must learn the kind of coordination that enables us to put to use the necessary equipment and to play without any trace of fatigue, no matter how demanding and difficult the passages we must perform.

Children and short people coordinate better.

Every normal living thing is born with the degree of coordination it needs to function within its environment and to survive. After only a few months, infants develop this quality remarkably well. In general, it is possible that children have even better coordination than adults, as a result of their small stature. Shorter people, too, are often better coordinated than tall ones. They move more effectively and with greater agility and ease.

Some of the most outstanding virtuosos were short and had small hands; Godowsky, Hofmann, and Friedman, just to name a few, were great artists who were of small stature. Obviously, tall people can also be great pianists, but it is well known that some child prodigies possess a miraculous ability to coordinate, and thus they are able to perform the most demanding and seemingly strenuous technical feats with the greatest ease.

Instinctive coordination

I mention this because it seems clear that when a child begins his musical studies, he usually possesses a considerable amount of innate coordination. If a teacher can take good advantage of this and doesn't interfere with it, he can shape a much better and happier pianist. When a child plays loudly, he instinctively throws his whole arm and body into action, and most likely he plays without any effort. I am not sure this is the case with advanced pianists, with grown-ups! Many of them are constrained because of their practice habits, and they are often handicapped by all kinds of inhibiting ideas. Very often their main concern is how to regain the innate coordination that they lost on their way to becoming advanced pianists. The most common cause for this loss of coordination is an overuse of drills designed to make the fingers independent and to strengthen the weak "wrist" muscles. Many adult pianists were required to suffer through finger exercises in order to develop "strong muscles." They gained a certain degree of finger independence at the expense of interdependence and coordination. Often psychological factors also inhibit performers. For now, however, let us concentrate on the purely technical aspects of piano playing. Independence of the fingers is essential; but instead of trying to acquire it by forced and muscle-stiffening exercises, our fundamental approach to technical solutions is to search for the correct positions in which the right equipment helps the fingers work independently and provides them with the power they need. This approach seems to be the most sensible way to avoid forcing and fatigue in the forearm muscles that move the fingers and to produce a good tone.

Activation of stronger muscles

When the larger muscles are mobilized, the effort required to play the piano will be distributed in such a way that the necessary expenditure of energy will hardly be felt or seen. May I emphasize here that

Distribution
and reduction óf
motions

this extreme reduction of energy must not be mistaken for "relaxation." It is a simple matter of utilizing muscles so expeditiously that hardly any effort need be used. As mentioned previously, total relaxation when playing the piano doesn't exist, since even the raising of a finger or hand must activate some muscles. Relative relaxation may be felt because most of the muscles are making no effort; the ones that work can handle their chores easily since they are being helped by the stronger muscles.

Avoid stiffness
rather than
remedy it by
relaxation

Compared to finger exercising, with its resulting strained and stiff muscles, the large and loose motions of weight technique certainly must have felt enjoyable. The term *relaxation* (see Breithaupt) sounds alluring, but however pleasurable large and loose motions may be, they are not the solution for our technical problems. If we weren't so tense, we wouldn't need relaxation either as a remedy or as prevention. If we utilize the optimal combination of certain muscles, we will never become stiff and tense. We don't want to relax; we want to make music and to be involved in all its drama and emotions—but with no physical strain!

Understand the
total equipment;
use only the
necessary
equipment.

Our aim here is to identify and apply all the necessary motion patterns that are the tools for piano playing in order to play effortlessly and expressively without inflammation of muscles and tendons. We will learn all about active and passive motions and about the exact role of the fingers, hand, wrist, forearm, upper arm, and body. Since it is only the fingers that are in actual contact with the keys, all other activities will be geared and limited to the role of helping them. We don't execute motions for motions' sake. Instead of bogging down with strenuous fingerwork or with exaggerated, circular "relaxing" gestures, we will carefully select the appropriate motion patterns and activate the proper sets of muscles.

Muscles

Before we describe these muscular activities, let us first examine how a muscle works. A muscle contracts voluntarily or involuntarily on orders from our nerve centers; when it contracts, it gets shorter and thicker. As it shortens, it pulls the portion of the anatomy to which its farther end is affixed toward its other point of attachment (figure 1). This is the only thing that a muscle can do: it can pull a limb or part of the body to which its tendon is attached toward itself. It can never return the pulled-in portion to its original position. This movement is made by the antagonistic muscle or by the force of gravity or by both. However, after the muscle has been contracted and put to work, it needs to return to its original shape in order to function again.

Warning;
consequences of
unheeded
warning

If it doesn't return to its original shape, it can respond to another nervous stimulus and contract still more, but it will be under strain. When this happens, fatigue sets in, in proportion to the degree of strain. This state of strain is the response the muscle uses to warn the

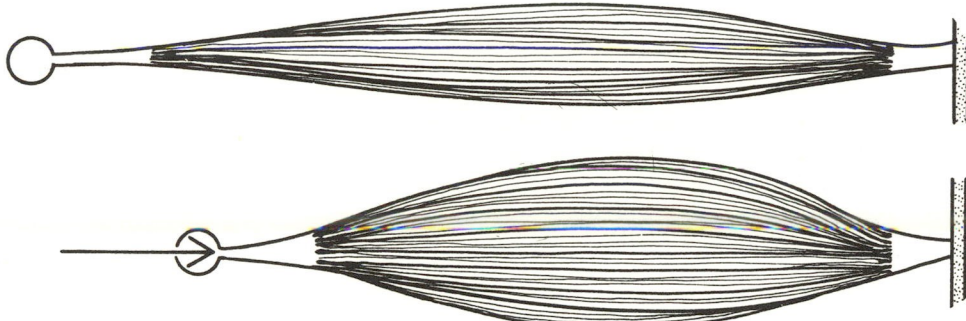

Figure 1. Muscle before and during contraction

nerve centers that help is needed. When help comes, the muscle can regain its original shape and go to work again. If help does not arrive, the muscle will work under greater strain and the warning signal will become more acute. Fatigue will increase; then stiffening, numbness, and more pain will occur; and in due time there will be chronic aches and inflammation of the tendons. Once tendonitis sets in, one must stop playing, sometimes for as long as three or four months or more.

Let us therefore remember that muscles need to return to their normal state after contraction; at this point the alternate (antagonistic) muscles should take over. This alternate activity ensures the needed relaxation of previously contracted muscles and enables the system to work continuously.

The forearm is the home of the muscles that move the fingers up and down. To raise the fingers we have a set of muscles on the upper (dorsal) side of the forearm called the *extensor* muscles. As long as these extensor muscles are contracted, the fingers stay up. If these muscles relax, the fingers come down with the partial help of the force of gravity. If we want to pull them down actively, we must contract a set of muscles on the lower (volar) side of the forearm called the *flexor* muscles. When this happens, the previously used (antagonistic) extensor muscles have a chance to relax and become slightly stretched. This relaxing and stretching enables them to be in perfect condition to contract again. In other words, the up-and-down motion of the fingers is executed by the antagonistic sets of extensor and flexor muscles that work and relax alternately. As long as antagonistic muscles work alternately, they can go on indefinitely! There are frequent occasions, however, when the antagonistic muscles have to contract simultaneously, but here the fixation must be instantaneous, not extended. If the contraction is extended, there will be excessive tension in the muscles. This undue strain must be avoided.*

Flexors and extensors in the forearm lift and depress the fingers.

* Within the framework of this book I don't believe it to be necessary to discuss the role of lactic

To move the
forearm use the
biceps and
triceps; to move
the upper arm
use the
shoulder and
back muscles.

To pull in the forearm, we activate the *biceps* and for the opposite motion we use the *triceps*. Both these muscles are located on the upper arm, and they are much stronger than the muscles of the forearm. To raise the upper arm we use some of the shoulder and back muscles. To direct the upper arm downward, the chest, back, and body muscles are activated. These muscles are among the strongest in the human body. By using all these strong muscles we can easily avoid fatigue. Once our coordination is right and there is no extended contraction of the antagonistic muscles, a practically unlimited source of muscular energy is available. I say "unlimited" because we are concerned with piano playing and not with breaking the world record in weight lifting or pull-ups. The frailest, thinnest human being has all the sources of energy he needs to play the most strenuous pianistic passages as loudly as possible. May I remind you that the resistance of the piano key is only about two or three ounces.

No muscle building

When we feel fatigue, we should deactivate the contracted muscles and utilize others; under no circumstances do we strain and "build up" the suffering muscles with torturous exercises. On the contrary, we don't want to desensitize our muscles—we want them to warn us when they are overworked and malfunctioning. We need these warning devices; they enable us to achieve closer and more successful coordination with our entire anatomy. I utterly disagree with the notion that muscle endurance has to be developed for playing the violin, piano, or any other musical instrument. Forcing muscles may be needed in athletics, where not only coordination but extreme strength and endurance are essential. In music, however, coordination is the name of the game; the strength that is already available in our muscles is sufficient, and we must consciously strive to conserve their sensitivity. Whatever might be gained by forcing the muscles will prove to be costly. Not only will our coordination suffer, but so will tone production.

Range of activities: central area preferred

Now that we are familiar with the work of the muscle (pulling by contraction), with the role of antagonistic muscles (alternate activities of opposite muscles), and with their partial relaxation, let us examine the exact range of activities of the playing apparatus (that is, of the fingers, hand, forearm, upper arm, and shoulder). An understanding of this range is of great importance in determining why, how, and to what degree these components should be activated in order to achieve optimum results in both technique and interpretation. It is a definite advantage to remain within the central areas of the available ranges as much as possible and to avoid the extremes whenever possible.

---

acid in causing a sensation of tiredness in the contracted muscles. Our concerns are the mechanical causes and remedies of tiredness.

The fingers   Although each of the fingers is different in length and shape, four
of them (the index finger, and the third, fourth, and fifth fingers) are
similar in structure. However the thumb is different in structure as
well as in length and shape. I call attention to this seemingly obvious
fact simply because unevenness in scale and arpeggio playing is usually caused by the misuse of the thumb. The thumb needs special
attention, and moreover it requires a different wrist, hand, and arm
position than the other fingers (see chapter five for a fuller discussion
of the thumb).

The thumb has two phalanxes, while all the other fingers have
three each. The fingers are attached to the hand (*metacarpal*) bones,
and four of these metacarpal bones (from the index to the fifth finger)
are closely tied by ligaments. The thumb, however, is freely movable,
as you can see in Figure 2. Again, the thumb is different.

Figure 2. Skeletal structure of the hand

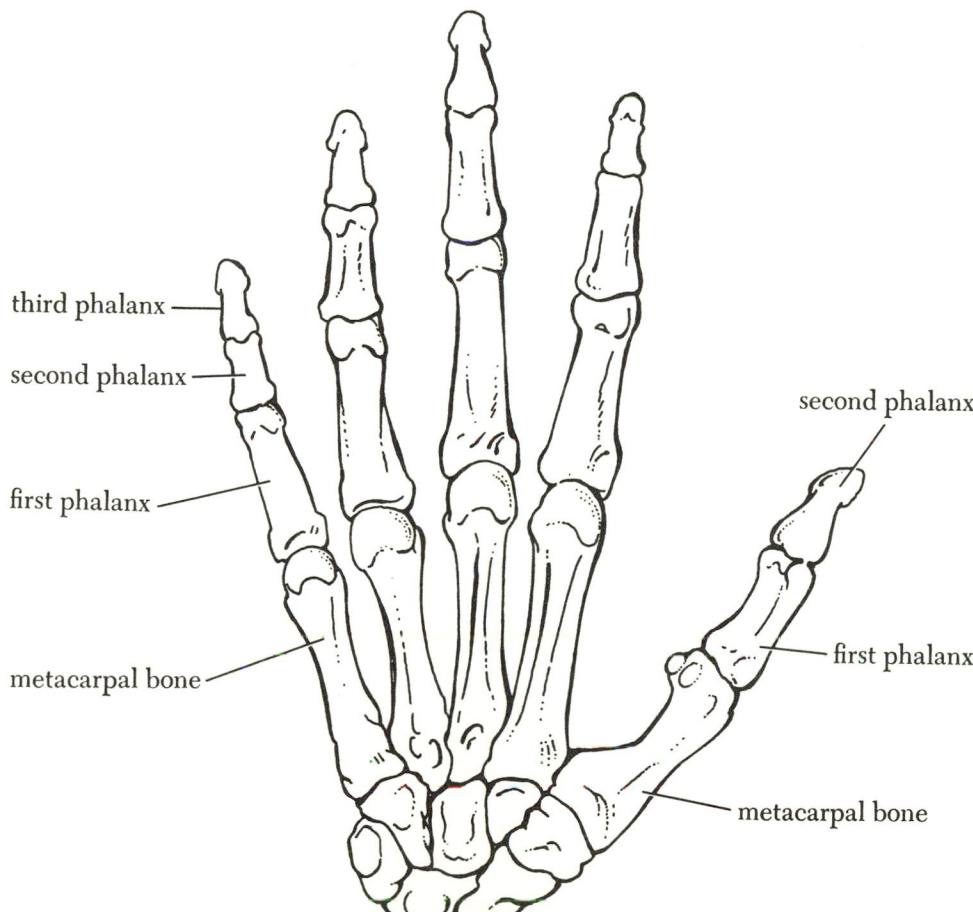

Horizontal arm adjustments

All vertical finger motions are executed by antagonistic muscles located on the forearm, as described before. Therefore a finger's position is correct only if it is placed as if it were an extension of its corresponding muscles; it will be moved in a direct line with these muscles too. This means that there must be a slight horizontal adjustment in the position of the arm for each finger. There can be no fixed wrist position for all five fingers unless they play simultaneously (that is, unless they play chords). To achieve the particular position that is optimal for each finger, the arm (including the wrist and hand) must be shifted continuously in the horizontal dimension. Figure 3 shows the central position of the arm and fingers. When the fingers are called into play, the horizontal shifts will be very small; otherwise the fingers will get out of line. We don't want to exaggerate the adjusting motion, since an unnecessarily large motion again causes friction and wastes energy within the tendons that move the finger.

The description of the equally important vertical adjusting motions is given in chapter five.

Movement of the piano key: a vertical path

Before we examine the range of action of the fingers, I would like to describe the way in which the piano key is set in motion by the finger. The piano key moves up and down in a straight vertical line, except for the negligible curve, which is caused by the fulcrum. Therefore the position of the last phalanx of the finger should be as close to vertical as possible at landing on the key so that energy can be transferred in the most direct manner. Any slanted approach to the keys results in a certain detraction of energy, and the amount of energy wasted depends on the angle of the vertical component. Sometimes we intentionally slant our fingers on the keys in order to avoid an overly direct attack (espressivo playing).

Figure 3. Central position of the arm and fingers

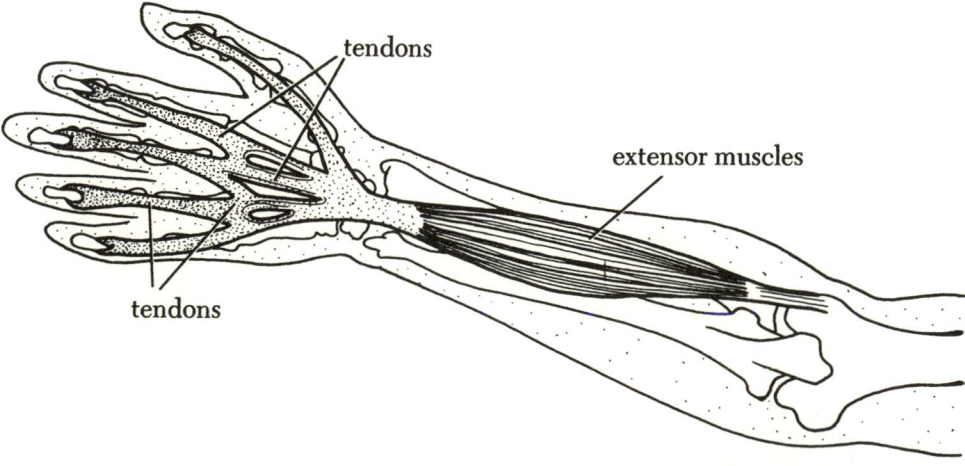

We know that the fingers, like the hand, arm, and the rest of the human anatomy, always move in a curved line because they are affixed to certain points of support; they act as the radius of a circle. Therefore we must modify the wrist position so that the last phalanx of the finger is able to approximate a perpendicular direction to the key. Each finger requires this adjustment, especially when we shift from white keys to black keys and from black keys to white keys.

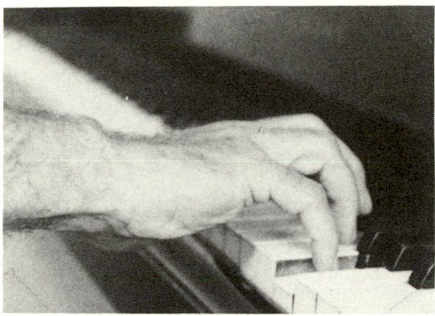

Figure 4. Correct position of the fifth finger; last phalanx placed vertically

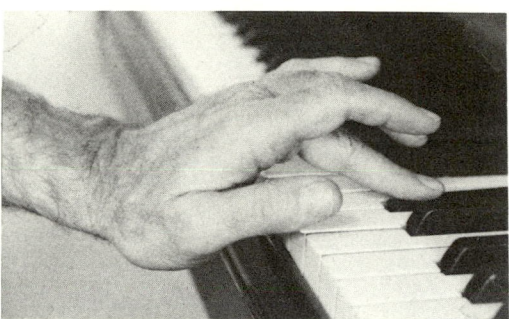

Figure 5. Incorrect position; third finger slanted, pulling outward

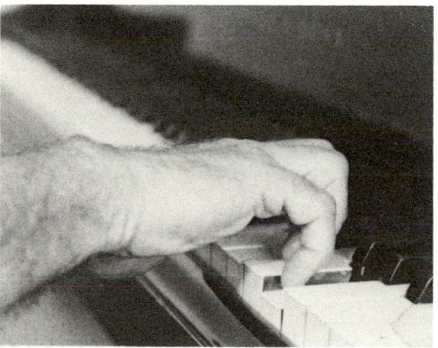

Figure 6. Incorrect position; fifth finger pulled in excessively, last phalanx slanted

Extreme and central ranges of the fingers, hand, and arm

Figures 7 and 8 show the positions of the thumb and the other fingers in their extreme ranges; figures 9 through 13 illustrate other extreme ranges of the hand and the wrist. Somewhere in the middle of these extremes we find the central areas, where we can function comfortably and avoid any forced positions.

With the cooperation of the rest of the playing mechanism, we can accommodate practically any of the components and avoid strain.

Avoid fixed and extreme positions.

Figures 9 through 11 show the extreme ranges of the wrist in the vertical, lateral, and circular directions. The dotted lines indicate the complete range, and the thick line shows the central area where the

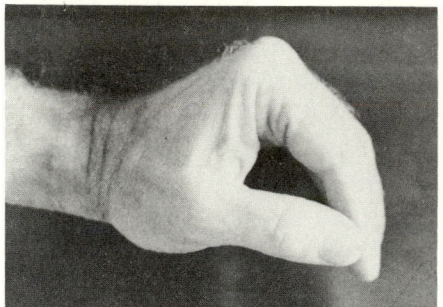

Figure 7. Extremely contracted thumb and finger position; comfortable area somewhat higher

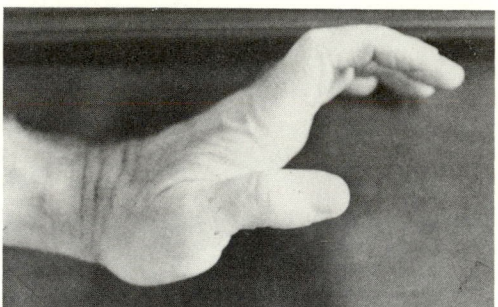

Figure 8. Extremely raised thumb and fingers; comfortable area somewhat lower

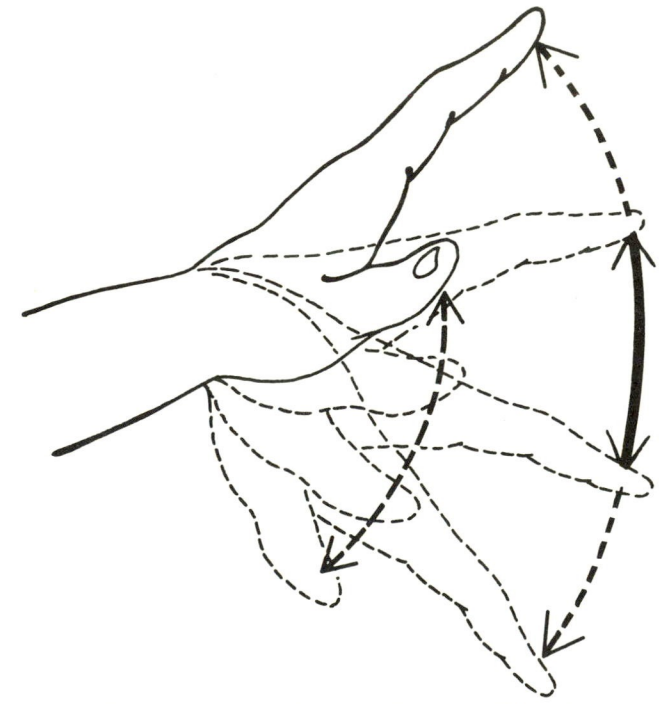

Figure 9. Vertical range of wrist and hand; central area marked

hand functions comfortably. Our aim is to bring the wrist, the fingers, and the arm within or close to these central areas, where they move with ease.

The horizontal motions of the fingers (open and closed position of the hand) are executed by muscles located on the hand. The fingers' vertical motions, as said before, are done by the antagonistic muscles of the forearm. None of these motions are done by "finger muscles" because nothing can move itself; the muscles that do the work are always found at the adjoining component of the human apparatus. The

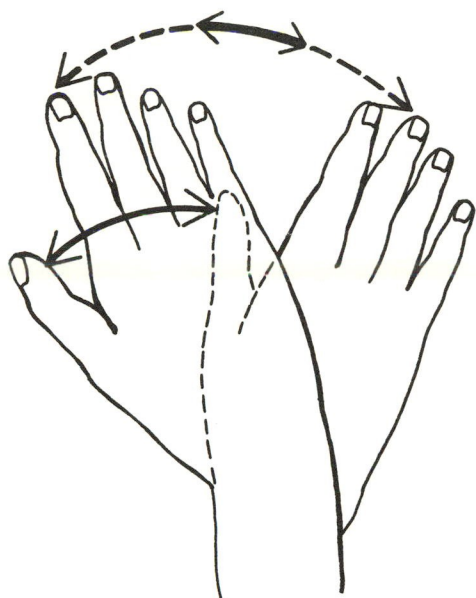

Figure 10. Lateral range of wrist and hand; central area marked

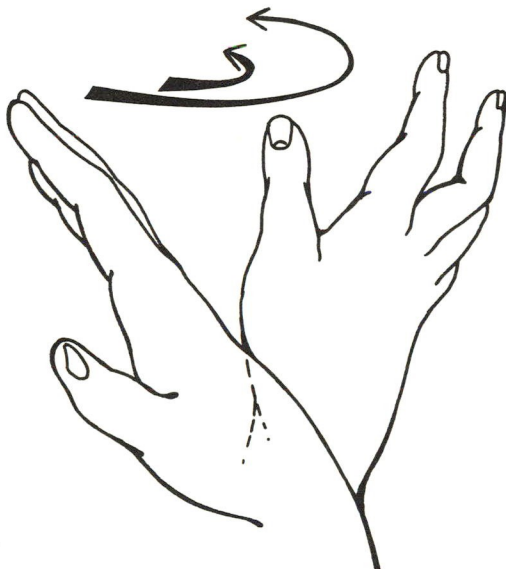

Figure 11. Circular range of wrist and hand; central area marked

hand is moved by the forearm muscles, the forearm by the upper-arm muscles, the upper arm by the back and chest muscles, etc. None of the muscles should stay extremely contracted for an extended time, and this is particularly important to observe when the hand is in a wide stretch. It will be necessary to permit the fingers to approximate their normal position as soon and as often as possible, even if one has only a split-second time to achieve this. This is the case with rapid staccato octaves too (see chapter seven).

With the help of the horizontal and vertical adjusting motions the fingers can avoid most extreme or fixed positions and operate within their central areas of activity. The rest of the playing mechanism is also helped by the respective adjusting motions of the adjacent members.

Let us give the exact listing of the capabilities of the various components that execute motions. These motions are described within the three dimensions—vertical, horizontal, and depth (depth refers to the plane from the back of the key to its edge). However, the combination of this limited number of motions provides an infinitely varied gamut of motions, sounds, and shadings of sounds!

The *fingers* can execute vertical and horizontal motions (see figures 7 and 8). They are moved by the flexor-extensor muscles of the forearm and by the abductor-adductor muscles of the hand. They can execute circular motions by combining the vertical and horizontal motions.

The *hand* can be moved vertically, horizontally, and circularly by the forearm muscles. It cannot execute rotary motions, which are the motions of the forearm (see figures 9, 10, and 11).

The *forearm* can be moved vertically by the upper-arm muscles (the biceps and triceps). With the help of muscles attached to the upper arm and forearm, it can rotate on its own axis by the pronation and supination of the ulna and radius. It cannot move laterally; this motion is made by the rotation of the upper arm.

The *upper arm* can move vertically, horizontally, and circularly as well as rotate with the help of the back, shoulder, and chest muscles. It is one of the most mobile members of the human body.

The *shoulder* can move vertically, forward and backward, and circularly. It seldom moves actively, but it supports and moves the entire arm.

Occasionally we refer to the position and motions of the trunk, in terms of the sideways, forward and backward, and rotational motions of the backbone. We also refer to the participation of the legs and feet in supporting and balancing the body and ensuring its stability, mobility, and equilibrium. Of course, the feet also manipulate the pedals. No discussion of the anatomy is complete without mention of the neck and head. However, their roles are negligible in piano playing, except that the head does all the thinking!

This list constitutes a complete inventory of the components used in piano playing and of all their possible motions. It shows that the number of ingredients is remarkably limited. However, with these motions and their combinations we can meet all pianistic demands.

They form the basic ingredients of our technique; we must know them and we must master them. The syntax of our technical language is composed of the various motion patterns that evolve from these motion components. We will combine them into synchronized activities of the fingers, hand, and arm. By understanding the basic motions clearly, how they are executed and what equipment is to be utilized, we can spot any malfunction and correct it immediately.

Curved lines result in straight vertical lines.

We have referred previously to the curved paths of every component and to the need of manipulating them in a manner that they result in a straight vertical line of the fingertip when landing on the keys. This is the optimal transference of speed to the vertically moving keys and hammers.

If we want the fingertips to descend in a straight vertical line, we must activate the upper arm. The fingers, hand, and forearm must be lifted with a simultaneous forward motion of the upper arm; when these components descend, we let the upper arm move back to its original position. The ultimate result of the four slight curves (finger, hand, forearm, and upper arm) will be a completely straight line at the fingertips, if the upper arm doesn't move too little or too much.

Figures 12 and 13 show the results of insufficient and excessive

Figure 12. Curved descent of the fingertip. When the upper arm is immobile, the path traced by the fingertip is a curve.

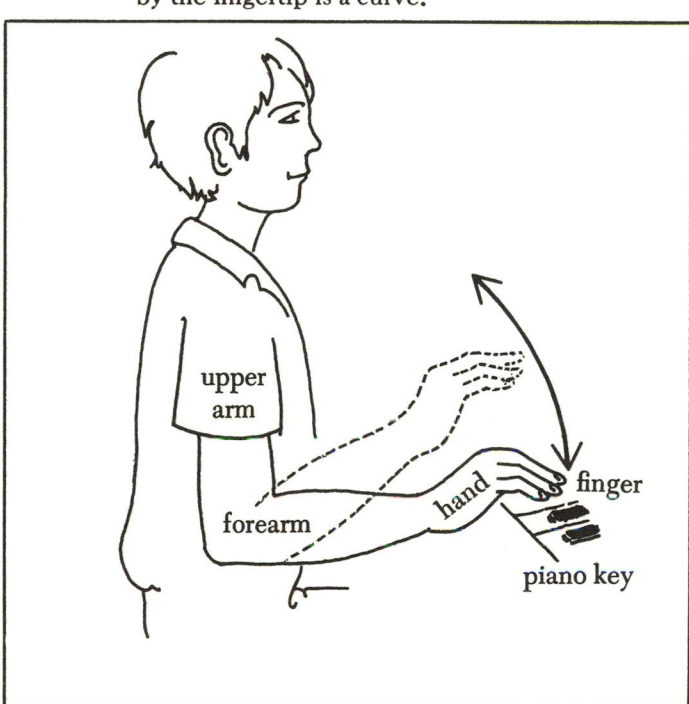

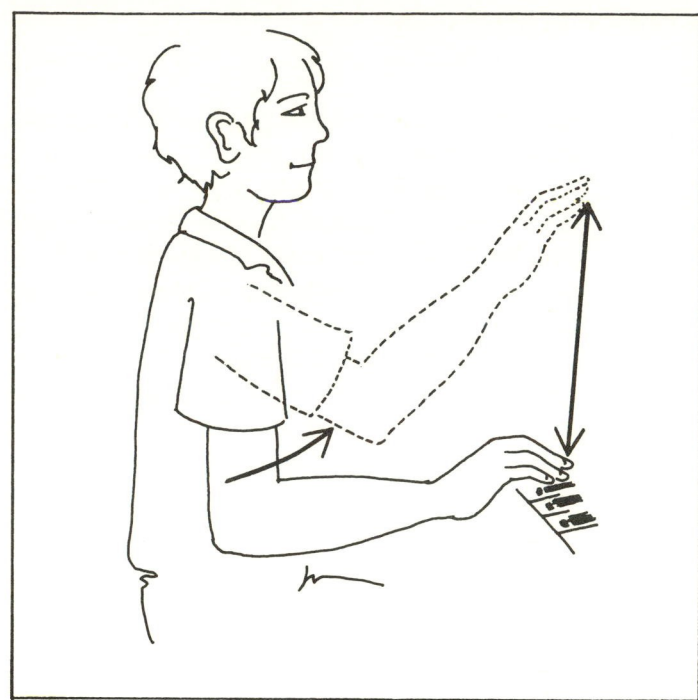

Figure 13. Slanted descent of the fingertip caused by excessive upper-arm motion

Figure 14. Vertical descent of the fingertip is the result of correct upper-arm participation

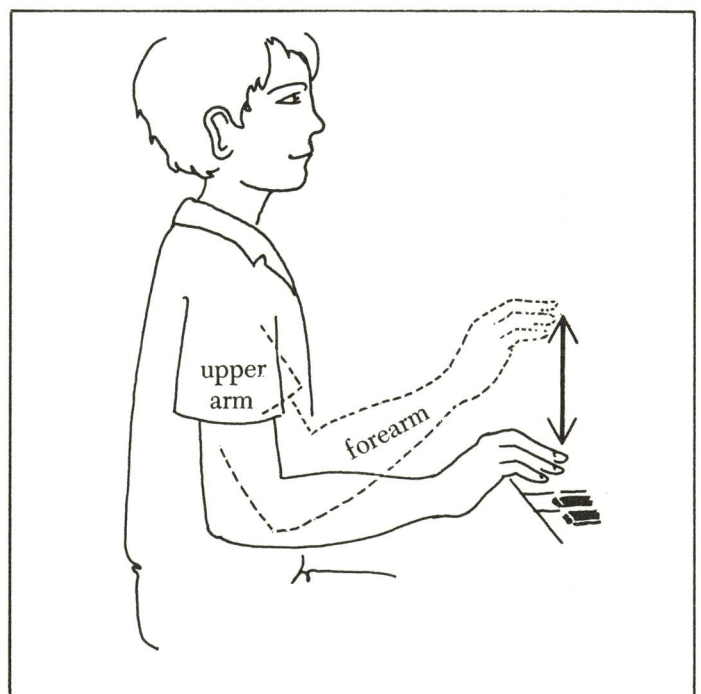

upper-arm participation; figure 14 shows the correct position of the upper arm.

Once again I must warn you against extreme positions. Overly raised fingers, straight fingers, overly curved fingers, extremely low and high wrists, extremely bent hands (in or out), pulled-in elbows, and stretched arms should all be avoided. All of these positions cause trouble.

Intense music, tense muscles

Sometimes it is the emotional intensity of the music that causes tense muscles. We should try to temper this condition. Today, more than ever, audiences mistake the excessively tense muscular activities of the performer for an intense musical experience, and all too often we see the public impressed and awed by convulsive contortions and spastic gyrations. What is worse than that is that these excesses are often inflicted on the unsuspecting audiences quite incongruously, when the music happens to be lyrical, serene, and gentle. One should indeed distinguish between purposeful and overcharged muscular activities.

The shoulder

The shoulder's main role is to lift the arm and to carry, guide, and control its weight. As a rule, the shoulder is not supposed to move much, and as a result of this, a feeling of strain may be experienced. To remedy this, all one has to do is to move it slightly, either circularly or toward the opposite position in which it was before. Even the shoulder, chest, and back muscles need relief, strong as they may be. Since it is the shoulder that carries the full weight of the arm continuously, it should rest occasionally; this happens during the free fall of the arm, when gravity takes over and when the arm drops close to the body. Sometimes a deep breath brings all the relief it needs. All in all, the shoulder has sufficient opportunities to rest temporarily and there is no need for it to tire.

Interplay between the shoulder and the fingers ("feelers")

Actually there is a continuous interplay that occurs between the shoulder and the fingertips. The power (or weight in motion) of the whole arm can be either completely held by the shoulder or fully transferred to the fingertips (beware of that!), or it can be partially held and partially transferred. The extremely sensitive tactile nerve endings on the fingertips regulate this activity by sending messages through the nervous system. It is because of this acute sensitivity of the fingertips that so many pianists enjoy staying in continuous contact with the keys, practically never abandoning them. They continuously "feel" the keys, and this physical stimulation by the surface of the keys helps them to generate more intensity in their feelings. Unfortunately there is a drawback to this habit: because the fingertips are touching the surface of the keys, they are unable to generate the speed that is possible when they are at a distance from the keys and allowed to fall. Their weight is not exploited because they cannot be moved by the force of gravity: they are already on the keys! The tone quality of the "touching fingers" is never harsh, of course, but the volume is insufficient unless one adds big swinging arm motions, which may then disrupt the musical phrasing.

Let me warn you against transferring the full weight of the arm to the fingers for an extended period of time. The transfer of weight to the fingers should be instantaneous, and the shoulder should immediately resume carrying the full weight of the arm in order to avoid excessive strain on the fingers. It is simply too much for the fingers to carry the full weight of the arm, and it is harmful to get used to applying pressure on the keys.

The torso

We can greatly benefit from the positive participation of the rest of the torso and its powerful muscles, one that is a purposeful and not an inhibitive participation. By the latter I mean that the body muscles may tense up, immobilize the performer and let his arms alone to do all the work. Sometimes not even the arms work, only the hands, while the rest of the equipment is immobilized and is fighting itself. The constructive role of the body muscles is to accommodate the arms while helping to keep the body in a mobile but secure condition.

Excessive body motion

Excessive body motion, the opposite of this immobility, is not commendable either, but at least it seldom causes exhaustion or tension, only puzzling vistas and sounds, to say the least.

Chest and back muscles

The chest muscles, which execute all downward and inward motions of the arms, are very helpful in certain kinds of chord playing. Of course, there are other groups of muscles involved in these motions too. Some back muscles are active in lifting the arms and the shoulders, others in pulling them down and they enable the body to lean backward and sideways.

The diaphragm

One of our most important muscles is the diaphragm. Because this muscle is totally hidden, many of us are unaware of its role, but it is crucial because it also regulates our breathing. When it becomes tense and rigid, this muscle (that practically divides the human body in two halves) keeps the lungs from expanding properly, and it can cause a sensation of utter discomfort and tension. When the lungs cannot function freely, breathing becomes faster and shorter in order to supply all the oxygen needed. During a performance the pianist needs more oxygen than usual because his body functions are accelerated and increased. Therefore the effects of a tense diaphragm and lungs can be quite disturbing. Needless to say, this impaired breathing has a harmful effect on the musical phrasing that becomes hectic and hasty. Unfortunately, the more tense the muscles get, the tighter the diaphragm will be. The closest connecting link between the performing apparatus and music itself is the breathing, which guides and controls both the phrasing and the pace of muscular activities. If inner tension can cause rigidity in the diaphragm, so can a faulty and tense technique; one trouble feeds on the other. A deep breath sometimes helps; it presses the diaphragm down and lets it expand so that normal breathing can be reestablished. If the playing mechanism recovers, and its respiratory system is not handicapped by continuous tension in either the diaphragm or other muscles, we have the setting for proper music making. By the way, one of the most familiar symptoms of stage fright is a tense, tight diaphragm that inhibits the entire body and spirit. Try a few deep breaths; they will help the diaphragm return to normal functioning.

Sitting

When we examine the correct way to sit at the piano we have to deal with two sets of factors: with the constant and with the variable. The constants include the size and shape of the piano and the height of the keyboard. The variables include all the things that relate to the performer. Not only his height and weight, but the infinite diversity within the proportions of his anatomy vary tremendously. The shape and size of his fingers, hands, forearm, arm, torso—all these influence the ideal sitting position. Even if two people of exactly the same height use a piano bench, its height may have to be changed. Even though two people may be the same height, if the lengths of their upper arms or the lengths of their torsos differ, their hands and fingers will be in a different position. Obviously there is no one way to sit at the piano; that is why adjustable benches had to be invented.

Stability, mobility

Instead of setting up rules, I would like to offer certain principles for consideration. In maintaining our balance at the piano, we seek both stability and mobility; we also seek minimum effort in maintaining balance at the piano. By *stability* I mean a position that enables us to sit comfortably, and by *mobility* I mean a position that enables us to move freely and effortlessly all over the keyboard. Most of the body weight rests on the bench, but some of it is supported by the feet, especially when the body is in motion. Whenever our hands or arms are in motion, the balance of the body changes, even though the change is very slight. The body assists the arms and hands and brings them to the position where they can act to their best advantage.

Equilibrium

This means, of course, that there is a continuous change of equilibrium. Most of the time the change is minimal or even invisible, but unless we move slightly, we will be off balance. An off-balance body position causes a certain tension in both the torso and the limbs. As I have said before many times, any fixed position is caused by and causes tension. But a change of position practically guarantees relief in the contracted muscles. The real reason why we always seek equilibrium is that we can remain in that position with the minimum effort. With any shift our balance changes and needs to be reestablished by a compensating shift of other components of the body. Total immobility is uncalled for, since there is no music without motion, and where there is motion, there will be a change of equilibrium. We will sit at the piano in a mobile manner, moving continuously but never in excess. Energy is wasted both through tension (in order to maintain a fixed position) and through moving too much. We have to maintain equilibrium, however, whether we are sitting still or in motion.

No uniform sitting position

No two pianists look alike at the piano. If we observe Horowitz's supereconomical ways of keeping anchored but mobile while performing the most hair-raising feats of virtuosity or watch Richter undulating continuously while he plays the simplest melodies, we find only one thing in common—their uncanny sense of balance and coordination. They sit and move completely differently, but at the same time each pianist takes the best advantage of his constitution and reflexes.

The feet

When we move from one extreme of the piano to the other, our feet can help to balance these motions of the body either by moving one foot in the opposite direction or by turning the other heel in the direction the body is leaning, thereby supporting it more effectively.

White and black keys

When you move from the white keys to the black keys, it is necessary to lean slightly forward and to raise the elbow (upper arm) so as to bring the wrist and fingers to an identical or very similar position to that used in playing on white keys. There is no reason why one should be uncomfortable when playing on the black keys, even though the

Figure 15. Leaning backward

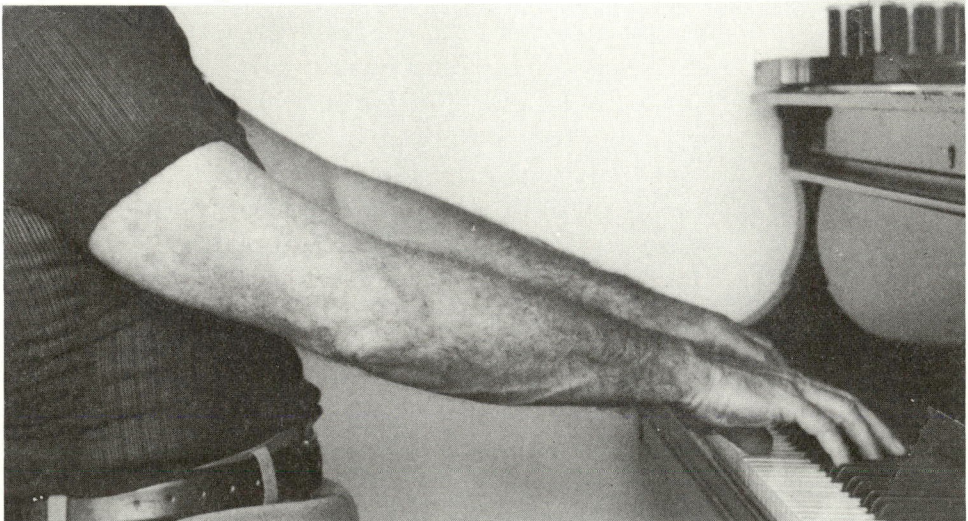

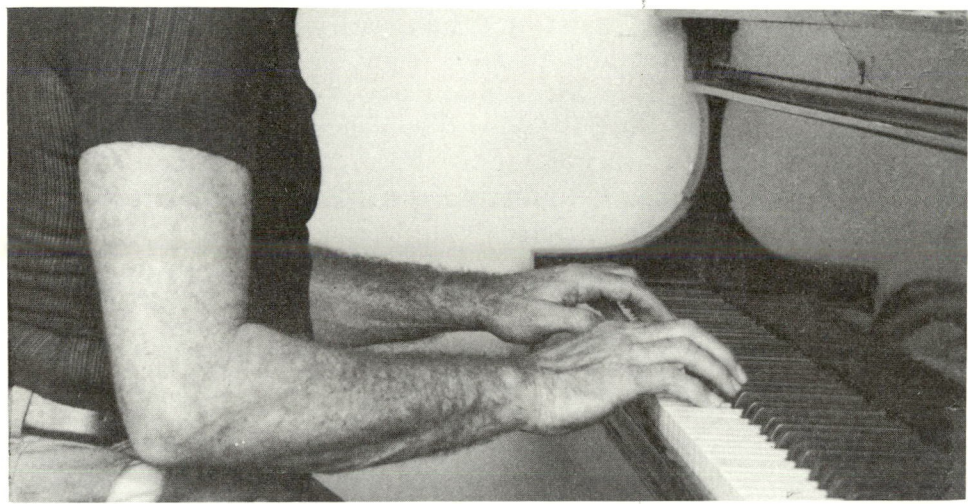

Figure 16. Leaning forward

keys are narrower. By raising the elbow the wrist has room to move up and down. When we alternate black and white key positions continuously, the body may assume a "central" position between the two extremes. However a continuous and slight change of position of the body is always beneficial; it helps one to keep the "tone" of the muscles alive and lets us breathe freely.

The bench   Every pianist should set the height of the bench and its distance from the piano to his own liking. As long as the playing is comfortable and not handicapped, the position is right. Quite a number of excellent pianists choose to sit extremely low, and they are nonetheless able to transfer all the necessary power and skill to the keyboard. The same is true for those who sit unusually high. There seems to be a generally accepted rule that the forearm ought to be completely horizontal and on the same level as the keys, but even this simple rule is not valid for every pianist. For instance, if the upper arm is extremely short, it is preferable to have the forearm at a slight angle to the keys, but if the upper arm is long, it may bring the elbow (forearm) to a low position. We have only to accept one ground rule—that of convenience and ease. When we practice pieces like the Chopin *Etudes*, opus 10 no. 1 and opus 25 no. 12, where most of the main notes of the melody and the bass are on the far left side of the keyboard, we will be more comfortable if we consider moving the bench a bit to the left of the center of the keyboard. It will be easier to lean to the far right and forward from this secure position rather than to be seated in the central position and to be continually off balance while weaving to the right and the left. Since the left foot does not have to be on the left pedal, it can conveniently be placed in positions where it can support and balance the body.

Ease and comfort have priority over everything else because unless the body is well balanced and supported, the diaphragm and other body muscles must tense up; tension in these muscles affects our breathing and technique, and while this handicap is hardly visible, it certainly takes its toll. During the countless hours that we spend practicing, any unnecessary activity adds up to a formidable expenditure of precious energy. We must be adamant in avoiding and correcting this pitfall of tensing up our muscles. Furthermore, continuous inner muscular tension is quite habit forming and damaging.

PART TWO

Basic Technical Patterns

All human
motions can be
systematized.

Part Two of this book presents a set of technical, or motion, patterns that are fundamental to piano playing. They are comprehensive in the sense that these patterns and their combinations serve as technical solutions to any and all pianistic writing. It may seem pretentious to claim that a few technical formulas will answer any pianistic problems, but, in the final analysis, it is possible to reduce and condense any and all movements of the human body into a very limited number of motion patterns. If Linnaeus and Darwin were capable of organizing the entire flora and fauna of the earth into clearly definable groups, we might manage to do something similar with the seemingly endless variety of human motions and gestures. The types of motions will be classified according to which part or parts of anatomy are involved and in what manner. Then we need to establish the best, most economical and expressive ways to execute these motions. Then we must assimilate them (practicing) and employ them in their proper contexts (interpretation). Simple, isn't it? Well, it's not that easy since technical difficulties such as speed, accuracy, and control still do exist, and matters of interpretation are, fortunately, wide open to different tastes and approaches. However, technical problems as such must be resolved unequivocally since the basic motion patterns and their combinations do provide solutions.

Therefore my aim is, first, to define these motion patterns; second, to describe their execution; and, finally, to point out where, when, and how they are to be employed. Since technical and musical patterns are definitely correlated, in that technical patterns should correspond to and express the music, the musical text will tell us with surprising clarity which technical pattern to employ. In a broader sense, correct reading of music includes identifying not only the notes to be played but also the corresponding technical solutions. This is the case in any style of music from Bach to Bartók.

4 Free Fall

Two sources of
energy: gravity
and our own
muscular system

The first and most available source of energy we can draw from is the force of gravity. Its presence is universal; it exists wherever matter is present. It influences all matter. Anything that is free to move moves toward the center of the earth. It is not that we are preoccupied with every aspect of this centripetal force, but it is a force that we must consider whenever we deal with anything that moves. Because it turns mass into weight, we are obliged to think of it whether we build a house, fly a plane, or play the piano. Since technique is organized motion and motions are our concern here, we recognize this inexhaustible source of energy; we try to tap it whenever possible, and put it to our own use. Since it is ever present, it is futile to ignore it: we might as well cooperate with it and save our own energy wherever possible.

The other source of energy is our own muscular system. As I stated earlier, the list ends here. There are no other physical sources of energy available to us. The force of gravity and our muscles will accomplish anything we require. Most of the time we combine the two, but it is obvious that it is more economical to utilize the force of gravity whenever possible and save our own energy. One exception to this principle is the *thrust* (see chapter eight).

Finger
technique vs.
Breithaupt's
weight
technique

In effect, the so-called modern school of piano playing was initiated by Rudolf Breithaupt when he published his book *Die Grundlage der natürliche Klaviertechnik* ("Natural Piano Technique"), whose first edition appeared in 1905. This work gave great and sometimes excessive importance to the role of relaxation and of weight in reaction against the old schools, which used and abused "finger technique." There was a need for new ideas because it was evident that the modern piano could not be mastered by sheer muscular force and especially not by the relatively weak forearm muscles that move the fingers. Breithaupt's technical terminology spread rapidly, but it was employed in a rather confused and confusing way.

Not more
weight but
longer leverage
for more sound

Breithaupt advocated the substitution of force by weight; in his view the volume of sound produced is in proportion to the quantity of weight employed: more weight, more sound. However, the volume of sound depends exclusively on the speed with which the hammer hits the strings, regardless of weight that generates that speed. To achieve this speed the muscles and the force of gravity combine in a way that activates the arms, hands, and fingers; they in turn transfer this speed to the keys and hammers. Whether the speed is generated by a small or a large weight is immaterial: the fact is that the rate of acceleration produced by the force of gravity is exactly the same whether the weight is small or large. (The factor of air resistance is negligible in this situation.) Therefore it is more economical to use as little weight as possible. The notion that the full weight of the arm produces more sound than a lighter weight is erroneous: the fact is that the activation of a longer lever generates more speed than a shorter one and therefore we add the upper arm to the forearm. The activation of the whole arm serves to increase the speed of the fingertips in a whiplike action. *We should not equate great tonal volume with a larger weight but rather with the speed that a longer lever can generate.* Ideally we should combine minimal weight and maximal leverage for extreme speed; we can increase the acceleration that is brought about by the force of gravity by using a slight muscular activity (throw) in an elongated arm. One might be tempted to rename weight technique as "speed technique."

Figure 17. Arm ready to fall

When describing the motion and technique of the *free fall*, let us bear in mind that although the force of gravity does most of the work, gravity is active in only one phase of the motion. Before the arm drops, it must be lifted actively by muscles, and at the moment when it lands on the keys, the impact is transferred and cushioned by an instantaneous muscular contraction. Therefore total relaxation occurs only between these two stages—between lifting and landing—during the

Figure 18. Arm landing: wrist assumes its lowest position and will rebound instantaneously as shown in Figure 19

Figure 19. Wrist rebounding

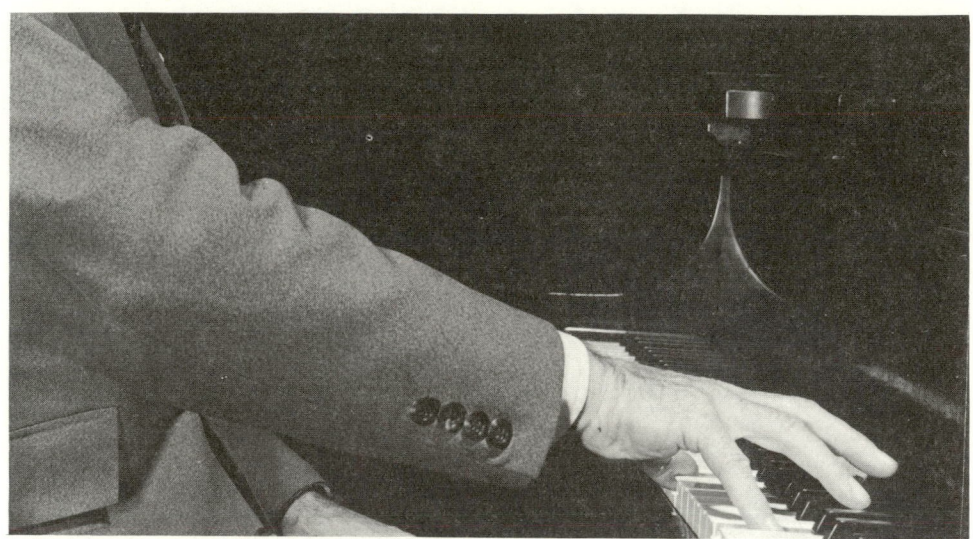

Figure 20. Successive raising of the upper arm, wrist, and hand

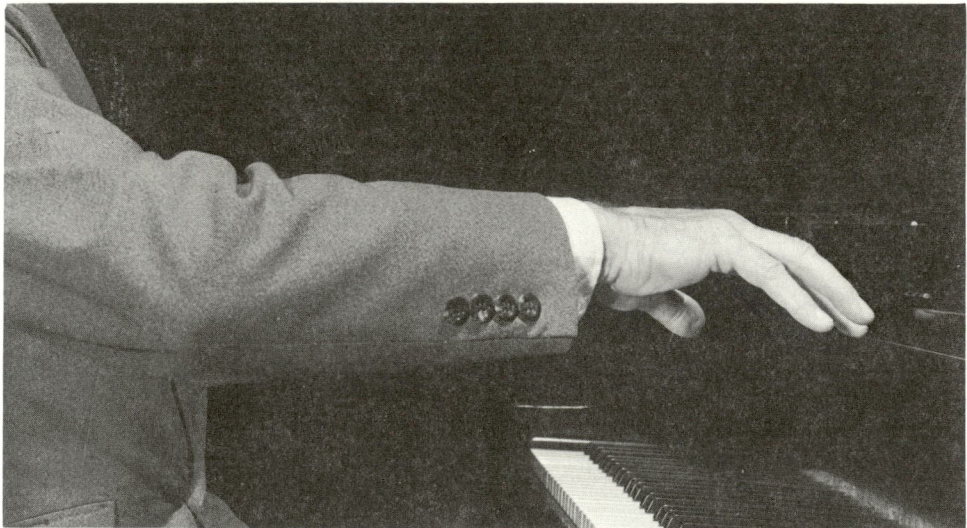

Figure 21. Position before fall: note far-out position of elbow. The upper arm must
assume position closer to body (Figure 22) before falling.

short time the arm is falling. I mention this to point out that even the
action that is most dependent on gravity, the free fall, is not a totally
relaxed activity. It is only when the fingers, hands, and arm have been
lifted and set in the proper position for falling that we let go and let
the force of gravity take over. We must learn not to interfere with the
acceleration by slowing it down or increasing it with a throw. We must
acquire the ability to let any part (or parts) of the arm fall freely as
though it were an object that didn't belong to us. In other words, we

Figure 22. Arm ready to fall again

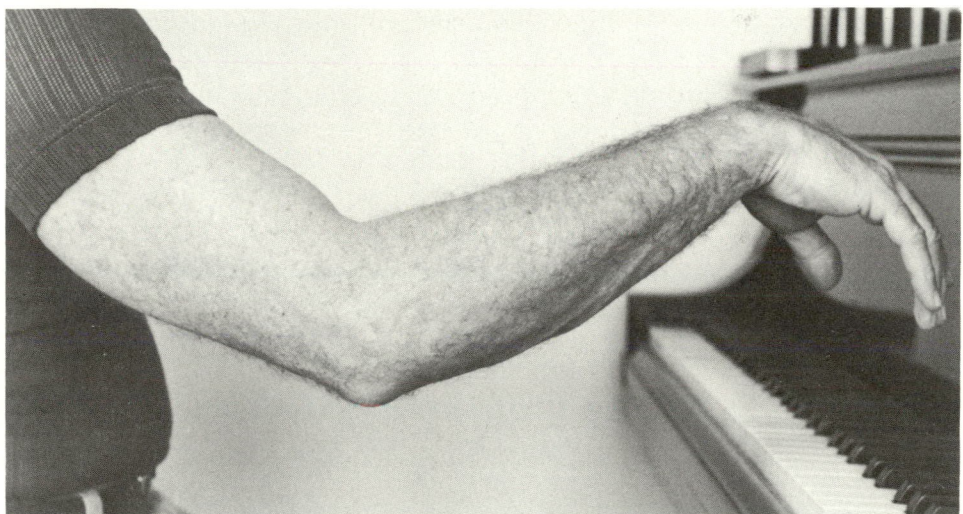

Figure 23. Wrong position for the wrist before free fall; wrist should be low

must be able to let the sheer force of gravity act upon it. We can practice this motion with the fingers alone, with the hand, the forearm, and the upper arm and then combine them in any way. As said before, the longer the equipment we use, the greater the speed we can generate.

Three stages of free fall—first stage: lifting

The free-fall motion consists of three stages. The first stage of the free fall is the lifting of the equipment. As always we strive for the least expenditure of energy. Therefore we initiate the upward motion with a slight upper-arm movement; this is immediately followed by the upward motion of the forearm, which in turn raises the hand and the fingers. It is not a simultaneous motion but a successive one. When ready to fall, the distance from the keys to the fingertips is approximately ten inches; at this point the elbow should be slightly lowered so that the fall of the wrist and fingertips will be completely vertical (see figures 17 through 22). It is very important to have the entire arm and hand completely immobile before the drop starts so as not to interfere with the force of gravity either by increasing the acceleration or by decreasing it. Please note the slightly curved position of the fingers and wrist; this position insures that at the moment of landing all the joints will be able to cushion elastically and transfer the energy to the keys correctly. Every one of the joints—the two joints between the phalanxes of the finger, the knuckle, the wrist, and, to a lesser extent, the elbow and shoulder joints—has a share in regulating the energy transference. The quality of the sound—its fullness, harshness, or weakness—depends on the degree to which the joints have been fixed. If they are loose, hardly any sound will come through; if they are rigid and stiff, we get a harsh, *martellato* sound. The joints must be resilient and firm, and they should be fixed only at the instant the finger depresses the key. While the lifting is a successive motion, the falling and landing is simultaneous for all the elements involved.

Second stage: drop

In the second stage, the arm, hand, and fingers fall at the same time. While the lifting was done by *active* muscles, this stage is completely passive, and there should be no interference with the acceleration caused by the force of gravity. During the fraction of a second that the equipment is falling, we are totally relaxed—yes, this is the time to relax.

Third stage: landing, rebound

Now comes the third stage—the landing. At this point there is a slight, instantaneous fixation in all the respective joints. This fixation causes the transference of energy into the keys and a slight rebound of the hand and fingers, and, notably, of the wrist. It is essential that this fixation be instantaneous, not extended, and that there be no sensation of continuous pressure in the fingertips. On the contrary, the moment the rebound of the hand takes place, the shoulder muscles begin to raise the upper arm (bringing it back to stage one), thereby relieving any extended pressure on the fingertips. During most of the lifting, the fingertips remain on the keys, since we don't want a staccato or an abrupt ending to the sound. Also we want a complete change of position in every joint after the sudden impact (and fixation of joints) at landing. If we use this sequence of motions, there will be an easy, flexible upward motion in the whole arm, and we will be ready for the next free fall. Our movement fits in with one of our basic principles—the avoidance of any prolongation of any fixed position. A very important detail to watch out for is that the wrist must be in a relatively low position at landing so that it can cushion naturally. If the wrist is high and loose, it will have an excessive "dead" run downward; if it is put in a fixed position, we get a harsh, hard sound. If the wrist is high, it will not be able to cushion properly (see figure 23).

White keys, black keys

The free-fall movement may be used on single notes, intervals, and chords, and ought to be practiced accordingly. When the arm drops on black keys, it is essential to assume a slightly higher arm position so that when the fingers land on the keys, the wrist has enough room to cushion and to rebound, just as when the fingers land on white keys. Unless we raise the upper arm (not the shoulder), the wrist won't have the needed extra space. The "feel" in the hands and fingers should be the same on the black keys as it is on the white keys.

Distance

Every pianist should determine for himself or herself the point from which the arm should fall. If we are too near the keys, the arm cannot accelerate enough; if we're too far away, we'll crash on the keys and may miss the key we're aiming at entirely. We must be sure that none of the components are in an extremely contracted or stretched position, that none of the knuckles stick out or collapse, and that the wrist is neither too high nor too low.

No exaggeration

I am afraid that this warning will have to be repeated many times, since we must try to avoid any excesses and exaggerations throughout our pianistic activities. Often one hears that, while practicing, one must exaggerate the "right" motion, but how can one exaggerate balance, equilibrium, effortless playing, and proper placing of the equipment?

When to use free fall

Gravity works on its own terms and unless enough time and distance are given for acceleration, insufficient speed will be generated

Figure 24. General position of arm when playing on white keys

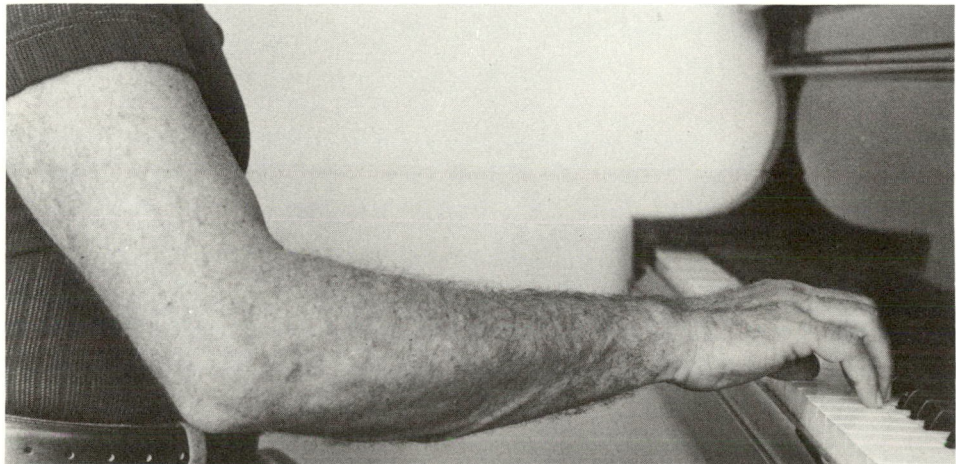

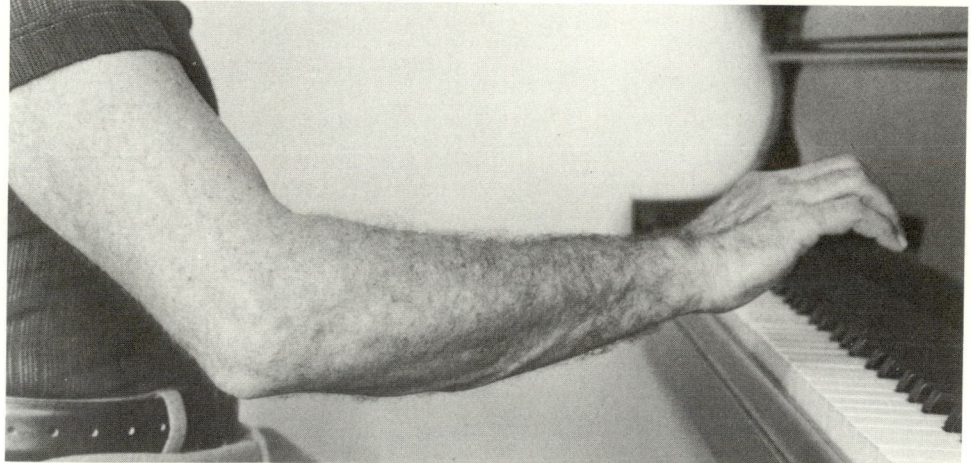

Figure 25. Raising the arm and hand over white keys

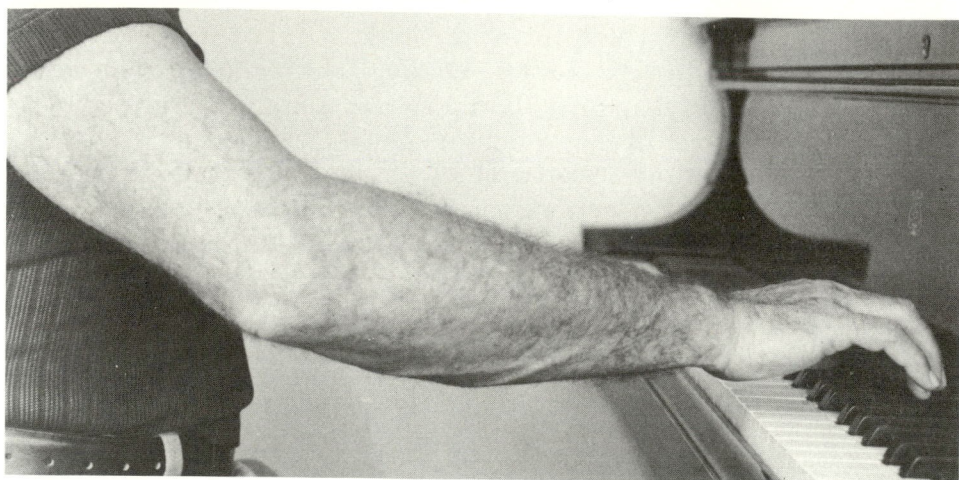

Figure 26. General position of arm when playing on black keys

Figure 27. Raising the arm and hand over black keys

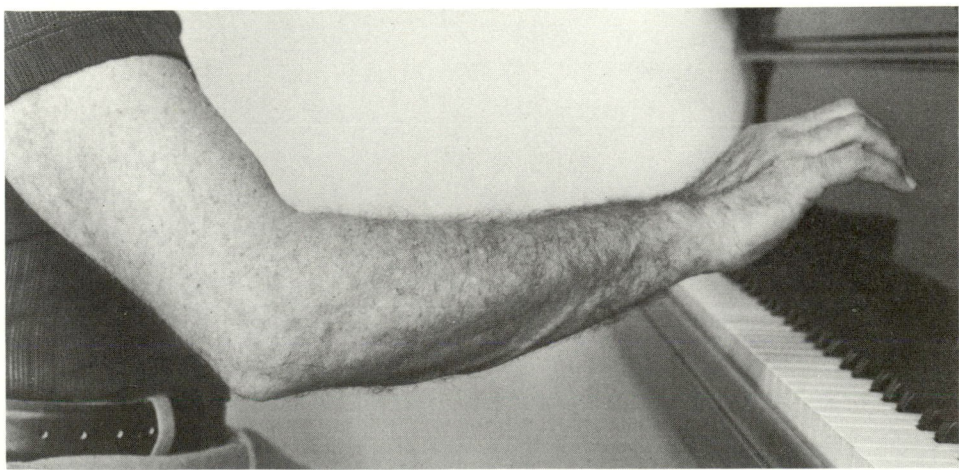

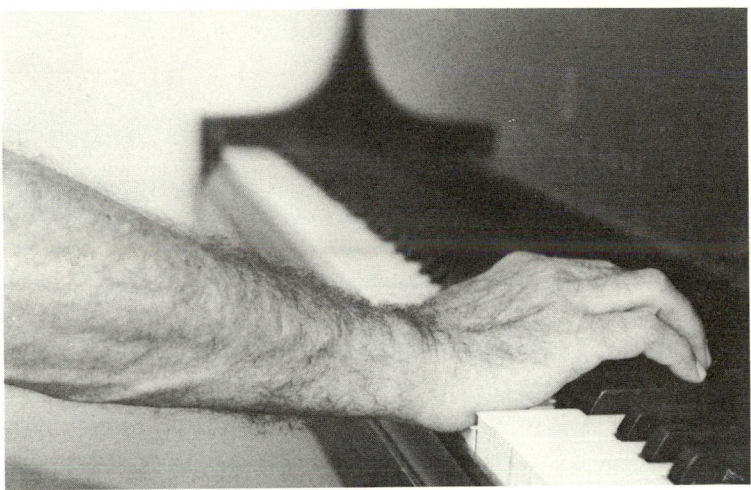

Figure 28. The palm touches the keys when the upper arm is not raised enough for free fall on black keys (wrong position).

in free fall without the addition of a throw. Therefore we can only employ free fall in passages in moderate tempo. Nothing can "drop" fast! For instance, the left hand of the Chopin *Etude*, opus 10 no. 1 and the opening of the Tchaikovsky *Piano Concerto No. 1* are ideal spots for free fall. However free fall is not very practical for chords that require a wide reach because the stretched hand that is needed for these chords tends to alter the acceleration of the falling hand. Here we had better use another type of motion—the *thrust* (for a full discussion of this motion see chapter eight).

In free fall we utilize the force of gravity alone (only in the falling stage, of course). In other situations we may use it only partially. But first we must master it in its original, unaltered form—a premise that is true of any of the basic patterns we are going to investigate. Only after we have clearly understood and assimilated these motions will we be successful in varying and combining them. Before we play these patterns quickly, we should practice and master the motions in slow tempo in their purest form. In fast playing almost everything looks alike; the motions become small, and all we can see are tiny, blurred finger movements very near the keys or rapid tremolo-like activities. These blurs are all reductions or distillations of the larger, well-defined movements we have described. Considerable patience is required in slow practicing, since our attention must be divided among all the participating components at all times; there are at least four components—the fingers, hand, forearm, and upper arm—that we should be aware of at all times. This slow beginning should bring good results; once the ingredients are in good shape and function well, our natural coordination easily synchronizes the motions, and they become second nature.

Guidelines for
free fall

Here are a few guidelines for the free fall:

1. The shoulder should not participate actively in the free fall. It should not move; it merely holds and releases the arm.
2. The upper arm must be active; the forearm should not act alone since full impact will result only in conjunction with the upper arm.
3. Don't sit too near the piano or too far away from it; the correct position is the one in which the fingertips fall completely vertical with the fingers slightly curved.
4. The head and body should not participate actively in the motion; they are immobile during the free fall.
5. Do not slide your fingers on the keys after they have landed—and certainly not while they are landing. In stage one the fingers should be brought up vertically by the combined upper arm, forearm, and hand motion.
6. There should be no pressure on the keys after the instantaneous impact nor while the fingers are in process of being lifted by the upper arm. Simply hold the key down with a minimum amount of weight until you abandon it. The shoulder will carry the full weight of the arm during lifting.
7. The joints of the fingers and wrist should be elastic, neither stiff nor loose.
8. Avoid supination (see forearm rotation, p. 79) of the forearm while raising it.
9. Differentiate between white and black key position by changing upper arm level.
10. It is most important that you do not influence the speed generated by the force of gravity, either by acceleration or by slowing down.
11. Since the fingertips have to move up and down in a perfectly vertical line, be sure that you observe the proper ratio of motion for the hand, forearm, and upper arm. Too much forearm motion raises the fingers in the shape of an arch away from the piano; too much upper-arm motion brings them too far forward. Also make sure that the fingers are lifted no more than about ten inches from the keys.
12. Lifting the arm is a successive, not a simultaneous, motion of the equipment, while dropping is synchronized.

There is no question that the piano's biggest sonorities can be achieved by the free-fall motion. The force of gravity does most of the work, and the rate of acceleration of any falling body is the same, regardless of its weight. Therefore the size, weight, and strength of the performer are of no consequence. All we have to do is to raise the arm to the proper position where the force of gravity can act on it in the best possible way—and let go! Another equally effective but quite different way to produce big sonorities is described in the chapter on thrust (chapter eight). In this gesture we put to use the largest and strongest muscles of the body and arm. The thrust is also totally effortless. If the right coordination of the entire body is achieved, the tiniest or frailest person can develop a powerful sound and technique—without a trace of forcing and without any muscle-building exercises.

As I mentioned earlier, many of the greatest piano virtuosos (Hofmann, Godowsky, Friedman, Schnabel, Bartók, and de Larrocha, for example) were and are of small stature. All of them produced powerful sonorities at will. It is also true that there were and are many tall or heavy-set pianists (Gieseking, Bachauer, Johannesen, Cliburn, Rachmaninoff), and they all had superb coordination, a highly refined sense of tone production based on a total lack of forcing, and a wonderful ear and tactile sense that enabled them to manipulate every gradation of weight, speed, and energy and to bring out the best of the piano and of themselves. If anything, one must guard against using too much power because of the limits of elasticity in the instrument. In the case of free fall, one must not drop the arm from too high a position, since its speed accelerates by its square per second under the pull of gravity.

Exercises for free fall

The following free-fall exercises are extremely simple; they enable us to exercise the required motions, but they do not induce us to practice mechanically.

Example 4. Sixth chords on white keys; play them hands separate and together

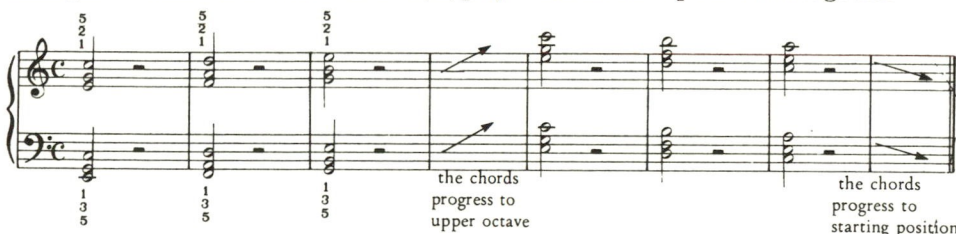

1. *Sixth chords on white keys, hands separate and together.* Practice the three distinct stages of the movement. Do not interfere with the force of gravity.

2. *Sixth chords on black keys, hands separate and together.* When you practice sixth chords on black keys, adjust the body and arm posi-

tion: *Lean* slightly forward; the wrist and fingers should be in same position as they are on the white keys.

Example 5. Chords on black keys; play them hands separate and together

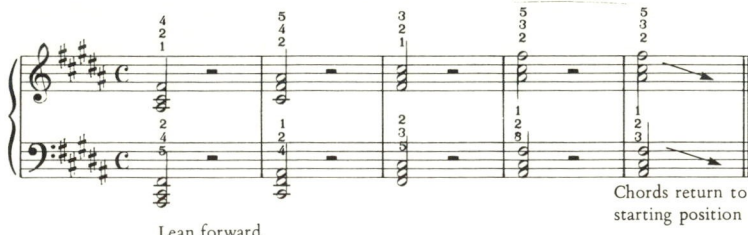

3. *One hand is on the white keys and the other is on the black keys, then vice versa.* The body turns slightly to adjust to the proper position. In example 6, the left shoulder moves slightly forward; in example 7, the right shoulder moves forward.

Example 6. Right hand on white keys; left hand on black keys; left shoulder slightly forward

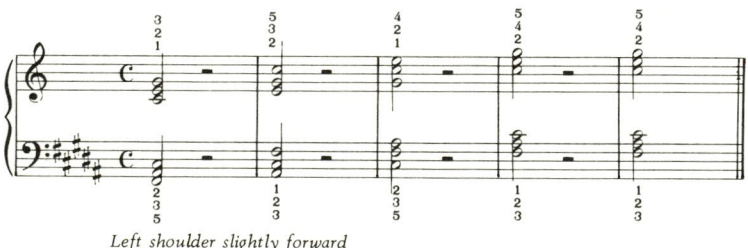

Example 7. Right hand on black keys; left hand on white keys; right shoulder slightly forward

Right shoulder slightly forward
Exercise of same pattern as previous examples (up and down)

4. Exercise both hands at central and extreme locations of the keyboard (on white and black keys), always adjusting the position of the body and arms.

5. In chords that contain a combination of white and black keys, adjust the arm and body to the most comfortable position. As you alter

the position of your upper arms, maintain the correct hand and wrist angles.

Example 8. Parallel shift of upper arms

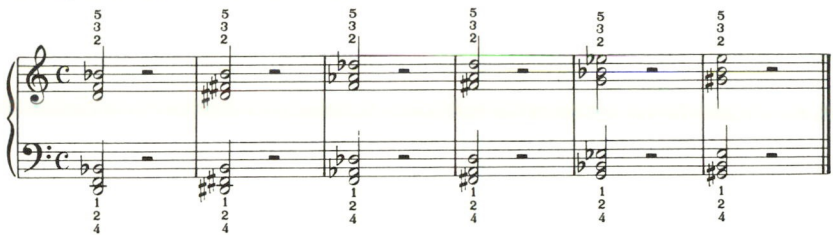

Parallel upper arms shift up, down, and sideways *(not wrist)*.

Example 9. Symmetrical shift of upper arms

Symmetrical upper arms shift up, down, and sideways *(not wrist)*.

6. This exercise may include any combination of white, black, and mixed chords. At the third stage (the landing) make sure that the wrist has ample room to cushion the impact and that it can bounce down and up from the keys with no interference.

After having mastered the free-fall motion on intervals smaller than the octave, we should achieve the same freedom and elasticity of joints with the extended fingers that octaves require. The main goal is to expose the hand freely to the force of gravity in an unhindered way and to place the whole playing apparatus in its optimal position. After the fingers leave the keys, the hands should assume their central positions.

7. At first practice octaves on white keys only and on black keys only, with the hands separate and the proper body adjustment; you should be aware of the three stages and all these instructions. Then practice them combined, using the same exercises given for sixths.

Examples for
free fall

The examples for the use of the free-fall motion are from the standard piano literature. I have indicated the points at which free fall is to be used by the symbol A. The motion of thrust is indicated by E (see chapter eight).

Symbols

A   *free fall*   E   thrust
B   five-fingers, scales, and arpeggios   ↓   low wrist
C   rotation   ↑   high wrist
D   staccato

Example 10. Chopin, *Etude*, opus 10 no. 1

Example 11. Bach, *Italian Concerto*, first movement

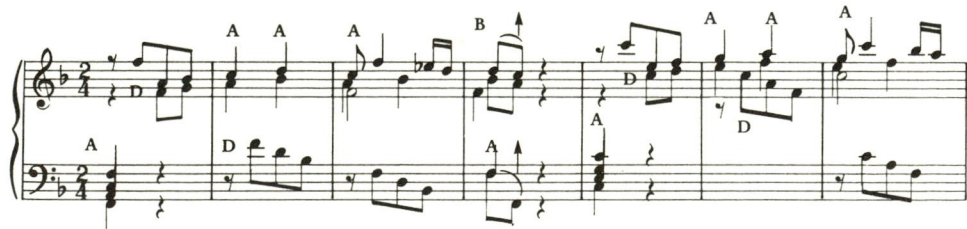

Example 12. Liszt, *Sonata in B Minor*

Example 13. Chopin, *Sonata in B Minor*, opus 58, fourth movement

Example 14. Chopin, *Sonata in B Flat Minor*, opus 35, first movement

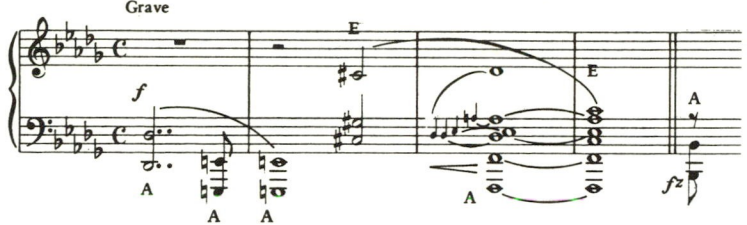

CHAPTER

5 Five-Fingers, Scales, and Arpeggios

Five-fingers,
scales,
arpeggios

In the free fall the role of the fingers was minimal; they acted mainly as a recoil mechanism. Now, however, we are going to examine the characteristics and functions of the fingers carefully. Their role is of foremost importance and they must be coordinated with, and helped by, the entire playing apparatus and the force of gravity. They are extremely important both in their active and passive roles because they are the "executors": they alone are in touch with the keys. Actually all our arm and body motions serve no other purpose than to help and to cooperate with the fingers.

Fingers:
extension of
forearm muscles

It is most important that we regard the fingers not as isolated units but as the extension and continuation of the forearm muscles and tendons that move them. I would like to make this point very clear: no finger exercise will ever give us true independence of the fingers unless each finger is helped by the proper placement and adjustment of the forearm and upper arm. True independence can be achieved only by cultivating *interdependence* with the forearm and upper arm muscles and not by maintaining a fixed hand (or wrist) position that brings the fingers into a forced, unnatural situation. In the long run these fixed positions will cause tension, fatigue, pain, and acute or chronic ailments. Worst of all, they produce a poor piano sound.

Adjustment of
arm for each
finger; flexible
wrist

Although the fingers are different in size, shape, and (in the case of the thumb) even in anatomy, we strive for evenness of sound in playing and practicing our scales and arpeggios. If we assume fixed hand and wrist positions and don't accommodate each one of the fingers, the unevenness of the fingers manifests itself in a most pronounced way: the short and thin fifth finger and the bulky, two-phalanxed thumb will never sound the same. We can force them to behave in a similar way, but we will have to keep on forcing them to do so all our life; they will never sound identically with a fixed wrist. Instead of a uniform, fixed hand position, the fingers need continuous adjusting motions by the wrist, the forearm, and the upper arm to accommodate the fingers and enable them to move freely, without hindrance and forcing, to produce the kind of motions that these components are capable of making.

Anatomy of the fingers; the thumb is different.

The thumb differs greatly from the other four fingers; it has only two phalanxes, while the others have three of them. It is the strongest and most agile finger; it can move alongside the hand and pass under the other fingers, and it is much more independent than the others. Its metacarpal bone is free from the other bones and is not tied to them by ligaments. The vertical motion of the other fingers originates where their first phalanx hinges on the metacarpal bone, but the thumb moves vertically from the point where its metacarpal bone is attached to the wrist (see figure 29).

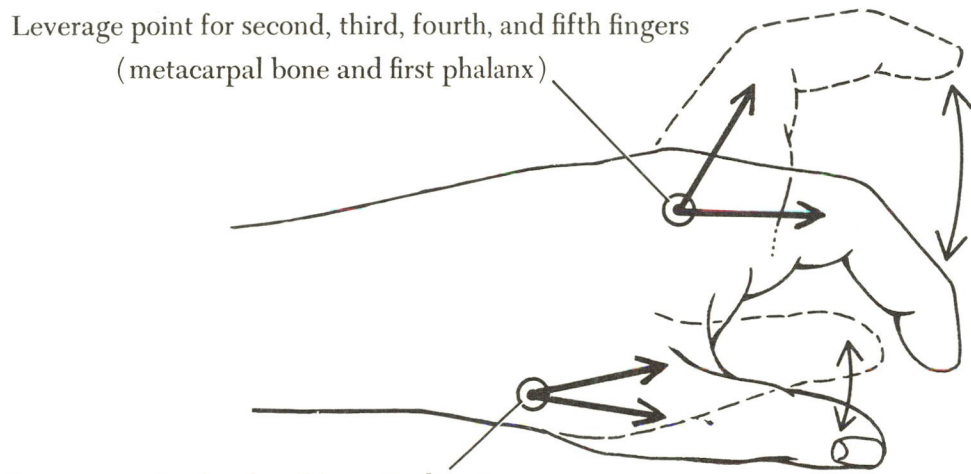

Leverage point for second, third, fourth, and fifth fingers (metacarpal bone and first phalanx)

Leverage point for thumb's vertical motion (from metacarpal bone and wrist)

Figure 29. Leverage points for the fingers

Always lower the wrist for the thumb.

The obvious consequence of this anatomical difference is that when the thumb moves vertically, it requires a different wrist position: the wrist must be placed considerably lower. If the wrist remained in the higher position suitable for the other fingers, the thumb's vertical motion would consist of an outward arch instead of a perpendicular one (see figures 30–33).

We must enable every one of the fingertips to descend vertically because the keys themselves move exclusively in a vertical direction. Therefore any diverted and slanted direction of the fingers toward the keys is uneconomical.

Horizontal adjusting motion

There are two equally indispensable adjusting motions of the arm and wrist that enable them to collaborate with each of the fingers; they are (1) movement in the vertical plane and (2) movement in the hori-

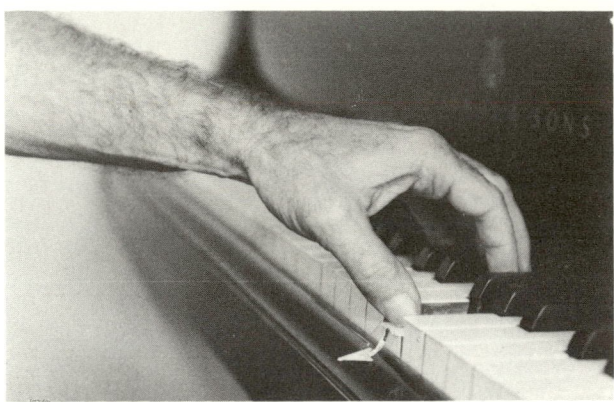

Figure 30. Wrist too high: thumb unable to move vertically

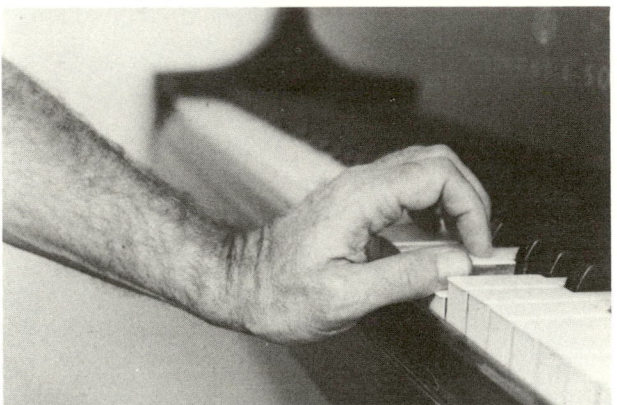

Figure 31. Wrist too low

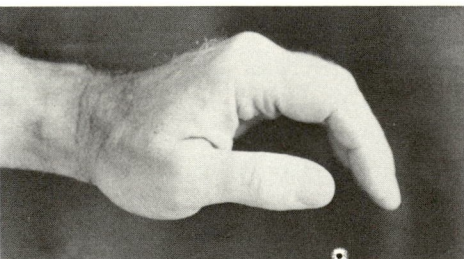

Figure 32. Low wrist enables thumb to move vertically

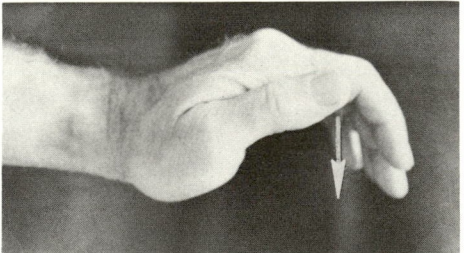

Figure 33. Thumb raised for vertical descent

zontal plane. Since we want to place the fingers in line with their respective forearm muscles (the flexors and extensors), there will be a slight lateral (or horizontal) change in the position of the wrist and forearm for each finger (see figure 34).

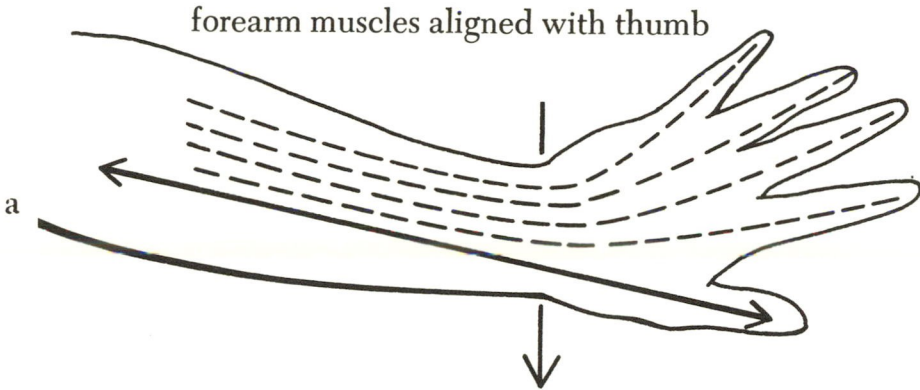

forearm muscles aligned with thumb

a

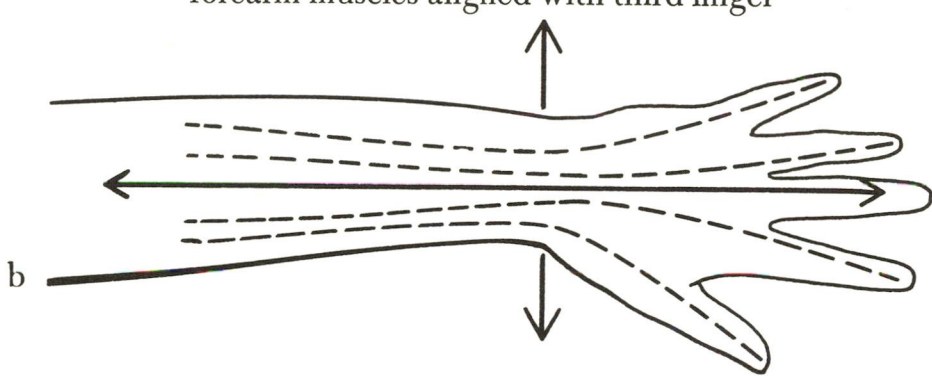

forearm muscles aligned with third finger

b

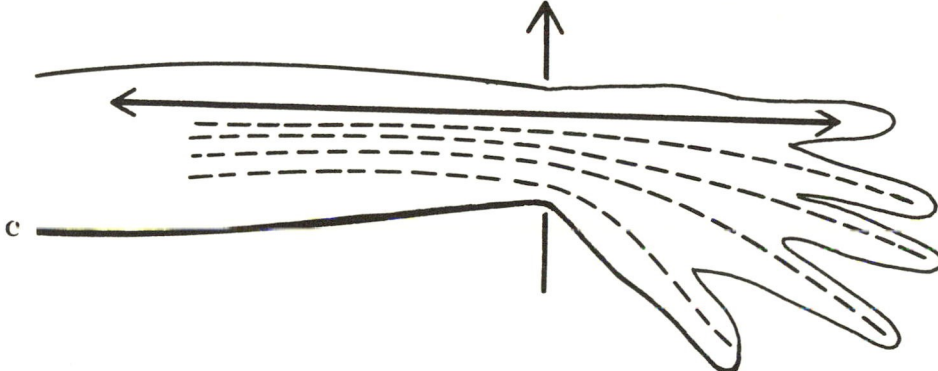

forearm muscles aligned with fifth finger

c

Figure 34. Horizontal alignment of forearm with (a) the thumb, (b) the third finger (and with 2–4 and 1–5 pairs of fingers), and (c) the fifth finger. The aligning and adjusting should be *continuous* and *exact*; overdoing it would put the finger out of line again!

Both the vertical and horizontal alignings (adjusting) should be continuous and precise: overdoing them would put the finger out of line again.

Figure 35 shows lateral views of the horizontally adjusted position for each finger. In figure 35e, the arm assumes the proper position for the fifth finger; that causes the thumb to find itself away from the keys, which is correct.

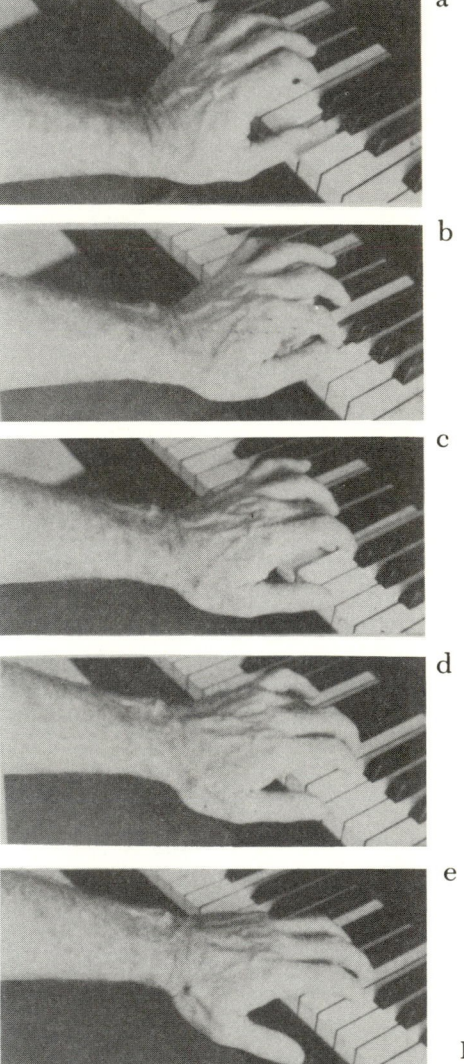

Figure 35. Lateral view of the horizontally adjusted position for each finger

Figure 36 provides an overhead view of these horizontally adjusted positions.

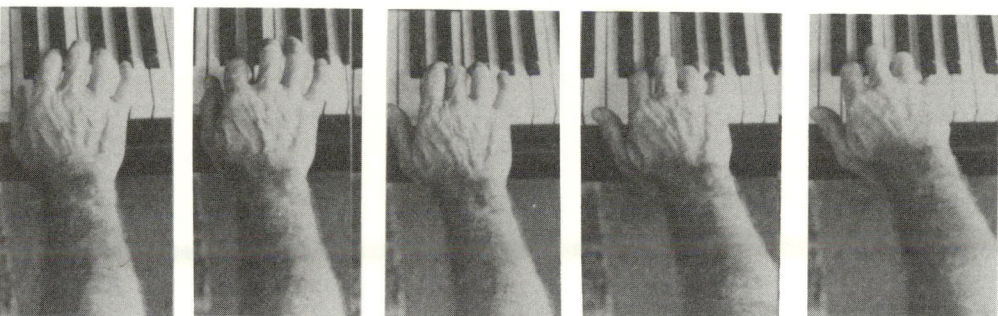

Figure 36. Overhead view of the horizontally adjusted position for each finger

Vertical adjusting motion

Whenever the thumb plays, the wrist should be lowered. When we proceed to the second finger we raise the wrist slightly, because the second finger's first phalanx and metacarpal bone join at a higher point than the place where the thumb's metacarpal bone and wrist meet. The thumb and the second finger can only execute their vertical motions from these points.* In the case of the third, fourth, and fifth fingers the wrist and forearm continue to rise, reaching their highest positions with the fifth finger. (Remember that a horizontal adjusting motion is also continuously occurring.) Both vertical and horizontal adjustments are essential, and the fingers should always be aligned with their respective higher or lower wrist positions with the thumb at the lowest point and the fifth finger at the highest. If both horizontal and vertical adjustments are accomplished, the fingers will be in their optimal positions.

Although we need not become experts in anatomy and physiology, we should know something about the structure of the equipment we use constantly—the fingers, hand, forearm, and upper arm. This knowledge will help to clear up fundamental misconceptions and will bring common sense into the nebulous world of the "art of piano playing." Remember that musical interpretation is an art but piano playing, per se, is not an art but a skill! There are too many false traditions, taboos, and fetishes—too many do's and don'ts, most of them based on anatomic nonsense—and they impede the development of the skill of piano playing.

Thumb; *never* under the palm

One of the most damaging technical errors is the habit of placing the thumb under the palm. It is usually done when playing scales and

*It is impossible to move the thumb vertically from the point where its first phalanx and metacarpal bone meet: it can move only horizontally (that is, toward and away from the palm). Its vertical motion is executed from the point where its metacarpal bone joins the wrist, and therefore we must lower the wrist when the thumb plays.

passages. This widespread and erroneous routine causes most of the problems in piano playing. Uneven passage-work, involuntary accents, a cramped feeling in the hand, and clumsiness and unsureness are caused by the fact that once the thumb is placed under the palm it is not only in an uncomfortable position but it simply has no equipment, no muscles available to bring it down vertically (see figure 37). You have to press, to push it down with the wrist or perform rapid shifts with the forearm, and inevitably there's the bump—the accent and uneven notes! How can one play an even effortless scale when one of the fingers is cramped or needs so many extra motions? This strenuous situation can be avoided altogether simply by not ever permitting the thumb to go under the palm. It must function in an unhindered way and be free to fall vertically; this is possible only if it is kept alongside the hand, out of the palm, and the wrist is lowered to accommodate it (see figure 38).

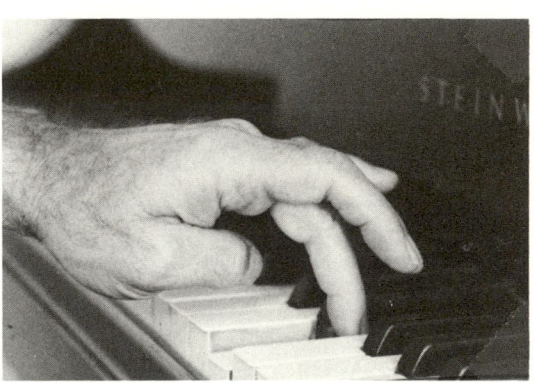

Figure 37. Thumb forced under the palm: wrong

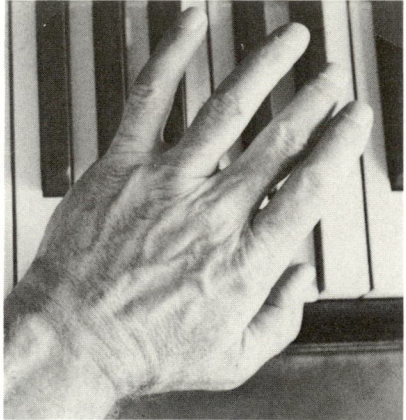

Figure 38. Thumb alongside the hand, enabling it to descend vertically: correct

Characteristics of the fingers

Before we describe scale playing in detail, let us examine the rest of the fingers individually. While the other four fingers differ distinctly from the thumb, they also vary among themselves. They differ in shape and size and, although they have adequate muscles, they are not equal in strength. The fourth finger, in particular, feels weak, but not because it lacks strong muscles. However its flexors and extensors are wrapped together with the third finger's muscles: hence these two fingers tend to contract and extend together. The fourth finger cannot be totally independent of the third. But it is possible to make the horizontal and vertical adjusting motions so precise, so accurate that the activation of the fourth finger can be done effortlessly. Without these adjustments the fourth finger is indeed handicapped. Contrary to common belief the fifth finger is one of the stronger fingers. It is true that it is the smallest one, but, in addition to the forearm muscles, it has a special set of strong muscles at the outer side of the hand. These muscles can develop substantially and give added power to the "pinky." It certainly needs this strength since most of the fundamental bass notes are played by the left, and the melodies by the right hand's fifth finger, as well as most of the "virtuoso" octave passages.

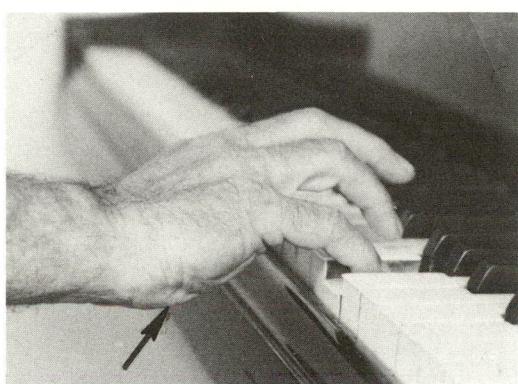

Figure 39. Extra sets of muscles on the outer side of the hand for the fifth finger

Lack of adjusting motions causes friction.

The forearm muscles that move the fingers are relatively small compared to the upper arm, shoulder, and chest muscles. Hence, if they are not utilized effectively—if they cannot transfer their full energy to the respective fingers—they tire quickly. If the fingers are not placed to form a fairly straight, continuous line with their forearm muscles and tendons, there is unnecessary friction alongside the tendons. Energy is wasted because the contracted muscles pull the finger sideways instead of directly. In order to achieve this close-to-straight line between the fingers and the elbow, the adjusting motions of the wrist should not be excessive; otherwise a bent line occurs again. Incidentally, these slight changes in the position of the arm are good, not only because they line up the fingers, but also because the slight but continuous changes prevent fixation and stiffness in the wrist. Thus we continually employ fresh, unused muscles and fibers.

Distinct positions

Each finger has its optimal position when it is properly lined up with its muscles. However what is ideal for the thumb is way off for the fourth or fifth finger. Actually we must think in terms of five slightly different "ideal" positions—one for each finger. We find, for instance, that when we are in the fifth-finger position, the thumb is actually removed from the keys (see figure 35e). Here the upper arm moves away from the body slightly; this motion brings the forearm and wrist slightly up, creating the fitting position for the fifth finger and displacing the thumb. When we use the thumb, the opposite happens; the arm and wrist are low, and the fifth finger is displaced. The point is that we should establish an ideal position for each finger. If we play several notes at the same time, the position of the arm and wrist should be central: that is, it should be halfway between the extreme fingers. For example, if we use the thumb and the fifth finger at the same time, the arm position will be that of the third finger, and for a combination of the third and fifth fingers the arm will be in position for the fourth finger.

Third adjusting motion: in and out, for white and black keys

When the wrist is adjusted for the use of the fifth finger, its upward motion is the consequence of the upper arm being moved away from the body. The upper arm also aids in shifting levels from white to black keys and from black keys to white. This is the third adjusting motion, of the in-and-out dimension (in depth), which together with the horizontal and vertical adjustments sets up the fingers for their optimal functionings, relieving them from excessive work.

All nonplaying fingers slightly raised

It is imperative that fingers that are not playing be raised slightly from the keys. They should not be pulled up too high and strained, and they should be ready to come down from a slight distance as soon as the arm and hand are lined up for the next finger's action. There are two important reasons for lifting the inactive fingers. First, the actual weight of the finger, no matter how small, can be utilized only if it is set in motion from a certain distance from the key. Once the finger rests on the key, the force of gravity cannot pull it down because it is down already. Its action must then be generated purely by the muscular energy stimulated by the tactile nerve endings of the fingertips. It is true that when our fingers rest on the keys, they have a relaxed sensation in them, and it is also true that if we feel the keys, we won't play wrong notes. But a slightly raised finger is secure and it feels under control too. Moreover it is ready to act effortlessly with the combined help of the force of gravity and the muscles. When the finger is slightly raised, it is possible to alternate contractions between the flexors and extensors, and the slightly raised fingers can receive any added throwing motion by the hand and arm that accelerates their speed by the vertical adjusting motions much more effectively than the motion of a finger touching the key. (For a further discussion of throwing motions see chapter seven.)

The "feelers"

The "feelers," those pianists who like to stay close to the keys at all times, usually produce sounds that are never too harsh, but their playing hardly goes beyond mezzo forte. For them volume can be increased only by forcing, mainly because the force of gravity has been mostly eliminated. Furthermore, the tone quality tends to become rather bland and dull. Another drawback to constant contact with the keys is the tendency to press. When we press the keys, extended contraction of certain muscles occurs; this contraction causes stiffness, and besides it is totally unnecessary. Because the pressure is continuous, one tends to pull the elbows (and the upper arm) toward the body. Thus one immediately creates an obstructed hand position characterized by excessive pronation (see page 79), a severe handicap that causes unnecessary tension and fatigue in the forearm. The only justification for "feeling" the keys is in pianissimo and legatissimo playing—but I wouldn't use it then either.

Again, the thumb

I have emphasized the importance of not placing or squeezing the thumb under the palm. When playing scales, also, we must raise the thumb alongside the hand while turning the elbow outward; then we must immediately lower the wrist in order to arrive at the position the thumb should be in before it descends on the key (a position in which the wrist is low). In this way we can avoid pulling the thumb under the palm. This motion is slightly bigger when the thumb passes under the fourth finger. Also the size of this motion decreases as the speed increases because the down motion of the wrist (before the thumb plays) helps to throw the thumb, instead of placing it, toward the correct position for its descent. It is helpful to place the third or fourth finger toward the back area of the keys when it is played before the thumb so that the elbow doesn't have to move too far out and the thumb can be placed more easily.

Guidelines

1. The finger that plays should be in a straight line with its flexor and extensor muscles.

2. The hand, wrist, and arm should slightly adjust within the vertical and horizontal planes to place each finger in the position where its muscles can contract effectively and where the hand and arm are in equilibrium over the finger that plays.

3. This slight change of position eliminates any fixed, tense situation in the joints and muscles and guarantees their readiness to be put to use again.

4. Any change of position enables the hand and arm to transmit a throw to the fingers, thereby allowing them to augment their speed and power.

5. The location of the forearm for double notes and chords is somewhere in the middle, between the extreme fingers.

6. When you play on the black keys, your upper arm should assume a slightly higher and more forward position so that the hand, wrist, and fingers can maintain the same relative position as on the white keys. The wrist should be in a normal position; it is the arm, not the wrist, that is higher than normal.

Figure 40. Arm position for white keys   **Figure 41.** Arm position for black keys

7. When you change the arm position, under no circumstances should you use any rotary motion of the forearm. This type of motion is used amply in other technical patterns, but not in five-finger, scale, or arpeggio movements.

8. Fingers should always be slightly raised before they play; they have to share the work with the rest of the equipment. However, the arm's adjusting motions are intended not to take over the fingers' work but to assist it. One of the most common mistakes is to use either the fingers alone or only wrist and arm motions. Fingers and arms are supposed to complement, not to substitute for, each other. Obviously relying on the fingers alone causes overwork in the forearm muscles, while the use of only the wrist and arm produces sloppy, inaccurate, and inarticulate playing.

9. Each finger must encounter, acquire, and ingrain the specific finger-hand-forearm-upper arm line-up unique and characteristic to that particular finger. When you play, each finger endeavors to assume, or to approximate, that particular position.

Scales and arpeggios

We have determined that specific conditions are characteristic for each finger and that the fingers must be coordinated and lined up with the muscles that place and move them. When we play scales and arpeggios, we try to establish or to approximate these optimal positions, modifying them according to specific conditions.

From the point of view of piano technique we group scales and arpeggios together, since arpeggios are essentially magnified, amplified scales. The only difference between them is that in arpeggios the intervals between the notes are larger than the intervals in scales. The technique is identical, but the connecting and adjusting motions between the notes and fingers are larger and wider in arpeggios than they are in scales.

Toward the extremes of the keyboard: right-hand-upward and left-hand-downward scales. More on the thumb!

Compared to the five-finger activities previously described, scales and arpeggios are complicated by the role of the thumb after the use of the third and fourth finger in right-hand-ascending scales and left-hand-descending scales and by the use of the third or the fourth finger after the thumb in right-hand-descending scales and left-hand-ascending scales. Here again I must set a negative goal: we have to avoid placing the thumb under the palm of the hand at all costs. Unfortunately placing the thumb under the palm is the most widespread method of teaching scales; we must protest against it vigorously. The thumb is our strongest and best-equipped finger, that has a special, husky extra muscle that pulls it toward the palm. But once it is pulled under the palm, it lacks the equipment to pull its second phalanx downward. Although it is most agile and can move in any direction while it is alongside the hand, the thumb is totally handicapped and cramped when it is pulled in. In no way can it match the other four fingers in their freedom to move downward from their respective knuckles. Since we want our scales and passages to be even and effortless, we should never create a situation where one of the fingers is severely restrained. This is exactly what happens to the thumb when it is forced under the palm. As I have mentioned before, the thumb always needs special attention and even when it is alongside the hand, it requires a lowered wrist position to descend on the key vertically and to function within its central area. If we force it into that unnatural and tight position (under the palm), we practically incapacitate it, and we lose all hope of achieving even, fluent playing. Once it is in that awkward, impossible position, the only way to bring it down is to push the whole wrist down and pretend that the inevitable clumsy, bumpy accent did not happen! You may try to camouflage it with a cautious, extra motion, but this motion would also interfere with the fluent motions of the other fingers. This is no way to play scales—this is no way to play the piano! No wonder that practicing scales becomes such an unpleasant, frustrating chore, both for children and adults.

The solution is natural and effortless. When a child or an untaught adult attempts his first scale, what does he do? First he sticks out his elbow and tries to reach the note with his thumb sideways. But then, he will be told, disciplined, cajoled, or beaten into the habit of raising his wrist, pressing his arm down, and forcing his thumb into that nasty little nest that the palm of the hand becomes. It is much better to allow the elbow to swing out and the thumb to reach its note in an unrestricted way than to restrain it by forcing it under the palm. When the critical moment comes for the thumb to follow the third or fourth finger, let us anticipate the event with a slight outward motion of the upper arm (and elbow), a slight lift of the thumb alongside the hand, a slight lowering of the wrist in preparation for the thumb, and then a quiet descent of the thumb to the next note. The size of these individual motions is minimal. This preparation is a perfectly natural, easy motion to execute, and there should be no problem with the timing of all the described activities.

The body helps

Also there is nothing wrong with a slight motion of the body in the direction of the scale: it accommodates and reduces the elbow motion. As you can see, it is better to mobilize the entire human apparatus than to isolate its components and force them! We encourage the participation of as many components as necessary to save the thumb from being immobilized. Further, the more we can distribute the motions amongst the components, the more reduced they will become in size until they are practically invisible. We cannot give precise measurements of the size of the motions; we can only indicate their direction. But as long as total coordination exists, the individual motions may be only millimeters in size.

The thumb: used on a white key after a black key and on a white key after a white key

The topography of the keyboard must be considered too. It is always easier for the thumb to play on a white key when the previous finger has played on a black key. Since the white key is lower, a lowered wrist position for the thumb comes about quite naturally. It is harder to move with the thumb from white key to white key and even more difficult to move from white key to black key. But these moves can be simplified if we use the simultaneous motions described. It is easier to play a D, A, E, or B major scale than the C major scale because the former scales allow the thumb to play a white key after a black key.

We use the same motions in fast scales, but there these motions are reduced, and we throw the fingers instead of placing them. Still, small as these motions are, we need the participation of every component.

Toward the center of the keyboard: right-hand-downward and left-hand-upward scales

So far we have described the thumb's role in the right-hand-ascending and left-hand-descending scales. In scales that move from the extremities of the keyboard toward the center we encounter a different situation. When the third or fourth finger follows the thumb, it tends to reach over it, cramping the thumb under the palm of the hand. This happens inevitably when the upper arm remains close to the body. When you play a descending scale with the right hand or an ascending scale with the left hand, the solution is simply to hold out the upper arm (and elbow). This way the third or fourth finger reaches over the thumb comfortably. The upper arm stays out, and the wrist moves down and up continuously, to accommodate the thumb (down) and the third and fourth fingers (up). Do watch that the thumb is raised both before and after playing! When the upper arm is lifted, all the fingers, including the thumb, will be parallel to each other.

Function of the
upper arm in
scales

Let us summarize the ground rules for scale playing. In scales that move toward the extremes of the keyboard, the upper arm, forearm, and wrist go down when the thumb is used and up when the other fingers are used. The fingers are always slightly raised when they are not playing. In scales that move toward the center of the keyboard, however, the upper arm must stay out continuously, and only the forearm and wrist go up and down, according to the fingers used.

Motions of the
body in scales

Do not mix the two motions: the role of the upper arm is totally different in each. In scales toward the extremes of the keyboard the upper arm uses small, pendulumlike motions while the body moves forward; in scales toward the center it will stay out at all times, away from the body as far as necessary while the body leans backward. Activating the upper arm is the only way to accommodate the fingers. Obviously the same rules apply to arpeggio playing, where the motions are slightly magnified.

If the upper arm stays out for an extended period, and it will during the above scales, the shoulder muscles need relief; they find it by occasionally lowering the arm toward the torso. If both hands start from the opposite extremes of the keyboard, the body must lean forward to accommodate the arms; then, as we proceed toward the center, the body leans backward. This forward-and-backward motion is the usual adjustment of the body; it moves to keep the arms from a stretched or overly bent position.

Symmetrical vs.
parallel motions

We see now why symmetrical motions are easier to execute than parallel ones: in symmetrical passages the motions of both arms are identical; in parallel ones we must synchronize two distinct motions. Furthermore in parallel passages the body has to move sideways, not backward and forward, according to the location. This sideways motion often causes an imbalance of the body, too.

Adjusting
motions to aid
the fingers

The adjusting motions of the hand, arm, and body serve exclusively to help the fingers. They are called upon depending on which finger is to be used and where it plays: the black keys or the white keys, the extremities of the keyboard or its center. The direction of the motions we described as being horizontal, vertical, forward and backward, circular, and rotary motions. Most components act simultaneously; therefore, although the size of each motion is minimal, their synchronization is sufficient to accomplish the task at hand.

Central areas

Preferably, each component should be used within the central area of its range, not at its extremes. We constantly refer to these central areas because this is where all the components function with no strain or excessive muscular tension and are easy to coordinate. It is this type of activity that serves our aim: to make piano playing a perfectly coordinated, totally effortless, and natural activity.

Arpeggios

The motions described pertain to arpeggios as well. In arpeggios the distances are wider and the adjusting motions are somewhat larger. Interestingly enough, the advocates of the thumb-under-the-palm cause less damage here. Because of the larger intervals, it is unrealistic and less tempting to squeeze the thumb under. The forced motion is usually replaced by a quick lateral shift with a fixed hand position. This type of motion is less damaging, but it is not the right solution either. The sudden shift tends to create an accent; furthermore it obstructs the flexible flow of movement, no matter how cleverly it is camouflaged. Also, it makes no sense to practice sudden shifting in slow tempo. There should be no sudden motions in slow practice, ever; how can you later accelerate an already fast motion? Anyway, no need exists for a sudden shift, since we have a smooth, well-synchronized upper arm-forearm-wrist-finger motion for any of these passages.

Shifts for wide skips

Incidentally we do use sudden shifts for *wide* lateral skips under special circumstances but we don't use them for ordinary scale and arpeggio passages.

Grouping of notes; legato playing

Thus far we have established a few pianistic concepts and have described certain positions and technical patterns as accurately as possible. We must now introduce a formula that is of the utmost importance; we will refer to it continually. It concerns the grouping of notes, both musically and technically. Its validity is such that it supersedes any other formulas that may seem to be in conflict with it.

Groupings, musical and technical

This unpretentious word, *grouping*, applies to many areas of piano playing. It has to do with legato playing, with phrasing, and with the execution of groups of motions (or technical formulas). It affects the position of the hand, wrist, forearm, and upper arm, and it is analogous to string players' bowing and singers' and wind players' breathing. It is an extremely meaningful activity for pianists, since the piano, essentially, is a percussion instrument and notes tend to sound isolated from one another. The grouping of notes is vitally important, both musically and technically.

The piano has another disadvantage compared to other instruments; its tone decays rapidly. The volume of a note or chord can be crashingly loud at first impact, but soon it is barely audible. To connect notes that by their nature represent instantaneous decrescendos, to shape melodic lines, to sustain intensity, and to produce a series of sounds that we hear as one phrase is an art in itself (see chapter sixteen). The technical solution for legato playing and grouping notes can be as well defined as the problem itself; it consists of an easily executed set of motion patterns. Incidentally we must distinguish between technical and musical groupings, for the two groupings do not necessarily coincide. By technical grouping I mean the connection of several notes in one motion, while the musical phrase sometimes doesn't end with the completion of the technical motion but continues on.

Legato markings   Grouping is often indicated in the score either directly or indirectly. Most of the time we see a slur ⌒ tying two or more notes together; sometimes the word *legato* is written. Sometimes nothing is written, but we recognize easily the technical and musical groupings of the notes.

Technique of   Legato playing is one of the mysteries of piano playing. Almost **legato playing** everybody knows the objective, but there are many theories about the best way to achieve a true legato. The mind, inspiration, and imagination have much to do with it, but the actual legato effect must be accomplished by physical means. By "physical means" I don't mean by the fingers, and certainly not by the fingers alone. There is no way to play a real legato by the fingers alone! No matter how tightly one grips the keys, trying not to release one note before the next is played, an imperfect legato results. Actually, if one note slightly overlaps the next (this is how legato is attempted by many), a series of short, instantaneous dissonances results; melodies very often consist of a sequence of scalelike notes, and these overlapping intervals of seconds are dissonances. A real legato, a real grouping of notes, can be accomplished only by a unifying motion of the arm (that is, of the forearm and upper arm). When we see a slur, or assume the presence of one, we begin the phrase with a relatively low wrist position and end it with a somewhat higher wrist. By low or high wrist I imply a low or high forearm position that often involves the upper arm too. The fingers act in their usual manner; they are slightly raised before and after playing. Let us take a group of two notes ♪ or a group of three notes ♪♪ and apply any kind of fingering (1-2, 2-3, 3-4 or 3-2-1, 5-4-3, 2-3-4, for example). Regardless of which finger plays, always initiate the group with a relatively low wrist position and move gradually higher until the last note of the group has been played! In our examples the highest wrist position is on the second note in the two-note group and on the third note in the three-note group (when I say "highest," I mean a slight elevation). We must avoid an extremely low or high wrist position. The fingers move up and down with slight motions, and extremes should be avoided for them as well. When we combine motions, which we do all the time, each motion must be reduced to its minimum. If we raise the fingers slightly and if we apply the usual horizontal, vertical, and in-depth adjusting motions of the arm and wrist, we can easily obtain a perfect legato.

A seeming
contradiction

You may have noticed that there seems to be a contradiction between our latest formula (raise the wrist at the end of a group) and the rule that the wrist must be low whenever the thumb plays and higher whenever the fifth finger plays. There is indeed a contradiction, because we just said that in legato the wrist must be low at the beginning of the group and high at the end, regardless of the finger in use. Does this rule mean that if the phrase begins with the fifth finger and ends with the thumb, the wrist will be in a higher position for the thumb than for the fifth finger? Yes, this is exactly the case! And, as I said before, this latter rule supersedes the first one (see figures 42 and 43).

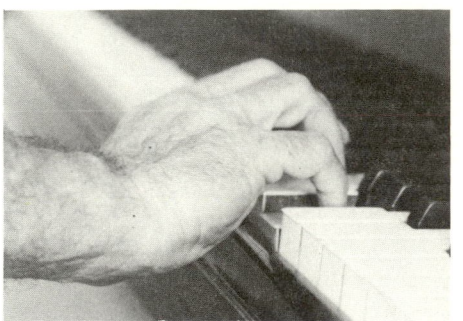

Figure 42. Group starts with fifth finger: low wrist

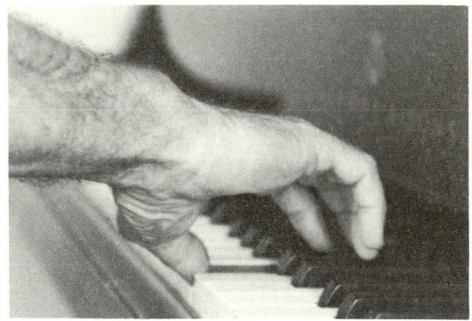

Figure 43. Group ends with thumb: higher wrist

However, the first rule is still valid. Considering that the thumb is more comfortable with a lower wrist and the fifth finger with a higher wrist, the upward motion of the wrist is definitely influenced by the former "thumb" rule; the relative height of the wrist at the ending of the group is a little lower than it would be if the phrase had ended on the fifth finger. As an example let us compare two phrases: one ends on the thumb, the other on the fifth finger. The phrase that ends with the fifth finger will have a somewhat higher wrist position than the phrase that ends with the thumb. Thus, although we do accept the rule for grouping notes (with the wrist raised at the end of the phrase), we also respect the primary need of the thumb for a relatively lower wrist position than that required by the other fingers. So much for the seeming contradiction.

I suggested before that the fingers alone can never produce a true legato. Legato demands that a note must blend into the next note without a break or any overlapping. The break does not occur when we hold over the previous note, but overlapping does occur. Since overlapping causes a trace of dissonance in scalewise motion, a better solution must be found. We'd prefer the previous note to fade away when the following note comes into existence, and blend into it.

The first note must cease sounding in due time, but not in a sudden, brusque manner, because suddenness in itself is contrary to the character of legato.

At this point, it is necessary to examine the essential role of the use of the damper in legato playing in producing the fading or blending effect I mentioned above. The damper (or *sordino*) is the mechanism that was affixed to the overgrown length of the piano strings during the second half of the 18th century. Its role is to stop the excessive reverberation of these longer strings. Before Mozart there was no need for the damper because the strings were shorter, the sound weaker, and one didn't mind a little extra reverberation. Actually, it made the sound of the old instruments richer, because it incorporated the harmonics of all the strings. But the piano soon reached adolescence and then developed into the Lisztian and contemporary nine- to ten-foot concert grand. Now the damper became a must, a life saver! Imagine how a concert grand piano would sound without that safeguard to stop its unwanted vibrations (for a further discussion of the pedal and pedal effects see chapter twelve). Let us return now to the damper's role in legato playing, and to the role of the fingers in manipulating it.

The speed with which the damper falls back on the string to stop its vibrations results from the speed with which the finger *abandons* the key; that is, if we raise the finger abruptly, the damper drops abruptly and stops the sound instantaneously. By the same token, if we leave the key slowly, the damper halts the strings gently and gradually, and the sound seems to fade away. Therefore we have to cultivate a technique of abandoning the key gradually. Since legato playing requires that notes blend into one another, we must rely on the mechanical device that can help to achieve this blending. As you will see, a combination of the damper, the fingers, and the arm is needed to enable us to play a real legato. This approach to legato playing is not yet understood and people seem to be too concerned with the activities of the fingers only.

Our goal is to let the fingers abandon the keys slowly, but this task is a difficult one for the fingers alone; it is hard to raise one finger slowly and lower the next one at normal speed. The solution to this problem is to raise the arm slightly. This arm motion gently lifts the finger that has just played, and the slow abandoning of the key retards the damper, which thereby halts the sound gently. By this gradual fading away of the previous note one creates not an illusionary but a true legato. If the next note enters gently, it will blend easily with the previous note. Therefore do not attempt legato playing with inhibited, repressed finger motions alone or with a motionless and fixed arm and wrist. Avoid large circular "relaxed" motions of the whole arm on each note too; they will have the effect of isolating, not connecting, notes. Instead guide smooth and slight finger motions with a smooth, unifying, and slightly upward motion of the whole arm. Remember, there is only one upward arm motion for the entire group of notes! No pressure is required, and no excessive finger or arm activities are needed, just a slight lifting of the arm toward the end of each group is all that is necessary.

Why upward?

Why is the arm moved upward rather than downward? The reason is that a quietly tapered phrase ending is achieved by lifting the weight of the arm rather than by lowering it into the keys. The upward arm motion retards the fall of the damper and slows down the finger, while a downward arm motion would accelerate it.

Phrase endings: touchstone of musicianship

If we acquire this easy, smooth technique of combining fingers, arm, and damper during and at the end of a phrase, our musical diction will improve significantly. One of the telling earmarks of good musicianship is the manner with which one ends a phrase: does the performer end the phrase gently or abruptly, does he use suitable or excessive motions?

Tense playing affects tone quality too.

Some may think that it is easier to achieve control with tensed-up muscles and with fixed hands and fingers, but under these circumstances not only the flow of music suffers, but the tone quality as well. We must be aware of the fact that in piano playing, just as in science, poetry, or sports, the ultimate can be achieved only by utmost economy and purposefulness, with no waste of the media. In a well-coordinated system of music making, the fingers work together with the arms, the arms work with the body, and they all mesh with our breathing. Occasionally we associate upward motions with inhaling and downward motions with exhaling. Breathing affects phrasing, and this is what interpretation is mostly about: how to phrase music! The mechanical, respiratory, and interpretative activities must be completely integrated. If our efforts and motions are continuously shared by the active but minute participation of the entire apparatus, only then can we develop a totally effortless technique, and our own, unmistakably individual tone quality.

Guidelines for five-fingers, scales and arpeggios

To sum up, here are a few guidelines for five-fingers, scale and arpeggio playing:

1. Each finger has its own characteristics.

2. Each finger is to be helped by the rest of the playing apparatus, which assumes a corresponding position suitable to that particular finger.

3. The need for changing positions for each finger results in continuous adjusting movements of the arm.

4. In general, the wrist is at its lowest point when the thumb is used and at its highest point when the fifth finger is used.

5. Guideline 4 is modified when grouping of notes is involved; in groups the lowest wrist position is assumed at the beginning of the phrase, no matter which finger plays, and the highest position is assumed at the end of the phrase. However the relative height is influenced by guideline 4.

6. When we play scales, we should avoid placing the thumb under the palm; instead we should place it alongside the hand. A combined finger-wrist-arm motion prevents a cramped and uncomfortable position for the thumb.

7. Whenever the hand is in the playing position, we should avoid an extreme pronation of the radius and ulna (of the forearm) by slightly raising the upper arm.

8. The technique for scales and arpeggios is fundamentally the same, except that in arpeggios wider intervals are covered with slightly larger arm motions than those used in scales.

9. The height of the upper arm should be modified for playing on black keys or white keys: it should be higher on black keys and lower on white keys. Thus we can maintain exactly the same position for the wrist, hand, and fingers in both situations.

10. When the speed of playing increases, the size of the motions decreases. The types of motions, however, remain unchanged. In a slow tempo we place the fingers in their proper position; in a fast tempo, we throw them toward the desired position. It is with this throw that the fingers can reduce their motion and achieve the increased speed, balance, and volume of sound even though the distance from which they approach the keys may be small. However, we cannot throw slowly, so in a slow practice we must *place* them in position.

11. In order to facilitate the passing of the thumb it is advisable to let the third or fourth finger play closer to the back of the key. In this way the upper arm can move less and still keep the thumb outside the palm of the hand.

Exercises for five-fingers, scales and arpeggios

The five-finger exercises given here should make the fingers independent, not from the arms, but from each other! By insisting on a specific position for each finger and collaboration with its equipment, we will establish conditions for each finger's independence and, at the same time, for being interdependent with the arm. Therefore these exercises are intended to activate the finger not in spite of its mobiliz-

Exercises serve
to ingrain the
appropriate arm
position for
each finger

ers but in conjunction with them. All the fingers should be lined up
with their respective forearm muscles by using the adjusting motions.

The following simple set of exercises serves to bring about typical,
characteristic constellation of the finger, arm, forearm, upper arm, and
torso position that is unique for each finger. Each of the fingers will
assume and ingrain its own distinct arm position, and whenever and
wherever any of the fingers play, we will have to bring about this
particular position automatically.

The slight changes that bring about these conditions for each finger, the adjusting motions, are in the horizontal, vertical, and depth
dimensions. The process of establishing and ingraining the quality,
size, and timing of the motions must be very carefully controlled. In a
nutshell, when we move from the thumb toward the fifth finger and
back, there is a gradual and precisely measured change laterally, vertically, and in depth in the arm position. The value of these exercises
lies not so much in what we play as in how we play. Therefore the
following few notes suffice for our purposes:

Example 15. Five-finger exercises on any keys

You may add a sharp or flat to any of the notes (as indicated),
thereby creating different situations for each finger. As you know, the
general position of the arm and body should be altered when you play
on the black keys. It is important that you do not practice the exercises
mechanically. With the conscious control of the mind you can establish and ingrain these rather complex motions quickly and effectively.
Once you have mastered these motions don't bother practicing exercises any more: go right on to the repertoire. The reason why I have
not submitted here the usual, copious assortment of exercises (see
Cortot's edition of the Chopin *Études*) is because they might induce
mechanical practicing, which is mostly a waste of time.

The exercises in example 16 include the same notes as before;
however here they are grouped in various ways. It is these grouping
signs that indicate the differences in the technique employed, in the
position of the wrist and arm. We must begin each group with a lower
wrist position and end with a relatively higher one, regardless of
which finger plays. It is as simple as that. Again we don't need different sets of exercises; all we need is to alter the slurs, to tie notes in
various combinations, and to use combinations of black and white keys

to form smaller and larger intervals, using this one group of notes. Help yourself: the idea is, not to practice exercises for their own sake, not to "practice" but to master the motion itself; once you have mastered this technique, apply it to the repertoire. We must avoid mechanical practicing, even if conscious practice is more strenuous on the mind: we are concerned with avoiding strain to the muscular system —not to the mind!

Example 16. Five-finger groups, phrased

Examples for five-fingers, scales and arpeggios

The list of all symbols used in the musical examples is given again here so that you may become familiar with them.

Symbols

A	free fall		E	thrust
B	*five-fingers, scales and arpeggios*		↓	low wrist
C	rotation		↑	high wrist
D	staccato			

B indicates the type of motion treated in this chapter. Free fall (A) was discussed in chapter four. Since rotation, staccato, and thrust have not yet been described, concentrate mainly on A and B in examples 17–28.

Example 17. Bach, *Partita No. 5 in G Major.* "Praeambulum"

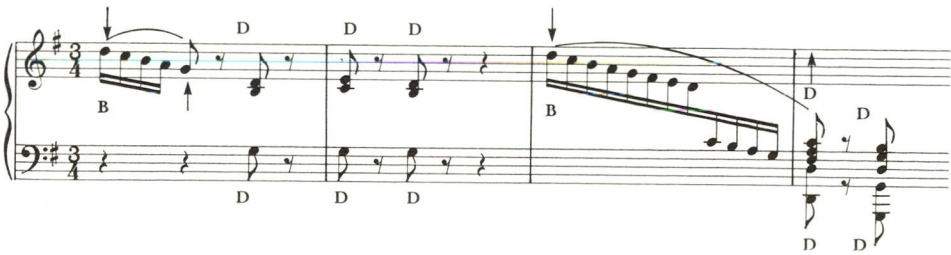

Example 18. Beethoven, *Sonata*, opus 2 no. 2, first movement

Example 19. Beethoven, *Sonata*, opus 14 no. 2, third movement

Example 20. Bach, *Chromatic Fantasy and Fugue*

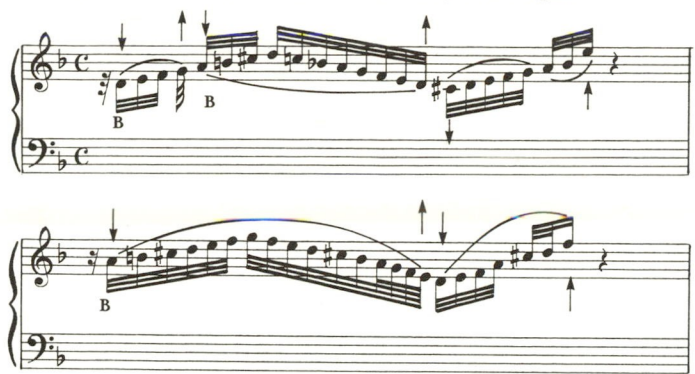

Example 21. Beethoven, *Sonata*, opus 31 no. 3, first movement

Example 22. Chopin, *Prelude in B Flat Minor*, opus 28 no. 16

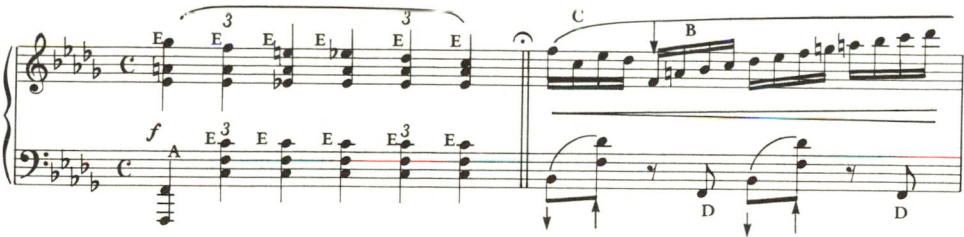

(Example 22 continued)

Example 23. Chopin, *Etude*, opus 25 no. 2

Example 24. Chopin, *Sonata in B Minor*, opus 58, second movement

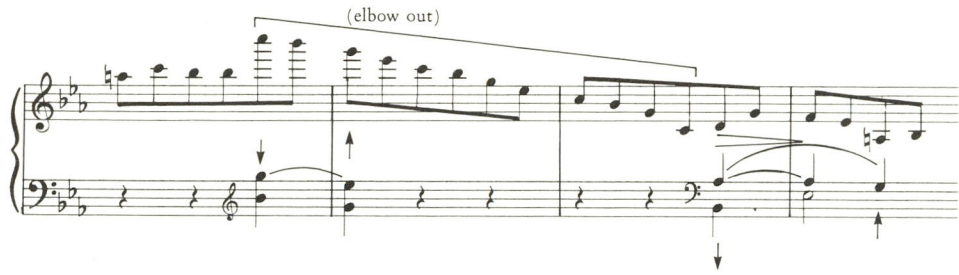

Example 25. Chopin, *Sonata in B Minor*, opus 58, fourth movement

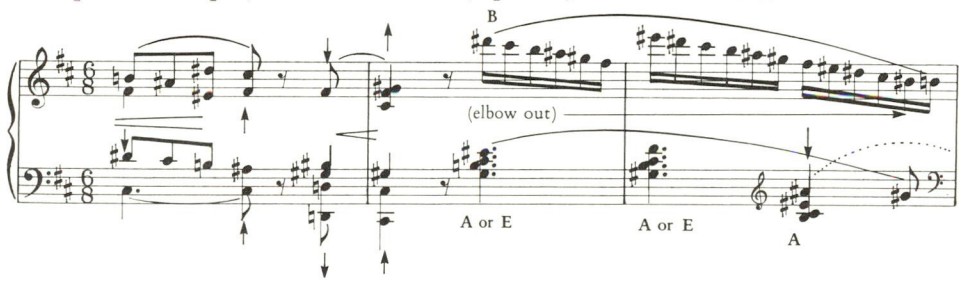

Example 26. Liszt, *Concert Etude No. 2 in F Minor* ("La Leggierezza")

Example 27. Chopin, *Prelude in F Major,* opus 28 no. 23

Example 28. Liszt, *Spanish Rhapsody*

6 Rotation

Rotation

Scales and arpeggios constitute a large part of piano playing, and the technique required in this activity takes care of a major share of pianistic problems. Rotary motion of the forearm, however, is eminently important too. We call it simply *rotation* because we are seldom concerned with the rotary motion of any other part of the playing mechanism. Only occasionally will I refer to the rotation of the torso and to the upper-arm rotation that participates in the lateral motion of the forearm.

Rotation is very helpful in adding power and speed to the fingers; if it is properly done, there will be no strain in the arm whatsoever. In general, the scale motion (B) is used when several notes proceed in one direction (either up or down the keyboard). Rotary motion (C) is applied whenever notes go zig-zagging, up and down alternately.

Example 29. Rotation patterns

These and similar passages indicate that the use of rotary motion is the technical solution.

Pronation; supination

Before I describe the technique of rotation, let me mention the role of the ulna and the radius, the two bones of the forearm. When the arm hangs freely next to the body, these two bones are in a parallel position. This is the forearm's most natural position. Because the two bones are in their central position, they can move into pronation or supination quite comfortably. In this central position the thumb points forward. *Pronation* results in turning the thumb toward the body, *supination* in turning the fifth finger toward the body. Now when we raise the forearm from this central position, the thumb points upward. This is roughly the position of the arm and hand used in playing the harp. We, however, want to play the piano, not the harp! Therefore we must bring the hand into a horizontal position with its palm down; this is done by pronation. You will notice now that when you put the hand in a completely horizontal position, you will feel considerable tension in the inner portion of the forearm (that is, in the flexors). Unless you move the upper arm away from the body, the forearm will be brought into its extreme position in which the ulna and radius will be crossed to their utmost and the pronation will be complete. This stiff, rigid position will cause severe tension in the forearm even before you play a single note. If you hold your hand and arm like this for a few seconds, even without playing, you will feel fatigue in the forearm flexor area. However when the upper arm is raised, the ulna and radius will be removed from their extreme position and relieved of tension, and the hand can assume its horizontal position without extreme pronation.

Therefore our ground rule is: whenever you sit down to play the piano, do not press the upper arm toward the body. The old school advocated an upper arm motionless and close to the body; it even demanded that a book be held under the arm or that a penny be placed on the hand in this cramped position. It disregarded the basic anatomic facts of the ulna and radius mentioned above and made you start off to play the piano under extreme handicap. The underarm was stiff to begin with and the immobilized upper arm was unable to adjust and help the fingers; as a result, one felt continuous tension and fatigue in the forearm. The teachers of the old school wanted to eliminate the sensation of fatigue by strengthening the forearm muscles (they called them "finger muscles") with "finger exercises." No wonder fatigue was the result! They put your arm muscles in a straitjacket before you even started to play "Chopsticks."

It is essential to avoid such excessive pronation of the forearm. Actually avoiding it is quite simple—just don't do it! Don't press down the upper arm. Raise your upper arm slightly, and the extreme tension caused by an excessive pronation will disappear. The other extreme —that of excessive supination—is no threat because we don't ever reach that position when playing the piano.

Once the upper arm is in position, the forearm, wrist, and fingers can easily line up, and you can start to play the piano effortlessly. So please remember: don't lock the upper arm in; move it away from the body and make it accomplish all the adjusting motions the finger requires in cooperation with the forearm and the wrist.

Axial rotation: active and passive participants

Rotation is primarily a forearm motion executed by muscles that adhere to the upper arm and forearm. During the axial rotation of the forearm the upper arm's role is passive; the upper arm merely places the forearm in the position where it can actively execute the rotary motion, and where it transmits its effect to the fingers. Only the forearm and the fingers are active; the upper arm and the wrist are both passive. The wrist doesn't participate in the motion at all; it doesn't move up or down or else it would obstruct the rotary motion. The eventual movement of the upper arm during rotation is a purely passive one; it is merely a response to the activities of the moving forearm. I wish to emphasize this fact because it is erroneous to think that the upper arm is an active participant in pure forearm rotary motion. The upper arm becomes active only when it adds a lateral dimension to the axial forearm motion in order to reach wider intervals; it is not active in pure axial forearm rotation.

Role of the fingers and the forearm

Pure axial forearm rotation is used for small intervals, up to about a sixth or a seventh, depending on the size of the hand. The role of the forearm's axial activity is to add power and speed to the fingers, which must be active at all times. The fingers should be slightly raised before playing, and both pronation and supination will add distance from the keys to the finger that is about to play. The forearm should be located in the center in relation to the fingers that play. For instance, if the thumb and fifth finger rotate, the forearm should be in a position where it is aligned with the third finger; it should also be in this position for the 2-4 combination. If you use the 2-5 combination while you rotate, the forearm will be somewhere between the third and fourth finger positions. When you use 3-5, you should be in the fourth-finger position, etc. While rotating double notes, the forearm should be in a central position between the two innermost fingers.

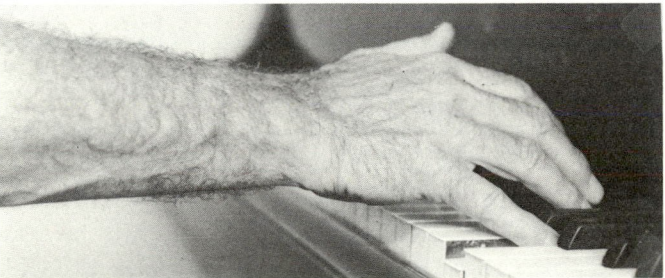

Figure 44. Supination on the fifth finger

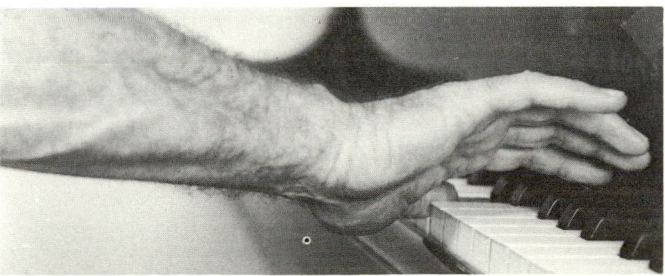

Figure 45. Pronation on the thumb

For extreme
distances:
lateral motion of
the upper arm

As I mentioned before, when the interval to be rotated increases over six or seven notes, we add a lateral component to the motion of the forearm. This lateral motion of the forearm is possible only if we make an axial rotation of the upper arm that enables the forearm to move horizontally also. Its size conforms with the increased interval. Moreover, in very wide distances the upper arm may make a lateral motion (from the shoulder down) in addition to its axial rotation. We can cover practically the whole keyboard with this motion.

Example 30. Liszt, *Mozart, Don Juan Fantasy*

Both fingers and
forearm must be
active.

In both the purely axial and the combined rotary motions, the forearm rolls from one side to the other. When it is at the thumb's side (pronation), the fifth finger must be slightly (actively) raised and ready to receive the subsequent throw (supination) that will roll the arm over to the fifth finger's side. When the arm is rolled over to the fifth finger, the thumb will be raised and ready for its turn to be thrown by pronation. It is a composite motion; one cannot rotate purely by the forearm with the fingers staying passive, nor if the fingers are overactive and the forearm is inactive. Proper coordination and timing are needed; the fingers and the forearm have to complement one another. The rolling movement of the forearm is steady; it is *not sudden*, but rolls from one side to the other with steady speed. When we increase speed, the size of the motions will be reduced. But the motions should never be sudden and jerky. The fingers are moved by the arm in an arch, and when the tempo increases, the arch becomes flatter; at maximum speed the arch resembles a straight line. However, as I said before, the fingers are slightly active at all times, while receiving the throw from the forearm in their ready (raised) position.

Location of the
elbow

We must be sure that the elbow is placed correctly; it doesn't change its location unless the intervals and notes change. It must be equidistant from the extreme fingers that play. Rotation is fundamentally a symmetrical motion that provides equal throw to the fingers. If we want to emphasize a certain finger so it can be heard more, we raise it slightly and thus it can receive more throw from the forearm;

we increase its distance from the keys by turning the forearm more toward the opposite finger. This may seem puzzling, but it really is quite simple: we don't produce more sound by more weight, but by greater speed from a greater distance from the keys. Since the element of time is the same for both notes, speed will be increased by increasing the distance. So, if you want to feature the fifth finger, turn the arm more toward the thumb.

Elbow shift   When we rotate on black keys, the general arm position is higher, and the upper arm is placed slightly forward and sideways (just as it is adjusted in free fall and scales). This position maintains the straight line between the elbow and the fingers. If the rotation is on one black and one white key, the position of the elbow must be changed accordingly. If the right thumb is on a black key and the fifth finger on a white key, the elbow moves closer to the body; if the reverse is true, the elbow moves outward. If we play a descending chromatic sixth sequence, the elbow will be very busy moving right and left, to conform with the above conditions. If the elbow fails to adjust, the hand and fingers will stiffen and play unevenly, skipping notes. If the elbow's continuous shifting is well executed, ease and evenness for the fingers and the elimination of stiffness are guaranteed. These adjusting motions of the elbow should be minimal and very precise. They should be noticeable only in slow tempo. At high speed they

Figure 46. Pure axial rotation: (a) pronation, (b) supination

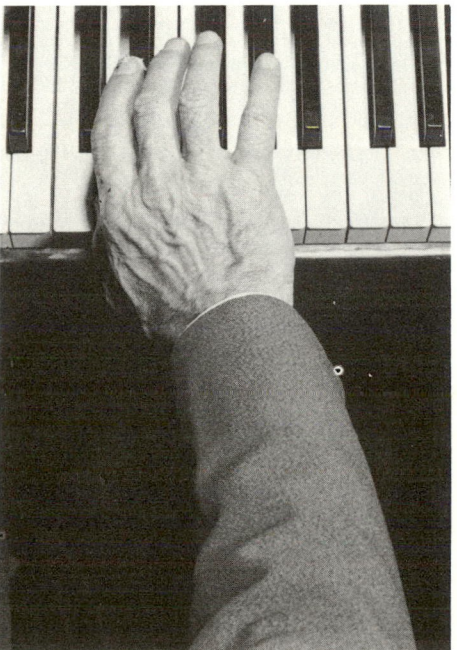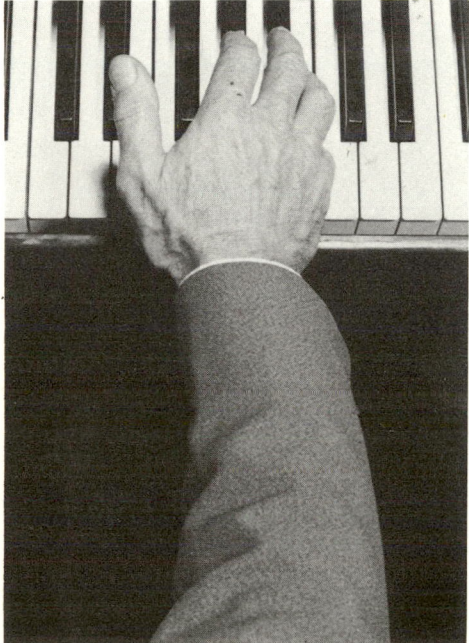

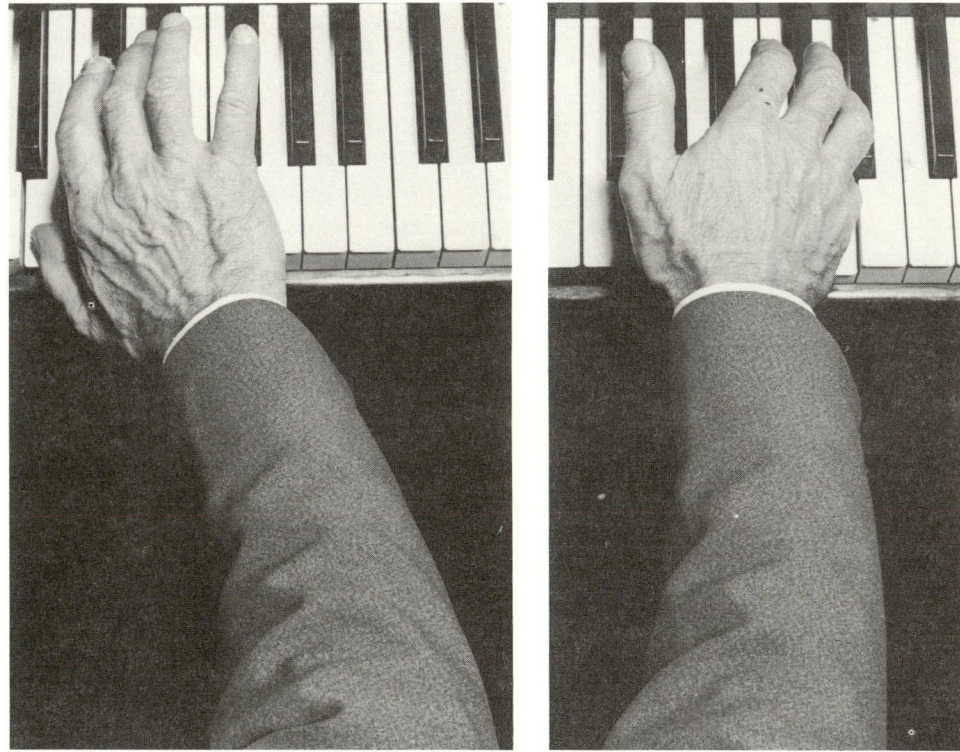

Figure 47. When larger intervals are played, lateral motion of the forearm is added to axial rotation.

become practically invisible, but they are nonetheless there. The reason that we go into such detail is that we are concerned with the learning processes, and it is in the slow tempo we use for practicing that these motions must be brought into play; however they are essential in any tempo.

Here are a few reminders. The wrist must be inactive, and it must avoid any twisting motions. It holds the hand steadily, in straight continuation of the forearm. The fingers must be active, but they must never reach out to the next note. Reaching out is one of the most common errors, and it must be watched carefully: the finger must be slightly raised, but it must stay on the same side where the arm is rotated until the arm begins its turn in the opposite direction and transmits its throw to the finger. If the finger reaches away toward the next note, it loses distance from the next key to be played; there will be tension, and, worst of all, the motion will originate from the finger: it will disrupt forearm rotation, decrease the distance and speed, and the finger begins to force. Here's a final hint: if there is an extended loud rotation passage, we can always alter the position of the arm and

The fingers should never reach out toward the next key.

elbow, going up or down slightly, in order to avoid a fixed position and prevent fatigue.

Guidelines for using rotation follow:

1. Find the right position for the arm, hand, and fingers. Silently press down the keys to be played; the elbow should be in a central position. Now test the pronation position by raising the fifth finger; most likely your elbow will rise to the point where the upper arm can remain static during rotation. This point is the right location for the elbow (upper arm) for these particular notes. The elbow should move from this position only when you change notes.

2. The wrist functions only as an inactive connecting joint; it should never move independently and it should not twist. It aligns the hand with the forearm according to the fingers used, and it helps to establish the elbow in its central position between the two or more fingers involved. If there are more than two fingers in action, the elbow is equidistant from the two inner fingers.

3. The fingers' role can never be replaced by the rotating forearm; it can only be complemented by it. For instance, if the second and fifth fingers rotate in pronation, the fifth finger must be raised slightly but actively; if they rotate in supination, the second finger must be raised. Even in fast rotation the fingers must be raised actively somewhat before and after playing.

4. When rotation takes place in the middle of the keyboard, the upper arm is jammed in, and it will feel stiff. To avoid this uncomfortable situation we should move the body slightly away from the upper arm; if both arms are engaged, the body should lean slightly backward. By the same token, if both arms rotate simultaneously at the opposite, outer extremes of the keyboard, the body should lean forward to avoid stretching the arms unduly and placing the hands at an extreme angle.

The essence of rotary motion lies in a passive upper arm, an active forearm, an inactive hand and wrist, and slightly active fingers. The hand and fingers receive the side-swinging effects of the axially rotating forearm. When the intervals increase and the axial rotation of the forearm no longer suffices to reach the notes comfortably, we add lateral motion to the rotation of the forearm by rotating the upper arm on its own axis. The forearm and finger motions are complementary: neither can substitute for the other. The elbow must be placed equidistant between the extreme fingers; it will be perpendicular to the imaginary line that connects the points where the two extreme fingers

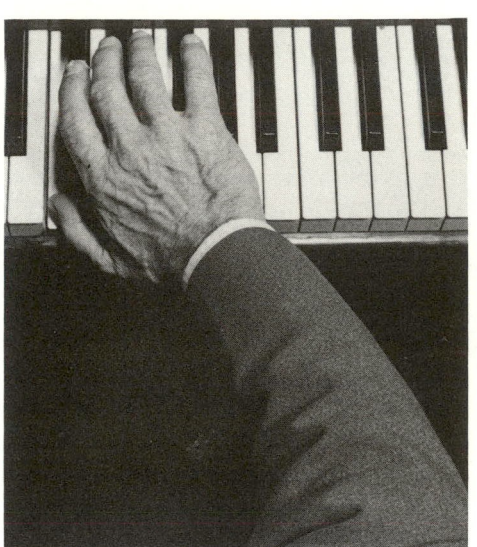 

Figure 48. Rotation from white keys to black keys: elbow out

Figure 49. Rotation from black keys to white keys: elbow in

 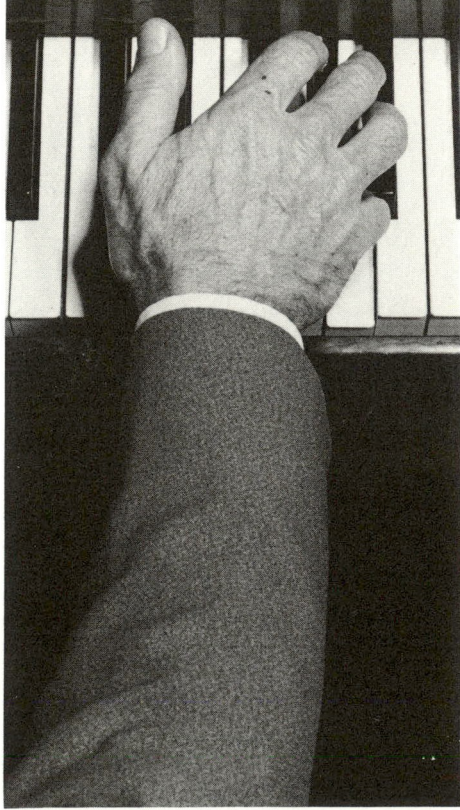

touch the keys. When we rotate on two black or two white keys, the position of the elbow is central between the two notes engaged. When one of the notes is white and the other black, the elbow shifts to be perpendicular to the center of the previously mentioned imaginary line that connects the fingers and adjusts its distance from the body, according to the keys and fingers.

Elementary Exercises

Avoid shifting the elbow and watch the size and curve of rotation. The fingers should be raised, but they should not reach out toward the next note. The upper arm is immobile, and the wrist does not participate actively in the motion.

Example 31. Purely axial forearm rotation

Do these exercises with the left hand too; play them two octaves lower than in example 31 so that the arm is free and not too close to the body. Add sharps and flats, play them hands together in both a parallel and symmetrical manner, and start the exercises from any note and any register of the piano; watch your elbow and body position here also.

Use the same type of motions for double notes and chords in rotation. Do the exercise with the left hand too; alter notes at will in order to avoid playing mechanically. Symmetrical motions for both hands are easier than parallel ones.

Example 32. Rotation of double notes and chords

Where intervals are larger, we add a forearm lateral motion, produced by the axial rotation of the upper arm (see figure 47). The fingers must not reach out to the next note (they couldn't reach it anyway), and the wrist must still remain inactive. With the help of upper-arm

(margin note, left) Axial forearm rotation

(margin note, left) Lateral motion of forearm added to axial rotation

rotation, the forearm is brought to the position where it can throw the fingers exactly as it does with smaller intervals. For distances up to two octaves (approximately) the elbow doesn't have to change location; for larger intervals the entire upper arm moves laterally too. However this type of movement is most unusual.

Add sharps and flats to example 33 also; use any larger intervals and any register of the piano.

Examples for
rotation

Example 33. Lateral motion added to axial rotation

Symbols

A	free fall	D	staccato
B	five-fingers, scales, arpeggios	E	thrust
C	*rotation*	↓	low wrist
		↑	high wrist

C is the symbol used for rotation, the motion discussed in this chapter. You are already familiar with A and B. D and E are discussed in chapters seven and eight, respectively.

Example 34. Bach, *Well-Tempered Clavier*, book 2, Prelude No. 15 in G Major

Example 35. Haydn, *Sonata in E Minor*, third movement

Example 36. Mozart, *Sonata in A Minor*, K. 310, first movement

(Example 36 continued)

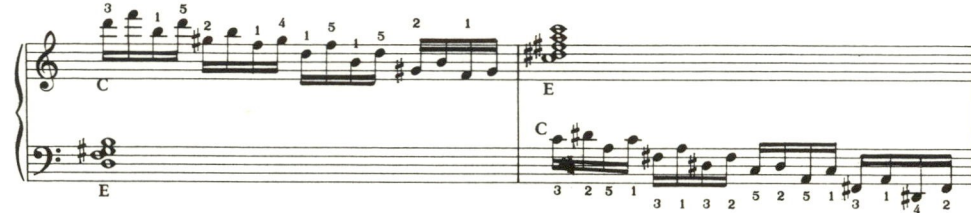

Example 37. Beethoven, *Piano Concerto in G Major*, opus 58, third movement

Example 38. Beethoven, *Sonata*, opus 26, fourth movement

Example 39. Chopin, *Etude*, opus 25 no. 1

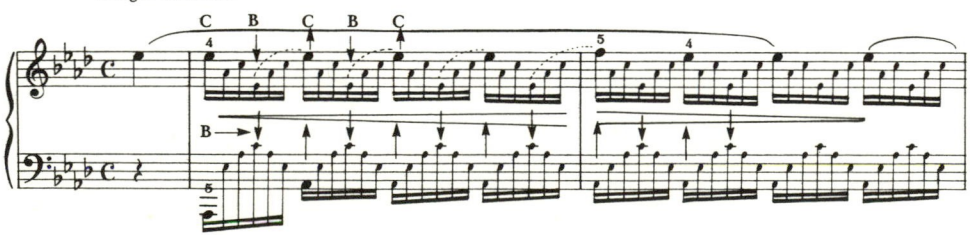

Example 40. Brahms, *Variations on a Theme by Paganini*, opus 35, book 1 variation 4

Example 41. Schumann, *Carnaval*, opus 9, "Paganini"

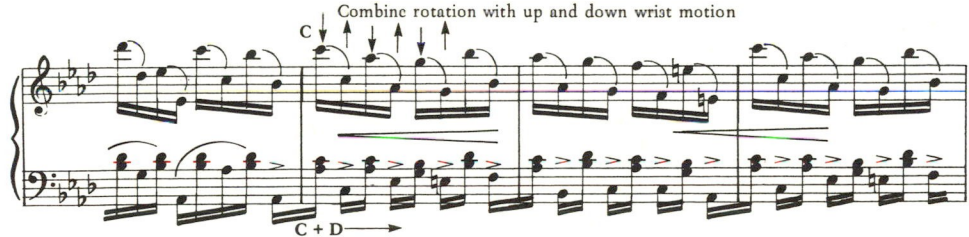

Combine rotation with up and down wrist motion

(Example 41 continued)

Example 42. Ginastera, *Sonata,* second movement

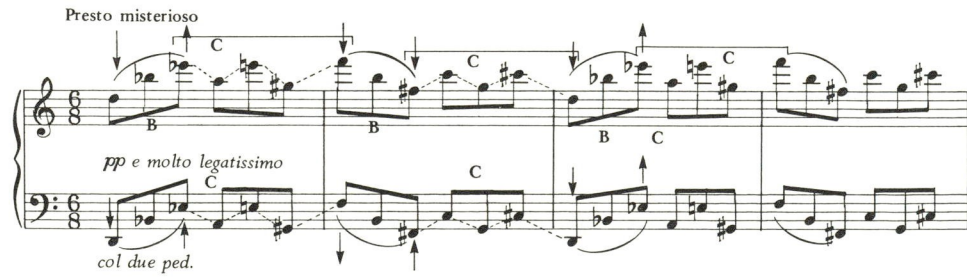

7   Staccato

Octaves are one of the most spectacular activities in piano playing. Professionals and amateurs alike seem to be fascinated and impressed by octaves, possibly because of the stormy, dynamic quality and the immense volume of sound that is produced by some virtuosos. Undoubtedly one often experiences a quasi-hypnotic effect when listening to the excitement and the irresistible sweep of crescendos in Liszt's "Funérailles," Balakirev's *Islamey*, and Chopin's *Polonaise in A Flat Major*, opus 53.

Same technique for staccato single notes, double notes, and chords

In our attempts to simplify and classify technical formulas, we will equate the motions of *octave technique* with those of the ordinary *staccato*—grandiose as these sound effects may be. While we realize that legato octaves and pianissimo octaves also exist, we nevertheless maintain that even in them the fundamental motion pattern is identical to that of staccato single notes, double notes, and chords (with certain modification, of course). The technique of staccato involves an active and coordinated arm, wrist, hand, and finger motion in which all the components participate simultaneously. By sharing this motion, extreme speed and volume can be achieved with complete effortlessness. Again our aim is not relaxation but a minimal expenditure of energy with optimal results. If the arm in its totality functions well and if it is activated by the strongest muscles of the body (the chest, back, stomach, and diaphragm), we can achieve maximum speed and volume with no strain. Actually the maximum speed with which we can play staccato octaves is about the same as that of a wind player playing staccato notes. It is a matter of coordination and reflexes; a well-synchronized mechanism can create wonders.

Entire arm active at all times

In scales and arpeggios and in rotation, most muscular activities take place within the forearm area, and they are helped, actively or passively, by the upper arm. However in the staccato motion the entire arm, including the upper arm, is actively engaged at all times. In addition to the fingers, hand, wrist, and forearm, we must activate the upper arm continuously; it gives us an added source of power that is essential to this motion. Since in all composite motions both the nature and size of the movements involved must be determined correctly, it is necessary to define the exact role of the upper arm as well as that of the rest of the components. Remember that the upper arm is the link that connects the strongest body muscles to the fingers.

Throwing must come from the upper arm; fallacy of the "wrist" staccato

Essentially staccato motion is a throwing motion. The throw has to involve the entire arm, the hand, and the fingers. We are familiar with the conditions of making sounds on the piano: the keys move vertically, and therefore the most effective way to transfer energy to the keys is in the vertical direction. The fallacy of playing a "wrist staccato" is manifold: first, if we use the wrist alone, we are utilizing exclusively and overburdening our comparatively weak forearm muscles. Furthermore, when the lever that is used (the hand) is very short, the curved line traced by the fingertips is rather pronounced; consequently the desired straight vertical descent of the fingertips cannot be attained.

Figure 50 shows the synchronized action of the upper arm, forearm, hand, and fingers in the staccato motion that enables the fingertips to descend vertically. The greatest amount of movement takes place in the hand and fingers, and there is a minimum of movement in the upper arm.

Figure 50. Synchronized action of the upper arm, forearm, hand, and fingers in the staccato motion

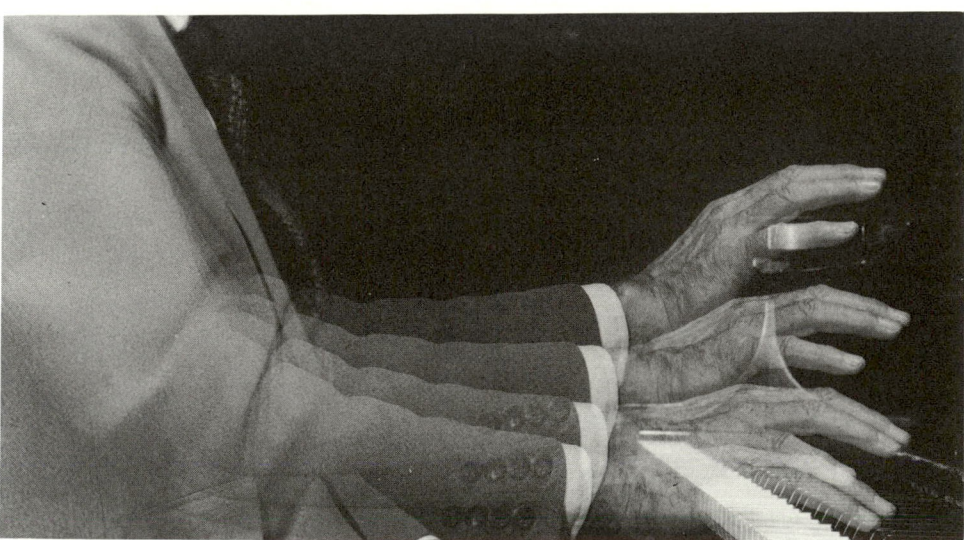

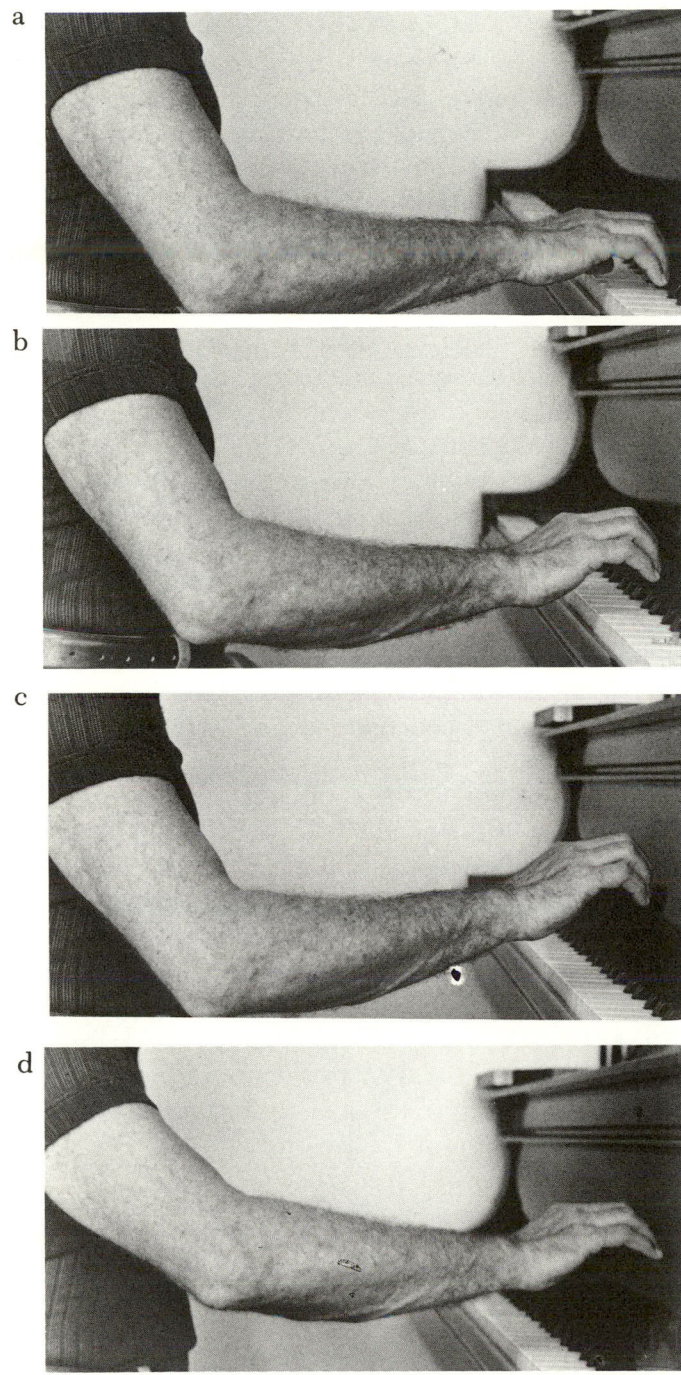

Figure 51. Staccato: simultaneous, gradual lifting of the
(a) fingers, (b) hand, (c) forearm, and (d) upper
arm

Optimal throw
of the fingertip
by activation of
the hand,
forearm, and
upper arm

If we add the forearm to the wrist motion, we are somewhat better off since we are utilizing stronger muscles—the upper-arm muscles that move the forearm (the biceps and triceps). Although the path traced by the descending fingertips is a less extreme curve, it is still not a straight line. Also, we still have no chance to activate the body muscles. The only way to produce a straight vertical line for the descent of the last phalanx of the finger is to activate the upper arm. And only with the aid of the upper arm can the strongest body muscles (the shoulder, back, chest, stomach, and diaphragm) participate in the throw. It now becomes obvious that the reason we get tired when using the wrist staccato is that the forearm muscles are relatively small and weak; they need help from the stronger body muscles.

Coordination is
essential.

We must therefore learn how to activate and cooperate with these larger muscles and generate the throw from the body itself. No ball player would dream of using only his wrist unless he wished to throw the ball a minimal distance. A pitcher's hand is thrown by the forearm, the forearm is thrown by the upper arm, and the upper arm is activated with the help of a strong twisting motion of the entire body. These motions involve the utmost coordination and efficiency. What happens in piano playing is that we throw the fingers toward the keys in a similar coordinated and effortless way. Our hand is thrown by the forearm, the forearm is thrown by the upper arm, and the upper arm is thrown by the powerful muscles of the body (no twisting motion though!). We then lift the fingers with the same active apparatus. In the loudest and fastest staccatos we can also take advantage of the rebound from the keyboard.

Four
components at
all times

By using a considerably longer and larger equipment than the hand alone, by distributing the up-and-down motions among four components instead of two, and by using the powerful muscles of the shoulder and chest instead of the weak forearm muscles, we are infinitely better off in terms of economy, endurance, and tone quality. Because of the efficient cooperation of the total equipment there is no trace of fatigue even in the most demanding passages, and there is a much better sound and greater identification with the music.

Upward and
downward
synchronization
of the entire
equipment

Let us examine the above points one by one. The activation of a *longer lever* obviously helps to generate greater speed at the extremity of the playing equipment; the result is a larger sound that is produced in a more economical way. The distribution of the motions is also advantageous; for example, if we want to raise the fingertips eight inches above the keys using the wrist alone, the hand will move about thirty-five degrees (see figure 52). Now, if we wish to cover the same distance by distributing the upward motion so that all components of the arm participate, we will only use a tiny motion by the fingers, a

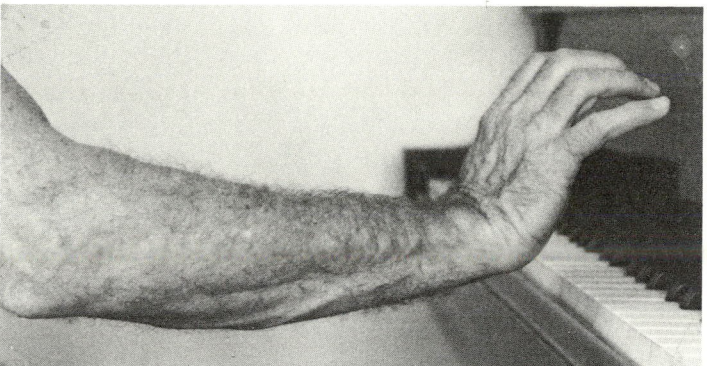

Figure 52. Excessive raising of the hand while keeping the forearm immobile causes excessive tension (wrong position).

tiny motion by the hand, a smaller motion by the forearm, and a still smaller one by the upper arm. The individual motions are minuscule, but with the correct synchronization, the result will be perfect and effortless. If we can get up to eight inches of height with minimal motions, how much less we'll have to move in rapid tempos when we need to come up only a fraction of an inch. All this is achieved by the distributed motions within a synchronized equipment. The synchronization of the motions both up and down is essential. When we go up, there must be a slight simultaneous rise of the finger, hand, forearm, and upper arm. The size of the individual motions is not only small but smaller and smaller as we proceed toward the larger ingredients: the upper arm moves the least. When we go down, all four components again move simultaneously. This condition is absolutely necessary. One error that is frequently made in playing staccato is that the arm is lifted but the hand is allowed to hang down passively, "relaxedly." The passive hand obstructs the throw motion! The hand and fingers must come up together with the rest of the equipment.

Active motion by all four components

Let us now examine the various stages of the staccato motion. We have discussed how to raise the arm, getting it into position before the throw begins. In the free-fall motion we prepared and lifted the arm and then simply inactivated the shoulder muscles to let the arm drop freely by the force of gravity, without interference or throw. The staccato motion differs from free fall in that here we actively throw the arm with the help of the shoulder and chest muscles: the throw is minimal, but it is active. The force of gravity also contributes to the downward motion but the main source of energy is one's own muscles. Also, in high speed the path covered is extremely short, so there is no time for the gradual acceleration caused by gravity. All the components are active and they execute very tiny motions. They receive a throw that originates from the upper arm, with the muscles of the shoulder and chest. When landing on the key and on the way back, all components must go through a minimal but definite change in every one of their joints. This minimal change guarantees that the muscles will not get fixed and stiff. Obviously these changes will be totally invisible in fast tempos, but they will be there! Please do not exaggerate any of these changes either, otherwise the relationship among the four components will be affected: the distribution has to be right. We can verify that we are performing the motions correctly by seeing that the fingertips move in a completely straight vertical line in the up-down motion.

We must be careful to avoid the following: stretched fingers at the landing, overly drawn-in fingers, a wrist either too high or too low, excessive forearm action, an immobilized forearm, excessive upper-arm motion (which causes excessive forward motion of the hand that disrupts the vertical approach to the keys), and insufficient movement of the upper arm.

Time spent on keys is minimal.

Since we are playing staccato, we spend as little time as possible on the surface of the keys; when landing on the keys, the time spent on the surface will be a mere fraction of a second. The moment the fingers touch the keys, we immediately lift the entire equipment (the fingers, hand, and arm), raising it to its original position to receive the next throw. The hand and fingers must bounce back immediately as if dribbling a ball, or as if the keys were sizzling hot!

Entire equipment is lifted simultaneously.

It is also important to lift up the entire arm simultaneously—not the arm first and then the hand as in the free-fall lifting, but the whole unit together. This motion is essential. We must place them again in a position where they can best receive the throw which is within their central range.

Rebound from keybed

Since we want to utilize any help we can get, we also take advantage of the rebound from the bottom of the key. When we play loud and fast, we throw the fingers to the bottom of the keys; since the keybed is made of elastic material, it responds with considerable rebound. When we come down with vigor, we feel quite a strong recoil. This counteraction to our action can be of considerable advantage in lifting the equipment, our next chore before throwing it down again. An elastic hand and arm, therefore, receive considerable help from the keybed itself. Therefore in extreme fortissimo passages played at top speed the staccato action may be reduced to a purely downward active throw; the upward motion is automatically taken care of by this upward rebound. This is the way to play some of the most spectacularly rapid fortissimo octaves and chords.

Innumerable
variants in
combinations of
the four
components

After we acquire the habit of using the entire arm for staccato, we can explore innumerable variants of this motion. They are innumerable because, although only four components are involved, we can vary their speed, height, and position, and we can vary the prominence given to the fingers, hand, forearm, and upper arm or to any combination of these components. While we always use the entire apparatus, we may alter slightly the amount of finger action, wrist action, forearm action, and upper-arm action; we may also vary a combination of any two or three components (forearm-fingers, wrist-fingers, forearm-wrist, and so on). The potential for variety in sound production is also unlimited since sound is the result of motions that generate it and you will have different tone qualities and quantities according to the way the equipment is used. Obviously a light sound results from using more finger and wrist action than forearm and upper-arm action. We may choose the components to emphasize, but it must be the entire mechanism that always works. No "wrist staccato," please—don't use the wrist exclusively.

White and black
keys

Concerning white and black keys, the same considerations are valid as for the free fall, scales and arpeggios, and rotation. Because of the topography of the keyboard the playing equipment has to be placed higher when you play on the black keys. If they are used extensively, the forward position of the arms is helped by a slight leaning forward of the trunk; that position can reduce the forward motion of the arm.

The body moves.

If we keep on changing the position of the body continuously, we help to free joints of any fixed, immobile condition. Don't move too much, though; just move a little—in the direction where you play: the less the better.

Adjusting
motions: lining
up the fingers
with their
muscles

To line up the fingers with their respective forearm muscles is just as necessary in staccato playing as in scale and free-fall playing. Lining them up is done by a horizontal, vertical, and in-depth adjusting motion. Because of this alignment the throw from the upper arm is received much more directly, and it is transmitted through the fingers straight to the keys.

Legato octaves

Legato octaves require basically the same up-and-down motions of the arm as staccato octaves, except for two things: first, the up-down motions (used on each note) are as gentle and small as possible, and, second, the fingers stay on the keys until the end of the metric value of the note. The legato effect is produced by the gentle depression of the key in the down motion while the next note will be connected by the slow descent of the damper caused by the slow-up motion of the arm. Incidentally notes are grouped together with the help of an upward motion of the arm, just as in ordinary legato playing. Whether the

Volume: joints

sequence of the notes is white followed by black or black followed by white, we don't have to go up-down on each note; we lower the arm gently on the first key and raise it on the key that ends the group.

The volume of the sound of legato octaves is regulated the same way as it is in staccato octaves: soft joints are used for soft sounds; resistant and resilient joints are used for louder sounds. Any fixation of the joints in forte playing should always be instantaneous and not prolonged.

The motion for legato-octave playing is more like a shift than a throw (see figure 53). The octave passages in examples 43 and 44 illustrate the contrast between the two types of playing motion; the Liszt sixth rhapsody calls for the staccato throwing motion, while the Chopin etude requires the shift of the legato octave motion. Bear in mind that this is not a wrist motion: the entire arm must always participate, helped by the body.

Example 43. Liszt, *Hungarian Rhapsody No. 6*

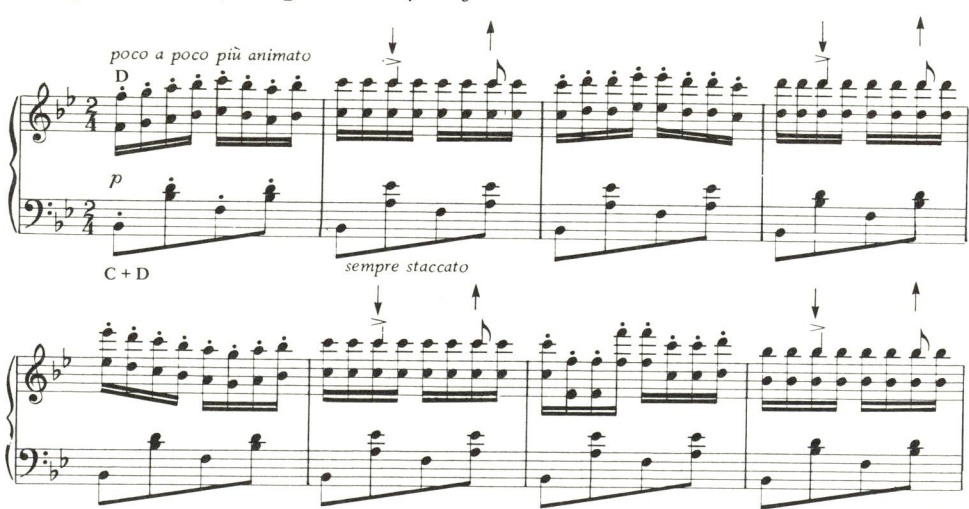

Example 44. Chopin, *Etude*, opus 25 no. 10

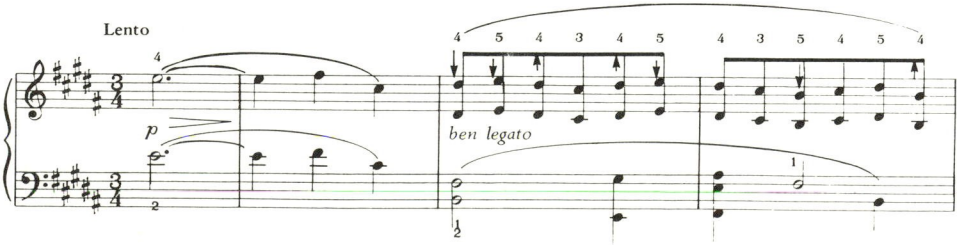

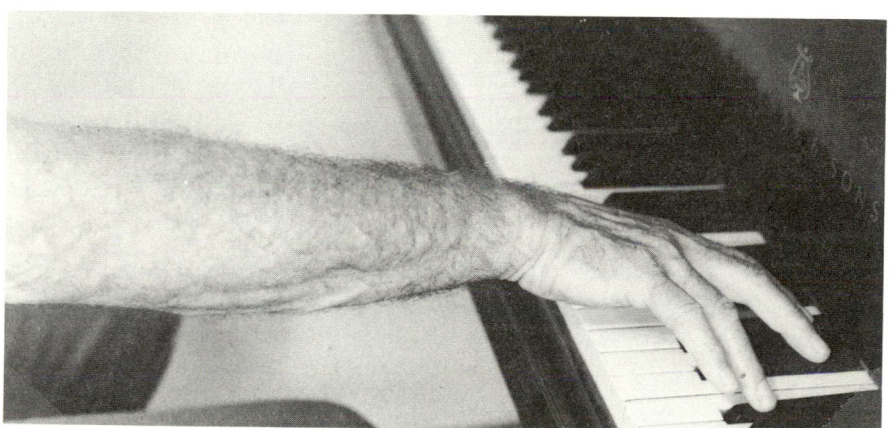

Figure 53. Elevation of the wrist for legato octaves on black keys

Eliminate strain.   If we adopt these ideas and live or, rather, play by them, the use of the strongest muscles of the body and the distribution of the movements will enable us to play without any strain. The need to strengthen the smaller muscles will be eliminated; instead of exercising muscles we will aim for coordination, synchronizing the small muscles with the powerful ones and enabling them to receive help. The resistance of the keys is not more than two ounces: if we tap the available powerful muscles, we have no excuse for feeling tired in our arms—or anywhere else. The force of gravity is always present, and will help us if we allow it to do so.

First practice
individual
components;
then
combinations.

Change in
motion when
accelerating

It is advisable to begin practicing the staccato motion with an awareness of all the components; at first concentrate only on the slight raising and lowering of the fingers, then of the hand, then of the forearm, and the upper arm. Next, synchronize them in two's and three's, before you attempt to master all four of them.

In the summary of basic technical patterns I will describe a certain change in the motions of the arm while accelerating the staccato motion. In the meantime let us concentrate on the correct assimilation of the fundamental motion itself (see page 104).

Guidelines for
staccato

1. Single notes, intervals, and chords all require the same throwing motion when they are played staccato. Therefore octaves can be played just as quickly as the fastest single notes. Because the throw comes from the strongest body muscles, which transmit their energy through the entire arm, the entire arm must always be activated in the staccato motion.

2. The throw is initiated by the upper arm. Both in the down motion and the up motion the components act simultaneously. The speed of the motions is the same in both directions. The time spent on the surface of the keys (whether we "hit bottom" or not) should be as short as possible—a mere fraction of a second is all the time necessary—except in legato octaves, where we stay on the keys with the fingers.

3. The staccato motion is never sudden or jerky; if we want a louder sound, we make the joints more resilient or increase the distance of the throw, or we combine these actions.

4. When we move from finger to finger and from key to key, we must make a continuous adjustment in the arm and body position in order to prevent any fixed, stiff position. If we have to repeat the same notes with the same fingers for an extended time, we prevent fixation by slight changes of position of some or all of the components.

5. In legato octaves, we complement a minimal arm-throw motion with active fingerwork to connect the notes more easily. The throw is so small that the finger doesn't have to leave the key.

6. The staccato motion is often combined with other basic motions: scales (horizontal and vertical adjustment of the arm) and rotation are the most common ones.

7. There is no need to concentrate on and exercise the activities of the shoulder, chest, and stomach muscles; it is sufficient to practice the complete synchronization of the four elements of the arm (finger, hand, forearm, and upper arm). Once the body position is well established, the control of the active components of the arm is all that is

needed. If the arm works well, the strong muscles will step in when they are needed.

8. Every participating member of the playing apparatus should endeavor to operate within its central range; and should also continuously and purposefully change its position to let the antagonist muscles be activated.

9. Once the body muscles that help the arm in staccato motion are activated, the diaphragm can participate on its own. In a sense, it "initiates" the motion by means of its rapid contractions. The diaphragm can generate maximum speed—the same speed that singers and wind players can attain in their staccatos!

Exercises for staccato

1. Most faults in staccato (octave) playing are caused by the lack or excess of action in some components of the playing apparatus. As I have repeatedly stated, the upper arm, forearm, hand, and fingers must all be actively involved in this motion. The exercises aim primarily at achieving correct coordination by establishing at what rate each unit should move. The simplest way to test the correctness of the total movement is to check whether the up-and-down motion of the arm results in a vertical path of the fingertips. If there is too much or too little activity in any of the ingredients, this line will deviate from a line perpendicular to the keys. We must make sure that the adjusting motions of the forearm line up the fingers with their respective forearm muscles. Remember that all motions of the arm serve only one purpose—to help the fingers receive and transmit their throw. After wide stretches (octaves or ninths) be sure that the hand has a chance to regain its central position: this is achieved by raising the hands and slightly pulling in the fingers. The wrist should not remain in a fixed position.

2. Use fingers 1, 2, 3, 4, and 5 successively (watch their forearm-adjusting motions); first play the exercises hands separately; then hands together, using both parallel and symmetrical motions. Play them on white and black keys, simultaneously and alternately. Graduate the volume from pianissimo to fortissimo. Use the same exercises for intervals of all sizes and chords. As the speed increases, the size of the motion will decrease.

Shift of sequence of arm motion in rapid staccato

3. Although staccato motion can be considered a simultaneous throw of all the components involved, there is nevertheless an infinitesimal time lapse between the initiation of the throw by the shoulder and its reception by the fingers. Therefore in fast tempos a slight

shift in the sequence and appearance of the staccato motion occurs. In slow tempos the fingers, hand, forearm, and upper arm move up or down simultaneously. In fast tempo, that minimal lapse of time will cause the fingers, hand, and forearm to go downward, while the upper arm moves forward (or up); when the first three components move upward, the upper arm moves back (or down). This slight alteration happens only beyond a certain fast tempo, and it occurs automatically. Do not be concerned with it; under no circumstance should you try to practice the staccato motion that way in slower tempos. All four components must move in the same direction and simultaneously, and the altered motion must come about involuntarily. When you become aware of this change, do not interfere with it, nor should you try to bring it about consciously either. As a matter of fact, when you play fast and are about to slow down, be sure that the original motion (the simultaneous one) returns. Then, when you accelerate beyond a certain speed, let the resultant motion come about automatically. You might have some doubts about this, but experience will validate my observations.

Example 45. Staccato patterns (single, double)

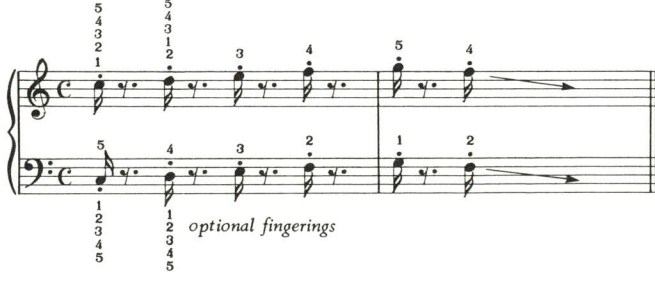

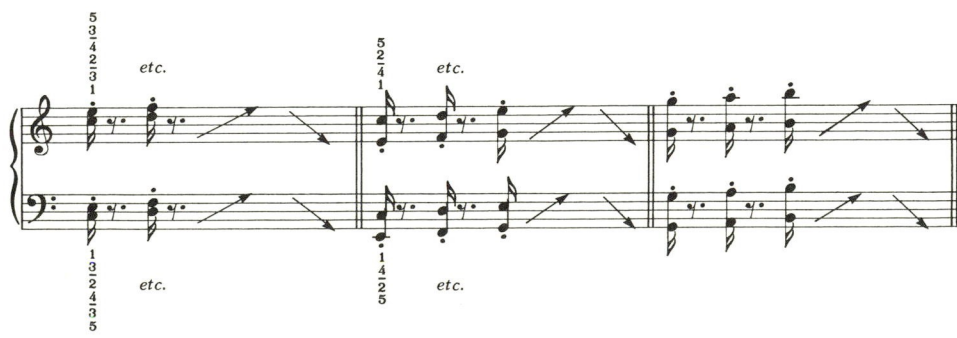

Symbols

Examples for
staccato

A	free fall	D	*staccato*
B	five-fingers, scales, arpeggios	E	thrust
C	rotation	↓	low wrist
		↑	high wrist

Example 46. Beethoven, *Sonata*, opus 14 no. 2, second movement

Example 47. Brahms, *Variations and Fugue on a Theme by Handel*, opus 24, variation 22

Example 48. Liszt, *Sonata in B Minor*

Example 49. Liszt, *Transcendental Etude No. 4* ("Mazeppa")

Example 50. Liszt, *Spanish Rhapsody*

Example 51. Liszt, *Transcendental Etude No. 7* ("Eroica")

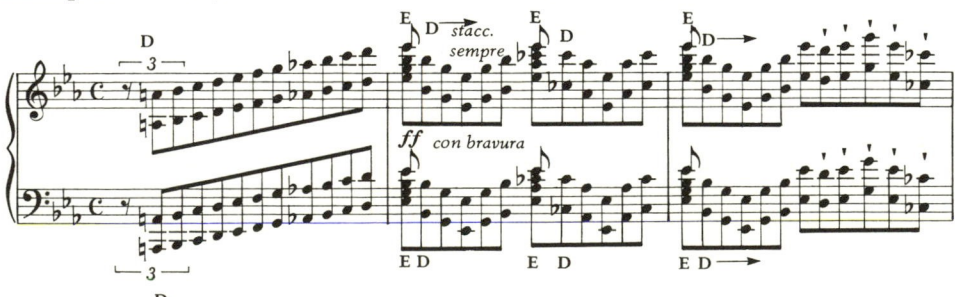

Example 52. Chopin, *Etude*, opus 25 no. 10

CHAPTER

8　Thrust

Thrust vs. free
fall

In the chapter on free fall (chapter four) we explained the technique of producing large sonorities primarily with the help of the force of gravity. The active involvement of the muscular system was limited to (1) lifting the playing equipment (the arms and the hands) and placing it in the proper position where the force of gravity could activate its downward fall, and (2) the instantaneous fixating of the forearm muscles when contact is made with the keys, enabling the fingers to transfer the full impact of the fall to the keys. After this split-second fixation the shoulder muscles immediately lift the arm to prepare it for the next fall. In the free fall muscles do not participate during the downward motion of the arm; its fall and acceleration are caused exclusively by the force of gravity.

Thrust:
maximum
power and fast
reflexes from
the surface of
the keys

The technique we will examine now, the *thrust*, is executed purely by active muscles, and neither the force of gravity nor weight are employed. Instead of raising the arm, hand, and fingers and exposing them to the gradual acceleration of the force of gravity, we place the fingers right on the surface of the keys and push the keys down with a sudden instantaneous contraction of some of the strongest body and arm muscles (the chest, stomach, back triceps, and forearm flexor muscles). This action generates maximum speed in the fingertips. In the thrust, unlike the techniques described before, the fingers are in constant contact with the keys; they touch the keys before, during and after the actual sudden muscle contraction takes place. The speed our powerful muscles generate by this lightninglike contraction is such that, were we to create distance between the fingers and keys, a crude, harsh and forced sound would result. Within the limits of the elasticity of the materials the piano is made of, the maximum sonorities of the instrument can be produced by this thrust from the surface of the keys. Since we use our strongest equipment only for a split second, the motion feels totally effortless, and since the muscles return to their original condition and shape immediately, they are ready at once for the next thrust.

We do not want to mix the thrust with either the free fall or with any throw motion. We must train the entire muscular system for this sudden electric-shocklike contraction during which the body appears to be motionless. First we must assume the right position for this action, and then we must not budge while the thrust takes place. The fingers stay on the surface of the keys, and the arms are slightly bent. The thrust must go vertically *down* into the keys, and the body must remain immobile to resist the rebound that takes place from the keybed. No matter how sudden and rapid the thrust, it will not produce a hard sound, since the fingers are in direct contact with the keys and their acceleration will not surpass the optimum speed for maximum volume. This last condition is essential; otherwise the speed of the thrust would compel the piano to produce a forced sound. A good, sensitive piano should never be forced!

No extended contraction or fixation. Downward direction

In executing the thrust motion there is absolutely no need to push the arm upward, no need to lean during the motion, and no need to push the head forward. Also any prolonged fixation should be avoided at all costs. The contraction must be as sudden and as short as possible; otherwise stiffness and rigidity will occur.

As usual, the position of the body and arms is adjusted for playing on white or black keys (see figures 54 and 55).

When to use thrust

The thrust lends itself to moderately fast passages and slow chord sequences. The sudden contraction followed by the total relaxation of the muscles obviously takes more time than a rapid succession of throw motions. However the sound is powerful and effortless. This technique is also ideal for wide stretches and chords, where the free-fall motion would be risky. Of course, the degree and speed of contraction is optional: in fortissimos we utilize the maximum speed of contraction; otherwise we apportion speed according to the volume of sound we want to produce.

Figure 54. Position for thrust on white keys   **Figure 55.** Position for thrust on black keys

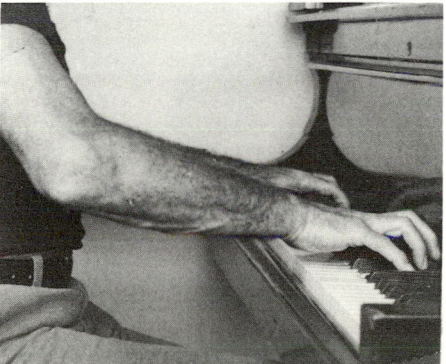

Summary

Here is a summary of the basic principles involved in the thrust:

1. The fingers must be in touch with the keys before, during, and sometimes after the push. Even at the loudest fortissimos, the muscular contraction is instantaneous and as brief as possible. The direction of the push is vertical, not slanted or upward. If we abide by these conditions, we will be able to produce the loudest sonorities without a trace of tension or fatigue. The speed of our reflexes can be developed by practice.

2. The suddenness of the contraction can be regulated at will. We need not think in terms of excessive fortes at all times; the thrust can serve mezzo forte or piano sonorities as well. The dynamic level depends on the abruptness of the attack. This motion is regulated by the extremely sensitive, tactile nerve endings of the fingertips, which are in continuous touch with the keys, and the volume is influenced by the degree of softness and elasticity of the joints at the moment of impact.

3. For large, extended chords thrust is preferable to free fall. There is less risk of hitting wrong notes; moreover a stretched hand position usually interferes with the free acceleration of the fall.

4. During the thrust the shoulders and body support the active role of the arms; they remain immobile when the thrust goes into the keyboard. Unless we hold the shoulders and body firmly in place, they will bounce backward by resistance from the keybed; during the thrust they should remain still. Visually, this activity appears surprisingly low key because the body remains immobile and the arms move downward only about a half inch. But it can generate the loudest bang the piano can produce!

Exercises for thrust

None needed! Apply the technique of thrust as it is described here to any chord or interval; and then apply it to any portion of the literature that calls for it. Some sample passages that call for thrust are given in the following examples.

Examples for thrust

Symbols

A free fall
B five-fingers, scales, arpeggios
C rotation
D staccato

E   *thrust*
↑   high wrist
↓   low wrist

Example 53. Chopin, *Prelude in C Minor,* opus 28 no. 20

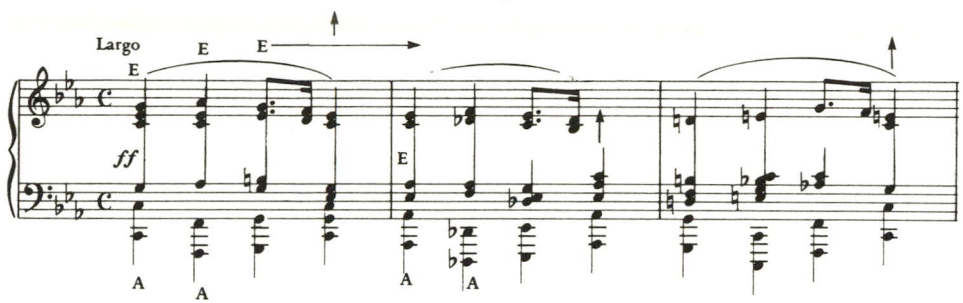

Example 54. Liszt, *Années de Pèlerinage,* "Après une lecture de Dante"

Example 55. Liszt, *Spanish Rhapsody*

Example 56. Brahms, *Variations and Fugue on a Theme by Handel*, opus 24
variation 9

Example 57. Beethoven, *Piano Concerto No. 5* ("Emperor"), opus 83, first movement

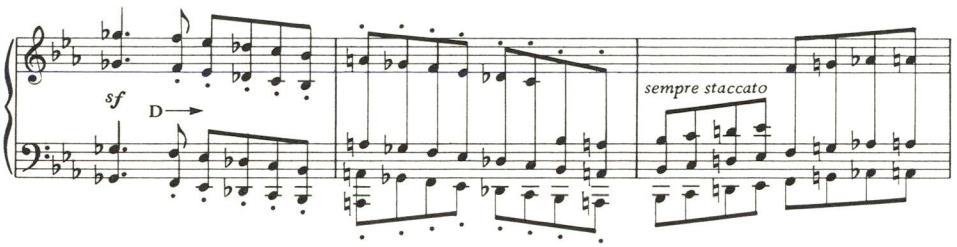

Example 58. Liszt, *Transcendental Etude No. 7* ("Eroica")

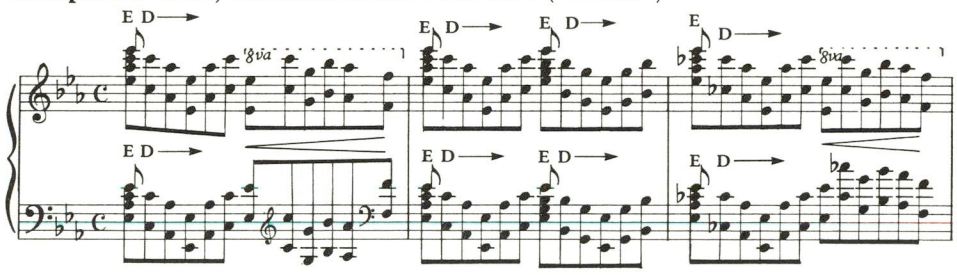

Example 59. Beethoven, *Sonata*, opus 106, first movement

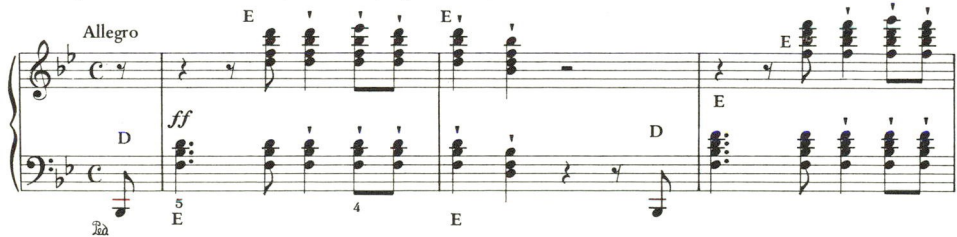

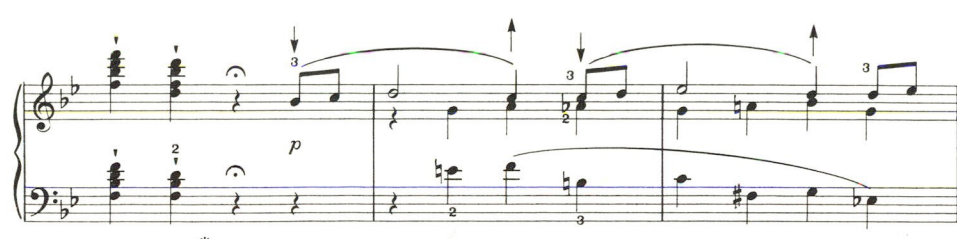

Example 60. Tchaikovsky, *Piano Concerto No. 1,* first movement

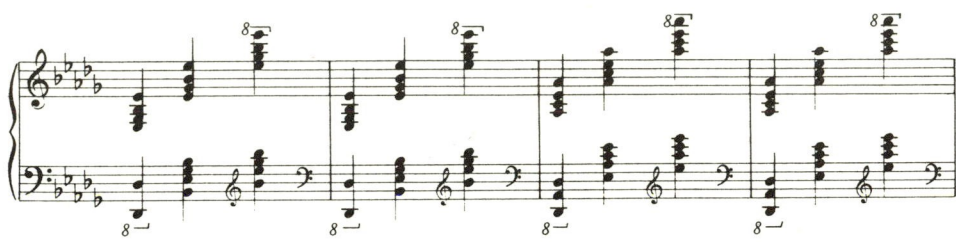

9 Summary of the Basic Technical Patterns

Fundamental motion patterns, individually or combined, provide the solution to all technical problems.

The preceding chapters have listed five basic motion patterns and their symbols: (A) free fall; (B) five-fingers, scales, and arpeggios; (C) rotation; (D) staccato (octaves); and (E) thrust.

We contend that these five fundamental patterns offer a solution for most, if not all, technical problems in piano playing when they are applied individually or in combination with one another. This is not to say that all difficulties will be eliminated; rather, it means that no passage should leave us puzzled about the type of motion to apply in resolving the technical problem posed. The difficulties of playing with extreme speed, accuracy, and control still exist, but we now know how to resolve technical problems and how to practice even the most complex and challenging passages. One may not be able to duplicate the nearly incredible feat of Richter's performance of Liszt's "Feux Follets," but the technical solutions are available; the rest depends on our perseverance, imagination, and talent.

Score indicates the motions to be applied.

All of these basic technical patterns are recognizable and indicated within the written score. The patterns of musical notation indicate unequivocally the basic formula or formulas to be applied. Indeed, any sequence of notes, phrasing indication, or touch forms (legato, staccato, portato, and tenuto) can and must be matched with its own technical equivalent. Once we have identified the type of motions to be used (after the indications in the score), our only concern is its proper execution.

Individuality and variety in every action

I must emphasize that the recognition and application of these basic patterns by no means limit the variety and richness of expression we are seeking. Rudimentary as they may be, these patterns lend themselves to an unlimited variety of shadings according to how they are graduated, how they are combined and what each performer's anatomy, reflexes, temperament, tactile sensibilities, weight, and size are. If I accent a note or if I retard or accelerate a passage, these actions reflect my own reflexes, responses, and personality. Similarly any motion pattern will be characterized by the performer's constitution and anatomy, and so will the quality of his tone. There is no need to search for individualizing performances, because the individual is manifested in every breath and every gesture. Once the technical doubts and obstacles are removed, there is unlimited opportunity for spontaneous responses, where originality, talent, or genius can manifest themselves.

These observations apply to the interpretation and execution of the written text. The text will be realized through the application of the appropriate, basic motion patterns—the technical formulas explained in the preceding chapters. A summary of the technical, mechanical aspects of piano playing will be followed by an explanation of the way to translate the visual patterns of a score into motion patterns—that is, the way to transform the score into technique. Although free fall was the first motion discussed, we will begin our review with the five-finger, scale, and arpeggio movement (B), because it is the motion pattern that is used most often.

Five-fingers require five characteristic hand and arm positions

First, let us remember that each of the fingers has a characteristic position in which it functions at its best. It should be placed in a straight line with its respective forearm muscles. We know that the thumb generically requires a lower wrist position than the other fingers and that the wrist and arm gradually rise as we progress toward the fifth finger. We call these motions that align the fingers with their forearm muscles adjusting motions; they can be made horizontally, vertically, and in depth (from the edge of the key to its back). They accommodate the fingers with small changes of position and thus eliminate any fixed positions of the wrist and arm. Therefore a sequence of notes in the score not only dictates the notes' location on the keyboard and the finger action that makes them sound, but it automatically specifies all the simultaneous, coordinated arm and wrist actions appropriate to the playing mechanism. There is a slight and continuous change in the position of the equipment while we move from one finger to the other; it is not an aimless wandering, but a purposeful one. Bear in mind that we are actually dealing with five slightly different arm-hand-finger positions that come about as the occasion requires. Of course, these positions are modified according to whether we play on white or black keys, whether at the central or extreme areas of the keyboard. The body leans forward or sideways, and the wrist position changes to avoid any unnecessary strain.

Let us examine these simple note patterns:

Example 61. Unslurred five-finger pattern

Score indicates
the location of
the notes and
the motion
patterns to be
used.

Their visual image at once evokes the five-finger technical solution. We immediately equate (in both hands) the first C with a low wrist position (the thumb calls for it), a forearm position that falls in line with the thumb, and a gentle finger motion. The next note, the D, calls for a slightly higher wrist for the index finger, and it also demands a slight lateral shift of the forearm to line up the second finger with its muscles. At this point we lift the thumb to join the other fingers that are not playing. In other words, this sequence of notes in the score indicates the action to be taken, not only by the fingers, but by the wrist, forearm, and upper arm; it also tells us how to proceed to the following note. By the time we reach the note to be played by the fourth finger, the forearm and wrist are in exactly the position the fourth finger requires—that is, farther out and up. The highest position for the wrist and arm is at the fifth note (avoid being too far out), after which the upper arm, forearm, and wrist gradually return to original position, reaching the lowest point at the thumb. Remember that each finger must do its own share; only one is on a key; the other fingers are slightly raised, ready to come down as soon as the rest of the equipment (the wrist and arm) are brought into position. These principles apply to both hands.

A slur modifies
technique.

The notes in example 62 follow the same ascending and descending stepwise pattern as those in example 61. However here the slurs unite the notes into groups.

Example 62. Slurred five-finger pattern

These slurs thoroughly modify the technical interpretation of the notes. In example 61 our only concern was placing the arm, fingers, and wrist in the precise position required for each finger, with the lowest wrist for the thumb and the highest for the fifth finger. In example 62 the slur indicates a grouping that alters the technical solution to the passage. We must tie these notes together; to do so we use the technique of legato playing.

Arm and wrist
always lower at
beginning of a
group, higher at
end

We have stated that a real legato cannot be achieved solely by finger activity (even though, as usual, the fingers have an active role); for the notes tied together by a slur, we use an upward motion of the arm and hand. At the beginning, we always use a relatively low wrist, hand, and arm position, and at the end of a group, the wrist, hand, and arm position is higher; this is a firm rule with no exceptions.

Now this rule seems to contradict our first basic rule; actually it only complements it. We still line up the forearm with each finger, and we still have a relatively low position for the thumb and a higher one for the fifth finger; however while we play the notes within the slur, the upper arm gradually raises the whole apparatus slightly. At the end of the slur the forearm, hand, and fingers abandon the keys with an upward motion, regardless of which finger is ending the phrase. Any group of notes that is perceived to be a technical or musical group should be played with this ascending arm motion whether the slur has actually been notated or not. The extent of the lift is determined by the usual factors: whether we end the group on black or white keys, what is the location of the passage on the keyboard, and which one of the fingers ends the group.

Therefore the technical interpretation of example 62 demands: a low wrist position for the first note, a higher position for the next, and the highest position at the last note (not too high, please!) On the next note, at the beginning of the new slur, a low wrist position is used for the fifth finger; a gradually higher position is used for the next note, and the highest position is used for the last note, which is played by the thumb. Again the technical interpretation is the same for both hands.

Phrase endings

Please remember that no matter which finger plays—whether it is the thumb or the fifth finger—at the beginning of the phrase the wrist is low and at the end of the phrase, it is higher. The reasons for these categorical statements can be found in the chapter on legato playing, if you wish to refresh your memory. No matter how many notes there are in the group, there is always an upward motion at the end of the group. In a very long legato passage smaller subdivisions may be found where we can employ this upward movement; at the end of the phrase the upward motion will again be in evidence. Of course, anything that goes up has to come down; so be sure that the wrist returns to its low point when you begin the next group. These groupings are sometimes technical and sometimes musical; the two aspects do not always coincide. Also the groupings are not always marked in the score. Nevertheless, whether we play Bach or Bartok, slowly or quickly, loudly or softly, the binding of notes into groups is accomplished by upward arm motions.

Example 63. Beethoven, *Sonata*, opus 53 ("Waldstein"), first movement

In example 63 the dotted slurs represent subdivisions of the printed slur. Use a lower wrist at the beginning and a higher wrist at the end of each of these subdivisions.

By the way, when we end a phrase, the length of the last note is the performer's choice; it can be short, medium, or long. This note's length is determined by the amount of time the finger remains on the key and is indicated by the score. An upward arm motion regulates this motion too. Do not make all your phrase endings uniform; we have all the tools we need to vary the touch, color, and dynamics. A satisfactorily working apparatus in which all the components function within, or close to, the central areas of their range is all that is necessary.

One word of caution: whenever the wrist, hand, and arm are in action, watch the fingers. They tend to become passive, motionless, and to hang over the keys. There must be a coordinated action between the fingers and the rest of the apparatus; the fingers must always be *slightly* raised before playing, and they should be constantly active. Only in maximum speed does the finger action become so tiny that it is invisible. Another word of warning: whenever the fingers are active (especially when they are overactive), the wrist may freeze; it tends to become fixed and stiff. Both of these threats are real, and many pianistic problems and absurdities result from these two mistakes. We must synchronize our actions so that *each component does its own work*, thereby reducing all motions to their minimum. But one does not substitute the work of any one component for the work of another. You will find that if one is inactive or overactive, the other components will compensate for it. Avoid excessive motions, don't raise the fingers too high, and don't make large circular motions with the wrist, forearm, or upper arm. Don't fix and stiffen the wrist, don't press the upper arm to the body, or hold your fingers glued to the keys.

Examples 61–63 are extremely simple, but they are quite characteristic of passages in complex scores. The five-finger, scale, and arpeggio formulas should be applied in any passage where the notes move in the same direction in groups of three or more notes. No matter which direction they move in, what the style of the piece is, what the dynamics are, or whether the notes are single, double, or chords, the scale and arpeggio technique applies. However, if the notes are marked staccato, tenuto, or portato, we must employ the respective touch forms.

Here are a few examples of passages where the scale technique can be applied:

Each component must do its work; no compensation by other members of the team

Recognize patterns containing notes moving in the same direction (scales, arpeggios).

Examples

Example 64. Chopin, *Etude*, opus 10 no. 2

Example 65. Chopin, *Etude*, opus 10 no. 4

Example 66. Chopin, *Etude,* opus 10 no. 8

Example 67. Chopin, *Etude*, opus 10 no. 12

Example 68. Chopin, *Etude*, opus 25 no. 2

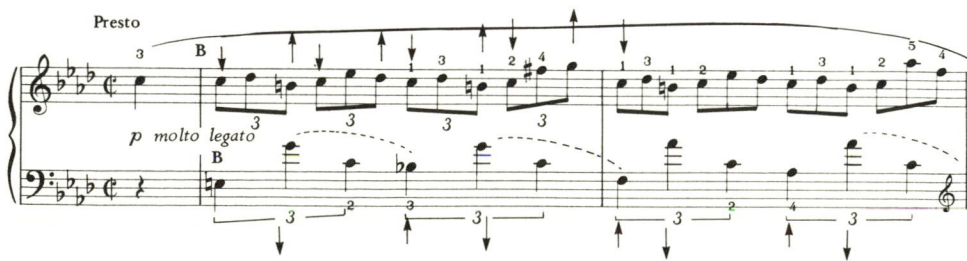

Example 69. Chopin, *Etude,* opus 25 no. 12

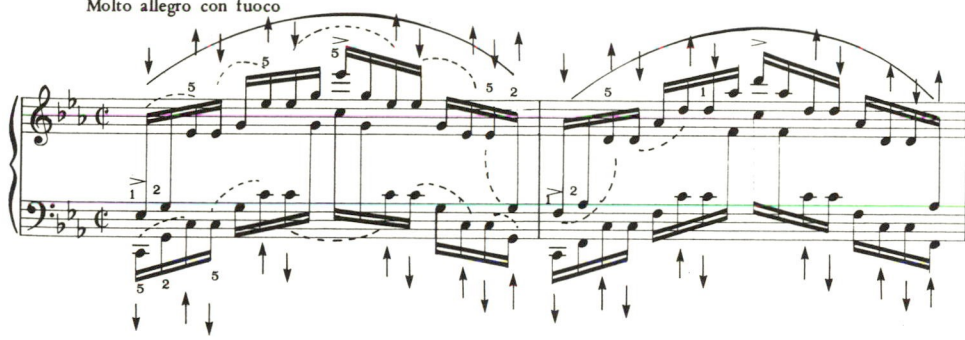

Example 70. Mendelssohn, *Etude in F Major,* opus 104

Example 71. Liszt, *Concert Etude No. 2 in F Minor* ("La Leggierezza")

The thumb and upper arm

Scales and arpeggios are basically five-finger motions with the added complication that the thumb passes under or over the third or fourth finger. In scales and arpeggios avoid keeping the thumb under the palm of the hand and allow it to function alongside the hand by lifting the upper arm slightly away from the body. When the hand moves away from the center of the keyboard, the elbow must move away from the body just before the thumb is about to play, and the wrist must be lowered. Then the position appropriate to the next finger is assumed. The elbow swings back and forth continuously during runs in which the right hand goes up and the left hand goes down. However, when you move from the extremities of the keyboard toward its center, the upper arm must stay out all the time, and it is the wrist that goes down and up depending on the note grouping and the fingers that play. The degree to which the upper arm stays up depends on the location of the notes on the keyboard: at the extremes the elbow must stay farther out. In arpeggios, where the intervals between notes are large, the elbow must stay even farther out to facilitate the fingers' passing over the thumb. The size of the motions, as always, depends on the speed at which we play. It diminishes as speed increases, and grows as the tempo gets slower. However each component must contribute its full share of aid to the fingers.

Rotation suggested by the score

Identifying musical patterns where rotation is applied is a simple matter; rotation is used whenever notes go up-down-up or down-up-down. The obvious examples of this motion are tremolos and tremolo-like passages.

Example 72. Bach, *Organ Toccata and Fugue in D Minor*

You will recall how carefully one must modify the size of the rotary motions when the size of the interval, the dynamics, or the location on the keyboard is changed or when there is a change from white keys to black.

Other examples in which rotation should be applied include:

Example 73. Chopin, *Etude*, opus 10 no. 5

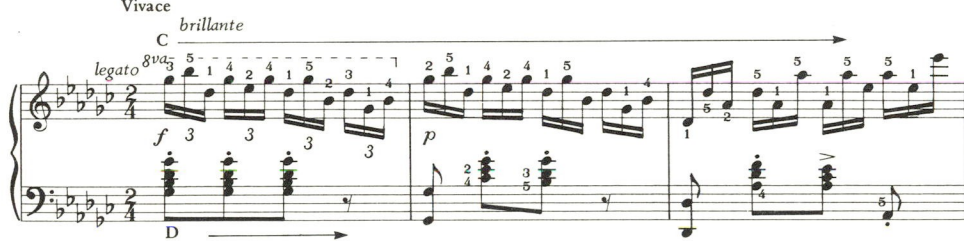

Example 74. Chopin, *Etude*, opus 10 no. 10

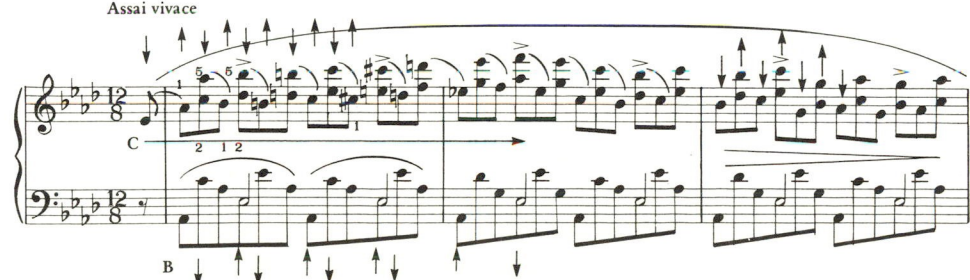

(Example 74 continued)

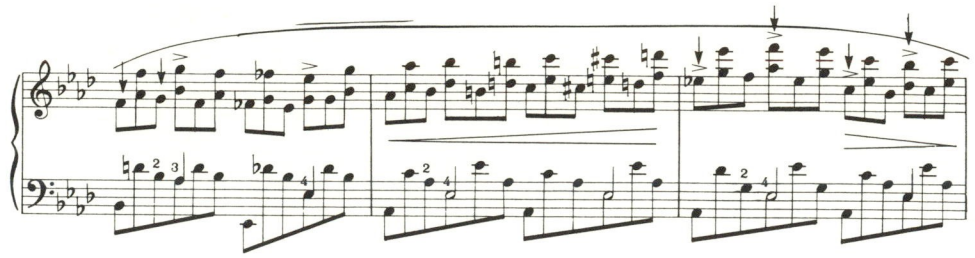

Example 75. Chopin, *Etude*, opus 25 no. 11

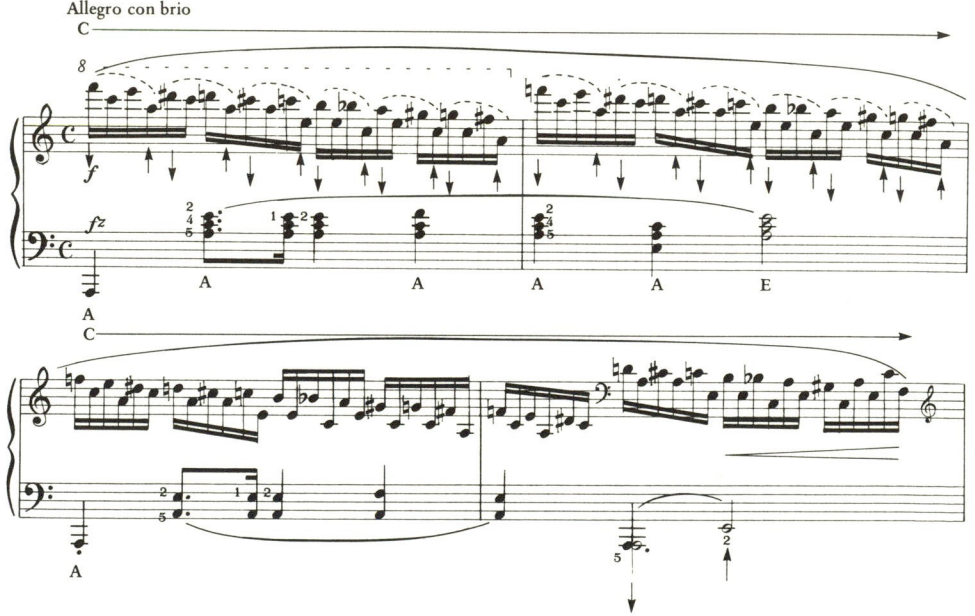

Example 76. Liszt, *Paganini Etude No. 3* ("La Campanella")

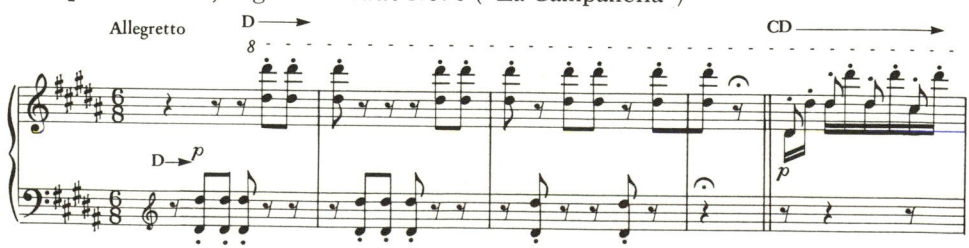

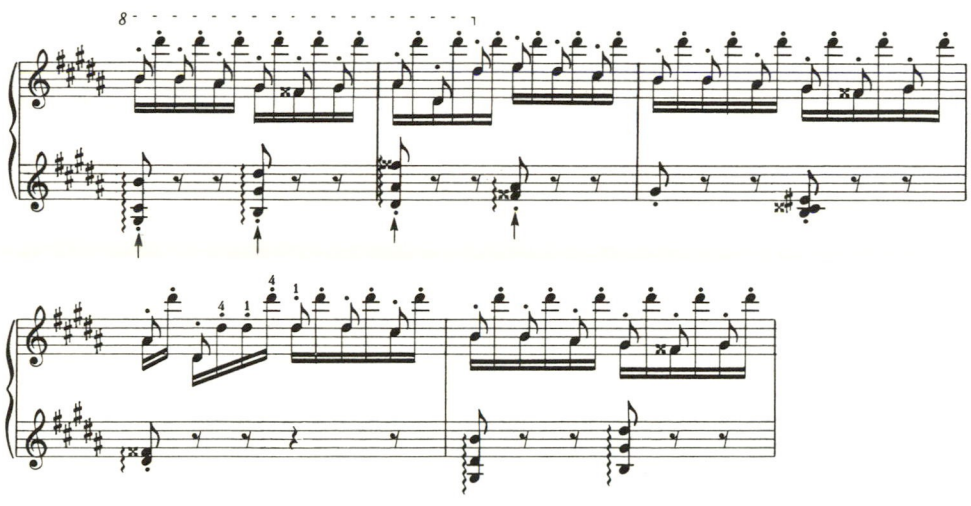

Example 77. Beethoven, *Sonata*, opus 13, first movement

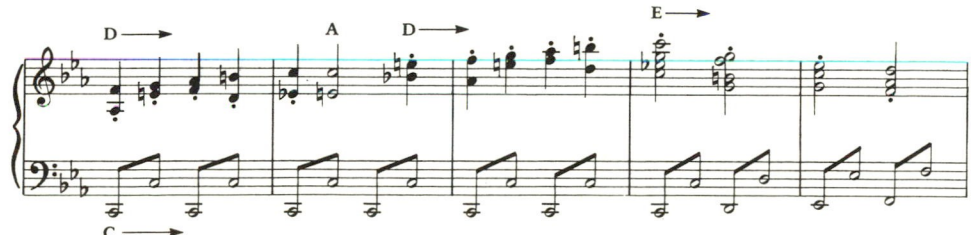

Example 78. Beethoven, *Sonata,* opus 26, fourth movement

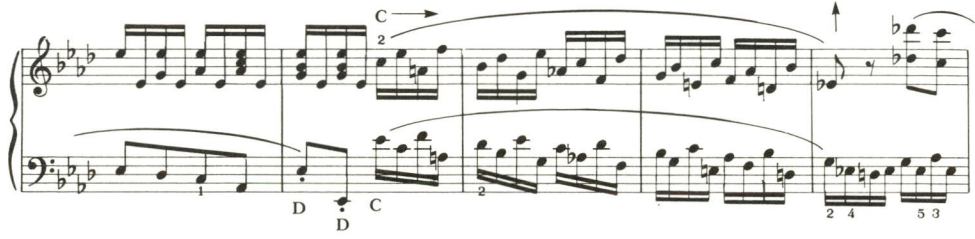

Trills

In all these examples, rotary motion prevails and it can be easily recognized from the score. Many trills can be executed with this motion, especially when the 1–3, 2–4, or 3–5 fingerings are used. It is essential that the forearm rotation be transmitted to the fingers, which should be slightly raised in anticipation of the axial throw of the forearm. Forearm rotation must be used judiciously—too much activity may immobilize the fingers; too little activity strains them as they try to do most of the work.

I mentioned earlier that the technical grouping of a passage may not coincide with its musical grouping. In the Chopin *Etude,* opus 25 no. 11 (example 75) the rotary motion must be applied in groups of four, according to the technical demands of the passage, in spite of the fact that the notes are written in groups of six. In example 79, the quadruple grouping of the rotary action is indicated by dotted slurs.

Example 79. Chopin, *Etude,* opus 25 no. 11

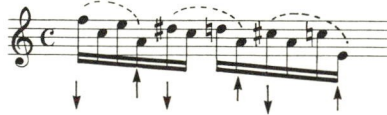

A slight downward position must be assumed on the first note of each group, and a slight upward motion of the wrist is needed toward the fourth note of each group. These cyclic motions do not coincide with the musical grouping of the passage and with the bass, but they are required to increase the fast, loud, and effortless activities of the fingers. Besides the forearm's rotary motion, the fingers need the extra up-down motion of the wrist to add maximum speed and power to their activities.

Rotation plus lateral movement and in combination with staccato

Many passages in piano music call for rotation. Whenever the notes constantly reverse their direction, rotation is the motion pattern to use. When the intervals grow wider and when axial rotation is insufficient, a lateral movement of the forearm has to be added. On some occasions rotation must be combined with a staccato motion; for example, see Liszt's "La Campanella" (example 76) and "Paganini" in Schumann's *Carnaval*.

Staccato

The vertical throw of staccato motion is most often employed for isolated sounds; its visual symbol in the score is a dot or a wedge, but it is often not indicated in the score. That little dot represents a fairly complex throwing motion that originates from the shoulder and actively involves the entire arm, hand, and fingers. It is complex in that several components of the playing mechanism must act, but the motion itself amounts to nothing more than a straight throw. That is the essence of the staccato: the upper arm transmits a throw through the forearm and hands toward the fingers, which transmit this impulse to the keys. The fingers and the rest of the equipment return immediately to the position from which the throw began. Since this activity is so thoroughly distributed, the motions of the participating components are minimal and effortless, regardless of the tempo or dynamics of the passage. Incidentally, a distinction between the *dot* and the *wedge* should be made only after the Baroque period. In the days when quill feathers were used for writing, there was simply no way to write a dot, therefore a wedge became the symbol for staccato. Later on, especially in the Romantic period, the wedge was identified as the sign for a sharper staccato and the dot stood for a regular staccato. However, this distinction should not be made for music written before the 19th century.

Staccato not always indicated in score

The beginning of Beethoven's "Waldstein" Sonata, opus 53 is an example of a passage in which staccato is required but the dot is missing in the score. This passage requires a light throw with no excessive sharpness or abruptness in the sound. Many of the formidable octave passages in Liszt's *Sonata in B Minor* are not marked staccato either, but they obviously call for this type of motion.

Infinite variety in the application of staccato

As mentioned before, the execution of staccato and octaves can be varied infinitely. Although the entire apparatus must always participate, we can increase or decrease the role of the fingers, hand, forearm, upper arm, and any combination of these components. If we desire a shorter, crisper sound, we may activate the fingers and the hand slightly more; if we want a heavier and more massive sound, we use more forearm and upper arm action.

No muscle
building!

In all of these variants the entire equipment must be actively involved at all times. The motion is a highly coordinated and integrated
activity. Total effortlessness is achieved by a sensible distribution of
energy and not by strengthening some of the congenitally weaker muscles of the wrist or forearm. There is nothing more harmful and unpleasant for pianists than the "wrist-building" exercises some people
advocate: the pianist usually ends up with tendonitis as he works
diligently on his way to develop a hard and wooden sound.

The famous octave passages in Chopin's *Polonaise in A Flat Major*,
opus 53 and Liszt's "Funérailles" require staccato technique, as do all
of the following examples:

Example 80. Liszt, *Hungarian Rhapsody No. 6*

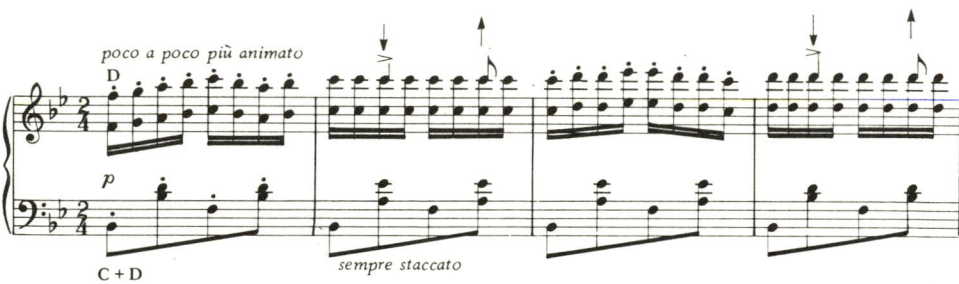

Example 81. Anton Rubinstein, *Etude*, opus 23 no. 2 ("Staccato Etude")

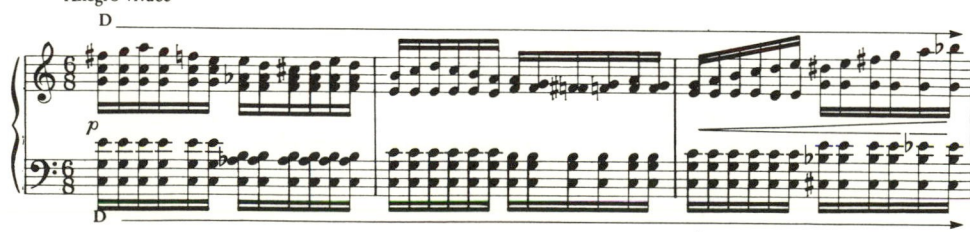

Example 82. Schumann, *Toccata*, opus 7

Example 83. Prokofiev, *Toccata*, opus 11

Example 84. Ravel, *Le Tombeau de Couperin,* "Toccata"

In many of these examples the staccato motion is combined with other motions, particularly with rotary motion. However our first purpose is to develop a staccato motion in its purest form!

Legato octaves will be played with the staccato-type motion, provided that it will be tempered by extra finger work; extra wrist motion is important too, especially in alternating white and black keys. This is the case in Chopin's *Etude,* opus 25 no. 10:

Example 85. Chopin, *Etude,* opus 25 no. 10

The Rondo from Beethoven's "Waldstein" Sonata calls for a greatly concentrated and rapid series of octave movements:

Example 86. Beethoven, *Sonata*, opus 53, third movement

It is obvious that once extreme speed is attained, distinctions between a true legato and a true staccato disappear and all we have is a semi-staccato.

Free fall and thrust

Free fall and thrust are quite interchangeable even though the former motion is produced mainly by the force of gravity while the latter is generated solely by the muscles. Both motions produce big, massive sonorities, and they are used mainly for this purpose. It should be remembered that thrust is more appropriate for chords with wide intervals, while free fall is called for in passages in slow or moderate tempo.

Examples   Either motion may be used in examples 87 and 88:

Example 87. Schubert, *Fantasy in C Major*, opus 15 ("Wanderer")

Example 88. Tchaikovsky, *Piano Concerto No. 1*, first movement

While both thrust and free fall will serve in the Chopin *Prelude in C Minor* in example 89, thrust may be more suitable for producing the character specified in the opening phrase:

Example 89. Chopin, *Prelude in C Minor*, opus 28 no. 20

Free fall is recommended for the bass of examples 90 and 91:

Example 90. Chopin, *Etude*, opus 10 no. 1

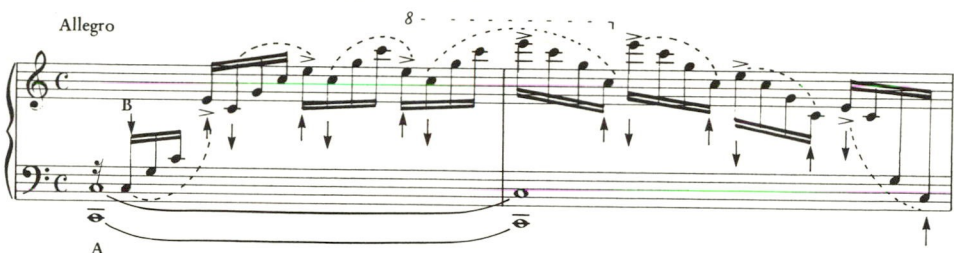

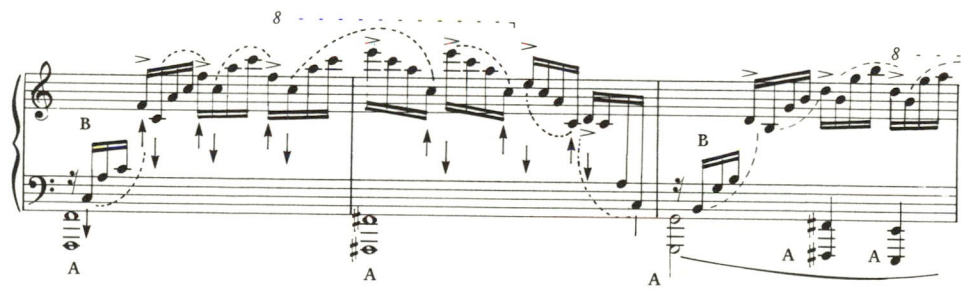

Example 91. Beethoven, *Sonata*, opus 109, second movement

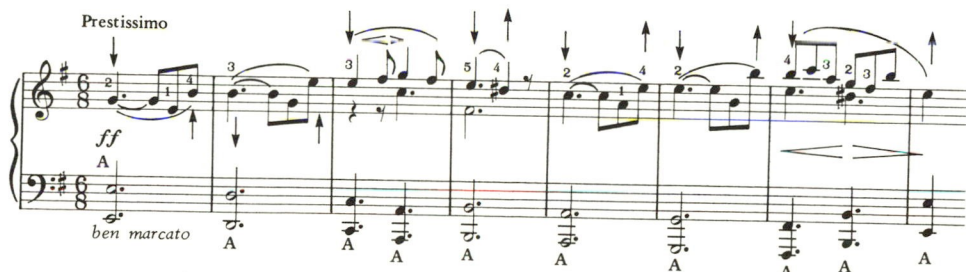

Avoid creating a combination of the two motions; do not lean into a free fall and do not employ thrust from a distance. Neither the piano nor your knuckles can endure these actions! When the whole arm is freely accelerating from a sufficient distance, its speed is more than enough to produce the greatest possible sound. If you increase the speed of the arm with a throw, no good or sensitive piano can respond to the onslaught; there is a limit to the elasticity of felt, wood, and strings. The maximum sound can be produced either by the sheer force of gravity or by the sudden contraction of our strongest and biggest muscles. Do not combine the two!

Trills

As an appendix to our discussion of the five basic motion patterns, I add a few words on trills, a subject conspicuous for its absence in the preceding discussion of piano technique. Trills are an important part of piano playing since they are found in every style of piano music. When they are properly executed they create an impressive effect, but formulating a clear-cut solution to the technical problem they pose is difficult because they seem to be executed in rather elusive and highly personal ways. In this respect they resemble an important device used by all string players, the *vibrato*. It is difficult to define a formula for practicing either the trill or the vibrato, and it is almost impossible to teach these devices. However it is possible to create the conditions that enable one to produce either a good trill or a sensitively applied vibrato: if the ingredients of a well-coordinated and smoothly functioning playing apparatus are working properly, effortlessly, and resiliently, they won't let us down!

Finger combinations

Experience shows that almost any combination of fingers can produce a fine trill. Some players are most comfortable with a 3-5 combination, while others prefer 1-3, even 3-4, or complex combinations like 1-4-2-3 or 1-3-2-4. Some prefer the left hand to the right hand and medium speed to fast speed, and some excel at very fast and loud, even shrill trills! This highly individual activity results from a combination of reflex and adjusting motions, and the teacher's main task is to ensure a free mobilization of all the components involved—the fingers, wrist, and forearm.

Speed of the trill

It is best to start a trill at a moderate tempo with slightly articulated finger and forearm motions. The speed of the trill should be gradually accelerated while the player carefully guards against tension in the arm, hand, and fingers. At excessive speed coordination is lost, forcing occurs, and the trill freezes in its tracks. Trills need not be executed at a frantic pace; those that are played effortlessly at a moderate tempo are often completely satisfying.

Execution

A trill may be comfortably executed in a variety of ways: the fingers can be either curved or extended, the wrist can be low or high, and a variety of finger combinations can be used. The same may also be said for double thirds. It is important to place the arm in a comfortable position, to align the fingers with their respective forearm muscles, and to use the usual adjusting motions of the wrist and arm. In order to prevent tension, it is especially important to attend to both the vertical and horizontal adjusting motions that we use whenever the fingers are in action; these motions diminish as the speed of the trill increases.

In example 92 a variety of fingerings are furnished for a single-note trill:

In example 93 four fingerings are provided for the same brief excerpt from Chopin's etude in thirds. The changes of fingering in the fourth variant allow a cyclic adjusting motion to be made for every group of eight thirds played.

Example 93. Chopin, *Etude*, opus 25 no. 6

PART THREE

Technique Becomes Music

10 Identification and Application of the Basic Technical Patterns

Symbols for
basic patterns,
wrist positions,
and touch forms

We have reduced piano technique to five basic motion patterns and their combinations. We contend that the musical text clearly indicates which to select as the appropriate technical solution. Now we will submit an extended musical example indicating the technical formulas to apply both in practice and in performance (see example 94).

The symbols for the five motion patterns and for low and high wrist are joined by symbols for the four touch forms.

Symbols

free fall   A

five-fingers, scales and arpeggios   B

rotation   C

staccato   D

thrust   E

low wrist   ↓

high wrist   ↑

legato   ⌒

portato   ⌒. . . .

tenuto   – – – – –

staccato · · · · or ᵎ ᵎ ᵎ ᵎ

marcato > ʌ ⋀

sf = sforzato: sharp accent, or intense expressivo (especially in slow passages)

Tenuto

Besides staccato and legato there are two other touch forms: the tenuto and the portato. The tenuto marking – – – – – indicates that the note is to be held for its full value; if there are several tenuto notes in succession, they should not be as closely connected as they would be if they were marked legato. In legato we connect the notes with an upward arm motion and by letting the dampers fall slowly; in tenuto we let the dampers fall freely. This will create a slight disconnection between the notes that is characteristic to tenuto. The slight finger motion is helped by the usual horizontal and vertical adjustment of the forearm, but the raising of the fingers is not slowed down by an upward grouping motion of the arm as it is in legato playing. The damper falls without impediment, and the sound ends distinctly with the lifting of the finger. Incidentally, the tenuto sign does not necessarily indicate an accent!

Portato

The portato (sometimes incorrectly called "portamento") marking ⌒‥‥‥ indicates sort of a semilegato or semistaccato; the notes are not tied but gently separated. When tenuto is called for, a horizontal arm motion with a clear upward articulation of the fingers is used, and the almost imperceptible separation of the notes is accomplished by the free fall of the damper. The portato indicates a vertical wrist motion on each note and gentle finger activity. This subtle down-up motion of the wrist slows the action of the dampers to the point where the notes are barely separated gradually, not suddenly. Legato, staccato, portato, and tenuto are the four distinct touch forms; an understanding of the differences among them helps in finding the exact motion patterns with which to produce the appropriate sounds.

Skill

We have a clear concept of the five basic motion patterns and their method of execution; we understand the four touch forms and how they can be produced; we know our sources of energy and how to tap them; we know what the location factors are that modify the positions and actions of our torso, arms, and feet in order to adjust to the use of black and white keys and different sections of the keyboard. Now our task is to translate the notational patterns in the score into their corresponding motion patterns. Technique in a broader sense is the application of movements to produce sounds according to the specifications of the written text—technique is not artistry; it is a mechanical and intellectual skill.

Artistry

Art and artistry are manifested by a highly aesthetic, original, personal, and convincing approach that reveals the true and deeper aspects of the music and by the mastery of the performer. To approach and to achieve artistry we must develop a superior skill, a complete pianistic mastery, that can lift us to artistic heights. Art and interpretation are intangible and indefinable, full of unpredictable and improvisatory elements, but piano playing is not. The ingredients of piano technique are clearly definable; they include the anatomy and motions of the human body, the mechanics of the instrument, and the force of gravity. Nonetheless, these motions that comprise piano technique must correspond to their musical counterparts: this is indispensable if we are to interrelate motions with the corresponding emotions!

Conscious, not mechanical, practicing

The musical example is the exposition of the first movement of Beethoven's *Sonata*, opus 53 ("Waldstein"). As in the previous examples the symbols of the basic motion patterns are included, and arrows indicate a high or low wrist position. The measure numbers are also given. In the excerpt from the "Waldstein" Sonata, with the help of the indications inherent in the score, we will use the list of symbols to indicate performance techniques. The multiplicity and synchronization of the various ingredients require intense concentration, especially at first. Compared to mechanical practice, this kind of practicing is strenuous: we must control several ingredients at the same time. It may be easy to pay attention to the thumb alone, but it is more difficult to control the wrist, the forearm, and upper arm, and the size of each of their motions all at the same time. But as our practice methods improve, more can be achieved with less and less mental and physical effort. Furthermore, once technique is established and acquired, don't practice it anymore—ever! With the basic formulas at our disposal we merely adapt them to particular passages and apply them. It is like learning the alphabet. As a child, one must learn and practice every letter, but once the letters are ingrained, there is no longer any need to practice them—one simply uses them for writing. The writing continues to improve and becomes more and more one's own means of expression, whether it is used for poetry, the weather report, or a recipe. Similarly our scales, octaves, and tremolos improve with use, and they become more and more characteristic of our own manner of performing (for more hints about how to practice technique see chapter fourteen).

The "Waldstein" Sonata: first movement, exposition

Here is the exposition of the first movement of Beethoven's "Waldstein" Sonata. I indicate the basic motion patterns as well as the touch forms and technical solutions suggested by the score. The composer's score markings are the basis for our interpretation: the added dotted slurs indicate technical groupings.

Example 94. Beethoven, *Sonata*, opus 53 ("Waldstein"), first movement, exposition

The first two measures are played with staccato motion (D). The left hand continues playing staccato through the tenth measure. In the

third measure the right hand starts the legato (B) with a low wrist and ends it on the third beat with a higher wrist. The fourth measure is played the same way as the third measure; however here the trunk moves slightly forward and to the right to enable the right arm to reach the high notes comfortably.

(Example 94 continued)

Measures 5–8 are played the same way as measures 1–4. At beginning of bar 9 lean slightly forward in order to reach the top note comfortably. The right hand uses a typical five-finger motion for measures 9–10, with a lower wrist at the thumb, a higher wrist at the fifth finger, and the standard lateral adjusting motion for each finger in order to line it up with its respective muscles. Beginning with the second beat of measure 11, the right elbow is kept in a raised position until the end of the bar to accommodate the fingers during the downward scale, while the trunk moves gradually toward the central position. The left hand uses free fall (A) for the first two beats of measure 11 and then it ascends toward the downbeat of the next measure—a typical motion for a group ending. The right hand carries out this same motion on the downbeat of bar 12, after which both hands are thrown gently, with staccato (D) motion. In bar 13 use a gentle free fall (A) for both hands.

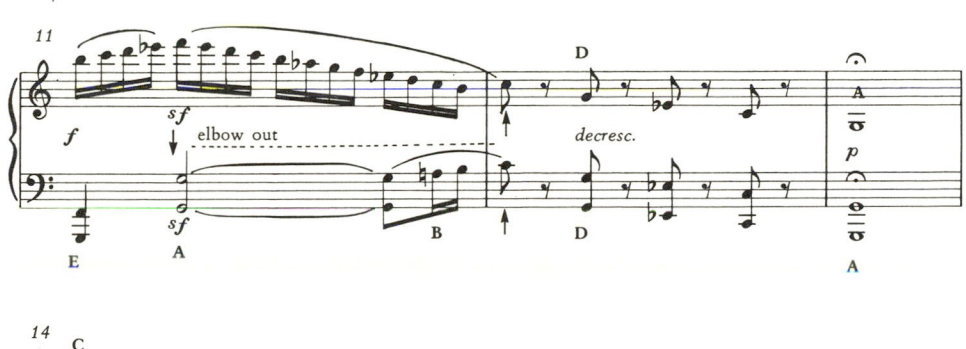

In measure 14 the left hand begins with a slight throw (using staccato) on the first note and then it joins the right hand with a forearm rotation (C). The right arm rotates until bar 16, and the left arm continues until bar 18; then after one staccato motion, it continues to the end of bar 22. The right hand uses legato motion in bars 16–17 (the wrist uses a down-up motion) and at bar 18 resumes rotation until end of bar 19. In bars 20–21 the right hand is legato. From bar 23 until the end of bar 30 both hands use scale and arpeggio motions, grouping them according to the slurs marked. In bar 29 the left hand uses thrust (E) for the chord.

From bar 31 to the end of bar 34 both the right and left hands use staccato combined with rotation. From bar 35 to end of bar 41 both hands use legato for the slurred notes. At measure 42 the right hand uses scale technique. From measure 43 to end of measure 57 the same technique is used as in measures 35–41.

(Example 94 continued)

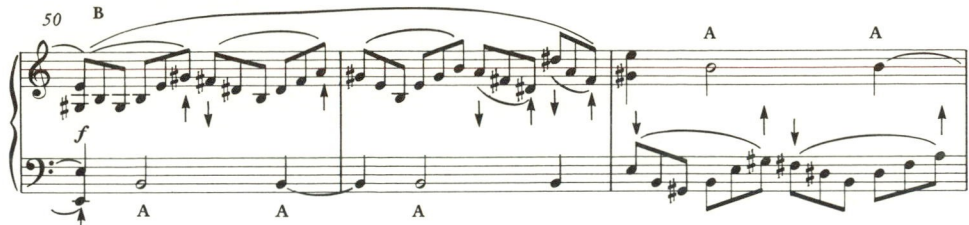

From bar 58 to end of bar 61 the left hand uses rotation. On the first and third beats of bar 58 the right hand uses legato-arpeggio technique, and on the second and fourth beats it uses rotation; rotation is also used in bars 59–60. In bar 61 the right hand uses a descending scale motion with the upper arm out. In bars 62–65 the right hand groups scale motion according to the slurs, and the left hand plays staccato. In bars 66–67 the right hand plays staccato, and the left hand uses arpeggio motion until the third beat of measure 67; then it uses staccato.

In bars 68–73 the right hand uses rotation, and the left hand uses staccato. The left hand trills from measure 72 to the end of measure 73 (with a slight rotation if it is convenient). In measure 74 the first beat is a thrust for both hands; then the right hand proceeds with scale motion (which is grouped according to the slurs) until the third beat of measure 76. At this point use legato arpeggio according to the slurs until the end of measure 77. Bars 78–85 use the same motions as bars 74–77. Bars 86–87 use staccato as they are a repetition of the first two measures of the piece.

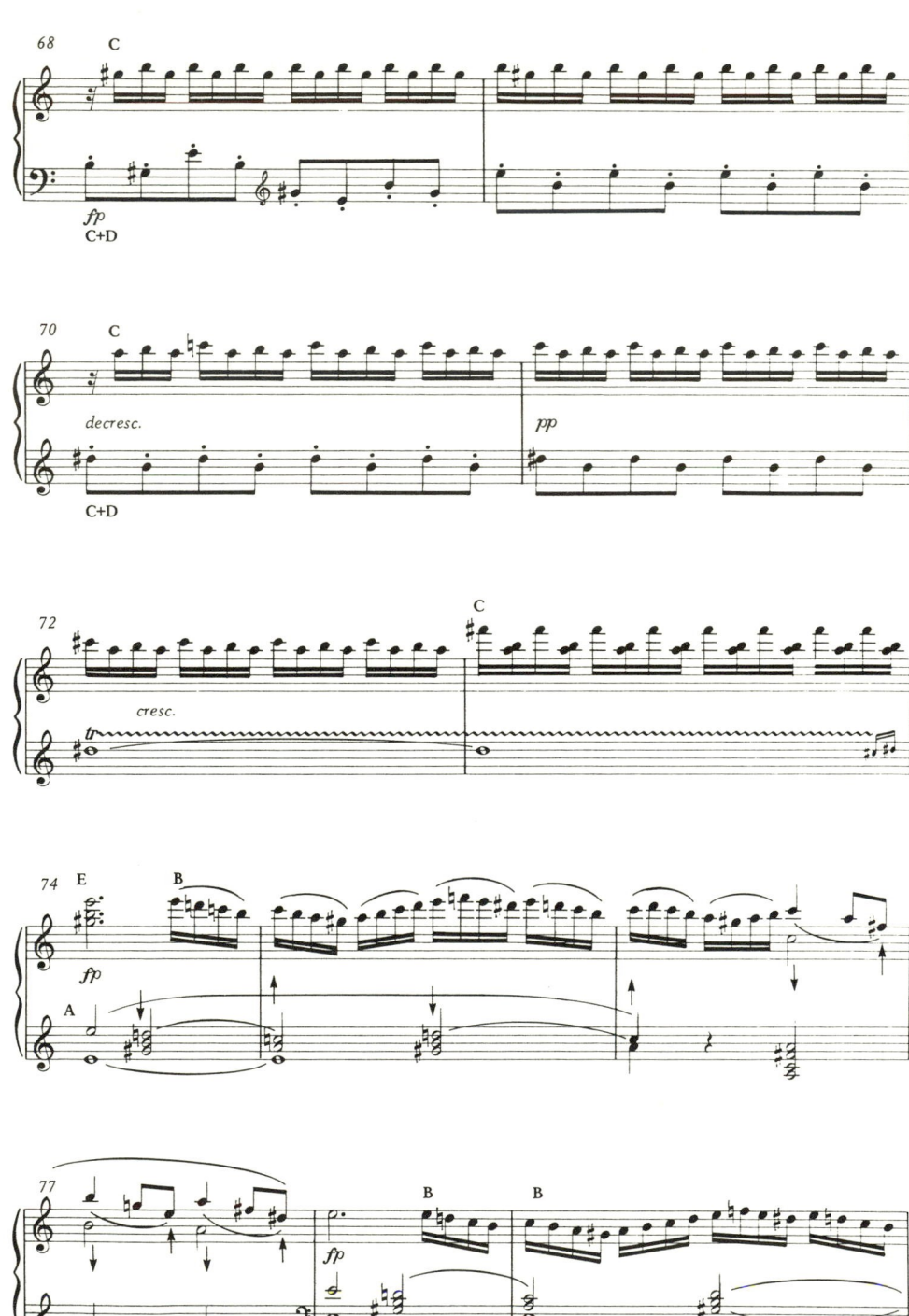

Our only concern in example 94 is to indicate technical solutions (or motion patterns) that are suggested by the written text. There is no attempt whatsoever to suggest our own ideas of interpretation, only to "translate" visual patterns to motion patterns. However interpretation and individuality do manifest themselves even at these initial stages because dynamics, tempo changes, accents, phrasing, and quality of touch (just to mention a few factors) reflect our own, personal responses. At this point our aim is only to recognize the formulas, to diagnose technical solutions, and to execute them in the correct manner. We must always remember that every one of the motions is complex; it is the result of coordinated activities of the fingers, hand, wrist, forearm, upper arm, and often the trunk. Furthermore the size of the motions and the degree of muscular intensity must be considered: they must be reduced to the very minimum to create an efficient collaboration among all the participating members. We know that totally relaxed playing does not exist, but totally effortless playing is our aim. Total emotional involvement is very desirable, but physical involvement should be minimal. If we cultivate interdependence within the playing apparatus and eliminate excessive effort, we can avoid impairing our breathing and phrasing, and we will be in a position to serve music better. As stated earlier, excitement and exaltation should be felt and generated not by muscular strain and tension but by the music itself. Obviously, excitement and exaltation can cause muscular tension and strain, but conscious control of our playing mechanism should help to reduce this strain and prevent it from interfering with our technical processes. Many performances suffer from continuously "turned on," exaggeratedly tense physical activities and gestures that simulate the intense involvement of the artist even when the music at hand is serene and lyrical.

Rapid up-down motion converts to in-out motion.

One technical process that has not yet been discussed is a variant of a familiar basic motion. In rapid double-note passages the up-down motion of the forearm and wrist that accommodates the thumb changes to an in-and-out motion. The upper arm executes a slight to-and-fro motion that causes the forearm, hand, and fingers to vibrate back and forth. This process is applicable to the passages in examples 95 to 99 and will facilitate greatly the performances of these rather difficult works.

Example 95. Schumann, *Toccata*, opus 7

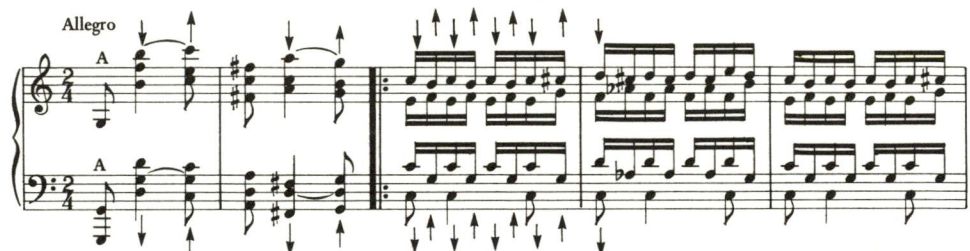

Example 96. Liszt, *Transcendental Etude No. 5* ("Feux Follets")

In Chopin's *Etude* in C major, opus 10 no. 7 as well as in the other examples, the wrist is lowered for the notes played by the thumb and raised for the following ones. However, in fast tempo this up-and-down motion is transformed into a forward-back movement of the upper arm. Thus the original vertical motion of the wrist is converted into another motion that serves us better. As in all motions executed in conjunction with finger motions, this motion adds to the speed of the fingers by means of an extra throw. The fingers, as always, must be slightly raised in order to receive the throw. Be sure, however, that in slow or medium-fast tempo you insist on the *up-down* wrist motion. The in-and-out motion must happen only at increased speed, and always involuntarily.

Example 97. Chopin, *Etude,* opus 10 no. 7

Example 98. Brahms, *Variations on a Theme by Paganini,* opus 35, book 1, variation 1

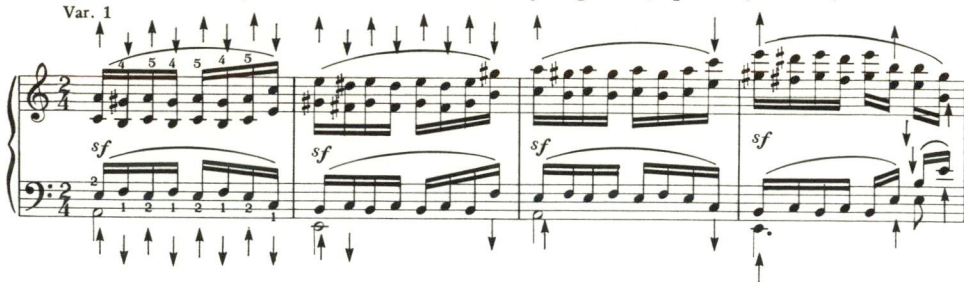

Example 99. Chopin, *Etude,* opus 25 no. 8

11 Independence and Interdependence

Coordination, not muscle building, is main goal.

In discussing piano technique I have favored the coordination, synchronization, and interdependence of the human anatomy over the development of muscular strength and the isolation of the components of the playing mechanism. During the endless hours of practicing pianists tend to give too much importance to the development of muscles that help the independence of the fingers, wrist, and the forearm. Of course, independence of the fingers is tremendously important; the question is how to achieve it. The wrong kind of practice for independence breeds complications and fails to resolve the inherent problem —the weakness and unevenness of finger action.

The reason usually given for grueling, tedious finger exercises is that the fingers play unevenly and weakly because they are weak and therefore need strengthening. The truth is that they function unsatisfactorily because the fingers are not placed in positions where their own muscles can help them satisfactorily, and therefore the stronger muscles of the body cannot be activated: they are simply not coordinated with the total equipment.

We are all born with a considerable ability to coordinate—we could not survive otherwise. Most beginners at the piano start off with a normal, natural position and disposition. Later they are told to "build up the strength of the fingers, especially the fourth finger," or to "strengthen the wrist," a joint that tires after a series of forced motions. Children usually begin with broad arm and body motions that help their "strength" but soon their fingers are glued to the keys in exercises in which four of the five fingers must hold on to the keys, while the fifth finger goes through its forced and senseless "muscle building." Coordination is thereby destroyed!

This manner of practicing goes on for years; this kind of practicing must go on indefinitely because it goes against the nature of the human anatomy and of normal coordination. You must keep on working at it to maintain these strenuous and wasteful habits. While you may gain a certain independence of the fingers, you fail to use your entire playing apparatus interdependently: the fortified but isolated units are detached from the larger equipment that could pass on power to them if only the fingers were ready to cooperate.

Practicing to achieve independence is beneficial only if it is carried on within the framework of *interdependence.* Finger exercises are useful only if the position and participation of the arm (that is, the forearm and upper arm) are considered. The fingers must be lined up with their respective forearm muscles, and the upper arm must participate in placing the entire equipment where it belongs. Without a continuous but always slight adjusting activity of the arm, coordination is spoiled. We really cannot strengthen "finger muscles" because it is the forearm muscles that move the fingers. However unless these arm muscles are properly lined up with the fingers and upper arm, they work under a handicap. By the same token, if the whole apparatus works under proper conditions, there is no need to strengthen the forearm muscles—or any other muscles, for that matter. The strong muscles supply all the help the weak ones need; above all, the slight changes in the arm's position eliminate stiffness in the wrist.

Principal adjusting motions

The principal adjusting motions are: (1) horizontal (lateral) adjusting motions, which line up the fingers with their respective flexor and extensor forearm muscles; (2) vertical motions, which raise the wrist from the low thumb position toward the higher fifth-finger position, and (3) depth motions (forward and backward from the edge to the back of the key), which adjust the fingers to white and black keys with the help of the upper arm: the position of the upper arm for black keys is somewhat higher and more forward than the position for white keys. We may add to these the movements of the body: sideways, axially and forward-backward, according to need.

The purpose of these motions (which should be neither too large nor too small) is to accommodate the fingers. Most of these motions may occur automatically and instinctively. This is fine when it happens, but unfortunately we cannot always rely on instinct alone. It is possible that "doing what comes naturally" will take us a long way, but it won't take us all the way. When problems arise, we must know how to help ourselves. Fortunately, in due time most conscious activities become subconscious, and then they become automatic, when they are completely mastered. It is not necessary to be aware of everything all the time—God forbid! But in case we need it, our knowledge can come to our assistance.

No pressure

The ever-present adjusting motions enable us not only to place the equipment properly and to activate any and all of the necessary muscular resources, but they eliminate extended fixation, stiffness, and rigidity in the muscles and joints—the most common source of trouble in technique and tone production. The continuous alternation of antagonistic sets of muscles automatically relaxes the previously engaged muscles while the opposite muscles work. Of course, we only relax to a certain extent; we don't do it completely. But whenever the joints and muscles must be fixed, the fixing must be only momentary, not only because our muscles prefer it, but because of the nature of the piano. When the hammer is activated to its proper speed, it hits the strings in a split-second throw, bounces back and never applies pressure on the strings. Pressure on the keys may be habit-forming and gratifying (see chapter thirteen), but it is unnecessary and wasteful. If we are not addicted to it, we can easily eliminate it and not indulge in "relaxing" motions, for instantaneous fixation is totally effortless.

Vibrato on string instruments

Extended pressure is necessary only for playing string instruments; this is one of the reasons why string players welcome and feature the vibrato. In addition to its beauty vibrato also serves to relieve muscle tension through a continuous shifting in position. Stiffness caused by extended tension is removed by the rapid alternation in the use of antagonistic muscles. It also helps to reduce intonation problems; furthermore, the sound itself is improved by the physiologically advantageous muscular actions.

Another even more important purpose of the adjusting motions is to add speed and power to the fingers. No matter how small these adjusting motions are, when they are timed correctly, the synchronized vertical, horizontal, and in-and-out motions add a considerable throw to the fingers, sufficient to increase their speed. This occurs in fast tempo as well, even though the motions are so small that they are invisible.

Direction, but not size, of motions is being specified.

While we can clearly define the directions of the motions (up and down, side to side, back and forth, and axial), everyone has to determine their size according to his or her anatomy. A long upper arm and short fingers move differently than a short upper arm and long fingers; all we know for certain is the general direction of the movement. Similarly the adjusting motions of the body serve the pianist to maintain his balance, and the size of movements depends on the size of the various sections of his anatomy. We must be concerned with the proper placing of the entire mechanism (torso, legs, head) and with the height of the stool and its distance from the piano.

The five basic motions contain the following active and passive movements:

Chart of active and passive motions

Free fall: The entire arm, hand, and fingers are *actively* engaged during lifting and landing. Not the body and the head.

Five-finger motion, scales, and arpeggios: Here, too, the entire arm, hand, and fingers are actively engaged; and we move the body according to the location of the hands on the keyboard.

Rotation: Only the forearm and the fingers are actively engaged in the forearm's axial rotation, not the wrist and the upper arm. In wider rotation the upper arm rotates axially and brings about a lateral motion of the forearm, and in extremely wide distances the upper arm moves laterally too.

Staccato: The entire arm, hand, and fingers are active at all times. Not the head and body.

Thrust: The muscles of the entire body are active, and the force of gravity is not involved. The slight motion of the forearm and hand is barely visible. The head, torso, and feet are immobile; they support the thrust and resist the rebound caused by the keys. There are no passive motions.

Besides active motions there are passive ones that come about indirectly:

Free fall: During the arm's downward motion that is caused by the force of gravity, the falling arm is totally passive.

Five-finger motion, scales, and arpeggios: This motion is totally active; there are no passive motions.

Rotation: In the forearm's axial rotation the upper arm simply holds the rest of the arm; otherwise it is passive. It may "shake along," but it doesn't participate in the motion itself. It is active only in wide intervals.

Staccato: There are no passive motions except during the rebound in extremely fast and loud playing.

Thrust: There are no passive motions.

Finger exercises to "build muscles"

As we stated earlier, our aim is to develop independence within the framework of interdependence; this is why we have referred so often to interdependence in this chapter.

We must examine now the harmful effects of forced finger exercises when interdependence is not taken into consideration. The exercises in examples 100 and 101 are typical of those that aim to develop independence at the expense of interdependence.

Example 100. Five-finger exercise (harmful: fixed position)

Example 101. Five-finger exercise (harmful: fixed position)

The victim, or student, is supposed to press down four notes, raise the finger that plays, and repeat the down-and-up motion until he feels considerable tension and stiffness in the forearm. He then proceeds to the next finger and lets the previously active one join the others in pressing down the keys. During the entire procedure the arm and wrist are supposed to be held immobile in a fixed position by tightening up both the flexor and the extensor muscles of the forearm. This type of exercise is a rather unpleasant experience, but it is supposed to make us better pianists. If we practice example 101, the experience is not only unpleasant but painful too since the intervals are wider and the tension will be greater in the arm. Moreover, in due time it becomes quite harmful. Nevertheless, we feel good; we pay our debt to society, to Art and to our teacher: we work "hard!" The chronic pain doesn't stop us as yet, but now there is a fair chance that tendonitis will develop. If we insist on continuing this masochistic pastime, we will indeed develop chronic tendonitis—which becomes the "coup de grâce" that will liberate us from any further undue suffering. We will then have to give up the piano completely!

There is a great deal wrong with this approach. The role of the forearm muscles is to act as an antagonistic set—the flexors pull the fingers down, and extensors raise them. When the four inactive fingers in these exercises continually press down the keys instead of resting, their flexors are under continuous tension; this state is not only unnecessary but harmful. Furthermore, because the arm and wrist are fixed and immobile, the active finger cannot find a correct position in line with its muscles. Therefore not only the finger but the muscles that move it must function under a handicap. We know that each finger has an optimal position where it can work effortlessly; by not permitting the wrist and arm to move, we make it impossible for the finger to assume this position. We need the horizontal, vertical, and depth adjusting motions to place the finger properly—a fixed wrist prohibits this. Thus what could be a continuous enjoyable flow of activities (going from the thumb to the fifth finger and back) becomes agonizing drudgery.

The warning system

It is true that in due time the pain diminishes because the muscles become tough and insensitive (so does the sound), but this in turn causes further damage: (1) the coordination and interdependence of the system become impaired, and (2) the desensitized muscles lose the ability to warn us when forcing takes place. In short, the muscles have been strengthened and desensitized. This is a bad situation because the first symptom of incorrect, forced activity should be fatigue and tension in the abused muscles; when these symptoms occur, the "big brother" muscles should rush in to help. So we have a vicious circle: we try to strengthen the weak muscles, and in doing so we eliminate the instinctive activation of the stronger ones; with no help from the strong muscles we have to keep on strengthening the weaker ones. As a result numbness and pain afflict the muscles. The worst of it is that an ugly tone is a direct result of the malfunctioning apparatus.

In contrast to finger exercises that stress independence alone, finger exercises that incorporate correct arm participation can be really useful. Evenness and power can be achieved in the fingers without strain if you use the correct arm motions. Instead of building muscles, it is much more beneficial to learn how to coordinate the weaker muscles with the stronger ones. Sensations of fatigue in the muscles are not necessarily signs of weakness but a call for help. In all truth, one ought to cultivate this warning system instead of desensitizing it.

Blood
circulation

In spite of all the damage they do, it must be conceded that these painful, athletic muscle-building exercises, like all exercises, help to increase blood supply and circulation. When these strenuous exercises stop, the fingers feel relief and move with more ease for a while. The reason they are used as warming-up exercises is that some people think they need them in order to loosen up when they begin practicing. My contention, however, is that by activating the entire body—by distributing motions and effort among all the participating members—one hardly needs any warming-up exercises. After all, the pianist is using the same equipment that he uses constantly for lifting a chair, for opening a door, or for writing, and he doesn't need warming-up exercises for any of these activities. When piano playing becomes totally effortless, the need for warming up vanishes. You can always rub your fingers together or stretch your arms if you feel sluggish, but you don't need anything else. If you enjoy stretching exercises at the piano, by all means go ahead and use them, but don't overburden the muscles.

Independence of fingers is best achieved by feeling and ingraining the arm and wrist position appropriate to each individual finger; every finger should assume its optimal position when called to duty.

Although we have emphasized the interdependence of the arm, hand, and fingers in this discussion, it is obvious that the entire body thrives on interdependence. In order to maintain balance and support the body, we often change the position of the feet and the head. The more interaction within the entire body, the more effortless and economical the playing becomes. When the body is totally involved in participating and the muscular action is totally distributed among its components, the performer hardly seems to be moving at all; yet he may play with lightning speed and produce thundering sounds.

CHAPTER
12 The Pedals

Pedals were needed to mute the longer strings.

As the piano evolved into its present form, and especially as it increased in range and size, various alterations and additions were needed to cope with the duration of its sound, volume of the sound and the control of the volume of sound. The strings constantly grew longer and finally, around the time of Mozart, the excessive reverberations of these longer strings had to be curbed. Dissonant and transient notes were not objectionable on the earlier short-stringed instruments because the sounds didn't last long enough to drown out the fundamental harmonies and basses.

Damper originally operated by knee, then foot.

Near the midpoint of the eighteenth century, when the strings had become quite long, matters seemed to have gotten out of hand. So a mechanism operated by the knees that served as a mute was affixed to the piano to stop the sound of these unwanted cacophonies. This device, which was known as the *sordino,* or *damper,* was added to the strings, enabling the performer to stop its vibrations at will. In due time the feet took over from the knee, and the device came to be known as the *pedal.* Pianists now had a very effective device that allowed them to clear sonorities or to mix them. The pianist's repertoire of effects was expanded since he could weaken sonorities, strengthen them, feature them, blend them, and create sounds that could be magical or ghastly, depending on the artistry of the performer.

Two or three pedals now

Considerable evolution in the development of the pedal led eventually to excess; in the early nineteenth century pianos had as many as six to eight pedals, some of which imitated drums and cymbals. Later the number of pedals was reduced to two or three.

Pedal nomenclature

A comprehensive history of the evolution of the pedal can be found in many excellent books and sources of reference on the subject; but it will not be given here. Nor is it necessary to describe the pedal; we are all familiar with it. However the nomenclature associated with this device is confusing. Several different names are applied to the three pedals, and often we find ourselves in the perplexing situation of not knowing which pedal people are discussing. Before I list some of these confusing names, I would suggest using just one name for each of them. For convenience's sake let us call them the *right, left,* and *middle* pedals.

The right pedal is sometimes called the *forte* pedal; it is also called the *loud* pedal, and the *sustaining* pedal—or just *pedal.* The middle pedal is called the *sostenuto* pedal, the *organ point* pedal, and the *sustaining* pedal. The left pedal is occasionally called the *sordino* pedal, the *damper* pedal, the *una corda* pedal, the *due corde* pedal, and the *muted* pedal; most often it is called the *soft* pedal. Depending on the part of the world you come from, you may use any of these terms. What adds to the confusion in a spectacular way is that in some countries the damper was originally called *sordino* because it muted the strings. In many of Beethoven's scores we find the indications *con sordino* and *senza sordino*; these terms appear in the Urtext edition of the second movement of the third piano concerto, for instance. Since in Italian *con* means "with," and *senza* means "without," the semi-knowledgeable understood *con sordino* to mean "with pedal" and *senza sordino* to mean "without pedal"; of course, this was not the case. By *sordino* Beethoven meant the damper, not the pedal. Therefore in this case *con sordino* means "with damper" (without pedal) and *senza sordino* means "without damper" (with pedal). Confusing, isn't it!

"Sordino"

Whatever name we give to the pedals (and we might as well settle for *right, middle,* and *left* pedals), their role is extremely important. They enhance sonorities and can help to produce sound effects that make a performance memorable and unique.

The right pedal: a richer sound

The right pedal is sometimes called the loud pedal because it actually increases the volume of the sound. When the pedal is depressed with a note or chord, sympathetic vibrations are generated in all the strings of the piano. (Sympathetic vibrations are produced by vibrations in neighboring bodies of the same wavelength.) Without the pedal we hear the vibrations of only those strings that are hit by the hammers, because they are the only strings whose dampers are raised. If we play middle C without pedal, only the harmonics of this string participate in the sound produced. On the other hand, if we put the right pedal down while playing the C, *all* the other strings of the piano —some two hundred from top to bottom—join in with sympathetic vibrations. When several notes or chords are played, the sympathetic vibrations are even richer; they prolong the sound and add to it an aura of many more harmonics.

Registers

There are no hard and fast rules governing the use of the right pedal, but there are several valid guiding principles. In general, much more pedal can be used for the higher strings than for the lower strings. Actually the highest notes on the piano have no dampers at all. Because the sound is so short, the dissonances don't bother us. It is perfectly feasible to play a scale in the high register with the pedal down; this same procedure is impossible in the bass. The farther down we go, the more cacophonic any simultaneous sound will be. A major third is a perfect consonance, but if it is played in the lowest register, it turns into a sinister rumble—with or without the pedal.

Harmonics

As a general guideline, one can safely pedal any number of notes that form the harmonics of an audible fundamental note.

Example 102. Harmonics of A; all notes can be pedaled with the bass note.

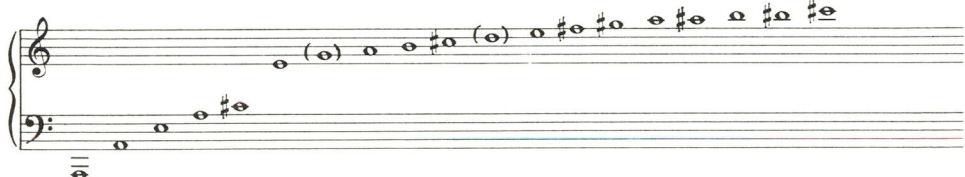

As we go up the harmonics ladder from bass to treble, the intervals gradually diminish; the octave is followed by the fifth, fourth, major third, minor third, and major second, etc. Even though some of these intervals are not in tune with the piano (tempered or not), they may be pedaled together as long as their root notes (that is, their lowest notes) lie above the lower limit of human hearing. As I mentioned before, intervals played in the lower register sound "bad" because their fundamental notes are far below the limits of human hearing. It is safe to pedal notes in the higher register, especially when the fundamental note is also played and heard.

Example 103. Harmonics of C; emphasizing different harmonics' combinations

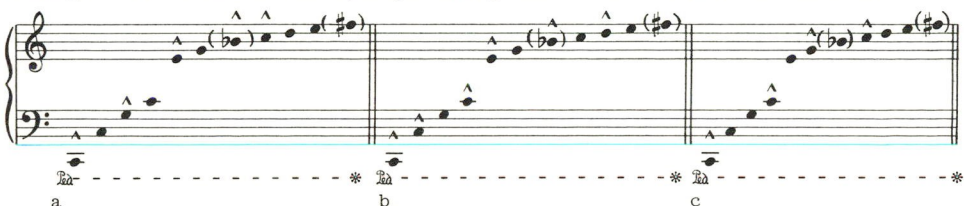

Timing

In general, one applies the right pedal immediately after depressing the keys. It is preferable to capture the sound *after* the hammer hits the strings and after the dampers are raised. In this way we can prolong the pure sound and exclude the noise of the hammer, the keybed, and the damper. Minimal as they may be, these noises influence the purity of the sound. The moment at which to put the pedal down is determined by the registers: the lower register requires more time than the middle register to produce a pure sound; therefore we put the pedal down a bit later. The ear is the best and only judge of how much pedal to use. If we listen carefully, we can time our pedaling well. Because every piano and every hall is slightly different, we must listen very carefully, especially when harmonics change, when a dissonance overlaps, and when a voice must be brought out; we may or may not wish to mix sonorities. There should be a split-second delay between the depression of the keys and the depression of the pedal; but that split-second is subject to changes.

Partial pedals   Soon after the invention of the pedal, composers began to include pedal markings in their scores. We should heed these indications when we are certain that they are the composer's markings because they are both authentic and sometimes quite explicit. However there are a number of uncertainties in these pedal marks: first, most of the markings merely indicate when the pedal should be depressed but not whether it should be depressed partially or completely. One can use a half pedal, or even one-third or one-fifth of the pedal's capacity. If we depress the pedal completely, the dampers clear the strings completely; a partial pedal mutes the strings only partly, and this type of pedaling produces a totally different sound effect.

The size of the instrument also has a bearing on its sound, for the length of the strings varies with the length of the piano. In Mozart's and Beethoven's time piano sound was weaker and decayed more rapidly than the sound of the larger pianos of Liszt's day and our own time. Beethoven indicated long pedals in the following well-known examples:

Example 104. Beethoven, *Sonata*, opus 53, last movement

Example 105. Beethoven, *Sonata*, opus 31 no. 2, first movement

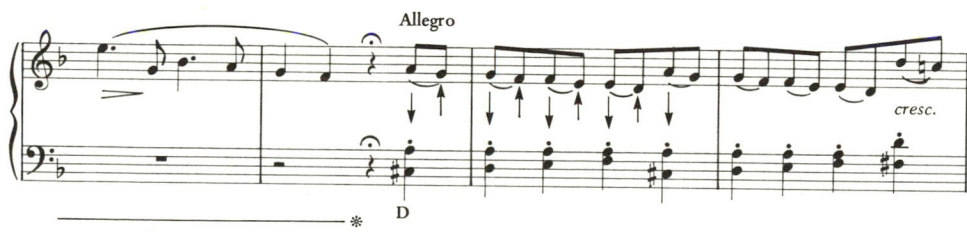

Example 107. Beethoven, *Sonata,* opus 53, last movement

Example 108. Beethoven, *Concerto No. 4,* opus 58, third movement

Blending bass, middle, and top registers over an organ point

The art of pedaling hinges on our ability to blend harmonics. For example, just take one set of harmonics: by accentuating and coloring different harmonics within the same column, we create innumerable sound effects, even without varying the dynamics. When you consider the fact that you can also alter the dynamics, touch, speed, and rhythm of the harmonics of one note, you can indeed see that a great variety of effects can be created within the same column of harmonics.

It was a traditional device even in Bach's time to blend certain harmonies, especially the tonic and the dominant, in a tempered and aesthetic way. But discretion must be used. For instance, if we play the bass note softly and the middle register more loudly in a passage of mixed harmonies, we will produce a muddy and generally unpleasant effect. But if we gently accent the bass, underplay the middle register, and bring out the top notes, the blend of chords can be beautiful.

The ear is the judge.

One must not take the pedal markings in the Beethoven examples we cited literally: instead we must search for the real meaning behind the indications in all pedal markings. Some contemporary composers (Bartók and Prokofiev, for example) are more specific in their pedal markings; for instance, half pedal signs and pedal tremolo signs are indicated in their work. But in general composers often supply no markings at all.

On today's piano it would be pedantic and naïve to depress the pedal completely and hold it to the bitter end just because "Beethoven said so." The sounds would become blurred and cacophonic, while all Beethoven wanted was a blended effect with two or more harmonies merging over a fundamental note or chord. We must remember that his piano had much shorter strings than ours and that he never did specify how far the pedal should be depressed.

The pedal tremolo

The pedal *tremolo* is an effective device that may be used quite often both to mix and to clear sonorities. It is used frequently in Impressionist and modern music, but there is room for it in any style. Some good examples of pedal *vibrato* (as the tremolo is often called) are the following:

Example 109. Chopin, *Etude*, opus 25 no. 2

Example 110. Chopin, *Sonata in B Flat Minor*, opus 35, fourth movement

Example 111. Ginastera, *Sonata*, second movement

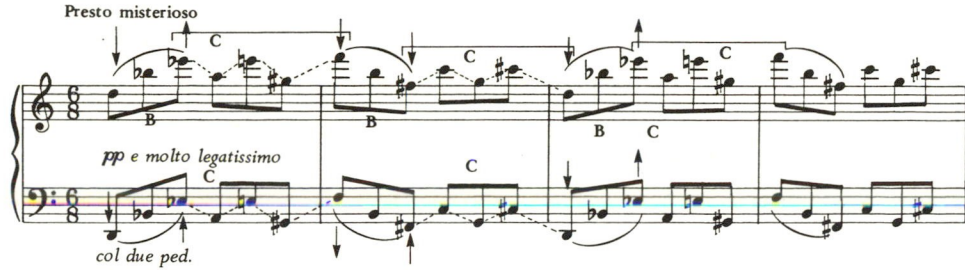

Example 112. Debussy, "Feux d'artifice"

Incidentally the pedal vibrato may be applied as rapidly, regularly or irregularly as one chooses, depending on one's ear and coloristic imagination.

Crescendo effect

Another effective way of using the right pedal is in crescendo effects in both loud and soft passages. The right pedal augments a crescendo by generating sympathetic vibrations in all the strings. It is effective for short glissando-type runs in both pianissimo and fortissimo passages like the ones in examples 113 and 114:

Example 113. Mozart, *Concerto in D Minor*, K. 466, first movement

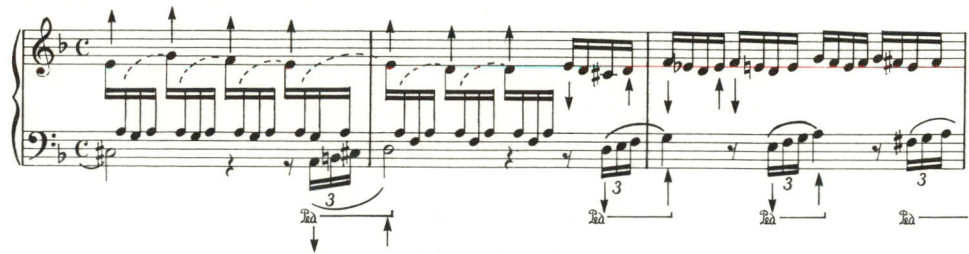

Example 114. Liszt, "Mephisto Waltz"

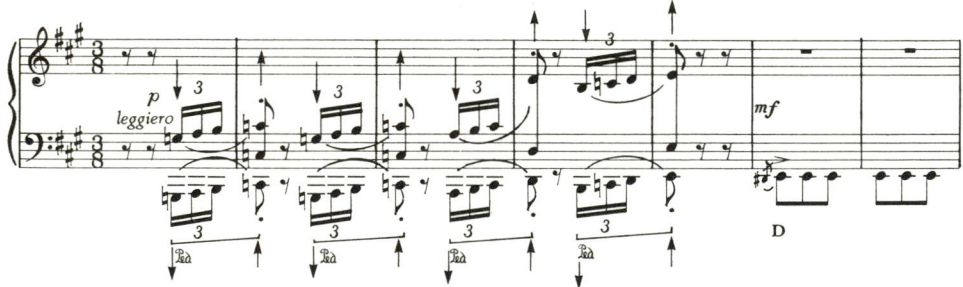

Harmony

Since the right pedal helps to synchronize sounds, chords, and harmonies, a thorough knowledge of harmony is desirable for its effective manipulation. The pedal is also very helpful in contemporary music where the main notes and harmonies are often obscured by neighboring or derived (sharpened, flattened) notes; the pedal can help a great deal to underline structurally important notes. All in all, it is advisable to use as much pedal as possible. The pedal can be regarded as a device that can restore the piano to its previous happy state, when no damper interfered with the rich sympathetic vibrations of its entire string system. Let us use the dampers ("con sordino") only when overlapping sonorities necessitate a "blotter" to soak up and eliminate unwanted sounds. The dampers, in effect, can choke off the vibrations of the strings quite suddenly; this abrupt quality is sometimes undesirable, especially at phrase endings. Here a smooth pedaling and a gentle lifting of the fingers with the help of the arm is preferable. I would fully concur with the response of a fine pianist who was asked when he uses the right pedal. His answer was, "Whenever it doesn't sound bad." Indeed it is a good idea to use a little pedal on the last note of every phrase ending.

Pedal indications

There are several ways to indicate pedaling. Most frequently the 𝄢. sign indicates the point where the pedal should be depressed. An asterisk ❋ is often used where the pedal is to be lifted. Sometimes this sign is used: └────────┘ ; the first vertical line indicates the depressing of the pedal, and the second vertical line indicates its lifting.

Example 115. Pedal marking

Sometimes dots are used for the duration of the pedal: 𝄢 . . . . . "½ Pedal" or "⅓ Pedal" is used occasionally. For pedal tremolo or vibrato we sometimes find either the words printed or the following: 𝄢

Another indication for the right pedal—one that was often used by Beethoven—is *tutte corde*. In some instances, however, this term is a substitute for *tre corde,* and it should be interpreted merely in the sequence beginning with *una corda* and *due corde*; in this case it means to let all three strings of a note sound, and is used after the left pedal has been lifted. In due time, however, *tutte corde* became an indication that all strings should be freed of their dampers: it simply means that the right pedal should be depressed.

Senza sordino; con sordino

As we mentioned earlier, the term *senza sordino* is also a right pedal sign; it was frequently used by Beethoven. The end of his indication is *con sordino,* a term that means the dampers are to be dropped on the strings to stop the sound, by releasing the pedal.

Example 116. Beethoven, *Piano Concerto No. 3*, opus 37, second movement

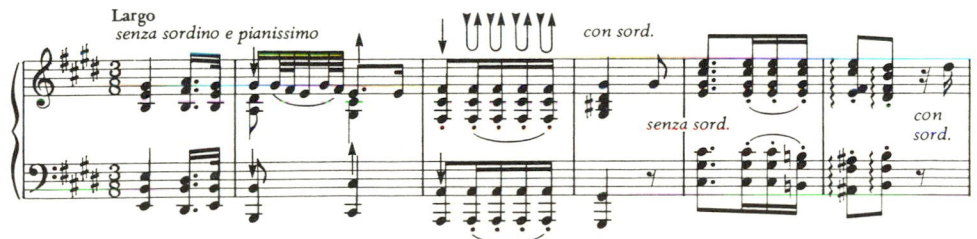

(Example 116 continued)

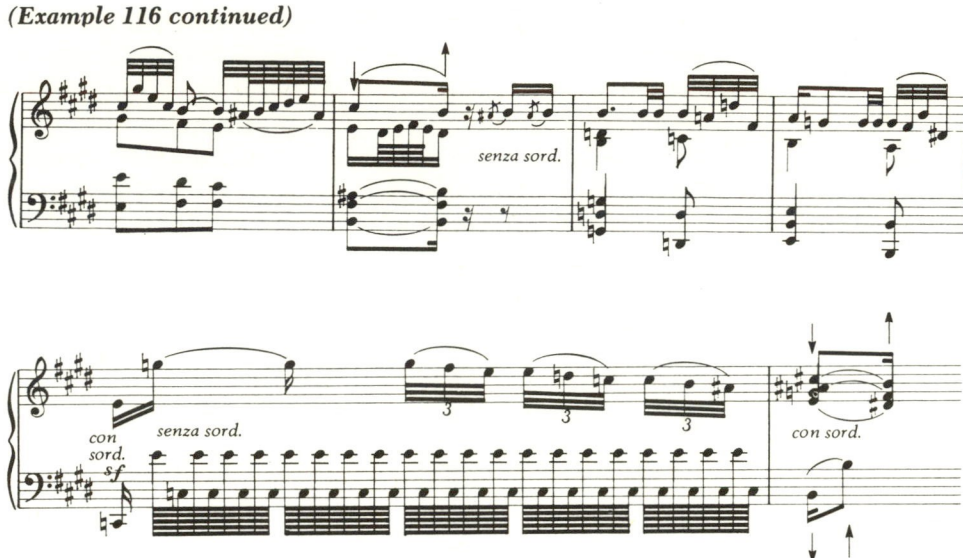

The pedal in Baroque and pre-Baroque music

Even when no pedal indication appears in the score, we should still use the pedal unless there is a special reason not to do so. As I said before, the ear is the judge. Even though Baroque music was written before the piano and its pedals were invented, we are fully justified in using anything and everything possible to make it sound the way that best serves our musical purposes. The piano was not invented as a whim or as a superfluous addition to some already-existing and totally satisfactory family of instruments. On the contrary, it was invented because there was a need for it; its predecessors left a great deal to be desired, and composers created music that necessitated an evolution in keyboard instruments. The increased volume and expressiveness of the piano was a step ahead of its forebears, and the pedal added to its already richer tonal palette. Arpeggios, runs, and tremolos sound better with the pedal in any period or style, be it Baroque, Classic, Romantic, or contemporary. The pedal can also enhance polyphonic music if it is handled judiciously.

Middle pedal: invaluable for isolating and blending certain notes

The middle pedal is a relatively new addition to the piano. Actually it was an American invention, and only recently has it been adopted by some of the European and Asian piano factories. It certainly is a most welcome improvement. It enables us to sustain any particular note or notes that we wish to feature or include in subsequent passages, without having all the strings vibrating sympathetically. Its role is very, very important. When properly used, it equals the right pedal, and I personally use it nearly as much as the right pedal. It should be activated just *after* the key (or keys) is pressed down and held; the respective dampers are then suspended in the up position, permitting the strings to vibrate until the dampers are released again.

Since the middle pedal prolongs only the notes we wish to hold, it is ideal for organ points and sustained notes whenever we don't want to submerge the rest of the notes in one pedal. For instance, we can sustain a whole column of harmonics of a chord and let these notes, and only these, generate sympathetic vibrations to the other notes played. The harmonics of the chord feed on each other's vibrations; they reinforce the pure harmony held by the middle pedal and keep it emerging clearly beyond all the other nonharmonic notes that are played. The effect of the middle pedal is much more evident in the lower registers, where the strings are longer than those of the treble.

We can and should develop the technique of applying the middle pedal during runs, passages, and scales. We can hold certain notes that are organically part of the main harmony with the fingers, sustain them with the middle pedal, and highlight the chord as a structural part of the music. Once these pure harmonies emerge, we can then use the right pedal to incorporate them and improve the overall sonority. Thus the middle pedal can act as a filter that passes on the "purified harmonic product" to the musical texture. This technique is very useful in any style of music. In conventional music the harmonies can emerge from scale passages, and in contemporary music we can choose to feature the structural notes that are often obscured by grace notes or passing notes. Used either overtly or covertly the middle pedal is a great improvement to the modern piano, and it is well worth cultivating.

One of the more sophisticated uses of the middle pedal involves the use of harmonics. If we want the harmonics of some notes to sound and to envelop other sonorities, we can press down these notes mutely and catch them with the middle pedal even before we start to play the piece. The harmonics of the sustained notes will come to life through sympathetic vibrations; sometimes they produce an eerie and strangely beautiful sonority. This device is well employed in bagpipe music (musettes) and in music-box imitations. One of Bartók's compositions, "Harmonics," exploits this technique in a most imaginative way:

Example 117. Bartok, *Mikrokosmos*, vol. 4, "Harmonics"

Chord held down mute

By the way, we must be watchful to release the middle pedal at the right time in order to avoid mixing (and catching) unwanted sounds if the harmony changes.

A classic example of the use of harmonics is in Schumann's *Carnaval:*

Example 118. Schumann, *Carnaval*, opus 9, "Paganini"

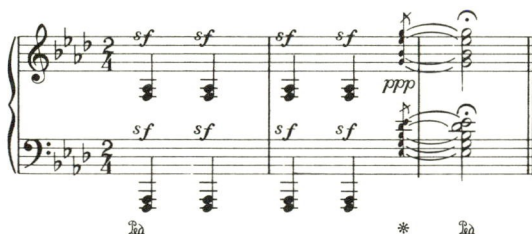

The last chord of "Paganini" is to be depressed mutely while the previous fortissimo chords still sound and generate sympathetic vibrations in the strings.

The middle pedal can be used with or without the right pedal for effects like the long pedals of Beethoven. Another obvious passage in which the middle pedal is used is the extended A-flat-major harmony with its recitative-like cadenza at the end of Chopin's *Fantasy*, opus 49. The middle pedal can be held throughout the long fermatas.

Example 119. Chopin, *Fantasy*, opus 49

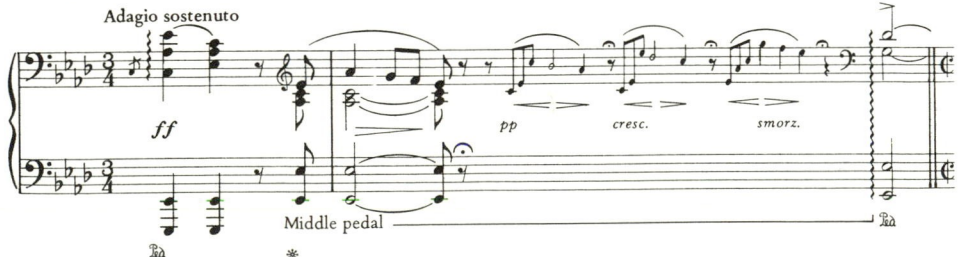

Middle pedal

Still another ideal spot for both pedals is the coda of the *Chromatic Fantasy* by Bach.

Example 120. Bach, *Chromatic Fantasy and Fugue*

From the beginning of the Coda: middle pedal for low D, plus some right pedal until end of the Fantasy.

Wide stretches

We can accomplish much with the middle pedal in wide stretches; it is easier to hold notes with the pedal than to strain the hand. At the beginning of the third movement of Beethoven's *Sonata*, opus 31 no. 2 ("Tempest") it is quite possible to hold the sustained A in the left hand with the middle pedal; you can depress its key mutely before starting the piece and then activate the middle pedal. The note must be released when the harmony changes and then caught again when it recurs.

Example 121. Beethoven, *Sonata*, opus 31 no. 2, third movement

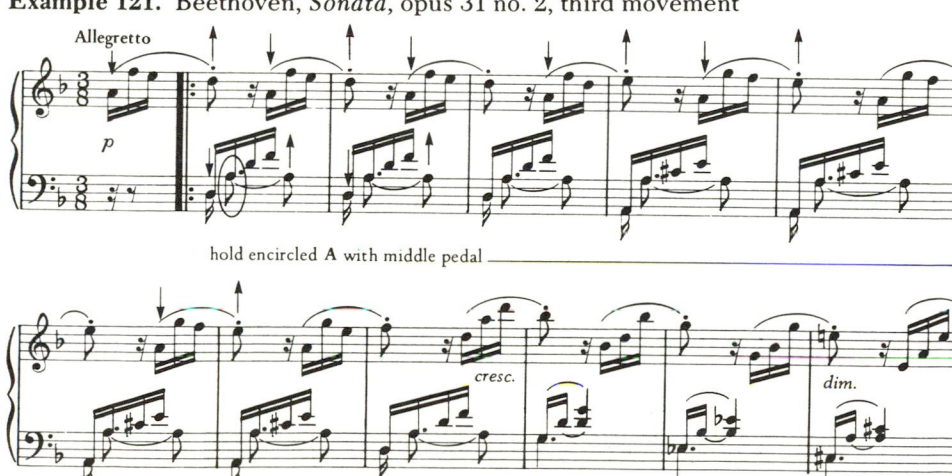

Sometimes the middle pedal can be used more subtly. In example 122 one's first impulse might be to catch the low C with the middle pedal and sustain it through the harmony. If you did this you would soon notice that this low C is overwhelmingly loud because of the dynamic marking. A much better effect results when the C of the octave higher is sustained. The tonic note is still sustained, but it is done in a much more attractive manner.

Example 122. Beethoven, *Sonata*, opus 53, last movement

(Middle pedal for encircled C; right pedal as before)

Una corda; due corde

The left pedal, which is often called the soft pedal, una corda, or due corde, helps us to produce softer sonorities by mechanical means. When we use the left pedal, the entire mechanism of the piano shifts to the right so that the hammers do not hit all three strings but only one or two; the number of strings hit depends on when the piano was built. When the shifting device was first applied in the eighteenth century, the mechanism went far enough to the right for the hammer to play only one string: it could be shifted back gradually to touch two strings and then back to its normal position, where the hammer hit all three strings. Beethoven often indicated una corda, due corde, and tutte corde. Today's instruments do not shift quite as far to the right as those of Beethoven's day, and the left pedal activates two strings. Even so, the difference in the volume of two strings is quite noticeable when it is compared to the sound produced by three strings. Since the lowest bass notes have only one string each, their sound is not reduced by the use of the left pedal. However there might be some difference in volume and in the tone quality because a softer portion of the felt contacts the string when the left pedal is depressed.

A different
timbre too

And this brings up an interesting topic: if the piano has new hammers, the shifting of the mechanism merely reduces volume of the sound because two strings are struck instead of three. Most of the time, however, the hammers are "played in," and the felt has grooves on it. Therefore when the left pedal is depressed and the piano mechanism shifts, a less-used portion of the felt contacts the strings and this alters the *tone quality*. Although the purpose of this pedal is not a change in tone quality, everyone now associates the left pedal with both a reduced sound and a new timbre. We might as well accept this fact and use the left pedal also as a coloring device that enriches our tonal palette. But let us bear in mind that it is preferable to rely on touch quality created by the fingers rather than the feet.

"Riding" the
left pedal

The shifting of the hammers to a softer-sounding portion of the felt tempts many pianists to use the left pedal excessively. Indeed with it the piano does sound gentler, and it is easier to control in soft passages. At public performances, when one often must play an unfamiliar and imperfect instrument, the left pedal can safeguard against unpleasant surprises in sonority. Another cause of "riding" the left pedal continuously may be nerves, a problem we will discuss in chapter eighteen.

I believe that the use of the left pedal in Baroque music is as valid as in that of any other period. There is no reason to believe that Bach and his contemporaries did not occasionally desire extremely soft or extremely loud sonorities; they certainly asked for loud moments in music for the organ, voice, and strings; moreover the sound of the clavichord, a very popular Baroque keyboard instrument, was very soft and gentle. It seems to me that the gentlest of pianissimos is entirely appropriate in music like this prelude by Bach; if this work doesn't call for pianissimo, I don't know what does:

Example 123. Bach, *Well-Tempered Clavier*, book 1, Prelude No. 8 in E Flat Minor

Depress early
and fully.

Here the left pedal is certainly an asset.

Unlike the other two pedals, the left pedal is applied just *before* we play the note. The mechanism should already be in position when the hammer hits the strings so that it doesn't slide at the moment of attack. Unless you are playing one of the older instruments with una corda, due corde, and tre corde options, you should keep the left pedal fully depressed at all times while in use.

We have three pedals but only two feet. A problem arises on those occasions when we must depress all three pedals simultaneously. Performers with broader feet have less of a problem than those with narrow feet. But for both types it might be useful to turn the left heel outward so that a larger portion of the sole covers the left and middle pedals. The right foot is reserved for just one pedal for the obvious reason that the right pedal is used most frequently; therefore the right foot must be more mobile.

The ear is
master.

Fortunately foot technique is not terribly strenuous—at least nobody ever complained of tired or tense feet while playing the piano. But I must emphasize that the manner, frequency, quantity, and intensity of pedal work must be guided primarily by the ear: constant listening, awareness, and control are needed to produce the desired sounds. Every piano is different, and acoustic conditions vary greatly; therefore you cannot preplan your pedaling at home to make it perfect anywhere. The only constant is the sound image we want to create; but even this aspect of playing frequently changes on the spur of the moment. It is essential for performers to familiarize themselves with the concert instrument, especially by experimenting with extreme pianissimos and extreme fortissimos. Some of the lowest bass strings, for example, have the tendency to shift to horizontal vibrations in extreme fortissimos. Thus they touch the metal portion of the damper and surprise you with an infernal rattling and metallic sound. You simply cannot guess whether the piano does this or not! Obviously, you may find the opposite too: no response to your extreme pianissimos. The only way to find out is by rehearsing on the piano.

CHAPTER

13   Singing Tone

Expressive
capability of the
piano

Although the piano is primarily a percussion instrument, it has the ability to talk, to sing, and to shout if necessary, as well as to whisper. Its mechanism is so ingenious that somehow it can respond to, and generate, the widest range of human emotions. Nobody doubts its ability to graduate dynamics, but some often question its ability to vary tone quality. Is it capable of responding to changes of touch, and, if so, how do we achieve this? First, let me assure you that the piano is indeed responsive to various touches, and it can produce a singing tone, as anyone who has heard the varied piano sounds of Horowitz, Rubinstein, or Richter can testify. But how can we produce a singing tone?

The piano produces a sound that reflects the voicing of its hammers. A very fine piano does much more than that: it responds sensitively to the way the pianist plays. A pianist's sound is the direct result of his technique—of the motions he uses; a sensitive instrument reflects not only his manner of playing but also his personality. A very fine piano does what a musical instrument is supposed to do; it acts as a vehicle for the performer through which he expresses himself by his personal interpretation of the music.

Role of the
equipment

Our concern here is the quality of sound that results from the player's technique rather than the piano's intrinsic sound. It is correct to assume that a hard sound results from a hard equipment (or from fixed joints of the performer), while a soft, singing sound is produced by a soft mechanism (that is, resilient joints). This seems to be a rather simplistic statement, but it is nonetheless true. If the attack on the piano is sudden, angular, and produced with a stiff wrist, a hard, harsh sound is inevitable. If we want a round, sonorous sound, we must activate a well-cushioned elastic human mechanism. We must not force this mechanism on the piano, but throw it or drop it with a responsive springy action in the wrist and the other joints. Under any circumstances the sound reflects both the quality of the playing equipment and the technique utilized, as well as the tone quality of the piano.

If a hard sound results from a nonresilient mechanism and a soft sound results from a yielding one, how does one produce a *singing tone*? The essential quality in a singing tone is intensity, and this is true for soft as well as for loud sounds. The sound should carry; it should have body, it should be expressive, and it should have lasting quality. The playing mechanism, therefore, should be neither too hard nor too soft; the joints of the fingers, wrist, and hand must be supple, resilient, and elastic. They should cushion the descending energy in order to eliminate sudden impacts, and they should reduce the speed with which the fingertip contacts the key. If all the joints (including the joints between the phalanges of the fingers) are resilient, a singing tone will result.

You will notice that when I discuss the joints, I use the term *elastic* instead of *limp*. Limpness produces an anemic sound, not a soft sound, because the energy directed toward the keys is not transferred properly. Hard, stiff joints do have one use: they are reserved for *martellato* or "hammered" effects.

The degree of hardness and stiffness in our joints, or resistance, can be controlled. For an extreme pianissimo, the resistance of our joints is minimal. The degree of resistance can be different from one joint to the other; this variety does also affect our tone quality. For example, we can use very loose finger joints with a rather fixed wrist or rather firm finger joints and a very supple wrist; resistance can be varied almost infinitely. The use of the entire arm and very flexible joints produces an extremely light and gentle sound. You may utilize only the forearm or you may feature only the hands and fingers: you have all the choices in the world!

When you play a singing melody, observe the descending and lifting motions of your arm; they are slow, quiet, and effortless. The character of the motion must correspond to that of the sound; this is the essence of piano playing. Technique, sound, and motions are indivisible: they affect, influence, and create one another.

We should fully realize that these cushioned, gentle motions resemble, and alarmingly so, that which is popularly called "pressure." Pressure, a word frequently applied to piano technique, is, if I may say so, the most abused, the most misplaced and unattractive activity in piano playing. First, it is totally inappropriate to an instrument that produces its sounds by an instantaneous hammer action. Once the sound is made, pressure has no influence whatsoever on it. It should be obvious that any activity on the key after the sound has been heard is wasted. Moreover, it hinders free tone production for the following note, because of an excessively prolonged tension in the muscles.

Spiritual or
carnal
experience: the
piano as "love
object"

Extended pressure tightens up the muscles, and, what is still worse, it is habit forming. It affects the flow of the music with an uncalled-for exaggerated intensity that usually has very little to do with the music's content. Often it is used as an added energizing factor in performance. There is no doubt that pressure produces a strong physical sensation in the muscles; it also stimulates the tactile nerve endings of the fingertips—not a negligible factor in terms of carnal gratification! But pressing on the keys just isn't the thing to do! The piano is a musical instrument, and although these pleasurable activities in the human physical equipment are part of the enjoyment of making music, they should not become a habitual outlet or a substitute for pent-up energy. Carnal gratification is best achieved in other, more pleasurable, activities! Frankly speaking, those long lonely hours spent in practicing the piano do not justify transforming the instrument into an object of love making, no matter how handy (excuse the pun) it may seem. An extremely widespread "method" of practicing urges us to lean on, to press, and to squeeze the keys—to generate stimulation in the physical sense and to equate these activities with spiritual sensations! Instead of indulging in these misplaced activities one should build a technique sensibly, without forcing, and should then use this physical equipment as a means of creating genuinely spiritual and sublimated experiences.

Shoulder, not
the fingers,
carries the
weight.

Singing tone is produced when the cushioning activities of the joints slow down the descending arm speed, thus making it possible for only a portion of the speed and weight to be transferred to the keys. The shoulder muscles, not the fingertips, should always carry most of the arm weight. The "relaxed but massive sensation" in the fingertips that the advocates of pressure aim for should be replaced by the gentle, resilient feeling of a light and effortless weight transference. This partial weight of the arm produces an intense, warm singing tone without excessive and damaging pressure on the fingertips. In the delicate balance between spiritual intensity and physical intensity, the former should have priority. The gentle, slowed-down cushioning activity of the joints should not be mistaken for pressure. Mind you, we do not want to eliminate the physical gratification inherent in piano playing; on the contrary, we do want to activate the physical equipment, but we want to do it properly and without using it as a source for physical excitation and pseudospiritual self-stimulation. Let the piano be a tool for musical expression and not an object for muscular gratification.

Breithaupt:
weight addict

One of Breithaupt's fundamental errors was to misunderstand and overemphasize the role of weight in piano technique. He sought to reduce active muscle work by letting the fingers carry an overload of weight, and thus he exposed them to constant pressure and strain.

There are two problems with his approach: first, the finger muscles located in the forearm are not intended to carry excess weight; their role is to transfer energy instantaneously to the fingers and to the hammers. Second, it is the shoulder muscles that should carry most of the weight of the whole arm at all times.

Difference
between
cushioning and
pressure

The essential difference between the *cushioning* technique and *pressure* is that in cushioning, the joints are essentially passive and under minimal strain. However, when pressure is applied, both the flexors and extensors of the forearm become tightly contracted for an extended time and the fingers are forced to carry too much weight. These excessive muscular activities are habit-forming. Many pianists get so used to them that they actually enjoy them: they feel busy and "involved." In actuality excessive muscular activities are strenuous and, in a way, damaging to the technique and to the sound.

CHAPTER

14   **Practicing**

Practicing: one
phase of
learning

Before we discuss conditions, difficulties and problems of public performances, we will examine what practicing is, how to practice and the results of correct and faulty practicing. If we think of the endless hours we spend practicing and compare these hours with the time actually spent performing in public, we realize the high priority of our concern with practice itself. Granted, the proof is in the performance, which is like the icing on the cake. But to mix our metaphors, performance is the tip of the iceberg that is visible above the surface of the water, while practicing represents the immense and invisible bulk that is underneath the "icing." Efficient practice and wasteful practicing yield entirely different results, and the time one can save by avoiding wasteful practicing is spectacular! We should try to develop practice habits that are productive—that is, habits that are based on minimum effort and maximum efficiency. We will find it gratifying that we can steadily improve this technique of learning; indeed, there is no limit to what is possible. One's learning capacity can be developed to an impressive degree.

Learning
processes

Practicing is that phase of learning in which we acquire motion habits through repetition. Other stages of learning include the readings of the piece, the search for its meaning, and its memorization. We practice when we sit at the keyboard and execute motions according to the text. We repeat these motions until we secure the desired speed, dynamics, interpretation, and mood of the music. We try to ingrain certain motion patterns, and then we apply them in their respective passages. After we have reached the point where we can execute these motions automatically, we can concentrate exclusively on interpretation.

Learning by
conscious effort

Now let us examine the learning processes themselves. It has been proven that the amount of time required to memorize a text can vary dramatically, depending on whether or not attention is paid to its content. If we read a text mechanically, without concentration and without being aware of its content, we may never memorize it, no matter how many times we go through it. On the other hand, if the text is given to us to be memorized, and if we read this text with total concentration on its meaning, we may be able to memorize it after just a few readings. The difference between the mechanical and the conscious approach is quite striking; the number of repetitions needed to ingrain habits is infinitely smaller when we concentrate.

The same holds true for practicing the piano. Conscious and carefully executed motions are learned and retained very rapidly; sometimes only a few repetitions are needed to master a passage. Since the mind registers any experience indelibly, the speed with which it ingrains motions depends on the sameness, frequency and intensity of the repeated motions. Therefore, if we repeat a certain motion with great concentration and play it the same way on every repetition, the process of ingraining the material will be very rapid, and the results will be lasting. The mind can be compared with the smooth, flat surface of a record; its grooves deepen continuously if the needle always follows the same path. However, if the needle is continuously sidetracked, its grooves do not deepen, and when the record is played again, the needle wanders off to any one of the grooves engraved on the record's surface. If while practicing the motions we execute constantly vary, the engraving process of our mind will be slow and unreliable. Not only memory problems but technical insecurity are the result of this approach. This is why haphazard practicing brings such poor results.

Mechanical vs. conscious practicing

The advantages of conscious practice and the waste in mechanical work can be seen clearly. Mechanical practice obviously produces some results, but they are achieved in a time-consuming and inefficient way. One never feels sure of the results of purely mechanical practice—one never "knows" the passage, and consequently one easily forgets it. All practicing should be done consciously. One could say that the worst practicing is no practice at all, but I am not so sure about that! Mechanical practicing can form detrimental habits that have to be eliminated sooner or later.

Varying rhythmic patterns?

A commonly used practice method is one in which passages are repeated with varying rhythmic patterns. For several reasons, I do not advocate this type of practice; the use of a rhythmic formula tends to make practicing mechanical, and when patterns with dotted notes are used, the short notes usually don't receive sufficient time and attention. It is better to practice the notes as they are originally written and ingrain the text as you want it engraved in your mind.

Example 124. Varying rhythmic patterns; (a) original, (b) variations

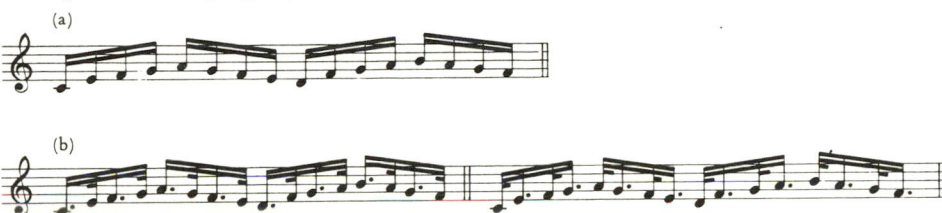

As learning
process
improves, fewer
repetitions are
necessary.

Since we talked about good and bad practice methods, why not mention the ideal one? If we know exactly what motion to learn, if we know how to execute it, and if we concentrate intensely on repeating the motion correctly and in exactly the same way for a sufficient number of times, we will engrave it in minimum time. To carry the analogy with the record further, the engraving will be ideal; there will be no conflict or divergence in the groove because there will be only one groove. The depth of the groove will become sufficient after a few practice sessions. For instance, if we practice a new passage twelve times at the first practice session, we may find that at the beginning of the second practice session it feels as if we had never seen it before. But after five or six repeats it will go as well as it did at the end of the twelve repetitions in the first practice session. The third session will require two or three repetitions, and most likely you will know the passage the fourth time you try it. But we want to accomplish more than just this! The number of repetitions applies only to the basic learning processes; additional repetitions should enable us to improve the passage interpretatively as well as technically. If the basic foundation is well established, continuous improvement will follow. This is the reason it is so very important to employ the correct motions with conscious attention.

Slow practice
most helpful,
but not the goal

Slow practice is very helpful; it enables us to execute every aspect of the motion effortlessly and with absolute accuracy. However, a word of caution is necessary. We advocate slow practice because the mind requires sufficient time to make the mechanism execute and control the motions. When a passage is new and difficult, considerable time is needed for these processes. Sometimes we have to spend extra time on a group of notes, or even on a single note. Then again, the next note may be easily manageable, and consequently it requires much less time. Our aim is slow practice, not for its own sake, but for the sake of executing the required motions with sufficient control and awareness. Consequently, if a certain passage is well under control, easy to execute, and in no need of extra time, then we just move on.

We give the time necessary to any passage, or any note, that needs it. But we do not spend time playing it over and over in slow and even tempo, just because we began slowly; this activity would waste our time. We must make the seemingly contradictory statement that practicing should be as fast as possible; by this we mean that it should be as fast as possible *while completely controlling the intended motions.* The statement makes sense because our aim is to achieve awareness and control. With sufficient repetition we need less and less time to exercise this control, and thus we will be able to play faster and correctly all the time. The important thing is to avoid playing a passage any faster than we can control it. Being aware of the degree of control we have is really a matter of inner discipline—something we must work on all the time.

Uneven practice
most
economical

There is one last point to be made about slow practice. If we follow these suggestions and give the necessary time (no more and no less) to each note, we will find ourselves playing totally uneven metric values because the amount of time it takes to master each note or passage varies with its difficulty! This unevenness is quite different from mechanical practicing, in which the poor victim repeats everything with mechanical regularity. It is not that I advocate unevenness in performance, but if the needed time given to each note while learning a work results from the continuous watchfulness of the mind, it is a most welcome sign of intelligent practicing. Mechanical practicing can be compared to an assembly line where the speed is constant regardless of the tasks to be accomplished; too much time is allotted for simple operations, and not enough time is allotted for the complex ones. Conscious practice, on the other hand, provides all the time needed for complex situations and very little time for the simple ones. To develop this continuous control is really a matter of inner discipline that is well worth cultivating.

Role of the
conscious mind

Much has been said about the importance and effectiveness of the conscious mind during the learning process; it is undeniable that conscious practicing has a considerable edge over mechanical practicing. Conscious practicing is analogous to a spotlight that focuses on a relatively small area and illuminates it thoroughly. It then proceeds to other problem areas and finally is able to integrate the examined areas. It can observe and resolve many things that the subconscious and automatic centers couldn't handle at all. However, we must realize that the conscious mind soon tires and concentration cannot be maintained for extended periods: for most people the limit is about twenty minutes. However, with a little rest it can recuperate and, with proper training, it can be strengthened considerably. Nevertheless, it seems that a short break after practicing twenty minutes is advisable; because we insist on conscious practicing, we should use the mind at its best.

Conscious, subconscious, and automatic centers

If the conscious mind is like a spotlight, the subconscious is similar to a large dimly lit cave; the spotlight can enter it and pinpoint small spots, but it can never illuminate the entire area at once. It is in the subconscious mind that we store most of our experiences, and it is also the place where most of our memories are submerged. There is still another region where most of the vital bodily processes are controlled by the unconscious and automatic nerve centers; the conscious mind has hardly any control over these centers.

Two-way traffic

A primarily one-way connection exists between the conscious, subconscious, and unconscious minds. In due time conscious activities pass to the realm of the subconscious; many of them continue to the unconscious region. However this sequence can be reversed, for much traffic moves between the subconscious and conscious mind. Most of what we have learned and stored in the subconscious can be brought back to our awareness at will, and it seems that having been in storage didn't hurt it a bit! We may often be surprised how much better a piece feels, both musically and technically, after it has been "put away" for a long period. A well-learned piece may take very little time, or no time at all, to revive. Sometimes we can remember and replay it with every detail instantly recalled.

Conscious mind acquires experiences; subconscious mind stores them.

With its three layers (the conscious, subconscious, and unconscious levels) the human mind is eminently capable of coping with most human experiences; in any case, that's all we have. The role of these layers of the mind in learning, in storing the learned experience, and in recalling it corresponds to its role in music—practicing, memorizing, and performing a composition.

The unconscious mind stores and manipulates most of the innate and instinctive processes related to our vital functions, and it also stores the acquired skills that have become automatic; this level of the mind has little to do with the processes of learning and acquiring. It is the conscious mind that is responsible for selecting, analyzing, and finding the best ways to assimilate the material or skill to be acquired. The latter's role, therefore, is to make us aware of the material, to make us understand it, and to enable us to master it. In learning new music, the conscious mind converts the written image of the notes into its respective technical patterns and then finds the best ways to apply these technical formulas.

Conscious mind is inhibitive, not creative.

However, although the conscious mind can analyze problems, find solutions to these problems, and can help to acquire skills and put them to use, it cannot take part in creative processes. Its role is intellectual and inhibitive; it hinders all spontaneous, improvisatory, and instinctive processes. But at the same time as it prevents these processes it feeds the subconscious and automatic mind. Once a skill has been learned and assimilated, it inevitably sinks into the subconscious and unconscious levels. The conscious mind's valuable role is irreplaceable, for it continues to enrich and develop us during our entire lifetime; it is in charge of learning. On the other hand, the creative processes are the product of the subconscious and unconscious mind; they produce the spontaneous and involuntary activities. All that has been said about the vital role of the conscious mind refers to the learning processes: creativity is not a function of the conscious mind.

Conscious mind should not interfere with acquired skills.

The use of the conscious mind is limited to acquiring the skill of piano playing. The conscious process establishes the correct mental concept of the motions and controls the practice methods in which we apply and assimilate the motion patterns. After these motions are learned, we no longer need the supervision of the conscious mind; the skill of piano playing will have become "second nature," and from here on it belongs to the subconscious and unconscious layers of the mind. Once the skill becomes a habit, not only do we not need the control of the conscious mind, but we must discourage it, for it interferes with the natural flow of happenings. When we know a passage and can play it freely, we should not be concerned with the details of raising our wrist or elbow.

Practice technique only when correction is necessary.

The critical mind is only helpful in establishing new habits and in eliminating bad ones; these activities belong to the conscious process of learning (or unlearning), but they are not part of the uninhibited, unconscious flow of automatic processes. Once our technique is ingrained and is automatic, it is in the domain of the subconscious and the unconscious—and that is where it should be. Once we possess a good technique, we use it; we don't have to practice it. Once you have learned to walk, to bicycle, to write, or to talk, you don't practice these automatic skills; instead you use them in the best possible way. Only if one of these skills fails will you use your conscious processes to correct it.

This is the sequence of events: once we have acquired skill in piano playing, the subconscious and unconscious mind provides us with an automated technique for performing familiar musical patterns and imbues them with spontaneous and creative improvisations. The role of the conscious mind is to help us acquire unfamiliar repertoire and technical know-how; it also enables us to recall, supervise, and improve old repertoire and technical formulas, all under the revealing "spotlight" of our awareness.

Practice is conscious; performance spontaneous.

There is truth in the old saying: when you practice alone, you should be as aware of every note and motion as if you were on the stage of Carnegie Hall, being watched by two thousand people. But when you actually perform there, you should play as if you were at home, alone. Practicing should be conscious, performing mostly spontaneous. In this chapter we have discussed the first half of this saying —that is, when you practice, you must be fully aware and conscious of everything you do so that you can conceive the correct motion patterns, ingrain them, and execute them perfectly. Mind you, this manner of working is much more strenuous mentally than mechanical practicing, but the results are achieved in an incomparably shorter time; furthermore the results of attentive practicing are reliable and permanent, and they eliminate any further need for practicing the already-acquired technique. When you have a good technique, your practice should then center on the application of this effortless, reliable, and automatic technique directly to the repertoire.

No "etudes"; only essential exercises

Now that we have thoroughly examined the "how" of practicing, the next question to consider is "what" to practice. Since I do not believe in mechanical practicing, I recommend eliminating most studies that feature technique and not music (Hanon, Pischna, Czerny). Exercises and technical studies that employ certain technical patterns repetitiously tend to lead us to mechanical practicing. It is much more productive to assimilate a technical formula in its purest form and, when it is learned correctly, to employ it at once in a musical composition by adapting it to the specific demands of the piece. The piano repertoire is so immense—there is so much to learn—that it is foolish to spend time with inferior music when the same technical development can be achieved by working on great music. Etudes by Chopin and Liszt are masterpieces of the first order and merit the most serious study; in previous chapters we supplied examples from great works of music in which the various motions should be applied. The literature is filled with technical formulas, and I urge that you apply what you have learned to real music rather than to "etudes" concocted by innumerable nameless composers.

Of course, I am not saying that we should avoid any technical practice and learn only pieces of music. On the contrary, it is imperative to learn first the technical formulas impeccably though the necessary exercises and only then proceed to their application in the repertory.

Motion patterns

Since most of you who are interested in these pianistic observations must have certain familiarity with piano playing, I would recommend, as a practical consideration, that you examine and assimilate the five motion patterns successively, and not all at once. Conscious practice and controlled application of these formulas require consid-erable mental strain. It is better to learn first the free fall motion alone, and look for repertory where it can be applied: you will find numerous opportunities to use it. Then, continue with the five-finger, scale and arpeggio motion, and proceed the same way. Here, of course, you will find an inexhaustible area to explore. Follow through then with rota-tion, staccato and the thrust. Obviously, this is not an overnight ven-ture and it may take quite a few months' time. However, the time will be well spent and the results ought to be conclusive.

Mental practice

Now that we have established a clear concept of piano playing, and in particular of its five basic motion patterns, we can practice very successfully away from the piano. When the execution of these basic formulas is completely mastered, their application to the text will be direct, immediate, and unequivocal. If the music calls for rotary mo-tion, we understand its technique and we are capable of doing it (it is not enough to know how to do something; one must be able to do it!). As we look at a musical passage we associate it with its technical solution, and thus we can go through the motion mentally; this whole sequence of events can become almost automatic. We can imagine the motion without actually performing it at the piano; you may be sur-prised to find that it is perfectly feasible to practice and learn a com-position in this manner. Furthermore, when we practice mentally, we don't play wrong notes, we don't miss notes, we don't play mechani-cally, and we waste no time or energy. What we need is intense con-centration—an activity that is strenuous but efficient and fast working. In mental practice the mind engraves these immediate, clear associa-tions and processes (reading the score and associating the visual ma-terial with the motoric activities) with great ease, and the "replay" will occur without interference.

Mental practice can be developed to the highest degree. It is true that at first the strain is considerable, but it gradually decreases, and after a short while spectacular results can be achieved. We should not ignore the piano and rely purely on mental practice; but we will find that by combining mental practice and conventional practice, we can absorb and master repertoire much more securely in a much shorter time. The ideal way to practice is to combine the two approaches. When a pianist is on a concert tour, he will often have no access to a piano; mental practice can be a lifesaver. Obviously singers, violinists, and flutists are luckier than those of us who choose the piano, since they can carry their instruments with them; but some of the advantages of mental practicing apply to them too. The musicians who work with the most complex scores, the orchestra conductors, are obliged to rely exclusively on mental learning and practice—at least until they have

Conductors and
mental practice

an orchestra at their command. It is most useful to be able to imagine the sound of music without the aid of an instrument, and it is enjoyable as well. One learns to read the score like a book! Since mechanical practicing is taboo (it is time consuming and it usually doesn't resolve technical problems), you should favor practicing consciously whether you are at the piano or away from it.

15   Memorization

Why memorize?

Since Liszt introduced the practice more than a century ago, it has become customary to perform from memory in public. Toscanini established the same standard for conductors. Most of us go along with this practice, but we must realize that the quality of a performance has nothing to do with the use of a score; it is possible that some of the very best recordings were made with a wide-open score and that some of the poorest concert performances were performed by memory.

There are many arguments both for and against performing without the music. Some say that by the time you know a piece really well, you have it memorized; others say that the absence of music puts more pressure and tension on the already quite tenuous existence of the artist. Chamber-music players practically always use music at public performances. Most of us soloists play by memory most of the time, but some of us do not. Mitropoulos conducted extremely complex contemporary scores, and he did not even use the score at rehearsals! As you can see, there is no uniformity on this subject. In any case, because it is possible to memorize practically anything and because almost everybody wants to, or must, perform by memory, the technique of memorization warrants consideration.

In essence memorization implies not only the ability to store music but also the ability to bring it back—to perform it. It is one thing to recognize a melody when one hears it and quite another thing to remember it or sing it. A much lesser degree of prior engraving of the music in the mind is sufficient for recognition than that required for active reproduction.

Technique of memorization

Memory is something we were born with, but, to develop it, a technique of memorization must be acquired; like conscious practicing, it can be developed to a remarkable degree. The mind can be trained and strengthened the same way that an athlete can develop his muscles. There are many ways to improve memory; according to some mnemotechnicians the most impressive memorization feats can be achieved by the average human being, if his training is right.

Memorize only when properly prepared.

It is advisable to concentrate on memorization only when the material is ready to be stored—that is, when most of the technical and musical problems have been cleared. It is possible to modify passages once they have been memorized, but these alterations will conflict with the material already retained. For ideal memorization, we should repeat every note and every motion while practicing in exactly the same way. In this way we can ingrain the entire product unequivocally and uniquely; we would then come as close as possible to an infallible system of memorization, and there would be no conflict during replay. One should attempt to approximate this ideal situation, even if we know that this is hardly ever possible; in any case, the less conflict we create in the mind, the better we can memorize.

Too early memorization

Some of us memorize so easily that we retain the material even during the first practice sessions, when the solutions of all the problems have not been achieved. The subsequent practice sessions are then spent on activities that may conflict with the original "storing"; because of these conflicts there may be difficulties during the replay. The concentrated and intentional memorization of the finished product is much more effective and faster in the long run than the instantaneous procedure of the overly fast memorizer. We should memorize music intentionally at the point when it is almost completely prepared.

Memorize while young.

There are two valid observations that can be made about memory. First, the earlier in life we learn something, the longer and more securely we retain it. Things that we have ingrained in our early childhood are always going to be remembered. The same principle applies to music; we feel much more secure with music we memorized in our teens than with pieces that we memorized in our thirties or forties. However we cannot determine the exact age at which this or that will happen, and it is possible to learn something more thoroughly and more intelligently in middle age than in youth! We can compensate for age with improved learning techniques and purposefulness; in spite of this, it is of great advantage for a young artist to have a repertoire built at an early age and to store it for future use.

No memory is infallible.

The other observation that we can make with certainty is that, unfortunately, no memory is infallible. You may know a piece forward and backward, you may be able to write every note of it, you may know its structure, you may have practiced it and performed it innumerable times; but there is always the possibility of a blank, of a wrong connection, a faulty association of sequences, and—you forget! In retrospect we often know the reasons. We may be able to cope with the things that went wrong one by one, but not with all of them all at once and always. We cannot be absolutely perfect, like machines; and, as a matter of fact, even machines may go wrong!

The four ingredients

While memorization is not infallible and, it must be admitted, is a rather mysterious process, we do know something about it, and we should be able to improve it considerably. Four ingredients share in the process of memorization, and although all of them may be equally important, their roles do vary in the individual musician. The four elements are: (1) visual memory; (2) acoustic or aural memory; (3) motoric or kinetic memory; and (4) intellectual or analytical memory. Everyone uses these four elements in memorizing, but most of us rely more on only two of them (for example, a combination of visual-motoric, aural-motoric, or aural-intellectual elements), while the other two elements are used somewhat less. Of course, this is a generalized observation, but it is one that is well documented.

Visual memory

People with *visual memory* retain primarily by sight. For instance, many of us remember the exact location of a passage in the text (upper left page, second line, small print), and we can memorize a whole page just by looking at it. In actuality many of the most spectacular memories are "photographic," or purely visual. Experiments have been made in which a seven-digit number is covered with the hand. The hand is then raised for a split second and immediately lowered, permitting the number to be seen for an instant. The picture of the number is engraved on the mind like a flash and it can be recalled instantly. This kind of memory can be trained and developed, and the number of digits can be considerably increased. Some conductors have prodigiously trained minds; they can remember entire pages of fully orchestrated scores purely by visual memory.

Acoustic memory

Acoustic memory is obviously very important for musicians. Many "popular" musicians learn and retain their music purely by ear; "serious" music can be learned in the same way, but only up to a certain point. Classical music can be so complex—with its voice crossings, complicated harmonies and rhythms, and the enormous structures of symphonies and sonatas—that we need the help of all four memory ingredients. Acoustic memory is quite valuable, and it can be greatly helped by ear training. Perfect pitch is very helpful, but it is not essential; good relative pitch is sometimes even better, especially when you are dealing with transposing instruments or when the general pitch of an instrument (or singer) you are working with is half a note off. A knowledge of harmony and theory helps us to recognize chords and structures, to organize them, and to retain them with greater ease.

Motoric memory

Motoric memory is of utmost significance especially for instrumentalists. One may tend to disparage it and to consider it a mechanical activity, but it is more than that. It is the memorization of all the motions executed while making music. Remember, we started off learning them consciously with the intention of ingraining them. Only after thorough learning will they become automatic, after they have been stored quite securely. We find ourselves playing fluently, without hesitation, even without being aware of the notes that we are playing. Actually motoric memory may be reliable enough to carry us through intricate passages that we have not learned and memorized securely by means of the other three components of the process. Because the habits of the performing apparatus are well ingrained, they may pull us through the performance. This situation is not ideal, but it is better than stopping in the middle of a passage to think what comes next! However motoric memory is *not* reliable, and we must endeavor to reinforce it with the other three ingredients.

Intellectual memory

The role of *intellectual memory* is obvious. By analyzing and understanding form and harmonic structure, by organizing the material and determining where climaxes, low points, dynamic fluctuations, ornaments, pedal effects, and modulatory processes take place, we reinforce our memory and allow it to contribute its share to a flawless performance. There are often places in the music where we have to count measures, repetitions, and pauses; this is especially true when we play contemporary music or when we play with orchestras or ensembles. All these processes are intellectual activities and complement the other three factors effectively.

Reinforce all four memory components.

By understanding these four ingredients and by identifying the two that are our best skills, we will learn how to reinforce our memory. If you are an audio-motoric type of memorizer (a very common combination) and you repeatedly have many unexpected lapses that always occur in different places when you play from memory, it is very likely that the visual and intellectual aspects have not contributed enough support. The memory lapses occur because of the performer's failure to reread the music. It may only be necessary to read through the score carefully a few times in order to reinforce the visual component. It could also be possible that you have looked at the music but haven't reanalyzed it. In this case, your intellectual memory has weakened. Maybe you haven't practiced enough, and your motoric memory has suffered—there are any number of reasons for a memory lapse.

The solution to this problem is to reinforce all four components with all the conscious attention they require. Check the structure of the music carefully, listen to it with attention, employ and correct the technical patterns with care, and read through the music with intense concentration. If these four essential memory ingredients receive enough attention, you will have done your best to consolidate your memory.

Memory slips: causes

One reason no memory is infallible is that we often encounter factors beyond our control. We may have practiced and mastered a piece, using the most apt technical solutions; we may have performed it faultlessly any number of times. Then we play the piece in public on another piano with an unexpectedly different action. The result is an immediate interference with our motoric and acoustic memory that affects the usual flow of motions. We may feel that we have to force the piano (which creates more tension in the muscles) or use smaller motions (which will inhibit us). A memory lapse does not mean that we do not know the piece well enough. Our timing and reflexes have been disturbed, and the flow of our feelings and our motoric memory is also upset. Sometimes the visual circumstances, such as the lighting of the hall and stage, are disturbing. At other times the acoustic conditions, or the temperature in the hall, or the noise of the audience shake us up. Innumerable details we cannot anticipate distract us, and sometimes we cannot cope with them. These things can affect our memory in a split second; sometimes our lapse is noticeable, and sometimes it is not. This is understandable, because a concert performance happens not only in space but in time. A performance must have a certain flow—a continuity and timing with no obstructions. As the composer writes down his music, he may stop for a second between notes or scribble as fast as he can; what counts is not the flow and regularity with which he writes but what he puts down on paper. In a performance it is not only the "what" and "how" that counts but the "when." You may know the music, you may know the next note, but not at this instant—sorry, too late!

Never mind; it can and does happen to everybody. This is the reason some of the finest artists (Myra Hess and Béla Bartók, for example) used music when they concertized. Nobody really objected to it. All performers can do is try their best: reinforce the memory with its four ingredients and use a consistently good and well-ingrained technique. Remember that playing the piece over and over probably will not help; try to find the weakest of the four ingredients, work on it, and then follow through with the others. Familiarize yourself with the conditions under which you will perform and try to avoid unforeseen happenings—rehearse at the hall!

Psychological factors

There are many factors besides physical and pianistic reasons that affect memory; emotional complexes, inhibitions, and stage fright are among them. It is beyond the scope of this book to examine these aspects in detail. Obviously our past experiences, the vast reservoir of the subconscious, our drives, our urges, our conditioned reflexes, our frustrations and successes, and our anticipated failures and punishments all influence the flow of our actions. A human being is the sum total of present, past, and distant experiences: our childhood experiences, and even our prenatal and atavistic influences, have a profound effect on our lives. It is no wonder that our actions and reactions are not always predictable and seem to be quite often unexplainable. Still, with all of these unknown and intangible factors to contend with, we can, and must, lean on knowledge and experience that we can exploit. For this reason I have defined certain principles in memorization and their manner of application, calling attention to the vast resources we can mobilize if the stage is adequately set for them.

16 Musical Diction

Music evokes feelings; it does not communicate information.

The language of music differs from other languages; unlike verbal languages, it does not have precise means for dealing with facts, objects, and abstract concepts. We cannot say in music: "Today the temperature is eighty-two degrees, and the air is very humid." We cannot use it to communicate facts or convey ideas. What music can do is generate and communicate moods—the emotional responses that accompany facts and ideas. In a rather mysterious way music can represent and evoke emotions that correspond to circumstances, events, and actions that have not even taken place. A direct and immediate connection exists between certain combinations of sounds and certain feelings. When we hear Beethoven's "Moonlight Sonata" or Debussy's *Clair de Lune* we do not actually have to see the moon, but we can perhaps feel its presence and respond emotionally to the mood created by moonlight! We may feel elated at some parts of the *Eroica* Symphony and depressed by its "Funeral March" without knowing what actually "happened." Actually, nothing "happened." The authenticity of the plot that inspired Beethoven is of no importance. When Beethoven got disillusioned with Napoleon, who originally inspired him to write the *Eroica* Symphony, he simply substituted him with another, imagined hero, who remained nameless, but evoked the same heroic and dramatic moods. Music will circumvent events, communications and information, and will evoke emotional responses by direct aural contact, whether they are stimulating, soothing or depressing. Unquestionably sound alone can represent and affect the entire human emotional gamut.

Notation is rudimentary.

The scope of this book does not permit us to go into detail concerning the why and how of all this; however, consonances, dissonances, and harmonic overtones that blend or clash do have the role of creating tension and release. The subject of musical diction—the means by which music communicates—can be very controversial. Nonetheless we can set certain norms about this important area concerning interpretation. First, it is clear that musical notation is rudimentary: it is rigid and imperfect as to shadings, flexibilities and freedom of phrasing, rhythm, dynamics and pedaling.

Pianists are less flexible than other instrumentalists.

Also, singers, string players, and wind players are much freer in their interpretation of notes and especially in metric values than pianists. Their instruments are more expressive and sensitive than ours, and through bowing and breathing they can make much more use of slight delays, suspenses and accelerandos. Keyboard musicians deal with mechanically regulated pitches; they tend to articulate evenly, instantly, and precisely; unfortunately their diction also tends to be monotonous, square, and lifeless. However, pianists should not merely rattle off the notes; they should be as flexible on their instruments as those who achieve subtlety with breathing or bowing—in other words, they should be musicians. They too can find the meaningful notes in the score and emphasize them; their use of emphasis determines whether their musical diction is convincing and beautiful or dull and artificial.

Downbeats and upbeats; the mazurka

Most music is divided into bars, and within the bars the notes are grouped into cyclic patterns of heavy and light beats. No matter how many beats there are in a bar (and some pieces have continually changing numbers of beats in the bar, while other pieces have no barlines at all), certain notes need emphasis. The obvious note of emphasis in each measure is the downbeat, the first beat of the bar. In a four-beat measure the third beat is the second-heaviest one, while the second and fourth beats are lighter. In a three-beat measure the downbeat is the emphasized note, and the second and third beats vary in intensity. When measures are syncopated, the upbeats are emphasized. In mazurkas, for example, the emphasis may be on *any* beat of the bar; the melody may have its own accent on the first and third beats, and the accompaniment may have several voices, each with its own accents. (Contrary to popular belief the mazurka does not always have an accent on the second beat; although the second beat is often important, there is no hard-and-fast rule for its accentuation, and many mazurkas don't even have a note on the second beat!) No matter how many beats there are in a measure, other notes besides the downbeat may be important for melodic, harmonic, coloristic, or rhythmic reasons; and any of them may have free rubatos too! As a matter of fact, in the mazurka the metric length of some notes must vary too, not only their volume.

Means of emphasis

Certain types of notes by their nature should be very lightly played. They include passing notes, some grace notes, notes that fill in an interval, and ornamental notes. Emphasis can be given to a note by an added length of time we hold it; accented notes are likely to be slightly longer than unaccented ones.

It is impossible to list the innumerable species of notes; all I wish to say is that in music some notes are more important than others. Our musical diction will not be right unless we register these differences in our performances. Some performers can emphasize instinctively; others proceed in a more deliberate fashion. The way that we emphasize is also an individual matter; we may call attention to a note by playing it louder or softer or by slightly prolonging it or delaying it. We can make it stand out by applying a different touch—staccato, legato, portato, or tenuto. Besides the addition of ornaments (which was general practice during the Baroque period) or an octave or two (upper or lower), one may add other harmonics also or shift register. The score also includes marcatos, sforzatos, subito pianos, etc. Besides these, our musical sensitivity and spontaneous reactions will find their way to give subtle meaning to certain notes.

Flexibility

Because the piano, unlike the organ and the harpsichord, responds to "touch" we need not depend on extreme agogy or rhythmic freedom the way harpsichord players often do. On the other hand, our rhythm should be flexible and free; we should not be slaves to the notated rhythmic values. Some music is meant to be motoric (for example, certain toccatas and etudes), but in general one never should play with inflexible evenness.

The most important factor in musical diction on the piano is the nature of the sound of the piano itself. After the hammer has struck the strings, the intensity of the sound immediately diminishes whether we played loudly or softly. If we want to connect the second note of the bar to the downbeat that preceded it, we must realize that this second note is an upbeat—that is, it occurs in a weaker part of the bar than the note on the downbeat. Therefore the second note should have less volume than the downbeat. Also, because of the decrease in intensity of the piano sound, this lesser volume note must be geared to the volume the first note has at the moment when the second note is about to sound. This means we must use still less volume when connecting upbeats on the piano than on other instruments with better sustaining powers.

Maintaining the same dynamic level for an entire group of notes

If we play upbeats with the same intensity as downbeats, we appear to be accenting the weak part of the bar; melodies played this way sound syncopated. If we ignore this fact, at best we project a series of clearly articulated sounds, not a melody; at worst we have a series of unrelated, poorly articulated notes. Since each note on the piano decays rapidly, upbeat notes can be connected satisfactorily only if the dynamic level of the attack of subsequent notes is lower than the dynamic level of the previous note was at its inception. Equal emphasis on the second (lighter) beat produces a crescendo, if the next downbeat is played louder than the first one was. A decrescendo on the piano is easier to produce: the next downbeat will have to be softer than the previous one was. These slight alterations in dynamic level can ensure continuity in the melodic line:

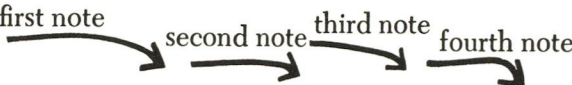

Figure 56. Dynamic manipulation of a melody

You will notice that the third note starts on a higher dynamic level than the end of the second note. The flow of the melody is not obstructed by this change because the third note is the next-heaviest beat after the downbeat, and it lends itself to more emphasis than the second or fourth beat of the measure.

Crescendo

This formula is rather primitive, but it works. If we want to give the impression of playing four notes on the same dynamic level, we have to play the second and fourth notes softer than the first note, and the third note nearly as loud as the first. In other words, the downbeat usually dominates the measure, both harmonically and melodically. Because the downbeat receives more emphasis, it unifies the whole measure. We only play the upbeats as loud as the heavy parts of the bar if we intend to give the impression of a crescendo; in this case the next downbeat is actually played louder than the preceding one.

Upbeats are lighter than downbeats.

The next formula for achieving continuity with dynamics is simple indeed; if a melody starts on an upbeat, or if a note that preceded it is a long note, its dynamic level must be much lower than the downbeat's. There is an inherent, slight crescendo in such passages that start in an upbeat and lead to a downbeat.

Example 125. Bach, *Well-Tempered Clavier*, book 2, Prelude No. 8 in E Flat Minor

(Example 125 continued)

"Negative accents"

Such crescendos are often marked by the composer, but sometimes they are not. Occasionally we find a certain indication quite characteristic of Beethoven—an upbeat crescendo ending with an unexpected piano on the downbeat. Here the emphasis to the featured note is given by a "negative accent": it is quite legitimate, since the "subito piano" calls attention to the note.

Example 126. Beethoven, *Sonata*, opus 31 no. 2, second movement

Positive (convex) and negative (concave) climaxes

The device of calling attention to a note by using less rather than more volume is justified, especially in gentle, lyrical passages; it is just as convincing as the conventional loud accent. In a more aggressive, virile kind of music, however, melodic and harmonic climaxes are better served by a positive accent. Obviously there are many ways to call attention to meaningful moments in music, and personality and temperament are the qualities that determine our means of expression. Actually, the highlights and climaxes of certain melodies can be emphasized in totally opposite ways. The plasticity in a bas-relief is such that the features of a face in it can be prominent in both a convex and concave manner; what matters is that the extreme features are emphasized. It seems to be an oversimplification to say that the positive emphasis (convex) is masculine, while the negative emphasis (concave), with a decrescendo toward the climax, is feminine. In today's "unisex" and "chauvinistic-versus-liberated" societies such a statement may seem provocative. Nevertheless this diagnosis of masculine-feminine approaches toward a musical climax is not totally out of place! In any case, what matters in music is the sum total of tension and release; everyone is entitled to a personal interpretation as long as it is sound and convincing and based on sufficient knowledge and good taste.

Ornamental passages: less volume

We often find ornamental passages—turns, trills, grace notes, and so on—within a melody; many of them appear in small print. It is quite safe to play these notes with less volume than the main notes whether or not they appear in small print.

Example 127. Chopin, *Concerto No. 2*, opus 21, second movement

Fiorituras

The role of these notes is to connect and feature the main notes, to prolong their sound, and to delay their entrance slightly; in this way they call attention to the main note. Since they are not organic to the melodies, they should be played unobtrusively, gently, and flexibly, and their dynamic level should always be somewhat lower than that of the main notes. We find many of these embellishments not only in Baroque but also in Classical and Romantic music. Actually, some of the most beautiful melodies of Chopin are essentially elaborate fiorituras (or embellishments); by expanding them and filling them with chromatic and transient notes of all kinds, Chopin managed to write sublime music. Obviously these "emancipated" embellishments that have been transformed into such expressive melodies must be treated more emphatically than simple ornamental notes. However, many of them are subject to the same interpretative principles we have mentioned.

The physical means for holding these melodies together is the legato technique, which was described in chapter five.

Appoggiaturas

Appoggiaturas are essentially dissonances that resolve on the following note. They always should be emphasized because of their harmonic function. Appoggiaturas must always receive a positive accent, never a negative one; accentuate the first note and play the resolution with less volume.

Example 128. Mozart, *Sonata in A Minor*, K. 310, second movement

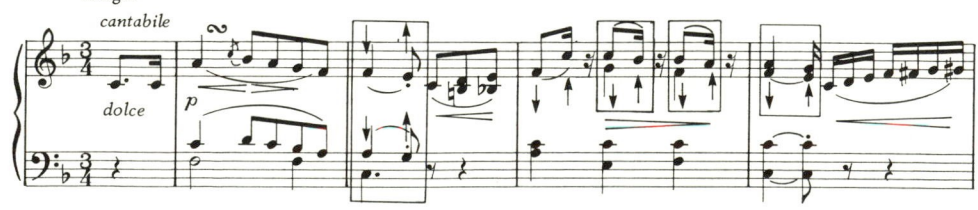

Example 129. Beethoven, *Sonata*, opus 2 no. 1, second movement

There are few exceptions to this rule, and sometimes a crescendo is marked after an appoggiatura or dissonance; usually this dynamic is indicated in the text.

Example 130. Beethoven, *Sonata*, opus 10 no. 2, second movement

Example 131. Beethoven, *Sonata*, opus 81a, first movement

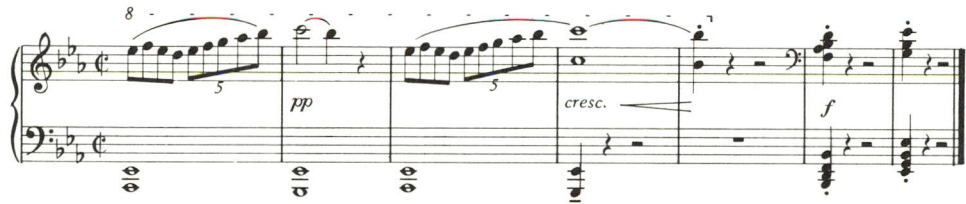

Consonant grace note never to be emphasized; main note receives its full value.

A widespread, glaring, and most unmusical mistake is often encountered in the execution of consonant grace notes. It is common knowledge that grace notes are to be played on the downbeat simultaneously with the bass. However this doesn't mean that they should be accentuated and featured. Their role is to call attention to the following note by slightly delaying its appearance and, of course, it is the *main note*—never the grace note—that is emphasized. As a matter of fact, the grace note must be played considerably softer than the main note, and, even more important, the main note must be held for its full metric duration. We must *never* deduct the metric value of the grace note from that of the main note and shorten it; instead we should add the value of the grace note to the value of the beat. The fact that it extends the metric value of the bass is no cause for alarm; this effect may be exactly what the composer intended and the reason he uses the grace note. One should not be a slave to "counting" at the expense of musical content; instead one should base one's rubatos and *agogic accents* on the live pulsation of the music, especially in slower music. When string players and singers interpret meaningful passages, they are usually flexible and free of metronomic rigidity that affects pianists. Only an unmusical violinist would arpeggiate the opening of Beethoven's "Kreutzer" Sonata in such a way that the top A loses some of its value:

Example 132. Beethoven, *Sonata for Piano and Violin*, opus 47 ("Kreutzer"), first movement

Yet when pianists encounter the same problem, as we do in the third movement of Beethoven's *Sonata*, opus 109, we seldom hear the correct solution. Example 133a shows the opening of a slow, expressive phrase as it was notated by Beethoven. Some pianists interpret this measure as indicated in example 133c, and the least musical perform it as it appears in example 133d. The correct way to play it is shown in example 133b; the high B receives its full value as a half note.

Example 133. Beethoven, *Sonata*, opus 109, third movement

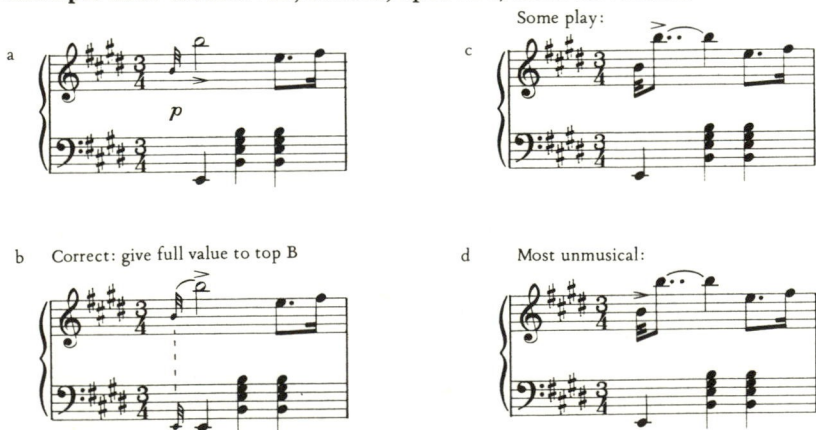

This musical anomaly stems from the valid rule that grace notes are to be played on the beat and not before it so that the value of the note that precedes the grace note is not shortened. But it is also necessary that the grace note not disturb the melodic flow, and the main note should certainly not be cheated of its full metric value, especially since it is considered important enough to merit the adding of an ornamental tone. The solution is to play a soft, unobtrusive grace note on the beat and a main note with its metric value *intact*. A slight flexible extension of the entire beat will sound fine.

Dissonant grace notes

Dissonant grace notes, the most common of which are appoggiaturas, are played on the beat; they should be emphasized, they add spice to music, but the degree to which they are emphasized is subject to the discretion of the performer.

Example 134. Mozart, *Sonata in A Minor*, K. 310, first movement

Two types of grace notes

A distinction must be made between the two types of grace notes —the ones that pertain to the beat and the ones that connect two notes. A grace note that belongs to a beat is usually characterized by a slur tying it to the next note; a grace note that connects two notes is printed between them, usually without a slur and sometimes before the barline. While the former is played on the beat, the latter is played between the beats. The notation of the first type of grace note varies

Example 135. Prokofieff, *Sonata No. 4*, first movement

greatly; in Baroque and Classical music some of these notes are slashed to indicate that they are short, while those without a slash are held to their full printed value—sometimes even longer. This notation is not consistent, however, and the performance of these notes is open to debate. Some grace notes without a slash are abbreviated, while other slashed grace notes (especially appoggiaturas) are given their full value, or even double their value. In the Baroque period connecting grace notes are often marked by a thin diagonal line indicating a glissando-like connection.

Example 136. Different types of grace notes

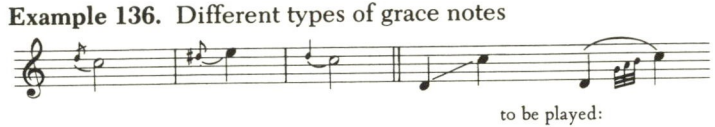

to be played:

Ritardando and accelerando

Composers most frequently use the terms *ritardando* and *accelerando* to introduce rhythmic flexibility into their music. As in all interpretive matters, the manner in which these tempo changes are applied determines their artistic validity. The word ritardando (ritenente or ritenuto) implies a slowing down. But with all such directions, the problem is how much, when, and at what rate? When there is a series of ritardandos in the course of a phrase, they should not be treated in the same way: the ones that occur in the middle of the phrase should be less pronounced than those at the end of the phrase.

Structural considerations should guide us. An indication can be interpreted in many different ways, and we possess much leeway in the evaluation of the text.

Even articulation vs. expressiveness

One actor may say the same words as another, but he will bring out their meaning in his own way. His diction is different. The volume of his voice, his pauses, and his use of emphasis all differ from those of the other actor. As different as these two actors may be, if they are good actors, they have one thing in common: they do not recite the text mechanically or in a clearly enunciated but noncommittal way. Instead they emphasize the meaningful portions of the text positively or negatively and play down the unimportant ones.

It is frustrating to listen to an articulate, note-perfect performance that lacks flexibility and imagination. The essentials are not emphasized, the right mood is not created, and the entire performance amounts to little more than a succession of pleasant sounds. A flexible, imaginative performance requires a minute but continuous modification of the metric values printed in the music; it includes color gradation and variety in the use of dynamics, pedaling, and rubato, elements that are indicated in the score only rudimentarily.

The intangibles

Musical diction involves the many tangibles and intangibles that allow us to fashion our own mode of musical speech. We must learn to call attention to the heavy beats and to treat nonharmonic tones effectively. All altered chords, like the Neapolitan-sixth, the diminished, and augmented chords must be recognized and treated according to the tension they represent. Notes that have auxiliary roles should be played unobtrusively. These notes of lesser importance include consonant grace notes, upbeat figures, passages that start as upbeats, the short notes in dotted figures, notes printed in small type, and connecting notes, resolutions of dissonances, accompaniment figures in general, and arpeggio figures that lead to a principal note.

Tension and release; the role of dissonance

Music can produce powerful effects on us; it can make us feel extremely stimulated or extremely depressed. These effects are brought about by the alternation of tension and release of tension, and those states are created by dissonances and consonances, fast and slow tempos, loud and soft dynamics, accelerandos and ritardandos, crescendos and diminuendos, counterpoint and homophony, rhythmic irregularities and regularities, and asymmetry and symmetry. The fact that a minor chord depresses us, while a major chord does not, is not a matter of upbringing or tradition but is based on an unalterable physical condition: some harmonics in the overtone series of the minor chord clash, while those of the major chord do not. This clash causes tensions, a slight discomfort in the hearing apparatus, and a depressing effect on the human organism. Since major chords correspond to actual overtones of the fundamental note, no such conflict is present, and their effect is restful, even stimulating.

Tension corresponds to dissonance, but dissonance is a relative matter; when a strongly dissonant chord is followed by a relatively less dissonant chord, it provides relief. In contemporary music a minor chord is certainly not considered a dissonance. However, in the Baroque period the minor chord was a dissonance, and very few works in this period end on a minor chord: it fails to provide a total release of tensions the way the major chord does. In earlier periods not even a major third was restful enough to resolve conflicts. Pure fifths were used at cadences, and in even earlier times pieces were required to end on an octave or a unison. Over the centuries we have become used to the higher tones in the overtone series, and today we tolerate, and even enjoy, a wide variety of dissonances—even those that remain unresolved.

In the nineteenth century it was considered most daring for Cho-

pin to end a prelude with a cadence in which the seventh of the chord
was allowed to linger on:

Example 137. Chopin, *Prelude No. 23 in F Major*, opus 28

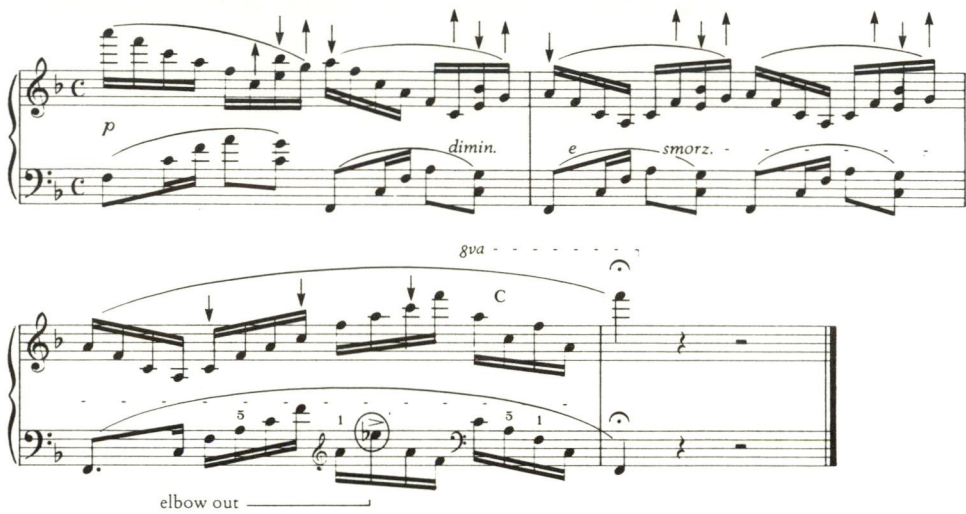

Today we fully accept the use of any of the twelve notes of the chromatic scale with the tonic, as this composition by Bartók illustrates:

Example 138. Bartók, *Sonata* (1926), first movement

The art of piano
playing

Present-day listeners respond to the same stimuli as did musicians
of past eras. Musical tension and release still result from the clash and
resolution of overtones, and the more our musical diction reflects an
awareness of these elements, the more convincingly will we communicate our musical impulses. It is up to our sensibility to respond to
the limitless shadings inherent in the score. The art of piano playing
really begins at the point when we can translate the score into the
motion patterns necessary for the communication of the subtlest musical impulses.

Orchestrate the piano!

The piano is comparable to the orchestra in its wealth and variety of sound. The color potential of the piano often tempts us to "orchestrate" many of the compositions we play. The piano works, the string quartets and symphonies of Beethoven or the ones of Brahms share many common features beyond the obvious horn and woodwind effects and timpani rolls. The coloring effects we can evoke from the piano make it very tempting to think of "orchestration." The orchestral effects of Liszt's piano music come instantly to mind. Try to think of the bassoon or the viola—or the organ, harpsichord, or snare drum. Think of anything besides the piano! You have already mastered the technique of piano playing; now try to enrich your sound by imitating the voice or the sound of other instruments.

The human voice

The human voice is surely the most expressive instrument of all; to say that a pianist "sings" as he plays is the supreme compliment. We can and should sing, and we can acquire the expressiveness and flexibility of the human voice: we should not hesitate to prolong or shorten a note when its meaning calls for it and breathe like singers do. We can learn much from listening to and watching good singers, who breathe, phrase, and shape music with more freedom and spontaneity than can any instrumentalist.

Problems of the singer

However, I wouldn't go so far as to say that the only source of music is the human voice. Admirable a musical instrument as it is, we must realize that, in a way, it is tremendously limited. Not only is its range limited, its dynamics too; also, it is a purely homophonic instrument. But, besides these limitations, its great weakness is that the singer can produce a sound only when he exhales. When he runs out of air he must inhale in order to fill his lungs so that he can sing again: singing is a "one-way" activity! While he is inhaling, everything must stop. He must inhale extremely rapidly and make every effort to exhale the air as slowly as possible so that he can use it for as many notes as possible. If the musical phrase ends where his breath ends, all is well! But, if not, all kinds of efforts are needed to cover up this sudden inhaling. His natural inclination would be to start singing high and loud and then to descend both in pitch and in volume; incidentally most ancient folk music does exactly this. Ascending melodies and extended crescendos are against the nature of the human voice. Obviously a singer must acquire superb breath control in order to surmount these basic difficulties inherent to singing. A fine singer is able to control ascending lines and crescendos, with their extended rise in tension. But he must always fight the limitation of his own lung capacity: he must breathe!

Breathing and singing

I mention this, not because I lack affection and respect for singers, but to call attention to a fundamental quality in music. Besides sound, music expresses and consists of motion above all else. I say "above all else" because sound itself is nothing other than the product of motion. As mentioned at the beginning of this book, music is motion within fluctuations of pitch, volume and timbre. It is best served by instruments that function in a continuous manner and can produce extended tensions both in crescendos and diminuendos without the need to gasp for breath. It is breathing rather than singing that represents the kinetic quality in music. The string player also can carry on a melody indefinitely with the up-and-down movements of his bow. Although a slight break must occur when the bow changes direction, this can be covered up and is negligible and inconspicuous compared to the gasp for breath of the singer. When he runs out of air he has to camouflage his need to breathe to convince us that his long phrase has not been interrupted by the well-covered gasp. If we think of the extended passages that lead to some of the irresistible climaxes of the orchestral and piano literature—passages during which we hold our breath and gasp for air—we realize just how difficult it is for the singer to maintain musical momentum and the long line of the melody while exhaling. It is, indeed, contrary to the upward sweep of such music to equate it with exhaling. How I would cherish a singer who is capable of inhaling and exhaling incessantly while he sings.

Singing tone at any cost?

Music represents a series of motions and changes that results in widely varying sounds. It is true that many of these sounds are best expressed by the human voice, but others are not. While it is desirable to equate some of our music with singing, we shouldn't think in these terms exclusively. Music is more than just a combination of lovely sounds. It must express the entire human emotional gamut, from the sublime to the vicious and from the serene to the hysterical, if necessary. We need not sugarcoat everything with a "lovely singing quality": often a certain passage should be hummed, whispered, or even shouted out. The insistence of cultivating a sensuous and warm singing tone for all music brings to mind the woman who was hired as an announcer for one of our radio stations because of her deepthroated sexy voice—and who ended up being a weather forecaster and a stock-market announcer, bless her soul.

Elements of musical diction

1. Downbeats
2. Upbeats
3. Melodic high and low points (to be emphasized either positively or negatively)
4. Harmonic tensions and releases (dissonances and consonances)
5. Rhythmic patterns (long and short)

6. Passing notes
7. Filling notes
8. Grace notes (consonant, dissonant, on the beat, transient, no emphasis)
9. Ornaments (mordents, trills, and turns; these may start on the main note, the upper note, or the lower note)
10. Ornamented passages (amplified turns, etc.)
11. Anticipatory arpeggios
12. Decreasing intensity of piano sound (tying melodies)
13. Upbeat passages leading to downbeats (inherent crescendo, subito piano after crescendo)
14. Endings of phrases, groups of notes
15. Ritardandos and accelerandos
16. Rubato and agogy
17. Suspense, delay
18. Accents (> ⋀ ; two kinds of sforzatos and fp)
19. Precipitation toward accents
20. Fermatas and series of fermatas
21. Appoggiaturas
22. Adding grace note values to beats
23. Small print (transient, ornamental notes, fiorituras)
24. Accompanying figures

Most of these elements have been discussed in this chapter and, of course, many other ingredients in music can be interpreted at the performer's discretion. Some of the items on this list need further explanation.

Harmonic tensions and releases

Harmonic Tensions and Releases. In general, the further harmonies wander away from the tonic, the more tension they create, especially when they contain altered notes. Altered notes tend to strain the tonal frame and anticipate or cause a change of key; for example, the secondary dominant in any key creates more tension than the dominant. Any diminished-seventh chord of a major scale contains notes that don't belong to the diatonic scale: this means tension! The Neapolitan-sixth chord's altered notes cause a jolting, dramatic effect. The direction of alteration causes uplifting or depressing effects (sharps uplift; flats depress) not only in the notes, but in our spirit too. This statement sounds superficial, but it is true. All over the world humans respond in a similar way to constellations of sounds. Notes altered by a flat within the key, minor chords, and diminished chords have a depressing effect. Sharps have the opposite effect; change a minor chord to a major chord, and you'll see what I mean. Augmented chords have a disconcerting effect; they create suspense, uncertainty, and considerable tension and vagueness because of lack of tonal direction. In the symbolic language of music our emotions are affected by the physiological stimuli caused by the ups and downs (the sharps and flats) of the text; it is as simple as that. Obviously other factors like tempo, loudness, pulsation, intensity, and timbre, etc., influence us too, but none influence us more than these intervallic factors.

Ornaments

Ornaments. The role of an ornament is to call attention to a note. Ornaments are used mainly by instruments that do not have the capacity to emphasize a single note by dynamics or timbre and therefore must synchronize dissonant notes with the main note. The harpsichord and the organ are examples of this type of instrument, but the clavichord and the piano are not. Therefore other criteria are to be used for ornaments on the latter instruments. There is a school of thought —and a very valid one—according to which most ornaments should be dispensed with on the clavichord and the piano. Incidentally the often-debated question of where to start the trill (on the upper or main note) is totally inconsequential when it is applied to the piano. On the harpsichord and organ it is obvious that ornaments start on the upper note because the main note, being part of the harmony of the bass, could not be emphasized and would be inaudible.

Rubato and agogic effects

Rubato and Agogic Effects. Rubato and agogic effects are essentially free, imaginative alterations of metric values that create flexible enunciation and parlando effects. They are necessary and justified in practically any style of music, with the exception of an intentionally motoric composition; however they must be made in good taste, and the style of the music must be taken into consideration in deciding the amount of rubato to use. One of the ultimate tests of an artistic interpretation is the skillful use of rubatos.

Accents

Accents. The intensity of accents is indicated by the design of the wedge: a wedge that points upward is usually stronger than one that is horizontal. The "extended" wedge, a wedge that applies to a group of several notes, was occasionally used by Liszt.

Example 139. Accent markings > ∧

The sforzato (*sf*) can be interpreted in two different ways. In fast dynamic pieces the sforzato ordinarily calls for a sudden accent that may be either witty or violent, depending on the text. However it must always be executed in accord with the actual dynamic level: it is poor taste to play a fortissimo *sforzato* in a mezzo forte or piano passage. These loud accents in relatively quiet passages are heard all too often, and they leave a spastic, even hysterical, impression. The other kind of *sforzato*, which is usually found in melodious slow passages, is not so much a quantitative accent as an *espressivo* emphasis. It should sound somewhat louder than the other notes, but the effect should be more intense than loud. Think of this *sforzato* as an *espressivo* sign rather than as an accent. Both *sforzatos* use the same sign (*sf*); we must use our own judgment in interpreting them according to their contexts.

Crescendo sounds like accelerando.

Precipitation Toward Accents. It is an acoustical phenomenon that a sudden, steep crescendo played in a steady tempo gives the impression of a precipitated *accelerando*. The accumulation of steadily increasing, crowding sonorities seems to have an extra dynamic effect. We must avoid making an *accelerando*, because it actually weakens the climax of the crescendo by causing the passage to sound hurried and overrushed. It is necessary to keep the crescendo steady and not accelerate the tempo.

Fermatas

Fermatas. The official value of the fermata is approximately one and a half times that of the written note. Its correct length depends on its location in the phrase—whether it occurs in the middle of a phrase, at the end of a phrase, or at the end of a section. The coda of the first movement of Beethoven's "Waldstein" Sonata provides an interesting example of fermatas in series: the three fermatas have different roles, and obviously the last one should be the longest.

Example 140. Beethoven, *Sonata*, opus 53, first movement

We find a very long fermata at the end of the recitative in Chopin's *Fantasy:*

Example 141. Chopin, *Fantasy*, opus 49

There are innumerable passages in which a prolonged pause is desirable, and they are not always marked in the score. Such halts and hesitations are meaningful in our musical diction; they should be used like well-timed pauses in a speech, but, of course, they should not be overdone.

Slurs

Phrasing signs, and slurs in particular, were inherited from string music. Slurs were originally used as bowing signs for the purpose of indicating those notes that should be played in one bow. In string scores, when slurs appear in an extended melody, they should be regarded purely as a prescription for bowing and not as an indication that the musical phrase is to be segmented. The bowing often indicates the number of notes grouped together, but not necessarily separated groups. A great many pianists, however, seem to be obsessed with observing the end of slurs with breathless, hiccup-like separations, even within the musical phrases.

Slurs indicate connection, not separation, except at the ends of phrases.

Slurs were adapted for use in keyboard music, indicating technical rather than musical groupings. Some pianists mistakenly regard the slur not so much as a connecting sign between notes but as an indication to separate one group from the next. This notion is totally absurd in most cases: string players strive for the completely opposite effect; they try their utmost to make their bow changes unnoticeable in order to avoid disrupting the musical phrasing. Instead of calling attention to the end of a technical slur, pianists should also try to connect it with the rest of the melody. Unless the end of the slur comes at the end of the musical phrase, we should regard the slur exclusively as a connecting sign and not as a separating device. In examples 142 and 143 the dotted slurs show the musical phrasing.

Example 142. Haydn, *Sonata in E Minor*, second movement

Example 143. Beethoven, *Sonata,* opus 31 no. 2, second movement

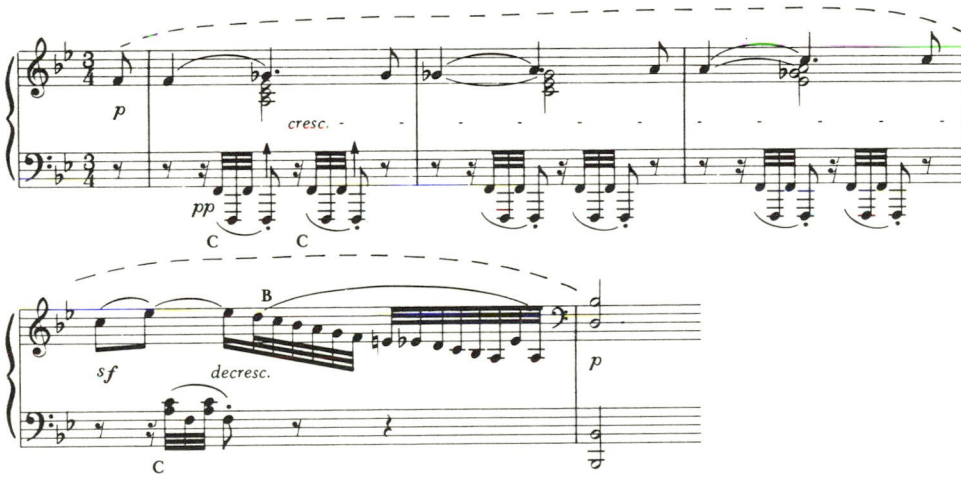

Remember that the real musical phrasing signs are often not notated, especially when they extend over the full length of the line.

National characteristics: French vs. Hungarian

Music is not a language in the sense that French, Spanish, or English is; it deals with sounds that represent, stimulate, and are generated by universal human emotions. Nonetheless certain characteristics of musical diction can be related to the performer's national background. Let us take two extremes. The French language and the Hungarian language, for instance, have very different kinds of inflection. French sounds as if almost every word had an upward inflection; the end of the word ascends both in pitch and in emphasis. On the other hand, Hungarian characteristically emphasizes the first syllable of a word; you can hear a descent toward the end of every word, as if it were actually marked decrescendo! If we consider two important aspects of musical diction, strong downbeats and light downbeats, we can easily see how these tendencies manifest themselves in music. I don't mean that every Hungarian emphasizes the downbeat more strongly than every Frenchman, but I would be somewhat surprised to hear a Magyar emphasize an upbeat, and I would expect more upbeat emphasis from a Frenchman.

A national rhythmic formula

An example of this phenomenon can be seen in a very characteristic Hungarian rhythmic formula. You will find many examples of it in Liszt's Hungarian rhapsodies, in the music of Bartók and Kodály, and in some of the Hungarian inspirations of Brahms and Sarasate; it also occurs in Polish music. This is the formula:  ; it corresponds to Hungarian enunciation, with its short, strong accent on the first note and its altered metric value. The first note is actually played *shorter* than the written text indicates. This rhythmic alteration is valid in many cases; for example, it can be applied to passages like this:

Example 144. Bartok, *Piano Concerto No. 3,* third movement

Although Bartók wrote strict eighth notes and quarter notes in ⅜ measures, the eighth notes in these measures should be slightly shortened when they are downbeats. (But beware! When the quarter notes are on the downbeat, they will be slightly lengthened.) Accents should be applied to all downbeats whether they are eighths or quarters, but we should see to it that all downbeats are altered metrically as I have described.

Individual contributions

Even though the differences among most languages are not as striking as those between Hungarian and French, languages do have varying rules on accentuation. Certain nationalistic traits can add flavor to an individual's musical diction; sometimes the effect can be most welcome. However, although regional contributions can enhance a performance, it is the feelings and thoughts of the individual, as they are expressed in his inflection, that are most valuable; of course it is important that they be tasteful and serve the music loyally. Although music is a universal language, there is obviously room for collective and individual influences and for all temperaments and tastes. The most intriguing and beautiful musical diction is still that of the gifted individual of any nationality.

17 Public Performance

Performing is the ultimate issue.

Since music is a performing art, our ultimate goal is to present definitive renditions of the compositions we play—renditions that convey our own interpretations. We want to reach audiences whether we play live concerts or make recordings or films. While it is true that nowadays there is more lecturing about and writing on music than ever before, our ultimate goal is to make music audible—to play it.

Performing teachers are more effective.

Everything this book has covered so far is designed to prepare us for performing. All of our study of analysis, composition, technique, interpretation, theory, how to memorize, how to practice, and how to develop a suitable musical diction has as its goal making pianists better performers. In fact, performing is a form of teaching; a teacher who can demonstrate what he preaches is incomparably more effective than one who can't.

Learn from performances, live and canned.

It is an essential part of the pianist's course of study to listen to as many performances and concerts as possible (preferably to the best ones, of course). However, one may learn from practically any experience; because interpretations vary greatly and because almost every performer plays differently every time, we have unlimited opportunities and challenges to learn from performances, live or canned.

The expected and the unexpected conditions at live concerts

The great challenge in performing in public comes from the way the environment of a live concert differs from your practice room. There are many anticipated as well as unexpected circumstances at a live concert, and some of the unexpected ones may be unfortunately beyond our control. The condition of the piano, the acoustics, noises during the concert, photographers, problems with our health, an emotional shock before and during the performance—all these can take their toll. But we should also be wary of the conditions we can anticipate and prepare for.

The stage affects almost everyone.

First and foremost, almost everyone feels somewhat different when he is on the stage—and this is an understatement! The degree of tension and pressure varies, of course; but in some shape or form it is ever present, and it does affect the performer. Ideally it will affect the pianist in a positive, inspiring way that enables him to surpass himself, but the reverse may happen too.

The performer feels differently on stage because he or she is affected by a number of physical, physiological, and psychological changes. The most obvious ones are the altered rate of pulse, respiration, metabolic processes, and the reflexes. The functioning of the glandular system, the flow of thought associations (both conscious and subconscious), inhibitive and repressive processes, spontaneous and improvisatory activities are also affected. Often we experience apprehension, anxiety, fear, and even panic. Sounds like more than a bit of misery, doesn't it?

Basic tempo conforms to the pulse.

Even if playing in public is not all that bad, it is worthwhile to explore the reasons for these symptoms. It is obvious that since our pulse and breathing accelerate (in some rare instances they slow down), our sense of timing and tempo must be affected. Tempo and timing are closely related to our normal pulse rate. Normally, if the beat unit of a piece is slower than our pulse, we perceive the music as slow and, of course, the reverse is also true. Also if the tempo is a bit slower than our heartbeat, it has a soothing effect; if it is faster, it stimulates us. When we are on stage, our pulse may be faster than normal. Will this change affect our sense of timing and our rate of playing? Of course it will!

Listen carefully.

The first priority in performing is to establish the proper tempo—the one we established in the practice room when our pulse was normal. On stage this tempo may feel slow. For the same reason, the tempo that feels right on stage may actually be too fast. Fortunately, if we are trained to listen carefully, we can adjust to our accelerated physical processes and still maintain the proper tempo in the pieces we play. Remember that what really counts is not what you feel but what you hear. With experience the discrepancy between the two will disappear. If you belong to the select minority that slows down under pressure, again listen carefully and make the necessary adjustment.

To slow down, magnify motions.

Our knowledge of the technical processes of piano playing helps us while we're on stage. To establish a slower tempo we can magnify all of our arm, forearm, hand, and finger motions so that everything takes just a bit more time. Prolong the pauses slightly, and try to breathe more slowly and deeply. We must regulate our motions according to the degree of tension we feel. In fact, if the pieces are well under control and if we know exactly what we want to do, we can get the upper hand in no time. Furthermore, if we are able to overcome the negative effects of pressure, tension may turn into an asset by adding that extra improvisatory quality that can make a performance memorable.

I don't pretend to offer an instant cure for all performance prob-

Familiarity eases fear.

lems; we all have our share of ups and downs at concerts. But I'd like to define certain factors that cause and that can remedy problems. Those negative factors that we can anticipate in public performance are threatening because they can be just as hard to handle as the unforeseen ones. We can count on having butterflies in the stomach, on not knowing the piano, the acoustics, the lights of the hall, and we can cope with them more easily if we understand them. The fears that lead to queasy stomachs are anticipated but are primarily related to the unfamiliarity of the performance situation; if one were to play the same pieces several times in a row under exactly the same circumstances, the stress and pressure would diminish to a great degree. Once our pulse, breathing, and metabolic processes return to normal, we can regain the control we have in the practice room, and we can play as we always do. In other words, the frequency with which we perform the same piece adds much to the quality of performance. Actually, a too-often performed piece under overly familiar circumstances can dull the rendition. This, however, is all too seldom, and one always can experiment with new interpretative ideas.

Character and mood

We can see how anxiety can affect the tempo of a performance; what's even more important is that stress can have an effect on the projection of the mood of the music. Sometimes the inhibiting factors are excessive, and the playing becomes bland; but usually projection and intensity become exaggerated. This tendency is prevalent today, incidentally, and much music performed in the concert halls suffers from tense overprojection. Simple melodies are played in an exalted, feverish manner, and these exaggerations, of course, distort the true meaning of the music. If climaxes are slightly exaggerated, they might still be inoffensive, but serene melodies suffer the most.

Spastic intensity at performances

I am puzzled when I see a perfectly quiet, civilized human being become totally transformed and frenzied when he sits down at the piano to perform, let us say, a tender, gentle Brahms intermezzo. Suddenly his breathing becomes heavy, the eyes roll, the lips pucker, the diaphragm stiffens, the left foot starts to scrub the floor, the right shoulder moves forward, and the head swings right and left, up and down (see chapter eighteen). All this transpires in the name of artistry and exaltation, poetry and lyricism! What a show it is, and what a tremendous expenditure of energy, totally uncalled for by the mood of the music. It is quite a sight—honestly—and it does impress the layman. Perhaps in this age of visual media communication (television) there is a trend to replace acoustic pleasures with optical ones.

Conscious mind can interfere with habits.

Although practicing must be essentially a conscious activity, public performance combines automatic, subconscious, and minimally conscious processes. When automatic activities are well established, spontaneous, improvisatory, and creative elements manifest themselves in an uninhibited manner, and the most meaningful interpretative ideas can emerge on the spot. At performances the conscious mind must not interfere with subconscious processes: it should occupy itself with more general or peripheral ingredients. Do not concentrate on the individual notes or technical patterns, but rather on the form and structure of the piece—the dynamic high and low points, suspenses and the length of the fermatas. In other words, pay conscious attention to those aspects of the music that don't interfere with the automatic habits. Memory troubles may arise when the conscious and inhibitive mind interferes with already established, automatic motion patterns.

Composers: craftsmanship vs. dilettantism

Composers learn the techniques of composition with great care and in great detail by applying conscious discipline. But after they have mastered the craft of composition, they put it in the service of their creative and subconscious impulses. For the actual creative process is never conscious—it simply happens; craftsmanship exercises its control later. Remember that technique without creative processes amounts only to craftsmanship, and creative processes without technique amount to amateurism and dilettantism.

The performer's lot is similar to that of the composer. To be outstanding, a performer needs a well-laid-out, well-ingrained technique that he can trust in creative spontaneous moments.

Recorded and live performances

The conductor: purely visual

There is considerable difference between the manner of playing live concerts and playing for recordings. First, the visual factor is nonexistent in a recording, while at live concerts it plays a great role. The most obvious proof of the impact and importance of the visual factor is that of the conductor. He doesn't produce a single sound, still he is the main interpreter of the music. Obviously he needs an orchestra, but a fine conductor, simply by supplying the visual, kinetic element, can interpret music in a most effective way, both to the musicians of his orchestra and to the public. His motion patterns spring from the content of the music and help him to communicate his ideas about the music. The facial expressions of Toscanini were never seen by the audience while he was conducting, except on television, but they conveyed innumerable meaningful interpretive details of the music, that sounds alone never could achieve!

No exaggerations!

Just as a conductor can reveal much about music through his gestures and facial expressions, the performing pianist, violinist, or singer can complement the interpretation of the music he performs with visually convincing and revelatory expressions and movements. Needless to say, the slightest exaggeration or affectation may spoil everything; nothing puts off a sensitive listener more than banalities and "corn." Only a judicious use of the visual element can enhance a musical performance.

Besides the total lack of visual contributions, several other condi-

Limited range
of dynamics of
recordings

tions make live concerts differ greatly from recording sessions. First, the range of dynamics on recordings is extremely limited compared to that of the concert stage. Even today, when we enjoy the benefits of high-fidelity technology, pianissimos are never soft enough, and fortissimos never register fully on the microphone as they do in life. Some of the most effective and memorable effects in a concert hall are the nearly inaudible sounds and the crashing crescendos and fortissimos that the microphone can never reproduce. When you "turn up" the fortissimos in a recording, they will be distorted, and up goes the pianissimo too! The average listener doesn't own super-stereo equipment, therefore the dynamic range he hears is significantly narrower than in real life. This means most of the musical climaxes and low points are misplaced.

The telling
pause

Another important aspect of live performance is the telling pause —a split-second suspense between passages of a piece during which the hand and arm move appropriately. In a live performance the visible gesture fills in the time between notes and makes it convincing, and the visual factor convincingly complements the auditory. If one makes the same gestures while recording, they will remain unseen, and the suspenses become a blank, black hole, a long and unjustified pause. Therefore all such rhetorical pauses should be modified when a recording is being made. The inability of the microphone to capture extreme dynamics makes these subtle, prolonged suspenses illogical in one's interpretation. Therefore, if one attempts to adjust one's suspenses to the reduced dynamic range, the process of making records will represent a flattening and a homogenizing of all the best attributes of a performance.

The loss of
touch

One of the most important ingredients, the "timbre" or touch of the performer, suffers greatly by the electronic conversion of sound. Most of one's individual colorings suffer by it.

Standardization
inevitable when
recording.

Indeed this homogenization is worse when diction and interpretation are considered. Actually one soon realizes that a certain degree of standardization is indispensable; the reason for it is very simple and quite inevitable. Suppose that during a live concert you have a most memorable and startling inspiration, and on the spur of the moment you create a totally unexpected effect in phrasing, accentuation, or rhythm. The element of surprise—an unpredictable little turn—gives the audience a unique and memorable experience. Suppose the same thing happens on a recording; the startling, unexpected little happening will be engraved—recorded forever, which means the listener will hear it exactly the same way whenever he listens to this recording. When the listener hears it the first time, he is just as enchanted as the audience at the live performance. When he hears it again: this time he knows what is about to happen, and he anticipates the thrill of hearing it again. At the next hearing, the surprise is replaced by familiarity. When he hears it for the fifth, eighth, and ninth time, when the "unexpected" happens in exactly the same way, the darned passage may well become merely irritating. What at first sounded like a startlingly beautiful surprise wears off sooner than you think. Unfortunately what is impressive as a "one-shot" experience at a live performance will not do in a canned performance. If you want to satisfy reviewers and your colleagues, you'd better learn to stay fairly close to conventional low-key interpretations. This is not my preference, of course, but is an observation I'd like to pass on to you.

Wrong notes are taboo!

If an unusual but beautifully played passage can prove irritating after repeated hearings, a wrong note provokes even more wrath. Wrong notes are strictly taboo in recordings, however tolerable they may be in a live performance if the interpretation is satisfying. After all, any child or amateur can hear a "sour" note, even if they don't notice the wrong interpretation.

To sum it all up, the order of priorities in a *live performance* is:

Criteria for a live performance

1. Original, personal, and convincing interpretations that are as spontaneous and creative as possible
2. Touch of the finest quality with the most varied range
3. Dynamics of the widest possible range
4. Pauses in proportion to the acoustics of the hall; more is better than less
5. Notes are emphasized according to their importance. Accompanying runs, passages, and filling-in notes should be underplayed; grace notes and derived notes should be treated as complementary ingredients.
6. No wrong notes, but beware of playing every right note in an overly articulated way.

The order of priorities for *recorded performance* is:

Criteria for a good recording

1. No wrong notes
2. No extremely soft or loud playing
3. No excessive (out-of-the-ordinary) rubatos
4. Compared to live performances, every pause, especially the ones between sections, should be shortened.
5. Every note should be clearly articulated even in accompaniments or fill-in notes.
6. Enunciation should be clear.
7. Gradations exist for the most part by volume. The individual touch is homogenized by the electronic equipment, and therefore it is of little value.

Poor balance in recordings of concert performances

It can be seen clearly that the priorities for live and recorded performances are different, and we ought to abide by them. Unfortunately the recording of live performance is more and more widespread today, and, with few exceptions, the result is most unfair both to the performer and to the listener. In addition to the considerations already discussed, most on-the-spot recordings are distorted by poor balance between the bass and treble. One is often shocked on hearing tapes of outstanding live performances.

Analogy with theater and films

A parallel situation exists in the world of theater and films. These two modes of acting also differ: they serve different purposes, and they suffer if they are treated in the same way. Theater performances must be scaled to the dimensions of the stage, while film is concerned with details and close-ups, as well as with settings that transcend the limitations of the theater. We need not dwell on this analogy; the correspondences are obvious.

Recordings and live performances are complementary; the audiovisual film, a welcome innovation.

Recordings today are much more widespread than live concerts. Both forms complement one another, but one will never replace the other. The live concert will never provide the availability, the scope, and the learning possibilities of the recording, and the recording can never give you the creative, spontaneous, and thrilling experiences of a live concert. The two will continue to coexist, and hopefully they will soon be joined by an innovative and overwhelmingly superior companion, the audiovisual film.

18 Mannerisms and Excess Energy

Mannerisms: manifestations of excess energy

One could write a whole book (and a quite amusing one, I am sure) on the many idiosyncrasies, mannerisms, "showmanship," and affectations of performers past and present. However it must be acknowledged that mannerisms can be valid. At best they are in fact manifestations of excess energy, reserve energy, personal peculiarities and temperament, and they may even enhance the process of self-expression. Music being what it is can bring us to a high degree of stimulation and exaltation. When we consider that only a relatively small portion of our physical energy is needed to execute even the most demanding pianistic feats, we may wonder where does the remaining energy go. Especially if our technique is effortless and we are not fighting ourselves and the instrument, our excess energy will require an outlet.

Spontaneous and cultivated mannerisms

Let us discuss those performers who are oblivious of audiences—who do "things," even when they practice alone and unobserved. They are unaware of their excess energy and excess motions and don't use them for ulterior motives like calling attention to themselves. It might be pretentious to assume that one knows the whys and wherefores of another person's actions, but one can distinguish between spontaneous, cultivated, and assumed mannerisms. We see examples of these mannerisms wherever we look. We also see "negative" mannerisms: repressed spontaneity, total lack of nonessential motions, impersonal behavior and interpretations, etc. Some performers who cultivate mannerisms do it in the name of "showmanship," to impress audiences. Both types are defended by those who adopt them: the first group is more numerous and "successful" because they cultivate "Romantic" or "dynamic" attitudes, while the other is puritanically "Classical" or "Baroque" in attitude. There are others who tend to cultivate unattractive, grotesque gestures: these represent phoney spontaneity. But they do the job because they call attention to the performer. Obviously all cultivated mannerisms are motivated by a desire to attract attention. This is somewhat true in many areas today: certainly in fashion, hairdos, obscenities shouted out "spontaneously." Anything goes in this crowded world that calls attention to the otherwise stereotype individual. Some performers are just plain nervous and act this out their own personal way. In any case, we don't wish to judge them but will examine those who have developed a consistent pattern of nonessential motions, noises, and gestures.

Mannerisms can be symptoms of a malfunctioning technique.

Mannerisms must also be classified on the basis of their being symptoms of an adequately functioning or a malfunctioning playing mechanism. And both types of these symptoms can be spontaneous or assumed. As diverse as these mannerisms may be, they belong to two main categories: (1) the ones that are the byproduct of a well-functioning, responsive, and expressive playing mechanism and that do not interfere with technique and tone production; and (2) those that are caused by excessive physical and emotional strain, as a result of a poorly functioning, wastefully operating equipment. The second group is stuck with frustration and continuous strain: the contorted, spastic motions and facial expressions are symptoms of forced and poor technique that will impair tone quality. Healthy mannerisms may evolve into an extra means of expressing the varying moods of the text —happy or unhappy as they may be. But the latter group of mannerisms dooms the performers to discomfort and frustration, no matter what the musical content may be. It is true that this suffering may be sublimated into "spirituality" in due time (then it is called "deep artistry"), but the fact remains that the source of all this self-inflicted suffering is simply an unnatural, painfully operating, and physiologically unsound human apparatus.

Audience reaction to "showmanship"

Whether they are a byproduct of a faulty mechanism or a well-functioning one, the forms that mannerisms take are unpredictable. Both types are certainly very much in evidence, and audiences appear to be very impressed by them. Ambition and an instinct for good showmanship may cause the performer to exploit this potent ingredient for success, and we occasionally witness quite a display of cultivated "involuntary" gestures on the concert stage. However the cultivation of mannerisms is objectionable for many obvious reasons, and most sensitive people react negatively to these rehearsed "spontaneities." The fact is that truly spontaneous reflex motions may occur at any time; they need not be cultivated and they are convincing.

Some mannerisms are not objectionable.

If a well-functioning human organism possesses excess energy, it will generate its own intriguing mannerisms. Nobody resented Gieseking's grunting, Toscanini's humming (mostly out-of-tune, too), or the grimaces of Horowitz or Heifetz: they were (and are) all artists, graced with a strong personality, technical perfection and lovely sound.

Some
mannerisms
provide relief
from tension.

Some excess motions may be beneficial, since any change of position prevents stiffness in the muscles. Many younger pianists cultivate a motion that is technically beneficial; it consists of a slow, gentle lifting of the arm with the thumb pointing upward, and it is usually accompanied by a suggestive, caressing motion. Because this motion (supination) enables the two bones of the forearm to return to a parallel situation, the tension caused by excessive crossing of the ulna and radius (pronation) will be relieved. This tension is particularly noticeable when the upper arm has been held too close to the body. Whether this mannerism is consciously executed or is sheer imitation is of no importance: it is beneficial, and therefore welcome, because it usually causes a pleasant relief in the forearm.

Most slow,
flexible motions
are welcome.

From the technical point of view slow and flexible extra motions may be of value, whether they are instinctive or consciously cultivated. And, unless the music happens to call for them, violent, spastic motions are not only unattractive and obtrusive, but they spring from an overtense, faultily functioning physical or emotional mechanism. The antagonistic sets of arm muscles are so excessively contracted that they respond only to violent stimuli. When the technique itself is corrected, these symptoms disappear. You will notice that I avoid psychological processes as the cause for mannerisms: they certainly are in evidence but my main concern, within the scope of this book, is the physical factors.

A mannerism
sampler

It is undeniable that among susceptible young and older pianists and audiences certain unattractive mannerisms are just as appealing as are attractive mannerisms. We could name a number of these spastic movements such as "catching flies," a sudden, upward circular motion of the forearms at the end of a phrase, with clenched fists; or "relay running," with one arm thrown violently backward at the end of a phrase and the other sharply forward, the eyes peering with a visionary stare toward infinity. When "relay running" or "catching flies" occurs after a dramatic crescendo, this is not too bad. But when an idyllic, lyrical melody by Schubert or an aria by Bach is disrupted by such violent, spastic convulsions, one begins to wonder! Both of these mannerisms are disconcerting and unnecessary, but maybe that's "show business."

"Yes-yes" vs.
"no-no"

Certain head motions are both widespread and harmless. Swinging the head horizontally (like saying "no-no") is evoked by and supposedly represents a lyrical, reflective mood, while a vertical movement of the head ("yes-yes") illustrates a dynamic and aggressive mood. Therefore the horizontal headshaker ("no-no") is categorized as "poetic," while the vertical headshaker ("yes-yes") qualifies as the steel-fingered, irresistible virtuoso. On a lucky day we may "see" a pianist who is complete: he goes "no-no" and "yes-yes" with equal abandon.

Another sight that is fun to watch is the "silent muncher," whose lips pucker at an uncontrollable but rhythmic beat: one puff for each note played.

Walking on and off stage

Walking on and off stage can provide quite a show too. We have the "tiptoeist," who walks with light and rapid steps and with a slow and deliberate bow toward the audience. He holds one elbow tightly to his midriff, while the other arm swings to and fro. His facial expression may range from the humble but grateful look of the shy schoolboy to the victorious, triumphant stare of the gladiator, who has just overpowered his black, three-legged opponent with great ease and relish. Others proceed with firm, deliberate steps toward the piano, fixing their eyes securely on the audience while walking: if they are lucky, most of these "starers" make it to the piano in spite of the hazards of an unfamiliar stage floor. Indeed, one has a broad selection of "walkers" to emulate. None was more impressive than the eighty-four-year-old Moritz Rosenthal (God bless his soul), who took seven minutes to reach the piano stool, fifty seconds to play the "Minute Waltz" by Chopin and another eight minutes to exit. The fifty seconds made the experience quite unforgettable.

Beware of excess energy!

Most mannerisms are really harmless. But it is objectionable when all our energies go right into the keyboard, when forcing, hitting, pressing, and massaging the keys become a habit and an outlet for the tension and hostilities of the performer. The piano simply cannot cope with all this explosive energy channeled into it. Its tone quality will suffer and so will the music. Sometimes this forcing and pressuring is well camouflaged, but both the sound of the piano and the muscular equipment of the pianist will be adversely affected.

So you may walk on and off stage in any way; you may groan, snore, and roll your head and eyes horizontally, vertically, or circularly; you may even catch flies and scrub the floor with your left foot (a very popular pastime), as long as you don't violate the piano and its sound in the process. Once your body has been conditioned as a well-functioning, coordinated mechanism and you have found safety valves for your excess energy in the form of mannerisms that are superimposed over correct motion patterns, the means for artistic self-expression is yours.

Index

D

E

F

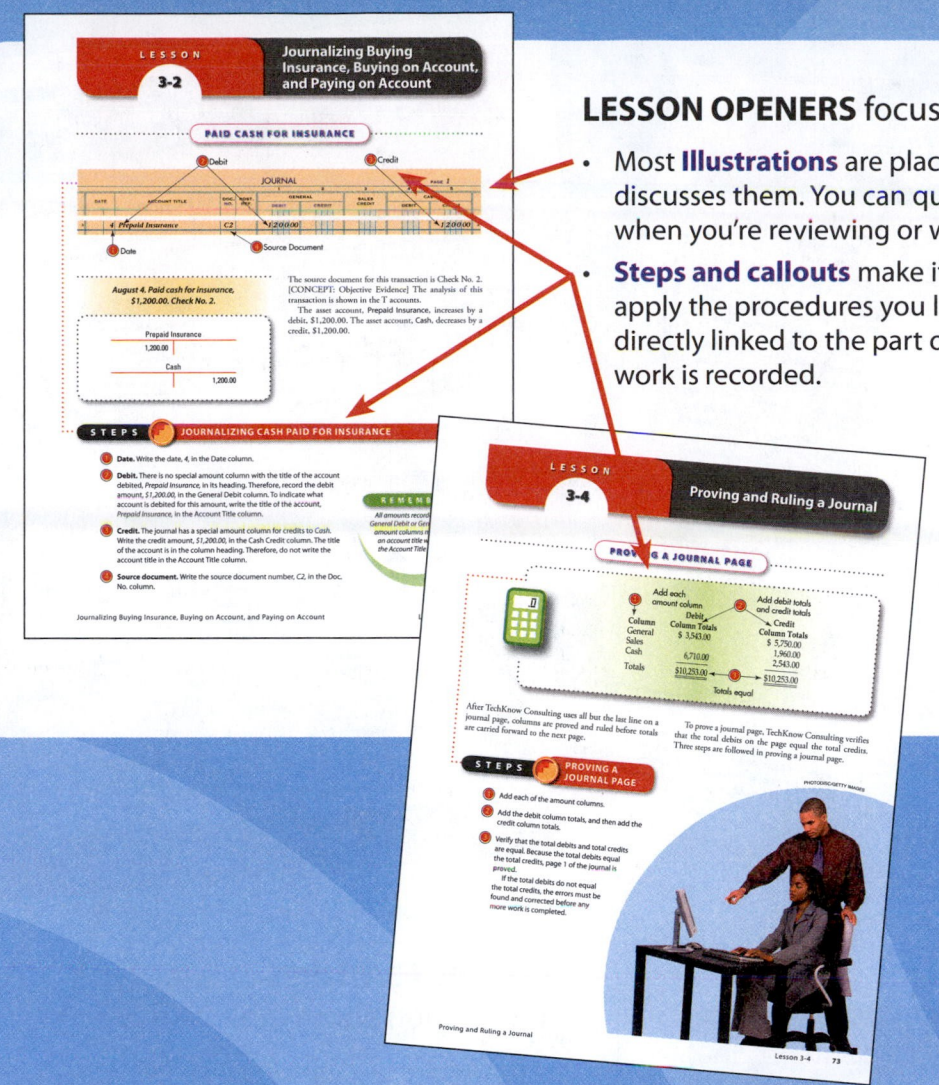

LESSON OPENERS focus on one or two topics.

- Most **Illustrations** are placed above the text that discusses them. You can quickly find the illustrations when you're reviewing or working problems.

- **Steps and callouts** make it easy to understand and apply the procedures you learn. Clear instructions are directly linked to the part of the illustration where the work is recorded.

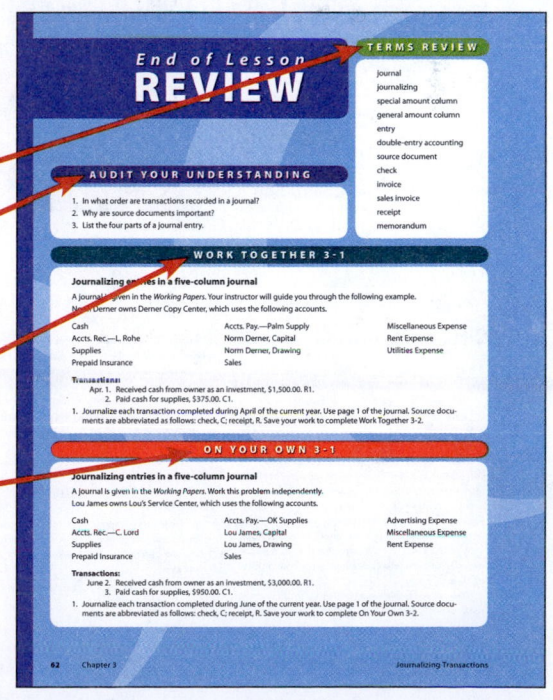

END-OF-LESSON REVIEW PAGES help you fully understand all concepts and procedures before moving on to the next lesson:

- **Terms Review** lists all the new words learned in the lesson.

- **Audit Your Understanding** asks two or more questions about the lesson material. You can check your answers in the Appendix.

- **Work Together** gives you guided practice through hands-on application of the lesson's procedures and concepts.

- **On Your Own** challenges you to complete problems by yourself.

Business, Management & Administration

Rita J. Cowans, Internal Auditor

As a highly respected employee at FedEx Corporation, Rita J. Cowans is a Manager in the Internal Audit Department. During her tenure at FedEx, Rita has held various positions in financial, operational, international, and information systems audit. Presently she is responsible for the financial, information systems, and international audit activities for FedEx Worldwide operations.

Her audit team conducts business process reviews, integrated financial and information system reviews, international entity reviews, fraud examinations, and vendor audits. Rita has been a leader in developing and promoting best practices as an integral part of the Internal Audit Department. "It's my responsibility to ensure that the employees and management of FedEx are effectively safeguarding the

assets of the corporation, complying with all laws and regulations, and accomplishing the corporate strategic objectives as established by senior management."

While in high school, Rita developed a love for mathematics and accounting. "I became a very critical and detail-oriented thinker and excelled at analyzing information and solving problems." With her parents' direction and strong support, she continued her education and graduated with a bachelor's degree in accounting. In addition, she successfully earned her Certified Internal Auditor (CIA) and Certified Information Systems Auditor (CISA) professional designations. "Being certified in the area of accounting in which you work is critical to your professional success. Certifications demonstrate that you are committed to your profession and communicate to others that you are an expert in your field."

Certifications also enable you to become active in organizations that provide educational opportunities for their members. Rita is a member of the Institute of Internal Auditors and Information Systems Audit and Control Association.

As a member of the FedEx Services Diversity Council, Rita works to ensure that individuals from every background have the opportunity to excel at FedEx. Ultimately, "having a passion for what you do and setting high standards will determine your level of success."

Salary Range: $30,000–$130,000 and up. Can lead to high-level careers at public accounting firms, private and public corporations, and government agencies, such as the Internal Revenue Service (IRS Auditor).

Qualifications: Bachelor's degree in accounting, finance, and information systems for entry-level position, plus normally five years of auditing experience for senior level or above. Professional Certifications preferred (CPA, CIA, CISA, CFE, etc.). Familiarity with business, information technology, and legal concepts and procedures is beneficial.

Occupational Outlook: The Sarbanes-Oxley Act of 2002 requires public corporations to expand the documentation and testing of their accounting systems. Internal auditors are an integral part of corporations' compliance with this law. As a result, the demand for internal auditors will be strong for years to come.

COURTESY OF RITA J. COWANS

Analyzing How Transactions Affect Owner's Equity Accounts

Lesson 2-3 **43**

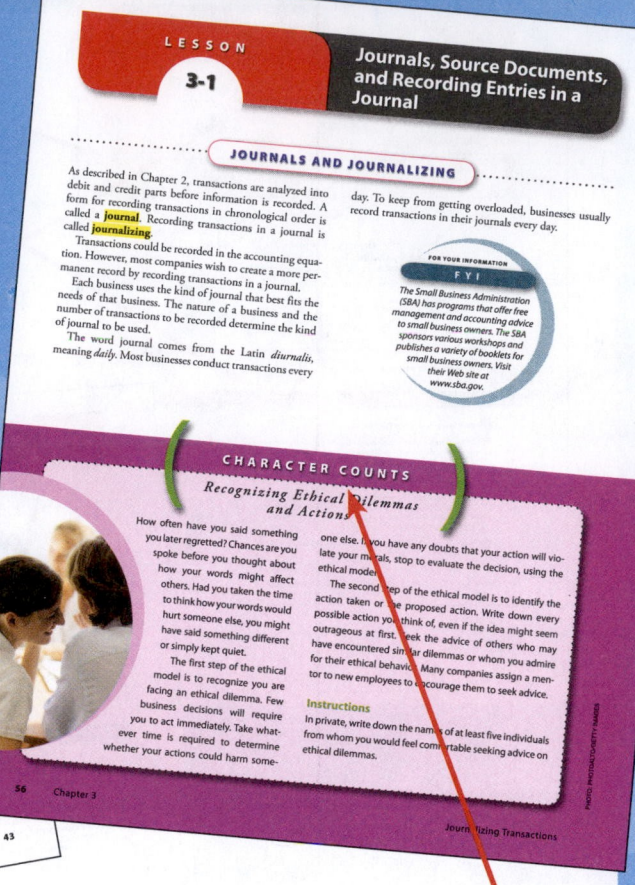

JOURNALS AND JOURNALIZING

As described in Chapter 2, transactions are analyzed into debit and credit parts before information is recorded. A form for recording transactions in chronological order is called a **journal**. Recording transactions in a journal is called **journalizing**.

Transactions could be recorded in the accounting equation. However, most companies wish to create a more permanent record by recording transactions in a journal.

Each business uses the kind of journal that best fits the needs of that business. The nature of a business and the number of transactions to be recorded determine the kind of journal to be used.

The word *journal* comes from the Latin *diurnalis*, meaning *daily*. Most businesses conduct transactions every

day. To keep from getting overloaded, businesses usually record transactions in their journals every day.

FOR YOUR INFORMATION
F Y I

The Small Business Administration (SBA) has programs that offer free management and accounting advice to small business owners. The SBA sponsors various workshops and publishes a variety of booklets for small business owners. Visit their Web site at www.sba.gov.

CHARACTER COUNTS

Recognizing Ethical Dilemmas and Actions

How often have you said something you later regretted? Chances are you spoke before you thought about how your words might affect others. Had you taken the time to think how your words would hurt someone else, you might have said something different or simply kept quiet.

The first step of the ethical model is to recognize you are facing an ethical dilemma. Few business decisions will require you to act immediately. Take whatever time is required to determine whether your actions could harm someone else. If you have any doubts that your action will violate your morals, stop to evaluate the decision, using the ethical model.

The second step of the ethical model is to identify the action taken or the proposed action. Write down every possible action you think of, even if the idea might seem outrageous at first. Seek the advice of others who may have encountered similar dilemmas or whom you admire for their ethical behavior. Many companies assign a mentor to new employees to encourage them to seek advice.

Instructions

In private, write down the names of at least five individuals from whom you would feel comfortable seeking advice on ethical dilemmas.

PHOTO: PHOTODISC/GETTY IMAGES

56 Chapter 3

Journalizing Transactions

MERCHANDISING BUSINESSES

TechKnow Consulting, the business described in Part 1, is a service business; it sells services for a fee. However, many other businesses purchase goods to sell. Goods that a business purchases to sell are called **merchandise**. A business that purchases and sells goods is called a **merchandising business**. A merchandising business that sells to those who use or consume the goods is called a **retail merchandising business**. A business that buys and resells merchandise to retail merchandising businesses is called a **wholesale merchandising business**. Service and merchandising businesses use many of the same accounts. A merchandising business has additional accounts on the balance sheet and income statement to account for the purchase and sale of merchandise.

BLEND IMAGES/GETTY IMAGES

BUSINESS STRUCTURES

Forming a Corporation

Many businesses need amounts of capital that cannot be easily provided by a proprietorship. These businesses choose to organize using another form of business. An organization with the legal rights of a person and which many persons may own is called a **corporation**. A corporation is formed by receiving approval from a state or federal agency. Each unit of ownership in a corporation is called a **share of stock**. Total shares of ownership in a corporation are called **capital stock**. An owner of one or more shares of a corporation is called a **stockholder**.

A corporation is a business organization that has the legal rights of a person. A corporation can own property, incur liabilities, and enter into contracts in its own name. A corporation may also sell ownership in itself. A person becomes an owner of a corporation by purchasing shares of stock.

The principal difference between the accounting records of proprietorships and corporations is in the capital accounts. Proprietorships have a single capital and drawing account for the owner. A corporation has separate capital accounts for the stock issued and for the earnings kept in the business, which will be explained in more detail in Chapter 16. As in proprietorships, information in a corporation's accounting system is kept separate from the personal records of its owners. [CONCEPT: Business Entity] Periodic financial statements must be sent to the stockholders of the corporation to report the financial activities of the business.

Critical Thinking

1. The names of many corporations include the words *Corporation, Incorporated, Corp.,* or *Inc.* in their names. Based on their names, identify several corporations in your area.

2. Why do you think many very large companies are organized as corporations?

PHOTO: PHOTODISC/GETTY IMAGES

234 Chapter 9

Journalizing Purchases and Cash Payments

SPECIAL FEATURES provide information about real-life issues:

- **Careers in Accounting** introduces you to actual people working in accounting or in positions where accounting knowledge is useful. This feature includes entry-level job requirements, career tracks, and projected trends for the future.

- **Character Counts** helps you understand complicated issues in the business world, such as confidentiality and integrity.

- **Business Structures** provides information on characteristics of proprietorships, corporations, and partnerships.

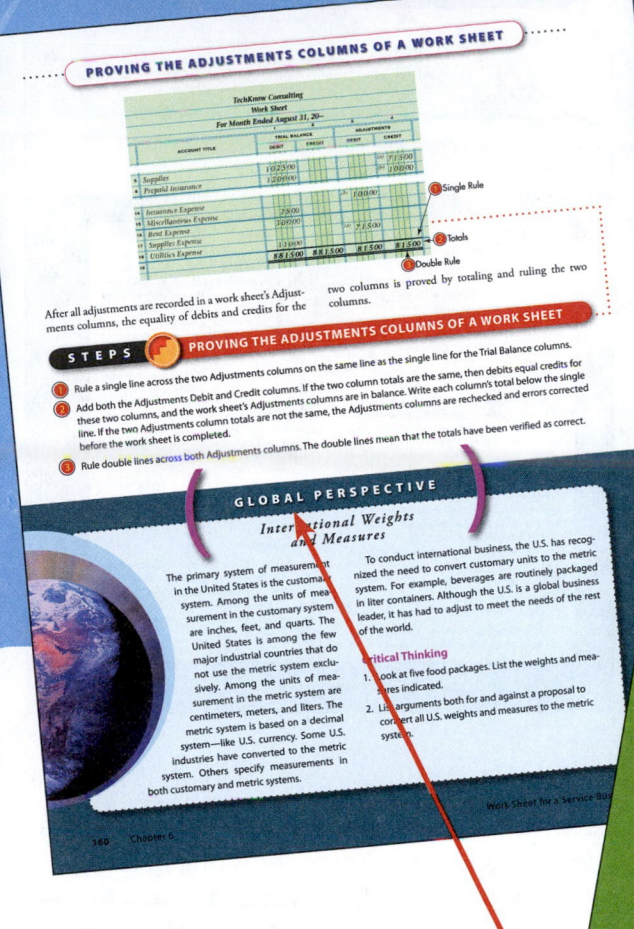

TechKnow Consulting
Work Sheet
For Month Ended August 31, 20--

After all adjustments are recorded in a work sheet's Adjustments columns, the equality of debits and credits for the two columns is proved by totaling and ruling the two columns.

1. Rule a single line across the two Adjustments columns on the same line as the single line for the Trial Balance columns.
2. Add both the Adjustments Debit and Credit columns. If the two column totals are the same, then debits equal credits for these two columns, and the work sheet's Adjustments columns are in balance. Write each column's total below the single line. If the two Adjustments column totals are not the same, the Adjustments columns are rechecked and errors corrected before the work sheet is completed.
3. Rule double lines across both Adjustments columns. The double lines mean that the totals have been verified as correct.

GLOBAL PERSPECTIVE

International Weights and Measures

The primary system of measurement in the United States is the customary system. Among the units of measurement in the customary system are inches, feet, and quarts. The United States is among the few major industrial countries that do not use the metric system exclusively. Among the units of measurement in the metric system are centimeters, meters, and liters. The metric system is based on a decimal system—like U.S. currency. Some U.S. industries have converted to the metric system. Others specify measurements in both customary and metric systems.

To conduct international business, the U.S. has recognized the need to convert customary units to the metric system. For example, beverages are routinely packaged in liter containers. Although the U.S. is a global business leader, it has had to adjust to meet the needs of the rest of the world.

Critical Thinking
1. Look at five food packages. List the weights and measures indicated.
2. List arguments both for and against a proposal to convert all U.S. weights and measures to the metric system.

CALCULATING CASH RECEIPTS ON ACCOUNT WITH SALES DISCOUNT

To encourage early payment for a sale on account, a deduction on the invoice amount may be allowed. A deduction that a vendor allows on the invoice amount to encourage prompt payment is known as a cash discount. A cash discount on sales is called a sales discount. When a sales discount is taken, a customer pays less cash than the invoice amount previously recorded in the sales account.

To encourage prompt payment, Hobby Shack gives credit terms of 2/10, n/30. When a customer pays the amount owed within 10 days, the sales invoice amount is reduced 2%. Otherwise, the net amount is due in 30 days.

On October 30, Hobby Shack sold merchandise on account to Cumberland Center for $1,200.00. On November 7, Hobby Shack received payment for this sale on account within the discount period. Because the payment is received within the discount period, the amount received is reduced by the amount of the sales discount.

Sales Invoice Amount	×	Sales Discount Rate	=	Sales Discount
$1,200.00	×	2%	=	$24.00

FINANCIAL LITERACY

Credit Cards

Buying goods with a credit card is a great way to take advantage of sales or to purchase an unplanned necessity such as an appliance. However, this convenience has a price—the interest that is applied to any unpaid balance on the account.

Interest rates and credit terms vary from card to card, so it is important to investigate and compare before choosing a card. Find out how the interest is calculated and when the interest starts on a purchase. For some companies, interest starts on the day of purchase. Sometimes interest doesn't start until 20 to 25 days after the end of a billing cycle. If you pay your bill in full by the due date, no interest will be charged. If you are charged interest, it is usually calculated based on the average daily unpaid balance of your account.

Some credit card companies entice you to switch to their card by offering very low introductory interest rates—but only for a specific period of time. Once the introductory period expires, the interest rate increases.

Other companies offer cash back or other rewards such as miles or points that can be used for the purchase of airline tickets or other items. Again, these programs vary greatly between credit cards. Make sure you understand the terms of such reward programs.

Credit cards can be a wonderful convenience as long as you understand the rules of the card you choose.

Activities
1. Using the Internet or other resources, compare the interest rates on two credit cards. If either card offers an introductory rate, find out the terms of the introductory rate and the interest rate after the introductory period is over. Present your findings in written form.
2. Using the Internet or other resources, find out how the interest is calculated for two different credit cards. Summarize your findings in a written report.

SPECIAL FEATURES introduce key concepts in realistic settings:

- **Global Perspective** will expose you to some of the ways in which accounting and business differ in other countries.
- **Financial Literacy** teaches you about managing your personal finances.
- **Cultural Diversity** explains how different cultures have contributed to the field of accounting.

OPENING AN ACCOUNT IN A GENERAL LEDGER

① Account Title   ② Account Number

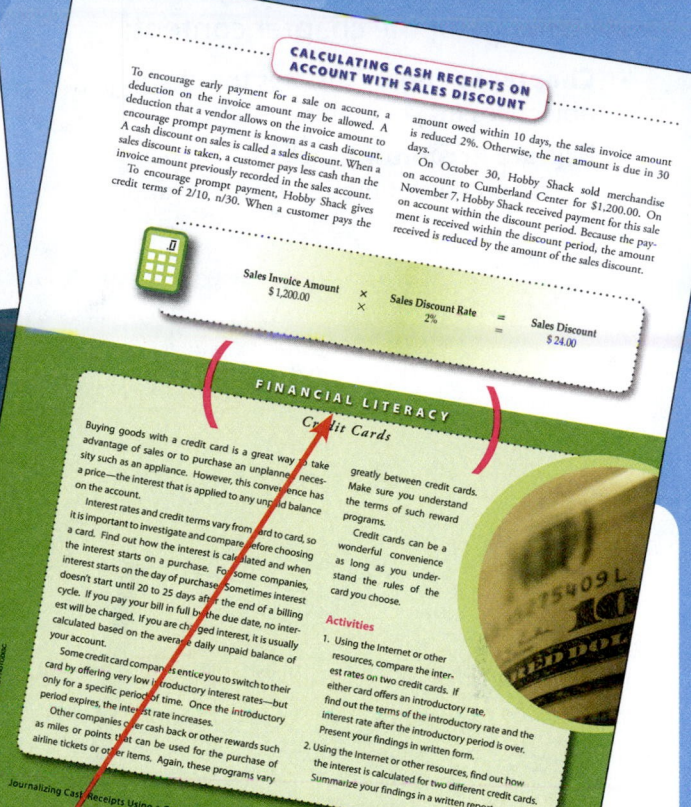

ACCOUNT *Cash*   ACCOUNT NO. **110**

Writing an account title and number on the heading of an account is called **opening an account**. A general ledger account is opened for each account listed on a chart of accounts. Accounts are opened and arranged in a general ledger in the same order as on the chart of accounts.

Cash, account number 110, is the first account on TechKnow Consulting's chart of accounts. The cash account is opened using the steps shown below. The same procedure is used to open all accounts listed on TechKnow Consulting's chart of accounts.

1. Write the account title, *Cash*, after the word *Account* in the heading.
2. Write the account number, *110*, after the words *Account No.* in the heading.

CULTURAL DIVERSITY

Accounting in Ancient Civilizations

In the ancient civilizations of Asia Minor and northern Africa, most citizens were illiterate. The scribe, who could read and write, became a very important person in the society. Of ancient Hebrew origin, the scribe has been called the forerunner of today's accountant.

Public scribes often recorded transactions as citizens arrived to do business. Most scribes recorded transactions on moist clay tablets that were then dried in the sun. Therefore, permanent records of transactions were not possible until scribes could write them down on clay tablets.

The Greeks invented coined money around 630 B.C., which facilitated assigning values to transactions.

The Babylonians in Asia Minor used an early form of banking. They transferred funds with a system resembling our modern-day checking accounts, one of the first uses of business documents.

These early practices provided the foundation for today's financial system and recordkeeping methods.

Critical Thinking
1. Estimate how many transactions might occur in a single day in a modern grocery store with which you are familiar.
2. List the number of different methods of payments that are accepted by modern grocery stores.

END-OF-CHAPTER PAGES give you opportunities to check your knowledge of the chapter content:

- **Chapter Summary** restates the chapter objectives for your reference.
- **Explore Accounting** includes opportunities for higher-level learning.

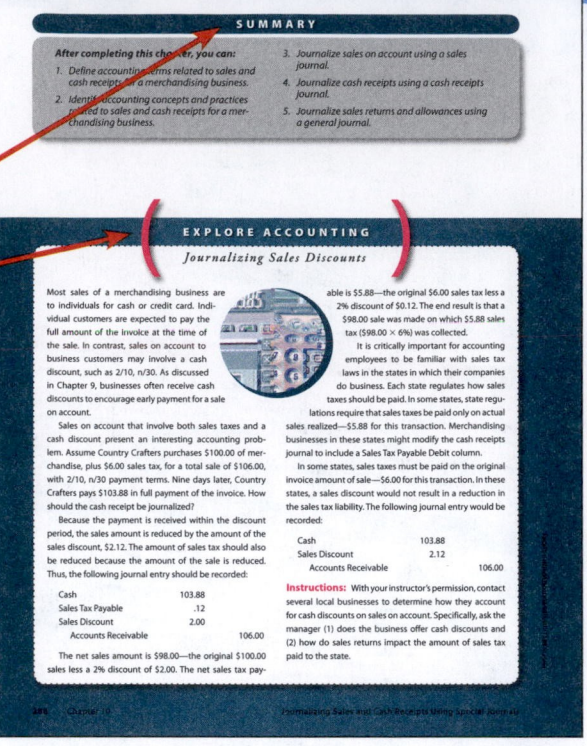

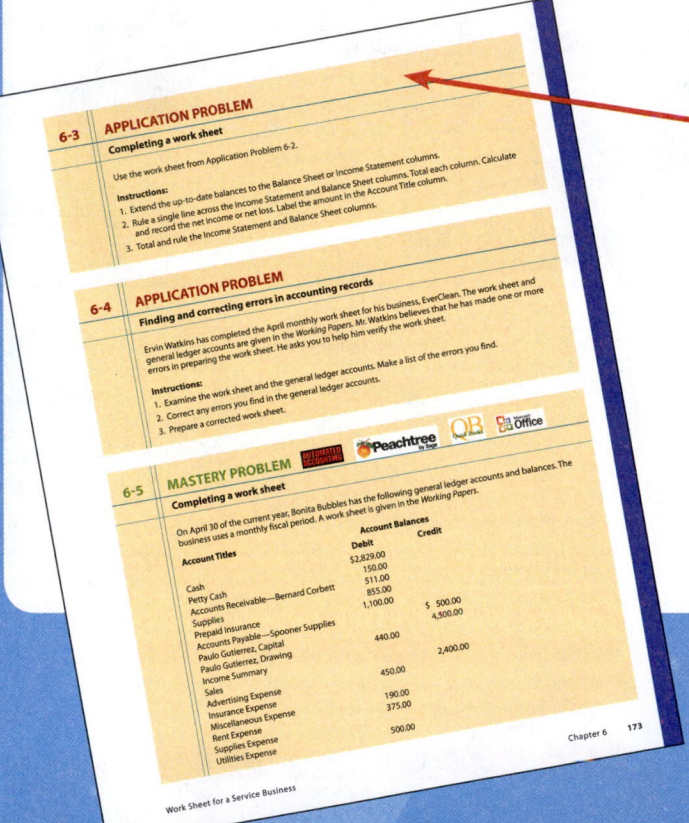

- Exercises contain at least one **Application Problem** for each lesson, plus one **Mastery Problem** and one **Challenge Problem** to test your understanding of the entire chapter. Many of these problems can also be worked using accounting software: **Automated Accounting, Peachtree®, QuickBooks®,** and **Microsoft® Excel!**

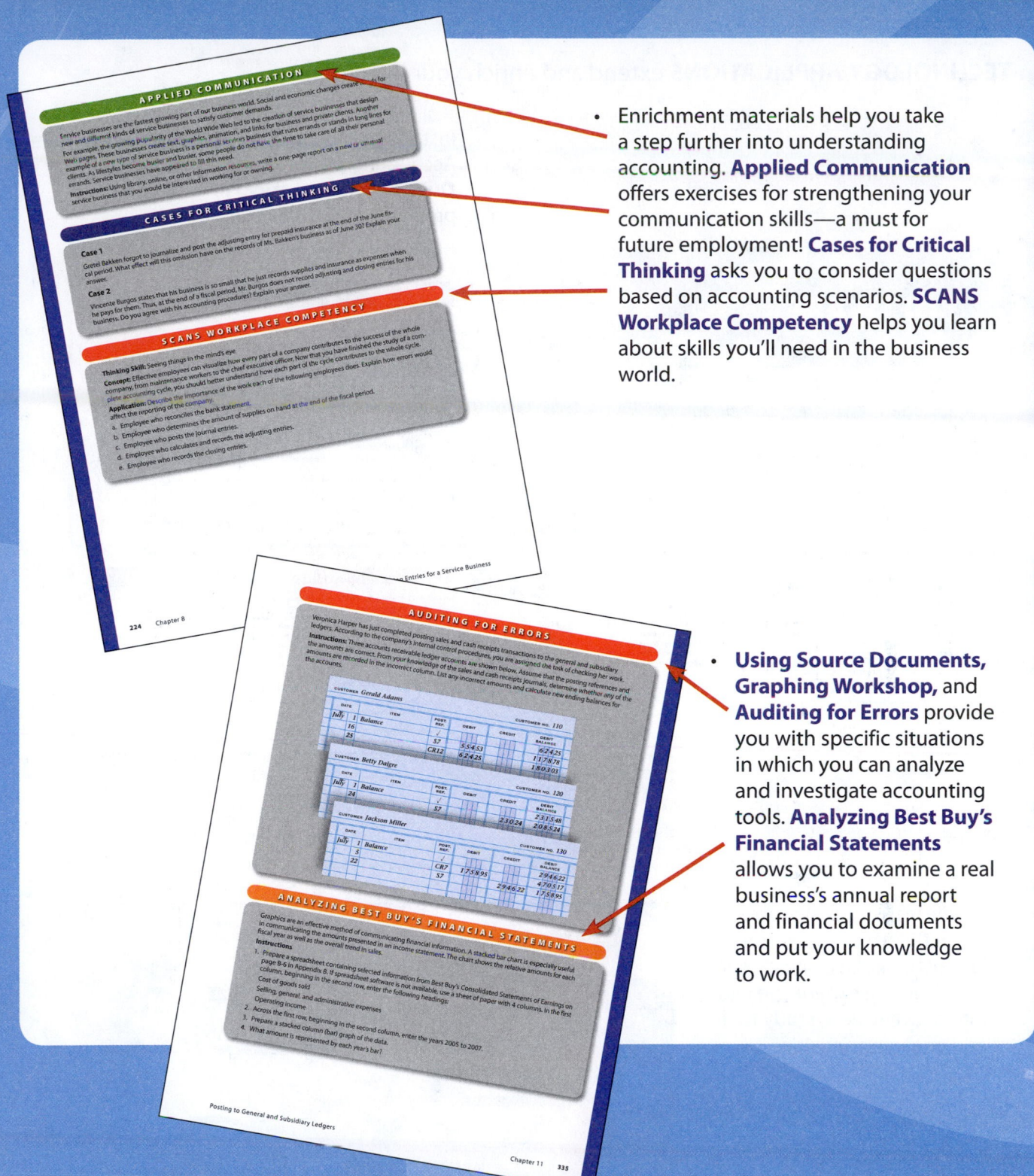

- Enrichment materials help you take a step further into understanding accounting. **Applied Communication** offers exercises for strengthening your communication skills—a must for future employment! **Cases for Critical Thinking** asks you to consider questions based on accounting scenarios. **SCANS Workplace Competency** helps you learn about skills you'll need in the business world.

- **Using Source Documents, Graphing Workshop,** and **Auditing for Errors** provide you with specific situations in which you can analyze and investigate accounting tools. **Analyzing Best Buy's Financial Statements** allows you to examine a real business's annual report and financial documents and put your knowledge to work.

Go Beyond the Book
For more information go to www.C21accounting.com

www.C21accounting.com offers a variety of resources and activities for you to explore. As you use this textbook, watch for the web site icons that will lead you to your online accounting connection!

TECHNOLOGY APPLICATIONS extend and enrich your learning:

- Instructions for completing Century 21 Accounting problems using **Peachtree, Quickbooks,** and **Microsoft Excel** are provided in each chapter.

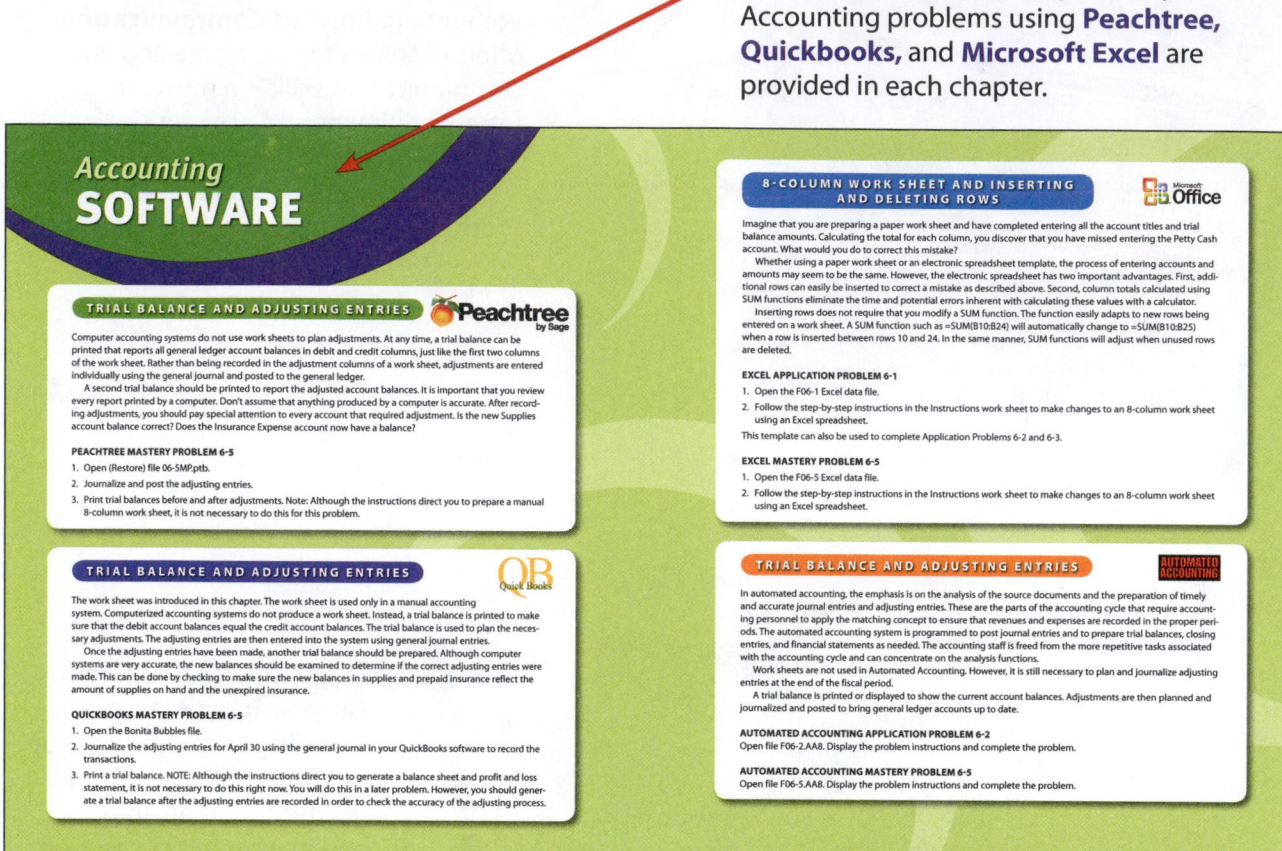

Accounting SOFTWARE

TRIAL BALANCE AND ADJUSTING ENTRIES — Peachtree by Sage

Computer accounting systems do not use work sheets to plan adjustments. At any time, a trial balance can be printed that reports all general ledger account balances in debit and credit columns, just like the first two columns of the work sheet. Rather than being recorded in the adjustment columns of a work sheet, adjustments are entered individually using the general journal and posted to the general ledger.

A second trial balance should be printed to report the adjusted account balances. It is important that you review every report printed by a computer. Don't assume that anything produced by a computer is accurate. After recording adjustments, you should pay special attention to every account that required adjustment. Is the new Supplies account balance correct? Does the Insurance Expense account now have a balance?

PEACHTREE MASTERY PROBLEM 6-5

1. Open (Restore) file 06-5MP.ptb.
2. Journalize and post the adjusting entries.
3. Print trial balances before and after adjustments. Note: Although the instructions direct you to prepare a manual 8-column work sheet, it is not necessary to do this for this problem.

TRIAL BALANCE AND ADJUSTING ENTRIES — QB QuickBooks

The work sheet was introduced in this chapter. The work sheet is used only in a manual accounting system. Computerized accounting systems do not produce a work sheet. Instead, a trial balance is printed to make sure that the debit account balances equal the credit account balances. The trial balance is used to plan the necessary adjustments. The adjusting entries are then entered into the system using general journal entries.

Once the adjusting entries have been made, another trial balance should be prepared. Although computer systems are very accurate, the new balances should be examined to determine if the correct adjusting entries were made. This can be done by checking to make sure the new balances in supplies and prepaid insurance reflect the amount of supplies on hand and the unexpired insurance.

QUICKBOOKS MASTERY PROBLEM 6-5

1. Open the Bonita Bubbles file.
2. Journalize the adjusting entries for April 30 using the general journal in your QuickBooks software to record the transactions.
3. Print a trial balance. NOTE: Although the instructions direct you to generate a balance sheet and profit and loss statement, it is not necessary to do this right now. You will do this in a later problem. However, you should generate a trial balance after the adjusting entries are recorded in order to check the accuracy of the adjusting process.

8-COLUMN WORK SHEET AND INSERTING AND DELETING ROWS — Microsoft Office

Imagine that you are preparing a paper work sheet and have completed entering all the account titles and trial balance amounts. Calculating the total for each column, you discover that you have missed entering the Petty Cash account. What would you do to correct this mistake?

Whether using a paper work sheet or an electronic spreadsheet template, the process of entering accounts and amounts may seem to be the same. However, the electronic spreadsheet has two important advantages. First, additional rows can easily be inserted to correct a mistake as described above. Second, column totals calculated using SUM functions eliminate the time and potential errors inherent with calculating these values with a calculator.

Inserting rows does not require that you modify a SUM function. The function easily adapts to new rows being entered on a work sheet. A SUM function such as =SUM(B10:B24) will automatically change to =SUM(B10:B25) when a row is inserted between rows 10 and 24. In the same manner, SUM functions will adjust when unused rows are deleted.

EXCEL APPLICATION PROBLEM 6-1

1. Open the F06-1 Excel data file.
2. Follow the step-by-step instructions in the Instructions work sheet to make changes to an 8-column work sheet using an Excel spreadsheet.

This template can also be used to complete Application Problems 6-2 and 6-3.

EXCEL MASTERY PROBLEM 6-5

1. Open the F06-5 Excel data file.
2. Follow the step-by-step instructions in the Instructions work sheet to make changes to an 8-column work sheet using an Excel spreadsheet.

TRIAL BALANCE AND ADJUSTING ENTRIES — AUTOMATED ACCOUNTING

In automated accounting, the emphasis is on the analysis of the source documents and the preparation of timely and accurate journal entries and adjusting entries. These are the parts of the accounting cycle that require accounting personnel to apply the matching concept to ensure that revenues and expenses are recorded in the proper periods. The automated accounting system is programmed to post journal entries and to prepare trial balances, closing entries, and financial statements as needed. The accounting staff is freed from the more repetitive tasks associated with the accounting cycle and can concentrate on the analysis functions.

Work sheets are not used in Automated Accounting. However, it is still necessary to plan and journalize adjusting entries at the end of the fiscal period.

A trial balance is printed or displayed to show the current account balances. Adjustments are then planned and journalized and posted to bring general ledger accounts up to date.

AUTOMATED ACCOUNTING APPLICATION PROBLEM 6-2

Open file F06-2.AA8. Display the problem instructions and complete the problem.

AUTOMATED ACCOUNTING MASTERY PROBLEM 6-5

Open file F06-5.AA8. Display the problem instructions and complete the problem.

- Online learning is available at **www.C21accounting.com**. This dynamic web site extends your learning experience with interactive review, study tools, and engaging activities.

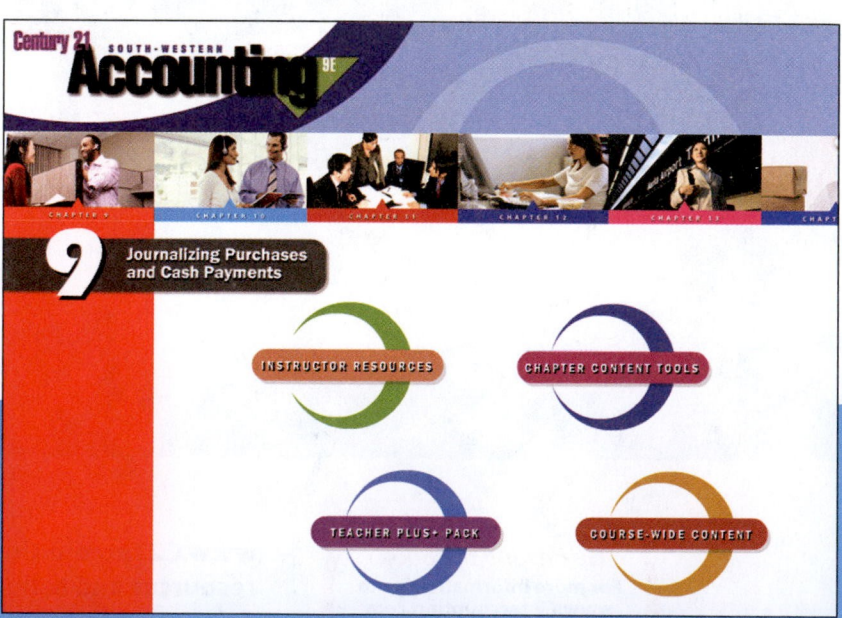

CONTENTS

PART 1
Accounting for a Service Business Organized as a Proprietorship

PART 2
Accounting for a Merchandising Business Organized as a Corporation

PART 3
Accounting for a Merchandising Business Organized as a Corporation— Adjustments and Valuation

PART 4
Additional Accounting Procedures

ADDITIONAL FEATURES IN THIS BOOK

CHAPTER REVIEW AND PRACTICE

Reviewers

Jon Abel, Salem, OR
*Marilyn Achelpohl, Orion, IL
Abe Aleman, Levelland, TX
*Cindy Anderson, Wyndmere, ND
Kathy Andreason, Salt Lake City, UT
Cynthia S. Aycock, Eagle Lake, FL
*Carolyn Balis, Northfield, OH
*Betty A. Banks-Burke, Hudson, OH
Tiffannie Barden, Phoenix, AZ
Jim Bauer, Cincinnati, OH
Reta Bell, Garden City, TX
Rose Berta, Redwood City, CA
Anne Berten, Portland, OR
Chad E. Bobb, Indianapolis, IN
*Debra L. Bushey, Derry, PA
*Monica Caillouet, Gonzales, LA
Ellen Clizbe, Moreno Valley, CA
Tony Composto, Brooklyn, NY
Becky Cornacchia, Naples, FL
Alicia E. Censi Corso, Los Angeles, CA
David Damme, Eureka, CA
*Debbie Darnell, Huntington, IN
Donna Davis, Charlotte, NC
Paula Davis, Atlanta, GA
Sylvia Davis, Lakewood, CA
Dana Dingell, Vienna, VA
Kathy Dixon, Richmond, VA
*Daniel Doseck, Albany, OH
Keith Downs, Dallastown, PA
Dr. Judith A. Drager-McCoy, Lititz, PA
Ann Droptini, Gladewater, TX
Kathy Dunaway, Erlanger, KY
Jean Eckert, Wexford, PA
Julie Eckhart, Salem, WI
*Fahryka Elliott, Richmond, VA
Carrie English, Woodbridge, VA
Barbara Erwin, Orlando, FL
*Jennie Ewert, Beaverton, MI
K. Skip Fabritius, Olympia, WA
*Erika Ferranti, Stoneham, MA
Debbie Fischer, St. Petersburg, FL
Matt Flanagan, Longmeadow, MA
Kathryn Focht, West Lawn, PA
Kathleen Ford, Rochester, MI
Lance B. Garvin, Indianapolis, IN
*Debbie Gentene, Mason, OH
Wendy Gentry, Garden Grove, CA
*Donna Gernert, Palm Coast, FL
Andy Gilley, Hendersonville, TN

*Sandy Giuliani, Grafton, WI
Kathy Goos, Moreno Valley, CA
Bonnie Graman, Hamilton, OH
Madge Gregg, Hoover, AL
Tracy Gutierrez, Garden Grove, CA
Stan Harder, Factoryville, PA
Kathy Harenka, Mukwonago, WI
Liz Hargis, Cincinnati, OH
*Jean Harms, Port Orange, FL
Cindy Hiester, Astoria, OR
Beth Hubbard, Virginia Beach, VA
Lisa Huddlestun, Kansas, IL
Steve Ingmire, Indianapolis, IN
Gladys Jackson, Woodbridge, NJ
Beverly Kaesar, Neenah, WI
Sheryl Kirby, Philadelphia, PA
*Trish Klinger, Steelton, PA
*Jane Knaub, York, PA
*Alvin Kroon, Mukilteo, WA
Jim Littenhoff, Cincinnati, OH
Darlene Londo, Appleton, WI
Fran Loos, Salt Lake City, UT
Ann M. Ludlow, St. Louis, MO
*Dennis Macy, Elkton, MD
Frances Mallard, Brentwood, TN
Diane Malley, Londonderry, NH
H. Jean Malonson, Hayward, CA
Lee C. Marcroux, Hartford, CT
Chris Marshall, Denver, CO
*Claire Martin, Onida, SD
Libby Martin, Chattanooga, TN
Sally M. Graham Martin,
    Nokesville, VA
Marge Marvell, Madison, IN
Barb Mason, Paris, MO
*Ronda Matthews, Gonzales, LA
Susan McClements, Nappanee, IN
Robin McCluggage, Cincinnati, OH
Kelvin Meeks, Memphis, TN
*Jane Melroy, Pratt, KS
Lori Meseke, CPA, Vandalia, IL
*Theresa Molltarls, Bridgeville, PA
*John Mondshein, Allentown, PA
Susan Moore, Meriden, CT
Heather Moraru, Suwanee, GA
Jennifer Mundy, O'Fallon, IL
Jospeh Nero, Red Hook, NY
Barb Nichols, Evansville, IN
*Julie Nguyen, West Chester, OH

*James O'Connell, Pittsburgh, PA
Carol Pearsall, Houston TX
Beverly Pettit, Willow Springs, MO
*Dick Pettit, Ovilla, TX
*Matt Pohlman, Latimer, IA
Katherine Prange, Breese, IL
Eleanor Rankin, Rio Rico, AZ
*Howard W. Rankin, MBA,
    Monticello, KY
Suzanne Rechenberg, Cincinnati, OH
Dr. Andrea B. Reiter, Dingman's
    Falls, PA
Nicole Reitz-Larson, Salt Lake
    City, UT
Dr. Harriet D. Rogers, Whitewater, WI
Tim Rohlinger, Kewaskum, WI
George Roth, Prairie du Sac, WI
Joyce Rowe, Lubbock, TX
Sam Sanchez, Laredo, TX
*Rob Schumacher, Middletown, DE
Peggy J. Scott, Chesapeke, VA
*Mark Sears, Winter Garden, FL
Christopher G. Shaffer,
    Cincinnati, OH
Janet Shaw, Bailey, NC
Mary Ann Shea, Amherst, MA
Jenny V. Shippy, Naples, FL
*Alice Sineath, Advance, NC
Sherri Small, Las Vegas, NV
H. Leland Smith, Racine, WI
Tommie Stanaland, Perry, FL
Dottie Starkey, Milford, DE
Laurel Stein, Wall, NJ
Jeynelle Strickland, Savanah, GA
*Diane Tanner, Jacksonville, FL
Susan Thie, Hamilton, OH
Claire Thoke, Glendale, CA
John Tingley, Bradley, IL
Linda Underwood, Gilcrest, CO
*Eileen Wascisin, Bellingham, WA
Jennifer Wegner, Mishicot, WI
Linda White, Fayetteville, PA
Parnell Wiggins, Memphis, TN
Lonnie Wilson, Evansville, IN
Vicki Winchester, Highland, KS
Vickie Wolfe, Glenns Ferry, ID
Kathy Woodard, Coventry, RI

* content verifier

PART 1

Accounting for a Service Business Organized as a Proprietorship

THE BUSINESS— TECHKNOW CONSULTING

TechKnow Consulting is the business that will be used in the chapters in Part 1 to illustrate the accounting concepts and procedures for a service business organized as a proprietorship. TechKnow rents the office space in which the business is located as well as the equipment used. The service provided by the business involves setting up and troubleshooting network problems for a variety of clients.

CHAPTER 1

CHAPTER 2

CHAPTER 5

CHAPTER 6

PHOTOS: STOCKBYTE, BLEND IMAGES, DIGITAL VISION (ALL GETTY IMAGES)

TECHKNOW CONSULTING CHART OF ACCOUNTS

GENERAL LEDGER

Balance Sheet Accounts

(100) ASSETS
110 Cash
120 Petty Cash
130 Accounts Receivable—Oakdale School
140 Accounts Receivable—Campus Internet Cafe
150 Supplies
160 Prepaid Insurance

(200) LIABILITIES
210 Accounts Payable—Supply Depot
220 Accounts Payable—Thomas Supply Company

(300) OWNER'S EQUITY
310 Kim Park, Capital
320 Kim Park, Drawing
330 Income Summary

Income Statement Accounts

(400) REVENUE
410 Sales

(500) EXPENSES
510 Advertising Expense
520 Insurance Expense
530 Miscellaneous Expense
540 Rent Expense
550 Supplies Expense
560 Utilities Expense

The chart of accounts for TechKnow Consulting is illustrated for ready reference as you study the accounting cycle for a proprietorship in this textbook.

CHAPTER 3

CHAPTER 4

CHAPTER 7

CHAPTER 8

STOCKBYTE/GETTY IMAGES

CHAPTER 1

Starting a Proprietorship: Changes That Affect the Accounting Equation

OBJECTIVES

After studying Chapter 1, you will be able to:

1. Define accounting terms related to starting a service business organized as a proprietorship and to changes that affect the accounting equation.

2. Identify accounting concepts and practices related to starting a service business organized as a proprietorship and to changes that affect the accounting equation.

3. Classify accounts as assets, liabilities, or owner's equity and demonstrate their relationships in the accounting equation.

4. Analyze how transactions affect accounts in an accounting equation.

KEY TERMS

- accounting
- accounting system
- accounting records
- financial statements
- service business
- proprietorship
- asset
- equities
- liability
- owner's equity
- accounting equation
- ethics
- business ethics
- transaction
- account
- account title
- account balance
- capital
- revenue
- sale on account
- expense
- withdrawals

Point Your Browser
www.C21accounting.com

Gold's Gym

Gold's Gym and the Importance of Location

Are you ready for a good workout? With so many labor-saving devices available today, many people look to fitness facilities for their daily physical exercise. For a fee, a member can make use of a variety of cardiovascular machines, weightlifting/resistance equipment, free weights, and indoor tracks. Many facilities offer classes and personal trainers. You can even shop for specialty food and workout clothing.

Gold's Gym is a franchise operation, meaning that individuals or groups buy the right to open and operate a Gold's Gym. The first Gold's Gym opened in 1965 in Venice, California. Since then, more than 650 Gold's Gyms have opened in the United States and in 23 countries around the world.

©GOLD'S GYM INTERNATIONAL

When considering the possibility of opening a new Gold's Gym, there are many decisions that have to be made. These decisions include where to locate the gym, how big the facility should be, what equipment to include, and how to let people know about the new facility.

Critical Thinking

1. Why is the location of a business important to the success of that business?

2. What things would you consider when deciding where to locate a business such as Gold's Gym?

Source: www.goldsgym.com

DIGITAL VISION/GETTY IMAGES

INTERNET ACTIVITY

Small Business Administration

Go to the homepage for the Small Business Administration, a government organization designed to help small businesses in the United States. Search the site for advice about starting a business. Use the link www.sba.gov, or do a search for the Small Business Administration if the link is no longer accurate.

Instructions

1. List at least five aids that the Small Business Administration site provides to help a person start a business.

2. Briefly explain which aid you feel is most helpful.

The Accounting Equation

WHAT IS ACCOUNTING?

Planning, recording, analyzing, and interpreting financial information is called **accounting**. A planned process for providing financial information that will be useful to management is called an **accounting system**. Organized summaries of a business's financial activities are called **accounting records**.

Accounting is the language of business. Many individuals in a business complete accounting forms and prepare accounting reports. Owners, managers, and accounting personnel use their knowledge of accounting to understand the information provided in the accounting reports. Regardless of their responsibilities within an organization, individuals can perform their jobs more efficiently if they know the language of business—accounting.

Suppliers that are considering extending credit to a business and institutions that are considering extending loans to a business are also interested in a business's financial activities. Financial reports that summarize the financial condition and operations of a business are called **financial statements**. Business owners and managers also use financial statements to make business decisions.

Inaccurate accounting records often contribute to business failure and bankruptcy. Failure to understand accounting information can result in poor business decisions for both businesses and nonprofit organizations. Understanding accounting helps managers and owners make better business decisions.

In addition, nearly everyone in the United States earns money and must submit income tax reports to the federal and state governments. Everyone must plan ways to keep spending within available income in both their personal and business lives.

THE BUSINESS—TECHKNOW CONSULTING

A business that performs an activity for a fee is called a **service business**. Kim Park decided to start her own business, helping set up and troubleshoot computer networks. A business owned by one person is called a **proprietorship**. A proprietorship is also referred to as a *sole proprietorship*. Kim named her new proprietorship "TechKnow Consulting." TechKnow Consulting will rent office space and the equipment needed to troubleshoot network problems.

Since TechKnow Consulting is a new business, Kim must design the accounting system that will be used to keep TechKnow Consulting's accounting records. Kim must be careful to keep these accounting records separate from her own personal financial records. For example, Kim owns a house and a personal car. TechKnow Consulting's financial records must not include information about Kim's house, car, or other personal belongings. Kim must use one checking account for her personal expenses and another checking account for TechKnow Consulting. The accounting concept *Business Entity* is applied when a business's financial information is recorded and reported separately from the owner's personal financial information. [CONCEPT: Business Entity]

Accounting concepts are described throughout this textbook when an application of a concept first occurs. When additional applications occur, a concept reference, such as [CONCEPT: Business Entity], indicates an application of a specific accounting concept. A brief description of each accounting concept used in this text is also provided on the *Century 21 Accounting* web site at www.C21accounting.com.

After completing a computer networking program at a local community college, Kim decided to start her own business so she would have more control over her daily schedule. After only two months, she has made all the arrangements and is ready to begin.

Kim enjoys both helping schools, businesses, and individuals set up a computer network and troubleshooting a network that is not working properly. She also enjoys being her own boss. She gets satisfaction from keeping her own accounting records and seeing that she is making money every month.

PHOTODISC/GETTY IMAGES

BUSINESS STRUCTURES

Forming and Dissolving a Proprietorship

A proprietorship is a business owned and controlled by one person. The advantages of a proprietorship include:

- *Ease of formation.*
- *Total control by the owner.*
- *Profits that are not shared.*

However, there are some disadvantages of organizing a proprietorship:

- *Limited resources.* The owner is the only person who can invest cash and other assets in the business.

- *Unlimited liability.* The owner is totally responsible for the liabilities of the business. Personal assets, such as a car, can be claimed by creditors to pay the business's liabilities.

- *Limited expertise.* Limited time, energy, and experience can be put into the business by the owner.

- *Limited life.* A proprietorship must be dissolved when the owner dies or decides to stop doing business.

- *Obligation to follow the laws of both the federal government and the state and city in which the business is formed.* Most cities and states have few, if any, legal procedures to follow. Once any legal requirements are met, the proprietorship can begin business. Should

the owner decide to dissolve the proprietorship, he or she merely needs to stop doing business. Noncash assets can be sold, with the cash used to pay any outstanding liabilities.

Critical Thinking

1. Why do you think more businesses are organized as proprietorships than any other form of business organization?

2. What kinds of people do you think would be most successful as owners of a proprietorship?

PHOTO: PHOTODISC/GETTY IMAGES

Assets	=	Liabilities + Owner's Equity
Left side amount		Right side amounts
$0	=	$0 + $0

TechKnow Consulting will own items such as cash and supplies that will be used to conduct daily operations. Anything of value that is owned is called an **asset**. Assets have value because they can be used either to acquire other assets or to operate a business. For example, TechKnow Consulting will use cash to buy supplies for the business. TechKnow Consulting will then use the asset—supplies—in the operation of the computer consulting business.

Financial rights to the assets of a business are called **equities**. A business has two types of equities: (1) *Equity of those to whom money is owed.* For example, TechKnow Consulting may buy some supplies and agree to pay for the supplies at a later date. The business from whom supplies are bought will have a right to some of TechKnow's assets until TechKnow pays for the supplies. An amount owed by a business is called a **liability**. (2) *Equity of the owner.* Kim will own TechKnow Consulting and invest in the assets of the business. Therefore, she will have a right to decide how the assets will be used. The amount remaining after the value of all liabilities is subtracted from the value of all assets is called **owner's equity**.

The relationship among assets, liabilities, and owner's equity can be written as an equation. An equation showing the relationship among assets, liabilities, and owner's equity is called the **accounting equation**. The accounting equation is most often stated as:

$$\text{Assets} = \text{Liabilities} + \text{Owner's Equity}$$

The accounting equation must be in balance. The total of the amounts on the left side must always equal the total of the amounts on the right side. Before a business starts, its accounting equation would show all zeros.

CHARACTER COUNTS

Accounting Scandals Rock the Financial World

Entering the 21st century, Enron, World-Com, and Andersen were three of the most celebrated names in corporate America. But the actions of a few individuals forced financial mammoths Enron and WorldCom into bankruptcy. Andersen, once one of the prestigious "Big 5" accounting firms, was forced out of business. These accounting scandals caused hundreds of thousands of employees to lose their jobs and millions of individuals to lose billions of dollars in investment and retirement accounts. The scandals rocked the public's confidence in the accounting profession and the stock markets.

The principles of right and wrong that guide an individual in making decisions are called **ethics**. The use of ethics in making business decisions is called **business ethics**.

Making ethical business decisions is a skill you can learn. Each chapter of this textbook contains a feature on business ethics. In Part 1, you will explore a model that guides your evaluation of business decisions. In later chapters, you will apply that model to make ethical business decisions. You will also be exposed to sources that will enable you to continue learning about business ethics long after you have completed this accounting course.

Instructions

Obtain an article that describes an accounting scandal such as Enron, WorldCom, Adelphia, Healthcorp South, or Parmalat. Write a one-paragraph summary that describes what happened and the individuals involved.

accounting

accounting system

accounting records

financial statements

service business

proprietorship

asset

equities

liability

owner's equity

accounting equation

ethics

business ethics

AUDIT YOUR UNDERSTANDING

1. What is accounting?
2. Give two examples of service businesses.
3. What is a proprietorship?
4. State the accounting equation.

WORK TOGETHER 1-1

Completing the accounting equation

Write the answers to the following problem in the *Working Papers*. Your instructor will guide you through the following example.

1. For each line, fill in the missing amount to complete the accounting equation.

Assets	=	Liabilities	+	Owner's Equity
?		3,000		8,000
10,000		?		6,000
63,000		35,000		?

ON YOUR OWN 1-1

Completing the accounting equation

Write the answers to the following problem in the *Working Papers*. Work this problem independently.

1. For each line, fill in the missing amount to complete the accounting equation.

Assets	=	Liabilities	+	Owner's Equity
30,000		?		13,000
?		60,000		20,000
51,000		25,000		?

.... **RECEIVING CASH** ....

	Assets	=	Liabilities	+	Owner's Equity
	Cash	=			Kim Park, Capital
Beginning Balances	$0		$0		$0
Received cash from owner as an investment	+5,000				+5,000
New Balances	$5,000		$0		$5,000

Business activities change the amounts in the accounting equation. A business activity that changes assets, liabilities, or owner's equity is called a **transaction**. For example, a business that pays cash for supplies is engaging in a transaction. After each transaction, the accounting equation must remain in balance.

The accounting concept *Unit of Measurement* is applied when business transactions are stated in numbers that have common values—that is, using a common unit of measurement. [CONCEPT: Unit of Measurement] For example, in the United States, business transactions are recorded in dollars. The unit of measurement concept is followed so that the financial reports of businesses can be clearly stated and understood in numbers that have comparable values.

Received Cash Investment from Owner
Ms. Park uses $5,000.00 of her own money to invest in TechKnow Consulting. TechKnow Consulting should be concerned only with the effect of this transaction on TechKnow Consulting's records. The business should not be concerned about Ms. Park's personal records. [CONCEPT: Business Entity]

....

Transaction 1 *August 1. Received cash from owner as an investment, $5,000.00.*

....

A record summarizing all the information pertaining to a single item in the accounting equation is called an **account**. The name given to an account is called an **account title**. Each part of the accounting equation consists of one or more accounts.

In the accounting equation shown above, the asset account, Cash, is increased by $5,000.00, the amount of cash received by the business. This increase is on the left side of the accounting equation. The amount in an account is called the **account balance**. Before the owner's investment, the account balance of Cash was zero. After the owner's investment, the account balance of Cash is $5,000.00.

The account used to summarize the owner's equity in a business is called **capital**. The capital account is an owner's equity account. In the accounting equation shown above, the owner's equity account, Kim Park, Capital, is increased by $5,000.00. This increase is on the right side of the accounting equation. Before the owner's investment, the account balance of Kim Park, Capital was zero. After the owner's investment, the account balance of Kim Park, Capital is $5,000.00.

The accounting equation has changed as a result of the receipt of cash. However, both sides of the equation are changed by the same amount. The $5,000.00 increase on the left side of the equation equals the $5,000.00 increase on the right side of the equation. Therefore, the accounting equation is still in balance.

	Assets			= Liabilities +	Owner's Equity
	Cash +	Supplies +	Prepaid Insurance =		Kim Park, Capital
Balances	$5,000	$0	$0	$0	$5,000
Paid cash for supplies	−275	+275			
Balances	$4,725	$275	$0	$0	$5,000
Paid cash for insurance	−1,200		+1,200		
New Balances	$3,525	$275	$1,200	$0	$5,000

TechKnow Consulting pays cash for supplies and insurance.

Paid Cash for Supplies
TechKnow Consulting needs supplies to operate the business. Kim Park uses some of TechKnow Consulting's cash to buy supplies.

· ·

Transaction 2 *August 3. Paid cash for supplies, $275.00.*

· ·

In this transaction, two asset accounts are changed. One asset, cash, has been exchanged for another asset, supplies. The asset account, Cash, is decreased by $275.00, the amount of cash paid out. This decrease is on the left side of the accounting equation. The asset account, Supplies, is increased by $275.00, the amount of supplies bought. This increase is also on the left side of the accounting equation.

For this transaction, two assets are changed. Therefore, the two changes are both on the left side of the accounting equation. When changes are made on only one side of the accounting equation, the equation must still be in balance. Therefore, if one account is increased, another account on the same side of the equation must be decreased. After this transaction, the new account balance of Cash is $4,725.00. The new account balance of Supplies is $275.00. The sum of the amounts on the left side is $5,000.00 (Cash, $4,725.00 + Supplies, $275.00). The amount on the right side is also $5,000.00. Therefore, the accounting equation is still in balance.

Paid Cash for Insurance
Insurance premiums must be paid in advance. For example, TechKnow Consulting pays a $1,200.00 insurance premium for future insurance coverage.

· ·

Transaction 3 *August 4. Paid cash for insurance, $1,200.00.*

· ·

In return for this payment, TechKnow Consulting is entitled to insurance coverage for the length of the policy. The insurance coverage is something of value owned by TechKnow Consulting. Therefore, the insurance coverage is an asset. Because insurance premiums are paid in advance, or prepaid, the premiums are recorded in an asset account titled Prepaid Insurance.

In this transaction, two assets are changed. One asset, cash, has been exchanged for another asset, prepaid insurance. The asset account, Cash, is decreased by $1,200.00, the amount of cash paid out. The asset account, Prepaid Insurance, is increased by $1,200.00, the amount of insurance bought.

After this transaction, the new account balance of Cash is $3,525.00. The new account balance of Prepaid Insurance is $1,200.00. The sum of the amounts on the left side is $5,000.00 (Cash, $3,525.00 + Supplies, $275.00 + Prepaid Insurance, $1,200.00). The amount on the right side is also $5,000.00. Therefore, the accounting equation is still in balance.

	Assets			= Liabilities +	Owner's Equity
	Cash +	Supplies +	Prepaid Insurance =	Accts. Pay.—Supply Depot +	Kim Park, Capital
Balances	$3,525	$275	$1,200	$0	$5,000
Bought supplies on account		+500		+500	
New Balances	$3,525	$775	$1,200	$500	$5,000
Paid cash on account	−300			−300	
New Balances	$3,225	$775	$1,200	$200	$5,000

Bought Supplies on Account

TechKnow Consulting needs to buy additional supplies. The supplies are obtained from Supply Depot, and Tech-Know arranges to pay for them at the end of the month. It is a common business practice to buy items and pay for them at a future date. Another way to state this activity is to say that these items are bought *on account.*

Transaction 4 *August 7. Bought supplies on account from Supply Depot, $500.00.*

In this transaction, one asset and one liability are changed. The asset account, Supplies, is increased by $500.00, the amount of supplies bought. Supply Depot will have a claim against some of TechKnow Consulting's assets until TechKnow Consulting pays for the supplies bought. Therefore, Accounts Payable—Supply Depot is a liability account. The liability account, Accounts Payable—Supply Depot, is increased by $500.00, the amount owed for the supplies.

After this transaction, the new account balance of Supplies is $775.00. The new account balance of Accounts Payable—Supply Depot is $500.00. The sum of the amounts on the left side is $5,500.00 (Cash, $3,525.00 + Supplies, $775.00 + Prepaid Insurance, $1,200.00). The sum of the amounts on the right side is also $5,500.00 (Accounts Payable—Supply Depot, $500.00 + Kim Park, Capital, $5,000.00). Therefore, the accounting equation is still in balance.

Paid Cash on Account

Since TechKnow Consulting is a new business, Supply Depot has not done business with TechKnow Consulting before. Supply Depot allows TechKnow Consulting to buy supplies on account but requires TechKnow Consulting to send a check for $300.00 immediately. TechKnow Consulting will pay the remaining portion of this liability at a later date.

Transaction 5 *August 11. Paid cash on account to Supply Depot, $300.00.*

In this transaction, one asset and one liability are changed. The asset account, Cash, is decreased by $300.00, the amount of cash paid out. After this payment, Tech-Know Consulting owes less money to Supply Depot. Therefore, the liability account, Accounts Payable—Supply Depot, is decreased by $300.00, the amount paid on account.

After this transaction, the new account balance of Cash is $3,225.00. The new account balance of Accounts Payable—Supply Depot is $200.00. The sum of the amounts on the left side is $5,200.00 (Cash, $3,225.00 + Supplies, $775.00 + Prepaid Insurance, $1,200.00). The sum of the amounts on the right side is also $5,200.00 (Accounts Payable—Supply Depot, $200.00 + Kim Park, Capital, $5,000.00). Therefore, the accounting equation is still in balance.

REMEMBER

The left side of the accounting equation (assets) must always equal the right side (liabilities plus owner's equity).

TERMS REVIEW

transaction

account

account title

account balance

capital

AUDIT YOUR UNDERSTANDING

1. What must be done if a transaction increases the left side of the accounting equation?
2. How can a transaction affect only one side of the accounting equation?
3. To what does the phrase *on account* refer?

WORK TOGETHER 1-2

Determining how transactions change an accounting equation

Write the answers to the following problem in the *Working Papers*. Your instructor will guide you through the following example.

Trans. No.	Assets	=	Liabilities	+	Owner's Equity
1.					

1. For each transaction, place a plus (+) in the appropriate column if the classification is increased. Place a minus (−) in the appropriate column if the classification is decreased.

Transactions:

1. Bought supplies on account.
2. Received cash from owner as an investment.
3. Paid cash for insurance.
4. Paid cash on account.

ON YOUR OWN 1-2

Determining how transactions change an accounting equation

Write the answers to the following problem in the *Working Papers*. Work this problem independently.

Trans. No.	Assets	=	Liabilities	+	Owner's Equity
1.					

1. For each transaction, place a plus (+) in the appropriate column if the classification is increased. Place a minus (−) in the appropriate column if the classification is decreased.

Transactions:

1. Received cash from owner as an investment.
2. Bought supplies on account.
3. Paid cash for supplies.
4. Paid cash for insurance.
5. Paid cash on account.

REVENUE TRANSACTIONS

	Assets				= Liabilities +	Owner's Equity
	Cash +	Accts. Rec.—Oakdale School	+ Supplies +	Prepaid Insurance =	Accts. Pay.—Supply Depot +	Kim Park, Capital
Balances	$3,225	$0	$775	$1,200	$200	$5,000
Received cash from sales	+295					+295 (revenue)
New Balances	$3,520	$0	$775	$1,200	$200	$5,295
Sold services on account		+350				+350 (revenue)
New Balances	$3,520	$350	$775	$1,200	$200	$5,645

Total of left side:
$3,520 + $350 + $775 + $1,200 = $5,845

Total of right side:
$200 + $5,645 = $5,845

Received Cash from Sales

A transaction for the sale of goods or services results in an increase in owner's equity. An increase in owner's equity resulting from the operation of a business is called **revenue**. When cash is received from a sale, the total amount of both assets and owner's equity is increased.

Transaction 6 *August 12. Received cash from sales, $295.00.*

When TechKnow Consulting receives cash for services performed, the asset account, Cash, is increased by the amount of cash received, $295.00. This increase is on the left side of the equation. The owner's equity account, Kim Park, Capital, is also increased by $295.00. This increase is on the right side of the equation. After this transaction is recorded, the equation is still in balance.

In this chapter, three different kinds of transactions that affect owner's equity are described. Therefore, a description of the transaction is shown in parentheses to the right of the amount in the accounting equation.

Sold Services on Account

A sale for which cash will be received at a later date is called a **sale on account**, or a *charge sale*. TechKnow Consulting contracts with a school and an Internet cafe to provide consulting services for payment at a later date. All other customers must pay cash at the time of the service. Regardless of when payment is made, the revenue should be recorded at the time of a sale. The accounting concept *Realization of Revenue* is applied when revenue is recorded at the time goods or services are sold. [CONCEPT: Realization of Revenue]

Transaction 7 *August 12. Sold services on account to Oakdale School, $350.00.*

When TechKnow Consulting sells services on account, the asset account, Accounts Receivable—Oakdale School, is increased by $350.00, the amount of cash that will be received.

This increase is on the left side of the equation. The owner's equity account, Kim Park, Capital, is also increased by $350.00 on the right side of the equation. The equation is still in balance.

		Assets			=	Liabilities	+	Owner's Equity
		Accts. Rec.—				Accts. Pay.—		
		Oakdale		Prepaid		Supply		Kim Park,
	Cash +	School	+ Supplies +	Insurance	=	Depot	+	Capital
Balances	$3,520	$350	$775	$1,200		$200		$5,645
Paid cash for rent	−300							−300 (expense)
New Balances	$3,220	$350	$775	$1,200		$200		$5,345
Paid cash for telephone bill	−40							−40 (expense)
New Balances	$3,180	$350	$775	$1,200		$200		$5,305

Total of left side:
$3,180 + $350 + $775 + $1,200 = $5,505

Total of right side:
$200 + $5,305 = $5,505

A transaction to pay for goods or services needed to operate a business results in a decrease in owner's equity. A decrease in owner's equity resulting from the operation of a business is called an **expense**. When cash is paid for expenses, the business has less cash. Therefore, the asset account, Cash, is decreased. The owner's equity account, Kim Park, Capital, is also decreased by the same amount.

Paid Cash for Rent

Transaction 8 *August 12. Paid cash for rent, $300.00.*

The asset account, Cash, is decreased by $300.00, the amount of cash paid out. This decrease is on the left side of the equation. The owner's equity account, Kim Park, Capital, is also decreased by $300.00. This decrease is on the right side of the equation. After this transaction is recorded, the equation is still in balance.

Paid Cash for Telephone Bill

Transaction 9 *August 12. Paid cash for telephone bill, $40.00.*

The asset account, Cash, is decreased by $40.00, the amount of cash paid out. This decrease is on the left side of the equation. The owner's equity account, Kim Park, Capital, is also decreased by $40.00. This decrease is on the right side of the equation. After this transaction is recorded, the equation is still in balance.

Other expense transactions might be for advertising, equipment rental or repairs, charitable contributions, and other miscellaneous items. All expense transactions affect the accounting equation in the same way as in Transactions 8 and 9.

PHOTODISC/GETTY IMAGES

	Assets				= Liabilities +	Owner's Equity
	Cash +	Accts. Rec.—Oakdale School	+ Supplies +	Prepaid Insurance =	Accts. Pay.—Supply Depot +	Kim Park, Capital
Balances	$3,180	$350	$775	$1,200	$200	$5,305
Received cash on account	+200	−200				
New Balances	$3,380	$150	$775	$1,200	$200	$5,305
Paid cash to owner for personal use	−125					−125 (withdrawal)
New Balances	$3,255	$150	$775	$1,200	$200	$5,180

Total of left side:
$3,255 + $150 + $775 + $1,200 = $5,380

Total of right side:
$200 + $5,180 = $5,380

Received Cash on Account

When a business receives cash from a customer for a prior sale, the transaction increases the cash account balance and decreases the accounts receivable balance.

Transaction 10 *August 18. Received cash on account from Oakdale School, $200.00.*

The asset account, Cash, is increased by $200.00. This increase is on the left side of the equation. The asset account, Accounts Receivable—Oakdale School, is decreased by $200.00. This decrease is also on the left side of the equation. After this transaction is recorded, the equation is still in balance.

Paid Cash to Owner for Personal Use

Assets taken out of a business for the owner's personal use are called **withdrawals**. A withdrawal decreases owner's equity. Although an owner may withdraw any kind of asset, usually an owner withdraws cash. The withdrawal decreases the account balance of the withdrawn asset, such as Cash.

Transaction 11 *August 18. Paid cash to owner for personal use, $125.00.*

The asset account, Cash, is decreased by $125.00. This decrease is on the left side of the accounting equation. The owner's equity account, Kim Park, Capital, is also decreased by $125.00. This decrease is on the right side of the equation. After this transaction is recorded, the equation is still in balance.

A decrease in owner's equity because of a withdrawal is not a result of the normal operations of a business. Therefore, a withdrawal is not considered an expense.

Summary of Changes in Owner's Equity

Immediately after recording the beginning investment used to start TechKnow Consulting, the total owner's equity was $5,000.00, which represented the investment by the owner, Kim Park. Since that initial investment, five additional transactions that changed owner's equity were recorded in the accounting equation.

These transactions increased owner's equity by $180.00, from $5,000.00 to $5,180.00. Transaction 10, cash received on account, is not listed because it affects two accounts that are both on the left side of the accounting equation.

Transaction Number	Kind of Transaction	Change in Owner's Equity
6	Revenue (cash)	+295.00
7	Revenue (on account)	+350.00
8	Expense (rent)	−300.00
9	Expense (telephone)	− 40.00
11	Withdrawal	−125.00
Net change in owner's equity		+180.00

End of Lesson
REVIEW

TERMS REVIEW

revenue

sale on account

expense

withdrawals

AUDIT YOUR UNDERSTANDING

1. How is owner's equity affected when cash is received from sales?
2. How is owner's equity affected when services are sold on account?
3. How is owner's equity affected when cash is paid for expenses?

WORK TOGETHER 1-3

Determining how transactions change an accounting equation

Write the answers to the following problem in the *Working Papers*. Your instructor will guide you through the following example.

1. Place a plus (+) in the appropriate column if the account is increased. Place a minus (−) in the appropriate column if the account is decreased.

		Assets			=	Liabilities	+	Owner's Equity
Trans. No.	Cash +	Accts. Rec.—Bowman Co. +	Supplies +	Prepaid Insurance	=	Accts. Pay.—Maxwell Co.	+	Susan Sanders, Capital
1.								

Transactions:

1. Received cash from sales.
2. Sold services on account to Bowman Company.
3. Paid cash for telephone bill.
4. Received cash on account from Bowman Company.
5. Paid cash to owner for personal use.

ON YOUR OWN 1-3

Determining how transactions change an accounting equation

Write the answers to the following problem in the *Working Papers*. Work this problem independently.

1. Place a plus (+) in the appropriate column if the account is increased. Place a minus (−) in the appropriate column if the account is decreased.

		Assets			=	Liabilities	+	Owner's Equity
Trans. No.	Cash +	Accts. Rec.—Navarro Co. +	Supplies +	Prepaid Insurance	=	Accts. Pay.—Barrett Co.	+	Vincent Orr, Capital
1.								

Transactions:

1. Sold services on account to Navarro Company.
2. Received cash from sales.
3. Received cash on account from Navarro Company.
4. Paid cash to owner for personal use.
5. Paid cash for rent.

After completing this chapter, you can:

1. Define accounting terms related to starting a service business organized as a proprietorship and to changes that affect the accounting equation.

2. Identify accounting concepts and practices related to starting a service business organized as a proprietorship and to changes that affect the accounting equation.

3. Classify accounts as assets, liabilities, or owner's equity and demonstrate their relationships in the accounting equation.

4. Analyze how transactions affect accounts in an accounting equation.

EXPLORE ACCOUNTING

What Is GAAP?

The standards and rules that accountants follow while recording and reporting financial activities are commonly referred to as *generally accepted accounting principles*, or *GAAP*. These rules have not been developed by any one group of rule makers but have instead evolved over time and from many sources.

By law, the Securities and Exchange Commission (SEC) has the authority to establish GAAP. The SEC, however, has allowed a series of private organizations to determine GAAP. Currently, the organization that has the authority to set accounting standards is the Financial Accounting Standards Board (FASB), which was established in 1973.

The standard-setting process includes getting input and feedback from many sources. FASB listens to this feedback and considers all sides of each issue.

Why Is GAAP Necessary?

Users of financial statements rely on the information those statements contain. If the preparers of financial statements were allowed to follow any measurement, recording, and reporting rules, the users of the statements would have no way to determine if the financial statements present fairly the financial position of the business.

By requiring the financial statement preparers to consistently follow certain standards and rules—such as GAAP—the users are able to compare the financial statements of several companies and to track the results of one company over several time periods.

Discussion: Why would a group of people disagree with a proposed accounting standard?

Research: Using your local library or the Internet, find additional information about the FASB. Write a one-page report on your findings.

APPLICATION PROBLEM

Completing the accounting equation

Instructions:
For each line, fill in the missing amount to complete the accounting equation. Use the form in your *Working Papers* to complete this problem.

Assets	=	Liabilities	+	Owner's Equity
95,000		51,000		?
?		44,000		20,000
4,000		?		2,500
138,000		70,000		?
19,000		?		11,000
?		4,000		12,000
35,000		13,000		?
?		120,000		49,000
8,000		?		3,200
86,000		48,000		?
12,000		?		7,000
?		8,000		22,000
47,000		24,000		?
?		29,000		13,000
57,000		?		36,000
125,000		69,000		?
11,000		?		6,000
?		2,000		3,300

1-2

APPLICATION PROBLEM

Determining how transactions change an accounting equation

Calvin Parish is starting Parish Repair Shop, a small service business. Parish Repair Shop uses the accounts shown in the following accounting equation. Use the form in your *Working Papers* to complete this problem.

| Trans. No. | Assets | | | = | Liabilities | | + | Owner's Equity |
	Cash +	Supplies +	Prepaid Insurance =		Accts. Pay.— Five Star Supply +	Accts. Pay.— Riverland Company +		Calvin Parish, Capital
Beg. Bal.	0	0	0		0	0		0
1.	+3,000							+3,000
New Bal.	3,000	0	0		0	0		3,000
2.								

Go Beyond the Book
For more information go to
www.C21accounting.com

Transactions:

1. Received cash from owner as an investment, $3,000.00.
2. Paid cash for insurance, $1,600.00.
3. Bought supplies on account from Five Star Supply, $700.00.
4. Bought supplies on account from Riverland Company, $300.00.
5. Paid cash on account to Five Star Supply, $700.00.
6. Paid cash on account to Riverland Company, $200.00.
7. Paid cash for supplies, $100.00.
8. Received cash from owner as an investment, $1,500.00.

Instructions:

For each transaction, complete the following. Transaction 1 is given as an example.

a. Analyze the transaction to determine which accounts in the accounting equation are affected.

b. Write the amount in the appropriate columns using a plus (+) if the account increases or a minus (−) if the account decreases.

c. Calculate the new balance for each account in the accounting equation.

d. Before going on to the next transaction, determine that the accounting equation is still in balance.

1-3 APPLICATION PROBLEM

Determining how revenue, expense, and withdrawal transactions change an accounting equation

Peter Smith operates a service business called Peter's Service Company. Peter's Service Company uses the accounts shown in the following accounting equation. Use the form in your *Working Papers* to complete this problem.

| Trans. No. | Assets | | | | = | Liabilities | + | Owner's Equity |
	Cash	+	Accts. Rec.— Lisa Lee	+ Supplies +	Prepaid Insurance	=	Accts. Pay.— Kline Co.	+	Peter Smith, Capital
Beg. Bal.	625	0	375	300	200	1,100
1.	−300					−300 (expense)
New Bal.	325	0	375	300	200	800
2.						

Transactions:

1. Paid cash for rent, $300.00.
2. Paid cash to owner for personal use, $150.00.
3. Received cash from sales, $800.00.
4. Paid cash for equipment repairs, $100.00.
5. Sold services on account to Lisa Lee, $400.00.
6. Received cash from sales, $650.00.
7. Paid cash for charitable contributions, $35.00.
8. Received cash on account from Lisa Lee, $300.00.

Instructions:

For each transaction, complete the following. Transaction 1 is given as an example.

a. Analyze the transaction to determine which accounts in the accounting equation are affected.

b. Write the amount in the appropriate columns, using a plus (+) if the account increases or a minus (−) if the account decreases.

c. For transactions that change owner's equity, write in parentheses a description of the transaction to the right of the amount.

d. Calculate the new balance for each account in the accounting equation.

e. Before going on to the next transaction, determine that the accounting equation is still in balance.

1-4 | MASTERY PROBLEM

Determining how transactions change an accounting equation

Marion Cassidy operates a service business called Cassidy Company. Cassidy Company uses the accounts shown in the following accounting equation. Use the form in your *Working Papers* to complete this problem.

Trans. No.	Cash	+	Accts. Rec.— Ana Santiago	+ Supplies +	Prepaid Insurance	=	Accts. Pay.— Delta Co.	+	Marion Cassidy, Capital
			Assets			**=**	**Liabilities**	**+**	**Owner's Equity**
Beg. Bal.	2,300		0	200	100		1,800		800
1.	−400								−400 (expense)
New Bal.	1,900		0	200	100		1,800		400
2.									

Transactions:

1. Paid cash for rent, $400.00.
2. Received cash from owner as an investment, $500.00.
3. Paid cash for telephone bill, $50.00.
4. Received cash from sales, $1,025.00.
5. Bought supplies on account from Delta Company, $450.00.
6. Sold services on account to Ana Santiago, $730.00.
7. Paid cash for advertising, $660.00.
8. Paid cash for supplies, $150.00.
9. Received cash on account from Ana Santiago, $400.00.
10. Paid cash on account to Delta Company, $1,500.00.
11. Paid cash for one month of insurance, $100.00.
12. Received cash from sales, $1,230.00.
13. Paid cash to owner for personal use, $1,200.00.

Instructions:

For each transaction, complete the following. Transaction 1 is given as an example.

a. Analyze the transaction to determine which accounts in the accounting equation are affected.

b. Write the amount in the appropriate columns, using a plus (+) if the account increases or a minus (−) if the account decreases.

c. For transactions that change owner's equity, write in parentheses a description of the transaction to the right of the amount.

d. Calculate the new balance for each account in the accounting equation.

e. Before going on to the next transaction, determine that the accounting equation is still in balance.

Determining how transactions change an accounting equation

Zachary Martin owns Zachary's Repair Shop. On February 1, Zachary's Repair Shop's accounting equation indicated the following account balances. Use the form in your *Working Papers* to complete this problem.

Trans. No.	Assets				=	Liabilities	+	Owner's Equity
	Cash +	Accts. Rec.— Mary Lou Pier +	Supplies +	Prepaid Insurance =		Accts. Pay.— Kollasch Co. +		Zachary Martin, Capital
Beg. Bal. 1.	8,552	1,748	1,485	615		3,145		9,255

Transactions:

1. Took $400.00 of supplies for personal use.
2. Had equipment repaired at Kollasch Company and agreed to pay Kollasch Company at a later date, $250.00.
3. Mr. Martin had some personal property, which he sold for $500.00 cash.
4. Paid Kollasch Company $120.00 on account.

Instructions:

1. For each transaction, complete the following.
   a. Analyze the transaction to determine which accounts in the accounting equation are affected.
   b. Write the amount in the appropriate columns, using a plus (+) if the account increases or a minus (−) if the account decreases.
   c. For transactions that change owner's equity, write in parentheses a description of the transaction to the right of the amount.
   d. Calculate the new balance for each account in the accounting equation.
   e. Before going on to the next transaction, determine that the accounting equation is still in balance.
2. Answer the following questions.
   a. Why can the owner of a business withdraw assets from that business for personal use?
   b. Why would the owner withdraw assets other than cash?

APPLIED COMMUNICATION

A resume provides a statement of your education, experience, and qualifications for a prospective employer. Your resume should be accurate, honest, and perfect in every respect. It should include all work experience along with the companies and dates of employment. Education, activities, and interests are all important items that should be covered.

Instructions:

Research how to prepare an appropriate resume using the library or the Internet. Then prepare a resume that you could send to a prospective employer.

Case 1

Akira Shinoda starts a new business. Mr. Shinoda uses his personal car in the business with the expectation that later the business can buy a car. All expenses for operating the car, including license plates, gasoline, oil, tune-ups, and new tires, are paid for out of business funds. Is this an acceptable procedure? Explain.

Case 2

At the end of the first day of business, Quick Clean Laundry has the assets and liabilities shown below.

The owner, Anh Vu, wants to know the amount of her equity in Quick Clean Laundry. Determine this amount and explain what this amount represents.

Assets		Liabilities	
Cash	$3,500.00	A/P—Smith Office Supplies	$ 750.00
Supplies	950.00	A/P—Super Supplies Company	1,500.00
Prepaid Insurance	1,200.00		

GRAPHING WORKSHOP

The assets, liabilities, and owner's equity for three different companies are given in the graph at right.

Analyze the graph to answer the following questions.

1. Which category is largest?
2. Why will assets always be 50% of the total?

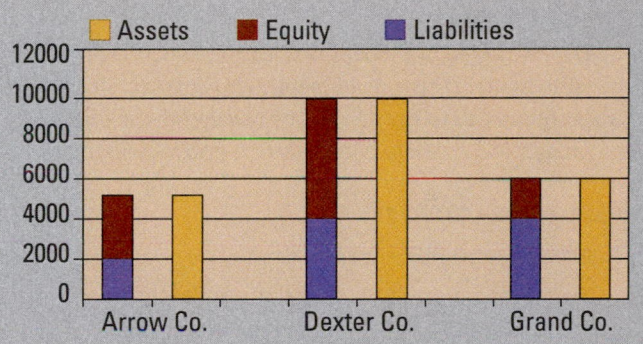

ANALYZING BEST BUY'S FINANCIAL STATEMENTS

Selected published financial information for Best Buy Co., Inc., is reproduced in Appendix B. Look at pages B-5 through B-8, where you will find Best Buy's financial statements. Under the heading on each page, you will see the phrase "$ in millions." This means that all dollar amounts are rounded to the nearest million. Therefore, an amount such as $174 actually means $174,000,000. Another way to think of this is that you can calculate the actual amount by multiplying the rounded amount by 1,000,000 ($174 × 1,000,000 = $174,000,000).

Not all companies round the amounts in their financial statements to the nearest million. Many companies round to the nearest thousand.

Instructions

1. List the actual amount of Accounts Payable and Revenue for Best Buy for 2007.
2. The financial statements for Barnes & Noble include the phrase "thousands of dollars." In 2005, the financial statements included Accounts Payable, $828,852, and Sales, $5,103,004. List the actual amount of Accounts Payable and Sales.

Accounting
SOFTWARE

ACCOUNTING SOFTWARE

As you begin your journey into the exciting world of accounting, it is important that you also experience how today's businesses use personal computers to record their transactions and prepare financial statements. How are transactions entered onto computer screens? How does the computer keep track of the total of the Cash account? How is the information that is collected reported on financial statements?

At the end of every chapter, this feature will introduce you to Peachtree, one of the most widely recognized brands of computer accounting systems. Your teacher may also have you complete selected end-of-chapter problems using Peachtree. You will discover that the knowledge of accounting you learn in this textbook will enable you to understand how Peachtree operates and provides management with the information it needs to make good business decisions.

The Peachtree brand was first introduced in 1976, a time when personal computers were just beginning to become available to individuals and businesses. Since then, Peachtree Software has merged with many other software companies to form Sage Software. With millions of customers in the United States and Canada, Sage Software provides a wide variety of accounting and management software to small and medium-sized businesses.

PEACHTREE ACTIVITY*

1. Access the Sage Software web site at www.sagesoftware.com.

2. Identify the most current versions of Peachtree that are available.

3. Identify what version of Peachtree is available at your school.

ACCOUNTING SOFTWARE

During your study of accounting, your instructor may introduce you to an accounting software program called QuickBooks. Accounting software programs are more efficient and can be much more accurate than completing tasks manually. Many companies require new employees to have some knowledge of accounting software programs. Therefore, learning how to use QuickBooks can make you more employable.

QuickBooks accounting software was developed by the Intuit Company, which was founded in 1983. The software is available in many versions. The version used by a company depends on the tasks that the company wishes to complete electronically. However, all versions of QuickBooks have general items in common. During your study of accounting, you will learn how to manually complete an accounting task. You may then be asked to complete the same task using QuickBooks. It is important to understand the manual tasks before using accounting software so that you can understand what the software is doing. An understanding of accounting also allows you to review the information that is produced electronically and check it for accuracy.

QUICKBOOKS ACTIVITY*

1. Access the Intuit web site at www.quickbooks.intuit.com.

2. Identify the most current versions of QuickBooks that are available.

3. Identify what version of QuickBooks is available at your school.

ACCOUNTING SOFTWARE

Electronic spreadsheets are one of the most popular software programs used by accountants. The reason is simple—the row and column structure of an electronic spreadsheet resembles the journal paper used by accountants for decades, some say even centuries.

It is not surprising, then, that publications read by accountants frequently contain articles about electronic spreadsheets. The *Journal of Accountancy*, published by the American Institute of Certified Public Accountants, is sent to over 300,000 accountants. The *Journal* regularly publishes articles that provide detailed instructions for using electronic spreadsheet features. More importantly, the articles provide examples of accounting applications of the features.

As you study accounting in this course, you will have the opportunity to complete several problems on an electronic spreadsheet. Along the way, you will learn a variety of helpful features. In some cases, you will be able to try out these features in your exercises.

EXCEL ACTIVITY*

1. Identify what electronic spreadsheet version is available at your school.

2. Access the *Journal of Accountancy* online at www.aicpa.org/pubs/jofa/joahome.htm. Perform a search for the name of your electronic spreadsheet.

3. Select one of the articles in the search results. Write a short summary of the feature described in the article.

ACCOUNTING SOFTWARE

Automated Accounting was developed by Warren Allen and Dale Klooster in the late 1970s for use in their accounting classrooms. They were pioneers in the use of computer technology in the classroom. The software includes a complete accounting system, with modules for specialized activities such as bank statement reconciliation, plant assets, inventory, and payroll. The software was so comprehensive and easy to use that some small businesses also used the software for their business needs. South-Western acquired the software in the early 1980s as a companion to its *Century 21 Accounting* textbooks. Automated Accounting has been revised and updated continuously since then.

AUTOMATED ACCOUNTING ACTIVITY*

1. Consider the problems you have worked in Chapter 1. If you used a computerized accounting system to work the problems, what kinds of errors would the computerized accounting system prevent?

2. For the problems in Chapter 1, what kinds of errors would not be prevented by using a computerized accounting system?

*COMPUTER SAFETY AND HEALTH BASICS

There are some basic safety and health precautions for using computer equipment.
Read the safety and health tips on the *Century 21 Accounting* web site.

BLEND IMAGES/GETTY IMAGES

CHAPTER 2

Analyzing Transactions into Debit and Credit Parts

OBJECTIVES

After studying Chapter 2, you will be able to:

1. Define accounting terms related to analyzing transactions into debit and credit parts.

2. Identify accounting practices related to analyzing transactions into debit and credit parts.

3. Use T accounts to analyze transactions showing which accounts are debited or credited for each transaction.

4. Analyze how transactions to set up a business affect accounts.

5. Analyze how transactions affect owner's equity accounts.

KEY TERMS

- T account
- debit
- credit
- normal balance
- chart of accounts

Point Your Browser
www.C21accounting.com

American Automobile Association (AAA)

Traveling with the American Automobile Association (AAA)

Picture yourself driving on a dark, deserted road. Suddenly your car stalls. You pull over to the side of the road. What do you do next? If you are a member of the American Automobile Association (AAA), you can pick up your cell phone and call for emergency roadside assistance.

Many people realize the benefits of a membership with the AAA. However, not many people know that the AAA was instrumental in starting the nationwide School Safety Patrol program back in 1920. In 1930, the AAA pioneered the driver education program still in existence in many high schools. As early as 1916, the AAA was fighting for federal dollars to be used to construct a national highway system.

The AAA sells memberships to individuals and families. In exchange for the membership fee, the AAA provides an array of benefits including emergency roadside assistance, travel services, insurance services, driver protection services, and even emergency check cashing services.

©AAA, WWW.AAANEWSROOM.NET, ABOUT AAA, 2004

Critical Thinking

1. What asset and liability accounts might the AAA use to record its transactions?

2. List at least two transactions that the AAA might record.

Source: www.aaa.com

INTERNET ACTIVITY

Company Headquarters

Go to the homepage of a company of your choice.

Instructions

Search the site to find when the company was started and where its headquarters (or home office) is located. This information is typically found under one of the following headings: "About Us," "Investor Relations," "History," or "Contact Us."

ANALYZING THE ACCOUNTING EQUATION

Even though the effects of transactions can be recorded in an accounting equation, the procedure is not practical in an actual accounting system. The number of accounts used by most businesses would make the accounting equation cumbersome to use as a major financial record. Therefore, a separate record is commonly used for each account. The accounting equation can be represented as a T, as shown below.

Assets	=	Liabilities	+	Owner's Equity
Left side		Right side		

The values of all things owned (assets) are on the left side of the accounting equation. The values of all equities or claims against the assets (liabilities and owner's equity) are on the right side of the accounting equation. The total of amounts on the left side of the accounting equation must always equal the total of amounts on the right side. Therefore, the total of all assets on the left side of the accounting equation must always equal the total of all liabilities and owner's equity on the right side.

CHARACTER COUNTS

Ethics Versus Morality

Ethics and morality—these words are often used to refer to an individual's ability to "do what is right." These synonymous English words were derived from different languages. "Ethics" is derived from Greek, and "morality" is derived from Latin. Over time, our society has given a slightly different meaning to each word.

Over 100 years ago, C. C. Everett wrote, "Ethics is the science of morality." Morality is the standard of conduct that is acceptable in a society. Ethics is an organized method that relies on our morality to make moral decisions. Science students learn the scientific method—a model that guides how a proper experiment should be conducted. In the same manner, many ethical models have been proposed to guide individuals in applying their morality to business decisions.

The following ethical model will be used in this textbook:

1. Recognize you are facing an ethical dilemma.
2. Identify the action taken or the proposed action.
3. Analyze the action.
   a. Is the action illegal?
   b. Does the action violate company or professional standards?
   c. Who is affected, and how, by the action?
4. Determine if the action is ethical.

Instructions

Prepare a short report that contrasts the ethical model with the scientific method. How are the models similar? How are they different?

PHOTO: ASIAPIX/GETTY IMAGES

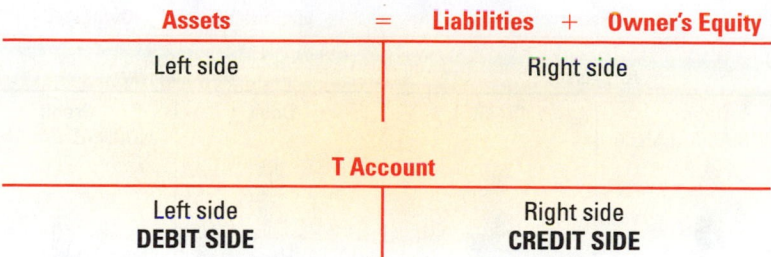

A record summarizing all the information pertaining to a single item in the accounting equation is known as an *account*. Transactions change the balances of accounts in the accounting equation. Accounting transactions must be analyzed to determine how account balances are changed. An accounting device used to analyze transactions is called a **T account**.

There are special names for amounts recorded on the left and right sides of a T account. An amount recorded on the left side is called a **debit**. An amount recorded on the right side is called a **credit**. The words debit and credit come from the Latin and Italian words *debere* and *credere*. Common abbreviations are *dr.* for debit and *cr.* for credit.

ACCOUNT BALANCES

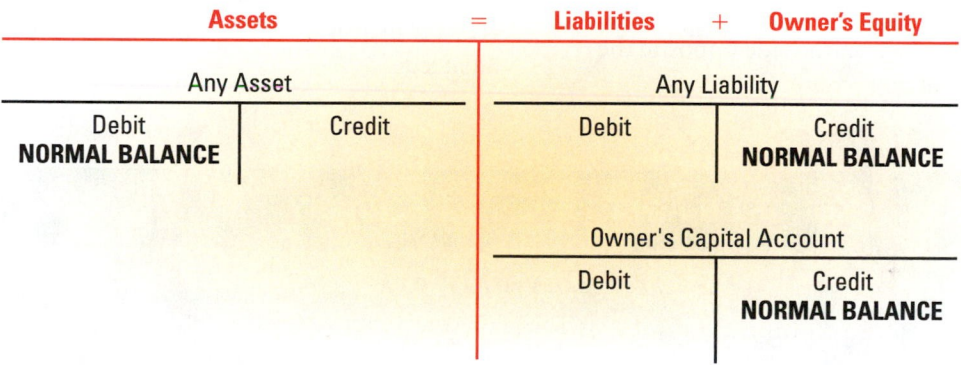

The side of the account that is increased is called the **normal balance**. The process of increasing or decreasing account balances is discussed on the next page. Assets are on the left side of the accounting equation and have normal debit balances (left side). Liabilities are on the right side of the accounting equation and have normal credit balances (right side). The owner's capital account is on the right side of the accounting equation and has a normal credit balance (right side).

Assets = Liabilities + Owner's Equity

Any Asset

Debit NORMAL BALANCE	Credit
Increase ↑	Decrease ↓

Any Liability

Debit	Credit NORMAL BALANCE
Decrease ↓	Increase ↑

Owner's Capital Account

Debit	Credit NORMAL BALANCE
Decrease ↓	Increase ↑

The sides of a T account are used to show increases and decreases in account balances.

Two basic accounting rules regulate increases and decreases of account balances.

1. Account balances increase on the normal balance side of an account.
2. Account balances decrease on the side opposite the normal balance side of an account.

Asset accounts have normal debit balances; therefore, asset accounts increase on the debit side and decrease on the credit side. Liability accounts have normal credit balances; therefore, liability accounts increase on the credit side and decrease on the debit side. The owner's capital account has a normal credit balance; therefore, the capital account increases on the credit side and decreases on the debit side.

FINANCIAL LITERACY

First Day at Work

It is your first day at a new job. You feel you are totally prepared. But when you arrive, you are directed to the Human Resources Department, where you are asked many questions for which you do not know the answer. Which health plan do you want? How many dependents will you claim? Do you want to participate in the 401(k) plan? Do you want to buy additional life and/or disability insurance? These are just a few of the questions you could be asked as you begin a new job.

Many companies offer some form of health insurance. You may need to decide your level of coverage and who is to be covered by the insurance. Life insurance and disability insurance are sometimes provided by an employer, but additional levels of coverage may be available for purchase. Your employer may match your contributions into

a retirement plan such as a 401(k), but you need to decide how much you can afford to contribute into the plan.

There may also be numerous forms to complete. For tax purposes, you need to know how many dependents you claim. You may need to fill out medical information, provide picture identification and a social security number, and compile a list of emergency contacts and phone numbers.

Activities

1. Set up an appointment with someone in the Human Resources Department at a local company. Ask what decisions must be made by a new employee. Summarize your findings in a written report.

2. Give a list of typical benefits to 10 people. Have each person identify the three benefits most important to him/her. Summarize your findings in a chart or table.

End of Lesson REVIEW

TERMS REVIEW

T account

debit

credit

normal balance

AUDIT YOUR UNDERSTANDING

1. Draw the accounting equation on a T account.
2. What are the two accounting rules that regulate increases and decreases of account balances?

WORK TOGETHER 2-1

Determining the normal balance and increase and decrease sides for accounts

Write the answers to the following problems in the *Working Papers*. Your instructor will guide you through the following examples.

Cash

Accounts Receivable—Christine Kelly

Supplies

Prepaid Insurance

Accounts Payable—Miller Supplies

Accounts Payable—Wayne Office Supplies

Jeff Dixon, Capital

For each of the accounts, complete the following:

1. Prepare a T account.
2. Label the debit and credit sides.
3. Label each side of the T account using the following labels:
   a. Normal Balance
   b. Increase
   c. Decrease

ON YOUR OWN 2-1

Determining the normal balance and increase and decrease sides for accounts

Write the answers to the following problems in the *Working Papers*. Work this problem independently.

Cash

Accounts Receivable—Lee McCann

Accounts Receivable—Sonya Lopez

Supplies

Prepaid Insurance

Accounts Payable—Topline Supplies

Vickie Monson, Capital

For each of the accounts, complete the following:

1. Prepare a T account.
2. Label the debit and credit sides.
3. Label each side of the T account using the following labels:
   a. Normal Balance
   b. Increase
   c. Decrease

RECEIVED CASH FROM OWNER AS AN INVESTMENT

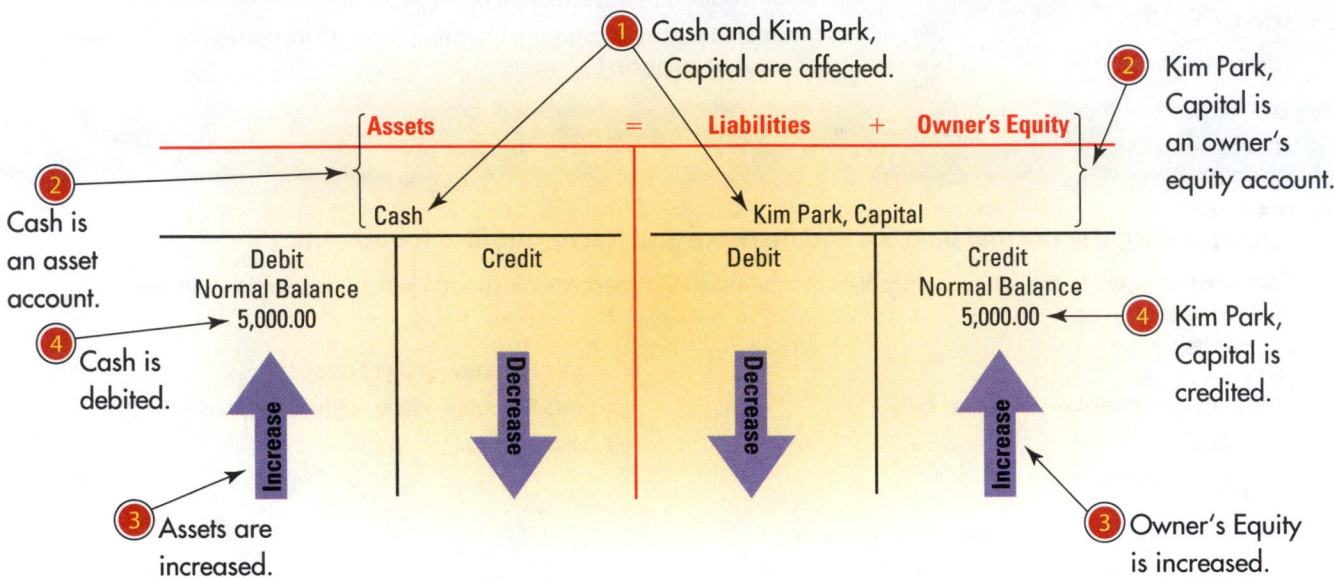

① Cash and Kim Park, Capital are affected.

② Kim Park, Capital is an owner's equity account.

② Cash is an asset account.

④ Cash is debited.

③ Assets are increased.

④ Kim Park, Capital is credited.

③ Owner's Equity is increased.

| Assets | = | Liabilities | + | Owner's Equity |

Cash

| Debit Normal Balance 5,000.00 | Credit |

Kim Park, Capital

| Debit | Credit Normal Balance 5,000.00 |

August 1. Received cash from owner as an investment, $5,000.00.

The effect of this transaction is shown in the illustration. Before a transaction is recorded in the records of a business, the information is analyzed to determine which accounts are changed and how. Each transaction changes the balances of at least two accounts. A list of accounts used by a business is called a **chart of accounts**. The chart of accounts for TechKnow Consulting is found on page 3.

When accounts are analyzed, debits must equal credits for each transaction. In addition, after a transaction is recorded, total debits must equal total credits.

The same four questions are used every time a transaction is analyzed into its debit and credit parts.

STEPS

QUESTIONS FOR ANALYZING A TRANSACTION INTO ITS DEBIT AND CREDIT PARTS

① Which accounts are affected?
Cash and *Kim Park, Capital*

② How is each account classified?
Cash is an asset account. *Kim Park, Capital* is an owner's equity account.

③ How is each classification changed?
Assets increase. Owner's equity increases.

④ How is each amount entered in the accounts?
Assets increase on the debit side. Therefore, debit the asset account, *Cash*. Owner's equity accounts increase on the credit side. Therefore, credit the owner's equity account, *Kim Park, Capital*.

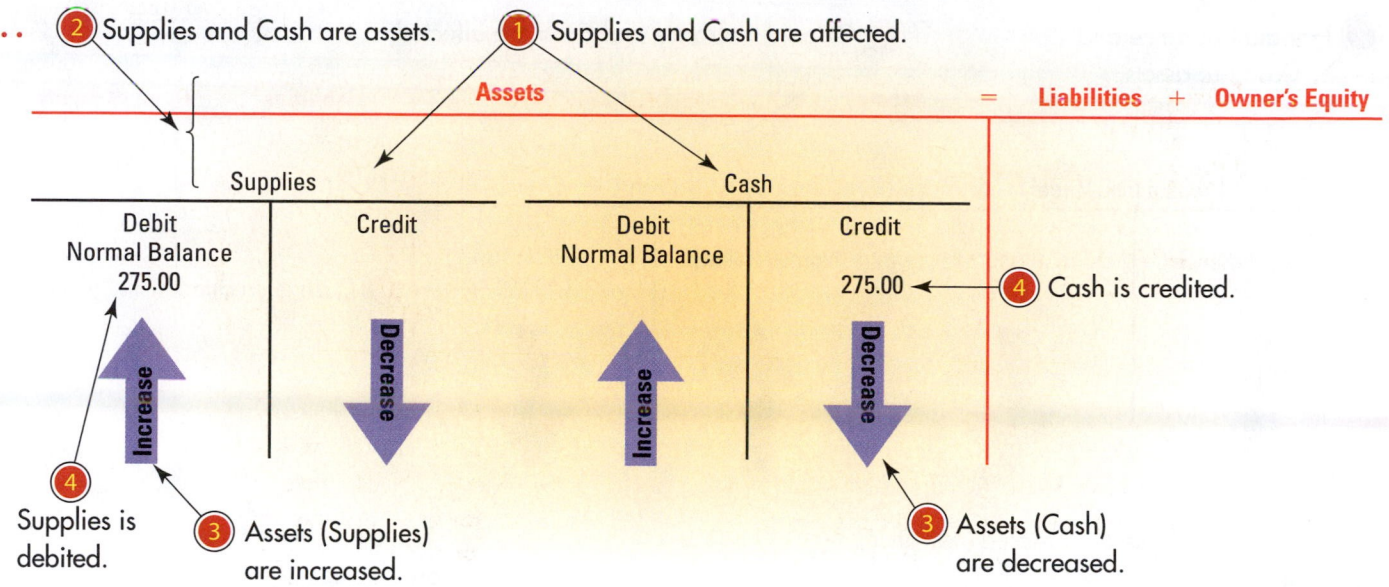

② Supplies and Cash are assets.   ① Supplies and Cash are affected.

Assets = **Liabilities** + **Owner's Equity**

Supplies | Cash

Debit Normal Balance 275.00 | Credit *(Decrease)* | Debit Normal Balance | Credit *(Decrease)* 275.00 ← ④ Cash is credited.

Increase

④ Supplies is debited.   ③ Assets (Supplies) are increased.   ③ Assets (Cash) are decreased.

August 3. Paid cash for supplies, $275.00.

The effect of this transaction on the accounting equation is shown in the illustration. In this transaction, two asset accounts are changed. One asset, cash, has been exchanged for another asset, supplies. The asset account, Cash, decreases by $275.00, the amount of cash paid out. This decrease is on the left side of the accounting equation. The asset account, Supplies, increases by $275.00, the amount of supplies bought. This increase is also on the left side of the accounting equation.

The two changes are both on the left side of the accounting equation. When changes are made on only one side of the accounting equation, the equation must still be in balance. Therefore, if one account is increased, another account on the same side of the equation must be decreased.

As you have seen, transactions must be carefully analyzed. A transaction may affect accounts from both sides of the accounting equation. Or, a transaction may affect accounts that are on the same side of the accounting equation, as is true in this example. A common error is to assume that every transaction must affect accounts on both sides of the accounting equation.

STEPS   QUESTIONS FOR ANALYZING A TRANSACTION INTO ITS DEBIT AND CREDIT PARTS

① Which accounts are affected?
Supplies and *Cash*

② How is each account classified?
Supplies is an asset account. *Cash* is an asset account.

③ How is each classification changed?
One asset (*Supplies*) increases and another asset (*Cash*) decreases.

④ How is each amount entered in the accounts?
Assets increase on the debit side. Therefore, debit the asset account, *Supplies*. Assets decrease on the credit side. Therefore, credit the asset account, *Cash*.

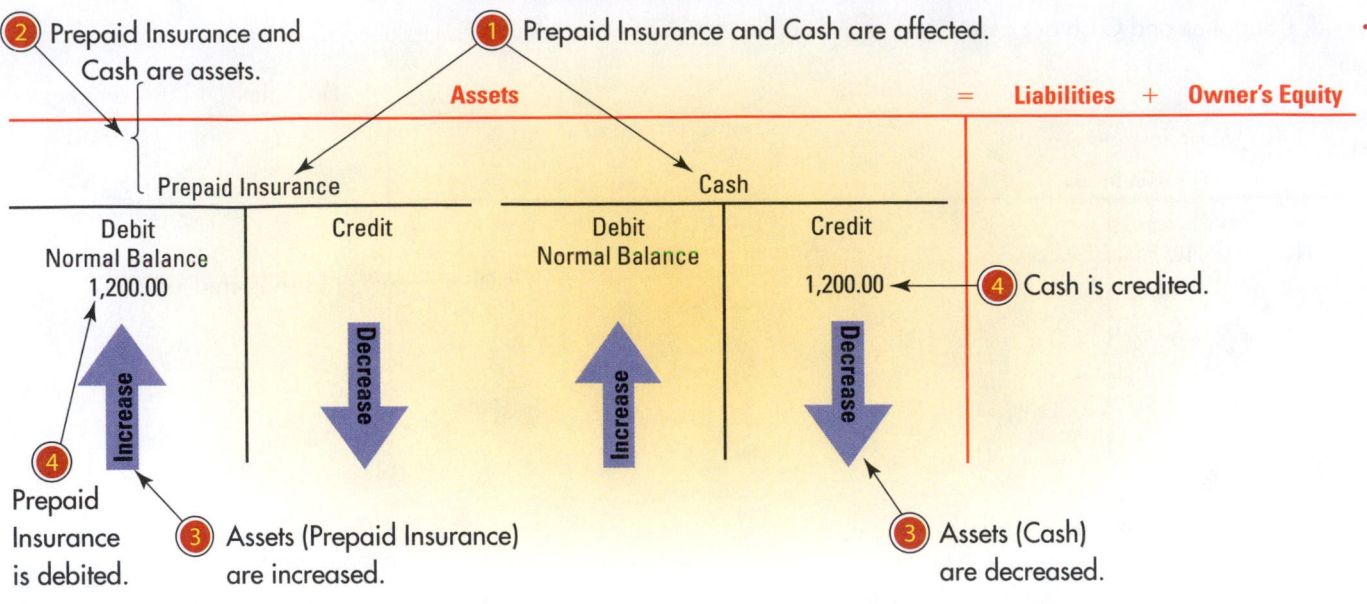

② Prepaid Insurance and Cash are assets.

① Prepaid Insurance and Cash are affected.

Assets = **Liabilities** + **Owner's Equity**

Prepaid Insurance

| Debit Normal Balance 1,200.00 | Credit |

Cash

| Debit Normal Balance | Credit 1,200.00 |

④ Cash is credited.

④ Prepaid Insurance is debited.

Increase

Decrease

Increase

Decrease

③ Assets (Prepaid Insurance) are increased.

③ Assets (Cash) are decreased.

August 4. Paid cash for insurance, $1,200.00.

Paying cash for insurance is very similar to paying cash for supplies. One asset is increased and one asset is decreased.

The effect of this transaction on the accounting equation is shown in the illustration. In this transaction, two assets are changed. One asset, cash, has been exchanged for another asset, prepaid insurance. The asset account, Cash, decreases by $1,200.00, the amount of cash paid out. This decrease is on the left side of the accounting equation. The asset account, *Prepaid Insurance*, increases by $1,200.00, the amount of insurance bought. This increase is also on the left side of the accounting equation.

FOR YOUR INFORMATION

F Y I

T accounts get their name from the arrangement of the lines making up the account. The horizontal line on top of the centered vertical line looks like a capital "T."

FOR YOUR INFORMATION

F Y I

Paying cash for insurance and buying supplies for cash are examples of transactions that affect only one side of the accounting equation. All the accounts involved in these transactions are assets.

STEPS **QUESTIONS FOR ANALYZING A TRANSACTION INTO ITS DEBIT AND CREDIT PARTS**

① Which accounts are affected?
Prepaid Insurance and *Cash*

② How is each account classified?
Prepaid Insurance is an asset account. *Cash* is an asset account.

③ How is each classification changed?
One asset (*Prepaid Insurance*) increases and another asset (*Cash*) decreases.

④ How is each amount entered in the accounts?
Assets increase on the debit side. Therefore, debit the asset account, *Prepaid Insurance*.
Assets decrease on the credit side. Therefore, credit the asset account, *Cash*.

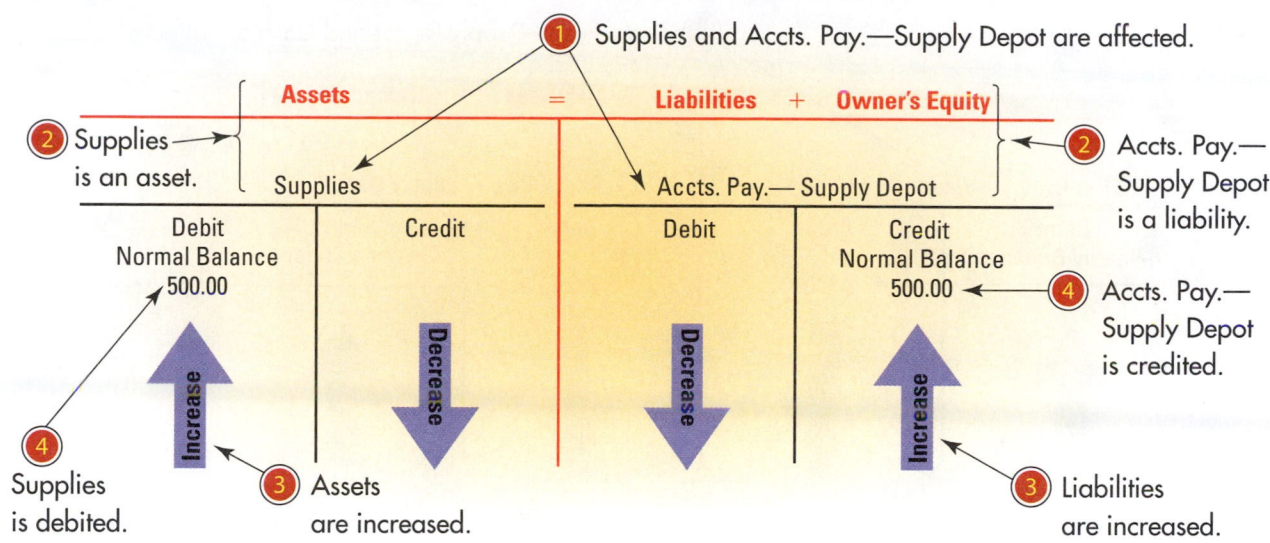

① Supplies and Accts. Pay.—Supply Depot are affected.

② Supplies is an asset.

② Accts. Pay.— Supply Depot is a liability.

Assets = **Liabilities** + **Owner's Equity**

Supplies | Accts. Pay.— Supply Depot

Debit Normal Balance 500.00 | Credit | Debit | Credit Normal Balance 500.00

④ Accts. Pay.— Supply Depot is credited.

④ Supplies is debited.

③ Assets are increased.

③ Liabilities are increased.

August 7. Bought supplies on account from Supply Depot, $500.00.

The effect of this transaction on the accounting equation is shown in the illustration. In this transaction, one asset and one liability are changed. The asset account, Supplies, increases by $500.00, the amount of supplies bought. This increase is on the left side of the accounting equation. Supply Depot will have a claim against some of TechKnow Consulting's assets until TechKnow Consulting pays for the supplies bought. Therefore, Accounts Payable—Supply Depot is a liability account. The liability account, Accounts Payable—Supply Depot, increases by $500.00, the amount owed for the supplies. This increase is on the right side of the accounting equation.

S T E P S QUESTIONS FOR ANALYZING A TRANSACTION INTO ITS DEBIT AND CREDIT PARTS

PHOTODISC/GETTY IMAGES

① Which accounts are affected?
Supplies and *Accounts Payable—Supply Depot*

② How is each account classified?
Supplies is an asset account. *Accounts Payable—Supply Depot* is a liability account.

③ How is each classification changed?
Assets increase. Liabilities increase.

④ How is each amount entered in the accounts?
Assets increase on the debit side. Therefore, debit the asset account, *Supplies*. Liabilities increase on the credit side. Therefore, credit the liability account, *Accounts Payable—Supply Depot*.

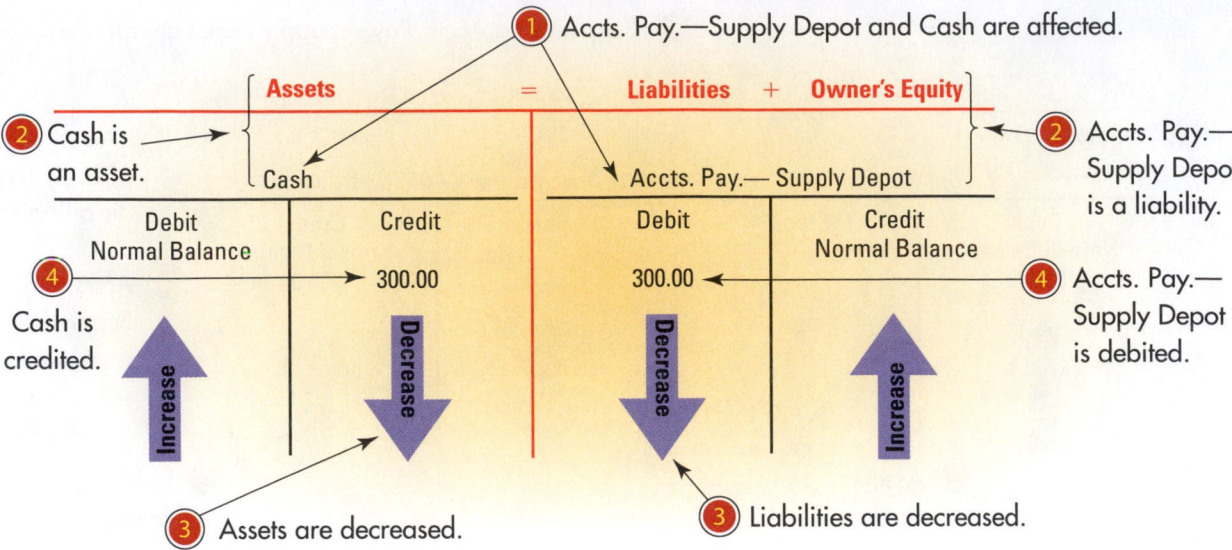

① Accts. Pay.—Supply Depot and Cash are affected.

② Cash is an asset.

② Accts. Pay.—Supply Depot is a liability.

④ Cash is credited.

④ Accts. Pay.—Supply Depot is debited.

③ Assets are decreased.

③ Liabilities are decreased.

August 11. Paid cash on account to Supply Depot, $300.00.

The effect of this transaction on the accounting equation is shown in the illustration. In this transaction, one asset and one liability are changed. The asset account, Cash, is decreased by $300.00, the amount of cash paid out. This decrease is on the left side of the accounting equation. After this payment, TechKnow Consulting owes less money to Supply Depot. Therefore, the liability account, Accounts Payable—Supply Depot, is decreased by $300.00, the amount paid on account. The decrease is on the right side of the accounting equation.

STEPS

QUESTIONS FOR ANALYZING A TRANSACTION INTO ITS DEBIT AND CREDIT PARTS

① Which accounts are affected?
Accounts Payable—Supply Depot and *Cash*

② How is each account classified?
Accounts Payable—Supply Depot is a liability account. *Cash* is an asset account.

③ How is each classification changed?
Liabilities decrease. Assets decrease.

④ How is each amount entered in the accounts?
Liabilities decrease on the debit side. Therefore, debit the liability account, *Accounts Payable—Supply Depot*. Assets decrease on the credit side. Therefore, credit the asset account, *Cash*.

REMEMBER

When you decrease an account balance, record the decrease on the side opposite the normal balance side of the account. The side opposite the normal balance side can be on the left or the right, depending on the type of account.

TERM REVIEW

chart of accounts

AUDIT YOUR UNDERSTANDING

1. State the four questions used to analyze a transaction.
2. What two accounts are affected when a business pays cash for supplies?

WORK TOGETHER 2-2

Analyzing transactions into debit and credit parts

T accounts are given in the *Working Papers*. Your instructor will guide you through the following examples. Kathy Bergum owns Bergum Services. Bergum Services uses the following accounts. Some of the accounts will be explained in Lesson 2-3.

Cash	Accts. Pay.—Bales Supplies	Sales
Accts. Rec.—Sam Erickson	Kathy Bergum, Capital	Advertising Expense
Supplies	Kathy Bergum, Drawing	Rent Expense
Prepaid Insurance		

Transactions:

Apr. 1. Received cash from owner as an investment, $5,000.00.
    2. Paid cash for supplies, $50.00.
    5. Paid cash for insurance, $75.00.
    6. Bought supplies on account from Bales Supplies, $100.00.
    9. Paid cash on account to Bales Supplies, $50.00.

1. Prepare two T accounts for each transaction. On each T account, write the account title of one of the accounts affected by the transaction.

2. Write the debit or credit amount in each T account to show the transaction's effect.

ON YOUR OWN 2-2

Analyzing transactions into debit and credit parts

T accounts are given in the *Working Papers*. Work this problem independently. Derrick Hoffman owns Hoffman Accounting Service. Hoffman Accounting Service uses the following accounts. Some of the accounts will be explained in Lesson 2-3.

Cash	Accts. Pay.—Nash Supply	Sales
Accts. Rec.—Jon Roe	Derrick Hoffman, Capital	Miscellaneous Expense
Supplies	Derrick Hoffman, Drawing	Utilities Expense
Prepaid Insurance		

Transactions:

Sept. 1. Received cash from owner as an investment, $2,000.00.
    4. Paid cash for insurance, $300.00.
    5. Paid cash for supplies, $100.00.
    6. Bought supplies on account from Nash Supply, $230.00.
    11. Paid cash on account to Nash Supply, $115.00.

1. Prepare two T accounts for each transaction. On each T account, write the account title of one of the accounts affected by the transaction.

2. Write the debit or credit amount in each T account to show the transaction's effect.

RECEIVED CASH FROM SALES

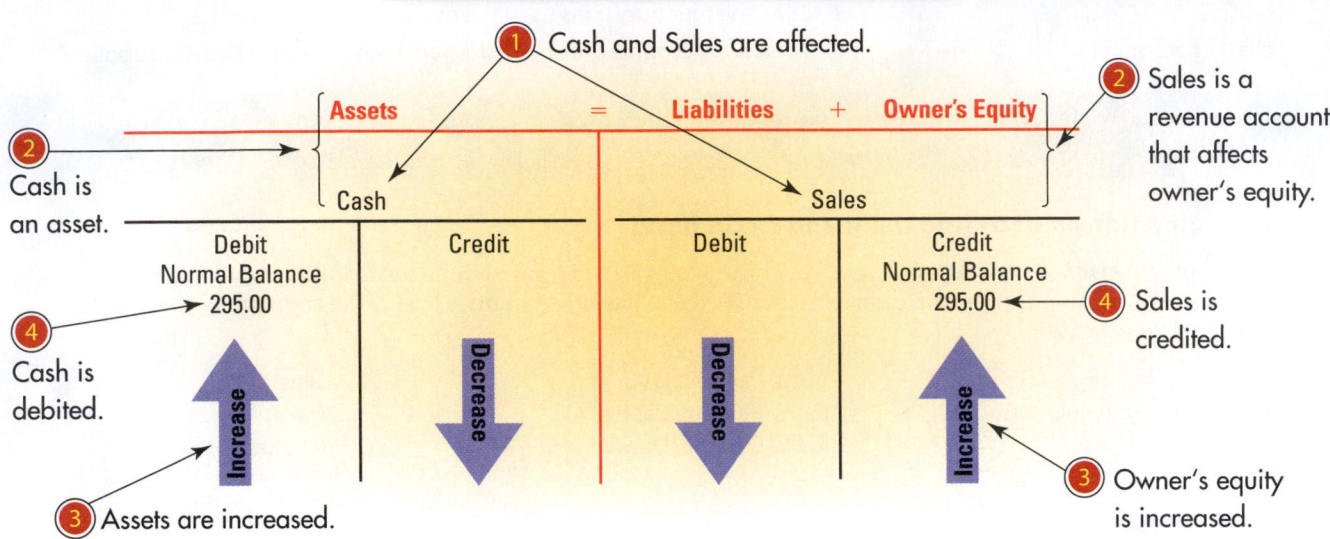

① Cash and Sales are affected.

② Sales is a revenue account that affects owner's equity.

② Cash is an asset.

④ Cash is debited.

③ Assets are increased.

④ Sales is credited.

③ Owner's equity is increased.

Assets = Liabilities + Owner's Equity

Cash — Debit Normal Balance 295.00 — Credit — Decrease

Sales — Debit — Decrease — Credit Normal Balance 295.00

August 12. Received cash from sales, $295.00.

Revenue increases owner's equity. The increases from revenue could be recorded directly in the owner's capital account. However, to avoid a capital account with a large number of entries and to summarize revenue information separately from the other records, TechKnow Consulting uses a separate revenue account titled Sales.

The owner's capital account has a normal credit balance. Increases in the owner's capital account are shown as credits. Because revenue increases owner's equity, increases in revenue are also recorded as credits. Therefore, a revenue account has a normal credit balance.

STEPS   QUESTIONS FOR ANALYZING A TRANSACTION INTO ITS DEBIT AND CREDIT PARTS

① Which accounts are affected?
Cash and *Sales*

② How is each account classified?
Cash is an asset account. *Sales* is a revenue account that affects owner's equity.

③ How is each classification changed?
Assets increase. Owner's equity increases.

④ How is each amount entered in the accounts?
Assets increase on the debit side. Therefore, debit the asset account, *Cash*. Owner's equity accounts increase on the credit side. Revenue increases owner's equity. Therefore, credit the revenue account, *Sales*.

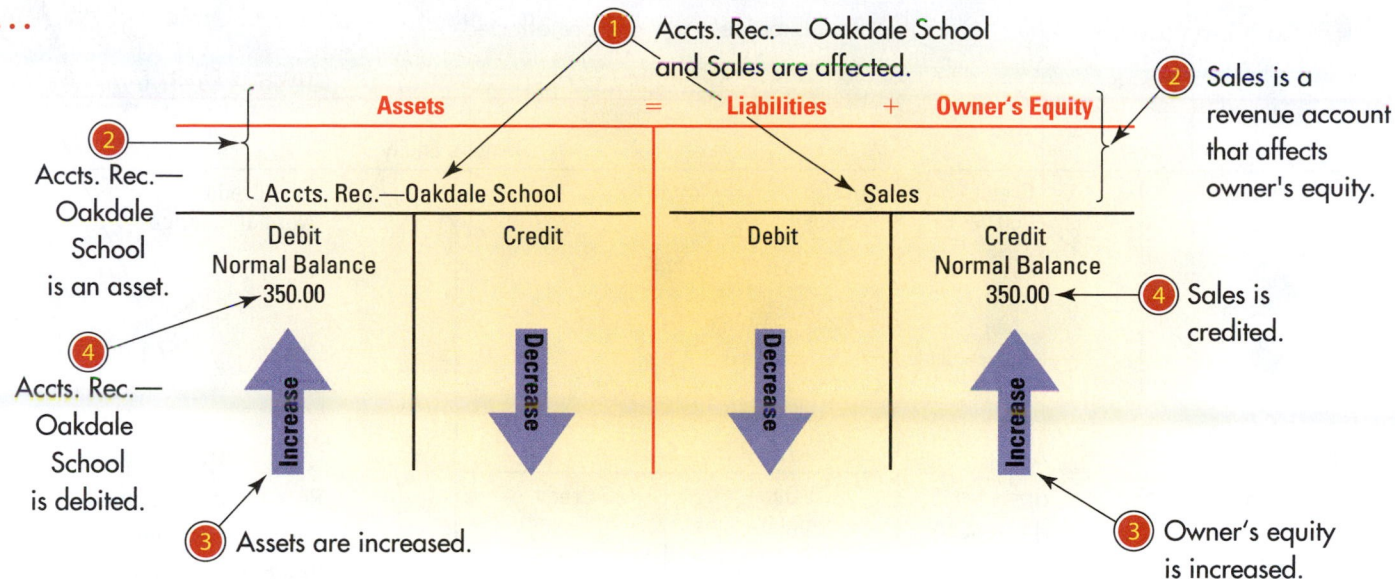

Accts. Rec.—Oakdale School is an asset.

Accts. Rec.—Oakdale School is debited.

Assets are increased.

Accts. Rec.— Oakdale School and Sales are affected.

Sales is a revenue account that affects owner's equity.

Sales is credited.

Owner's equity is increased.

August 12. Sold services on account to Oakdale School, $350.00.

The analysis for selling services on account is similar to that for selling services for cash. The only difference is

that cash is not received at this time; therefore, the cash account is not affected by the transaction. Instead, this transaction increases an accounts receivable account. The same four questions are used to analyze this transaction into its debit and credit parts.

STEPS — QUESTIONS FOR ANALYZING A TRANSACTION INTO ITS DEBIT AND CREDIT PARTS

1. Which accounts are affected?
   Accounts Receivable—Oakdale School and *Sales*

2. How is each account classified?
   Accounts Receivable—Oakdale School is an asset account. *Sales* is a revenue account that affects owner's equity.

3. How is each classification changed?
   Assets increase. Owner's equity increases.

4. How is each amount entered in the accounts?
   Assets increase on the debit side. Therefore, debit the asset account, *Accounts Receivable—Oakdale School*. Owner's equity accounts increase on the credit side. Revenue increases owner's equity. Therefore, credit the revenue account, *Sales*.

REMEMBER

Owner's equity is recorded on the right side of the accounting equation. The right side of a T account is the credit side. Therefore, owner's equity has a normal credit balance.

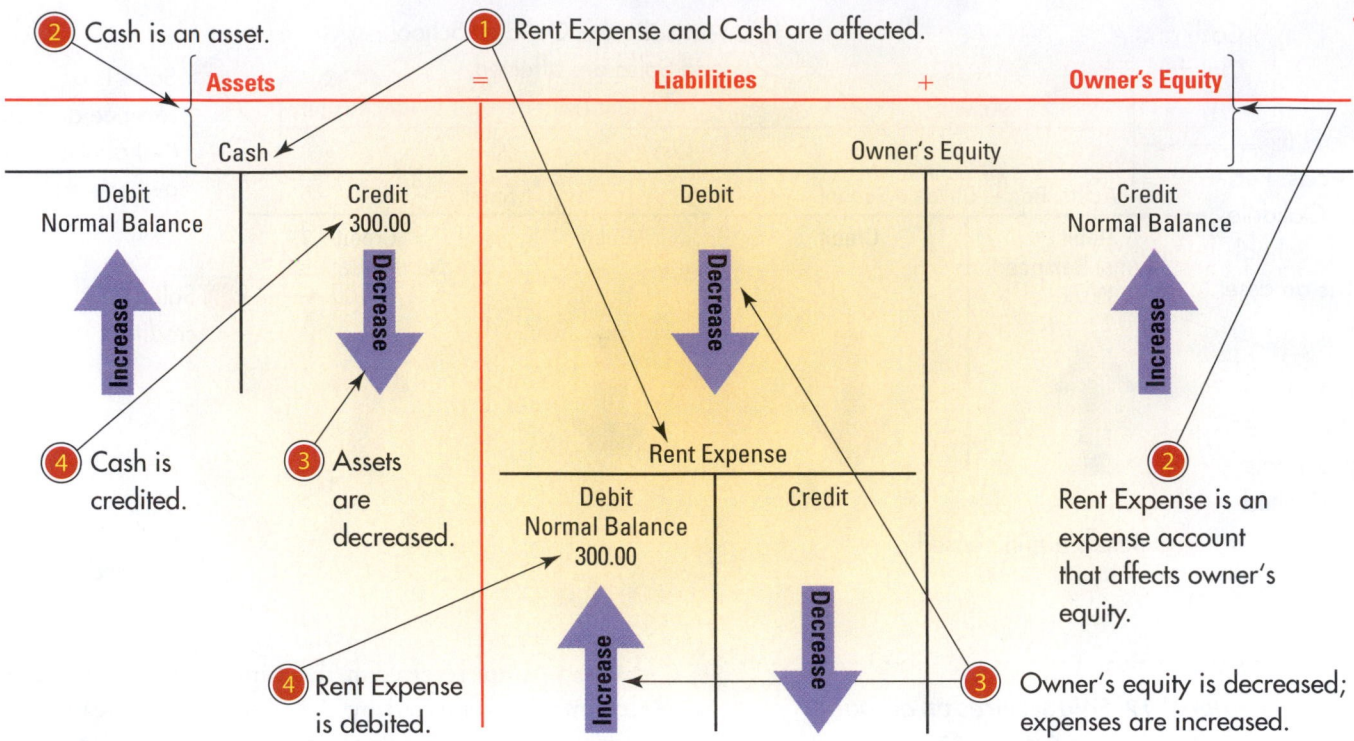

② Cash is an asset.

① Rent Expense and Cash are affected.

| Assets | = | Liabilities | + | Owner's Equity |

④ Cash is credited.

③ Assets are decreased.

④ Rent Expense is debited.

② Rent Expense is an expense account that affects owner's equity.

③ Owner's equity is decreased; expenses are increased.

August 12. Paid cash for rent, $300.00.

Expenses decrease owner's equity. The decreases from expenses could be recorded directly in the owner's capital account. However, to avoid a capital account with a large number of entries and to summarize expense information separately from the other records, TechKnow Consulting uses separate expense accounts.

The titles of TechKnow Consulting's expense accounts are shown on its chart of accounts. The expense account Rent Expense is used to record all payments for rent.

The owner's capital account has a normal credit balance. Decreases in the owner's capital account are shown as debits. Therefore, an expense account has a normal debit balance. Because expenses decrease owner's equity, increases in expenses are recorded as debits.

All expense transactions are recorded in a similar manner.

STEPS  QUESTIONS FOR ANALYZING A TRANSACTION INTO ITS DEBIT AND CREDIT PARTS

① Which accounts are affected?
Rent Expense and *Cash*

② How is each account classified?
Rent Expense is an expense account that affects owner's equity. *Cash* is an asset account.

③ How is each classification changed?
Owner's equity decreases from an increase in expenses. Assets decrease.

④ How is each amount entered in the accounts?
Owner's equity accounts decrease on the debit side. An increase in expenses decreases owner's equity. Expense accounts have normal debit balances. Therefore, debit the expense account, *Rent Expense*. Assets decrease on the credit side. Therefore, credit the asset account, *Cash*.

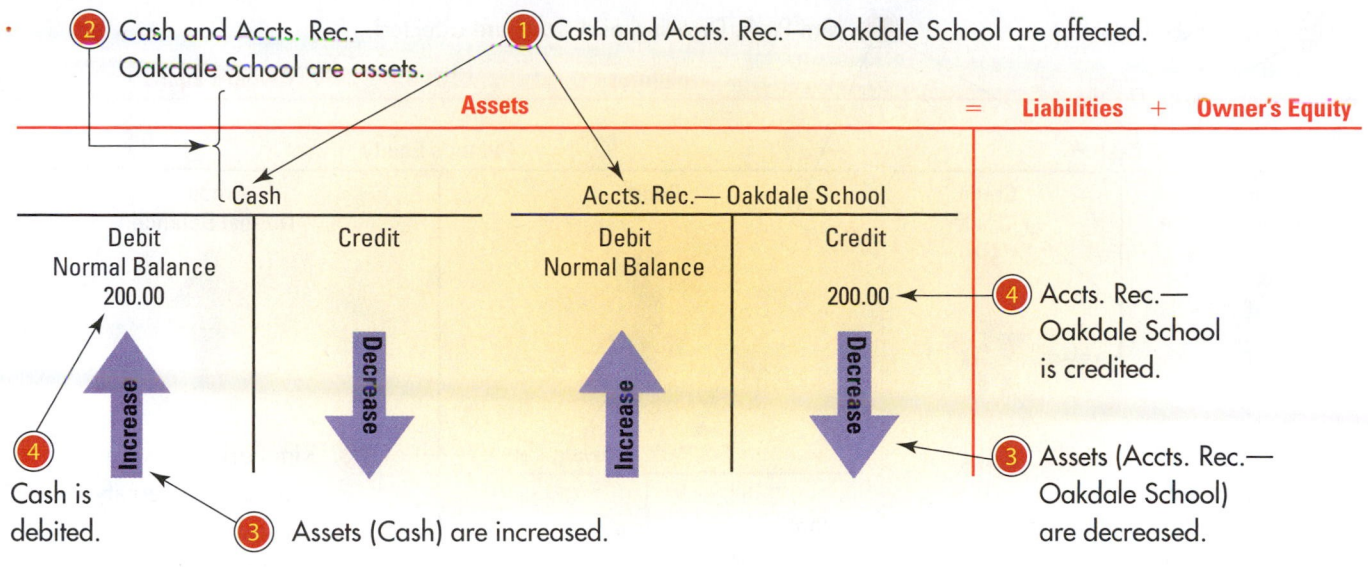

② Cash and Accts. Rec.— Oakdale School are assets.

① Cash and Accts. Rec.— Oakdale School are affected.

Assets = **Liabilities** + **Owner's Equity**

Cash   Accts. Rec.— Oakdale School

| Debit Normal Balance 200.00 | Credit | Debit Normal Balance | Credit 200.00 |

Increase / *Decrease* / *Increase* / *Decrease*

④ Cash is debited.

③ Assets (Cash) are increased.

④ Accts. Rec.— Oakdale School is credited.

③ Assets (Accts. Rec.— Oakdale School) are decreased.

August 18. Received cash on account from Oakdale School, $200.00.

STEPS — QUESTIONS FOR ANALYZING A TRANSACTION INTO ITS DEBIT AND CREDIT PARTS

① Which accounts are affected?
Cash and *Accounts Receivable—Oakdale School*

② How is each account classified?
Cash is an asset account. *Accounts Receivable—Oakdale School* is an asset account.

③ How is each classification changed?
One asset (*Cash*) increases and another asset (*Accounts Receivable—Oakdale School*) decreases.

④ How is each amount entered in the accounts?
Assets increase on the debit side. Therefore, debit the asset account, *Cash*. Assets decrease on the credit side. Therefore, credit the asset account, *Accounts Receivable—Oakdale School*.

PHOTODISC/GETTY IMAGES

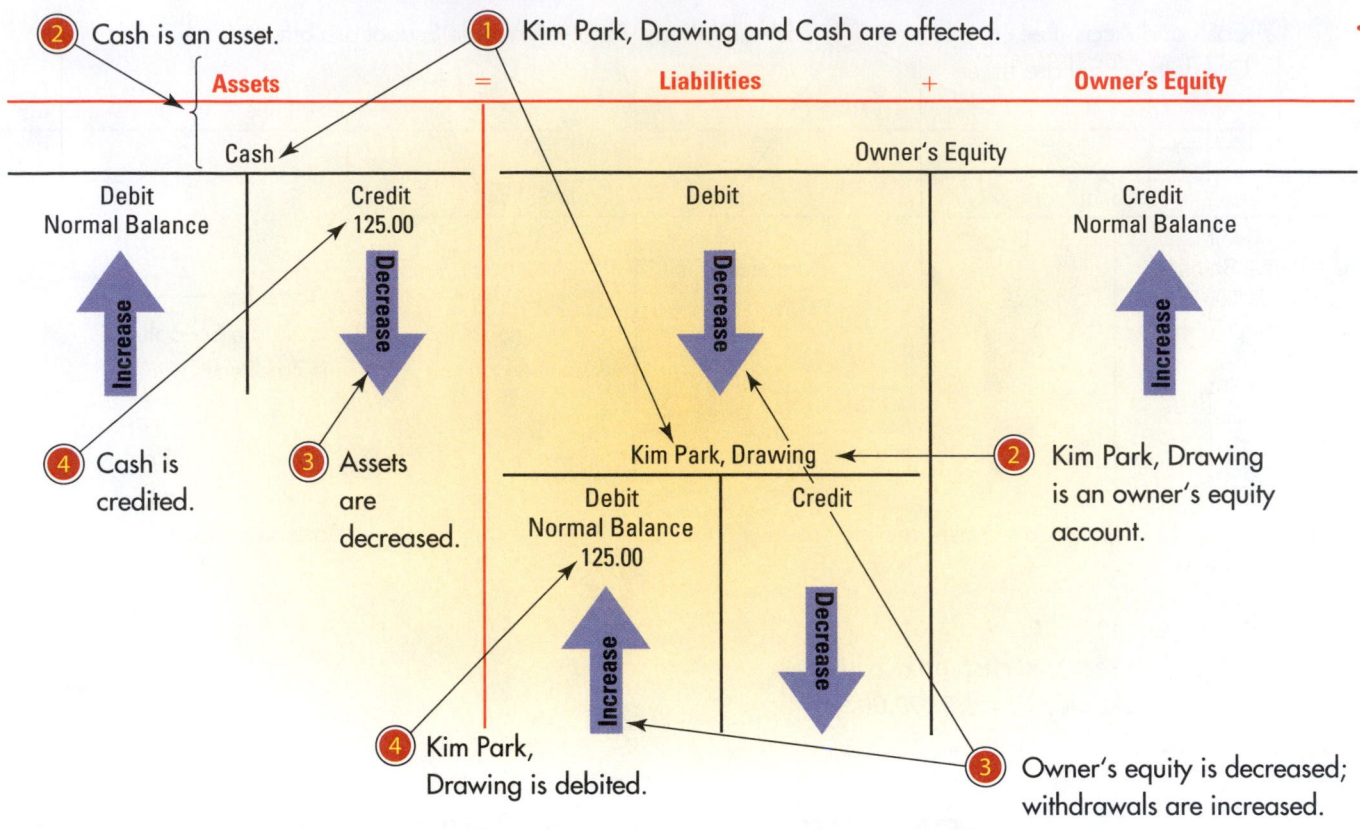

② Cash is an asset.

① Kim Park, Drawing and Cash are affected.

Assets	=	Liabilities	+	Owner's Equity

Cash

Debit Normal Balance	Credit 125.00

Increase ↑   *Decrease* ↓

④ Cash is credited.

③ Assets are decreased.

Owner's Equity

Debit	Credit Normal Balance

Decrease ↓   *Increase* ↑

Kim Park, Drawing

Debit Normal Balance 125.00	Credit

Increase ↑   *Decrease* ↓

② Kim Park, Drawing is an owner's equity account.

④ Kim Park, Drawing is debited.

③ Owner's equity is decreased; withdrawals are increased.

August 18. Paid cash to owner for personal use, $125.00.

Withdrawals decrease owner's equity. Withdrawals could be recorded directly in the owner's capital account. However, to avoid a capital account with a large number of entries and to summarize withdrawal information separately from the other records, TechKnow Consulting uses a separate withdrawal account titled Kim Park, Drawing.

FOR YOUR INFORMATION

FYI

When drawing T accounts to analyze transactions, stack the accounts instead of writing them horizontally. Stacking the accounts will make it easier to recognize debits and credits.

STEPS **QUESTIONS FOR ANALYZING A TRANSACTION INTO ITS DEBIT AND CREDIT PARTS**

① Which accounts are affected?
Kim Park, Drawing and *Cash*

② How is each account classified?
Kim Park, Drawing is an owner's equity account. *Cash* is an asset account.

③ How is each classification changed?
Owner's equity decreases from an increase in withdrawals. Assets decrease.

④ How is each amount entered in the accounts?
Owner's equity accounts decrease on the debit side. An increase in withdrawals decreases owner's equity. Withdrawal accounts have normal debit balances. Therefore, debit the owner's equity account, *Kim Park, Drawing*. Assets decrease on the credit side. Therefore, credit the asset account, *Cash*.

Business, Management & Administration

Rita J. Cowans, Internal Auditor

COURTESY OF RITA J. COWANS

As a highly respected employee at FedEx Corporation, Rita J. Cowans is a Manager in the Internal Audit Department. During her tenure at FedEx, Rita has held various positions in financial, operational, international, and information systems audit. Presently she is responsible for the financial, information systems, and international audit activities for FedEx Worldwide operations.

Her audit team conducts business process reviews, integrated financial and information system reviews, international entity reviews, fraud examinations, and vendor audits. Rita has been a leader in developing and promoting best practices as an integral part of the Internal Audit Department. "It's my responsibility to ensure that the employees and management of FedEx are effectively safeguarding the assets of the corporation, complying with all laws and regulations, and accomplishing the corporate strategic objectives as established by senior management."

While in high school, Rita developed a love for mathematics and accounting. "I became a very critical and detail-oriented thinker and excelled at analyzing information and solving problems." With her parents' direction and strong support, she continued her education and graduated with a bachelor's degree in accounting. In addition, she successfully earned her Certified Internal Auditor (CIA) and Certified Information Systems Auditor (CISA) professional designations. "Being certified in the area of accounting in which you work is critical to your professional success. Certifications demonstrate that you are committed to your profession and communicate to others that you are an expert in your field."

Certifications also enable you to become active in organizations that provide educational opportunities for their members. Rita is a member of the Institute of Internal Auditors and Information Systems Audit and Control Association.

As a member of the FedEx Services Diversity Council, Rita works to ensure that individuals from every background have the opportunity to excel at FedEx. Ultimately, "having a passion for what you do and setting high standards will determine your level of success."

Salary Range: $30,000–$130,000 and up. Can lead to high-level careers at public accounting firms, private and public corporations, and government agencies, such as the Internal Revenue Service (IRS Auditor).

Qualifications: Bachelor's degree in accounting, finance, and information systems for entry-level position, plus normally five years of auditing experience for senior level or above. Professional Certifications preferred (CPA, CIA, CISA, CFE, etc). Familiarity with business, information technology, and legal concepts and procedures is beneficial.

Occupational Outlook: The Sarbanes-Oxley Act of 2002 requires public corporations to expand the documentation and testing of their accounting systems. Internal auditors are an integral part of corporations' compliance with this law. As a result, the demand for internal auditors will be strong for years to come.

End of Lesson REVIEW

1. What two accounts are affected when a business receives cash from sales?
2. What two accounts are affected when services are sold on account?
3. What two accounts are affected when a business pays cash to the owner for personal use?
4. Are revenue accounts increased on the debit side or credit side? Explain why.
5. Are expense accounts increased on the debit side or credit side? Explain why.

WORK TOGETHER 2-3

Analyzing revenue, expense, and withdrawal transactions into debit and credit parts

T accounts are given in the *Working Papers*. Your instructor will guide you through the following examples.

Use the chart of accounts for Bergum Services in Work Together 2-2.

Transactions:

Apr. 10. Received cash from sales, $600.00.
    11. Sold services on account to Sam Erickson, $850.00.
    14. Paid cash for rent, $250.00.
    18. Received cash on account from Sam Erickson, $425.00.
    20. Paid cash to owner for personal use, $300.00.

1. Prepare two T accounts for each transaction. In each T account, write the account title of one of the accounts affected by the transaction.
2. Write the debit or credit amount in each T account to show the transaction's effect.

ON YOUR OWN 2-3

Analyzing revenue, expense, and withdrawal transactions into debit and credit parts

T accounts are given in the *Working Papers*. Work this problem independently.

Use the chart of accounts for Hoffman Accounting Service in On Your Own 2-2.

Transactions:

Sept. 13. Received cash from sales, $1,500.00.
    15. Sold services on account to Jon Roe, $500.00.
    16. Paid cash for utilities, $450.00.
    18. Received cash on account from Jon Roe, $250.00.
    21. Paid cash to owner for personal use, $700.00.

1. Prepare two T accounts for each transaction. On each T account, write the account title of one of the accounts affected by the transaction.
2. Write the debit or credit amount in each T account to show the transaction's effect.

After completing this chapter, you can:

1. Define accounting terms related to analyzing transactions into debit and credit parts.

2. Identify accounting practices related to analyzing transactions into debit and credit parts.

3. Use T accounts to analyze transactions, showing which accounts are debited or credited for each transaction.

4. Analyze how transactions to set up a business affect accounts.

5. Analyze how transactions affect owner's equity accounts.

EXPLORE ACCOUNTING

Owner Withdrawals

Employee salaries are considered an expense that reduces the net income of a company. When the owner withdraws cash from the company, this withdrawal is not considered an expense. The income of a business is calculated by subtracting total expenses from total revenue. Since withdrawals are not considered to be an expense, they do not affect the business's income.

A business owned by one person is called a proprietorship. The Internal Revenue Service does not require the proprietorship, itself, to pay taxes. However, the owner of the proprietorship must include the net income of the proprietorship in his or her own taxable income.

Because the income of a proprietorship is not affected by owner withdrawals, the income tax paid by the owner is not affected by how much cash the owner withdraws from the business. If Wang Accounting Services has revenues

of $2,500.00 and expenses of $1,100.00, its income is $1,400.00 ($2,500.00 − $1,100.00). Wang Accounting Services will have income of $1,400.00 regardless of whether the owner withdraws $100.00 or $1,000.00 from the business during that period.

Discussion

1. Hector Moya owns ESW Party Service. He is considering giving his employees a raise that would increase total salaries by $15,000.00 per year. What effect would this raise have on Mr. Moya's income tax?

2. Mr. Moya is also considering withdrawing $5,000.00 from ESW Party Service for his personal use. What effect would this withdrawal have on the income tax Mr. Moya must pay this year?

PHOTO: PHOTOGRAPHER'S CHOICE/GETTY IMAGES

2-1 APPLICATION PROBLEM

Determining the normal balance and increase and decrease sides for accounts

Write the answers for the following problem in the *Working Papers*.

Cash

Accounts Receivable—Jens Olefson

Accounts Receivable—Toni Nolan

Supplies

Prepaid Insurance

Accounts Payable—United Company

Juan Reo, Capital

1	2	3	4	5	6	7	8
Account	Account Classification	Account's Normal Balance		Increase Side		Decrease Side	
		Debit	Credit	Debit	Credit	Debit	Credit
Cash	Asset	✓		✓			✓

Instructions:

Do the following for each account. The cash account is given as an example.

1. Write the account title in Column 1.
2. Write the account classification in Column 2.
3. Place a check mark in either Column 3 or 4 to indicate the normal balance of the account.
4. Place a check mark in either Column 5 or 6 to indicate the increase side of the account.
5. Place a check mark in either Column 7 or 8 to indicate the decrease side of the account.

2-2 APPLICATION PROBLEM

Analyzing transactions into debit and credit parts

Hal Rosen owns Hal's Marketing Services, which uses the following accounts.

Cash

Supplies

Prepaid Insurance

Accounts Receivable—Dominik Field

Accounts Payable—All Star Company

Hal Rosen, Capital

Hal Rosen, Drawing

Sales

Advertising Expense

Rent Expense

Transactions:

Mar. 1. Received cash from owner as an investment, $1,000.00.

   1. Paid cash for insurance, $400.00.

   3. Bought supplies on account from All Star Company, $600.00.

   5. Paid cash for supplies, $100.00.

   8. Paid cash on account to All Star Company, $400.00.

Go Beyond the Book
For more information go to
www.C21accounting.com

Instructions:

1. Prepare two T accounts for each transaction. On each T account, write the account title of one of the accounts affected by the transaction. Use the forms in your *Working Papers*.

2. Write the debit or credit amount in each T account to show how the transaction affected that account. T accounts for the first transaction are given as an example.

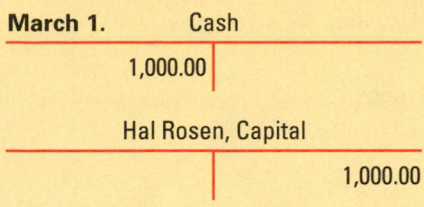

March 1.

Cash

1,000.00

Hal Rosen, Capital

1,000.00

2-3 | APPLICATION PROBLEM

Analyzing revenue, expense, and withdrawal transactions into debit and credit parts

Use the chart of accounts for Hal's Marketing Services given in Application Problem 2-2.

Transactions:

Mar. 11. Received cash from sales, $2,200.00.
12. Paid cash for advertising, $150.00.
14. Sold services on account to Dominik Field, $1,700.00.
18. Paid cash to owner for personal use, $500.00.
19. Received cash on account from Dominik Field, $1,000.00.

Instructions:

1. Prepare two T accounts for each transaction. On each T account, write the account title of one of the accounts affected by the transaction. Use the forms in your *Working Papers*.

2. Write the debit or credit amount in each T account to show how the transaction affected that account.

2-4 | APPLICATION PROBLEM

Analyzing revenue, expense, and withdrawal transactions into debit and credit parts

Use the chart of accounts for Hal's Marketing Services given in Application Problem 2-2.

Transactions:

Mar. 25. Sold services for cash, $1,100.00.
26. Performed $500.00 of services for Dominik Field on account.
27. Ran an ad in the local newspaper. Paid $125.00 cash.
28. Hal Rosen withdrew $450.00 for his personal use.
29. Received a $250.00 check from Dominik Field on account.

Instructions:

1. Prepare two T accounts for each transaction. On each T account, write the account title of one of the accounts affected by the transaction. Use the forms in your *Working Papers*.

2. Write the debit or credit amount in each T account to show how the transaction affected that account.

MASTERY PROBLEM

Analyzing transactions into debit and credit parts

Vickie Lands owns a business called LandScape. LandScape uses the following accounts.

Cash	Vickie Lands, Drawing
Accounts Receivable—Alston Goff	Sales
Accounts Receivable—Josie Leveson	Advertising Expense
Supplies	Miscellaneous Expense
Prepaid Insurance	Rent Expense
Accounts Payable—North End Supplies	Repair Expense
Accounts Payable—Bethany Supplies	Utilities Expense
Vickie Lands, Capital	

Instructions:

1. Prepare a T account for each account. Use the forms in your *Working Papers*.

2. Analyze each transaction into its debit and credit parts. Write the debit and credit amounts in the proper T accounts to show how each transaction changes account balances. Write the date of the transaction in parentheses before each amount.

Transactions:

June 1. Received cash from owner as an investment, $2,700.00.
      2. Paid cash for rent, $500.00.
      4. Paid cash for supplies, $300.00.
      4. Received cash from sales, $850.00.
      5. Paid cash for insurance, $275.00.
      8. Sold services on account to Alston Goff, $700.00.
      9. Bought supplies on account from Bethany Supplies, $200.00.
    10. Paid cash for repairs, $75.00.
    11. Received cash from owner as an investment, $1,900.00.
    11. Received cash from sales, $900.00.
    12. Bought supplies on account from North End Supplies, $130.00.
    13. Received cash on account from Alston Goff, $500.00.
    15. Paid cash for miscellaneous expense, $25.00.
    16. Paid cash on account to Bethany Supplies, $50.00.
    22. Paid cash for electric bill (utilities expense), $55.00.
    23. Paid cash for advertising, $95.00.
    25. Sold services on account to Josie Leveson, $450.00.
    26. Paid cash to owner for personal use, $400.00.
    30. Received cash on account from Josie Leveson, $200.00.

CHALLENGE PROBLEM

Analyzing transactions recorded in T accounts

Adriana Janek owns a business for which the following T accounts show the current financial situation. Write the answers for the following problem in the *Working Papers*.

Cash		
(1) 6,000.00	(2)	100.00
(5) 700.00	(3)	65.00
(8) 400.00	(6)	75.00
(9) 900.00	(7)	900.00
	(10)	600.00
	(11)	550.00
	(12)	500.00

Sales	
(5)	700.00
(8)	400.00
(9)	900.00
(13)	225.00

Accts. Rec.—Ralph Dahl	
(13) 225.00	

Advertising Expense	
(6) 75.00	

Supplies	
(4) 1,100.00	
(10) 600.00	

Miscellaneous Expense	
(3) 65.00	

Accts. Pay.—Tri City Supplies	
(11) 550.00	(4) 1,100.00

Rent Expense	
(7) 900.00	

Adriana Janek, Capital	
	(1) 6,000.00

Utilities Expense	
(2) 100.00	

Adriana Janek, Drawing	
(12) 500.00	

1	2	3	4	5	6
Trans. No.	Accounts Affected	Account Classification	Entered in Account as a — Debit	Credit	Description of Transaction
1.	*Cash* *Adriana Janek, Capital*	*Asset* *Owner's Equity*	√	√	*Received cash from owner as an investment*

Instructions:

1. Analyze each numbered transaction in the T accounts. Write the titles of accounts affected in Column 2. For each account, write the classification of the account in Column 3.

2. For each account, place a check mark in either Column 4 or 5 to indicate if the account is affected by a debit or a credit.

3. For each transaction, write a brief statement in Column 6 describing the transaction. Information for Transaction 1 is given as an example.

APPLIED COMMUNICATION

An entrepreneur is a person who attempts to earn a profit by taking the risk of operating a business. You have expressed an interest in starting your own business after graduation. Your family has agreed to help finance your new business if you can convince them that you would be successful.

Instructions: Develop a formal plan outlining the details of the business you would operate. Describe the type of business, the equipment or resources needed, and financial information, such as start-up costs and expenses. Write clear and persuasive sentences.

CASES FOR CRITICAL THINKING

Case 1

Aruna Patel records all cash receipts as revenue and all cash payments as expenses. Is Ms. Patel recording her cash receipts and cash payments correctly? Explain your answer.

Case 2

Thomas Bueler records all investments, revenue, expenses, and withdrawals in his capital account. At the end of each month, Mr. Bueler sorts the information to prepare a summary of what has caused the changes in his capital account balance. To help Mr. Bueler prepare this summary in the future, what changes would you suggest he make in his records?

SCANS WORKPLACE COMPETENCY

Resource Competency: Ranking Activities

Concept: Employers need workers who can identify tasks to be completed and prioritize them so that time is spent on tasks that are the most productive. It is human nature to do the tasks that are enjoyable or easy to complete first; however, these tasks are not necessarily the ones that contribute most to the success of a business.

Application: Use the planning sheet on the website (www.C21accounting.com) or create your own form for prioritizing tasks. The form should have four narrow columns labeled *A, B, C,* and ✓ and a wider column for tasks that need to be completed. List all the tasks or activities you need to do tomorrow or this week in the wide column. Then place a check mark in one of the three columns for each item on the list to show whether it is of the highest priority (*A*), medium priority (*B*), or low priority (*C*). Place a check mark in the column labeled ✓ as each task is completed.

The bookkeeper for Lyons Company used T accounts to analyze three transactions as follows.

Transaction 1:

Cash		Ruth Lyons, Capital	
200.00			200.00

Transaction 2:

Accounts Payable		Supplies	
	500.00		500.00

Transaction 3:

Accounts Receivable		Sales	
100.00			100.00

Review the three sets of T accounts and answer the following questions.

1. Which T account analysis is incorrect? How did you determine it was incorrect?
2. What information would you need to determine the correct T account analysis for this transaction?

ANALYZING BEST BUY'S FINANCIAL STATEMENTS

The Best Buy financial statement on Appendix B page B-5 lists the assets, liabilities, and shareholder's equity of Best Buy. Shareholder's equity for a corporation is the same as capital for a proprietorship.

Instructions: Find the total assets, total liabilities, and total equity for Best Buy for 2006 and 2007. Put your answer in the form of an accounting equation. You will have to add the total current liabilities, long-term liabilities, and long-term debt to find the total liabilities. Minority interest, which is a special type of account, should be added to total liabilities and total equity in the accounting equation.

PHOTODISC/GETTY IMAGES

Accounting
SOFTWARE

OPENING SOFTWARE AND PROBLEM FILES

Your first opportunity to enter transactions in Peachtree will be in Chapter 4. The first step in using Peachtree is to learn how to open the software and then open a problem data file. Problem data files have the chart of accounts and beginning account balances already set up. Therefore, once the data file is open, you are ready to begin entering transactions to solve a problem.

Each problem you will complete has an individual problem or data file. Detailed instructions for opening files and completing problems are provided on the *Century 21 Accounting* web site (www.C21accounting.com).

Peachtree uses unique terminology for opening data files. Rather than opening a file, the software will *restore* a file. The procedures for opening a problem data file depend on how your software is installed.

PEACHTREE ACTIVITY

1. Locate and open your Peachtree software. Depending on how the software was installed, you may be able to open Peachtree from your Start menu or you may have a Peachtree icon on your desktop.

2. Open the data file for Mastery Problem 4-5 (filename: 04-5MP.ptb).

3. Close the data file and exit the software.

OPENING SOFTWARE AND PROBLEM FILES

Your first opportunity to enter transactions in QuickBooks will be in Chapter 4. Learning some basic skills for using the software now will prepare you to complete these problems accurately and efficiently. Detailed instructions for opening files and completing problems are provided on the *Century 21 Accounting* web site (www.C21accounting.com).

Each problem you will complete has an individual problem or data file. The file is already set up for QuickBooks and includes company information and the chart of accounts and beginning balances at the point the problem begins.

QUICKBOOKS ACTIVITY

1. Locate and open your QuickBooks software. Depending on how the software was installed, you may be able to open QuickBooks from your Start menu or you may have a QuickBooks icon on your desktop.

2. Open the data file for Mastery Problem 4-5. QuickBooks uses the company name as the filename, so look for the file named O'Kalla Lawn and Garden.qbw.

3. Close the data file and exit the software.

OPENING SOFTWARE AND PROBLEM FILES

The birth of the electronic spreadsheet can be traced back to Dan Bricklin, a student at Harvard Business School, who was preparing a written worksheet analysis for a case study. Knowing that there must be a better alternative, Bricklin began programming an electronic version. His goal was to create a program in which the user could visualize the worksheet as it was created.

By 1979, Bricklin was marketing his program under the name *VisiCalc*, short for *visible calc*ulator. The program was an instant success and is credited with providing businesses a reason to finally purchase their first personal computer, an expensive purchase at that time.

This program had a dramatic impact in business. No longer were individuals required to create worksheets by hand, calculating each value with adding machines. Most important, if any number on the worksheet changed, other numbers calculated with formulas automatically changed. This power instantly transformed how businesses created budgets, analyzed financial statements, and performed "what if" analyses.

EXCEL ACTIVITY

1. Locate and open your Excel software. Depending on how the software was installed, you may be able to open Excel from your Start menu or you may have an Excel icon on your desktop.

2. Open the data file for Application Problem 5-2 (filename: F05-2.xls). Your instructor may have already copied the data files to your computer. They may also be downloaded from the *Century 21 Accounting* web site (www.C21accounting.com).

3. Close the data file and exit the software.

OPENING SOFTWARE AND PROBLEM FILES

Using computer software to process accounting data can be an efficient and effective way to control the financial information of a business. In order to use the software, it is important to have a general understanding of computer and software terminology. Keyboarding skills are also essential for entering data. The more skilled you are and the greater your understanding, the better able you will be to accurately process financial information.

Automated Accounting software is used to teach students about computerized accounting principles. Accounting software is a set of instructions that operate the computer and enable the user to enter financial information and create reports, spreadsheets, graphs, and documents. Specifically, Automated Accounting can process transactions for:

- The purchase of assets, supplies, services, and the related payments.

- Investments in the business.

- Sales, cash receipts, and noncash transactions.

There are many other types of transactions that can be entered into an automated accounting system. Many of the various types of transactions will be studied in this course.

AUTOMATED ACCOUNTING ACTIVITY

1. Locate and open your Automated Accounting software. Depending on how the software was installed, you may be able to open Automated Accounting from your Start menu or you may have an Automated Accounting icon on your desktop. They may also be downloaded from the *Century 21 Accounting* web site (www.C21accounting.com).

2. Open the data file for Application Problem 3-5 (filename: F03-5.AA8). To open the data file, click the Open button on the toolbar. Then look in the C21 1st Year folder and double-click the appropriate filename.

3. Close the data file and exit the software.

DIGITAL VISION/GETTY IMAGES

CHAPTER 3

Journalizing Transactions

OBJECTIVES

After studying Chapter 3, you will be able to:

1. Define accounting terms related to journalizing transactions.

2. Identify accounting concepts and practices related to journalizing transactions.

3. Record transactions to set up a business in a five-column journal.

4. Record transactions to buy insurance for cash and supplies on account in a five-column journal.

5. Record transactions that affect owner's equity and receiving cash on account in a five-column journal.

6. Prove and rule a five-column journal and prove cash.

KEY TERMS

- journal
- journalizing
- special amount column
- general amount column
- entry
- double-entry accounting
- source document
- check
- invoice
- sales invoice
- receipt
- memorandum
- proving cash

Point Your Browser
www.C21accounting.com

Travelocity

Taking Travel to a Better Place—Travelocity

Do you sometimes feel that you need a vacation but are unsure about how to coordinate airline, hotel, and ground transportation reservations? That's where a company like Travelocity can help. Travelocity can also help with cruises, rail travel, and mini travel guides.

Maybe you want to take an inexpensive vacation, and you don't have a specific destination in mind. By searching the Travelocity web site, you can quickly find the "top deals" in airfares, cruises, hotels, rental cars, and total vacation packages. You can even find suggestions about what to see and do at your destination.

Want to travel throughout Europe? Travelocity will help you arrange rail travel across Europe, arrange for a place to stay, and help you get there. That's full service at its best.

All of this activity needs to be recorded in the accounting records of Travelocity.

©PR NEWSWIRE/TRAVELOCITY

Critical Thinking

1. What account would Travelocity credit when you make a reservation with them? What account would be debited?

2. Why do you think Travelocity might be able to get less expensive airline tickets than you, as an individual, could get?

Source: www.travelocity.com

INTERNET ACTIVITY

AICPA

Go to the homepage for the American Institute of Certified Public Accountants (AICPA) (www.aicpa.org). Search the site for information about the AICPA Mission Statement.

Instructions

1. Summarize the mission statement and the objectives of the AICPA.

2. Expand the search by looking at other pages. List three additional resources provided by the AICPA.

Journals, Source Documents, and Recording Entries in a Journal

JOURNALS AND JOURNALIZING

As described in Chapter 2, transactions are analyzed into debit and credit parts before information is recorded. A form for recording transactions in chronological order is called a **journal**. Recording transactions in a journal is called **journalizing**.

Transactions could be recorded in the accounting equation. However, most companies wish to create a more permanent record by recording transactions in a journal.

Each business uses the kind of journal that best fits the needs of that business. The nature of a business and the number of transactions to be recorded determine the kind of journal to be used.

The word journal comes from the Latin *diurnalis*, meaning *daily*. Most businesses conduct transactions every day. To keep from getting overloaded, businesses usually record transactions in their journals every day.

FOR YOUR INFORMATION

F Y I

The Small Business Administration (SBA) has programs that offer free management and accounting advice to small business owners. The SBA sponsors various workshops and publishes a variety of booklets for small business owners. Visit their Web site at www.sba.gov.

CHARACTER COUNTS

Recognizing Ethical Dilemmas and Actions

How often have you said something you later regretted? Chances are you spoke before you thought about how your words might affect others. Had you taken the time to think how your words would hurt someone else, you might have said something different or simply kept quiet.

The first step of the ethical model is to recognize you are facing an ethical dilemma. Few business decisions will require you to act immediately. Take whatever time is required to determine whether your actions could harm some-

one else. If you have any doubts that your action will violate your morals, stop to evaluate the decision, using the ethical model.

The second step of the ethical model is to identify the action taken or the proposed action. Write down every possible action you think of, even if the idea might seem outrageous at first. Seek the advice of others who may have encountered similar dilemmas or whom you admire for their ethical behavior. Many companies assign a mentor to new employees to encourage them to seek advice.

Instructions

In private, write down the names of at least five individuals from whom you would feel comfortable seeking advice on ethical dilemmas.

PHOTO: PHOTOALTO/GETTY IMAGES

					JOURNAL					PAGE	
					1	2		3	4	5	
	DATE	ACCOUNT TITLE	DOC. NO.	POST. REF.	GENERAL		SALES CREDIT	CASH			
					DEBIT	CREDIT		DEBIT	CREDIT		
1											1
2											2
3											3

Using a Journal

TechKnow Consulting uses a multicolumn journal that has five amount columns: General Debit, General Credit, Sales Credit, Cash Debit, and Cash Credit. A journal amount column headed with an account title is called a **special amount column**. These columns are used for transactions that occur frequently. For example, most of TechKnow Consulting's transactions involve receipt or payment of cash. A large number of the transactions involve receiving cash from sales. Therefore, TechKnow Consulting uses three special amount columns in its journal: Sales Credit, Cash Debit, and Cash Credit. Using special amount columns eliminates writing an account title in the Account Title column and saves time.

A journal amount column that is not headed with an account title is called a **general amount column**. In TechKnow Consulting's journal, the General Debit and General Credit columns are general amount columns.

Accuracy

Information recorded in a journal includes the debit and credit parts of each transaction recorded in one place. The information can be verified by comparing the data in the journal with the transaction data.

Chronological Record

Transactions are recorded in a journal in order by date. All information about a transaction is recorded in one place, making the information for a specific transaction easy to locate.

Double-Entry Accounting

Information for each transaction recorded in a journal is called an **entry**. The recording of debit and credit parts of a transaction is called **double-entry accounting**. In double-entry accounting, each transaction affects at least two accounts. Both the debit and the credit parts are recorded, reflecting the dual effect of each transaction on the business's records. Double-entry accounting assures that debits equal credits.

Source Documents

A business paper from which information is obtained for a journal entry is called a **source document**. Each transaction is described by a source document that proves that the transaction did occur. For example, TechKnow Consulting prepares a check stub for each cash payment made. The check stub describes information about the cash payment transaction for which the check is prepared. The accounting concept *Objective Evidence* is applied when a source document is prepared for each transaction. [CONCEPT: Objective Evidence]

A transaction should be journalized only if it actually occurs. The amounts recorded must be accurate and true. Nearly all transactions result in the preparation of a source document. TechKnow Consulting uses five source documents: checks, sales invoices, receipts, calculator tapes, and memorandums.

NO. 1 $ _275.00_	
Date _August 3_ .... 20 _--_	
To _Port City Supply_	
For _Supplies_	

BAL. BRO'T. FOR'D.	0	00
AMT. DEPOSITED ... 8 / 1 / -- Date	5,000	00
SUBTOTAL	5,000	00
OTHER:		
SUBTOTAL	5,000	00
AMT. THIS CHECK	275	00
BAL. CAR'D. FOR'D.	4,725	00

TechKnow Consulting
7549 Broadway
Portland, OR 97202-2531

NO. 1   24-317 / 1230

August 3,   20 _--_

PAY TO THE ORDER OF _Port City Supply_ $ _275.00_

Two hundred seventy-five no/100 ——————— DOLLARS

Pacific national bank
Portland, OR

For Classroom Use Only

FOR _Supplies_   _Kim Park_

⑆123003175⑆ 43‖452119‖

A business form ordering a bank to pay cash from a bank account is called a **check**. The source document for cash payments is a check. TechKnow Consulting makes all cash payments by check. The checks are prenumbered to help TechKnow Consulting account for all checks. TechKnow Consulting's record of information on a check is the check stub prepared at the same time as the check.

Procedures for preparing checks and check stubs are described in Chapter 5.

TechKnow Consulting
7549 Broadway
Portland, OR 97202-2531

Sold to: Oakdale School
5211 SE Oak Street
Portland, OR 97208-5392

No. **1**
Date 8/12/--
Terms 30 days

Description	Amount
Computer Network Setup	$350.00
Total	$350.00

When services are sold on account, the seller prepares a form showing information about the sale. A form describing the goods or services sold, the quantity, and the price is called an **invoice**. An invoice used as a source document for recording a sale on account is called a **sales invoice**. A sales invoice is also referred to as a *sales ticket* or a *sales slip*.

A sales invoice is prepared in duplicate. The original is given to the customer. The copy is used as the source document for the sale on account transaction. [CONCEPT: Objective Evidence] Sales invoices are prenumbered in sequence to help account for all sales invoices.

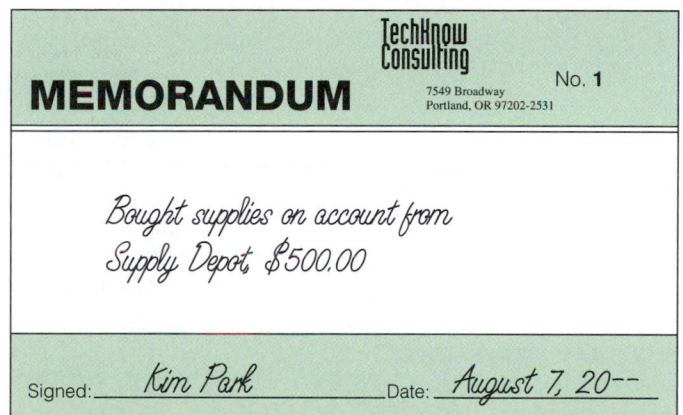

No. **1**

Date _August 1,_ 20 _--_

From _Kim Park_

For _Investment_

$ 5,000 | 00

Receipt No. **1**

August 1, 20 _--_

Rec'd from _Kim Park_

For _Investment_

Five thousand and no/100 _____ Dollars

TechKnow Consulting

Amount $ 5,000 | 00

Kim Park

Received By

7549 Broadway
Portland, OR 97202-2531

Receipts

A business form giving written acknowledgement for cash received is called a ==receipt==. When cash is received from sources other than sales, TechKnow Consulting prepares a receipt. The receipts are prenumbered to help account for all of the receipts. A receipt is the source document for cash received from transactions other than sales. [CONCEPT: Objective Evidence]

MEMORANDUM

TechKnow Consulting
7549 Broadway
Portland, OR 97202-2531

No. 1

_Bought supplies on account from
Supply Depot, $500.00_

Signed: _Kim Park_   Date: _August 7, 20--_

Memorandums

A form on which a brief message is written describing a transaction is called a ==memorandum==. When no other source document is prepared for a transaction, or when an additional explanation is needed about a transaction, TechKnow Consulting prepares a memorandum. [CONCEPT: Objective Evidence] TechKnow Consulting's memorandums are prenumbered to help account for all memorandums. A brief note is written on the memorandum to describe the transaction.

Calculator Tapes

TechKnow Consulting collects cash at the time services are rendered to customers. At the end of each day, TechKnow Consulting uses a printing electronic calculator to total the amount of cash received from sales for that day. By totaling all the individual sales, a single source document is produced for the total sales of the day. Thus, time and space are saved by recording only one entry for all of a day's sales. The calculator tape is the source document for daily sales. [CONCEPT: Objective Evidence] A calculator tape used as a source document is shown here.

TechKnow Consulting dates and numbers each calculator tape. For example, in the illustration, the number _T12_ indicates that the tape is for the twelfth day of the month.

0•00 *
Aug. 12, 20-- 150•00 +
35•00 +
_T12_ 110•00 +
295•00 *

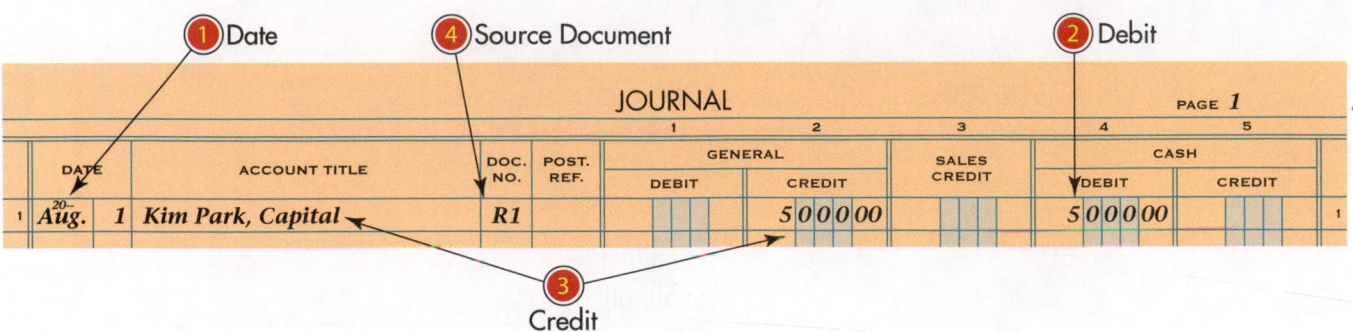

① Date ④ Source Document ② Debit

③ Credit

DATE	ACCOUNT TITLE	DOC. NO.	POST. REF.	GENERAL DEBIT	GENERAL CREDIT	SALES CREDIT	CASH DEBIT	CASH CREDIT	
¹Aug. 1	Kim Park, Capital	R1			5 000 00		5 000 00		1

JOURNAL — PAGE 1

Information for each transaction recorded in a journal is known as an entry. An entry consists of four parts: (1) date, (2) debit, (3) credit, and (4) source document. Before a transaction is recorded in a journal, the transaction is analyzed into its debit and credit parts.

The source document for this transaction is Receipt No. 1. [CONCEPT: Objective Evidence] The analysis of this transaction is shown in the T accounts.

The asset account, Cash, increases by a debit, $5,000.00. The owner's capital account, Kim Park, Capital, increases by a credit, $5,000.00.

August 1. Received cash from owner as an investment, $5,000.00. Receipt No. 1.

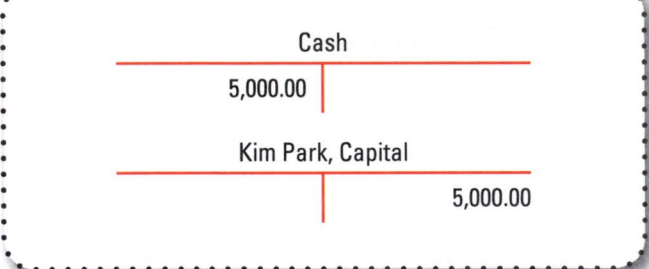

Cash	
5,000.00	

Kim Park, Capital	
	5,000.00

FOR YOUR INFORMATION

FYI

Dollars and cents signs and decimal points are not used when writing amounts on ruled accounting paper. Sometimes a color tint or a heavy vertical rule is used on printed accounting paper to separate the dollars and cents columns.

STEPS **JOURNALIZING CASH RECEIVED FROM OWNER AS AN INVESTMENT**

① **Date.** Write the date, *20--, Aug. 1,* in the Date column. This entry is the first one on this journal page. Therefore, write both the year and the month for this entry. Do not write either the year or the month again on the same page.

② **Debit.** The journal has a special amount column for debits to *Cash.* Write the debit amount, *$5,000.00,* in the Cash Debit column. The title of the account is in the column heading. Therefore, you do not need to write the account title in the Account Title column.

③ **Credit.** There is no special amount column with the title of the account credited, *Kim Park, Capital,* in its heading. Therefore, record the credit amount, *$5,000.00,* in the General Credit column. To indicate what account is credited for this amount, write the title of the account, *Kim Park, Capital,* in the Account Title column. (All amounts recorded in the General Debit or General Credit amount columns must have an account title written in the Account Title column.)

④ **Source document.** Write the source document number, *R1,* in the Doc. No. column. The source document number, *R1,* indicates that this is Receipt No. 1. (The source document number is a cross reference from the journal to the source document. Receipt No. 1 is filed in case more details about this transaction are needed.)

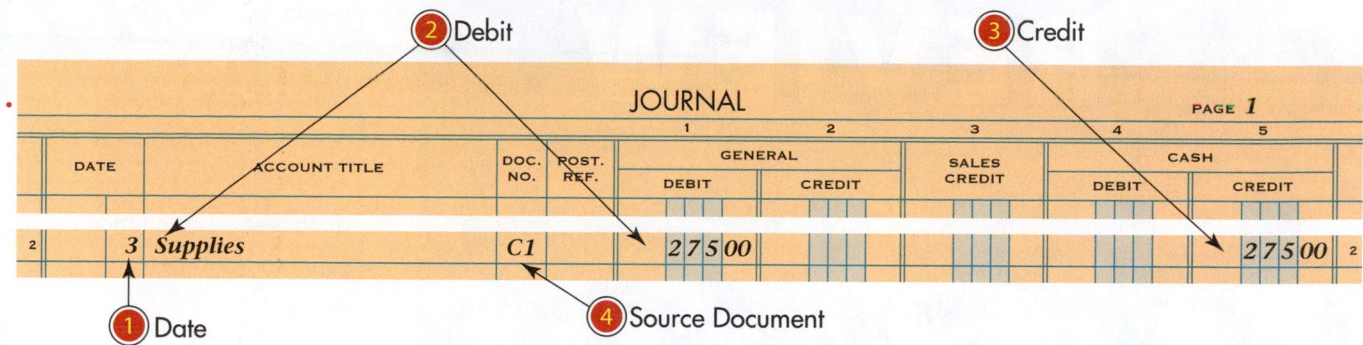

② Debit ③ Credit

		JOURNAL									PAGE 1
					1	2	3	4	5		
DATE	ACCOUNT TITLE	DOC. NO.	POST. REF.	GENERAL		SALES CREDIT	CASH				
				DEBIT	CREDIT		DEBIT	CREDIT			
3	*Supplies*	*C1*		2 7 5 00				2 7 5 00			2

① Date ④ Source Document

August 3. Paid cash for supplies, $275.00. Check No. 1.

The asset account, Supplies, increases by a debit, $275.00. The asset account, Cash, decreases by a credit, $275.00.

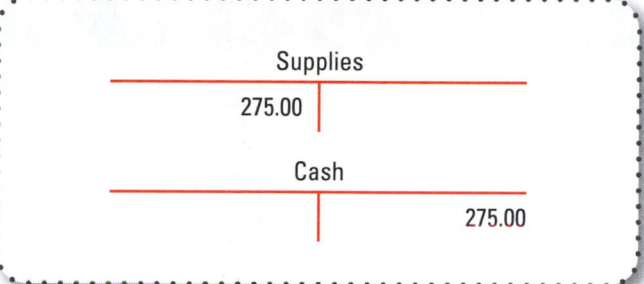

Supplies
| 275.00 | |

Cash
| | 275.00 |

The source document for this transaction is Check No. 1. [CONCEPT: Objective Evidence] The analysis of this transaction is shown in the T accounts.

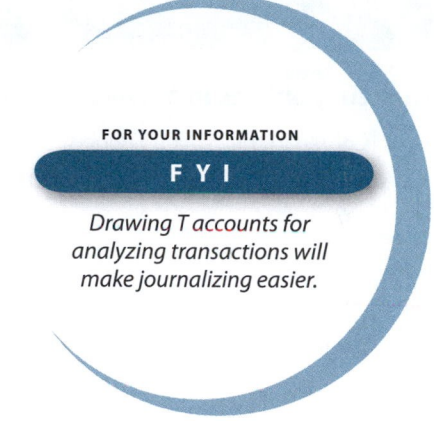

FOR YOUR INFORMATION

FYI

Drawing T accounts for analyzing transactions will make journalizing easier.

STEPS **JOURNALIZING CASH PAID FOR SUPPLIES**

① **Date.** Write the date, *3*, in the Date column. This is not the first entry on the journal page. Therefore, do not write the year and month for this entry.

② **Debit.** There is no special amount column with the title of the account debited, *Supplies*, in its heading. Therefore, record the debit amount, *$275.00*, in the General Debit column. In order to indicate what account is debited for this amount, write the title of the account, *Supplies*, in the Account Title column.

③ **Credit.** The journal has a special amount column for credits to *Cash*. Write the credit amount, *$275.00*, in the Cash Credit column. The title of the account is in the column heading. Therefore, do not write the account title in the Account Title column.

④ **Source document.** Write the source document number, *C1*, in the Doc. No. column. The source document number, C1, indicates that this is Check No. 1.

REMEMBER

When an account such as Cash is used frequently, it can be time-consuming to write the account title over and over. Using a special amount column for a frequently-used account saves time.

End of Lesson REVIEW

TERMS REVIEW

- journal
- journalizing
- special amount column
- general amount column
- entry
- double-entry accounting
- source document
- check
- invoice
- sales invoice
- receipt
- memorandum

AUDIT YOUR UNDERSTANDING

1. In what order are transactions recorded in a journal?
2. Why are source documents important?
3. List the four parts of a journal entry.

WORK TOGETHER 3-1

Journalizing entries in a five-column journal

A journal is given in the *Working Papers*. Your instructor will guide you through the following example.

Norm Derner owns Derner Copy Center, which uses the following accounts.

Cash	Accts. Pay.—Palm Supply	Miscellaneous Expense
Accts. Rec.—L. Rohe	Norm Derner, Capital	Rent Expense
Supplies	Norm Derner, Drawing	Utilities Expense
Prepaid Insurance	Sales	

Transactions:

Apr. 1. Received cash from owner as an investment, $1,500.00. R1.
2. Paid cash for supplies, $375.00. C1.

1. Journalize each transaction completed during April of the current year. Use page 1 of the journal. Source documents are abbreviated as follows: check, C; receipt, R. Save your work to complete Work Together 3-2.

ON YOUR OWN 3-1

Journalizing entries in a five-column journal

A journal is given in the *Working Papers*. Work this problem independently.

Lou James owns Lou's Service Center, which uses the following accounts.

Cash	Accts. Pay.—OK Supplies	Advertising Expense
Accts. Rec.—C. Lord	Lou James, Capital	Miscellaneous Expense
Supplies	Lou James, Drawing	Rent Expense
Prepaid Insurance	Sales	

Transactions:

June 2. Received cash from owner as an investment, $3,000.00. R1.
3. Paid cash for supplies, $950.00. C1.

1. Journalize each transaction completed during June of the current year. Use page 1 of the journal. Source documents are abbreviated as follows: check, C; receipt, R. Save your work to complete On Your Own 3-2.

Journalizing Buying Insurance, Buying on Account, and Paying on Account

PAID CASH FOR INSURANCE

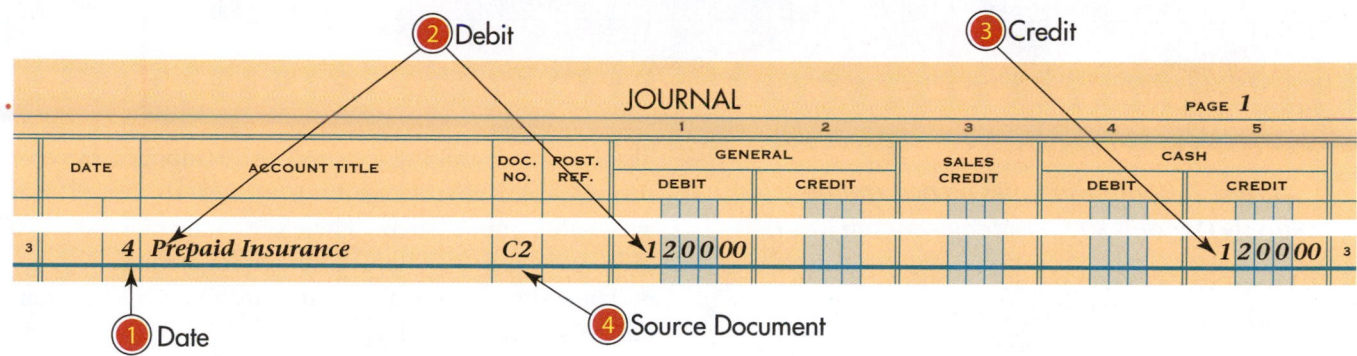

The source document for this transaction is Check No. 2. [CONCEPT: Objective Evidence] The analysis of this transaction is shown in the T accounts.

The asset account, Prepaid Insurance, increases by a debit, $1,200.00. The asset account, Cash, decreases by a credit, $1,200.00.

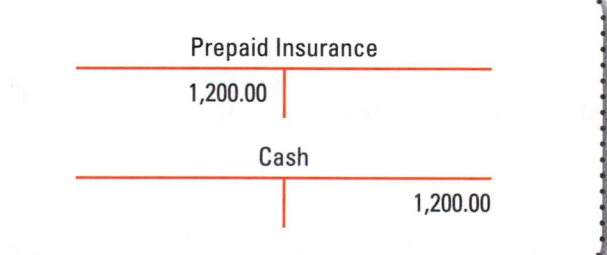

August 4. Paid cash for insurance, $1,200.00. Check No. 2.

Prepaid Insurance

| 1,200.00 | |

Cash

| | 1,200.00 |

STEPS JOURNALIZING CASH PAID FOR INSURANCE

1 **Date.** Write the date, *4*, in the Date column.

2 **Debit.** There is no special amount column with the title of the account debited, *Prepaid Insurance,* in its heading. Therefore, record the debit amount, *$1,200.00,* in the General Debit column. To indicate what account is debited for this amount, write the title of the account, *Prepaid Insurance,* in the Account Title column.

3 **Credit.** The journal has a special amount column for credits to *Cash.* Write the credit amount, *$1,200.00,* in the Cash Credit column. The title of the account is in the column heading. Therefore, do not write the account title in the Account Title column.

4 **Source document.** Write the source document number, *C2,* in the Doc. No. column.

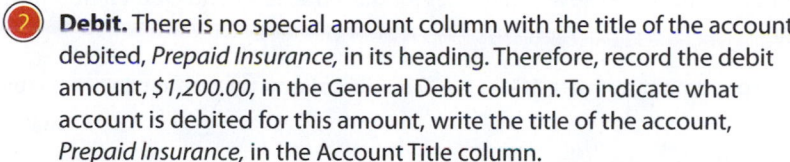

REMEMBER

All amounts recorded in the General Debit or General Credit amount columns must have an account title written in the Account Title column.

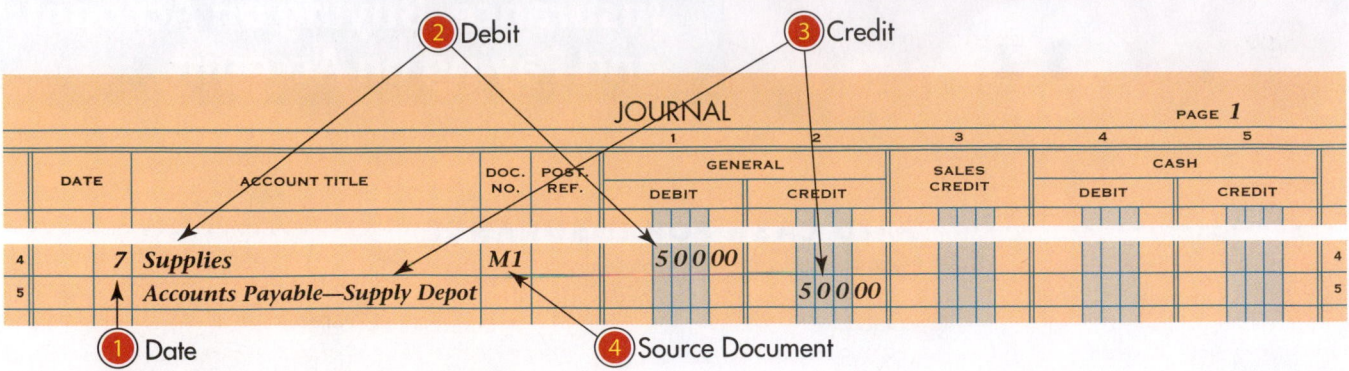

② Debit ③ Credit

JOURNAL PAGE 1

	DATE	ACCOUNT TITLE	DOC. NO.	POST. REF.	GENERAL DEBIT	GENERAL CREDIT	SALES CREDIT	CASH DEBIT	CASH CREDIT	
4	7	Supplies	M1		500 00					4
5		Accounts Payable—Supply Depot				500 00				5

① Date ④ Source Document

August 7. Bought supplies on account from Supply Depot, $500.00. Memorandum No. 1.

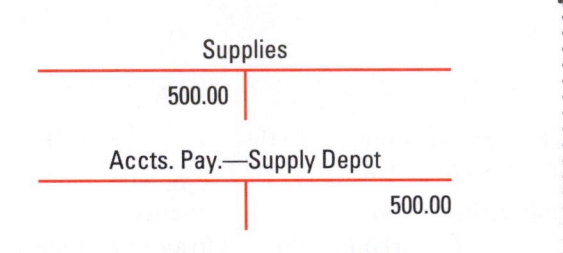

Supplies

500.00

Accts. Pay.—Supply Depot

500.00

TechKnow Consulting ordered these supplies by telephone. TechKnow Consulting wishes to record this transaction immediately. Therefore, a memorandum is prepared that shows supplies bought on account.

The source document for this transaction is Memorandum No. 1. [CONCEPT: Objective Evidence] The analysis of this transaction is shown in the T accounts.

The asset account, Supplies, increases by a debit, $500.00. The liability account, Accounts Payable—Supply Depot, increases by a credit, $500.00.

STEPS JOURNALIZING SUPPLIES BOUGHT ON ACCOUNT

① **Date.** Write the date, *7*, in the Date column.

② **Debit.** There is no special amount column with the title of the account debited, *Supplies,* in its heading. Therefore, record the debit amount, *$500.00,* in the General Debit column. In order to indicate what account is to be debited for this amount, write the title of the account, *Supplies*, in the Account Title column.

③ **Credit.** There is no special amount column with the title of the account credited, *Accounts Payable—Supply Depot,* in its heading. Therefore, record the credit amount, *$500.00,* on the next line in the General Credit column. To indicate what account is credited for this amount, write the title of the account, *Accounts Payable—Supply Depot,* in the Account Title column on the same line as the credit amount.

This entry requires two lines in the journal because account titles for both the debit and credit amounts must be written in the Account Title column.

④ **Source document.** Write the source document number, *M1,* in the Doc. No. column on the first line of the entry.

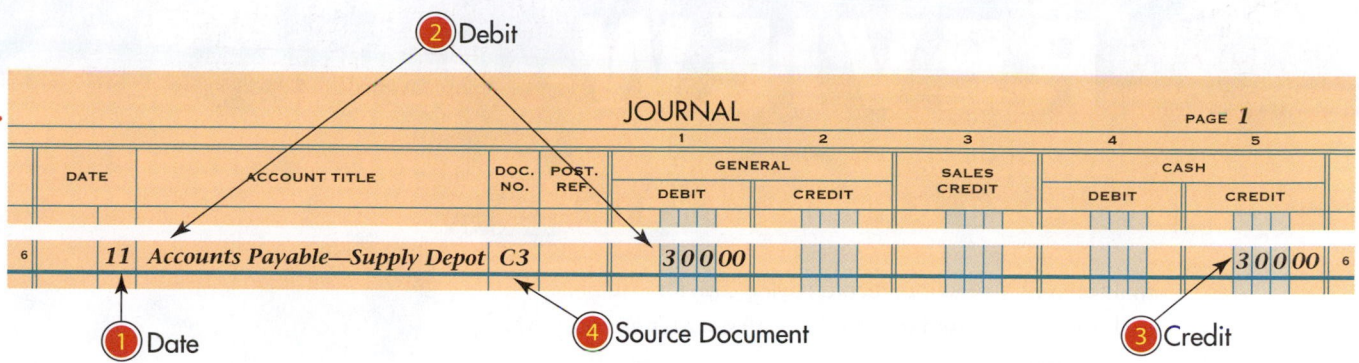

② Debit

					GENERAL		SALES	CASH	
	DATE	ACCOUNT TITLE	DOC. NO.	POST. REF.	DEBIT	CREDIT	CREDIT	DEBIT	CREDIT	
6	11	Accounts Payable—Supply Depot	C3		30000				30000	6

① Date   **④ Source Document**   **③ Credit**

August 11. Paid cash on account to Supply Depot, $300.00. Check No. 3.

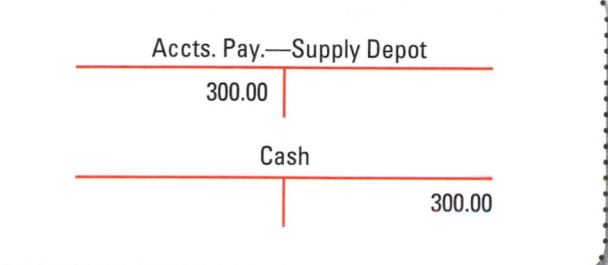

The source document for this transaction is Check No. 3. [CONCEPT: Objective Evidence] The analysis of this transaction is shown in the T accounts.

The liability account, Accounts Payable—Supply Depot, decreases by a debit, $300.00. The asset account, Cash, decreases by a credit, $300.00.

PHOTODISC/GETTY IMAGES

S T E P S   **JOURNALIZING CASH PAID ON ACCOUNT**

① **Date.** Write the date, *11*, in the Date column.

② **Debit.** There is no special amount column with the title of the account debited, *Accounts Payable—Supply Depot,* in its heading. Therefore, record the debit amount, *$300.00,* in the General Debit column. In order to indicate what account is debited for this amount, write the title of the account, *Accounts Payable—Supply Depot,* in the Account Title column.

③ **Credit.** The journal has a special amount column for credits to *Cash.* Write the credit amount, *$300.00,* in the Cash Credit column. The title of the account is in the column heading. Therefore, do not write the account title in the Account Title column.

④ **Source document.** Write the source document number, *C3,* in the Doc. No. column.

AUDIT YOUR UNDERSTANDING

1. Which journal columns are used to record paying cash for insurance?
2. Which journal columns are used to record buying supplies on account?
3. Which journal columns are used to record paying cash on account?

WORK TOGETHER 3-2

Journalizing entries in a five-column journal

Use the journal that you started for Work Together 3-1. Your instructor will guide you through the following example.

Norm Derner owns Derner Copy Center, which uses the following accounts.

Cash	Accts. Pay.—Palm Supply	Miscellaneous Expense
Accts. Rec.—L. Rohe	Norm Derner, Capital	Rent Expense
Supplies	Norm Derner, Drawing	Utilities Expense
Prepaid Insurance	Sales	

Transactions:

Apr. 5. Bought supplies on account from Palm Supply, $500.00. M1.
   7. Paid cash for insurance, $300.00. C2.
   9. Paid cash on account to Palm Supply, $250.00. C3.

1. Journalize the transactions continuing on the next blank line of page 1 of the journal. Source documents are abbreviated as follows: check, C; memorandum, M. Save your work to complete Work Together 3-3.

ON YOUR OWN 3-2

Journalizing entries in a five-column journal

Use the chart of accounts below and the journal that you started for On Your Own 3-1. Work this problem independently.

Lou James owns Lou's Service Center, which uses the following accounts.

Cash	Accts. Pay.—OK Supplies	Advertising Expense
Accts. Rec.—C. Lord	Lou James, Capital	Miscellaneous Expense
Supplies	Lou James, Drawing	Rent Expense
Prepaid Insurance	Sales	

Transactions:

June 5. Paid cash for insurance, $400.00. C2.
   9. Bought supplies on account from OK Supplies, $300.00. M1.
  10. Paid cash on account to OK Supplies, $300.00. C3.

1. Journalize the transactions continuing on the next blank line of page 1 of the journal. Source documents are abbreviated as follows: check, C; memorandum, M. Save your work to complete On Your Own 3-3.

RECEIVED CASH FROM SALES

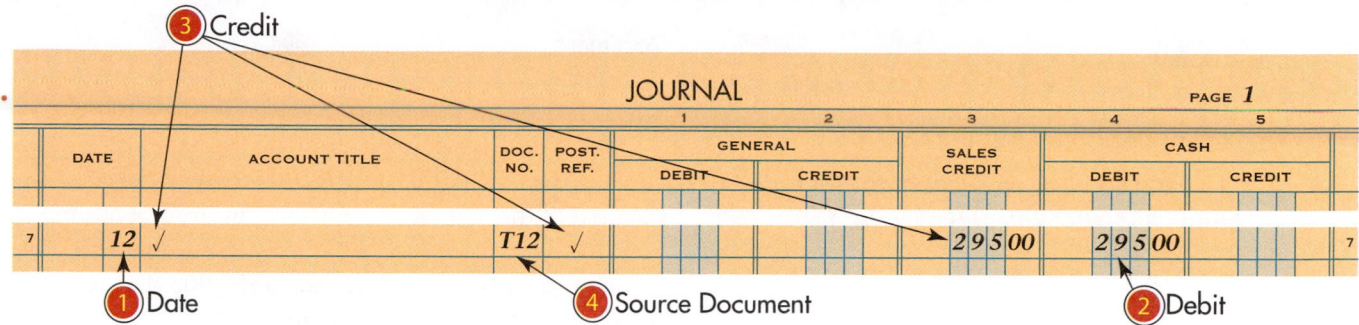

③ Credit   ① Date   ④ Source Document   ② Debit

August 12. Received cash from sales, $295.00. Tape No. 12.

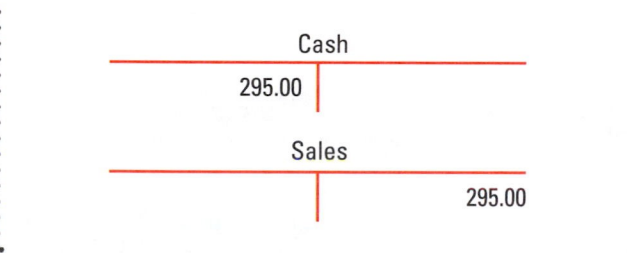

Cash

295.00 |

Sales

| 295.00

The source document for this transaction is Calculator Tape No. 12. [CONCEPT: Objective Evidence] The analysis of this transaction is shown in the T accounts.

The asset account, Cash, is increased by a debit, $295.00. The revenue account, Sales, is increased by a credit, $295.00.

The reason that Sales increases by a credit is discussed in the previous chapter. The owner's capital account has a normal credit balance. Increases in the owner's capital account are shown as credits. Because revenue increases owner's equity, increases in revenue are recorded as credits. A revenue account, therefore, has a normal credit balance.

STEPS JOURNALIZING CASH RECEIVED FROM SALES

① **Date.** Write the date, *12,* in the Date column.

② **Debit.** The journal has a special amount column for debits to *Cash.* Write the debit amount, *$295.00,* in the Cash Debit column. The title of the account is in the column heading. Therefore, do not write the account title in the Account Title column.

③ **Credit.** The journal also has a special amount column for credits to *Sales.* Write the credit amount, *$295.00,* in the Sales Credit column. The title of the account is in the column heading. Therefore, do not write the account title in the Account title column.

Because both amounts for this entry are recorded in special amount columns, no account titles are written in the Account Title column. Therefore, place a check mark in the Account Title column to show that no account titles need to be written for this transaction. A check mark is also placed in the Post. Ref. column.

The use of the Post. Ref. column is described in Chapter 4.

④ **Source document.** Write the source document number, *T12,* in the Doc. No. column.

SOLD SERVICES ON ACCOUNT

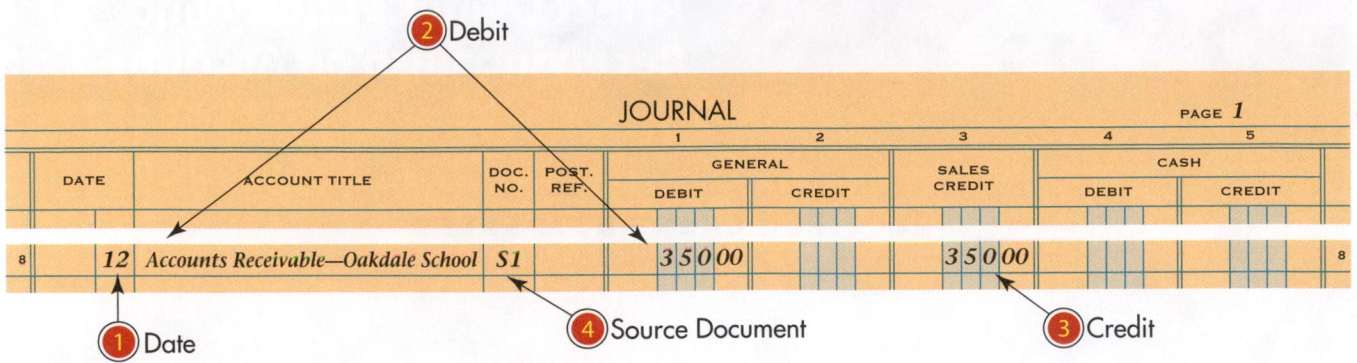

② Debit

	DATE	ACCOUNT TITLE	DOC. NO.	POST. REF.	GENERAL DEBIT	GENERAL CREDIT	SALES CREDIT	CASH DEBIT	CASH CREDIT	
8	12	Accounts Receivable—Oakdale School	S1		3 5 0 00		3 5 0 00			8

① Date **④** Source Document **③** Credit

August 12. Sold services on account to Oakdale School, $350.00. Sales Invoice No. 1.

Accts. Rec.—Oakdale School

350.00	

Sales

	350.00

The source document for this transaction is Sales Invoice No. 1. [CONCEPT: Objective Evidence] The analysis of this transaction is shown in the T accounts.

The asset account, Accounts Receivable—Oakdale School, increases by a debit, $350.00. The revenue account, Sales, increases by a credit, $350.00.

STEPS JOURNALIZING SERVICES SOLD ON ACCOUNT

① **Date.** Write the date, *12*, in the Date column.

② **Debit.** There is no special amount column with the title of the account debited, *Accounts Receivable—Oakdale School*, in its heading. Therefore, record the debit amount, *$350.00*, in the General Debit column. To indicate what account is debited for this amount, write the title of the account, *Accounts Receivable—Oakdale School*, in the Account Title column.

③ **Credit.** The journal has a special amount column for credits to *Sales*. Write the credit amount, *$350.00*, in the Sales Credit column. The title of the account is in the column heading. Therefore, do not write the account title in the Account Title column.

④ **Source document.** Write the source document number, *S1*, in the Doc. No. column.

PHOTODISC/GETTY IMAGES

FOR YOUR INFORMATION

F Y I

Accounting is not just for accountants. For example, a performing artist earns revenue from providing a service. Financial decisions must be made such as the cost of doing a performance, the percentage of revenue paid to a manager, travel expenses, and the cost of rehearsal space.

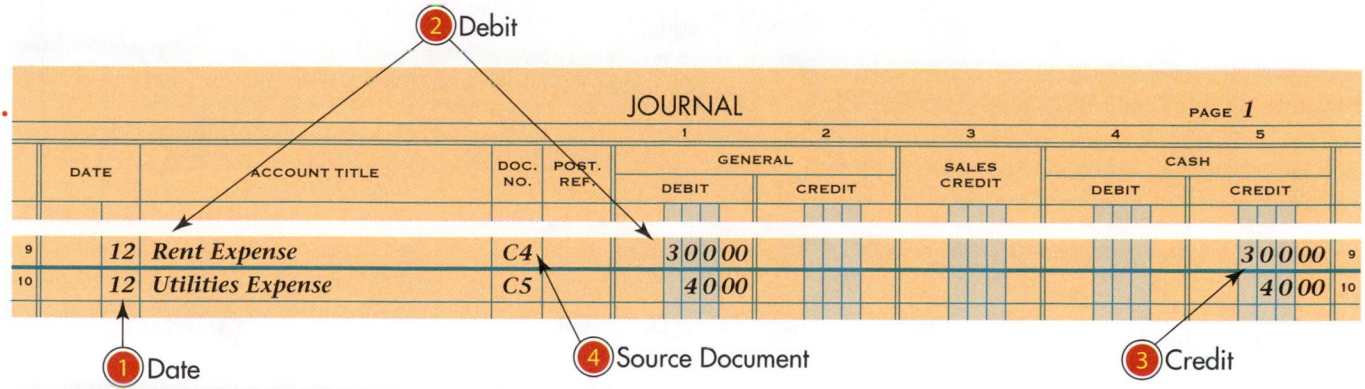

	DATE	ACCOUNT TITLE	DOC. NO.	POST. REF.	GENERAL		SALES CREDIT	CASH		
					1 DEBIT	2 CREDIT	3	4 DEBIT	5 CREDIT	
9	12	Rent Expense	C4		3 0 0 00				3 0 0 00	9
10	12	Utilities Expense	C5		4 0 00				4 0 00	10

August 12. Paid cash for rent, $300.00. Check No. 4.

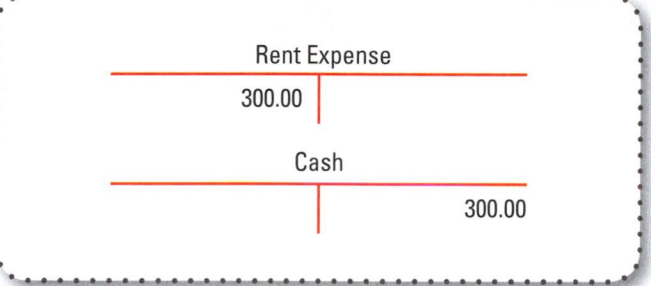

Rent Expense

300.00 |

Cash

| 300.00

The source document for this transaction is Check No. 4. [CONCEPT: Objective Evidence] The analysis of this transaction is shown in the T accounts.

The expense account, Rent Expense, increases by a debit, $300.00. The asset account, Cash, decreases by a credit, $300.00.

The reason that Rent Expense is increased by a debit is discussed in the previous chapter. The owner's capital account has a normal credit balance. Decreases in the owner's capital account are shown as debits.

Because expenses decrease owner's equity, increases in expenses are recorded as debits. An expense account, therefore, has a normal debit balance.

Whenever cash is paid for an expense, the journal entry is similar to the entry discussed above. Therefore, the journal entry to record paying cash for utilities is also illustrated.

STEPS — JOURNALIZING CASH PAID FOR AN EXPENSE

1. **Date.** Write the date, *12*, in the Date column.

2. **Debit.** There is no special amount column with the title of the account debited, *Rent Expense*, in its heading. Therefore, write the debit amount, *$300.00*, in the General Debit column. To indicate what account is to be debited for this amount, write the title of the account, *Rent Expense*, in the Account Title column.

3. **Credit.** The journal has a special amount column for credits to *Cash*. Write the credit amount, *$300.00*, in the Cash Credit column. The title of the account is in the column heading. Therefore, do not write the account title in the Account Title column.

4. **Source document.** Write the source document number, *C4*, in the Doc. No. column.

FOR YOUR INFORMATION

F Y I

Source documents can be critically important in tracking down errors. Businesses file their source documents so they can be referred to if it is necessary to verify information entered into their journals.

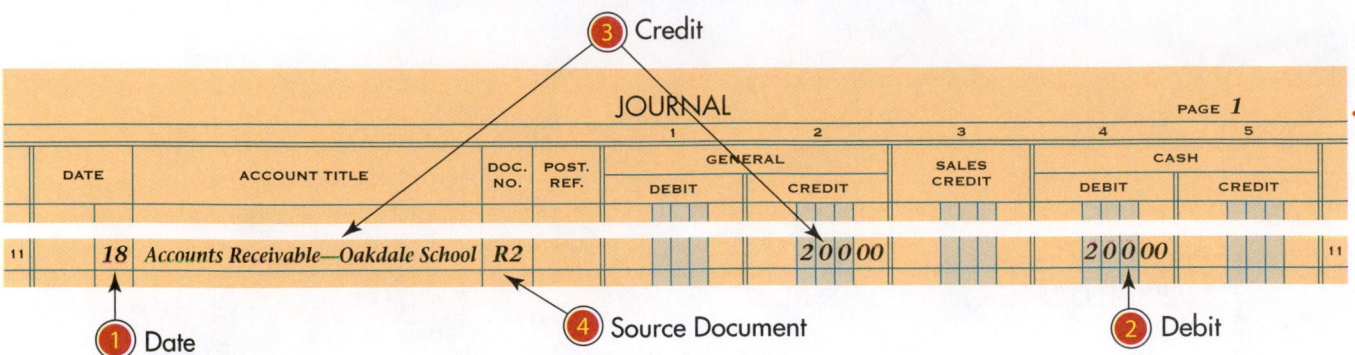

③ Credit

	DATE	ACCOUNT TITLE	DOC. NO.	POST. REF.	GENERAL DEBIT	GENERAL CREDIT	SALES CREDIT	CASH DEBIT	CASH CREDIT	
11	18	Accounts Receivable—Oakdale School	R2			2 0 0 00		2 0 0 00		11

JOURNAL   PAGE *1*

① Date   ④ Source Document   ② Debit

August 18. Received cash on account from Oakdale School, $200.00. Receipt No. 2.

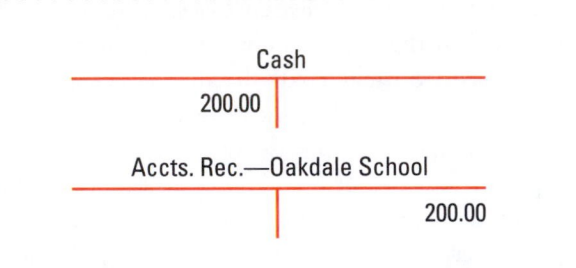

Cash

200.00

Accts. Rec.—Oakdale School

200.00

The source document for this transaction is Receipt No. 2. [CONCEPT: Objective Evidence] The analysis of this transaction is shown in the T accounts.

The asset account, Cash, increases by a debit, $200.00. The asset account, Accounts Receivable—Oakdale School, decreases by a credit, $200.00.

STEPS JOURNALIZING CASH RECEIVED ON ACCOUNT

① **Date.** Write the date, *18*, in the Date column.

② **Debit.** The journal has a special amount column for debits to *Cash*. Write the debit amount, *$200.00,* in the Cash Debit column. The title of the account is in the column heading. Therefore, do not write the account title in the Account Title column.

③ **Credit.** There is no special amount column with the title of the account credited, *Accounts Receivable—Oakdale School,* in its heading. Therefore, record the credit amount, *$200.00,* in the General Credit column. To indicate what account is to be credited for this amount, write the title of the account, *Accounts Receivable—Oakdale School,* in the Account Title column.

④ **Source document.** Write the source document number, *R2,* in the Doc. No. column.

REMEMBER

If you misspell words in your written communications, people may mistrust the quality of your accounting skills. Note that in the word receipt, the "e" comes before the "i" and there is a silent "p" before the "t" at the end of the word.

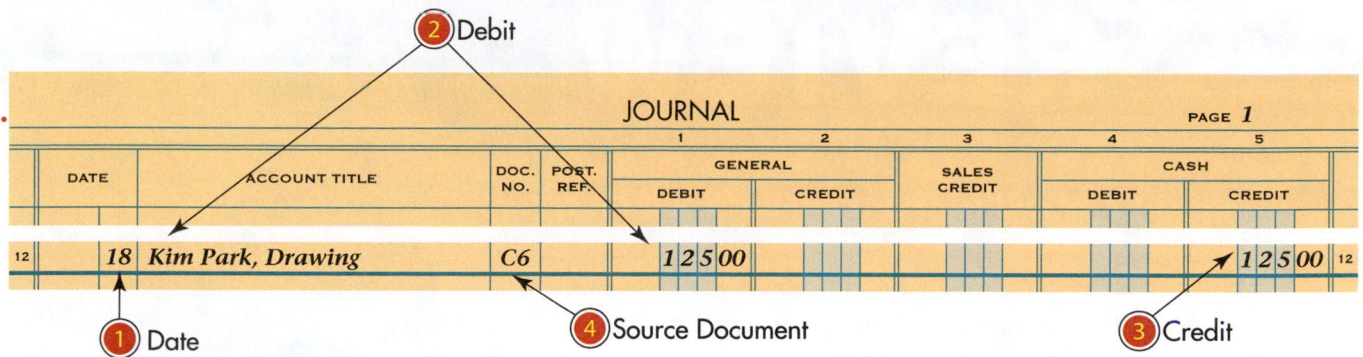

② Debit

	DATE	ACCOUNT TITLE	DOC. NO.	POST. REF.	GENERAL DEBIT	GENERAL CREDIT	SALES CREDIT	CASH DEBIT	CASH CREDIT	
12	18	*Kim Park, Drawing*	C6		1 2 5 00				1 2 5 00	12

① Date   **④ Source Document**   **③ Credit**

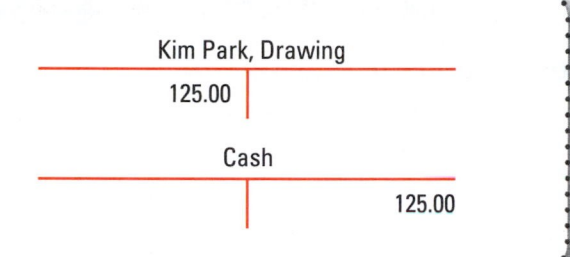

August 18. Paid cash to owner for personal use, $125.00. Check No. 6.

Kim Park, Drawing

125.00 |

Cash

| 125.00

The source document for this transaction is Check No. 6. [CONCEPT: Objective Evidence] The analysis of this transaction is shown in the T accounts.

The reason that Kim Park, Drawing increased by a debit is discussed in the previous chapter. Decreases in the owner's capital account are shown as debits. Because withdrawals decrease owner's equity, increases in withdrawals are recorded as debits. A withdrawal account, therefore, has a normal debit balance.

STEPS   JOURNALIZING CASH PAID TO OWNER FOR PERSONAL USE

① **Date.** Write the date, *18,* in the Date column.

② **Debit.** There is no special amount column with the title of the account debited, *Kim Park, Drawing,* in its heading. Therefore, record the debit amount, *$125.00,* in the General Debit column. To indicate what account is debited for this amount, write the title of the account, *Kim Park, Drawing,* in the Account Title column.

③ **Credit.** The journal has a special amount column for credits to *Cash.* Write the credit amount, *$125.00,* in the Cash Credit column. The title of the account is in the column heading. Therefore, do not write the account title in the Account Title column.

④ **Source document.** Write the source document number, *C6,* in the Doc. No. column.

SMALL BUSINESS

SPOTLIGHT

Successful small business owners typically have the following characteristics: confidence to make decisions, determination to keep trying during hard times for the business, willingness to take risks, creativity to surpass the competition, and an inner need to achieve.

End of Lesson REVIEW

AUDIT YOUR UNDERSTANDING

1. Which journal columns are used to record receiving cash from sales?
2. Which journal columns are used to record sales on account?
3. Which journal columns are used to record paying cash for an expense?
4. Which journal columns are used to record receiving cash on account?
5. Which journal columns are used to record paying cash to the owner for personal use?

WORK TOGETHER 3-3

Journalizing transactions that affect owner's equity in a five-column journal

Use the chart of accounts and journal from Work Together 3-2. Your instructor will guide you through the following example.

Transactions:

Apr. 12. Paid cash for rent, $1,000.00. C4.
13. Received cash from sales, $2,500.00. T13.
14. Sold services on account to L. Rohe, $510.00. S1.
19. Paid cash for electric bill, $148.00. C5.
20. Received cash on account from L. Rohe, $255.00. R2.
21. Paid cash to owner for personal use, $1,000.00. C6.

1. Journalize the transactions continuing on the next blank line of page 1 of the journal. Source documents are abbreviated as follows: check, C; receipt, R; sales invoice, S; calculator tape, T. Save your work to complete Work Together 3-4.

ON YOUR OWN 3-3

Journalizing transactions that affect owner's equity in a five-column journal

Use the chart of accounts and journal from On Your Own 3-2. Work this problem independently.

Transactions:

June 11. Paid cash for rent, $525.00. C4.
12. Sold services on account to C. Lord, $700.00. S1.
16. Received cash from sales, $2,300.00. T16.
17. Paid cash for postage (Miscellaneous Expense), $37.00. C5.
19. Received cash on account from C. Lord, $350.00. R2.
20. Paid cash to owner for personal use, $850.00. C6.

1. Journalize the transactions continuing on the next blank line of page 1 of the journal. Source documents are abbreviated as follows: check, C; receipt, R; sales invoice, S; calculator tape, T. Save your work to complete On Your Own 3-4.

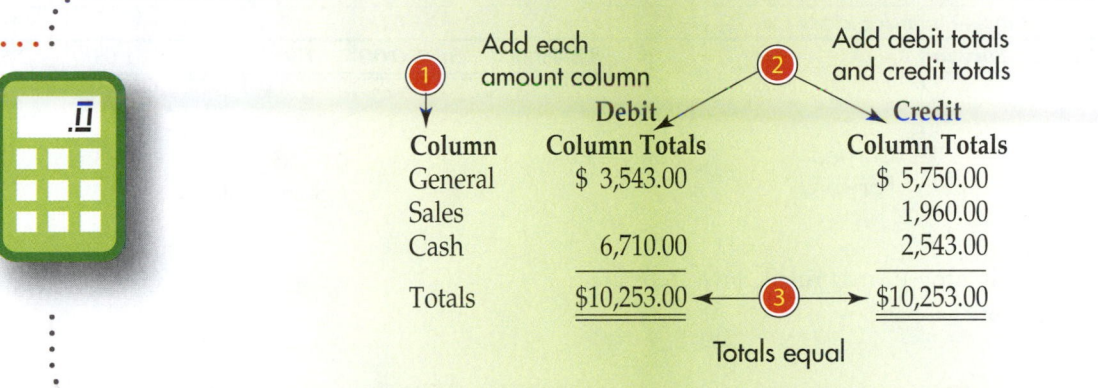

························· **PROVING A JOURNAL PAGE** ·········

	Add each amount column	Add debit totals and credit totals	
Column	Debit Column Totals	Credit Column Totals	
General	$ 3,543.00	$ 5,750.00	
Sales		1,960.00	
Cash	6,710.00	2,543.00	
Totals	$10,253.00	$10,253.00	

Totals equal

After TechKnow Consulting uses all but the last line on a journal page, columns are proved and ruled before totals are carried forward to the next page.

To prove a journal page, TechKnow Consulting verifies that the total debits on the page equal the total credits. Three steps are followed in proving a journal page.

STEPS **PROVING A JOURNAL PAGE**

1 Add each of the amount columns.

2 Add the debit column totals, and then add the credit column totals.

3 Verify that the total debits and total credits are equal. Because the total debits equal the total credits, page 1 of the journal is proved.

   If the total debits do not equal the total credits, the errors must be found and corrected before any more work is completed.

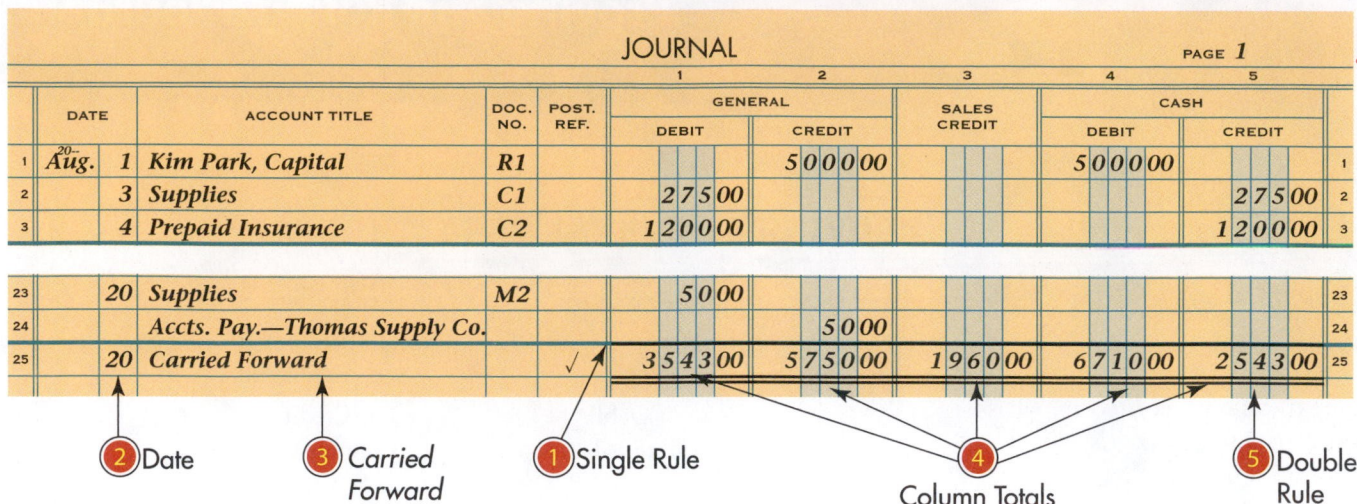

	DATE		ACCOUNT TITLE	DOC. NO.	POST. REF.	GENERAL		SALES CREDIT	CASH		
						DEBIT (1)	CREDIT (2)	(3)	DEBIT (4)	CREDIT (5)	
1	20– Aug.	1	Kim Park, Capital	R1			5 0 0 0 00		5 0 0 0 00		1
2		3	Supplies	C1		2 7 5 00				2 7 5 00	2
3		4	Prepaid Insurance	C2		1 2 0 0 00				1 2 0 0 00	3
23		20	Supplies	M2		5 0 00					23
24			Accts. Pay.—Thomas Supply Co.				5 0 00				24
25		20	Carried Forward		✓	3 5 4 3 00	5 7 5 0 00	1 9 6 0 00	6 7 1 0 00	2 5 4 3 00	25

② Date ③ Carried Forward ① Single Rule ④ Column Totals ⑤ Double Rule

After a journal page is proved, it is ruled. Five steps are followed in ruling a journal page.

STEPS — RULING A JOURNAL PAGE

① Rule a single line across all amount columns directly below the last entry to indicate that columns are to be totaled.

② On the next line, write the date, *20,* in the Date column.

③ Write *Carried Forward* in the Account Title column. Place a check mark in the Post. Ref. column. The use of the Post. Ref. column is described in Chapter 4.

④ Write each column total below the single line.

⑤ Rule double lines below the column totals across all amount columns. A double rule in a journal indicates that the amounts are totals and that the sum of the debit totals equals the sum of the credit totals.

PHOTODISC/GETTY IMAGES

FOR YOUR INFORMATION
FYI

Account titles in accounting records should always be written so that there is no question about the meaning. The usual practice is to write the full account title. If a title is long, however, and the space is short, an account title may sometimes have to be abbreviated.

STARTING A NEW JOURNAL PAGE

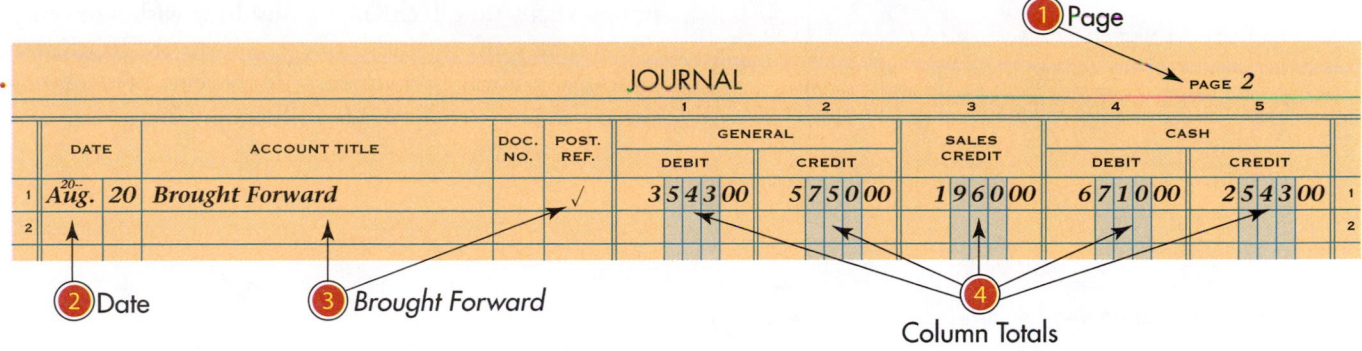

① Page

② Date   **③ Brought Forward**

④ Column Totals

The column totals from the previous page are carried forward to a new page. The totals are recorded on the first line of the new page, using the following four steps.

STEPS STARTING A NEW JOURNAL PAGE

① Write the page number, *2*, at the top of the journal.

② Write the date, *20--, Aug. 20*, in the Date column. Because this is the first time that a date is written on page 2, the year, month, and day are all written in the Date column.

③ Write *Brought Forward* in the Account Title column. A check mark is also placed in the Post. Ref. column.

④ Record the column totals brought forward from the previous page.

PROVING AND RULING A JOURNAL AT THE END OF A MONTH

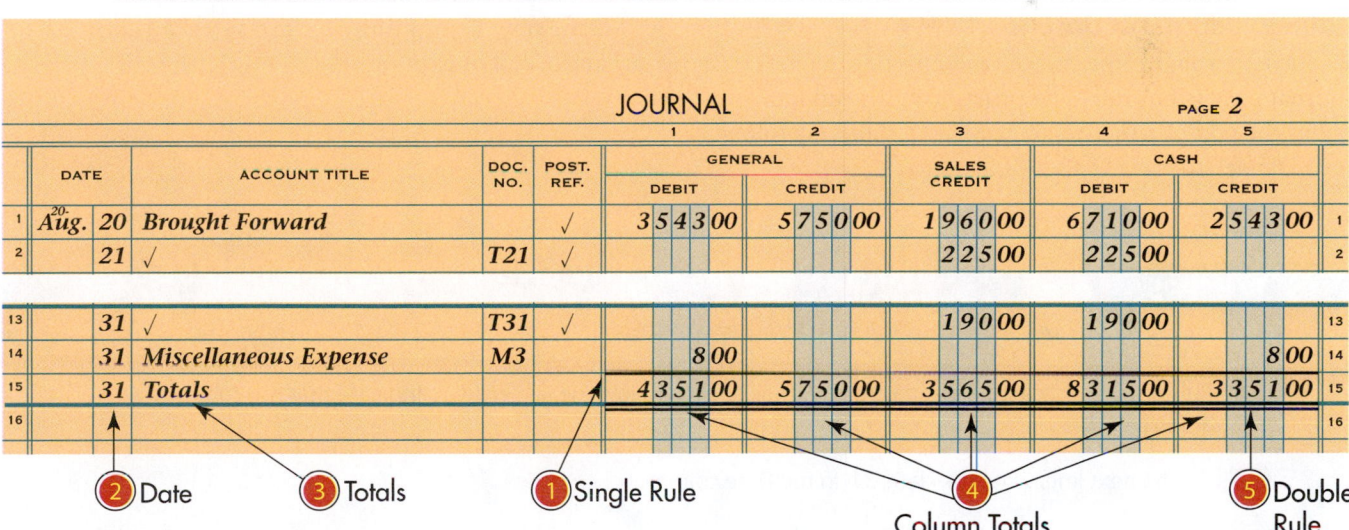

② Date   **③ Totals**   **① Single Rule**   **④ Column Totals**   **⑤ Double Rule**

TechKnow Consulting always proves and rules a journal at the end of each month, even if the last page for the month is not full.

The last page of a journal for a month is proved using the same steps previously described. Then, cash is proved and the journal is ruled. The proof of page 2 of TechKnow Consulting's journal is completed as shown on the next page. Proving cash is also discussed on the next page.

Page 2 of TechKnow Consulting's journal is proved because the total debits are equal to the total credits, $12,666.00.

Column	Debit Column Totals	Credit Column Totals
General	$ 4,351.00	$ 5,750.00
Sales		3,565.00
Cash	8,315.00	3,351.00
Totals	$12,666.00	$12,666.00

Proving Cash

Determining that the amount of cash agrees with the accounting records is called **proving cash**. Cash can be proved at any time TechKnow Consulting wishes to verify the accuracy of the cash records. However, TechKnow Consulting always proves cash at the end of a month when the journal is proved. TechKnow Consulting uses two steps to prove cash.

1. Calculate the cash balance.

Cash on hand at the beginning of the month. . . . . $ 0.00

TechKnow Consulting began the month with no cash balance. Ms. Park invested the initial cash on August 1.

Plus total cash received during the month. . . . . +8,315.00

This amount is the total of the journal's Cash Debit column.

Equals total . . . . $ 8,315.00

Less total cash paid during the month . . . . −3,351.00

This amount is the total of the journal's Cash Credit column.

Equals cash balance at the end of the month . . . . $ 4,964.00

2. Verify that the cash balance equals the checkbook balance on the next unused check stub in the checkbook. Because the cash balance calculated using the journal and the checkbook balance are the same, $4,964.00, cash is proved.

Checkbook balance on the next unused check stub . . . . $ 4,964.00

The double rules in the calculations above indicate that the amounts are totals and the work is proved.

Ruling a Journal at the End of a Month

A journal is ruled at the end of each month even if the last journal page is not full. The procedures for ruling a journal at the end of a month are similar to those for ruling a journal page to carry the totals forward.

TechKnow Consulting uses five steps in ruling a journal at the end of each month.

STEPS — RULING A JOURNAL AT THE END OF A MONTH (THESE STEPS ARE ILLUSTRATED ON THE PREVIOUS PAGE)

1. Rule a single line across all amount columns directly below the last entry to indicate that the columns are to be added.

2. On the next line, write the date, *31,* in the Date column.

3. Write the word *Totals* in the Account Title column.
   A check mark is not placed in the Post. Ref. column for this line. More information about the Totals line will be provided in Chapter 4.

4. Write each column total below the single line.

5. Rule double lines below the column totals across all amount columns. The double lines mean that the amounts are totals and that the debit totals equal the credit totals.

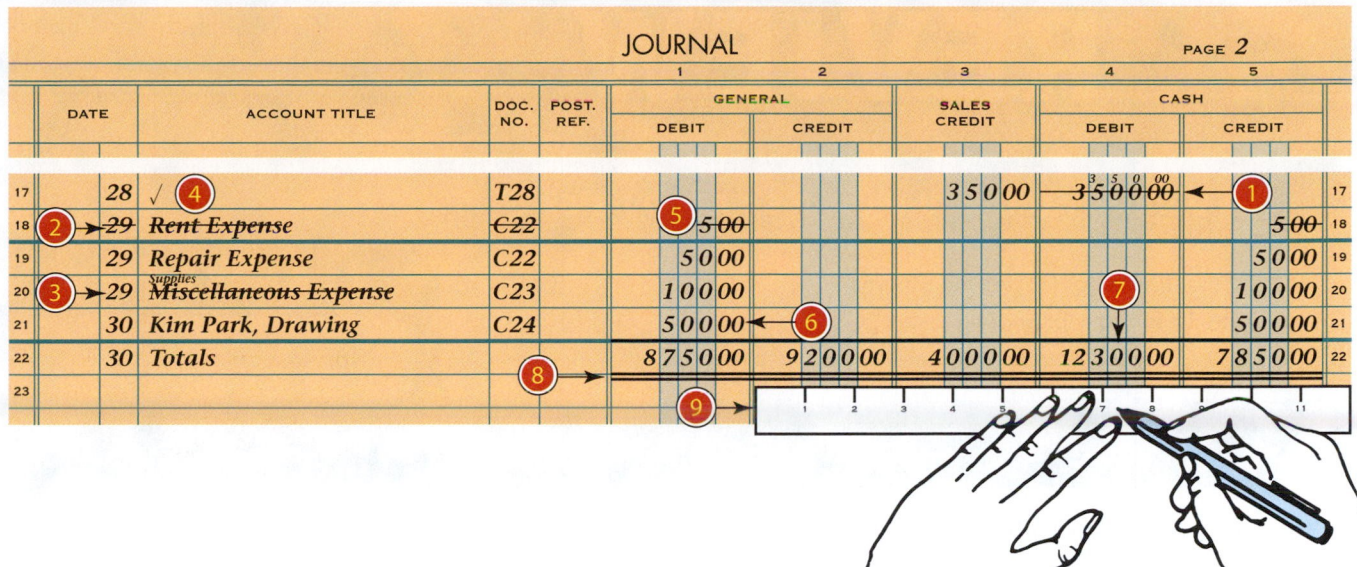

JOURNAL   PAGE 2

	DATE	ACCOUNT TITLE	DOC. NO.	POST. REF.	GENERAL DEBIT	GENERAL CREDIT	SALES CREDIT	CASH DEBIT	CASH CREDIT	
17	28	✓	T28				3 5 0 00	3 5 0 00		17
18	29	Rent Expense	C22		5 00				5 00	18
19	29	Repair Expense	C22		5 0 00				5 0 00	19
20	29	Supplies / Miscellaneous Expense	C23		1 0 0 00				1 0 0 00	20
21	30	Kim Park, Drawing	C24		5 0 0 00				5 0 0 00	21
22	30	Totals			8 7 5 0 00	9 2 0 0 00	4 0 0 0 00	12 3 0 0 00	7 8 5 0 00	22
23										23

In completing accounting work, TechKnow Consulting follows standard accounting practices. These practices include procedures for error corrections, abbreviating words, writing dollar and cents signs, and ruling columns.

1. Errors are corrected in a way that does not cause doubts about what the correct information is. If an error is recorded, cancel the error by neatly drawing a line through the incorrect item. Write the correct item immediately above the canceled item.

2. Sometimes an entire entry is incorrect and is discovered before the next entry is journalized. Draw neat lines through all parts of the incorrect entry. Journalize the entry correctly on the next blank line.

3. Sometimes several correct entries are recorded after an incorrect entry is made. The next blank lines are several entries later. Draw neat lines through all incorrect parts of the entry. Record the correct items on the same lines as the incorrect items, directly above the canceled parts.

4. Words in accounting records are written in full when space permits. Words may be abbreviated only when space is limited. All items are written legibly.

5. Dollars and cents signs and decimal points are not used when writing amounts on ruled accounting paper. Sometimes a color tint or a heavy vertical rule is used on printed accounting paper to separate the dollars and cents columns.

6. Two zeros are written in the cents column when an amount is in even dollars, such as $500.00. If the cents column is left blank, doubts may arise later about the correct amount.

7. A single line is ruled across amount columns to indicate a calculation such as addition.

8. A double line is ruled across amount columns to indicate that the amounts are totals. In a journal the double rules also indicate that the debit totals equal the credit totals.

9. Neatness is very important in accounting records so that there is never any doubt about what information has been recorded. A ruler is used to make single and double lines.

End of Lesson
REVIEW

AUDIT YOUR UNDERSTANDING

1. List the three steps for proving a journal.
2. State the formula for proving cash.
3. List the five steps to rule a journal at the end of a month.

TERM REVIEW

proving cash

WORK TOGETHER 3-4

Proving and ruling a journal

Use the journal from Work Together 3-3. Your instructor will guide you through the following examples.

Transactions:

Apr. 23. Sold services on account to L. Rohe, $375.00. S2.
    27. Paid cash to owner for personal use, $500.00. C7.
    29. Received cash on account from L. Rohe, $300.00. R3.
    30. Received cash from sales, $544.00. T30.

1. Journalize the transactions for April 23 and 27. Source documents are abbreviated as follows: check, C; receipt, R; sales invoice, S; calculator tape, T.

2. Prove and rule page 1 of the journal. Carry the column totals forward to page 2 of the journal.

3. Use page 2 of the journal to journalize the rest of the transactions for April.

4. Prove page 2 of the journal.

5. Prove cash. The beginning cash balance on April 1 is zero. The balance on the next unused check stub is $1,526.00.

6. Rule page 2 of the journal.

ON YOUR OWN 3-4

Proving and ruling a journal

Use the journal from On Your Own 3-3. Work this problem independently.

Transactions:

June 23. Sold services on account to C. Lord, $400.00. S2.
    26. Paid cash for delivery charges (Miscellaneous Expense), $23.00. C7.
    27. Received cash on account from C. Lord, $200.00. R3.
    30. Received cash from sales, $422.00. T30.

1. Journalize the transactions for June 23 and 26. Source documents are abbreviated as follows: check, C; memorandum, M; receipt, R; sales invoice, S; calculator tape, T.

2. Prove and rule page 1 of the journal. Carry the column totals forward to page 2 of the journal.

3. Use page 2 of the journal to journalize the rest of the transactions for June.

4. Prove page 2 of the journal.

5. Prove cash. The beginning cash balance on June 1 is zero. The balance on the next unused check stub is $3,187.00.

6. Rule page 2 of the journal.

After completing this chapter, you can:

1. Define accounting terms related to journalizing transactions.

2. Identify accounting concepts and practices related to journalizing transactions.

3. Record transactions to set up a business in a five-column journal.

4. Record transactions to buy insurance for cash and supplies on account in a five-column journal.

5. Record transactions that affect owner's equity and receiving cash on account in a five-column journal.

6. Prove and rule a five-column journal and prove cash.

EXPLORE ACCOUNTING

Prenumbered Documents

As one way to control the operations of the business, a company often will use prenumbered documents. Such a document is one that has the form number printed on it in advance. The most common example in everyday life is the personal check.

Businesses use several prenumbered documents. Examples include business checks, sales invoices, receipts, and memorandums.

The use of prenumbered documents allows a simple way to ensure that all documents are recorded. For example, when a business records the checks written during a period of time, all check numbers should be accounted for in numeric order. The person recording the checks must watch to see that no numbers are skipped. In this way, the business is more confident that all checks are recorded.

By using several types of prenumbered documents, the business helps ensure that all transactions are properly recorded.

Another way a business tries to control operations is through the use of batch totals. When many (sometimes hundreds) of documents are being recorded, the total amount can be used to help ensure that all documents are recorded.

For example, when sales invoices are recorded, the total of all the invoices is calculated prior to the invoices being recorded. Once all invoices are recorded, another total can be calculated. If the two totals are equal, it is assumed that all invoices have been recorded. If the totals do not equal, it may indicate that a document was skipped.

Research: With your instructor's permission, contact a local business and ask what prenumbered documents are used there. Determine how the business uses the documents to ensure that all documents are recorded properly.

3-1   APPLICATION PROBLEM

Journalizing transactions in a five-column journal

Dennis Gilbert owns a service business called D & G Company, which uses the following accounts.

Cash	Accts. Pay.—Scott Supplies	Miscellaneous Expense
Accts. Rec.—Covey Company	Dennis Gilbert, Capital	Rent Expense
Supplies	Dennis Gilbert, Drawing	Utilities Expense
Prepaid Insurance	Sales	

Transactions:

Feb. 1. Received cash from owner as an investment, $10,000.00. R1.
    4. Paid cash for supplies, $3,000.00. C1.
    5. Paid cash for supplies, $250.00. C2.

Instructions:

Journalize the transactions completed during February of the current year. Use page 1 of the journal given in the *Working Papers*. Source documents are abbreviated as follows: check, C; receipt, R.
    Save your work to complete Application Problem 3-2.

3-2   APPLICATION PROBLEM

Journalizing buying insurance, buying on account, and paying on account in a five-column journal

Use the chart of accounts and journal from Application Problem 3-1.

Transactions:

Feb. 6. Paid cash for insurance, $600.00. C3.
    7. Bought supplies on account from Scott Supplies, $2,000.00. M1.
    8. Paid cash on account to Scott Supplies, $1,000.00. C4.
  12. Paid cash on account to Scott Supplies, $1,000.00. C5.

Instructions:

Journalize the transactions. Source documents are abbreviated as follows: check, C; memorandum, M. Save your work to complete Application Problem 3-3.

Go Beyond the Book
For more information go to
www.C21accounting.com

3-3 | APPLICATION PROBLEM

Journalizing transactions that affect owner's equity and receiving cash on account in a five-column journal

Use the chart of accounts given in Application Problem 3-1 and the journal from Application Problem 3-2.

Transactions:

Feb. 12. Paid cash for rent, $800.00. C6.
13. Received cash from sales, $500.00. T13.
14. Sold services on account to Covey Company, $450.00. S1.
15. Paid cash for telephone bill, $380.00. C7.
15. Paid cash to owner for personal use, $2,800.00. C8.
18. Received cash from sales, $278.00. T18.
19. Paid cash for postage (Miscellaneous Expense), $64.00. C9.
21. Received cash on account from Covey Company, $250.00. R2.
22. Received cash from sales, $700.00. T22.
22. Paid cash for heating bill, $329.00. C10.
25. Bought supplies on account from Scott Supplies, $340.00. M2.

Instructions:

Journalize the transactions. Source documents are abbreviated as follows: check, C; memorandum, M; receipt, R; sales invoice, S; calculator tape, T. Save your work to complete Application Problem 3-4.

3-4 | APPLICATION PROBLEM

Proving and ruling a journal

Use the chart of accounts given in Application Problem 3-1 and the journal from Application Problem 3-3.

Transactions:

Feb. 25. Received cash on account from Covey Company, $200.00. R3.
25. Paid cash for a delivery (Miscellaneous Expense), $25.00. C11.
26. Sold services on account to Covey Company, $800.00. S2.
26. Paid cash for supplies, $44.00. C12.
27. Paid cash for rent, $200.00. C13.
27. Paid cash for postage (Miscellaneous Expense), $37.00. C14.
28. Received cash from sales, $1,365.00. T28.
28. Paid cash to owner for personal use, $800.00. C15.

Instructions:

1. Journalize the transactions for February 25 and 26. Source documents are abbreviated as follows: check, C; receipt, R; sales invoice, S; calculator tape, T.
2. Prove and rule page 1 of the journal. Carry the column totals forward to page 2 of the journal.
3. Use page 2 of the journal to journalize the transactions for February 27 and 28.
4. Prove page 2 of the journal.
5. Prove cash. The beginning cash balance on February 1 is zero. The balance on the next unused check stub is $1,964.00.
6. Rule page 2 of the journal.

APPLICATION PROBLEM

Journalizing transactions and proving and ruling a five-column journal

Hans Schultz owns a service business called YardCare, which uses the following accounts.

Cash	Accts. Pay.—Midwest Supplies	Advertising Expense
Accts. Rec.—Frank Morris	Hans Schultz, Capital	Utilities Expense
Supplies	Hans Schultz, Drawing	
Prepaid Insurance	Sales	

Transactions:

Apr. 1. Hans Schultz invested $2,500.00 of his own money in the business. Receipt No. 1.
3. Used business cash to purchase supplies costing $105.00. Wrote Check No. 1.
4. Wrote Check No. 2 for insurance, $240.00.
5. Purchased supplies for $75.00 over the phone from Midwest Supplies, promising to send the check next week. Memo. No. 1.
11. Sent Check No. 3 to Midwest Supplies, $75.00.
12. Sent a check for the electricity bill, $65.00. Check No. 4.
15. Wrote a $700.00 check to Mr. Schultz for personal use. Used Check No. 5.
16. Sold services for $358.00 to Frank Morris, who agreed to pay for them within 10 days. Sales Invoice No. 1.
17. Recorded cash sales of $1,287.00.
18. Paid $90.00 for advertising. Wrote Check No. 6.
25. Received $358.00 from Frank Morris for the services performed last week. Wrote Receipt No. 2.

Instructions:

1. Journalize the transactions completed during April of the current year. Use page 1 of the journal given in the *Working Papers*. Remember to record appropriate source document numbers.

2. Prove and rule the journal.

3. Prove cash. The beginning cash balance on April 1 is zero. The balance on the next unused check stub is $2,870.00.

MASTERY PROBLEM

Journalizing transactions and proving and ruling a five-column journal

Jane Fernandez owns a service business called Jane's Car Wash, which uses the following accounts.

Cash	Accts. Pay.—Pine Supplies	Miscellaneous Expense
Accts. Rec.—Tony's Limos	Jane Fernandez, Capital	Rent Expense
Supplies	Jane Fernandez, Drawing	Repair Expense
Prepaid Insurance	Sales	Utilities Expense
Accts. Pay.—Atkin Supplies	Advertising Expense	

Transactions:

June 1. Received cash from owner as an investment, $16,000.00. R1.
2. Paid cash for supplies, $300.00. C1.
3. Paid cash for rent, $900.00. C2.
4. Bought supplies on account from Atkin Supplies, $1,700.00. M1.
5. Paid cash for electric bill, $146.00. C3.
8. Paid cash on account to Atkin Supplies, $1,000.00. C4.
8. Received cash from sales, $980.00. T8.
8. Sold services on account to Tony's Limos, $450.00. S1.

9. Paid cash for insurance, $1,200.00. C5.
10. Paid cash for repairs, $388.00. C6.
10. Received cash from sales, $476.00. T10.
11. Paid cash for miscellaneous expense, $15.00. C7.
11. Received cash from sales, $630.00. T11.
12. Received cash from sales, $900.00. T12.
15. Paid cash to owner for personal use, $400.00. C8.
15. Received cash from sales, $850.00. T15.
16. Paid cash for supplies, $1,100.00. C9.
17. Received cash on account from Tony's Limos, $225.00. R2.
17. Bought supplies on account from Pine Supplies, $600.00. M2.
17. Received cash from sales, $500.00. T17.
18. Received cash from sales, $800.00. T18.
19. Received cash from sales, $650.00. T19.
22. Bought supplies on account from Pine Supplies, $60.00. M3.
22. Received cash from sales, $610.00. T22.
23. Paid cash for telephone bill, $85.00. C10.
23. Sold services on account to Tony's Limos, $582.00. S2.
24. Paid cash for advertising, $125.00. C11.
24. Received cash from sales, $300.00. T24.
25. Received cash from sales, $770.00. T25.
26. Paid cash for supplies, $90.00. C12.
26. Received cash from sales, $300.00. T26.
29. Received cash on account from Tony's Limos, $350.00. R3.
30. Paid cash to owner for personal use, $450.00. C13.
30. Received cash from sales, $500.00. T30.

Instructions:

1. The journals for Jane's Car Wash are given in the *Working Papers*. Use page 1 of the journal to journalize the transactions for June 1 through June 19. Source documents are abbreviated as follows: check, C; memorandum, M; receipt, R; sales invoice, S; calculator tape, T.

2. Prove and rule page 1 of the journal. Carry the column totals forward to page 2 of the journal.

3. Use page 2 of the journal to journalize the transactions for the remainder of June.

4. Prove page 2 of the journal.

5. Prove cash. The beginning cash balance on June 1 is zero. The balance on the next unused check stub is $18,642.00.

6. Rule page 2 of the journal.

3-7 CHALLENGE PROBLEM

Journalizing transactions using a variation of the five-column journal

Tony Wirth owns a service business called Wirth's Tailors, which uses the following accounts.

Cash	Accts. Pay.—Marker Supplies	Rent Expense
Accts. Rec.—Amy's Uniforms	Tony Wirth, Capital	Utilities Expense
Supplies	Tony Wirth, Drawing	
Prepaid Insurance	Sales	

Transactions:

June 1. Received cash from owner as an investment, $17,000.00. R1.
2. Paid cash for insurance, $3,000.00. C1.
3. Bought supplies on account from Marker Supplies, $2,500.00. M1.
4. Paid cash for supplies, $1,400.00. C2.

8. Paid cash on account to Marker Supplies, $1,300.00. C3.
9. Paid cash for rent, $800.00. C4.
12. Received cash from sales, $550.00. T12.
15. Sold services on account to Amy's Uniforms, $300.00. S1.
16. Paid cash for telephone bill, $70.00. C5.
22. Received cash on account from Amy's Uniforms, $300.00. R2.
25. Paid cash to owner for personal use, $900.00. C6.

Instructions:

The journal for Wirth's Tailors is given in the *Working Papers*. Wirth's Tailors uses a journal with a column arrangement slightly different from the journal used in this chapter, as shown below.

1. Use page 1 of the journal to journalize the transactions. Source documents are abbreviated as follows: check, C; memorandum, M; receipt, R; sales invoice, S; calculator tape, T.

2. Prove and rule the journal.

3. Prove cash. The beginning cash balance on June 1 is zero. The balance on the next unused check stub is $10,380.00.

APPLIED COMMUNICATION

Careful research about careers will help prepare you for making career choices. There are several U.S. government publications that provide detailed descriptions of many job titles. Two that are available in most public libraries are the *Dictionary of Occupational Titles (DOT)* and the *Occupational Outlook Handbook*.

Instructions: Go to the library and, using one of the two publications listed or any other appropriate resource, find the description for any accounting-related job. Record information you find, such as qualifications needed, job outlook, and earnings. Write one paragraph describing the pros and cons of working in such a job. Be sure to write a topic sentence and a conclusion.

CASES FOR CRITICAL THINKING

Case 1

During the summer, Willard Kelly does a variety of small jobs for many different people in the community to earn money. Mr. Kelly keeps all his money in a single checking account. He writes checks to pay for personal items and for business expenses. These payments include personal clothing, school supplies, gasoline for his car, and recreation. Mr. Kelly uses his check stubs as his accounting records. Are Mr. Kelly's accounting procedures and records correct? Explain your answer.

Case 2

In her business, Monica Zapata uses a journal with the following columns: Date, Account Title, Check No., Cash Debit, and Cash Credit. Ms. Zapata's husband, Rodrigo, suggests that she needs three additional amount columns: General Debit, General Credit, and Sales Credit. Ms. Zapata states that all her business transactions are for cash, and she never buys on account. Therefore, she doesn't see the need for more than the Cash Debit and Cash Credit special amount columns. Who is correct, Ms. or Mr. Zapata? Explain your answer.

Basic Skill: Writing

Concept: Employers frequently cite the ability to communicate as one of the most important skills they require in employees. When communicating thoughts, ideas, and information, it is important to be clear and concise so that the intended receiver of the communication understands the message.

Application: Proprietorships are the most common form of business organization in the United States with over 17 million proprietorships filing tax returns. Review the advantages and disadvantages of proprietorships in Chapter 1 and write a paragraph describing why you think proprietorships are the most common form of business organization.

USING SOURCE DOCUMENTS

Journalizing transactions and proving and ruling a journal

Cy Sawyer owns a service business called Cy's Repair Service, which uses the following accounts.

Cash	Accts. Pay.—Atlas Supplies	Miscellaneous Expense
Accts. Rec.—J. Hutton	Cy Sawyer, Capital	Rent Expense
Supplies	Cy Sawyer, Drawing	Utilities Expense
Prepaid Insurance	Sales	

Source documents related to the transactions for Cy's Repair Service for May are provided in the *Working Papers*.

Instructions

1. The journal for Cy's Repair Service is given in the *Working Papers*. Use page 1 of the journal to journalize the transactions for May. Source documents are abbreviated as follows: check, C; memorandum, M; receipt, R; sales invoice, S; calculator tape, T.

2. Prove the journal.

3. Prove cash. The beginning cash balance on May 1 is zero. The balance on the next unused check stub is $5,223.00.

4. Rule the journal.

ANALYZING BEST BUY'S FINANCIAL STATEMENTS

To calculate what percentage one amount is of another amount, you divide the smaller amount by the total that contains the amount. Using Best Buy as an example, Cash for 2007 = $1,205,000,000. Total assets for 2007 = $13,570,000,000. To calculate what percentage cash is of total assets, use the following formula: Cash, 1,205,000,000 ÷ total assets, 13,570,000,000. The answer is .0888 or 8.88%.

Instructions

1. Use the information on page B-5 in Appendix B. Find the amount of Receivables and Total Assets for Best Buy for 2006 and 2007. Calculate what percentage Receivables are of Total Assets for 2006 and 2007.

2. Did the percentage increase or decrease over this period of time?

3. If this percentage would increase rapidly, what could be happening?

Accounting
SOFTWARE

TOOLBAR, MENUS, HELP, AND PROBLEM INSTRUCTIONS

Modern software usually has several features in common. These include a toolbar, menus, and a Help function. A toolbar is a set of icons or buttons that perform a single function, such as Open, Save, or Print. The kinds and number of toolbar buttons vary with the software. In addition to the toolbar buttons, there are menus that perform more detailed functions. Each menu item usually includes several options that display when the menu item is clicked. Different kinds of software have different kinds of menu options.

The Help menu provides information about how to perform different kinds of functions using the software. Experienced users of a particular kind of software rarely use the Help function. However, it can be very useful when you are starting out and need to look up how to do a particular task. There are often several different kinds of help available on the Help menu.

PEACHTREE ACTIVITY

1. Open (Restore) the data file for Mastery Problem 4-5 (filename: 04-5MP.ptb).

2. Click the Help menu. Note that several options are available. Click the different options to see what is available. Then, click Contents and Index and search for help on adding an account ("add account"). Write a brief description of the procedure.

3. Close the data file and exit the software.

TOOLBAR, MENUS, HELP, AND PROBLEM INSTRUCTIONS

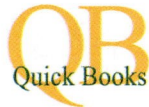

QuickBooks has toolbar, menu, and Help functions. A toolbar is a set of icons or buttons that perform a single function, such as Open, Save, or Print. The kinds and number of toolbar buttons vary with the software. In addition to the toolbar buttons, there are menus that perform more detailed functions. Each menu item usually includes several options that display when the menu item is clicked. Different kinds of software have different kinds of menu options.

The Help menu provides information about how to perform different kinds of functions using the software. Experienced users of a particular kind of software rarely use the Help function. However, it can be very useful when you are starting out and need to look up how to do a particular task. There are often several different kinds of help available on the Help menu.

QUICKBOOKS ACTIVITY

1. Open Mastery Problem 4-5 (filename: O'Kalla Lawn and Garden.qbw).

2. Click the Help menu. Note that several options are available. Click the different options to see what is available. Then, search for help on adding an account ("add account"). Write a brief description of the procedure.

3. Close the data file and exit the software.

BASIC SPREADSHEET TERMINOLOGY

A file containing an electronic spreadsheet is referred to as a *workbook*. A workbook can contain one or more work sheets, each containing the row and column cell structure in which text, numbers, and formulas are entered. A schedule or form created on a work sheet ready for data to be entered is referred to as a *template* or *data file*.

The Excel problem template files have at least two work sheets. One of the work sheets is labeled *Instructions*. The Instructions work sheet details the specific instructions for that problem. It is accessed by simply clicking the Instructions tab.

EXCEL ACTIVITY

1. Open the data file for Application Problem 5-2 (filename: F05-2.xls).
2. Click the Instructions tab and read the instructions for this problem. You will not complete this problem until Chapter 5.
3. Close the data file and exit the software.

HELP, PROBLEM INSTRUCTIONS, AND JOURNAL ENTRIES

The *Automated Accounting* software has a Help menu with features similar to all other software. The software also has a function that displays instructions for specific problems. Click the Browser toolbar button. This opens the default browser and displays the specific step-by-step instructions for a problem. The instructions may be displayed at any time they are needed. However, it is usually easier to simply minimize the browser with the instructions displayed and then maximize the browser when an instruction is needed.

Just as in manual accounting, transactions are recorded in a journal. A 2-column general journal is used for all problems in Part 1. The journal is accessed by clicking the Journal toolbar button and the General Journal tab. You may move to the next entry field with the Tab key or position with the mouse.

Date: Key the date or increase or decrease it with the + or − keys.

Refer.: The source document number and identifying letter abbreviation are keyed in the Refer. column.

Account: You may key the account number, select the account by clicking the chart of accounts button, or key part of the account title.

Debit: Key the debit amount in the debit column. Use the Tab key to advance to the next line for an additional account title.

Credit: Key the credit amount in the credit column.

Post: After all parts of a transaction are entered, click the Post button or press Enter in the last field of the entry. This prepares the software for a new transaction.

AUTOMATED ACCOUNTING ACTIVITY

1. Open your Automated Accounting software.
2. Open the data file for Application Problem 3-5 (filename: F03-5.AA8).
3. Click the Help button, then click Help Contents and Index.
4. Search for Help on adding a new account.
5. Keep the data file open to complete Application Problem 3-5.

AUTOMATED ACCOUNTING APPLICATION PROBLEM 3-5

Open file F03-5.AA8 if it is not already open. Display the problem instructions and complete the problem.

AUTOMATED ACCOUNTING MASTERY PROBLEM 3-6

Open file F03-6.AA8. Display the problem instructions and complete the problem.

REDCHOPSTICKS/GETTY IMAGES

CHAPTER 4

Posting to a General Ledger

After studying Chapter 4, you will be able to:

1. Define accounting terms related to posting from a journal to a general ledger.

2. Identify accounting concepts and practices related to posting from a journal to a general ledger.

3. Prepare a chart of accounts for a service business organized as a proprietorship.

4. Post separate amounts from a journal to a general ledger.

5. Post column totals from a journal to a general ledger.

6. Analyze and journalize correcting entries.

KEY TERMS

- ledger
- general ledger
- account number
- file maintenance
- opening an account
- posting
- correcting entry

Point Your Browser
www.C21accounting.com

88

AMAZON.COM

Record Sales Volume at Amazon.com

Have you ever realized the day before a special occasion that you forgot to purchase a gift for someone? Have you ever thought of going online, purchasing a gift, and getting it delivered the very next day?

On December 24 of a recent year, more than 70,000 gift certificates were ordered on Amazon.com. These certificates were delivered, via e-mail, on December 25. Recently Amazon.com, headquartered in Seattle, experienced its busiest holiday season and set a single-day record for items ordered—averaging 24 items per second!

©AP PHOTO/SCOTT SADY

In a letter to stockholders, Jeffrey P. Bezos, the founder and CEO of Amazon.com, explained about a Customer Review feature that had been established. This feature allows customers to rate both products and vendors. Mr. Bezos noted that "negative reviews cost us some sales in the short run." Also, an Instant Order Update feature reminds customers that they have already ordered an item if they order the same item again. Mr. Bezos stated that this feature "slightly reduced sales."

Critical Thinking

1. If the Customer Review feature and the Instant Order Update feature both reduce sales, why would Amazon.com continue to make these features available to its customers?

2. What problems might occur when Amazon.com receives orders at the rate of 24 items per second?

Source: www.amazon.com and Letter to Shareholders in 2003 Annual Report

DIGITAL VISION/GETTY IMAGES

INTERNET ACTIVITY

Securities and Exchange Commission

Go to the homepage for the Securities and Exchange Commission (SEC) at www.sec.gov. The SEC was created through two Acts of Congress. Search the site to find out more about these two Acts. This information is usually found under the headings such as "About the SEC" and/or "What We Do."

Instructions

1. List the names of the two Acts of Congress that created the SEC.

2. Briefly summarize the purposes of these two Acts.

Preparing a Chart of Accounts

ACCOUNT FORM

TechKnow Consulting records transactions in a journal, as described in Chapter 3. A journal is a permanent record of the debit and credit parts of each transaction with transactions recorded in chronological order. However, a journal does not show, in one place, all the changes in a single account.

If only a journal is used, a business must search through all journal pages to find items affecting a single account balance. For this reason, a form is used to summarize in one place all the changes to a single account. A separate form is used for each account.

CHARACTER COUNTS

Are Your Actions Legal?

"A man should be upright, not be kept upright." This famous statement by Marcus Aurelius suggests that, in a perfect world, everyone would always do the right thing. In the real world, however, governments have been forced to create complex systems of laws to force individuals to adhere to the social norm of right and wrong. We rely on these laws for our protection as well as the orderly operation of our society. For example, think about the chaos that might result if individuals could choose which side of the road to drive on! Many laws are common knowledge for individuals working in business:

- Employers may not discriminate on the basis of national origin.
- Customers may not be charged different prices for the same item.
- Taxes must be paid to the government.

Whether an action is legal is not always so obvious. Did you know:

- It may be illegal to sell certain items, such as computers and oil, to countries that violate global norms of conduct.
- An interviewer may not ask a prospective employee if he or she has children.
- Companies with more than $10 million in assets having more than 500 owners must file annual and other periodic reports with the government.

No one can be expected to know every law that might affect the operation of a business. To assist its managers, businesses hire lawyers to provide their managers with legal advice. Most large businesses have their own legal departments staffed with lawyers. Smaller businesses typically pay a retainer fee to an independent lawyer to provide legal advice when needed. All businesses should provide their managers with regular training on legal issues. Managers should be encouraged to consult the lawyers if there is any question whether an action might be illegal.

Instructions

Use an Internet or library source to prepare a list of questions that are illegal for an employer to ask during a job interview.

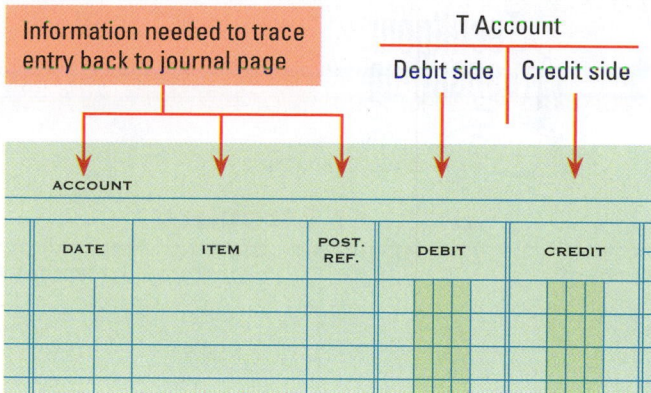

An account form is based on and includes the debit and credit sides of a T account. In addition to debit and credit columns, space is provided in the account form for recording the transaction date and journal page number. This information can be used to trace a specific entry back to where a transaction is recorded in a journal.

The major disadvantage of the account form illustrated above is that no current, up-to-date account balance is shown. If this form is used, an up-to-date balance must be calculated each time the account is examined. When an account has a large number of entries, the balance is difficult and time consuming to calculate. Therefore, a more commonly used account form has Debit and Credit Balance columns, as shown below.

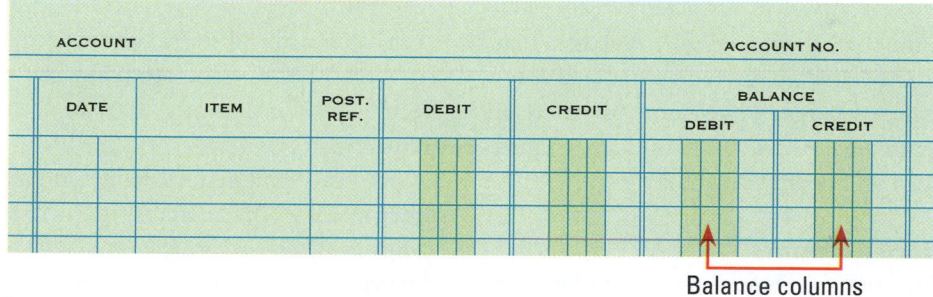

Because the form has columns for the debit and credit balance, it is often referred to as the *balance-ruled account form.*

The account balance is calculated and recorded as each entry is recorded in the account. Recording information in an account is described later in this chapter. The T account is a useful device for analyzing transactions into debit and credit parts. However, the balance-ruled account form is more useful than the T account as a permanent record of changes to account balances. TechKnow Consulting uses the balance-ruled account form.

PHOTODISC/GETTY IMAGES

TechKnow
Consulting

7549 Broadway
Portland, OR 97202-2531

CHART OF ACCOUNTS

Balance Sheet Accounts	Income Statement Accounts
(100) ASSETS	**(400) REVENUE**
110 Cash	410 Sales
120 Petty Cash	**(500) EXPENSES**
130 Accounts Receivable—Oakdale School	510 Advertising Expense
140 Accounts Receivable—Campus Internet Cafe	520 Insurance Expense
150 Supplies	530 Miscellaneous Expense
160 Prepaid Insurance	540 Rent Expense
(200) LIABILITIES	550 Supplies Expense
210 Accounts Payable—Supply Depot	560 Utilities Expense
220 Accounts Payable—Thomas Supply Co.	
(300) OWNER'S EQUITY	
310 Kim Park, Capital	
320 Kim Park, Drawing	
330 Income Summary	

A group of accounts is called a **ledger**. A ledger that contains all accounts needed to prepare financial statements is called a **general ledger**. The name given to an account is known as an *account title*. The number assigned to an account is called an **account number**.

Preparing a Chart of Accounts

A list of account titles and numbers showing the location of each account in a ledger is known as a *chart of accounts*.

TechKnow Consulting's chart of accounts is shown above. For ease of use while studying the chapters in Part 1, TechKnow Consulting's chart of accounts is also shown on page 3.

Accounts in a general ledger are arranged in the same order as they appear on financial statements. TechKnow Consulting's chart of accounts shows five general ledger divisions: (1) Assets, (2) Liabilities, (3) Owner's Equity, (4) Revenue, and (5) Expenses.

.... **ACCOUNT NUMBERS** ....

1   5   0   **Supplies**

General ledger division   Location within general ledger division

TechKnow Consulting assigns a three-digit account number to each account. For example, Supplies is assigned the number 150, as shown.

The first digit of each account number shows the general ledger division in which the account is located. For example, the asset division accounts are numbered in the 100s. Therefore, the number for the asset account, Supplies, begins with a 1.

The second two digits indicate the location of each account within a general ledger division. The 50 in the account number for Supplies indicates that the account is located between account number 140 and account number 160.

Assigning Account Numbers

TechKnow Consulting initially assigns account numbers by 10s so that new accounts can be added easily. Nine numbers are unused between each account on TechKnow Consulting's chart of accounts. For example, numbers 111 to 119 are unused between accounts numbered 110 and 120. New numbers can be assigned between existing account numbers without renumbering all existing accounts. The procedure for arranging accounts in a general ledger, assigning account numbers, and keeping records current is called **file maintenance**.

Unused account numbers are assigned to new accounts. TechKnow Consulting records payments for gasoline in Miscellaneous Expense. If Ms. Park found that the amount paid each month for gasoline had become a major expense, she might decide to use a separate account. The account might be titled Gasoline Expense. TechKnow Consulting arranges expense accounts in alphabetic order in its general ledger. Therefore, the new account would be inserted between Advertising Expense and Insurance Expense.

510	Advertising Expense	(Existing account)
	Gasoline Expense	**(New Account)**
520	Insurance Expense	(Existing account)

The number selected for the new account should leave some unused numbers on either side of it for other accounts that might need to be added. The middle, unused account number between existing numbers 510 and 520 is 515. Therefore, 515 is assigned as the account number for the new account.

510	Advertising Expense	(Existing account)
515	*Gasoline Expense*	*(New Account)*
520	Insurance Expense	(Existing account)

When an account is no longer needed, it is removed from the general ledger and the chart of accounts. For example, if TechKnow Consulting were to buy its own equipment and building, there would be no need for the rent expense account. The account numbered 540 would be removed, and that number would become unused and available to assign to another account if the need should arise.

When a new account is added at the end of a ledger division, the next number in a sequence of 10s is used. For example, suppose TechKnow Consulting needs to add another expense account, Water Expense, to show more detail about one of the utility expenses. The expense accounts are arranged in alphabetic order. Therefore, the new account would be added at the end of the expense section of the chart of accounts. The last used expense account number is 560, as shown on the chart of accounts. The next number in the sequence of 10s is 570, which is assigned as the number of the new account.

550	Supplies Expense	(Existing account)
560	Utilities Expense	(Existing account)
570	*Water Expense*	*(New Account)*

TechKnow Consulting has relatively few accounts in its general ledger and does not anticipate adding many new accounts in the future. Therefore, a three-digit account number adequately provides for the few account numbers that might be added. However, as the number of general ledger accounts increases, a business may change to four or more digits.

Charts of accounts with more than three digits are described in later chapters.

PHOTODISC/GETTY IMAGES

1 Account Title   **2** Account Number

ACCOUNT *Cash*						ACCOUNT NO. *110*	
DATE	ITEM	POST. REF.	DEBIT	CREDIT	BALANCE		
					DEBIT	CREDIT	

Writing an account title and number on the heading of an account is called **opening an account**. A general ledger account is opened for each account listed on a chart of accounts. Accounts are opened and arranged in a general ledger in the same order as on the chart of accounts.

Cash, account number 110, is the first account on Tech-Know Consulting's chart of accounts. The cash account is opened using the steps shown below. The same procedure is used to open all accounts listed on TechKnow Consulting's chart of accounts.

STEPS  **OPENING AN ACCOUNT IN A GENERAL LEDGER**

1 Write the account title, *Cash*, after the word *Account* in the heading.

2 Write the account number, *110*, after the words *Account No.* in the heading.

CULTURAL DIVERSITY

Accounting in Ancient Civilizations

In the ancient civilizations of Asia Minor and northern Africa, most citizens were illiterate. The scribe, who could read and write, became a very important person in the society. Of ancient Hebrew origin, the scribe has been called the forerunner of today's accountant.

Public scribes often recorded transactions as citizens arrived to do business. Most scribes recorded transactions on moist clay tablets that were then dried in the sun. Therefore, permanent records of transactions were not possible until scribes could write them down on clay tablets.

The Greeks invented coined money around 630 B.C., which facilitated assigning values to transactions.

The Babylonians in Asia Minor used an early form of banking. They transferred funds with a system resembling our modern-day checking accounts, one of the first uses of business documents.

These early practices provided the foundation for today's financial system and recordkeeping methods.

Critical Thinking

1. Estimate how many transactions might occur in a single day in a modern grocery store with which you are familiar.

2. List the number of different methods of payments that are accepted by modern grocery stores.

PHOTO: PHOTODISC/GETTY IMAGES

TERMS REVIEW

ledger
general ledger
account number
file maintenance
opening an account

AUDIT YOUR UNDERSTANDING

1. Describe the two parts of an account number.
2. List the two steps for opening an account.

WORK TOGETHER 4-1

Preparing a chart of accounts and opening an account

Forms are given in the *Working Papers*. Your instructor will guide you through the following examples.

Clara Ross owns a service business called Ross Company, which uses these accounts.

Accts. Pay.—Sherer Supplies	Miscellaneous Expense	Cash	Automobile Expense
Accts. Rec.—Tyler Link	Insurance Expense	Sales	Clara Ross, Capital
Accts. Pay.—Mid City Supplies	Prepaid Insurance	Supplies	Rent Expense
Accts. Rec.—Megan Alvarez	Clara Ross, Drawing	Supplies Expense	

1. Prepare a chart of accounts. Arrange expense accounts in alphabetical order. Use 3-digit account numbers and number the accounts within a division by 10s.
2. Two new accounts, Postage Expense and Utilities Expense, are to be added to the chart of accounts prepared in Instruction 1. Assign account numbers to the two new accounts.
3. Using the account form in the *Working Papers*, open Cash.

ON YOUR OWN 4-1

Preparing a chart of accounts and opening an account

Forms are given in the *Working Papers*. Work this problem independently.

Eric Roen owns a service business called Roen's Hair Care, which uses these accounts.

Accts. Pay.—Milton Company	Supplies Expense	Cash	Delivery Expense
Accts. Rec.—Superior Supplies	Insurance Expense	Sales	Accts. Pay.—North Star
Prepaid Insurance	Telephone Expense	Supplies	Accts. Rec.—M. Faller
Eric Roen, Drawing	Eric Roen, Capital		

1. Prepare a chart of accounts. Arrange expense accounts in alphabetical order. Use 3-digit account numbers and number the accounts within a division by 10s.
2. Two new accounts, Gasoline Expense and Water Expense, are to be added to the chart of accounts prepared in Instruction 1. Assign account numbers to the two new accounts.
3. Using the account form in the *Working Papers*, open Delivery Expense.

Posting Separate Amounts from a Journal to a General Ledger

POSTING AN AMOUNT FROM A GENERAL DEBIT COLUMN

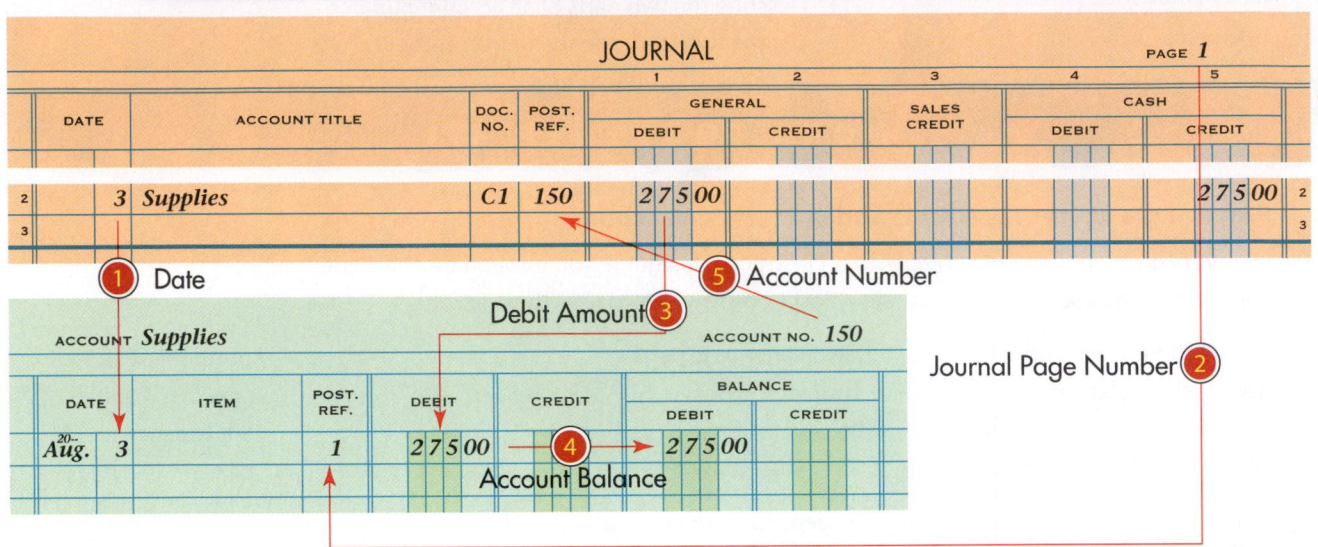

① Date ⑤ Account Number Debit Amount ③

② Journal Page Number

④ Account Balance

Transferring information from a journal entry to a ledger account is called **posting**. Posting sorts journal entries so that all debits and credits affecting each account are brought together. For example, all changes to Cash are brought together in the cash account.

Amounts in journal entries are recorded in either general amount columns or special amount columns. There are two rules for posting amounts from a journal: (1) Separate amounts in a journal's general amount columns are posted individually to the account written in the Account Title column. (2) Separate amounts in a journal's special amount columns are not posted individually. Instead, the special amount column totals are posted to the account named in the heading of the special amount column.

Posting a Separate Amount from a General Debit Column

For most journal entries, at least one separate amount is posted individually to a general ledger account. When an entry in a journal includes an amount in a general amount column, the amount is posted individually.

Each separate amount in the General Debit and General Credit columns of a journal is posted to the account written in the Account Title column.

STEPS

POSTING AN AMOUNT FROM A GENERAL DEBIT COLUMN

① Write the date, *20--, Aug. 3*, in the Date column of the account *Supplies*.

② Write the journal page number, *1*, in the Post. Ref. column of the account. *Post. Ref.* is an abbreviation for Posting Reference.

③ Write the debit amount, *$275.00*, in the Debit amount column.

④ Write the new account balance, *$275.00*, in the Balance Debit column. Because this entry is the first in the *Supplies* account, the previous balance is zero.

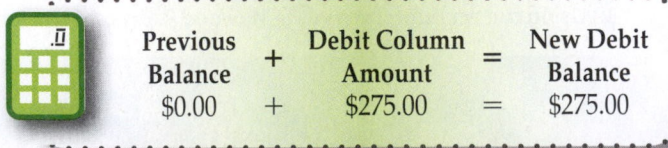

Previous Balance	+	Debit Column Amount	=	New Debit Balance
$0.00	+	$275.00	=	$275.00

⑤ Return to the journal and write the account number, *150*, in the Post. Ref. column of the journal.

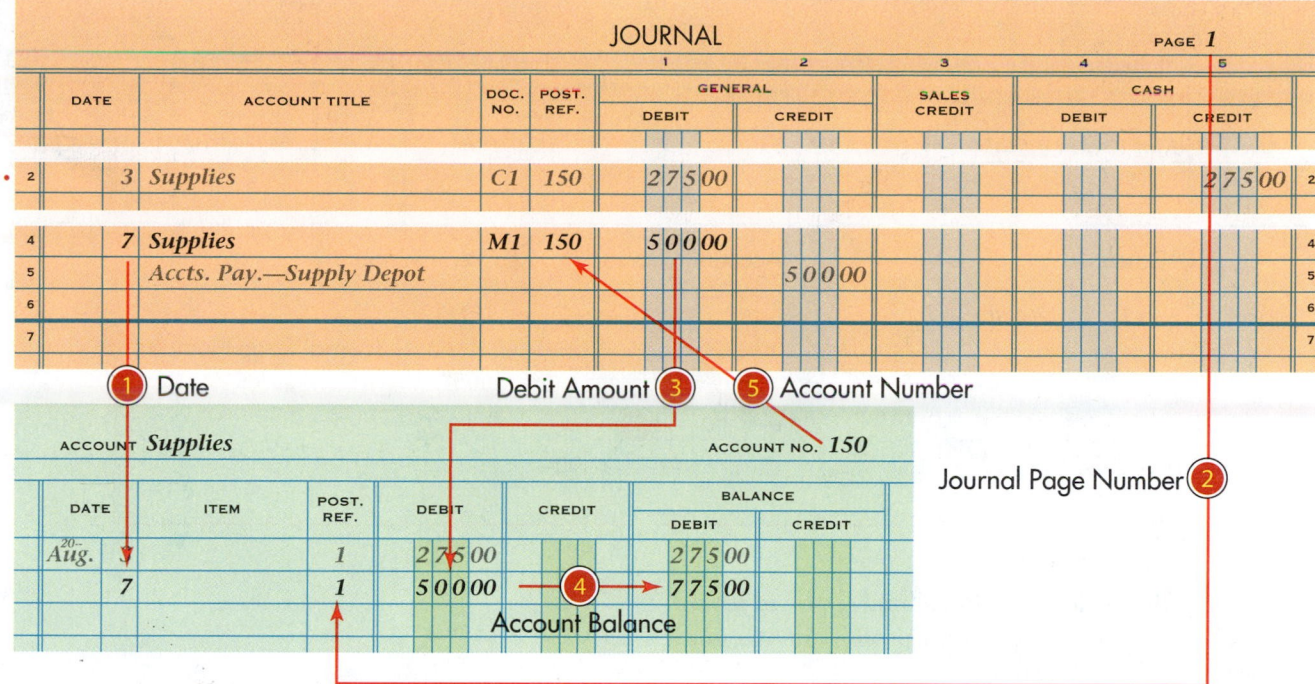

The numbers in the Post. Ref. columns of the general ledger account and the journal serve three purposes: (1) An entry in an account can be traced to its source in a journal. (2) An entry in a journal can be traced to where it was posted in an account. (3) If posting is interrupted, the accounting personnel can easily see which entries in the journal still need to be posted. A blank in the Post. Ref.

column of the journal indicates that posting for that line still needs to be completed. Therefore, the posting reference is always recorded in the journal as the last step in the posting procedure.

The same five steps are followed when a second amount is posted to an account.

 STEPS **POSTING A SECOND AMOUNT TO AN ACCOUNT**

1 Write the date, *7*, in the Date column of the account. The month and year are written only once on a page of a ledger account, unless the month or year changes.

2 Write the journal page number, *1*, in the Post. Ref. column of the account.

3 Write the debit amount, *$500.00*, in the Debit amount column.

Previous Debit Balance	+	Debit Column Amount	=	New Debit Balance
$275.00	+	$500.00	=	$775.00

4 Write the new account balance, *$775.00*, in the Balance Debit column.

5 Return to the journal and write the account number, *150*, in the Post. Ref. column of the journal.

REMEMBER

Each separate amount in the General Debit and Credit columns of a journal is posted individually. Therefore, the totals of these columns are not posted.

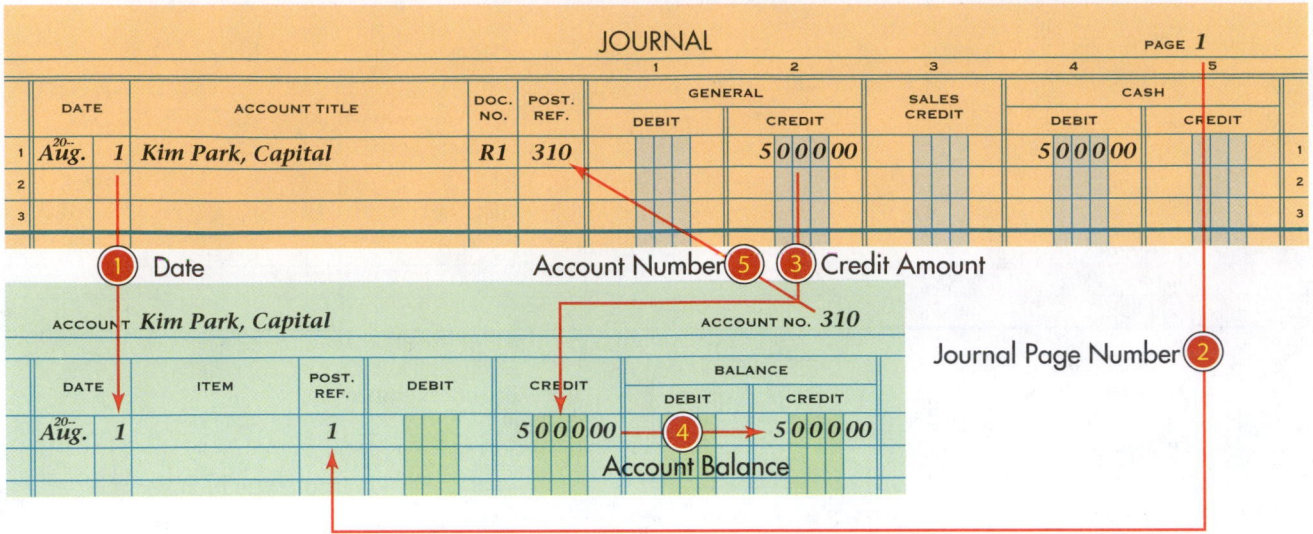

An amount in the General Credit column is posted separately. Five steps are followed when posting an amount from the General Credit column.

1. Write the date, 20--, Aug. 1, in the Date column of the account.

2. Write the journal page number, 1, in the Post. Ref. column of the account.

3. Write the credit amount, $5,000.00, in the Credit amount column.

4. Write the new account balance, $5,000.00, in the Balance Credit column.

Previous Balance	+	Credit Column Amount	=	New Credit Balance
$0.00	+	$5,000.00	=	$5,000.00

5. Return to the journal and write the account number, 310, in the Post. Ref. column of the journal.

PHOTODISC/GETTY IMAGES

AUDIT YOUR UNDERSTANDING

TERM REVIEW

posting

1. List the five steps of posting from the general columns of a journal to the general ledger.
2. Are the totals of the General Debit and General Credit columns posted? Why or why not?

WORK TOGETHER 4-2

Posting separate amounts to a general ledger

A completed journal and general ledger accounts are given in the *Working Papers*. Your instructor will guide you through the following example.

Leonard Witkowski owns a service business that uses the following accounts.

Assets	Owner's Equity
110 Cash	310 Leonard Witkowski, Capital
120 Accounts Receivable—Danielle Braastad	320 Leonard Witkowski, Drawing
130 Supplies	**Revenue**
140 Prepaid Insurance	410 Sales
Liabilities	**Expenses**
210 Accounts Payable—Joshua's Supplies	510 Rent Expense

1. Post the separate amounts (on each line of the journal) that need to be posted individually. Save your work to complete Work Together 4-3.

ON YOUR OWN 4-2

Posting separate amounts to a general ledger

A completed journal and general ledger accounts are given in the *Working Papers*. Work this problem independently.

Heather Hasley owns a service business, which uses the following accounts.

Assets	Owner's Equity
110 Cash	310 Heather Hasley, Capital
120 Accounts Receivable—Ken Garlie	320 Heather Hasley, Drawing
130 Supplies	**Revenue**
140 Prepaid Insurance	410 Sales
Liabilities	**Expenses**
210 Accounts Payable—Bodden Company	510 Advertising Expense

1. Post the separate amounts (on each line of the journal) that need to be posted individually. Save your work to complete On Your Own 4-3.

Posting Column Totals from a Journal to a General Ledger

CHECK MARKS SHOW THAT AMOUNTS ARE NOT POSTED

	DATE		ACCOUNT TITLE	DOC. NO.	POST. REF.	GENERAL		SALES CREDIT	CASH		
						DEBIT	CREDIT		DEBIT	CREDIT	
1	20-- Aug.	20	Brought Forward		✓	3 5 4 3 00	5 7 5 0 00	1 9 6 0 00	6 7 1 0 00	2 5 4 3 00	1
13		31	✓	T31	✓			1 9 0 00	1 9 0 00		13
14		31	Miscellaneous Expense	M3	↑	8 00				8 00	14
15		31	Totals			4 3 5 1 00	5 7 5 0 00	3 5 6 5 00	8 3 1 5 00	3 3 5 1 00	15
16						(✓)	(✓)				16
17											17

JOURNAL   PAGE 2

Check mark indicates that amounts ARE NOT posted individually.

Check marks indicate that general amount column totals ARE NOT posted.

Journal Entries That Are Not Posted Individually

Several lines in TechKnow Consulting's journal contain amounts that are not to be posted individually. These include forwarding totals and amounts recorded in special amount columns. The totals brought forward from page 1 are shown on line 1 of the journal. None of these separate total amounts on line 1 are posted individually to general ledger accounts. To assure that no postings are overlooked, no blank posting reference spaces should be left in the Post. Ref. column of the journal. Therefore, when the totals were forwarded to page 2 of the journal, a check mark was placed in the Post. Ref. column of line 1 to show that no separate amounts are posted individually.

Separate amounts in the special amount columns— Sales Credit, Cash Debit, and Cash Credit—are not posted individually. For example, on line 13 of the journal, two separate $190.00 amounts are recorded in two special amount columns, Sales Credit and Cash Debit.

A check mark was placed in the Post. Ref. column on line 13 when the entry was journalized. The check mark indicates that no separate amounts are posted individually from this line. Instead, the totals of the special amount columns are posted.

Totals of General Debit and General Credit Amount Columns

The General Debit and General Credit columns are not special amount columns because the column headings do not contain the name of an account. All of the separate amounts in the General Debit and General Credit amount columns are posted individually.

Therefore, the column totals are not posted. A check mark in parentheses is placed below each general amount column total as shown. The check mark indicates that the total of the General Debit column is not posted.

A check mark in the Post. Ref. column indicates that no amounts on that line are posted individually. On the totals line, the amounts in the special amount columns are posted. Therefore, a check mark is not placed in the Post. Ref. column for the totals line.

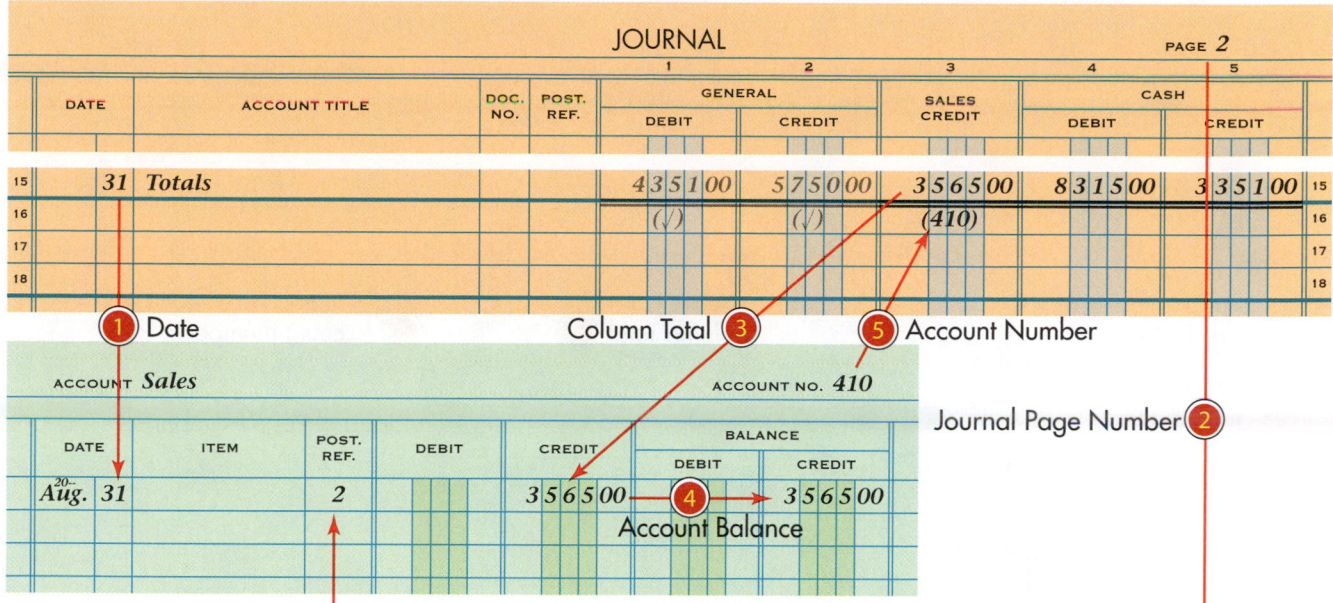

Separate amounts in special amount columns are not posted individually. The separate amounts are part of the special amount column totals. Only the totals of special amount columns are posted.

TechKnow Consulting's journal has three special amount columns for which only totals are posted: Sales Credit, Cash Debit, and Cash Credit.

The Sales Credit column of a journal is a special amount column with the account title **Sales** in the heading. Each separate amount in a special amount column could be posted individually. However, all of the separate amounts are debits or credits to the same account. Therefore, an advantage of a special amount column is that only the column total needs to be posted. For example, 16 separate sales transactions are recorded in the Sales Credit column of TechKnow Consulting's August journal. Instead of making 16 separate credit postings to **Sales**, only the column total is posted. As a result, only one posting is needed, which saves 15 postings. The smaller number of postings means 15 fewer opportunities to make a posting error. Posting special amount column totals saves time and results in greater accuracy.

STEPS   POSTING THE TOTAL OF THE SALES CREDIT COLUMN

1. Write the date, *20--, Aug. 31*, in the Date column of the account *Sales*.

2. Write the journal page number, *2*, in the Post. Ref. column of the account.

3. Write the column total, *$3,565.00*, in the Credit amount column.

4. Write the new account balance, *$3,565.00*, in the Balance Credit column.

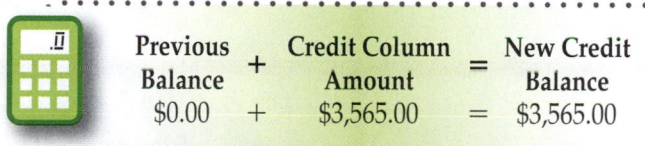

Previous Balance	+	Credit Column Amount	=	New Credit Balance
$0.00	+	$3,565.00	=	$3,565.00

5. Return to the journal and write the account number in parentheses, *(410)*, below the Sales Credit column total.

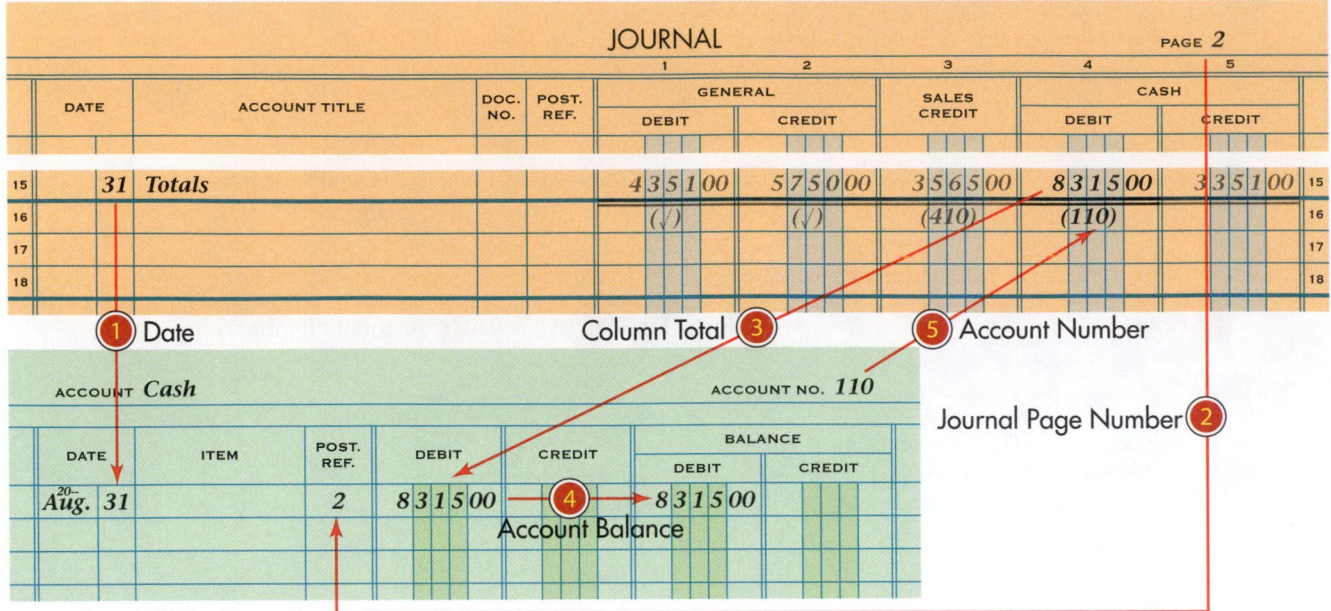

	DATE	ACCOUNT TITLE	DOC. NO.	POST. REF.	GENERAL DEBIT	GENERAL CREDIT	SALES CREDIT	CASH DEBIT	CASH CREDIT	
15	31	Totals			4 3 5 1 00	5 7 5 0 00	3 5 6 5 00	8 3 1 5 00	3 3 5 1 00	15
16					(✓)	(✓)	(410)	(110)		16
17										17
18										18

JOURNAL   PAGE **2**

① Date   Column Total ③   ⑤ Account Number

ACCOUNT **Cash**   ACCOUNT NO. **110**

Journal Page Number ②

DATE	ITEM	POST. REF.	DEBIT	CREDIT	BALANCE DEBIT	BALANCE CREDIT
20-- Aug. 31		2	8 3 1 5 00		8 3 1 5 00	

④ Account Balance

The Cash Debit column of a journal is a special amount column with the account title **Cash** in the heading.

The Cash Debit column is posted using the following steps.

STEPS   POSTING THE TOTAL OF THE CASH DEBIT COLUMN

① Write the date, *20--, Aug. 31*, in the Date column of the account *Cash*.

② Write the journal page number, *2*, in the Post. Ref. column of the account.

③ Write the column total, *$8,315.00*, in the Debit amount column.

④ Write the new account balance, *$8,315.00*, in the Balance Debit column.

Previous Balance	+	Debit Column Amount	=	New Debit Balance
$0.00	+	$8,315.00	=	$8,315.00

⑤ Return to the journal and write the account number in parentheses, *(110)*, below the Cash Debit column total.

REMEMBER

Errors are corrected in a way that does not cause doubts about what the correct information is. If an error is recorded, cancel the error by neatly drawing a line through the incorrect item. Write the correct items immediately above the canceled item.

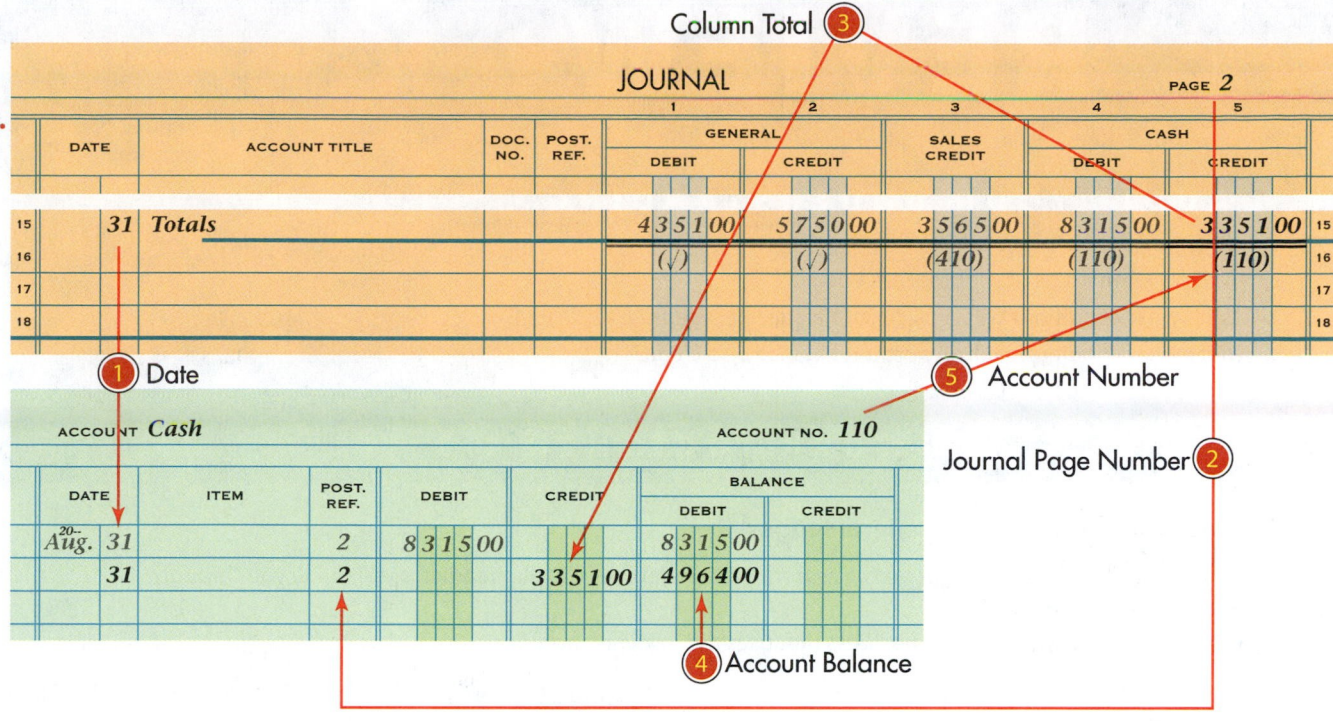

The Cash Credit column of a journal is a special amount column with the account title Cash in the heading. The Cash Credit column is posted using the following steps.

STEPS · POSTING THE TOTAL OF THE CASH CREDIT COLUMN

1. Write the date, *31*, in the Date column of the account *Cash*.

2. Write the journal page number, *2*, in the Post. Ref. column of the account.

3. Write the column total, *$3,351.00*, in the credit amount column.

4. Write the new account balance, *$4,964.00*, in the Balance Debit column.

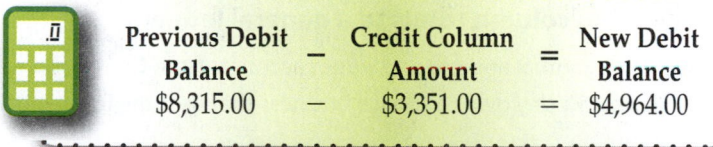

Previous Debit Balance	−	Credit Column Amount	=	New Debit Balance
$8,315.00	−	$3,351.00	=	$4,964.00

5. Return to the journal and write the account number in parentheses, *(110)*, below the Cash Credit column total.

REMEMBER

Whenever the debits in an account exceed the credits, the account balance is a debit. Whenever the credits in an account exceed the debits, the account balance is a credit.

End of Lesson REVIEW

AUDIT YOUR UNDERSTANDING

1. Which column totals of a journal are posted?
2. Under what conditions will an account balance be a debit?
3. Under what conditions will an account balance be a credit?

WORK TOGETHER 4-3

Posting column totals to a general ledger

Use the journal and general ledger accounts from Work Together 4-2. Your instructor will guide you through the following example.

Leonard Witkowski owns a service business that uses the following accounts.

Assets

110 Cash
120 Accounts Receivable—Danielle Braastad
130 Supplies
140 Prepaid Insurance

Liabilities

210 Accounts Payable—Joshua's Supplies

Owner's Equity

310 Leonard Witkowski, Capital
320 Leonard Witkowski, Drawing

Revenue

410 Sales

Expenses

510 Rent Expense

1. Post the journal's special amount column totals.

ON YOUR OWN 4-3

Posting column totals to a general ledger

Use the journal and general ledger accounts from On Your Own 4-2. Work this problem independently.

Heather Hasley owns a service business that uses the following accounts.

Assets

110 Cash
120 Accounts Receivable—Ken Garlie
130 Supplies
140 Prepaid Insurance

Liabilities

210 Accounts Payable—Bodden Company

Owner's Equity

310 Heather Hasley, Capital
320 Heather Hasley, Drawing

Revenue

410 Sales

Expenses

510 Advertising Expense

1. Post the journal's special amount column totals.

JOURNAL PAGE WITH POSTING COMPLETED

JOURNAL PAGE WITH POSTING COMPLETED

JOURNAL   PAGE 2

	DATE	ACCOUNT TITLE	DOC. NO.	POST. REF.	GENERAL DEBIT	GENERAL CREDIT	SALES CREDIT	CASH DEBIT	CASH CREDIT	
1	Aug. 20	Brought Forward		✓	3 5 4 3 00	5 7 5 0 00	1 9 6 0 00	6 7 1 0 00	2 5 4 3 00	1
2	21	✓	T21	✓			2 2 5 00	2 2 5 00		2
3	24	✓	T24	✓			2 0 5 00	2 0 5 00		3
4	25	✓	T25	✓			2 7 5 00	2 7 5 00		4
5	26	✓	T26	✓			2 9 0 00	2 9 0 00		5
6	27	Utilities Expense	C10	560	7 0 00				7 0 00	6
7	27	✓	T27	✓			2 0 5 00	2 0 5 00		7
8	28	Supplies	C11	150	2 0 0 00				2 0 0 00	8
9	28	✓	T28	✓			2 1 5 00	2 1 5 00		9
10	31	Miscellaneous Expense	C12	530	2 0 00				3 0 00	10
11		Advertising Expense		510	1 0 00					11
12	31	Kim Park, Drawing	C13	320	5 0 0 00				5 0 0 00	12
13	31	✓	T31	✓			1 9 0 00	1 9 0 00		13
14	31	Miscellaneous Expense	M3	530	8 00				8 00	14
15	31	Totals			4 3 5 1 00	5 7 5 0 00	3 5 6 5 00	8 3 1 5 00	3 3 5 1 00	15
16					(✓)	(✓)	(410)	(110)	(110)	16
17										17

Page 2 of TechKnow Consulting's August journal is shown after all posting has been completed. With the exception of the Totals line, notice that the Post. Ref. Column is completely filled in with either an account number or a check mark.

GENERAL LEDGER WITH POSTING COMPLETED

ACCOUNT Cash   ACCOUNT NO. 110

DATE	ITEM	POST. REF.	DEBIT	CREDIT	BALANCE DEBIT	BALANCE CREDIT
Aug. 31		2	8 3 1 5 00		8 3 1 5 00	
31		2		3 3 5 1 00	4 9 6 4 00	

ACCOUNT Petty Cash   ACCOUNT NO. 120

DATE	ITEM	POST. REF.	DEBIT	CREDIT	BALANCE DEBIT	BALANCE CREDIT
Aug. 19		1	1 0 0 00		1 0 0 00	

After all posting from the August journal is completed, TechKnow Consulting's general ledger is shown here and on the next several pages.

The use of the accounts Income Summary, Insurance Expense, and Supplies Expense is described in Chapter 6.

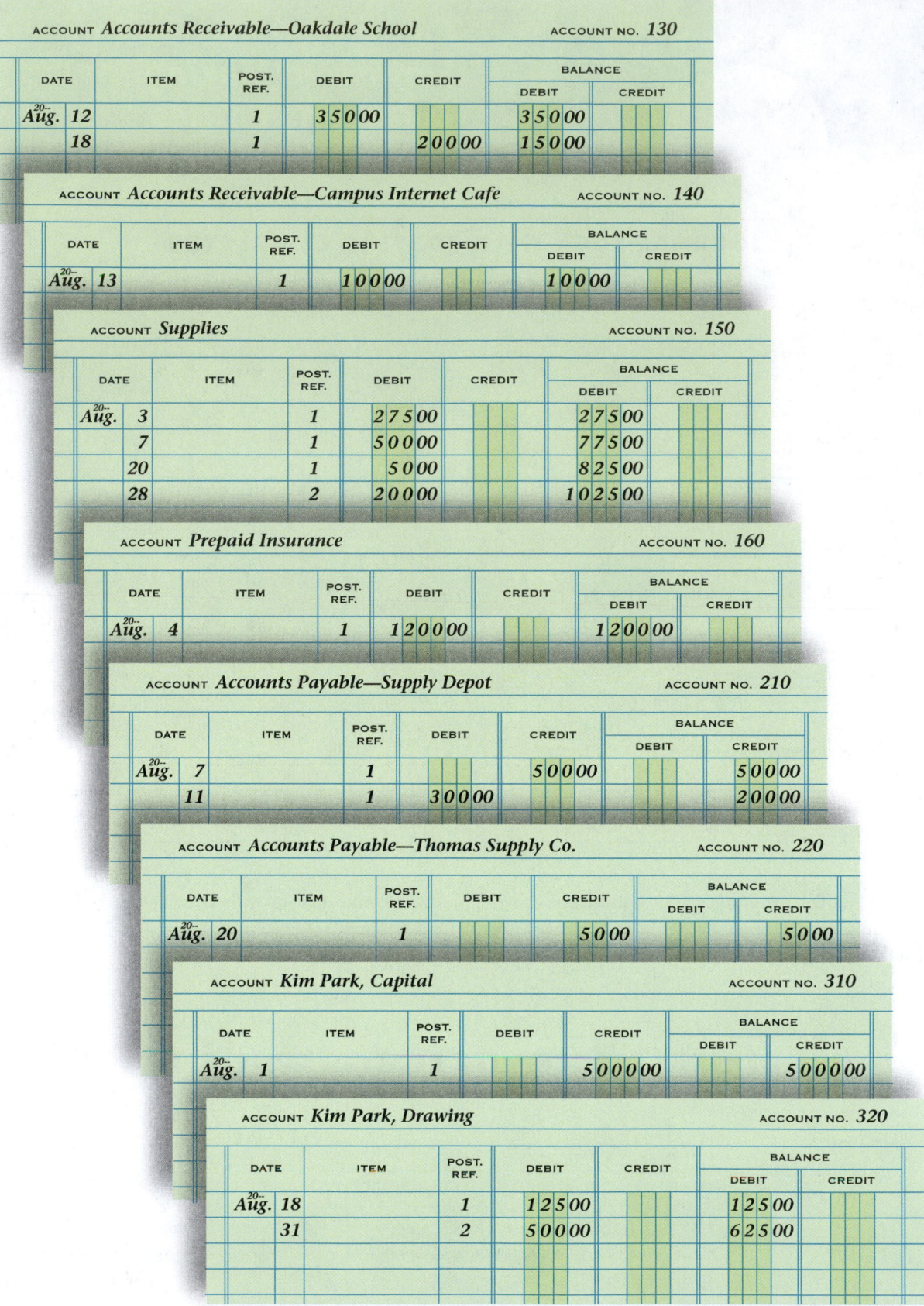

ACCOUNT *Accounts Receivable—Oakdale School*   **ACCOUNT NO.** *130*

DATE	ITEM	POST. REF.	DEBIT	CREDIT	BALANCE DEBIT	BALANCE CREDIT
Aug. 12		1	350 00		350 00	
18		1		200 00	150 00	

ACCOUNT *Accounts Receivable—Campus Internet Cafe*   **ACCOUNT NO.** *140*

DATE	ITEM	POST. REF.	DEBIT	CREDIT	BALANCE DEBIT	BALANCE CREDIT
Aug. 13		1	100 00		100 00	

ACCOUNT *Supplies*   **ACCOUNT NO.** *150*

DATE	ITEM	POST. REF.	DEBIT	CREDIT	BALANCE DEBIT	BALANCE CREDIT
Aug. 3		1	275 00		275 00	
7		1	500 00		775 00	
20		1	50 00		825 00	
28		2	200 00		1025 00	

ACCOUNT *Prepaid Insurance*   **ACCOUNT NO.** *160*

DATE	ITEM	POST. REF.	DEBIT	CREDIT	BALANCE DEBIT	BALANCE CREDIT
Aug. 4		1	1200 00		1200 00	

ACCOUNT *Accounts Payable—Supply Depot*   **ACCOUNT NO.** *210*

DATE	ITEM	POST. REF.	DEBIT	CREDIT	BALANCE DEBIT	BALANCE CREDIT
Aug. 7		1		500 00		500 00
11		1	300 00			200 00

ACCOUNT *Accounts Payable—Thomas Supply Co.*   **ACCOUNT NO.** *220*

DATE	ITEM	POST. REF.	DEBIT	CREDIT	BALANCE DEBIT	BALANCE CREDIT
Aug. 20		1		50 00		50 00

ACCOUNT *Kim Park, Capital*   **ACCOUNT NO.** *310*

DATE	ITEM	POST. REF.	DEBIT	CREDIT	BALANCE DEBIT	BALANCE CREDIT
Aug. 1		1		5000 00		5000 00

ACCOUNT *Kim Park, Drawing*   **ACCOUNT NO.** *320*

DATE	ITEM	POST. REF.	DEBIT	CREDIT	BALANCE DEBIT	BALANCE CREDIT
Aug. 18		1	125 00		125 00	
31		2	500 00		625 00	

A General Ledger after Posting Has Been Completed (continued)

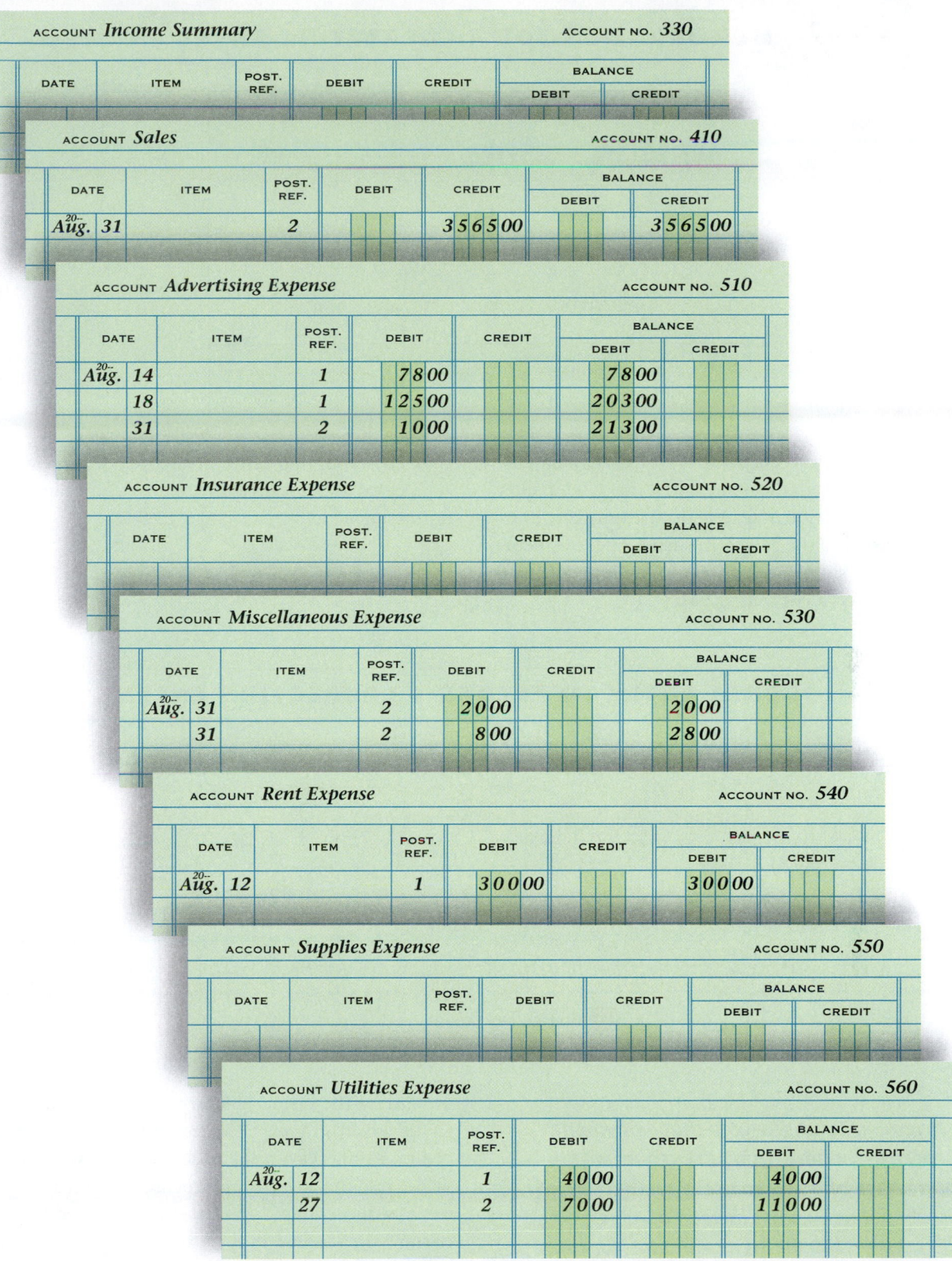

ACCOUNT *Income Summary* **ACCOUNT NO.** *330*

DATE	ITEM	POST. REF.	DEBIT	CREDIT	BALANCE DEBIT	BALANCE CREDIT

ACCOUNT *Sales* **ACCOUNT NO.** *410*

DATE	ITEM	POST. REF.	DEBIT	CREDIT	BALANCE DEBIT	BALANCE CREDIT
Aug. 31		2		3 5 6 5 00		3 5 6 5 00

ACCOUNT *Advertising Expense* **ACCOUNT NO.** *510*

DATE	ITEM	POST. REF.	DEBIT	CREDIT	BALANCE DEBIT	BALANCE CREDIT
Aug. 14		1	7 8 00		7 8 00	
18		1	1 2 5 00		2 0 3 00	
31		2	1 0 00		2 1 3 00	

ACCOUNT *Insurance Expense* **ACCOUNT NO.** *520*

DATE	ITEM	POST. REF.	DEBIT	CREDIT	BALANCE DEBIT	BALANCE CREDIT

ACCOUNT *Miscellaneous Expense* **ACCOUNT NO.** *530*

DATE	ITEM	POST. REF.	DEBIT	CREDIT	BALANCE DEBIT	BALANCE CREDIT
Aug. 31		2	2 0 00		2 0 00	
31		2	8 00		2 8 00	

ACCOUNT *Rent Expense* **ACCOUNT NO.** *540*

DATE	ITEM	POST. REF.	DEBIT	CREDIT	BALANCE DEBIT	BALANCE CREDIT
Aug. 12		1	3 0 0 00		3 0 0 00	

ACCOUNT *Supplies Expense* **ACCOUNT NO.** *550*

DATE	ITEM	POST. REF.	DEBIT	CREDIT	BALANCE DEBIT	BALANCE CREDIT

ACCOUNT *Utilities Expense* **ACCOUNT NO.** *560*

DATE	ITEM	POST. REF.	DEBIT	CREDIT	BALANCE DEBIT	BALANCE CREDIT
Aug. 12		1	4 0 00		4 0 00	
27		2	7 0 00		1 1 0 00	

A General Ledger after Posting Has Been Completed (concluded)

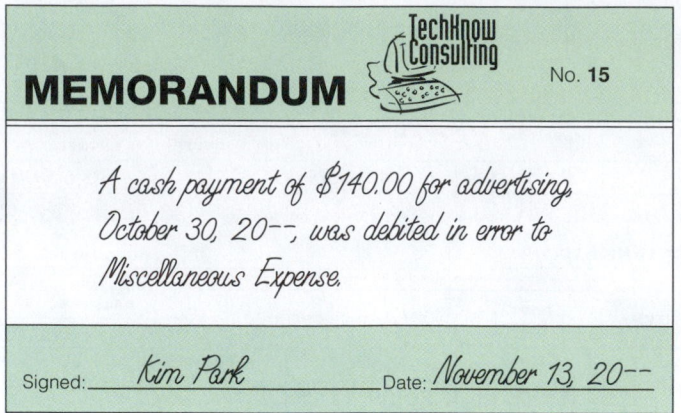

Errors discovered before entries are posted may be corrected by ruling through the item, as described in Chapter 3. However, a transaction may have been improperly journalized and posted to the ledger. In such a case, the incorrect journal entry should be corrected with an additional journal entry, called a **correcting entry**.

If an accounting error is discovered, a memorandum is prepared as the source document describing the correction to be made.

JOURNAL ENTRY TO RECORD A CORRECTING ENTRY

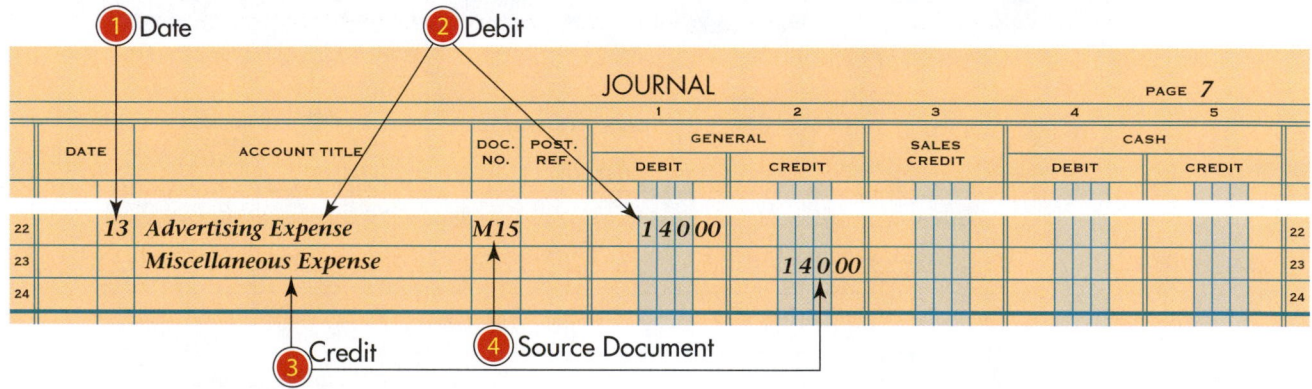

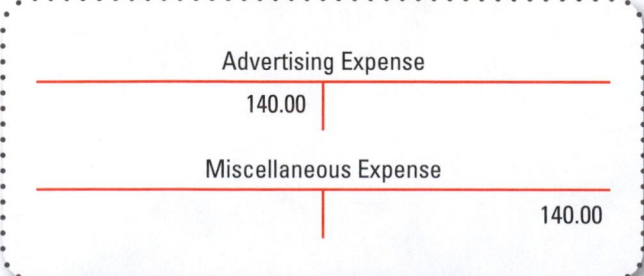

November 13. Discovered that a payment of cash for advertising in October was journalized and posted in error as a debit to Miscellaneous Expense instead of Advertising Expense, $140.00. Memorandum No. 15.

To correct the error, an entry is made to add $140.00 to the advertising expense account. The entry must also deduct $140.00 from the miscellaneous expense account.

Because the advertising expense account has a normal debit balance, Advertising Expense is debited for $140.00 to show the increase in this expense account. The miscellaneous expense account also has a normal debit balance. Therefore, Miscellaneous Expense is credited for $140.00 to show the decrease in this expense account.

End of Lesson REVIEW

1. What is a correcting entry?
2. When is a correcting entry necessary?
3. When an amount is journalized and posted as a debit to an incorrect expense account, why is the amount of the correcting entry debited to the correct expense account?
4. When an amount is journalized and posted as a debit to an incorrect expense account, why is the amount of the correcting entry credited to the incorrect expense account?

TERM REVIEW

correcting entry

WORK TOGETHER 4-4

Journalizing correcting entries

A journal is given in the *Working Papers*. Your instructor will guide you through the following example.

Transactions:

Nov. 1. Discovered that a transaction for supplies bought last month was journalized and posted in error as a debit to Prepaid Insurance instead of Supplies, $60.00. M15.

1. Discovered that a transaction for rent expense for last month was journalized and posted in error as a debit to Repair Expense instead of Rent Expense, $550.00. M16.

1. Journalize each correcting entry discovered during November of the current year. Use page 21 of the journal.

ON YOUR OWN 4-4

Journalizing correcting entries

A journal is given in the *Working Papers*. Work this problem independently.

Transactions:

June 1. Discovered that a transaction for supplies bought last month was journalized and posted in error as a debit to Prepaid Insurance instead of Supplies, $150.00. M23.

1. Discovered that a transaction for utilities expense for last month was journalized and posted in error as a debit to Miscellaneous Expense instead of Utilities Expense, $850.00. M24.

1. Journalize each correcting entry discovered during June of the current year. Use page 11 of the journal.

After completing this chapter, you can:

1. Define accounting terms related to posting from a journal to a general ledger.

2. Identify accounting concepts and practices related to posting from a journal to a general ledger.

3. Prepare a chart of accounts for a service business organized as a proprietorship.

4. Post separate amounts from a journal to a general ledger.

5. Post column totals from a journal to a general ledger.

6. Analyze and journalize correcting entries.

EXPLORE ACCOUNTING

Chart of Accounts

Each company designs its chart of accounts to meet the needs of that company. TechKnow Consulting, the company described in this section of the textbook, has a relatively simple chart of accounts, with a small number of accounts. Therefore, TechKnow Consulting can use a three-digit account number for each account. A company with more accounts may need to use a four- or five-digit account number for each account. The numbering system used by the company should ensure that each account can be assigned a unique number.

When setting up a chart of accounts, a company does not have to use a straight series of numbers. If a company has several departments, it may choose to use account numbers such as 12-150. The first two digits (12) can be used to designate a specific department. The last three digits (150) identify a unique account within that department. If this company has many departments or many accounts within each department, it may have to increase the number of digits in the account, such as 123-4567.

A large corporation made up of smaller companies may have one chart of accounts for the entire corporation. If the managers of the corporation also want to be able to separate out the accounts for each company, they may choose to set up the account numbers in an xx-yyy-zzzz format. The first two digits (xx) would be a unique number for each company, the second set of numbers (yyy) refers to a department number, and the third set of numbers (zzzz) is a unique account.

Another example would be a company that manufactures goods for its customers. Such a company may want to include the job order number in each account number, so that it can easily trace the cost of each job.

As you can see, there is an infinite number of possible systems that can be followed when assigning account numbers. A company should consider future growth when first setting up a system so that it can avoid having to renumber accounts at a later date.

Group Activity: Develop a chart of accounts for an imaginary business. Write a detailed description of the company and a rationale for the account numbering system you have developed.

4-1 APPLICATION PROBLEM AUTOMATED ACCOUNTING

Preparing a chart of accounts and opening an account

Lillian Deters owns a service business called Deters Duplicating, which uses the following accounts.

Accounts Receivable—Teegan Walters	Lillian Deters, Capital	Postage Expense	Supplies
Accounts Receivable—Austin Kirnyczuk	Lillian Deters, Drawing	Charitable Expense	Sales
Accounts Payable—Dakota Company	Prepaid Insurance	Rent Expense	Cash
Accounts Payable—Falls Supply	Advertising Expense		

Instructions:

1. Prepare a chart of accounts similar to the one described in this chapter. Arrange expense accounts in alphabetical order. Use 3-digit account numbers and number the accounts within a division by 10s.
2. Two new accounts, Delivery Expense and Telephone Expense, are to be added to the chart of accounts prepared in Instruction 1. Assign account numbers to the two new accounts.
3. Using the forms in the *Working Papers*, open the Prepaid Insurance and the Postage Expense accounts.

4-2 APPLICATION PROBLEM

Posting separate amounts to a general ledger

A completed journal and general ledger accounts are given in the *Working Papers*.
Alto Komoko owns a service business that uses the accounts given in the *Working Papers*.

Instructions:
Post the separate amounts (on each line of the journal) that need to be posted individually. Save your work to complete Application Problem 4-3.

4-3 APPLICATION PROBLEM

Posting column totals to a general ledger

Use the journal and general ledger from Application Problem 4-2.

Instructions:
Post the journal's special amount column totals.

Go Beyond the Book
For more information go to
www.C21accounting.com

4-4   APPLICATION PROBLEM

Journalizing correcting entries

The following errors were discovered after the incorrect entries were already journalized and posted.

Transactions:

Apr. 1. Discovered that a transaction for utilities expense was journalized and posted in error as a debit to Repairs Expense instead of Utilities Expense, $265.00. M66.

     5. Discovered that a cash investment by Manuel Ricardo, owner, was journalized and posted in error as a credit to Sales instead of Manuel Ricardo, Capital, $600.00. M67.

Instructions:

Journalize each correcting entry discovered during April of the current year. Use page 7 of the journal given in the *Working Papers*.

4-5   MASTERY PROBLEM   

Journalizing transactions and posting to a general ledger

Patrick O'Kalla owns a service business called O'Kalla Law n and Garden. O'Kalla Lawn and Garden's general ledger accounts are given in the *Working Papers*.

Transactions:

Nov. 1. Received cash from owner as an investment, $5,500.00. R1.
     3. Paid cash for supplies, $400.00. C1.
     5. Received cash from sales, $900.00. T5.
     6. Sold services on account to Merilda Domingo, $280.00. S1.
     9. Paid cash for rent, $600.00. C2.
     11. Paid cash for miscellaneous expense, $50.00. C3.
     13. Bought supplies on account from Park Supplies, $240.00. M1.
     13. Received cash from sales, $430.00. T13.
     16. Paid cash for advertising, $143.00. C4.
     18. Paid cash on account to Park Supplies, $140.00. C5.
     20. Paid cash for electric bill, $230.00. C6.
     20. Received cash on account from Merilda Domingo, $150.00. R2.
     25. Paid cash for supplies, $150.00. C7.
     27. Paid cash for supplies, $80.00. C8.
     27. Received cash from sales, $2,100.00. T27.
     30. Paid cash to owner for personal use, $500.00. C9.
     30. Received cash from sales, $110.00. T30.

Instructions:

1. Open an account for Utilities Expense. Use the 3-digit numbering system described in the chapter.

2. Journalize the transactions completed during November of the current year. Use page 1 of a journal. Source documents are abbreviated as follows: check, C; memorandum, M; receipt, R; sales invoice, S; calculator tape, T.

3. Prove the journal.

4. Prove cash. The beginning cash balance on November 1 is zero. The balance on the next unused check stub is $6,897.00.

5. Rule the journal.

6. Post from the journal to the general ledger.

4-6   CHALLENGE PROBLEM

Posting using a variation of the five-column journal

Frances Fessler owns a service business called HouseCare. HouseCare uses a five-column journal that is different from the journal used in this chapter. HouseCare's March journal and general ledger accounts (before posting) are given in the *Working Papers*.

Instructions:

1. Post the separate amounts (on each line of the journal) that need to be posted individually.
2. Post the journal's special amount column totals.

APPLIED COMMUNICATION

Instructions: Write a memorandum responding to the following scenario: Kim Park is at the bank, applying for a business loan. Ms. Park has just called you and asked that you fax or email her with the following information: Tech-Know Consulting's asset, liability, owner's equity, sales, and expense accounts, and their current balances. In your memorandum, include an introductory sentence or paragraph and end with a concluding statement.

CASE FOR CRITICAL THINKING

Trent Marvets does the accounting work for his business. When posting, he first transfers all of the information to the general ledger accounts. Then he returns to the journal and, all at one time, writes the account numbers in the Post. Ref. column of the journal. Eiko Harada also does the accounting work for her business. When posting, she writes all the account numbers in the Post. Ref. column of the journal before she transfers any information to the accounts. Is Mr. Marvets or Ms. Harada following the correct procedure? Explain your answer.

USING SOURCE DOCUMENTS

Journalizing transactions and posting to a general ledger

1. The journal for Darcia's School of Dance is given in the *Working Papers*. Use page 1 of the journal to journalize the transactions for July.
2. Prove the journal.
3. Prove cash. The beginning cash balance on July 1 is zero. The balance on the next unused check stub is $6,576.00.
4. Rule the journal.
5. Post from the journal to the general ledger.

ANALYZING BEST BUY'S FINANCIAL STATEMENTS

In order to move into smaller markets, Best Buy has intentionally planned smaller stores, with 20,000 to 30,000 square feet as compared to the standard Best Buy showroom, which is 45,000 square feet. In order to calculate the average total retail square footage per U.S. Best Buy store, divide the total retail square footage by the number of stores. You will find this data in the 5-Year Financial Highlights on Appendix page B-2.

Instructions

1. Calculate the average total retail square footage per store for U.S. Best Buy stores for 2003 through 2007.
2. Is Best Buy succeeding on the goal of smaller stores?

Accounting
SOFTWARE

CHART OF ACCOUNTS MAINTENANCE; JOURNALIZING TRANSACTIONS

In this chapter, you learned how to add a new account to a general ledger. The process of creating a new account in Peachtree is almost identical.

1. Select Maintain, Chart of Accounts from the menu bar.
2. Key the account number in the Account ID field, and press Enter.
3. Key the account title in the Description field, and press Enter.
4. Select Expenses in the Account Type field.
5. Click Save, and then click Close.

Transactions can now be posted to the new account through Peachtree's general journal. The new account will appear in the account list. When the transaction is saved, Peachtree automatically posts the transaction to the general ledger.

PEACHTREE MASTERY PROBLEM 4-5

1. Open (Restore) file 04-5MP.ptb.
2. Before you start journalizing, add Account No. 540, Utilities Expense, to O'Kalla Lawn and Garden's Chart of Accounts. Journalize and post the November transactions using General Journal Entry from the menu bar and selecting Tasks.
3. From the menu bar, select Reports and then General Ledger to print the general journal.
4. Print the general ledger from the Select a Report window.

CHART OF ACCOUNTS MAINTENANCE; JOURNALIZING TRANSACTIONS

In this chapter, you learned how to add a new account to a general ledger. The process of creating a new account in QuickBooks is almost identical.

1. Click on the Account drop-down box.
2. Click on New to bring up the Add New Account dialog box.
3. Select an account type and click on Continue.
4. Enter the account number, name, and any other appropriate information.
5. Click on Save and Close.

Posting Amounts to the General Ledger
When you make journal entries, QuickBooks automatically posts the entries to the ledger accounts when you select Save and New or Save and Close.

QUICKBOOKS MASTERY PROBLEM 4-5

1. Open the O'Kalla Lawn and Garden file if it is not already open.
2. Choose Make General Journal Entries from the Company menu, and enter the transactions.
3. Print the General Journal report from the Accountant & Taxes option from the Reports drop-down menu; choose Journal and date the report November 30.
4. Choose Company & Financial from the Reports drop-down menu; select Balance Sheet Standard, and print a report dated November 30.

A basic knowledge of electronic spreadsheets is required to complete the exercises in this textbook. For purposes of the exercises in this textbook, you need to be able to:

Open a workbook.

Enter numbers and text in a template.

Enter a formula.

Enter a SUM function.

Save the workbook.

Print a work sheet.

Switch between work sheets.

Each template contains an Instructions work sheet that contains the exercise number and title followed by a detailed list of instructions. A second work sheet contains a template that you will complete by entering numbers and text. Whenever a cell contains [F], that means that you are to create a formula in that cell.

EXCEL ACTIVITY

1. Access the spreadsheet files as instructed by your teacher.
2. Open several of these files to get acquainted with the style of the workbooks and the types of tasks that you will be performing.

CHART OF ACCOUNTS MAINTENANCE; JOURNALIZING TRANSACTIONS

Chart of Accounts Maintenance

Accounts can be added, deleted, or changed. The Account Maintenance window will appear when you choose the Maintain Accounts menu item from the Data drop-down list or click on the Accts. toolbar button.

Adding a New Account

1. Enter the account number in the Account column at the end of the list, then press the Tab key.
2. Enter the title for the new account.
3. For a departmentalized business, enter the department number.
4. Click the Add Account button.
5. Click the Close button to exit the Accounts window.

Changing an Account Title

1. Select the account that you wish to change.
2. Enter the correct account title or department number.
3. Click the Change button when the account title has been changed.

The account number cannot be changed. If an account number needs to be changed because of an incorrect account number, the account must be deleted, then added as a new account number.

Deleting an Account

1. Select the account that you wish to delete.
2. Click the Delete button. General ledger accounts cannot be deleted unless the account has a zero balance.
3. Click the OK button.

Posting Amounts to the General Ledger

In automated accounting, journal entries are automatically posted by clicking the Post button or pressing the Enter key after a transaction is entered in a journal.

AUTOMATED ACCOUNTING APPLICATION PROBLEM 4-1

Open file F04-1.AA8. Display the problem instructions and complete the problem.

AUTOMATED ACCOUNTING MASTERY PROBLEM 4-5

Open file F04-5.AA8. Display the problem instructions and complete the problem.

CHAPTER 5

Cash Control Systems

OBJECTIVES

After studying Chapter 5, you will be able to:

1. Define accounting terms related to using a checking account and a petty cash fund.

2. Identify accounting concepts and practices related to using a checking account.

3. Prepare business papers related to using a checking account.

4. Reconcile a bank statement.

5. Journalize dishonored checks and electronic banking transactions.

6. Establish and replenish a petty cash fund.

KEY TERMS

- code of conduct
- checking account
- endorsement
- blank endorsement
- special endorsement
- restrictive endorsement
- postdated check
- bank statement
- dishonored check
- electronic funds transfer
- debit card
- petty cash
- petty cash slip

Point Your Browser
www.C21accounting.com

Hard Rock Cafe

Hard Rock Really Rocks

"Hard Rock isn't just a name; it's a culture." These words are used on the Hard Rock website to describe the company. The culture that is Hard Rock is summed up in its mission, which is "to spread the spirit of rock 'n roll by creating authentic experiences that rock." As anyone who has visited a Hard Rock Cafe can tell you, it *is* all about rock and roll.

Each of the 121 Hard Rock Cafes, located in over 40 countries, features rock and roll memorabilia—over 60,000 pieces in total, as well as classic American food and good music. And, if your dining experience was a pleasant one, you can take a piece of it home with you by shopping at the on-site stores for articles that range from collector pins to one-of-a-kind guitars.

The Hard Rock culture is also evident in its mottos: "Love All—Serve All"; "All Is One"; "Save the Planet"; and "Take Time to Be Kind." Hard Rock lives out these mottos by contributing to many charitable organizations designed to make the earth a safer, healthier, and better place to live.

RISER/GETTY IMAGES

Critical Thinking

1. At Hard Rock Cafe, customers use cash or credit cards to make purchases. What control problems may occur when employees accept cash for a sale?

2. What can Hard Rock do, in its own cafes, to help support its "Save the Planet" motto?

Source: www.hardrock.com

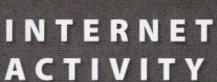

DIGITAL VISION/GETTY IMAGES

INTERNET ACTIVITY

Interest Rates

Banks offer many services, including savings accounts and loans. If you have a savings account with a bank, the bank pays you interest on the money in the account. If you take out a loan, you pay interest to the bank on the money you owe.

Go to the homepage for a bank of your choice.

Instructions

1. Find the range of interest the bank offers for its savings accounts.

2. Find the range of interest charged by the bank on an auto loan.

3. Compare the two rates. Why does the bank charge more interest on loans than it pays on savings accounts?

HOW BUSINESSES USE CASH

In accounting, money is usually referred to as cash. Most businesses make major cash payments by check. However, small cash payments for items such as postage and some supplies may be made from a cash fund kept at the place of business.

Because cash transactions occur more frequently than other types of transactions, more chances occur to make recording errors affecting cash. Cash can be transferred from one person to another without any question about ownership. Also, cash may be lost as it is moved from one place to another.

As a safety measure, TechKnow Consulting keeps most of its cash in a bank. Because all cash receipts are placed in a bank, TechKnow Consulting has written evidence to support its accounting records. TechKnow Consulting can compare its record of checks written with the bank's record of checks paid. Greater control of TechKnow Consulting's cash and greater accuracy of its cash records result from these procedures.

CHARACTER COUNTS

Business Codes of Conduct

A statement that guides the ethical behavior of a company and its employees is called a **code of conduct**. Merck & Co., Inc., a leading pharmaceutical company, makes its code of conduct available to its employees, consultants, and the public. The document, titled "Our Values and Standards," begins by stating:

At Merck, our values and standards have always formed the basis of our success. They inspire trust and confidence on the part of the medical community, government officials, regulatory agencies, financial markets, our customers and patients—all who are essential to our success.

The code of conduct contains sections that focus on Merck's relationship with customers, employees, shareholders, suppliers, and communities/society. Each section contains specific guidance on Merck policies. Common questions and answers are provided to expand on these policies. Throughout the document, individuals are encouraged to seek the guidance of upper-level managers, the Legal Department, and the Office of Ethics if they are unsure whether their actions comply with the code of conduct.

Instructions

Obtain access to Merck's code of conduct at www.merck.com. Assuming you are a Merck employee, may you:

1. Give a physician a gift consisting of a medical textbook?

2. Use your cellular phone to discuss new research methods with another Merck employee?

3. Accept a supplier's invitation to attend the Super Bowl?

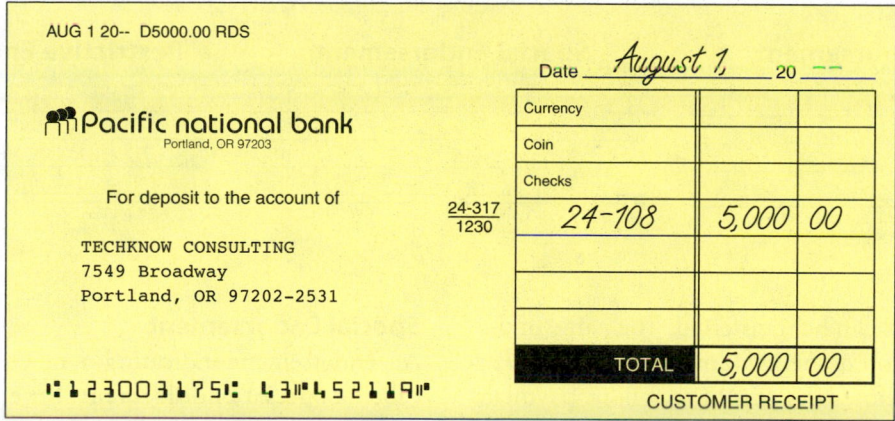

A business form ordering a bank to pay cash from a bank account is known as a check. A bank account from which payments can be ordered by a depositor is called a **checking account**.

When a checking account is opened, the bank customer must provide a signature on a signature card for the bank records. If several persons are authorized to sign checks, each person's signature must be on the signature card.

A bank customer prepares a deposit slip each time cash or checks are placed in a bank account. Deposit slips may differ slightly from one bank to another. Each bank designs its own deposit slips to fit the bank's recording machines. However, all deposit slips contain the same basic information.

Checks are listed on a deposit slip according to the bank routing number on each check. For example, the routing number 24-108 identifies the bank on which the $5,000.00 check is written.

When a deposit is made, a bank gives the depositor a receipt. Many banks use a copy of the deposit slip with a printed or stamped verification as the receipt. The printed verification, *Aug 1, 20-- D5000.00 RDS*, is printed along the top left edge of the deposit slip. This printed verification means that a total of $5,000.00 was deposited on August 1. The initials RDS next to the amount are those of the bank employee who accepted the deposit.

DEPOSIT RECORDED ON A CHECK STUB

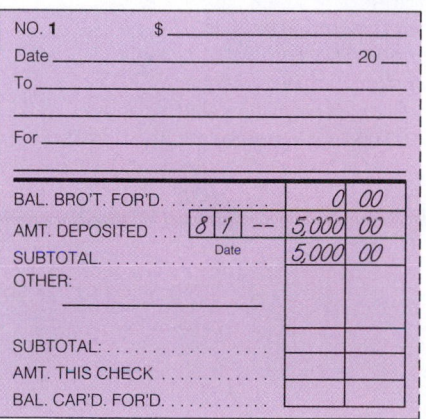

After the deposit is recorded on the check stub, a checkbook subtotal is calculated. The balance brought forward on Check Stub No. 1 is zero. The previous balance, $0.00, plus the deposit, $5,000.00, equals the subtotal, $5,000.00.

Cash receipts are journalized at the time cash is received. Later, the cash receipts are deposited in the checking account. Therefore, no journal entry is needed for deposits because the cash receipts have already been journalized.

Blank Endorsement

Endorse here
X   *Kim Park*

DO NOT WRITE, STAMP, OR SIGN BELOW THIS LINE
Reserved for Financial Institution Use

Special Endorsement

Endorse here
X   *Pay to the order of*
        Eleanor Johnson
        Kim Park

DO NOT WRITE, STAMP, OR SIGN BELOW THIS LINE
Reserved for Financial Institution Use

Restrictive Endorsement

Endorse here
X   For deposit only to
        the account of
        TECHKNOW CONSULTING
        Kim Park

DO NOT WRITE, STAMP, OR SIGN BELOW THIS LINE
Reserved for Financial Institution Use

Ownership of a check can be transferred. The name of the first owner is stated on a check following the words *Pay to the order of*. Therefore, the person to whom payment is to be made must indicate that ownership of the check is being transferred. One person transfers ownership to another person by signing on the back of a check. A signature or stamp on the back of a check transferring ownership is called an **endorsement**. Federal regulations require that an endorsement be confined to a limited amount of space that is indicated on the back of a check.

An endorsement should be signed exactly as the person's name appears on the front of the check. For example, a check made payable to K. A. Park is endorsed on the back as *K. A. Park*. Immediately below that endorsement, Ms. Park would write her official signature, *Kim Park*.

Ownership of a check might be transferred several times, resulting in several endorsements. Each endorser guarantees payment of the check. If a bank does not receive payment from the person who signed the check, each endorser is individually liable for payment.

Three types of endorsements are commonly used, each having a specific use in transferring ownership.

Blank Endorsement

An endorsement consisting only of the endorser's signature is called a **blank endorsement**. A blank endorsement indicates that the subsequent owner is whoever has the check.

If a check with a blank endorsement is lost or stolen, the check can be cashed by anyone who has possession of it. Ownership may be transferred without further endorsement. A blank endorsement should be used only when a person is at the bank ready to cash or deposit a check.

Special Endorsement

An endorsement indicating a new owner of a check is called a **special endorsement**. Special endorsements are sometimes known as *endorsements in full*.

Special endorsements include the words *Pay to the order of* and the name of the new check owner. Only the person or business named in a special endorsement can cash, deposit, or further transfer ownership of the check.

Restrictive Endorsement

An endorsement restricting further transfer of a check's ownership is called a **restrictive endorsement**. A restrictive endorsement limits use of the check to whatever purpose is stated in the endorsement.

Many businesses have a stamp prepared with a restrictive endorsement. When a check is received, it is immediately stamped with the restrictive endorsement. This prevents unauthorized persons from cashing the check if it is lost or stolen.

FOR YOUR INFORMATION

F Y I

The Federal Deposit Insurance Corporation (FDIC) protects depositors from banks that fail. Bank deposits are generally covered up to $100,000 per depositor.

TechKnow Consulting uses printed checks with check stubs attached. Consecutive numbers are preprinted on TechKnow Consulting's checks. Consecutive numbers on checks provide an easy way of identifying each check. Also, the numbers help keep track of all checks to assure that none are lost or misplaced.

A check stub is a business's record of each check written for a cash payment transaction. [CONCEPT: Objective Evidence] To avoid forgetting to prepare a check stub, the check stub is prepared before the check is written.

After the check stub is completed, the check is written.

STEPS PREPARING CHECK STUBS AND CHECKS

1. Write the amount of the check, *$275.00*, in the space after the dollar sign at the top of the stub.

2. Write the date of the check, *August 3, 20--*, on the Date line at the top of the stub.

3. Write to whom the check is to be paid, *Port City Supply Co.*, on the To line at the top of the stub.

4. Record the purpose of the check, *Supplies*, on the For line.

5. Write the amount of the check, *$275.00*, in the amount column at the bottom of the stub on the line with the words "Amt. This Check."

6. Calculate the new checking account balance, *$4,725.00*, and record the new balance in the amount column on the last line of the stub. The new balance is calculated as shown.

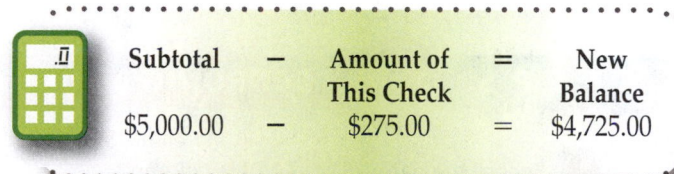

	Subtotal	−	Amount of This Check	=	New Balance
	$5,000.00	−	$275.00	=	$4,725.00

PREPARING CHECKS

7. Write the date, *August 3, 20--*, in the space provided. The date should be the month, day, and year on which the check is issued. A check with a future date on it is called a **postdated check**. Most banks will not accept postdated checks because money cannot be withdrawn from a depositor's account until the date on the check.

8. Write to whom the check is to be paid, *Port City Supply Co.*, following the words "Pay to the order of." If the person to whom a check is to be paid is a business, use the business's name rather than the owner's name. [CONCEPT: Business Entity] If the person to whom the check is to be paid is an individual, use that person's name.

9. Write the amount in figures, *$275.00*, following the dollar sign. Write the figures close to the printed dollar sign. This practice prevents anyone from writing another digit in front of the amount to change the amount of the check.

10. Write the amount in words, *Two hundred seventy-five and no/100*, on the line with the word "Dollars." This written amount verifies the amount written in figures after the dollar sign. Begin the words at the extreme left. Draw a line through the unused space up to the word "Dollars." This line prevents anyone from writing in additional words to change the amount. If the amounts in words and in figures are not the same, a bank may pay only the amount in words. Often, when the amounts do not agree, a bank will refuse to pay the check. (*continued on next page*)

11. Write the purpose of the check, *Supplies*, on the line labeled "For." (On some checks this space is labeled "Memo.") Some checks do not have a line for writing the purpose of the check.

12. Sign the check. A check should not be signed until each item on the check and its stub has been verified for accuracy.

RECORDING A VOIDED CHECK

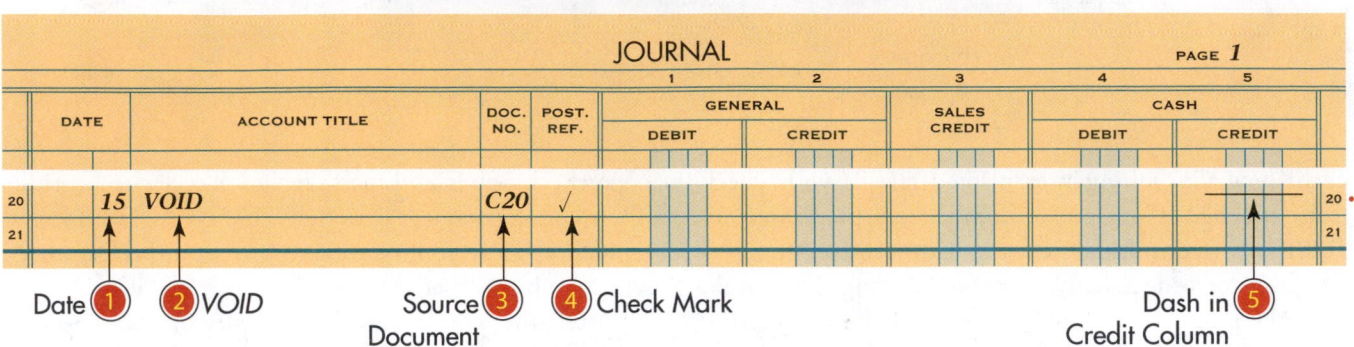

Date ① ② *VOID* Source ③ ④ Check Mark Dash in ⑤
Document Credit Column

Banks usually refuse to accept altered checks. If any kind of error is made in preparing a check, a new check should be prepared. Because checks are prenumbered, all checks not used should be retained for the records. This practice helps account for all checks and assures that no checks have been lost or stolen.

A check that contains errors must be marked so that others will know that it is not to be used. The word *VOID* is written in large letters across both the check and its stub.

When TechKnow Consulting records a check in its journal, the check number is placed in the journal's Doc. No. column. If a check number is missing from the Doc. No. column, there is a question whether all checks have been journalized. To assure that all check numbers are listed in the journal, TechKnow Consulting records voided checks in the journal.

STEPS RECORDING A VOIDED CHECK IN THE JOURNAL

① Record the date, *15*, in the Date column.

② Write the word *VOID* in the Account Title column.

③ Write the check number, *C20*, in the Doc. No. column.

④ Place a check mark in the Post. Ref. column.

⑤ Place a dash in the Cash Credit column.

REMEMBER

Always complete the check stub before writing the check. Otherwise you may forget to record the amount of the check on the check stub.

code of conduct

checking account

endorsement

blank endorsement

special endorsement

restrictive endorsement

postdated check

AUDIT YOUR UNDERSTANDING

1. List the three types of endorsements.
2. List the steps for preparing a check stub.
3. List the steps for preparing a check.

WORK TOGETHER 5-1

Endorsing and writing checks

Write the answers to the following problems in the *Working Papers*. Your instructor will guide you through the following examples. You are authorized to sign checks for Balsam Lake Accounting.

1. For each of these situations, prepare the appropriate endorsement.
   a. Write a blank endorsement.
   b. Write a special endorsement to transfer a check to Kelsey Sather.
   c. Write a restrictive endorsement to deposit a check in the account of Balsam Lake Accounting.
2. Record the balance brought forward on Check Stub No. 78, $1,805.75.
3. Record a deposit of $489.00 made on October 30 of the current year on Check Stub No. 78.
4. Prepare check stubs and write the following checks. Use October 30 of the current year as the date.
   a. Check No. 78 to Corner Garage for repairs, $162.00.
   b. Check No. 79 to St. Croix Supply for supplies, $92.00.

ON YOUR OWN 5-1

Endorsing and writing checks

Write the answers to the following problems in the *Working Papers*. Work these problems independently. You are authorized to sign checks for Centuria Hair Care.

1. For each of these situations, prepare the appropriate endorsement.
   a. Write a special endorsement to transfer a check to Kenneth Burleson.
   b. Write a restrictive endorsement to deposit a check in the account of Centuria Hair Care.
2. Record the balance brought forward on Check Stub No. 345, $2,106.53.
3. Record a deposit of $456.25 made on May 31 of the current year on Check Stub No. 345.
4. Prepare check stubs and write the following checks. Use May 31 of the current year as the date.
   a. Check No. 345 to Uniforms Plus for uniform rental, $355.00.
   b. Check No. 346 to HairWorld for supplies, $412.00.

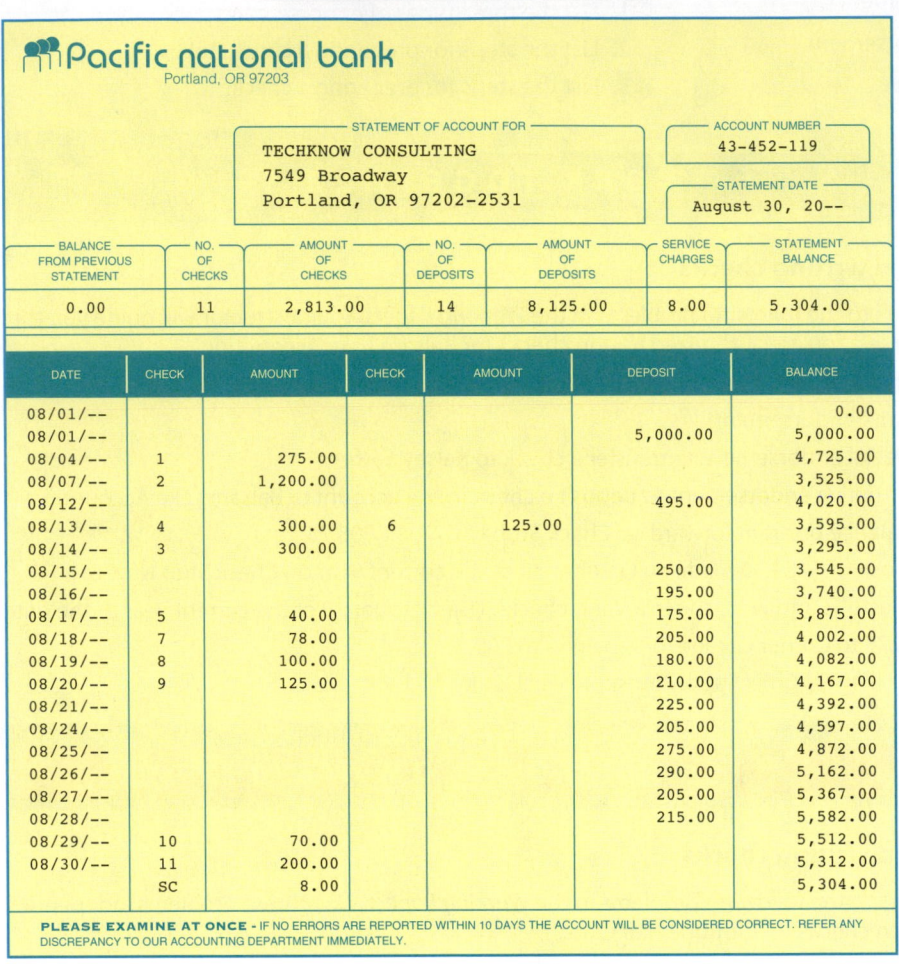

Pacific national bank
Portland, OR 97203

STATEMENT OF ACCOUNT FOR	ACCOUNT NUMBER
TECHKNOW CONSULTING 7549 Broadway Portland, OR 97202-2531	43-452-119 STATEMENT DATE August 30, 20--

BALANCE FROM PREVIOUS STATEMENT	NO. OF CHECKS	AMOUNT OF CHECKS	NO. OF DEPOSITS	AMOUNT OF DEPOSITS	SERVICE CHARGES	STATEMENT BALANCE
0.00	11	2,813.00	14	8,125.00	8.00	5,304.00

DATE	CHECK	AMOUNT	CHECK	AMOUNT	DEPOSIT	BALANCE
08/01/--						0.00
08/01/--					5,000.00	5,000.00
08/04/--	1	275.00				4,725.00
08/07/--	2	1,200.00				3,525.00
08/12/--					495.00	4,020.00
08/13/--	4	300.00	6	125.00		3,595.00
08/14/--	3	300.00				3,295.00
08/15/--					250.00	3,545.00
08/16/--					195.00	3,740.00
08/17/--	5	40.00			175.00	3,875.00
08/18/--	7	78.00			205.00	4,002.00
08/19/--	8	100.00			180.00	4,082.00
08/20/--	9	125.00			210.00	4,167.00
08/21/--					225.00	4,392.00
08/24/--					205.00	4,597.00
08/25/--					275.00	4,872.00
08/26/--					290.00	5,162.00
08/27/--					205.00	5,367.00
08/28/--					215.00	5,582.00
08/29/--	10	70.00				5,512.00
08/30/--	11	200.00				5,312.00
	SC	8.00				5,304.00

PLEASE EXAMINE AT ONCE - IF NO ERRORS ARE REPORTED WITHIN 10 DAYS THE ACCOUNT WILL BE CONSIDERED CORRECT. REFER ANY DISCREPANCY TO OUR ACCOUNTING DEPARTMENT IMMEDIATELY.

A report of deposits, withdrawals, and bank balances sent to a depositor by a bank is called a **bank statement**.

When a bank receives checks, the amount of each check is deducted from the depositor's account. The bank stamps the checks to indicate that the checks are canceled and are not to be transferred further. Canceled checks may be returned to a depositor with a bank statement or may be kept on record by the bank. Account service charges are also listed on a bank statement.

Although banks seldom make mistakes, occasionally a check or deposit might be recorded in a wrong account. If errors are discovered, the bank should be notified at once. However, a bank's records and a depositor's records may differ for several reasons:

1. A service charge may not have been recorded in the depositor's business records.
2. Outstanding deposits may be recorded in the depositor's records but not on a bank statement.
3. Outstanding checks may be recorded in the depositor's records but not on a bank statement.
4. A depositor may have made math or recording errors.

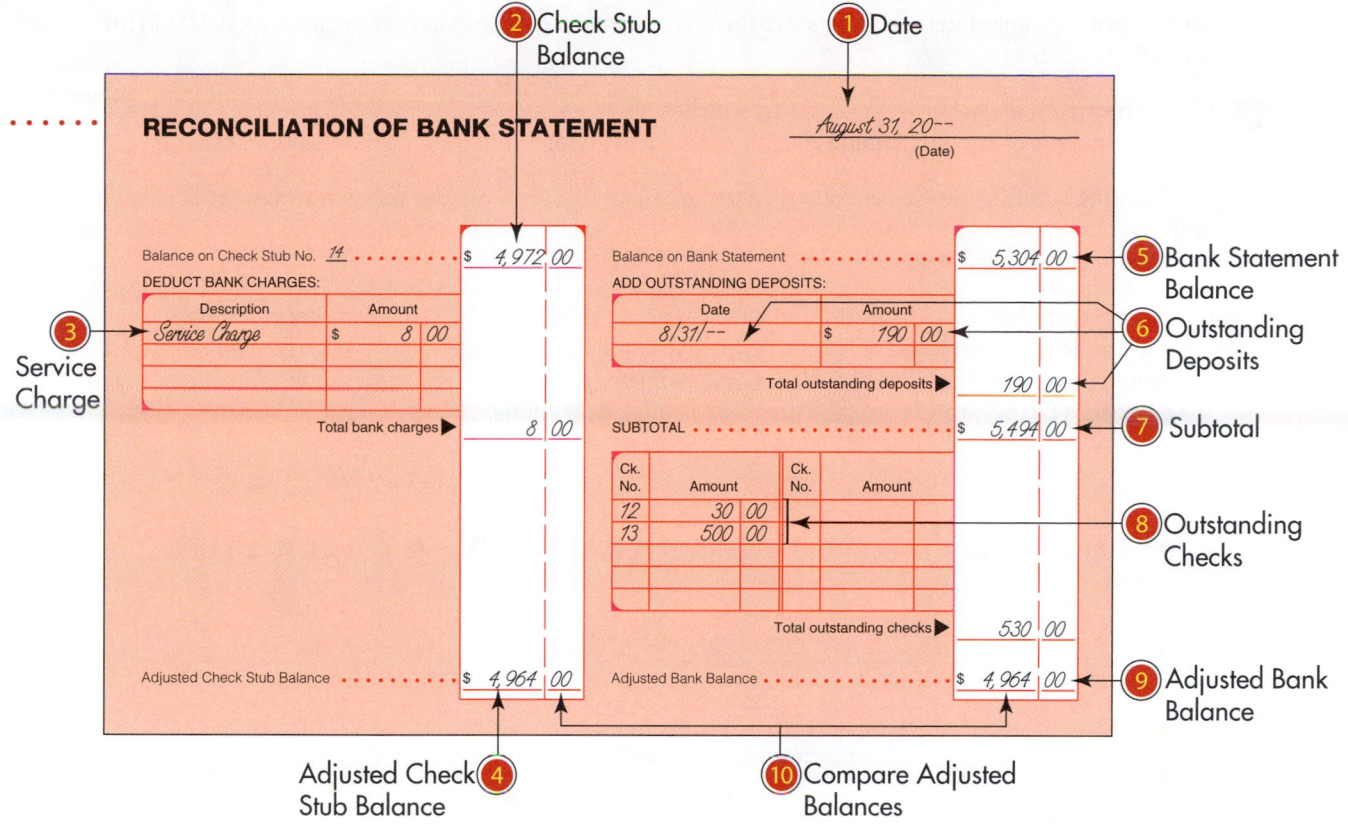

② Check Stub Balance ① Date

RECONCILIATION OF BANK STATEMENT   *August 31, 20--*
(Date)

Balance on Check Stub No. *14* . . . . $ 4,972 00   Balance on Bank Statement . . . . $ 5,304 00 ← ⑤ Bank Statement Balance
DEDUCT BANK CHARGES: ADD OUTSTANDING DEPOSITS:

③ Service Charge

Description	Amount
Service Charge	$ 8 00

Date	Amount
8/31/--	$ 190 00	← ⑥ Outstanding Deposits

Total outstanding deposits ▶ 190 00

Total bank charges ▶ 8 00

SUBTOTAL . . . . $ 5,494 00 ← ⑦ Subtotal

Ck. No.	Amount	Ck. No.	Amount
12	30 00		
13	500 00			← ⑧ Outstanding Checks

Total outstanding checks ▶ 530 00

Adjusted Check Stub Balance . . . . . . $ 4,964 00   Adjusted Bank Balance . . . . . . $ 4,964 00 ← ⑨ Adjusted Bank Balance

④ Adjusted Check Stub Balance   ⑩ Compare Adjusted Balances

A bank statement is reconciled by verifying that information on a bank statement and a checkbook are in agreement. Reconciling immediately is an important aspect of cash control.

TechKnow Consulting's canceled checks are kept on record at the bank. The bank statement is used to determine the canceled checks. For each canceled check listed on the bank statement, a check mark is placed on the corresponding check stub. A check stub with no check mark

indicates an outstanding check. Outstanding checks are those checks issued by a depositor but not yet reported on a bank statement. Outstanding deposits are those deposits made at a bank but not yet shown on a bank statement.

TechKnow Consulting receives a bank statement dated August 30 on August 31. TechKnow Consulting uses a reconciliation form printed on the back of the bank statement.

STEPS **RECONCILING A BANK STATEMENT**

① Write the date on which the reconciliation is prepared, *August 31, 20--*.

② In the left amount column, list the balance brought forward on Check Stub No. 14, the next unused check stub, *$4,972.00*.

③ In the space for bank charges, list any charges. The only such charge for TechKnow Consulting is the bank service charge, *$8.00*. The bank service charge is labeled "SC" on the bank statement.

④ Write the adjusted check stub balance, *$4,964.00*, in the space provided at the bottom of the left amount column. The balance on the check stub, $4,972.00, minus the bank's service charge, $8.00, equals the adjusted check stub balance, $4,964.00.

⑤ Write the ending balance shown on the bank statement, *$5,304.00*, in the right amount column. *(continued on next page)*

6. Write the date, *8/31/--*, and the amount, *$190.00*, of any outstanding deposits in the space provided. Add the outstanding deposits. Write the total outstanding deposits, *$190.00*, in the right amount column.

7. Add the ending bank statement balance to the total outstanding deposits. Write the total, *$5,494.00*, in the space for the Subtotal.

8. List the outstanding checks, Nos. *12* and *13*, and their amounts, *$30.00* and *$500.00*, in the space provided. Add the amounts of the outstanding checks, and write the total, *$530.00*, in the right amount column.

9. Calculate the adjusted bank balance, and write the amount, *$4,964.00*, in the space provided at the bottom of the right amount column. The subtotal, $5,494.00, minus the total outstanding checks, $530.00, equals the adjusted bank balance, $4,964.00.

10. Compare adjusted balances. The adjusted balances must be the same. The adjusted check stub balance is the same as the adjusted bank balance. Because the two amounts are the same, the bank statement is reconciled. The completed reconciliation form is filed for future reference. If the two adjusted balances are not the same, the error must be found and corrected before any more work is done.

RECORDING A BANK SERVICE CHARGE ON A CHECK STUB

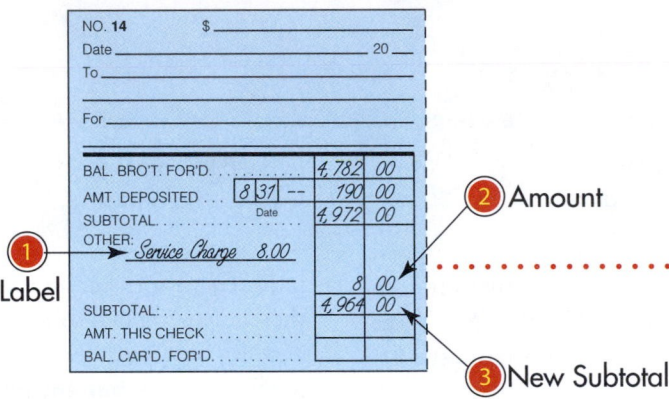

The bank deducts the service charge from TechKnow Consulting's checking account each month. Although TechKnow Consulting did not write a check for the bank service charge, this cash payment must be recorded in TechKnow Consulting's accounting records as a cash payment. TechKnow Consulting makes a record of a bank service charge on a check stub.

STEPS RECORDING A BANK SERVICE CHARGE ON A CHECK STUB

1. Write *Service Charge $8.00* on the check stub under the heading "Other."

2. Write the amount of the service charge, *$8.00*, in the amount column.

3. Calculate and record the new subtotal, *$4,964.00*, on the Subtotal line. A new Balance Carried Forward is not calculated until after Check No. 14 is written.

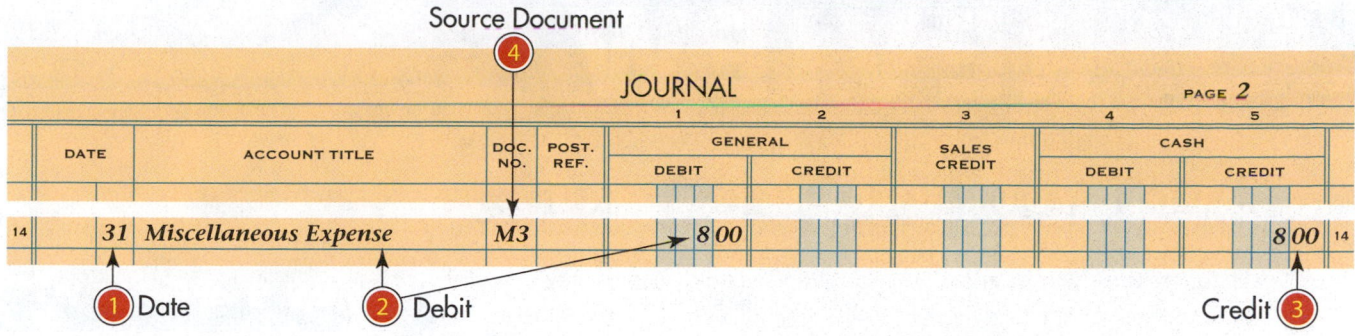

Source Document
④

JOURNAL   PAGE 2

	DATE	ACCOUNT TITLE	DOC. NO.	POST. REF.	GENERAL DEBIT	GENERAL CREDIT	SALES CREDIT	CASH DEBIT	CASH CREDIT	
14	31	*Miscellaneous Expense*	M3		8 00				8 00	14

① Date   ② Debit   Credit ③

Because the bank service charge is a cash payment for which no check is written, TechKnow Consulting prepares a memorandum as the source document. TechKnow Consulting's bank service charges are relatively small and occur only once a month. Therefore, a separate ledger account for the expense is not used. Instead, TechKnow Consulting records the bank service charge as a miscellaneous expense.

A memorandum is the source document for a bank service charge transaction. [CONCEPT: Objective Evidence] The analysis of this transaction is shown in the T accounts.

The expense account, Miscellaneous Expense, is debited for $8.00 to show the decrease in owner's equity. The asset account, Cash, is credited for $8.00 to show the decrease in assets.

August 31. Received bank statement showing August bank service charge, $8.00. Memorandum No. 3.

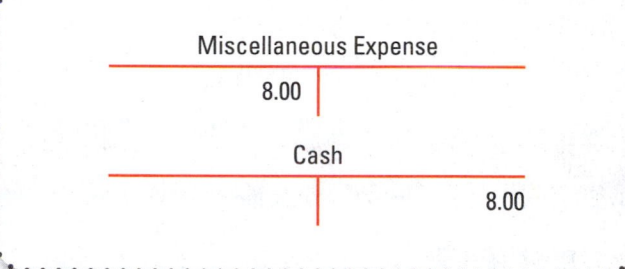

Miscellaneous Expense

8.00 |

Cash

| 8.00

STEPS ○ **JOURNALIZING A BANK SERVICE CHARGE**

① **Date.** Write the date, *31*, in the Date column.

② **Debit.** Write the title of the account to be debited, *Miscellaneous Expense*, in the Account Title column. Record the amount debited, $8.00, in the General Debit column.

③ **Credit.** Record the amount credited, *$8.00*, in the Cash Credit column.

④ **Source document.** Write the source document number, *M3*, in the Doc. No. column.

SMALL BUSINESS
SPOTLIGHT

Three factors generally motivate people to start a new business: the desire to control their own destinies, the desire to work more closely with customers, and the desire to achieve substantial profits.

End of Lesson REVIEW

AUDIT YOUR UNDERSTANDING

1. List four reasons why a depositor's records and a bank's records may differ.
2. If a check mark is placed on the check stub of each canceled check, what does a check stub with no check mark indicate?

TERM REVIEW

bank statement

WORK TOGETHER 5-2

Reconciling a bank statement and recording a bank service charge

Forms are given in the *Working Papers*. Your instructor will guide you through the following examples.

On July 29 of the current year, DeepClean received a bank statement dated July 28. The following information is obtained from the bank statement and from the records of the business.

Bank statement balance	$1,528.00	Outstanding checks:	
Bank service charge	2.00	No. 103	$ 70.00
Outstanding deposit, July 28	150.00	No. 105	35.00
		Checkbook balance on Check Stub No. 106	1,575.00

1. Prepare a bank statement reconciliation. Use July 29 of the current year as the date.
2. Record the service charge on check stub No. 106.
3. Record the service charge on journal page 14. Use Memorandum No. 44 as the source document.

ON YOUR OWN 5-2

Reconciling a bank statement and recording a bank service charge

Forms are given in the *Working Papers*. Work these problems independently.

On April 30 of the current year, Able Service Co. received a bank statement dated April 29. The following information is obtained from the bank statement and from the records of the business.

Bank statement balance	$3,184.00	Outstanding checks:	
Bank service charge	15.00	No. 115	$ 70.00
Outstanding deposits:		No. 117	313.00
April 29	360.00	No. 118	80.00
April 30	510.00		
		Checkbook balance on Check Stub No. 119	3,606.00

1. Prepare a bank statement reconciliation. Use April 30 of the current year as the date.
2. Record the service charge on check stub No. 119.
3. Record the service charge on journal page 8. Use Memorandum No. 84 as the source document.

Dishonored Checks and Electronic Banking

RECORDING A DISHONORED CHECK ON A CHECK STUB

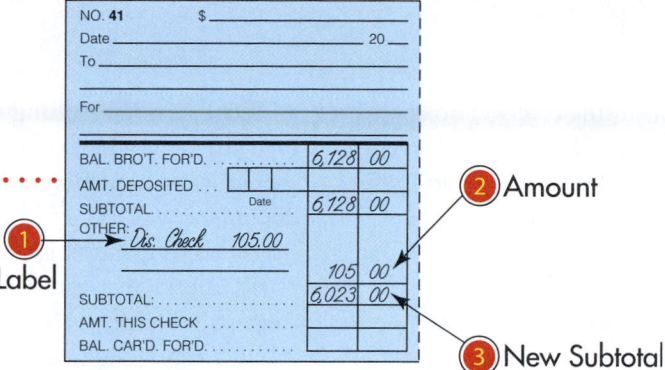

Label ①

② **Amount**

③ **New Subtotal**

A check that a bank refuses to pay is called a **dishonored check**. Banks dishonor a check when the account of the person who wrote the check has insufficient funds to pay the check. Banks may also dishonor a check for other reasons: (1) The check appears to be altered. (2) The signature of the person who signed the check does not match the one on the signature card at the bank. (3) The amounts written in figures and in words do not agree. (4) The check is postdated. (5) The person who wrote the check has stopped payment on the check.

Issuing a check on an account with insufficient funds is illegal. Altering or forging a check is also illegal. A dishonored check may affect the credit rating of the person or business that issued the check.

Sometimes money for a dishonored check can be collected directly from the person or business that wrote the check. Often, however, the value of a dishonored check cannot be recovered and becomes an expense to the business.

Most banks charge a fee for handling dishonored checks that have been previously accepted for deposit. This fee is an expense of the business receiving a dishonored check. TechKnow Consulting's bank charges a $35.00 fee for handling dishonored checks. TechKnow Consulting attempts to collect the $35.00 fee in addition to the amount of the dishonored check from the person or business that wrote the check.

When TechKnow Consulting receives a check, it records the check as a debit to Cash and deposits the check in the bank. When a check is dishonored, the bank deducts the amount of the check plus the fee, $35.00, from TechKnow Consulting's checking account. Therefore, TechKnow Consulting records a dishonored check as a cash payment transaction.

STEPS  RECORDING A DISHONORED CHECK ON A CHECK STUB

① Write *Dishonored check $105.00* on the line under the heading "Other." The amount is the amount of the dishonored check, $70.00, plus the service fee of $35.00.

② Write the total of the dishonored check, *$105.00*, in the amount column.

③ Calculate and record the new subtotal, *$6,023.00*, on the Subtotal line. A new Balance Carried Forward is not calculated until after Check No. 41 is written.

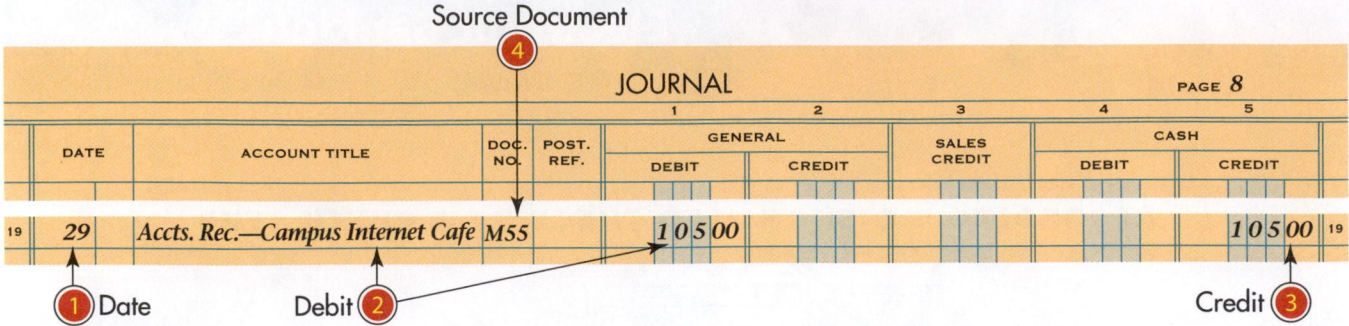

Source Document

During August, TechKnow Consulting received no checks that were subsequently dishonored. However, in November TechKnow Consulting did receive a check from Campus Internet Cafe that was eventually dishonored.

November 29. Received notice from the bank of a dishonored check from Campus Internet Cafe, $70.00, plus $35.00 fee; total, $105.00. Memorandum No. 55.

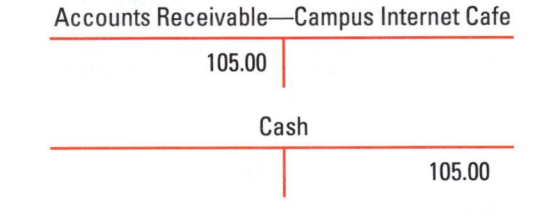

Accounts Receivable—Campus Internet Cafe
| 105.00 | |

Cash
| | 105.00 |

TechKnow Consulting receives a notice of the dishonored check and the fee from the bank. TechKnow attaches the notice to a memorandum, which is used as the source document. [CONCEPT: Objective Evidence] The analysis of this transaction is shown in the T accounts.

All checks received are deposited in TechKnow Consulting's checking account. The entry for each cash receipts transaction includes a debit to Cash. If a check is subsequently returned as dishonored, the previous cash debit for the amount of the check must be offset by a cash credit. The asset account, Cash, is credited for $105.00 to show the decrease in assets.

When TechKnow Consulting originally received the check from Campus Internet Cafe, Accounts Receivable—Campus Internet Cafe was credited to reduce the balance of the account. When TechKnow Consulting finds out that the check was not accepted by the bank, the account, Accounts Receivable—Campus Internet Cafe, must be increased to show that this amount, plus the bank charge, is still owed to TechKnow Consulting. The asset account, Accounts Receivable—Campus Internet Cafe, is debited for $105.00 to show the increase in assets.

STEPS — JOURNALIZING A DISHONORED CHECK

1. **Date.** Write the date, *29*, in the Date column.

2. **Debit.** Write the title of the account to be debited, *Accounts Receivable—Campus Internet Cafe*, in the Account Title column. Record the amount debited, $105.00, in the General Debit column.

3. **Credit.** Write the amount credited, *$105.00*, in the Cash Credit column.

4. **Source document.** Write the source document number, *M55*, in the Doc. No. column.

REMEMBER

Checking accounts and records should be maintained in such a way that all checks will be honored when presented to the bank.

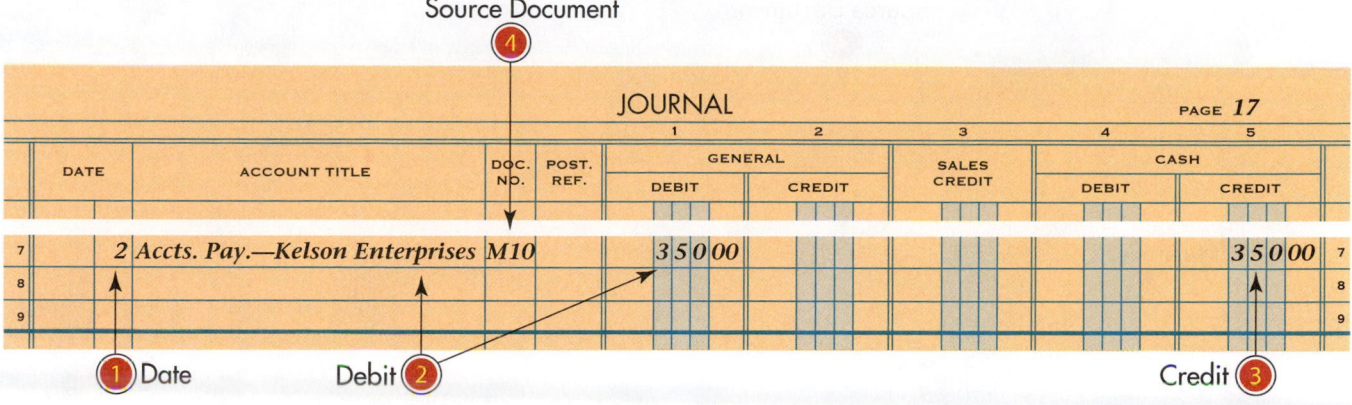

Source Document ④

	DATE	ACCOUNT TITLE	DOC. NO.	POST. REF.	GENERAL DEBIT	GENERAL CREDIT	SALES CREDIT	CASH DEBIT	CASH CREDIT	
7	2	Accts. Pay.—Kelson Enterprises	M10		350 00				350 00	7
8										8
9										9

JOURNAL   PAGE 17

① Date   Debit ②   Credit ③

A computerized cash payments system that transfers funds without the use of checks, currency, or other paper documents is called **electronic funds transfer.** Many businesses use electronic funds transfer (EFT) to pay vendors. To use EFT, a business makes arrangements with its bank to process EFT transactions. Arrangements are also made with vendors to accept EFT payments on account. Then a transfer of funds from the business's account to the vendor's account can be completed via the Internet or a telephone call.

To control cash payments through EFT, the person responsible for requesting transfers should be given a password. The bank should not accept EFT requests from any person unable to provide an established password.

Superior Cleaning Service uses electronic funds transfer to make payments on account to vendors. The journal entry for making payments on account through EFT is the same as when a check is written. The only change is the source document used for the transaction. Superior Cleaning Service uses a memorandum as the source document for an EFT. A note is written on the memorandum to describe the transaction.

The source document for this transaction is Memorandum No. 10. [CONCEPT: Objective Evidence] The analysis of this transaction is shown in the T accounts.

The liability account, Accounts Payable—Kelson Enterprises, is decreased by a debit, $350.00. The asset account, Cash, is decreased by a credit, $350.00.

A cash payment made by EFT is recorded on the check stub as "Other." This procedure keeps the checkbook in balance during the time lag from when the EFT is made until receipt of the bank statement. The EFT payments are verified as part of the regular bank statement reconciliation process. EFT payments are identified in the Check column of the bank statement by the notation "EFT," rather than by a check number.

STEPS  **JOURNALIZING AN ELECTRONIC FUNDS TRANSFER**

① **Date.** Write the date, 2, in the Date column.

② **Debit.** Write the title of the account to be debited, *Accounts Payable—Kelson Enterprises*, in the Account Title column. Record the amount debited, *$350.00*, in the General Debit column.

③ **Credit.** Record the amount credited, *$350.00*, in the Cash Credit column.

④ **Source document.** Write the source document number, *M10*, in the Doc. No. column.

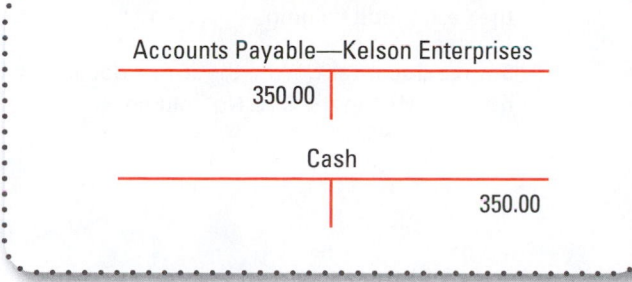

September 2. Paid cash on account to Kelson Enterprises, $350.00, using EFT. Memorandum No. 10.

Accounts Payable—Kelson Enterprises	
350.00	

Cash	
	350.00

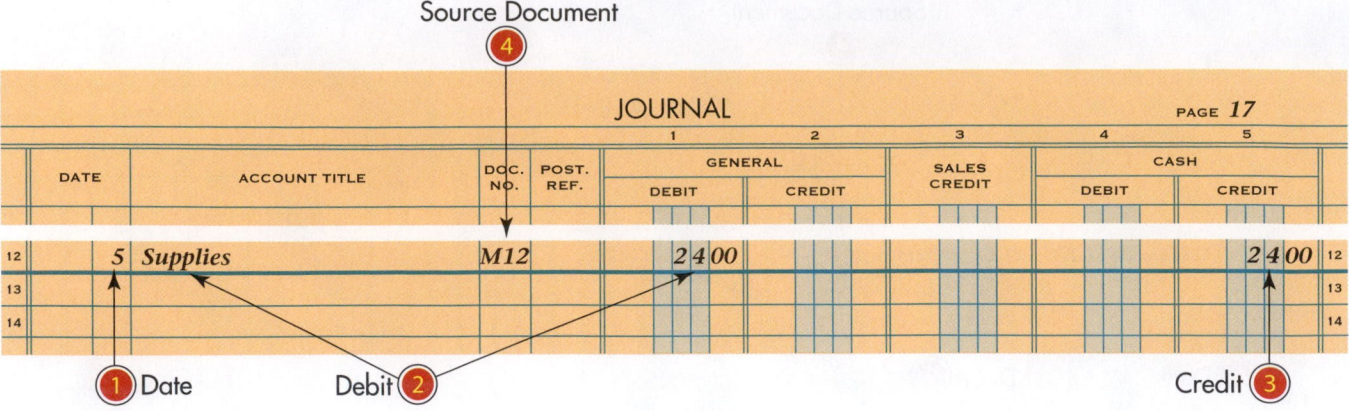

Source Document ④

	DATE	ACCOUNT TITLE	DOC. NO.	POST. REF.	GENERAL DEBIT	GENERAL CREDIT	SALES CREDIT	CASH DEBIT	CASH CREDIT	
12	5	*Supplies*	M12		2 4 00				2 4 00	12
13										13
14										14

① Date   Debit ②   Credit ③

A bank card that automatically deducts the amount of a purchase from the checking account of the cardholder is called a **debit card.** There is one major difference between a debit card and a credit card. When a purchase is made with a debit card, the amount of the purchase is automatically deducted from the checking account of the cardholder. A debit card eliminates the need to write a check for the purchase. However, the effect is the same. The checking account balance is reduced by the amount of the purchase. A debit card also eliminates the need to carry a checkbook.

When using a debit card, it is important to remember to record all purchases to avoid errors in the checking account.

Superior Cleaning Service uses a debit card to make some purchases. Recording a cash payment made by a debit card is similar to recording a cash payment made by electronic funds transfer.

Superior Cleaning Service uses a memorandum as the source document for a debit card purchase. A note is written on the memorandum to describe the transaction.

The source document for this transaction is Memorandum No. 12. [CONCEPT: Objective Evidence] The analysis of this transaction is shown in the T accounts.

The asset account, Supplies, is increased by a debit, $24.00. The asset account, Cash, is decreased by a credit, $24.00.

A cash payment made with a debit card is recorded on the check stub as "Other." This procedure keeps the checkbook in balance during the time lag from when the debit card payment is made until receipt of the bank statement. The debit card payments are verified as part of the regular bank statement reconciliation process. Debit card payments are identified as a Purchase on the bank statement, with the date, time, location, and the amount of the debit card transaction stated.

STEPS — JOURNALIZING A DEBIT CARD PURCHASE

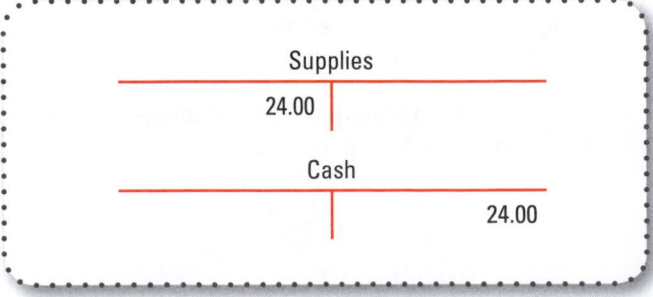

September 5. Purchased supplies, $24.00, using debit card. Memorandum No. 12.

Supplies	
24.00	

Cash	
	24.00

① **Date.** Write the date, *5*, in the Date column.

② **Debit.** Write the title of the account to be debited, *Supplies*, in the Account Title column. Record the amount debited, *$24.00*, in the General Debit column.

③ **Credit.** Record the amount credited, *$24.00*, in the Cash Credit column.

④ **Source document.** Write the source document number, *M12*, in the Doc. No. column.

End of Lesson
REVIEW

TERMS REVIEW

dishonored check

electronic funds transfer

debit card

1. List six reasons why a bank may dishonor a check.
2. What account is credited when electronic funds transfer is used to pay cash on account?
3. What account is credited when a debit card is used to purchase supplies?

WORK TOGETHER 5-3

Recording dishonored checks, electronic funds transfers, and debit card purchases

Write the answers to this problem in the *Working Papers*. Your instructor will guide you through the following example.

1. Enter the following transactions on page 6 of a journal.

Transactions:

March 15. Received notice from the bank of a dishonored check from Christopher Ikola, $63.00, plus $10.00 fee; total, $73.00. Memorandum No. 121.
16. Paid cash on account to Spinoza Enterprises, $135.00, using EFT. Memorandum No. 122.
17. Purchased supplies, $31.00, using a debit card. Memorandum No. 123.

ON YOUR OWN 5-3

Recording dishonored checks, electronic funds transfers, and debit card purchases

Write the answers to this problem in the *Working Papers*. Work this problem independently.

1. Enter the following transactions on page 12 of a journal.

Transactions:

June 12. Received notice from the bank of a dishonored check from Thomas Hofski, $65.00, plus $30.00 fee; total, $95.00. Memorandum No. 54.
13. Paid cash on account to Alfonso Company, $243.00, using EFT. Memorandum No. 55.
14. Purchased supplies, $65.00, using a debit card. Memorandum No. 56.

Petty Cash

ESTABLISHING A PETTY CASH FUND

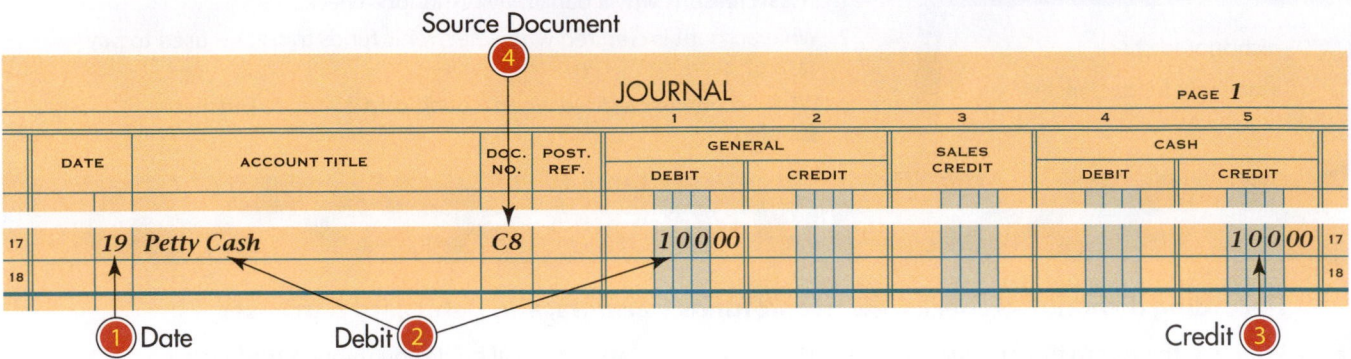

Source Document ④

JOURNAL — PAGE 1

① Date — ② Debit — ③ Credit

	DATE	ACCOUNT TITLE	DOC. NO.	POST. REF.	GENERAL DEBIT	GENERAL CREDIT	SALES CREDIT	CASH DEBIT	CASH CREDIT	
17	19	Petty Cash	C8		100 00				100 00	17
18										18

An amount of cash kept on hand and used for making small payments is called **petty cash.** A business usually has some small payments for which writing a check is not time or cost effective. Therefore, a business may maintain a separate cash fund for making small cash payments. The actual dollar amount considered to be a small payment differs from one business to another. Ms. Park has set $20.00 as the maximum amount to be paid at any one time from the petty cash fund.

The petty cash account is an asset with a normal debit balance. The balance of the petty cash account increases on the debit side and decreases on the credit side.

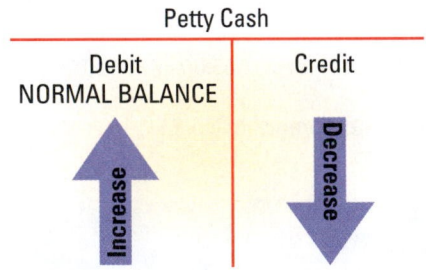

Petty Cash

Debit NORMAL BALANCE	Credit
Increase	Decrease

On August 19, Ms. Park decided that TechKnow Consulting needed a petty cash fund of $100.00. This amount should provide for small cash payments during a month.

August 19. Paid cash to establish a petty cash fund, $100.00. Check No. 8.

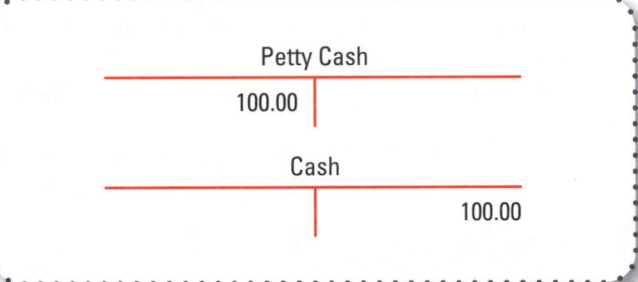

Petty Cash
100.00 |

Cash
| 100.00

The source document for this transaction is Check No. 8. [CONCEPT: Objective Evidence] The analysis is shown in the T accounts. Petty Cash is debited for $100.00 to show the increase in this asset account balance. Cash is credited for $100.00 to show the decrease in this asset account balance.

Ms. Park cashed the check and placed the $100.00 in a locked petty cash box at her place of business. Only she is authorized to make payments from the petty cash fund.

STEPS — ESTABLISHING A PETTY CASH FUND

① **Date.** Write the date, *19*, in the Date column.

② **Debit.** Write the title of the account to be debited, *Petty Cash*, in the Account Title column. Record the amount debited, *$100.00*, in the General Debit column.

③ **Credit.** Record the amount credited, *$100.00*, in the Cash Credit column.

④ **Source document.** Write the source document number, *C8*, in the Doc. No. column.

PETTY CASH SLIP	No. 1
Date: *August 19, 20--*	
Paid to: *Tribune*	
For: *Newspaper Ad*	$ *10.00*
Account: *Advertising Expense*	
Approved: *Kim Park*	

Each time a small payment is made from the petty cash fund, Ms. Park prepares a form showing the purpose and amount of the payment. A form showing proof of a petty cash payment is called a **petty cash slip**.

A petty cash slip shows the following information: (1) petty cash slip number; (2) date of petty cash payment; (3) to whom paid; (4) reason for the payment; (5) amount paid; (6) account in which amount is to be recorded; and (7) signature of person approving the petty cash payment.

The petty cash slips are kept in the petty cash box until the fund is replenished. No entries are made in the journal for the individual petty cash payments.

FINANCIAL LITERACY

Managing a Checking Account

The privilege of having a checking account brings with it the responsibility of managing that account. The cost of inefficient management can be high—especially if you write a "bad" check. A "bad" check, or insufficient-funds check, means that you don't have enough money in your account to cover the amount of the check written. If this happens, you may have to pay two fines, one to your bank and one to the company to whom you gave the bad check. These two fines could easily total over $100.

Managing a checking account is not difficult, but it involves recording all written checks, electronic funds transfers, and automatic payments; making regular deposits; recording all deposits, including electronic funds received; and reconciling your account each month.

Properly managing your checking account also means physically safeguarding your blank checks, your check registers, and monies waiting to be deposited. In addition, it requires safeguarding any account numbers and passwords used to log in to Internet banking sites.

Finally, efficiently managing a checking account means monitoring the costs and benefits of your account. Features of some accounts include interest on the balance, free electronic bill pay, Internet access to account information, electronic transfers between accounts, and free blank checks. Costs include monthly service fees, per-check charges, per-item charge on deposits, and overdraft charges.

Activities

1. Investigate the costs and features of checking accounts from three different banks. Present your findings to five people and ask each person which account would be best for his or her needs. Summarize your findings in a written report.

2. Visit a local bank and inquire about opening a checking account. Write a report outlining the steps involved.

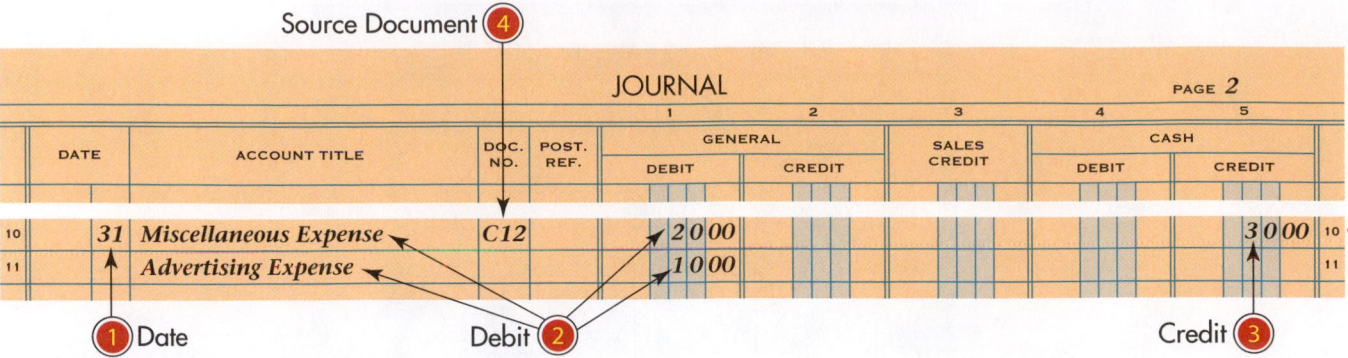

Source Document ④

JOURNAL PAGE 2

	DATE	ACCOUNT TITLE	DOC. NO.	POST. REF.	GENERAL DEBIT	GENERAL CREDIT	SALES CREDIT	CASH DEBIT	CASH CREDIT	
10	31	Miscellaneous Expense	C12		20 00				30 00	10
11		Advertising Expense			10 00					11

① Date   Debit ②   Credit ③

As petty cash is paid out, the amount in the petty cash box decreases. Eventually, the petty cash fund must be replenished and the petty cash payments recorded. TechKnow Consulting replenishes its petty cash fund whenever the amount on hand is reduced to $25.00. Also, the petty cash fund is always replenished at the end of each month so that all of the expenses are recorded in the month they are incurred.

Before petty cash is replenished, a proof of the fund must be completed.

Petty cash remaining in the petty cash fund $ 70.00
Plus total of petty cash slips . . . . + 30.00
Equals petty cash fund $100.00

The last line of the proof must show the same total as the original balance of the petty cash fund, $100.00. If petty cash does not prove, the errors must be found and corrected before any more work is done.

The proof shows that a total of $30.00 has been paid out of petty cash. An inspection of the petty cash slips shows that $20.00 has been paid for miscellaneous expenses and $10.00 has been paid for advertising. Therefore, an additional $30.00 must be placed in the fund. TechKnow Consulting will write a check to replenish the fund.

August 31. Paid cash to replenish the petty cash fund, $30.00: miscellaneous expense, $20.00; advertising, $10.00. Check No. 12.

Unless the petty cash fund is permanently increased or decreased, the balance of the account is always the original amount of the fund. The check issued to replenish petty cash is a credit to Cash and does not affect Petty Cash. When the check is cashed, the money is placed in the petty cash box. The amount in the petty cash box changes, as shown below.

Amount in petty cash box before fund
   is replenished . . . . $ 70.00
Amount from check issued to replenish
   petty cash . . . . + 30.00
Amount in petty cash box after fund
   is replenished $100.00

The total amount in the petty cash box, $100.00, is again the same as the balance of the petty cash account.

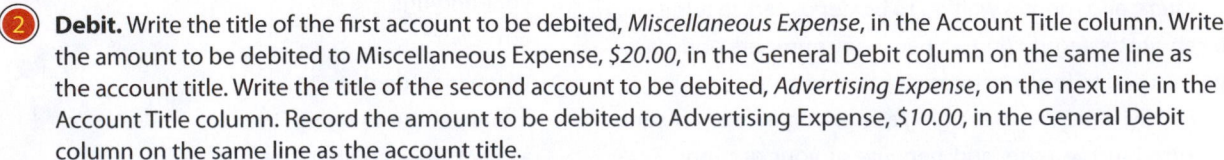

STEPS   JOURNALIZING THE ENTRY TO REPLENISH PETTY CASH

① **Date.** Write the date, *31*, in the Date column.

② **Debit.** Write the title of the first account to be debited, *Miscellaneous Expense*, in the Account Title column. Write the amount to be debited to Miscellaneous Expense, *$20.00*, in the General Debit column on the same line as the account title. Write the title of the second account to be debited, *Advertising Expense*, on the next line in the Account Title column. Record the amount to be debited to Advertising Expense, *$10.00*, in the General Debit column on the same line as the account title.

③ **Credit.** Record the amount to be credited, *$30.00*, in the Cash Credit column on the first line of this entry.

④ **Source document.** Write the source document number, *C12*, in the Doc. No. column on the first line of the entry.

Business, Management & Administration

Tim DuFrene, Sole Proprietor

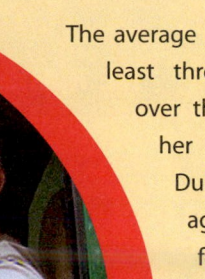

COURTESY OF TIM DUFRENE

The average person will make at least three career changes over the course of his or her working life. Tim DuFrene fits that average precisely. He has found that accounting is a transferable skill that has served him well throughout his multiple careers.

When Tim took accounting courses in high school and college, he saw himself preparing for a career in banking. His first full-time job was, in fact, in a bank. Working first as a teller, he used his accounting skills to balance cash and reconcile accounts. Advancing to the position of loan officer, Tim relied on his accounting knowledge to review business plans of loan applicants.

After a few years in banking, Tim was drawn into his second professional field—industrial construction. After several years of learning and applying a craft, Tim began working his way into management. Once again, accounting was an important aspect of his work responsibilities. As a project superintendent, he oversaw the construction of various industrial projects throughout the United States. Important accounting aspects of that job included bidding for projects, assessing estimated costs, and setting project budgets.

After 25 years in his second career of industrial construction, Tim became tired of the extensive travel associated with his job and decided to pursue a lifelong dream of owning his own business—career #3. In 2001, he launched Han-D-Man, a home maintenance and repair business that he runs from his home office. As a sole proprietor, he found his accounting skills to be especially important in setting up his business and tracking billing and income, managing expenses, and satisfying tax requirements. Tim says, "Owning my own business has allowed me to interact with many people and improve their quality of life through providing them with more pleasant, functional surroundings. I enjoy having more freedom now to pursue my hobbies, travel, and spend more time with my wife and children. My knowledge of accounting enabled me to change careers and be successful."

Salary Range: Self-employed individuals in a service industry set their desired hourly rate based on their expertise and geographic area. The time required to bid jobs, collect fees, and travel between jobs means that a service provider does not bill all of his or her work time. Thus, a service provider may bill about 1,600 hours during a year. Hourly billing rates between $25.00 and $50.00 per hour and a 1,600-hour work year yield an annual salary of $40,000 to $80,000, less expenses.

Qualifications: Self-employed individuals need three types of skills: (1) communication skills to interact with clients, (2) organizational skills to schedule jobs and manage the business, and (3) a specific skill to sell in the marketplace.

Occupational Outlook: In a career such as Tim's, the sustained growth of the housing market will cause individual homeowners to need more home repairs.

End of Lesson
REVIEW

AUDIT YOUR UNDERSTANDING

1. Why do businesses use petty cash funds?
2. Why is Cash and not Petty Cash credited when a petty cash fund is replenished?

TERMS REVIEW

petty cash

petty cash slip

WORK TOGETHER 5-4

Establishing and replenishing a petty cash fund

Write the answers to this problem in the *Working Papers*. Your instructor will guide you through the following example.

1. Journalize the following transactions completed during July of the current year. Use page 13 of a journal. The abbreviation for check is C.

Transactions:

July 3. Paid cash to establish a petty cash fund, $250.00. C57.
      31. Paid cash to replenish the petty cash fund, $78.00: supplies, $25.00; miscellaneous expense, $8.00; repairs, $45.00. C97.

ON YOUR OWN 5-4

Establishing and replenishing a petty cash fund

Write the answers to this problem in the *Working Papers*. Work this problem independently.

1. Journalize the following transactions completed during August of the current year. Use page 15 of a journal. The abbreviation for check is C.

Transactions:

Aug. 1. Paid cash to establish a petty cash fund, $200.00. C114.
      31. Paid cash to replenish the petty cash fund, $145.00: supplies, $72.00; advertising, $40.00; miscellaneous expense, $33.00. C157.

After completing this chapter, you can:

1. Define accounting terms related to using a checking account and a petty cash fund.

2. Identify accounting concepts and practices related to using a checking account.

3. Prepare business papers related to using a checking account.

4. Reconcile a bank statement.

5. Journalize dishonored checks and electronic banking transactions.

6. Establish and replenish a petty cash fund.

EXPLORE ACCOUNTING

Cash Controls

Cash transactions occur more frequently than other types of transactions. Because cash is easily transferred from one person to another, a business must try to safeguard its cash to protect it and other assets from errors.

An unintentional error occurs when someone mistakenly records an incorrect amount or forgets to record a transaction. An intentional error occurs when someone intentionally records an incorrect amount or does not record a transaction in order to cover up fraud or theft. Good cash control procedures should guard against both types of errors.

One common method of controlling cash is to insist that all cash payments over a certain amount be paid by check. In addition, checks should be prenumbered so that it is easy to account for each check. The document number column of a journal can be used to ensure that all checks issued are recorded in the journal. Other cash controls are to have one person responsible for authorizing all checks, and requiring a source document in support of each cash payment.

One of the best ways to safeguard assets is to separate duties so that one employee does not have total control of an entire set of processes. For example, one employee could receive and record the receipt of cash on account; a second employee could make and record deposits; and a third employee could reconcile the bank statement. By separating the duties, it is less likely that errors will be made.

A company that does not have enough employees to institute the separation of duties concept may hire a certified public accountant (CPA) to perform some of these duties on a regular basis.

Research Assignment: Talk to a businessperson to determine what kinds of controls are in place in his or her business to safeguard cash. Schools, hospitals, charitable organizations, and government offices as well as retail, wholesale, and service businesses should have established controls that are being followed. Summarize and present your findings to your class.

5-1 APPLICATION PROBLEM

Endorsing and writing checks

You are authorized to sign checks for Accounting Tutors. Forms are given in the *Working Papers*.

Instructions:

1. For each of the following situations, prepare the appropriate endorsement.
   a. Write a blank endorsement.
   b. Write a special endorsement to transfer a check to Vu Kim.
   c. Write a restrictive endorsement to deposit a check in the account of Accounting Tutors.
2. Record the balance brought forward on Check Stub No. 390, $6,711.62.
3. Record a deposit of $1,244.25 made on September 30 of the current year on Check Stub No. 390.
4. Prepare check stubs and write the following checks. Use September 30 of the current year as the date.
   a. Check No. 390 to Williamson Street Supplies for supplies, $945.00.
   b. Check No. 391 to Spring Park Tribune for advertising, $112.00.
   c. Check No. 392 to Bryce Wilton for rent, $250.00.

5-2 APPLICATION PROBLEM

Reconciling a bank statement and recording a bank service charge

Forms are given in the *Working Papers*. On May 31 of the current year, Parties Plus received a bank statement dated May 30. The following information is obtained from the bank statement and from the records of the business.

Bank statement balance	$1,927.00
Bank service charge	20.00
Outstanding deposit, May 30	756.25
Outstanding checks:	
No. 310	421.76
No. 311	150.50
Checkbook balance on Check Stub No. 312	2,130.99

Instructions:

1. Prepare a bank statement reconciliation. Use May 31 of the current year as the date.
2. Record the service charge on check stub No. 312.
3. Record the service charge on journal page 10. Use Memorandum No. 58 as the source document.

Go Beyond the Book
For more information go to
www.C21accounting.com

5-3 APPLICATION PROBLEM

Recording dishonored checks, electronic funds transfers, and debit card purchases

Enter the following transactions on page 8 of the journal given in the *Working Papers*.

Transactions:

Jan. 25. Received notice from the bank of a dishonored check from Ralston Eubanks, $125.00, plus $30.00 fee; total, $155.00. Memorandum No. 333.

26. Paid cash on account to Reed Rosman, $289.00, using EFT. Memorandum No. 334.

27. Purchased supplies, $54.00, using a debit card. Memorandum No. 335.

5-4 APPLICATION PROBLEM

Establishing and replenishing a petty cash fund

Journalize the following transactions completed during November of the current year. Use page 22 of the journal given in the *Working Papers*. The abbreviation for check is C.

Transactions:

Nov. 5. Paid cash to establish a petty cash fund, $300.00. C527.

30. Paid cash to replenish the petty cash fund, $165.00: supplies, $57.00; miscellaneous expense, $58.00; repairs, $40.00; postage (Postage Expense), $10.00. C555.

5-5 MASTERY PROBLEM   AUTOMATED ACCOUNTING   Peachtree by Sage   QB Quick Books

Reconciling a bank statement; journalizing a bank service charge, a dishonored check, and petty cash transactions

James Astrup owns a business called LawnMow. Selected general ledger accounts are given below.

110 Cash	140 Prepaid Insurance	535 Repair Expense
115 Petty Cash	320 James Astrup, Drawing	540 Supplies Expense
120 Accts. Rec.—Bruce Kassola	520 Miscellaneous Expense	550 Utilities Expense
130 Supplies	530 Rent Expense	

Instructions:

1. Journalize the following transactions completed during August of the current year. Use page 20 of the journal given in the *Working Papers*. Source documents are abbreviated as follows: check, C; memorandum, M; calculator tape, T.

Transactions:

Aug. 21. Paid cash to establish a petty cash fund, $300.00. C110.

24. Paid cash for repairs, $165.00. C111.

26. Paid cash for supplies, $60.00. C112.

27. Received notice from the bank of a dishonored check from Bruce Kassola, $140.00, plus $35.00 fee; total, $175.00. M33.

28. Paid cash for miscellaneous expense, $31.00. C113.

31. Paid cash to owner for personal use, $400.00. C114.

31. Paid cash to replenish the petty cash fund, $255.00: supplies, $125.00; miscellaneous expense, $130.00. C115.

31. Received cash from sales, $350.00. T31.

2. On August 31 of the current year, LawnMow received a bank statement dated August 30. Prepare a bank statement reconciliation. Use August 31 of the current year as the date. The following information is obtained from the August 30 bank statement and from the records of the business.

Bank statement balance	$2,721.00
Bank service charge	15.00
Outstanding deposit, August 31	350.00
Outstanding checks, Nos. 114 and 115	
Checkbook balance on Check Stub No. 116	2,431.00

3. Continue using the journal and journalize the following transaction:

Transaction:
Aug. 31. Received bank statement showing August bank service charge, $15.00. M34.

5-6   CHALLENGE PROBLEM 

Reconciling a bank statement and recording a bank service charge

Use the bank statement, canceled checks, and check stubs for GolfPro given in the *Working Papers*.

Instructions:

1. Compare the canceled checks with the check stubs. For each canceled check, place a check mark next to the appropriate check stub number. For each deposit shown on the bank statement, place a check mark next to the deposit amount on the appropriate check stub.

2. Prepare a bank statement reconciliation. Use August 29 of the current year as the date.

3. Record the following transactions on page 8 of a journal. The abbreviation for memorandum is M.

Transactions:
Sept. 1. Received bank statement showing August bank service charge, $5.00. M25.
    1. Received notice from the bank of a dishonored check from Sheldon Martindale, $170.00, plus $5.00 fee; total, $175.00. M26.
    4. Record the bank service charge and dishonored check on Check Stub No. 165.

APPLIED COMMUNICATION

All businesses are affected to some degree by issues and events that occur in the areas in which the businesses are located. For example, a city may gain an industry that will employ many people for a long time. Or, a town might build new roads or schools.

Instructions: Collect three to five newspaper or magazine articles about issues in your area that you think will affect local businesses. For each article, prepare a written list of consequences that a business might encounter.

CASES FOR CRITICAL THINKING

Case 1

Iris Velez and Suzanne Merker have personal checking accounts for which they receive a bank statement every month. Ms. Merker does not prepare a reconciliation; instead she records the balance on the bank statement as her new checkbook balance. Ms. Velez prepares a bank statement reconciliation for each bank statement received. Is Ms. Velez or Ms. Merker following the better procedure? Explain.

Case 2

Dorset Company decides to establish a petty cash fund. The owner, Edna Dorset, wants to establish a $100.00 petty cash fund and limit payments to $20.00 or less. The manager, Roy Evans, suggests a petty cash fund of $3,000.00 limited to payments of $50.00 or less. Mr. Evans claims this limit will help him avoid writing so many checks. Do you agree with Ms. Dorset or Mr. Evans? Explain.

SCANS WORKPLACE COMPETENCY

Personal Qualities: Responsibility

Concept: Employers seek individuals who exert a high level of effort and persevere toward goal attainment.

Application: Make a list of your responsibilities in this accounting course; then assess whether you meet these responsibilities with a low, medium, or high level of effort. Make a plan for how you can improve your performance on those responsibilities that you are not already fulfilling at a high level of effort.

A bar chart of the assets, liabilities, and owner's equity of Moua Company is shown here. Analyze the chart to answer the following questions.

1. What was the amount of total assets in May?
2. In what month were liabilities the lowest?

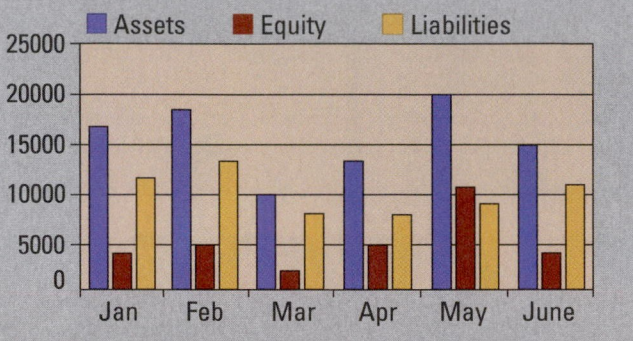

ANALYZING BEST BUY'S FINANCIAL STATEMENTS

On a financial statement, the term "Cash and cash equivalents" includes more than just cash on hand. Checking accounts, savings accounts, and even some very short-term investments are also included in this total. Best Buy's financial statement on Appendix B page B-5 shows the total "Cash and cash equivalents" for Best Buy for each year.

Published financial statements include notes that explain some of the titles and amounts used in the statements. Note 1 for Best Buy's financial statements begins on page B-9. Read the second page of Note 1.

Instructions: List the amount of Best Buy's cash and cash equivalents for 2006 and 2007. Look at Note 1 and list what Best Buy considers to be "cash and cash equivalents."

Accounting SOFTWARE

BANK STATEMENT RECONCILIATION; JOURNALIZING TRANSACTIONS

Preparing a bank reconciliation is an easy task with accounting software. Peachtree presents a list of all the checks and deposits so that a simple click identifies whether each transaction has cleared. Peachtree performs all calculations and clearly indicates any difference between the book and bank balances. Knowing that bank service charges must be journalized, Peachtree automatically generates the journal entry when the bank reconciliation is processed. You are only required to enter is the amount of the bank charge and the number of the general ledger account to be debited.

PEACHTREE MASTERY PROBLEM 5-5

1. Open (Restore) file 05-5MP.ptb.
2. Journalize and post the August cash transactions, including the journal entry for a dishonored check. Remember to save after each transaction.
3. From the menu bar, select Tasks, then Account Reconciliation to reconcile the bank statement; print a report.

PEACHTREE CHALLENGE PROBLEM 5-6

1. Open (Restore) file 05-6CP.ptb.
2. To complete account reconciliation, use the bank statement, canceled checks, check stubs, and transactions for Golf Pro. Journalize cash transactions and a dishonored check transaction.
3. Reconcile the bank statement and print a report.

BANK STATEMENT RECONCILIATION; JOURNALIZING TRANSACTIONS

QuickBooks can be used to prepare the monthly bank reconciliation. The bank statement can be reconciled to the checkbook balance in the following steps:

1. Choose Reconcile from the Banking menu. When the Begin Reconciliation dialog box appears, make sure Cash shows in the Account field, and enter the correct ending date.
2. Key in the required data in the Begin Reconciliation dialog box. Click Continue.
3. The Reconcile – Cash dialog box will display. Click in the blank field next to the Date field for all checks and deposits that have already cleared through the bank and appear on the bank statement. Verify that the amount next to Difference is 0.00. Make any necessary corrections. Click Reconcile Now.
4. The Select Reconciliation Report dialog box will appear.
   Choose which reports you want displayed. Click Display. The reports will display.

QUICKBOOKS MASTERY PROBLEM 5-5

1. Open the LawnMow file.
2. Journalize the transactions completed during August.
3. Choose Reconcile from the Banking menu to reconcile the bank statement.
4. From the Reconcile – Cash dialog box, click the Reconcile Now button to view the Reconciliation Summary report. Print this report.

QUICKBOOKS CHALLENGE PROBLEM 5-6

1. Open the GolfPro file.
2. Prepare a bank reconciliation for GolfPro.
3. Print the Reconciliation Summary and Reconciliation Detail reports.
4. Journalize the transaction for the dishonored check.
5. Print a Journal report for GolfPro for August 28 through September 30.

BANK STATEMENT RECONCILIATION

A bank reconciliation is a relatively easy procedure, yet it is a powerful tool to identify errors in the accounting records. A bank reconciliation provides proof that cash disbursements and receipts have been recorded the same way in the accounting records of both the business and the bank.

The spreadsheet template for Chapter 5 presents a replica of the bank reconciliation shown in this chapter. You will enter the description and amount of any bank charges identified on the bank statement. These are the items that will require a journal entry to record in the accounting records. On the opposite side of the template, you will enter the date and amount of all outstanding deposits, and the check number and amount of all outstanding checks.

By creating formulas to calculate the adjusted balances, you will be able to use the template for other reconciliations. Because the number of outstanding deposits and checks may differ from month to month, it may be necessary to add additional rows to the template. Thus, you should use the SUM function to calculate the total of bank charges, outstanding deposits, and outstanding checks.

EXCEL APPLICATION PROBLEM 5-2

1. Open the F05-2 Excel data file.
2. Follow the step-by-step instructions in the Instructions work sheet to reconcile a bank statement using an Excel spreadsheet.

BANK STATEMENT RECONCILIATION; JOURNALIZING TRANSACTIONS

The automated accounting system may be used to prepare the monthly bank reconciliation. Information maintained by the software, such as the checkbook balance and checks that were written during the period, will be automatically provided to make the reconciliation process simpler and more accurate.

While the *Automated Accounting* Help system contains detailed instructions, the bank statement can be reconciled to the checkbook balance in the following steps:

1. Choose the Other Activities menu item from the Data menu, or click on the Other toolbar button.
2. When the Reconciliation window appears, click on the Clear button to erase any previous data.
3. Enter the bank credits, bank charges, bank statement balance, and outstanding deposit amounts.
4. Checks written during the period are displayed in the Checks from the Journals list box. Select the outstanding checks by pointing and double-clicking. Each selected check will appear in the Outstanding Checks list, and the Adjusted Bank Balance will automatically be updated.
5. Click the Report command button in the Reconciliation window to see the completed reconciliation.
6. Click the Close command button to dismiss the report window.
7. When the Bank Reconciliation reappears, click the OK command button to record your data and end the Bank Reconciliation process.

AUTOMATED ACCOUNTING APPLICATION PROBLEM 5-2
Open file F05-2.AA8. Display the problem instructions and complete the problem.

AUTOMATED ACCOUNTING MASTERY PROBLEM 5-5
Open file F05-5.AA8. Display the problem instructions and complete the problem.

An Accounting Cycle for a Proprietorship: Journalizing and Posting Transactions

Reinforcement activities strengthen the learning of accounting concepts and procedures. Reinforcement Activity 1 is a single problem divided into two parts. Part A includes learning from Chapters 1 through 5. Part B includes learning from Chapters 6 through 8. An accounting cycle is completed in Parts A and B for a single business—Extreme Adventures.

EXTREME ADVENTURES

In May of the current year, Brian Dawson starts a service business called Extreme Adventures. The business provides adventure trips throughout the world, such as trekking in the Himalayas and helo skiing in Colorado. The business rents the facilities in which it operates, pays the utilities, and is responsible for maintenance. Extreme Adventures charges clients for each trip. Most of Extreme Adventures' sales are for cash. However, two private schools use Extreme Adventures for some physical education classes. These schools have an account with Extreme Adventures.

CHART OF ACCOUNTS

Extreme Adventures uses the following chart of accounts.

CHART OF ACCOUNTS

BALANCE SHEET ACCOUNTS

(100) ASSETS
110 Cash
120 Petty Cash
130 Accts. Rec.—Matterhorn University
140 Accts. Rec.—Midwest College
150 Supplies
160 Prepaid Insurance

(200) LIABILITIES
210 Accts. Pay.—Dunn Supplies
220 Accts. Pay.—Greenway Supplies

(300) OWNER'S EQUITY
310 Brian Dawson, Capital
320 Brian Dawson, Drawing
330 Income Summary

INCOME STATEMENT ACCOUNTS

(400) REVENUE
410 Sales

(500) EXPENSES
510 Advertising Expense
520 Insurance Expense
530 Miscellaneous Expense
540 Rent Expense
550 Repair Expense
560 Supplies Expense
570 Utilities Expense

RECORDING TRANSACTIONS

Instructions:

1. Journalize the following transactions completed during May of the current year. Use page 1 of the journal given in the *Working Papers*. Source documents are abbreviated as follows: check stub, C; memorandum, M; receipt, R; sales invoice, S; calculator tape, T.

May 1. Received cash from owner as an investment, $15,000.00. R1.
   1. Paid cash for rent, $1,800.00. C1.
   2. Paid cash for electric bill, $105.00. C2.
   4. Paid cash for supplies, $450.00. C3.
   4. Paid cash for insurance, $1,200.00. C4.
   7. Bought supplies on account from Dunn Supplies, $900.00. M1.
   11. Paid cash to establish a petty cash fund, $250.00. C5.
   12. Received cash from sales, $475.00. T12.
   13. Paid cash for repairs, $250.00. C6.
   13. Paid cash for miscellaneous expense, $40.00. C7.
   13. Received cash from sales, $235.00. T13.
   13. Sold services on account to Midwest College, $225.00. S1.
   14. Paid cash for advertising, $300.00. C8.
   15. Paid cash to owner for personal use, $200.00. C9.
   15. Paid cash on account to Dunn Supplies, $500.00. C10.
   15. Received cash from sales, $305.00. T15.
   15. Sold services on account to Matterhorn University, $425.00. S2.
   18. Paid cash for miscellaneous expense, $95.00. C11.
   18. Received cash on account from Midwest College, $125.00. R2.
   19. Received cash from sales, $480.00. T19.
   20. Paid cash for repairs, $160.00. C12.
   20. Bought supplies on account from Greenway Supplies, $120.00. M2.

2. Prove and rule page 1 of the journal. Carry the column totals forward to page 2 of the journal.

3. Post the separate amounts on each line of page 1 of the journal that need to be posted individually.

4. Use page 2 of the journal. Journalize the following transactions.

May 21. Paid cash for water bill, $265.00. C13.
   21. Received cash from sales, $620.00. T21.
   25. Paid cash for supplies, $25.00. C14.
   25. Received cash from sales, $605.00. T25.
   26. Paid cash for miscellaneous expense, $37.00. C15.
   26. Received cash on account from Matterhorn University, $250.00. R3.
   27. Received cash from sales, $715.00. T27.
   28. Paid cash for telephone bill, $245.00. C16.
   28. Received cash from sales, $650.00. T28.

5. Extreme Adventures received a bank statement dated May 27. The following information is obtained from the bank statement and from the records of the business. Prepare a bank statement reconciliation. Use May 29 as the date.

Bank statement balance	$13,180.00
Bank service charge	15.00
Outstanding deposit, May 28	650.00
Outstanding checks:	
No. 14	25.00
No. 15	37.00
No. 16	245.00
Checkbook balance on Check Stub No. 17	$13,538.00

6. Continue using page 2 of the journal, and journalize the following transactions.

May 29. Received bank statement showing May bank service charge, $15.00. M3.
    29. Paid cash for supplies, $30.00. C17.
    29. Received cash from sales, $695.00. T29.
    31. Paid cash to replenish the petty cash fund, $165.00: miscellaneous expense, $120.00; repairs, $45.00. C18.
    31. Paid cash to owner for personal use, $1,000.00. C19.
    31. Received cash from sales, $660.00. T31.

7. Prove page 2 of the journal.
8. Prove cash. The beginning cash balance on May 1 is zero. The balance on the next unused check stub is $13,683.00.
9. Rule page 2 of the journal.
10. Post the separate amounts on each line of page 2 of the journal that need to be posted individually.
11. Post the column totals on page 2 of the journal.

The general ledger prepared in Reinforcement Activity 1—Part A is needed to complete Reinforcement Activity 1—Part B.

PURESTOCK/GETTY IMAGES

DIGITAL VISION/GETTY IMAGES

CHAPTER 6

Work Sheet for a Service Business

Point Your Browser
www.C21accounting.com

150

The AICPA

Professionalism and the AICPA

The American Institute of Certified Public Accountants (AICPA) is America's leading professional CPA organization, with more than 340,000 members who work for public accounting firms, multinational corporations, small businesses, not-for-profit organizations, governmental agencies, and educational institutions.

Certified Public Accountants—CPAs—who work for public accounting firms provide many services to their clients, such as auditing financial statements, forensic accounting (sometimes called fraud auditing), consulting services, information technology services, evaluating operating performance, international accounting, and tax and financial planning services.

CPAs who are employed by corporations and businesses often work in finance and accounting departments as financial analysts and have the opportunity to rise up the ranks to positions such as controller and Chief Financial Officer (CFO), and even Chief Executive Officer (CEO). Others work in the areas of international finance, treasury, or internal auditing.

To find out more about CPA career opportunities, salary information, and the accounting profession, visit www.StartHereGoPlaces.com or www.aicpa .org, or e-mail the AICPA at educat@aicpa.org. In addition, each state has a CPA society or association that can provide you with more information. You can contact a state CPA society or association through the "CPA links" section of the AICPA web site.

Critical Thinking

1. If you were going to hire an accountant, why might you choose to hire a CPA?

2. If you were a CPA, why might you choose to join a professional association like the AICPA?

Source: www.aicpa.org

INTERNET ACTIVITY

AICPA Career Resources

Go to the homepage for the American Institute of Certified Public Accountants (AICPA) (www.aicpa.org). Search the site for information about career resources for students.

Instructions

1. List two resources provided by the AICPA designed to help students with career choices in the field of accounting.

2. Pick one of these two resources and examine it in more detail. List two interesting pieces of information you learned from this resource.

CONSISTENT REPORTING

General ledger accounts contain information needed by managers and owners. Before the information can be used, however, it must be analyzed, summarized, and reported in a meaningful way. The accounting concept *Consistent Reporting* is applied when the same accounting procedures are followed in the same way in each accounting period. [CONCEPT: Consistent Reporting] For example, in one year a delivery business might report the number of deliveries made. The next year, the same business reports the amount of revenue received for the deliveries made. The information for the two years cannot be compared because the business has not been consistent in reporting information about deliveries.

> A summary of preparing a work sheet is shown on the Work Sheet Overlay within this chapter.

FISCAL PERIODS

The length of time for which a business summarizes and reports financial information is called a **fiscal period** (also known as an accounting period). Businesses usually select a period of time for which to summarize and report financial information. The accounting concept *Accounting Period Cycle* is applied when changes in financial information are reported for a specific period of time in the form of financial statements. [CONCEPT: Accounting Period Cycle] Each business chooses a fiscal period length that meets its needs. Because federal and state tax reports are based on one year, most businesses use a one-year fiscal period. However, because TechKnow Consulting is a new business, Ms. Park wishes to have financial information reported frequently to help her make decisions. For this reason, TechKnow Consulting uses a one-month fiscal period.

A fiscal period can begin on any date. However, most businesses begin their fiscal periods on the first day of a month. TechKnow Consulting started business on August 1. Therefore, TechKnow Consulting's monthly fiscal period is for the period from August 1 through August 31, inclusive. Businesses often choose a one-year fiscal period that ends during a period of low business activity.

In this way, the end-of-year accounting work comes at a time when other business activities are the lightest.

Financial information may be analyzed, summarized, and reported on any date a business needs the information. However, financial information is always summarized and reported at the end of a fiscal period.

PHOTODISC/GETTY IMAGES

Work Sheet for a Service Business

A columnar accounting form used to summarize the general ledger information needed to prepare financial statements is called a **work sheet.**

Accountants use a work sheet for four reasons: (1) to summarize general ledger account balances to prove that debits equal credits; (2) to plan needed changes to general ledger accounts to bring account balances up to date; (3) to separate general ledger account balances according

to the financial statements to be prepared; and (4) to calculate the amount of net income or net loss for a fiscal period.

Journals and ledgers are permanent records of a business and are usually prepared in ink or printed by a computer. However, a work sheet is a planning tool and is not considered a permanent accounting record. Therefore, a work sheet is prepared in pencil.

• • • • • • • • • • • • • **PREPARING THE HEADING OF A WORK SHEET** • • • • • • • • • • • • •

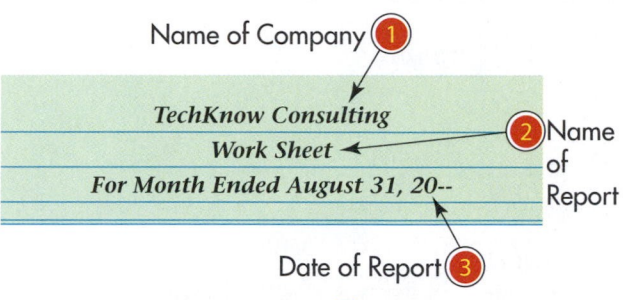

Name of Company ①

TechKnow Consulting
Work Sheet ← ② Name of Report
For Month Ended August 31, 20--

Date of Report ③

The heading on a work sheet consists of three lines and contains the name of the business, the name of the report, and the date of the report.

The date on TechKnow Consulting's work sheet indicates that the work sheet covers the 31 days from August 1 through and including August 31. If a work sheet were for a calendar year fiscal period, it might have a date stated as *For Year Ended December 31, 20--.*

CHARACTER COUNTS

Professional Codes of Conduct

Most professional organizations have a code of professional conduct to guide the actions of their members. One of the best-known codes of professional conduct is that of the American Institute of Certified Public Accountants (AICPA). A national organization of over 340,000 certified public accountants, the AICPA seeks to help its members provide professional services that benefit their employees, clients, and society. An important component of this mission is the AICPA Code of Professional Conduct.

The Code contains Rules of Conduct that its members must follow in their performance of professional services. The Rules address the topics of independence, integrity, objectivity, client relations, and colleague relations. Some Rules have Interpretations that provide further insight into the Rules. The Code is also supported by Ethics Rulings, a series of questions and answers that the AICPA elects to share with its members.

AICPA members who fail to adhere to the Code can be disciplined or expelled from the membership. Losing membership in the AICPA can result in serious consequences for a certified public accountant working in the profession.

Instructions

Access the AICPA's Code of Professional Conduct at www. aicpa.org. Citing the exact source of each answer, determine whether a member of the AICPA may:

1. Accept a gift from a client. (*Hint:* Search Independence Ethics Rulings)

2. Charge a client a fee based on the net income reported on the audited income statement. (*Hint:* Search Contingent Fees)

3. Advertise professional services in television commercials. (*Hint:* Search Other Professional Responsibilities and Practices, Advertising Interpretations)

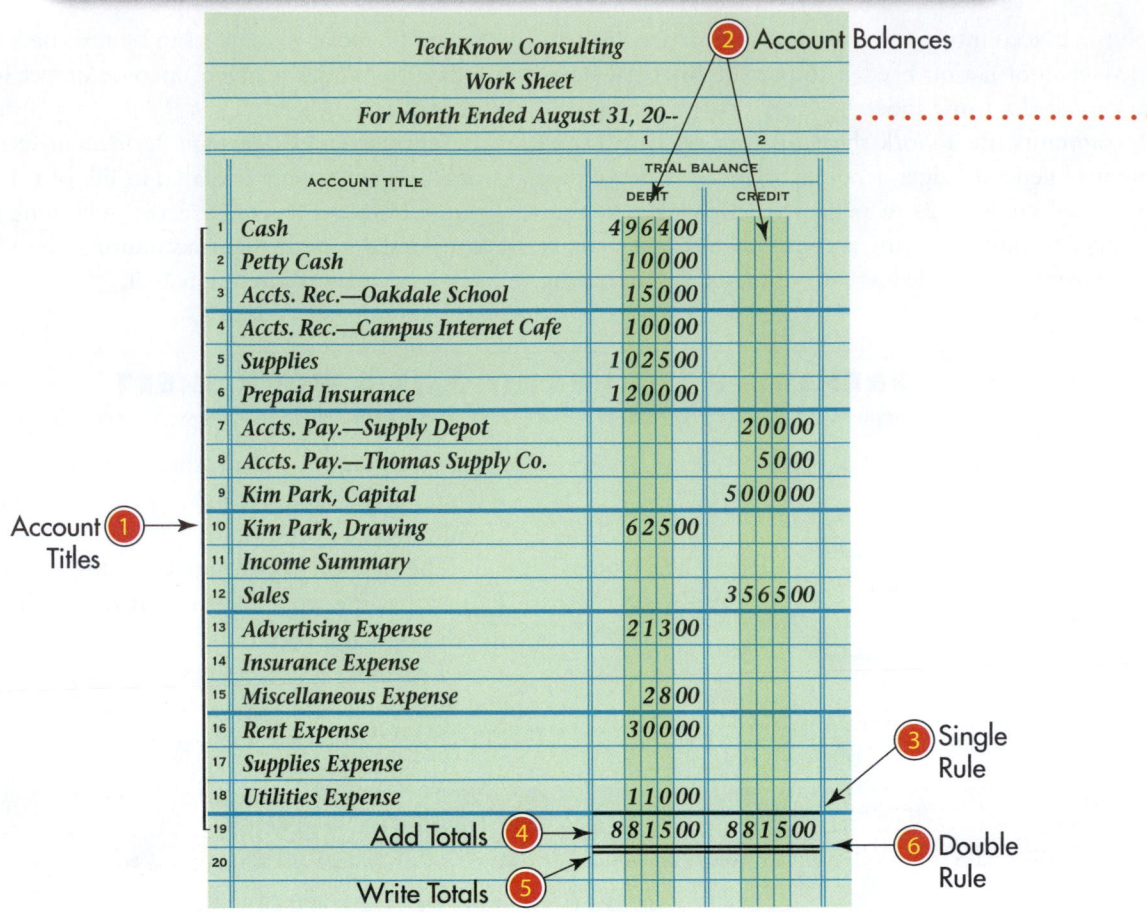

TechKnow Consulting
Work Sheet
For Month Ended August 31, 20--

②Account Balances

| | ACCOUNT TITLE | TRIAL BALANCE | |
		DEBIT	CREDIT
1	Cash	4 9 6 4 00	
2	Petty Cash	1 0 0 00	
3	Accts. Rec.—Oakdale School	1 5 0 00	
4	Accts. Rec.—Campus Internet Cafe	1 0 0 00	
5	Supplies	1 0 2 5 00	
6	Prepaid Insurance	1 2 0 0 00	
7	Accts. Pay.—Supply Depot		2 0 0 00
8	Accts. Pay.—Thomas Supply Co.		5 0 00
9	Kim Park, Capital		5 0 0 0 00
10	Kim Park, Drawing	6 2 5 00	
11	Income Summary		
12	Sales		3 5 6 5 00
13	Advertising Expense	2 1 3 00	
14	Insurance Expense		
15	Miscellaneous Expense	2 8 00	
16	Rent Expense	3 0 0 00	
17	Supplies Expense		
18	Utilities Expense	1 1 0 00	
19	Add Totals ④	8 8 1 5 00	8 8 1 5 00
20	Write Totals ⑤		

Account ① Titles

③Single Rule

⑥Double Rule

The total of all debit account balances must equal the total of all credit account balances. A proof of the equality of debits and credits in a general ledger is called a **trial balance.**

Information for the trial balance is taken from the general ledger. General ledger account titles are listed on a trial balance in the same order as they are listed on the chart of accounts. All the account titles are listed, even if some accounts do not have balances.

STEPS   PREPARING A TRIAL BALANCE ON A WORK SHEET

① Write the general ledger account titles in the work sheet's Account Title column.

② Write the general ledger debit account balances in the Trial Balance Debit column. Write the general ledger credit account balances in the Trial Balance Credit column. If an account does not have a balance, the space in the Trial Balance columns is left blank.

③ Rule a single line across the two Trial Balance columns below the last line on which an account title is written. This single line shows that each column is to be added.

④ Add both the Trial Balance Debit and Credit columns. If the two column totals are the same, then debits equal credits in the general ledger accounts. If the two column totals are not the same, recheck the Trial Balance columns to find the error. Other parts of a work sheet are not completed until the Trial Balance columns are proved. Suggestions for locating errors are described later in this chapter.

⑤ Write each column's total below the single line.

⑥ Rule double lines across both Trial Balance columns. The double lines mean that the Trial Balance column totals have been verified as correct.

End of Lesson
REVIEW

TERMS REVIEW

fiscal period

work sheet

trial balance

AUDIT YOUR UNDERSTANDING

1. What is written on the three-line heading on a work sheet?
2. What general ledger accounts are listed in the Trial Balance columns of a work sheet?

WORK TOGETHER 6-1

Recording the trial balance on a work sheet

Use the work sheet given in the *Working Papers*. Your instructor will guide you through the following example.

On February 28 of the current year, Golden Tan has the following general ledger accounts and balances. The business uses a monthly fiscal period.

Account Titles	Account Balances	
	Debit	**Credit**
Cash	$9,800.00	
Petty Cash	150.00	
Accounts Receivable—Ruby Prince	2,795.00	
Supplies	456.00	
Prepaid Insurance	750.00	
Accounts Payable—Richard Navarro		$ 555.00
Gary Baldwin, Capital		14,885.00
Gary Baldwin, Drawing	3,400.00	
Income Summary		
Sales		4,320.00
Advertising Expense	931.00	
Insurance Expense		
Miscellaneous Expense	378.00	
Supplies Expense		
Utilities Expense	1,100.00	

1. Prepare the heading and trial balance on a work sheet. Total and rule the Trial Balance columns. Save your work to complete Work Together 6-2.

Recording the trial balance on a work sheet

Use the work sheet given in the *Working Papers*. Work this problem independently.

On December 31 of the current year, Copa's Copies has the following general ledger accounts and balances. The business uses a monthly fiscal period.

Account Titles	Account Balances	
	Debit	Credit
Cash	$6,800.00	
Petty Cash	75.00	
Accounts Receivable—Burt Strog	1,498.00	
Supplies	238.00	
Prepaid Insurance	325.00	
Accounts Payable—Janet Dao		$ 298.00
Jabbo West, Capital		7,443.00
Jabbo West, Drawing	1,700.00	
Income Summary		
Sales		4,140.00
Advertising Expense	456.00	
Insurance Expense		
Miscellaneous Expense	189.00	
Supplies Expense		
Utilities Expense	600.00	

1. Prepare the heading and trial balance on a work sheet. Total and rule the Trial Balance columns. Save your work to complete On Your Own 6-2.

PLANNING ADJUSTMENTS ON A WORK SHEET

Sometimes a business will pay cash for an expense in one fiscal period, but the expense is not used until a later period. The expense should be reported in the same fiscal period that it is used to produce revenue. The accounting concept *Matching Expenses with Revenue* is applied when revenue from business activities and expenses associated with earning that revenue are recorded in the same accounting period. For example, TechKnow Consulting buys supplies in quantity in August, but some of the supplies are not used until September. Only the value of the supplies used in August should be reported as expenses in August. In this way, August revenue and the supplies expense associated with earning the August revenue are recorded in the same accounting period. [CONCEPT: Matching Expenses with Revenue]

In order to give accurate information on financial statements, some general ledger accounts must be brought up to date at the end of a fiscal period. For example, TechKnow Consulting debits an asset account, Supplies, each time supplies are bought. Supplies on hand are items of value owned by a business until the supplies are used. The value of supplies that are used becomes an expense to the business. However, recording an expense each time an individual supply, such as a pencil, is used would be impractical. Therefore, on August 31 the balance of the asset account, Supplies, is the value of all supplies bought rather than the value of only the supplies that have not yet been used. The amount of supplies that have been used must be deducted from the asset account, Supplies, and recorded in the expense account, Supplies Expense.

Likewise, the amount of insurance that has been used during the fiscal period is also an expense of the business. When the insurance premium for a year of insurance coverage is paid, the entire amount is debited to an asset account, Prepaid Insurance. Recording each day's amount of insurance used during August is impractical. Therefore, at the end of a fiscal period, the amount of the insurance coverage used must be deducted from the asset account, Prepaid Insurance, and recorded in the expense account, Insurance Expense.

Changes recorded on a work sheet to update general ledger accounts at the end of a fiscal period are called **adjustments**. The assets of a business, such as supplies and prepaid insurance, are used to earn revenue. The portions of the assets consumed in order to earn revenue become expenses of the business. The portions consumed are no longer assets but are now expenses. Therefore, adjustments must be made to both the asset and expense accounts for supplies and insurance. After the adjustments are made, the expenses incurred to earn revenue are reported in the same fiscal period as the revenue is earned and reported. [CONCEPT: Matching Expenses with Revenue]

A work sheet is used to plan adjustments. Changes are not made in general ledger accounts until adjustments are journalized and posted. The accuracy of the planning for adjustments is checked on a work sheet before adjustments are actually journalized.

Procedures for journalizing TechKnow Consulting's adjustments are described in Chapter 8.

REMEMBER

The ending balance of the asset account, Supplies, should represent the amount of supplies remaining on hand at the end of the fiscal period. The amount of supplies used during the period should be recorded in the expense account, Supplies Expense.

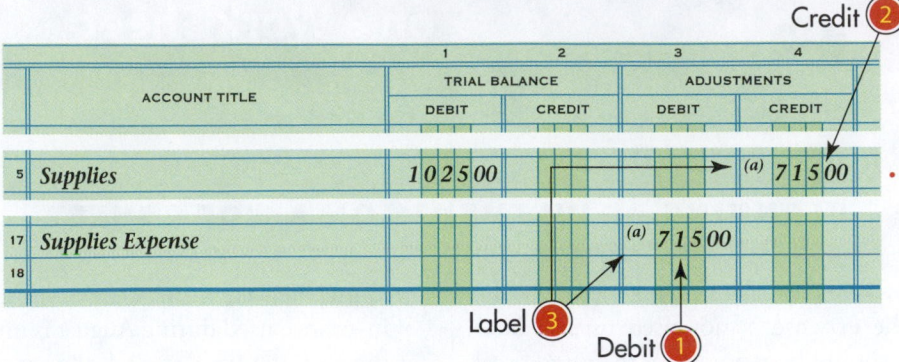

On August 31, before adjustments, the balance of Supplies is $1,025.00, and the balance of Supplies Expense is zero, as shown in the T accounts.

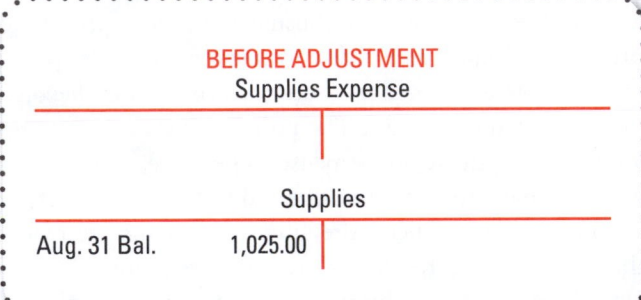

BEFORE ADJUSTMENT

Supplies Expense

Supplies

Aug. 31 Bal.	1,025.00

On August 31, Ms. Park counted the supplies on hand and found that the value of supplies still unused on that date was $310.00. The value of the supplies used is calculated as follows.

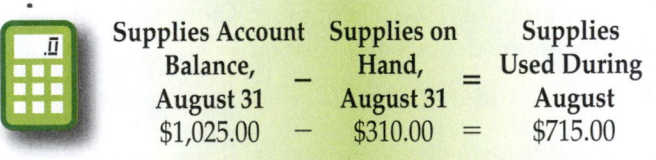

Supplies Account Balance, August 31	–	Supplies on Hand, August 31	=	Supplies Used During August
$1,025.00	–	$310.00	=	$715.00

Four questions are asked in analyzing the adjustment for the asset account, Supplies.

1. **What is the balance of *Supplies*?** *$1,025.00*
2. **What should the balance be for this account?**
   $310.00

3. **What must be done to correct the account balance?**
   Decrease $715.00
4. **What adjustment is made?**
   Debit Supplies Expense, *$715.00*
   Credit Supplies, *$715.00*

The expense account, Supplies Expense, is increased by a debit, $715.00, the value of supplies used. The balance of Supplies Expense, $715.00, is the value of supplies used during the fiscal period from August 1 to August 31. [CONCEPT: Matching Expenses with Revenue]

AFTER ADJUSTMENT

Supplies Expense

Adj. (a)	715.00

Supplies

Aug. 31 Bal.	1,025.00	Adj. (a)	715.00
(New Bal.	310.00)		

The asset account, Supplies, is decreased by a credit, $715.00, the value of supplies used. The debit balance, $1,025.00, less the credit adjustment, $715.00, equals the new balance, $310.00. The new balance of Supplies is the same as the value of supplies on hand on August 31.

STEPS  **RECORDING THE SUPPLIES ADJUSTMENT ON A WORK SHEET**

1. Write the debit amount, *$715.00,* in the work sheet's Adjustments Debit column on the line with the account title *Supplies Expense.*

2. Write the credit amount, *$715.00,* in the Adjustments Credit column on the line with the account title *Supplies.*

3. Label the two parts of this adjustment with a small letter *a* in parentheses, *(a)*. The letter *a* identifies the debit and credit amounts as part of the same adjustment.

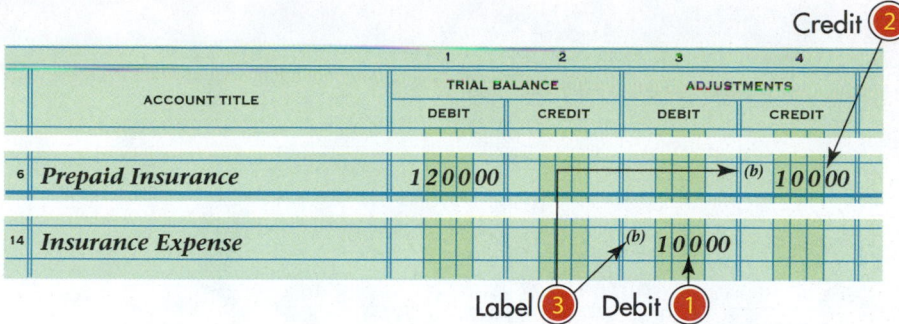

On August 31, before adjustments, the balance of Prepaid Insurance is $1,200.00 and the balance of Insurance Expense is zero.

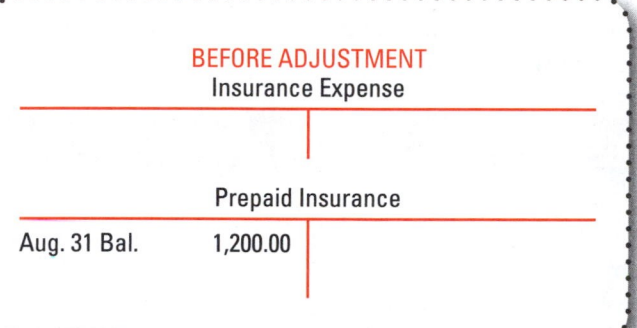

On August 31, Ms. Park checked the insurance records and found that the value of insurance coverage remaining was $1,100.00. The value of the insurance coverage used during the fiscal period is calculated as follows.

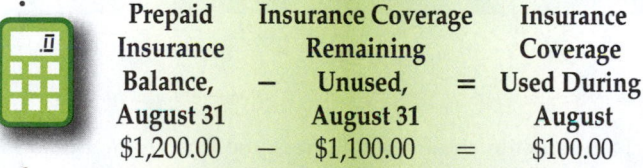

Prepaid Insurance Balance, August 31	–	Insurance Coverage Remaining Unused, August 31	=	Insurance Coverage Used During August
$1,200.00	–	$1,100.00	=	$100.00

Four questions are asked in analyzing the adjustment for the asset account, Prepaid Insurance.

1. **What is the balance of** Prepaid Insurance? *$1,200.00*

2. **What should the balance be for this account?**
$1,100.00
3. **What must be done to correct the account balance?**
Decrease $100.00
4. **What adjustment is made?**
Debit Insurance Expense, *$100.00*
Credit Prepaid Insurance, *$100.00*

The expense account, Insurance Expense, is increased by a debit, $100.00, the value of insurance used. The balance of Insurance Expense, $100.00, is the value of insurance coverage used from August 1 to August 31. [CONCEPT: Matching Expenses with Revenue]

AFTER ADJUSTMENT

Insurance Expense

Adj. (b)	100.00	

Prepaid Insurance

| Aug. 31 Bal. | 1,200.00 | Adj. (b) | 100.00 |
| (New Bal. | 1,100.00) | | |

The asset account, Prepaid Insurance, is decreased by a credit, $100.00, the value of insurance used. The debit balance, $1,200.00, less the credit adjustment, $100.00, equals the new balance, $1,100.00. The new balance of Prepaid Insurance is the same as the amount of insurance coverage unused on August 31.

STEPS — RECORDING THE PREPAID INSURANCE ADJUSTMENT ON A WORK SHEET

1. Write the debit amount, *$100.00,* in the work sheet's Adjustments Debit column on the line with the account title *Insurance Expense.*

2. Write the credit amount, *$100.00,* in the Adjustments Credit column on the line with the account title *Prepaid Insurance.*

3. Label the two parts of this adjustment with a small letter *b* in parentheses, *(b).* The letter *b* identifies the debit and credit amounts as part of the same adjustment.

TechKnow Consulting
Work Sheet
For Month Ended August 31, 20--

		1 TRIAL BALANCE DEBIT	2 TRIAL BALANCE CREDIT	3 ADJUSTMENTS DEBIT	4 ADJUSTMENTS CREDIT
5	Supplies	1 0 2 5 00			(a) 7 1 5 00
6	Prepaid Insurance	1 2 0 0 00			(b) 1 0 0 00
14	Insurance Expense			(b) 1 0 0 00	
15	Miscellaneous Expense	2 8 00			
16	Rent Expense	3 0 0 00			
17	Supplies Expense			(a) 7 1 5 00	
18	Utilities Expense	1 1 0 00			
19		8 8 1 5 00	8 8 1 5 00	8 1 5 00	8 1 5 00

1 Single Rule
2 Totals
3 Double Rule

After all adjustments are recorded in a work sheet's Adjustments columns, the equality of debits and credits for the two columns is proved by totaling and ruling the two columns.

1 Rule a single line across the two Adjustments columns on the same line as the single line for the Trial Balance columns.

2 Add both the Adjustments Debit and Credit columns. If the two column totals are the same, then debits equal credits for these two columns, and the work sheet's Adjustments columns are in balance. Write each column's total below the single line. If the two Adjustments column totals are not the same, the Adjustments columns are rechecked and errors corrected before the work sheet is completed.

3 Rule double lines across both Adjustments columns. The double lines mean that the totals have been verified as correct.

GLOBAL PERSPECTIVE

International Weights and Measures

The primary system of measurement in the United States is the customary system. Among the units of measurement in the customary system are inches, feet, and quarts. The United States is among the few major industrial countries that do not use the metric system exclusively. Among the units of measurement in the metric system are centimeters, meters, and liters. The metric system is based on a decimal system—like U.S. currency. Some U.S. industries have converted to the metric system. Others specify measurements in both customary and metric systems.

To conduct international business, the U.S. has recognized the need to convert customary units to the metric system. For example, beverages are routinely packaged in liter containers. Although the U.S. is a global business leader, it has had to adjust to meet the needs of the rest of the world.

Critical Thinking

1. Look at five food packages. List the weights and measures indicated.

2. List arguments both for and against a proposal to convert all U.S. weights and measures to the metric system.

The following overlay summarizes the preparation of a work sheet. Follow the directions below in using the overlay.

1. Before using the overlay, be sure the pages and transparent overlays are arranged correctly. The correct arrangement is shown below.

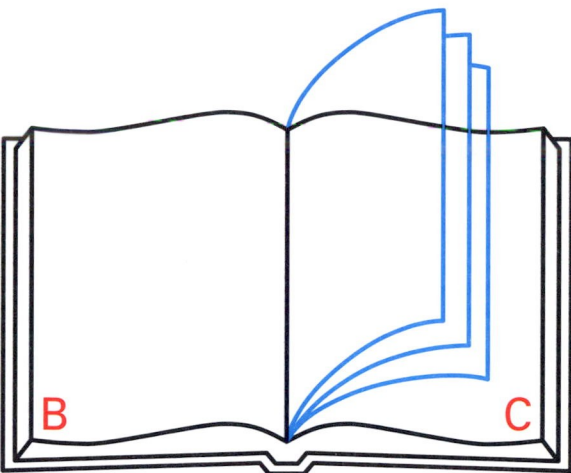

2. Place your book in a horizontal position. Study the steps on page C in preparing the work sheet. You will be able to read the text through the transparent overlays. When directed, carefully lift the transparent overlays and lay them over the work sheet as shown below.

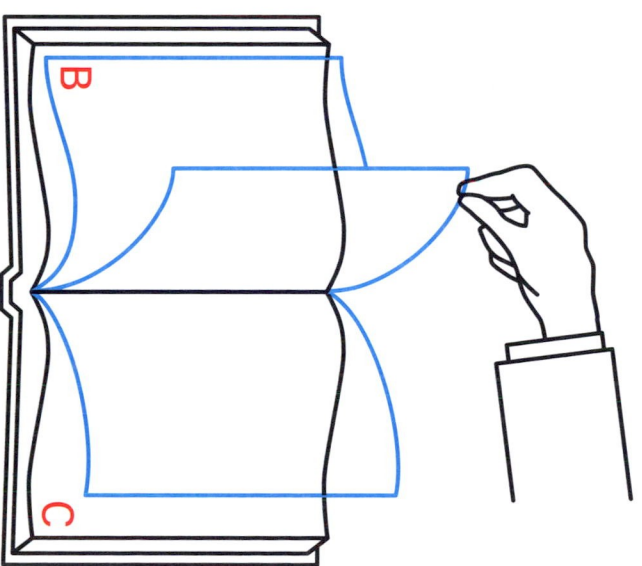

PREPARING A WORK SHEET

To correctly use the insert, read the steps on page C. Apply the transparent overlays when directed to do so in the steps.

TechKnow Consulting

Work Sheet

For Month Ended August 31, 20--

	ACCOUNT TITLE	TRIAL BALANCE		ADJUSTMENTS		INCOME STATEMENT		BALANCE SHEET	
		DEBIT	CREDIT	DEBIT	CREDIT	DEBIT	CREDIT	DEBIT	CREDIT
1	Cash	4 9 6 4 00							
2	Petty Cash	1 0 0 00							
3	Accts. Rec.—Oakdale School	1 5 0 00							
4	Accts. Rec.—Campus Internet Cafe	1 0 0 00							
5	Supplies	1 0 2 5 00							
6	Prepaid Insurance	1 2 0 0 00							
7	Accts. Pay.—Supply Depot		2 0 0 00						
8	Accts. Pay.—Thomas Supply Co.		5 0 00						
9	Kim Park, Capital		5 0 0 0 00						
10	Kim Park, Drawing	6 2 5 00							
11	Income Summary								
12	Sales		3 5 6 5 00						
13	Advertising Expense	2 1 3 00							
14	Insurance Expense								
15	Miscellaneous Expense	2 8 00							
16	Rent Expense	3 0 0 00							
17	Supplies Expense								
18	Utilities Expense	1 1 0 00							
19		8 8 1 5 00	8 8 1 5 00						
20									
21									

PREPARING A WORK SHEET

1. Write the heading.
2. Record the trial balance.
   - Write the general ledger account titles in the Account Title column.
   - Write the account balances in either the Trial Balance Debit or Credit column.
   - Rule a single line across the Trial Balance columns.
   - Add the Trial Balance columns and compare the totals.
   - Rule double lines across both Trial Balance columns.
   - *Carefully apply the first overlay.*
3. Record the supplies adjustment.
   - Write the debit amount in the Adjustments Debit column on the line with the account title Supplies Expense.
   - Write the credit amount in the Adjustments Credit column on the line with the account title Supplies.
   - Label this adjustment (*a*).
4. Record the prepaid insurance adjustment.
   - Write the debit amount in the Adjustments Debit column on the line with the account title Insurance Expense.
   - Write the credit amount in the Adjustments Credit column on the line with the account title Prepaid Insurance.
   - Label this adjustment (*b*).
5. Prove the Adjustments columns.
   - Rule a single line across the Adjustments columns.
   - Add the Adjustments columns and compare the totals to ensure that they are equal.
   - Write the proving totals below the single line.
   - Rule double lines across both Adjustments columns.
   - *Carefully apply the second overlay.*
6. Extend all balance sheet account balances.
   - Extend the up-to-date asset account balances to the Balance Sheet Debit column.
   - Extend the up-to-date liability account balances to the Balance Sheet Credit column.
   - Extend the owner's capital and drawing account balances to the Balance Sheet columns.
7. Extend all income statement account balances.
   - Extend the up-to-date revenue account balance to the Income Statement Credit column.
   - Extend the up-to-date expense account balances to the Income Statement Debit column.
   - *Carefully apply the third overlay.*
8. Calculate and record the net income (or net loss).
   - Rule a single line across the Income Statement and Balance Sheet columns.
   - Add the columns and write the totals below the single line.
   - Calculate the net income or net loss amount.
   - Write the amount of net income (or net loss) below the smaller of the two Income Statement column totals. Write the words *Net Income* or *Net Loss* in the Account Title column.
   - Extend the amount of net income (or net loss) to the Balance Sheet columns. Write the amount under the smaller of the two column totals. Write the amount on the same line as the words *Net Income* (or *Net Loss*).
9. Total and rule the Income Statement and Balance Sheet columns.
   - Rule a single line across the Income Statement and Balance Sheet columns immediately below the net income (or net loss) amounts.
   - Add the net income (or net loss) to the previous column totals. Compare the column totals to ensure that totals for each pair of columns are in balance.
   - Write the proving totals for each column below the single line.
   - Rule double lines across the Income Statement and Balance Sheet columns immediately below the proving totals.

C

Malpractice Liability of Accountants

Accountants are subject to the legal consequences of malpractice. They can be held financially liable for misconduct or improper practice in their profession.

Most lawsuits against public accountants involve audits of financial statements. Consider the following example. Best & Farrish, CPAs, audited the financial statements of Richmond, Inc. Relying on these statements, American Bank loaned $1,000,000 to Richmond. Unknown to the accountants, however, Richmond's president was involved in a scheme to steal cash. Richmond experienced financial difficulties and was unable to repay the loan to American Bank. The bank sued Best & Farrish for $1,000,000, claiming it was negligent for not detecting the president's fraud.

Should Best & Farrish be required to pay $1,000,000 to American Bank? Over many years, the courts have established four guidelines for determining whether accountants are liable for the financial losses of third parties.

1. *Financial loss.* Did the third party incur a financial loss? Answering this question is typically an easy task. American Bank lost $1,000,000 when Richmond did not repay its loan.

2. *Reliance on financial statements.* Did the third party actually rely on the financial statements for making its decision? Accountants should not be held liable unless the third party used the financial statements in making its decision. If American Bank received a copy of the financial statements but relied solely on other information obtained from Richmond's managers, then Best & Farrish should not be held liable for American Bank's loss.

3. *Level of negligence.* Accountants who fail to exhibit a reasonable level of care are guilty of ordinary negligence. Gross negligence occurs when an accountant's actions represent a flagrant violation of professional standards.

Professional standards recognize that accountants are not able to detect all frauds. Whether Best & Farrish was negligent in not detecting the president's fraud would depend on the facts of the case.

4. *Accountant-third party relationship.* Accountants have a contract with their clients; a client can sue the accountant for breach of contract. However, third parties do not have a contract with the accountant. Whether a third party can sue the accountant depends on whether the accountant specifically knew the third party intended to use the financial statements.

If Best & Farrish knew American Bank would use the audited financial statements to grant a loan, then American Bank could sue Best & Farrish for ordinary negligence. However, if Best & Farrish did not know Richmond even intended to obtain a bank loan, then gross negligence or fraud would need to be proven for American Bank to win its case.

Accountants must take great care in performing their professional services. Accountants who can prove the audit was performed in accordance with professional accounting standards will prevail against negligence lawsuits.

Instructions

Using your local library or online resources, locate an article describing a malpractice lawsuit against a public accounting firm. What were the main facts of this case? What is your opinion of the firm's liability?

EXTENDING INCOME STATEMENT ACCOUNT BALANCES ON A WORK SHEET

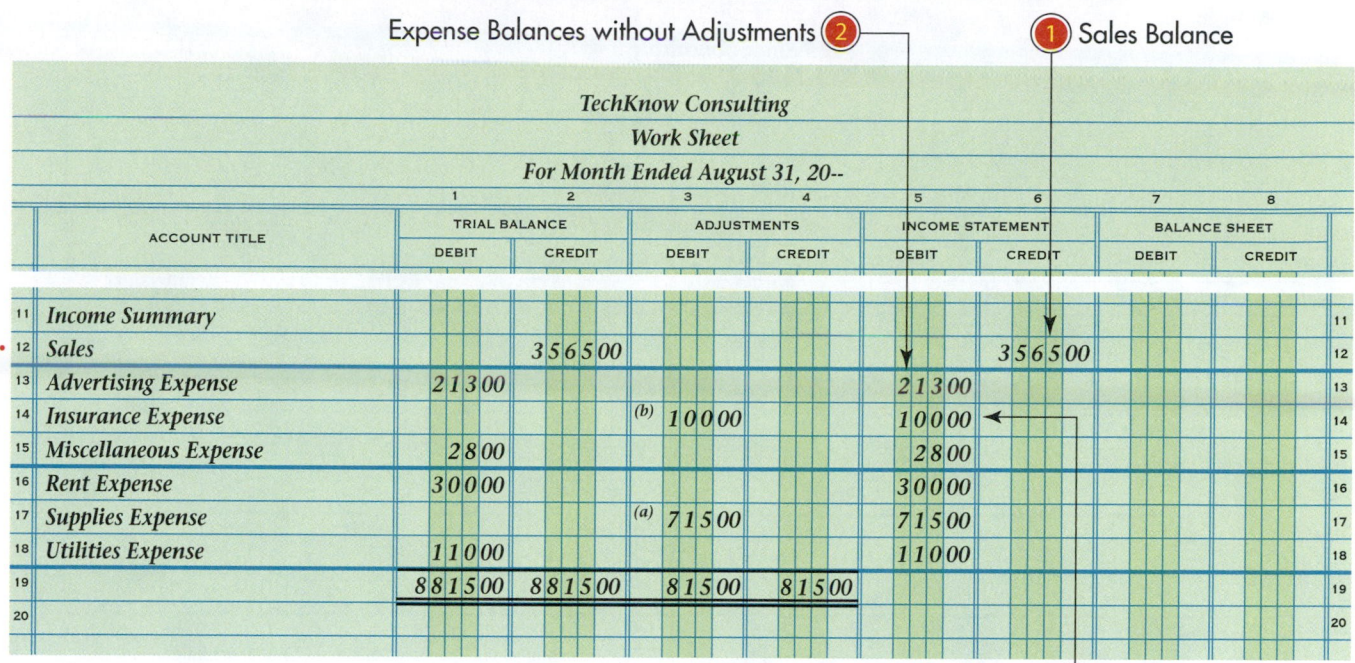

Expense Balances without Adjustments ②   ① Sales Balance

TechKnow Consulting

Work Sheet

For Month Ended August 31, 20--

	TRIAL BALANCE		ADJUSTMENTS		INCOME STATEMENT		BALANCE SHEET	
ACCOUNT TITLE	1 DEBIT	2 CREDIT	3 DEBIT	4 CREDIT	5 DEBIT	6 CREDIT	7 DEBIT	8 CREDIT
11 Income Summary								
12 Sales		3 5 6 5 00				3 5 6 5 00		
13 Advertising Expense	2 1 3 00				2 1 3 00			
14 Insurance Expense			(b) 1 0 0 00		1 0 0 00			
15 Miscellaneous Expense	2 8 00				2 8 00			
16 Rent Expense	3 0 0 00				3 0 0 00			
17 Supplies Expense			(a) 7 1 5 00		7 1 5 00			
18 Utilities Expense	1 1 0 00				1 1 0 00			
19	8 8 1 5 00	8 8 1 5 00	8 1 5 00	8 1 5 00				
20								

Expense Balances with Adjustments ③

A financial statement showing the revenue and expenses for a fiscal period is called an ==income statement.== TechKnow Consulting's income statement accounts are the revenue and expense accounts. Up-to-date income statement account balances are extended to the Income Statement Debit and Credit columns of the work sheet.

FOR YOUR INFORMATION

F Y I

Use a ruler when extending amounts on a work sheet to keep track of the line you are on.

FOR YOUR INFORMATION

F Y I

A work sheet is prepared in manual accounting to adjust the accounts and sort amounts needed to prepare financial statements. However, in automated accounting, adjustments are prepared from the trial balance, and the software automatically generates the financial statements with no need for a work sheet.

S T E P S EXTENDING INCOME STATEMENT ACCOUNT BALANCES ON A WORK SHEET

① Extend the balance of *Sales, $3,565.00,* to the Income Statement Credit column. The balance of *Sales* in the Trial Balance Credit column is up-to-date because no adjustment affects this account.

② Extend the balance of *Advertising Expense, $213.00,* to the Income Statement Debit column. The balance of *Advertising Expense* is up-to-date because no adjustment affects this account. Extend the balances of all expense accounts not affected by adjustments to the Income Statement Debit column.

③ Calculate the up-to-date adjusted balance of *Insurance Expense.* The balance of *Insurance Expense* in the Trial Balance Debit column is zero. This zero balance is not up-to-date because this account is affected by an adjustment. The debit balance, $0.00, plus the debit adjustment, $100.00, equals the adjusted balance, $100.00. Extend the up-to-date adjusted debit balance, *$100.00,* to the Income Statement Debit column. Using the same procedure, calculate and extend the up-to-date adjusted balance of each expense account affected by an adjustment.

TechKnow Consulting

Work Sheet

For Month Ended August 31, 20--

		ACCOUNT TITLE	TRIAL BALANCE		ADJUSTMENTS		INCOME STATEMENT		BALANCE SHEET		
			1 DEBIT	2 CREDIT	3 DEBIT	4 CREDIT	5 DEBIT	6 CREDIT	7 DEBIT	8 CREDIT	
1		Cash	4 9 6 4 00						4 9 6 4 00		1
2		Petty Cash	1 0 0 00						1 0 0 00		2
3		Accts. Rec.—Oakdale School	1 5 0 00						1 5 0 00		3
4		Accts. Rec.—Campus Internet Cafe	1 0 0 00						1 0 0 00		4
5		Supplies	1 0 2 5 00			(a) 7 1 5 00			3 1 0 00		5
6		Prepaid Insurance	1 2 0 0 00			(b) 1 0 0 00			1 1 0 0 00		6
7		Accts. Pay.—Supply Depot		2 0 0 00						2 0 0 00	7
8		Accts. Pay.—Thomas Supply Co.		5 0 00						5 0 00	8
9		Kim Park, Capital		5 0 0 0 00						5 0 0 0 00	9
10		Kim Park, Drawing	6 2 5 00						6 2 5 00		10
11		Income Summary									11
12		Sales		3 5 6 5 00				3 5 6 5 00			12
13		Advertising Expense	2 1 3 00				2 1 3 00				13
14		Insurance Expense			(b) 1 0 0 00		1 0 0 00				14
15		Miscellaneous Expense	2 8 00				2 8 00				15
16		Rent Expense	3 0 0 00				3 0 0 00				16
17		Supplies Expense			(a) 7 1 5 00		7 1 5 00				17
18		Utilities Expense	1 1 0 00				1 1 0 00				18
19			8 8 1 5 00	8 8 1 5 00	8 1 5 00	8 1 5 00	1 4 6 6 00	3 5 6 5 00	7 3 4 9 00	5 2 5 0 00	19
20		Net Income					2 0 9 9 00			2 0 9 9 00	20
21							3 5 6 5 00	3 5 6 5 00	7 3 4 9 00	7 3 4 9 00	21

Extend Net Income

Single Rule ①

Totals ②

④

⑤

Single Rule

③ Net Income

Totals ⑥

Double Rule ⑦

The difference between total revenue and total expenses when total revenue is greater is called **net income.** Before the work sheet is complete, net income must be calculated and the work sheet must be totaled and ruled. A summary of preparing a work sheet is shown on the Work Sheet Overlay.

STEPS

CALCULATING AND RECORDING NET INCOME ON A WORK SHEET; TOTALING AND RULING A WORK SHEET

① Rule a single line across the four income statement and balance sheet columns.

② Add both the Income Statement and Balance Sheet columns. Write the totals below the single line.

③ Calculate the net income. The Income Statement Credit column total, $3,565.00, minus the Income Statement Debit column total, $1,466.00, equals net income, $2,099.00. Write the amount of net income, *$2,099.00,* below the Income Statement Debit column total. Write the words *Net Income* on the same line in the Account Title column.

④ Extend the amount of net income, *$2,099.00,* to the Balance Sheet Credit column. Since the owner's equity account, *Kim Park, Capital,* increases by a credit, extend the net income amount to the Balance Sheet Credit column.

⑤ Rule a single line across the four Income Statement and Balance Sheet columns just below the net income amounts.

⑥ Add the subtotal and net income amount for each column to get proving totals for the Income Statement and Balance Sheet columns. Write the totals below the single line. Check the equality for each pair of columns.

⑦ Rule double lines across the Income Statement and Balance Sheet columns.

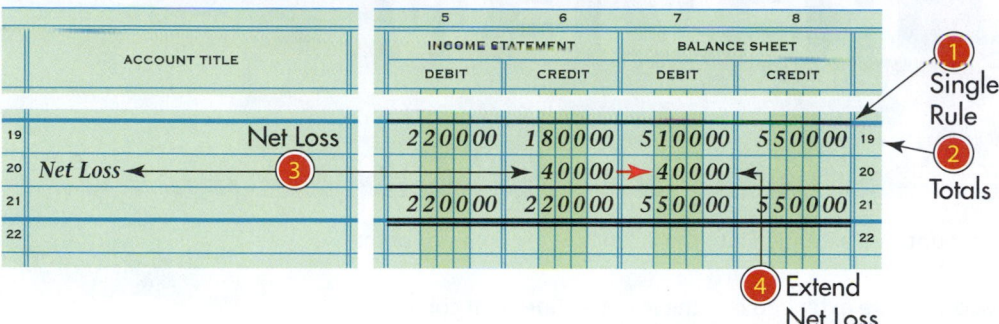

		5	6	7	8	
	ACCOUNT TITLE	INCOME STATEMENT		BALANCE SHEET		
		DEBIT	CREDIT	DEBIT	CREDIT	
19	Net Loss	2 200 00	1 800 00	5 100 00	5 500 00	19
20	Net Loss		40 00 00	40 00 00		20
21		2 200 00	2 200 00	5 500 00	5 500 00	21
22						22

① Single Rule
② Totals
③
④ Extend Net Loss

TechKnow Consulting's completed work sheet shows a net income. However, a business might have a net loss to report. The difference between total revenue and total expenses when total expenses are greater is called a **net loss.**

① Rule a single line across the four Income Statement and Balance Sheet columns.

② Add both the Income Statement and Balance Sheet columns. Write the totals below the single line.

③ Calculate the net loss. The Income Statement Debit column total, $2,200.00, minus the Income Statement Credit column total, $1,800.00, equals net loss, $400.00. The Income Statement Debit column total (expenses) is greater than the Income Statement Credit column total (revenue). Therefore, because expenses exceed revenue, there is a net loss. Write the amount of net loss, *$400.00,* below the Income Statement Credit column total. Write the words *Net Loss* on the same line in the Account Title column.

④ Extend the amount of net loss, *$400.00,* to the Balance Sheet Debit column on the same line as the words *Net Loss.* The owner's equity account, *Kim Park, Capital,* is decreased by a debit. Therefore, a net loss is extended to the Balance Sheet Debit column.

PHOTODISC/GETTY IMAGES

End of Lesson REVIEW

AUDIT YOUR UNDERSTANDING

1. Which accounts are extended into the Balance Sheet columns of the work sheet?
2. Which accounts are extended into the Income Statement columns of the work sheet?
3. In which Balance Sheet column do you record net income on the work sheet?
4. In which Balance Sheet column do you record net loss on the work sheet?

TERMS REVIEW

balance sheet

income statement

net income

net loss

WORK TOGETHER 6-3

Completing a work sheet

Use the work sheet from Work Together 6-2. Your instructor will guide you through the following examples.

1. Extend the up-to-date balances to the Balance Sheet and Income Statement columns.
2. Rule a single line across the Income Statement and Balance Sheet columns. Total each column. Calculate and record the net income or net loss. Label the amount in the Account Title column.
3. Total and rule the Income Statement and Balance Sheet columns.

ON YOUR OWN 6-3

Completing a work sheet

Use the work sheet from On Your Own 6-2. Work this problem independently.

1. Extend the up-to-date balances to the Balance Sheet or Income Statement columns.
2. Rule a single line across the Income Statement and Balance Sheet columns. Total each column. Calculate and record the net income or net loss. Label the amount in the Account Title column.
3. Total and rule the Income Statement and Balance Sheet columns.

Finding and Correcting Errors on the Work Sheet

CORRECTING ACCOUNTING ERRORS ON THE WORK SHEET

Some errors in accounting records are not discovered until a work sheet is prepared. For example, a debit to supplies may not have been posted from a journal to the general ledger supplies account. The omission may not be discovered until the work sheet's trial balance does not balance. Also, information may be transferred incorrectly from general ledger accounts to the work sheet's trial balance. Additional errors may be made, such as recording adjustment information incorrectly or adding columns

incorrectly. In addition, errors may be made in extending amounts to the Income Statement and Balance Sheet columns.

Any errors found on a work sheet should be corrected before any further work is completed. If an incorrect amount is found on a work sheet, erase the error and replace it with the correct amount. If an amount is written in an incorrect column, erase the amount and record it in the correct column.

CHECKING FOR TYPICAL CALCULATION ERRORS

When two column totals are not in balance, subtract the smaller total from the larger total to find the difference. Check the difference between the two amounts against the following guides.

1. **The difference is 1, such as $.01, $.10, $1.00, or $10.00.** For example, if the totals of the two columns are Debit, $14,657.00, and Credit, $14,658.00, the difference between the two columns is $1.00. The error is most likely in addition. Add the columns again.

2. **The difference can be divided evenly by 2.** For example, the difference between two column totals is $48.00, which can be divided by 2 with no remainder. Look for a $24.00 amount in the Trial Balance columns of the work sheet. If the amount is found, check to make sure it has been recorded in the correct Debit or Credit column. A $24.00 debit amount recorded in a credit column results in a difference between column totals of $48.00. If the error is not found on the work sheet, check the general ledger accounts and journal entries. An entry for $24.00 may have been recorded in an incorrect column in the journal or in an account.

3. **The difference can be divided evenly by 9.** For example, the difference between two columns is $45.00, which can be divided by 9 with no remainder. When the difference can be divided equally by 9, look for transposed numbers such as 54 written as 45 or 19 written as 91. Also, check for a "slide." A "slide" occurs when numbers are moved to the right or left in an amount column. For example, $12.00 is recorded as $120.00 or $350.00 is recorded as $35.00.

4. **The difference is an omitted amount.** Look for an amount equal to the difference. If the difference is $50.00, look for an account balance of $50.00 that has not been extended. Look for any $50.00 amount on the work sheet and determine if it has been handled correctly. Look in the accounts and journals for a $50.00 amount, and check if that amount has been handled correctly. Failure to record a $50.00 account balance will make a work sheet's column totals differ by $50.00.

CHECKING FOR ERRORS IN THE WORK SHEET

Check for Errors in the Trial Balance Column

1. Have all general ledger account balances been copied in the trial balance column correctly?
2. Have all general ledger account balances been recorded in the correct Trial Balance column?

Check for Errors in the Adjustments Columns

1. Do the debits equal the credits for each adjustment? Use the small letters that label each part of an adjustment to help check accuracy and equality of debits and credits.
2. Is the amount for each adjustment correct?

Check for Errors in the Income Statement and Balance Sheet Columns

1. Has each amount been copied correctly when extended to the Income Statement or Balance Sheet column?
2. Has each account balance been extended to the correct Income Statement or Balance Sheet column?
3. Has the net income or net loss been calculated correctly?
4. Has the net income or net loss been recorded in the correct Income Statement or Balance Sheet column?

For all three of these cases, correct any errors found and add the columns again.

CORRECTING AN ERROR IN POSTING TO THE WRONG ACCOUNT

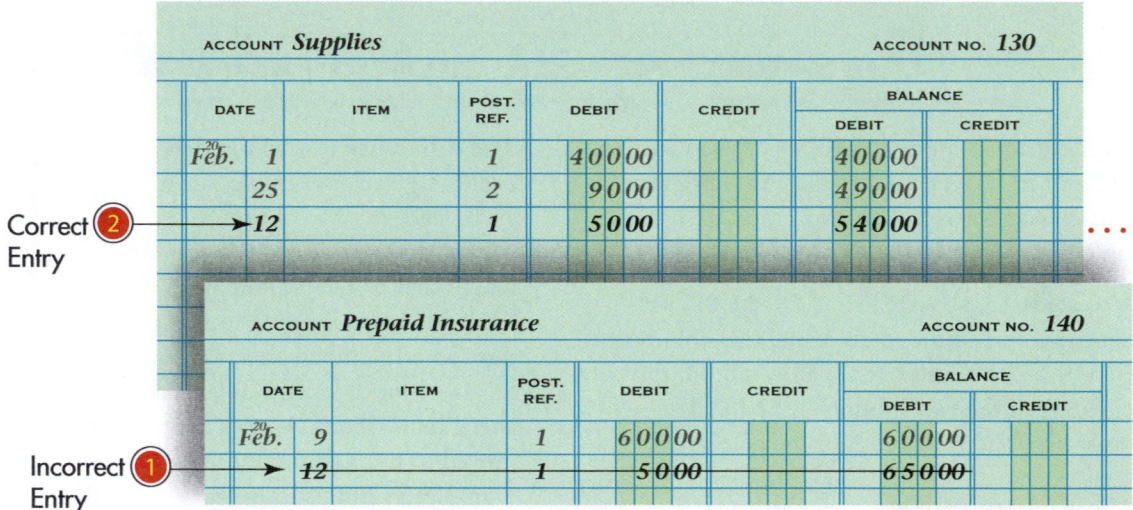

If a pair of work sheet columns does not balance and an error cannot be found on the work sheet, look for an error in posting from the journal to the general ledger accounts.

As each item in an account or a journal entry is verified, a check mark should be placed next to it. The check mark indicates that the item has been checked for accuracy.

1. Have all amounts that need to be posted actually been posted from the journal? To correct, complete the posting to the correct account. When posting is corrected, recalculate the account balance and correct it on the work sheet.
2. Have all amounts been posted to the correct accounts? To correct, follow these steps.

STEPS · **CORRECTING AN ERROR IN POSTING TO THE WRONG ACCOUNT**

1. Draw a line through the entire incorrect entry. Recalculate the account balance and correct the work sheet.

2. Record the posting in the correct account. Recalculate the account balance, and correct the work sheet.

CORRECTING AN INCORRECT AMOUNT AND AN AMOUNT POSTED TO THE WRONG COLUMN

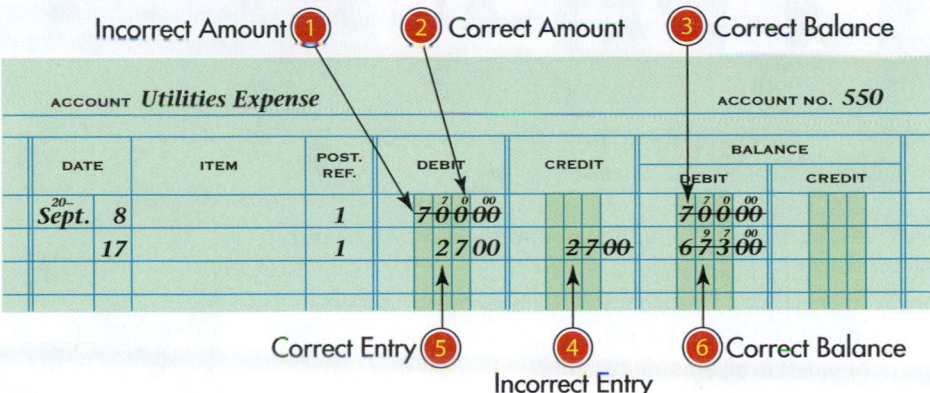

Errors can be made in writing amounts in general ledger accounts. Errors in permanent records should never be erased. Erasures in permanent records raise questions about whether important financial information has been altered.

STEPS **CORRECTING AN INCORRECT AMOUNT**

1. Draw a line through the incorrect amount.

2. Write the correct amount just above the correction in the same space.

3. Recalculate the account balance, and correct the account balance on the work sheet.

CORRECTING AN AMOUNT POSTED TO THE WRONG COLUMN

4. Draw a line through the incorrect item in the account.

5. Record the posting in the correct amount column.

6. Recalculate the account balance, and correct the work sheet.

CHECKING FOR ERRORS IN JOURNAL ENTRIES

1. Do debits equal credits in each journal entry?
2. Is each journal entry amount recorded in the correct journal column?
3. Is information in the Account Title column correct for each journal entry?
4. Are all of the journal amount column totals correct?

5. Does the sum of debit column totals equal the sum of credit column totals in the journal?
6. Have all transactions been recorded?

Some suggestions for correcting errors in journal entries are described in Chapter 3.

PREVENTING ERRORS

The best way to prevent errors is to work carefully. Check the work at each step in an accounting procedure. Most errors occur in doing arithmetic, especially in adding columns. When possible, use a calculator. When an error is discovered, do no more work until the cause of the error is found and corrections are made.

End of Lesson
REVIEW

1. What is the first step in checking for arithmetic errors when two column totals are not in balance?
2. What is one way to check for an error caused by transposed numbers?
3. What term is used to describe an error that occurs when numbers are moved to the right or left in an amount column?

WORK TOGETHER 6-4

Finding and correcting errors in accounting records

Paul Coty has completed the September monthly work sheet for his business, LeafyLift. The work sheet and general ledger accounts are given in the *Working Papers*. Mr. Coty believes that he has made one or more errors in preparing the work sheet. He asks you to help him verify the work sheet. Your instructor will guide you through the following examples.

1. Examine the work sheet and the general ledger accounts. Make a list of the errors you find.
2. Correct any errors you find in the general ledger accounts.
3. Prepare a corrected work sheet.

ON YOUR OWN 6-4

Finding and correcting errors in accounting records

Nadine Fritz has completed the November monthly work sheet for her business, Your Personal Trainer. The work sheet and general ledger accounts are given in the *Working Papers*. Ms. Fritz believes that she has made one or more errors in preparing the work sheet. She asks you to help her verify the work sheet. Work this problem independently.

1. Examine the work sheet and the general ledger accounts. Make a list of the errors you find.
2. Correct any errors you find in the general ledger accounts.
3. Prepare a corrected work sheet.

After completing this chapter, you can:

1. Define accounting terms related to a work sheet for a service business organized as a proprietorship.

2. Identify accounting concepts and practices related to a work sheet for a service business organized as a proprietorship.

3. Prepare a heading and a trial balance on a work sheet.

4. Plan adjustments for supplies and prepaid insurance.

5. Complete a work sheet for a service business organized as a proprietorship.

6. Identify selected procedures for finding and correcting errors in accounting records.

EXPLORE ACCOUNTING

Fiscal Periods

A fiscal period is the length of time for which a business summarizes and reports financial information. Since many companies are required to publish yearly annual reports, these companies choose a year for the fiscal period. In such a case, a company will prepare financial statements every year.

A fiscal year can be any consecutive 12-month period. The Internal Revenue Service (IRS) requires many companies to report taxable income for the fiscal year January 1 through December 31. A fiscal year beginning January 1 can also be called a calendar year. Because they use a calendar year for reporting taxable income, many companies choose to use the calendar year for issuing financial statements also.

However, there is no requirement to begin a fiscal year on January 1. Companies often choose a fiscal year that ends during a period of low business activity. Twelve consecutive months which end when business activities have reached the lowest point in their annual cycle are called a natural business year.

The following survey conducted on 600 businesses shows the number of companies that chose a fiscal year ending at the end of a specific month.

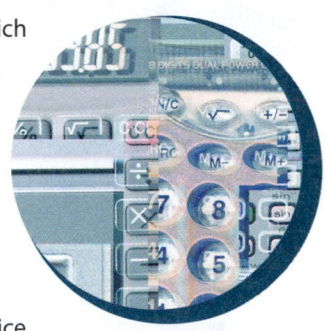

Fiscal Year End	No. of Companies
January	32
February	10
March	16
April	8
May	18
June	48
July	8
August	15
September	38
October	19
November	15
December	373

Activity: Assume you work for a company that makes snowmobiles. You must determine what fiscal year should be used. Make a written recommendation to the owner. Explain why your recommendation is preferable.

Source: Accounting Trends and Techniques, 2002, published by the American Institute of Certified Public Accountants.

6-1 APPLICATION PROBLEM  Office

Recording the trial balance on a work sheet

Use the work sheet given in the *Working Papers*. On June 30 of the current year, Roseville Rental has the following general ledger accounts and balances. The business uses a monthly fiscal period.

Account Titles	Account Balances	
	Debit	**Credit**
Cash	$11,620.00	
Petty Cash	100.00	
Accounts Receivable—Leslie Naples	855.00	
Supplies	690.00	
Prepaid Insurance	900.00	
Accounts Payable—Russell Goodland		$ 355.00
Sunthi Ling, Capital		12,926.00
Sunthi Ling, Drawing	500.00	
Income Summary		
Sales		2,270.00
Advertising Expense	340.00	
Insurance Expense		
Miscellaneous Expense	184.00	
Supplies Expense		
Utilities Expense	362.00	

Instructions:
Prepare the heading and trial balance on a work sheet. Total and rule the Trial Balance columns. Save your work to complete Application Problem 6-2.

6-2 APPLICATION PROBLEM AUTOMATED ACCOUNTING

Planning adjustments on a work sheet

Use the work sheet from Application Problem 6-1.

Instructions:

1. Analyze the following adjustment information into debit and credit parts. Record the adjustments on the work sheet.

Adjustment Information, June 30

Supplies on hand	$250.00
Value of prepaid insurance	750.00

2. Total and rule the Adjustments columns. Save your work to complete Application Problem 6-3.

(*Go Beyond the Book*)
For more information go to
www.C21accounting.com

6-3 APPLICATION PROBLEM

Completing a work sheet

Use the work sheet from Application Problem 6-2.

Instructions:

1. Extend the up-to-date balances to the Balance Sheet or Income Statement columns.
2. Rule a single line across the Income Statement and Balance Sheet columns. Total each column. Calculate and record the net income or net loss. Label the amount in the Account Title column.
3. Total and rule the Income Statement and Balance Sheet columns.

6-4 APPLICATION PROBLEM

Finding and correcting errors in accounting records

Ervin Watkins has completed the April monthly work sheet for his business, EverClean. The work sheet and general ledger accounts are given in the *Working Papers*. Mr. Watkins believes that he has made one or more errors in preparing the work sheet. He asks you to help him verify the work sheet.

Instructions:

1. Examine the work sheet and the general ledger accounts. Make a list of the errors you find.
2. Correct any errors you find in the general ledger accounts.
3. Prepare a corrected work sheet.

6-5 MASTERY PROBLEM   AUTOMATED ACCOUNTING   Peachtree by Sage   QB Quick Books   Microsoft Office

Completing a work sheet

On April 30 of the current year, Bonita Bubbles has the following general ledger accounts and balances. The business uses a monthly fiscal period. A work sheet is given in the *Working Papers*.

Account Titles	Account Balances	
	Debit	**Credit**
Cash	$2,829.00	
Petty Cash	150.00	
Accounts Receivable—Bernard Corbett	511.00	
Supplies	855.00	
Prepaid Insurance	1,100.00	
Accounts Payable—Spooner Supplies		$ 500.00
Paulo Gutierrez, Capital		4,500.00
Paulo Gutierrez, Drawing	440.00	
Income Summary		
Sales		2,400.00
Advertising Expense	450.00	
Insurance Expense		
Miscellaneous Expense	190.00	
Rent Expense	375.00	
Supplies Expense		
Utilities Expense	500.00	

Instructions:

1. Prepare the heading and trial balance on a work sheet. Total and rule the Trial Balance columns.
2. Analyze the following adjustment information into debit and credit parts. Record the adjustments on the work sheet.

   Adjustment Information, April 30

Supplies inventory	$220.00
Value of prepaid insurance	800.00

3. Total and rule the Adjustments columns.
4. Extend the up-to-date balances to the Balance Sheet or Income Statement columns.
5. Rule a single line across the Income Statement and Balance Sheet columns. Total each column. Calculate and record the net income or net loss. Label the amount in the Account Title column.
6. Total and rule the Income Statement and Balance Sheet columns.

6-6 · CHALLENGE PROBLEM

Completing a work sheet

LawnPro Company had a small fire in its office. The fire destroyed some of the accounting records. On November 30 of the current year, the end of a monthly fiscal period, the following information was constructed from the remaining records and other sources. A work sheet is given in the *Working Papers*.

Remains of the general ledger:

Account Titles	Account Balances
Accounts Receivable—C. Gabriel	$ 825.00
Supplies	700.00
Don Arnodt, Drawing	300.00
Sales	3,800.00
Advertising Expense	200.00
Rent Expense	600.00
Utilities Expense	390.00

Information from the business's checkbook:

Cash balance on last unused check stub	$3,119.00
Total payments for miscellaneous expense	50.00
Total payments for insurance	400.00

Information obtained through inquiries to other businesses:

Owed to St. Croix Supplies	$1,500.00
Value of prepaid insurance, November 30	250.00

Information obtained by counting supplies on hand after the fire:

Supplies on hand	$ 200.00

Instructions:

1. From the information given, prepare a heading and reconstruct a trial balance on a work sheet. The owner's capital account balance is the difference between the total of all debit account balances minus the total of all credit account balances.
2. Complete the work sheet.

Work Sheet for a Service Business

Accounting information is used by managers to make business decisions. But exactly what kind of decisions does the owner of a local business make? How does accounting information enable the manager to make better decisions?

Instructions: Identify a local business of personal interest to you. Write five questions you would ask the manager to learn how that person uses accounting information to make decisions. Interview the manager and write a one- or two-page summary of the interview.

CASE FOR CRITICAL THINKING

When posting amounts from a journal to general ledger accounts, a $10.00 debit to Supplies is mistakenly posted as a credit to Utilities Expense. Will this error be discovered when the work sheet is prepared? Explain.

AUDITING FOR ERRORS

The trial balance for Enfield Company is given below.

Account Titles	Account Balances	
	Debit	Credit
Cash	$ 4,391.00	
Petty Cash	300.00	
Accounts Receivable—Harned Co.		$2,950.00
Supplies	327.00	
Accounts Payable—Esby Inc.		1,250.00
Ervin Enfield, Capital	6,500.00	
Ervin Enfield, Drawing	600.00	
Income Summary		
Sales	2,500.00	
Advertising Expense	1,432.00	
Supplies Expense		
Rent Expense	250.00	
Totals	16,300.00	4,200.00

The debit column does not equal the credit column. The new bookkeeper knows that the amounts are correct but is not sure if the amounts are in the correct columns.

Instructions

1. Using what you know about the normal balance side of each account, find which amount(s) are in the wrong column.

2. On a separate piece of paper, copy the balances, putting them in the correct columns.

3. Total the columns to prove that debits now equal credits.

ANALYZING BEST BUY'S FINANCIAL STATEMENTS

The length of time for which a business summarizes and reports financial information is known as a *fiscal period*. Annual statements use a fiscal period equal to one year. However, the fiscal year does not necessarily begin on January 1 and end on December 31 (a calendar year). A company's fiscal year can begin on any date. Most companies choose a fiscal year that ends during a period of low business activity, often after a period of high activity, when inventories are low. Look at the second page of Note 1 to Best Buy's financial statements on Appendix B page B10.

Instructions

1. When does Best Buy's fiscal year end?

2. Why do you think Best Buy's management feels that this is a good time for a fiscal year end?

Accounting SOFTWARE

TRIAL BALANCE AND ADJUSTING ENTRIES

Computer accounting systems do not use work sheets to plan adjustments. At any time, a trial balance can be printed that reports all general ledger account balances in debit and credit columns, just like the first two columns of the work sheet. Rather than being recorded in the adjustment columns of a work sheet, adjustments are entered individually using the general journal and posted to the general ledger.

A second trial balance should be printed to report the adjusted account balances. It is important that you review every report printed by a computer. Don't assume that anything produced by a computer is accurate. After recording adjustments, you should pay special attention to every account that required adjustment. Is the new Supplies account balance correct? Does the Insurance Expense account now have a balance?

PEACHTREE MASTERY PROBLEM 6-5

1. Open (Restore) file 06-5MP.ptb.

2. Journalize and post the adjusting entries.

3. Print trial balances before and after adjustments. Note: Although the instructions direct you to prepare a manual 8-column work sheet, it is not necessary to do this for this problem.

TRIAL BALANCE AND ADJUSTING ENTRIES

The work sheet was introduced in this chapter. The work sheet is used only in a manual accounting system. Computerized accounting systems do not produce a work sheet. Instead, a trial balance is printed to make sure that the debit account balances equal the credit account balances. The trial balance is used to plan the necessary adjustments. The adjusting entries are then entered into the system using general journal entries.

Once the adjusting entries have been made, another trial balance should be prepared. Although computer systems are very accurate, the new balances should be examined to determine if the correct adjusting entries were made. This can be done by checking to make sure the new balances in supplies and prepaid insurance reflect the amount of supplies on hand and the unexpired insurance.

QUICKBOOKS MASTERY PROBLEM 6-5

1. Open the Bonita Bubbles file.

2. Journalize the adjusting entries for April 30 using the general journal in your QuickBooks software to record the transactions.

3. Print a trial balance. NOTE: Although the instructions direct you to generate a balance sheet and profit and loss statement, it is not necessary to do this right now. You will do this in a later problem. However, you should generate a trial balance after the adjusting entries are recorded in order to check the accuracy of the adjusting process.

8-COLUMN WORK SHEET AND INSERTING AND DELETING ROWS

Imagine that you are preparing a paper work sheet and have completed entering all the account titles and trial balance amounts. Calculating the total for each column, you discover that you have missed entering the Petty Cash account. What would you do to correct this mistake?

Whether using a paper work sheet or an electronic spreadsheet template, the process of entering accounts and amounts may seem to be the same. However, the electronic spreadsheet has two important advantages. First, additional rows can easily be inserted to correct a mistake as described above. Second, column totals calculated using SUM functions eliminate the time and potential errors inherent with calculating these values with a calculator.

Inserting rows does not require that you modify a SUM function. The function easily adapts to new rows being entered on a work sheet. A SUM function such as =SUM(B10:B24) will automatically change to =SUM(B10:B25) when a row is inserted between rows 10 and 24. In the same manner, SUM functions will adjust when unused rows are deleted.

EXCEL APPLICATION PROBLEM 6-1

1. Open the F06-1 Excel data file.

2. Follow the step-by-step instructions in the Instructions work sheet to make changes to an 8-column work sheet using an Excel spreadsheet.

This template can also be used to complete Application Problems 6-2 and 6-3.

EXCEL MASTERY PROBLEM 6-5

1. Open the F06-5 Excel data file.

2. Follow the step-by-step instructions in the Instructions work sheet to make changes to an 8-column work sheet using an Excel spreadsheet.

TRIAL BALANCE AND ADJUSTING ENTRIES

In automated accounting, the emphasis is on the analysis of the source documents and the preparation of timely and accurate journal entries and adjusting entries. These are the parts of the accounting cycle that require accounting personnel to apply the matching concept to ensure that revenues and expenses are recorded in the proper periods. The automated accounting system is programmed to post journal entries and to prepare trial balances, closing entries, and financial statements as needed. The accounting staff is freed from the more repetitive tasks associated with the accounting cycle and can concentrate on the analysis functions.

Work sheets are not used in Automated Accounting. However, it is still necessary to plan and journalize adjusting entries at the end of the fiscal period.

A trial balance is printed or displayed to show the current account balances. Adjustments are then planned and journalized and posted to bring general ledger accounts up to date.

AUTOMATED ACCOUNTING APPLICATION PROBLEM 6-2
Open file F06-2.AA8. Display the problem instructions and complete the problem.

AUTOMATED ACCOUNTING MASTERY PROBLEM 6-5
Open file F06-5.AA8. Display the problem instructions and complete the problem.

CHAPTER 7

Financial Statements for a Proprietorship

OBJECTIVES

After studying Chapter 7, you will be able to:

1. Define accounting terms related to financial statements for a service business organized as a proprietorship.

2. Identify accounting concepts and practices related to preparation of financial statements for a service business organized as a proprietorship.

3. Prepare an income statement for a service business organized as a proprietorship and analyze an income statement using component percentages.

4. Prepare a balance sheet for a service business organized as a proprietorship.

KEY TERMS

- stakeholders
- component percentage

Point Your Browser
www.C21accounting.com

American Eagle Outfitters

King of Jeans

If you have bought a pair of jeans at American Eagle (AE), you're not alone. American Eagle sells the most jeans of any U.S. specialty store brand. In 2006, the company sold over 6.5 million pairs of jeans. And, American Eagle doesn't sell only jeans. An AE T-shirt is sold every 10 seconds.

American Eagle describes the style of its brand as "laidback, current clothing" and targets 15-to-25-year-olds. It strives for high-quality merchandise while offering it at affordable prices. Their strategy seems to be working. Sales have increased from $1.39 billion in 2003 to $2.29 billion for the year ending February, 2007. These sales are from 911 stores in the U.S., Puerto Rico, and Canada as well as through ae.com.

In 2006, AE launched its new lifestyle brand under the name of Martin + OSA. This brand is described as being able to go from the workplace to leisure activities and is targeted at 25-to-40-year-olds. American Eagle hopes that this new brand will boost sales even more in the future.

Critical Thinking

1. What account titles might you find on a balance sheet for American Eagle?

2. Why would American Eagle start a new brand of sportswear focused on the 25-to-40-year-old market?

Source: www.ae.com

INTERNET ACTIVITY

Financial Statement Analysis

Choose two companies in the same industry. Go to the homepage for each company. Search each site for its most current financial statements.

Instructions

1. List the "Total Revenue," "Total Expenses," and "Net Income" or "Net Loss" for each company.

2. For each company, calculate and record the component percentages for total expenses and net income by dividing each item by the amount of net sales. Round percentage calculations to the nearest 0.1%.

3. Compare the component percentages for net income for each company. Which company has the better component percentage?

········· **REPORTING FINANCIAL INFORMATION** ·········

The financial information needed by managers and owners to make good business decisions can be found in the general ledger accounts. However, the information in the general ledger is very detailed. Therefore, to make this general ledger information more usable, the information is summarized, organized, and reported to the owners and managers.

Also, all financial information must be reported if good business decisions are to be made. A financial statement with incomplete information is similar to a book with missing pages. The complete story is not told. If a business has both rent and utilities expenses but reports only the rent expense, managers will have incomplete information on which to base decisions. The accounting concept *Adequate Disclosure* is applied when financial statements contain all information necessary to understand a business's financial condition. [CONCEPT: Adequate Disclosure]

TechKnow Consulting prepares two financial statements: an income statement and a balance sheet. TechKnow Consulting always prepares financial statements at the end of each monthly fiscal period. [CONCEPT: Accounting Period Cycle]

When a business is started, it is expected that the business will continue to operate indefinitely. For example, Kim Park assumes that she will own and operate TechKnow Consulting for many years. When she retires, she expects to sell TechKnow Consulting to someone else, who will continue its operation. The accounting concept *Going Concern* is applied when financial statements are prepared with the expectation that a business will remain in operation indefinitely. [CONCEPT: Going Concern]

PHOTODISC/GETTY IMAGES

Identifying Stakeholders

Many states now require motorcyclists to wear helmets—a law unpopular with individuals who believe they should have the freedom of choice. Most people recognize that wearing a helmet provides the rider with extra protection in a crash. But why not allow a rider to accept the extra risk of riding without a helmet?

A well-known ethical model, the utilitarian theory, states that an ethical action is one that provides the greatest balance of good over harm. Any persons or groups who will be affected by an action are called **stakeholders**. The impact of the action on all stakeholders should be analyzed. Major stakeholders include owners, employees, customers, local communities, and society. Not every type of stakeholder will apply in each decision. However, the list of stakeholders provides a useful guide for individuals to search beyond themselves for the impact of their actions.

Examine the table below, which analyzes the impact on stakeholders involved in a motorcyclist's decision to ride without a helmet.

This analysis clearly demonstrates how a seemingly personal decision—wearing a helmet—can affect many people. Individuals must make their own conclusions from this analysis. State legislators who have voted for helmet laws believed that benefits to the motorcyclist failed to offset the negative impact on so many stakeholders. Individuals who opposed helmet laws believe the benefits to the individual offset the negative impact on all other stakeholders.

Instructions

Most colleges and universities have minimum academic standards for admission. Create a table that analyzes the positive and negative impact of admission standards. Are admission standards ethical?

Impact on Stakeholders of a Motorcyclist's Decision to Ride Without a Helmet		
Stakeholders	**Negative Impact**	**Positive Impact**
Motorcyclist	• Likely to have to pay higher insurance premiums. • May incur more serious injuries or death.	• Enjoys the freedom of riding without the confinement of a helmet.
Automobile drivers	• May suffer higher mental anguish if motorcyclist incurs more serious injuries.	• May drive more cautiously when near motorcyclists without helmets.
Relatives	• Personal lives and careers may be negatively affected if accident disables motorcyclist.	
Emergency personnel	• Risks to emergency personnel are greater because they are more aggressive when responding to serious accidents.	
Insurance companies	• Higher medical bills resulting from more serious injuries will hopefully be offset by charging higher insurance premiums.	
State	• May be subject to lawsuits by individuals who believe state was negligent in not passing a helmet law. • More serious accidents require more emergency personnel and equipment, thus spending limited resources.	
Society	• Government programs will pay for medical bills and disability payments not provided by the motorcyclist's insurance.	

	ACCOUNT TITLE	INCOME STATEMENT		BALANCE SHEET		
		5 DEBIT	**6** CREDIT	**7** DEBIT	**8** CREDIT	
12	*Sales*		3 5 6 5 00			12
13	*Advertising Expense*	2 1 3 00				13
14	*Insurance Expense*	1 0 0 00				14
15	*Miscellaneous Expense*	2 8 00				15
16	*Rent Expense*	3 0 0 00				16
17	*Supplies Expense*	7 1 5 00				17
18	*Utilities Expense*	1 1 0 00				18
19		1 4 6 6 00	3 5 6 5 00			19
20	*Net Income*	2 0 9 9 00				20
21		3 5 6 5 00	3 5 6 5 00			21
22						22

An income statement reports financial information over a specific period of time, indicating the financial progress of a business in earning a net income or a net loss. Expenses are the amounts a business pays to operate the business and earn the revenue. The revenue earned and the expenses incurred to earn that revenue are reported in the same fiscal period. [CONCEPT: Matching Expenses with Revenue]

Information needed to prepare TechKnow Consulting's income statement is obtained from two places on the work sheet. Account titles are obtained from the work sheet's Account Title column. Account balances are obtained from the work sheet's Income Statement columns. The income statement for a service business has four sections: (1) heading, (2) revenue, (3) expenses, and (4) net income or net loss.

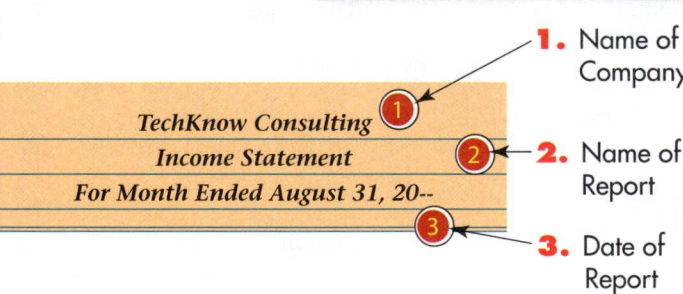

1. Name of Company

TechKnow Consulting ①
Income Statement ②
For Month Ended August 31, 20-- ③

2. Name of Report

3. Date of Report

PREPARING THE HEADING OF AN INCOME STATEMENT

S T E P S

The income statement's date shows that this income statement reports information for the one-month period from August 1 through August 31.

① Center the name of the company, *TechKnow Consulting*, on the first line.

② Center the name of the report, *Income Statement*, on the second line.

③ Center the date of the report, *For Month Ended August 31, 20--*, on the third line.

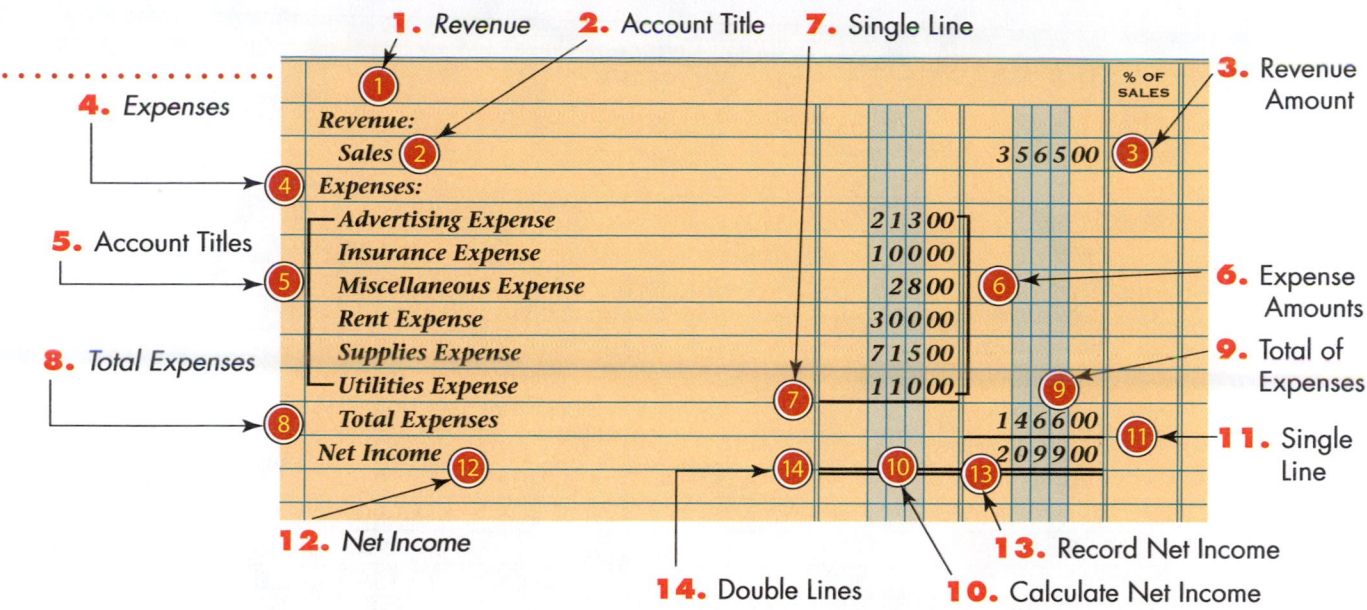

1. Revenue **2.** Account Title **7.** Single Line

4. Expenses

3. Revenue Amount

5. Account Titles

6. Expense Amounts

8. Total Expenses

9. Total of Expenses

11. Single Line

12. Net Income

13. Record Net Income

14. Double Lines

10. Calculate Net Income

STEPS **PREPARING THE REVENUE, EXPENSES, AND NET INCOME SECTIONS OF AN INCOME STATEMENT**

(1) Write the name of the first section, *Revenue:*, at the extreme left of the wide column on the first line.

(2) Write the title of the revenue account, *Sales*, on the next line, indented about one centimeter.

(3) Record the balance of the account, *$3,565.00*, on the same line in the second amount column.

(4) Write the name of the second section, *Expenses:*, on the next line at the extreme left of the wide column.

(5) Write the title of each expense account in the wide column, indented about one centimeter.

(6) Record the balance of each expense account in the first amount column on the same line as the account title.

(7) Rule a single line across the first amount column under the last expense account balance to indicate addition.

(8) Write the words *Total Expenses* on the next blank line in the wide column, indented about one centimeter.

(9) Record the amount of total expenses, *$1,466.00*, on the same line in the second amount column.

(10) Calculate and verify the amount of net income.
  a. Calculate net income from information on the income statement, as shown.
  b. Compare the amount of net income, $2,099.00, with the net income on the work sheet. If the two amounts are not the same, an error has been made.

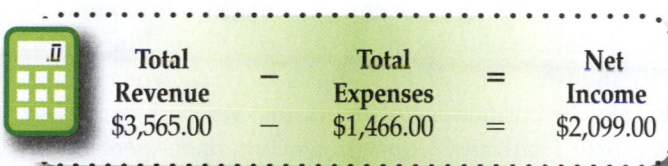

	Total Revenue	−	Total Expenses	=	Net Income
	$3,565.00	−	$1,466.00	=	$2,099.00

(11) Rule a single line across the second amount column just below the amount of total expenses.

(12) Write the words *Net Income* on the next line at the extreme left of the wide column.

(13) On the same line, record the amount of net income, *$2,099.00*, in the second amount column.

(14) Rule double lines across both amount columns below the amount of net income to show that the amount has been verified as correct.

TechKnow Consulting						
Income Statement						
For Month Ended August 31, 20--						
						% OF SALES
Revenue:						
Sales					3 5 6 5 00	100.0
Expenses:						
Advertising Expense		2 1 3 00				
Insurance Expense		1 0 0 00				
Miscellaneous Expense		2 8 00				
Rent Expense		3 0 0 00				
Supplies Expense		7 1 5 00				
Utilities Expense		1 1 0 00				
Total Expenses					1 4 6 6 00	41.1
Net Income					2 0 9 9 00	58.9

For a service business, the revenue reported on an income statement is compared to two components: (1) total expenses and (2) net income. To make decisions about future operations, a manager analyzes relationships between these two income statement components and the total sales. The percentage relationship between one financial statement item and the total that includes that item is called a **component percentage**. On an income statement, component percentages are calculated by dividing the amount of each component by the total amount of sales. TechKnow Consulting calculates a component percentage for total expenses and net income. The relationship between each component and total sales is shown in a separate column on the income statement at the right of the amount columns.

Acceptable Component Percentages

For a component percentage to be useful, Ms. Park needs to know what component percentages are acceptable for businesses similar to TechKnow Consulting. Various industry organizations publish average percentages for similar businesses. In the future, Ms. Park could also compare TechKnow Consulting's component percentages from one fiscal period with the percentages of previous fiscal periods.

Total Expenses Component Percentage

The total expenses component percentage, based on information from the August income statement, is calculated as shown. For businesses similar to TechKnow Consulting, an acceptable total expenses component percentage is not more than 55.0%. Therefore, TechKnow Consulting's percentage, 41.1%, is less than 55.0% and is acceptable.

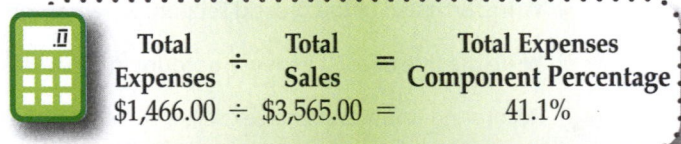

Total Expenses ÷ Total Sales = Total Expenses Component Percentage
$1,466.00 ÷ $3,565.00 = 41.1%

Net Income Component Percentage

The net income component percentage, based on information from the August income statement, is calculated as shown. For businesses similar to TechKnow Consulting, an acceptable net income component percentage is not less than 45.0%. Therefore TechKnow Consulting's percentage, 58.9%, is greater than 45.0% and is acceptable.

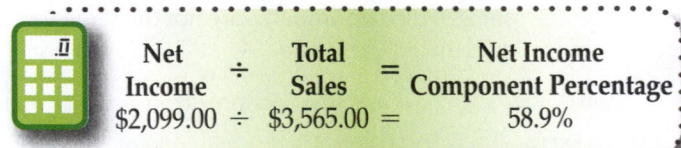

Net Income ÷ Total Sales = Net Income Component Percentage
$2,099.00 ÷ $3,565.00 = 58.9%

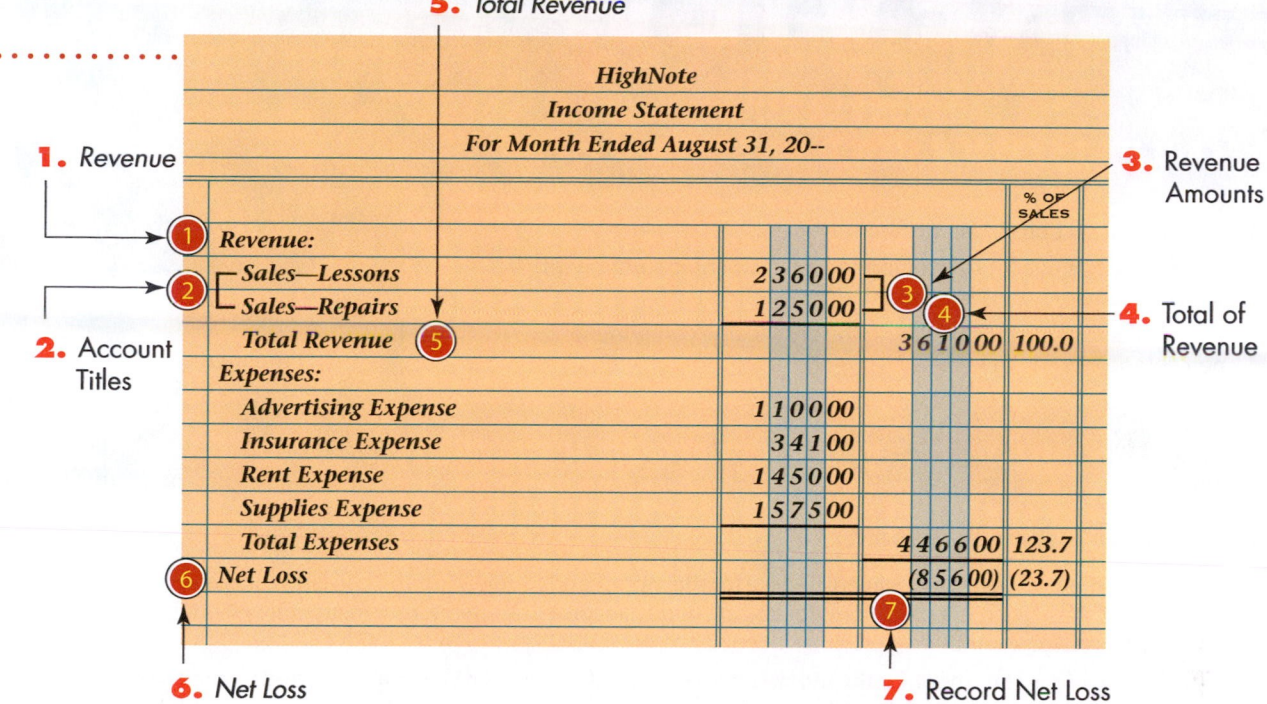

5. Total Revenue

1. Revenue

3. Revenue Amounts

4. Total of Revenue

2. Account Titles

6. Net Loss

7. Record Net Loss

The financial statement shown:

HighNote
Income Statement
For Month Ended August 31, 20--

			% OF SALES
Revenue:			
Sales—Lessons	2 3 6 0 00		
Sales—Repairs	1 2 5 0 00		
Total Revenue		3 6 1 0 00	100.0
Expenses:			
Advertising Expense	1 1 0 0 00		
Insurance Expense	3 4 1 00		
Rent Expense	1 4 5 0 00		
Supplies Expense	1 5 7 5 00		
Total Expenses		4 4 6 6 00	123.7
Net Loss		(8 5 6 00)	(23.7)

TechKnow Consulting receives revenue from only one source, the sale of services for setting up and troubleshooting computer networks. HighNote receives revenue from two sources, the sale of services for music lessons and the sale of services to repair musical instruments. The business's owner wants to know how much revenue is earned from each source. Therefore, the business uses two revenue accounts: Sales—Lessons and Sales—Repairs.

When an income statement is prepared for HighNote, both revenue accounts are listed. The revenue section of HighNote differs from the income statement prepared by TechKnow Consulting.

If total expenses exceed total revenue, a net loss is reported on an income statement. HighNote reported a net loss on its August income statement.

STEPS **PREPARING THE REVENUE SECTION OF AN INCOME STATEMENT WITH TWO SOURCES OF REVENUE**

1. Write the section heading, *Revenue:*, at the left of the wide column.

2. Write the titles of both revenue accounts in the wide column, indented about one centimeter.

3. Record the balance of each account in the first amount column on the same line as the account title.

4. Total the two revenue account balances. Write the total amount on the next line in the second amount column.

5. Write the words *Total Revenue* in the wide column, indented about one centimeter on the same line as the total revenue amount.

PREPARING THE NET LOSS SECTION OF AN INCOME STATEMENT

6. Write the words *Net Loss* at the extreme left of the wide column.

7. Subtract the total expenses from the revenue to calculate the net loss. Record the amount of net loss in the second amount column in parentheses. An amount written in parentheses on a financial statement indicates a negative amount.

End of Lesson REVIEW

AUDIT YOUR UNDERSTANDING

1. List the four sections of an income statement.
2. What is the formula for calculating the total expenses component percentage?
3. What is the formula for calculating the net income component percentage?

WORK TOGETHER 7-1

Preparing an income statement

A partial work sheet of Darlene's Delivery Service for the month ended July 31 of the current year is given in the *Working Papers*. Also given is a blank form for completing an income statement. Your instructor will guide you through the following example.

1. Prepare an income statement for the month ended July 31 of the current year. Calculate and record the component percentages for total expenses and net income. Round percentage calculations to the nearest 0.1%.

ON YOUR OWN 7-1

Preparing an income statement

A partial work sheet of Cuts by Kelley for the month ended February 28 of the current year is given in the *Working Papers*. Also given is a blank form for completing an income statement. Work this problem independently.

1. Prepare an income statement for the month ended February 28 of the current year. Calculate and record the component percentages for total expenses and net income. Round percentage calculations to the nearest 0.1%.

Balance Sheet Information on a Work Sheet

BALANCE SHEET

	ACCOUNT TITLE	7 BALANCE SHEET DEBIT	8 CREDIT	
1	Cash	4 9 6 4 00		1
2	Petty Cash	1 0 0 00		2
3	Accounts Receivable—Oakdale School	1 5 0 00		3
4	Accounts Receivable—Campus Internet Cafe	1 0 0 00		4
5	Supplies	3 1 0 00		5
6	Prepaid Insurance	1 1 0 0 00		6
7	Accounts Payable—Supply Depot		2 0 0 00	7
8	Accounts Payable—Thomas Supply Co.		5 0 00	8
9	Kim Park, Capital		5 0 0 0 00	9
10	Kim Park, Drawing	6 2 5 00		10
19		7 3 4 9 00	5 2 5 0 00	19
20	Net Income		2 0 9 9 00	20
21		7 3 4 9 00	7 3 4 9 00	21

A balance sheet reports financial information on a specific date, indicating the financial condition of a business. The financial condition of a business refers to its financial strength. If a business has adequate available assets and few liabilities, that business is financially strong. If the business's financial condition is not strong, adverse changes in the economy might cause the business to fail.

Information about assets, liabilities, and owner's equity might be obtained from the general ledger accounts or from a work sheet. However, the information is easier to use if reported in an organized manner such as on a balance sheet.

Information needed to prepare TechKnow Consulting's balance sheet is obtained from two places on the work sheet. Account titles are obtained from the work sheet's Account Title column. Account balances are obtained from the work sheet's Balance Sheet columns.

A balance sheet has four sections: (1) heading, (2) assets, (3) liabilities, and (4) owner's equity.

HEADING OF A BALANCE SHEET

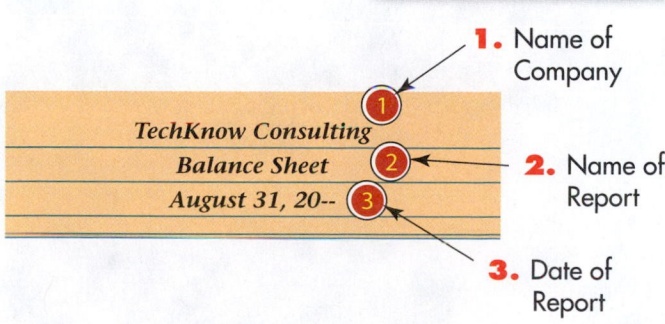

1. Name of Company

2. Name of Report

3. Date of Report

TechKnow Consulting
Balance Sheet
August 31, 20--

STEPS

PREPARING THE HEADING OF A BALANCE SHEET

1. Center the name of the company, *TechKnow Consulting*, on the first line.

2. Center the name of the report, *Balance Sheet*, on the second line.

3. Center the date of the report, *August 31, 20--*, on the third line.

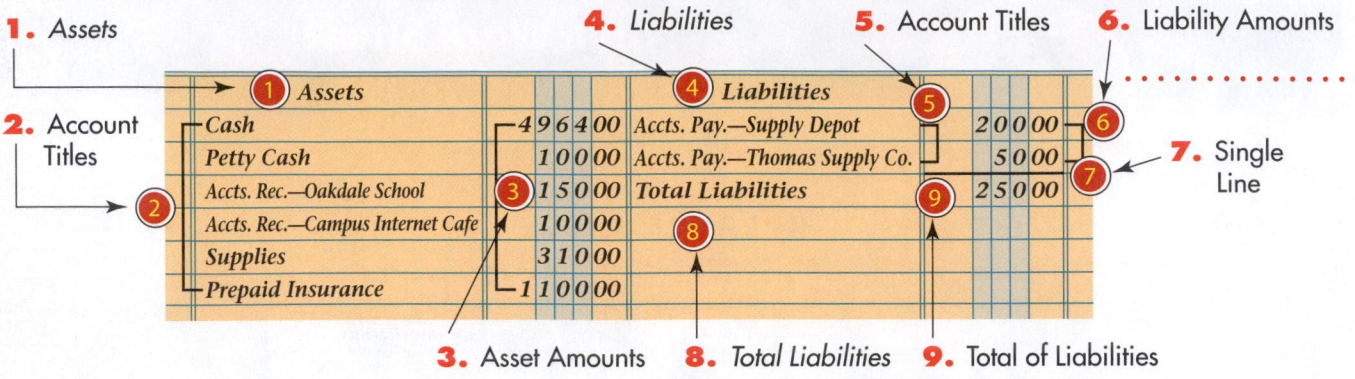

1. Assets   **4.** Liabilities   **5.** Account Titles   **6.** Liability Amounts

2. Account Titles

7. Single Line

(1) Assets		(4) Liabilities	
Cash	4 9 6 4 00	Accts. Pay.—Supply Depot	2 0 0 00
Petty Cash	1 0 0 00	Accts. Pay.—Thomas Supply Co.	5 0 00
Accts. Rec.—Oakdale School	1 5 0 00	Total Liabilities	2 5 0 00
Accts. Rec.—Campus Internet Cafe	1 0 0 00		
Supplies	3 1 0 00		
Prepaid Insurance	1 1 0 0 00		

3. Asset Amounts   **8.** Total Liabilities   **9.** Total of Liabilities

A balance sheet reports information about the elements of the accounting equation.

Assets = Liabilities + Owner's Equity

The assets are on the LEFT side of the accounting equation and on the LEFT side of TechKnow Consulting's balance sheet.

Two kinds of equities are reported on a balance sheet: (1) liabilities and (2) owner's equity. Liabilities and own-er's equity are on the RIGHT side of the accounting equation and on the RIGHT side of TechKnow Consulting's balance sheet.

The information needed to prepare the assets section is obtained from the work sheet's Account Title column and the Balance Sheet Debit column. The information needed to prepare the liabilities section is obtained from the work sheet's Account Title column and the Balance Sheet Credit column.

STEPS   PREPARING THE ASSETS AND LIABILITIES SECTIONS OF A BALANCE SHEET

(1) Write the title of the first section, *Assets*, in the middle of the left wide column.

(2) Write the titles of all asset accounts under the heading.

(3) Record the balance of each asset account in the left amount column on the same line as the account title.

(4) Write the title of the next section, *Liabilities*, in the middle of the right wide column.

(5) Write the titles of all liability accounts under the heading.

(6) Record the balance of each liability account in the right amount column on the same line as the account title.

(7) Rule a single line across the right amount column under the last amount, to indicate addition.

(8) Write the words *Total Liabilities* in the right wide column on the next blank line.

(9) Record the total of all liabilities, *$250.00*, in the right amount column.

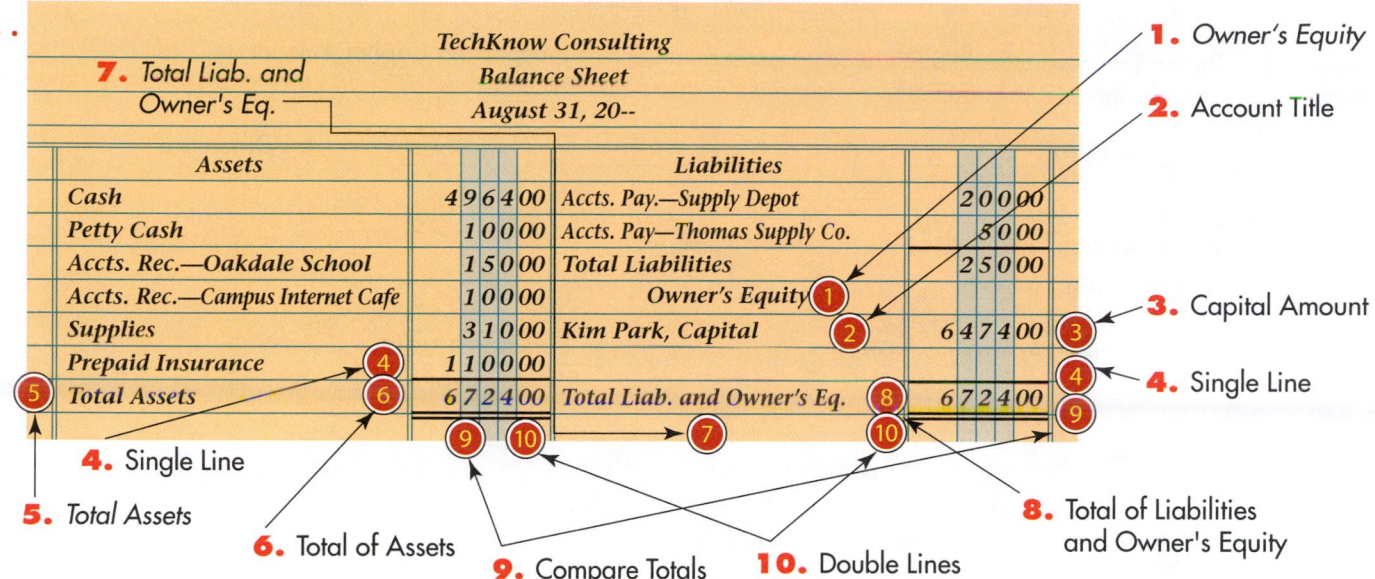

1. Owner's Equity

2. Account Title

3. Capital Amount

4. Single Line

4. Single Line

5. Total Assets

6. Total of Assets

7. Total Liab. and Owner's Eq.

8. Total of Liabilities and Owner's Equity

9. Compare Totals

10. Double Lines

Only the amount of current capital is reported on Tech-Know Consulting's balance sheet. The amounts needed to calculate the current capital are found in the work sheet's Balance Sheet columns. The amount of current capital is calculated as shown.

Capital Account Balance	+	Net Income	–	Drawing Account Balance	=	Current Capital
$5,000.00	+	$2,099.00	–	$625.00	=	$6,474.00

When a business has a net loss, current capital is calculated as shown. The current capital is reported on the balance sheet in the same way as when the business has a net income.

Capital Account Balance	–	Net Loss	–	Drawing Account Balance	=	Current Capital
$12,000.00	–	$200.00	–	$500.00	=	$11,300.00

STEPS · PREPARING THE OWNER'S EQUITY SECTION OF A BALANCE SHEET

1 Write the title of the section, *Owner's Equity*, in the middle of the right wide column on the next line below "Total Liabilities."

2 Write the title of the owner's capital account, *Kim Park, Capital*, on the next line.

3 Record the current amount of owner's equity, *$6,474.00*, in the right amount column.

4 Rule a single line under the last amount in the longer left amount column. Rule a single line in the right amount column on the same line.

5 Write the words *Total Assets* on the next line, in the left wide column.

6 Record the amount of total assets, *$6,724.00*, in the left amount column.

7 Write the words *Total Liab. and Owner's Eq.* in the right wide column on the same line as Total Assets.

8 Record the amount of total liabilities and owner's equity, *$6,724.00*, in the right amount column.

9 Compare the totals of the two amount columns. The totals are the same, so the balance sheet is in balance.

10 Rule double lines across both the left and right amount columns just below the column totals to show that the totals have been verified as correct.

OWNER'S EQUITY REPORTED IN DETAIL ON A BALANCE SHEET

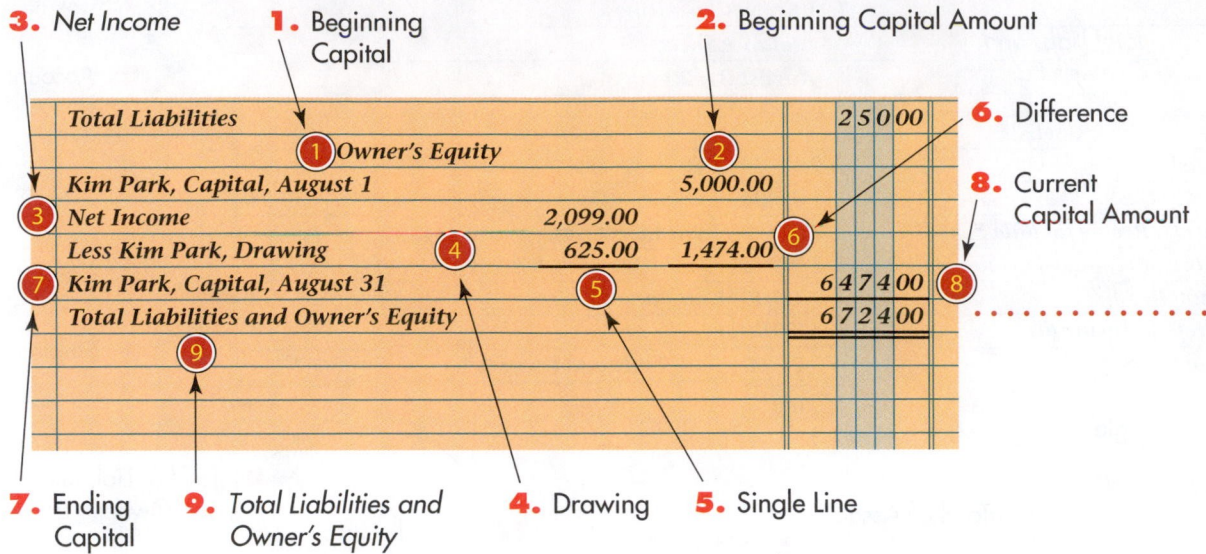

3. Net Income **1.** Beginning Capital **2.** Beginning Capital Amount **6.** Difference **8.** Current Capital Amount

7. Ending Capital **9.** Total Liabilities and Owner's Equity **4.** Drawing **5.** Single Line

TechKnow Consulting's balance sheet reports the current capital on August 31 but does not show how this amount was calculated. TechKnow Consulting is a small business with relatively few changes in owner's equity to report. Therefore, Kim Park decided that the business does not need to report all the details in the owner's equity sec-tion. However, some businesses prefer to report the details about how owner's equity is calculated.

If TechKnow Consulting were to report details about owner's equity, the owner's equity section of the balance sheet would be prepared as shown in the illustration.

STEPS PREPARING THE OWNER'S EQUITY SECTION REPORTED IN DETAIL ON A BALANCE SHEET

1. Write the words *Kim Park, Capital, August 1* on the first line under the words "Owner's Equity."

2. Record the owner's capital account balance on August 1, *$5,000.00*, in the wide column.

3. Write the words *Net Income* on the next line. Record the net income, *$2,099.00*, in the wide column to the left of the capital account balance.

4. Write the words *Less Kim Park, Drawing* on the next line. Record the balance of the drawing account, *$625.00*, in the wide column.

5. Rule a single line under the amount.

6. Subtract the balance of the drawing account from the net income. Record the difference, *$1,474.00*, in the wide column to the right of the drawing account balance.

7. Write the words *Kim Park, Capital, August 31* on the next line.

8. Add the August 1 capital amount, *$5,000.00*, and the difference between the net income and the drawing account, *$1,474.00*. Record the sum, *$6,474.00*, in the right amount column.

9. Write the words *Total Liabilities and Owner's Equity* on the next line. Record the amount of total liabilities and owner's equity, *$6,724.00*, in the right amount column.

> **REMEMBER**
>
> Capital is not copied from the work sheet to the balance sheet. Capital is calculated using beginning capital, plus net income or minus net loss, minus drawing.

Eric Feng, Entrepreneur/Franchisee

COURTESY OF ERIC FENG

Entrepreneurial spirit is the foundation of our economy. From Henry Ford to Sam Walton to Bill Gates, individuals have dreamed of controlling their destiny by starting their own business. These entrepreneurs identified a need in the marketplace and developed a product to fill that need. Through vision and determination, they created three of the best-known corporations in the world.

Eric Feng is an example of how an entrepreneurial spirit can launch a successful business. He says, "I wanted to be my own boss—a dream for many people—and we were no exception." Eric and his wife, Candy, came to the United States as foreign students to pursue advanced college degrees. Eric finished a master's degree in computer science, and Candy earned a degree in accounting. After several years of working for the local university, they decided it was time to turn their dream into reality.

"We took our first step when we decided to purchase a franchise for a quick-serve restaurant," Eric recalls. After researching numerous opportunities, they decided to pursue the purchase of an Arby's franchise. "We did not have any experience managing a company, much less a restaurant business, nor did we have any significant capital to invest in the business. What we did have, however, was our knowledge of accounting."

The Fengs prepared an extensive business plan that outlined in detail the amount of capital that would be required. The business plan included budgets of sales, expenses, and net income under several different sets of assumptions. They then submitted the business plan to the commercial loan officers of several local banks. "The loan officers at the National Bank of Commerce were confident enough in our business plan to provide us the financing we needed to make our dream come true. The reason, we were told later, was that we had a well-thought-out business plan that made good business sense. All business ventures involve risk. Thanks to the accounting and computer backgrounds we had, we were able to evaluate the business venture in financial accounting terms and demonstrate to the bank that it was a risk worth taking."

Like many entrepreneurs, the Fengs have expanded their operations beyond their initial restaurant. Now the owners of three Arby's units, Eric and Candy credit their success to their knowledge of accounting. "Business success is not a matter of luck. We owe what we have today to our knowledge of accounting and our insistence on quality in all we do."

Salary Range: Virtually unlimited, although the net income from a single unit of a franchise is limited by its physical size and location. However, like the Fengs, an entrepreneur can acquire many units of the same franchise.

Qualifications: Franchisors provide potential franchisees with information on qualifications, which may include specific levels of financial net worth, access to operating capital, and personal experience in the industry.

Occupational Outlook: On its web site (www. franchise.org), the International Franchise Association lists over 800 corporations that offer franchises. Each of these franchisors is actively seeking entrepreneurs to expand the number of company units in operation.

End of Lesson REVIEW

AUDIT YOUR UNDERSTANDING

1. List the four sections on a balance sheet.
2. What is the formula for calculating current capital?

WORK TOGETHER 7-2

Preparing a balance sheet

A partial work sheet of Ken's Carpet Cleaning for the month ended April 30 of the current year is given in the *Working Papers*. Also given is a blank form for completing a balance sheet. Your instructor will guide you through the following example.

1. Prepare a balance sheet for April 30 of the current year.

ON YOUR OWN 7-2

Preparing a balance sheet

A partial work sheet of Anne's Alterations for the month ended October 31 of the current year is given in the *Working Papers*. Also given is a blank form for completing a balance sheet. Work this problem independently.

1. Prepare a balance sheet for October 31 of the current year.

After completing this chapter, you can:

1. Define accounting terms related to financial statements for a service business organized as a proprietorship.

2. Identify accounting concepts and practices related to preparation of financial statements for a service business organized as a proprietorship.

3. Prepare an income statement for a service business organized as a proprietorship and analyze an income statement using component percentages.

4. Prepare a balance sheet for a service business organized as a proprietorship.

EXPLORE ACCOUNTING

Comparative and Interim Financial Statements

A corporation that trades its stock on a U.S. stock exchange must submit an annual report to the Securities and Exchange Commission (SEC). The SEC has specific requirements as to what must be included in the financial statements.

One requirement is that the financial statements included in the annual report must show amounts for more than one year. The balance sheet must show ending balances for the current and the previous year. The income statement and statement of stockholder's equity must show amounts for the current year and the two previous years. Financial statements providing information for multiple fiscal periods are called *comparative financial statements*.

These statements make it possible for a user to compare performance from year to year. For example, the net income for the current year can be compared to the net income for the two previous years. In this way, the user can determine if there is a positive or negative trend occurring in net income. On the balance sheet, the ending cash balance for the current year can be compared to the ending cash balance from the previous year to determine if the amount of cash on hand is increasing or decreasing.

Businesses that are required to submit an annual report to the SEC must also submit a quarterly report. This report is not as detailed as the annual report, but it must include the financial statements for the quarter. Financial statements providing information for a time period shorter than the fiscal year are called *interim financial statements*. Users of financial information are able to evaluate the progress of the firm every three months rather than waiting an entire year. The importance of interim financial statements can be verified by the fact that the results reported in these statements are often summarized and reported in financial news sources, such as *The Wall Street Journal* and CNBC.

Activity: Contact a corporation near you. Ask if the business prepares interim financial statements and, if it does, find out how often these statements are prepared.

7-1 APPLICATION PROBLEM

Preparing an income statement

A form is given in the *Working Papers*. The following information is obtained from the work sheet of Len's Laundry for the month ended August 31 of the current year.

	ACCOUNT TITLE	5 INCOME STATEMENT DEBIT	6 INCOME STATEMENT CREDIT	7 BALANCE SHEET DEBIT	8 BALANCE SHEET CREDIT	
11	Sales		6 2 3 3 00			11
12	Advertising Expense	8 0 0 00				12
13	Insurance Expense	2 0 0 00				13
14	Miscellaneous Expense	3 1 5 00				14
15	Supplies Expense	4 5 0 00				15
16	Utilities Expense	1 4 9 5 00				16
17		3 2 6 0 00	6 2 3 3 00	1 0 4 3 6 00	7 4 6 3 00	17
18	Net Income	2 9 7 3 00			2 9 7 3 00	18
19		6 2 3 3 00	6 2 3 3 00	1 0 4 3 6 00	1 0 4 3 6 00	19
20						20
21						21

Instructions:

1. Prepare an income statement for the month ended August 31 of the current year.

2. Calculate and record the component percentages for total expenses and net income. Round percentage calculations to the nearest 0.1%.

7-2 APPLICATION PROBLEM

Preparing a balance sheet

A form is given in the *Working Papers*. The following information is obtained from the work sheet of Len's Laundry for the month ended August 31 of the current year.

	ACCOUNT TITLE	7 BALANCE SHEET DEBIT	8 BALANCE SHEET CREDIT	
1	Cash	7 6 0 7 00		1
2	Accts. Rec.—Natasha Goodlad	7 0 0 00		2
3	Accts. Rec.—R. Henry	4 9 8 00		3
4	Supplies	4 3 1 00		4
5	Prepaid Insurance	2 0 0 00		5
6	Accts. Pay.—Tri-County Supplies		3 8 1 00	6
7	Accts. Pay.—West End Supply Co.		5 5 5 00	7
8	Leonard Long, Capital		6 5 2 7 00	8
9	Leonard Long, Drawing	1 0 0 0 00		9
10	Income Summary			10
17		1 0 4 3 6 00	7 4 6 3 00	17
18	Net Income		2 9 7 3 00	18
19		1 0 4 3 6 00	1 0 4 3 6 00	19
20				20

Instructions:

Prepare a balance sheet for August 31 of the current year.

7-3 MASTERY PROBLEM

Preparing financial statements with a net loss

Forms are given in the *Working Papers*. The following information is obtained from the work sheet of Rolstad Repair Service for the month ended September 30 of the current year.

	ACCOUNT TITLE	INCOME STATEMENT		BALANCE SHEET		
		DEBIT	CREDIT	DEBIT	CREDIT	
1	Cash			6 9 5 8 00		1
2	Petty Cash			1 5 0 00		2
3	Accts. Rec.—M. Hollerud			1 9 7 00		3
4	Supplies			7 8 0 00		4
5	Prepaid Insurance			8 0 0 00		5
6	Accts. Pay.—Tampa Supply				6 1 2 00	6
7	Ron Rolstad, Capital				9 3 3 7 00	7
8	Ron Rolstad, Drawing			6 0 0 00		8
9	Income Summary					9
10	Sales		3 2 6 9 00			10
11	Advertising Expense	4 5 0 00				11
12	Insurance Expense	1 5 7 00				12
13	Miscellaneous Expense	8 5 00				13
14	Supplies Expense	1 4 0 0 00				14
15	Utilities Expense	1 6 4 1 00				15
16		3 7 3 3 00	3 2 6 9 00	9 4 8 5 00	9 9 4 9 00	16
17	Net Loss		4 6 4 00	4 6 4 00		17
18		3 7 3 3 00	3 7 3 3 00	9 9 4 9 00	9 9 4 9 00	18
19						19
20						20

Instructions:

1. Prepare an income statement for the month ended September 30 of the current year.

2. Calculate and record the component percentages for total expenses and net loss. Place the percentage for net loss in parentheses to show that it is for a net loss. Round percentage calculations to the nearest 0.1%.

3. Prepare a balance sheet for September 30 of the current year.

CHALLENGE PROBLEM

Preparing financial statements with two sources of revenue and a net loss

Forms are given in the *Working Papers*. The information below is obtained from the work sheet of LawnMow for the month ended October 31 of the current year.

		5	6	7	8	
	ACCOUNT TITLE	INCOME STATEMENT		BALANCE SHEET		
		DEBIT	CREDIT	DEBIT	CREDIT	
1	Cash			1 8 9 8 00		1
2	Accts. Rec.—Sandra Rohe			9 5 00		2
3	Supplies			6 5 0 00		3
4	Prepaid Insurance			1 2 0 0 00		4
5	Accts. Pay.—Corner Garage				5 8 00	5
6	Accts. Pay.—Broadway Gas				1 1 0 00	6
7	Accts. Pay.—Esko Repair				2 1 5 00	7
8	Ryo Morrison, Capital				4 0 0 0 00	8
9	Ryo Morrison, Drawing			1 0 0 00		9
10	Income Summary					10
11	Sales—Lawn Care		4 9 0 0 00			11
12	Sales—Shrub Care		2 5 0 0 00			12
13	Advertising Expense	3 9 0 00				13
14	Insurance Expense	4 0 0 00				14
15	Miscellaneous Expense	5 5 0 00				15
16	Rent Expense	3 3 0 0 00				16
17	Supplies Expense	3 2 0 0 00				17
18		7 8 4 0 00	7 4 0 0 00	3 9 4 3 00	4 3 8 3 00	18
19	Net Loss		4 4 0 00	4 4 0 00		19
20		7 8 4 0 00	7 8 4 0 00	4 3 8 3 00	4 3 8 3 00	20
21						21

Instructions:

1. Prepare an income statement for the month ended October 31 of the current year.

2. Calculate and record the component percentages for total expenses and net loss. Place the percentage for net loss in parentheses to show that it is for a net loss. Round percentage calculations to the nearest 0.1%.

3. Prepare a balance sheet for October 31 of the current year.

Assume that you are the owner of a proprietorship, and you have just hired a new assistant. In the past, your assistants have had difficulty understanding the importance of financial statements to your business.

Instructions: Write down what you would say to your assistant about the importance of income statements and balance sheets in making financial decisions. Your statements should be no longer than one or two paragraphs.

CASE FOR CRITICAL THINKING

Romelle Woods and Ahti Indihar each own small businesses. Ms. Woods prepares an income statement and balance sheet at the end of each day for her business, in order to make business decisions. Mr. Indihar prepares an income statement and balance sheet for his business only at the end of each one-year fiscal period, when preparing tax reports. Which owner is using the better procedure? Explain your answer.

GRAPHING WORKSHOP

The net income figures for three companies for three years are given below.

	2005	2006	2007
Atlas Company	15,000	17,000	14,000
Mertzel Company	13,000	15,000	17,000
Tampeau Company	16,000	14,000	13,000

Develop a graph that will best illustrate the difference in the net income for each company each year. Decide for yourself which type of graph to use.

ANALYZING BEST BUY'S FINANCIAL STATEMENTS

Best Buy's financial reports include a consolidated statement of earnings, which is shown in Appendix B page B-6. This statement reports revenue, expenses, and operating income similar to an income statement for a proprietorship. Best Buy's statement of earnings is more complex than the income statement described in this chapter. Besides reporting net income (called *net earnings*), it also reports "Earnings from continuing operations." The difference between these two amounts is caused by discontinuing or selling a portion of the company or because of changes in accounting procedures.

Instructions

1. What are Best Buy's net earnings for each of the three years?

2. What are Best Buy's earnings from continuing operations for each of the three years?

3. Note 2 to the financial statements is on page B-20. Note 2 tells about discontinuing or selling a portion of the company. Read Note 2. What portion of the company was sold that caused the difference between net earnings and earnings from continuing operations in 2004?

Accounting
SOFTWARE

GENERATING FINANCIAL STATEMENTS

As an elementary student, you learned to add, subtract, multiply, and divide—the basic functions of math. In junior high and high school, you learned algebra and geometry—more complex and sophisticated levels of math.

Throughout this chapter, you have been learning the basic functions of accounting. When you use Peachtree to print an income statement and balance sheet, you will note some terms and headings that you have not yet learned, such as Cost of Goods Sold, Gross Profit, Current Assets, and Long-term Liabilities. Peachtree was developed assuming that you, the user, possess a more complete knowledge of accounting. Be patient; you will learn about these terms as you continue your accounting education.

PEACHTREE MASTERY PROBLEM 7-3

1. Open (Restore) file 07-3MP.ptb.
2. Print an income statement and balance sheet.

PEACHTREE CHALLENGE PROBLEM 7-4

1. Open (Restore) file 07-4CP.ptb.
2. Print an income statement and balance sheet.

GENERATING FINANCIAL STATEMENTS

Accounting terms vary from company to company. This chapter discussed the income statement, which shows net income or net loss. Another name for this statement is *profit and loss statement*. QuickBooks uses the title Profit & Loss to identify a statement that shows net income or net loss.

Financial statements also vary in format. The financial statements printed in QuickBooks may contain terms, such as current assets or current liabilities, that have not been covered in this course. These terms will be defined in a later chapter. Regardless of the terms used, the financial statements still provide the same basic information and can still be analyzed in the same way.

QUICKBOOKS MASTERY PROBLEM 7-3

Note: For all printouts, add a custom footer that includes your name and the problem number; print in portrait orientation

1. Open the Rolstad Repair Service file.
2. Print a profit and loss statement for the month ended September 30. Use the Reports menu and choose Company & Financial.
3. Modify the report to include component percentages for expenses and net loss as a percentage of sales.
4. Print a standard balance sheet as of September 30.

QUICKBOOKS CHALLENGE PROBLEM 7-4

1. Open the LawnMow file.
2. Print a profit and loss report for October 1 through October 31, including component percentages.
3. Generate a balance sheet for October 31.

GENERATING FINANCIAL STATEMENTS

Data and *information* are often considered synonymous terms. Accountants use the term *data* to refer to unorganized facts. In contrast, *information* is data that has been organized and is presented in a manner that can be understood by the reader.

An income statement organizes the current balances of revenue and expense accounts to inform the reader how effectively the business has operated during a fiscal period. For a business that has incurred a net loss, accountants have commonly reported negative amounts by using a hyphen in front of the number or by surrounding the number with parentheses.

Today's electronic spreadsheets provide accountants with an additional method of alerting the reader to a net loss. Negative values can also be displayed in red font. You have probably heard someone say "in the red" when referring to a business that is losing money. By allowing negative numbers to appear in red, the electronic spreadsheet uses this traditional association to further communicate that the business has incurred a net loss.

EXCEL MASTERY PROBLEM 7-3

1. Open the F07-3 Excel data file.

2. Follow the step-by-step instructions in the Instructions work sheet to change the cell format of the net loss amount.

GENERATING FINANCIAL STATEMENTS

One of the advantages of using accounting software is that once transaction data are entered, the software prepares financial statements automatically.

To display financial statements:

1. Click the Reports toolbar button, or choose the Report Selection menu item from the Report menu.

2. When the Report Selection dialog appears, choose the Financial Statements option from the Select a Report Group list.

3. Choose the financial statement report you would like to display from the Choose a Report to Display list.

4. Click the OK button.

The up-to-date account balances stored by the software are used to calculate and display the current financial statements. A component percentage is included for each dollar amount. Component percentages calculated on the income statement show the relationship of items to total sales.

The balance sheet reports information about assets, liabilities, and owner's equity on a specific date. Additional information about owner's equity can be obtained by selecting the Statement of Owner's Equity. This statement shows changes to the capital account during the period.

When a report is displayed in *Automated Accounting*, it can also be copied in word processor or spreadsheet format by pressing the Copy button at the bottom of the report window. The report can then be pasted into a word processing document or spreadsheet for additional processing or distribution. For example, if an income statement were pasted into a spreadsheet, amounts could be changed to perform "what-if" analysis, such as "What if sales increased by 25%: what would the effect on net income be?"

AUTOMATED ACCOUNTING APPLICATION PROBLEMS 7-1 AND 7-2

Open file F07-1.AA8. Display the problem instructions and complete the problems.

AUTOMATED ACCOUNTING CHALLENGE PROBLEM 7-4

Open file F07-4.AA8. Display the problem instructions and complete the problem.

DIGITAL VISION/GETTY IMAGES

CHAPTER 8

Recording Adjusting and Closing Entries for a Service Business

OBJECTIVES

After studying Chapter 8, you will be able to:

1. Define accounting terms related to adjusting and closing entries for a service business organized as a proprietorship.

2. Identify accounting concepts and practices related to adjusting and closing entries for a service business organized as a proprietorship.

3. Record adjusting entries for a service business organized as a proprietorship.

4. Record closing entries for a service business organized as a proprietorship.

5. Prepare a post-closing trial balance for a service business organized as a proprietorship.

KEY TERMS

- adjusting entries
- permanent accounts
- temporary accounts
- closing entries
- post-closing trial balance
- accounting cycle

Point Your Browser
www.C21accounting.com

The Walt Disney Company

Conservation Is Good Business at The Walt Disney Company

Say the word "Disney" and you may think of any one of hundreds of movies produced by Walt Disney Studios. You may think of a wild, exciting ride in one of the Disney theme parks around the world. You may even think of a fun-filled resort area within Walt Disney World in Orlando.

How many of you, however, would think of the environment when you hear the word "Disney"? In 1990, The Walt Disney Company introduced an initiative called "Environmentality." Disney Online describes Environmentality as "a fundamental ethic that blends business growth with the conservation of natural resources. Attention to the environment drives new business initiatives, demonstrating how environmental stewardship goes hand-in-hand with bottom-line cost savings." Environmentality goes beyond just complying with laws. It includes "purchasing recycled products, waste minimization, resource conservation, research and development, community involvement, and education" to make the program successful.

A 2003 report designed to highlight environmental accomplishments describes many examples of waste reductions and resource conservation. One example is a water-monitoring program in Disney's Animal Kingdom. The monitoring results identified areas where water usage could be reduced, saving an estimated 145,000,000 gallons of water each year.

©GREG E. MATHIESON/MAI/LANDOV

Critical Thinking

1. List at least two reasons why The Walt Disney Company would be interested in such environmental measures.

2. If The Walt Disney Company purchased equipment to help measure water usage, would that equipment be classified as an asset, liability, or owner's equity on the balance sheet? Why?

Source: disney.go.com

INTERNET ACTIVITY

Closing Entries

Go to the homepage for a company or corporation of your choice. Search the site for the most recent annual report. Go to the income statement.

Instructions

1. Looking at the categories of revenues on the income statement, list the accounts that may be included in the company's entry to close the revenue accounts.

2. Looking at the categories of expenses on the income statement, list the accounts that may be included in the company's entry to close the expense accounts.

ADJUSTING ENTRIES

TechKnow Consulting prepares a work sheet at the end of each fiscal period to summarize the general ledger information needed to prepare financial statements. [CONCEPT: Accounting Period Cycle] Financial statements are prepared from information on the work sheet. [CONCEPT: Adequate Disclosure]

TechKnow Consulting's adjustments are analyzed and planned on a work sheet. However, these adjustments must be journalized so they can be posted to the general ledger accounts. Journal entries recorded to update general ledger accounts at the end of a fiscal period are called **adjusting entries**.

Adjusting entries are recorded on the next journal page following the page on which the last daily transactions for the month are recorded.

ADJUSTING ENTRY FOR SUPPLIES

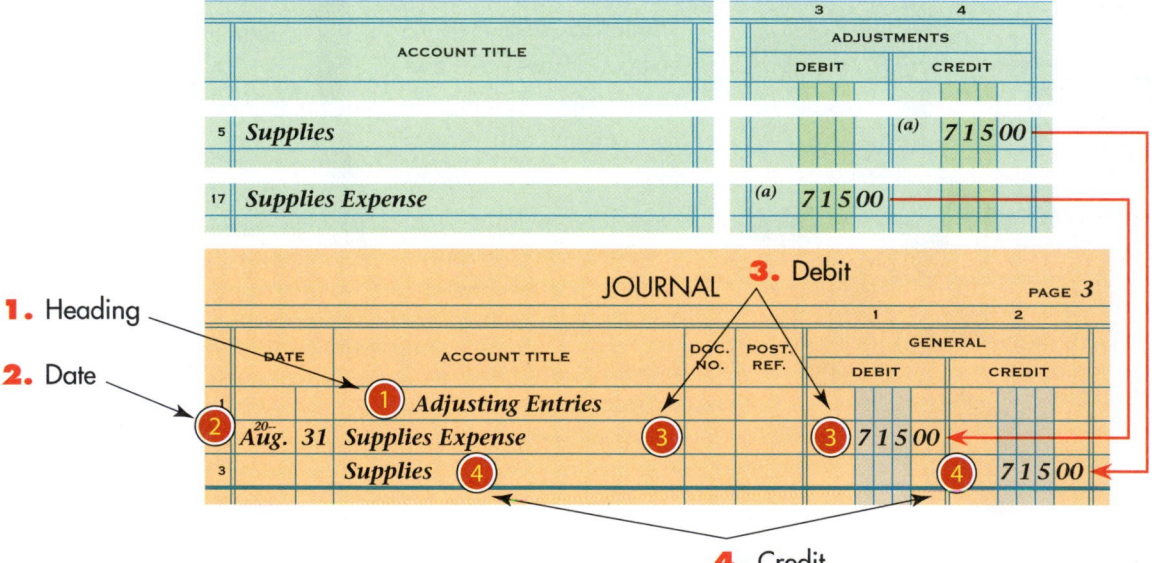

The information needed to journalize the adjusting entry for Supplies is obtained from lines 5 and 17 of the work sheet, as shown in the illustration. The entry must be recorded in a journal and posted to the general ledger accounts affected by the entry.

The effect of posting the adjusting entry for supplies to the general ledger accounts is shown in the T accounts.

Supplies Expense has an up-to-date balance of $715.00, which is the value of the supplies used during the fiscal period. [CONCEPT: Matching Expenses with Revenue]

Supplies has a new balance of $310.00, which is the cost of the supplies on hand at the end of the fiscal period.

Supplies Expense		
Adj. (a)	715.00	

Supplies		
Bal.	1,025.00	Adj. (a) 715.00
(New Bal.	310.00)	

1. Write the heading, *Adjusting Entries*, in the middle of the Account Title column of the journal. Because no source document is prepared for adjusting entries, the entries are identified with a heading in the journal. The heading is written only once for all adjusting entries.

2. Write the date, *20--, Aug. 31*, in the Date column.

3. Write the title of the account debited, *Supplies Expense*, in the Account Title column. Record the debit amount, *$715.00*, in the General Debit column on the same line as the account title.

4. Write the title of the account credited, *Supplies*, on the next line in the Account Title column. Record the credit amount, *$715.00*, in the General Credit column on the same line as the account title.

CHARACTER COUNTS

Can I Say This on My Resume?

Kendra Wheeler applied for a payroll clerk job with Hampton Group. She slightly exaggerated her work experience on her resume. She felt uncomfortable with this decision, but she was desperate to get a job.

Based on the resume, Kendra was hired. After one year, she received above-average ratings during her annual review. Then, her boss met Kendra's former supervisor and learned the truth.

Was Kendra's action unethical? Let's apply the ethical model to this situation.

1. *Recognize you are facing an ethical dilemma.* Kendra should have realized that her uncomfortable feelings were a sign that her actions might not be ethical.

2. *Identify the action taken or the proposed action.* Kendra could have stated her qualifications honestly. However, she elected to exaggerate her work experience. That action will be evaluated in the following steps.

3. *Analyze the action.*

a. *Is the action illegal?* No. Overstating qualifications is not illegal, but the employer could terminate her employment.

b. *Does the action violate company or professional standards?* No. Kendra was neither an employee of the company nor a member of any profession at the time she was hired.

c. *Who is affected, and how, by the action?*

Impact on Stakeholders of Exaggerating Work Experience on a Resume		
Stakeholders	**Negative**	**Positive**
Kendra	• She might be terminated. • If retained, she could have difficulty being promoted.	• She obtained employment.
Other applicants	• More highly qualified applicants lost an employment opportunity.	
Hampton Group	• The company lost the opportunity of receiving the benefits of a more qualified employee. • If Kendra is terminated, the company must train another employee. • If Kendra is retained, managers may hesitate to give Kendra responsibilities necessary for the efficient operation of the company.	

4. *Determine if the action is ethical.* Kendra's action was not ethical. Exaggerating her resume provided her with a short-term benefit. However, this benefit does not outweigh the negative impact on other applicants and the Hampton Group. In fact, Kendra's action could possibly cause her more harm in the long run.

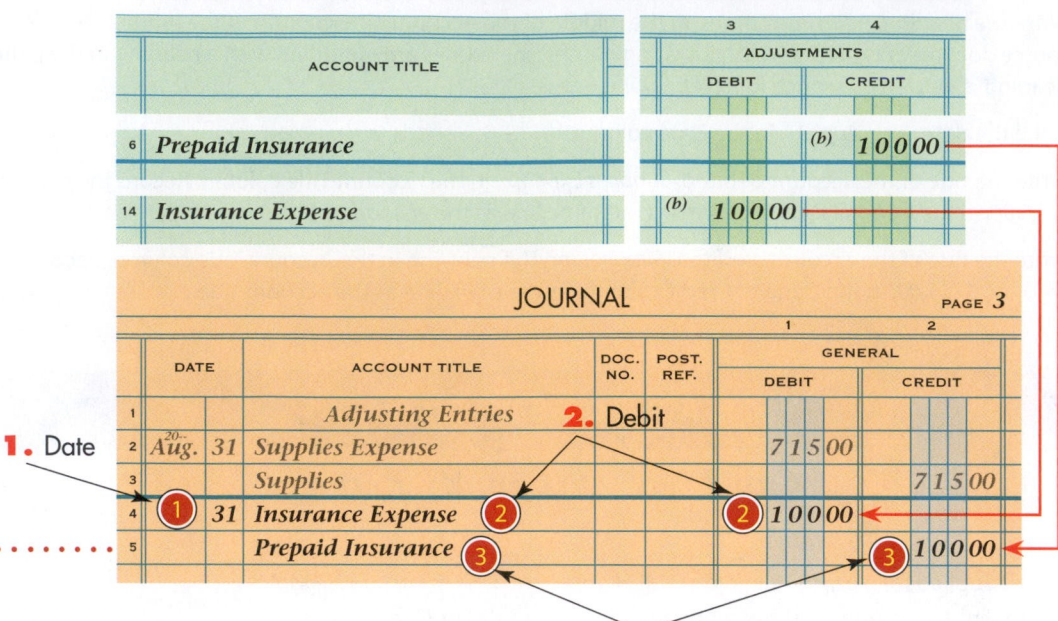

	ACCOUNT TITLE		ADJUSTMENTS	
			DEBIT	CREDIT
6	*Prepaid Insurance*			(b) 1 0 0 00
14	*Insurance Expense*		(b) 1 0 0 00	

JOURNAL   PAGE *3*

	DATE	ACCOUNT TITLE	DOC. NO.	POST. REF.	GENERAL DEBIT	GENERAL CREDIT
1		*Adjusting Entries*				
2	20-- Aug. 31	*Supplies Expense*			7 1 5 00	
3		*Supplies*				7 1 5 00
4	31	*Insurance Expense*			1 0 0 00	
5		*Prepaid Insurance*				1 0 0 00

1. Date   **2.** Debit   **3.** Credit

The information needed to journalize the adjusting entry for Prepaid Insurance is obtained from lines 6 and 14 of the work sheet. The entry must be recorded in a journal and posted to the general ledger accounts affected by the entry.

The effect of posting the adjusting entry for Prepaid Insurance to the general ledger accounts is shown in the T accounts.

| Insurance Expense | |
| Adj. (b)   100.00 | |

Prepaid Insurance	
Bal. 1,200.00	Adj. (b) 100.00
(New Bal. *1,100.00)*	

PHOTODISC/GETTY IMAGES

STEPS

ADJUSTING ENTRY FOR PREPAID INSURANCE

1. Write the date, *31*, in the Date column.

2. Write the title of the account debited, *Insurance Expense*, in the Account Title column. Record the debit amount, *$100.00*, in the General Debit column on the same line as the account title.

3. Write the title of the account credited, *Prepaid Insurance*, on the next line in the Account Title column. Record the credit amount, *$100.00*, in the General Credit column on the same line as the account title.

End of Lesson
REVIEW

TERM REVIEW

adjusting entries

1. Why are adjusting entries journalized?
2. Where is the information obtained to journalize adjusting entries?
3. What accounts are increased from zero balances after adjusting entries for supplies and prepaid insurance are journalized and posted?

WORK TOGETHER 8-1

Journalizing and posting adjusting entries

A partial work sheet of Darlene's Delivery Service for the month ended July 31 of the current year is given in the *Working Papers*. Also given are a journal and general ledger accounts. The general ledger accounts do not show all details for the fiscal period. The balance shown in each account is the account's balance before adjusting entries are posted. Your instructor will guide you through the following example.

1. Use page 4 of a journal. Journalize and post the adjusting entries. Save your work to complete Work Together 8-2.

ON YOUR OWN 8-1

Journalizing and posting adjusting entries

A partial work sheet of Cuts by Kelley for the month ended February 28 of the current year is given in the *Working Papers*. Also given are a journal and general ledger accounts. The general ledger accounts do not show all details for the fiscal period. The balance shown in each account is the account's balance before adjusting entries are posted. Work this problem independently.

1. Use page 8 of a journal. Journalize and post the adjusting entries. Save your work to complete On Your Own 8-2.

NEED FOR PERMANENT AND TEMPORARY ACCOUNTS

Accounts used to accumulate information from one fiscal period to the next are called **permanent accounts**. Permanent accounts are also referred to as *real accounts*. Permanent accounts include the asset and liability accounts and the owner's capital account. The ending account balances of permanent accounts for one fiscal period are the beginning account balances for the next fiscal period.

Accounts used to accumulate information until it is transferred to the owner's capital account are called

temporary accounts. Temporary accounts are also referred to as *nominal accounts*. Temporary accounts include the revenue, expense, and owner's drawing accounts plus the income summary account. Temporary accounts show changes in the owner's capital for a single fiscal period. Therefore, at the end of a fiscal period, the balances of temporary accounts are summarized and transferred to the owner's capital account. The temporary accounts begin a new fiscal period with zero balances.

NEED FOR CLOSING TEMPORARY ACCOUNTS

Journal entries used to prepare temporary accounts for a new fiscal period are called **closing entries**. The temporary account balances must be reduced to zero at the end of each fiscal period. This procedure prepares the

PHOTODISC/GETTY IMAGES

temporary accounts for recording information about the next fiscal period. Otherwise, the amounts for the next fiscal period would be added to amounts for previous fiscal periods. [CONCEPT: Matching Expenses with Revenue] The net income for the next fiscal period would be difficult to calculate because amounts from several fiscal periods remain in the accounts. Therefore, the temporary accounts must start each new fiscal period with zero balances.

To close a temporary account, an amount equal to its balance is recorded in the account on the side opposite to its balance. For example, if an account has a credit balance of $3,565.00, a debit of $3,565.00 is recorded to close the account.

Whenever a temporary account is closed, the closing entry must have equal debits and credits. If an account is debited for $3,000.00 to close the account, some other account must be credited for the same amount. A temporary account titled Income Summary is used to summarize the closing entries for the revenue and expense accounts.

The income summary account is unique because it does not have a normal balance side. The balance of this account is determined by the amounts posted to the account at the end of a fiscal period. When revenue is greater than total expenses, resulting in a net income, the income summary account has a credit balance, as shown in the T account.

Income Summary	
Debit	Credit
Total expenses	Revenue (greater than expenses)
	(Credit balance is the net income.)

When total expenses are greater than revenue, resulting in a net loss, the income summary account has a debit balance, as shown in the T account.

Income Summary	
Debit	Credit
Total expenses (greater than revenue)	Revenue
(Debit balance is the net loss.)	

Thus, whether the balance of the income summary account is a credit or a debit depends upon whether the business earns a net income or incurs a net loss. Because Income Summary is a temporary account, the account is also closed at the end of a fiscal period when the net income or net loss is recorded.

TechKnow Consulting records four closing entries: (1) an entry to close income statement accounts with credit balances; (2) an entry to close income statement accounts with debit balances; (3) an entry to record net income or net loss and close Income Summary; and (4) an entry to close the owner's drawing account.

Information needed to record the four closing entries is found in the Income Statement and Balance Sheet columns of the work sheet.

FOR YOUR INFORMATION

F Y I

Most small businesses use the calendar year as their fiscal year because it matches the way in which the owners have to file their personal income tax returns.

REMEMBER

TechKnow Consulting makes four closing entries: (1) Close income statement accounts with credit balances. (2) Close income statement accounts with debit balances. (3) Record net income or loss in the owner's capital account and close Income Summary. (4) Close the owner's drawing account.

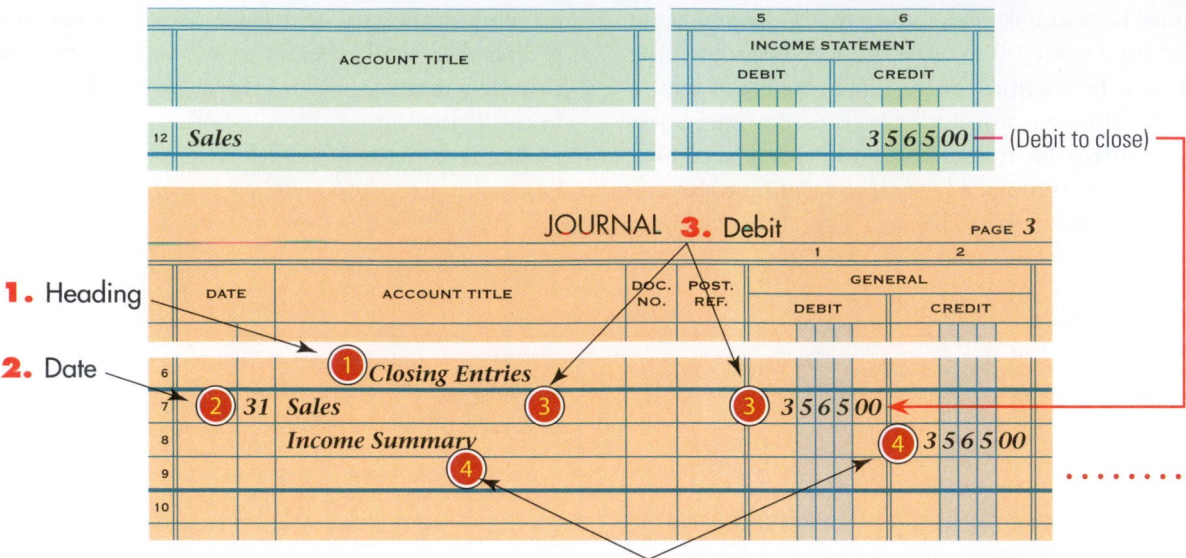

TechKnow Consulting has one income statement account with a credit balance, Sales. This credit balance must be reduced to zero to prepare the account for the next fiscal period. To reduce the balance to zero, Sales is debited for the amount of the balance. Because debits must equal credits for each journal entry, some other account must be credited. The account used for the credit part of this closing entry is Income Summary.

The effect of this closing entry on the general ledger accounts is shown in the T accounts.

The balance of Sales is now zero, and the account is ready for the next fiscal period. The credit balance of Sales is transferred to Income Summary.

Sales			
Closing	3,565.00	Bal.	3,565.00
		(New Bal. zero)	

Income Summary		
	Closing (revenue)	3,565.00

FOR YOUR INFORMATION

FYI

The reasons for recording closing entries can be compared to a trip odometer. Closing entries are recorded to prepare the temporary accounts for the next fiscal period by reducing their balances to zero. Likewise, a trip odometer must be reset to zero to begin recording the miles for the next trip.

STEPS **CLOSING ENTRY FOR AN INCOME STATEMENT ACCOUNT WITH A CREDIT BALANCE**

1. Write the heading, *Closing Entries*, in the middle of the Account Title column of the journal. For TechKnow Consulting, this heading is placed in the journal on the first blank line after the last adjusting entry.

2. Write the date, *31*, on the next line in the Date column.

3. Write the title of the account debited, *Sales*, in the Account Title column. Record the debit amount, *$3,565.00*, in the General Debit column on the same line as the account title.

4. Write the title of the account credited, *Income Summary*, on the next line in the Account Title column. Record the credit amount, *$3,565.00*, in the General Credit column on the same line as the account title.

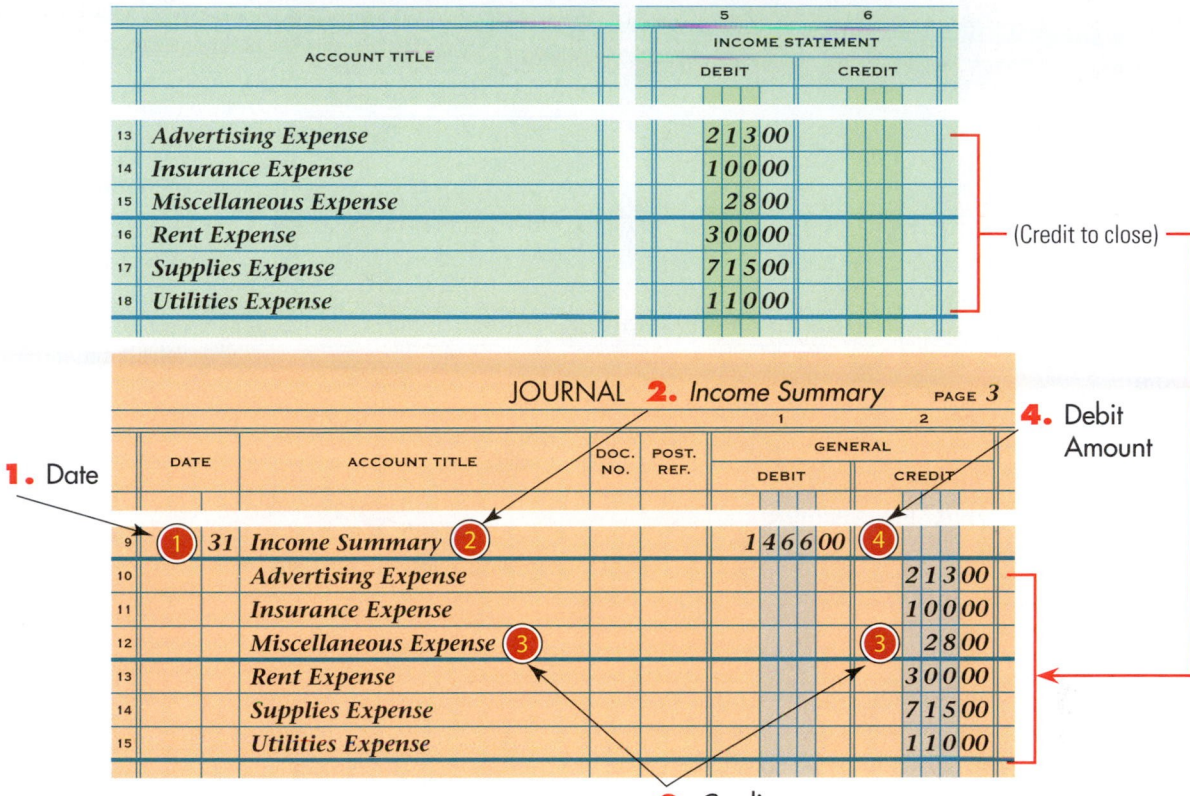

TechKnow Consulting has six income statement accounts with debit balances. The six expense accounts have normal debit balances at the end of a fiscal period. The balances of the expense accounts must be reduced to zero to prepare the accounts for the next fiscal period. Each expense account is credited for an amount equal to its balance. Income Summary is debited for the total of all the expense account balances. The amount debited to Income Summary is not entered in the amount column until all expenses have been journalized and the total amount calculated.

The effect of this closing entry on the general ledger accounts is shown in the T accounts. The balance of each expense account is returned to zero, and the accounts are ready for the next fiscal period. The balance of Income Summary is the net income for the fiscal period, $2,099.00.

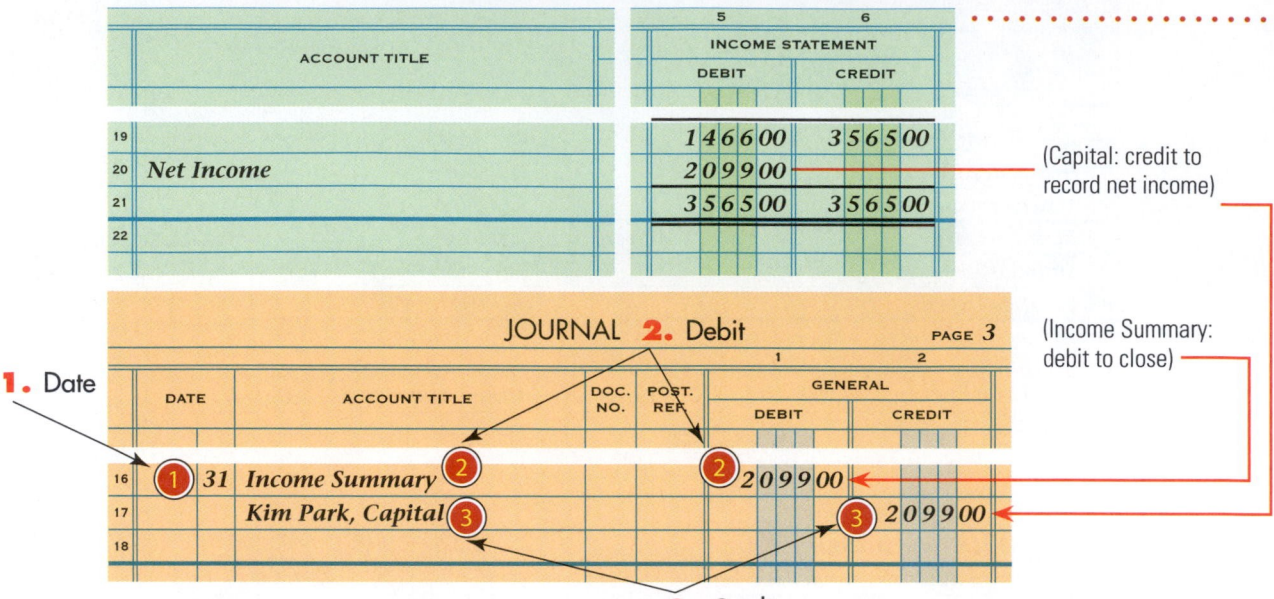

(Capital: credit to record net income)

(Income Summary: debit to close)

1. Date   **2.** Debit   **3.** Credit

TechKnow Consulting's net income appears on line 20 of the work sheet. The amount of net income increases the owner's capital and, therefore, must be credited to the owner's capital account. The balance of the temporary account, Income Summary, must be reduced to zero to prepare the account for the next fiscal period.

The effect of this closing entry on the general ledger accounts is shown in the T accounts. The debit to the income summary account, $2,099.00, reduces the account balance to zero and prepares the account for the next fiscal period. The credit, $2,099.00, increases the balance of the owner's capital account, Kim Park, Capital.

Income Summary			
Closing (expenses)	1,466.00	Closing (revenue)	3,565.00
Closing	2,099.00	*(New Bal. zero)*	

Kim Park, Capital			
		Bal.	5,000.00
		Closing (net inc.)	2,099.00
		(New Bal.	*7,099.00)*

If a business incurs a net loss, the closing entry is a debit to the owner's capital account and a credit to the income summary account.

STEPS   CLOSING ENTRY TO RECORD NET INCOME OR LOSS AND CLOSE THE INCOME SUMMARY ACCOUNT

1. Write the date, *31*, on the next line in the Date column.

2. Write the title of the account debited, *Income Summary*, in the Account Title column. Record the debit amount, *$2,099.00*, in the General Debit column on the same line as the account title.

3. Write the title of the account credited, *Kim Park, Capital*, on the next line in the Account Title column. Record the credit amount, *$2,099.00*, in the General Credit column on the same line as the account title.

REMEMBER

Amounts for closing entries are taken from the Income Statement and Balance Sheet columns of the work sheet.

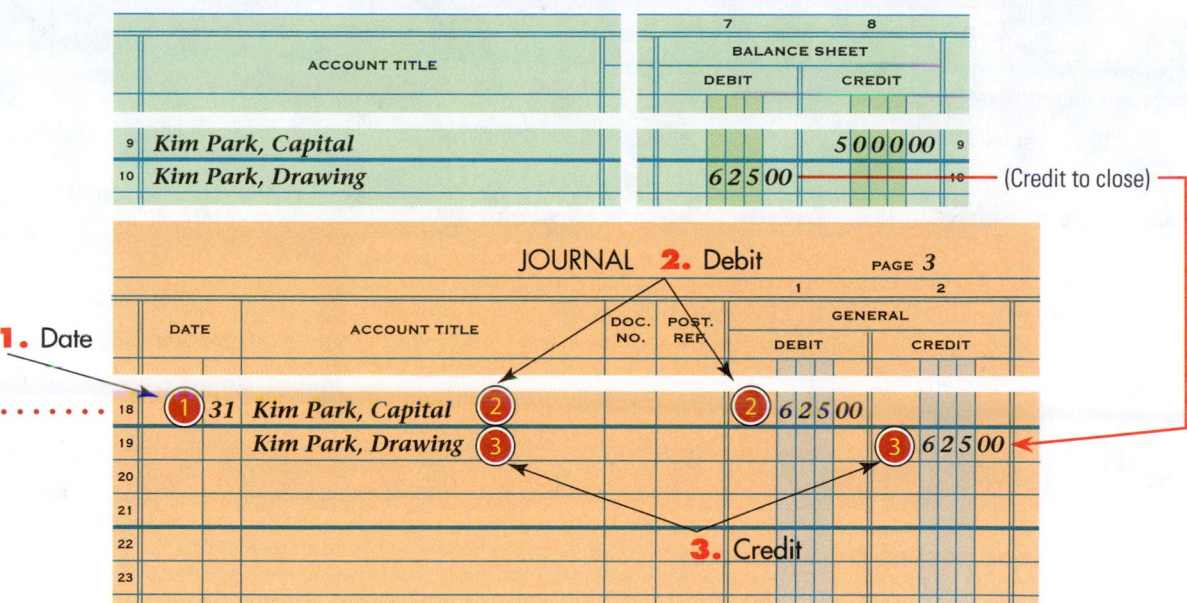

Withdrawals are assets that the owner takes out of a business and which decrease the amount of the owner's equity. The drawing account is a temporary account that accumulates information separately for each fiscal period. Therefore, the drawing account balance is reduced to zero at the end of one fiscal period to prepare the account for the next fiscal period.

The drawing account is neither a revenue nor an expense account. Therefore, the drawing account is not closed through Income Summary. The drawing account balance is closed directly to the owner's capital account.

The effect of the entry to close the drawing account is shown in the T accounts.

The drawing account has a zero balance and is ready for the next fiscal period. The capital account's new balance, $6,474.00, is verified by comparing the balance to the amount of capital shown on the balance sheet prepared at the end of the fiscal period. The capital account balance shown on TechKnow Consulting's balance sheet in Chapter 7 is $6,474.00. The two amounts are the same, and the capital account balance is verified.

Kim Park, Capital			
Closing (drawing)	625.00	Bal.	5,000.00
		Net Income	2,099.00
		(New Bal.	6,474.00)

Kim Park, Drawing			
Bal.	625.00	Closing	625.00
(New Bal. zero)			

 **STEPS** CLOSING ENTRY FOR THE OWNER'S DRAWING ACCOUNT

① Write the date, *31*, in the Date column.

② Write the title of the account debited, *Kim Park, Capital*, in the Account Title column. Record the debit amount, *$625.00*, in the General Debit column on the same line as the account title.

③ Write the title of the account credited, *Kim Park, Drawing*, in the Account Title column. Record the credit amount, *$625.00*, in the General Credit column on the same line as the account title.

End of Lesson
REVIEW

1. What do the ending balances of permanent accounts for one fiscal period represent at the beginning of the next fiscal period?
2. What do the balances of temporary accounts show?
3. List the four closing entries.

TERMS REVIEW

permanent accounts

temporary accounts

closing entries

WORK TOGETHER 8-2

Journalizing and posting closing entries

Use the journal and general ledger accounts from Work Together 8-1. A partial work sheet for the month ended July 31 of the current year is given in the *Working Papers*. Your instructor will guide you through the following example.

1. Continue on the same journal page. Journalize and post the closing entries. Save your work to complete Work Together 8-3.

ON YOUR OWN 8-2

Journalizing and posting closing entries

Use the journal and general ledger accounts from On Your Own 8-1. A partial work sheet for the month ended February 28 of the current year is given in the *Working Papers*. Work this problem independently.

1. Continue on the same journal page. Journalize and post the closing entries. Save your work to complete On Your Own 8-3.

GENERAL LEDGER ACCOUNTS AFTER ADJUSTING AND CLOSING ENTRIES ARE POSTED

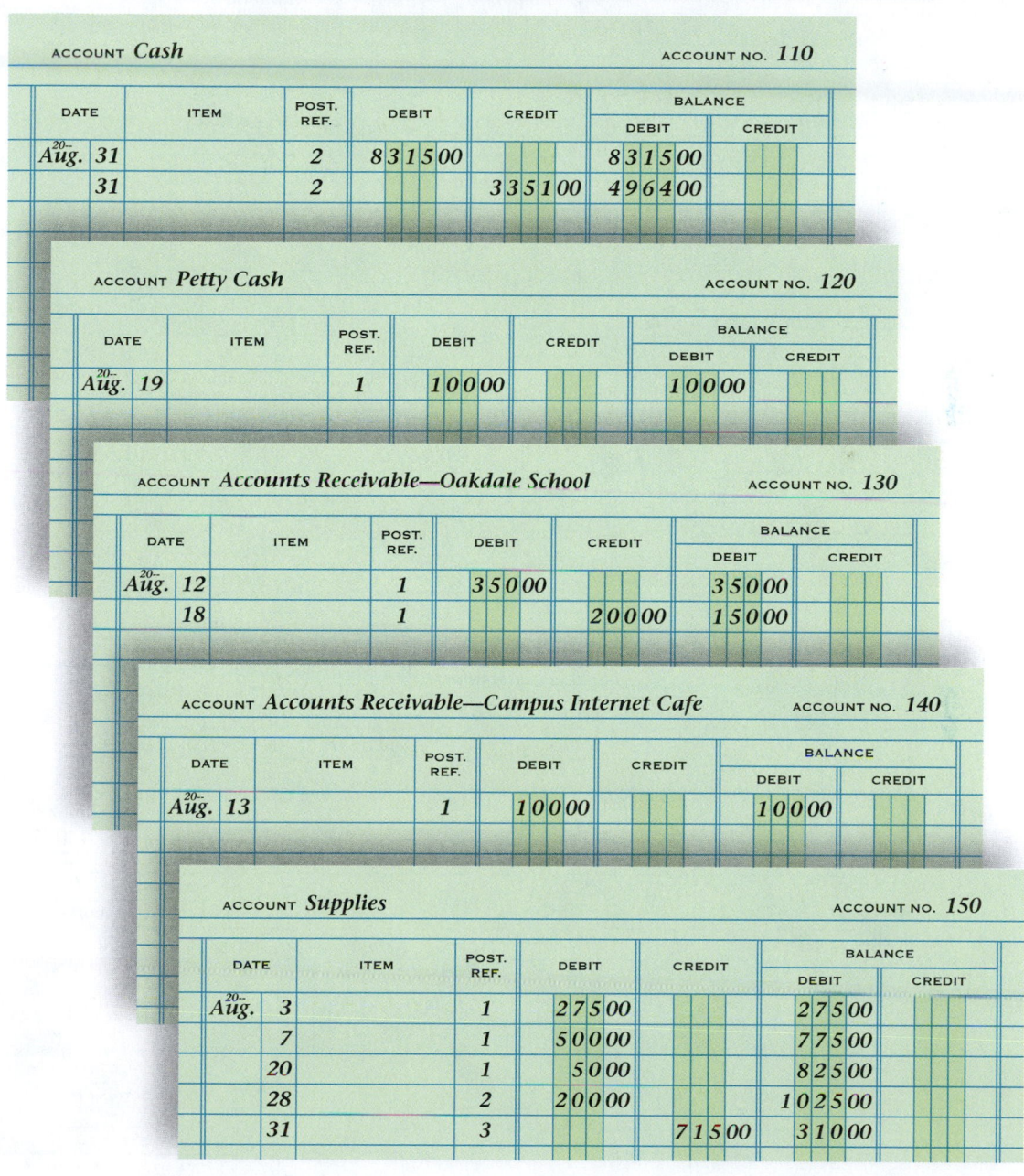

ACCOUNT *Cash*   ACCOUNT NO. *110*

DATE	ITEM	POST. REF.	DEBIT	CREDIT	BALANCE DEBIT	BALANCE CREDIT
Aug. 31		2	8 3 1 5 00		8 3 1 5 00	
31		2		3 3 5 1 00	4 9 6 4 00	

ACCOUNT *Petty Cash*   ACCOUNT NO. *120*

DATE	ITEM	POST. REF.	DEBIT	CREDIT	BALANCE DEBIT	BALANCE CREDIT
Aug. 19		1	1 0 0 00		1 0 0 00	

ACCOUNT *Accounts Receivable—Oakdale School*   ACCOUNT NO. *130*

DATE	ITEM	POST. REF.	DEBIT	CREDIT	BALANCE DEBIT	BALANCE CREDIT
Aug. 12		1	3 5 0 00		3 5 0 00	
18		1		2 0 0 00	1 5 0 00	

ACCOUNT *Accounts Receivable—Campus Internet Cafe*   ACCOUNT NO. *140*

DATE	ITEM	POST. REF.	DEBIT	CREDIT	BALANCE DEBIT	BALANCE CREDIT
Aug. 13		1	1 0 0 00		1 0 0 00	

ACCOUNT *Supplies*   ACCOUNT NO. *150*

DATE	ITEM	POST. REF.	DEBIT	CREDIT	BALANCE DEBIT	BALANCE CREDIT
Aug. 3		1	2 7 5 00		2 7 5 00	
7		1	5 0 0 00		7 7 5 00	
20		1	5 0 00		8 2 5 00	
28		2	2 0 0 00		1 0 2 5 00	
31		3		7 1 5 00	3 1 0 00	

TechKnow Consulting's general ledger, after the adjusting and closing entries are posted, is shown here and on the next several pages. When an account has a zero balance, lines are drawn in both the Balance Debit and Balance Credit columns. The lines assure a reader that a balance has not been omitted.

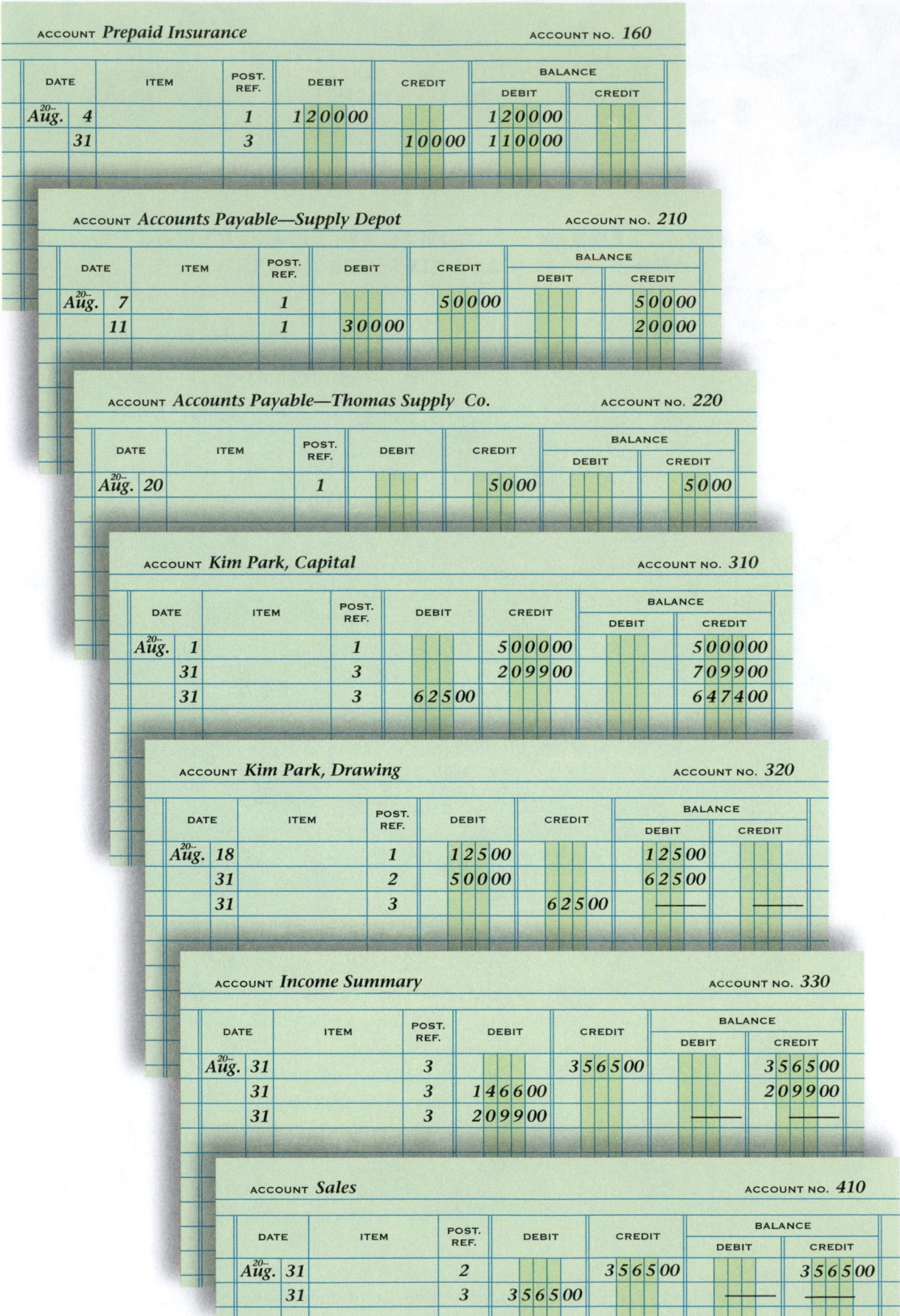

ACCOUNT *Prepaid Insurance*   **ACCOUNT NO.** *160*

DATE	ITEM	POST. REF.	DEBIT	CREDIT	BALANCE DEBIT	BALANCE CREDIT
Aug. 20-- 4		1	1 2 0 0 00		1 2 0 0 00	
31		3		1 0 0 00	1 1 0 0 00	

ACCOUNT *Accounts Payable—Supply Depot*   **ACCOUNT NO.** *210*

DATE	ITEM	POST. REF.	DEBIT	CREDIT	BALANCE DEBIT	BALANCE CREDIT
Aug. 20-- 7		1		5 0 0 00		5 0 0 00
11		1	3 0 0 00			2 0 0 00

ACCOUNT *Accounts Payable—Thomas Supply Co.*   **ACCOUNT NO.** *220*

DATE	ITEM	POST. REF.	DEBIT	CREDIT	BALANCE DEBIT	BALANCE CREDIT
Aug. 20-- 20		1		5 0 00		5 0 00

ACCOUNT *Kim Park, Capital*   **ACCOUNT NO.** *310*

DATE	ITEM	POST. REF.	DEBIT	CREDIT	BALANCE DEBIT	BALANCE CREDIT
Aug. 20-- 1		1		5 0 0 0 00		5 0 0 0 00
31		3		2 0 9 9 00		7 0 9 9 00
31		3	6 2 5 00			6 4 7 4 00

ACCOUNT *Kim Park, Drawing*   **ACCOUNT NO.** *320*

DATE	ITEM	POST. REF.	DEBIT	CREDIT	BALANCE DEBIT	BALANCE CREDIT
Aug. 20-- 18		1	1 2 5 00		1 2 5 00	
31		2	5 0 0 00		6 2 5 00	
31		3		6 2 5 00	—	

ACCOUNT *Income Summary*   **ACCOUNT NO.** *330*

DATE	ITEM	POST. REF.	DEBIT	CREDIT	BALANCE DEBIT	BALANCE CREDIT
Aug. 20-- 31		3		3 5 6 5 00		3 5 6 5 00
31		3	1 4 6 6 00			2 0 9 9 00
31		3	2 0 9 9 00		—	

ACCOUNT *Sales*   **ACCOUNT NO.** *410*

DATE	ITEM	POST. REF.	DEBIT	CREDIT	BALANCE DEBIT	BALANCE CREDIT
Aug. 20-- 31		2		3 5 6 5 00		3 5 6 5 00
31		3	3 5 6 5 00		—	

A General Ledger after Adjusting and Closing Entries Are Posted (continued)

ACCOUNT Advertising Expense   ACCOUNT NO. 510

DATE		ITEM	POST. REF.	DEBIT	CREDIT	BALANCE DEBIT	BALANCE CREDIT
Aug.	14		1	7 8 00		7 8 00	
	18		1	1 2 5 00		2 0 3 00	
	31		2	1 0 00		2 1 3 00	
	31		3		2 1 3 00	———	———

ACCOUNT Insurance Expense   ACCOUNT NO. 520

DATE		ITEM	POST. REF.	DEBIT	CREDIT	BALANCE DEBIT	BALANCE CREDIT
Aug.	31		3	1 0 0 00		1 0 0 00	
	31		3		1 0 0 00	———	———

ACCOUNT Miscellaneous Expense   ACCOUNT NO. 530

DATE		ITEM	POST. REF.	DEBIT	CREDIT	BALANCE DEBIT	BALANCE CREDIT
Aug.	31		2	2 0 00		2 0 00	
	31		2	8 00		2 8 00	
	31		3		2 8 00	———	———

ACCOUNT Rent Expense   ACCOUNT NO. 540

DATE		ITEM	POST. REF.	DEBIT	CREDIT	BALANCE DEBIT	BALANCE CREDIT
Aug.	12		1	3 0 0 00		3 0 0 00	
	31		3		3 0 0 00	———	———

ACCOUNT Supplies Expense   ACCOUNT NO. 550

DATE		ITEM	POST. REF.	DEBIT	CREDIT	BALANCE DEBIT	BALANCE CREDIT
Aug.	31		3	7 1 5 00		7 1 5 00	
	31		3		7 1 5 00	———	———

ACCOUNT Utilities Expense   ACCOUNT NO. 560

DATE		ITEM	POST. REF.	DEBIT	CREDIT	BALANCE DEBIT	BALANCE CREDIT
Aug.	12		1	4 0 00		4 0 00	
	27		2	7 0 00		1 1 0 00	
	31		3		1 1 0 00	———	———

A General Ledger after Adjusting and Closing Entries Are Posted (concluded)

2. Account Titles

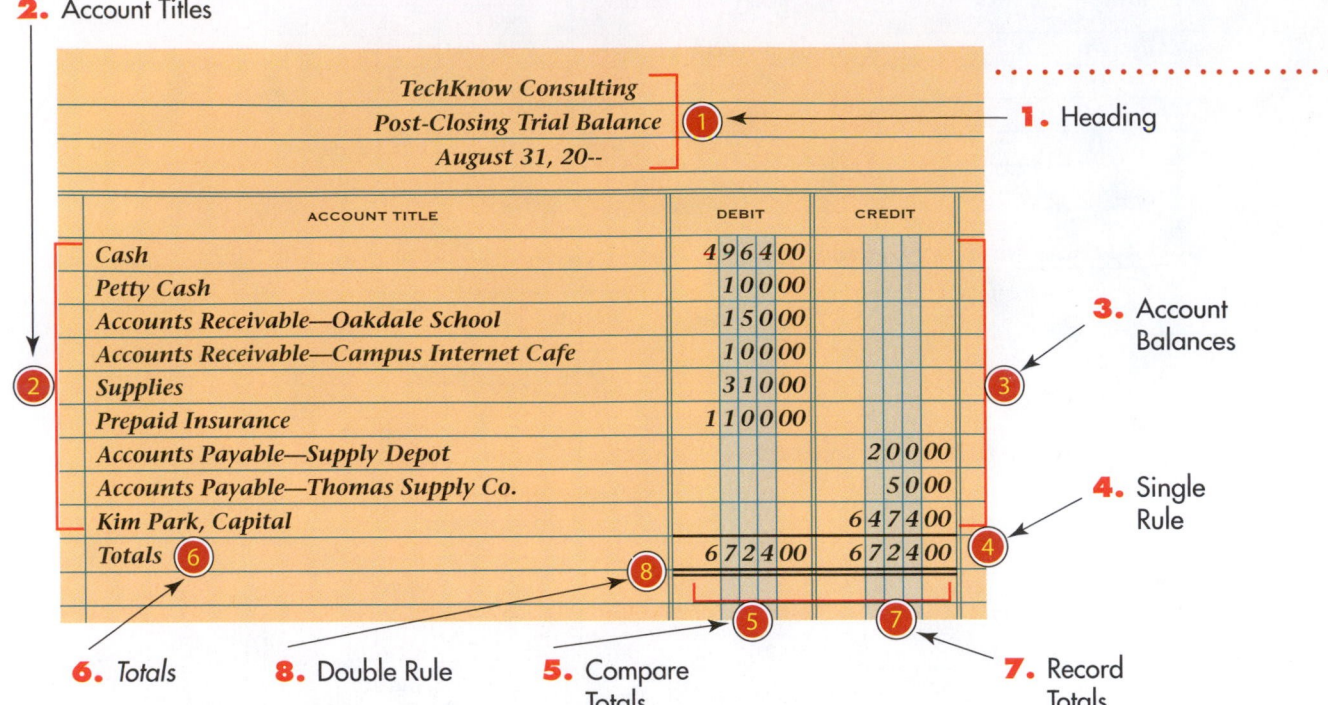

1. Heading

3. Account Balances

4. Single Rule

ACCOUNT TITLE	DEBIT	CREDIT
Cash	4 9 6 4 00	
Petty Cash	1 0 0 00	
Accounts Receivable—Oakdale School	1 5 0 00	
Accounts Receivable—Campus Internet Cafe	1 0 0 00	
Supplies	3 1 0 00	
Prepaid Insurance	1 1 0 0 00	
Accounts Payable—Supply Depot		2 0 0 00
Accounts Payable—Thomas Supply Co.		5 0 00
Kim Park, Capital		6 4 7 4 00
Totals ⑥	6 7 2 4 00	6 7 2 4 00

6. Totals

8. Double Rule

5. Compare Totals

7. Record Totals

After the closing entries are posted, TechKnow Consulting verifies that debits equal credits in the general ledger accounts by preparing a trial balance. A trial balance prepared after the closing entries are posted is called a **post-closing trial balance**.

Only general ledger accounts with balances are included on a post-closing trial balance. The permanent accounts (assets, liabilities, and owner's capital) have balances and do appear on a post-closing trial balance. Because the temporary accounts (income summary, revenue, expense, and drawing) are closed and have zero balances, they do not appear on a post-closing trial balance.

The total of all debits must equal the total of all credits in a general ledger. The totals of both columns on TechKnow Consulting's post-closing trial balance are the same, $6,724.00. TechKnow Consulting's post-closing trial balance shows that the general ledger account balances are in balance and ready for the new fiscal period.

STEPS      PREPARING A POST-CLOSING TRIAL BALANCE

① Write the heading on three lines.

② Write the titles of all general ledger accounts with balances in the Account Title column.

③ On the same line with each account title, write each account's balance in either the Debit or Credit column.

④ Rule a single line across both amount columns below the last amount, and add each amount column.

⑤ Compare the two column totals. The two column totals must be the same. If the two column totals are not the same, the errors must be found and corrected before any more work is completed.

⑥ Write the word *Totals* on the line below the last account title.

⑦ Write the column totals, *$6,724.00*, below the single line.

⑧ Rule double lines across both amount columns to show that the totals have been verified as correct.

Recording Adjusting and Closing Entries for a Service Business

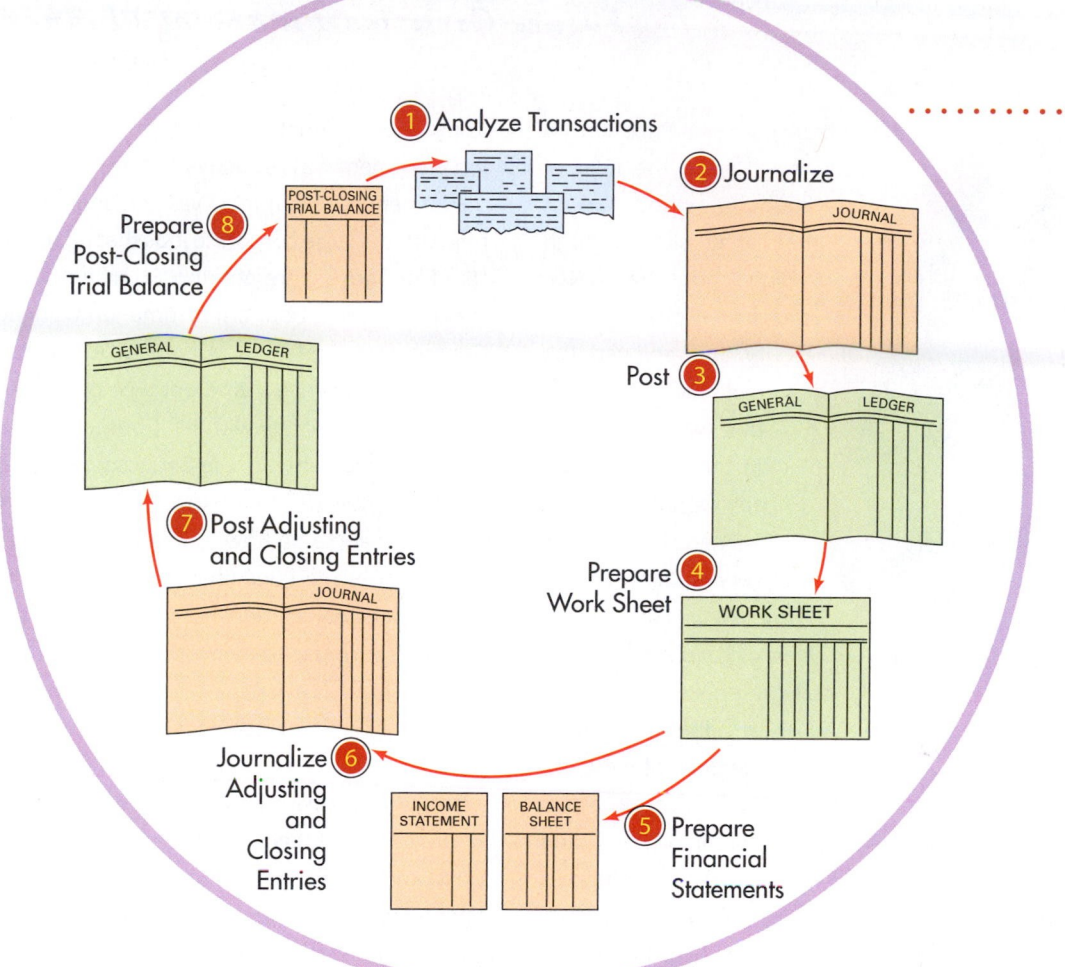

Chapters 1 through 8 describe TechKnow Consulting's accounting activities for a one-month fiscal period. The series of accounting activities included in recording financial information for a fiscal period is called an **accounting cycle**. [CONCEPT: Accounting Period Cycle]

For the next fiscal period, the cycle begins again at Step 1.

REMEMBER

The word post means after. The Post-Closing Trial Balance is prepared after closing entries.

STEPS

STEPS IN AN ACCOUNTING CYCLE

1. Source documents are checked for accuracy, and transactions are analyzed into debit and credit parts.

2. Transactions, from information on source documents, are recorded in a journal.

3. Journal entries are posted to the general ledger.

4. A work sheet, including a trial balance, is prepared from the general ledger.

5. Financial statements are prepared from the work sheet.

6. Adjusting and closing entries are journalized from the work sheet.

7. Adjusting and closing entries are posted to the general ledger.

8. A post-closing trial balance of the general ledger is prepared.

Anna McNeese Price, Future Certified Financial Planner

COURTESY OF ANNA MCNEESE PRICE

When Anna McNeese Price started college, entering the field of accounting wasn't part of her career plan. Through high school she worked at a mental health facility and enjoyed the personal contact she had with the clients in the physical therapy department. But an interest in business (and a sudden lack of interest in biology) led her to change majors as a college sophomore.

After considering the different business degrees offered, she decided to go into accounting. Anna recalls, "I knew I was interested in business, and I thought accounting would be the most challenging. I also heard about the great job market, and since I was going through school during the height of the World-Com/Enron scandals, any degree that could guarantee job placement was attractive."

But her desire to affect lives personally didn't seem to mix with the large corporate jobs that recruiters from the "Big Four" firms were offering. So when one of her professors told her about a part-time job working for Ernie George, a certified financial planner, Anna saw an opportunity to experience a different type of career.

By working closely with Mr. George and his assistant, Anna has been able to use her accounting background to better understand the stock market and what it takes to advise people on how to invest their money. She has found that as a certified financial planner, Mr. George has a close personal relationship with his clients and is able to make the impact that she dreamed of in her early college career.

"I will finish my bachelor's of accountancy next year and immediately enroll in the Master of Taxation program," Anna explains. "Within five years of graduation, I hope to have obtained my certified public accountant (CPA) and certified financial planner (CFP) certifications and go into private practice as a certified financial planner with professional tax expertise."

Salary Range: Median annual earnings of personal financial advisors were $62,700 in 2004, according to the *Occupational Outlook Handbook*. Over 25% of financial planners earn more than $100,000. (Source: Bureau of Labor Statistics, U.S. Department of Labor, *Occupational Outlook Handbook, 2006–07 Edition*; Financial Analysts and Personal Financial Advisors, on the Internet at www.bls.gov/oco/ocos259.htm [visited January 15, 2007].)

Qualifications: A college degree is required, and professional certification is recommended. Financial planners must have good communication skills. Because many financial planners are self-employed, they must also possess the skills necessary to manage a business.

Occupational Outlook: More and more people are choosing alternative ways to plan for retirement. The complexity of the stock market and the tax laws (which can limit how much you can save) have increased the need for professionals who can give sound advice to individuals interested in investing.

End of Lesson
REVIEW

TERMS REVIEW

post-closing trial balance

accounting cycle

AUDIT YOUR UNDERSTANDING

1. Why are lines drawn in both the Balance Debit and Balance Credit columns when an account has a zero balance?
2. Which accounts go on the post-closing trial balance?
3. Why are temporary accounts omitted from a post-closing trial balance?

WORK TOGETHER 8-3

Preparing a post-closing trial balance

Use the general ledger accounts from Work Together 8-2. Your instructor will guide you through the following example. A form to complete a post-closing trial balance is given in the *Working Papers*.

1. Prepare a post-closing trial balance for Darlene's Delivery Service on July 31 of the current year.

ON YOUR OWN 8-3

Preparing a post-closing trial balance

Use the general ledger accounts from On Your Own 8-2. Work this problem independently. A form to complete a post-closing trial balance is given in the *Working Papers*.

1. Prepare a post-closing trial balance for Cuts by Kelley on February 28 of the current year.

After completing this chapter, you can:

1. Define accounting terms related to adjusting and closing entries for a service business organized as a proprietorship.

2. Identify accounting concepts and practices related to adjusting and closing entries for a service business organized as a proprietorship.

3. Record adjusting entries for a service business organized as a proprietorship.

4. Record closing entries for a service business organized as a proprietorship.

5. Prepare a post-closing trial balance for a service business organized as a proprietorship.

EXPLORE ACCOUNTING

Public Accounting Firms

One type of business that helps other businesses with accounting issues is known as a *public accounting firm.*

The independent reviewing and issuing of an opinion on the reliability of accounting records is known as *auditing.*

When performing an audit for a client, the accounting firm looks closely at the client's financial statements and the way the client records transactions. The auditor's job is to determine if the financial statements fairly present the financial position of the client. The auditor issues an opinion, which is a statement as to whether the financial statements follow standard accounting rules (GAAP). (GAAP stands for *Generally Accepted Accounting Principles.*) This "opinion" is used by bankers deciding to lend money to the company. It is also used by investors when making investment decisions.

Auditing, however, is just one of many services provided by public accounting firms. Other services include tax preparation, tax advice, payroll services, bookkeeping services, financial statement preparation, and consulting services. These other services often make up a higher percentage of business for the accounting firm than performing audits.

Many accounting firms report that they are getting more requests for consulting services than for other services they can provide.

In many cases, consulting is also the area that produces the largest profit margin for the public accounting firm. Therefore, some firms are actively advertising their ability to provide management consulting services for clients.

Activity: Contact a public accounting firm in your area. Research what services the firm provides and which service area (if any) is growing. Present your findings to your class.

8-1 APPLICATION PROBLEM

Journalizing and posting adjusting entries

A journal and general ledger accounts for Len's Laundry are given in the *Working Papers*. A partial work sheet for the month ended April 30 of the current year is shown below.

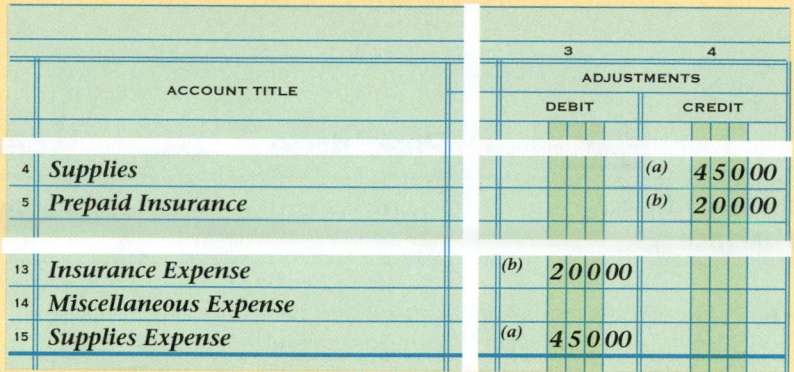

	ACCOUNT TITLE	ADJUSTMENTS	
		DEBIT	CREDIT
4	Supplies		(a) 4 5 0 00
5	Prepaid Insurance		(b) 2 0 0 00
13	Insurance Expense	(b) 2 0 0 00	
14	Miscellaneous Expense		
15	Supplies Expense	(a) 4 5 0 00	

Use page 12 of a journal. Journalize and post the adjusting entries. Save your work to complete Application Problem 8-2.

8-2 APPLICATION PROBLEM

Journalizing and posting closing entries

Use the journal and general ledger accounts for Len's Laundry from Application Problem 8-1. A partial work sheet for the month ended April 30 of the current year is shown below.

	ACCOUNT TITLE	INCOME STATEMENT		BALANCE SHEET		
		DEBIT	CREDIT	DEBIT	CREDIT	
1	Cash			7 6 0 7 00		1
2	Accounts Receivable—Natasha Goodlad			7 0 0 00		2
3	Accounts Receivable—R. Henry			4 9 8 00		3
4	Supplies			4 3 1 00		4
5	Prepaid Insurance			2 0 0 00		5
6	Accounts Payable—Tri-County Supplies				3 8 1 00	6
7	Accounts Payable—West End Supply Co.				5 5 5 00	7
8	Leonard Long, Capital				6 5 2 7 00	8
9	Leonard Long, Drawing			1 0 0 0 00		9
10	Income Summary					10
11	Sales		6 2 3 3 00			11
12	Advertising Expense	8 0 0 00				12
13	Insurance Expense	2 0 0 00				13
14	Miscellaneous Expense	3 1 5 00				14
15	Supplies Expense	4 5 0 00				15
16	Utilities Expense	1 4 9 5 00				16
17		3 2 6 0 00	6 2 3 3 00	10 4 3 6 00	7 4 6 3 00	17
18	Net Income	2 9 7 3 00			2 9 7 3 00	18
19		6 2 3 3 00	6 2 3 3 00	10 4 3 6 00	10 4 3 6 00	19
20						20

Continue on the same journal page. Journalize and post the closing entries. Save your work to complete Application Problem 8-3.

8-3 APPLICATION PROBLEM

Preparing a post-closing trial balance

Use the general ledger accounts for Len's Laundry from Application Problem 8-2. A form to complete a post-closing trial balance is given in the *Working Papers*.

Prepare a post-closing trial balance for Len's Laundry on April 30 of the current year.

8-4 MASTERY PROBLEM

Journalizing and posting adjusting and closing entries with a net loss; preparing a post-closing trial balance

Rolstad Repair Service's partial work sheet for the month ended October 31 of the current year is given below. The general ledger accounts are given in the *Working Papers*. The general ledger accounts do not show all details for the fiscal period. The Balance shown in each account is the account's balance before adjusting and closing entries are posted.

	ACCOUNT TITLE	ADJUSTMENTS DEBIT	ADJUSTMENTS CREDIT	INCOME STATEMENT DEBIT	INCOME STATEMENT CREDIT	BALANCE SHEET DEBIT	BALANCE SHEET CREDIT	
1	Cash					6 9 5 8 00		1
2	Petty Cash					1 5 0 00		2
3	Accts. Rec.—M. Hollerud					1 9 7 00		3
4	Supplies		(a) 1 4 0 0 00			7 8 0 00		4
5	Prepaid Insurance		(b) 1 5 7 00			8 0 0 00		5
6	Accts. Pay.—Tampa Supply						6 1 2 00	6
7	Ron Rolstad, Capital						9 3 3 7 00	7
8	Ron Rolstad, Drawing					6 0 0 00		8
9	Income Summary							9
10	Sales				3 2 6 9 00			10
11	Advertising Expense			4 5 0 00				11
12	Insurance Expense	(b) 1 5 7 00		1 5 7 00				12
13	Miscellaneous Expense			8 5 00				13
14	Supplies Expense	(a) 1 4 0 0 00		1 4 0 0 00				14
15	Utilities Expense			1 6 4 1 00				15
16		1 5 5 7 00	1 5 5 7 00	3 7 3 3 00	3 2 6 9 00	9 4 8 5 00	9 9 4 9 00	16
17	Net Loss				4 6 4 00	4 6 4 00		17
18				3 7 3 3 00	3 7 3 3 00	9 9 4 9 00	9 9 4 9 00	18
19								19

Instructions:

1. Use page 20 of a journal. Journalize and post the adjusting entries.
2. Continue to use page 20 of the journal. Journalize and post the closing entries.
3. Prepare a post-closing trial balance.

Go Beyond the Book
For more information go to
www.C21accounting.com

CHALLENGE PROBLEM

Journalizing and posting adjusting and closing entries with two revenue accounts and a net loss; preparing a post-closing trial balance

LawnMow's partial work sheet for the month ended September 30 of the current year is given below. The general ledger accounts are given in the *Working Papers*. The general ledger accounts do not show all details for the fiscal period. The Balance shown in each account is the account's balance before adjusting and closing entries are posted.

	ACCOUNT TITLE	ADJUSTMENTS DEBIT	ADJUSTMENTS CREDIT	INCOME STATEMENT DEBIT	INCOME STATEMENT CREDIT	BALANCE SHEET DEBIT	BALANCE SHEET CREDIT	
1	Cash					1 8 9 8 00		1
2	Accts. Rec.—Sandra Rohe					9 5 00		2
3	Supplies		(a) 3 2 0 0 00			6 5 0 00		3
4	Prepaid Insurance		(b) 4 0 0 00			1 2 0 0 00		4
5	Accts. Pay.—Corner Garage						5 8 00	5
6	Accts. Pay.—Broadway Gas						1 1 0 00	6
7	Accts. Pay.—Esko Repair						2 1 5 00	7
8	Ryo Morrison, Capital						4 0 0 0 00	8
9	Ryo Morrison, Drawing					1 0 0 00		9
10	Income Summary							10
11	Sales—Lawn Care				4 9 0 0 00			11
12	Sales—Shrub Care				2 5 0 0 00			12
13	Advertising Expense			3 9 0 00				13
14	Insurance Expense	(b) 4 0 0 00		4 0 0 00				14
15	Miscellaneous Expense			5 5 0 00				15
16	Rent Expense			3 3 0 0 00				16
17	Supplies Expense	(a) 3 2 0 0 00		3 2 0 0 00				17
18		3 6 0 0 00	3 6 0 0 00	7 8 4 0 00	7 4 0 0 00	3 9 4 3 00	4 3 8 3 00	18
19	Net Loss				4 4 0 00	4 4 0 00		19
20				7 8 4 0 00	7 8 4 0 00	4 3 8 3 00	4 3 8 3 00	20
21								21

Instructions:

1. Use page 18 of a journal. Journalize and post the adjusting entries.

2. Continue to use page 18 of the journal. Journalize and post the closing entries.

3. Prepare a post-closing trial balance.

4. Ryo Morrison, owner of LawnMow, is disappointed that his business incurred a net loss for September of the current year. Mr. Morrison would have preferred not to have to reduce his capital by $440.00. He knows that you are studying accounting, so Mr. Morrison asks you to analyze his work sheet for September. Based on your analysis of the work sheet, what would you suggest might have caused the net loss for LawnMow? What steps would you suggest so that Mr. Morrison can avoid a net loss in future months?

Service businesses are the fastest growing part of our business world. Social and economic changes create needs for new and different kinds of service businesses to satisfy customer demands.

For example, the growing popularity of the World Wide Web led to the creation of service businesses that design Web pages. These businesses create text, graphics, animation, and links for business and private clients. Another example of a new type of service business is a personal services business that runs errands or stands in long lines for clients. As lifestyles become busier and busier, some people do not have the time to take care of all their personal errands. Service businesses have appeared to fill this need.

Instructions: Using library, online, or other information resources, write a one-page report on a new or unusual service business that you would be interested in working for or owning.

CASES FOR CRITICAL THINKING

Case 1

Gretel Bakken forgot to journalize and post the adjusting entry for prepaid insurance at the end of the June fiscal period. What effect will this omission have on the records of Ms. Bakken's business as of June 30? Explain your answer.

Case 2

Vincente Burgos states that his business is so small that he just records supplies and insurance as expenses when he pays for them. Thus, at the end of a fiscal period, Mr. Burgos does not record adjusting and closing entries for his business. Do you agree with his accounting procedures? Explain your answer.

SCANS WORKPLACE COMPETENCY

Thinking Skill: Seeing things in the mind's eye

Concept: Effective employees can visualize how every part of a company contributes to the success of the whole company, from maintenance workers to the chief executive officer. Now that you have finished the study of a complete accounting cycle, you should better understand how each part of the cycle contributes to the whole cycle.

Application: Describe the importance of the work each of the following employees does. Explain how errors would affect the reporting of the company.

a. Employee who reconciles the bank statement.

b. Employee who determines the amount of supplies on hand at the end of the fiscal period.

c. Employee who posts the journal entries.

d. Employee who calculates and records the adjusting entries.

e. Employee who records the closing entries.

The closing entries for Greenlund Enterprises are given below. Assuming all account balances are correct, review the entries. List any errors you find.

Date	Account Title	Doc No.	Post Ref.	General Debit	Credit
20-- May 31	Income Summary			32,000	
	Sales				32,000
31	Income Summary			6,200	
	Insurance Expense			900	
	Rent Expense				2,500
	Supplies Expense				1,200
	Utilities Expense				3,400
31	Lionel Greenlund, Capital			38,200	
	Income Summary				38,200
31	Lionel Greenlund, Capital			4,500	
	Lionel Greenlund, Drawing				4,500

ANALYZING BEST BUY'S FINANCIAL STATEMENTS

Refer to Best Buy's consolidated statements of earnings on Appendix B page B-6. To calculate what percentage an item increased or decreased from one year to another, calculate the difference between the two amounts and divide this difference by the amount for the earlier year. For example, the percentage of increase in revenue from 2005 to 2006 would be calculated as follows: ($30,848,000,000 − $27,433,000,000) ÷ $27,433,000,000 = 12.45%.

Instructions

1. What is Best Buy's revenue (sales) for each of the three years? Is this a favorable or unfavorable trend?
2. Calculate the percentage of increase in revenue from 2006 to 2007.
3. How does the increase from 2006 to 2007 compare to the increase from 2005 to 2006?

Accounting
SOFTWARE

Accounting software does not require that you journalize closing entries. Rather, you can use a wizard to assist you in closing the accounts. A wizard is a series of windows that collect the information necessary to perform a specific task. Based on the information you enter, the wizard performs the selected functions automatically.

A wizard is especially useful for functions that are very complicated or rarely performed. In the case of closing entries, computerized accounting systems are only closed at the end of a fiscal year. Because you only perform this process once a year, it is helpful to have a wizard to assist you.

Once Peachtree closes an account, you no longer have the ability to examine or modify journal entries made in that fiscal year. For this reason, Peachtree allows you to have two fiscal years open at one time. This strategy provides you with ample opportunity to ensure that your journal entries from the past fiscal year are correct while you continue to record transactions for the current fiscal year.

PEACHTREE MASTERY PROBLEM 8-4

1. Open (Restore) file 08-4MP.ptb.
2. Journalize and post the adjusting and closing entries in Peachtree's general journal. Use the closing entries wizard to record the closing entries.
3. Print the October 31 general ledger.
4. Print a post-closing trial balance.

PEACHTREE CHALLENGE PROBLEM 8-5

1. Open (Restore) file 08-5CP.ptb.
2. Journalize and post the adjusting and closing entries in Peachtree's general journal. Use the closing entries wizard to record the closing entries.
3. Print the September 30 general ledger.
4. Print a post-closing trial balance.

CLOSING ENTRIES; POST-CLOSING TRIAL BALANCE

QuickBooks automatically closes all revenue and expense accounts into a summary account. However, the user must make entries to close this summary account into the capital account and to close the drawing account into the capital account.

Similar to manual accounting, it is a good idea to run a trial balance after the closing entries have been made and posted. Although computer systems are very accurate, the new balances should be examined to determine if the correct closing entries were made. The capital account should show the new ending balance, and all revenue and expense accounts should have a zero balance.

QUICKBOOKS MASTERY PROBLEM 8-4

1. Open the Rolstad Repair Service file and record the adjusting entries dated October 31.
2. Print a Profit & Loss report for October 1-31.
3. Print a Balance Sheet report and a Trial Balance report for the month ending October 31. Use the Accountant & Taxes Reports menu to print the Trial Balance report.
4. Using the information in the Trial Balance and the Profit & Loss reports, record the closing entries.
5. Print a Journal report containing both the adjusting and closing entries. Use October 31 for the date.
6. Print a post-closing trial balance from the Accountant & Taxes Reports menu.

QUICKBOOKS CHALLENGE PROBLEM 8-5

1. Open the LawnMow file and record the September 30 adjusting entries.
2. Print a Profit & Loss report for September 1-30.
3. Print a Balance Sheet report and Trial Balance report for the month ending September 30. Use the Accountant & Taxes Reports menu to print the Trial Balance report.
4. Using the information in the Trial Balance and the Profit & Loss reports, record the closing entries.
5. View and print a Journal report containing both the adjusting and closing entries, using September 30 for the To and From dates.
6. Print a post-closing trial balance from the Account & Taxes Reports menu.
7. Record the closing entries and print a post-closing trial balance.

CHARTS AND GRAPHS

A post-closing trial balance verifies that debits equal credits after posting adjustments and closing the accounts. The schedule reports the account balances of all permanent accounts at the beginning of the next fiscal period.

What if a manager asked you to provide a report of assets at the beginning of a fiscal period? Before preparing the answer, you should determine how the manager intends to use the information. Does the manager need to know the exact amount of every asset account? If so, a schedule of the asset accounts from the post-closing trial balance would provide the manager with the requested information.

However, the manager may not need to know the exact dollar amount of each asset. Instead, the manager may need only a general perception of the relative amount of each asset owned by the business. In this case, creating a chart of the data will provide the manager with better information than a detailed schedule of accounts.

EXCEL MASTERY PROBLEM 8-4

1. Complete Mastery Problem 8-4 using your Working Papers or accounting software. Prepare a post-closing trial balance.
2. In a new spreadsheet, list the asset accounts in one column and their balances in the next column.
3. Experiment with creating different types of charts of these accounts and balances (pie chart, bar chart, or line chart, for example).

CLOSING ENTRIES; POST-CLOSING TRIAL BALANCE

In an automated accounting system, closing entries are generated and posted by the software. The software automatically closes net income to the owner's capital account after closing the revenue and expense accounts. The drawing account is closed as well.

To perform a period-end closing:

1. Choose Generate Closing Journal Entries from the Options menu.
2. Click Yes to generate the closing entries.
3. The general journal will appear, containing the journal entries.
4. Click the Post button.

In *Automated Accounting*, once closing entries are posted, the journal entries of the period cannot be accessed to make corrections if errors are found later. Therefore, it is always a good practice to save your file before closing entries are generated; the letters *BC* (for *Before Closing*) can be added to the filename. After the closing entries are generated, add the letters *AC* (for After Closing) to the filename and save the file again. When this procedure is followed, if it is necessary to correct a journal entry, the file with *BC* in its name can be opened and corrected, and closing entries can be generated again.

AUTOMATED ACCOUNTING MASTERY PROBLEM 8-4
Open file F08-4.AA8. Display the problem instructions and complete the problem.

AUTOMATED ACCOUNTING CHALLENGE PROBLEM 8-5
Open file F08-5.AA8. Display the problem instructions and complete the problem.

An Accounting Cycle for a Proprietorship: End-of-Fiscal-Period Work

The general ledger prepared in Reinforcement Activity 1—Part A is needed to complete Reinforcement Activity 1—Part B. Reinforcement Activity 1—Part B includes end-of-fiscal-period activities studied in Chapters 6 through 8.

WORK SHEET

INSTRUCTIONS:

12. Prepare a trial balance on the work sheet given in the *Working Papers*. Use a one-month fiscal period ended May 31 of the current year.

13. Analyze the following adjustment information into debit and credit parts. Record the adjustments on the work sheet.

Adjustment Information, May 31	
Supplies on hand	$ 625.00
Value of prepaid insurance	1,100.00

14. Total and rule the Adjustments columns.

15. Extend the up-to-date account balances to the Balance Sheet and Income Statement columns.

16. Complete the work sheet.

FINANCIAL STATEMENTS

INSTRUCTIONS:

17. Prepare an income statement. Figure and record the component percentages for sales, total expenses, and net income. Round percentage calculations to the nearest 0.1%.

18. Prepare a balance sheet.

ADJUSTING ENTRIES

INSTRUCTIONS:

19. Use page 3 of the journal. Journalize and post the adjusting entries.

CLOSING ENTRIES

INSTRUCTIONS:

20. Continue using page 3 of the journal. Journalize and post the closing entries.

POST-CLOSING TRIAL BALANCE

INSTRUCTIONS:

21. Prepare a post-closing trial balance.

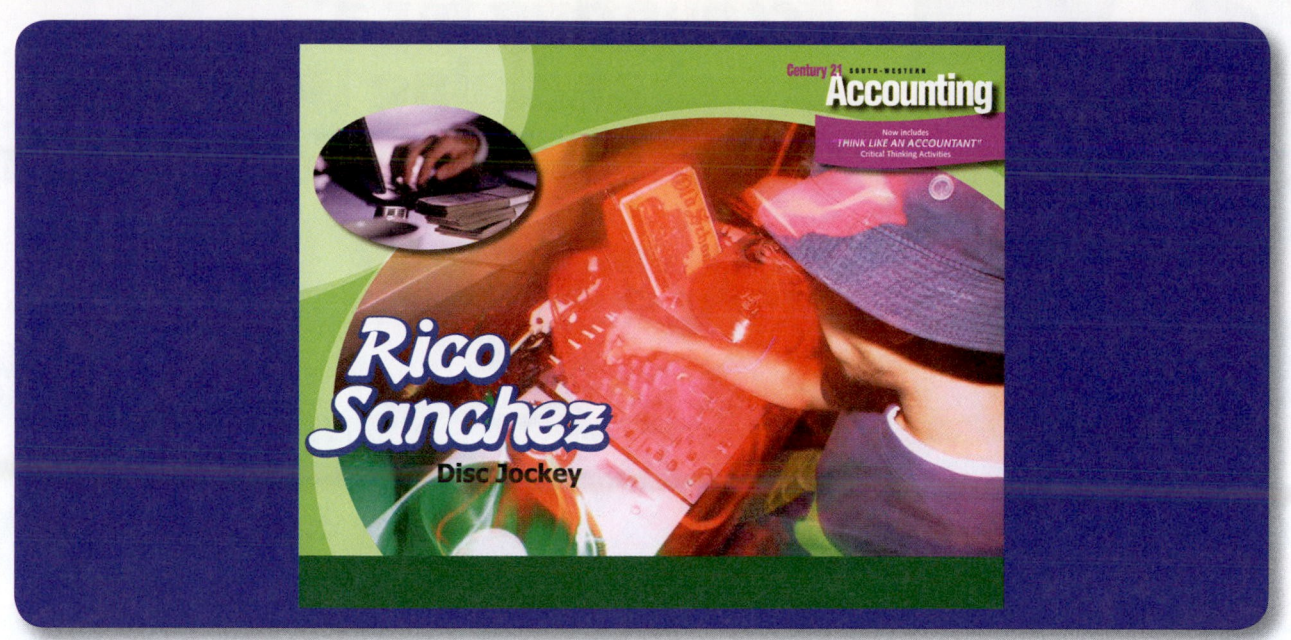

This simulation covers the transactions completed by Rico Sanchez, Disc Jockey, a service business organized as a proprietorship. On September 1 of the current year, Rico Sanchez, Disc Jockey, begins business. The owner, Rico Sanchez, performs as a disc jockey at clubs and private parties. He also specializes in karaoke when requested.

The activities included in the accounting cycle for Rico Sanchez, Disc Jockey, are listed below. The company uses a 5-column journal and a general ledger similar to those described for TechKnow in Cycle 1.

This simulation is available in manual and in automated versions, for use with *Automated Accounting* software.

The following activities are included in this simulation:

1 Journalizing transactions in a 5-column journal.

2 Preparing a bank statement reconciliation and recording a bank service charge.

3 Proving cash.

4 Posting from a journal to a general ledger.

5 Preparing a trial balance on a work sheet.

6 Recording adjustments on a work sheet.

7 Completing a work sheet.

8 Preparing financial statements (income statement and balance sheet).

9 Journalizing and posting adjusting entries.

10 Journalizing and posting closing entries.

11 Preparing a post-closing trial balance.

12 Completing Think Like an Accountant Financial Analysis activity.

Accounting for a Merchandising Business Organized as a Corporation

THE BUSINESS— HOBBY SHACK, INC.

Hobby Shack, Inc., the business described in Part 2, is a retail merchandising business organized as a corporation. The business purchases and sells a wide variety of craft and hobby items such as silk flowers, ceramics, paints, and jewelry. Hobby Shack purchases its merchandise directly from businesses that manufacture the items. Hobby Shack rents the building in which the business is located.

CHAPTER 9

CHAPTER 10

CHAPTER 13

CHAPTER 14

HOBBY SHACK, INC., CHART OF ACCOUNTS

GENERAL LEDGER

Balance Sheet Accounts

(1000) ASSETS

1100	Current Assets
1110	Cash
1120	Petty Cash
1130	Accounts Receivable
1135	Allowance for Uncollectible Accounts
1140	Merchandise Inventory
1145	Supplies—Office
1150	Supplies—Store
1160	Prepaid Insurance
1200	Plant Assets
1205	Office Equipment
1210	Accumulated Depreciation—Office Equipment
1215	Store Equipment
1220	Accumulated Depreciation—Store Equipment

(2000) LIABILITIES

2100	Current Liabilities
2110	Accounts Payable
2120	Federal Income Tax Payable
2130	Employee Income Tax Payable
2135	Social Security Tax Payable
2140	Medicare Tax Payable
2145	Sales Tax Payable
2150	Unemployment Tax Payable—Federal
2155	Unemployment Tax Payable—State
2160	Health Insurance Premiums Payable
2165	U.S. Savings Bonds Payable
2170	United Way Donations Payable
2180	Dividends Payable

(3000) STOCKHOLDERS' EQUITY

3110	Capital Stock
3120	Retained Earnings
3130	Dividends
3140	Income Summary

Income Statement Accounts

(4000) OPERATING REVENUE

4110	Sales
4120	Sales Discount
4130	Sales Returns and Allowances

(5000) COST OF MERCHANDISE

5110	Purchases
5120	Purchases Discount
5130	Purchases Returns and Allowances

(6000) OPERATING EXPENSES

6105	Advertising Expense
6110	Cash Short and Over
6115	Credit Card Fee Expense
6120	Depreciation Expense—Office Equipment
6125	Depreciation Expense—Store Equipment
6130	Insurance Expense
6135	Miscellaneous Expense
6140	Payroll Taxes Expense
6145	Rent Expense
6150	Salary Expense
6155	Supplies Expense—Office
6160	Supplies Expense—Store
6165	Uncollectible Accounts Expense
6170	Utilities Expense
6200	Income Tax Expense
6205	Federal Income Tax Expense

SUBSIDIARY LEDGERS

Accounts Receivable Ledger

110	Country Crafters
120	Cumberland Center
130	Fairview Church
140	Playtime Childcare
150	Village Crafts
160	Washington Schools

Accounts Payable Ledger

210	American Paint
220	Ceramic Supply
230	Crown Distributing
240	Floral Designs
250	Gulf Craft Supply
260	Synthetic Arts

The charts of accounts for Hobby Shack, Inc., are illustrated here for ready reference as you study Part 2 of this textbook.

CHAPTER 11

CHAPTER 12

CHAPTER 15

CHAPTER 16

PHOTOS: DIGITAL VISION, DIGITAL VISION, PHOTOGRAPHER'S CHOICE RF, STOCKBYTE (ALL GETTY IMAGES)

DIGITAL VISION/GETTY IMAGES

CHAPTER 9

Journalizing Purchases and Cash Payments

OBJECTIVES

After studying Chapter 9, you will be able to:

1. Define accounting terms related to purchases and cash payments for a merchandising business.

2. Identify accounting concepts and practices related to purchases and cash payments for a merchandising business.

3. Journalize purchases of merchandise using a purchases journal.

4. Journalize cash payments and cash discounts using a cash payments journal.

5. Prepare a petty cash report and journalize the reimbursement of the petty cash fund.

6. Total, prove, and rule a cash payments journal and start a new cash payments journal page.

7. Journalize purchases returns and allowances and other transactions using a general journal.

KEY TERMS

- merchandise
- merchandising business
- retail merchandising business
- wholesale merchandising business
- corporation
- share of stock
- capital stock
- stockholder
- special journal

- cost of merchandise
- markup
- vendor
- purchase on account
- purchases journal
- special amount column
- purchase invoice
- terms of sale
- cash payments journal
- cash discount

- purchases discount
- general amount column
- list price
- trade discount
- contra account
- cash short
- cash over
- purchases return
- purchases allowance
- debit memorandum

Point Your Browser
www.C21accounting.com

OfficeMax

Purchasing Synergies Benefit OfficeMax and Boise Office Solutions

Like the trees it manages, Boise Cascade Corporation has grown and evolved from its roots as a wood products company in Boise, Idaho. Building on its strength as a manufacturer of wood building products and paper, Boise established Boise Office Solutions to provide office supplies and furniture directly to businesses, government offices, and educational institutions.

In its 2002 annual report, Boise stated, "Boise Office Solutions' primary goal is profitable growth. This means winning new customers, selling more products to existing customers, and controlling operating costs."

©BLOOMBERG NEWS/LANDOV

Boise took a bold step to achieve that goal through the 2003 acquisition of OfficeMax, an office products company with nearly 1,000 retail outlets. The acquisition more than doubled sales in Boise's office products distribution business.

The company expects to use its combined purchasing power to lower the cost of the office products purchased from other manufacturers and to eliminate duplicate distribution facilities and marketing efforts. Boise expects the combined companies to achieve synergy benefits of $160 million a year.

Critical Thinking

1. How can purchasing more units of an item enable a company to purchase that item at a reduced cost?

2. Can you think of any two other companies that could reduce their operating costs by combining their businesses?

Source: www.bc.com

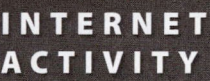

DIGITAL VISION/GETTY IMAGES

INTERNET ACTIVITY

C Corporations, S Corporations, and LLCs

There are several factors to consider when organizing a corporation. One of these is to determine what type of corporation you want to organize. Search the Internet for an explanation of each of the following types of corporations: C Corporation, S Corporation, and a Limited Liability Company (LLC).

Instructions

1. List the benefits and disadvantages of a C Corporation.

2. List the benefits and disadvantages of an S Corporation.

3. List the benefits and disadvantages of a Limited Liability Company.

Journalizing Purchases Using a Purchases Journal

• • • MERCHANDISING BUSINESSES • • •

TechKnow Consulting, the business described in Part 1, is a service business; it sells services for a fee. However, many other businesses purchase goods to sell. Goods that a business purchases to sell are called **merchandise**. A business that purchases and sells goods is called a **merchandising business**. A merchandising business that sells to those who use or consume the goods is called a **retail merchandising business**. A business that buys and resells merchandise to retail merchandising businesses is called a **wholesale merchandising business**. Service and merchandising businesses use many of the same accounts. A merchandising business has additional accounts on the balance sheet and income statement to account for the purchase and sale of merchandise.

BLEND IMAGES/GETTY IMAGES

BUSINESS STRUCTURES

Forming a Corporation

Many businesses need amounts of capital that cannot be easily provided by a proprietorship. These businesses choose to organize using another form of business. An organization with the legal rights of a person and which many persons may own is called a **corporation**. A corporation is formed by receiving approval from a state or federal agency. Each unit of ownership in a corporation is called a **share of stock**. Total shares of ownership in a corporation are called **capital stock**. An owner of one or more shares of a corporation is called a **stockholder**.

A corporation is a business organization that has the legal rights of a person. A corporation can own property, incur liabilities, and enter into contracts in its own name. A corporation may also sell ownership in itself. A person becomes an owner of a corporation by purchasing shares of stock.

The principal difference between the accounting records of proprietorships and corporations is in the capital accounts. Proprietorships have a single capital and drawing account for the owner. A corporation has separate capital accounts for the stock issued and for the earnings kept in the business, which will be explained in more detail in Chapter 16. As in proprietorships, information in a corporation's accounting system is kept separate from the personal records of its owners. [CONCEPT: Business Entity] Periodic financial statements must be sent to the stockholders of the corporation to report the financial activities of the business.

Critical Thinking

1. The names of many corporations include the words *Corporation*, *Incorporated*, *Corp.*, or *Inc.* in their names. Based on their names, identify several corporations in your area.

2. Why do you think many very large companies are organized as corporations?

PHOTO: PHOTODISC/GETTY IMAGES

Janice Kellogg decided to quit her full-time job and turn her ceramic hobby into a retail hobby business. She developed a plan to rent space in a shopping center and operate Hobby Shack six days a week. Hobby Shack would sell a wide variety of art and hobby supplies to individuals, schools, and businesses. Janice planned to expand the merchandise she offers, rent store and office equipment, and employ other individuals to work in the store. However, Janice did not personally have the capital to implement her plan. But with the help of a small group of investors, Janice formed a corporation called Hobby Shack, Inc. Each stockholder received a number of shares of stock based on the amount invested.

Unlike a proprietorship, a corporation exists independent of its owners. Janice expects the Hobby Shack to continue beyond her lifetime and plans to give her shares of stock to her children. [CONCEPT: Going Concern]

•••••••••••••••••••• **USING SPECIAL JOURNALS** ••••••••••••••••

A business with a limited number of daily transactions may record all entries in one journal. A business with many daily transactions may choose to use a separate journal for each kind of transaction. A journal used to record only one kind of transaction is called a **special journal**. Hobby Shack uses five journals to record daily transactions:

1. Purchases journal—for all purchases of merchandise on account
2. Cash payments journal—for all cash payments
3. Sales journal—for all sales of merchandise on account
4. Cash receipts journal—for all cash receipts
5. General journal—for all other transactions

Recording transactions in a sales journal and a cash receipts journal is described in Chapter 10.

CHARACTER COUNTS

Walking on Ethical Ice

Lockheed Martin is an international corporation engaged in the production of advanced technology systems. The company's largest customers are the U.S. Department of Defense and other U.S. federal government agencies.

Lockheed Martin is working to be a leader in ethical conduct. In its code of conduct, "Setting the Standard," the company provides its employees with detailed guidance on making ethical decisions. One method of assisting its employees to make ethical decisions is to provide a list of statements that are warning signs of unethical behavior, such as the following:

"Well, maybe just this once."
"No one will ever know."
"It doesn't matter how it gets done as long as it gets done."
"It sounds too good to be true."
"Everyone does it."

"Shred that document."
"We can hide it."
"No one will get hurt."
"What's in it for me?"
"This will destroy the competition."
"We didn't have this conversation."

Instructions
Think of statements you hear that are warning signs of unethical behavior.

Source: www.lockheedmartin.com

The price a business pays for goods it purchases to sell is called **cost of merchandise**. The selling price of merchandise must be greater than the cost of merchandise for a business to make a profit. The amount added to the cost of merchandise to establish the selling price is called **markup**. Revenue earned from the sale of merchandise includes both the cost of merchandise and markup. Only the markup increases capital. Accounts for the cost of merchandise are kept in a separate division of the general ledger. The cost of merchandise division is shown in Hobby Shack's chart of accounts on page 231.

In addition to purchasing merchandise to sell, a merchandising business also buys supplies and other assets for use in the business. A business from which merchandise is purchased or supplies or other assets are bought is called a **vendor**.

The account used for recording the cost of merchandise is titled Purchases. Purchases is classified as a cost account because it is in the cost of merchandise division in the chart of accounts. Purchases is a temporary account. Because the cost of merchandise reduces capital when the merchandise is purchased, Purchases has a normal debit balance. Therefore, the purchases account increases by a debit and decreases by a credit, as shown in the T account.

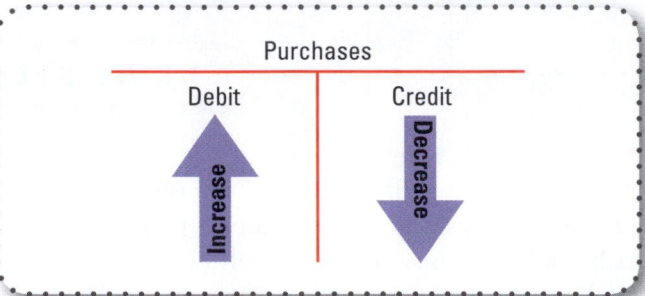

The cost account, Purchases, is used only to record the cost of merchandise purchased. No other items bought, such as supplies, are recorded in the purchases account. These items are recorded in other accounts, such as Supplies. Merchandise and other items bought are recorded and reported at the price agreed upon at the time the transactions occur. The accounting concept *Historical Cost* is applied when the actual amount paid for merchandise or other items bought is recorded. [CONCEPT: Historical Cost]

A transaction in which the merchandise purchased is to be paid for later is called a **purchase on account**. Some businesses that purchase on account from only a few vendors keep a separate general ledger account for each vendor. Businesses that purchase on account from many vendors will have many accounts for vendors. To avoid a bulky general ledger, the total amount owed to all vendors can be summarized in a single general ledger account.

A liability account that summarizes the amounts owed to all vendors is titled Accounts Payable. Hobby Shack uses an accounts payable account. The liability account, Accounts Payable, has a normal credit balance. Therefore, the accounts payable account increases by a credit and decreases by a debit, as shown in the T account.

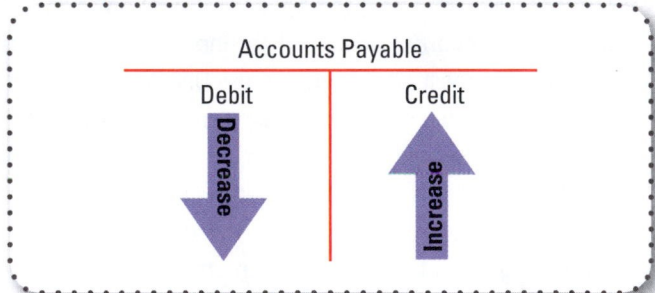

		PURCHASES JOURNAL		PAGE			
	DATE	ACCOUNT CREDITED	PURCH. NO.	POST. REF.	PURCHASES DR. ACCTS. PAY. CR.		
1							1
2							2

A special journal used to record only purchases of merchandise on account is called a **purchases journal**. A purchase on account transaction is recorded on only one line of Hobby Shack's purchases journal. The amount column has two account titles in its heading: *Purchases Dr.* and *Accts. Pay. Cr.* A journal amount column headed with an account title is called a **special amount column**. Special amount columns are used for frequently occurring transactions. All of Hobby Shack's purchase on account transactions involve a debit to Purchases and a credit to Accounts Payable. Therefore, Hobby Shack's special amount column in the purchases journal includes those accounts in the heading.

Using special amount columns eliminates writing general ledger account titles in the Account Title column. Recording entries in a journal with special amount columns saves time.

PURESTOCK/GETTY IMAGES

REMEMBER

All purchase on account transactions are recorded in the purchases journal. If a purchase is made for cash, the transaction is NOT recorded in the purchases journal.

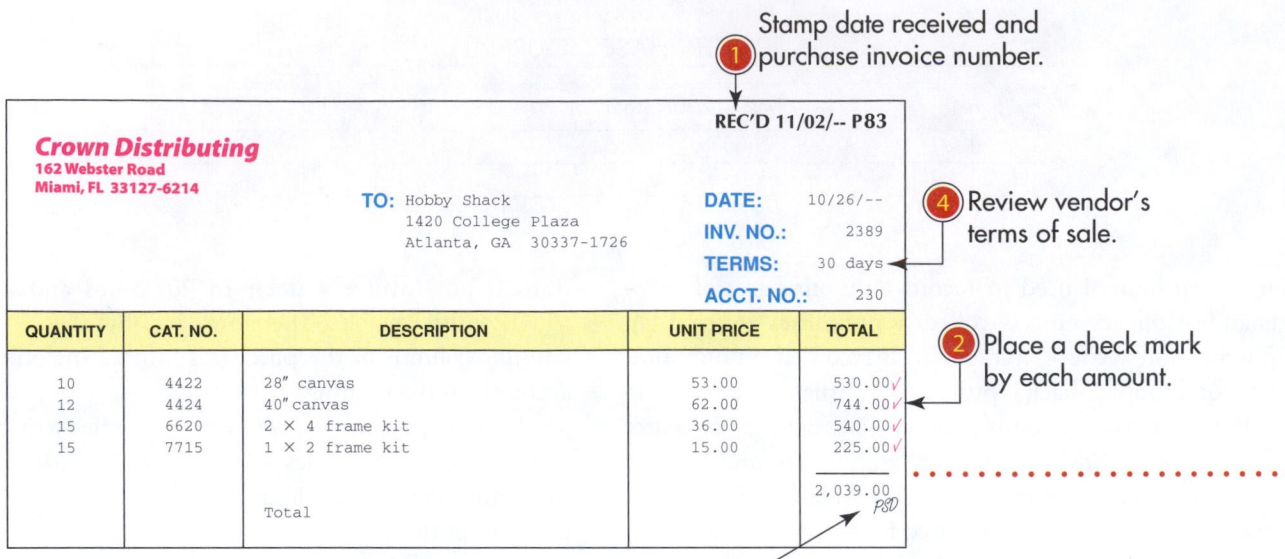

When a vendor sells merchandise to a buyer, the vendor prepares a form showing what has been sold. A form describing the goods sold, the quantity, and the price is known as an invoice. An invoice used as a source document for recording a purchase on account transaction is called a **purchase invoice**. [CONCEPT: Objective Evidence]

A purchase invoice lists the quantity, the description, the price of each item, and the total amount of the invoice. A purchase invoice provides the information needed for recording a purchase on account.

Hobby Shack takes the following actions when a purchase invoice is received.

STEPS   RECEIVING A PURCHASE INVOICE

1. Stamp the date received, *11/02/--*, and Hobby Shack's purchase invoice number, *P83*, in the upper right corner.

   This date should not be confused with the vendor's date on the invoice, *10/26*. Hobby Shack assigns numbers in sequence to easily identify all purchase invoices. The number stamped on the invoice, *P83*, is the number assigned by Hobby Shack to this purchase invoice. This number should not be confused with the invoice number, *2389*, assigned by the vendor. Each vendor uses a different numbering system. Therefore, vendor invoice numbers could not be recorded in sequence, which would make it impossible to detect a missing invoice.

2. Place a check mark by each of the amounts in the Total column to show that the items have been received and that amounts have been checked and are correct.

3. The person who checked the invoice should initial below the total amount in the Total column.

4. Review the vendor's terms. An agreement between a buyer and a seller about payment for merchandise is called the **terms of sale**. The terms of sale on the invoice are 30 days. These terms mean that payment is due within 30 days from the vendor's date of the invoice. The invoice is dated October 26. Therefore, payment must be made by November 25.

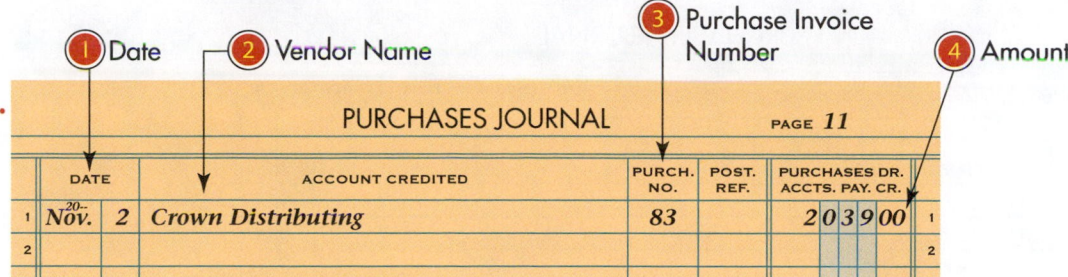

① Date ② Vendor Name ③ Purchase Invoice Number ④ Amount

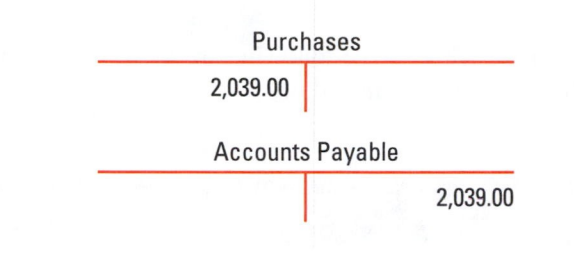

November 2. Purchased merchandise on account from Crown Distributing, $2,039.00. Purchase Invoice No. 83.

Purchases	
2,039.00	

Accounts Payable	
	2,039.00

A purchase on account transaction increases the amount owed to a vendor. This transaction increases the purchases account balance and increases the accounts payable account balance. Because the purchases account has a normal debit balance, Purchases is debited for $2,039.00 to show the increase in this cost account. The accounts payable account has a normal credit balance. Therefore, Accounts Payable is credited for $2,039.00 to show the increase in this liability account.

STEPS ⬤ JOURNALIZING A PURCHASE OF MERCHANDISE ON ACCOUNT

① Write the date, *20--, Nov. 2*, in the Date column.

② Write the vendor name, *Crown Distributing*, in the Account Credited column.

③ Write the purchase invoice number, *83*, in the Purch. No. column.

④ Write the amount of the invoice, *$2,039.00*, in the special amount column. This single amount is both a debit to *Purchases* and a credit to *Accounts Payable*. Therefore, it is not necessary to write the title of either general ledger account.

The way Hobby Shack keeps a record of the amount owed to each vendor is described in Chapter 11.

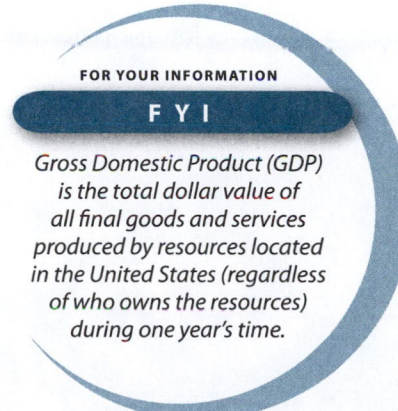

FOR YOUR INFORMATION

FYI

Gross Domestic Product (GDP) is the total dollar value of all final goods and services produced by resources located in the United States (regardless of who owns the resources) during one year's time.

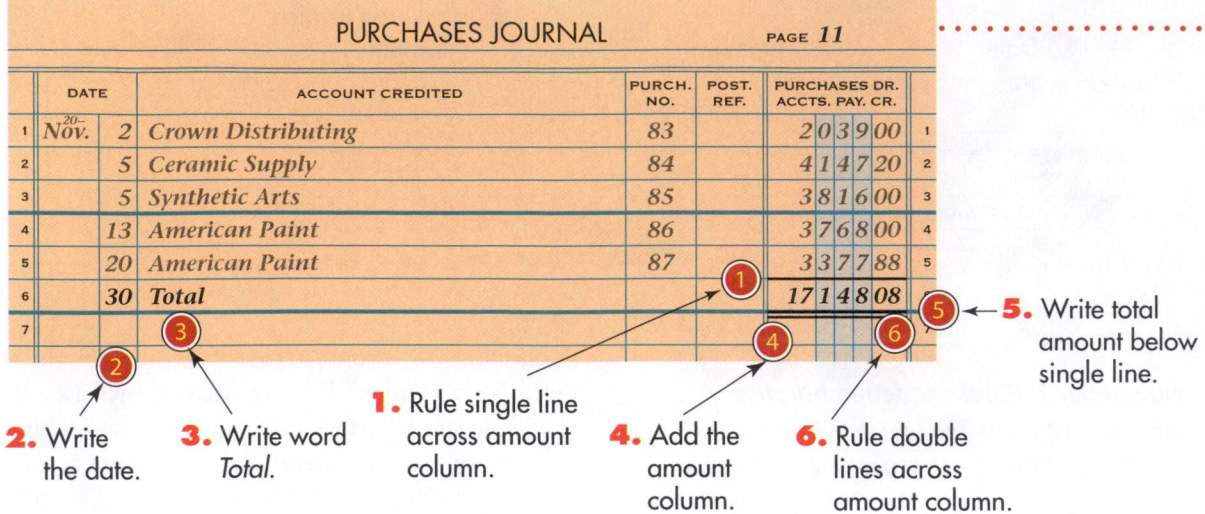

PURCHASES JOURNAL   PAGE *11*

	DATE		ACCOUNT CREDITED	PURCH. NO.	POST. REF.	PURCHASES DR. ACCTS. PAY. CR.	
1	*Nov.*	*2*	*Crown Distributing*	83		2 0 3 9 00	1
2		*5*	*Ceramic Supply*	84		4 1 4 7 20	2
3		*5*	*Synthetic Arts*	85		3 8 1 6 00	3
4		*13*	*American Paint*	86		3 7 6 8 00	4
5		*20*	*American Paint*	87		3 3 7 7 88	5
6		*30*	*Total*			17 1 4 8 08	6
7							7

1. Rule single line across amount column.

2. Write the date.

3. Write word *Total*.

4. Add the amount column.

5. Write total amount below single line.

6. Rule double lines across amount column.

Hobby Shack always rules its purchases journal at the end of each month, even if the page for the month is not full.

Hobby Shack uses the following six steps in ruling its purchases journal at the end of each month.

STEPS   **TOTALING AND RULING A PURCHASES JOURNAL**

① Rule a single line across the amount column under the last entry.

② Write the date, *30*, in the Date column.

③ Write the word *Total* in the Account Credited column.

④ Add the amount column. Verify the total by re-adding the column in reverse order.

⑤ Write the total, *$17,148.08*, directly below the single line in the amount column.

⑥ Rule double lines across the amount column directly below the total amount to show that the total has been verified as correct.

Posting from a purchases journal is described in Chapter 11.

merchandise

merchandising business

retail merchandising business

wholesale merchandising business

corporation

share of stock

capital stock

stockholder

special journal

cost of merchandise

markup

vendor

purchase on account

purchases journal

special amount column

purchase invoice

terms of sale

AUDIT YOUR UNDERSTANDING

1. What kinds of transactions are recorded in a purchases journal?
2. For what are special amount columns in a journal used?
3. Why are there two account titles in the amount column of the purchases journal?
4. What is the advantage of having special amount columns in a journal?

WORK TOGETHER 9-1

Journalizing purchases using a purchases journal

The purchases journal for Lambert Hardware is given in the *Working Papers*. Your instructor will guide you through the following examples.

1. Using the current year, journalize these transactions on page 10 of the purchases journal. Purchase invoices are abbreviated as P.

Transactions:

Oct. 2. Purchased merchandise on account from American Tools, $1,230.00. P116.
    7. Purchased merchandise on account from Harris Manufacturing, Inc., $480.00. P117.
   11. Purchased merchandise on account from Keasler Supply, $780.00. P118.

2. Total and rule the purchases journal.

ON YOUR OWN 9-1

Journalizing purchases using a purchases journal

The purchases journal for Classic Gifts, Inc., is given in the *Working Papers*. Work this problem independently.

1. Using the current year, journalize these transactions on page 11 of the purchases journal. Purchase invoices are abbreviated as P.

Transactions:

Nov. 4. Purchased merchandise on account from Ulman Supply, Inc., $670.00. P149.
    9. Purchased merchandise on account from Else Silver Co., $2,345.00. P150.
   18. Purchased merchandise on account from Pratt Paints, $1,150.00. P151.

2. Total and rule the purchases journal.

Journalizing Cash Payments Using a Cash Payments Journal

CASH PAYMENTS JOURNAL

			CK. NO.	POST. REF.	GENERAL		ACCOUNTS PAYABLE DEBIT	PURCHASES DISCOUNT CREDIT	CASH CREDIT	
	DATE	ACCOUNT TITLE			DEBIT	CREDIT				
1										1

CASH PAYMENTS JOURNAL   PAGE

A special journal used to record only cash payment transactions is called a **cash payments journal**. Only those columns needed to record cash payment transactions are included in Hobby Shack's cash payments journal. A cash payments journal may be designed to accommodate a business's frequent cash payment transactions. Since all cash payment transactions affect the cash account, a special amount column is provided for this general ledger account. In addition, Hobby Shack has many cash payment transactions affecting the accounts payable account. Therefore, a special amount column is provided in the cash payments journal for this general ledger account.

Normally, the total amount shown on a purchase invoice is the amount that a customer is expected to pay. To encourage early payment, however, a vendor may allow a deduction from the invoice amount. A deduction that a vendor allows on the invoice amount to encourage prompt payment is called a **cash discount**. A cash discount on purchases taken by a customer is called a **purchases discount**. When a purchases discount is taken, the customer pays less than the invoice amount previously recorded in the purchases account. Taking purchases discounts reduces the customer's cost of merchandise purchased. Because it often takes purchase discounts, Hobby Shack uses a cash payments journal with a Purchases Discount Credit column.

A journal amount column that is not headed with an account title is called a **general amount column**. Hobby Shack's cash payments journal has General Debit and General Credit columns for cash payment transactions that do not occur often, such as monthly rent.

All cash payments made by Hobby Shack are recorded in a cash payments journal. The source document for most cash payments is the check issued. A few payments, such as bank service charges, are made as direct withdrawals from the company's bank account. For payments not using a check, the source document is a memorandum. Most of Hobby Shack's cash payments are to vendors and for expenses that are paid by check.

REMEMBER

Only cash payment transactions are recorded in the cash payments journal.

1. Date   **2.** Account Title   **3.** Check Number   **4.** Debit   **5.** Credit

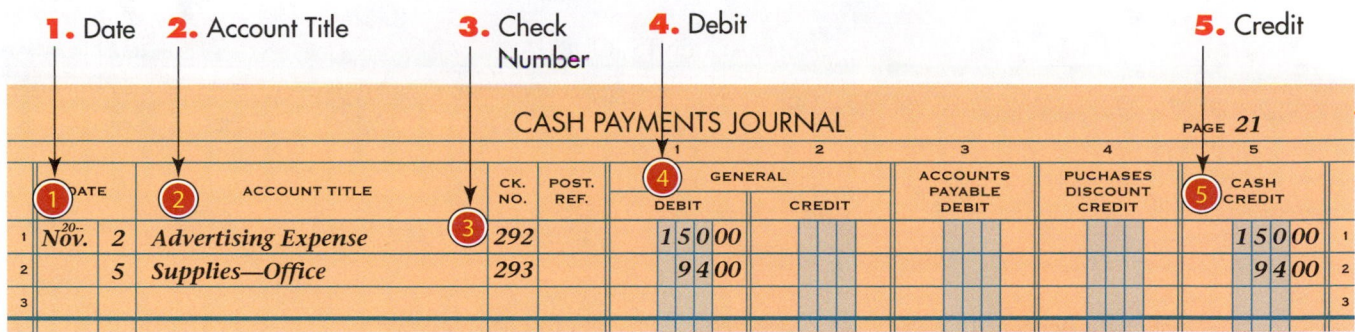

							1		2	3	4	5
	DATE	**ACCOUNT TITLE**	**CK. NO.**	**POST. REF.**		**GENERAL**			**ACCOUNTS PAYABLE DEBIT**	**PUCHASES DISCOUNT CREDIT**		**CASH CREDIT**

CASH PAYMENTS JOURNAL — PAGE 21

	DATE	ACCOUNT TITLE	CK. NO.	POST. REF.	GENERAL DEBIT	GENERAL CREDIT	ACCOUNTS PAYABLE DEBIT	PUCHASES DISCOUNT CREDIT	CASH CREDIT	
1	Nov. 20-- 2	Advertising Expense	292		150 00				150 00	1
2	5	Supplies—Office	293		94 00				94 00	2
3										3

November 2. Paid cash for advertising, $150.00. Check No. 292.

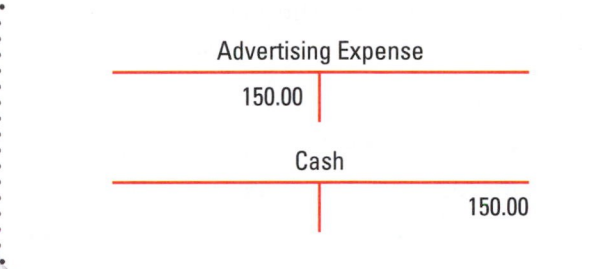

Advertising Expense
| 150.00 | |

Cash
| | 150.00 |

Hobby Shack usually pays for an expense at the time the transaction occurs.

This cash payment increases the advertising expense account balance and decreases the cash account balance. The expense account Advertising Expense has a normal debit balance and increases by a debit of $150.00. The asset account Cash also has a normal debit balance and decreases by a credit of $150.00.

STEPS · **JOURNALIZING A CASH PAYMENT OF AN EXPENSE**

1. Write the date, *20--, Nov. 2*, in the Date column.

2. Write the account title, *Advertising Expense*, in the Account Title column.

3. Write the check number, *292*, in the Ck. No. column.

4. Write the debit amount to Advertising Expense, *$150.00*, in the General Debit column.

5. Write the credit amount, *$150.00*, in the Cash Credit column.

. . . . **BUYING SUPPLIES FOR CASH** . . . .

November 5. Paid cash for office supplies, $94.00. Check No. 293.

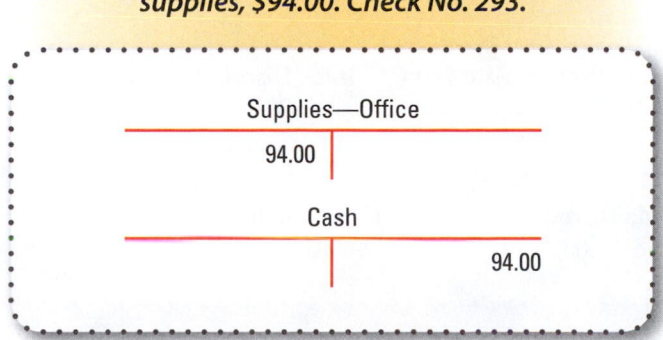

Supplies—Office
| 94.00 | |

Cash
| | 94.00 |

Hobby Shack buys supplies for use in the business. Supplies are not recorded in the purchases account because supplies are not intended for sale. Cash register tapes and price tags are examples of supplies used in a business.

This transaction increases the office supplies account balance and decreases the cash account balance. The steps for journalizing buying supplies for cash are similar to journalizing paying cash for an expense.

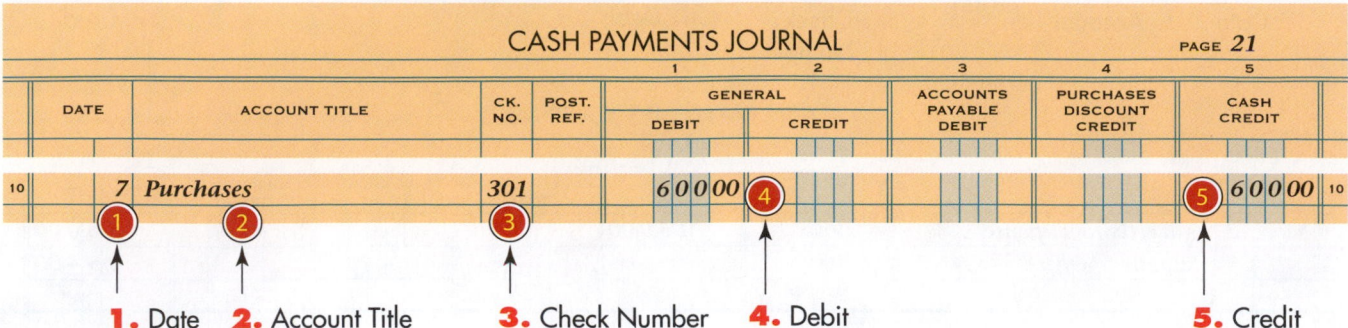

1. Date **2.** Account Title **3.** Check Number **4.** Debit **5.** Credit

Businesses usually purchase merchandise on account. However, vendors may not extend credit to all of their customers. Thus, these businesses must pay the vendor with a check before the merchandise is either shipped or delivered.

Trade Discount

Most manufacturers and wholesalers print catalogs and maintain Internet sites that describe their products. Generally, the prices listed are the manufacturers' suggested retail prices. The retail price listed in a catalog or on an Internet site is called a **list price**. When a merchandising business purchases a number of products from a manufacturer, the price frequently is quoted as "list price less trade discount." A reduction in the list price granted to customers is called a **trade discount**. Trade discounts are also used to quote different prices for different quantities purchased without changing catalog or list prices.

When a trade discount is granted, the seller's invoice shows the actual amount charged. This amount after the trade discount has been deducted from the list price is referred to as the *invoice amount*. Only the invoice amount is used in a journal entry. [CONCEPT: Historical Cost] No journal entry is made to show the amount of a trade discount.

Cash Purchases

Hobby Shack pays cash for 10 ceramic molds with an invoice amount of $600.00, the list price less a trade discount. Because the transaction involves a cash payment, it is recorded in the cash payments journal. Only purchases on account are recorded in the purchases journal.

November 7. Purchased merchandise for cash, $600.00. Check No. 301.

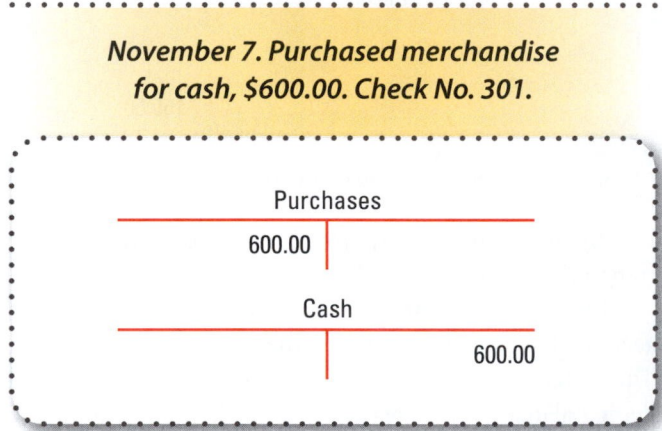

The list price for the 10 ceramic molds is $1,500.00. The invoice price is the list price, less a 60% trade discount. The total invoice amount is calculated in two steps, as follows.

STEP 1: Total				
List Price	×	Trade Discount Rate	=	Trade Discount
$1,500.00	×	60%	=	$900.00

STEP 2: Total				
List Price	−	Trade Discount	=	Invoice Amount
$1,500.00	−	$900.00	=	$600.00

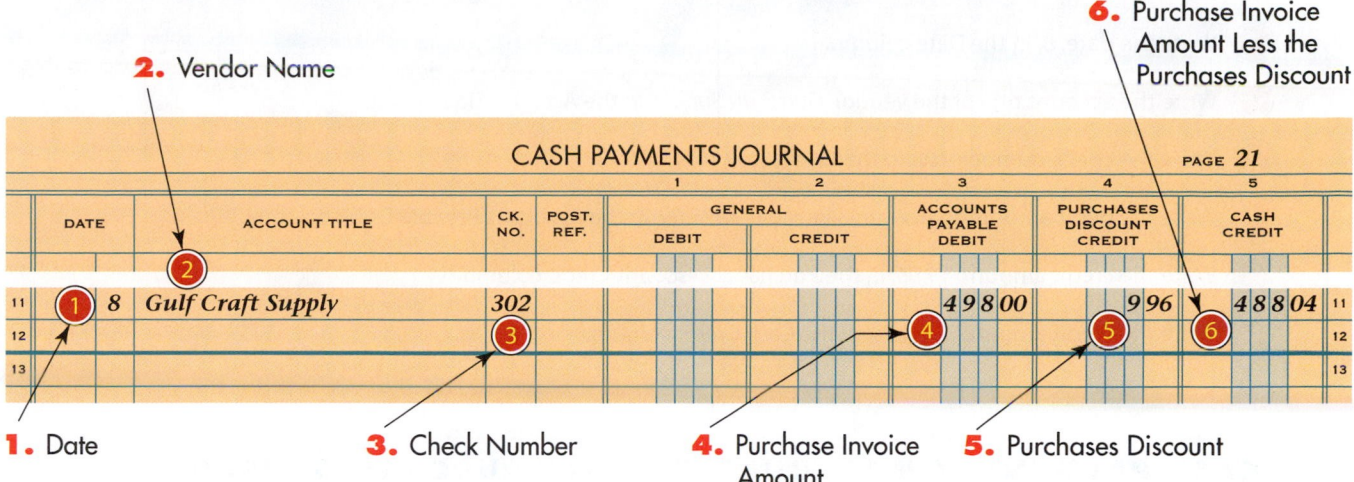

2. Vendor Name

6. Purchase Invoice Amount Less the Purchases Discount

1. Date

3. Check Number

4. Purchase Invoice Amount

5. Purchases Discount

A cash discount is stated as a percentage deducted from the invoice amount. For example, *2/10, n/30* is a common term of sale, which is read *two ten, net thirty*. *Two ten* means that 2% of the invoice amount may be deducted if the invoice is paid within 10 days of the invoice date. *Net thirty* means that the total invoice amount must be paid within 30 days.

Purchases discounts are recorded in a general ledger account titled Purchases Discount. An account that reduces a related account on a financial statement is called a **contra account**. Purchases Discount is a contra account to Purchases and is included in the cost of merchandise division of the general ledger. On an income statement, Purchases Discount is deducted from the balance of its related account, Purchases.

Since contra accounts are deductions from their related accounts, contra account normal balances are opposite the normal balances of their related accounts. The normal balance for Purchases is a debit. Therefore, the normal balance for Purchases Discount, a contra account to Purchases, is a credit. Trade discounts are not recorded; however, cash discounts are recorded as purchases discounts because they decrease the recorded invoice amount.

November 8. Paid cash on account to Gulf Craft Supply, $488.04, covering Purchase Invoice No. 82 for $498.00, less 2% discount, $9.96. Check No. 302.

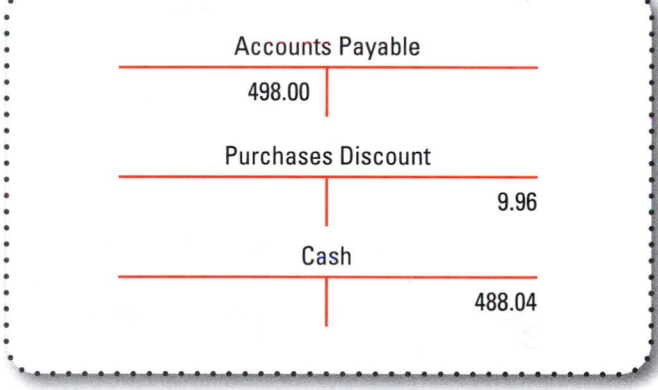

The way Hobby Shack keeps a record of the amount paid to each vendor is described in Chapter 11.

The steps, numbered above, are described on the top of page 246.

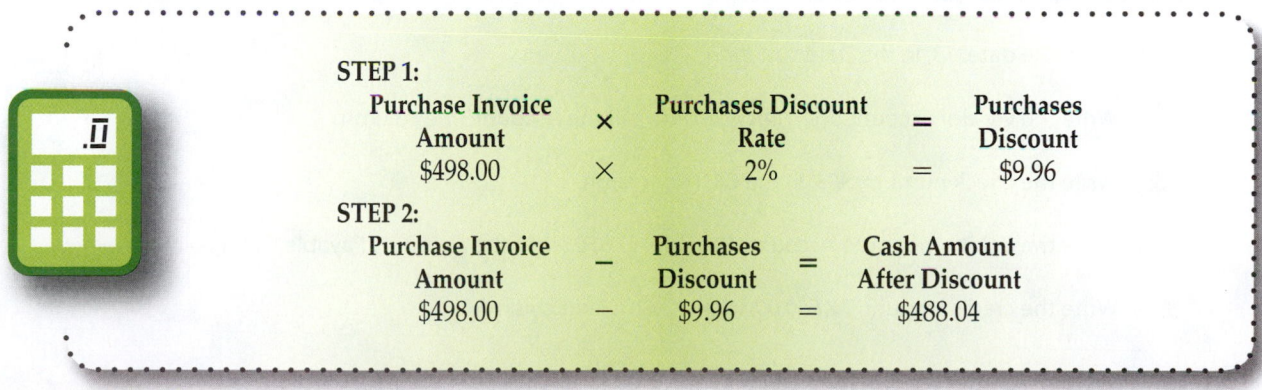

STEP 1:

Purchase Invoice Amount	×	Purchases Discount Rate	=	Purchases Discount
$498.00	×	2%	=	$9.96

STEP 2:

Purchase Invoice Amount	−	Purchases Discount	=	Cash Amount After Discount
$498.00	−	$9.96	=	$488.04

STEPS — JOURNALIZING A CASH PAYMENT ON ACCOUNT WITH PURCHASES DISCOUNT

1. Write the date, *8*, in the Date column.

2. Write the account title of the vendor, *Gulf Craft Supply*, in the Account Title column.

3. Write the check number, *302*, in the Ck. No. column.

4. Write the debit amount to Accounts Payable, *$498.00*, in the Accounts Payable Debit column.

5. Write the credit amount, *$9.96*, in the Purchases Discount Credit column.

6. Write the credit amount, *$488.04*, in the Cash Credit column.

CASH PAYMENTS ON ACCOUNT WITHOUT PURCHASES DISCOUNTS

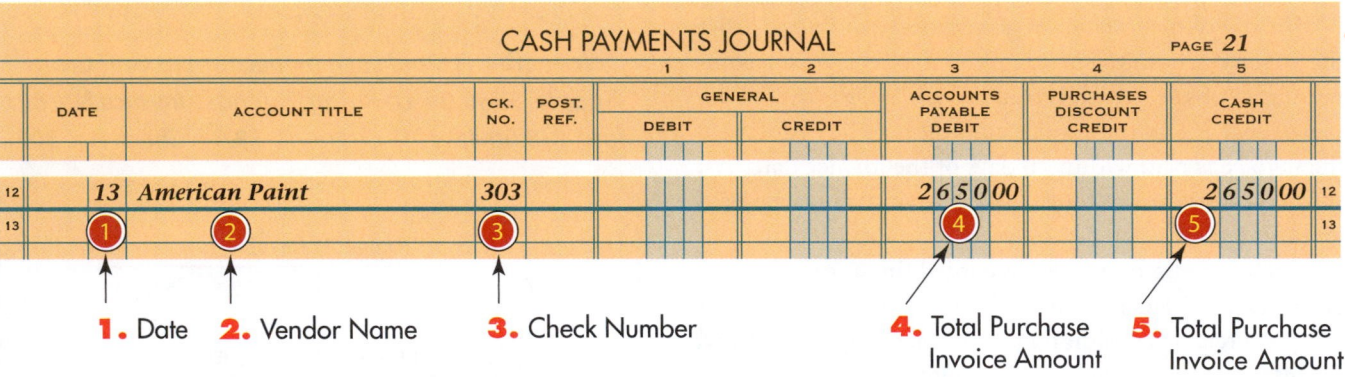

1. Date   **2.** Vendor Name   **3.** Check Number   **4.** Total Purchase Invoice Amount   **5.** Total Purchase Invoice Amount

Some vendors do not offer purchases discounts. Sometimes a business does not have the cash available to take advantage of a purchases discount. In both cases, the full purchase invoice amount is paid.

Hobby Shack purchased merchandise on account from American Paint on October 25. American Paint's credit terms are n/30. Therefore, Hobby Shack will pay the full amount of the purchase invoice, $2,650.00, within 30 days of the invoice date, October 25.

> *November 13. Paid cash on account to American Paint, $2,650.00, covering Purchase Invoice No. 77. Check No. 303.*

STEPS — JOURNALIZING A CASH PAYMENT OF AN EXPENSE

1. Write the date, *13*, in the Date column.

2. Write the vendor account title, *American Paint*, in the Account Title column.

3. Write the check number, *303*, in the Ck. No. column.

4. Write the debit amount to Accounts Payable, *$2,650.00*, in the Accounts Payable Debit column.

5. Write the credit amount, *$2,650.00*, in the Cash Credit column.

End of Lesson
REVIEW

TERMS REVIEW

- cash payments journal
- cash discount
- purchases discount
- general amount column
- list price
- trade discount
- contra account

AUDIT YOUR UNDERSTANDING

1. Why would a vendor offer a cash discount to a customer?
2. What is recorded in the general amount columns of the cash payments journal?
3. What is the difference between purchasing merchandise and buying supplies?
4. What is meant by terms of sale 2/10, n/30?

WORK TOGETHER 9-2

Journalizing cash payments using a cash payments journal

The cash payments journal for Franklin Lumber is given in the *Working Papers*. Your instructor will guide you through the following example.

1. Using the current year, journalize these transactions on page 10 of a cash payments journal. The checks used as source documents are abbreviated as C.

Transactions:

Oct. 1. Paid cash for telephone bill, $85.00. C321.
7. Paid cash for office supplies, $52.00. C322.
11. Paid cash to GMT Hardware for merchandise with a list price of $800.00, less a 60% trade discount. C323.
17. Paid cash on account to West Supply covering Purchase Invoice No. 199 for $3,420.00, less 2% discount. C324.
19. Paid cash on account to Quill Forest Products covering Purchase Invoice No. 182 for $4,380.00. No cash discount was offered. C325.

ON YOUR OWN 9-2

Journalizing cash payments using a cash payments journal

The cash payments journal for Rapid Auto Supply is given in the *Working Papers*. Work this problem independently.

1. Using the current year, journalize these transactions on page 11 of the cash payments journal. The checks used as source documents are abbreviated as C.

Transactions:

Nov. 2. Paid cash for the electric bill, $248.00. C432.
6. Paid cash for office supplies, $142.00. C433.
9. Paid cash to Zebra Metals for merchandise with a list price of $3,400.00, less a 40% trade discount. C434.
12. Paid cash on account to Racing Images covering Purchase Invoice No. 543 for $4,230.00, less 2% discount. C435.
14. Paid cash on account to SPL Renovations covering Purchase Invoice No. 182 for $2,573.00. No cash discount was offered. C436.

Performing Additional Cash Payments Journal Operations

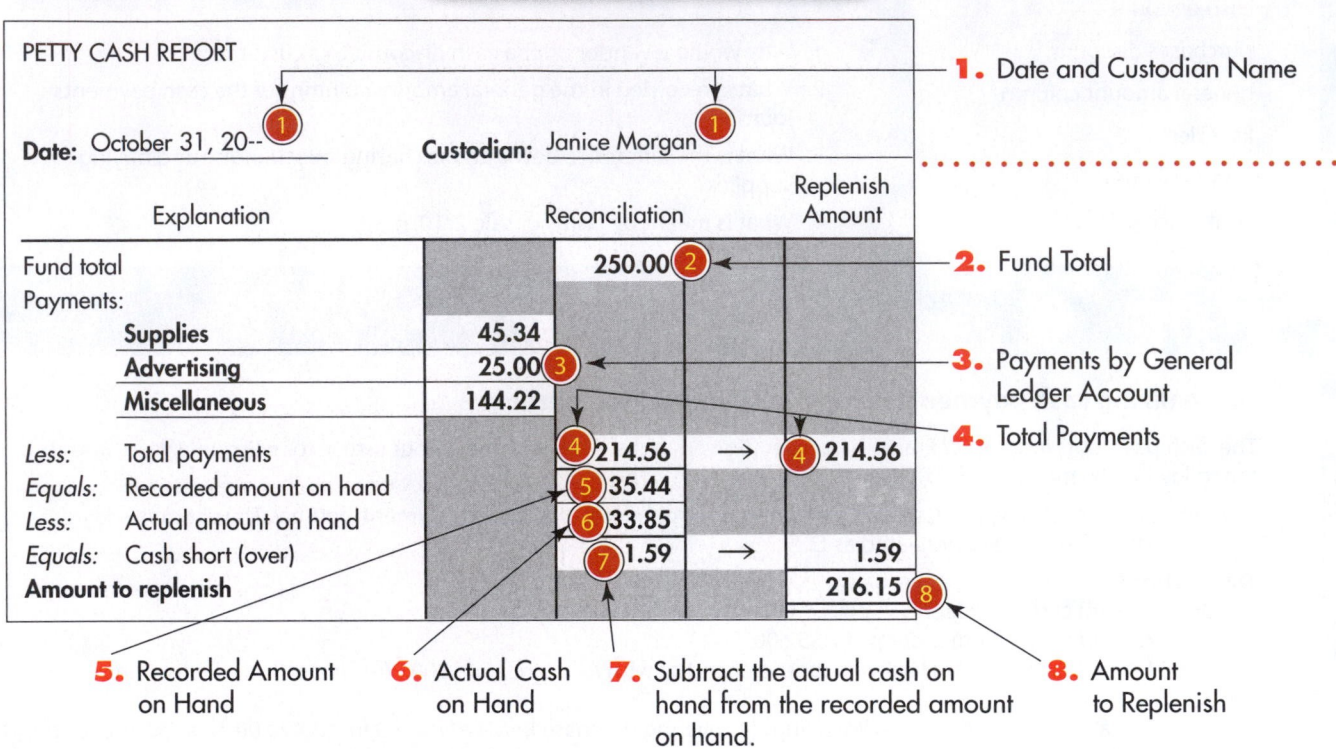

PETTY CASH REPORT

PETTY CASH REPORT

1. Date and Custodian Name

Date: October 31, 20-- ①   **Custodian:** Janice Morgan ①

Explanation		Reconciliation	Replenish Amount
Fund total		250.00 ②	
Payments:			
Supplies	45.34		
Advertising	25.00 ③		
Miscellaneous	144.22		
Less: Total payments		④ 214.56 →	④ 214.56
Equals: Recorded amount on hand		⑤ 35.44	
Less: Actual amount on hand		⑥ 33.85	
Equals: Cash short (over)		⑦ 1.59 →	1.59
Amount to replenish			216.15 ⑧

2. Fund Total

3. Payments by General Ledger Account

4. Total Payments

5. Recorded Amount on Hand

6. Actual Cash on Hand

7. Subtract the actual cash on hand from the recorded amount on hand.

8. Amount to Replenish

A petty cash fund enables a business to pay cash for small expenses without writing a check, as described in Chapter 5.

Errors may be made when making payments from a petty cash fund. These errors cause a difference between actual cash on hand and the record of the amount of cash that should be on hand. A petty cash on hand amount that is less than a recorded amount is called ==cash short==. A petty cash on hand amount that is more than a recorded amount is called ==cash over==.

The custodian prepares a petty cash report when the petty cash fund is to be replenished.

STEPS **PREPARING A PETTY CASH REPORT**

① Write the date, *October 31, 20--*, and custodian name, *Janice Morgan*, in the report heading.

② Write the fund total, *$250.00*, from the general ledger account.

③ Summarize petty cash payments by totals for each general ledger account.

④ Calculate and write the total payments, *$214.56*, in the Reconciliation and Replenish Amount columns.

⑤ Calculate and write the recorded amount on hand, *$35.44* ($250.00 − $214.56).

⑥ Write the actual amount of cash on hand, *$33.85*, in the Reconciliation column.

⑦ Subtract the actual amount on hand, *$33.85*, from the recorded amount on hand, $35.44, and write the amount, *$1.59*, in the Reconciliation and Replenish Amount columns. Note that petty cash is short by $1.59. The actual amount of petty cash on hand is $1.59 less than the recorded amount.

⑧ Write the total of the replenish amount, *$216.15*.

PETTY CASH REPORT

Date: November 18, 20--   **Custodian:** Janice Morgan

Explanation		Reconciliation		Replenish Amount
Fund total		250.00		
Payments:				
	Supplies—Office	32.33		
	Advertising	50.00		
	Miscellaneous	128.50		
Less:	Total payments		210.83 →	210.83
Equals:	Recorded amount on hand		39.17	
Less:	Actual amount on hand		41.34	
Equals:	Cash short (over)		(2.17) →	(2.17)
Amount to replenish				208.66

4. Expense Amounts ④

6. Total Cash Payment

CASH PAYMENTS JOURNAL

PAGE 21

					1 GENERAL	2	3 ACCOUNTS PAYABLE	4 PURCHASES DISCOUNT	5 CASH
	DATE	ACCOUNT TITLE	CK. NO.	POST. REF.	DEBIT	CREDIT	DEBIT	CREDIT	CREDIT
19	① 18	Supplies—Office	310		3 2 33				2 0 8 66
20		Advertising Expense			5 0 00				
21		Miscellaneous Expense	③		1 2 8 50				
22	②	Cash Short and Over				2 17			

1. Date   **2.** Account Titles   **3.** Check Number   **5.** Cash Short as a Debit, Cash Over as a Credit

Petty cash short and petty cash over are recorded in an account titled Cash Short and Over. The account is a temporary account. At the end of the fiscal year, the cash short and over account is closed to Income Summary.

The balance of Cash Short and Over can be either a debit or credit. However, the balance is usually a debit because the petty cash fund is more likely to be short than over. A cash shortage adds to the cost of operating a business. Thus, the account is classified as an operating expense. Note that in Step 5, the amount of petty cash over is recorded in the General Credit column. If petty cash were short, the amount would be recorded in the General Debit column.

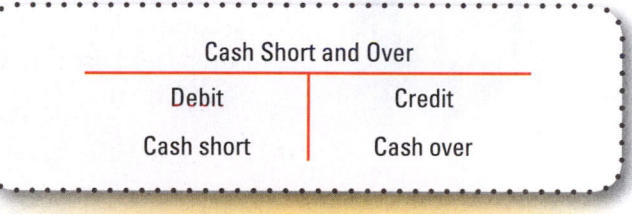

Cash Short and Over	
Debit	Credit
Cash short	Cash over

November 18. Paid cash to replenish the petty cash fund, $208.66: office supplies, $32.33; advertising, $50.00; miscellaneous, $128.50; cash over, $2.17. Check No. 310.

The petty cash fund is replenished for the amount paid out, $210.83, less cash over, $2.17. This total amount, $208.66, restores the fund's cash balance to its original amount, $250.00 ($210.83 − $2.17 + $41.34 cash on hand).

TOTALING, PROVING, AND RULING A CASH PAYMENTS JOURNAL PAGE TO CARRY TOTALS FORWARD

1. Rule a single line across all amount columns.

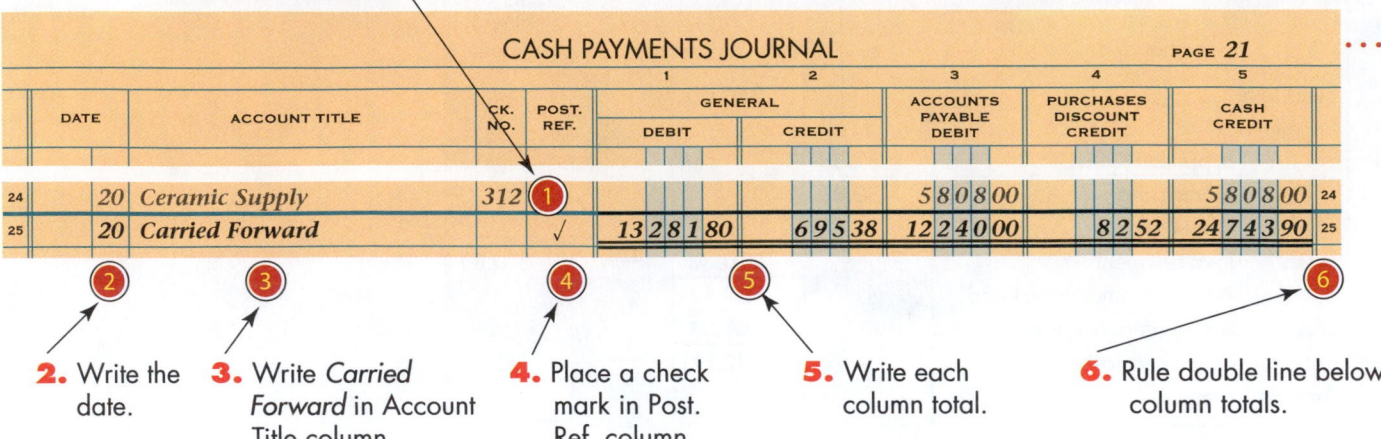

	DATE	ACCOUNT TITLE	CK. NO.	POST. REF.	GENERAL DEBIT	GENERAL CREDIT	ACCOUNTS PAYABLE DEBIT	PURCHASES DISCOUNT CREDIT	CASH CREDIT	
24	20	Ceramic Supply	312	①			5 8 0 8 00		5 8 0 8 00	24
25	20	Carried Forward		✓	13 2 8 1 80	6 9 5 38	12 2 4 0 00	8 2 52	24 7 4 3 90	25

2. Write the date.

3. Write *Carried Forward* in Account Title column.

4. Place a check mark in Post. Ref. column.

5. Write each column total.

6. Rule double line below column totals.

A journal is proved and ruled whenever a journal page is filled and always at the end of a month.

After all November 20 entries are recorded, page 21 of Hobby Shack's cash payments journal is filled. Column totals of page 21 are totaled and proved before being forwarded to page 22. The proof that Hobby Shack's debit totals equal the credit totals on page 21 of the journal is shown.

If the total debits do not equal the total credits, the errors must be found and corrected before any more work is completed.

After a journal page has been totaled and proved, the journal is ruled in preparation for forwarding to the next page.

Column Title	Debit Column Totals	Credit Column Totals
General Debit	$13,281.80	
General Credit		$ 695.38
Accounts Payable Debit	12,240.00	
Purchases Discount Credit.......		82.52
Cash Credit		24,743.90
Totals	$25,521.80	$25,521.80

STEPS · STEPS FOR RULING A CASH PAYMENTS JOURNAL

① Rule a single line across all amount columns directly below the last entry to indicate that all the columns are to be added.

② On the next line, write the date, *20*, in the Date column.

③ Write the words *Carried Forward* in the Account Title column.

④ Place a check mark in the Post. Ref. column to show that nothing on this line needs to be posted.

⑤ Write each column total below the single line.

⑥ Rule double lines below the column totals across all amount columns to show that the totals have been verified as correct.

2. Write the date.

3. Write *Brought Forward* in Account Title column.

1. Write the journal page number.

CASH PAYMENTS JOURNAL

PAGE 22 ①

	DATE		ACCOUNT TITLE	CK. NO.	POST. REF.	GENERAL DEBIT (1)	GENERAL CREDIT (2)	ACCOUNTS PAYABLE DEBIT (3)	PURCHASES DISCOUNT CREDIT (4)	CASH CREDIT (5)	
1	20-- Nov.	20 ③	*Brought Forward*		✓	13 28 1 80	69 5 38	12 2 40 00	8 2 52	24 7 4 3 90	1

4. Place a check mark in Post. Ref. column.

5. Record column totals brought forward from previous page.

The totals from the previous journal page are carried forward to the next journal page.

The totals are recorded on the first line of the new page.

STEPS  STEPS FOR FORWARDING TOTALS TO A NEW JOURNAL PAGE

① Write the journal page number, *22*, at the top of the journal.

② Write the date, *20--, Nov. 20*, in the Date column.

③ Write the words *Brought Forward* in the Account Title column.

④ Place a check mark in the Post. Ref. column to show that nothing on this line needs to be posted.

⑤ Record the column totals brought forward from page 21 of the journal.

GLOBAL PERSPECTIVE

Accountancy in Africa

The accounting profession in Africa has been influenced by the European colonial powers that formerly governed there. Most African nations gained independence in the mid-twentieth century.

In Nigeria, Kenya, Ghana, and Zimbabwe (formerly under British rule), accounting is seen as a tool for financial management and is oriented toward the needs of the enterprise. Tax authorities are concerned with account items that can be valued in different ways, such as fixed assets, inventories, and depreciation.

In Togo, Rwanda, and Gambia (formerly ruled by France), accountancy is regulated by charts of accounts that standardize financial transactions and annual financial statements.

In Angola, Cape Verde, and São Tomé and Principe (formerly ruled by Portugal), the accounting system also is based on charts of accounts that provide rules and regulations for companies. There are no professional accounting organizations in many African countries.

In the expanding economies of many developing African countries, the belief is that it is important to have well-qualified and experienced accountants and a sound accounting framework to sustain economic growth.

Critical Thinking

1. What should an investor consider when comparing financial statements of companies in Kenya and Gambia?

2. What would be the advantages of having a professional accounting organization in a country that does not currently have one?

1. Rule a single line across all amount columns.

CASH PAYMENTS JOURNAL   PAGE 22

	DATE	ACCOUNT TITLE	CK. NO.	POST. REF.	GENERAL DEBIT (1)	GENERAL CREDIT (2)	ACCOUNTS PAYABLE DEBIT (3)	PURCHASES DISCOUNT CREDIT (4)	CASH CREDIT (5)	
1	Nov. 20	Brought Forward		✓	13 2 8 1 80	6 9 5 38	12 2 4 0 00	8 2 52	24 7 4 3 90	1
8	29	Advertising Expense	319		1 5 0 0 00				1 5 0 0 00	8
9	30	Floral Designs	320				1 6 5 0 00	3 3 00	1 6 1 7 00	9
10	30	Rent Expense	321		6 0 0 00				6 0 0 00	10
11	30	Totals			16 4 6 2 99	1 3 9 0 75	17 9 8 4 00	1 5 4 84	32 9 0 1 40	11

2. Write the date.

3. Write *Totals* in Account Title column.

4. Write each column total.

5. Rule double line across all amount columns.

Equality of debits and credits in a journal is proved at the end of each month. Proof for Hobby Shack's cash payments journal for November is shown.

Column Title	Debit Column Totals	Credit Column Totals
General Debit	$16,462.99	
General Credit		$ 1,390.75
Accounts Payable Debit	17,984.00	
Purchases Discount Credit.......		154.84
Cash Credit		32,901.40
Totals	$34,446.99	$34,446.99

The two totals, $34,446.99, are equal. Equality of debits and credits in Hobby Shack's cash payments journal for November is proved.

After a cash payments journal has been totaled and proved at the end of the month, the journal is ruled.

STEPS   STEPS FOR RULING A CASH PAYMENTS JOURNAL AT THE END OF THE MONTH

1. Rule a single line across all amount columns directly below the last entry to indicate that all the columns are to be added.

2. On the next line write the date, *30*, in the date column.

3. Write the word *Totals* in the Account Title column.

4. Write each column total below the single line.

5. Rule double lines across all amount columns to show that the totals have been verified as correct.

Posting from a cash payments journal is described in Chapter 11.

End of Lesson
REVIEW

TERMS REVIEW

cash short

cash over

1. When journalizing a cash payment to replenish petty cash, what is entered in the Account Title column of the cash payments journal?
2. What is the usual balance of the account Cash Short and Over?
3. List the five steps for ruling a cash payments journal at the end of the month.

WORK TOGETHER 9-3

Performing other cash payments journal operations

The cash payments journals and petty cash report for Keller Lighting are given in the *Working Papers*. Your instructor will guide you through the following examples. The abbreviation for a check is C.

1. Rule page 5 of the cash payments journal using March 27 of the current year.
2. Begin page 6 of a cash payments journal.
3. Kevin Tomlinson is the custodian of a $200.00 petty cash account. On March 31, he had receipts for the following total payments: supplies—office, $45.23; supplies—store, $66.18; and miscellaneous, $49.25. A cash count shows $40.59 in the petty cash box. Prepare the petty cash report.
4. Record the replenishment of the fund on March 31. C536.
5. Total, prove, and rule the cash payments journal.

ON YOUR OWN 9-3

Performing other cash payments journal operations

The cash payments journals and petty cash report for Magic Music are given in the *Working Papers*. Work this problem independently. The abbreviation for a check is C.

1. Rule page 11 of the cash payments journal using June 28 of the current year.
2. Begin page 12 of a cash payments journal.
3. Jerri Harris is the custodian of a $250.00 petty cash account. On June 30, she had receipts for the following total payments: supplies—office, $56.21; supplies—store, $48.27; repairs, $82.25; and miscellaneous, $36.17. A cash count shows $26.48 in the petty cash box. Prepare the petty cash report.
4. Record the replenishment of the fund on June 30. C627.
5. Total, prove, and rule the cash payments journal.

GENERAL JOURNAL

Not all transactions can be recorded in special journals. Those transactions that cannot be recorded in a special journal are recorded in a general journal. For example, when Hobby Shack buys supplies on account, the transaction cannot be recorded in any of the special journals. Because the transaction is not a cash payment, it cannot be recorded in the cash payments journal. Since the transaction is not a purchase of merchandise on account, it cannot be recorded in the purchases journal.

REMEMBER

If a transaction cannot be recorded in one of the special journals, it must be recorded in the general journal.

MEMORANDUM FOR BUYING SUPPLIES ON ACCOUNT

When Hobby Shack buys store supplies on account, an invoice is received from the vendor. This invoice is similar to the purchase invoice received when merchandise is purchased. To assure that no mistake is made, a memorandum is attached to the invoice, noting that the invoice is for store supplies and not for purchases.

FOR YOUR INFORMATION

FYI

Office supplies purchased by an office supplies company to sell to its customers should be recorded as a merchandise purchase. However, office supplies bought by the company for use by employees in its store or office should be recorded as store supplies or office supplies.

IMAGEMORE/GETTY IMAGES

HOBBY SHACK, INC.　　**MEMORANDUM**

NO.　52

DATE　November 6, 20--

Attached invoice is for store supplies bought on account.

1. Write the date.

2. Write the account title.

3. Write the memorandum number.

4. Write the debit amount.

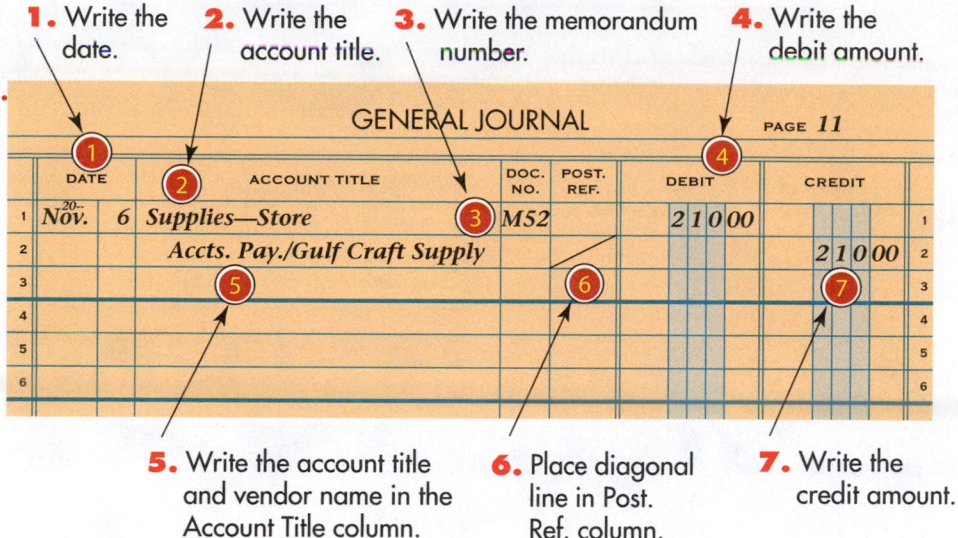

5. Write the account title and vendor name in the Account Title column.

6. Place diagonal line in Post. Ref. column.

7. Write the credit amount.

November 6. Bought store supplies on account from Gulf Craft Supply, $210.00. Memorandum No. 52.

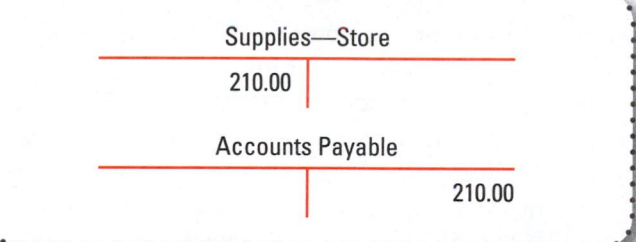

Hobby Shack usually buys supplies for cash. Occasionally, however, Hobby Shack buys some supplies on account.

This transaction increases the store supplies account balance and increases the accounts payable account balance. The asset account Supplies—Store has a normal debit balance and increases by a $210.00 debit. The liability account Accounts Payable has a normal credit balance and increases by a $210.00 credit.

The equality of debits and credits for each general journal entry is checked after each entry is recorded. For this entry, the amount of the debit entry, $210.00, is the same as the amount of the credit entry, $210.00. Therefore, debits equal credits for this entry.

STEPS — JOURNALIZING BUYING SUPPLIES ON ACCOUNT

 1. Write the date, 20--, Nov. 6, in the Date column.

2. Write the account title, *Supplies—Store*, in the Account Title column.

3. Write the memorandum number, *M52*, in the Doc. No. column.

4. Write the debit amount to Supplies—Store, *$210.00*, in the Debit column on the same line as the account title.

5. On the next line indented about one centimeter, write the account title and vendor name, *Accts. Pay./Gulf Craft Supply*, in the Account title column. Place a diagonal line between the two account titles.

6. Place a diagonal line in the Post. Ref. column on the same line to show that the single credit amount is posted to two accounts. Posting of a single amount in the general journal to two accounts is described in Chapter 11.

7. Write the credit amount to Accts. Pay./Gulf Craft Supply, *$210.00*, in the Credit column on the same line as the account titles.

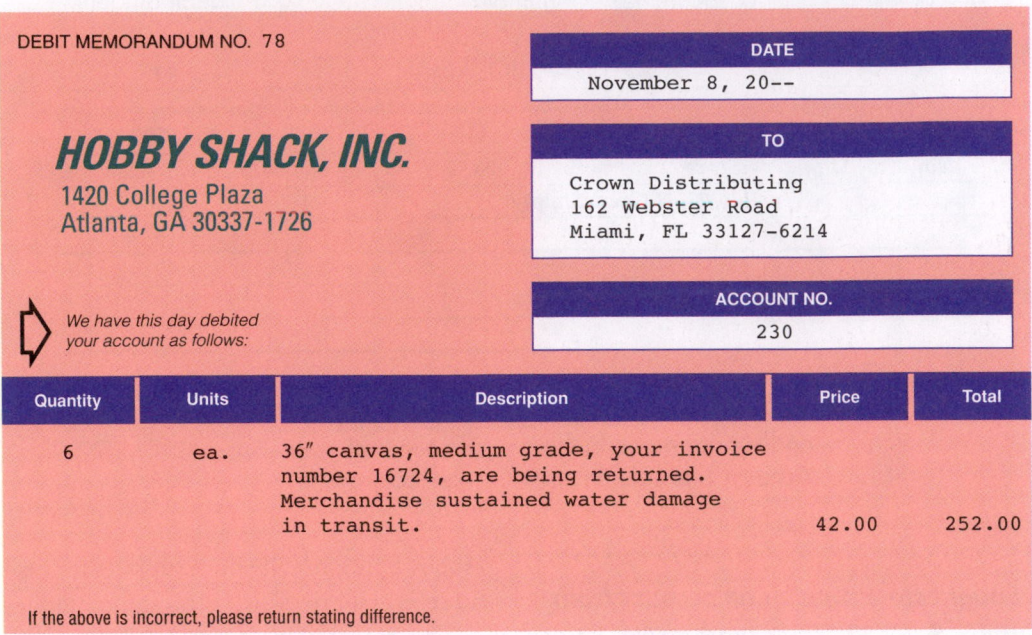

A customer may not want to keep merchandise that is inferior in quality or is damaged when received. A customer may be allowed to return part or all of the merchandise purchased. Credit allowed for the purchase price of returned merchandise, resulting in a decrease in the customer's accounts payable, is called a **purchases return**.

When merchandise is damaged but still usable or is of a different quality than that ordered, the vendor may let the customer keep the merchandise at a reduced price. Credit allowed for part of the purchase price of merchandise that is not returned, resulting in a decrease in the customer's accounts payable, is called a **purchases allowance**.

A purchases return or allowance should be confirmed in writing. A form prepared by the customer showing the price deduction taken by the customer for returns and allowances is called a **debit memorandum**. The form is called a debit memorandum because the customer records the amount as a debit (deduction) to the vendor account to show the decrease in the amount owed.

The customer may use a copy of the debit memorandum as the source document for journalizing purchases returns and allowances. However, the customer may wait for written confirmation from the vendor and use that confirmation as the source document. Hobby Shack issues a debit memorandum for each purchases return or allowance. This debit memorandum is used as the source document for purchases returns and allowances transactions. [CONCEPT: Objective Evidence] The transaction can be recorded immediately without waiting for written confirmation from the vendor. The original of the debit memorandum is sent to the vendor. A copy is kept by Hobby Shack.

Some businesses credit the purchases account for the amount of a purchases return or allowance. However, better information is provided if these amounts are credited to a separate account titled Purchases Returns and Allowances. A business can track the amount of purchases returns and allowances in a fiscal period if a separate account is used for recording them. The account enables a business to evaluate the effectiveness of its merchandise purchasing activities.

2. Write the account title and vendor name in the Account Title column.

1. Write the date.

3. Place a diagonal line in the Post. Ref. column.

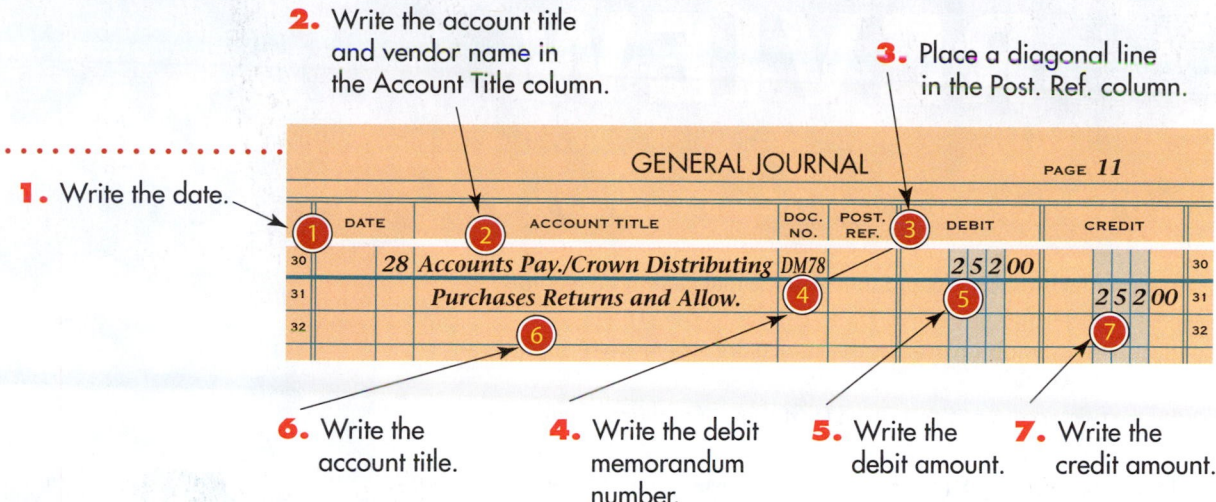

6. Write the account title.

4. Write the debit memorandum number.

5. Write the debit amount.

7. Write the credit amount.

Purchases returns and allowances decrease the amount of purchases. Therefore, Purchases Returns and Allowances is a contra account to Purchases. Thus, the normal account balance of Purchases Returns and Allowances is a credit, the opposite of the normal account balance of Purchases, a debit.

The account is in the cost of merchandise division of Hobby Shack's chart of accounts.

Accounts Payable	
252.00	

Purchases Returns and Allowances	
	252.00

November 28. Returned merchandise to Crown Distributing, $252.00, covering Purchase Invoice No. 80. Debit Memorandum No. 78.

STEPS JOURNALIZING PURCHASES RETURNS AND ALLOWANCES

1. Write the date, *28*, in the Date column.

2. Write the account title and vendor name, *Accounts Pay./Crown Distributing*, in the Account Title column. A diagonal line is placed between the two accounts.

3. Place a diagonal line in the Post. Ref. column to show that the single debit amount is posted to two accounts.

4. Write the debit memorandum number, *DM78*, in the Doc. No. column.

5. Write the amount, *$252.00*, in the Debit column of the first line.

6. On the next line indented about 1 centimeter, write *Purchases Returns and Allow.* in the Account Title column.

7. Write the amount, *$252.00*, in the Credit column of the second line.

FOR YOUR INFORMATION

FYI

Using the debit memorandum as a source document is a proper accounting procedure only if the business is confident that the vendor will honor the request for the purchases return or allowance.

End of Lesson REVIEW

AUDIT YOUR UNDERSTANDING

1. What journal is used to record transactions that cannot be recorded in special journals?
2. Why is a memorandum used as the source document when supplies are bought on account?
3. Why are two account titles written for the credit amount when supplies are bought on account?
4. When is the equality of debits and credits proved for a general journal?
5. If purchases returns and allowances are a decrease in purchases, why are returns and allowances credited to a separate account?
6. What is a primary difference between a purchases return and a purchases allowance?
7. When is a debit memorandum a proper source document for a purchases return or allowance?

TERMS REVIEW

purchases return

purchases allowance

debit memorandum

WORK TOGETHER 9-4

Journalizing other transactions using a general journal

A general journal for Rood Electric is given in the *Working Papers*. Your instructor will guide you through the following example.

1. Using the current year, journalize the following transactions on page 8 of the general journal. Source documents are abbreviated as follows: memorandum, M; debit memorandum, DM. Save your work to complete On Your Own 9-4.

Transactions:

Oct. 5. Bought store supplies on account from Designer Supplies, $180.00. M35.
7. Returned merchandise to Hendrix Products, $540.00. DM65.

ON YOUR OWN 9-4

Journalizing other transactions using a general journal

Use the general journal that you started for Work Together 9-4. Work this problem independently.

1. Using the current year, journalize the following transactions, continuing on the next blank line of page 8 of the general journal. Source documents are abbreviated as follows: memorandum, M; debit memorandum, DM.

Transactions:

Oct. 11. Bought office supplies on account from Office Express, $240.00. M36.
14. Returned merchandise to Fretz Industries, $1,239.00. DM66.

After completing this chapter, you can:

1. Define accounting terms related to purchases and cash payments for a merchandising business.

2. Identify accounting concepts and practices related to purchases and cash payments for a merchandising business.

3. Journalize purchases of merchandise using a purchases journal.

4. Journalize cash payments and cash discounts using a cash payments journal.

5. Prepare a petty cash report and journalize the reimbursement of the petty cash fund.

6. Total, prove, and rule a cash payments journal and start a new cash payments journal page.

7. Journalize purchases returns and allowances and other transactions using a general journal.

EXPLORE ACCOUNTING

Can Accounting Change the Course of History?

According to accounting historians, the start of the Industrial Revolution was delayed by nearly a century by restrictions on the use of the corporate form of organization. Events in Britain had a profound impact on the development of global commerce.

The scientific knowledge that was required to spur the Industrial Revolution began to emerge in the eighteenth century. The massive financial resources necessary to develop new industries could not be generated using partnerships, the traditional form of business organization. The British Parliament developed laws permitting the corporate form of organization, including limited liability for stockholders, as a means to enable these new industries to generate financial resources.

The financial collapse of one corporation caused Parliament to reverse the corporation laws. Financial losses, mismanagement, and improper accounting caused the financial collapse of the South Sea Company. The ensuing personal financial losses of investors generated a public outcry against the corporation laws. The South Sea Bubble Act of 1720 eliminated limited liability, effectively restricting the formation of corporations. Only a limited number of businesses, granted special charters by the British Parliament, were able to form as corporations during the remainder of the century.

During the early nineteenth century, a series of court cases and law changes gradually loosened the rules governing the granting of limited liability. Finally, the 1862 Companies Act completely removed all restrictions, permitting the corporate form of organization used today. Accounting historians believe that the spread of the Industrial Revolution was helped by the growing acceptance of the corporate form of organization.

Instructions: Research the start and growth of a major corporation in your state or region. Prepare a short report that discusses how the company generated the capital required to begin and expand the business. Would the company have been successful had it not been able to form as a corporation?

9-1   APPLICATION PROBLEM

Journalizing purchases using a purchases journal

Eupora Electric is a small appliance store.

Instructions:

1. Journalize the following transactions completed during September of the current year. Use page 9 of the purchases journal given in the *Working Papers*. The purchase invoices used as source documents are abbreviated as P.

Transactions:

Sept. 2. Purchased merchandise on account from Woodland Appliances, $2,600.00. P54.
      6. Purchased merchandise on account from Quality Wholesalers, $1,460.00. P55.
    12. Purchased merchandise on account from East Gate Appliances, $1,850.00. P56.
    18. Purchased merchandise on account from Winston, Inc., $2,300.00. P57.
    26. Purchased merchandise on account from Woodland Appliances, $3,800.00. P58.

2. Total and rule the purchases journal at the end of the month.

9-2   APPLICATION PROBLEM

Journalizing cash payments using a cash payments journal

Second Base is a sports equipment store that sells discontinued and damaged items.

Instructions:

Journalize the following transactions completed during November of the current year. Use page 22 of the cash payments journal given in the *Working Papers*. Source documents are abbreviated as follows: check, C; purchase invoice, P. Save your work to complete Application Problem 9-4.

Transactions:

Nov. 1. Paid cash for telephone bill, $96.00. C241.
      4. Paid cash on account to The Pro Shop, $1,250.00, covering P367, less 2% discount. C242.
      6. Paid cash for advertising, $75.00. C243.
      9. Paid cash on account to Athletic Center, $925.00, covering P362. No cash discount was offered. C244.
    11. Paid cash for office supplies, $50.00. C245.
    13. Paid cash to Tennis City for merchandise with a list price of $1,850.00, less a 50% trade discount. C246.
    18. Paid cash for store supplies, $125.00. C247.
    21. Purchased merchandise for cash from Trevor Industries, $250.00. C248.
    23. Purchased merchandise for cash from Paris Mfg. Co., $750.00, less a 60% trade discount. C249.
    25. Paid cash on account to Best Clothing, $925.00, covering P363. No cash discount was offered. C250.
    27. Paid cash on account to Trophy Sports, $2,100.00, covering P373, less 2% discount. C251.

Go Beyond the Book
For more information go to
www.C21accounting.com

9-3 APPLICATION PROBLEM **Microsoft Office**

Preparing a petty cash report

Kevin Tomlinson is the custodian of a $200.00 petty cash fund. On January 31 he had receipts for the following payments.

Payee	Description	Amount
City Office Supply	Computer disks	$ 5.95
KEWQ Radio	Voice fee for radio advertisement	50.00
Rocket Computers	Fix laser printer	45.95
Hooksville PTA	Advertisement in monthly newsletter	10.00
John Simmons	Pick up recyclable materials	8.00
Myers Hardware	Nails to repair outdoor sign	2.50
Books and More	Mouse pad	6.15

Instructions:

1. Classify each expense into one of the general ledger accounts used by Hobby Shack in this chapter.
2. Calculate the total of expenses by account.
3. Prepare the petty cash report given in the *Working Papers*. A cash count shows $70.67 in the petty cash box.

9-4 APPLICATION PROBLEM

Performing additional cash payments journal operations

Second Base is a sports equipment store that sells discontinued and damaged items. The cash payments journal used in Application Problem 9-2 is needed to complete this problem.

Instructions:

1. Total the amount columns of cash payments journal page 22 from Application Problem 9-2. Prove the equality of debits and credits.
2. Rule the cash payments journal.
3. Begin page 23 of a cash payments journal.
4. Wendy Morris is the custodian of a $250.00 petty cash account. On November 30, she had receipts for the following total payments: supplies—office, $45.31; supplies—store, $54.62; repairs, $75.82; and miscellaneous, $41.67. A cash count shows $31.05 in the petty cash box. Prepare the petty cash report.
5. Record the replenishment of the fund on November 30. C252.
6. Total the amount columns of the cash payments journal. Prove the equality of debits and credits.
7. Rule the cash payments journal.

APPLICATION PROBLEM

Journalizing other transactions using a general journal

Jenny's Designs is a bridal shop.

Instructions:
Journalize the following transactions completed during October of the current year. Use page 10 of the general journal given in the *Working Papers*. Source documents are abbreviated as follows: memorandum, M; debit memorandum, DM.

Transactions:
Oct. 5. Bought store supplies on account from Displays Warehouse, $275.00. M39.
       9. Returned merchandise to Hendrix Products, $640.00. DM25.
      13. Bought office supplies on account from Office Express, $215.00. M40.
      18. Returned merchandise to T-J Designs, $390.00. DM26.
      25. Bought store supplies on account from Classic Fixtures, $180.00. M41.

MASTERY PROBLEM

Journalizing purchases, cash payments, and other transactions

Mercury Computers sells computer parts and accessories.

Instructions:
1. Using the journals given in the *Working Papers*, journalize the following transactions completed during July of the current year. Use page 7 of a purchases journal, page 13 of a cash payments journal, and page 11 of a general journal. Source documents are abbreviated as follows: check, C; memorandum, M; purchase invoice, P; debit memorandum, DM.

Transactions:
Jul. 2. Purchased merchandise on account from Woodland Computers, $2,600.00. P354.
       4. Paid cash on account to Pacific Industries, $1,400.00, covering P367, less 2% discount. C242.
       6. Purchased merchandise on account from NewWave Electronics, $2,560.00. P355.
       8. Paid cash to WCKF Radio for advertising, $750.00. C243.
       8. Bought store supplies on account from Willcut & Bishop, $125.00. M39.
       9. Paid cash on account to American Semiconductor, $2,690.00, covering P352. No cash discount was offered. C244.
      10. Paid cash to Southern Bell for telephone bill, $136.00. C245.
      11. Paid cash on account to Woodland Computers, $2,600.00, covering P354, less 2% discount. C246.
      12. Returned merchandise to NewWave Electronics, $1,640.00. DM25.
      12. Purchased merchandise on account from Helms Supply, $550.00. P356.
      13. Paid cash to Edmondson Supply for office supplies, $126.00. C247.
      14. Paid cash to Deanes Electronics for merchandise with a list price of $3,480.00, less a 60% trade discount. C248.
      15. Bought office supplies on account from Office Express, $106.00. M40.
      15. Purchased merchandise on account from Keel, Inc., $3,480.00. P357.
      16. Paid cash on account to Farris Cable, $329.00, covering P353. No cash discount was offered. C249.
      18. Purchased merchandise for cash from Columbus Industries, $429.00. C250.
      20. Purchased merchandise for cash from Mena Mfg. Co., $260.00, less a 40% trade discount. C251.
      22. Paid cash on account to Keel, Inc., $3,480.00, covering P357, less 2% discount. C252.
      24. Paid cash to Williams Stores for store supplies, $94.00. C253.
      25. Paid cash on account to NewWave Electronics, $920.00, covering P355 less DM25. C254.
      27. Purchased merchandise on account from Woodland Computers, $3,200.00. P358.
      30. Returned merchandise to Woodland Computers, $120.00. DM26.

2. Total the amount columns of cash payments journal page 13. Prove the equality of debits and credits and rule the cash payments journal to carry the totals forward.

3. Record the totals brought forward from cash payments journal page 13 to line 1 of page 14 of the cash payments journal.

4. Journalize the following transactions.

Transactions:

Jul. 31. Paid cash on account to Helms Supply, $550.00, covering P356. No discount was offered. C255.

31. Paid cash to reimburse the petty cash fund, $181.75: supplies—office, $23.45; supplies—store, $84.32; miscellaneous, $74.34; and cash over, $0.36. C256.

5. Total and rule page 7 of the purchases journal.

6. Total the amount columns of cash payments journal page 14. Prove the equality of debits and credits of cash payments journal page 14.

7. Rule page 14 of the cash payments journal.

9-7 CHALLENGE PROBLEM

Journalizing purchases, cash payments, and other transactions

Fitness Connection is an exercise equipment store.

Instructions:

1. Using the journals given in the *Working Papers*, journalize the following transactions completed during November of the current year. Use page 12 of a purchases journal, page 26 of a cash payments journal, and page 11 of a general journal. Record the appropriate source documents in the journals.

Transactions:

Nov. 1. Wrote Check No. 363 for the monthly rent of $1,300.00.

2. Bought $120.00 worth of store supplies on account from Meda Store Supplies, recorded on Memo 43, with 2/10, n/30 payment terms.

3. Received an invoice, stamped Purchase Invoice 84, for merchandise on account from Central Fitness for $2,150.00, less a 60% trade discount.

4. Paid $150.00 to Pitman Industries with Check No. 364 for merchandise.

6. Wrote Check No. 365 for $1,020.00 to Pacer Equipment for Purchase Invoice 82's payment on account.

8. Returned $260.00 of the merchandise purchased on Purchase Invoice 84 to Central Fitness, recorded on Debit Memorandum 54.

9. Purchased $2,900.00 of merchandise on account from Trackmaster on Purchase Invoice 85, with 2/10, n/30 payment terms.

10. Paid $52.00 to myOffice for office supplies with Check No. 366.

11. Paid the balance of Purchase Invoice 84 less Debit Memorandum 54, to Central Fitness with Check No. 367, taking advantage of the 2/10, n/30 payment terms.

12. Wrote Check No. 368 for $290.00 to pay the monthly insurance premium.

16. Paid Trackmaster the amount owed on Purchase Invoice 85, writing Check No. 369.

29. Paid Meda Store Supplies for the Nov. 2 purchase of store supplies with Check No. 370.

30. Replenished the petty cash fund by writing Check No. 371 to the custodian for $207.00. Receipts were submitted for the following: office supplies, $48.00; store supplies, $24.00; advertising, $68.00; and miscellaneous, $66.00.

2. Evaluate and then write a response to the following questions.

a. The cash payments journal used in this problem has only three special amount columns. Under what circumstances would you recommend that additional special amount columns be added to a cash payments journal?

b. When insurance premiums are paid, should the debit entry be to the asset account, Prepaid Insurance, or to the expense account, Insurance Expense? Are there circumstances where either entry could be correct? Explain.

When you purchase merchandise for your business, you are considered a customer. Sometimes a customer might have a problem or complaint about the product. There are several ways to go about resolving the problem. One suggestion is to write to the person or company selling the product.

Instructions: Assume that you bought stereo speakers using the Internet site of a consumer electronics company. Unfortunately, the speakers make a strange static noise. Write a persuasive e-mail message to the company requesting a refund or a new set of speakers. Identify (1) information related to the purchase, such as invoice number and date, (2) the problem with the speakers, and (3) a request for a refund or a new set of speakers.

CASES FOR CRITICAL THINKING

Case 1

Trent Mercer owns and operates a music store in a mature shopping mall. When the largest store in the mall (often referred to as the *anchor*) moved two years ago, the traffic in the shopping center dramatically decreased. Mr. Mercer has an opportunity to move the business to a popular new shopping mall. Additional capital, however, is required to move and operate the business in a new location. The local bank has agreed to lend the money needed. His CPA has suggested that he consider forming a corporation and raise the necessary capital by selling capital stock to a small group of local investors. Should Mr. Mercer (1) borrow the money from the bank or (2) raise capital by creating a corporation? Explain your answer.

Case 2

Sophia Perez is a high school student who works part time in a local sports equipment store. As part of her duties, she records daily transactions in a journal. One day she asks the owner, "You use the purchase invoice as your source document for recording purchases of merchandise on account. You use a memorandum as your source document for recording the entry when supplies are bought on account. Why don't you use the invoice for both entries?" How would you respond to this question?

SCANS WORKPLACE COMPETENCY

Thinking Skill: Creative Thinking

Concept: Every business encounters problems that require new solutions. Methods of cutting costs, new promotions to increase sales, and changes in merchandising and product mix all require creative solutions. Employees who can "think outside the box" and generate new creative ideas are important resources to any company.

Application: Choose a retail merchandising business with which you are familiar. Study as much of the business as is visible to you. Generate new ideas that you think could increase sales for the company.

Journalizing purchases, cash payments, and other transactions from source documents

Messler Sailing sells sailboats, parts, and accessories. Source documents related to the purchases and cash payments of Messler Sailing for October are provided in the *Working Papers*.

Instructions

1. Using journals given in the *Working Papers*, journalize the transactions for October of the current year. Use page 10 of a purchases journal, page 15 of a cash payments journal, and page 14 of a general journal. Source documents are abbreviated as follows: check, C; memorandum, M; purchase invoice, P; debit memorandum, DM.

2. Total and rule the purchases journal.

3. Total the amount columns of cash payments journal page 15. Prove the equality of debits and credits and rule the cash payments journal.

ANALYZING BEST BUY'S FINANCIAL STATEMENTS

Best Buy has two types of stock—preferred and common. The company's Board of Directors must first authorize the issuance of each stock. The company then sells (issues) its stock on stock exchanges and can distribute shares to employees. On occasion, the company may repurchase shares, reducing the number of shares outstanding.

Instructions

1. Using page B-5 in Appendix B in this text, refer to Best Buy's balance sheet to determine the number of shares of preferred stock authorized, issued, and outstanding.

2. Identify the number of shares of common stock authorized, issued, and outstanding for 2007.

Accounting
SOFTWARE

Special journals eliminate the need for you to write most debit and credit account titles. Peachtree uses a different method to increase your efficiency when entering similar transactions, such as cash payments. Rather than using a cash payments journal, Peachtree has a unique input screen to record cash payments.

Cash payments should be made only to vendors that have been set up in Peachtree. When you are setting up a vendor, Peachtree requires that you enter the general ledger account to be debited when a payment is made to the vendor. For example, when "Castle Advertising" is set up, you would identify that cash payments should be debited to Advertising Expense. Thus, when entering a cash payment to Castle Advertising, Peachtree accesses the vendor's information and debits Advertising Expense. Peachtree also knows that cash payments require a credit to Cash. A window that displays the journal entry can be viewed before posting the transaction.

PEACHTREE MASTERY PROBLEM 9-6

1. Open (Restore) file 09-6MP.ptb.
2. Record purchases and cash payments. Use the July transactions to journalize and post to the purchase journal and cash disbursements journal in Peachtree.
3. Print the cash disbursements journal from the Reports menu (select Accounts Payable, Cash Disbursements Journal).
4. Print the purchases journal from the Report List.

PEACHTREE CHALLENGE PROBLEM 9-7

1. Open (Restore) file 09-7CP.ptb.
2. Journalize and post the November transactions in Peachtree's Purchase Journal and Cash Disbursements Journal.
3. Print the purchase journal.
4. Print the cash disbursements journal.

PURCHASES AND CASH PAYMENTS

QuickBooks does not use special journals. Instead, QuickBooks uses special screens designed to help make specific entries. These screens include one for entering bills, which is used to enter purchases on account, and one for paying bills, which is used to enter payments on account.

When you enter a purchase on account in QuickBooks, a vendor must be identified. That vendor must have already been entered into the company file. The software will credit both Accounts Payable and the specific vendor account. At the same time, an account to debit must be identified. For example, if buying supplies on account, the account—Supplies—would be identified in the entry and automatically debited. When a payment on account is entered, the software will automatically debit both Accounts Payable and the vendor, and credit Cash.

QUICKBOOKS MASTERY PROBLEM 9-6

1. Open the Mercury Computers file.
2. Journalize purchases, cash payments, and other transactions completed in July, using QuickBooks. Enter the Bills and Pay Bills windows for purchases and payments on account.
3. Print a Journal report using July 1 and July 31 as the dates.
4. Choose Vendors & Payables from the Reports menu, and print an Unpaid Bills Detail Report for July 31.

QUICKBOOKS CHALLENGE PROBLEM 9-7

1. Open the Fitness Connection file.
2. Journalize purchases, cash payments, and other transactions completed during November.
3. Print a Journal report, using November 1 and 30 for the dates.
4. Print an Unpaid Bills Detail report for November 30.

DISPLAYING CALCULATED AMOUNTS

When you think about a worksheet formula, it's natural to expect that the formula will perform a mathematical calculation using two or more numbers. However, a formula does not necessarily have to add, subtract, multiply, or divide.

When creating a petty cash report on an Excel worksheet, you will need to display a calculated amount in more than one cell. This task is accomplished with a single-cell formula or cell reference.

Assume the total amount of payments made out of the petty cash fund is calculated in cell D15. To complete the form, you want to display this amount in cell F15 to show how the amount to be replenished is calculated. The solution is to enter the formula +D15 in cell F15. The formula simply shows the same amount calculated in cell D15.

EXCEL APPLICATION PROBLEM 9-3

Open the F09-3 Excel data file. Follow the step-by-step instructions in the Instructions worksheet.
Note: This spreadsheet template may also be used to complete Instruction 4 of Application Problem 9-4.

PURCHASES AND CASH PAYMENTS

A merchandising business has many frequently occurring transactions that would require many entries in the general journal. Therefore, special journals are used to simplify the recording of these repetitive transactions. All transactions involving the payment of cash are recorded in the cash payments journal. All purchases of merchandise on account are recorded in the purchases journal.

Entering Purchases on Account in the Purchases Journal

1. Enter the transaction date and press Tab.
2. Enter the invoice number in the Refer. column and press Tab.
3. Enter the amount of the invoice in the Purchases Debit column and press Tab. The Accounts Payable credit amount is calculated and displayed automatically.
4. Choose a vendor name from the drop-down list.
5. Click the Post button.

Entering Cash Payments in the Cash Payments Journal

1. Enter the transaction date and press Tab. (Remember that the date can be increased and decreased by the + and − keys.)
2. Enter the check number in the Refer. column and press Tab.
3. For general debit or credit amounts, enter the account number and amount to debit or credit in the Debit or Credit columns. Enter other amounts in the special columns.
4. If making a payment on account, enter the Accounts Payable debit amount and choose the vendor from the drop-down vendor list. The Cash credit is automatically calculated and displayed by the computer.
5. If the transaction is correct, click the Post button.

AUTOMATED ACCOUNTING APPLICATION PROBLEM 9-2

Open file F09-2.AA8. Display the problem instructions and complete the problem.

AUTOMATED ACCOUNTING MASTERY PROBLEM 9-6

Open file F09-6.AA8. Display the problem instructions and complete the problem.

STOCKBYTE/GETTY IMAGES

CHAPTER 10

Journalizing Sales and Cash Receipts Using Special Journals

OBJECTIVES

After studying Chapter 10, you will be able to:

1. Define accounting terms related to sales and cash receipts for a merchandising business.

2. Identify accounting concepts and practices related to sales and cash receipts for a merchandising business.

3. Journalize sales on account using a sales journal.

4. Journalize cash receipts using a cash receipts journal.

5. Record sales returns and allowances using a general journal.

KEY TERMS

- customer
- sales tax
- sales journal
- cash sale
- credit card sale
- point-of-sale (POS) terminal
- terminal summary
- batch report
- batching out
- cash receipts journal
- sales discount
- sales return
- sales allowance
- credit memorandum

Point Your Browser
www.C21accounting.com

Best Buy

Best Buy—Increasing Sales Results

A sluggish economy had caused consumer spending to drop, especially in the sales of desktop computers and CDs. Growth in comparable store sales—the sales at stores open for more than a year—were disappointing. This was not the ideal time to assume leadership of a leading specialty retailer of consumer electronics, personal computers, entertainment software, and appliances. But that is exactly what faced Bradbury H. Anderson as he became the new chief executive officer of Best Buy.

©DANIEL ACKER/BLOOMBERG NEWS/LANDOV

So how did Best Buy overcome this challenge? It went digital. Recognizing changes in consumer preferences, Best Buy increased its assortment of digital cameras and digital, LCD, and projection TVs. Mr. Anderson and his new management team undertook other strategic plans to reduce product costs and store expenses. These changes enabled Best Buy to achieve a 2.5% increase in comparable store sales, a 13% increase in total revenue, and an 8% increase in net income.

Critical Thinking

1. How can a company have a 13% increase in total revenue with just a 2.5% increase in comparable store sales?

2. For any local company, such as a fast-food restaurant, suggest changes in the products they offer that you believe could increase sales.

Source: www.bestbuy.com

INTERNET ACTIVITY

State Sales Tax Rates

Go to the homepage for the Federation of Tax Administrators (www.taxadmin.org) or search the Internet for state sales tax rates. Look for a chart or table that compares the sales tax rate for each state.

Instructions

1. Make a chart comparing the sales tax rate for your state with the sales tax rate for 10 other states.

2. Highlight the highest and lowest rates.

DIGITAL VISION/GETTY IMAGES

Journalizing Sales on Account Using a Sales Journal

SALES TAX

Purchases and sales of merchandise are the two major activities of a merchandising business. A person or business to whom merchandise or services are sold is called a **customer**. Hobby Shack sells merchandise to a variety of customers, including individuals, schools, and churches. Hobby Shack uses the special journals described in this chapter to record transactions related to sales.

Laws of most states and some cities require that a tax be collected from customers for each sale made. A tax on a sale of merchandise or services is called a **sales tax**. Sales tax rates are usually stated as a percentage of sales. Regardless of the tax rates used, accounting procedures are the same.

Businesses must file reports with the proper government unit and pay the amount of sales tax collected. Every business collecting a sales tax needs accurate records of the amount of (1) total sales and (2) total sales tax collected. The amount of sales tax collected is a business liability until paid to the government agency. Therefore, the sales tax amount is recorded in a separate liability account titled Sales Tax Payable, which has a normal credit balance.

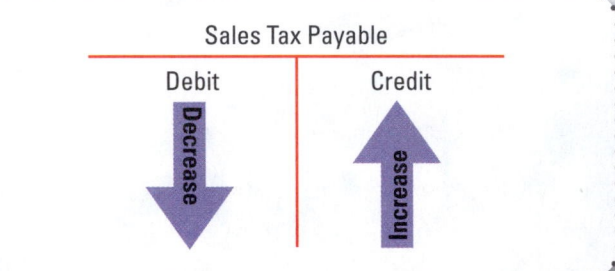

CHARACTER COUNTS

Integrity—Doing What's Right

What does the word *integrity* mean to you? The word is derived from a Latin word meaning "wholeness," "completeness," and "purity." Many companies include an interpretation of integrity in their code of conduct.

"We always try to do the right thing." —Procter & Gamble

"To say what we mean, to deliver what we promise, to fulfill our commitments, and to stand for what is right." —Lockheed Martin

"We do the right thing without compromise. We avoid even the appearance of impropriety." —Intel

Companies with integrity have an absolute commitment to do what is right in all business activities. Integrity is ultimately the most critical component to long-term business success. A business that fails to act with integrity will soon find it difficult to hire employees, deal with suppliers, and enjoy repeat customers.

The American Institute of Certified Public Accountants recognizes that integrity is critical for maintaining public confidence in its members' professional services. "Integrity is an element of character fundamental to professional recognition. It is the quality from which the public trust derives and the benchmark against which a member must ultimately test all decisions."

Instructions

In private, write down five qualities that you believe people of high integrity possess. Using a typical grading schedule (A+, A, A–, etc.), identify how you believe your friends, teachers, and others would rate your integrity. Do you have integrity as defined by the three companies above?

PHOTO: ASIAPIX/GETTY IMAGES

A sale of merchandise may be (1) on account or (2) for cash. A sale of merchandise increases the revenue of a business. Regardless of when payment is made, the revenue should be recorded at the time of a sale, not on the date cash is received. For example, on June 15 Hobby Shack sells merchandise on account to a customer. The customer pays Hobby Shack for the merchandise on July 12. Hobby Shack records the revenue on June 15, the date of the sale. The accounting concept *Realization of Revenue* is applied when revenue is recorded at the time goods or services are sold. [CONCEPT: Realization of Revenue]

A sale for which cash will be received at a later date is known as a sale on account. A sale on account is also referred to as a charge sale. Hobby Shack summarizes the total due from all charge customers in a general ledger

account titled Accounts Receivable. Accounts Receivable is an asset account with a normal debit balance. Therefore, the accounts receivable account is increased by a debit and decreased by a credit.

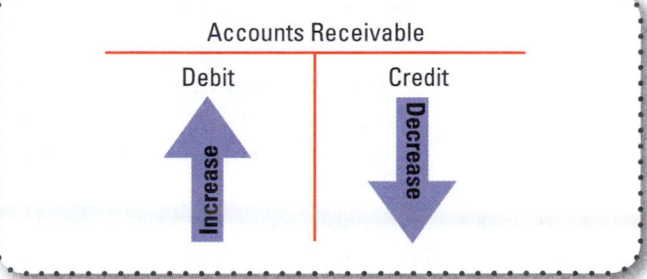

BUSINESS STRUCTURES

Advantages and Disadvantages of a Corporation

Organizing a corporation is as simple as filing an application with the appropriate state agency. The approved application establishes the corporation as a legal entity, giving the corporation many of the same legal rights and risks as individuals, including owning assets, borrowing money, paying taxes, and being sued.

The corporate form of business organization has several advantages over a sole proprietorship:

- *Limited liability*. The liability of stockholders is limited to their investment in the corporation.
- *Supply of capital*. Individuals are more willing to invest in a corporation because their personal assets are protected by limited liability.

However, there are also some disadvantages to a corporation:

- *Shared decision making*. Significant business decisions must be approved by a vote of the stockholders.
- *Shared profits*. The earnings of the corporation are divided among the stockholders.
- *Taxation*. The earnings of a corporation may be subject to federal and state income taxes. When the earnings of the corporation are distributed to the stockholders, individual stockholders may also have to pay income taxes on the distributions. Thus, the earnings of a

corporation can be taxed twice, a concept known as double taxation.

Proper planning can offer stockholders the advantage of limited liability while avoiding the disadvantage of double taxation. Thus, although the organization application can be prepared without the help of an attorney or accountant, consulting with these professionals is recommended.

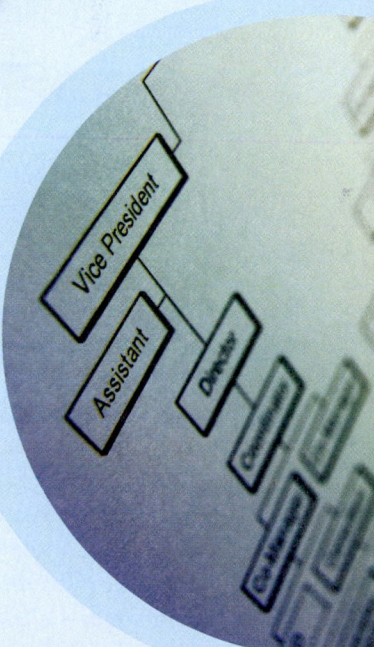

Critical Thinking

1. Think of two businesses you might be interested in starting. Describe whether the proprietorship or corporation form of organization would be better suited for this business.

2. Often a person who has started a proprietorship and run it successfully for many years sells the business to a corporation. Why would a corporation be interested in buying such a business?

SALES JOURNAL

	DATE	ACCOUNT DEBITED	SALE NO.	POST. REF.	ACCOUNTS RECEIVABLE DEBIT (1)	SALES CREDIT (2)	SALES TAX PAYABLE CREDIT (3)	
1								1
2								2

Hobby Shack uses a special journal to record only sales of merchandise on account transactions. A special journal used to record only sales of merchandise on account is called a **sales journal**.

The special amount columns in this sales journal are Accounts Receivable Debit, Sales Credit, and Sales Tax Payable Credit. With these special amount columns, each sale on account transaction can be recorded on one line of the sales journal.

SALES INVOICE

HOBBY SHACK, INC.				
1420 College Plaza Atlanta, GA 30337-1726	Sold to: Village Crafts 120 Mountain Road Marietta, GA 30060-1320		No. 76 Date 11/3/-- Terms 30 days	
	Cust. No. 150			

Stock No.	Description	Quantity	Unit Price	Amount
4422	Deer and fawn bisque	25	12.00	300.00
7710	Lighthouse, 6" -- bisque	30	8.00	240.00
			Subtotal	540.00
Customer's Signature Max Schindler		Salesclerk S.A.	Sales Tax	32.40
			Total	572.40

When merchandise is sold on account, the seller prepares a form showing what has been sold. A form describing the goods or services sold, the quantity, and the price is known as an *invoice*. An invoice used as a source document for recording a sale on account is known as a *sales invoice*. [CONCEPT: Objective Evidence] A sales invoice is also referred to as a *sales ticket* or a *sales slip*.

The seller considers an invoice for a sale on account to be a sales invoice. The same invoice is considered by the customer to be a purchase invoice.

In the case of Hobby Shack, three copies of a sales invoice are prepared. The original copy is given to the customer. The second copy goes to Hobby Shack's shipping department. The third copy is used as the source document for the sale on account transaction. [CONCEPT: Objective Evidence] Sales invoices are numbered in sequence. Number 76 is the number of the sales invoice issued to Village Crafts.

Hobby Shack operates in a state with a 6% sales tax rate. The total amount of the sale of merchandise in the invoice above is calculated as follows.

Price of Goods	×	Sales Tax Rate	=	Sales Tax
$540.00	×	6%	=	$32.40
Price of Goods	**+**	**Sales Tax**	**=**	**Total Amount**
$540.00	+	$32.40	=	$572.40

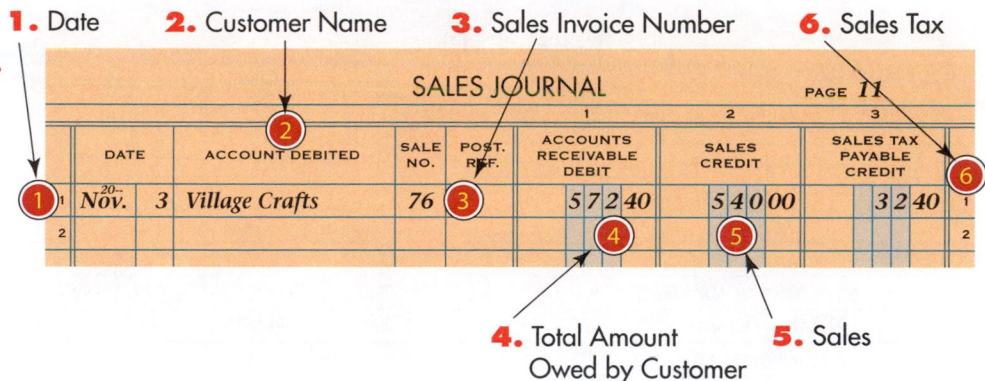

1. Date   **2.** Customer Name   **3.** Sales Invoice Number   **6.** Sales Tax

4. Total Amount Owed by Customer   **5.** Sales

Hobby Shack sells on account only to businesses. Other customers must either pay cash or use a credit card.

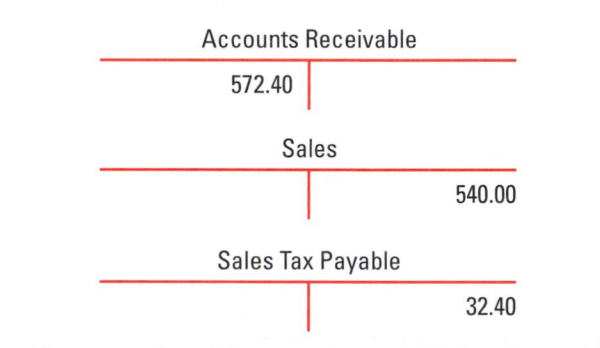

November 3. Sold merchandise on account to Village Crafts, $540.00, plus sales tax, $32.40; total, $572.40. Sales Invoice No. 76.

Accounts Receivable	
572.40	

Sales	
	540.00

Sales Tax Payable	
	32.40

A sale on account transaction increases the amount to be collected later from a customer. Payment for this sale will be received at a later date. However, the sale is recorded at the time the sale is made because the sale has taken place and payment is due to Hobby Shack. [CONCEPT: Realization of Revenue]

Because Accounts Receivable has a normal debit balance, Accounts Receivable is debited for the total sales and sales tax, $572.40, to show the increase in this asset account. Sales has a normal credit balance. Therefore, Sales is credited for the price of the goods, $540.00, to show the increase in this revenue account. The sales tax payable account also has a normal credit balance. Therefore, Sales Tax Payable is credited for the amount of sales tax, $32.40, to show the increase in this liability account.

STEPS   JOURNALIZING A SALE ON ACCOUNT

1 Write the date, *20--, Nov. 3*, in the Date column.

2 Write the customer name, *Village Crafts*, in the Account Debited column. The debit and credit amounts are recorded in special amount columns. Therefore, writing the titles of the general ledger accounts in the Account Debited column is not necessary. However, the name of the customer is written in the Account Debited column to show from whom the amount is due. Hobby Shack's procedures for keeping records of the amounts to be collected from each customer are described in Chapter 11.

3 Write the sales invoice number, *76*, in the Sale No. column.

4 Write the total amount owed by the customer, *$572.40*, in the Accounts Receivable Debit column.

5 Write the sales amount, *$540.00*, in the Sales Credit column.

6 Write the sales tax amount, *$32.40*, in the Sales Tax Payable Credit column.
Some states exempt schools and other organizations from paying sales tax. A sale to a tax-exempt organization would be recorded using the same amount in the Sales Credit and Accounts Receivable Debit columns. No amount would be entered in the Sales Tax Payable Credit column.

	DATE	ACCOUNT DEBITED	SALE NO.	POST. REF.	ACCOUNTS RECEIVABLE DEBIT	SALES CREDIT	SALES TAX PAYABLE CREDIT	
					1	2	3	
1	Nov. 20-- 3	Village Crafts	76		5 7 2 40	5 4 0 00	3 2 40	1
2	5	Fairview Church	77		1 9 0 8 00	1 9 0 8 00		2
3	9	Washington Schools	78		5 7 2 00	5 7 2 00		3
4	11	Country Crafters	79		7 6 8 50	7 2 5 00	4 3 50	4
5	16	Playtime Childcare	80		1 7 5 2 18	1 6 5 3 00	9 9 18	5
6	19	Village Crafts	81		2 5 4 9 30	2 4 0 5 00	1 4 4 30	6
7	24	Cumberland Center	82		1 5 8 00	1 5 8 00		7
8	24	Washington Schools	83		3 3 4 00	3 3 4 00		8
9	29	Country Crafters	84		4 5 3 68	4 2 8 00	2 5 68	9
10	30	Totals			9 0 6 8 06	8 7 2 3 00	3 4 5 06	10

SALES JOURNAL   PAGE *11*

At the end of each month, Hobby Shack totals, proves, and rules its sales journal. The procedures for proving and ruling a sales journal are the same as the procedures described for Hobby Shack's cash payments journal in Chapter 9.

The proof for Hobby Shack's sales journal is calculated as follows.

Col. No.	Column Title	Debit Totals	Credit Totals
1	Accounts Receivable Debit	$9,068.06	
2	Sales Credit		$8,723.00
3	Sales Tax Payable Credit		345.06
	Totals	$9,068.06	$9,068.06

The two totals, $9,068.06, are equal. Equality of debits and credits in Hobby Shack's sales journal for November is proved.

Posting from a sales journal is described in Chapter 11.

FOR YOUR INFORMATION

F Y I

Many states exempt food and drug sales for all customers. some states even exempt clothing sales from sales tax.

Journalizing Sales and Cash Receipts Using Special Journals

End of Lesson
REVIEW

TERMS REVIEW

customer

sales tax

sales journal

1. How does a merchandising business differ from a service business?
2. How are sales tax rates usually stated?
3. Why is sales tax collected considered a liability?
4. What is the title of the general ledger account used to summarize the total amount due from all charge customers?

WORK TOGETHER 10-1

Journalizing sales on account; proving and ruling a sales journal

The sales journal for Distinctive Appliances is given in the *Working Papers*. Your instructor will guide you through the following examples.

1. Using the current year, journalize the following transactions on page 9 of the sales journal. The sales invoice source document is abbreviated as S.

Transactions:

Sept. 1. Sold merchandise on account to Adrian Makowski, $800.00, plus sales tax, $48.00; total, $848.00. S104.
     11. Sold merchandise on account to Columbus City Schools, $875.00. Columbus City Schools is exempt from sales taxes. S105.
     28. Sold merchandise on account to Swiss Delight, $1,460.00, plus sales tax, $87.60; total, $1,547.60. S106.

2. Total, prove, and rule the sales journal.

ON YOUR OWN 10-1

Journalizing sales on account; proving and ruling a sales journal

The sales journal for Parris Supplies is given in the *Working Papers*. Work this problem independently.

1. Using the current year, journalize the following transactions on page 6 of the sales journal. The sales invoice source document is abbreviated as S.

Transactions:

Jun. 5. Sold merchandise on account to Peter Gallaher, $650.00, plus sales tax, $39.00; total, $689.00. S410.
    12. Sold merchandise on account to Spann Auto Supply, $590.00, plus sales tax, $35.40; total, $625.40. S411.
    24. Sold merchandise on account to Fleming College, $545.00. Fleming College is exempt from sales taxes. S412.

2. Total, prove, and rule the sales journal.

PROCESSING SALES TRANSACTIONS

Hobby Shack sells most of its merchandise for cash. A sale in which cash is received for the total amount of the sale at the time of the transaction is called a **cash sale**. Hobby Shack also sells merchandise to customers who have a bank-approved credit card. A sale in which a credit card is used for the total amount of the sale at the time of the transaction is called a **credit card sale**. Major bank-approved credit cards include VISA, MasterCard, and Discover Card. A customer who uses a credit card promises to pay the amount due for the credit card transaction to the bank issuing the credit card.

Some small businesses continue to use the traditional cash register to process sales transactions. After entering the price marked on each item sold, the sales clerk pushes a button instructing the cash register to total the sale, including any sales tax, and produce a cash register receipt for the customer. A typical cash register receipt is shown on the next page. At the end of every day, the cash register prints a summary of the sales recorded. The summary is adequate for journalizing the sales transaction, but it is unable to provide the business with information about what merchandise was sold, when it was sold, and to which customers.

Hobby Shack installed a modern version of a cash register. A computer used to collect, store, and report all the information of a sales transaction is called a **point-of-sale (POS) terminal**. Before any sale is entered, the number, description, price, and quantity on hand of each item of merchandise are stored in the POS terminal. When processing a sale, the sales clerk uses a scanning device to scan the universal product code (UPC) symbol on the item.

The POS terminal matches the number represented by the UPC symbol with the merchandise number to obtain the description and price of the merchandise. When all the merchandise has been scanned, the sales clerk enters the customer's method of payment. For a cash sale, the sales clerk enters the cash tendered by the customer and the POS terminal computes the amount of change. For a credit card sale, the customer swipes the credit card in the card scanner. The POS system produces a receipt that contains detailed information about the sale. A customer receipt from a POS terminal is shown on the next page.

Periodically, Hobby Shack instructs the point-of-sale terminal to print a report of all cash and credit card sales. The report that summarizes the cash and credit card sales of a point-of-sale terminal is called a **terminal summary**. Hobby Shack uses the terminal summary as the source document for recording sales in its journals. [CONCEPT: Objective Evidence] A terminal summary is shown on the next page.

At any time, the POS system can produce a variety of informational reports to help management make decisions. For example:

1. A report of sales by sales clerk would assist management to analyze a sales clerk's efficiency.
2. A report of sales by time of day would assist management in scheduling sales clerks to match busy periods.
3. A report of merchandise having a quantity on hand below a predetermined reorder point alerts management to purchase additional merchandise.

UPC (Universal Product Code) symbol on merchandise is scanned to enter data into a point-of-sale (POS) terminal

7 805386 774629

```
        Antique Shop
      123 Eagle Street
        Hanson, Iowa

                        13.23
                         2.45
                         2.45
                        10.34
      Subtotal          28.47
      Tax                1.71
      Total             30.18
```

Cash register receipt from a traditional cash register

```
        Hobby Shack, Inc.
        1420 College Plaza
         Atlanta, Georgia

    latex paint, blue 1 oz.
        5 @ $1.45              7.25
    paint brush, 3/4 glaze
        3 @ $3.25              9.75
    Subtotal 1               17.00
    Tax                       1.02
    TOTAL                    18.02

            VISA RECEIPT
    Jan Windham        XXXXXXXX1122
    Exp 02/--            Ref3534423
    04/01/--
    Register #: 002    Cashier #: 010


        Thanks, Come Again
```

Point-of-sale (POS) terminal receipt

```
            TERMINAL
            SUMMARY
        Hobby Shack, Inc.
```

Code:	34
Date:	11/27/--
Time:	18:24
Visa	034
Sales	295.38
Sales Tax	17.72
Total	313.10
MasterCard	042
Sales	107.21
Sales Tax	6.43
Total	113.64
Cash	152
Sales	5,057.41
Sales Tax	303.45
Total	5,360.86
Totals	
Sales	5,460.00
Sales Tax	327.60
Total	5,787.60

Terminal summary printed by POS terminal, used as source document for journalizing cash and credit card sales

```
            BATCH REPORT
    MERCHANT   02938493  234
    TERMINAL   923874
    DATE       04/03/--TIME 18:45
    BATCH      45

    VISA
    COUNT    =       007
    SALES    = $   325.23
    RETURNS  = $    12.13
    NET      = $   313.10

    MASTERCARD
    COUNT    =       003
    SALES    = $   145.86
    RETURNS  = $    32.22
    NET      = $   113.64

    TOTALS
    COUNT    =       010
    SALES    = $   471.09
    RETURNS  = $    44.35
    NET      = $   426.74

    CONTROL NUMBER: 0938904235343
```

Batch Report for credit card sales printed by POS terminal (as discussed on page 278)

Sales information for credit card sales is stored in the POS terminal. When Hobby Shack produces the terminal summary, it also instructs the point-of-sale terminal to print a report of credit card sales. A report of credit card sales produced by a point-of-sale terminal is called a **batch report**. A batch report can be detailed, showing each credit card sale, or it can provide a summary of the number and total of sales by credit card type. The process of preparing a batch report of credit card sales from a point-of-sale terminal is called **batching out**. A batch report for credit card sales is shown on the previous page.

Hobby Shack has contracted with its bank, First American, to process its credit card sales. When Hobby Shack batches out, the POS terminal electronically transmits a summary batch report to First American. The bank combines the batch reports for all of its customers and submits the information to the nearest Federal Reserve Bank. The funds are transferred among the banks issuing the credit cards, similar to the way checks are transferred between banks.

For example, suppose a customer having a VISA card issued by Capital National Bank buys $500.00 worth of merchandise from Hobby Shack. When Hobby Shack batches out, an electronic message is sent to First American with the credit card number and amount of the sale. When the Federal Reserve Bank receives the information, $500.00 is transferred from Capital National's account to First American's account. First American then credits Hobby Shack's account for the sale. The cash is deposited in Hobby Shack's account 2–3 business days after the sale. However, Hobby Shack records the transaction on the date it occurs.

CASH RECEIPTS JOURNAL

					GENERAL		ACCOUNTS RECEIVABLE CREDIT	SALES CREDIT	SALES TAX PAYABLE CREDIT	SALES DISCOUNT DEBIT	CASH DEBIT
	DATE	ACCOUNT TITLE	DOC. NO.	POST. REF.	DEBIT	CREDIT					
1											
2											
3											

Hobby Shack, Inc., has many transactions involving the receipt of cash. Because of the number of transactions, Hobby Shack uses a special journal for recording only cash receipts. A special journal used to record only cash receipt transactions is called a **cash receipts journal**.

Only those columns needed to record cash receipt transactions are included in Hobby Shack's cash receipts journal. Since all cash receipt transactions affect the cash account, a special column is provided for this general ledger account. In addition, Hobby Shack has many cash receipt transactions affecting the accounts receivable account, the sales account, and the sales tax payable account. Therefore, special columns are provided in Hobby Shack's cash receipts journal for these general ledger accounts.

To encourage early payment, Hobby Shack allows customers who purchase merchandise on account to take a deduction from the invoice amount. A cash discount on sales taken by a customer is called a **sales discount**. When a sales discount is taken, the customer pays less than the invoice amount previously recorded in the sales account. Sales discounts reduce the amount of cash Hobby Shack receives on sales on account. Because customers often take these discounts, Hobby Shack's cash receipts journal has a special column titled Sales Discount Debit. Because of these special columns, most of Hobby Shack's cash receipt transactions can be recorded on one line in the cash receipts journal. Cash receipts that do not occur often are recorded in the General columns.

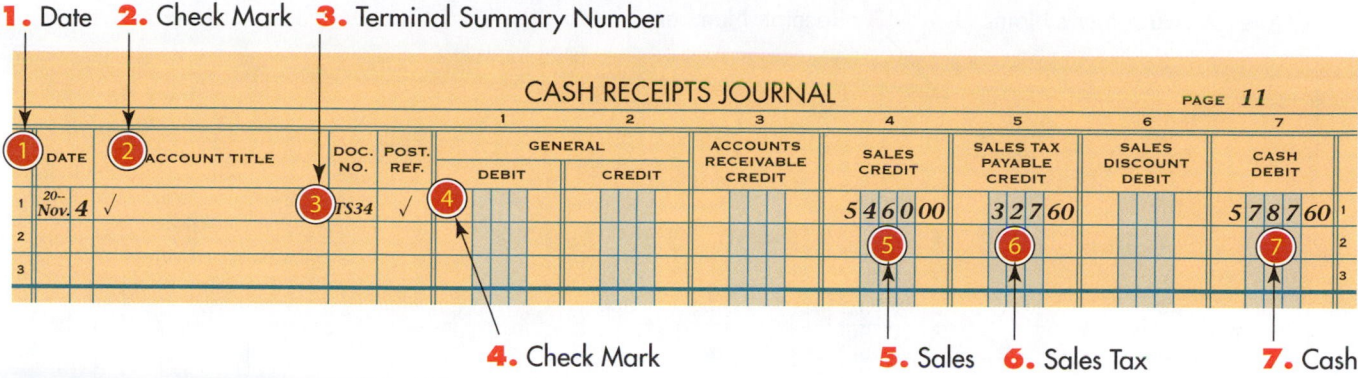

1. Date **2.** Check Mark **3.** Terminal Summary Number

4. Check Mark **5.** Sales **6.** Sales Tax **7.** Cash

Hobby Shack's POS terminal combines cash and credit card sales in the terminal summary. The total of the terminal summary is recorded as a single cash sales transaction.

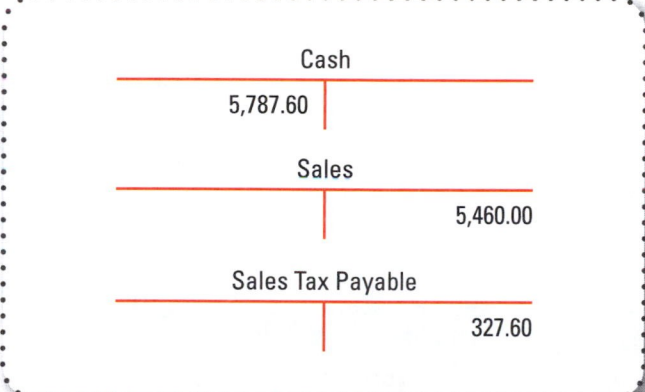

November 4. Recorded cash and credit card sales, $5,460.00, plus sales tax, $327.60; total, $5,787.60. Terminal Summary 34.

Cash	
5,787.60	

Sales	
	5,460.00

Sales Tax Payable	
	327.60

At the end of each week, Hobby Shack batches out and prints a terminal summary. The POS terminal assigns the summary a sequential number. The terminal summary is used by Hobby Shack as the source document for weekly cash and credit card sales transactions. [CONCEPT: Objective Evidence] Sales are also totaled at the end of each month so Hobby Shack can analyze monthly sales.

Management is responsible for determining how often the business should batch out, deposit cash, and record sales in the sales journal. Most businesses perform these tasks at the end of every business day. (The weekly processing demonstrated in this textbook was selected to simplify the textbook illustrations and problems.)

Because the asset account, Cash, has a normal debit balance, Cash is debited for the total sales and sales tax, $5,787.60, to show the increase in this asset account. The sales account has a normal credit balance. Therefore, Sales is credited for the total price of all goods sold, $5,460.00, to show the increase in this revenue account. The sales tax payable account also has a normal credit balance. Therefore, Sales Tax Payable is credited for the total sales tax, $327.60, to show the increase in this liability account.

STEPS **JOURNALIZING CASH AND CREDIT CARD SALES**

1 Write the date, *20--, Nov. 4*, in the Date column.

2 Place a check mark in the Account Title column to show that no account title needs to be written. The debit and credit amounts will be recorded in special amount columns.

3 Write the terminal summary document number, *TS34*, in the Doc. No. column.

4 Place a check mark in the Post. Ref. column to show that amounts on this line are not to be posted individually.

5 Write the sales amount, *$5,460.00*, in the Sales Credit column.

6 Write the sales tax amount, *$327.60*, in the Sales Tax Payable Credit column.

7 Write the cash amount, *$5,787.60*, in the Cash Debit column.

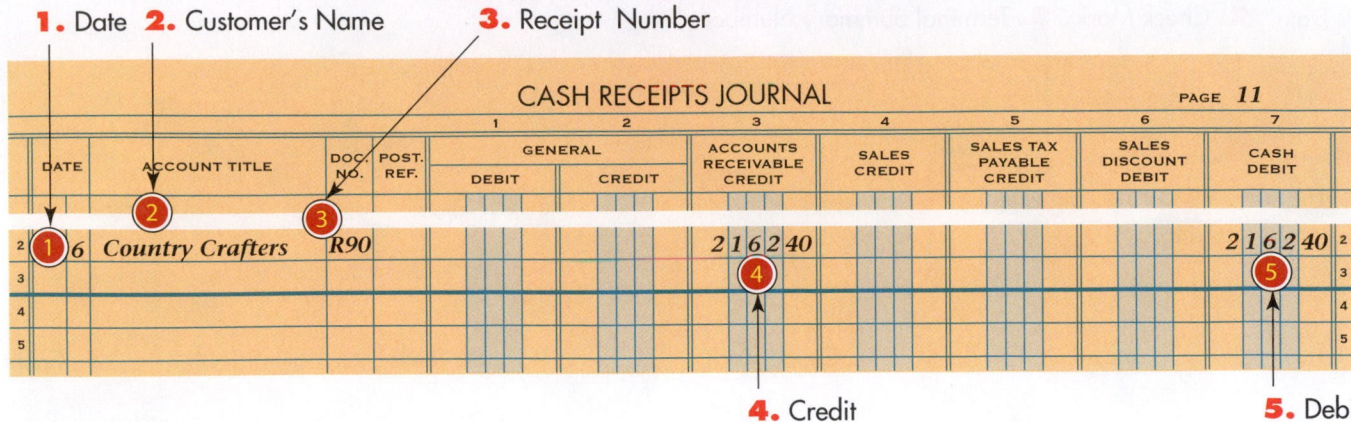

1. Date **2.** Customer's Name **3.** Receipt Number

4. Credit **5.** Debit

When cash is received on account from a customer, Hobby Shack prepares a receipt. The receipts are prenumbered so that all receipts can be accounted for. Receipts are prepared in duplicate. The original receipt is given to the customer. The copy of the receipt is used as the source document for the cash receipt on account transaction. [CONCEPT: Objective Evidence]

> **November 6. Received cash on account from Country Crafters, $2,162.40, covering S69. Receipt No. 90.**

A cash receipt on account transaction decreases future amounts to be collected from a customer. This transaction increases the cash account balance and decreases the accounts receivable account balance. Because the cash account has a normal debit balance, Cash is debited for the amount of cash received, $2,162.40, to show the increase in this asset account. The accounts receivable account also has a normal debit balance. Therefore, Accounts Receivable is credited for $2,162.40 to show the decrease in this asset account.

Hobby Shack's procedures for keeping records of the amounts received from customers are described in Chapter 11. Posting procedures are also described in Chapter 11.

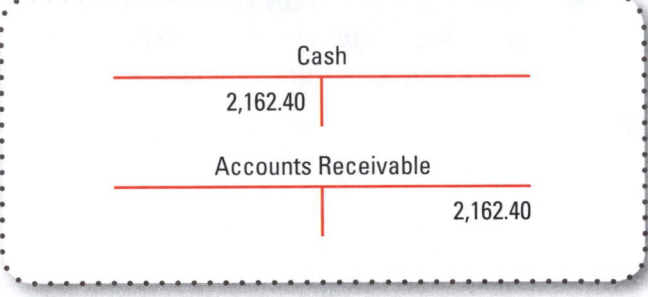

FOR YOUR INFORMATION

FYI

All cash receipts are recorded in a cash receipts journal. Most cash receipts are for (1) cash received from customers on account and (2) cash and credit card sales.

STEPS JOURNALIZING CASH RECEIPTS ON ACCOUNT

① Write the date, *6*, in the Date column.

② Write only the customer's name, *Country Crafters*, in the Account Title column. The debit and credit amounts are entered in special amount columns. Therefore, the titles of the two general ledger accounts do not need to be written in the Account Title column.

③ Write the receipt number, *R90*, in the Doc. No. column.

④ Write the credit amount, *$2,162.40*, in the Accounts Receivable Credit column.

⑤ Write the debit amount, *$2,162.40*, in the Cash Debit column.

To encourage early payment for a sale on account, a deduction on the invoice amount may be allowed. A deduction that a vendor allows on the invoice amount to encourage prompt payment is known as a cash discount. A cash discount on sales is called a sales discount. When a sales discount is taken, a customer pays less cash than the invoice amount previously recorded in the sales account.

To encourage prompt payment, Hobby Shack gives credit terms of 2/10, n/30. When a customer pays the amount owed within 10 days, the sales invoice amount is reduced 2%. Otherwise, the net amount is due in 30 days.

On October 30, Hobby Shack sold merchandise on account to Cumberland Center for $1,200.00. On November 7, Hobby Shack received payment for this sale on account within the discount period. Because the payment is received within the discount period, the amount received is reduced by the amount of the sales discount.

Sales Invoice Amount	×	Sales Discount Rate	=	Sales Discount
$ 1,200.00	×	2%	=	$ 24.00

FINANCIAL LITERACY

Credit Cards

Buying goods with a credit card is a great way to take advantage of sales or to purchase an unplanned necessity such as an appliance. However, this convenience has a price—the interest that is applied to any unpaid balance on the account.

Interest rates and credit terms vary from card to card, so it is important to investigate and compare before choosing a card. Find out how the interest is calculated and when the interest starts on a purchase. For some companies, interest starts on the day of purchase. Sometimes interest doesn't start until 20 to 25 days after the end of a billing cycle. If you pay your bill in full by the due date, no interest will be charged. If you are charged interest, it is usually calculated based on the average daily unpaid balance of your account.

Some credit card companies entice you to switch to their card by offering very low introductory interest rates—but only for a specific period of time. Once the introductory period expires, the interest rate increases.

Other companies offer cash back or other rewards such as miles or points that can be used for the purchase of airline tickets or other items. Again, these programs vary greatly between credit cards. Make sure you understand the terms of such reward programs.

Credit cards can be a wonderful convenience as long as you understand the rules of the card you choose.

Activities

1. Using the Internet or other resources, compare the interest rates on two credit cards. If either card offers an introductory rate, find out the terms of the introductory rate and the interest rate after the introductory period is over. Present your findings in written form.

2. Using the Internet or other resources, find out how the interest is calculated for two different credit cards. Summarize your findings in a written report.

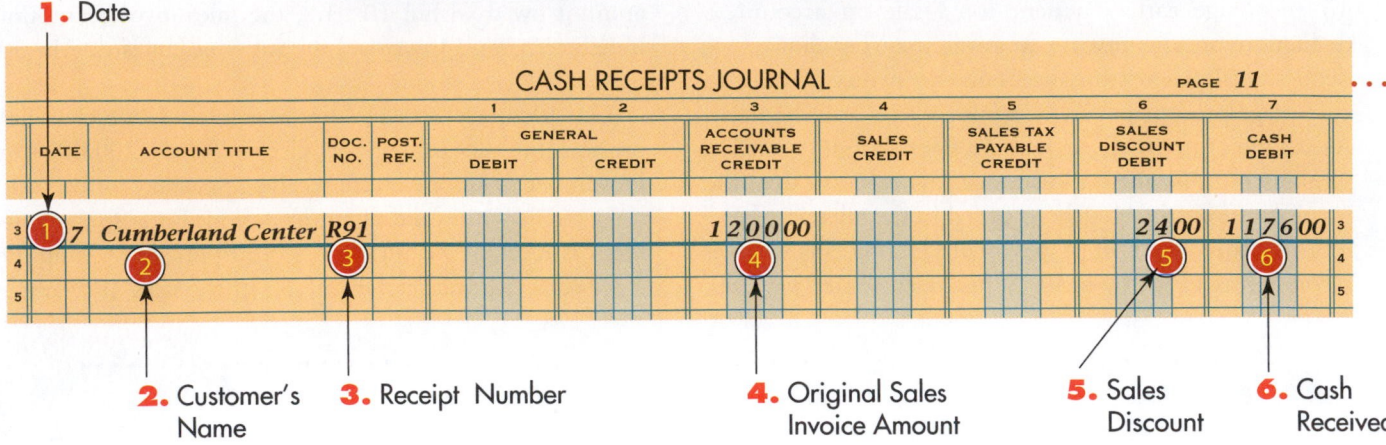

1. Date

2. Customer's Name

3. Receipt Number

4. Original Sales Invoice Amount

5. Sales Discount

6. Cash Received

Sales discounts are recorded in a general ledger account titled Sales Discount. Since sales discounts decrease sales, the account Sales Discount is a contra account to Sales.

A business could debit Sales for the amount of the sales discount. However, better information is provided if these amounts are debited to Sales Discount. A separate account provides business managers with more information to evaluate whether a sales discount is a cost-effective method of encouraging early payments of sales on account.

> **November 7. Received cash on account from Cumberland Center, $1,176.00, covering Sales Invoice No. 74 for $1,200.00, less 2% discount, $24.00. Receipt No. 91.**

Cash	
Nov. 7 1,176.00	

Accounts Receivable	
	Nov. 7 1,200.00

Sales Discount	
Nov. 7 24.00	

If a customer does not pay the amount owed within the sales discount period, the full invoice amount is due. If Cumberland Center had not taken the sales discount, the journal entry would be a debit to Cash, $1,200.00, and a credit to Accounts Receivable, $1,200.00.

STEPS | **JOURNALIZING CASH RECEIPTS ON ACCOUNT WITH SALES DISCOUNTS**

1. Write the date, *7*, in the Date column.

2. Write the customer's name, *Cumberland Center*, in the Account Title column.

3. Write the receipt number, *R91*, in the Doc. No. column.

4. Write the original invoice amount, *$1,200.00*, in the Accounts Receivable Credit column.

5. Write the amount of sales discount, *$24.00*, in the Sales Discount Debit column.

6. Write the debit to *Cash*, *$1,176.00*, in the Cash Debit column.

TOTALING, PROVING, AND RULING A CASH RECEIPTS JOURNAL

	DATE	ACCOUNT TITLE	DOC. NO.	POST. REF.	GENERAL DEBIT	GENERAL CREDIT	ACCOUNTS RECEIVABLE CREDIT	SALES CREDIT	SALES TAX PAYABLE CREDIT	SALES DISCOUNT DEBIT	CASH DEBIT	
					1	2	3	4	5	6	7	
22	30	✓	T38	✓				1380 00	82 80		1462 80	22
23	30	Totals					9540 00	27532 50	1648 80	52 50	38668 80	23
24												24

CASH RECEIPTS JOURNAL PAGE 11

The procedures for totaling, proving, and ruling a cash receipts journal are the same as the procedures described for Hobby Shack's cash payments journal in Chapter 9. The use of the General Debit and General Credit columns is described in Part 3.

The proof for Hobby Shack's cash receipts journal for November is calculated as shown below. The two totals, $38,721.30, are equal. Equality of debits and credits is proved.

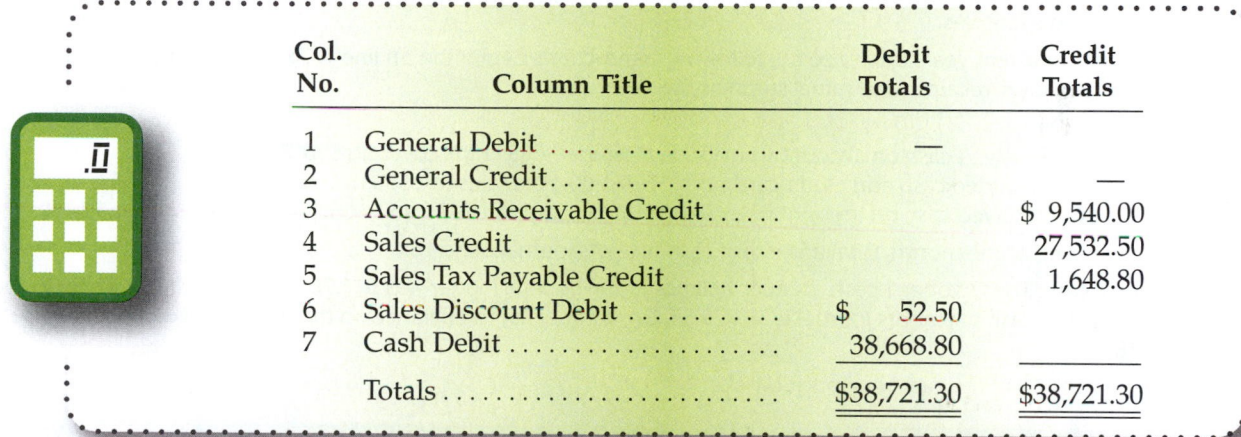

Col. No.	Column Title	Debit Totals	Credit Totals
1	General Debit	—	
2	General Credit		—
3	Accounts Receivable Credit		$ 9,540.00
4	Sales Credit		27,532.50
5	Sales Tax Payable Credit		1,648.80
6	Sales Discount Debit	$ 52.50	
7	Cash Debit	38,668.80	
	Totals	$38,721.30	$38,721.30

PROVING CASH AT THE END OF A MONTH

After the cash receipts journal is proved at the end of each month, cash is proved. Hobby Shack's cash proof at the end of November is calculated as shown.

The balance on the next unused check stub is $23,414.84. Since the balance on the next unused check stub is the same as the cash proof, cash is proved.

Cash on hand at the beginning of the month $17,647.44
    (Nov. 1 balance of general ledger cash account)
Plus total cash received during the month 38,668.80
    (Cash Debit column total, cash receipts journal)
Equals total $56,316.24
Less total cash paid during the month 32,901.40
    (Cash Credit column total, cash payments journal, Chapter 9)
Equals cash balance on hand at end of the month $23,414.84

Checkbook balance on the next unused check stub $23,414.84

End of Lesson REVIEW

TERMS REVIEW

- cash sale
- credit card sale
- point-of-sale (POS) terminal
- terminal summary
- batch report
- batching out
- cash receipts journal
- sales discount

AUDIT YOUR UNDERSTANDING

1. What is the difference in the receipt received by a customer from a cash register versus a point-of-sale terminal?
2. What are the two types of batch reports?
3. Who transfers funds between banks involved in the credit card sales?

WORK TOGETHER 10-2

Journalizing cash receipts; proving and ruling a cash receipts journal

Cash receipts journal page 16 for Graphics Co. is given in the *Working Papers*. Your instructor will guide you through the following examples.

1. Using the current year, journalize the following transactions beginning on line 1. Source documents are abbreviated as follows: receipt, R; terminal summary, TS.

Transactions:

Oct. 4. Received cash on account from Oakley Company, $371.00, covering S96. R144.
    13. Recorded cash and credit card sales, $8,361.60, plus sales tax, $501.70; total, $8,863.30. TS43.
    30. Received cash on account from Sierra Supply, covering S97 for $5,989.00, less 2% discount. R145.

2. For the end of the month, total and prove cash receipts journal page 16.

3. Prove cash. The October 1 cash account balance in the general ledger was $11,764.96. The October 31 cash credit total in the cash payments journal is $8,779.53. On October 31, the balance on the next unused check stub was $18,088.95.

4. Rule page 16 of the cash receipts journal.

ON YOUR OWN 10-2

Journalizing cash receipts; proving and ruling a cash receipts journal

Cash receipts journal page 17 for Holloman Auto Parts is given in the *Working Papers*. Work this problem independently.

1. Using the current year, journalize the following transactions beginning on line 1. Source documents are abbreviated as follows: receipt, R; terminal summary, TS.

Transactions:

Nov. 2. Received cash on account from Wakeman Auto, $425.00, covering S298. R312.
    13. Recorded cash and credit card sales, $3,254.30, plus sales tax, $189.55; total, $3,443.85. TS48.
    27. Received cash on account from Cooley Used Cars, covering S295 for $1,459.00, less 2% discount. R313.

2. For the end of the month, total and prove cash receipts journal page 17.

3. Prove cash. The November 1 cash account balance in the general ledger was $2,848.10. The November 30 cash credit total in the cash payments journal is $4,284.25. On November 30, the balance on the next unused check stub was $3,862.52.

4. Rule page 17 of the cash receipts journal.

CREDIT MEMORANDUM FOR SALES RETURNS AND ALLOWANCES

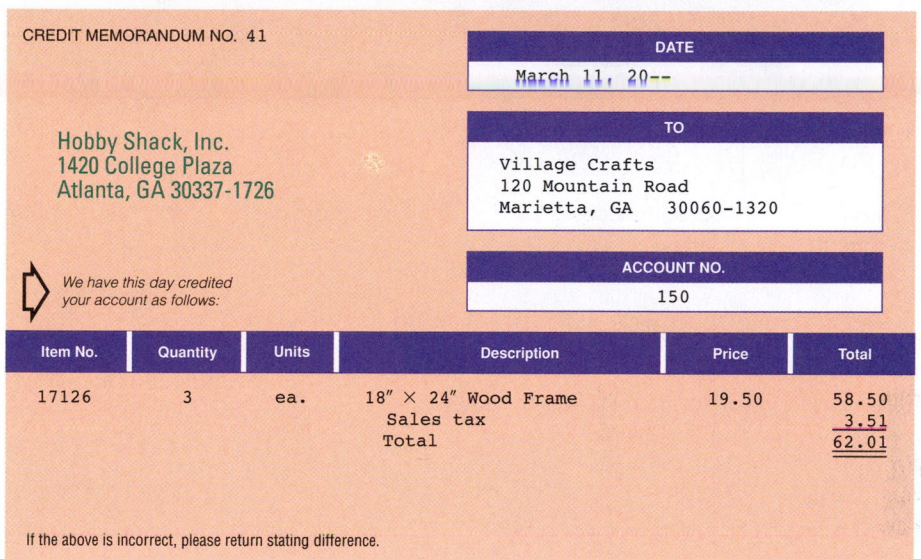

CREDIT MEMORANDUM NO. 41

DATE						
March 11, 20--						

Hobby Shack, Inc.
1420 College Plaza
Atlanta, GA 30337-1726

TO

Village Crafts
120 Mountain Road
Marietta, GA 30060-1320

We have this day credited
your account as follows:

ACCOUNT NO.

150

Item No.	Quantity	Units	Description	Price	Total
17126	3	ea.	18″ × 24″ Wood Frame	19.50	58.50
			Sales tax		3.51
			Total		62.01

If the above is incorrect, please return stating difference.

In Chapter 9, purchases-related transactions other than purchases and cash payments were recorded in a general journal. Hobby Shack has a sales-related transaction that is recorded in a general journal rather than either the sales or the cash receipts journals.

Sales Returns and Allowances

Most merchandising businesses expect to have some merchandise returned. A customer may have received the wrong item or damaged goods. A customer may return merchandise for a credit on account or a cash refund. Credit allowed a customer for the sales price of returned merchandise, resulting in a decrease in the vendor's accounts receivable, is called a **sales return**.

Credit may be granted to a customer without requiring the return of merchandise. Credit also may be given because of a shortage in a shipment. Credit allowed a customer for part of the sales price of merchandise that is not returned, resulting in a decrease in the vendor's accounts receivable, is called a **sales allowance**.

A vendor usually informs a customer in writing when a sales return or a sales allowance is granted. A form pre-

pared by the vendor showing the amount deducted for returns and allowances is called a **credit memorandum**. The original of a credit memorandum is given to the customer. The copy is used as the source document for recording the sales returns and allowances transaction. [CONCEPT: Objective Evidence]

Sales returns and sales allowances decrease the amount of sales. Therefore, the account Sales Returns and Allowances is a contra account to the revenue account Sales. Thus, the normal account balance of Sales Returns and Allowances is a debit, the opposite of the normal balance of Sales, a credit.

A business could debit the sales account for the amount of a return or allowance. However, better information is provided if these amounts are debited to Sales Returns and Allowances. This contra account enables management to quickly identify if the amount of sales returns and allowances compared to sales is greater than expected.

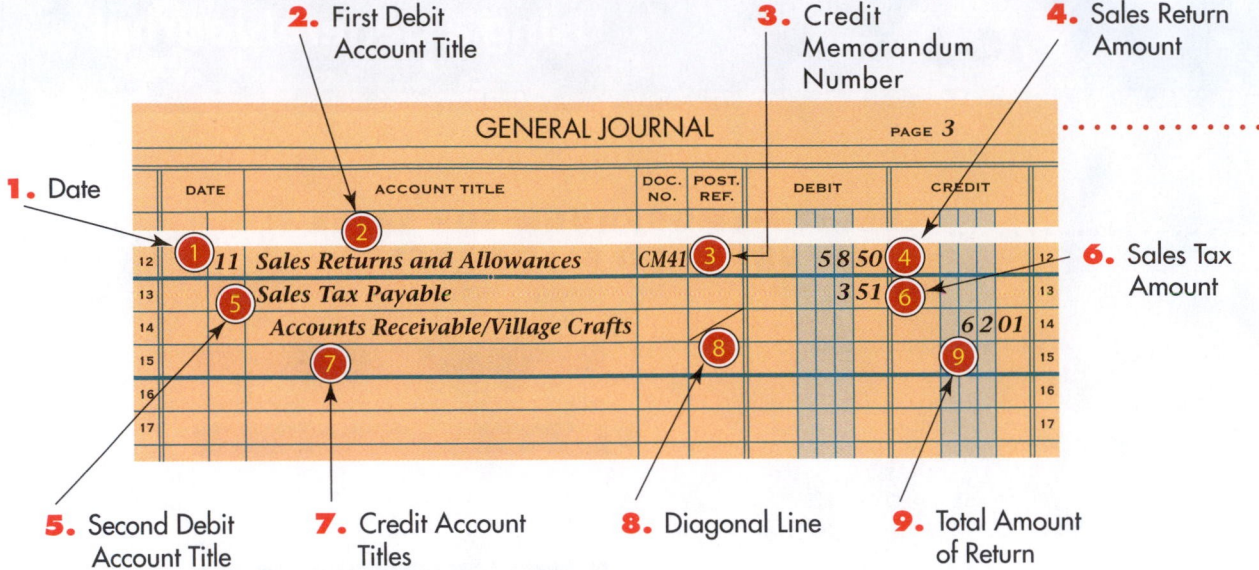

1. Date
2. First Debit Account Title
3. Credit Memorandum Number
4. Sales Return Amount
5. Second Debit Account Title
6. Sales Tax Amount
7. Credit Account Titles
8. Diagonal Line
9. Total Amount of Return

On March 8, Hobby Shack sold merchandise on account to Village Crafts for $503.50 ($475.00 sales plus $28.50 sales tax). Later, Village Crafts returned part of the merchandise. The sales return reduces the amount owed by Village Crafts by $62.01.

March 11. Granted credit to Village Crafts for merchandise returned, $58.50, plus sales tax, $3.51, from S160; total, $62.01. Credit Memorandum No. 41.

Sales Returns and Allowances	
Mar. 11 58.50	

Sales Tax Payable	
Mar. 11 3.51	Mar. 8 28.50

Accounts Receivable	
Mar. 8 503.50	Mar. 11 62.01

STEPS **JOURNALIZING SALES RETURNS AND ALLOWANCES**

1. Write the date, *11*, in the Date column.

2. Write *Sales Returns and Allowances* in the Account Title column.

3. Write *CM* and the credit memorandum number, *41*, in the Doc. No. column.

4. Write the amount of the sales return, *$58.50*, in the Debit column.

5. Write *Sales Tax Payable* on the next line in the Account Title column.

6. Write the sales tax amount, *$3.51*, in the Debit column.

7. On the next line, indented about 1 centimeter, write the accounts to be credited, *Accounts Receivable/Village Crafts*, in the Account Title column. Hobby Shack's procedures for keeping records of the amounts to be collected from each customer are described in Chapter 11.

8. Draw a diagonal line in the Post. Ref. column.

9. Write the total accounts receivable amount, *$62.01*, in the Credit column.

End of Lesson
REVIEW

AUDIT YOUR UNDERSTANDING

TERMS REVIEW

sales return

sales allowance

credit memorandum

1. What is the difference between a sales return and a sales allowance?
2. What is the source document for journalizing sales returns and allowances?
3. What general ledger accounts are affected, and how, by a sales returns and allowances transaction?
4. Why are sales returns and allowances not debited to the Sales account?

WORK TOGETHER 10-3

Journalizing sales returns and allowances using a general journal

The general journal for Cline Interiors is given in the *Working Papers*. Your instructor will guide you through the following examples.

1. Using the current year, journalize the following transactions on page 6 of a general journal. Source documents are abbreviated as: credit memorandum, CM; sales invoice, S.

Transactions:

June 3. Granted credit to Wilbanks and Associates for merchandise returned, $457.00, plus sales tax, $36.56, from S356; total, $493.56. CM41.
6. Granted credit to Westfall High School for damaged merchandise, $67.00 (no sales tax), from S345. CM42.

ON YOUR OWN 10-3

Journalizing sales returns and allowances using a general journal

The general journal for City Lighting is given in the *Working Papers*. Work this problem independently.

1. Using the current year, journalize the following transactions on page 7 of a general journal. Source documents are abbreviated as: credit memorandum, CM; sales invoice, S.

Transactions:

July 3. Granted credit to Carver High School for damaged merchandise, $46.00 (no sales tax), from S642. CM86.
4. Granted credit to Karen's Fine Gifts for merchandise returned, $425.00, plus sales tax, $25.50, from S623; total, $450.50. CM87.

After completing this chapter, you can:

1. Define accounting terms related to sales and cash receipts for a merchandising business.

2. Identify accounting concepts and practices related to sales and cash receipts for a merchandising business.

3. Journalize sales on account using a sales journal.

4. Journalize cash receipts using a cash receipts journal.

5. Journalize sales returns and allowances using a general journal.

EXPLORE ACCOUNTING

Journalizing Sales Discounts

Most sales of a merchandising business are to individuals for cash or credit card. Individual customers are expected to pay the full amount of the invoice at the time of the sale. In contrast, sales on account to business customers may involve a cash discount, such as 2/10, n/30. As discussed in Chapter 9, businesses often receive cash discounts to encourage early payment for a sale on account.

Sales on account that involve both sales taxes and a cash discount present an interesting accounting problem. Assume Country Crafters purchases $100.00 of merchandise, plus $6.00 sales tax, for a total sale of $106.00, with 2/10, n/30 payment terms. Nine days later, Country Crafters pays $103.88 in full payment of the invoice. How should the cash receipt be journalized?

Because the payment is received within the discount period, the sales amount is reduced by the amount of the sales discount, $2.12. The amount of sales tax should also be reduced because the amount of the sale is reduced. Thus, the following journal entry should be recorded:

Cash	103.88	
Sales Tax Payable	.12	
Sales Discount	2.00	
Accounts Receivable		106.00

The net sales amount is $98.00—the original $100.00 sales less a 2% discount of $2.00. The net sales tax pay-

able is $5.88—the original $6.00 sales tax less a 2% discount of $0.12. The end result is that a $98.00 sale was made on which $5.88 sales tax ($98.00 × 6%) was collected.

It is critically important for accounting employees to be familiar with sales tax laws in the states in which their companies do business. Each state regulates how sales taxes should be paid. In some states, state regulations require that sales taxes be paid only on actual sales realized—$5.88 for this transaction. Merchandising businesses in these states might modify the cash receipts journal to include a Sales Tax Payable Debit column.

In some states, sales taxes must be paid on the original invoice amount of sale—$6.00 for this transaction. In these states, a sales discount would not result in a reduction in the sales tax liability. The following journal entry would be recorded:

Cash	103.88	
Sales Discount	2.12	
Accounts Receivable		106.00

Instructions: With your instructor's permission, contact several local businesses to determine how they account for cash discounts on sales on account. Specifically, ask the manager (1) does the business offer cash discounts and (2) how do sales returns impact the amount of sales tax paid to the state.

10-1 APPLICATION PROBLEM

Journalizing sales on account; proving and ruling a sales journal

Audio Engineering is an electronics store specializing in sound systems.

Instructions:

1. Journalize the following transactions completed during September of the current year on page 10 of the sales journal given in the *Working Papers*. The sales invoice source document is abbreviated as S.

Transactions:

Sep. 2. Sold merchandise on account to Ketchum Clothing, $457.50, plus sales tax, $27.45; total, $484.95. S134.

5. Sold merchandise on account to Norton Industries, $345.00, plus sales tax, $20.70; total, $365.70. S135.

10. Sold merchandise on account to Jackson City Schools, $426.00. Jackson City Schools is exempt from paying sales tax. S136.

17. Sold merchandise on account to Riley & Slay, CPAs, $522.00, plus sales tax, $31.32; total, $553.32. S137.

23. Sold merchandise on account to Meadowbrook Church, $453.00. Meadowbrook Church is exempt from paying sales tax. S138.

30. Sold merchandise on account to Tang Construction, $512.00, plus sales tax, $30.72; total, $542.72. S139.

2. Total, prove, and rule page 10 of the sales journal.

10-2 APPLICATION PROBLEM

Journalizing cash receipts; proving and ruling a cash receipts journal

In Focus is a camera and film shop.

Instructions:

1. Journalize the following transactions completed during August of the current year on page 15 of the cash receipts journal given in the *Working Papers*. Source documents are abbreviated as follows: receipt, R; terminal summary, TS.

Transactions:

Aug. 1. Received cash on account from Reader Advertising, $345.60, covering S357. R288.

3. Recorded cash and credit card sales, $2,534.00, plus sales tax, $145.54; total, $2,679.54. TS28.

8. Received cash on account from WXGS Television, $312.60, covering S358. R289.

10. Recorded cash and credit card sales, $2,650.00, plus sales tax, $140.80; total, $2,790.80. TS29.

15. Received cash on account from Lambert News, covering S360 for $204.30, less 2% discount. R290.

17. Recorded cash and credit card sales, $2,372.00, plus sales tax, $132.43; total, $2,504.43. TS30.

24. Received cash on account from Kelly Modeling Agency, $236.96, covering S359. R291.

24. Recorded cash and credit card sales, $3,180.00, plus sales tax, $170.80; total, $3,350.80. TS31.

30. Received cash on account from JGN Industries, covering S361 for $201.40, less 2% discount. R292.

31. Recorded cash and credit card sales, $2,100.00, plus sales tax, $104.25; total, $2,204.25. TS32.

2. Total and prove the equality of debits and credits for cash receipts journal page 15.

Go Beyond the Book
For more information go to
www.C21accounting.com

3. Prove cash. The August 1 cash account balance in the general ledger was $2,548.25. The August 31 cash credit total in the cash payments journal was $15,485.25. On August 31, the balance on the next unused check stub was $1,885.56.

4. Rule page 15 of the cash receipts journal.

10-3   APPLICATION PROBLEM

Journalizing sales returns and allowances using a general journal

VanHorn Designs sells custom logo products.

Instructions:

1. Journalize the following transactions affecting sales completed during July of the current year. Use page 14 of the general journal given in the *Working Papers*. Source documents are abbreviated as follows: credit memorandum, CM; receipt, R; sales invoice, S.

Transactions:

July 2. Granted credit to Tahai Industries for merchandise returned, $253.00, plus sales tax, $15.18, from S456; total, $268.18. CM61.

4. Granted credit to Allergy Associates for damaged merchandise, $235.00, plus sales tax, $14.10, from S455; total, $249.10. CM62.

12. Granted credit to Jefferson School for damaged merchandise, $134.25, from S458. CM63.

10-4   MASTERY PROBLEM

Journalizing sales and cash receipts transactions; proving and ruling journals

Aqua Center installs and maintains swimming pools and spas.
   Use page 19 of a sales journal, page 20 of a cash receipts journal, and page 14 of a general journal. Balances brought forward are provided on line 1 of each journal in the *Working Papers*.

Instructions:

1. Journalize the following transactions completed during the remainder of October in the appropriate journal. The sales tax rate is 4%. Source documents are abbreviated as follows: receipt, R; sales invoice, S; terminal summary, TS.

Transactions:

Oct. 26. Received cash on account from Slumber Inns, covering S435 for $1,356.00, less a 2% discount. R293.

27. Sold merchandise on account to County Hospital, $489.50, plus sales tax, $19.58; total, $509.08. S443.

28. Recorded cash and credit card sales, $4,315.00, plus sales tax, $126.60; total, $4,441.60. TS44.

29. Received cash on account from Summit Lodge, $467.24, covering S438. R294.

29. Granted credit to Slumber Inns for merchandise returned, $124.00, plus sales tax, $4.96, from S293; total, $128.96. CM54.

30. Sold merchandise on account to Southeastern University, $3,643.50. Southeastern University is exempt from sales tax. S444.

31. Recorded cash and credit card sales, $1,232.00, plus sales tax, $42.22; total, $1,274.22. TS45.

2. Total and prove the equality of debits and credits for the sales journal.

3. Rule the sales journal.

4. Total and prove the equality of debits and credits for the cash receipts journal.

5. Prove cash. The October 1 cash account balance in the general ledger was $4,483.25. The October 31 cash credit total in the cash payments journal was $39,315.22. On October 31, the balance on the next unused check stub was $8,918.50.

6. Rule the cash receipts journal.

CHALLENGE PROBLEM

Journalizing transactions; proving and ruling special journals

Zone 6 is a lawn and garden store.

Instructions:

1. Journalize in the appropriate journal the following transactions completed during May of the current year. Use page 5 of a purchases and sales journal, page 8 of a cash payments journal, page 9 of a cash receipts journal, and page 7 of a general journal given in the *Working Papers*. The sales tax rate is 8%. Calculate and add the appropriate sales tax amount to each sale. Source documents are abbreviated as follows: check, C; credit memorandum, CM; purchase invoice, P; receipt, R; sales invoice, S; terminal summary, TS.

Transactions:

May 1. Paid cash for rent, $1,400.00. C344.
   3. Paid cash for electric bill, $186.00. C345.
   3. Granted credit to Slippery Rock Inn for merchandise returned, $235.00, plus sales tax, $18.80, from S493; total, $253.80. CM67.
   3. Purchased merchandise on account from Angelo Lawn Supplies, $1,340.00. P91.
   4. Bought $120.00 worth of store supplies on account from Mosby Store Supplies, recorded on Memo 43, with 2/10, n/30 payment terms.
   4. Paid cash on account to Northeast Nurseries, $7,632.00, covering P87. C346.
   4. Sold merchandise on account to First National Bank, $546.00, plus sales tax. S567.
   5. Bought office supplies for cash, $35.45. C347.
   5. Paid cash for some merchandise, $89.40. C348.
   6. Recorded cash and credit card sales, $3,235.00, plus sales tax of $239.40. TS23.
   7. Received an invoice, stamped Purchase Invoice 92, for merchandise on account from Forde Collectibles for $3,250.00, less a 60% trade discount.
   7. Houston Landscaping paid its $545.65 balance, less 2% discount. R490.
   8. Bought office supplies on account from Office Mart, $81.60. M44.
  10. Returned $260.00 of the merchandise purchased on Purchase Invoice 92 to Forde Collectibles, recorded on Debit Memorandum 23.
  11. Paid the remaining balance of Purchase Invoice 92, less Debit Memorandum 23, to Forde Collectibles with Check No. 349, taking advantage of the 2/10, n/30 payment terms.
  13. Cash and credit card sales for the week were $3,216.00, plus sales tax of $206.70. TS24.
  14. Jackson Public Schools bought merchandise on account for $450.00. S568.
  16. Purchased $2,900.00 of merchandise on account from Tom's Sod Farm on Purchase Invoice 93, with 2/10, n/30 payment terms.
  17. Paid cash on account to Office Mart, $81.60, covering M44. C350.
  20. Cash and credit card sales for the week were $2,554.00, plus sales tax, $184.23. TS25.
  22. First National Bank paid $589.68 cash on its account, covering S567. R491.
  23. SDR Investment Trust bought merchandise on account for $1,456.00, plus sales tax. S569.
  23. Purchased merchandise on account from LawnScapes, Inc., $4,488.00. P94.
  25. Paid $102.00 cash for advertising. C351.
  27. Cash and credit card sales for the week were $2,742.00, plus sales tax, $184.25. TS26.
  29. Slippery Rock Inn paid $2,345.64 on its account, covering S493. R492.
  29. Granted credit to SDR Investment Trust for damaged merchandise, $45.00, plus sales tax, from S455. CM68.
  31. Paid cash to replenish the petty cash fund, $361.60: office supplies, $74.40; store supplies, $85.00; advertising, $105.00; miscellaneous, $96.00. C352.
  31. Recorded cash and credit card sales, $768.00, plus sales tax, $49.45. TS27.

2. Total the purchases, cash payments, sales, and cash receipts journals.

3. Prove the equality of debits and credits for the cash payments, sales, and cash receipts journals.

4. Prove cash. The May 1 cash account balance in the general ledger was $2,464.60. On May 31, the balance on the next unused check stub was $8,406.44.

5. Rule the purchases, cash payments, sales, and cash receipts journals.

The tendency for prices to increase over time is referred to as *inflation*. Increasing prices reduce what an individual or company can purchase with the same amount of money.

Instructions: The following table represents the prices for selected consumer goods in 1990. Copy the table and add a column for the current year and a column for the percent of change. Use the newspaper and identify current prices for the products listed. Determine the percentage change in the price of each item. If an item decreased in price, can you explain the reason for the decrease?

Comparison of Prices for Selected Consumer Items

Item	1990 Price
19-inch color television	$149.00
Cassette tape	13.50
Milk (gallon)	1.99
Ground beef (pound)	1.69
Eggs, medium (dozen)	.99
Raisin bran	1.99
Film, 24 exposures	3.88
Theater ticket	6.50
Motor oil (quart)	.84
Refrigerator (19.1 cu. ft.)	790.00

Roshonda Compton, an accountant for an office supplies store, has noted a major increase in overdue amounts from charge customers. All invoice amounts from sales on account are due within 30 days. The amounts due have reduced the amount of cash available for the day-to-day operation of the business. Ms. Compton recommends that the business (1) stop all sales on account and (2) begin accepting bank credit cards. The owner is reluctant to accept the recommendations because the business might lose some reliable customers who do not have credit cards. Also, the business will have increased expenses because of the credit card fee. How would you respond to Ms. Compton's recommendations? What alternatives might the owner consider?

Basic Skill: Reading

Concept: Employers need employees at all levels who can read well. Reading includes locating, understanding, and interpreting written information. The written information may be in documents such as manuals, graphs, schedules, or even in software "Help" windows.

Application: Open a software application with which you are familiar, such as word processing, spreadsheet, or accounting software. Using either printed documentation or the Help function of the software, locate a software feature with which you are not familiar. Read the document and create a file in which you can practice applying this previously unknown feature. Write a statement about situations in which this new feature could save time.

Journalizing sales and cash receipts transactions; proving and ruling journals

Golfer's Paradise sells golf and other recreational equipment. Source documents related to the sales and cash receipts are provided in the *Working Papers*.

Sales journal page 18, cash receipts journal page 24, and general journal page 15 for Golfer's Paradise are given in the *Working Papers*. Balances brought forward are provided on line 1 of each journal.

Instructions

1. Journalize the transactions shown in the source documents in the appropriate journal. The sales tax rate is 8%.

2. Total and prove the equality of debits and credits for the sales journal.

3. Rule the sales journal.

4. Total and prove the equality of debits and credits for the cash receipts journal.

5. Prove cash. The November 1 cash account balance in the general ledger was $2,551.18. The November 30 cash credit total in the cash payments journal was $49,158.84. On November 30, the balance on the next unused check stub was $5,106.41.

6. Rule the cash receipts journal.

ANALYZING BEST BUY'S FINANCIAL STATEMENTS

Comparable store sales—the sales at stores open for more than a year—is one of the best measures of financial success for a retail business. An increase in comparable store sales can be achieved by a combination of raising unit sales prices and selling more units. Regardless of the reason, an increase in comparable store sales demonstrates that the company's products are in demand.

Instructions

1. Use Best Buy's 5-Year Financial Highlights on page B-2 in Appendix B to identify the comparable store sales change for 2005–2007.

2. Use the 5-Year Financial Highlights to identify the types and number of stores open at the end of 2006 and 2007.

Accounting
SOFTWARE

SALES AND CASH RECEIPTS

Accounting software enables you to create a sales invoice by entering sales information directly into the computer. Peachtree provides you with a computer screen that closely resembles a paper sales invoice. Peachtree enhances the process by assigning a document number, automatically entering a transaction date, providing you with a list of customers and inventory items, and calculating the total sale. These features increase the efficiency of creating a sales invoice and reduce the number of errors.

PEACHTREE MASTERY PROBLEM 10-4

1. Open (Restore) file 10-4MP.ptb.
2. Use the Receipts task to journalize and record cash receipts transactions. (Peachtree will automatically debit Cash; the offsetting credit goes to Sales or the account you specify.)
3. Use the Sales/Invoicing task to record a credit sale. (Peachtree automatically debits the customer's account and Accounts Receivable; the credit side defaults to Sales.)
4. Use the Credit Memos task to record sales returns. This transaction will post to the Sales Journal.
5. Print the sales journal from the Reports, Accounts Receivable Report List.
6. Print the cash receipts journal from the Report List.

PEACHTREE CHALLENGE PROBLEM 10-5

1. Open (Restore) file 10-5CP.ptb.
2. Record sales and cash receipts. The sales tax rate is 8%.
3. Print the purchase journal, cash disbursements journal, sales journal, and cash receipts journal.

SALES AND CASH RECEIPTS

New screens will be used to record receiving cash on account, selling merchandise on account, recording cash and credit card sales, granting credit for sales returns, and making cash payments. By filling in all the data required on these screens, the report generated will have much more information than can be provided by special journals. QuickBooks also provides many shortcuts to make entering the data more efficient and accurate. Dropdown lists are available for account titles and customer and vendor names. The software program automatically fills in much of the data on many screens.

QUICKBOOKS MASTERY PROBLEM 10-4

1. Open the Aqua Center file.
2. Use the Receive Payment option from the Customers menu to record payments on account.
3. Use the Create Invoices option from the Customers menu to record sales on account.
4. Use the Enter Sales Receipts window to record cash and credit card sales.
5. Record customer returns in the Create Credit Memos/Refunds feature.
6. Print a Journal report.

QUICKBOOKS CHALLENGE PROBLEM 10-5

1. Open the Zone file.
2. Use the Enter Bills and Pay Bills features to record purchases, payments, and vendor returns on account.
3. Use the Receive Payments and Create Invoices features to record cash receipts and sales on account.
4. Use the Create Credit Memos/Returns feature to record customer returns.
5. Use the Write Checks feature to record cash payments.
6. Use the Enter Sales Receipts feature to record cash and credit card sales.
7. Print a Journal report, a Customer Balance Summary report, a Vendor Balance Summary report, and a Trial Balance report.

SORTING AND FILTERING DATA

Effective managers use sales information to understand sales trends and target potential customers. In other words, sales information should be used to help increase sales. The sales journal reports sales for a period of time. Knowing the customers involved in the largest sales can provide managers with ideas to increase sales to other customers. Managers can learn how these sales were made and apply that knowledge when making sales to other customers.

Electronic spreadsheets have the ability to sort and filter data. Data can be sorted in ascending or descending order by numbers or text. Filters display the information that meets certain criteria, such as amounts that are greater than 10,000.

OPTIONAL SPREADSHEET ACTIVITY

Open the file F10-OPT. Complete the instructions provided to sort and filter the sales data.

SALES AND CASH RECEIPTS

To record transactions in the sales journal

1. Enter the transaction date.
2. Enter the invoice number in the Refer. column.
3. Enter the amount of the invoice in the Sales Credit column. The Accounts Receivable debit amount is calculated and displayed automatically.
4. If the transaction involves sales tax, enter the amount in the Sales Tax Credit column.
5. Choose a customer name from the Customer drop-down list.
6. Click the Post button.

The cash receipts journal is used to enter all cash receipt transactions. The debit to cash is automatically calculated and displayed by the computer. There are two types of cash receipts:

- Cash and credit card sales are cash receipts that do not affect Accounts Receivable.
- Receipts on account are cash receipts that do affect Accounts Receivable.

To record transactions in the cash receipts journal

1. Enter the transaction date.
2. Enter the transaction reference.
3. If recording a cash or credit card sale, enter the sales amount of the merchandise sold. Enter the amount of sales tax in the Sales Tax Payable Credit column. The debit to Cash is automatically calculated and displayed.
4. If recording a receipt on account, enter the amount in the A.R. Credit column. Choose the customer from the Customer drop-down list.
5. Click the Post button.

AUTOMATED ACCOUNTING APPLICATION PROBLEM 10-2

Open file F10-2.AA8. Display the problem instructions and complete the problem.

AUTOMATED ACCOUNTING MASTERY PROBLEM 10-4

Open file F10-4.AA8. Display the problem instructions and complete the problem.

DIGITAL VISION/GETTY IMAGES

CHAPTER 11

Posting to General and Subsidiary Ledgers

OBJECTIVES

After studying Chapter 11, you will be able to:

1. Define accounting terms related to posting to ledgers.

2. Identify accounting practices related to posting to ledgers.

3. Post separate items from a purchases, cash payments, and general journal to an accounts payable ledger.

4. Post separate items from a sales, cash receipts, and general journal to an accounts receivable ledger.

5. Post separate items from a cash payments and general journal to a general ledger.

6. Post special journal column totals to a general ledger.

7. Journalize and post correcting entries affecting customer accounts.

KEY TERMS

- subsidiary ledger
- accounts payable ledger
- accounts receivable ledger
- controlling account
- schedule of accounts payable
- schedule of accounts receivable

Point Your Browser
www.C21accounting.com

eBay, Inc.

eBay Conquers the Online Marketplace

Cleaning out your closet and finding things you don't need? Don't trash it, eBay it!

From its beginning in 1995, eBay has become an integral part of today's society, boasting 222 million registered users as of December 31, 2006. Innovative thinking has fueled eBay's dynamic growth of its online marketplace, where individuals and businesses bought and sold a staggering $52 billion worth of goods during 2006.

eBay is more than just an online marketplace. The company has been quick to identify and purchase companies that have developed services that take advantage of the Internet. PayPal, purchased in 2002, provides a platform for the online payment of eBay transactions. Purchased in 2005, Skype provides voice and video communications. Shopping.com provides comparison shopping for new products, and Rent.com lists apartments from more than 20,000 properties.

With every change in its business, eBay must change its accounting system. New accounts and different methods for combining those accounts are required to create financial statements.

GETTY IMAGES NEWS

DIGITAL VISION/GETTY IMAGES

INTERNET ACTIVITY

AICPA—Student Resources

Go to the homepage for the American Institute of Certified Public Accountants (AICPA) (www.aicpa.org).

Instructions

1. Search for "Accounting Fun Facts." Find and list three of the fun facts given.

2. Click on the "About the AICPA" link. Under the "Frequently Asked Questions (FAQ)" link, read through the questions and answers. List one question and summarize the answer to the question.

Critical Thinking

1. Many businesses begin as a sole proprietorship and later transform into a corporation. What changes might occur in the chart of accounts when a business changes from being a sole proprietorship to a corporation?

2. Identify another business that has experienced changes in its corporate structure. What motivated the change(s)?

Source: http://pages.ebay.com/aboutebay/thecompany/companyoverview.html

LEDGERS AND CONTROLLING ACCOUNTS

A business's size, number of transactions, and type of transactions determine the number of ledgers used in an accounting system.

General Ledger

Hobby Shack's general ledger chart of accounts is on page 231. However, because of the business's size and the number and type of transactions, Hobby Shack also uses additional ledgers in its accounting system.

Subsidiary Ledgers

A business needs to know the amount owed each vendor as well as the amount to be collected from each charge customer. Therefore, a separate account is needed for each vendor and each customer. Hobby Shack keeps a separate ledger for vendors and a separate ledger for customers.

Each separate ledger is summarized in a single general ledger account. A ledger that is summarized in a single general ledger account is called a **subsidiary ledger**. A subsidiary ledger containing only accounts for vendors from whom merchandise or other items are purchased on account is called an **accounts payable ledger**. A subsidiary ledger containing only accounts for charge customers is called an **accounts receivable ledger**. Total amounts are summarized in single general ledger accounts: Accounts Payable for vendors and Accounts Receivable for charge customers. An account in a general ledger that summarizes all accounts in a subsidiary ledger is called a **controlling account**. The balance of a controlling account equals the total of all account balances in its related subsidiary ledger.

CHARACTER COUNTS

Whose Computer Is It Really?

John Melton is an accounting manager at Stegall Industries. John frequently walks through his department to make himself readily available for his employees to ask questions and provide feedback. With increasing frequency, John has observed that his employees have Internet auction sites open while they are working on their computers. Concerned that productivity in his department is suffering, he is considering installing some sort of monitoring system to gather evidence of the employees' computer usage.

In accordance with company policy, John began his planning by examining the company's code of conduct. Two statements appear relevant: "Employees should be treated with mutual respect, free from the threat of harassment and discrimination."

"Employees may occasionally use company computer systems, such as Internet and e-mail, for personal use. Such use should be on a limited basis and should not result in a measurable cost to the Company."

Instructions

Use the ethical model to evaluate John's proposed action to monitor his employees' Internet usage. Do you have any recommendations for John?

PHOTO: DIGITAL VISION/GETTY IMAGES

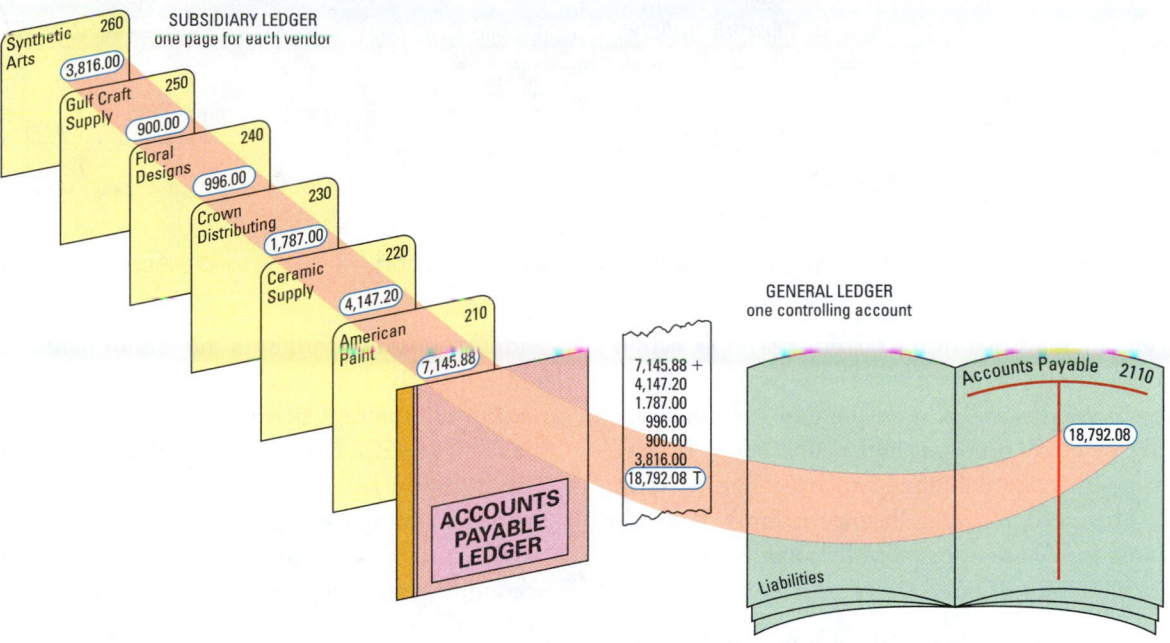

SUBSIDIARY LEDGER
one page for each vendor

Synthetic Arts 260 3,816.00
Gulf Craft Supply 250 900.00
Floral Designs 240 996.00
Crown Distributing 230 1,787.00
Ceramic Supply 220 4,147.20
American Paint 210 7,145.88

ACCOUNTS PAYABLE LEDGER

7,145.88 +
4,147.20
1.787.00
996.00
900.00
3,816.00
18,792.08 T

GENERAL LEDGER
one controlling account

Accounts Payable 2110
18,792.08

Liabilities

Hobby Shack assigns a vendor number to each account in the accounts payable ledger. A three-digit number is used. The first digit identifies the division in which the controlling account appears in the general ledger. The second two digits show each account's location within a subsidiary ledger. Accounts are assigned by 10s, beginning with the second digit. Accounts in the subsidiary ledgers can be located by either number or name.

The vendor number for American Paint is 210. The first digit, *2*, shows that the controlling account is a liability, Accounts Payable. The second and third digits, *10*, show the vendor number assigned to American Paint.

The procedure for adding new accounts to subsidiary ledgers is the same as described for TechKnow Consulting's general ledger in Chapter 4. Accounts are arranged in alphabetical order within the subsidiary ledgers. New accounts are assigned an unused middle number. If the proper alphabetical order places a new account as the last account, the next number in the sequence of 10s is assigned. Hobby Shack's chart of accounts for the subsidiary ledgers is on page 231.

When the balance of a vendor account in an accounts payable ledger is changed, the balance of the controlling account, Accounts Payable, is also changed. The total of all vendor account balances in the accounts payable ledger equals the balance of the controlling account, Accounts Payable.

STOCKBYTE/GETTY IMAGES

REMEMBER

The total amount owed to all vendors is summarized in a single general ledger account, Accounts Payable.

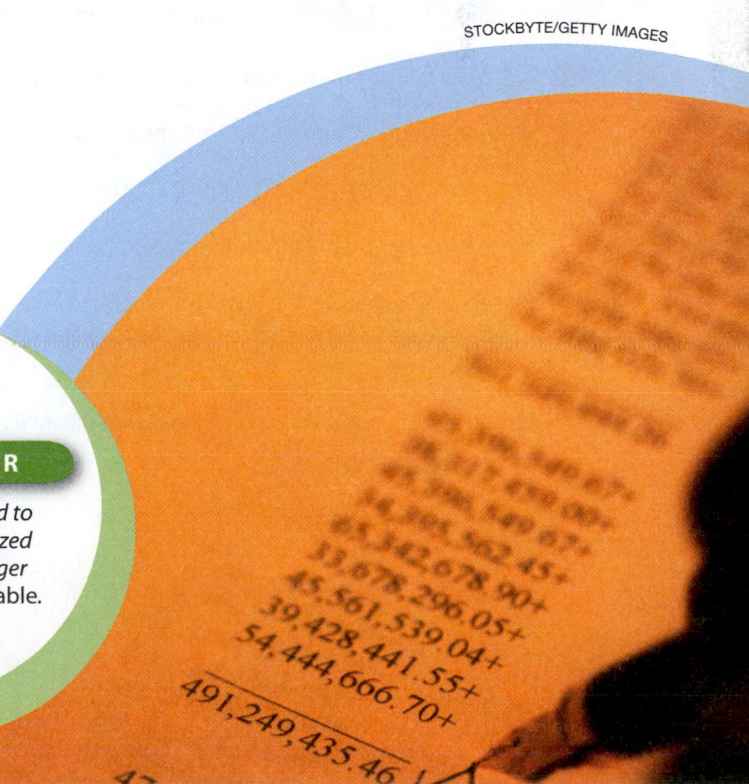

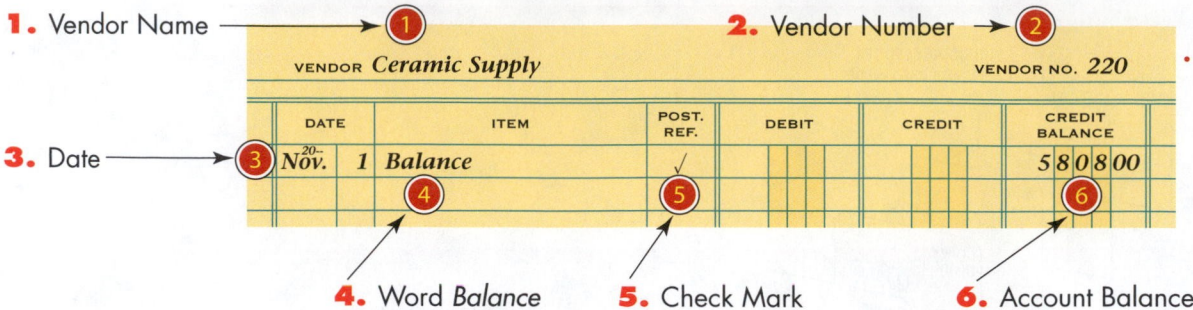

1. Vendor Name
2. Vendor Number
3. Date
4. Word *Balance*
5. Check Mark
6. Account Balance

Hobby Shack uses a 3-column accounts payable subsidiary account form. Information to be recorded in the accounts payable ledger includes the date, posting reference, debit or credit amount, and new account balance. Accounts payable are liabilities and have normal credit balances. Therefore, a Debit Balance column is usually not included in the accounts payable ledger accounts.

Each new account is opened by:

1. Writing the vendor name on the heading of the ledger account.
2. Writing the vendor number on the heading of the ledger account.

The vendor name is obtained from the first purchase invoice received. The vendor number is assigned using the three-digit numbering system previously described.

Some businesses record both the vendor name and vendor address on the ledger form. However, the address information is usually kept in a separate name and address file. This practice eliminates having to record the vendor address on the ledger form each time a new ledger page is opened or the address changes.

The number of entries that may be recorded on each account form depends on the number of lines provided. When all lines have been used, a new page is prepared. The vendor name, vendor number, and account balance are recorded on the new page.

On November 1, Hobby Shack prepared a new page for Ceramic Supply in the accounts payable ledger because the existing page was full. On that day, the account balance was $5,808.00.

 STEPS STARTING A NEW PAGE IN THE ACCOUNTS PAYABLE LEDGER

1. Write the vendor name, *Ceramic Supply*, on the Vendor line.

2. Write the vendor number, *220*, on the Vendor No. line.

3. Write the date, *20--, Nov. 1*, in the Date column.

4. Write the word *Balance* in the Item column.

5. Place a check mark in the Post. Ref. column to show that the amount has been carried forward from a previous page rather than posted from a journal.

6. Write the balance, *$5,808.00*, in the Credit Balance column.

REMEMBER

A new vendor account is opened by writing the vendor name and vendor number on the heading of the ledger account and placing it in alphabetical order.

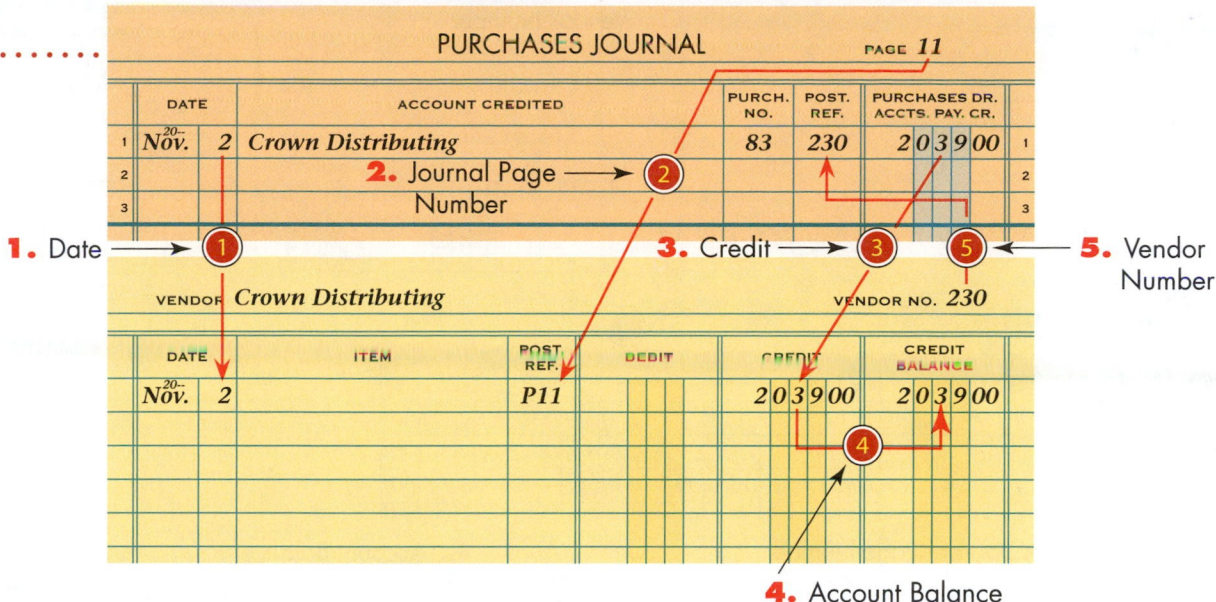

1. Date

2. Journal Page Number

3. Credit

4. Account Balance

5. Vendor Number

Each entry in the purchases journal affects the account of the vendor named in the Account Credited column. The amount on each line of a purchases journal is posted as a credit to a vendor account in the accounts payable ledger. Hobby Shack posts frequently to the accounts payable ledger. Posting frequently keeps each vendor account balance up to date.

STEPS **POSTING FROM A PURCHASES JOURNAL TO AN ACCOUNTS PAYABLE LEDGER**

① Write the date, *20--, Nov. 2*, in the Date column of the vendor account.

② Write the journal page number, *P11*, in the Post. Ref. column of the account. When several journals are used, an abbreviation is used to show the journal from which the posting is made. *P* is the abbreviation used for the purchases journal. The abbreviation *P11* means page 11 of the purchases journal.

③ Write the credit amount, *$2,039.00*, in the Credit column of the account for *Crown Distributing*.

④ Add the amount in the Credit column to the previous balance in the Credit Balance column. (*Crown Distributing* has no previous balance; therefore, $0 + $2,039.00 = $2,039.00.) Write the new account balance, *$2,039.00*, in the Credit Balance column.

⑤ Write the vendor number, *230*, in the Post. Ref. column of the journal. The vendor number shows that the posting for this entry is complete.

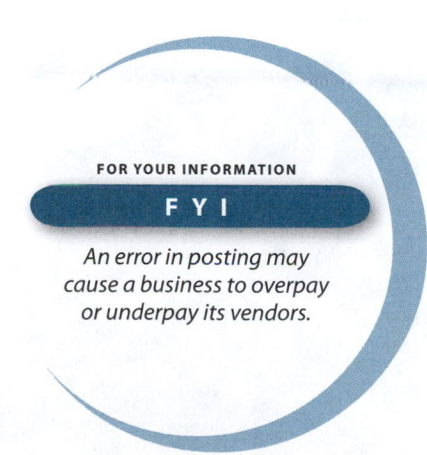

FOR YOUR INFORMATION

F Y I

An error in posting may cause a business to overpay or underpay its vendors.

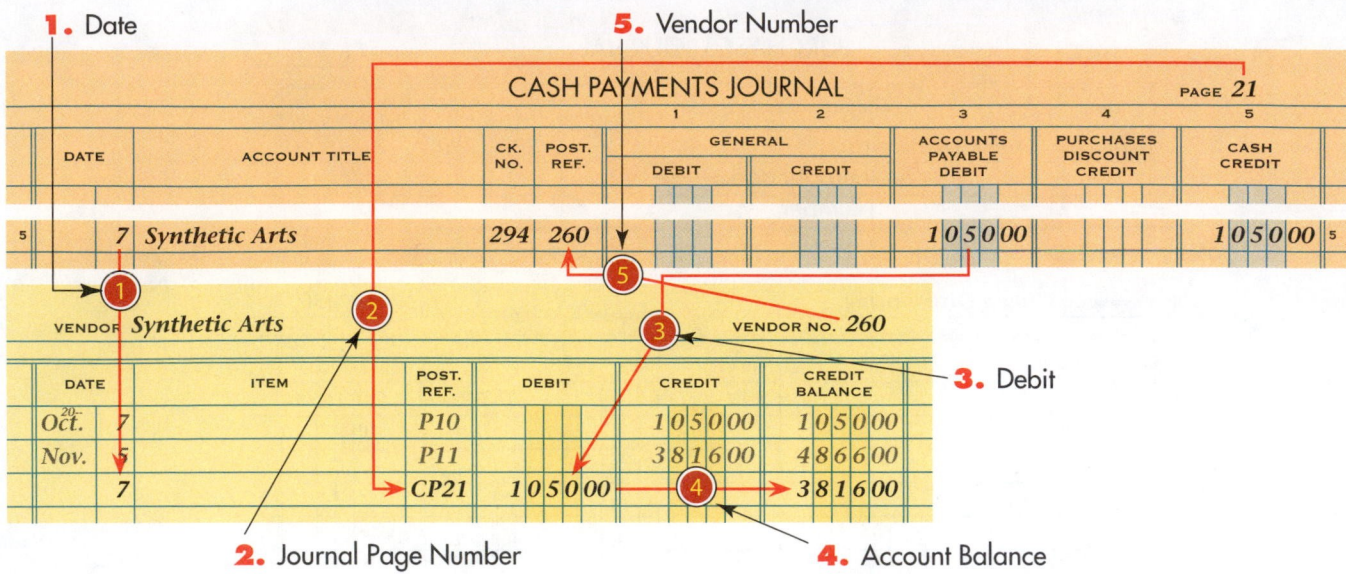

1. Date

5. Vendor Number

2. Journal Page Number

3. Debit

4. Account Balance

Each entry in the Accounts Payable Debit column of a cash payments journal affects a vendor account. Individual amounts in the Accounts Payable Debit column are posted frequently to the proper vendor account in the accounts payable ledger. Posting frequently keeps each vendor account balance up to date.

STEPS

POSTING FROM A CASH PAYMENTS JOURNAL TO AN ACCOUNTS PAYABLE LEDGER

1. Write the date, *7*, in the Date column of the vendor account.

2. Write the journal page number, *CP21*, in the Post. Ref. column of the account. The abbreviation *CP21* means page 21 of the cash payments journal.

3. Write the debit amount, *$1,050.00*, in the Debit column of the vendor account.

4. Subtract the amount in the Debit column from the previous balance in the Credit Balance column ($4,866.00 − $1,050.00 = $3,816.00). Write the new balance, *$3,816.00*, in the Credit Balance column.

5. Write the vendor number, *260*, in the Post. Ref. column of the cash payments journal.

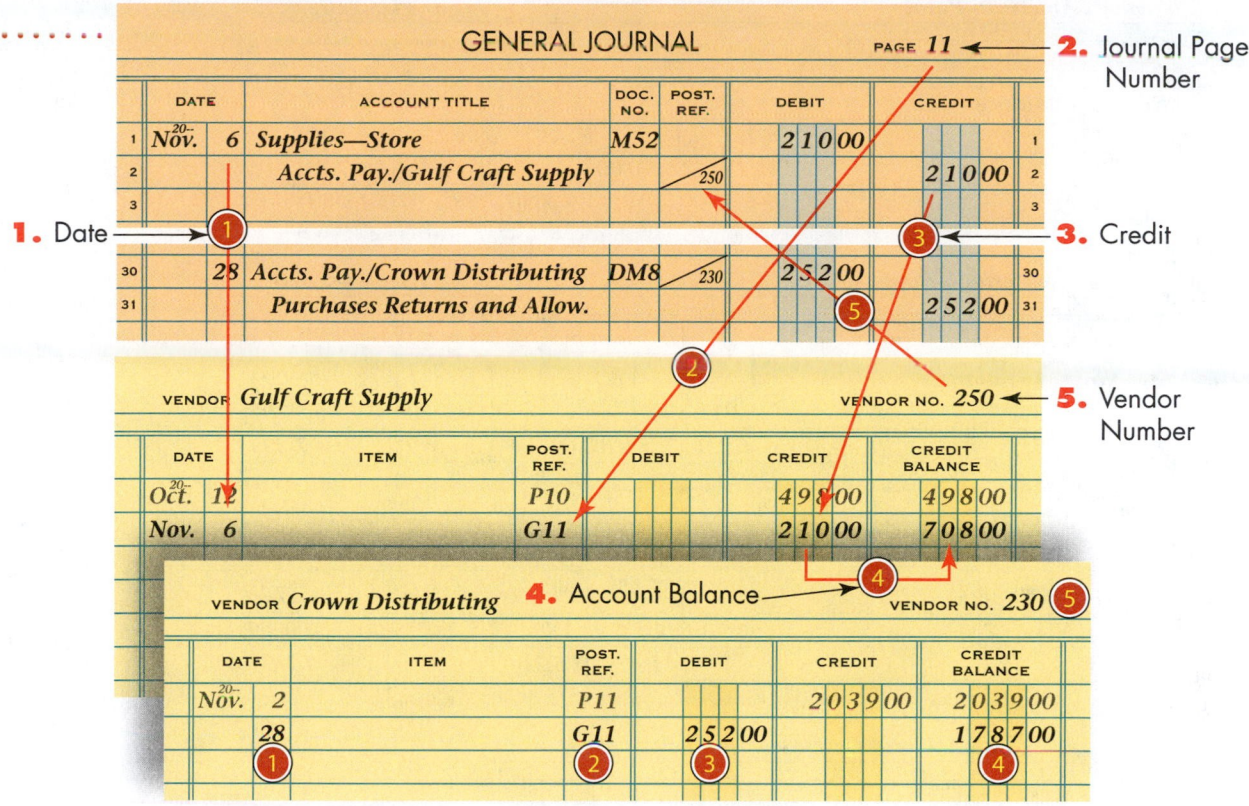

2. Journal Page Number

1. Date

3. Credit

5. Vendor Number

4. Account Balance

Entries in a general journal may affect account balances in a general ledger and an accounts payable ledger. Posting from a general journal to a general ledger is described on pages 317–318.

POSTING DEBIT AND CREDIT ENTRIES FROM A GENERAL JOURNAL TO AN ACCOUNTS PAYABLE LEDGER

POSTING A CREDIT ENTRY FOR SUPPLIES BOUGHT ON ACCOUNT

1. Write the date, *Nov. 6*, in the Date column of the vendor account.

2. Write the general journal page number, *G11*, in the Post. Ref. column of the account. The abbreviation *G11* means page 11 of the general journal.

3. Write the amount, *$210.00*, in the Credit column of the vendor account.

4. Add the amount in the Credit column to the previous balance in the Credit Balance column ($498.00 + $210.00 = $708.00). Write the new balance, *$708.00*, in the Credit Balance column.

5. Write the vendor number, *250*, to the right of the diagonal line in the Post. Ref. column of the general journal.

POSTING A DEBIT ENTRY FOR A PURCHASES RETURN OR ALLOWANCE

1. Write the date, *28*, in the Date column of the vendor account.

2. Write the general journal page number, *G11*, in the Post. Ref. column of the account.

3. Write the amount, *$252.00*, in the Debit column of the vendor account.

4. Subtract the amount in the Debit column from the previous balance in the Credit Balance column ($2,039.00 − $252.00 = $1,787.00). Write the new balance, *$1,787.00*, in the Credit Balance column.

5. Write the vendor number, *230*, to the right of the diagonal line in the Post. Ref. column of the general journal.

VENDOR *American Paint*   **VENDOR NO.** *210*

DATE		ITEM	POST. REF.	DEBIT	CREDIT	CREDIT BALANCE
Nov.	1	Balance	✓			2 6 5 0 00
	13		P11		3 7 6 8 00	6 4 1 8 00
	13		CP21	2 6 5 0 00		3 7 6 8 00
	20		P11		3 3 7 7 88	7 1 4 5 88

VENDOR *Ceramic Supply*   **VENDOR NO.** *220*

DATE		ITEM	POST. REF.	DEBIT	CREDIT	CREDIT BALANCE
Nov.	1	Balance	✓			5 8 0 8 00
	5		P11		4 1 4 7 20	9 9 5 5 20
	20		CP21	5 8 0 8 00		4 1 4 7 20

VENDOR *Crown Distributing*   **VENDOR NO.** *230*

DATE		ITEM	POST. REF.	DEBIT	CREDIT	CREDIT BALANCE
Nov.	2		P11		2 0 3 9 00	2 0 3 9 00
	28		G11	2 5 2 00		1 7 8 7 00

VENDOR *Floral Designs*   **VENDOR NO.** *240*

DATE		ITEM	POST. REF.	DEBIT	CREDIT	CREDIT BALANCE
Nov.	1	Balance	✓			7 4 4 00
	23		CP22	7 4 4 00		—
	24		G11		1 6 5 0 00	1 6 5 0 00
	26		G11		9 9 6 00	2 6 4 6 00
	30		CP22	1 6 5 0 00		9 9 6 00

VENDOR *Gulf Craft Supply*   **VENDOR NO.** *250*

DATE		ITEM	POST. REF.	DEBIT	CREDIT	CREDIT BALANCE
Nov.	1	Balance	✓			4 9 8 00
	6		G11		2 1 0 00	7 0 8 00
	8		CP21	4 9 8 00		2 1 0 00
	23		G11		6 9 0 00	9 0 0 00

VENDOR *Synthetic Arts*   **VENDOR NO.** *260*

DATE		ITEM	POST. REF.	DEBIT	CREDIT	CREDIT BALANCE
Nov.	1	Balance	✓			1 0 5 0 00
	5		P11		3 8 1 6 00	4 8 6 6 00
	7		CP21	1 0 5 0 00		3 8 1 6 00

Hobby Shack's accounts payable ledger has been posted for the month of November.

Hobby Shack, Inc. Schedule of Accounts Payable November 30, 20--	
American Paint	7 1 4 5 88
Ceramic Supply	4 1 4 7 20
Crown Distributing	1 7 8 7 00
Floral Designs	9 9 6 00
Gulf Craft Supply	9 0 0 00
Synthetic Arts	3 8 1 6 00
Total Accounts Payable	18 7 9 2 08

A controlling account balance in a general ledger must equal the sum of all account balances in a subsidiary ledger. Hobby Shack proves subsidiary ledgers at the end of each month.

A listing of vendor accounts, account balances, and total amount due all vendors is called a **schedule of accounts payable**. A schedule of accounts payable is prepared after all entries in a journal are posted. The balance of Accounts Payable in the general ledger is $18,792.08. The total of the schedule of accounts payable is $18,792.08. Because the two amounts are the same, the accounts payable ledger is proved.

GLOBAL PERSPECTIVE

The International Business Day

American business offices normally operate Monday through Friday, eight hours a day, with a 30- to 60-minute lunch break. This is not necessarily true in other countries, however. In the People's Republic of China, for example, employees usually work Monday through Saturday, eight hours a day, with lunch from 1:00 p.m. to 2:00 p.m.

When doing business internationally, both time zone differences and cultural factors affecting the business day must be taken into consideration. For example, in Spain, many businesses close at 2:00 p.m. so that employees may eat lunch with their families. The office reopens at 5:00 p.m. and stays open until about 8:00 p.m. Spain is in a time zone that is five hours ahead of Eastern Standard Time (EST), the time zone along the eastern coast of the United States. If doing business with a company in Spain, it would not be a good idea to try to call at 9:00 a.m. EST because the business might just be closing for lunch. A better time to call Spain from the EST time zone would be between noon and 3:00 p.m.

Critical Thinking

1. What are some ways you could reference time zones if you had to make frequent international phone calls?

2. If you work for a company with offices and customers all over the world, how could that affect the way you schedule projects?

PHOTO: STOCKBYTE/GETTY IMAGES

End of Lesson
REVIEW

TERMS REVIEW

- subsidiary ledger
- accounts payable ledger
- accounts receivable ledger
- controlling account
- schedule of accounts payable

AUDIT YOUR UNDERSTANDING

1. What is the relationship between a controlling account and a subsidiary ledger?
2. In which column of the cash payments journal are the amounts that are posted individually to the accounts payable ledger?

WORK TOGETHER 11-1

Posting to an accounts payable ledger

Partial purchases, cash payments, and general journals for Graphics, Inc., are given in the *Working Papers*. Also given in the *Working Papers* are accounts payable ledger account forms for selected accounts and a blank form for a schedule of accounts payable. Your instructor will guide you through the following examples.

1. Start a new page for an accounts payable ledger account for Regal Designs. The account number is 240 and the balance on October 1 of the current year is $877.00.
2. Post the Accounts Payable Credit entry on line 7 of the purchases journal to the accounts payable account for Regal Designs.
3. Post the Accounts Payable Debit entry on line 15 of the cash payments journal to the accounts payable account for Electro-Graphics Supply.
4. Post the credit entry on line 5 of the general journal to the accounts payable account for Electro-Graphics Supply. Post the debit entry on line 6 of the general journal to the accounts payable account for Art and Things.
5. Prepare a schedule of accounts payable for Graphics, Inc., on October 31 of the current year for these selected accounts. Accounts Payable balance in the general ledger on October 31 is $6,558.20. Save your work to complete Work Together 11-2, 11-3, and 11-4.

ON YOUR OWN 11-1

Posting to an accounts payable ledger

Partial purchases, cash payments, and general journals for Amatera, Inc., are given in the *Working Papers*. Also given in the *Working Papers* are accounts payable ledger account forms for selected accounts and a blank form for a schedule of accounts payable. Work this problem independently.

1. Start a new page for an accounts payable ledger account for Swann Industries. The account number is 240 and the balance on September 1 of the current year is $1,248.00.
2. Post the Accounts Payable Credit entry on line 11 of the purchases journal to the accounts payable account for Swann Industries.
3. Post the Accounts Payable Debit entry on line 19 of the cash payments journal to the accounts payable account for Miller Supply.
4. Post the credit entry on line 5 of the general journal to the accounts payable account for Miller Supply. Post the debit entry on line 6 of the general journal to the accounts payable account for Franklin Mfg. Corp.
5. Prepare a schedule of accounts payable for Amatera, Inc., on September 30 of the current year for these selected accounts. Accounts Payable balance in the general ledger on September 30 is $9,142.25. Save your work to complete On Your Own 11-2, 11-3, and 11-4.

ACCOUNTS RECEIVABLE LEDGER AND GENERAL LEDGER CONTROLLING ACCOUNT

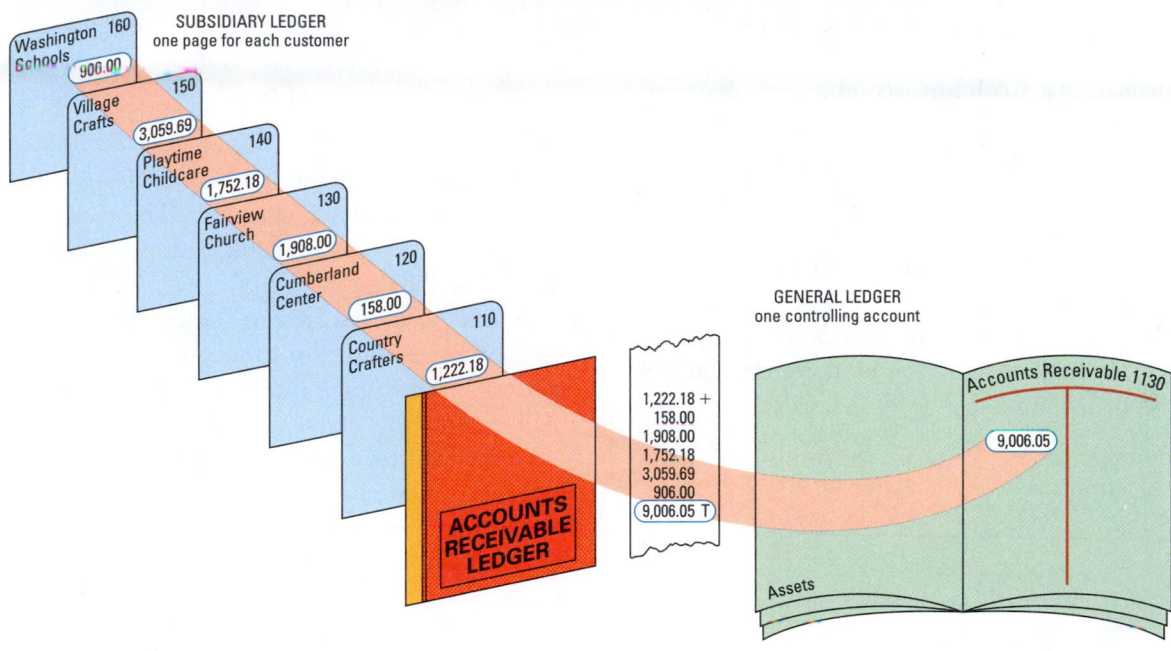

SUBSIDIARY LEDGER
one page for each customer

Washington Schools 160
906.00

Village Crafts 150
3,059.69

Playtime Childcare 140
1,752.18

Fairview Church 130
1,908.00

Cumberland Center 120
158.00

Country Crafters 110
1,222.18

ACCOUNTS RECEIVABLE LEDGER

1,222.18 +
158.00
1,908.00
1,752.18
3,059.69
906.00
9,006.05 T

GENERAL LEDGER
one controlling account

Accounts Receivable 1130
9,006.05

Assets

Hobby Shack assigns a customer number to each account in the accounts receivable ledger. A three-digit number is used.

The customer number for Country Crafters is 110. The first digit, *1*, shows that the controlling account is an asset, Accounts Receivable. The second and third digits, *10*, show the customer number assigned to Country Crafters.

When the balance of a customer account in an accounts receivable ledger is changed, the balance of the controlling account, Accounts Receivable, is also changed. The total of all customer account balances in the accounts receivable ledger equals the balance of the controlling account, Accounts Receivable.

PHOTODISC/GETTY IMAGES

REMEMBER

The total amount to be collected from all charge customers is summarized in a single general ledger account, Accounts Receivable.

1. Customer Name → ①   **2.** Customer Number → ②

CUSTOMER *Cumberland Center*   CUSTOMER NO. *120*

DATE	ITEM	POST. REF.	DEBIT	CREDIT	DEBIT BALANCE

Hobby Shack uses a 3-column accounts receivable subsidiary account form. The accounts receivable account form is similar to the one used for the accounts payable ledger. Accounts receivable are assets, and assets have normal debit balances. Therefore, the form used in the accounts receivable ledger has a Debit Balance column instead of a Credit Balance column.

Procedures for opening customer accounts are similar to those used for opening vendor accounts. Each new account is opened by:

1. Writing the customer name on the heading of the ledger account.

2. Writing the customer number on the heading of the ledger account.

The customer name is obtained from the first sales invoice prepared for a customer. The customer number is assigned using the three-digit numbering system previously described.

Some businesses record both the customer name and customer address on the ledger form. However, the address information is usually kept in a separate name and address file. This practice eliminates having to record the customer address on the ledger form each time a new ledger page is started or the address changes.

DIGITAL VISION/GETTY IMAGES

FOR YOUR INFORMATION

F Y I

When an account that is no longer used is removed from the accounts receivable ledger, that customer number is available for assignment to a new customer.

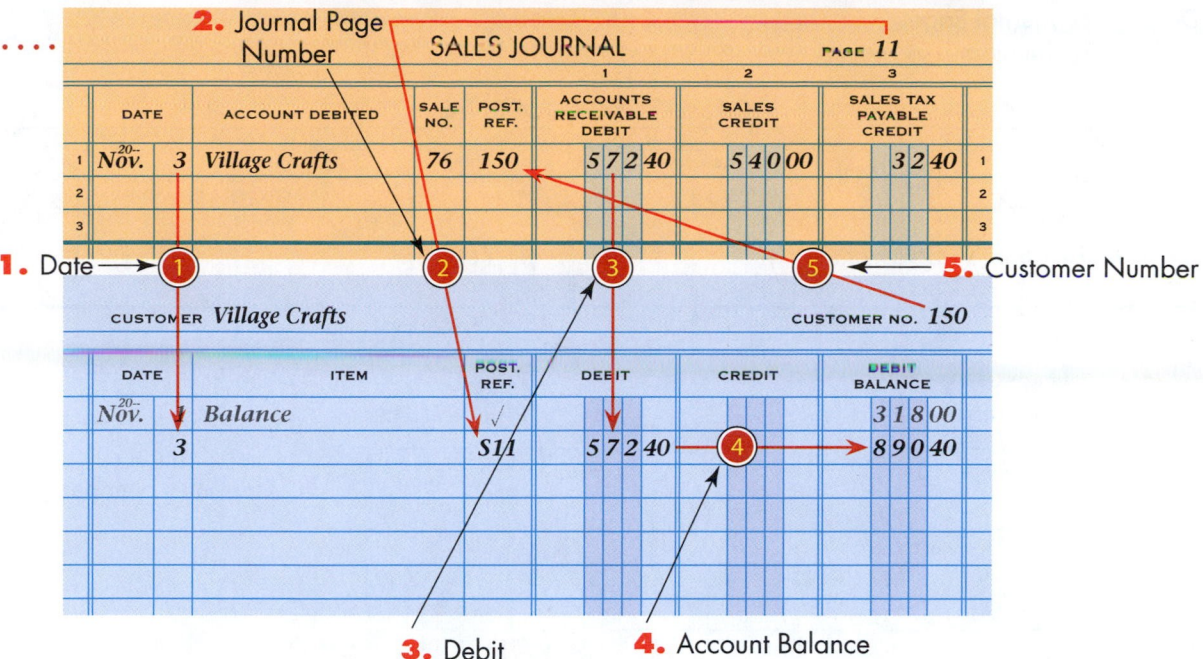

2. Journal Page Number

1. Date → ①   ②   ③   ⑤   **5.** Customer Number

3. Debit   **4.** Account Balance

Each amount in a sales journal's Accounts Receivable Debit column is posted to the accounts receivable ledger. Each amount is posted as a debit to the customer account listed in the Account Debited column. Hobby Shack posts frequently to the accounts receivable ledger so that each customer account will show an up-to-date balance.

The controlling account in the general ledger, **Accounts Receivable**, is also increased by this entry. At the end of the month, the journal's Accounts Receivable Debit column total is posted to the controlling account, **Accounts Receivable**.

STEPS POSTING FROM A SALES JOURNAL TO AN ACCOUNTS RECEIVABLE LEDGER

① Write the date, *3*, in the Date column of the account.

② Write the sales journal page number, *S11*, in the Post. Ref. column of the account. *S* is the abbreviation used for the sales journal.

③ Write the debit amount, *$572.40*, in the Debit column of the customer account.

④ Add the amount in the Debit column to the previous balance in the Debit Balance column ($318.00 + $572.40 = $890.40). Write the new account balance, *$890.40*, in the Debit Balance column.

⑤ Write the customer number, *150*, in the Post. Ref. column of the sales journal. The customer number shows that the posting for this entry is complete.

FOR YOUR INFORMATION

FYI

Individual amounts in the Accounts Receivable Debit column are posted frequently to customer accounts in the accounts receivable ledger.

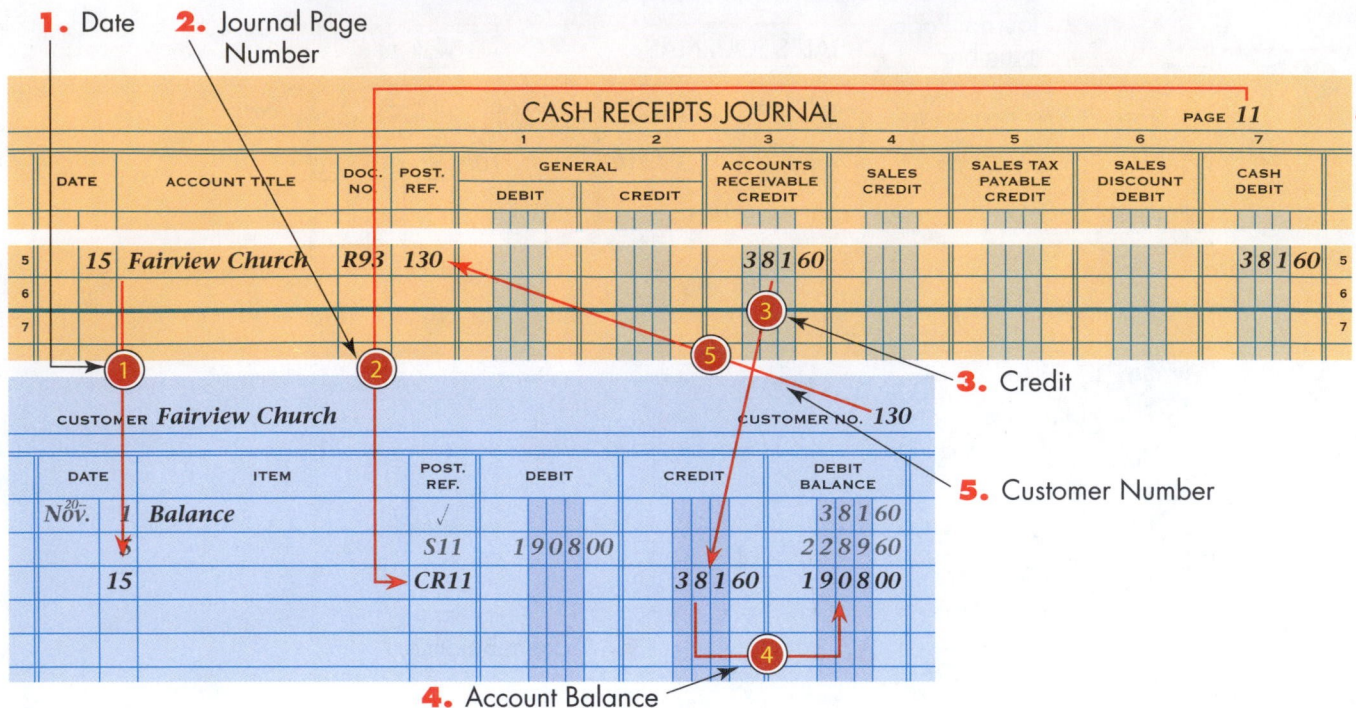

1. Date **2.** Journal Page Number

3. Credit

5. Customer Number

4. Account Balance

Each entry in the Accounts Receivable Credit column affects the customer named in the Account Title column. Each amount listed in the Accounts Receivable Credit column is posted to the proper customer account in the accounts receivable ledger. Hobby Shack posts frequently to the accounts receivable ledger so that each customer account will show an up-to-date balance.

STEPS POSTING FROM A CASH RECEIPTS JOURNAL TO AN ACCOUNTS RECEIVABLE LEDGER

1. Write the date, *15*, in the Date column of the account.

2. Write the cash receipts journal page number, *CR11*, in the Post. Ref. column of the account. *CR* is the abbreviation for the cash receipts journal.

3. Write the credit amount, *$381.60*, in the Credit column of the customer account.

4. Subtract the amount in the Credit column from the previous balance in the Debit Balance column ($2,289.60 − $381.60 = $1,908.00). Write the new balance, *$1,908.00*, in the Debit Balance column.

5. Write the customer number, *130*, in the Post. Ref. column of the cash receipts journal.

STOCKBYTE/GETTY IMAGES

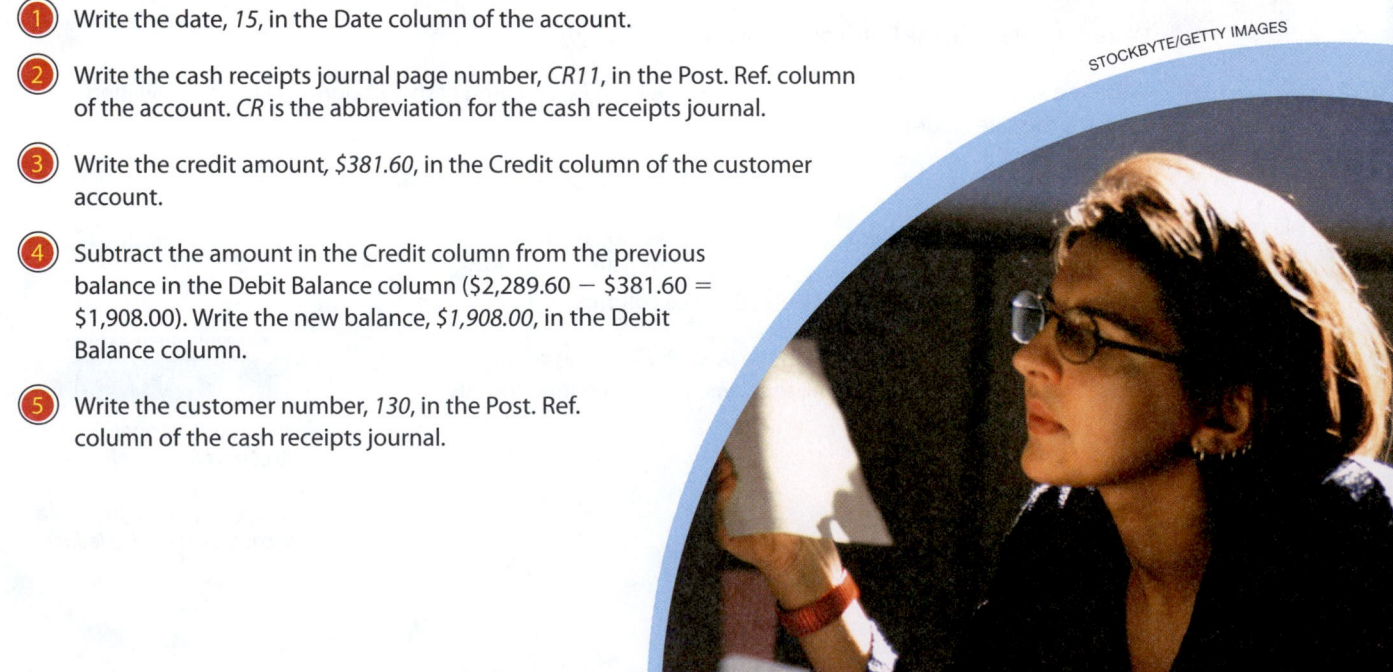

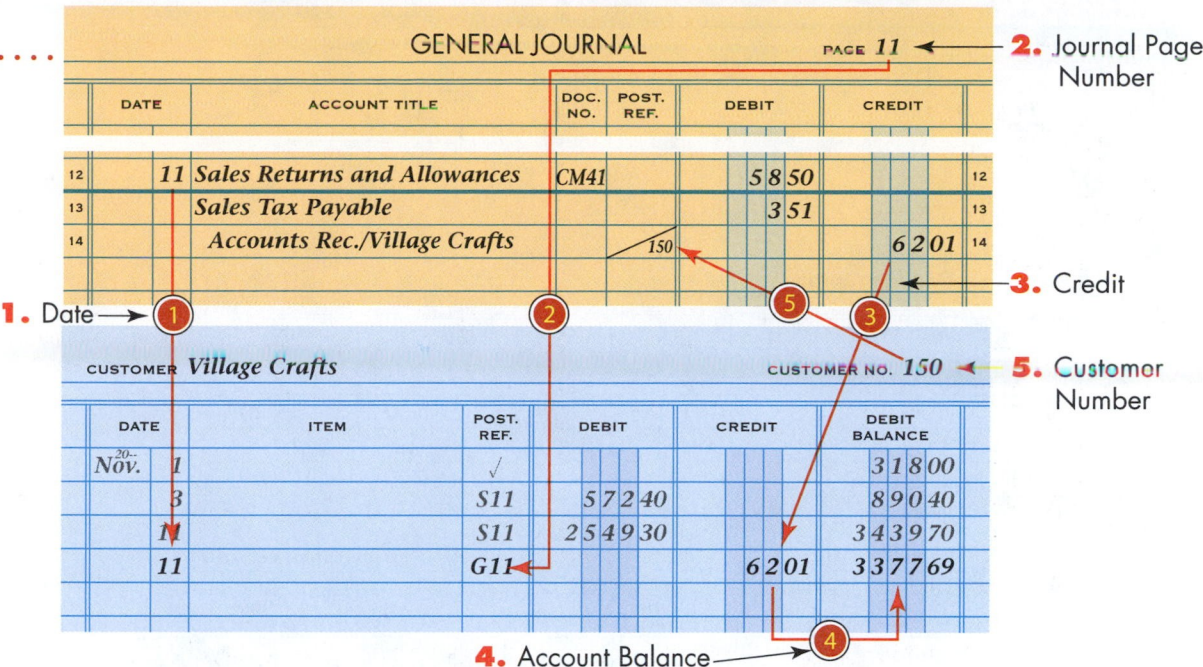

2. Journal Page Number

GENERAL JOURNAL PAGE *11*

DATE	ACCOUNT TITLE	DOC. NO.	POST. REF.	DEBIT	CREDIT
11	*Sales Returns and Allowances*	CM41		5 8 50	
	Sales Tax Payable			3 51	
	Accounts Rec./Village Crafts		150		6 2 01

1. Date

3. Credit

5. Customer Number

CUSTOMER *Village Crafts*   CUSTOMER NO. *150*

DATE	ITEM	POST. REF.	DEBIT	CREDIT	DEBIT BALANCE
Nov. 1		✓			3 1 8 00
3		S11	5 7 2 40		8 9 0 40
11		S11	2 5 4 9 30		3 4 3 9 70
11		G11		6 2 01	3 3 7 7 69

4. Account Balance

Entries in a general journal may affect account balances in a general ledger and an accounts receivable ledger. Posting from a general journal to a general ledger is described on pages 317–318.

STEPS POSTING A CREDIT ENTRY FOR SALES RETURNS AND ALLOWANCES FROM A GENERAL JOURNAL TO AN ACCOUNTS RECEIVABLE LEDGER

1. Write the date, *Nov. 11*, in the Date column of the customer account.

2. Write the general journal page number, *G11*, in the Post. Ref. column of the account. The abbreviation *G11* means page 11 of the general journal.

3. Write the amount, *$62.01*, in the Credit column of the customer account.

4. Subtract the amount in the Credit column from the previous balance in the Debit Balance column ($3,439.70 − $62.01 = $3,377.69). Write the new balance, *$3,377.69*, in the Debit Balance column.

5. Write the customer number, *150*, to the right of the diagonal line in the Post. Ref. column of the general journal.

CUSTOMER **Country Crafters**   CUSTOMER NO. 110

DATE	ITEM	POST. REF.	DEBIT	CREDIT	DEBIT BALANCE
Nov. 1	Balance	✓			2 1 6 2 40
6		CR11		2 1 6 2 40	—
11		S11	7 6 8 50		7 6 8 50
29		S11	4 5 3 68		1 2 2 2 18

CUSTOMER **Cumberland Center**   CUSTOMER NO. 120

DATE	ITEM	POST. REF.	DEBIT	CREDIT	DEBIT BALANCE
Nov. 1	Balance	✓			4 1 8 9 20
7		CR11		1 2 0 0 00	2 9 8 9 20
24		S11	1 5 8 00		3 1 4 7 20
25		CR11		2 9 8 9 20	1 5 8 00

CUSTOMER **Fairview Church**   CUSTOMER NO. 130

DATE	ITEM	POST. REF.	DEBIT	CREDIT	DEBIT BALANCE
Nov. 1	Balance	✓			3 8 1 60
5		S11	1 9 0 8 00		2 2 8 9 60
15		CR11		3 8 1 60	1 9 0 8 00

CUSTOMER **Playtime Childcare**   CUSTOMER NO. 140

DATE	ITEM	POST. REF.	DEBIT	CREDIT	DEBIT BALANCE
Nov. 1	Balance	✓			1 1 4 4 80
16		S11	1 7 5 2 18		2 8 9 6 98
18		CR11		1 1 4 4 80	1 7 5 2 18

CUSTOMER **Village Crafts**   CUSTOMER NO. 150

DATE	ITEM	POST. REF.	DEBIT	CREDIT	DEBIT BALANCE
Nov. 1	Balance	✓			3 1 8 00
3		S11	5 7 2 40		8 9 0 40
11		S11	2 5 4 9 30		3 4 3 9 70
11		G11		6 2 01	3 3 7 7 69
19		CR11		3 1 8 00	3 0 5 9 69

CUSTOMER **Washington Schools**   CUSTOMER NO. 160

DATE	ITEM	POST. REF.	DEBIT	CREDIT	DEBIT BALANCE
Nov. 1	Balance	✓			2 5 4 4 00
9		S11	5 7 2 00		3 1 1 6 00
12		CR11		2 5 4 4 00	5 7 2 00
24		S11	3 3 4 00		9 0 6 00

Hobby Shack's accounts receivable ledger has been posted for the month of November.

Hobby Shack, Inc.	
Schedule of Accounts Receivable	
November 30, 20--	
Country Crafters	1 2 2 2 18
Cumberland Center	1 5 8 00
Fairview Church	1 9 0 8 00
Playtime Childcare	1 7 5 2 18
Village Crafts	3 0 5 9 69
Washington Schools	9 0 6 00
Total Accounts Receivable	9 0 0 6 05

A listing of customer accounts, account balances, and total amount due from all customers is called a **schedule of accounts receivable**. A schedule of accounts receivable is prepared after all entries in a journal are posted. The balance of Accounts Receivable in the general ledger is $9,006.05. The total of the schedule of accounts receivable is $9,006.05. Because the two amounts are the same, the accounts receivable ledger is proved.

FINANCIAL LITERACY

Account Reconciliations

"I don't ever reconcile my accounts. I just trust the bank." Many people feel this way about reconciling checking accounts. Yet mistakes can be made—even by the bank.

Savings accounts as well as checking accounts should be reconciled regularly. Internet account access makes it possible to reconcile your accounts frequently. This can uncover errors more quickly—therefore preventing overdraft charges that otherwise may be applied.

Many banks include a reconciliation form on the back of the monthly statements sent to each account owner. The forms give directions for completing the reconciliation. The steps are: (1) Go through the statement, marking deposits and checks that have cleared the bank and recording any charges and/or automatic withdrawals/deposits that are listed on the statement. (2) List the account balance as printed on the bank statement. (3) Add any deposits made that have not cleared the bank. (4) Subtract any checks that have been written but have not cleared the bank. (5) Verify that the new subtotal equals the balance as recorded in your records.

If you find errors in your records, make the necessary corrections and clearly note the reason for the correction.

This will make it easier to understand the corrections if you need to refer to them in the future.

Activities

1. Survey 10 people to determine if they regularly perform an account reconciliation. If so, ask them how often they find an error that they made and how often they find an error made by their bank. Report your findings to your class in a presentation.

2. Interview a bank employee who helps clients with bank reconciliations. Ask him or her what are the most common errors made by the account owner and by the bank. Summarize your findings in a written report.

End of Lesson REVIEW

AUDIT YOUR UNDERSTANDING

1. To which accounts are the separate amounts in the sales journal posted individually?
2. In which column of the cash receipts journal are the amounts that are posted individually to the accounts receivable ledger?
3. What accounts are listed on a schedule of accounts receivable?

TERM REVIEW

schedule of accounts receivable

WORK TOGETHER 11-2

Posting to an accounts receivable ledger

Partial sales and cash receipts journals for Graphics, Inc. are given in the *Working Papers*. Also given in the *Working Papers* are one blank accounts receivable ledger account form and a blank form for preparation of a schedule of accounts receivable. You will also need the general journal from Work Together 11-1. Your instructor will guide you through the following examples.

1. Start a new page for an accounts receivable ledger account for Brandee Sparks. The account number is 140, and the balance for October 1 of the current year is $212.00.
2. Post the Accounts Receivable Debit entry on line 5 of the sales journal to the accounts receivable account for Brandee Sparks.
3. Post the Accounts Receivable Credit entry on line 9 of the cash receipts journal to the accounts receivable account for Alfredo Lopez.
4. Post the credit entry on line 3 of the general journal to the accounts receivable account for David Bishop.
5. Prepare a schedule of accounts receivable for Graphics, Inc., on October 31 of the current year. Accounts Receivable balance in the general ledger on October 31 is $2,530.22. Save your work to complete Work Together 11-4.

ON YOUR OWN 11-2

Posting to an accounts receivable ledger

Partial sales and cash receipts journals for Amatera, Inc. are given in the *Working Papers*. Also given in the *Working Papers* are one blank accounts receivable ledger account form and a blank form for preparation of a schedule of accounts receivable. You will also need the general journal from On Your Own 11-1. Work this problem independently.

1. Start a new page for an accounts receivable ledger account for Davis Sullivan. The account number is 140, and the balance for September 1 of the current year is $564.00.
2. Post the Accounts Receivable Debit entry on line 8 of the sales journal to the accounts receivable account for Davis Sullivan.
3. Post the Accounts Receivable Credit entry on line 21 of the cash receipts journal to the accounts receivable account for Harris Evans.
4. Post the credit entry on line 3 of the general journal to the accounts receivable account for Mary Burgin.
5. Prepare a schedule of accounts receivable for Amatera, Inc., on September 30 of the current year. Accounts Receivable balance in the general ledger on September 30 is $5,986.80. Save your work to complete On Your Own 11-4.

Posting from Journals to a General Ledger

STARTING A NEW PAGE FOR AN ACCOUNT IN A GENERAL LEDGER

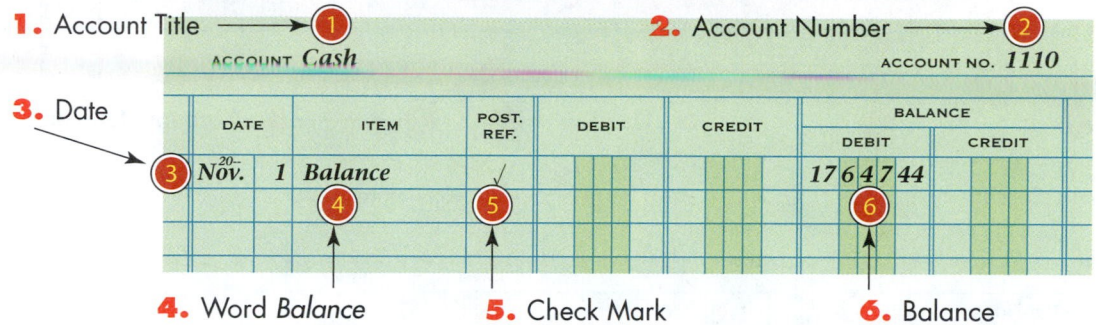

1. Account Title → ①
2. Account Number → ②

ACCOUNT *Cash*   ACCOUNT NO. *1110*

3. Date

	DATE	ITEM	POST. REF.	DEBIT	CREDIT	BALANCE	
						DEBIT	CREDIT
③	20-- Nov. 1	*Balance*	✓			17 6 4 7 44	
		④	⑤			⑥	

4. Word *Balance*
5. Check Mark
6. Balance

The number of entries that may be recorded on each general ledger account form depends on the number of lines provided. When all lines have been used, a new page is prepared. The account name, account number, and account balance are recorded on the new page.

On November 1, Hobby Shack prepared a new page for Cash in the general ledger because the existing page was full. On that day, the account balance was $17,647.44.

STEPS ● STARTING A NEW PAGE FOR A GENERAL LEDGER ACCOUNT

① Write the account title, *Cash*, at the top of the page.

② Write the account number, *1110*, at the top of the page.

③ Write the date, *20--, Nov. 1*, in the Date column.

④ Write the word *Balance* in the Item column.

⑤ Place a check mark in the Post. Ref. column to show that the amount has been carried forward from a previous page rather than posted from a journal.

⑥ Write the balance, *$17,647.44*, in the Balance Debit column.

2. Journal Page Number

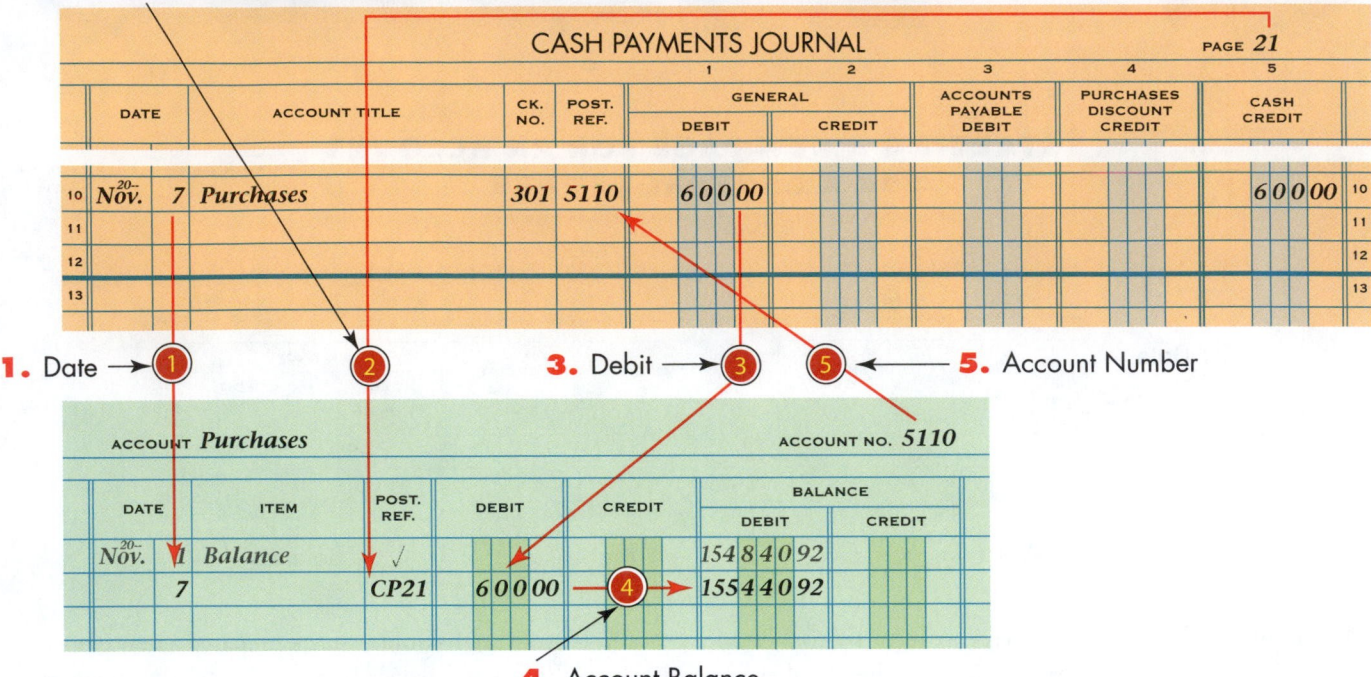

1. Date

3. Debit

5. Account Number

4. Account Balance

Amounts in cash payments journal entries are recorded in either general amount columns or special amount columns. Each amount in the General columns of a cash payments journal is posted individually to the general ledger account written in the Account Title column. However, only the monthly total of each special amount column is posted to a general ledger account.

STEPS — **POSTING FROM THE GENERAL AMOUNT COLUMNS OF A CASH PAYMENTS JOURNAL TO A GENERAL LEDGER**

① Write the date, *7*, in the Date column of the account.

② Write the journal page number, *CP21*, in the Post. Ref. column of the account. The abbreviation *CP21* means page 21 of the cash payments journal.

③ Write the debit amount, *$600.00*, in the account's Debit column. (A credit amount would be written in the Credit column.)

④ Add the amount in the Debit column to the previous balance in the Balance Debit column ($600.00 + $154,840.92 = $155,440.92). Write the new account balance, *$155,440.92*, in the Balance Debit column of the account.

⑤ Write the general ledger account number, *5110*, in the Post. Ref. column of the cash payments journal.

REMEMBER

Separate amounts listed in special amount columns of a special journal are not posted individually to the general ledger—only the totals are posted.

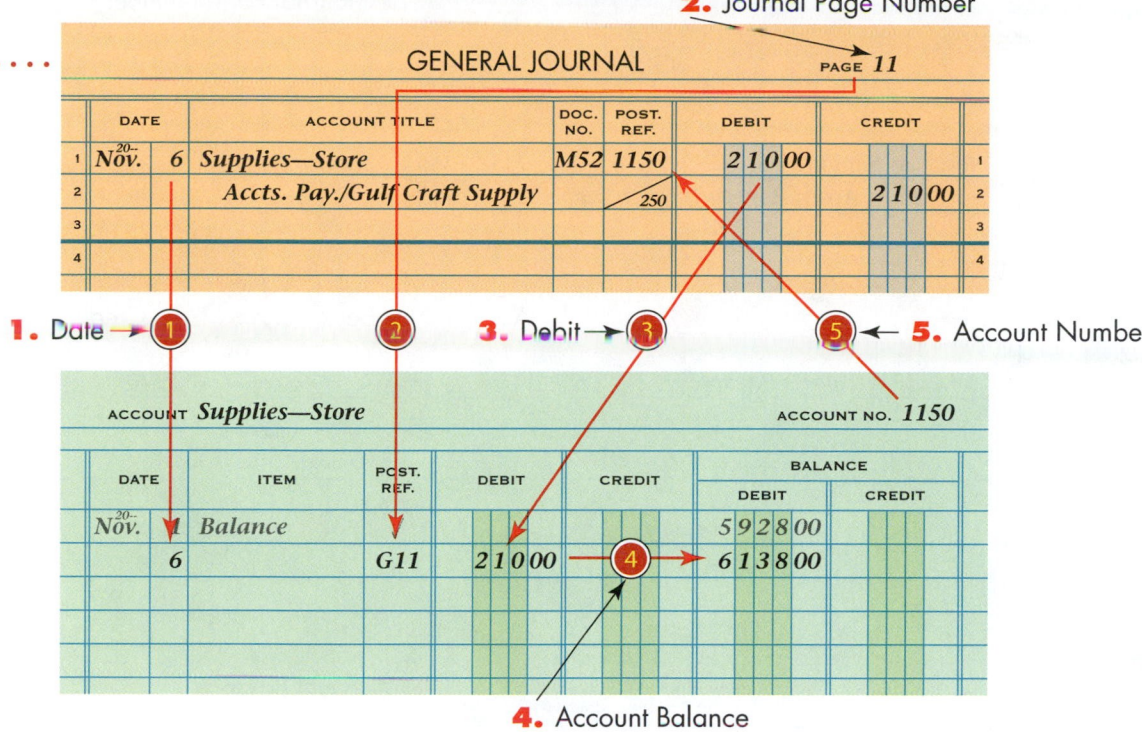

2. Journal Page Number

1. Date   **3.** Debit   **5.** Account Number

4. Account Balance

STEPS — POSTING A DEBIT AMOUNT FROM A GENERAL JOURNAL TO A GENERAL LEDGER

① Write the date, *6*, in the Date column of the account.

② Write the general journal page number, *G11*, in the Post. Ref. column of the account. The abbreviation *G11* means page 11 of the general journal.

③ Write the amount, *$210.00*, in the Debit column of the account.

④ Calculate and write the new account balance, *$6,138.00*, in the Balance Debit column of the account.

⑤ Write the general ledger account number, *1150*, in the Post. Ref. column of the general journal.

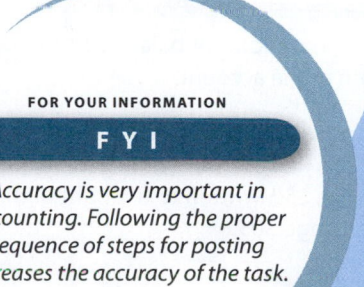

DIGITAL VISION/GETTY IMAGES

FOR YOUR INFORMATION

FYI

Accuracy is very important in accounting. Following the proper sequence of steps for posting increases the accuracy of the task.

2. Journal Page Number

GENERAL JOURNAL — PAGE 11

	DATE	ACCOUNT TITLE	DOC. NO.	POST. REF.	DEBIT	CREDIT	
1	Nov. 20-- 6	Supplies—Store	M52	1150	2 1 0 00		1
2		Accts. Pay./Gulf Craft Supply		2110 / 250		2 1 0 00	2
3							3
4							4

1. Date → ①   ②   **5.** Account Number   ⑤   ③   **3.** Credit

ACCOUNT Accounts Payable   ACCOUNT NO. 2110

DATE	ITEM	POST. REF.	DEBIT	CREDIT	BALANCE DEBIT	BALANCE CREDIT
Nov. 20-- 1	Balance					12 9 8 4 00
6		G11		2 1 0 00		13 1 9 4 00

4. Account Balance

Transactions recorded in a general journal can affect both subsidiary ledger and general ledger accounts. Buying supplies on account, for example, results in a credit to **Accounts Payable**. The purchase should also be recorded as a credit in the subsidiary ledger account of the vendor, Gulf Craft Supply.

The diagonal line in the Post. Ref. column allows the posting reference of both the general ledger and subsidiary ledger account to be recorded.

STEPS **POSTING A CREDIT AMOUNT FROM A GENERAL JOURNAL TO A GENERAL LEDGER**

① Write the date, *6*, in the Date column of the account.

② Write the general journal page number, *G11*, in the Post. Ref. column of the account.

③ Write the amount, *$210.00*, in the Credit column of the account.

④ Calculate and write the new account balance, *$13,194.00*, in the Balance Credit column of the account.

⑤ Write the general ledger account number, *2110*, to the left of the diagonal line in the Post. Ref. column of the general journal. The vendor account number, *250*, written to the right of the diagonal line, was described on page 303.

SMALL BUSINESS

SPOTLIGHT

The major ways of starting a new small business are:
1. *Buy an existing business.*
2. *Buy a franchise.*
3. *Start a business from scratch.*

End of Lesson REVIEW

1. Which amounts in a general journal are posted individually?
2. List the five steps for posting to a general ledger account.

WORK TOGETHER 11-3

Posting to a general ledger

Use the partial cash payments and general journals from Work Together 11-1. General ledger account forms are given in the *Working Papers*. Your instructor will guide you through the following examples.

1. Start a new page for a general ledger account for Supplies—Office. The account number is 1145, and the balance for October 1 of the current year is $3,824.00.
2. Post the October 19 General Debit entry of the cash payments journal to the appropriate general ledger account.
3. Post the October 12 general journal entry to the appropriate general ledger accounts.
4. Post the October 26 general journal entry to the appropriate general ledger accounts.
5. Post the October 28 general journal entry to the appropriate general ledger accounts. Save the general ledger accounts to complete Work Together 11-4.

ON YOUR OWN 11-3

Posting to a general ledger

Use the partial cash payments and general journals from On Your Own 11-1. General ledger account forms are given in the *Working Papers*. Work this problem independently.

1. Start a new page for a general ledger account for Supplies—Store. The account number is 1150, and the balance for September 1 of the current year is $3,158.00.
2. Post the September 21 General Debit entry of the cash payments journal to the appropriate general ledger account.
3. Post the September 15 general journal entry to the appropriate general ledger accounts.
4. Post the September 27 general journal entry to the appropriate general ledger accounts.
5. Post the September 29 general journal entry to the appropriate general ledger accounts. Save the general ledger accounts to complete On Your Own 11-4.

Posting Special Journal Totals to a General Ledger

POSTING TOTALS OF A SALES JOURNAL TO A GENERAL LEDGER

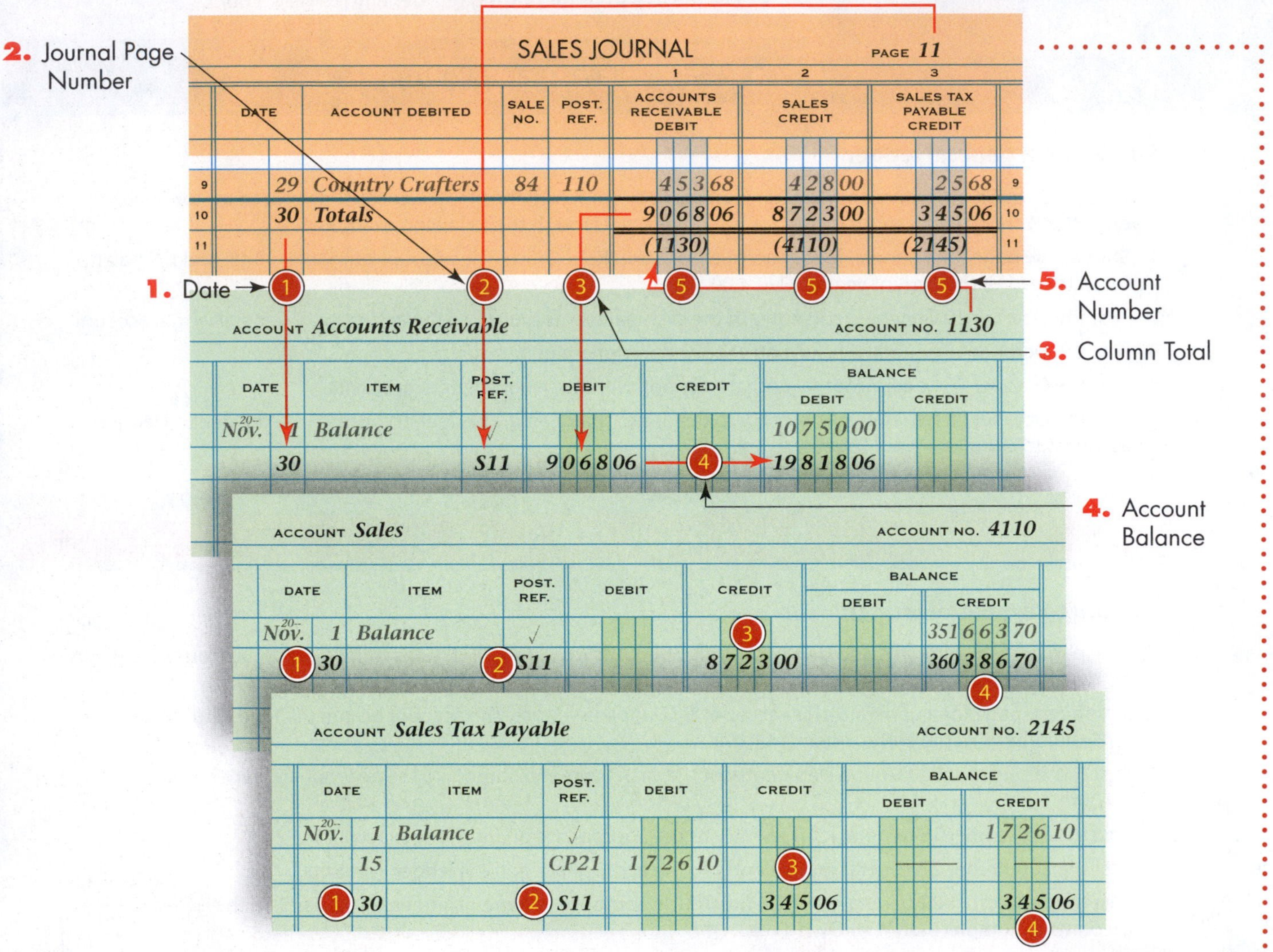

2. Journal Page Number

SALES JOURNAL PAGE 11

	DATE	ACCOUNT DEBITED	SALE NO.	POST. REF.	1 ACCOUNTS RECEIVABLE DEBIT	2 SALES CREDIT	3 SALES TAX PAYABLE CREDIT	
9	29	Country Crafters	84	110	4 5 3 68	4 2 8 00	2 5 68	9
10	30	Totals			9 0 6 8 06	8 7 2 3 00	3 4 5 06	10
11					(1130)	(4110)	(2145)	11

1. Date →
5. Account Number
3. Column Total

ACCOUNT **Accounts Receivable** ACCOUNT NO. **1130**

DATE	ITEM	POST. REF.	DEBIT	CREDIT	BALANCE DEBIT	BALANCE CREDIT
Nov. 20-- 1	Balance	√			10 7 5 0 00	
30		S11	9 0 6 8 06		19 8 1 8 06	

4. Account Balance

ACCOUNT **Sales** ACCOUNT NO. **4110**

DATE	ITEM	POST. REF.	DEBIT	CREDIT	BALANCE DEBIT	BALANCE CREDIT
Nov. 20-- 1	Balance	√				351 6 6 3 70
30		S11		8 7 2 3 00		360 3 8 6 70

ACCOUNT **Sales Tax Payable** ACCOUNT NO. **2145**

DATE	ITEM	POST. REF.	DEBIT	CREDIT	BALANCE DEBIT	BALANCE CREDIT
Nov. 20-- 1	Balance	√				1 7 2 6 10
15		CP21	1 7 2 6 10			
30		S11		3 4 5 06		3 4 5 06

STEPS **POSTING EACH SPECIAL AMOUNT COLUMN TOTAL OF A SALES JOURNAL**

1. Write the date, *30*, in the Date columns of the accounts.

2. Write the sales journal page number, *S11*, in the Post. Ref. columns of the accounts.

3. For each column and account, write the column total in the Debit or Credit column of the account.

4. For each account, calculate and write the new account balance in the Balance Debit or Credit column.

5. In the sales journal, write the general ledger account number in parentheses below each column total.

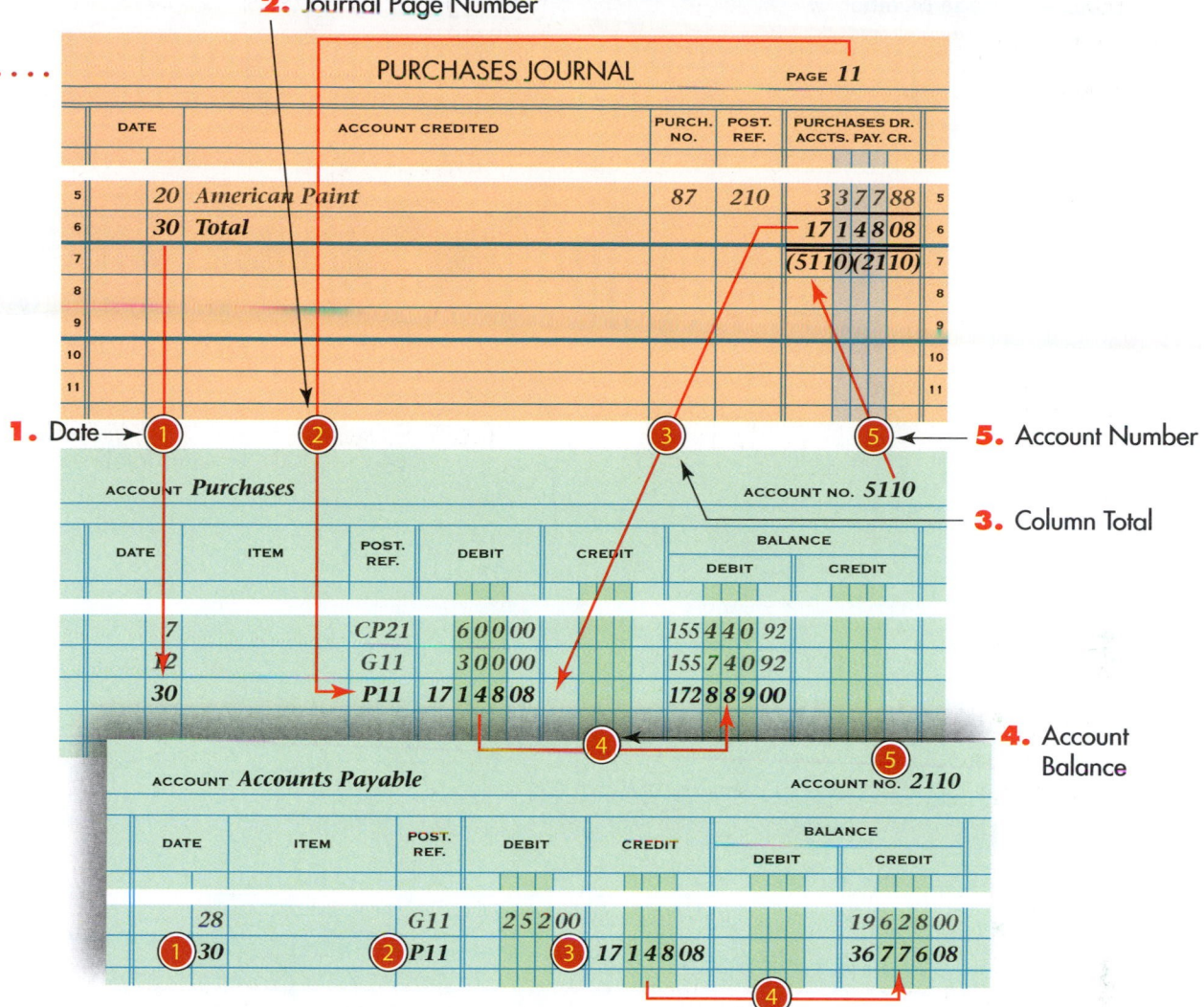

2. Journal Page Number

1. Date

5. Account Number

3. Column Total

4. Account Balance

A purchases journal is totaled and ruled at the end of each month as described in Chapter 9. The total amount of the purchases journal is then posted to two general ledger accounts, Purchases and Accounts Payable.

STEPS **POSTING THE TOTAL OF A PURCHASES JOURNAL TO THE TWO GENERAL LEDGER ACCOUNTS**

1. Write the date, *30*, in the Date columns of the accounts.

2. Write the purchases journal page number, *P11*, in the Post. Ref. columns of the accounts. The abbreviation *P11* means page 11 of the purchases journal.

3. For each account, write the purchases journal column total, *$17,148.08*, in the Debit or Credit column.

4. For each account, calculate and write the new account balance in the Balance Debit or Credit column.

5. Return to the purchases journal and write the purchases general ledger account number, *(5110)*, and the accounts payable general ledger account number, *(2110)*, in parentheses below the column total.

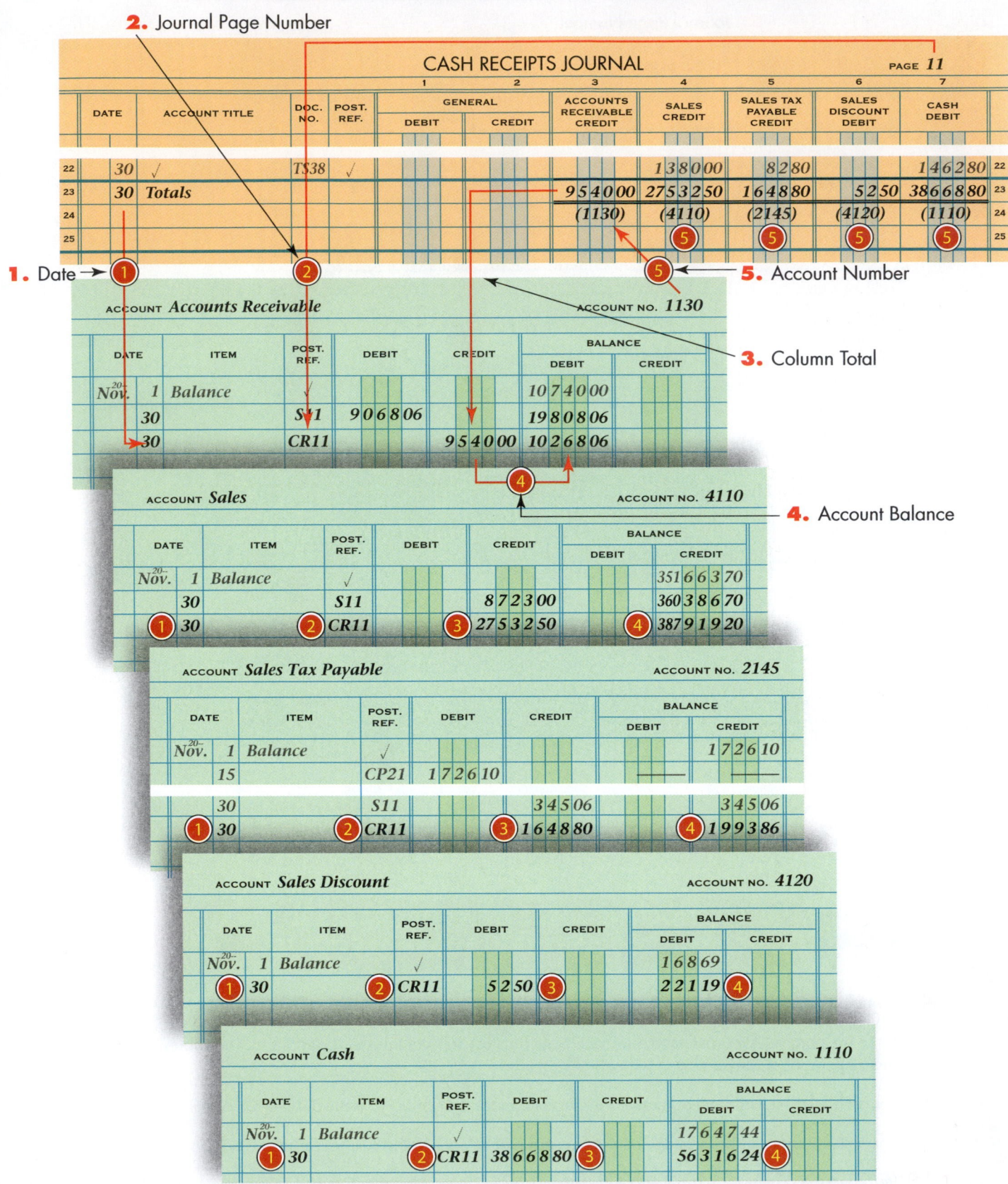

2. Journal Page Number

1. Date

5. Account Number

3. Column Total

4. Account Balance

At the end of each month, equality of debits and credits is proved for a cash receipts journal. Cash is then proved as described in Chapter 10. After cash is proved, the cash receipts journal is ruled as described in Chapter 10. The total of each special amount column is then posted to the corresponding general ledger account.

STEPS POSTING EACH SPECIAL AMOUNT COLUMN TOTAL OF A CASH RECEIPTS JOURNAL

1. Write the date, *30*, in the Date columns of the accounts.

2. Write the cash receipts journal page number, *CR11*, in the Post. Ref. columns of the accounts. The abbreviation *CR11* means page 11 of the cash receipts journal.

3. For each special amount column and account, write the special amount column total in the Debit or Credit column of the account.

4. For each account, calculate and write the new account balance in the Balance Debit or Credit column.

5. Return to the cash receipts journal and write the general ledger account number in parentheses below each special amount column total.

CULTURAL DIVERSITY

Timeless Tools

Throughout history, people of different cultures and civilizations have devised tools for counting, calculating, and recordkeeping.

The Jibaro Indians living in the Amazon rain forest in South America use the most basic counting tools of all—their fingers. Jibaros use phrases to express the numbers five and ten that translate to "I have finished one hand" and "I have finished both hands."

A more complex device of ancient origin is the abacus. The abacus is a calculating device that developed in several different cultures. The Babylonians in Asia Minor had an early form of abacus, as did the Egyptians in northern Africa. The first abacus was known in China as early as the 6th century B.C. This abacus was a flat piece of wood divided into squares. Its use spread to the rest of the Asian world.

The abacus may be used to add, subtract, multiply, and divide. Twelfth-century Chinese mathematicians used the abacus to solve algebraic equations. Today some highly skilled people, particularly of Asian descent, still use the abacus for calculations.

Recordkeepers in the Incan civilization (in present-day Peru) memorized business transactions and recited them when necessary. Incan record-keepers used small ropes of different colors and sizes and knotted and joined them in different ways to help remember financial data. These ropes, called *quipu*, were one of the earliest means of recording transactions.

Accounting tools have changed over the course of history. They will continue to evolve with future advances in technology.

Critical Thinking

1. What tools do most accounting workers today use for calculations?

2. Discuss whether the use of modern calculating tools results in the creation of more complex accounting transactions.

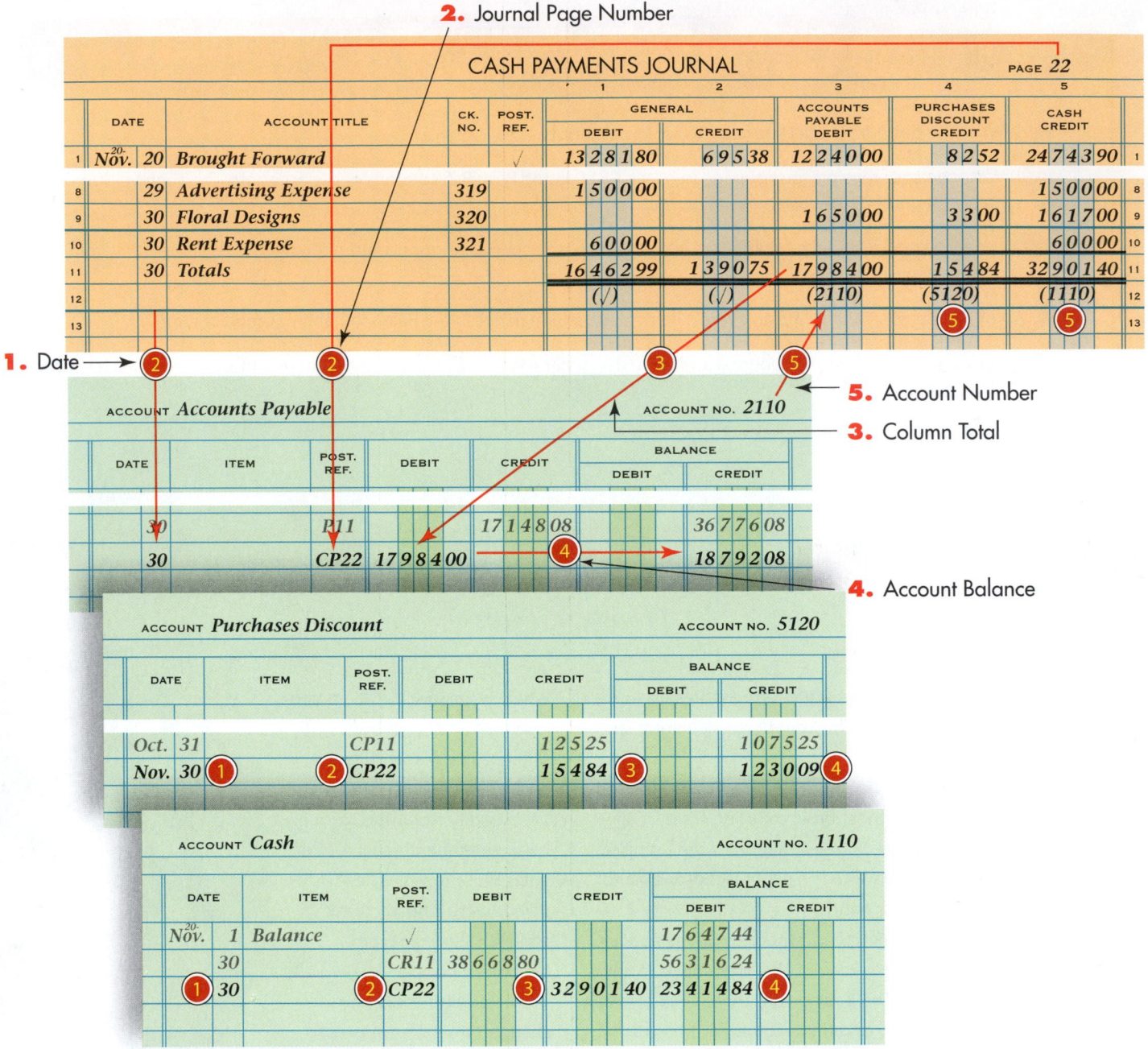

The cash payments journal is totaled and ruled at the end of each month as described in Chapter 9. The total of each special column is then posted to a general ledger account. The total of each special amount column is posted to the account named in the journal's column headings.

The totals of the General amount columns are not posted. Each amount in these columns was posted individually to a general ledger account. To indicate that these totals are not to be posted, a check mark is placed in parentheses below each column total.

STEPS — POSTING THE TOTALS OF EACH SPECIAL AMOUNT COLUMN TO THE GENERAL LEDGER ACCOUNT

1. Write the date, *30*, in the Date columns of the accounts.

2. Write the cash payments journal page number, *CP22*, in the Post. Ref. columns of the accounts.

3. For each special amount column and account, write the special amount column total in the Debit or Credit column of the account.

4. For each account, calculate and write the new account balance in the Balance Debit or Credit column.

5. Return to the cash payments journal and write the general ledger account number in parentheses below each special amount column total.

ORDER OF POSTING FROM SPECIAL JOURNALS

Items affecting customer or vendor accounts are posted periodically during the month. Hobby Shack posts frequently so that the balances of the subsidiary ledger accounts will be up to date. Since general ledger account balances are needed only when financial statements are prepared, the general ledger accounts are posted less often during the month. All items, including the totals of special columns, must be posted before a trial balance is prepared. Hobby Shack posts special amount column totals monthly.

The journals should be posted in the following order:

1. Sales journal.
2. Purchases journal.
3. General journal.
4. Cash receipts journal.
5. Cash payments journal.

DIGITAL VISION/GETTY IMAGES

FOR YOUR INFORMATION

F Y I

It is important to post the journals in the proper sequence. However, sometimes the entries will be out of chronological order. For example, if subsidiary accounts are posted for the week ended June 24, it is possible for a June 23 entry from the sales journal to appear before a June 20 entry from the cash receipts journal.

PAYING EMPLOYEES

Hobby Shack employs several people to work in the business. These employees record the time they work for Hobby Shack each day. Periodically, Hobby Shack pays its employees for the number of hours each employee has worked. The money paid for employee services is called a **salary**. The period covered by a salary payment is called a **pay period**. A business may decide to pay employee salaries every week, every two weeks, twice a month, or once a month. Hobby Shack uses a semimonthly pay period. Employees are paid twice a month, on the 15th and last day of each month.

The total amount earned by all employees for a pay period is called a **payroll**. The payroll is reduced by state and federal taxes and other deductions, such as health insurance, to determine the amount paid to all employees. Special payroll records support the recording of payroll transactions in a journal. The business also uses these records to inform employees of their annual earnings and to prepare payroll reports for the government.

FOR YOUR INFORMATION
FYI

Salaries are usually stated as a fixed amount on a weekly, biweekly, semimonthly, or monthly basis. Salaried workers do not normally receive overtime pay. Money paid to employees on an hourly, daily, or even weekly basis is often referred to as wages. In practice, the terms wages and salary are often used interchangeably.

CHARACTER COUNTS

Is It Discrimination or Poor Judgment?

Your group at CyberMarket has an opening for a research analyst. You are on the search committee to pick candidates to be interviewed. Your company has a code of conduct that states the company will not discriminate on the basis of "race, color, religion, national origin, sex, sexual orientation or group affiliation, age, disability, or veteran status." In a recent meeting, committee members gave the following reasons for wanting to eliminate two candidates.

Candidate A: "She graduated from college before I was born. She can't possibly know anything about our business."

Candidate B: "The ad said two to five years of experience, but we really need someone with more than two years of experience."

Instructions

Use the ethical model to help evaluate hiring decisions based on each of the statements above. Use online sources, as appropriate, to determine whether any actions are illegal.

Hobby Shack

EMPLOYEE NO. 3

NAME Rick E. Selby

PAY PERIOD ENDED December 15, 20--

MORNING		AFTERNOON		OVERTIME		HOURS	
IN	OUT	IN	OUT	IN	OUT	REG	OT
7⁵⁸	12⁰²	12⁵⁹	5⁰⁶				

A payroll system must include an accurate record of the time each employee has worked. Several methods are used for keeping time records. One of the more frequently used methods is a time card. Time cards are used as the basic source of information to prepare a payroll.

Some time cards require employees to record only the total hours worked each day. Employees who record the total hours worked each day usually complete time cards by hand.

A business may use a time card that requires employees to record their arrival and departure times. Hobby Shack uses a time clock to record the daily arrival and departure times of its employees.

The time card shown here is for Rick E. Selby. Mr. Selby's employee number is at the top of the card. Below the employee number are the employee name and the ending date of the pay period.

Hobby Shack's time cards have three sections (Morning, Afternoon, and Overtime) with In and Out columns under each section. When Mr. Selby reported for work on December 1, he inserted the card in the time clock. The clock recorded his time of arrival, 7:58, on the first line of the time card. The other entries on this line indicate that he left for lunch at 12:02. He returned at 12:59 and left for the day at 5:06.

Hobby Shack calculates overtime pay for each employee who works more than 8 hours in one day. No employee works more than 5 days in any one week.

DIGITAL VISION/GETTY IMAGES

FOR YOUR INFORMATION

FYI

Larger companies can afford more expensive systems to record employee arrival and departure times. A popular system requires employees to scan a personal identification card through a card scanner. At the end of the pay period, the system prints a report similar to the time card.

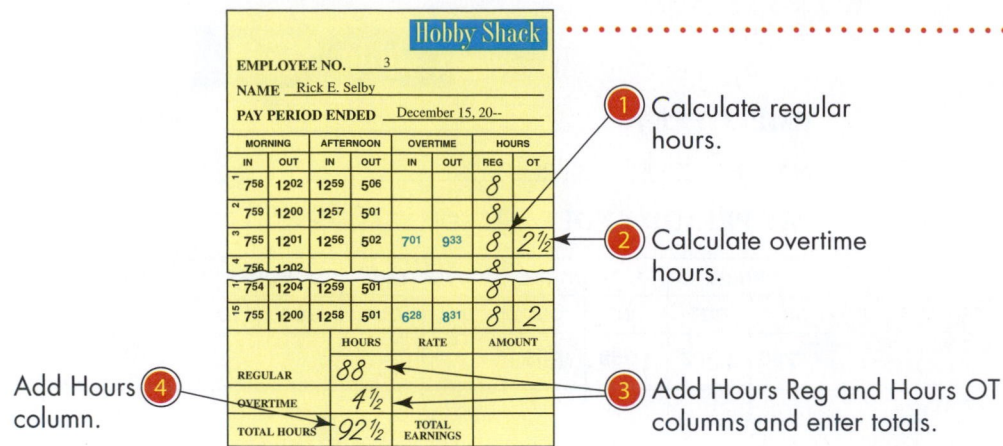

1 Calculate regular hours.

2 Calculate overtime hours.

Add Hours 4 column.

3 Add Hours Reg and Hours OT columns and enter totals.

The first task in preparing a payroll is to calculate the number of hours worked by each employee. When calculating hours worked, Hobby Shack rounds arrival and departure times to the nearest quarter hour.

STEPS CALCULATING EMPLOYEE HOURS WORKED

1 Calculate the number of regular hours for each day and enter the amounts in the Hours Reg column. Mr. Selby works 8 hours during a normal day. The hours worked on December 3, the third line of the time card, are calculated using the arrival and departure times imprinted on the time card.

The hours worked in the morning and afternoon are calculated separately. The morning departure time of 12:01 is rounded to the nearest quarter hour, 12:00. The rounded arrival time, 8:00, subtracted from the departure time, 12:00,

	Departure Time	−	Arrival Time	=	Hours Worked
Morning:					
Time card	12:01		7:55		
Nearest quarter hour	12:00	−	8:00	=	4:00
Afternoon:					
Time card	5:02		12:56		
Nearest quarter hour	5:00	−	1:00	=	4:00
Total regular hours worked on December 3					8:00

equals the morning hours worked. Hours worked of 4:00 means that Mr. Selby worked 4 hours and no (00) minutes. The total regular hours worked, 8, is recorded in the Hours Reg column.

2 Calculate the number of overtime hours for each day and enter the amounts in the Hours OT column. Overtime hours for December 3 are calculated using the same procedure as for regular hours.

	Departure Time	−	Arrival Time	=	Hours Worked
Time card	9:33		7:01		
Nearest quarter hour	9:30	−	7:00	=	2:30

The hours worked of 2:30 means that Mr. Selby worked 2 hours and 30 minutes ($1/2$ hour) of overtime.

3 Add the hours worked in the Hours Reg and Hours OT columns and enter the totals in the spaces provided at the bottom of the time card. Mr. Selby worked 88 regular hours (8 hours × 11 days) and $4^{1}/_{2}$ overtime hours during the semimonthly pay period.

4 Add the Hours column to calculate the total hours. Enter the total in the Hours column at the bottom of the time card. Mr. Selby worked 88 regular hours and $4^{1}/_{2}$ overtime hours for a total of $92^{1}/_{2}$ hours.

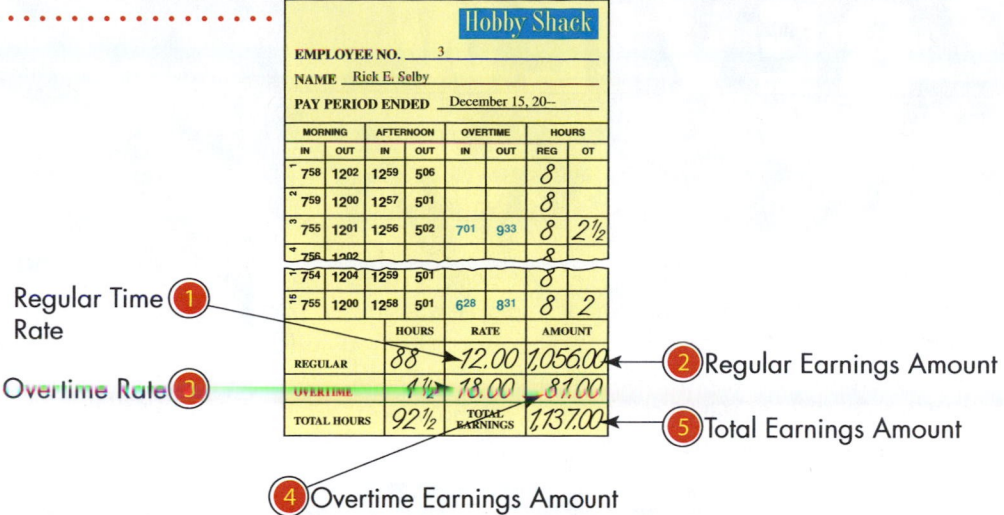

Regular Time ① Rate

Overtime Rate ③

② Regular Earnings Amount

⑤ Total Earnings Amount

④ Overtime Earnings Amount

Once the total regular and overtime hours are determined, employee earnings can be calculated. The total pay due for a pay period before deductions is called **total earnings**. Total earnings are sometimes referred to as gross pay or gross earnings.

Hobby Shack owes Mr. Selby $1,137.00 for his work during the pay period ending December 15. However, taxes and other deductions must be subtracted from total earnings to determine the actual amount Hobby Shack will pay Mr. Selby.

S T E P S **CALCULATING AN EMPLOYEE'S TOTAL EARNINGS**

① Enter the rate for regular time in the Rate column. Mr. Selby's regular hourly rate is *$12.00*.

② Calculate the regular earnings by multiplying regular hours times the regular rate. Enter the amount of regular earnings, *$1,056.00*, in the Regular Amount space.

③ Enter the rate for overtime, *$18.00*, in the Rate column. Mr. Selby is paid $1\frac{1}{2}$ times his regular rate for overtime work.

④ Calculate the overtime earnings by multiplying overtime hours times the overtime rate. Enter the amount of overtime earnings, *$81.00*, in the Overtime Amount space.

⑤ Add the Amount column to calculate the total earnings. Enter the amount of total earnings, *$1,137.00*, in the Total Earnings space.

Regular Hours	×	Regular Rate	=	Regular Earnings
88	×	$12.00	=	$1,056.00

Regular Rate	×	$1\frac{1}{2}$	=	Overtime Rate
$12.00	×	$1\frac{1}{2}$	=	$18.00

Overtime Hours	×	Overtime Rate	=	Overtime Earnings
$4\frac{1}{2}$	×	$18.00	=	$81.00

End of Lesson REVIEW

AUDIT YOUR UNDERSTANDING

1. What is a payroll?
2. How many hours were worked by a Hobby Shack employee who arrived at 8:29 and departed at 12:02?
3. How does Hobby Shack calculate overtime earnings?
4. What are the total earnings of a Hobby Shack employee who worked 44 hours in a week and earns $11.00 per hour?

TERMS REVIEW

salary

pay period

payroll

total earnings

WORK TOGETHER 12-1

Calculating total earnings

Information taken from employee time cards is provided in the *Working Papers*. Your instructor will guide you through the following example.

1. For each employee, calculate the amount of regular, overtime, and total earnings. Overtime hours are paid at $1\frac{1}{2}$ times the regular rate.

ON YOUR OWN 12-1

Calculating total earnings

Information taken from employee time cards is provided in the *Working Papers*. Work this problem independently.

1. For each employee, calculate the amount of regular, overtime, and total earnings. Overtime hours are paid at $1\frac{1}{2}$ times the regular rate.

Taxes based on the payroll of a business are called ==payroll taxes==. A business is required by law to withhold certain payroll taxes from employee salaries. All payroll taxes are based on employee total earnings. Therefore, accurate and detailed payroll records must be maintained. Errors in payroll records could cause incorrect payroll tax payments. Federal and state governments may charge a business a penalty for failure to pay correct payroll taxes when they are due. Payroll taxes withheld represent a liability for the employer until payment is made to the government.

Employee Income Tax

A business must withhold federal income taxes from employee total earnings. Federal income taxes withheld must be forwarded periodically to the federal government. Federal income tax is withheld from employee earnings in all 50 states. Employers in many states also are required to withhold state, city, or county income taxes from employee earnings.

BUSINESS STRUCTURES

Selecting a Corporate Form

There are several forms of corporations, each designed to meet the specific needs of its stockholders. The appropriate form is generally dependent on the size of the business and may be changed as the business grows.

1. *General Corporations.* Corporations that have more than 30 stockholders or offer to sell stock to the public must organize as a general or "C" corporation. These corporations must have a board of directors, conduct annual stockholders meetings, and publish financial reports with certain government agencies, such as the Securities and Exchange Commission. Large, well-known companies, such as Wal-Mart and General Motors, are C Corporations.

2. *Close Corporations.* In some states, corporations having fewer than 30 stockholders may elect to be a close corporation. This form of corporation reduces the governance requirements of a C Corporation. For example, a board of directors or annual stockholder meetings may not be required. Less than half of the states recognize this form of corporation.

3. *Subchapter S Corporation.* Named for the related section of the Internal Revenue Code, the Subchapter S or *"S"* Corporation is a special tax status available to

C corporations. Unlike with C Corporations, distributions of earnings are not taxed to the stockholders, thus eliminating the "double taxation" of corporate earnings and distributions. Having 75 or fewer stockholders is the primary requirement for electing S corporation status.

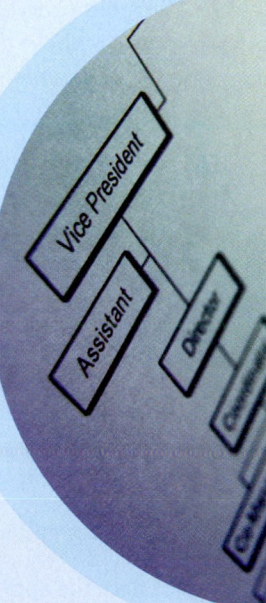

Critical Thinking

1. You plan to expand your small proprietorship with an investment from several family members who will be stockholders. Which form of corporation would you probably use?

2. Considering your answer to question 1, what is the advantage to you? To your investors?

3. Marital Status

2. Social Security Number

1. Name and Address

4. Withholding Allowances

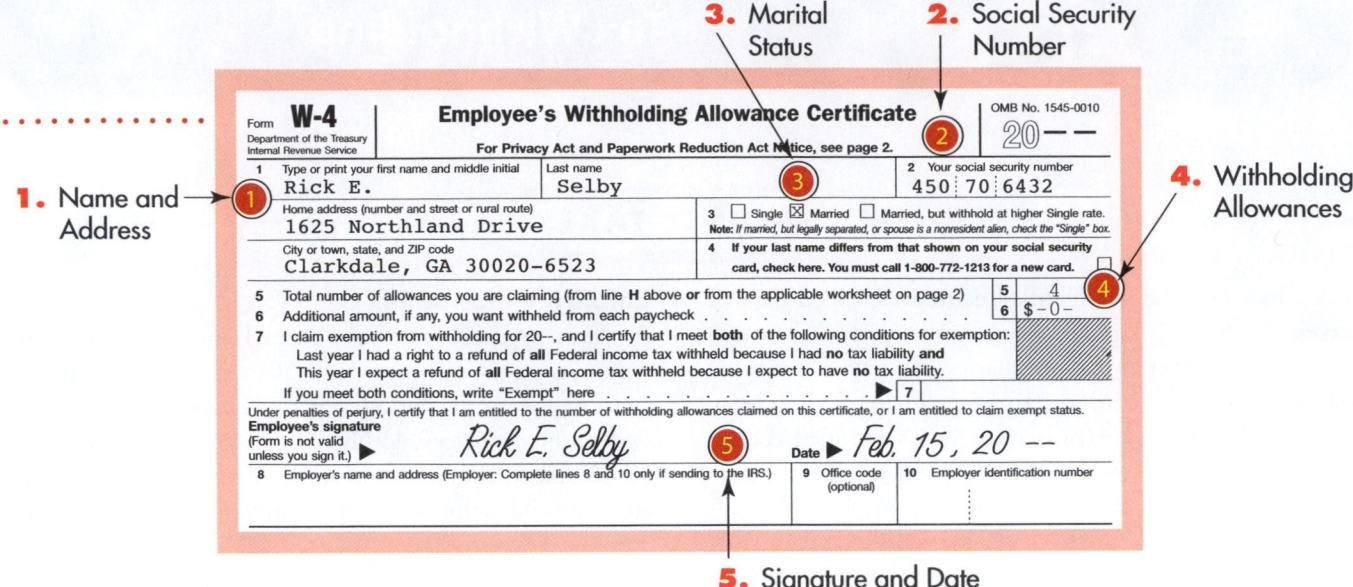

5. Signature and Date

The information used to determine the amount of income tax withheld is identified on Form W-4, Employee's Withholding Allowance Certificate. A deduction from total earnings for each person legally supported by a taxpayer, including the employee, is called a ==withholding allowance==. Employers are required to have a current Form W-4 on file for all employees. The amount of income tax withheld is based on employee marital status and number of withholding allowances. A married employee will have less income tax withheld than a single employee with the same total earnings. The larger the number of withholding allowances claimed, the smaller the amount of income tax withheld.

Most employees are required to have federal income taxes withheld from their salaries. An exemption from withholding is available for certain low-income and part-time employees. The employee must meet the requirements listed in item 7 of the Form W-4. However, individuals cannot claim exemption from withholding if (1) their income exceeds $750 and includes more than $250 of unearned income such as interest and dividends and (2) another person can claim them as a dependent on their tax return.

PREPARING AN EMPLOYEE'S WITHHOLDING ALLOWANCE CERTIFICATE

FOR YOUR INFORMATION

F Y I

Each employee must have a social security number. Current law ensures that most infants who are at least one year old by the end of a tax year will have a social security number. Therefore, most employees will have received their social security number as a child. Employees without social security numbers can apply for a number at the nearest Social Security office.

① Write the employee's name and address.

② Write the employee's social security number.

③ Check the appropriate marital status block. Mr. Selby checked the married box for item 3.

④ Write the total number of withholding allowances claimed. Mr. Selby claimed four withholding allowances, one each for himself, his wife, and his two children.

⑤ The employee signs and dates the form.

FOR YOUR INFORMATION

F Y I

Employees are responsible for contacting their employer when the number of their dependents changes. A new W-4 form should be completed and a copy of the form sent to the Internal Revenue Service.

SINGLE Persons—SEMIMONTHLY Payroll Period

If the wages are— At least	But less than	0	1	2	3	4	5	6	7	8	9	10
		The amount of income tax to be withheld is—										
$0	$115	$0	$0	$0	$0	$0	$0	$0	$0	$0	$0	$0
115	120	1	0	0	0	0	0	0	0	0	0	0
120	125	1	0	0	0	0	0	0	0	0	0	0
125	130	2	0	0	0	0	0	0	0	0	0	0
130	135	2	0	0	0	0	0	0	0	0	0	0
235	240	13	0	0	0	0	0	0	0	0	0	0
240	245	13	0	0	0	0	0	0	0	0	0	0
245	250	14	1	0	0	0	0	0	0	0	0	0
250	260	14	2	0	0	0	0	0	0	0	0	0
260	270	15	3	0	0	0	0	0	0	0	0	0
540	560	51	32	18	5	0	0	0	0	0	0	0
560	580	54	35	20	7	0	0	0	0	0	0	0
580	600	57	38	22	9	0	0	0	0	0	0	0
600	620	60	41	24	11	0	0	0	0	0	0	0
620	640	63	44	26	13	0	0	0	0	0	0	0
640	660	66	47	28	15	2	0	0	0	0	0	0
660	680	69	50	31	17	4	0	0	0	0	0	0
680	700	72	53	34	19	6	0	0	0	0	0	0
700	720	75	56	37	21	8	0	0	0	0	0	0
720	740	78	59	40	23	10	0	0	0	0	0	0
740	760	81	62	43	25	12	0	0	0	0	0	0
760	780	84	65	46	27	14	1	0	0	0	0	0
780	800	87	68	49	29	16	3	0	0	0	0	0
800	820	90	71	52	32	18	5	0	0	0	0	0
820	840	93	74	55	35	20	7	0	0	0	0	0
840	860	96	77	58	38	22	9	0	0	0	0	0
860	880	99	80	61	41	24	11	0	0	0	0	0
880	900	102	83	64	44	26	13	0	0	0	0	0
900	920	105	86	67	47	28	15	2	0	0	0	0
920	940	108	89	70	50	31	17	4	0	0	0	0
940	960	111	92	73	53	34	19	6	0	0	0	0
960	980	114	95	76	56	37	21	8	0	0	0	0
980	1,000	117	98	79	59	40	23	10	0	0	0	0
1,000	1,020	120	101	82	62	43	25	12	0	0	0	0
1,020	1,040	123	104	85	65	46	27	14	2	0	0	0
1,040	1,060	126	107	88	68	49	29	16	4	0	0	0
1,060	1,080	129	110	91	71	52	32	18	6	0	0	0
1,080	1,100	132	113	94	74	55	35	20	8	0	0	0
1,100	1,120	135	116	97	77	58	38	22	10	0	0	0
1,120	1,140	138	119	100	80	61	41	24	12	0	0	0
1,140	1,160	141	122	103	83	64	44	26	14	1	0	0
1,160	1,180	144	125	106	86	67	47	28	16	3	0	0
1,180	1,200	147	128	109	89	70	50	31	18	5	0	0
1,200	1,220	150	131	112	92	73	53	34	20	7	0	0
1,220	1,240	153	134	115	95	76	56	37	22	9	0	0
1,240	1,260	156	137	118	98	79	59	40	24	11	0	0
1,260	1,280	159	140	121	101	82	62	43	26	13	0	0
1,280	1,300	163	143	124	104	85	65	46	28	15	2	0
1,300	1,320	168	146	127	107	88	68	49	30	17	4	0
1,320	1,340	173	149	130	110	91	71	52	33	19	6	0

The amount of federal income tax withheld from each employee's total earnings is determined from withholding tables prepared by the Internal Revenue Service. These withholding tables are revised each year and are available from the Internal Revenue Service in Publication 15 (Circular E), Employer's Tax Guide. The withholding tables shown in this chapter are those available when this textbook was prepared.

Tables are prepared for various payroll periods—monthly, semimonthly, biweekly, weekly, and daily. Single persons are taxed at different levels of income than married persons. Therefore, one table is available for single persons and another table is available for married persons for each pay period.

Hobby Shack's pay period is semimonthly, so Hobby Shack uses the semimonthly withholding tables.

MARRIED Persons—SEMIMONTHLY Payroll Period

(1) Select the appropriate table.

If the wages are—		And the number of withholding allowances claimed is—										
At least	But less than	0	1	2	3	4	5	6	7	8	9	10
		The amount of income tax to be withheld is—										
720	740	40	27	14	1	0	0	0	0	0	0	0
740	760	42	29	16	3	0	0	0	0	0	0	0
760	780	44	31	18	5	0	0	0	0	0	0	0
780	800	46	33	20	7	0	0	0	0	0	0	0
800	820	48	35	22	9	0	0	0	0	0	0	0
820	840	50	37	24	11	0	0	0	0	0	0	0
840	860	52	39	26	13	0	0	0	0	0	0	0
860	880	54	41	28	15	2	0	0	0	0	0	0
880	900	56	43	30	17	4	0	0	0	0	0	0
900	920	58	45	32	19	6	0	0	0	0	0	0
920	940	60	47	34	21	8	0	0	0	0	0	0
940	960	63	49	36	23	10	0	0	0	0	0	0
960	980	66	51	38	25	12	0	0	0	0	0	0
980	1,000	69	53	40	27	14	1	0	0	0	0	0
1,000	1,020	72	55	42	29	16	3	0	0	0	0	0
1,020	1,040	75	57	44	31	18	5	0	0	0	0	0
1,040	1,060	78	59	46	33	20	7	0	0	0	0	0
1,060	1,080	81	61	48	35	22	9	0	0	0	0	0
1,080	1,100	84	64	50	37	24	11	0	0	0	0	0
1,100	1,120	87	67	52	39	26	13	0	0	0	0	0
1,120	1,140	90	70	54	41	28	15	2	0	0	0	0
1,140	1,160	93	73	56	43	30	17	4	0	0	0	0
1,160	1,180	96	76	58	45	32	19	6	0	0	0	0
1,180	1,200	99	79	60	47	34	21	8	0	0	0	0
1,200	1,220	102	82	63	49	36	23	10	0	0	0	0
1,220	1,240	105	85	66	51	38	25	12	0	0	0	0
1,240	1,260	108	88	69	53	40	27	14	1	0	0	0
1,260	1,280	111	91	72	55	42	29	16	3	0	0	0
1,280	1,300	114	94	75	57	44	31	18	5	0	0	0
1,300	1,320	117	97	78	59	46	33	20	7	0	0	0
1,320	1,340	120	100	81	62	48	35	22	9	0	0	0
1,340	1,360	123	103	84	65	50	37	24	11	0	0	0
1,360	1,380	126	106	87	68	52	39	26	13	0	0	0
1,380	1,400	129	109	90	71	54	41	28	15	2	0	0
1,400	1,420	132	112	93	74	56	43	30	17	4	0	0
1,420	1,440	135	115	96	77	58	45	32	19	6	0	0
1,440	1,460	138	118	99	80	60	47	34	21	8	0	0
1,460	1,480	141	121	102	83	63	49	36	23	10	0	0
1,480	1,500	144	124	105	86	66	51	38	25	12	0	0
1,500	1,520	147	127	108	89	69	53	40	27	14	1	0
1,820	1,840	195	175	156	137	117	98	78	59	46	33	21
1,840	1,860	198	178	159	140	120	101	81	62	48	35	23
1,860	1,880	201	181	162	143	123	104	84	65	50	37	25
1,880	1,900	204	184	165	146	126	107	87	68	52	39	27
1,900	1,920	207	187	168	149	129	110	90	71	54	41	29

(2) Locate employee's total earnings.

(3) Intersection of wages and number of withholding allowances column.

STEPS DETERMINING AN EMPLOYEE'S INCOME TAX WITHHOLDING

(1) Select the appropriate table. Married Persons—Semimonthly Payroll Period is selected to determine income tax withholding for employee Rick E. Selby.

(2) Locate the employee's total earnings between the appropriate lines of the At Least and But Less Than columns. Mr. Selby's total earnings for the pay period ended December 15, 20--, are $1,137.00. Locate the line At Least $1,120.00 But Less Than $1,140.00.

(3) Follow the selected wages line across to the column headed by the employee's number of withholding allowances. The amount listed at the intersection of the wages line and number of withholding allowances column is the employee's amount of income tax withholding. Mr. Selby's federal income tax withholding, with total earnings of $1,137.00 and withholding allowances of four, is $28.00 for the semimonthly pay period ended December 15, 20--.

The Federal Insurance Contributions Act (FICA) provides for a federal system of old-age, survivors, disability, and hospital insurance. A federal tax paid for old-age, survivors, and disability insurance is called **social security tax**. A federal tax paid for hospital insurance is called **Medicare tax**. Each of these taxes is accounted for and reported separately.

Social security and Medicare taxes are paid by both employees and employer. Employers are required to withhold and deposit the employees' part of the taxes and pay a matching amount of these taxes.

Social security tax is calculated on employee earnings up to a maximum paid in a calendar year. The maximum amount of earnings on which a tax is calculated is called a **tax base**. Congress sets the tax base and the tax rates for social security tax. An act of Congress can change the tax base and tax rate at any time. The social security tax rate and base used in this text are 6.2% of earnings up to a maximum of $87,000.00 in each calendar year.

Between January 1 and December 15, Mr. Selby's earnings are less than the social security tax base. Therefore,

Mr. Selby's social security tax deduction for the semimonthly pay period ended December 15, 20--, is calculated as shown.

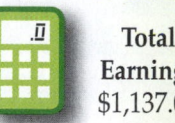

Total Earnings	×	Social Security Tax Rate	=	Social Security Tax Deduction
$1,137.00	×	6.2%	=	$70.49

Medicare does not have a tax base. Therefore, Medicare tax is calculated on total employee earnings. The Medicare tax rate used in this text is 1.45% of total employee earnings.

Rick E. Selby's Medicare tax deduction for the semimonthly pay period ended December 15, 20--, is calculated as shown.

Total Earnings	×	Medicare Tax Rate	=	Medicare Tax Deduction
$1,137.00	×	1.45%	=	$16.49

DAJ/GETTY IMAGES

FOR YOUR INFORMATION

FYI

Accounting procedures are the same regardless of changes in the tax base and tax rate. The social security tax rate and the tax base shown above are assumed for all payroll calculations in this textbook.

REMEMBER

When an employee's earnings exceed the tax base, no more social security tax is deducted.

End of Lesson
REVIEW

AUDIT YOUR UNDERSTANDING

1. Where does an employer get the information used to determine the amount of federal income tax to withhold from employees' earnings?
2. Employee federal income tax withholdings are based on what two factors?
3. Does the employer or employee pay social security tax and Medicare tax?

TERMS REVIEW

payroll taxes

withholding allowance

social security tax

Medicare tax

tax base

WORK TOGETHER 12-2

Determining payroll tax withholding

Information taken from a semimonthly payroll is given in the *Working Papers*. Your instructor will guide you through the following examples.

1. For each employee, determine the federal income tax that must be withheld. Use the tax withholding tables in this lesson.
2. Calculate the amount of social security tax and Medicare tax that must be withheld for each employee. Use a social security tax rate of 6.2% and a Medicare tax rate of 1.45%. None of the employees has accumulated earnings greater than the tax base.

ON YOUR OWN 12-2

Determining payroll tax withholding

Information taken from a semimonthly payroll is given in the *Working Papers*. Work this problem independently.

1. For each employee, determine the federal income tax that must be withheld. Use the tax withholding tables in this lesson.
2. Calculate the amount of social security tax and Medicare tax that must be withheld for each employee. Use a social security tax rate of 6.2% and a Medicare tax rate of 1.45%. None of the employees has accumulated earnings greater than the tax base.

Preparing Payroll Records

······· **PAYROLL REGISTER** ·······

3. Employee Personal Data

6. Social Security Tax

8. Health Insurance

2. Payment Date

1. Pay Period Date

4. Earnings

5. Federal Income Tax

7. Medicare Tax

9. Other Deductions

① SEMIMONTHLY PERIOD ENDED *December 15, 20--*   PAYROLL REGISTER   DATE OF PAYMENT *December 15, 20--* ②

	EMPL. NO.	EMPLOYEE'S NAME	MARITAL STATUS	NO. OF ALLOWANCES	EARNINGS			DEDUCTIONS						NET PAY	CHECK NO.	
					1	2	3	4	5	6	7	8	9	10		
					REGULAR	OVERTIME	TOTAL	FEDERAL INCOME TAX	SOC. SEC. TAX	MEDICARE TAX	HEALTH INSURANCE	OTHER	TOTAL	NET PAY	CHECK NO.	
1	2	Aranda, Susan A.	M	2	968 00		968 00	38 00	60 02	14 04	45 00	B 10 00	167 06	800 94	482	1
2	5	Drew, Paul S.	S	1	550 00		550 00	32 00	34 10	7 98	38 00		112 08	437 92	483	2
3	1	Kellogg, Janice P.	M	1	1760 00	150 00	1910 00	187 00	118 42	27 70	38 00	UW 20 00	391 12	1518 88	484	3
4	6	Mendel, Ann M.	S	1	240 00		240 00		14 88	3 48			18 36	221 64	485	4
5	3	Selby, Rick E.	M	4	1056 00	81 00	1137 00	28 00	70 49	16 49	60 00	B 10 00 UW 10 00	194 98	942 02	486	5
6	4	Young, Justin L.	S	1	906 40		906 40	86 00	56 20	13 14	38 00	B 15 00 UW 10 00	218 34	688 06	487	6
7		Totals			5480 40	231 00	5711 40	371 00	354 11	82 83	219 00	B 35 00 UW 40 00	1101 94	4609 46	⑬	7
8													⑩	⑪		8
9								⑫								9

12. Total, Prove, and Rule

11. Net Pay

10. Total Deductions

13. Check Number

A business form used to record payroll information is called a **payroll register**. A payroll register summarizes the payroll for one pay period and shows total earnings, payroll withholdings, and net pay of all employees. Hobby Shack prepares a separate payroll register for each semimonthly payroll.

S T E P S   PREPARING A PAYROLL REGISTER

① Enter the last date of the semimonthly payroll period, *December 15, 20--*, at the top of the payroll register.

② Enter the date of payment, *December 15, 20--*, also at the top of the payroll register.

③ For each employee, enter employee number, name, marital status, and number of allowances. This information is taken from personnel records. Entries for Rick E. Selby are on line 5 of the register.

④ Enter regular earnings, overtime earnings, and total earnings for each employee in columns 1, 2, and 3 of the payroll register. This information is taken from each employee's time card.

(5) Enter in column 4 the federal income tax withheld from each employee. Mr. Selby's federal tax withholding is *$28.00*.

(6) Enter in column 5 of the payroll register the social security tax withheld from each employee. Mr. Selby's social security tax deduction, *$70.49*, is recorded in column 5 of the payroll register. Mr. Selby's total earnings for the year have not exceeded the social security tax base, so his total earnings for the pay period are taxed.

(7) Enter in column 6 the Medicare tax withheld from each employee. Mr. Selby's Medicare tax deduction is *$16.49*.

(8) Enter in column 7 the health insurance premium deductions. Full-time employees of Hobby Shack participate in a group health insurance plan to take advantage of lower group rates. Mr. Selby's semimonthly health insurance premium is *$60.00*. Premiums are set by the insurance company and are usually based on the employee marital status and whether coverage is for an individual or a family. Some health insurance premiums may be based on the number of individuals covered.

(9) Enter in column 8 all other employee payroll deductions. The Other column is used to record voluntary deductions requested by an employee. Entries are identified by code letters. Hobby Shack uses the letter *B* to identify amounts withheld for buying U.S. Savings Bonds. *UW* is used to identify amounts withheld for employee contributions to United Way. Mr. Selby has authorized Hobby Shack to withhold *$10.00* each pay period to buy U.S. Savings Bonds for him. Mr. Selby has also authorized that *$10.00* be withheld as a contribution to the United Way.

(10) After all deductions are entered in the payroll register, add all the deduction amounts for each employee and enter the totals in column 9. Mr. Selby's total deductions, *$194.98*, are calculated as shown.

Federal Income Tax	+	Social Security Tax	+	Medicare Tax	+	Health Insurance	+	Other	=	Total Deductions
$28.00	+	$70.49	+	$16.49	+	$60.00	+	$20.00	=	$194.98

(11) Determine the net pay for each employee. The total earnings paid to an employee after payroll taxes and other deductions is called **net pay**. Subtract the total deductions, column 9, from total earnings, column 3, to determine net pay. Enter net pay in column 10. Mr. Selby's net pay, *$942.02*, is calculated as shown.

Total Earnings	−	Total Deductions	=	Net Pay
$1,137.00	−	$194.98	=	$942.02

(12) Total, prove, and rule the payroll register. Total each amount column. Subtract the Total Deductions column from the Total Earnings column. The result should equal the total of the Net Pay column. If the totals do not agree, the errors must be found and corrected. Proving the accuracy of Hobby Shack's payroll register for the pay period ended December 15, 20--, is shown.

Total Earnings	−	Total Deductions	=	Net Pay
$5,711.40	−	$1,101.94	=	$4,609.46

The net pay, $4,609.46, is the same as the total of the Net Pay column. The payroll register is proved. After the payroll register is proved, rule double lines below all amount column totals to show the totals have been verified as correct.

(13) Payroll checks are written after payroll calculations are verified and a manager approves the payroll. Write the payroll check numbers in the Check No. column.

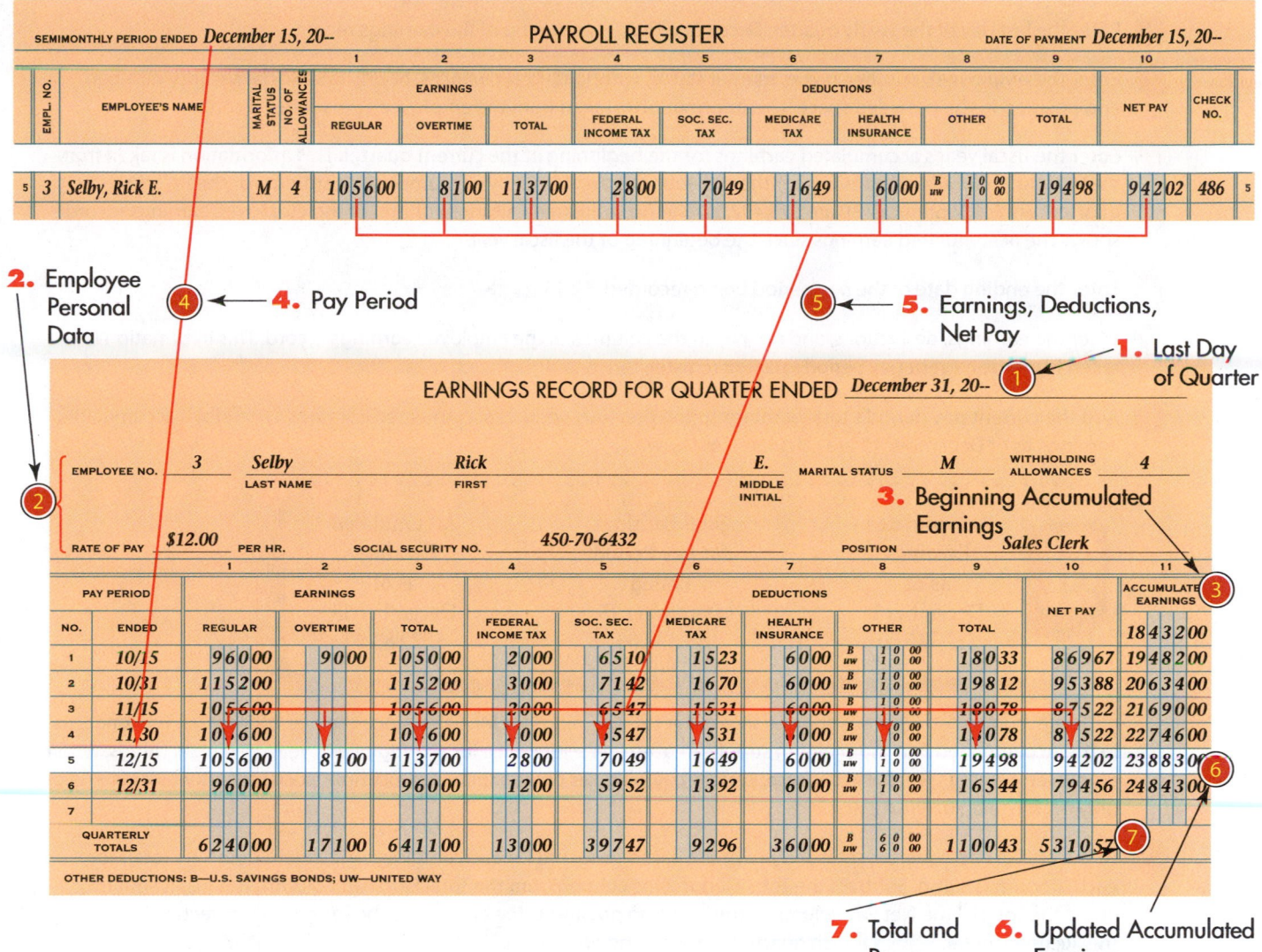

2. Employee Personal Data

4. Pay Period

5. Earnings, Deductions, Net Pay

1. Last Day of Quarter

3. Beginning Accumulated Earnings

7. Total and Prove **6.** Updated Accumulated Earnings

A business must send a quarterly report to federal and state governments showing employee taxable earnings and taxes withheld from employee earnings. Detailed information about each employee's earnings is summarized in a single record for each employee. A business form used to record details affecting payments made to an employee is called an **employee earnings record**. An employee's earnings and deductions for each pay period are summarized on one line of the employee earnings record. A new earnings record is prepared for each employee each quarter. Rick E. Selby's earnings record for the fourth quarter is shown.

The steps for completing the employee earnings record are on the next page.

FOR YOUR INFORMATION

FYI

The federal income tax withholding tables on pages 347–348 contain a column for 0 dependents. How can an employee have 0 dependents if the employee is a dependent? Some employees claim fewer dependents than they are allowed—even as low as zero—to increase the amount of tax withheld. An employee who has other taxable income, such as interest and dividends, can use payroll withholding to pay the additional income taxes owed on this income. As a result, the employee avoids having a large income tax payment when the tax return is filed.

1. Enter the last day of the yearly quarter, *December 31, 20--*, at the top of the earnings record.

2. Enter the employee's number, name, marital status, withholding allowances, hourly rate, social security number, and position in the provided space. This information is taken from the employee's personnel records.

3. Enter the fiscal year's accumulated earnings for the beginning of the current quarter. This information is taken from the ending accumulated earnings for the previous quarter. Mr. Selby's accumulated earnings for the first three quarters ended September 30 are *$18,432.00*. The Accumulated Earnings column of the employee earnings record shows the accumulated earnings since the beginning of the fiscal year.

4. Enter the ending date of the pay period being recorded, *12/15*.

5. Enter the earnings, deductions, and net pay in the columns of the employee earnings record. This information is taken from the current pay period's payroll register.

6. Add the current pay period's total earnings to the previous period's accumulated earnings. Mr. Selby's accumulated earnings as of December 15 are calculated as shown.

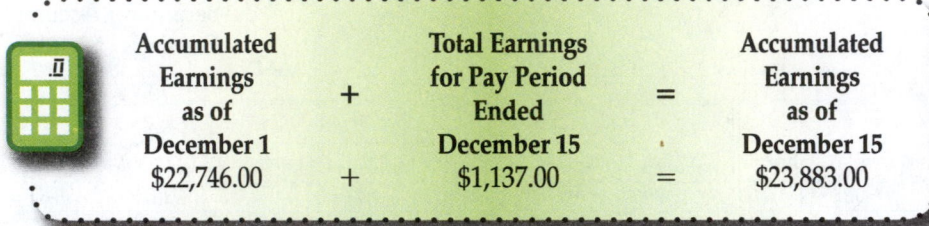

Accumulated Earnings as of December 1	+	Total Earnings for Pay Period Ended December 15	=	Accumulated Earnings as of December 15
$22,746.00	+	$1,137.00	=	$23,883.00

The Accumulated Earnings column shows the total earnings for Mr. Selby since the first of the year. The amounts in the Accumulated Earnings column supply an up-to-date reference for an employee's year-to-date earnings. When employee earnings reach the tax base, certain payroll taxes do not apply. For example, social security taxes are paid only on the first $87,000 of earnings.

7. At the end of each quarter, total and prove the earnings record for each employee. Calculate quarterly totals for each amount column. Subtract the Total Deductions column from the Total Earnings column. The result should equal the total of the Net Pay column. If the totals do not agree, the errors must be found and corrected. Proving the accuracy of Mr. Selby's fourth quarterly totals is shown.

Total Earnings	−	Total Deductions	=	Net Pay
$6,411.00	−	$1,100.43	=	$5,310.57

The net pay, *$5,310.57*, is compared to the total of the Net Pay column. The earnings record is proved because these amounts are equal. These totals are needed to prepare required government reports.

REMEMBER

Total earnings, not net pay, are added to the previous accumulated earnings amount on the earnings record. Total earnings is the amount compared to the tax base to determine whether social security taxes should be withheld.

End of Lesson REVIEW

AUDIT YOUR UNDERSTANDING

1. What does the payroll register summarize?
2. How is net pay calculated?
3. Why do companies complete employee earnings records?

WORK TOGETHER 12-3

Preparing payroll records

Selected payroll data for Antique Shop are provided in a payroll register in the *Working Papers*. Your instructor will guide you through the following examples.

1. Complete the payroll register entries for Judy Hensley and Mike McCune for the semimonthly pay period ended July 15, 20--. Use the tax withholding tables shown in Lesson 12-2. Use tax rates of 6.2% for social security tax and 1.45% for Medicare tax. Neither employee has reached the tax base. For each employee, withhold $60.00 for health insurance and $15.00 for U.S. Savings bonds, per pay period.

2. Total all the amount columns of the payroll register. Prove the payroll register.

3. Prepare a quarterly earnings record for Ms. Hensley for the quarter ended September 30, 20--, and enter the July 15 payroll information. Ms. Hensley's employee number is 5; rate of pay is $13.00; social security number is 543-69-0123; position is sales clerk. Accumulated earnings at the end of the second quarter are $13,520.00. Save your work to complete Work Together 12-4.

ON YOUR OWN 12-3

Preparing payroll records

Selected payroll data for Prosser Company are provided in a payroll register in the *Working Papers*. Work this problem independently.

1. Complete the payroll register entries for Allen P. Best and Tammy S. Edwards for the semimonthly pay period ended July 15, 20--. Use the tax withholding tables shown in Lesson 12-2. Use tax rates of 6.2% for social security tax and 1.45% for Medicare tax. For each employee, withhold $60.00 for health insurance and $10.00 for U.S. Savings Bonds per pay period. For Ms. Edwards, also withhold $20.00 for United Way per pay period.

2. Total all the amount columns of the payroll register. Prove the payroll register.

3. Prepare a quarterly earnings record for Mr. Best for the quarter ended September 30, 20--, and enter the July 15 payroll information. Mr. Best's employee number is 4; rate of pay is $12.25; social security number is 301-69-1427; position is sales clerk. Accumulated earnings at the end of the second quarter are $28,692.00. Save your work to complete On Your Own 12-4.

······· PAYROLL BANK ACCOUNT ·······

1. Prepare the check stub.

2. Prepare the check.

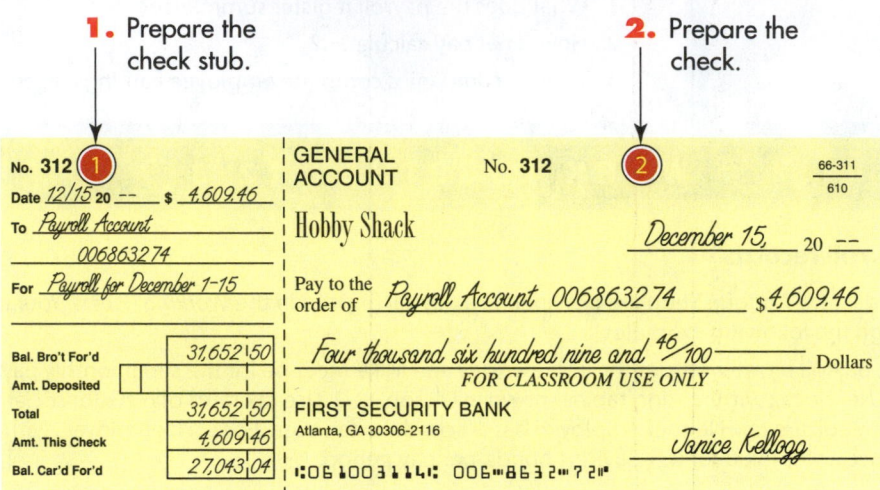

No. **312** ①
Date _12/15_ 20 _--_ $ _4,609.46_
To _Payroll Account_
_006863274_
For _Payroll for December 1–15_

Bal. Bro't For'd	31,652	50
Amt. Deposited		
Total	31,652	50
Amt. This Check	4,609	46
Bal. Car'd For'd	27,043	04

GENERAL ACCOUNT   No. **312** ②

66-311
610

Hobby Shack

December 15, 20 _--_

Pay to the order of _Payroll Account 006863274_ $_4,609.46_

Four thousand six hundred nine and ⁴⁶/₁₀₀ —————— Dollars

FOR CLASSROOM USE ONLY

FIRST SECURITY BANK
Atlanta, GA 30306-2116

Janice Kellogg

⑆061003114⑆ 006⑈8632⑉72⑈

Hobby Shack pays its employees with checks written on a special payroll checking account. A check for the total net pay is written on Hobby Shack's general checking account. The check is deposited in the payroll checking account.

A separate checking account for payroll checks helps to protect and control payroll payments. The exact amount needed to pay the payroll is deposited in the special payroll checking account. If amounts on checks are altered or unauthorized payroll checks are prepared, the amount in the special payroll account would be insufficient to cover all the checks. Thus, the bank and Hobby Shack would be alerted quickly to an unauthorized payroll check. Also, since payroll checks are drawn on the separate account, any balance in this account will correspond to the sum of outstanding payroll checks.

STEPS   **PREPARING A CHECK FOR TOTAL NET PAY**

① Prepare the check stub. The date of the check is *12/15*. The amount, *$4,609.46*, is the total of the Net Pay column of the payroll register. The check is payable to *Payroll Account 006863274*, Hobby Shack's special payroll checking account. The payment is for the payroll period from December 1 to 15. Calculate and record the new general checking account balance.

② Prepare the check from the information on the check stub. Hobby Shack's check is drawn on the company's general account and is signed by Janice Kellogg.

REMEMBER

Using a separate checking account for payroll checks provides internal control and helps to prevent fraud.

1. Enter on check stub information from payroll register.

2. Prepare employee's payroll check for net amount of earnings.

① Check No. **486**			
PERIOD ENDING	12	15	20--
EARNINGS	$	1,137.00	
REG.	$	1,056.00	
O.T.	$	81.00	
DEDUCTIONS	$	194.98	
INC. TAX	$	28.00	
SOC. SEC. TAX	$	70.49	
MED. TAX	$	16.49	
HEALTH INS.	$	60.00	
OTHER	$	B 10.00 UW 10.00	
NET PAY	$	942.02	

PAYROLL ACCOUNT

66-311 / 610

December 15, 20 --

No. **486**

Pay to the order of _Rick E. Selby_ $ _942.02_

Nine hundred forty-two and $^{02}/_{100}$ _____ Dollars

FOR CLASSROOM USE ONLY

FIRST SECURITY BANK
Atlanta, GA 30306-2116

Hobby Shack

Janice Kellogg

⑆061003114⑆ 006⑈8632⑈74⑆

The information used to prepare payroll checks is taken from a payroll register. A special payroll check form is used that has a detachable stub for recording earnings and amounts deducted. Employees keep the stubs for a record of deductions and cash received.

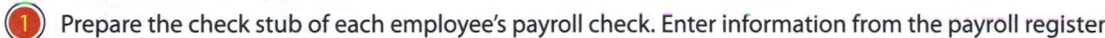
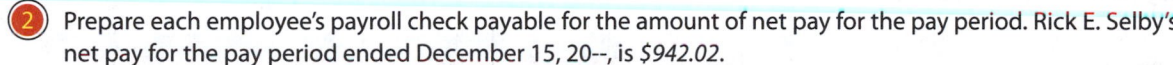

STEPS PREPARING AN EMPLOYEE'S PAYROLL CHECK

① Prepare the check stub of each employee's payroll check. Enter information from the payroll register.

② Prepare each employee's payroll check payable for the amount of net pay for the pay period. Rick E. Selby's net pay for the pay period ended December 15, 20--, is *$942.02*.

PHOTODISC/GETTY IMAGES

A computerized cash payments system that transfers funds without the use of checks, currency, or other paper documents is known as electronic funds transfer (EFT). Some businesses deposit employee net pay directly to each employee bank account by using EFT. When EFT is used, the bank's computer deducts the amount of net pay from the business's bank account and adds the amount to each employee bank account. The payroll must still be calculated, but individual checks are not written and do not have to be distributed. Under this system, each employee receives a statement of earnings and deductions similar to the detachable stub on a payroll check.

End of Lesson REVIEW

1. Why does Hobby Shack have a separate checking account for payroll checks?
2. What is the source of the information that is recorded on each employee's payroll check stub?
3. How do payroll procedures differ for employees who request that their pay be deposited through electronic funds transfer?

WORK TOGETHER 12-4

Preparing payroll checks

Use the payroll register from Work Together 12-3. In the *Working Papers* are three blank checks: one General Account check and two Payroll Account checks. Your instructor will guide you through the following examples.

1. Prepare Antique Shop's General Account check for the pay period ended July 15, 20--. The payment date is July 15. Balance brought forward from the previous check is $16,542.00. The Payroll Account number is 0639583. Sign your name as the manager of Antique Shop.
2. For the pay period ended July 15, 20--, prepare payroll checks for Judy Hensley and Mike McCune. The payment date is July 15. Sign your name as the manager of Antique Shop. Record the two payroll check numbers in the payroll register.

ON YOUR OWN 12-4

Preparing payroll checks

Use the payroll register from On Your Own 12-3. In the *Working Papers* are three blank checks: one General Account check and two Payroll Account checks. Work this problem independently.

1. Prepare Prosser Company's General Account check for the pay period ended July 15, 20--. The payment date is July 15. Balance carried forward from the previous check is $12,421.90. The Payroll Account number is 146-7219-6. Sign your name as the manager of Prosser Company.
2. For the pay period ended July 15, 20--, prepare payroll checks for Allen P. Best and Tammy S. Edwards. The payment date is July 15. Sign your name as the manager of Prosser Company. Record the two payroll checks in the payroll register.

SUMMARY

After completing this chapter, you can:

1. Define accounting terms related to payroll records.

2. Identify accounting practices related to payroll records.

3. Complete a payroll time card.

4. Calculate payroll taxes.

5. Complete a payroll register and an employee earnings record.

6. Prepare payroll checks.

Go Beyond the Book
For more information go to
www.C21accounting.com

EXPLORE ACCOUNTING

Employee vs. Independent Contractor

A business sometimes contracts with individuals to perform specified services for the business. Determining whether such an individual is an employee or a self-employed independent contractor is an important issue.

If the person is found to be an employee, the employer must withhold and submit employee income tax, social security tax, and Medicare tax to the Internal Revenue Service (IRS). The employer must pay an equal amount of social security and Medicare tax. Also, the employer will pay unemployment taxes (discussed in Chapter 13) and be subject to various employer reporting requirements.

A person who is found to be a self-employed independent contractor must pay an amount of social security and Medicare tax that is equivalent to both the employer and employee taxes.

If an employer incorrectly treats an employee as a self-employed independent contractor, the penalties can be severe. Therefore, it is important to a business to make an accurate determination of the status of all individuals performing work for the business. The IRS has provided guidelines to help businesses make the distinction. Every

individual who performs services subject to the will and control of an employer both as to what shall be done and how it shall be done is considered an employee for withholding purposes. The major determining factor is whether the employer has the legal right to control both the method and result of the services. If the business has the right to control only the result of the service performed and not the means and methods of accomplishing the result, the individual is probably a self-employed independent contractor.

Research: Review federal tax publications or interview local businesses on the issues below. Then prepare a written or oral report to present to your class. (1) Why is it important to determine an individual's status? What is at stake for the individual, the employer, and the IRS? (2) What are the advantages and disadvantages of determining an individual to be an employee or independent contractor—to the individual? to the employer? to the IRS?

12-1 APPLICATION PROBLEM

Preparing payroll time cards

Employee time cards are given in the *Working Papers*.

Instructions:
1. Calculate the regular, overtime, and total hours worked by each employee. Any hours over the regular 8-hour day are considered overtime. Record the hours on the time cards.
2. Determine the regular, overtime, and total earnings for each employee. The overtime rate is $1\frac{1}{2}$ times the regular rate. Complete the time cards.

12-2 APPLICATION PROBLEM

Determining payroll tax withholding

Information taken from the semimonthly payroll register is given in the *Working Papers*.

Instructions:
1. Determine the federal income tax that must be withheld for each of the eight employees. Use the tax withholding tables shown in Lesson 12-2.
2. Calculate the amount of social security tax and Medicare tax that must be withheld for each employee using 6.2% and 1.45% tax rates, respectively. None of the eight employees has accumulated earnings greater than the tax base.

12-3 APPLICATION PROBLEM Microsoft Office

Preparing a payroll register

The information for the semimonthly pay period October 1–15 of the current year is given in the *Working Papers*.

Instructions:
Complete a payroll register for Perez Company. The date of payment is October 15. Use the tax withholding tables shown in Lesson 12-2 for the income tax withholding for each employee. Calculate social security and Medicare taxes withholding using 6.2% and 1.45% tax rates, respectively. None of the employees has accumulated earnings greater than the social security tax base.

12-4 APPLICATION PROBLEM Microsoft Office

Preparing an employee earnings record

Grady R. Hurley's earnings for the six semimonthly pay periods in July, August, and September of the current year are given in the *Working Papers*. Deductions and net pay have been completed for July and August.

The following additional data about Grady R. Hurley are needed to complete the employee earnings record.

1. Employee number: 28
2. Marital status: married
3. Withholding allowances: 2
4. Rate of pay: regular, $15.00
5. Social security number: 462-81-5823
6. Position: service manager
7. Accumulated earnings for the end of second quarter: $15,750.00

8. Deductions from total earnings:
   a. Health insurance: $60.00 each semimonthly pay period
   b. U.S. Savings Bonds: $20.00 each semimonthly pay period
   c. Federal income tax: determined each pay period by using the withholding tables in Lesson 12-2
   d. Social security taxes: 6.2% of total earnings each pay period
   e. Medicare taxes: 1.45% of total earnings each pay period

Instructions:
1. Calculate and record the accumulated earnings for the July and August pay periods.
2. Complete the earnings record for the pay periods ended September 15 and September 30.
3. Total all amount columns on the earnings record.
4. Verify the accuracy of the completed employee earnings record. The Quarter Total for Regular and Overtime Earnings should equal the Quarter Total for Net Pay plus Total Deductions. The Quarter Total for Total Earnings should equal the end-of-quarter Accumulated Earnings minus the beginning-of-quarter Accumulated Earnings.

12-5 APPLICATION PROBLEM

Preparing payroll checks

Royal Appliances' net payroll for the semimonthly pay period ended May 15, 20--, is $7,498.80. Payroll checks are prepared May 15, 20--. Blank checks are provided in the *Working Papers*.

Instructions:
1. Prepare a General Account check for the total amount of the net pay. Make the check payable to Payroll Account 018-65-4237, and sign your name as manager of Royal Appliances. The beginning check stub balance is $10,138.95.
2. Prepare payroll checks for two employees of Royal Appliances. Payroll information for the two employees is as follows. Sign your name as a manager of Royal Appliances.

a. Wanda M. Curtis		b. Kevin R. Hayes	
Check No. 823		Check No. 827	
Regular Earnings	$740.00	Regular Earnings	$920.00
Overtime Earnings	40.00	Overtime Earnings	30.00
Deductions:		Deductions:	
Federal Income Tax	$ 33.00	Federal Income Tax	$ 23.00
Social Security Tax	48.36	Social Security Tax	58.90
Medicare Tax	11.31	Medicare Tax	13.78
Health Insurance	35.00	Health Insurance	60.00
		Savings Bond	20.00

12-6 MASTERY PROBLEM

Preparing a semimonthly payroll

The following information for Arrow Company is for the semimonthly pay period August 16–31 of the current year. Forms are given in the *Working Papers*.

EMPL. NO.	EMPLOYEE'S NAME	MARITAL STATUS	NO. OF ALLOWANCES	EARNINGS REGULAR	EARNINGS OVERTIME	DEDUCTIONS HEALTH INSURANCE	DEDUCTIONS SAVINGS BONDS
5	Acron, Peter C.	M	3	1 1 2 6 40	1 1 5 20	60 00	10 00
7	Barenis, Mary P.	S	1	1 1 5 5 00		25 00	
6	Epps, John P.	M	2	7 9 2 00		40 00	10 00
1	Goforth, Alice A.	S	2	1 1 3 5 20	7 7 40	40 00	
8	Hiett, Franklin B.	M	3	1 1 8 8 00		60 00	10 00
9	Land, Keith	S	1	9 5 4 60		25 00	10 00
2	Malone, Lillie L.	S	1	1 0 8 3 60		25 00	
4	Rivers, Linda K.	M	2	1 0 9 1 20	9 3 00	40 00	
10	Sowell, Jacob S.	M	2	1 1 6 1 60		40 00	10 00
3	Vole, Ryan V.	M	5	1 0 7 5 00		80 00	10 00

Instructions:

1. Prepare a payroll register. The date of payment is August 31. Use the income tax withholding tables shown in Lesson 12-2 to find the income tax withholding for each employee. Calculate social security and Medicare tax withholdings using 6.2% and 1.45% tax rates, respectively. None of the employees has accumulated earnings greater than the social security tax base.
2. Prepare a check for the total amount of the net pay. Make the check payable to Payroll Account 59-721-65, and sign your name as the manager of Arrow Company. The beginning check stub balance is $16,216.90.
3. Prepare payroll checks for Peter C. Acron, Check No. 1692, and Franklin B. Hiett, Check No. 1696. Sign your name as the manager of Arrow Company. Record the two payroll check numbers in the payroll register.

12-7 CHALLENGE PROBLEM

Calculating piecework wages

Production workers in factories are frequently paid on the basis of the number of units they produce. This payroll method is referred to as the *piecework incentive wage plan*. Most piecework incentive wage plans include a guaranteed hourly rate to employees regardless of the number of units they produce. This guaranteed hourly rate is referred to as the *base rate*.

Time and motion study engineers usually determine the standard time required for producing a single unit. Assume, for example, that time studies determine that one-third of an hour is the standard time required to produce a unit. Then the standard rate for an 8-hour day would be 24 units (8 hours divided by 1/3 hour = 24 units per day). If a worker's daily base pay is $96.00, the incentive rate per unit is $4.00 ($96.00 divided by 24 units × $4.00 per unit). Therefore, the worker who produces 24 or fewer units per day is paid the base pay, $96.00. However, each worker is paid an additional $4.00 for each unit over 24 produced each day.

Draker Furniture Company has eight employees in production departments that are paid on a piecework incentive wage plan. The following standard and incentive wage rates are listed by department.

Department	Standard Production per Employee	Incentive Rate per Unit
Cutting	32 units per day	$3.50
Assembly	20 units per day	$5.75
Finishing	45 units per day	$2.00

A payroll register is given in the *Working Papers*. Each employee worked eight hours a day during the semimonthly pay period, May 1–15. Payroll records for May 1–15 are summarized in the following table.

Employee No.	Employee Name	Marital Status	No. of Allowances	Guaranteed Daily Rate	2	3	4	5	6	9	10	11	12	13
	Cutting Department													
C3	Bell, Julie M.	M	4	$112.00	33	30	28	32	32	32	32	33	35	33
C6	Hairston, Gary P.	M	2	$112.00	29	35	29	32	31	33	32	33	30	30
C9	Reeves, John M.	S	1	$112.00	31	30	35	34	34	31	35	28	31	32
	Assembly Department													
A2	Bullock, Amy C.	S	2	$115.00	22	20	20	20	22	22	22	22	23	20
A6	Green, Steven P.	S	1	$115.00	20	23	23	20	22	21	20	20	20	20
A9	Prine, Jacob R.	M	4	$115.00	23	22	21	22	22	21	22	22	20	23
	Finishing Department													
F5	Gerez, Dave A.	M	2	$90.00	39	47	38	47	43	41	40	41	39	46
F2	Kyle, Ryan G.	S	1	$90.00	41	43	47	38	42	39	43	39	43	39

Header note: *Units Produced per Day — Pay Period May 1–15*

Instructions:

Prepare a payroll register. The earnings column Incentive is used instead of Overtime. The date of payment is May 15. Use the income tax withholding tables shown in Lesson 12-2. Calculate the employee social security and Medicare tax withholdings using 6.2% and 1.45% tax rates, respectively. None of the employees has health insurance or other deductions. None of the employees has accumulated earnings greater than the social security tax base.

The employees of Kaden Company currently use time cards and a time clock to record their arrival and departure times. Management plans to replace the time clock with a device that reads a magnetic strip on the back of each employee's name badge. The badge is scanned by a reader in the same manner that credit cards are scanned. Because the badge reader is connected to a computer, the information is recorded directly to a computer file. Thus, the new system will enable management to make daily analyses of employee hours and productivity. This information should allow managers to make more timely decisions and increase profits.

Instructions: Assume you work in the payroll department for Kaden Company. Write a memo to the employees informing them of the new system. Because some employees may not be happy with this new system, be sure to include reasons why the policy is being implemented.

CASE FOR CRITICAL THINKING

Vadillo Lumber currently requires each employee to inform the accounting clerk of the total hours worked each day during the pay period. The total number of hours worked by all employees has been steadily increasing during the prior pay periods. The new store manager has suggested that a time clock be installed to record arrival and departure times. The accounting clerk believes the current system is satisfactory. Do you agree with the new manager or the accounting clerk? Explain your response.

GRAPHING WORKSHOP

Distribution of Gross Wages

The chart depicts data from the payroll register of Alectra Corporation. Analyze the graph to answer the following questions.

1. What was the largest payroll deduction?
2. What percent of employees' wages are withheld for taxes?
3. What amount is represented by the entire pie graph?

Payroll Distribution

- 6.3%
- 6.2%
- 1.5%
- 4.3%
- 0.9%
- 80.8%

- Federal Income Tax
- Social Security Tax
- Medicare Tax
- Health Insurance
- Other Deductions
- Net Pay

ANALYZING BEST BUY'S FINANCIAL STATEMENTS

Annual reports contain a report by management designed to inform potential investors and business partners about how the financial statements were prepared. The report describes, in detail, accounting and management policies that are followed to ensure that the amounts on the financial statements can be relied upon for making business decisions.

Instructions: Use Management's Report on the Financial Statements and Management's Report on Internal Control over Financial Reporting on page B-4 in Appendix B to answer the following questions.

1. Who is responsible for the preparation of Best Buy's financial statements?
2. What is the system of internal control designed to do?
3. Can internal controls prevent or detect all misstatements?

Accounting
SOFTWARE

RECORDING PAYROLL

Review the payroll calculations for: (1) gross wages, (2) federal income tax withholding, (3) FICA taxes, considering whether the employee has reached the tax base, (4) Medicare taxes, and (5) net wages. Peachtree can perform all the calculations required to prepare payroll checks.

Before preparing payroll checks, an employee's personal record must be up to date. The personal record contains the employee's regular and overtime wage rates, filing status (single or married), withholding allowances, and any optional deductions. When the number of hours worked is entered, Peachtree calculates all required amounts and prints the payroll check. The journal entry is automatically recorded when the payroll check is printed. Peachtree records each payroll check as a separate journal entry.

PEACHTREE APPLICATION PROBLEM 12-5
1. Open (Restore) file 12-5AP.ptb.
2. Use Peachtree's Payments task to journalize the May 15 transactions to establish the payroll account for the amount of the net payroll; post the Payments entry.
3. Record the May 15 paychecks for the two employees. Post the Payments entries.

PEACHTREE MASTERY PROBLEM 12-6
1. Open (Restore) file 12-6MP.ptb.
2. Prepare a payroll register.
3. Record the check for the net payroll for the pay period August 16-31.
4. Journalize and post payroll checks for the two employees.
5. Print the cash disbursements journal.

RECORDING PAYROLL

The benefit of an automated payroll package is that it usually calculates all the deductions and the net pay for each employee. In QuickBooks, the payroll function is a special package to which a company can subscribe.

A company that does not subscribe to the payroll function will still use QuickBooks for payroll but will have to calculate the deductions and net pay manually. The payroll check will be entered into QuickBooks similar to other checks, which will automatically make a journal entry for the check. Since each employee will receive a separate check, a separate entry will be made for each employee. This is different from the method illustrated in this chapter, where the payroll register totals are used to journalize the payroll.

QUICKBOOKS APPLICATION PROBLEM 12-5
1. Open the Royal Appliances file if it is not already open.
2. Record the deposit in the Payroll account using the Make Deposits feature.
3. Write the payroll checks using the Write Checks feature for the two employees.
4. Print a Journal report for May 1 through May 15.

QUICKBOOKS MASTERY PROBLEM 12-6
1. Open the Arrow Company file.
2. Record the payroll deposit.
3. Write the payroll checks for the two employees.
4. Print a Journal report for August 16 through August 31.

USING THE ROUND FUNCTION

Can 4.00 + 3.00 equal 6.99? It can on an electronic spreadsheet! Users of such spreadsheets typically apply cell formatting to display dollar amounts to two-decimal-place accuracy. If they do not account for rounding, this kind of error can occur.

Shown below are two employees' FICA tax calculations. Each actual number in the first column is rounded to display to the nearest cent when it is displayed in the second column. This is done by using the ROUND function. The function =ROUND(Cell, Number of places) rounds the contents of the Cell to a specified Number of decimals. Thus, the function doesn't just display a number to a specified decimal-place accuracy, it actually rounds the number.

To get a correct total of the individual rounded amounts in Cell C5, simply add the rounded amounts in cells C3 and C4. You may use +C3+C4 or SUM(C3:C4), but do not round the total.

	A	B	C	D
1		Actual	Formatted (to two	=ROUND (to two
2		Number	decimal places)	decimal places)
3	Sanders, Jim	3.996	$4.00	4.00
4	Keller, Danielle	2.997	$3.00	3.00
5	Totals	6.993	$6.99	7.00

EXCEL APPLICATION PROBLEM 12-3
Open the F12-3 Excel data file. Follow the step-by-step instructions in the Instructions worksheet.

EXCEL APPLICATION PROBLEM 12-4
Open the F12-4 Excel data file. Follow the step-by-step instructions in the Instructions worksheet.

RECORDING PAYROLL

In an automated payroll system, the computer is used to maintain the employee database, to record payroll transactions at the end of each pay period, to calculate withholding taxes, and to create all the related journal entries. The employee database identifies each employee by employee number. Other data required for each employee includes the employee's name, social security number, marital status, number of withholding allowances, pay rate, and voluntary deductions. Employee accounts may be added, changed, or deleted from the accounting system.

Entering Payroll Transactions
1. Click the Other toolbar button.
2. Click the Payroll tab.
3. Enter the date of the check.
4. Select the employee from the employee drop-down list.
5. Verify that the check number displayed is correct, or key the correct number.
6. For salaried employees, the salary amount will be automatically displayed. For hourly employees, enter the regular and overtime hours worked during the current payroll period.
7. Click the Calculate Taxes button to direct the software to calculate the employee taxes.
8. Enter the employee's voluntary deductions.
9. Click OK to generate and display the payroll check.
10. Click the Close button to dismiss the check and continue, or click Print to print the check.

AUTOMATED ACCOUNTING MASTERY PROBLEM 12-6
Open file F12-6.AA8. Display the problem instructions and complete the problem.

CHAPTER 13

Payroll Accounting, Taxes, and Reports

PHOTODISC/GETTY IMAGES

OBJECTIVES

After studying Chapter 13, you will be able to:

1. Define accounting terms related to payroll accounting, taxes, and reports.

2. Identify accounting concepts and practices related to payroll accounting, taxes, and reports.

3. Analyze payroll transactions and record a payroll.

4. Record employer payroll taxes.

5. Prepare selected payroll tax reports.

6. Pay and record withholding and payroll taxes.

KEY TERMS

- federal unemployment tax
- state unemployment tax
- lookback period

Point Your Browser
www.C21accounting.com

Google

Employee Benefits at Google

Innovative thinking comes from creative minds. Technology companies must continually develop new products and applications for those products in order to stay competitive in today's rapidly changing marketplace. To maintain a creative workforce, companies must create a comfortable work environment that encourages and rewards creativity.

Google offers many innovative benefits designed to make its employees' lives healthier, less complicated, and simply more fun. Beyond traditional medical, vacation, and retirement benefits, employees at Google's Mountain View, California headquarters can ride to work in a shuttle that serves the San Francisco area. Once at work, employees can:

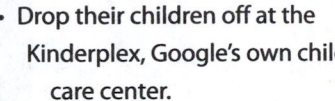

- Drop their children off at the Kinderplex, Google's own child care center.
- Eat a free lunch or dinner cooked by gourmet chefs.
- Visit a doctor or receive a massage.
- Have their laundry dry cleaned.
- Exercise in the gym.

Google is family friendly. New mothers receive 12 weeks of paid (75%) maternity leave. Fathers also receive between 2 and 6 weeks of parental leave. New parents are reimbursed for up to $500 for take-out meals during the first four weeks the new baby is home. Google also provides financial assistance to pay the legal and other fees in the adoption of a child.

From ski trips to parking-lot roller hockey, Google makes working fun.

Critical Thinking

1. Google has offices all over the world. Identify three services you would suggest any company offer that would uniquely serve employees living in your city or state.

2. Why do you think Google employees are offered financial planning classes?

Source: www.google.com

©JUSTIN SULLIVAN/GETTY IMAGES

DIGITAL VISION/GETTY IMAGES

INTERNET ACTIVITY

IRS Forms Online

(NOTE: You will need to have Adobe Acrobat Reader on your computer to complete this activity.)

The Internal Revenue Service (IRS) makes some tax forms available online. Go to the homepage for the IRS (www.irs.gov). Click on "Forms and Publications." A W-4 Form is the form you fill out for your employer when you are hired. A 1040EZ Form is the form you use to file your income tax return each year.

Instructions

1. Search the site for a W-4 Form. Print out the form.

2. Search the site for a 1040EZ Form. Print out the form.

3. List one additional form that is available on the IRS site.

Recording a Payroll

······ **DIFFERENT FORMS OF PAYROLL INFORMATION** ······

Payroll information for each pay period is recorded in a payroll register. Each pay period the payroll information for each employee is also recorded on each employee earnings record. Separate payroll accounts for each employee are not kept in the general ledger. Instead, accounts are kept in the general ledger to summarize total earnings and deductions for all employees.

The payroll register and employee earnings records provide all the payroll information needed to prepare payroll and payroll tax reports. Journal entries are made to record the payment of the payroll and the employer payroll taxes. In addition, various quarterly and annual payroll tax reports are required to report the payment of payroll taxes.

IMAGE SOURCE/GETTY IMAGES

CHARACTER COUNTS

Your Call May Be Recorded

Janice Whitehead has just been fired for violating her employer's code of conduct. Over the last few months, Janice has been using her office phone to call former classmates to inform them of an upcoming class reunion. She believes her firing is unethical and is considering legal action against the company.

Cobb Manufacturing has the following statement in its code of conduct:

"Company telephones are to be used exclusively for company business. Employees needing to make personal phone calls should use their personal cellular phones."

During an ethics training program, employees were informed that the company uses a pen register. The device creates a list of all outgoing calls and the length of each call. Janice signed a statement that she understood the company has a "no tolerance" approach toward topics discussed in the training program.

Instructions

Was it ethical for Cobb Manufacturing to fire Janice for making personal phone calls?

PHOTO: DIGITAL VISION/GETTY IMAGES

SEMIMONTHLY PERIOD ENDED December 15, 20--			PAYROLL REGISTER								DATE OF PAYMENT December 15, 20--		
				1	2	3	4	5	6	7	8	9	10
EMPL. NO.	EMPLOYEE'S NAME	MARITAL STATUS	NO. OF ALLOWANCES	EARNINGS			DEDUCTIONS					NET PAY	CHECK NO.
				REGULAR	OVERTIME	TOTAL	FEDERAL INCOME TAX	SOC. SEC. TAX	MEDICARE TAX	HEALTH INSURANCE	OTHER	TOTAL	
2	Aranda, Susan A.	M	2	968 00		968 00	38 00	60 02	14 04	45 00	B 10 00	167 06	800 94	482
5	Drew, Paul S.	S	1	550 00		550 00	32 00	34 10	7 98	38 00		112 08	437 92	483
1	Kellogg, Janice P.	M	1	1760 00	150 00	1910 00	187 00	118 42	27 70	38 00	UW 20 00	391 12	1518 88	484
6	Mendel, Ann M.	S	1	240 00		240 00		14 88	3 48			18 36	221 64	485
3	Selby, Rick E.	M	4	1056 00	81 00	1137 00	28 00	70 49	16 49	60 00	B 10 00 / UW 10 00	194 98	942 02	486
4	Young, Justin L.	S	1	906 40		906 40	86 00	56 20	13 14	38 00	B 15 00 / UW 10 00	218 34	688 06	487
	Totals			5480 40	231 00	5711 40	371 00	354 11	82 83	219 00	B 35 00 / UW 40 00	1101 94	4609 46	

Similar to a special journal, the column totals of a payroll register provide the debit and credit amounts needed to journalize a payroll.

As you will learn in this chapter, the payroll journal entry is based on the totals of the Earnings Total column, each deduction column, and the Net Pay column. The totals of the Earnings Regular, Earnings Overtime, and Deductions Total columns are not used to journalize the payroll.

FINANCIAL LITERACY

Taxes

An old saying goes, "Only two things are certain in life—death and taxes!" Depending on where you live, you may encounter a few or many different taxes. In the United States, there is a federal tax on the income you earn. Some states also impose a tax on personal income. Many states and some cities have a sales tax, but the list of taxable items varies greatly. Some states and cities charge a sales tax on nearly everything, while others may exclude specific items such as food, clothing, medical items, etc. If you own property, you may have to pay a state property tax and/or a city property tax.

The major purpose of most taxes is to provide funds for services supplied by the government such as schools, roadways, emergency services, water and sewer systems, public transportation systems, and public parks.

However, some taxes are designed to encourage us to behave in certain ways. If the United States government wants us to save more money, it can make certain payments to savings and investment accounts tax deductible, which means those amounts are not subject to tax. If the government wants to encourage home ownership, it can make interest on home mortgages tax deductible.

Activities

1. Using tables provided by the Internal Revenue Service for the most current year (which can be found on the Internet), determine how much federal income tax would be due from a single taxpayer with no additional deductions, who earned $26,000.

2. Write a report on your state's sales tax, including the amount of the tax and what items are subject to this tax. If your state does not have a sales tax, pick a neighboring state that has a sales tax.

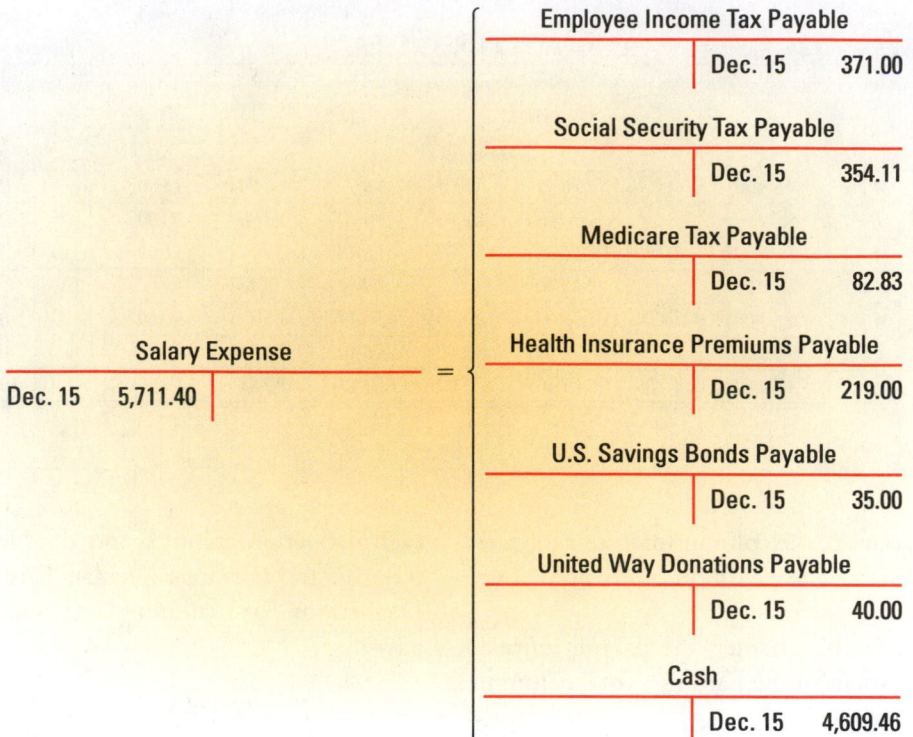

Data about Hobby Shack's semimonthly pay period ended December 15, obtained from the payroll register, are summarized in the T accounts.

The Total Earnings column total, $5,711.40, is the salary expense for the period. **Salary Expense** is debited for this amount.

The Federal Income Tax column total, $371.00, is the amount withheld from employee salaries for federal income tax. The amount withheld is a liability of the business until the taxes are sent to the federal government. **Employee Income Tax Payable** is credited for $371.00 to record this liability.

The Social Security Tax column total, $354.11, is the amount withheld for social security tax. The amount is a liability of the business until the tax is paid to the government. **Social Security Tax Payable** is credited for $354.11.

The Medicare Tax column total, $82.83, is the amount withheld for Medicare tax. The amount is a liability of the business until the tax is paid to the government. **Medicare Tax Payable** is credited for $82.83.

The Health Insurance column total, $219.00, is the amount withheld for health insurance premiums. The amount is a liability of the business until the premiums are paid to the insurance company. **Health Insurance Premiums Payable** is credited for $219.00 to record this liability.

Two types of Other deductions are recorded in Hobby Shack's payroll register. The $35.00 Other column total identified with the letter *B* is withheld to buy savings bonds for employees. The $40.00 total identified with the letters *UW* is withheld for employee United Way pledges. Until these amounts have been paid by the employer, they are liabilities of the business. **U.S. Savings Bonds Payable** is credited for $35.00. **United Way Donations Payable** is credited for $40.00.

The Net Pay column total, $4,609.46, is the net amount paid to employees. **Cash** is credited for $4,609.46. A check for the total net pay amount, $4,609.46, is written on Hobby Shack's general checking account and is deposited in a special payroll checking account. Individual payroll checks are then written on the special payroll checking account.

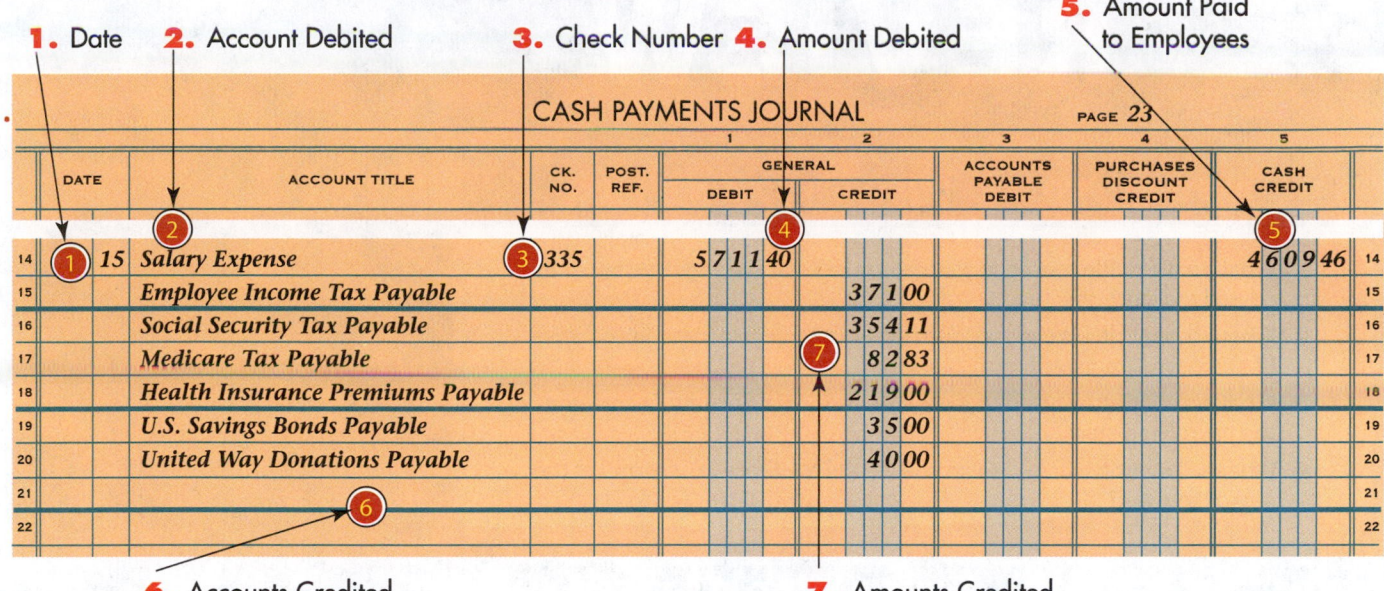

1. Date **2.** Account Debited **3.** Check Number **4.** Amount Debited **5.** Amount Paid to Employees

CASH PAYMENTS JOURNAL PAGE 23

	DATE	ACCOUNT TITLE	CK. NO.	POST. REF.	GENERAL DEBIT	GENERAL CREDIT	ACCOUNTS PAYABLE DEBIT	PURCHASES DISCOUNT CREDIT	CASH CREDIT	
14	15	Salary Expense	335		5 7 1 1 40				4 6 0 9 46	14
15		Employee Income Tax Payable				3 7 1 00				15
16		Social Security Tax Payable				3 5 4 11				16
17		Medicare Tax Payable				8 2 83				17
18		Health Insurance Premiums Payable				2 1 9 00				18
19		U.S. Savings Bonds Payable				3 5 00				19
20		United Way Donations Payable				4 0 00				20
21										21
22										22

6. Accounts Credited   **7.** Amounts Credited

Hobby Shack journalized the company's payroll for the semimonthly period ended December 15, 20--.

> December 15. Paid cash for semimonthly payroll, $4,609.46 (total payroll, $5,711.40, less deductions: employee income tax, $371.00; social security tax, $354.11; Medicare tax, $82.83; health insurance premiums, $219.00; U.S. Savings Bonds, $35.00; United Way donations, $40.00). Check No. 335.

Amounts recorded in the General columns of a cash payments journal are posted individually to general ledger accounts. The credit to Cash, *$4,609.46*, is not posted separately to the cash account. The amount is included in the journal's Cash Credit column total that is posted at the end of the month. The same procedures are followed to post this journal entry to the appropriate accounts as were described in Chapter 11.

STEPS JOURNALIZING PAYMENT OF A PAYROLL

1. Write the date, *15*, in the Date column.

2. Write the title of the account debited, *Salary Expense*, in the Account Title column.

3. Write the check number, *335*, in the Ck. No. column.

4. Write the amount debited to Salary Expense, *$5,711.40*, in the General Debit column.

5. On the same line, write the total amount paid to employees, *$4,609.46*, in the Cash Credit column.

6. On the next six lines, write the titles of the accounts credited, *Employee Income Tax Payable, Social Security Tax Payable, Medicare Tax Payable, Health Insurance Premiums Payable, U.S. Savings Bonds Payable*, and *United Way Donations Payable*, in the Account Title column.

7. On the same six lines, write the amounts credited to the corresponding liability accounts, *$371.00, $354.11, $82.83, $219.00, $35.00*, and *$40.00*, in the General Credit column.

REMEMBER

Total Earnings is the debit amount for Salary Expense. Net Pay is the credit amount for cash.

End of Lesson REVIEW

1. What account title is used to journalize the Total Earnings column of the payroll register?
2. What account title is used to journalize the Federal Income Tax column of the payroll register?
3. What account title is used to journalize the Social Security Tax column of the payroll register?
4. What account title is used to journalize the Medicare Tax column of the payroll register?

WORK TOGETHER 13-1

Recording a payroll

Metro Company's payroll register has the following totals for the semimonthly pay period, July 1–15 of the current year. T accounts and a cash payments journal page are provided in the *Working Papers*. Your instructor will guide you through the following examples.

Total Earnings	Federal Income Tax Withheld	Social Security Tax Withheld	Medicare Withheld
$12,600.00	$1,186.00	$781.20	$182.70

1. Use the T accounts provided to analyze Metro's July 1–15 payroll.
2. Journalize the payment of Metro's July 1–15 payroll on page 15 of the cash payments journal. The payroll was paid by Check No. 455 on July 15 of the current year.

ON YOUR OWN 13-1

Recording a payroll

Butler Company's payroll register has the following totals for the semimonthly pay period, August 16–31 of the current year. T accounts and a cash payments journal page are provided in the *Working Papers*. Work this problem independently.

Total Earnings	Federal Income Tax Withheld	Social Security Tax Withheld	Medicare Withheld
$14,260.00	$1,562.00	$884.12	$206.77

1. Use the T accounts provided to analyze Butler's August 16–31 payroll.
2. Journalize the payment of Butler's August 16–31 payroll on page 16 of a cash payments journal. The payroll was paid by Check No. 628 on August 31 of the current year.

Recording Employer Payroll Taxes

CALCULATING EMPLOYER PAYROLL TAXES

Employers must pay to the government the taxes withheld from employee earnings. Hobby Shack has withheld federal income tax, social security tax, and Medicare tax from employee salaries. The amounts withheld are liabilities to the business until they are actually paid to the government. In addition, employers must pay several of their own payroll taxes. Employer payroll taxes are business expenses.

Most employers must pay four separate payroll taxes. These taxes are (1) social security tax, (2) Medicare tax, (3) federal unemployment tax, and (4) state unemployment tax. Employer payroll taxes expense is based on a percentage of employee earnings.

Employer Social Security and Medicare Taxes

The social security and Medicare taxes are the only payroll taxes paid by both the employees and the employer. Hobby Shack withheld $354.11 in social security tax and $82.83 in Medicare tax from employee wages for the pay period ended December 15. Hobby Shack owes the same amount of social security and Medicare taxes as the amount withheld from employees. Therefore, Hobby Shack's social security and Medicare taxes for the pay period ended December 15 are also $354.11 and $82.83 respectively.

Congress sets the social security and Medicare tax rates for employees and employers. Periodically, Congress may change the tax rates and tax base. The social security tax rate and base used in this text are 6.2% of earnings up to a maximum of $87,000.00 in each calendar year. Medicare does not have a tax base. Therefore, Medicare tax is calculated on total employee earnings. The Medicare tax rate used in this text is 1.45% of total employee earnings.

REDCHOPSTICKS/GETTY IMAGES

REMEMBER

Employers must pay four taxes on employee earnings—social security tax, Medicare tax, federal unemployment tax, and state unemployment tax.

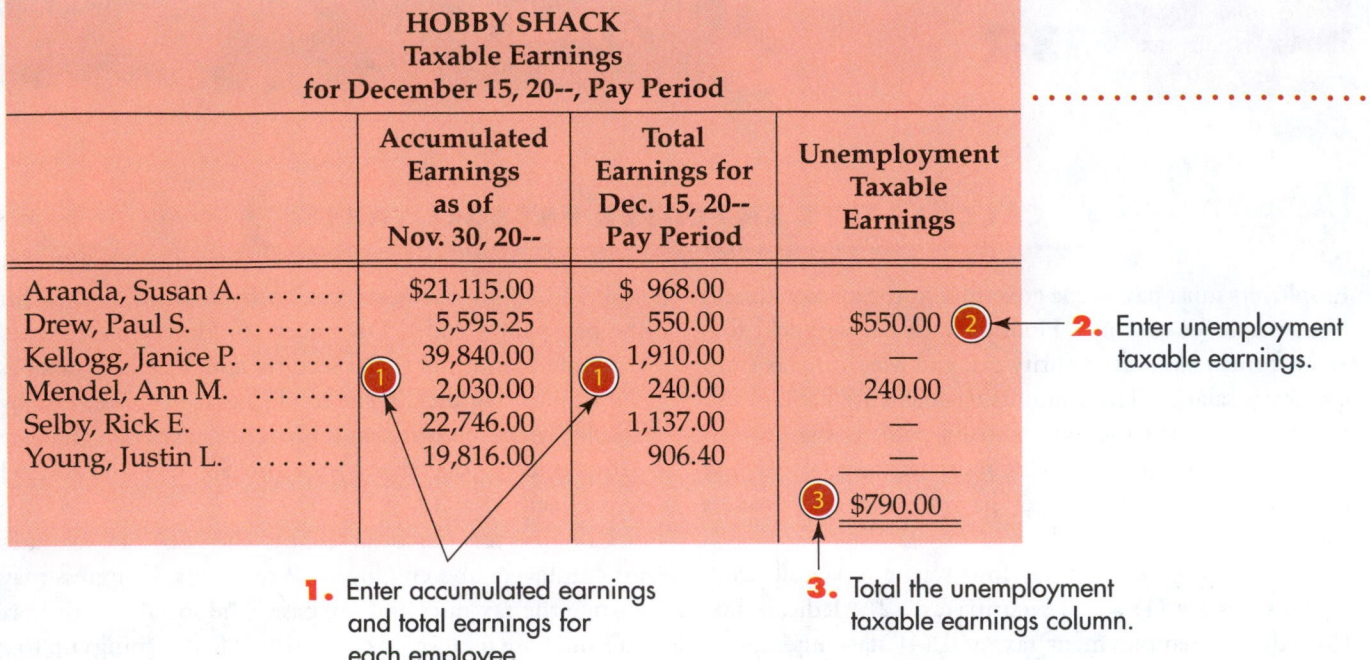

HOBBY SHACK
Taxable Earnings
for December 15, 20--, Pay Period

	Accumulated Earnings as of Nov. 30, 20--	Total Earnings for Dec. 15, 20-- Pay Period	Unemployment Taxable Earnings	
Aranda, Susan A.	$21,115.00	$ 968.00	—	
Drew, Paul S.	5,595.25	550.00	$550.00	2
Kellogg, Janice P.	39,840.00	1,910.00	—	
Mendel, Ann M.	2,030.00	240.00	240.00	
Selby, Rick E.	22,746.00	1,137.00	—	
Young, Justin L.	19,816.00	906.40	—	
			$790.00	3

2. Enter unemployment taxable earnings.

1. Enter accumulated earnings and total earnings for each employee.

3. Total the unemployment taxable earnings column.

Federal unemployment insurance laws require that employers pay taxes for unemployment compensation. These tax funds are used to pay workers' benefits for limited periods of unemployment and to administer the unemployment compensation program.

The total earnings subject to unemployment tax is referred to as *unemployment taxable earnings*. The unemployment tax is applied to the first $7,000.00 earned by each employee for each calendar year. The amount of unemployment taxable earnings for Hobby Shack's pay period ended December 15, 20--, is shown in the illustration.

STEPS **CALCULATING UNEMPLOYMENT TAXABLE EARNINGS**

1 For each employee, enter accumulated earnings as of November 30 and total earnings for the December 15 pay period. These amounts are taken from each employee earnings record. Rick E. Selby's accumulated earnings as of November 30, *$22,746.00*, are recorded in the first column. His total earnings for the December 15 pay period, *$1,137.00*, are recorded in the second column.

2 Enter unemployment taxable earnings for the pay period in the Unemployment Taxable Earnings column for employees whose accumulated earnings are less than $7,000.00. The November 30 accumulated earnings for Paul S. Drew, *$5,595.25*, plus the December 15 earnings, *$550.00*, equal $6,145.25 and are less than $7,000.00. Therefore, his total earnings for the December 15 pay period, *$550.00*, are subject to unemployment tax and are recorded in the Unemployment Taxable Earnings column. Since the accumulated earnings for Mr. Selby are greater than $7,000.00, none of his current earnings are subject to unemployment tax. Thus, the amount of unemployment taxable earnings recorded in the third column is zero, which is represented by a dash.

3 Total the Unemployment Taxable Earnings column. This total amount, *$790.00*, is used to calculate the unemployment tax.

Hobby Shack pays two unemployment taxes, federal unemployment tax and state unemployment tax.

Federal Unemployment Tax

A federal tax used for state and federal administrative expenses of the unemployment program is called **federal unemployment tax**. The federal unemployment tax is 6.2% of the first $7,000.00 earned by each employee. An employer generally can deduct from federal unemployment payments the amounts paid to state unemployment funds. This deduction cannot be more than 5.4% of taxable earnings. The effective federal unemployment tax rate in most states is, therefore, 0.8% on the first $7,000.00 earned by each employee. (Federal, 6.2% − deductible for state, 5.4% = 0.8%.) All of the unemployment tax on the first $7,000.00 of salary is paid by the employer.

Hobby Shack's federal unemployment tax for the pay period ended December 15, 20--, is calculated as shown.

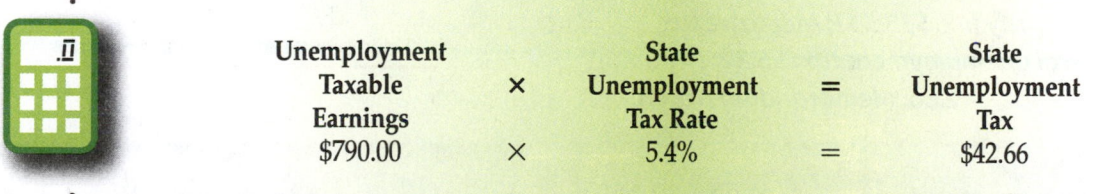

	Unemployment Taxable Earnings	×	Federal Unemployment Tax Rate	=	Federal Unemployment Tax
	$790.00	×	0.8%	=	$6.32

State Unemployment Tax

A state tax used to pay benefits to unemployed workers is called **state unemployment tax**. The Social Security Act specifies certain standards for unemployment compensation laws. Therefore, a high degree of uniformity exists in state unemployment laws. However, details of state unemployment laws do differ. Because of these differences, employers must know the requirements of the states in which they operate.

Many states require that employers pay unemployment tax of 5.4% on the first $7,000.00 earned by each employee. The unemployment taxable earnings used to calculate the federal unemployment tax are also used to calculate the state unemployment tax. Hobby Shack's state unemployment tax for the pay period ended December 15, 20--, is calculated as shown.

	Unemployment Taxable Earnings	×	State Unemployment Tax Rate	=	State Unemployment Tax
	$790.00	×	5.4%	=	$42.66

DIGITAL VISION/GETTY IMAGES

1. Date   **2.** Account Debited   **3.** Memorandum Number   **4.** Amount Debited

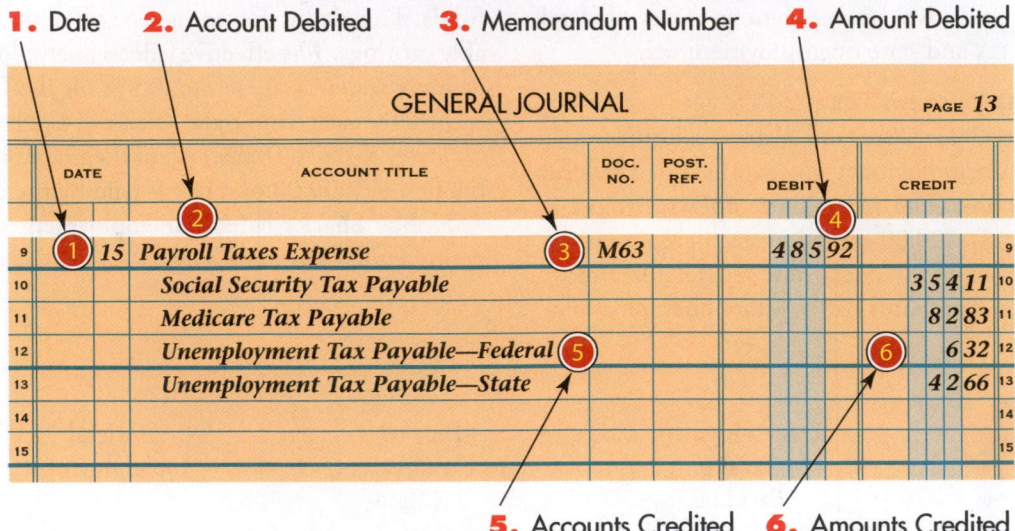

5. Accounts Credited   **6.** Amounts Credited

Employer payroll taxes are paid to the government at a later date. However, the liability is incurred when salaries are paid. Therefore, the transaction to record employer payroll taxes expense is journalized on the same date the payroll is journalized. The salary expense and the employer payroll taxes expense are, therefore, both recorded in the same accounting period.

> *December 15. Recorded employer payroll taxes expense, $485.92, for the semimonthly pay period ended December 15. Taxes owed are: social security tax, $354.11; Medicare tax, $82.83; federal unemployment tax, $6.32; state unemployment tax, $42.66. Memorandum No. 63.*

Payroll Taxes Expense is debited for $485.92 to show the increase in the balance of this expense account. Four liability accounts are credited to show the increase in payroll tax liabilities.

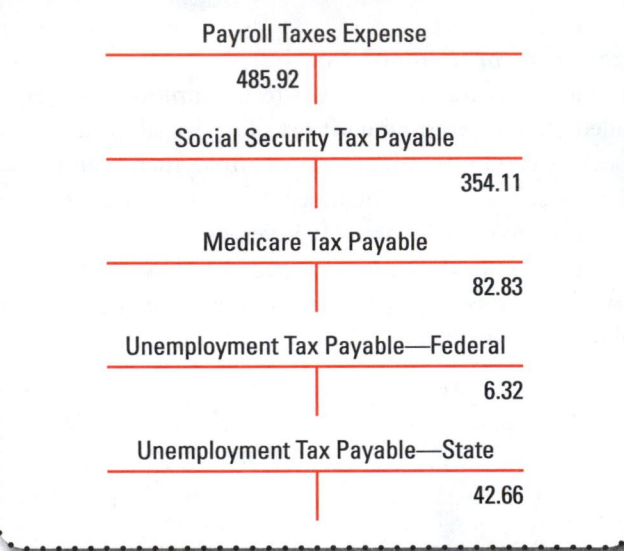

Amounts recorded in the general journal are posted individually to general ledger accounts. The same procedures are followed to post this journal entry to the appropriate accounts as were described in Chapter 11.

STEPS ⬢ **JOURNALIZING EMPLOYER PAYROLL TAXES**

1. Write the date, *15*, in the Date column.

2. Write the title of the expense account debited, *Payroll Taxes Expense*, in the Account Title column.

3. Write the memorandum number, *M63*, in the Doc. No. column.

4. Write the debit amount, *$485.92*, in the Debit column.

5. Write the titles of the liability accounts credited, *Social Security Tax Payable, Medicare Tax Payable, Unemployment Tax Payable—Federal,* and *Unemployment Tax Payable—State,* on the next four lines of the Account Title column, indented about 1 centimeter.

6. Write the credit amounts, *$354.11, $82.83, $6.32,* and *$42.66,* respectively, in the Credit column.

TERMS REVIEW

federal unemployment tax

state unemployment tax

1. What is the tax rate Hobby Shack must pay on employees for each of the following taxes: social security, Medicare, federal unemployment, and state unemployment?

2. What is the amount of each employee's earnings that is subject to federal and state unemployment taxes at Hobby Shack?

WORK TOGETHER 13-2

Recording employer payroll taxes

Payroll information taken from employee earnings records is given below. A form and general journal page are provided in the *Working Papers*. Your instructor will guide you through the following examples.

Employee Name	Accumulated Earnings, April 30	Total Earnings for May 1–15 Pay Period
Beltran, Tamela C.	$5,100.00	$637.50
Cintron, Irma V.	7,350.00	920.00

1. Calculate the amount of earnings subject to unemployment taxes. Unemployment taxes are owed on the first $7,000.00 of earnings for each employee.

2. Calculate the amount of employer payroll taxes owed for the May 1–15 pay period. Use the employer payroll tax rates shown in this chapter.

3. Journalize the employer's payroll taxes for the May 1–15 pay period on May 15 of the current year. Use general journal page 10 and Memorandum No. 46.

ON YOUR OWN 13-2

Recording employer payroll taxes

Payroll information taken from employee earnings records is given below. A form and general journal page are provided in the *Working Papers*. Work this problem independently.

Employee Name	Accumulated Earnings, May 31	Total Earnings for June 1–15 Pay Period
Caldwell, Sarah H.	$6,020.00	$ 580.00
Easley, Benjamin P.	5,450.00	620.00
Franks, John J.	8,420.00	1,000.00

1. Calculate the amount of earnings subject to unemployment taxes. Unemployment taxes are owed on the first $7,000.00 of earnings for each employee.

2. Calculate the amount of employer payroll taxes owed for the June 1–15 pay period. Use the employer payroll tax rates shown in this chapter.

3. Journalize the employer's payroll taxes for the June 1–15 pay period on June 15 of the current year. Use general journal page 12 and Memorandum No. 83.

a Control number	22222	Void ☐	For Official Use Only ▶ OMB No. 1545-0008	

b Employer identification number 31-0429632	1 Wages, tips, other compensation 24,843.00	2 Federal income tax withheld 648.00
c Employer's name, address, and ZIP code	3 Social security wages 24,843.00	4 Social security tax withheld 1,540.27
Hobby Shack, Inc. 1420 College Plaza	5 Medicare wages and tips 24,843.00	6 Medicare tax withheld 360.22
Atlanta, GA 30337-1726	7 Social security tips	8 Allocated tips
d Employee's social security number 450-70-6432	9 Advance EIC payment	10 Dependent care benefits

e Employee's first name and initial Rick E.	Last name Selby	11 Nonqualified plans	12a See instructions for box 12
		13 Statutory employee ☐ Retirement plan ☐ Third-party sick pay ☐	12b
1625 Northland Drive		14 Other	12c
Clarkdale, GA 30020-6523			12d
f Employee's address and ZIP code			

15 State Employer's state ID number	16 State wages, tips, etc.	17 State income tax	18 Local wages, tips, etc.	19 Local income tax	20 Locality name

Form **W-2** Wage and Tax Statement

20 - -

Department of the Treasury—Internal Revenue Service

Copy A For Social Security Administration — Send this entire page with Form W-3 to the Social Security Administration; photocopies are **not** acceptable.

Cat. No. 10134D

For Privacy Act and Paperwork Reduction Act Notice, see back of Copy D.

Each employer who withholds income tax, social security tax, and Medicare tax from employee earnings must furnish each employee with an annual report of these withholdings. The report shows total year's earnings and the amounts withheld for taxes for an employee. These amounts are obtained from the employee earnings records. The report is prepared on the Internal Revenue Service Form W-2, Wage and Tax Statement. The Form W-2 prepared by Hobby Shack for Rick E. Selby is shown.

Employers are required to furnish Form W-2 to each employee by January 31 of the next year. If an employee ends employment before December 31, Form W-2 must be furnished within 30 days of the last date of employment.

Four copies (A to D) of Form W-2 are prepared for each employee. Copies B and C are given to the employee. The employee attaches Copy B to a personal federal income tax return and keeps Copy C for a personal record. The employer sends Copy A to the Social Security Administration and keeps Copy D for the business's records.

Businesses in states with state income tax must prepare additional copies of Form W-2. The employee attaches the additional copy to the personal state income tax return.

1. Heading

Form 941
(Rev. January 2004)
Department of the Treasury
Internal Revenue Service (99)

Employer's Quarterly Federal Tax Return

▶ See separate instructions revised January 2004 for information on completing this return.

Please type or print.

Enter state code for state in which deposits were made **only** if different from state in address to the right ▶ [ ] (see page 2 of separate instructions).

1

Name (as distinguished from trade name)
Hobby Shack, Inc.
Trade name, if any

Address (number and street)
1420 College Plaza

Date quarter ended
December 31, 20--
Employer identification number
31-0429632
City, state, and ZIP code
Atlanta GA
30337-1726

OMB No. 1545-0029

T	
FF	
FD	
FP	
I	
T	

If address is different from prior return, check here ▶ [ ]

IRS Use

1 1 1 1 1 1 1 1 1 1   2   3 3 3 3 3 3   4 4 4   5 5 5

6   7   8 8 8 8 8 8 8   9 9 9 9   10 10 10 10 10 10 10 10 10

2. Number of Employees

3. Total Quarterly Earnings

4. Income Tax Withheld

A If you **do not have to file** returns in the future, check here ▶ [ ] and enter date final wages paid ▶

B If you are a seasonal employer, see **Seasonal employers** on page 1 of the instructions and check here ▶ [ ]

1	Number of employees in the pay period that includes March 12th ▶	1	6
2	Total wages and tips, plus other compensation (see separate instructions)	2	3 2 , 9 8 0 00
3	Total income tax withheld from wages, tips, and sick pay	3	2 , 1 6 8 00
4	Adjustment of withheld income tax for preceding quarters of **this calendar year**	4	– 0 –
5	Adjusted total of income tax withheld (line 3 as adjusted by line 4)	5	2 , 1 6 8 00
6	Taxable social security wages 6a	3 2 , 9 8 0 00 × 12.4% (.124) =	6b	4 , 0 8 9 52
	Taxable social security tips 6c	– 0 – × 12.4% (.124) =	6d	– 0 –
7	Taxable Medicare wages and tips . . . 7a	3 2 , 9 8 0 00 × 2.9% (.029) =	7b	9 5 6 42
8	Total social security and Medicare taxes (add lines 6b, 6d, and 7b). **Check here if wages are not subject to social security and/or Medicare tax** . . . . ▶ [ ]	8	5 , 0 4 5 94
9	Adjustment of social security and Medicare taxes (see instructions for required explanation) Sick Pay $ _____ ± Fractions of Cents $ _____ ± Other $ _____ =	9	– 0 –
10	Adjusted total of social security and Medicare taxes (line 8 as adjusted by line 9) . . .	10	5 , 0 4 5 94
11	**Total taxes** (add lines 5 and 10)	11	7 , 2 1 3 94
12	Advance earned income credit (EIC) payments made to employees (see instructions) .	12	– 0 –
13	Net taxes (subtract line 12 from line 11). **If $2,500 or more, this must equal line 17, column (d) below (or line D of Schedule B (Form 941))**	13	7 , 2 1 3 94
14	Total deposits for quarter, including overpayment applied from a prior quarter	14	7 , 2 1 3 94
15	**Balance due** (subtract line 14 from line 13). See instructions	15	– 0 –
16	**Overpayment.** If line 14 is more than line 13, enter excess here ▶ $ _____ and check if to be: [ ] Applied to next return **or** [ ] Refunded.		

5. Employee and Employer Social Security and Medicare Taxes

6. Total Social Security plus Medicare Taxes

7. Total Taxes

• **All filers:** If line 13 is less than $2,500, **do not** complete line 17 or Schedule B (Form 941).

• **Semiweekly schedule depositors:** Complete Schedule B (Form 941) and check here . . . . ▶ [ ]

• **Monthly schedule depositors:** Complete line 17, columns (a) through (d), and check here. . . . . ▶ [X]

17	Monthly Summary of Federal Tax Liability. (Complete **Schedule B (Form 941)** instead, if you were a semiweekly schedule depositor.)			
	(a) First month liability	**(b)** Second month liability	**(c)** Third month liability	**(d)** Total liability for quarter
	2,271.44	2,394.70	2,547.80	7,213.94

9. Total Taxes

Third Party Designee

Do you want to allow another person to discuss this return with the IRS (see separate instructions)? [ ] **Yes.** Complete the following. [ ] **No**

Designee's name ▶
Phone no. ▶ ( )
Personal identification number (PIN) ▶

Sign Here

Under penalties of perjury, I declare that I have examined this return, including accompanying schedules and statements, and to the best of my knowledge and belief, it is true, correct, and complete.

Signature ▶ *Janice Kellogg*
Print Your Name and Title ▶ Janice Kellogg, Manager
Date ▶ 1/24/--

For Privacy Act and Paperwork Reduction Act Notice, see back of Payment Voucher.
Cat. No. 17001Z
Form **941** (Rev. 1-2004)

8. Total Taxes for Each Month

Each employer is required by law to periodically report the payroll taxes withheld from employee salaries and the employer payroll taxes due the government. Some reports are submitted quarterly and others, annually.

Each employer must file a quarterly federal tax return showing the federal income tax, social security tax, and Medicare tax due the government. This information is submitted every three months on Form 941, Employer's Quarterly Federal Tax Return. Form 941 is filed before the last day of the month following the end of a calendar quarter. Hobby Shack's Form 941 for the quarter ended December 31 is shown on the previous page. The information needed to prepare Form 941 is obtained from employee earnings records.

STEPS — PREPARING AN EMPLOYER'S QUARTERLY FEDERAL TAX RETURN

1 Enter the company name, address, employer identification number, and the date the quarter ended in the heading section of Form 941.

2 Enter the number of employees, *6*, on line 1.

3 Enter total quarterly earnings, *$32,980.00*, on line 2. This amount is the sum of the fourth quarter total earnings of all employees. Total earnings, *$32,980.00*, is also recorded on lines 6a and 7a.

4 Enter the income tax withheld, *$2,168.00*, on line 3. The amount is the total of the fourth quarter federal income tax withheld from all employees. The same amount is entered on line 5.

5 Enter the quarterly employee and employer social security taxes, *$4,089.52*, and Medicare taxes, *$956.42*, on lines 6b and 7b, respectively. The taxes due are calculated as shown.

	Total Earnings	×	Tax Rate	=	Tax
Social Security	$32,980.00	×	12.4%	=	$4,089.52
Medicare	$32,980.00	×	2.9%	=	$ 956.42

The 12.4% tax rate is the sum of the employee 6.2% and the employer 6.2% social security tax rates. The 2.9% tax rate is the sum of the employee 1.45% and the employer 1.45% Medicare tax rates.

6 Enter the total social security tax plus Medicare tax, *$5,045.94* ($4,089.52 + $956.42 = $5,045.94), on line 8. Since Hobby Shack has no adjustment to its taxes, the total is also entered on line 10.

7 Enter the total taxes, *$7,213.94*, on lines 11 and 13. Hobby Shack is required to pay the federal government the sum of the federal income tax withheld and the employee and employer's shares of the social security tax and Medicare tax.

8 Enter on lines 17a, 17b, and 17c the total amounts of employee income tax withheld and employee and employer social security and Medicare taxes for each month of the quarter. For the month of December, the amount of taxes owed is calculated as shown and recorded on line 17c.

	Federal Income Tax Withheld	+	Employee Social Security and Medicare Tax	+	Employer Social Security and Medicare Tax	=	Federal Tax Liability
Dec. 1–15	$371.00	+	$436.94	+	$436.94	=	$1,244.88
Dec. 16–31	$386.00	+	$458.46	+	$458.46	=	$1,302.92
Totals	$757.00	+	$895.40	+	$895.40	=	$2,547.80

9 Enter the total quarterly withholding and payroll taxes, *$7,213.94*, on line 17d. This total is the sum of the three monthly totals reported on line 17 ($2,271.44 + $2,394.70 + $2,547.80 = $7,213.94).

DO NOT STAPLE OR FOLD

a Control number	33333	For Official Use Only ▶ OMB No. 1545-0008		

b Kind of Payer ▶	941 [X] Military [ ] 943 [ ] CT-1 [ ] Hshld. emp. [ ] Medicare govt. emp. [ ] Third-party sick pay [ ]	1 Wages, tips, other compensation 104,525.00	2 Federal income tax withheld 6,790.00
		3 Social security wages 104,525.00	4 Social security tax withheld 6,480.55
c Total number of Forms W-2	d Establishment number	5 Medicare wages and tips 104,525.00	6 Medicare tax withheld 1,515.61
e Employer identification number 31-0429632		7 Social security tips	8 Allocated tips
f Employer's name Hobby Shack, Inc. 1420 College Plaza Atlanta, GA 30337-1726		9 Advance EIC payments	10 Dependent care benefits
		11 Nonqualified plans	12 Deferred compensation
		13 For third-party sick pay use only	
		14 Income tax withheld by payer of third-party sick pay	
g Employer's address and ZIP code			
h Other EIN used this year			
15 State Employer's state ID number		16 State wages, tips, etc.	17 State income tax
		18 Local wages, tips, etc.	19 Local income tax
Contact person Janice Kellogg		Telephone number (404) 555-9368	For Official Use Only
Email address jkellogg@hobbyshack.com		Fax number ( )	

Under penalties of perjury, I declare that I have examined this return and accompanying documents, and, to the best of my knowledge and belief, they are true, correct, and complete.

Signature ▶ *Janice Kellogg*   Title ▶ *Manager*   Date ▶ *2/27/--*

Form **W-3** Transmittal of Wage and Tax Statements   **20 --**   Department of the Treasury Internal Revenue Service

Send this entire page with the entire Copy A page of Form(s) W-2 to the Social Security Administration. Photocopies are not acceptable.

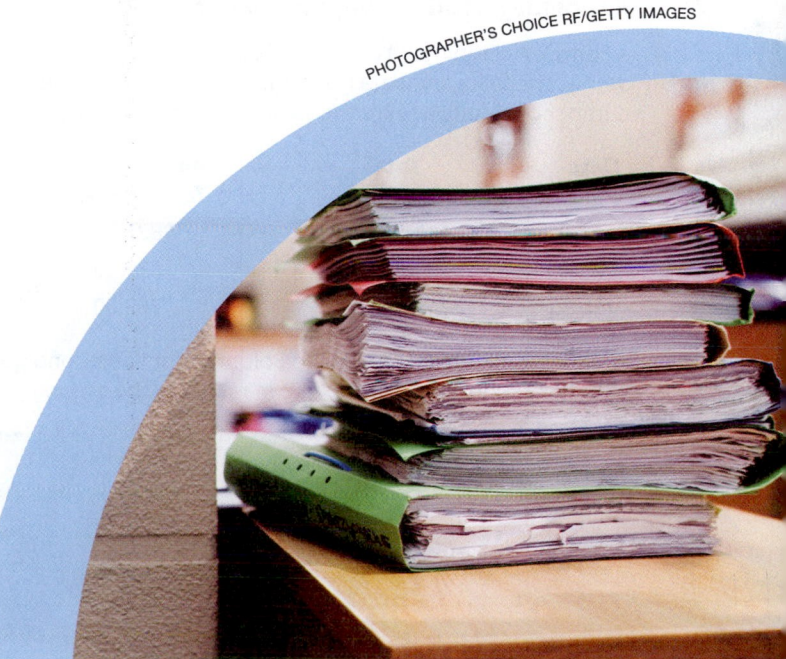

Form W-3, Transmittal of Wage and Tax Statements, is sent to the Social Security Administration by February 28 each year. Form W-3 reports the previous year's earnings and payroll taxes withheld for all employees. Attached to Form W-3 is Copy A of each employee Form W-2. Employers with more than 250 employees must send the information to the Internal Revenue Service in computer files rather than the actual Forms W-2 and W-3.

At the end of a calendar year, employers must also report to the federal and state governments a summary of all earnings paid to employees during the twelve months.

End of Lesson
REVIEW

1. When must employers furnish a W-2 statement to their employees?
2. What taxes are included in the quarterly federal tax return filed by the employer?

WORK TOGETHER 13-3

Reporting withholding and payroll taxes

A Form 941, Employer's Quarterly Federal Tax Return, is given in the *Working Papers*. Your instructor will guide you through the following example. The following data is for Audio Solutions.

Date Paid	Total Earnings	Federal Income Tax Withheld	Employee Social Security Tax Withheld	Employee Medicare Tax Withheld
Jan. 31	$10,440.00	$731.00	$647.28	$151.38
Feb. 28	10,960.00	767.00	679.52	158.92
Mar. 31	12,400.00	868.00	768.80	179.80

a. Company address: 625 Sandpiper Street, Ormond Beach, Florida 32074-4060

b. Employer identification number: 70-7818356

c. Number of employees: 6

1. Prepare a Form 941 for Audio Solutions for the first quarter of the current year. Use the preparation date of April 24. Sign your name as the manager of the company.

ON YOUR OWN 13-3

Reporting withholding and payroll taxes

A Form 941, Employer's Quarterly Federal Tax Return, is given in the *Working Papers*. Work this problem independently. The following data is for Audio Solutions. The company address, employer identification number, and number of employees are the same as in Work Together 13-3.

Date Paid	Total Earnings	Federal Income Tax Withheld	Employee Social Security Tax Withheld	Employee Medicare Tax Withheld
Apr. 30	$11,760.00	$823.00	$729.12	$170.52
May 31	11,820.00	827.00	732.84	171.39
June 30	10,900.00	763.00	675.80	158.05

1. Prepare a Form 941 for Audio Solutions for the second quarter of the current year. Use the preparation date of July 22. Sign your name as the manager of the company.

Paying Withholding and Payroll Taxes

PAYING THE LIABILITY FOR EMPLOYEE INCOME TAX, SOCIAL SECURITY TAX, AND MEDICARE TAX

Employers must pay to the federal, state, and local governments all payroll taxes withheld from employee earnings as well as the employer payroll taxes. The payment of payroll taxes with the government is referred to as a *deposit*. Two amounts determine how often deposits are made to the federal government: (1) the amount of payroll taxes collected during the current deposit period and (2) the amount of payroll taxes owed during a prior 12-month period. The 12-month period that ends on June 30th of the prior year is called the lookback period. The Internal Revenue Service provides businesses with the following flowchart to assist them in determining when to make tax deposits.

When to Deposit Form 941 Employment Taxes

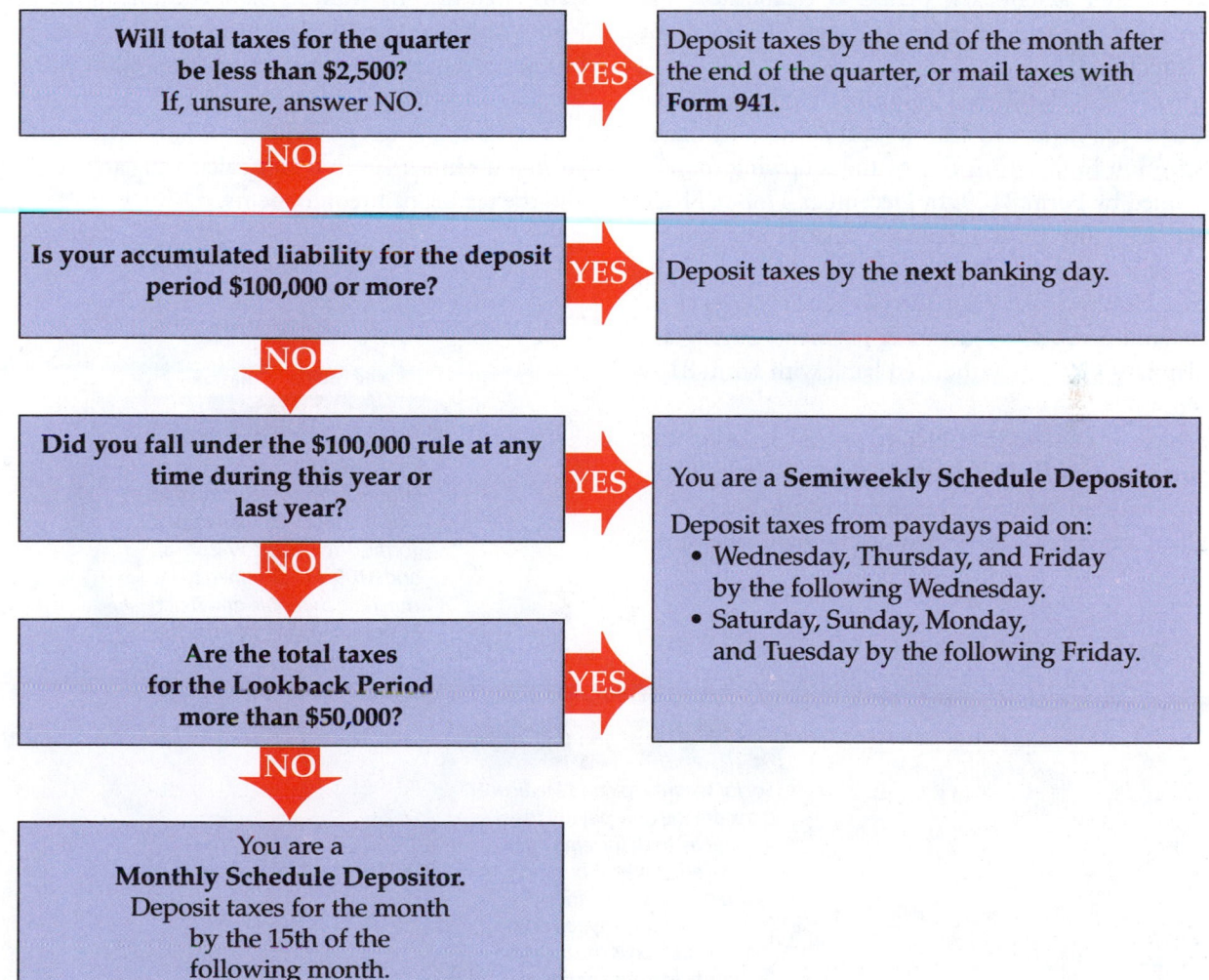

Will total taxes for the quarter be less than $2,500? If, unsure, answer NO.	**YES**	Deposit taxes by the end of the month after the end of the quarter, or mail taxes with **Form 941.**

NO

Is your accumulated liability for the deposit period $100,000 or more?	**YES**	Deposit taxes by the **next** banking day.

NO

Did you fall under the $100,000 rule at any time during this year or last year?	**YES**	You are a **Semiweekly Schedule Depositor.** Deposit taxes from paydays paid on: • Wednesday, Thursday, and Friday by the following Wednesday. • Saturday, Sunday, Monday, and Tuesday by the following Friday.

NO

Are the total taxes for the Lookback Period more than $50,000?	**YES**	

NO

You are a
Monthly Schedule Depositor.
Deposit taxes for the month
by the 15th of the
following month.

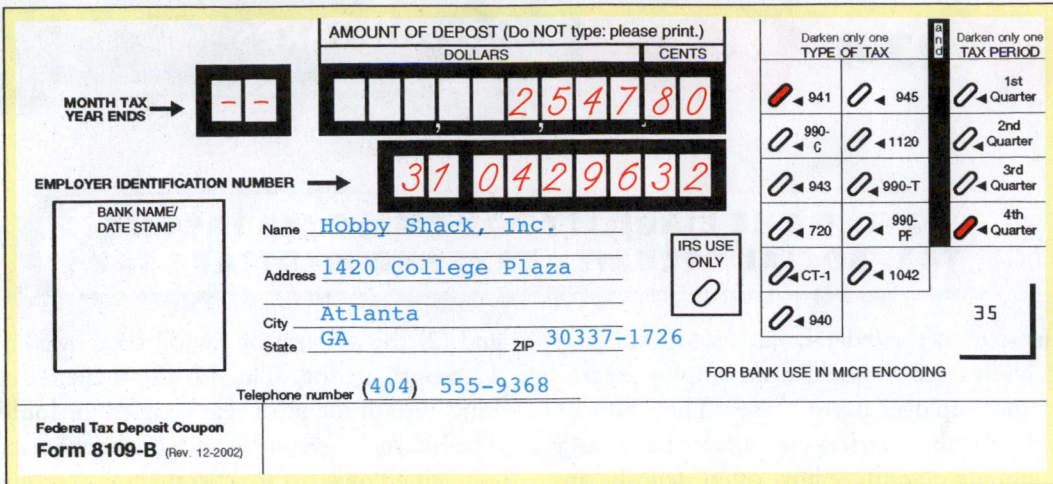

New employers are monthly schedule depositors for the first calendar year of business. The Internal Revenue Service issues a monthly Form 8109 coupon book to new employers. After a lookback period is established, the business must evaluate whether a change in its deposit period is required.

Hobby Shack is classified as a monthly depositor. So, the payroll taxes are deposited with a local authorized financial institution by the 15th day of the following month, accompanied by Form 8109. In December, Hobby Shack withheld $757.00 from employee salaries for federal income taxes and $895.40 for social security and Medicare taxes. Hobby Shack must also pay the employer share of the payroll taxes. The federal tax payment, $2,547.80, is sent January 15 to an authorized bank with Form 8109 as shown.

The type of tax—federal income, social security, and Medicare—is identified by marking the 941 circle. These taxes are reported to the government using Form 941. The calendar quarter is identified on the right side of the form.

Deposits can also be made using the Electronic Federal Tax Payment System (EFTPS). Using either a personal computer or telephone, the business can have the deposit transferred directly from its bank account to the government. Although any business can enroll in the EFTPS, businesses having deposits of more than $200,000 during the past calendar year must use the EFTPS.

Tax rules change periodically. Always check the most current tax information before calculating any tax amount and the tax deposit requirements.

FOR YOUR INFORMATION

FYI

Some federal tax forms can be printed from copies available on the Internet. Other tax forms, such as the W-2, W-3, and 8109, are designed to be machine readable and must be obtained directly from the Internal Revenue Service.

REMEMBER

Social security tax and Medicare tax are the only payroll taxes paid by both the employer and employee. A business pays the same amount of social security tax and Medicare tax as the amount withheld from employees.

JOURNALIZING PAYMENT OF LIABILITY FOR EMPLOYEE INCOME TAX, SOCIAL SECURITY TAX, AND MEDICARE TAX

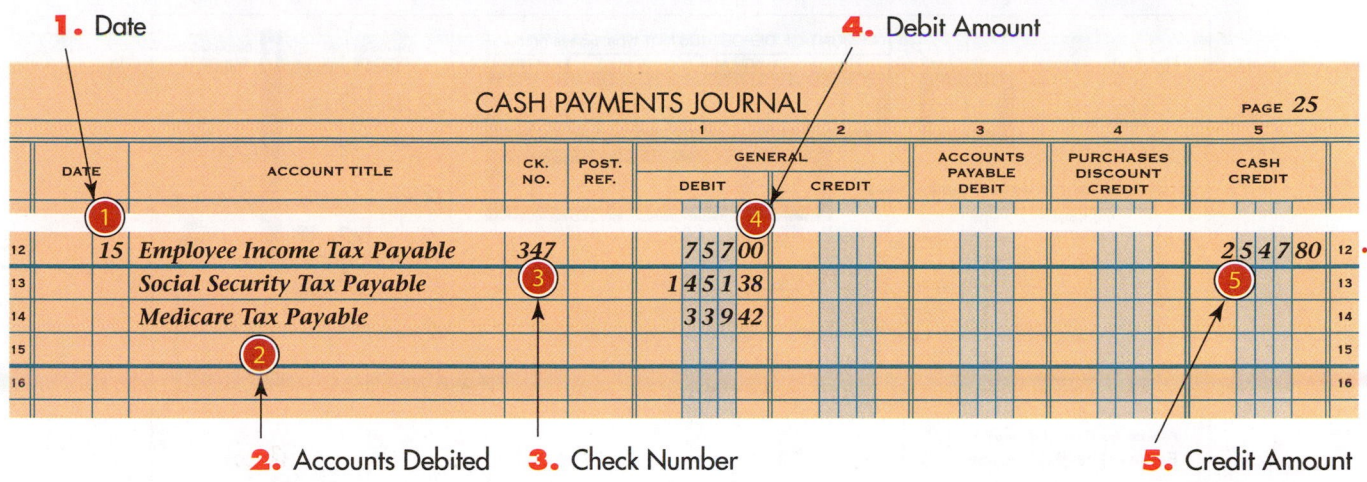

1. Date   **4.** Debit Amount

	DATE	ACCOUNT TITLE	CK. NO.	POST. REF.	GENERAL DEBIT	GENERAL CREDIT	ACCOUNTS PAYABLE DEBIT	PURCHASES DISCOUNT CREDIT	CASH CREDIT	
12	15	Employee Income Tax Payable	347		757 00				2 5 4 7 80	12
13		Social Security Tax Payable			1 4 5 1 38					13
14		Medicare Tax Payable			3 3 9 42					14
15										15
16										16

2. Accounts Debited   **3.** Check Number   **5.** Credit Amount

---

January 15. Paid cash for liability for employee income tax, $757.00; social security tax, $1,451.38; and Medicare tax, $339.42; total, $2,547.80. Check No. 347.

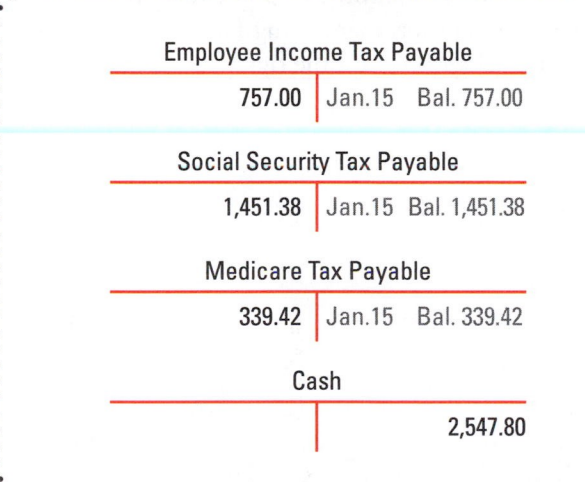

Employee Income Tax Payable	
757.00	Jan.15 Bal. 757.00

Social Security Tax Payable	
1,451.38	Jan.15 Bal. 1,451.38

Medicare Tax Payable	
339.42	Jan.15 Bal. 339.42

Cash	
	2,547.80

The balances of the liability accounts are reduced by this transaction. Therefore, Employee Income Tax Payable is debited for $757.00. Social Security Tax Payable is debited for $1,451.38. Medicare Tax Payable is debited for $339.42. The balance of Cash is decreased by a credit for the total payment, $2,547.80.

STEPS

JOURNALIZING A PAYMENT OF LIABILITY FOR EMPLOYEE INCOME TAX, SOCIAL SECURITY TAX, AND MEDICARE TAX

① Write the date, *15*, in the Date column.

② Write the titles of the three accounts debited, *Employee Income Tax Payable, Social Security Tax Payable*, and *Medicare Tax Payable*, in the Account Title column.

③ Write the check number, *347*, in the Ck. No. column.

④ Write the three debit amounts, *$757.00, $1,451.38*, and *$339.42*, in the General Debit column.

⑤ Write the amount of the credit to *Cash, $2,547.80*, in the Cash Credit column.

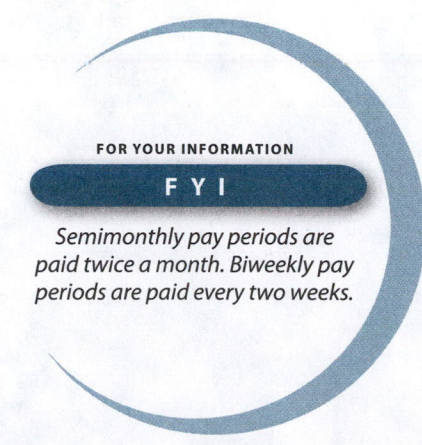

FOR YOUR INFORMATION

FYI

Semimonthly pay periods are paid twice a month. Biweekly pay periods are paid every two weeks.

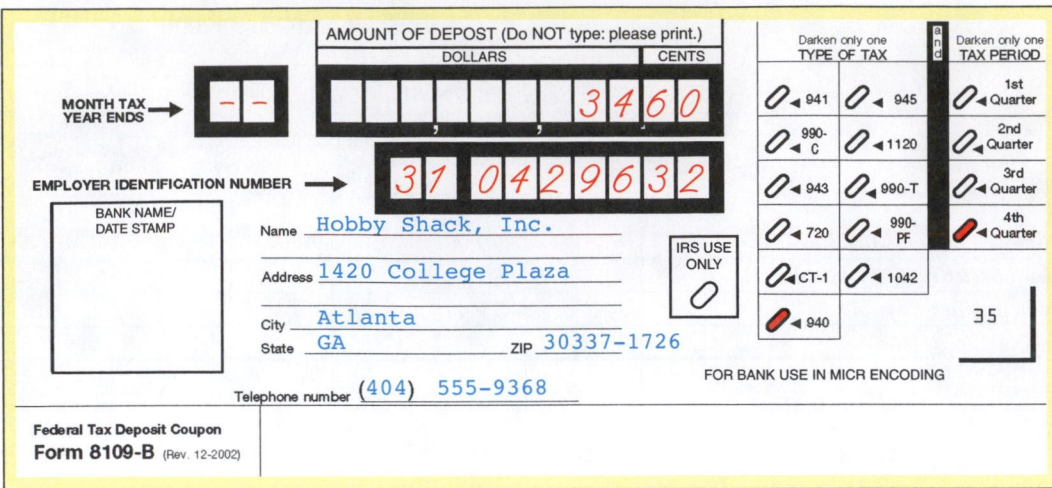

Federal unemployment insurance is paid by the end of the month following each quarter if the liability amount is more than $100. However, all unemployment tax liabilities outstanding at the end of a calendar year should be paid. Federal unemployment tax is paid to the federal government by making a tax deposit with an authorized bank. The deposit for federal unemployment tax is similar to the deposit required for income tax, social security tax, and Medicare tax. Form 8109, Federal Tax Deposit Coupon accompanies the unemployment tax deposit.

The total of federal unemployment taxes paid during a calendar year is reported on Form 940. Hobby Shack's federal unemployment tax liability at the end of December 31 is $34.60. Hobby Shack's Form 8109 for the fourth quarter is shown. The type of tax, federal unemployment tax, is identified by marking the 940 circle since this tax is reported to the government using Form 940. The calendar quarter is identified on the right side of the form.

JOURNALIZING PAYMENT OF LIABILITY FOR FEDERAL UNEMPLOYMENT TAX

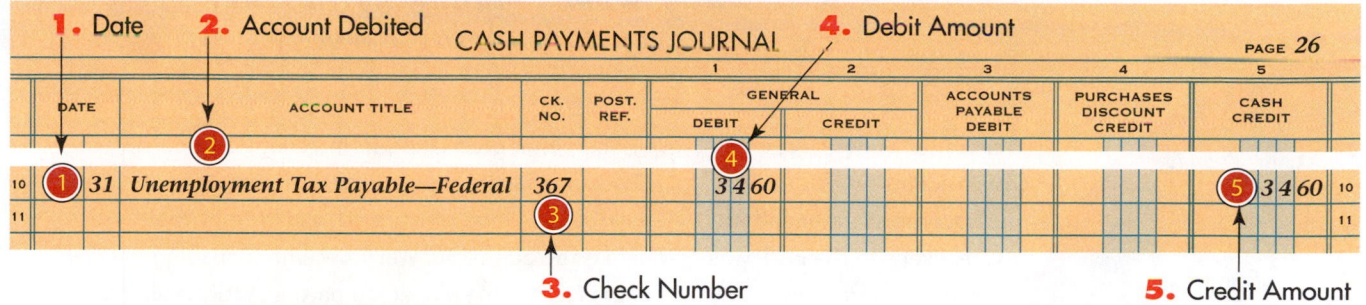

1. Date **2.** Account Debited **4.** Debit Amount

3. Check Number **5.** Credit Amount

January 31. Paid cash for federal unemployment tax liability for quarter ended December 31, $34.60. Check No. 367.

The balance of the liability account is reduced by this transaction. Therefore, Unemployment Tax Payable—Federal is debited for $34.60. The balance of the asset account, Cash, is decreased by a credit for the payment, $34.60.

Unemployment Tax Payable—Federal	
34.60	Jan. 31 Bal. 34.60

Cash	
	34.60

STEPS **JOURNALIZING A PAYMENT OF LIABILITY FOR FEDERAL UNEMPLOYMENT TAX**

1. Write the date, *31*, in the Date column.

2. Write the title of the account debited, *Unemployment Tax Payable—Federal*, in the Account Title column.

3. Write the check number, *367*, in the Ck. No. column.

4. Write the debit amount, *$34.60*, in the General Debit column.

5. Write the amount of the credit to Cash, *$34.60*, in the Cash Credit column.

JOURNALIZING PAYMENT OF LIABILITY FOR STATE UNEMPLOYMENT TAX

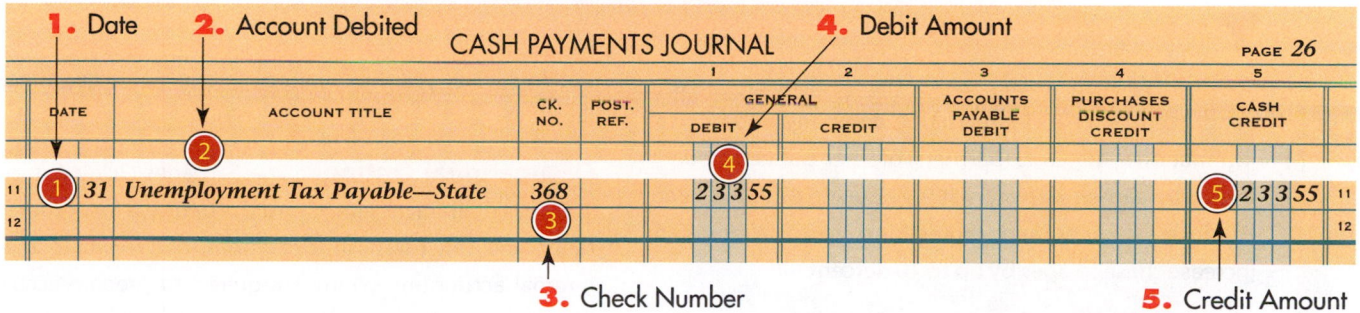

1. Date **2.** Account Debited **4.** Debit Amount

3. Check Number **5.** Credit Amount

The same steps are followed as for federal unemployment tax. State requirements for reporting and paying state unemployment taxes vary. In general, employers are required to pay the state unemployment tax during the month following each calendar quarter.

January 31. Paid cash for state unemployment tax liability for quarter ended December 31, $233.55. Check No. 368.

CAREERS IN ACCOUNTING

Wally Wood, Managing Partner of Accounting Firm

COURTESY OF WALLY WOOD

Stop a farmer as he harvests his crop. Ask him how he decided to become a farmer and you are likely to hear, "I was born to be a farmer. My grandfather started this farm. My father worked this farm. I've never thought of doing anything else."

Likewise, Wally Wood was born into the accounting profession. Wally began working part-time for his father, K. Dale Wood, CPA, in 1973 at the age of 16. He started his accounting career doing write-up work for clients, recording their accounting transactions in accounting records, and preparing their financial statements. He also began preparing short tax returns.

After graduating from high school, he became a full-time employee of his father's accounting firm while majoring in accounting at the local university. "After about two years, due to circumstances beyond our control, I became the in-charge on several tax and small write-up clients. By the time I graduated from college, I was responsible for the majority of the tax and write-up clients."

Soon after graduating from college and passing the CPA examination, Wally became a partner in the firm, now called Wood and Wood, Ltd. Within three years, before the age of 30, Wally became managing partner of the firm. As the managing partner, Wally is ultimately responsible for the quality of all services provided by the firm. A managing partner also markets the firm's services to obtain new clients. Like the owner of any small business, the managing partner manages the firm's employees, technology, equipment, and accounting records.

The firm recently expanded by buying another CPA firm, becoming Wood, Wood and Taylor, Ltd. Wally notes, "As a small firm, we are uniquely positioned to provide personalized tax, audit, and consulting services to our clients, including individuals, small businesses, and government agencies. We also perform peer reviews for other accounting firms, evaluating their work to ensure that proper accounting and auditing standards are being applied."

As managing partner of an accounting firm, Wally recognizes his obligation to be involved in the growth and governance of his profession. As a member of several committees of his state society of certified public accountants, he is working to ensure that accountants provide quality services to their clients.

Salary Range: According to the 2005 salary survey conducted by financial recruiting company Robert Half International, directors (partners) of small public accounting firms earned between $69,000 and $87,750 a year. Graduate degrees and professional certifications can increase these salaries by up to 10 percent.

Qualifications: Starting your own accounting firm requires a combination of expertise and experience. After earning a Certified Public Accountant license, you should

obtain several years' experience in another accounting firm.

Occupational Outlook: The Sarbanes-Oxley Act of 2002 has dramatically increased the demand for accountants who can establish, document, and evaluate the internal accounting controls required to prepare accurate financial statements. Clients continue to need tax planning and other consulting services.

End of Lesson REVIEW

AUDIT YOUR UNDERSTANDING

TERM REVIEW

lookback period

1. For a monthly schedule depositor, when are payroll taxes paid to the federal government?
2. What are two different uses for Form 8109?

WORK TOGETHER 13-4

Paying withholding and payroll taxes

A cash payments journal page is given in the *Working Papers*. Your instructor will guide you through the following examples. The following payroll data is for Digital Supplies for the monthly pay period ended March 31 of the current year.

Date Paid	Federal Income Tax Withheld	Employee Social Security Tax Withheld	Employee Medicare Tax Withheld
Mar. 31	$1,386.00	$1,322.05	$309.25

Credit balances on March 31 for the unemployment tax accounts for the first quarter are as follows: Unemployment Tax Payable—Federal, $511.75; Unemployment Tax Payable—State, $3,454.34. Digital Supplies pays both unemployment taxes each quarter.

1. Prepare a journal entry for payment of the withheld taxes. Digital Supplies is a monthly schedule depositor. Journalize Check No. 383 on cash payments journal page 14 using the date the taxes are due to the federal government.
2. Prepare journal entries for payment of the federal and state unemployment taxes liability. Assume both checks were prepared on the due date for the federal tax deposit. Check Nos. 401 and 402.

ON YOUR OWN 13-4

Paying withholding and payroll taxes

A cash payments journal page is given in the *Working Papers*. Work this problem independently. The following payroll data is for River Hardware for the monthly pay period ended June 30 of the current year.

Date Paid	Federal Income Tax Withheld	Employee Social Security Tax Withheld	Employee Medicare Tax Withheld
June 30	$1,052.00	$1,004.40	$234.95

Credit balances on June 30 for the unemployment tax accounts for the second quarter are as follows: Unemployment Tax Payable—Federal, $274.80; Unemployment Tax Payable—State, $1,922.40. River Hardware pays both unemployment taxes each quarter, regardless of the amount owed.

1. Prepare a journal entry for payment of the withheld taxes. River Hardware is a monthly schedule depositor. Journalize Check No. 678 on cash payments journal page 19 using the date the taxes are due to the federal government.
2. Prepare journal entries for payment of the federal and state unemployment taxes liability. Assume both checks were prepared on the due date for the federal tax deposit. Check Nos. 711 and 712.

After completing this chapter, you can:

1. Define accounting terms related to payroll accounting, taxes, and reports.

2. Identify accounting concepts and practices related to payroll accounting, taxes, and reports.

3. Analyze payroll transactions and record a payroll.

4. Record employer payroll taxes.

5. Prepare selected payroll tax reports.

6. Pay and record withholding and payroll taxes.

EXPLORE ACCOUNTING

Net Income vs. Taxable Income

Financial statements should provide important information that is accurate, reliable, comparable, and consistent. Over the years, a set of principles and concepts for maintaining accounting records and preparing financial statements has been developed. These guidelines are known as Generally Accepted Accounting Principles (GAAP). Most businesses use GAAP in preparing their financial statements and determining their net income.

The Internal Revenue Service (IRS) is responsible for collecting money to operate the federal government. Federal income taxes are calculated as a percentage of business or individual income. To accomplish its task, the IRS prepares Internal Revenue Service Regulations.

The objectives of the accounting profession and business community, however, are not necessarily the same as those of the federal government and the IRS. For example, a GAAP concept, Matching Expenses with Revenue, requires that the cost of business equipment be allocated over the usable life of the equipment. However, to encourage businesses to replace equipment more rapidly, IRS Regulations may permit the cost of equipment to be allocated more rapidly. Thus, in a certain year the expense for allocating cost would be greater for tax purposes than for financial reporting purposes. These types of differences create different amounts reported as net income for financial reporting purposes and for tax reporting purposes.

Thus, most businesses follow GAAP in preparing their financial statements but must follow IRS Regulations in preparing their tax returns. As a result, net income on financial statements generally differs from taxable income reported on tax returns.

Research: Examine several company annual reports. Study the financial statements and the notes connected with those statements. Is there any information indicating a difference between net income reported on the financial statements and taxable income for tax purposes? What are they, if any?

13-1 APPLICATION PROBLEM

Recording a payroll

Dana's payroll register has the following totals for two semimonthly pay periods, July 1–15 and July 16–31 of the current year.

Period	Total Earnings	Deductions					Net Pay
		Federal Income Tax	Social Security Tax	Medicare Tax	Other	Total	
July 1–15	$6,970.00	$685.00	$432.14	$101.07	B $180.00	$1,398.21	$5,571.79
July 16–31	6,040.00	572.00	374.48	87.58	B 150.00	1,184.06	4,855.94

Other Deductions: B—U.S. Savings Bonds

Instructions:

Journalize payment of the two payrolls on page 15 of the cash payments journal given in the *Working Papers*. The first payroll was paid by Check No. 547 on July 15 of the current year. The second payroll was paid by Check No. 568 on July 31 of the current year.

13-2 APPLICATION PROBLEM

Recording employer payroll taxes

Use Malone's selected payroll information for the two semimonthly pay periods, April 1–15 and April 16–30 of the current year. Forms and a general journal are given in the *Working Papers*.

Employee Name	Accumulated Earnings, March 31	Total Earnings for April 1–15 Pay Period	Total Earnings for April 16–30 Pay Period
Bolser, Frank T.	$4,860.00	$ 810.00	$ 795.00
Denham, Beth R.	5,670.00	945.00	980.00
Harjo, Teresa S.	7,500.00	1,250.00	1,250.00
Knutzen, John L.	3,720.00	620.00	635.00
Prescott, Laura F.	4,560.00	760.00	740.00
Schmidt, Ian T.	6,900.00	1,150.00	1,125.00

Employer payroll tax rates are as follows: social security, 6.2%; Medicare, 1.45%; federal unemployment, 0.8%; state unemployment, 5.4%. Unemployment taxes are owed on the first $7,000.00 of earnings for each employee.

Instructions:

1. Calculate the amount of earnings subject to unemployment taxes for the April 1–15 pay period. Note that Ian T. Schmidt has accumulated earnings on March 31 of $6,900.00. Therefore, only $100.00 ($7,000.00 – $6,900.00) of his April 1–15 earnings is subject to unemployment tax.
2. Calculate the employer payroll tax amounts for the April 1–15 pay period.

Go Beyond the Book
For more information go to www.C21accounting.com

3. Journalize the employer payroll taxes on page 16 of a general journal. Use the date of April 15 of the current year. The source document is Memorandum No. 69.

4. Calculate the employer payroll taxes for the April 16–30 pay period. Calculate April 15 accumulated earnings by adding total earnings for the April 1–15 pay period to the March 31 accumulated earnings. Note that only part of Beth R. Denham's earnings for April 16–30 are subject to unemployment tax.

5. Journalize the employer payroll taxes on page 16 of a general journal. Use the date of April 30 of the current year. The source document is Memorandum No. 76.

13-3   APPLICATION PROBLEM

Reporting withholding and payroll taxes

The following payroll data is for Eagle Toys for the second quarter of the current year.

Date Paid	Total Earnings	Federal Income Tax Withheld	Employee Social Security Tax Withheld	Employee Medicare Tax Withheld
Apr. 30	$ 9,166.00	$654.00	$568.29	$132.91
May 31	10,382.00	687.00	643.68	150.54
June 30	9,872.00	718.00	612.06	143.14

Additional data:

1. Company address: 784 McDonald Street, Mesa, AZ 85201-5874

2. Employer identification number: 80-7818356

3. Number of employees: 5

4. Federal tax payments have been made on May 15, June 15, and July 15.

Instructions:
Prepare the Form 941, Employer's Quarterly Federal Tax Return, given in the *Working Papers*. Use the date July 21. Sign your name as the manager of the company. Amounts on lines 13 and 17d may not equal, due to rounding.

13-4   APPLICATION PROBLEM

Paying withholding and payroll taxes

The following payroll data is for Zimmerman Company for the first quarter of the current year.

Period	Total Earnings	Federal Income Tax Withheld
March	$17,560.00	$1,548.00
First Quarter	$52,210.00	—

In addition, total earnings are subject to 6.2% employee and 6.2% employer social security tax, plus 1.45% employee and 1.45% employer Medicare tax. The federal unemployment tax rate is 0.8% and the state unemployment tax rate is 5.4% of total earnings. No total earnings have exceeded the tax base for calculating unemployment taxes.

Instructions:

1. Calculate the appropriate liability amount of social security and Medicare taxes for March. Journalize the payment of the withheld taxes on page 8 of the cash payments journal given in the *Working Papers*. The taxes were paid by Check No. 813 on April 15 of the current year.

2. Calculate the appropriate federal unemployment tax liability for the first quarter. Journalize payment of this liability in the cash payments journal. The tax was paid by Check No. 830 on April 30 of the current year.

3. Calculate the appropriate state unemployment tax liability for the first quarter. Journalize payment of this liability in the cash payments journal. The tax was paid by Check No. 831 on April 30 of the current year.

13-5 MASTERY PROBLEM

Journalizing payroll transactions

Keller Systems, Inc., completed payroll transactions during the period May 1 to June 15 of the current year. Payroll tax rates are as follows: social security, 6.2%; Medicare, 1.45%; federal unemployment, 0.8%; state unemployment, 5.4%. The company buys savings bonds for employees as accumulated withholdings reach the necessary amount to purchase a bond. No total earnings have exceeded the tax base for calculating unemployment taxes. Keller Systems is a monthly schedule depositor for payroll taxes.

Instructions:

1. Journalize the following transactions on page 14 of the cash payments journal and page 10 of the general journal given in the *Working Papers*. Source documents are abbreviated as follows: check, C, and memorandum, M.

Transactions:

May 15. Paid cash for April's payroll tax liability. Withheld taxes from April payrolls: employee income tax, $532.00; social security tax, $634.88; and Medicare tax, $148.48. C421.

15. Paid cash for semimonthly payroll. Total earnings, $5,250.00; withholdings: employee income tax, $273.00; U.S. Savings Bonds, $60.00 (calculate the social security and Medicare deductions). C422.

15. Recorded employer payroll taxes expense for the May 15 payroll. M42.

15. Paid cash for U.S. Savings Bonds for employees, $300.00. C423.

31. Paid cash for semimonthly payroll. Gross wages, $5,310.00; withholdings: employee income tax, $276.00; U.S. Savings Bonds, $60.00. C461.

31. Recorded employer payroll taxes expense for the May 31 payroll. M46.

31. Paid cash for federal unemployment tax liability for quarter ended March 31, $245.76. C462.

31. Paid cash for state unemployment tax liability for quarter ended March 31, $1,658.88. C463.

June 15. Paid cash for the May liability for employee income tax, social security tax, and Medicare tax, C487. (Calculate the social security and Medicare tax liabilities by multiplying total earnings for the period by 12.4% for social security tax and 2.9% for Medicare tax.)

15. Paid cash for semimonthly payroll. Gross wages, $5,280.00; withholdings: employee income tax, $274.00; U.S. Savings Bonds, $75.00. C488.

15. Recorded employer payroll taxes expense. M53.

2. Prove and rule the cash payments journal.

13-6 CHALLENGE PROBLEM

Journalizing and posting payroll transactions

Golf Design, Inc., completed payroll transactions during the period January 1 to April 30 of the current year. Payroll tax rates are as follows: social security, 6.2%; Medicare, 1.45%; federal unemployment, 0.8%; and state unemployment, 5.4%. The company buys savings bonds for employees as the accumulated withholdings reach the necessary amount to purchase a bond. No total earnings have exceeded the tax base for calculating unemployment taxes.

The balances in the general ledger as of January 1 of the current year are recorded in the *Working Papers*.

Chart of Accounts

Account Number	Account Title
2120	Employee Income Tax Payable
2130	Social Security Tax Payable
2140	Medicare Tax Payable
2150	Unemployment Tax Payable—Federal
2160	Unemployment Tax Payable—State
2180	U.S. Savings Bonds Payable
6150	Payroll Taxes Expense
6170	Salary Expense

Instructions:

1. Journalize the following transactions on page 1 of the cash payments journal and the general journal given in the Working Papers. Payroll withholdings for employee income tax and U.S. Savings Bonds are provided. Calculate other payroll withholdings using the tax rates provided. Source documents are abbreviated as follows: check, C, and memorandum, M.

Transactions:

Jan. 2. Wrote a check for 15 U.S. Savings Bonds at $25.00 each for employees. C195.

15. Paid the December liability for employee income tax, social security tax, and Medicare tax. C204.

31. Wrote a check for federal unemployment tax liability for quarter ended December 31. C210.

31. Wrote a check for state unemployment tax liability for quarter ended December 31. C211.

31. Paid January payroll (total payroll, $12,200.00, less deductions: employee income tax, $805.00; U.S. Savings Bonds, $125.00). C216.

31. Recorded employer payroll taxes expense. M98.

Posting. Post the items that are to be posted individually.

Feb. 15. Wrote a check for January liability for employee income tax and for social security tax and Medicare tax. C222.

28. Paid February payroll (total payroll, $12,360.00, less deductions: employee income tax, $816.00; U.S. Savings Bonds, $125.00). C232.

28. Recorded employer payroll taxes expense. M107.

Posting. Post the items that are to be posted individually.

2. Prove and rule cash payments journal page 1. Carry the column totals forward to page 2 of the cash payments journal.

3. Journalize the following transactions on page 2 of the cash payments journal and continuing on page 1 of the general journal.

Transactions:

Mar. 15. Wrote a check for February liability for employee income tax, social security tax, and Medicare tax. C237.

31. Paid March payroll (total payroll, $11,860.00, less deductions: employee income tax, $783.00; U.S. Savings Bonds, $125.00). C258.

31. Recorded employer payroll taxes expense. M116.

Posting. Post the items that are to be posted individually.

Apr. 1. Paid cash for 15 U.S. Savings Bonds at $25.00 each for employees. C259.

15. Wrote a check for March liability for employee income tax, social security tax, and Medicare tax. C270.

30. Wrote a check for federal unemployment tax liability for quarter ended March 31. C276.

30. Wrote a check for state unemployment tax liability for quarter ended March 31. C277.

Posting. Post the items that are to be posted individually.

4. Prove and rule cash payments journal page 2.

One of the unwritten rules of business is that payroll information is private and confidential. People usually do not want their co-workers to know how much they are paid. This common business practice presents a challenge for employees responsible for payroll accounting. Payroll workers handle many different types of data. The payroll department records personal information about employees, such as addresses and social security numbers, and verifies and totals time cards. In addition, each pay period, payroll accountants calculate each employee's earnings, deductions, and net pay. It is important for payroll employees to be trustworthy and able to maintain confidentiality.

Instructions: In the form of a memorandum, write a statement of a company's policy regarding the confidentiality of payroll information. The memorandum should be addressed to the employees of the payroll department.

CASE FOR CRITICAL THINKING

Wyatt Company has decided to hire a sales representative. The business can afford to pay the representative a salary of only $30,000.00. The accounting assistant informs the manager that hiring the representative will cost the business more than the $30,000.00 salary. Do you agree with the accounting assistant? Explain your response.

AUDITING FOR ERRORS

In June, the liability for federal and state unemployment tax for Excelsior Corporation is recorded at about the same amount as for previous months. Jackie Blette suggests that it usually begins to decrease in June, except when many new graduates are hired that month. You have been asked to investigate the payroll data to discover whether there is a problem.

Instructions

1. Why would the liability for unemployment tax begin to decline in June?
2. If there is an error in the unemployment liability amounts, what is the likely cause?
3. Examine the information below and on a separate sheet of paper write the correct amounts for the unemployment tax liabilities.

Accumulated Earnings Jan.–May	June Total Earnings	Federal Unemployment Tax	State Unemployment Tax
$4,260.00	$ 810.00	$ 6.48	$43.74
5,200.00	1,100.00	8.80	59.40
6,450.00	1,250.00	10.00	67.50
6,800.00	1,350.00	10.80	72.90
3,600.00	1,200.00	9.60	64.80

ANALYZING BEST BUY'S FINANCIAL STATEMENTS

Best Buy plans for current-year claims against it as well as any claims that might occur in the future. Best Buy estimates an amount for claims it expects to pay in the future that relate to activities of the current fiscal year.

Instructions: Use the Insurance section in Note 1 of Best Buy's financial statements in Appendix B, page B-14 , to answer the following questions.

1. How does Best Buy insure against losses?
2. For what types of losses does Best Buy self-insure?
3. Does Best Buy purchase insurance?
4. How does Best Buy estimate its claims?
5. How are accrued claims reported on the March 3, 2007 financial statements?

Accounting SOFTWARE

RECORDING PAYROLL TAXES

The government does not send an invoice for the amount of payroll taxes due. Businesses must keep accurate records of the payroll taxes withheld and employer payroll taxes to ensure the correct amount is paid. The payroll tax liability accounts provide a record of all payroll taxes due. The balance in the account is the amount that should be paid to the government.

Peachtree provides two methods to obtain the outstanding balances of general ledger accounts. A report of general ledger accounts presents each transaction and the ending balance of every account. Another window reports only the monthly total debits and credits and balance for a single account.

PEACHTREE MASTERY PROBLEM 13-5
1. Open (Restore) file 13-5MP.ptb.
2. Journalize and post the May 15 and May 31 transactions in the cash disbursements journal. Use the general journal to record the employer payroll taxes expense for May 15 and May 31.
3. Before you journalize and post the June 15 transactions, remember to change the accounting periods (Tasks, System, Change Accounting Period).
4. Journalize and post the June 15 transactions. Use the general journal for the payroll tax expense transactions.
5. Print the May 15 through June 15 cash disbursements journal.

PEACHTREE CHALLENGE PROBLEM 13-6
1. Open (Restore) file 13-6CP.ptb.
2. Journalize and post the payroll transactions. Use the general journal to record the employer payroll taxes expense.
3. Print the January through April cash disbursements journal.
4. Print the January 2 through March general journal.
5. Print the January through April general ledger.

RECORDING PAYROLL TAXES

When paying payroll taxes and other payroll liabilities in this chapter, the amounts were clearly stated in the transaction. In a company, there are no bills received stating payroll liability amounts and due date. The payroll employee must determine how much needs to be paid for each liability and when the amount is due. The electronic records contain all the data needed to determine the correct amounts, but they must be accessed in order to be of help. QuickBooks has several ways to determine the balance of various accounts.

A trial balance can be run to show the balance in each account. In most cases, the balance of the account is the amount that is due the government for the payroll tax liability. To get more detail, a general ledger can be printed or displayed. The general ledger can be displayed in two forms—one showing only the account balances and one showing all the entries in each account along with the account balance.

QUICKBOOKS MASTERY PROBLEM 13-5
1. Open the Keller Systems Inc file.
2. Journalize the transactions completed during May 15 through June 15. Use the Write Checks option for all cash payments. Use the Make General Journal Entries window for all other transactions.
3. Print a Journal report. Use May 15 and June 15 for the dates.

QUICKBOOKS CHALLENGE PROBLEM 13-6
1. Open the Golf Design Inc file.
2. Journalize the transactions completed during January through April.
3. Print a Journal report. Use January 1 and April 30 for the dates.

CALCULATING UNEMPLOYMENT TAX

Determining the amount of unemployment taxable earnings can be difficult. The calculation is especially difficult in the pay period in which an employee's accumulated earnings reach $7,000. Mistakes can easily be made calculating these amounts. The solution is to create a template on an electronic spreadsheet.

A formula using a combination of IF and MIN functions is required to calculate unemployment taxable earnings. An IF function compares two numbers and enters one of two values in the cell. The syntax of the IF function is =IF(logical_test, true_value, false_value). A MIN function calculates the minimum of two or more values. The syntax of the MIN function is =MIN(value1, value2, …)

Suppose an employee's accumulated earnings are $6,200 (cell C8) and earnings for the pay period are $500 (cell D8). The function to calculate the unemployment taxable earnings would be

=IF(C8>7000,0,MIN(D8,7000-C8))

The logical_test is false; C8 is not greater than $7,000. Therefore, the MIN function then calculates the lesser of (1) $500 in D8 or (2) $800, the difference between $7,000 and the accumulated earnings, $6,200. As you can see, using IF functions can be complex and will require you to have a full understanding how unemployment taxes are calculated.

OPTIONAL SPREADSHEET ACTIVITY
Open the file F13-OPT. Follow the step-by-step instructions in the Instructions worksheet to use the IF and MIN functions to calculate unemployment taxable earnings.

RECORDING PAYROLL TAXES

In an automated payroll system, the computer is used to maintain the employee database, to record payroll transactions at the end of each pay period, and to display and print various payroll reports.

Generating Payroll Journal Entries
Automated Accounting can generate the current payroll journal entry.
1. Choose the Current Payroll Journal Entry menu item from the Options menu. Note that you must first have a payroll entered into the system before payroll journal entries can be generated.
2. When the confirmation dialog box appears, click Yes.
3. Click the Post button.

Generating the Employer's Payroll Taxes Journal Entries
Automated Accounting can also generate the current payroll taxes journal entry.
1. Choose the Employer's Payroll Taxes menu item from the Options menu.
2. When the confirmation dialog box appears, click Yes.
3. Click the Post button.

AUTOMATED ACCOUNTING MASTERY PROBLEM 13-5
Open file F13-5.AA8. Display the problem instructions and complete the problem.

An Accounting Cycle for a Corporation: Journalizing and Posting Transactions

Reinforcement Activity 2 reinforces learning from Part 2, Chapters 9 through 16. Activities cover a complete accounting cycle for a merchandising business organized as a corporation. Reinforcement Activity 2 is a single problem divided into two parts. Part A includes learning from Chapters 9 through 13. Part B includes learning from Chapters 14 through 16.

The accounting work of a single merchandising business for the last month of a yearly fiscal period is used in this reinforcement activity. The records kept and reports prepared, however, illustrate the application of accounting concepts for all merchandising businesses.

MEDICAL SERVICES COMPANY (MSC)

Medical Services Company (MSC), a merchandising business, is organized as a corporation. The business sells a complete line of medical accessories, from crutches to lift chairs. MSC is located in a medical office plaza adjacent to the hospital and is open for business Monday through Saturday. A monthly rent is paid for the building. MSC accepts credit cards from customers.

CHART OF ACCOUNTS

MSC uses the chart of accounts shown on the next page.

JOURNALS AND LEDGERS

The journals and ledgers used by MSC are listed below. Models of the journals and ledgers are shown in the text-book chapters indicated.

Journals and Ledgers	Chapter
Purchases journal	9
Cash payments journal	9
General journal	9
Sales journal	10
Cash receipts journal	10
Accounts payable ledger	11
Accounts receivable ledger	11
General ledger	11

CHART OF ACCOUNTS
GENERAL LEDGER

Balance Sheet Accounts

(1000) ASSETS

1100 Current Assets

1110 Cash

1120 Petty Cash

1130 Accounts Receivable

1135 Allowance for Uncollectible Accounts

1140 Merchandise Inventory

1145 Supplies—Office

1150 Supplies—Store

1160 Prepaid Insurance

1200 Plant Assets

1210 Office Equipment

1220 Accumulated Depreciation—Office Equipment

1230 Store Equipment

1240 Accumulated Depreciation—Store Equipment

(2000) LIABILITIES

2100 Current Liabilities

2110 Accounts Payable

2115 Federal Income Tax Payable

2120 Employee Income Tax Payable

2130 Social Security Tax Payable

2135 Medicare Tax Payable

2140 Sales Tax Payable

2150 Unemployment Tax Payable—Federal

2160 Unemployment Tax Payable—State

2170 Health Insurance Premiums Payable

2180 U.S. Savings Bonds Payable

2190 United Way Donations Payable

2195 Dividends Payable

(3000) OWNERS' EQUITY

3110 Capital Stock

3120 Retained Earnings

3130 Dividends

3140 Income Summary

Income Statement Accounts

(4000) OPERATING REVENUE

4110 Sales

4120 Sales Discount

4130 Sales Returns and Allowances

(5000) COST OF MERCHANDISE

5110 Purchases

5120 Purchases Discount

5130 Purchases Returns and Allowances

(6000) OPERATING EXPENSES

6110 Advertising Expense

6115 Cash Short and Over

6120 Credit Card Fee Expense

6125 Depreciation Expense—Office Equipment

6130 Depreciation Expense—Store Equipment

6135 Insurance Expense

6140 Miscellaneous Expense

6150 Payroll Taxes Expense

6160 Rent Expense

6165 Repairs Expense

6170 Salary Expense

6175 Supplies Expense—Office

6180 Supplies Expense—Store

6185 Uncollectible Accounts Expense

6190 Utilities Expense

(7000) INCOME TAX EXPENSE

7105 Federal Income Tax Expense

SUBSIDIARY LEDGERS

Accounts Receivable Ledger

110 Bratton Clinic

120 Clegg Medical Center

130 Glenmore School

140 Jamacus Clinic

150 Odom Daycare

160 Treet Retirement Home

Accounts Payable Ledger

210 Armstrong Medical

220 Cross Office Supply

230 Evans Supply

240 Ogden Instruments

250 Spencer Industries

260 Ziegler, Inc.

RECORDING TRANSACTIONS

The December 1 account balances for the general and subsidiary ledgers are given in the *Working Papers*.

Instructions:

1. Journalize the following transactions completed during December of the current year. Use page 12 of a sales journal, page 12 of a purchases journal, page 12 of a general journal, page 12 of a cash receipts journal, and page 23 of a cash payments journal. MSC offers sales terms of 2/10, n/30. The sales tax rate is 6%. Source documents are abbreviated as follows: check, C; memorandum, M; purchase invoice, P; receipt, R; sales invoice, S; terminal summary, TS; debit memorandum, DM; credit memorandum, CM.

Dec. 1. Paid cash for rent, $1,200.00. C372.

     2. Paid cash for electric bill, $346.20. C373.

     2. Received cash on account from Clegg Medical Center, covering S64 for $413.40, less 2% sales discount. R92.

     3. Paid cash for miscellaneous expense, $72.00. C374.

     3. Paid cash on account to Spencer Industries, covering P73 for $580.00, less 2% discount. C375.

     4. Sold merchandise on account to Bratton Clinic, $450.00, plus sales tax, $27.00; total, $477.00. S67.

     5. Recorded cash and credit card sales, $5,796.00, plus sales tax, $347.76; total, $6,143.76. TS45.
       Posting. Post the items that are to be posted individually. Post the journals in this order: sales journal, purchases journal, general journal, cash receipts journal, and cash payments journal.

    7. Sold merchandise on account to Glenmore School, $462.00. Glenmore School is exempt from sales tax. S68.

    7. Received cash on account from Treet Retirement Home, $432.48, covering S65. R93.

    8. Bought office supplies on account from Cross Office Supply, $351.60. M43.

    9. Purchased merchandise on account from Ogden Instruments, $2,250, less a 40% trade discount. P77.

    9. Bought store supplies on account from Ziegler, Inc., $330.00. M44.

  10. Paid cash for office supplies, $174.00. C376.

  11. Paid cash on account to Evans Supply, $1,170.00, covering P74. C377.

  11. Purchased merchandise on account from Spencer Industries, $1,032.00. P78.

  12. Paid cash for store supplies, $264.00. C378.

  12. Recorded cash and credit card sales, $7,125.00, plus sales tax, $427.50; total, $7,552.50. TS46.
       Posting. Post the items that are to be posted individually.

  14. Purchased merchandise on account from Evans Supply, $3,276.00. P79.

  14. Sold merchandise on account to Odom Daycare, $170.00, plus sales tax, $10.20; total, $180.20. S69.

  14. Paid cash for advertising, $415.00. C379.

  15. Returned $226.00 of merchandise to Evans Supply from P79, $226.00. DM4.

  15. Paid cash on account to Armstrong Medical, $1,272.00, covering P75. C380.

  15. Received cash on account from Jamacus Clinic, $821.50, covering S66. R94.

  15. Sold merchandise on account to Clegg Medical Center, $490.00, plus sales tax, $29.40; total, $519.40. S70.

  15. Paid cash for liability for employee income tax, $342.00, social security tax, $767.00, and Medicare tax, $179.38; total, $1,288.38. C381.

  15. Paid cash for semimonthly payroll, $2,313.85 (total payroll, $2,930.00, less deductions: employee income tax, $162.00; social security tax, $181.66; Medicare tax, $42.49; health insurance, $170.00; U.S. Savings Bonds, $30.00; United Way donations, $30.00). C382.

  15. Recorded employer payroll taxes, $248.95, for the semimonthly pay period ended December 15. Taxes owed are: social security tax, $181.66; Medicare tax, $42.49; federal unemployment tax, $3.20; and state unemployment tax, $21.60. M45.

  19. Recorded cash and credit card sales, $6,925.00, plus sales tax, $415.50; total, $7,340.50. TS47.
       Posting. Post the items that are to be posted individually.

  23. Paid cash on account to Ogden Instruments, $2,200.00, covering P76. C383.

  24. Received cash on account from Odom Daycare, covering S69 for $180.20, less 2% discount. R95.

  24. Granted credit to Clegg Medical Center for merchandise returned, $120.00, plus sales tax, $7.20, from S70; total, $127.20. CM5.

  26. Recorded cash and credit card sales, $6,980.00, plus sales tax, $418.80; total, $7,398.80. TS48.
       Posting. Post the items that are to be posted individually.

MSC's bank charges a fee for handling the collection of credit card sales deposited during the month. The credit card fee is deducted from MSC's bank account. The amount is then shown on the bank statement. The credit card fee is recorded in the cash payments journal as a reduction in cash.

Dec. 28. Recorded credit card fee expense, $342.00. M46. (Debit Credit Card Fee Expense; credit Cash.)

2. Prove and rule page 23 of the cash payments journal.

3. Carry the column totals forward to page 24 of the cash payments journal.

4. Journalize the following transactions.

Dec. 30. Purchased merchandise on account from Armstrong Medical, $1,940.00. P80.
31. Paid cash to replenish the petty cash fund, $145.20: office supplies, $35.00; store supplies, $19.00; advertising, $64.00; miscellaneous, $26.00; cash short, $1.20. C384.
31. Paid cash for semimonthly payroll, $2,462.32 (total payroll, $3,120.00, less deductions: employee income tax, $189.00; social security tax, $193.44; Medicare tax, $45.24; health insurance, $170.00; U.S. Savings Bonds, $30.00; United Way donations, $30.00). C385.
31. Recorded employer payroll taxes, $263.48, for the semimonthly pay period ended December 31. Taxes owed are: social security tax, $193.44: Medicare tax, $45.24; federal unemployment tax, $3.20; and state unemployment tax, $21.60. M47.
31. Recorded cash and credit card sales, $3,890.00, plus sales tax, $233.40; total, $4,123.40. TS49.
Posting. Post the items that are to be posted individually.

5. Prove and rule the sales journal. Post the totals of the special columns.

6. Total and rule the purchases journal. Post the total.

7. Prove the equality of debits and credits for the cash receipts and cash payments journals.

8. Prove cash. The balance on the next unused check stub is $40,126.14.

9. Rule the cash receipts journal. Post the totals of the special columns.

10. Rule the cash payments journal. Post the totals of the special columns.

11. Prepare a schedule of accounts receivable and a schedule of accounts payable. Prove the accuracy of the subsidiary ledgers by comparing the schedule totals with the balances of the controlling accounts in the general ledger. If the totals are not the same, find and correct the errors.

The ledgers used in Reinforcement Activity 2—Part A are needed to complete Reinforcement Activity 2—Part B.

14

CHAPTER 14

Distributing Dividends and Preparing a Work Sheet for a Merchandising Business

TETRA IMAGES/GETTY IMAGES

OBJECTIVES

After studying Chapter 14, you will be able to:

1. Define accounting terms related to distributing dividends and preparing a work sheet for a merchandising business.

2. Identify accounting concepts and practices related to distributing dividends and preparing a work sheet for a merchandising business.

3. Journalize the declaration and payment of a dividend.

4. Begin a work sheet for a merchandising business.

5. Plan work sheet adjustments for merchandise inventory, supplies, prepaid expenses, uncollectible accounts, and depreciation.

6. Calculate federal income tax and plan the work sheet adjustment for federal income tax.

7. Complete a work sheet for a merchandising business.

KEY TERMS

- retained earnings
- dividends
- board of directors
- declaring a dividend
- merchandise inventory
- uncollectible accounts
- allowance method of recording losses from uncollectible accounts
- book value
- book value of accounts receivable
- current assets
- plant assets
- depreciation expense
- estimated salvage value
- straight-line method of depreciation
- accumulated depreciation
- book value of a plant asset

Point Your Browser
www.C21accounting.com

Lowe's

Lowe's—the Good Neighbor

Welcome to the neighborhood! That's the reaction Lowe's wants when it opens a store in your neighborhood. Lowe's is working to make home improvement more convenient for its customers. By providing the right products at the right price, whether in local stores or at Lowes.com, the company seeks to make it easy for its customers to improve the quality and value of their homes.

Lowe's is also investing in its community. The company provides relief supplies to victims of natural disasters, financial support for Habitat for Humanity, and educational grants to K-12 public education systems.

Community involvement is important to the employees at Lowe's. The company encourages volunteerism through Lowe's Heroes, a program focused on home safety. Looking out for your neighbor—that's what being a good neighbor is all about.

Critical Thinking

1. Beyond having quality products at a fair price, how do Lowe's and other home improvement companies assist customers to improve their homes?

2. How should Lowe's account for a donation of lumber to a Habitat for Humanity house?

Source: www.lowes.com

INTERNET ACTIVITY

Finding Stock Prices

Many company web sites give a history of the stock prices for the company's stock. Go to the homepage for a company of your choice. Look under a heading such as "About Us" or "Investor Relations" to find information about the price of the company's stock.

Instructions

1. Find the closing stock price from the previous day's trading.

2. Find the highest price for which the stock sold on the previous day.

3. Find the lowest price for which the stock sold on the previous day.

Distributing Corporate Earnings to Stockholders

FINANCIAL INFORMATION

Management decisions about future business operations are often based on financial information. This information shows whether a profit is being made or a loss is being incurred. Profit or loss information helps an owner or manager determine future changes. Financial information is also needed to prepare required tax reports.

Hobby Shack uses a fiscal year that begins on January 1 and ends on December 31. Therefore, Hobby Shack summarizes its financial information on December 31 of each year.

DIGITAL VISION/GETTY IMAGES

CHARACTER COUNTS

He's Guilty!

A company that believes one of its employees is stealing may obtain the services of a Certified Fraud Examiner (CFE). The CFE is trained to examine accounting records and obtain other evidence related to the alleged theft. CFEs often serve as expert witnesses in court. The Code of Professional Ethics of the Association of Certified Fraud Examiners provides its members with guidance on how to serve as an expert witness. The Code states that the CFE should obtain evidence that provides a reasonable basis for his or her opinion. However, the CFE should never express an opinion on the guilt or innocence of any person.

Instructions

Access the ACFE Code of Professional Ethics of the Association of Certified Fraud Examiners at www.cfenet.com. Citing the section, what other advice does the Code provide a CFE when serving as an expert witness?

PHOTO: STOCKBYTE/GETTY IMAGES

(3000) STOCKHOLDERS' EQUITY
3110 Capital Stock
3120 Retained Earnings
3130 Dividends
3140 Income Summary

A corporation's ownership is divided into units. Each unit of ownership in a corporation is known as a *share of stock*. An owner of one or more shares of a corporation is known as a *stockholder*. Each stockholder is an owner of a corporation.

Owners' equity accounts for a corporation normally are listed under a major chart of accounts division titled Stockholders' Equity.

Most corporations have many stockholders. It is not practical to have a separate owner's equity account for each stockholder. Instead, a single owners' equity account, titled Capital Stock, is used for the investment of all owners.

A second stockholders' equity account is used to record a corporation's earnings. Net income increases a corporation's total stockholders' equity. Some income may be retained by a corporation for business expansion. An amount earned by a corporation and not yet distributed to stockholders is called **retained earnings**. Retained Earnings is the title of the account used to record a corporation's earnings.

Some income may be given to stockholders as a return on their investments. A third stockholders' equity account is used to record the distribution of a corporation's earnings to stockholders. Earnings distributed to stockholders are called **dividends**. A corporation's dividend account is a temporary account similar to a proprietorship's drawing account. Each time a dividend is declared, an account titled Dividends is debited. At the end of each fiscal period, the balance in the dividends account is closed to Retained Earnings.

PHOTOGRAPHER'S CHOICE RF/GETTY IMAGES

REMEMBER

Dividends *is a temporary account that is closed to* Retained Earnings *at the end of the fiscal period.*

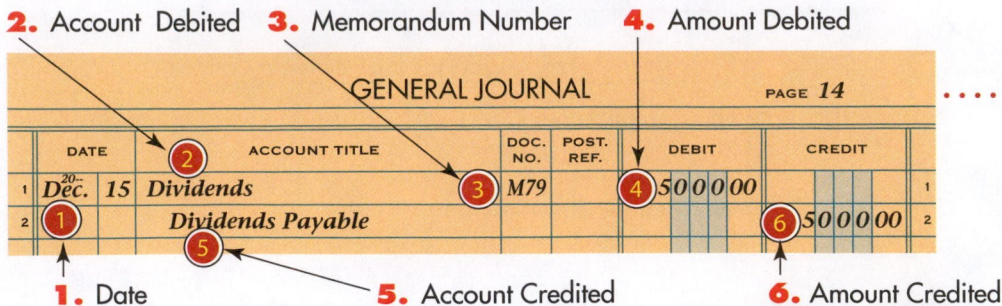

2. Account Debited   **3.** Memorandum Number   **4.** Amount Debited

1. Date   **5.** Account Credited   **6.** Amount Credited

A group of persons elected by the stockholders to manage a corporation is called a **board of directors**. Dividends can be distributed to stockholders only by formal action of a corporation's board of directors. [CONCEPT: Business Entity]

Action by a board of directors to distribute corporate earnings to stockholders is called **declaring a dividend**. Dividends normally are declared on one date and paid on a later date. If a board of directors declares a dividend, the corporation is then obligated to pay the dividend. The dividend is a liability that must be recorded in the corporation's accounts.

Hobby Shack declares dividends each March 15, June 15, September 15, and December 15. The dividends are then paid on the 15th of the following month.

The stockholders' equity account, Dividends, has a normal debit balance and is increased by a $5,000.00 debit. Dividends Payable is credited for $5,000.00 to show the increase in this liability account.

December 15. Hobby Shack's board of directors declared a quarterly dividend of $2.00 per share; capital stock issued is 2,500 shares; total dividend, $5,000.00. Date of payment is January 15. Memorandum No. 79.

Dividends	
3/15 Decl.	5,000.00
6/15 Decl.	5,000.00
9/15 Decl.	5,000.00
12/15 Decl.	**5,000.00**

Dividends Payable			
4/15 Paid	5,000.00	3/15 Decl.	5,000.00
7/15 Paid	5,000.00	6/15 Decl.	5,000.00
10/15 Paid	5,000.00	9/15 Decl.	5,000.00
		12/15 Decl.	**5,000.00**

	Number of Shares Outstanding		Quarterly Dividend per Share		Total Quarterly Dividend
	2,500	×	$2.00	=	$5,000.00

STEPS ● **JOURNALIZING DECLARING A DIVIDEND**

① Write the date, *20--, Dec. 15*, in the Date column.

② Write the title of the account debited, *Dividends*, in the Account Title column.

③ Write the memorandum number, *M79*, in the Doc. No. column.

④ Write the debit amount, *$5,000.00*, in the Debit column.

⑤ Write the title of the account credited, *Dividends Payable*, on the next line of the Account Title column, indented about 1 centimeter.

⑥ Write the credit amount, *$5,000.00*, in the Credit column.

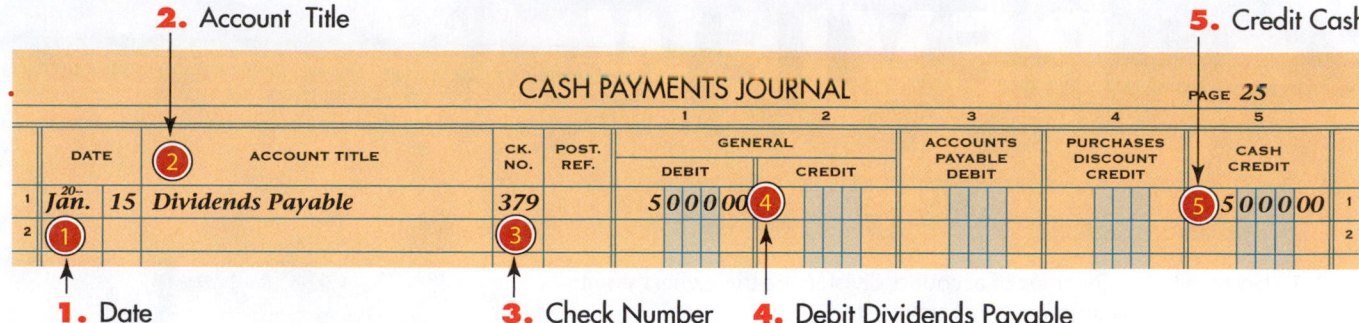

2. Account Title

5. Credit Cash

| | DATE | ACCOUNT TITLE | CK. NO. | POST. REF. | GENERAL | | ACCOUNTS PAYABLE DEBIT | PURCHASES DISCOUNT CREDIT | CASH CREDIT | |
					DEBIT	CREDIT				
1	Jan. 15	Dividends Payable	379		5 0 0 0 00				5 0 0 0 00	1
2										2

1. Date **3.** Check Number **4.** Debit Dividends Payable

Hobby Shack issues one check for the amount of the total dividend to be paid. This check is deposited in a special dividend checking account. A separate check for each stockholder is drawn on this special account. The special account avoids a large number of cash payments journal entries and also reserves cash specifically for paying dividends.

A check is often made payable to an agent, such as a bank. The agent then handles the details of sending dividend checks to individual stockholders.

January 15. Paid cash for quarterly dividend declared December 15, $5,000.00. Check No. 379.

Dividends Payable			
4/15 Paid	5,000.00	3/15 Decl.	5,000.00
7/15 Paid	5,000.00	6/15 Decl.	5,000.00
10/15 Paid	5,000.00	9/15 Decl.	5,000.00
1/15 Paid	5,000.00	12/15 Decl.	5,000.00

Cash			
		1/15 Paid	5,000.00

When this entry is posted, the dividends payable account has a zero balance.

STEPS JOURNALIZING THE PAYMENT OF DIVIDENDS

 Write the date, *20--, Jan. 15*, in the Date column.

② Write the account title, *Dividends Payable*, in the Account Title column.

③ Write the check number, *379*, in the Ck. No. column.

④ Write the debit amount, *$5,000.00*, in the General Debit column.

⑤ Write the credit amount, *$5,000.00*, in the Cash Credit column.

FOR YOUR INFORMATION

FYI

Dividends are declared on one date and paid on a later date. Only stockholders owning the stock on the date of record specified by the board of directors receive the dividend. Stockholders owning the stock on the date of record receive the entire dividend, regardless of how long they have owned the stock.

End of Lesson REVIEW

1. Under what major chart of accounts division are the owners' equity accounts for a corporation normally listed?
2. How many accounts are kept for the investment of all owners of a corporation?
3. What account does a corporation use to record earnings not yet distributed to stockholders?
4. What action is required before a corporation can distribute income to its stockholders?

TERMS REVIEW

retained earnings

dividends

board of directors

declaring a dividend

WORK TOGETHER 14-1

Journalizing dividends

Journals are given in the *Working Papers*. Your instructor will guide you through the following examples.

Coastal Aquatics completed the following transactions during December of the current year and January of the next year.

Transactions:

Dec. 15. The board of directors declared a dividend of $3.00 per share; capital stock issued is 1,750 shares. M162.

Jan. 15. Paid cash for dividend declared December 15. C687.

1. Use page 14 of a general journal. Journalize the dividend declared on December 15.
2. Use page 21 of a cash payments journal. Journalize payment of the dividend on January 15.

ON YOUR OWN 14-1

Journalizing dividends

Journals are given in the *Working Papers*. Work this problem independently.

Sonoma Treasures completed the following transactions during December of the current year and January of the next year.

Transactions:

Dec. 15. The board of directors declared a dividend of $1.00 per share; capital stock issued is 21,000 shares. M321.

Jan. 15. Paid cash for dividend declared December 15. C721.

1. Use page 22 of a general journal. Journalize the dividend declared on December 15.
2. Use page 24 of a cash payments journal. Journalize payment of the dividend.

Beginning an 8-Column Work Sheet for a Merchandising Business

A columnar accounting form on which the financial information needed to prepare financial statements is summarized is known as a *work sheet*. A work sheet is used to plan adjustments and summarize the information nec-essary to prepare financial statements. The steps used to prepare a work sheet are similar for proprietorships and corporations.

ENTERING A TRIAL BALANCE ON A WORK SHEET

To prepare a work sheet, a trial balance is first entered in the Trial Balance columns. All general ledger accounts and balances are listed in the same order as they appear in the general ledger. Trial Balance columns are totaled to prove equality of debits and credits.

The worksheet for Hobby Shack is different from the work sheet completed for TechKnow in Chapter 6. Unlike a service business, a merchandising business will have an account for merchandise inventory. A corporation's accounts are similar to those of a proprietorship except for the capital stock, retained earnings, dividends, and federal income tax accounts.

PLANNING ADJUSTMENTS ON A WORK SHEET

Some general ledger accounts need to be brought up to date before financial statements are prepared. Accounts are brought up to date by planning and entering adjust-ments on a work sheet. Adjustments are planned in the Adjustments columns of a work sheet. Adjustments recorded on a work sheet are for planning purposes only. The general ledger account balances are not changed until entries are journalized and posted. Journal entries made to bring general ledger accounts up to date are known as *adjusting entries*.

Hobby Shack's adjustments for supplies and prepaid insurance are the same as those for TechKnow described in Chapter 6. Hobby Shack also makes adjustments to these accounts: (1) Merchandise Inventory, (2) Uncollect-ible Accounts Expense, (3) Depreciation Expense, and (4) Federal Income Tax Expense.

The adjustment for merchandise inventory is unique to a merchandising business. Adjustments for uncollect-ible accounts expense and depreciation expense could also be made by a service business. The adjustment for federal income tax is unique to corporations. This adjustment is not made for a proprietorship because taxes are paid by the owner, not the business.

SMALL BUSINESS

SPOTLIGHT

Small businesses represent approximately 99 percent of employers, employ nearly 50 percent of non-government employees, and are responsible for about two-thirds to three-quarters of net new jobs, according to the Office of Advocacy of the U.S. Small Business Administration.

1. Account Titles

ACCOUNT	Cash						ACCOUNT NO. 1110	

DATE	ITEM	POST. REF.	DEBIT	CREDIT	BALANCE DEBIT	BALANCE CREDIT
Dec. 20-- 1	Balance	✓			2826000	
31		CR12	3718080		6544080	
31		CP24		3636052	2908028	

2. Account Balances

Hobby Shack, Inc.
Work Sheet
For Year Ended December 31, 20--

		1 TRIAL BALANCE DEBIT	2 TRIAL BALANCE CREDIT
	ACCOUNT TITLE	DEBIT	CREDIT
1	Cash	2908028	
2	Petty Cash	30000	
3	Accounts Receivable	1469840	
4	Allow. for Uncoll. Accts.		12752
5	Merchandise Inventory	14048000	
6	Supplies—Office	348000	
7	Supplies—Store	394400	
8	Prepaid Insurance	580000	
9	Office Equipment	3586450	
10	Acc. Depr.—Office Equipment		649700
11	Store Equipment	4084950	
12	Acc. Depr.—Store Equipment		506900
13	Accounts Payable		1158303
14	Federal Income Tax Payable		
40	Insurance Expense		
41	Miscellaneous Expense	256490	
42	Payroll Taxes Expense	910500	
43	Rent Expense	1800000	
44	Salary Expense	10452500	
45	Supplies Expense—Office		
46	Supplies Expense—Store		
47	Uncollectible Accounts Expense		
48	Utilities Expense	382000	
49	Federal Income Tax Expense	1800000	
50		67086159	67086159

3. Total, prove and rule the debit and credit columns.

STEPS RECORDING A TRIAL BALANCE ON A WORK SHEET

1 Write the title of each general ledger account in the work sheet's Account Title column in the same order they appear in the general ledger. All accounts are listed regardless of whether there is a balance or not. Listing all accounts reduces the possibility of overlooking an account that needs to be brought up to date.

2 Write the balance of each account in the appropriate work sheet's Trial Balance Debit or Credit column. The amounts are taken from the general ledger accounts.

3 Total, prove, and rule the Trial Balance Debit and Credit columns of the work sheet.

The balance of Supplies—Office in the trial balance, $3,480.00, is the cost of office supplies on hand at the beginning of the year plus the office supplies purchased during the year. The supplies on hand on December 31 are counted and determined to be $750.00. The difference is the value of office supplies used during the year, which is an expense.

Likewise, the balance of Supplies—Store in the trial balance, $3,944.00, is the cost of store supplies on hand at the beginning of the year plus the store supplies purchased during the year. The value of store supplies on hand on December 31 is determined to be $1,034.00.

Analyzing Supplies Adjustments

Four questions are asked to analyze the adjustments for the supplies accounts.

1. **What is the balance of the Supplies accounts?**
   Supplies—Office, *$3,480.00*
   Supplies—Store, *$3,944.00*
2. **What should the balance be for these accounts?**
   Supplies—Office, *$750.00*
   Supplies—Store, *$1,034.00*
3. **What must be done to correct the account balances?**
   Decrease Supplies—Office, *$2,730.00 ($3,480.00 − 750.00)*
   Decrease Supplies—Store, *$2,910.00 ($3,944.00 − 1,034.00)*
4. **What adjustment is made?**
   Debit:
   Supplies Expense—Office, *$2,730.00*
   Supplies Expense—Store, *$2,910.00*
   Credit:
   Supplies—Office, *$2,730.00*
   Supplies—Store, *$2,910.00*

The supplies adjustments are shown in the T accounts. The December 31 balance shown in faded type is the balance before the adjustments.

Supplies Expense—Office	
Adj. (a) 2,730.00	

Supplies—Office	
Dec. 31 Bal. 3,480.00	Adj. (a) 2,730.00
(Adj. Bal. 750.00)	

Supplies Expense—Store	
Adj. (b) 2,910.00	

Supplies—Store	
Dec. 31 Bal. 3,944.00	Adj. (b) 2,910.00
(Adj Bal. 1,034.00)	

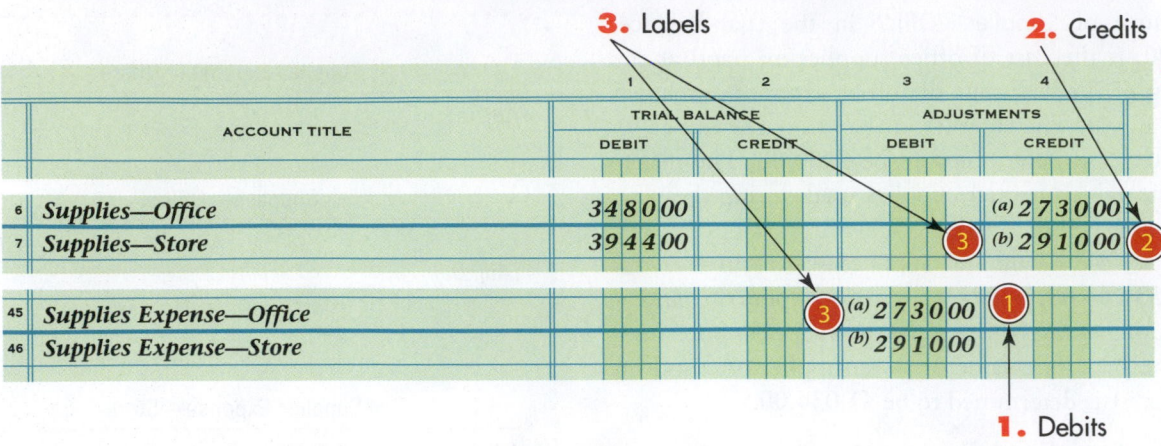

3. Labels **2. Credits**

	ACCOUNT TITLE	TRIAL BALANCE		ADJUSTMENTS	
		DEBIT	CREDIT	DEBIT	CREDIT
6	Supplies—Office	3 4 8 0 00			(a) 2 7 3 0 00
7	Supplies—Store	3 9 4 4 00		③	(b) 2 9 1 0 00 ②
45	Supplies Expense—Office			③ (a) 2 7 3 0 00 ①	
46	Supplies Expense—Store			(b) 2 9 1 0 00	

1. Debits

STEPS — RECORDING WORK SHEET ADJUSTMENTS FOR SUPPLIES

① Write the debit amounts in the Adjustments Debit column on the lines with the appropriate account titles: $2,730.00 with *Supplies Expense—Office* and $2,910.00 with *Supplies Expense—Store*.

② Write the credit amounts in the Adjustments Credit column on the lines with the appropriate account titles: $2,730.00 with *Supplies—Office* and $2,910.00 with *Supplies—Store*.

③ Label the two parts of the *Supplies—Office* adjustment with a small letter *a* in parentheses, *(a)*. Label the two parts of the *Supplies—Store* adjustment with a small letter *b* in parentheses, *(b)*.

Insurance premiums are debited to a prepaid insurance account when paid. During the year, Hobby Shack paid $5,800.00 of insurance premiums.

Analyzing a Prepaid Insurance Adjustment

Hobby Shack determined that the value of prepaid insurance on December 31 is $2,630.00. Therefore, the value of insurance used during the year is $3,170.00 ($5,800.00 − $2,630.00). This difference is the amount of insurance expense for the year. Prepaid Insurance is credited and Insurance Expense is debited at the end of the fiscal period for the value of insurance used.

The prepaid insurance adjustment is shown in the T accounts. The December 31 balance shown in faded type is the balance before the adjustment.

1. **What is the balance of** Prepaid Insurance?
   $5,800.00

2. **What should the balance be for this account?**
   $2,630.00

3. **What must be done to correct the account balance?**
   Decrease $3,170.00 ($5,800.00 − $2,630.00)

4. **What adjustment is made?**
   Debit Insurance Expense, *$3,170.00*
   Credit Prepaid Insurance, *$3,170.00*

Insurance Expense	
Adj. (c) 3,170.00	

Prepaid Insurance	
Dec. 31 Bal. 5,800.00	Adj. (c) 3,170.00
(New Bal. 2,630.00)	

Recording a Prepaid Insurance Adjustment

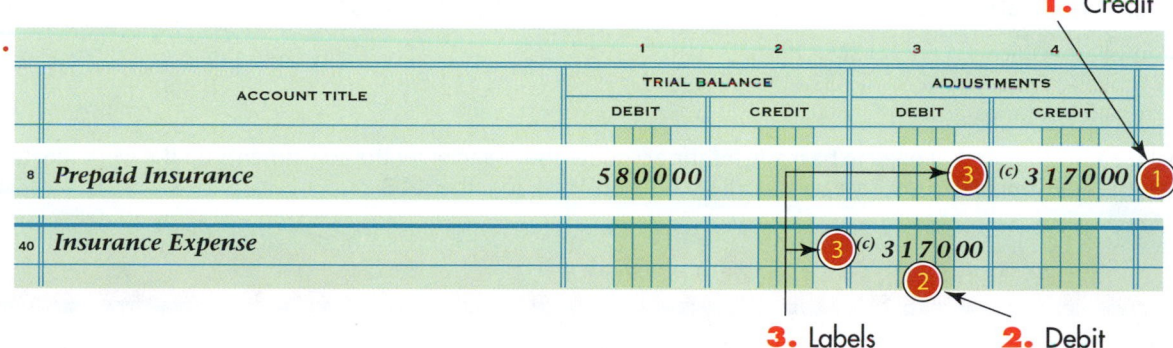

1. Credit

3. Labels   **2.** Debit

STEPS — RECORDING WORK SHEET ADJUSTMENTS FOR PREPAID INSURANCE

1. Enter the amount of insurance used, *$3,170.00*, in the Adjustments Credit column on the Prepaid Insurance line of the work sheet.

2. Enter the same amount, *$3,170.00*, in the Adjustments Debit column on the Insurance Expense line of the work sheet.

3. Label the two parts of the adjustment with a small letter *c* in parentheses, *(c)*.

End of Lesson
REVIEW

AUDIT YOUR UNDERSTANDING

1. What accounts are used for the adjustment to office supplies?
2. What accounts are used for the adjustment to prepaid insurance?

WORK TOGETHER 14-2

Beginning an 8-column work sheet for a merchandising business

A partially completed work sheet for Coastal Aquatics is given in the *Working Papers*. Four general ledger accounts are shown below. Your instructor will guide you through the following examples.

1. Enter the accounts and account balances on the following lines.

Line	Account	Account Balance
3	Accounts Receivable	$ 15,485.25
13	Accounts Payable	18,482.28
29	Sales	845,828.09
32	Purchases	389,184.01

2. Total, prove, and rule the trial balance.

3. From a physical count of the following, December 31 balances are determined to be:

Supplies—Office	$657.15
Supplies—Store	633.11
Prepaid Insurance	800.00

Analyze adjustments that need to be made for the accounts above and enter the adjustments on the work sheet. Label the adjustments *(a)–(c)*. Save your work to complete Work Together 14-3.

ON YOUR OWN 14-2

Beginning an 8-column work sheet for a merchandising business

A partially completed work sheet for Sonoma Treasures is given in the *Working Papers*. Four general ledger accounts are shown below. Work this problem independently.

1. Enter the accounts and account balances on the following lines.

Line	Account	Account Balance
8	Prepaid Insurance	$ 12,000.00
25	Capital Stock	210,000.00
30	Sales Discount	715.25
43	Rent Expense	30,000.00

2. Total, prove, and rule the trial balance.

3. From a physical count of the following, December 31 balances are determined to be:

Supplies—Office	$ 633.61
Supplies—Store	983.36
Prepaid Insurance	3,000.00

Analyze adjustments that need to be made for the accounts above and enter the adjustments on the work sheet. Label the adjustments *(a)–(c)*. Save your work to complete On Your Own 14-3.

Planning and Recording a Merchandise Inventory Adjustment

MERCHANDISE INVENTORY

In addition to supplies and prepaid insurance, Hobby Shack needs to adjust the merchandise inventory account. Planning the adjustment is similar to the adjustment for supplies. However, the adjusting entry includes a new account.

The amount of goods on hand for sale to customers is called **merchandise inventory**. The general ledger account in which merchandise inventory is recorded is titled Merchandise Inventory. Merchandise Inventory is an asset account with a normal debit balance.

Merchandise Inventory

Debit	Credit
Increase	Decrease

Hobby Shack's merchandise inventory account on January 1, the beginning of the fiscal year, has a debit balance of $140,480.00.

Merchandise Inventory

Jan. 1 Bal.	140,480.00

The balance of the merchandise inventory account on December 31, the end of the fiscal year, is the same amount, $140,480.00. The January 1 and December 31 balances are the same because no entries have been made in the account during the fiscal year. The changes in inventory resulting from purchases and sales transactions have not been recorded in the merchandise inventory account.

During a fiscal period, the amount of merchandise on hand increases each time merchandise is purchased. However, all purchases are recorded in the purchases account. The amount of merchandise on hand decreases each time merchandise is sold. However, all sales are recorded in the sales account. This procedure makes it easier to determine the total purchases and sales during a fiscal period. The merchandise inventory account balance, therefore, must be adjusted to reflect the changes resulting from purchases and sales during a fiscal period.

STOCKBYTE/GETTY IMAGES

3. Label

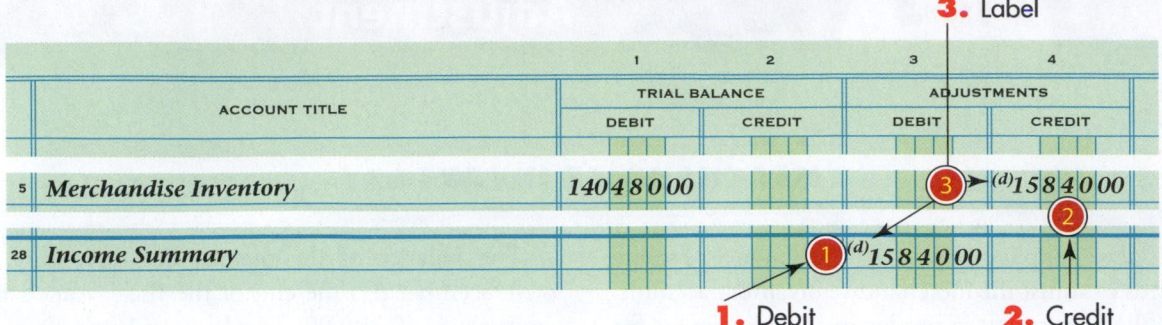

	ACCOUNT TITLE	TRIAL BALANCE		ADJUSTMENTS	
		DEBIT	CREDIT	DEBIT	CREDIT
5	*Merchandise Inventory*	140 4 8 0 00		③	(d)15 8 4 0 00 ②
28	*Income Summary*			① (d)15 8 4 0 00	

1. Debit   **2.** Credit

The two accounts used to adjust the merchandise inventory are Merchandise Inventory and Income Summary.

Before the adjustment, the merchandise inventory account has a January 1 debit balance of $140,480.00. The merchandise inventory account balance, however, is not up-to-date. The actual count of merchandise on December 31 shows that the inventory is valued at $124,640.00. Therefore, the merchandise inventory account balance must be adjusted to show the current value of merchandise on hand.

Most accounts needing adjustment at the end of a fiscal period have a related temporary account. For example, when the account Prepaid Insurance is adjusted, Insurance Expense is the related expense account, a temporary account. Merchandise Inventory, however, does not have a related expense account. Therefore, Income Summary, a temporary account, is used to adjust the merchandise inventory account at the end of a fiscal period.

Four questions are asked in analyzing the adjustment for merchandise inventory.

1. **What is the balance of** Merchandise Inventory?
   $140,480.00

2. **What should the balance be for this account?**
   $124,640.00

3. **What must be done to correct the account balance?**
   Decrease $15,840.00

4. **What adjustment is made?**
   Debit Income Summary, *$15,840.00*
   Credit Merchandise Inventory, *$15,840.00*

Merchandise Inventory			
Jan. 1 Bal.	140,480.00	Adj. (d)	15,840.00
(New Bal.	124,640.00)		

Income Summary			
Adj. (d)	15,840.00		

Income Summary is debited and Merchandise Inventory is credited for $15,840.00. The beginning debit balance of Merchandise Inventory, *$140,480.00*, minus the adjustment credit amount, *$15,840.00*, equals the ending debit balance of Merchandise Inventory, *$124,640.00*.

STEPS

RECORDING A WORK SHEET ADJUSTMENT FOR MERCHANDISE INVENTORY

① Write the debit amount, *$15,840.00*, in the Adjustments Debit column on the line with the account title *Income Summary*.

② Write the credit amount, *$15,840.00*, in the Adjustments Credit column on the line with the account title *Merchandise Inventory*.

③ Label the two parts of this adjustment with a small letter *d* in parentheses, *(d)*.

If the amount of merchandise inventory on hand is greater than the January 1 balance of Merchandise Inventory, opposite entries would be made—debit Merchandise Inventory and credit Income Summary. For example, Venable Company's merchandise inventory account on January 1 has a debit balance of $294,700.00. The count of merchandise on December 31 shows that the inventory is valued at $298,900.00. The merchandise on hand is $4,200.00 greater than the January 1 balance of Merchandise Inventory.

Four questions are asked in analyzing the adjustment for merchandise inventory.

1. **What is the balance of** Merchandise Inventory?
   $294,700.00
2. **What should the balance be for this account?**
   $298,900.00
3. **What must be done to correct the account balance?**
   Increase $4,200.00
4. **What adjustment is made?**
   Debit Merchandise Inventory, *$4,200.00*
   Credit Income Summary, *$4,200.00*

The merchandise inventory adjustment is shown in the T accounts.

Merchandise Inventory		
Jan. 1 Bal.	294,700.00	
Adj. (d)	4,200.00	
(New Bal.	298,900.00)	

Income Summary	
	Adj. (d) 4,200.00

Merchandise Inventory is debited and Income Summary is credited for $4,200.00. The beginning debit balance of Merchandise Inventory, *$294,700.00*, plus the adjustment debit amount, *$4,200.00*, equals the ending debit balance of Merchandise Inventory, *$298,900.00*.

DIGITAL VISION/GETTY IMAGES

REMEMBER

When an account that requires adjusting does not have a related expense account, the temporary account Income Summary is used.

End of Lesson
REVIEW

AUDIT YOUR UNDERSTANDING

1. In what order should general ledger accounts be listed on a work sheet?
2. What accounts are used for the adjustment for merchandise inventory?
3. What adjusting entry is entered on a work sheet when the ending merchandise inventory is less than the beginning value?
4. When is the temporary account Income Summary used?

TERM REVIEW

merchandise inventory

WORK TOGETHER 14-3

Analyzing and recording an adjustment for merchandise inventory

Use the work sheet from Work Together 14-2. Your instructor will guide you through the following example.

1. From a physical count of merchandise inventory, the December 31 balance is determined to be $234,904.20. Analyze the merchandise inventory adjustment and enter the adjustment on the work sheet. Label the adjustment (d). Save your work to complete Work Together 14-4.

ON YOUR OWN 14-3

Analyzing and recording an adjustment for merchandise inventory

Use the work sheet from On Your Own 14-2. Work this problem independently.

1. From a physical count of merchandise inventory, the December 31 balance is determined to be $261,089.97. Analyze the merchandise inventory adjustment and enter the adjustment on the work sheet. Label the adjustment (d). Save your work to complete On Your Own 14-4.

Planning and Recording an Allowance for Uncollectible Accounts Adjustment

ALLOWANCE METHOD OF RECORDING LOSSES FROM UNCOLLECTIBLE ACCOUNTS

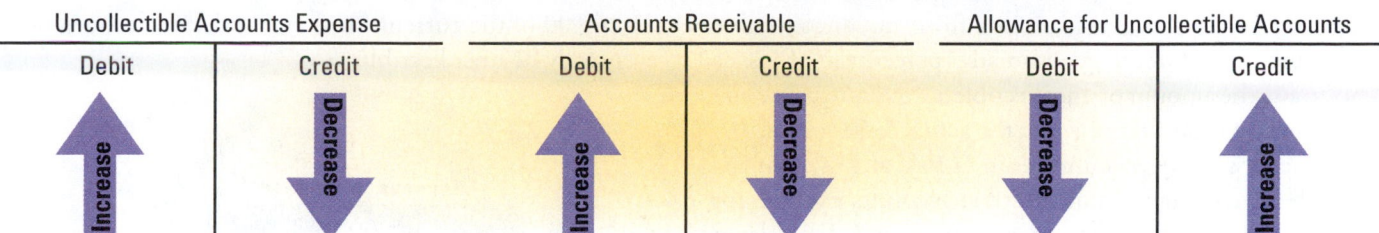

With each sale on account, a business takes a risk that customers will not pay their accounts. Accounts receivable that cannot be collected are called **uncollectible accounts**. This risk is a cost of doing business that should be recorded as an expense in the same accounting period that the revenue is earned. Accurate financial reporting requires that expenses be recorded in the fiscal period in which the expenses contribute to earning revenue. [CONCEPT: Matching Expenses with Revenue]

At the end of a fiscal year, a business does not know which customer accounts will become uncollectible. If a business knew exactly which accounts would become uncollectible, it could credit Accounts Receivable and each customer account for the uncollectible amounts and debit Uncollectible Accounts Expense for the same amounts.

To solve this accounting problem, a business can calculate and record an estimated amount of uncollectible accounts expense. Estimating uncollectible accounts expense at the end of a fiscal period accomplishes two objectives:

1. It reports a balance sheet amount for Accounts Receivable that reflects the amount the business expects to collect in the future.
2. It recognizes the expense of uncollectible accounts in the same period in which the related revenue is recorded.

To record estimated uncollectible accounts, an adjusting entry is made affecting two accounts. The estimated amount of uncollectible accounts is debited to Uncollectible Accounts Expense and credited to an account titled Allowance for Uncollectible Accounts.

An account that reduces a related account is known as a *contra account*. Allowance for Uncollectible Accounts is a contra account to its related asset account, Accounts Receivable.

Crediting the estimated value of uncollectible accounts to a contra account is called the **allowance method of recording losses from uncollectible accounts**. The difference between an asset's account balance and its related contra account balance is called **book value**. The difference between the balance of Accounts Receivable and its contra account, Allowance for Uncollectible Accounts, is called the **book value of accounts receivable**. The book value of accounts receivable, which is reported on the balance sheet, represents the total amount of accounts receivable the business expects to collect in the future.

A contra account is usually assigned the next number of the account number sequence after its related account in the chart of accounts. Hobby Shack's Accounts Receivable account is numbered 1130 and the Allowance for Uncollectible Accounts contra account is numbered 1135.

Total Sales on Account	×	Percentage	=	Estimated Uncollectible Accounts Expense
$124,500.00	×	1%	=	$1,245.00

Many businesses use a percentage of total sales on account to estimate uncollectible accounts expense. Each sale on account represents a risk of loss from an uncollectible account. Therefore, if the estimated percentage of loss is accurate, the amount of uncollectible accounts expense will be accurate regardless of when the actual losses occur.

Since a sale on account creates a risk of loss, estimating the percentage of uncollectible accounts expense for the same period matches sales revenue with the related uncollectible accounts expense. [CONCEPT: Matching Expenses with Revenue]

Hobby Shack estimates uncollectible accounts expense by calculating a percentage of total sales on account. A review of Hobby Shack's previous experience in collecting sales on account shows that actual uncollectible accounts expense has been about 1% of total sales on account. The company's total sales on account for the year is $124,500.00. Thus, Hobby Shack estimates that $1,245.00 of the current fiscal year's sales on account will eventually be uncollectible.

FOR YOUR INFORMATION

FYI

Allowance for Bad Debts *and* Allowance for Doubtful Accounts *are account titles sometimes used instead of* Allowance for Uncollectible Accounts.

FINANCIAL LITERACY

Personal Budgets

Mention the word "budget" to most people and many negative thoughts come to mind. However, a budget does not have to be restrictive or inflexible. In fact, a budget may give you more freedom.

A budget is merely a plan that helps you achieve your goals. When getting ready to prepare a budget, you not only need to gather income and expense data, but you also need to determine and prioritize your goals. For example, suppose you want to take a trip during spring break, but you also like to have all the latest clothing styles. If you can't do both, which is more important to you? No one can answer this question for you. Financial goals are very personal.

One of the major benefits of a budget is that any "leftover" money you have is used to fund your goals in their order of priority. This may mean that instead of spending money on the latest fashions, you may choose to save it to fund your spring-break trip—but only because you determined the trip was more important. You are in control, and your budget can change as your goals change.

Think of a budget as a flexible spending plan that helps you achieve your goals, and you will be more likely to follow your budget and actually be able to take that trip!

Activities

1. One way to gather expense data for your budget is to write down all of your expenses for a period of time. Do this for one week. Try to pick a typical week, and remember to include all expenses. Then categorize what you've spent into "needs" and "wants."

2. Survey five adults. Ask each one if he or she has a budget. If that person has a budget, ask if he or she follows it. What does he or she feel are the advantages and disadvantages of having a budget? Summarize your findings in a written report.

PHOTO: PHOTODISC/GETTY IMAGES

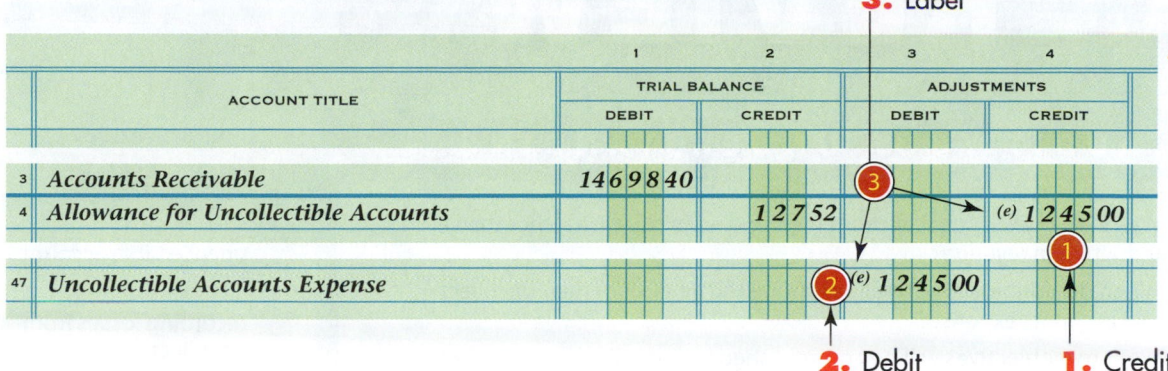

3. Label

	1	2	3	4
ACCOUNT TITLE	TRIAL BALANCE		ADJUSTMENTS	
	DEBIT	CREDIT	DEBIT	CREDIT
3 *Accounts Receivable*	14 6 9 8 40		③	
4 *Allowance for Uncollectible Accounts*		1 2 7 52		(e) 1 2 4 5 00
47 *Uncollectible Accounts Expense*			② (e) 1 2 4 5 00	①

2. Debit   **1.** Credit

The percentage of total sales on account method of estimating uncollectible accounts expense assumes that a portion of every sale on account dollar will become uncollectible. Hobby Shack has estimated that 1% of its $124,500.00 sales on account, or $1,245.00, will eventually become uncollectible.

At the end of a fiscal period, an adjustment for uncollectible accounts expense is planned on a work sheet.

The Allowance for Uncollectible Accounts balance in the Trial Balance Credit column, $127.52, is the allowance estimate from the previous fiscal period that has not yet been identified as uncollectible.

When the allowance account has a previous credit balance, the amount of the adjustment is added to the previous balance.

This new balance of the allowance account, $1,372.52, is the estimated amount of accounts receivable that will eventually become uncollectible. This amount, subtracted from the accounts receivable account balance, $14,698.40, is the book value of accounts receivable. Notice in the T accounts that Accounts Receivable is not affected by this adjustment. Also notice that Uncollectible Accounts Expense did not have a balance before the adjustment.

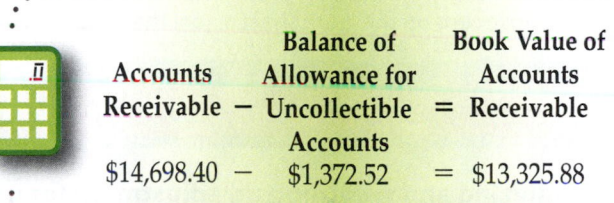

	Accounts Receivable	−	Balance of Allowance for Uncollectible Accounts	=	Book Value of Accounts Receivable
	$14,698.40	−	$1,372.52	=	$13,325.88

Hobby Shack estimates that it will collect $13,325.88 from its outstanding accounts receivable.

Accounts Receivable

Dec. 31 Bal.	14,698.40	

Uncollectible Accounts Expense

Adj. (e)	1,245.00	

Allowance for Uncollectible Accounts

	Bal.	127.52
	Adj. (e)	1,245.00
	(New Bal.	*1,372.52)*

STEPS

RECORDING A WORK SHEET ADJUSTMENT FOR UNCOLLECTIBLE ACCOUNTS

① Enter the estimated uncollectible amount, *$1,245.00*, in the Adjustments Credit column on the *Allowance for Uncollectible Accounts* line of the work sheet.

② Enter the same amount, *$1,245.00*, in the Adjustments Debit column on the *Uncollectible Accounts Expense* line of the work sheet.

③ Label the two parts of this adjustment with a small letter *e* in parentheses, *(e)*.

End of Lesson REVIEW

AUDIT YOUR UNDERSTANDING

1. Why is an uncollectible account recorded as an expense rather than a reduction in revenue?
2. When do businesses normally estimate the amount of their uncollectible accounts expense?
3. What two objectives will be accomplished by recording an estimated amount of uncollectible accounts expense?
4. Why is *Allowance for Uncollectible Accounts* called a *contra account*?
5. How is the book value of accounts receivable calculated?

TERMS REVIEW

uncollectible accounts

allowance method of recording losses from uncollectible accounts

book value

book value of accounts receivable

WORK TOGETHER 14-4

Analyzing and recording an adjustment for uncollectible accounts expense

Use the work sheet from Work Together 14-3. Your instructor will guide you through the following example.

1. Coastal Aquatics estimates uncollectible accounts expense as 0.5% of its total sales on account. During the current year, Coastal Aquatics had sales on account of $424,000.00. Record the uncollectible accounts expense adjustment on the work sheet. Label the adjustment *(e)*. Save your work to complete Work Together 14-5.

ON YOUR OWN 14-4

Analyzing and recording an adjustment for uncollectible accounts expense

Use the work sheet from On Your Own 14-3. Work this problem independently.

1. Sonoma Treasures estimates uncollectible accounts expense as 0.4% of its total sales on account. During the current year, Sonoma Treasures had sales on account of $462,500.00. Record the uncollectible accounts expense adjustment on the work sheet. Label the adjustment *(e)*. Save your work to complete On Your Own 14-5.

Planning and Recording Depreciation Adjustments

CATEGORIES OF ASSETS

Most businesses use two broad categories of assets in their operations. Cash and other assets expected to be exchanged for cash or consumed within a year are called **current assets**. Assets that will be used for a number of years in the operation of a business are called **plant assets**. Some of Hobby Shack's plant assets are computers, cash registers, sales display cases, and furniture.

Businesses may have three major types of plant assets—equipment, buildings, and land. Hobby Shack records its equipment in two different equipment accounts—**Office Equipment** and **Store Equipment**. Because it rents the building and the land where the business is located, Hobby Shack does not need plant asset accounts for buildings and land. [CONCEPT: Adequate Disclosure]

Depreciating Plant Assets

A business buys plant assets to use in earning revenue. Hobby Shack bought a new lighted display case. Hobby Shack knows that the display case will be useful only for a limited period of time. After several years, most display cases become worn from use and no longer attractively display the products. Hobby Shack will replace worn display cases with newer models. Thus, each display case has a limited useful life to the business.

In order to match revenue with the expenses used to earn the revenue, the cost of a plant asset should be expensed over the plant asset's useful life. A portion of a plant asset's cost is transferred to an expense account in each fiscal period that a plant asset is used to earn revenue. [CONCEPT: Matching Expenses with Revenue] The portion of a plant asset's cost that is transferred to an expense account in each fiscal period during a plant asset's useful life is called **depreciation expense**.

Three factors are considered in calculating the annual amount of depreciation expense for a plant asset.

1. *Original Cost.* The original cost of a plant asset includes all costs paid to make the asset usable to a business. These costs include the price of the asset, delivery costs, and any necessary installation costs.

2. *Estimated Salvage Value.* Generally, a business removes a plant asset from use and disposes of it when the asset is no longer usable. The amount that will be received for an asset at the time of its disposal is not known when the asset is bought. Thus, the amount that may be received at disposal must be estimated. The amount an owner expects to receive when a plant asset is removed from use is called **estimated salvage value**. Estimated salvage value may also be referred to as *residual value* or *scrap value*.

3. *Estimated Useful Life.* The total amount of depreciation expense is distributed over the estimated useful life of a plant asset. When a plant asset is bought, the exact length of useful life is not known. Therefore, the number of years of useful life must be estimated. Two factors affect the useful life of a plant asset: (1) physical depreciation and (2) functional depreciation. Physical depreciation is caused by wear from use and deterioration from aging and weathering. Functional depreciation occurs when a plant asset becomes inadequate or obsolete. An asset is inadequate when it can no longer satisfactorily perform the needed service. An asset is obsolete when a newer asset can operate more efficiently or produce better service.

CALCULATING DEPRECIATION EXPENSE AND BOOK VALUE

Straight-Line Depreciation

Charging an equal amount of depreciation expense for a plant asset in each year of useful life is called the **straight-line method of depreciation**.

Hobby Shack summarizes the depreciation expense for each plant asset to calculate the total depreciation expense recorded on the work sheet.

On January 2, 20X1, Hobby Shack bought a lighted display case for $1,250.00, with an estimated salvage value of $250.00 and an estimated useful life of 5 years. Using the straight-line method of depreciation, the annual depreciation expense, $200.00, is the same for each year in which the asset is used.

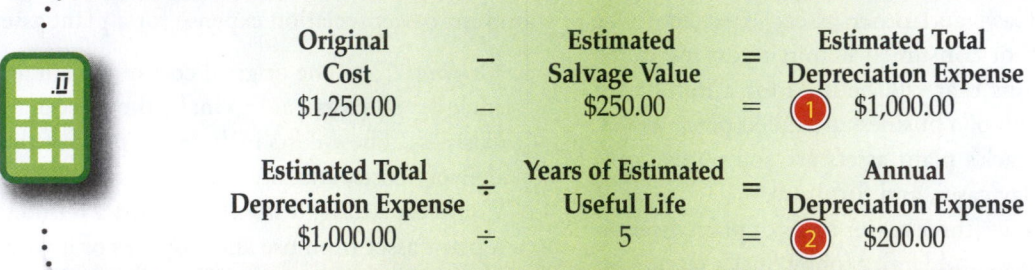

Original Cost	−	Estimated Salvage Value	=	Estimated Total Depreciation Expense
$1,250.00	−	$250.00	=	① $1,000.00

Estimated Total Depreciation Expense	÷	Years of Estimated Useful Life	=	Annual Depreciation Expense
$1,000.00	÷	5	=	② $200.00

STEPS — CALCULATING ANNUAL DEPRECIATION EXPENSE

① Subtract the asset's estimated salvage value from the asset's original cost. This difference is the estimated total depreciation expense for the asset's entire useful life.

② Divide the estimated total depreciation expense by the years of estimated useful life. The result is the annual depreciation expense.

Calculating Accumulated Depreciation

The total amount of depreciation expense that has been recorded since the purchase of a plant asset is called **accumulated depreciation**. The amount accumulates each year of the plant asset's useful life.

First, the depreciation expense that has accumulated over all prior years is determined. Second, the depreciation expense for the current year is calculated. Third, the prior accumulated depreciation and the current depreciation expense are added.

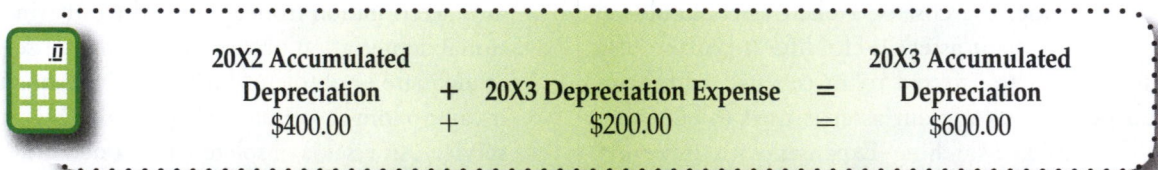

20X2 Accumulated Depreciation	+	20X3 Depreciation Expense	=	20X3 Accumulated Depreciation
$400.00	+	$200.00	=	$600.00

Calculating Book Value

The original cost of a plant asset minus accumulated depreciation is called the **book value of a plant asset**. The book value is calculated by subtracting the accumulated depreciation from the original cost of the asset.

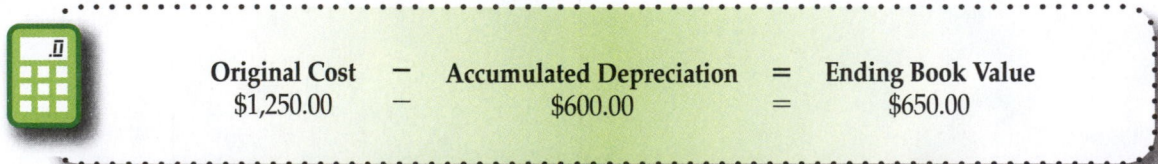

Original Cost	−	Accumulated Depreciation	=	Ending Book Value
$1,250.00	−	$600.00	=	$650.00

Procedures for recording the accumulated depreciation and book value of individual assets are presented in Chapter 18.

ANALYZING AND RECORDING ADJUSTMENTS FOR DEPRECIATION EXPENSE

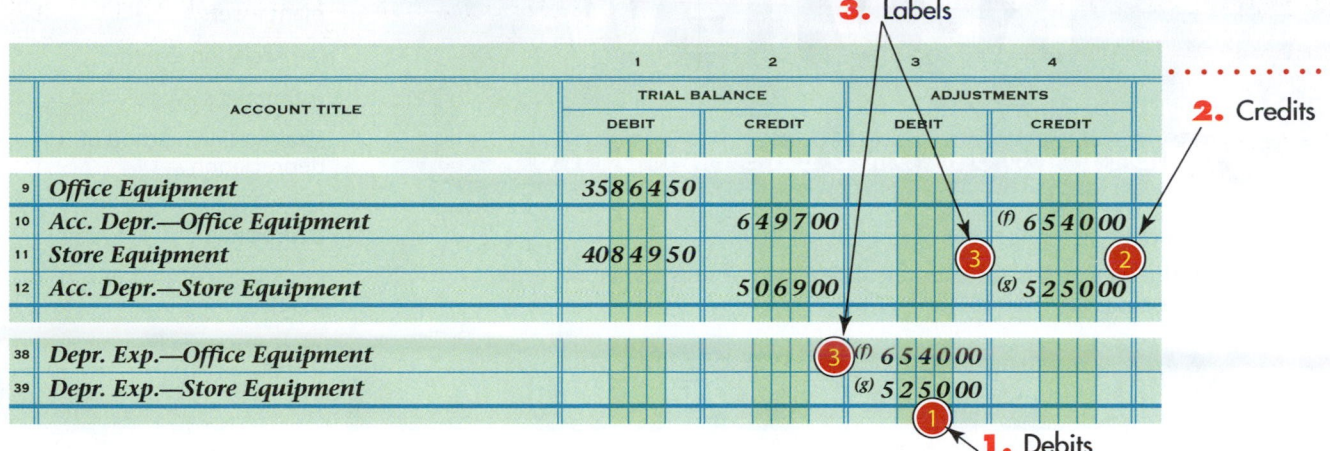

3. Labels

2. Credits

1. Debits

At the end of the fiscal year, Hobby Shack calculates the depreciation expense for each plant asset. Hobby Shack determined that total depreciation expense is $6,540.00 for office equipment and $5,250.00 for store equipment. Adjustments are planned in the Adjustments columns of the work sheet.

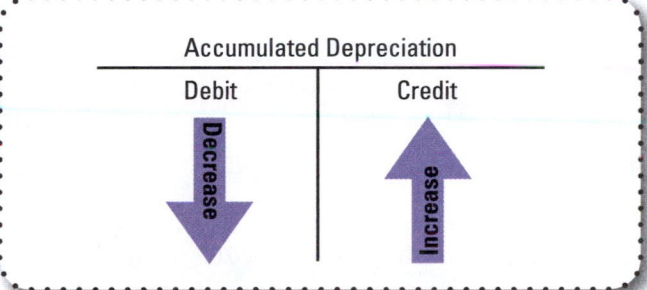

Accumulated Depreciation	
Debit	Credit
Decrease	Increase

It is important to retain original cost information for plant assets. Therefore, rather than credit the plant asset account, depreciation is recorded in the contra asset account Accumulated Depreciation.

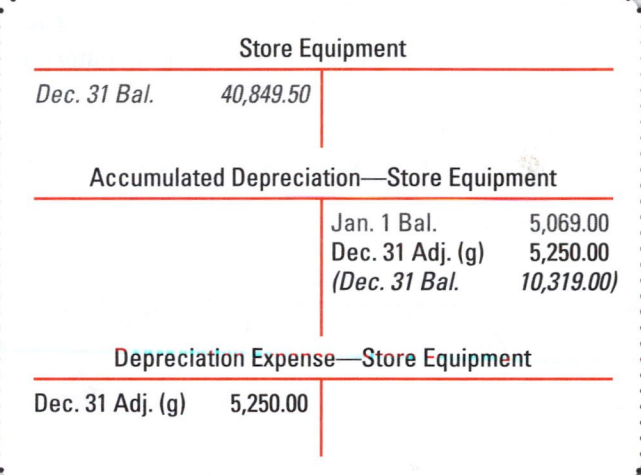

Store Equipment	
Dec. 31 Bal. 40,849.50	

Accumulated Depreciation—Store Equipment	
	Jan. 1 Bal. 5,069.00
	Dec. 31 Adj. (g) 5,250.00
	(Dec. 31 Bal. 10,319.00)

Depreciation Expense—Store Equipment	
Dec. 31 Adj. (g) 5,250.00	

At any time, the book value of plant assets can be calculated by subtracting Accumulated Depreciation from its related plant asset account.

Office Equipment	
Dec. 31 Bal. 35,864.50	

Accumulated Depreciation—Office Equipment	
	Jan. 1 Bal. 6,497.00
	Dec. 31 Adj. (f) 6,540.00
	(Dec. 31 Bal. 13,037.00)

Depreciation Expense—Office Equipment	
Dec. 31 Adj. (f) 6,540.00	

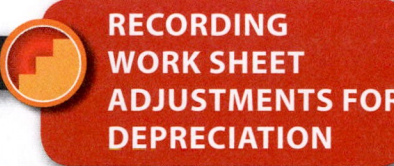

STEPS — **RECORDING WORK SHEET ADJUSTMENTS FOR DEPRECIATION**

1. Write the debit amounts in the Adjustments Debit column on the lines with the appropriate account titles: $6,540.00 with *Depreciation Expense—Office Equipment* and $5,250.00 with *Depreciation Expense—Store Equipment*.

2. Write the credit amounts in the Adjustments Credit column on the lines with the appropriate account titles: $6,540.00 with *Accumulated Depreciation—Office Equipment* and $5,250.00 with *Accumulated Depreciation—Store Equipment*.

3. Label the two parts of the Office Equipment adjustment with a small letter *f* in parentheses, *(f)*. Label the two parts of the Store Equipment adjustment with a small letter *g* in parentheses, *(g)*.

End of Lesson REVIEW

AUDIT YOUR UNDERSTANDING

1. What are the two categories of assets?
2. What three factors are used to calculate a plant asset's annual depreciation expense?

WORK TOGETHER 14-5

Planning and recording adjustments for depreciation

Use the work sheet from Work Together 14-4. Your instructor will guide you through the following example.

1. Calculate depreciation expense for a computer printer costing $1,600.00; estimated salvage value, $100.00, useful life, 5 years.
2. Calculate the book value of the computer printer at the end of its second year of service.
3. On December 31, Coastal Aquatics determined the total depreciation expense: office equipment, $6,120.00; store equipment, $5,060.00. Plan the work sheet adjustments and label the adjustments *(f)* and *(g)*. Save your work to complete Work Together 14-6.

ON YOUR OWN 14-5

Planning and recording adjustments for depreciation

Use the work sheet from On Your Own 14-4. Work this problem independently.

1. Calculate depreciation expense for a display rack costing $2,350.00; estimated salvage value, $600.00, useful life, 7 years.
2. Calculate the book value of the display rack at the end of its third year of service.
3. On December 31, Sonoma Treasures determined the total depreciation expense: office equipment, $5,184.00; store equipment, $6,480.00. Plan the work sheet adjustments and label the adjustments *(f)* and *(g)*. Save your work to complete On Your Own 14-6.

FEDERAL INCOME TAX EXPENSE ADJUSTMENT

Corporations anticipating annual federal income taxes of $500.00 or more are required to pay their estimated taxes each quarter. Estimated income tax is paid in quarterly installments in April, June, September, and December. However, the actual federal income tax owed is calculated at the end of a fiscal year. Based on the actual income tax owed for a year, a corporation must file an annual return. Any additional tax owed that was not paid in quarterly installments must be paid when the final return is filed.

Early in the current year, Hobby Shack estimated $18,000.00 federal income tax for the year. Hobby Shack paid $4,500.00 in each quarterly installment for a total of $18,000.00. Each tax payment is recorded as a debit to Federal Income Tax Expense and a credit to Cash.

Federal income tax is an expense of a corporation. However, the amount of tax depends on net income before the tax is recorded.

Federal Income Tax Expense is an expense account. The account appears under a major division titled *Income*

Tax Expense in Hobby Shack's chart of accounts. Federal Income Tax Payable, a liability account, appears under the heading *Current Liabilities*.

In order to make adjustments to federal income tax, you must first determine the net income before federal income tax expense. To calculate, follow these steps:

1. Complete all other adjustments on a work sheet.
2. Extend all amounts except Federal Income Tax Expense to the Income Statement or Balance Sheet columns.
3. On a separate sheet of paper, total the work sheet's Income Statement columns.
4. Calculate the difference between the Income Statement Debit column total and the Income Statement Credit column total. This difference between the totals of these two income statement columns is the net income before federal income tax expense.

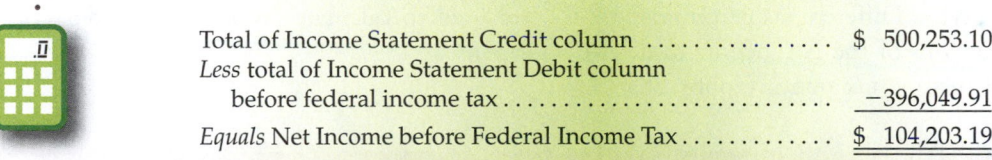

Total of Income Statement Credit column	$ 500,253.10
Less total of Income Statement Debit column before federal income tax	−396,049.91
Equals Net Income before Federal Income Tax	$ 104,203.19

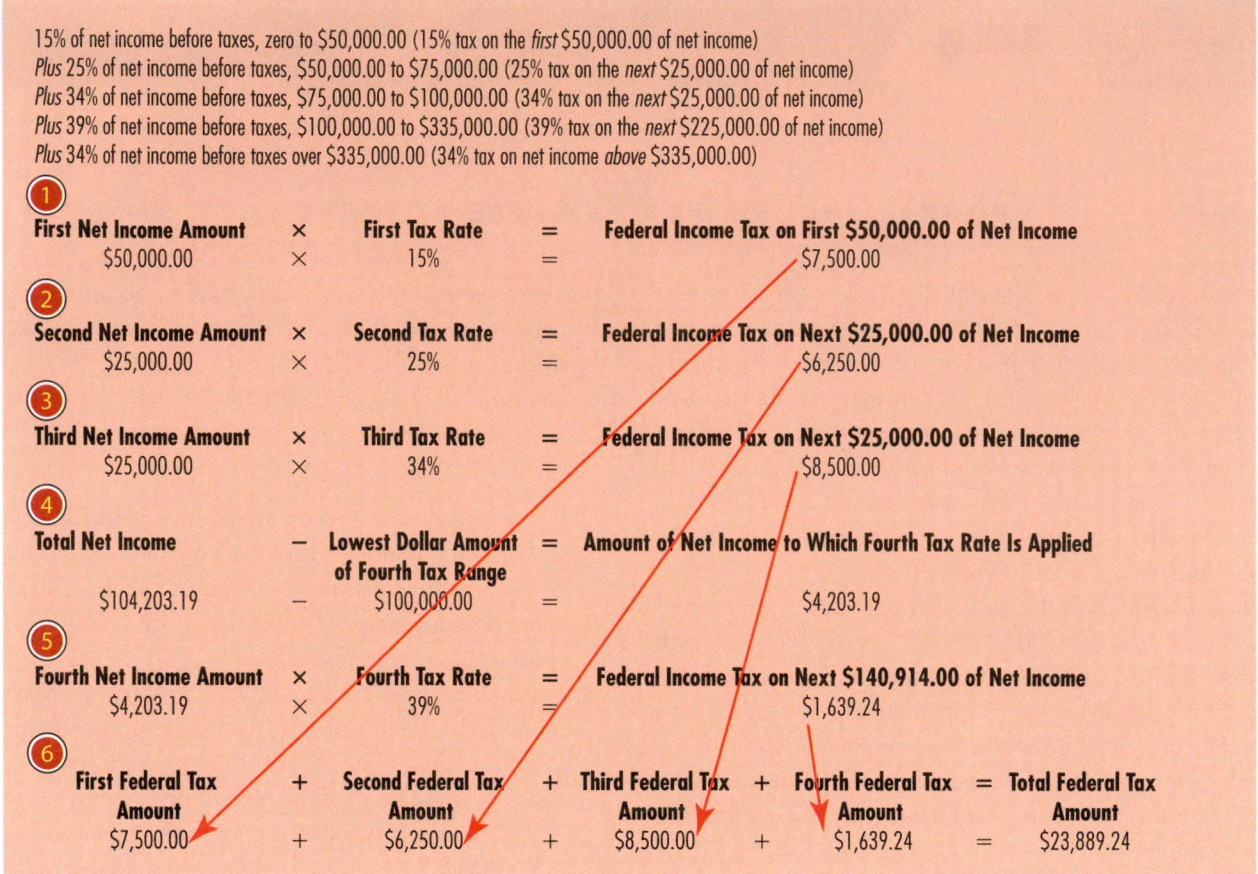

15% of net income before taxes, zero to $50,000.00 (15% tax on the *first* $50,000.00 of net income)
Plus 25% of net income before taxes, $50,000.00 to $75,000.00 (25% tax on the *next* $25,000.00 of net income)
Plus 34% of net income before taxes, $75,000.00 to $100,000.00 (34% tax on the *next* $25,000.00 of net income)
Plus 39% of net income before taxes, $100,000.00 to $335,000.00 (39% tax on the *next* $225,000.00 of net income)
Plus 34% of net income before taxes over $335,000.00 (34% tax on net income *above* $335,000.00)

①

| First Net Income Amount | × | First Tax Rate | = | Federal Income Tax on First $50,000.00 of Net Income |
| $50,000.00 | × | 15% | = | $7,500.00 |

②

| Second Net Income Amount | × | Second Tax Rate | = | Federal Income Tax on Next $25,000.00 of Net Income |
| $25,000.00 | × | 25% | = | $6,250.00 |

③

| Third Net Income Amount | × | Third Tax Rate | = | Federal Income Tax on Next $25,000.00 of Net Income |
| $25,000.00 | × | 34% | = | $8,500.00 |

④

| Total Net Income | − | Lowest Dollar Amount of Fourth Tax Range | = | Amount of Net Income to Which Fourth Tax Rate Is Applied |
| $104,203.19 | − | $100,000.00 | = | $4,203.19 |

⑤

| Fourth Net Income Amount | × | Fourth Tax Rate | = | Federal Income Tax on Next $140,914.00 of Net Income |
| $4,203.19 | × | 39% | = | $1,639.24 |

⑥

| First Federal Tax Amount | + | Second Federal Tax Amount | + | Third Federal Tax Amount | + | Fourth Federal Tax Amount | = | Total Federal Tax Amount |
| $7,500.00 | + | $6,250.00 | + | $8,500.00 | + | $1,639.24 | = | $23,889.24 |

The amount of federal income tax expense a corporation must pay is calculated using a tax rate table furnished by the Internal Revenue Service. Different tax percentages are applied to different portions of the net income to determine the total federal income tax owed. Hobby Shack's net income before federal income tax is $104,203.19. Corporation tax rates in effect when this text was written are used to calculate Hobby Shack's federal income tax expense.

STEPS   CALCULATING FEDERAL INCOME TAX

① Multiply $50,000.00 by a tax rate of 15% to calculate the first federal income tax amount. This is the tax Hobby Shack must pay on its first $50,000.00 of net income.

② Multiply $25,000.00 by a tax rate of 25% to calculate the second federal income tax amount. This is the tax Hobby Shack must pay on the next $25,000.00 of net income.

③ Multiply $25,000.00 by a tax rate of 34% to calculate the third federal income tax amount. This is the tax Hobby Shack must pay on the next $25,000.00 of net income.

④ The tax rate of 39% applies to all net income that falls in the range of $100,000.00 to $335,000.00. Hobby Shack's net income is $104,203.19. When the net income does not equal or exceed the highest dollar amount given in a range, the amount of net income to which the tax rate is applied is determined by subtracting the lowest dollar amount in the range from the total net income. ($104,203.19 − $100,000.00 = $4,203.19)

⑤ Multiply $4,203.19 by a tax rate of 39% to calculate the fourth federal income tax amount, $1,639.24. This is the tax Hobby Shack must pay on the remainder of its net income.

⑥ Add the four tax amounts together to determine Hobby Shack's federal income tax expense for the fiscal year.

		1	2	3	4	5	6	7	8	
	ACCOUNT TITLE	TRIAL BALANCE		ADJUSTMENTS		INCOME STATEMENT		BALANCE SHEET		
		DEBIT	CREDIT	DEBIT	CREDIT	DEBIT	CREDIT	DEBIT	CREDIT	
9	Office Equipment	35 864 50						35 864 50		9
10	Acc. Depr.—Office Equipment		6 497 00		(f) 6 540 00				13 037 00	10
11	Store Equipment	40 849 50						40 849 50		11
12	Acc. Depr.—Store Equipment		5 069 00		(g) 5 250 00				10 319 00	12
13	Accounts Payable		11 583 03						11 583 03	13
14	Federal Income Tax Payable			①	(h) 5 889 24				③ 5 889 24	14
46	Supplies Expense—Store			(b) 2 910 00		2 910 00				46
47	Uncollectible Accounts Expense			(e) 1 245 00		1 245 00				47
48	Utilities Expense	3 820 00				3 820 00				48
49	Federal Income Tax Expense	18 000 00		① (h) 5 889 24		③ 23 889 24				49
50		670 861 59	670 861 59	43 574 24	43 574 24					50
51					②					51

1. Calculate and enter the federal income tax adjustment.

2. Total and rule the adjustment columns.

3. Extend the account balances.

STEPS — RECORDING A WORK SHEET ADJUSTMENT FOR FEDERAL INCOME TAX EXPENSE

① Calculate the amount of the federal income tax expense adjustment. The adjustment is the difference between the federal income tax for the year and the taxes paid during the year.

Federal Income Tax.	$23,889.24
Less Total of Quarterly Installments	−18,000.00
Equals Federal Income Tax Adjustment	$ 5,889.24

Enter the federal income tax expense adjustment, *$5,889.24*, in the Adjustments Credit column on the *Federal Income Tax Payable* line of the work sheet. Enter the same amount in the Adjustments Debit column of the *Federal Income Tax Expense* line of the work sheet. Label both parts of the adjustment *(h)*.

② Total and rule the Adjustments columns.

③ Extend the *Federal Income Tax Expense* account balance, *$23,889.24*, to the Income Statement Debit column. Extend the amount for *Federal Income Tax Payable*, *$5,889.24*, to the Balance Sheet Credit column.

Federal Income Tax Expense

4/15	4,500.00		
6/15	4,500.00		
9/15	4,500.00		
12/15	4,500.00		
(12/15 Bal.	*18,000.00)*		
12/31 Adj. (h)	5,889.24		
(New Bal.	*23,889.24)*		

Federal Income Tax Payable

		12/31 Adj. (h)	5,889.24

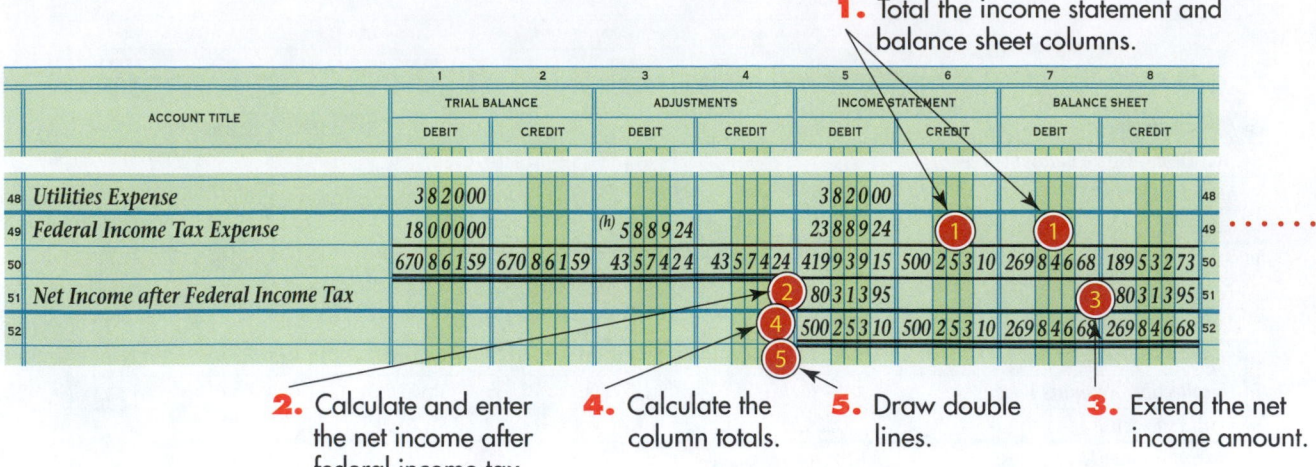

1. Total the income statement and balance sheet columns.

2. Calculate and enter the net income after federal income tax.

4. Calculate the column totals.

5. Draw double lines.

3. Extend the net income amount.

After the adjustment for federal income tax expense has been recorded, the work sheet is ready to be completed. Income Statement column totals are used to calculate net income after federal income tax.

Hobby Shack follows the same procedures for completing a work sheet as described for TechKnow in Chapter 6, with the exception of the Income Summary account. TechKnow sells a service, not merchandise. Therefore, TechKnow has no amount recorded in the Income Summary account, a related account used to adjust Merchandise Inventory. Hobby Shack sells merchandise. Therefore, the Income Summary account is used as the related account

to adjust Merchandise Inventory. The merchandise inventory adjustment reflects the increases and decreases in the amount of goods on hand resulting from purchases and sales. Therefore, the amount recorded in Income Summary is extended to the work sheet's Income Statement Debit or Credit column. An Income Summary debit amount is extended to the Income Statement Debit column. An Income Summary credit amount is extended to the Income Statement Credit column.

Hobby Shack's completed work sheet for the year ended December 31, 20--, is shown on pages 432–433.

STEPS   COMPLETING A WORK SHEET

1. Total the Income Statement and Balance Sheet columns.

2. Write the words *Net Income after Federal Income Tax* on line 51 of the work sheet. Calculate and enter the net income after federal income tax, *$80,313.95*, in the Income Statement Debit column on this new line of the work sheet.

Total of Income Statement Credit column	$500,253.10
Less Total of Income Statement Debit column	−419,939.15
Equals Net Income after Federal Income Tax	$ 80,313.95

3. Extend the net income after federal income tax amount, *$80,313.95*, to the Balance Sheet Credit column.

4. Total the four Income Statement and Balance Sheet columns. Determine that the totals of each pair of columns are in balance.

5. Rule double lines across the Income Statement and Balance Sheet columns to show that the totals have been verified as correct.

Everlyn Johnson, Small Business Owner

COURTESY OF EVERLYN JOHNSON

By the age of 18, you will have gained experiences that will change your life in ways you might never imagine. These experiences may come from an extracurricular activity, a part-time job, or a hobby, and they may influence the direction of your career or retirement.

For Everlyn Johnson, the youthful experience that would affect her life was learning to sew. Her mother taught her the basics when Everlyn was 11. Advancing from quilts to doll clothes to her prom dress, Everlyn learned that human sciences (formerly home economics) would lead her to a fulfilling career. Earning bachelor's, master's, and doctoral degrees in the area, Dr. Johnson worked with her state's cooperative extension service for over 27 years. In her role as a county agent, she was responsible for educating the public on home living skills—including sewing. Later she advanced to a position where she was responsible for gathering and communicating current knowledge and research with other county agents.

Most people plan to relax in their retirement. But not Dr. Johnson. She says, "I constantly heard people say that they wish they knew how to sew. I saw a niche that needed filling and decided I was the person to fulfill it." So after just three years of retirement, Everlyn decided to open a fabric store.

One of her first tasks to prepare for the store opening was to enroll in an income tax course at the local university. She recalls, "I felt the tax course would help me do a better job of keeping the records of the business and would ensure that I planned the business to take advantage of tax laws." Then she started doing her homework, meeting with a variety of small business owners to learn the rewards and pitfalls of small business ownership.

Everlyn visited fabric stores outside her market area. "The owners of many stores painted less than a rosy picture of the prospect of opening a store," she remarks. "I felt they were missing something—that main ingredient that would make the store successful. Then I visited two stores that were constantly conducting sewing classes. It was clear to see that these classes were the key to the success of the stores. Perfect!" Having spent most of her career teaching classes, Everlyn now plans sewing classes, teaching some herself, to serve her customers and to promote the sale of fabric and accessories in her store.

Salary: Approximately $70,000, depending on experience.

Qualifications: A master's degree requires one year of university courses beyond the bachelor's degree. Most doctoral programs require another four years of university study and research.

Occupational Outlook: The budgetary constraints of county, state, and federal governments have reduced the financial resources devoted to cooperative education. Thus, the opportunities for individuals in this career have been declining. However, in Dr. Johnson's situation, she was able to use her background to move into a successful business venture.

Hobby Shack, Inc.

Work Sheet

For Year Ended December 31, 20--

	1 TRIAL BALANCE DEBIT	2 TRIAL BALANCE CREDIT	3 ADJUSTMENTS DEBIT	4 ADJUSTMENTS CREDIT	5 INCOME STATEMENT DEBIT	6 INCOME STATEMENT CREDIT	7 BALANCE SHEET DEBIT	8 BALANCE SHEET CREDIT	
ACCOUNT TITLE									
1 Cash	2908028						2908028		1
2 Petty Cash	30000						30000		2
3 Accounts Receivable	1469840						1469840		3
4 Allow. for Uncoll. Accts.		12752		(e) 124500				137252	4
5 Merchandise Inventory	14048000			(d) 1584000			12464000		5
6 Supplies—Office	348000			(a) 273000			75000		6
7 Supplies—Store	394400			(b) 291000			103400		7
8 Prepaid Insurance	580000			(c) 317000			263000		8
9 Office Equipment	3586450						3586450		9
10 Acc. Depr.—Office Equipment		649700		(f) 654000				1303700	10
11 Store Equipment	4084950						4084950		11
12 Acc. Depr.—Store Equipment		506900		(g) 525000				1031900	12
13 Accounts Payable		1158303						1158303	13
14 Federal Income Tax Payable				(h) 588924				588924	14
15 Employee Income Tax Payable		75700						75700	15
16 Social Security Tax Payable		145138						145138	16
17 Medicare Tax Payable		39942						39942	17
18 Sales Tax Payable		255670						255670	18
19 Unemployment Tax Payable—Federal		3460						3460	19
20 Unemployment Tax Payable—State		23355						23355	20
21 Health Insurance Premiums Payable		100800						100800	21
22 U.S. Savings Bonds Payable		6000						6000	22
23 United Way Donations Payable		7000						7000	23
24 Dividends Payable		500000						500000	24
25 Capital Stock		125000000						125000000	25
26 Retained Earnings		1076129						1076129	26
27 Dividends	2000000						2000000		27
28 Income Summary			(d) 1584000		1584000				28

	Account Title	Trial Balance Debit	Trial Balance Credit	Adjustments Debit	Adjustments Credit	Income Statement Debit	Income Statement Credit	Balance Sheet Debit	Balance Sheet Credit
29	Sales		49512000				49512000		
30	Sales Discount	25848				25848			
31	Sales Returns and Allowances	312728				312728			
32	Purchases	20996000				20996000			
33	Purchases Discount		164815				164815		
34	Purch. Returns and Allowances		348495				348495		
35	Advertising Expense	360000				360000			
36	Cash Short and Over	1925				1925			
37	Credit Card Fee Expense	338500				338500			
38	Depr. Exp.—Office Equipment			(f) 654000		654000			
39	Depr. Exp.—Store Equipment			(g) 525000		525000			
40	Insurance Expense			(c) 317000		317000			
41	Miscellaneous Expense	256490				256490			
42	Payroll Taxes Expense	910500				910500			
43	Rent Expense	1800000				1800000			
44	Salary Expense	10452500				10452500			
45	Supplies Expense—Office			(a) 273000		273000			
46	Supplies Expense—Store			(b) 291000		291000			
47	Uncollectible Accounts Expense			(e) 124500		124500			
48	Utilities Expense	382000				382000			
49	Federal Income Tax Expense	1800000		(h) 589824		2388924			
50		67086159	67086159	4357424	4357424	41993915	50025310	26984668	18953273
51	Net Income after Federal Income Tax					8031395			8031395
52						50025310	50025310	26984668	26984668

1. Trial balance   **2. Adjustments**   **3. Extend Adjusted Balances**

Hobby Shack, Inc.

Work Sheet

For Year Ended December 31, 20--

	1 TRIAL BALANCE DEBIT	2 TRIAL BALANCE CREDIT	3 ADJUSTMENTS DEBIT	4 ADJUSTMENTS CREDIT	5 ADJUSTED TRIAL BALANCE DEBIT	6 ADJUSTED TRIAL BALANCE CREDIT
ACCOUNT TITLE						
1 Cash	2908028				2908028	
2 Petty Cash	30000				30000	
3 Accounts Receivable	1469840				1469840	
4 Allow. for Uncoll. Accts.		12752		(e) 124500		137252
5 Merchandise Inventory	14048000			(d)1584000	12464000	
6 Supplies—Office	348000			(a) 273000	75000	
7 Supplies—Store	394400			(b) 291000	103400	
8 Prepaid Insurance	580000			(c) 317000	263000	
9 Office Equipment	3586450				3586450	
10 Acc. Depr.—Office Equipment		649700		(f) 654000		1303700
11 Store Equipment	4084950				4084950	
12 Acc. Depr.—Store Equipment		506900		(g) 525000		1031900
13 Accounts Payable		1158303				1158303
14 Federal Income Tax Payable				(h) 588924		588924
24 Dividends Payable		500000				500000
25 Capital Stock		12500000				12500000
26 Retained Earnings		1076129				1076129
27 Dividends	2000000				2000000	
28 Income Summary			(d)1584000		1584000	
29 Sales		49512000				49512000
30 Sales Discount	25848				25848	
31 Sales Returns and Allowances	312728				312728	
32 Purchases	20996000				20996000	
33 Purchases Discount		164815				164815
34 Purch. Returns and Allowances		348495				348495
35 Advertising Expense	360000				360000	
36 Cash Short and Over	1925				1925	
37 Credit Card Fee Expense	338500				338500	
38 Depr. Exp.—Office Equipment			(f) 654000		654000	
39 Depr. Exp.—Store Equipment			(g) 525000		525000	
40 Insurance Expense			(c) 317000		317000	
41 Miscellaneous Expense	256490				256490	
42 Payroll Taxes Expense	910500				910500	
43 Rent Expense	1800000				1800000	
44 Salary Expense	10452500				10452500	
45 Supplies Expense—Office			(a) 273000		273000	
46 Supplies Expense—Store			(b) 291000		291000	
47 Uncollectible Accounts Expense			(e) 124500		124500	
48 Utilities Expense	382000				382000	
49 Federal Income Tax Expense	1800000		(h) 588924		2388924	
50	67086159	67086159	4357424	4357424	68978583	68978583
51 Net Income after Federal Income Tax						
52						

4. Total, prove, and rule

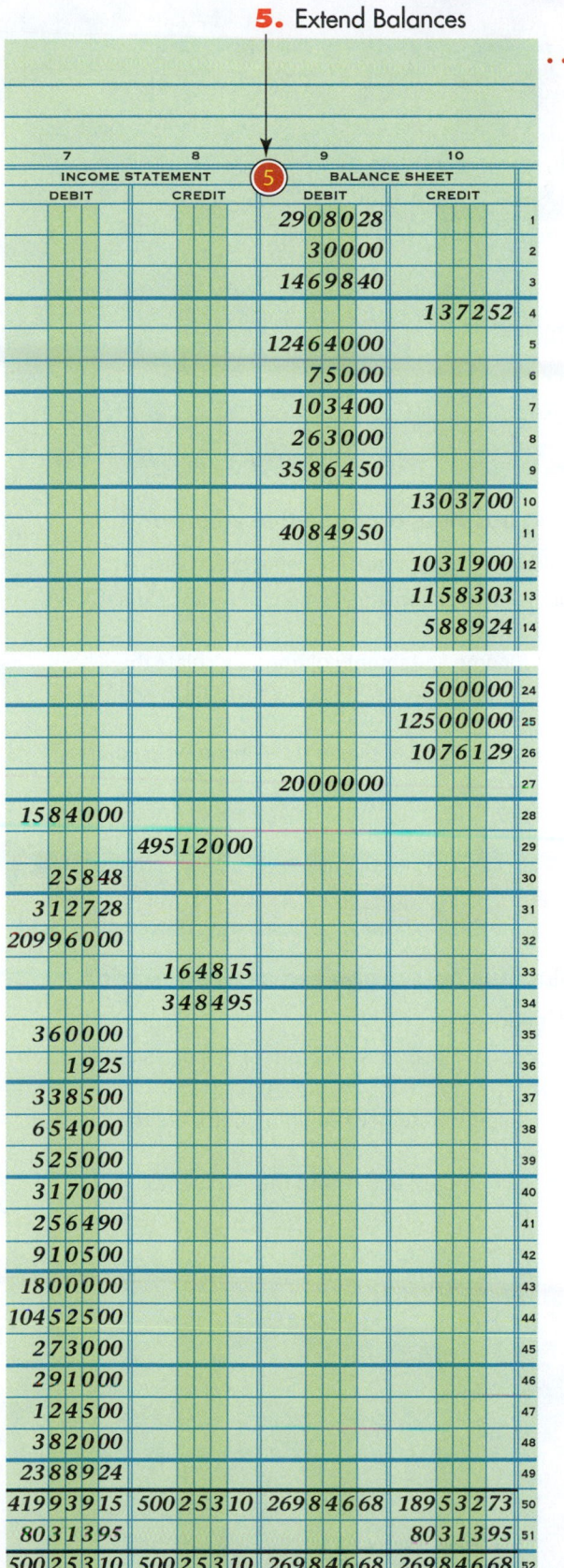

5. Extend Balances

6. Calculate net income; total, prove, and rule

Some large businesses with many accounts to be adjusted at the end of a fiscal period may use a 10-column work sheet. A 10-column work sheet includes an additional pair of amount columns titled Adjusted Trial Balance.

Any business with adjustments to make at the end of a fiscal period could use either an 8-column or a 10-column work sheet. However, completing two extra amount columns when most of the account balances are not adjusted requires extra time and work. Account balances not adjusted must be extended from the Trial Balance columns to the Adjusted Trial Balance columns; whereas, with an 8-column work sheet, account balances not adjusted are extended directly to the Balance Sheet or Income Statement columns.

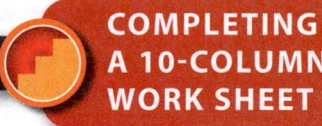

STEPS COMPLETING A 10-COLUMN WORK SHEET

1. Record the trial balance on the work sheet.

2. Plan the adjustments on the work sheet.

3. Extend the balances in the Trial Balance Debit and Credit columns to the Adjusted Trial Balance Debit and Credit columns. Calculate up-to-date adjusted balances for all accounts affected by adjustments.

4. Total, prove, and rule the Adjusted Trial Balance Debit and Credit columns.

5. Extend the amounts in the Adjusted Trial Balance Debit and Credit columns to the appropriate Income Statement and Balance Sheet columns.

6. Calculate net income and total, prove, and rule the Income Statement and Balance Sheet columns in the same way as on an 8-column work sheet.

REMEMBER

A 10-column work sheet is often used by large merchandising companies with many accounts to be adjusted.

Calculating Federal Income Tax and Completing a Work Sheet

End of Lesson
REVIEW

1. In what column is the Income Summary amount extended?
2. To which Balance Sheet column is a net loss amount extended?
3. What extra step is required when a 10-column work sheet is prepared instead of an 8-column work sheet?

WORK TOGETHER 14-6

Completing an 8-column work sheet for a merchandising business organized as a corporation

Use the work sheet from Work Together 14-5. Your instructor will guide you through the following examples.

1. Extend all amounts except Federal Income Tax Expense to the appropriate Income Statement or Balance Sheet columns. Do not total the columns.
2. On the form provided in the *Working Papers*, total the work sheet's Income Statement columns. Calculate the difference between the debit and credit totals. This difference becomes the net income before federal income tax expense.
3. Using the tax table shown in this chapter, calculate federal income tax expense and record the income tax adjustment on the work sheet. Label the adjustment *(h)*.
4. Complete the work sheet.

ON YOUR OWN 14-6

Completing an 8-column work sheet for a merchandising business organized as a corporation

Use the work sheet from On Your Own 14-5. Work this problem independently.

1. Extend all amounts except Federal Income Tax Expense to the appropriate Income Statement or Balance Sheet columns. Do not total the columns.
2. On the form provided in the *Working Papers*, total the work sheet's Income Statement columns. Calculate the difference between the debit and credit totals.
3. Using the tax table shown in this chapter, calculate federal income tax expense and record the income tax adjustment on the work sheet. Label the adjustment *(h)*.
4. Complete the work sheet.

After completing this chapter, you can:

1. Define accounting terms related to distributing dividends and preparing a work sheet for a merchandising business.

2. Identify accounting concepts and practices related to distributing dividends and preparing a work sheet for a merchandising business.

3. Journalize the declaration and payment of a dividend.

4. Begin a work sheet for a merchandising business.

5. Plan work sheet adjustments for merchandise inventory, supplies, prepaid expenses, uncollectible accounts, and depreciation.

6. Calculate federal income tax and plan the work sheet adjustment for federal income tax.

7. Complete a work sheet for a merchandising business.

Go Beyond the Book
For more information go to
www.C21accounting.com

EXPLORE ACCOUNTING

Accounting Systems Design

An important role of accountants is to prepare financial statements for businesses. In addition, many accountants design accounting systems used to prepare the various financial reports important to successful business operations.

An accounting system should be designed to meet the needs of the business it serves. Factors to consider are size of the company, number of facility locations, geographic area of operations (local, statewide, national, international), number of employees, and type of organization (service, merchandising, manufacturing). Also to be considered are the intended uses of the information: traditional financial statements (income statement, balance sheet, cash flow statement), income tax information, management decision information, management control information, and product pricing information.

An accounting system is built around a chart of accounts, which provides the organizational system around which information will be collected, filed, and made available for various types of financial reports.

A small business owned and operated by one person may not need detailed information. However, as a business grows in size and complexity, more detailed information is required. Large international businesses need very complex accounting systems with thousands of accounts to furnish management with the information needed to make decisions and the data for various reports required by governments and other agencies. As businesses grow, accountants constantly look for ways to provide better information. Thus, accountants play a key role in the successful growth of a business.

Activity: Assume Hobby Shack has made the decision to change from a merchandising business to a manufacturing business. It will create its own ceramic molds that will enable it to produce its own line of ceramic images. As the accountant, how would you recommend the chart of accounts be modified to meet the changing needs of the company?

14-1 APPLICATION PROBLEM

Journalizing dividends

Drake Corporation completed the following transactions during December of the current year and January of the next year.

Instructions:

1. Use page 17 of a general journal. Journalize the dividend declared on December 15.

2. Use page 28 of a cash payments journal. Journalize payment of the dividend on January 15.

Transactions:

Dec. 15. The board of directors declared a dividend of $1.50 per share; capital stock issued is 2,100 shares. M258.

Jan. 15. Paid cash for dividend declared December 15. C721.

14-2 APPLICATION PROBLEM

Beginning an 8-column work sheet for a merchandising business

A partially completed work sheet for Branson Amusement Company is given in the *Working Papers*. Four general ledger accounts are shown below.

Instructions:

1. Enter the accounts and account balances on the following lines.

Line	Account	Account Balance
6	Supplies—Office	$ 5,210.98
13	Accounts Payable	17,558.16
33	Purchases Discount	5,155.28
44	Salary Expense	193,971.80

2. Total, prove, and rule the trial balance.

3. From a physical count of the following, December 31 balances are determined to be:

Supplies—Office	$489.73
Supplies—Store	701.19
Prepaid Insurance	500.00

Analyze the supplies and prepaid insurance adjustments and enter the adjustments on the work sheet. Label the adjustments *(a)–(c)*. Save your work to complete Application Problem 14-3.

14-3 APPLICATION PROBLEM

Analyzing and recording a merchandise inventory adjustment on a work sheet

Use the work sheet prepared in Application Problem 14-2.

Instructions:

1. From a physical count of merchandise inventory, the December 31 balance is determined to be $226,766.38. Analyze the merchandise inventory adjustment and enter the adjustment on the work sheet. Label the adjustment *(d)*. Save your work to complete Application Problem 14-4.

14-4 APPLICATION PROBLEM

Analyzing and recording an allowance for uncollectible accounts adjustment on a work sheet

Use the work sheet prepared in Application Problem 14-3.

Instructions:

1. Branson Amusement Company estimates uncollectible accounts expense as 0.8% of its total sales on account. During the current year, Branson had credit sales of $248,500.00. As of December 31, record the uncollectible accounts expense adjustment on the work sheet and label the adjustment *(e)*. Save your work to complete Application Problem 14-5.

14-5 APPLICATION PROBLEM

Planning and recording adjustments for depreciation

Use the work sheet prepared in Application Problem 14-4.

Instructions:

1. Wave Dive Company tests scuba equipment. Calculate depreciation expense for scuba testing equipment costing $10,540.00; estimated salvage value, $2,500.00; useful life, 3 years.
2. Calculate the book value of the scuba testing equipment at the end of its second year of service.
3. On December 31, Branson Amusement Company determined total depreciation expense: office equipment, $5,850.00; store equipment, $5,250.00. Plan the work sheet adjustments and label the adjustments *(f)* and *(g)*. Save your work to complete Application Problem 14-6.

14-6 APPLICATION PROBLEM

Calculating federal income tax and completing an 8-column work sheet for a merchandising business

Use the work sheet prepared in Application Problem 14-5.

Instructions:

1. Extend all amounts except Federal Income Tax Expense to the appropriate Income Statement or Balance Sheet columns. Do not total the columns.
2. On the form provided in the *Working Papers*, calculate the net income before federal income tax expense.
3. Using the tax table shown in this chapter, calculate federal income tax expense and record the income tax adjustment on the work sheet. Label the adjustment *(h)*.
4. Finish the work sheet.

14-7 MASTERY PROBLEM   Peachtree by Sage   QB Quick Books

Preparing an 8-column work sheet for a merchandising business

The trial balance for Carol's Closet as of December 31 of the current year is recorded on a work sheet in the *Working Papers*.

Instructions:

1. Analyze the following adjustment information collected on December 31 and record the adjustments on the work sheet. Label each adjustment using labels *(a)* through *(g)*.

   a. Office supplies inventory .... $ 1,407.00

   b. Store supplies inventory 570.11

   c. Merchandise inventory 238,830.61

   d. Uncollectible accounts are 1.2% of credit sales of: 458,200.00

   e. Value of prepaid insurance 2,000.00

   f. Estimate of office equipment depreciation 5,216.00

   g. Estimate of store equipment depreciation 4,820.00

2. Using the tax table shown in this chapter, calculate federal income tax expense and record the income tax adjustment on the work sheet. Label the adjustment *(h)*.

3. Complete the work sheet.

14-8 CHALLENGE PROBLEM

Preparing a 10-column work sheet for a merchandising business

Hillside Ski Shop's trial balance as of December 31 of the current year is recorded on a work sheet in the *Working Papers*.

Instructions:

1. Analyze the following adjustment information collected on December 31 and record the adjustments on the work sheet. Label each adjustment using labels *(a)* through *(g)*.

   a. Office supplies inventory .... $ 343.42

   b. Store supplies inventory 309.41

   c. Merchandise inventory 167,000.46

   d. Uncollectible accounts are 1.0% of credit sales of: 158,900.00

   e. Value of prepaid insurance 3,000.00

   f. Estimate of office equipment depreciation 3,890.00

   g. Estimate of store equipment depreciation 3,460.00

2. Using the tax table shown in this chapter, calculate federal income tax expense and record the income tax adjustment on the work sheet. Label the adjustment *(h)*.

3. Complete the work sheet.

APPLIED COMMUNICATION

Sometimes a credit customer does not pay off the amount due on an account receivable by the deadline specified in the terms of the sale on account. In this situation, a business wants to (1) receive the amount owed and (2) preserve a long-term relationship so there can be repeated sales to that customer.

Instructions: Write a first-notice letter to a customer who has not yet paid an amount due. Balance your business's need to receive payment with the desire to keep the customer's goodwill now and in the future. Use a supportive opening and closing.

After completing a work sheet, Park's Boutique finds that garment bags worth $600.00 were overlooked in the supplies inventory. Jerry Park suggests that the oversight does not have any effect on balancing the Income Statement and Balance Sheet columns of the work sheet. He adds that the oversight will be corrected when the store supplies are counted at the end of the next fiscal period. The accountant recommends that the work sheet be redone to reflect the recalculated supplies inventory. Do you agree with Mr. Park or the accountant? Explain your answer.

AUDITING FOR ERRORS

Martin Grotte has just completed the year-end work sheet for Lancing Corporation. Part of the work sheet is shown below.

	Trial Balance		Adjustments	
Account Title	Debit	Credit	Debit	Credit
Accounts Receivable	42,518.25			
Allow. for Uncoll. Accts.		251.66		(e) 496.41
Merchandise Inventory	251,486.36		(d) 9,548.25	
Supplies—Office	5,141.84			(a) 4,154.22
Supplies—Store	3,148.28			(b) 2,974.22
Prepaid Insurance	6,000.00			(c) 5,000.00
Office Equipment	28,550.00			
Acc. Depr.—Office Equipment		12,480.00		(f) 5,210.00
Store Equipment	58,940.00			
Acc. Depr.—Store Equipment		16,420.00		(g) 8,420.00
Federal Income Tax Payable				(h) 45,813.38
Sales		992,818.10		
Utilities Expense	5,485.22			
Federal Income Tax Expense	60,000.00		(h) 45,813.38	

Martin used the following information to prepare the work sheet adjustments:
a. Uncollectible accounts are estimated to be 0.5% of gross sales (the amount of sales before discounts and returns and allowances are subtracted).
b. Office supplies inventory on hand, $987.62.
c. Store supplies inventory on hand, $174.06.
d. Merchandise inventory on hand, $241,938.11.
e. The six-month insurance premium was paid on July 1.
f. Office equipment has a 5-year useful life and a $2,500 salvage value.
g. Store equipment has a 7-year useful life and a $3,500 salvage value.

Instructions

Audit the work sheet to determine if the work sheet adjustments were recorded properly. Prepare a list that describes any errors you discover and how they should be corrected.

ANALYZING BEST BUY'S FINANCIAL STATEMENTS

Investors use a ratio known as the *dividend yield* when making investment decisions. The dividend yield is calculated as follows:

$$\text{Dividend Yield} = \frac{\text{Dividend per Share}}{\text{Market Price per Share}}$$

Companies with large dividend yields (greater than 3%) are typically considered to be *income stocks*, meaning that investors own the stock primarily to earn the dividend. In contrast, companies with small dividend yields (less than 2%) are often referred to as *growth stocks*, meaning that investors are counting on the market value of the stock to increase over time.

Instructions: Use Best Buy's Statement of Changes in Shareholders' Equity on page B-8 in Appendix B to answer the following questions.

1. Calculate the 2006 dividend yield for Best Buy, assuming the current market price is $50.00 per share.
2. Would you classify Best Buy as an income or growth stock?

Accounting
SOFTWARE

JOURNALIZING ADJUSTING ENTRIES

Peachtree has a working trial balance report that is similar to a work sheet. The report presents each account, the account balance as of the end of the last fiscal period, and the current balance.

Like the work sheet, the printed working trial balance has blank debit and credit columns where adjustments can be planned. The completed report provides the support for adjustments of allowance for uncollectible accounts, inventory, prepaid insurance, and accumulated depreciation accounts. After the adjustments are entered in Peachtree, an income statement is printed to obtain the required pretax net income amount needed for calculating federal income taxes.

PEACHTREE APPLICATION PROBLEM 14-1
1. Open (Restore) file 14-1AP.ptb.
2. Journalize and post the dividend declared on December 15 in the general journal.
3. Change the accounting periods from Period 12 to Period 13.
4. Using the Write Checks task, journalize and post the payment of the dividend on January 16.
5. Print the December 15 general journal.
6. Print the January 15 cash disbursements journal.

PEACHTREE MASTERY PROBLEM 14-7
1. Open (Restore) file 14-7MP.ptb.
2. Journalize and post the adjusting entries in the general journal.
3. Display or print Peachtree's general ledger trial balance to see the account balances.
4. Print the December 31 general journal, the income statement and the balance sheet.

JOURNALIZING ADJUSTING ENTRIES

As discussed in this chapter, many corporations pay cash dividends to their shareholders. The number of shareholders receiving checks could number in the thousands. Similar to how many companies use a special payroll account, some companies deposit the total amount of the cash dividend to a special dividend bank account. The check to each shareholder is written from that special dividend account.

Also covered in this chapter is the calculating and recording of adjusting entries. If a work sheet is not used, the adjusting entries must be planned using other means. A trial balance can be printed out and used to plan the adjusting entries. The trial balance, however, will not provide the amount of pretax net income needed to calculate the federal income tax adjustment. To determine this amount, it is necessary to enter all the other adjusting entries, print out a profit & loss statement, and use the net income amount on that profit & loss statement to calculate the adjusting entry for federal income taxes.

QUICKBOOKS APPLICATION PROBLEM 14-1
1. Open the Drake Corporation file.
2. Record the dividend transactions. Use the Write Checks option for all cash payments; use the Make General Journal Entries window for all other transactions.
3. Print a Journal report, using December 15 and January 15 for the dates. Change column widths as needed to display all of the data.

QUICKBOOKS MASTERY PROBLEM 14-7
1. Open the Carol's Closet file.
2. Journalize the adjusting entries, using the Make General Journal Entries window for all transactions.
3. View a Profit & Loss Standard report, using January 1 and December 31 for the dates; close without printing.
4. Print a Journal report for Carol's Closet, using December 1 and December 31 for the dates.
5. Print a Trial Balance report, using December 31 for the dates.

LOGICAL RELATIONSHIPS

In Chapter 9, you learned that a formula can consist of a reference to a single cell. A formula can also determine the logical relationship between two numbers. Some common logical relationships are equal to (=), less than, (<), greater than or equal to (>=), and not equal to (<>).

Debit and credit columns of a worksheet must be equal. As the numbers get larger, it becomes more likely that you may miss an error. Examine the following section of a worksheet.

	A	B	C
56	Utilities Expense	4,051.06	0.00
57	Fed. Income Tax Expense	48,000.00	0.00
58		1,058,513.74	1,059,513.74
59	Net Inc. after Fed. Income Tax		
60			

How long did it take you to detect that the column totals are not equal? Rather than relying on yourself to determine if the columns are equal, you can enter a formula, such as +B58=C58, to compare the two amounts. If the amounts are equal, the cells will display TRUE; if the amounts are not equal, FALSE.

EXCEL APPLICATION PROBLEM 14-2

Open the F14-2 Excel data file. Follow the step-by-step instructions in the Instructions worksheet. Use the logical functions to ensure that each pair of column totals are equal.

EXCEL APPLICATION PROBLEM 14-3

Open the F14-3 Excel data file. Follow the step-by-step instructions in the Instructions worksheet. Use the logical functions to ensure that each pair of column totals are equal.

CREATING CHARTS AND GRAPHS

Charts and graphs provide a picture of numeric data. To be effective, charts and graphs should be clearly labeled. They are commonly used to track sales goals, monitor expenses, identify trends, and make forecasts.

Different styles of graphs are used to display different types of financial information. A pie graph is used to illustrate parts of a whole, such as cost of goods sold, operating expenses, and net income as percentages of net sales. Bar graphs are used to show the relative size of related items, such as expenses. Line graphs are used to illustrate trends, such as net sales or net income over a period of years.

To prepare a graph based on financial data when a data file is open, choose the Graph Selection menu item from the Reports menu or click the Graphs toolbar button. Then click the type of graph you would like to display.

AUTOMATED ACCOUNTING GRAPHING PROBLEM (OPTIONAL)

1. Open the data file that is your solution to Automated Accounting Problem F11-5. There is no Help file available for this optional graphing problem.
2. Click the Graphs toolbar button.
3. Click the Income Statement button to display a graph of the income statement.
4. View the other graphs available. Note that some are not very meaningful because this particular problem does not have a wide range of data available for graphing.
5. Exit Automated Accounting without saving your file.

PHOTOGRAPHER'S CHOICE RF/GETTY IMAGES

CHAPTER 15

Financial Statements for a Corporation

OBJECTIVES

After studying Chapter 15, you will be able to:

1. Define accounting terms related to financial statements for a merchandising business organized as a corporation.

2. Identify accounting concepts and practices related to financial statements for a merchandising business organized as a corporation.

3. Prepare an income statement for a merchandising business organized as a corporation.

4. Analyze an income statement using component percentages and financial ratios.

5. Prepare a statement of stockholders' equity for a merchandising business organized as a corporation.

6. Prepare a balance sheet for a merchandising business organized as a corporation.

KEY TERMS

- net sales
- cost of merchandise sold
- gross profit on sales
- financial ratio
- earnings per share
- price-earnings ratio
- statement of stockholders' equity
- par value
- current liabilities
- long-term liabilities
- supporting schedule

Point Your Browser
www.C21accounting.com

Gap, Inc.

The Evolution of Gap, Inc.

Many of today's most notable companies had very humble beginnings. Gap, Inc., began in 1969 when Don and Doris Fisher opened a clothing store in San Francisco. The company grew quickly, becoming a publicly traded company in just seven years.

The company expanded beyond its Gap store concept in 1983 by purchasing Banana Republic, a small safari and travel clothing company. Gap further extended its penetration into the clothing market by introducing the Old Navy brand in 1994. The rest, as they say, is history. With over 3,000 stores, Gap, Inc., is now a major force in the apparel industry.

©GETTY IMAGES

Each of its clothing brands targets different customers. The original Gap brand targets style-conscious customers in the casual specialty market. Banana Republic targets men and women who want more sophisticated seasonal fashions, shoes, personal care products, intimate apparel, and gifts for the home. Old Navy is more value focused, providing families with great fashions at affordable prices.

Critical Thinking

1. Should a single set of financial statements be prepared for Gap Inc., or should financial statements be prepared for each brand?
2. How would the chart of accounts differ among the three brands?

Source: www.gapinc.com

DIGITAL VISION/GETTY IMAGES

INTERNET ACTIVITY

EDGAR—Part 1

Go to the homepage for the Securities and Exchange Commission (SEC) (www.sec.gov). The SEC provides almost instant access to forms filed with the SEC. Investors can access these forms through a system called EDGAR. Click on "Filings and Forms (EDGAR)." Search the site to find out more about EDGAR.

Instructions

1. Each letter in "EDGAR" is an abbreviation for a word. List the word connected with each letter in EDGAR.
2. Briefly state how EDGAR helps investors.

Preparing an Income Statement

USES OF FINANCIAL STATEMENTS

Financial statements provide the primary source of information needed by owners and managers to make decisions on the future activity of a business. All financial information must be reported in order to make sound business decisions. The financial statements should provide information about a business's financial condition, changes in this financial condition, and the progress of operations. [CONCEPT: Adequate Disclosure]

Comparing financial condition and progress for more than one fiscal period also helps owners and managers make sound business decisions. Therefore, financial information must be reported the same way from one fiscal period to the next. [CONCEPT: Consistent Reporting]

Hobby Shack prepares three financial statements to report financial progress and condition. A corporation prepares an income statement and a balance sheet similar to those used by a proprietorship. A corporation also prepares a statement of stockholders' equity.

HOLA IMAGES/GETTY IMAGES

CHARACTER COUNTS

Can You Share Client Names?

After working six years with a national public accounting firm, Raymond Steele decided to venture out on his own. Raymond's new firm, Steele Consulting, specializes in helping companies that are facing severe financial difficulties. When delivering proposals to potential clients, Raymond proudly lists the names of his current clients.

The Code of Professional Conduct for the American Institute of Certified Public Accountants "prohibits a member in public practice from disclosing confidential information without the client's consent." Raymond is aware of the rule but believes he is not violating this rule.

Instruction

Access the AICPA Code of Professional Conduct. Determine if Raymond's actions violate the confidentiality rule. (Hint: Remember that the Code includes rules, interpretations, and ethics rulings.)

PHOTO: STOCKBYTE/GETTY IMAGES

Ken Harrison, Computer and Information Systems Manager

COURTESY OF KEN HARRISON

As a high school student, Ken Harrison knew he didn't want to do the same thing for his entire career. Ken recalls, "I was the only one in my college freshman orientation group who firmly knew their intended major. 'Accounting!' I proudly responded to our group leader." Ken had been advised that an accounting degree was a good background for law school. However, when presented with attractive accounting job offers in the first semester of his senior year, he thought that "perhaps law school could wait!"

Ken began his career with PricewaterhouseCoopers. During five years in public accounting, he was exposed to numerous accounting issues and became acquainted with the upper-level managers and officers of his clients.

Networking in his profession and community has brought Ken numerous opportunities. At age 28, he was offered the chief financial officer (CFO) position for a start-up general aviation company. Later, as its general manager, he was involved in sales, marketing, human resources, finance, and information technology. "As a successful entrepreneurial business, our little company soon became the target of larger companies in the industry. I hadn't studied much about mergers and acquisitions in college, but 'deal making' soon became a requirement." The sale of the company to a much larger out-of-state corporation, which brought in their own leadership, resulted in Ken's position being eliminated.

Another opportunity soon appeared—to go to work for a publicly held client who needed a CPA familiar with mergers and acquisitions. Seven years later, when Ken's personal desires turned to a more humanitarian calling, he accepted the CFO position of an international not-for-profit organization working to provide impoverished people with the skills and means to improve their lives. In that role, he experienced different and interesting challenges, including travel to many developing countries. "Who would have imagined an accounting degree would take me to remote Africa!" he remarks.

Ken is now working in state government for another former colleague. He explains, "Our mission is to help improve business processes of the state government by installing and supporting an enterprise resource planning (ERP) system." Ken helps direct 80 individuals who assist the users of the ERP throughout the government.

Salary Range: Earnings for computer and information systems managers vary by specialty and level of responsibility. The median annual salary for these managers was $92,570 in 2004 (Bureau of Labor Statistics, *Occupational Outlook Handbook, 2006-07*, at www.bls.gov [visited January 15, 2007]).

Qualifications: Ken believes networking is the key to opportunity. Developing relationships with colleagues and individuals in professional and civic organizations will open doors to opportunities in the most unexpected places. A Certified Public Accountant (CPA) license and public accounting experience provide a solid foundation. Communication skills and a willingness to work in every aspect of the organization, from sales to technology, are important to take advantage of job opportunities.

Occupational Outlook: The U.S. Department of Labor expects jobs for computer and information systems managers to increase much faster than the national average for all occupations. The continued application of technology to business operations will increase the number of jobs that use computer technology, thus requiring more individuals to manage the technology.

Hobby Shack, Inc.

Work Sheet

For Year Ended December 31, 20--

	ACCOUNT TITLE	1 TRIAL BALANCE DEBIT	2 TRIAL BALANCE CREDIT	3 ADJUSTMENTS DEBIT	4 ADJUSTMENTS CREDIT	5 INCOME STATEMENT DEBIT	6 INCOME STATEMENT CREDIT	7 BALANCE SHEET DEBIT	8 BALANCE SHEET CREDIT	
5	Merchandise Inventory	14048000			(d)1584000			12464000		5
29	Sales		49512000				49512000			29
30	Sales Discount	25848				25848				30
31	Sales Returns and Allowances	312728				312728				31
32	Purchases	20996000				20996000				32
33	Purchases Discount		164815				164815			33
34	Purch. Returns and Allowances		348495				348495			34
35	Advertising Expense	360000				360000				35
36	Cash Short and Over	1925				1925				36
37	Credit Card Fee Expense	338500				338500				37
38	Depr. Exp.—Office Equipment			(f) 654000		654000				38
39	Depr. Exp.—Store Equipment			(g) 525000		525000				39
40	Insurance Expense			(c) 317000		317000				40
41	Miscellaneous Expense	256490				256490				41
42	Payroll Taxes Expense	910500				910500				42
43	Rent Expense	1800000				1800000				43
44	Salary Expense	10452500				10452500				44
45	Supplies Expense—Office			(a) 273000		273000				45
46	Supplies Expense—Store			(b) 291000		291000				46
47	Uncollectible Accounts Expense			(e) 124500		124500				47
48	Utilities Expense	382000				382000				48
49	Federal Income Tax Expense	1800000		(h) 588924		2388924				49
50		67086159	67086159	4357424	4357424	41993915	50025310	26984668	18953273	50
51	Net Income after Federal Income Tax					8031395			8031395	51
52						50025310	50025310	26984668	26984668	52

An income statement is used to report a business's financial progress. Merchandising businesses report revenue, cost of merchandise sold, gross profit on sales, expenses, and net income or loss. Current and previous income statements can be compared to determine the reasons for increases or decreases in net income. This comparison is helpful in making management decisions about future operations.

Information from a completed work sheet is used to prepare an income statement. Amounts in all revenue and expense accounts and Merchandise Inventory are reported on an income statement.

The income statement of a merchandising business has three main sections: (1) revenue section, (2) cost of merchandise sold section, and (3) expenses section.

REVENUE SECTION OF AN INCOME STATEMENT FOR A MERCHANDISING BUSINESS

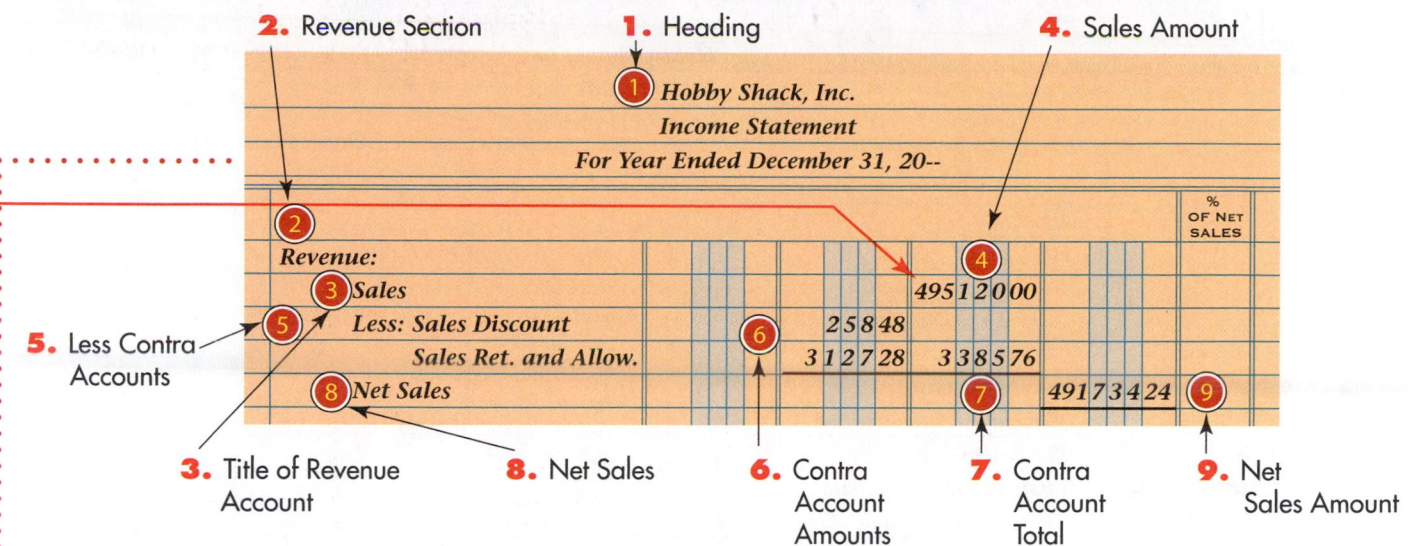

2. Revenue Section
1. Heading
4. Sales Amount

5. Less Contra Accounts

3. Title of Revenue Account
8. Net Sales
6. Contra Account Amounts
7. Contra Account Total
9. Net Sales Amount

Hobby Shack's income statement differs from TechKnow's income statement shown in Part 1. Hobby Shack has more accounts to report on the income statement. The account Sales and its contra accounts, Sales Discount and Sales Returns and Allowances, are reported in the Revenue section. Total sales less sales discount and sales returns and allowances is called **net sales**.

S T E P S — **PREPARING THE REVENUE SECTION OF AN INCOME STATEMENT**

1. Write the income statement heading on three lines.

2. Write the name of this section, *Revenue:*, at the extreme left of the wide column on the first line.

3. Write the title of the revenue account, *Sales*, on the next line, indented about one centimeter.

4. Write the balance of the sales account, *$495,120.00*, in the third amount column.

5. Write *Less:* on the next line, indented about one centimeter, followed by *Sales Discount* and *Sales Returns and Allowances* on the next line.

6. Write the balances of the sales discount account, *$258.48*, and sales returns and allowances account, *$3,127.28*, in the second amount column.

7. Add sales discounts, *$258.48*, and sales returns and allowances, *$3,127.28*, and write the amount, *$3,385.76*, in the third amount column.

8. Write *Net Sales* on the next line, indented about one centimeter.

9. Subtract the total of the contra accounts, *$3,385.76*, from sales, *$495,120.00*, to calculate net sales, *$491,734.24*. Write this amount in the fourth amount column.

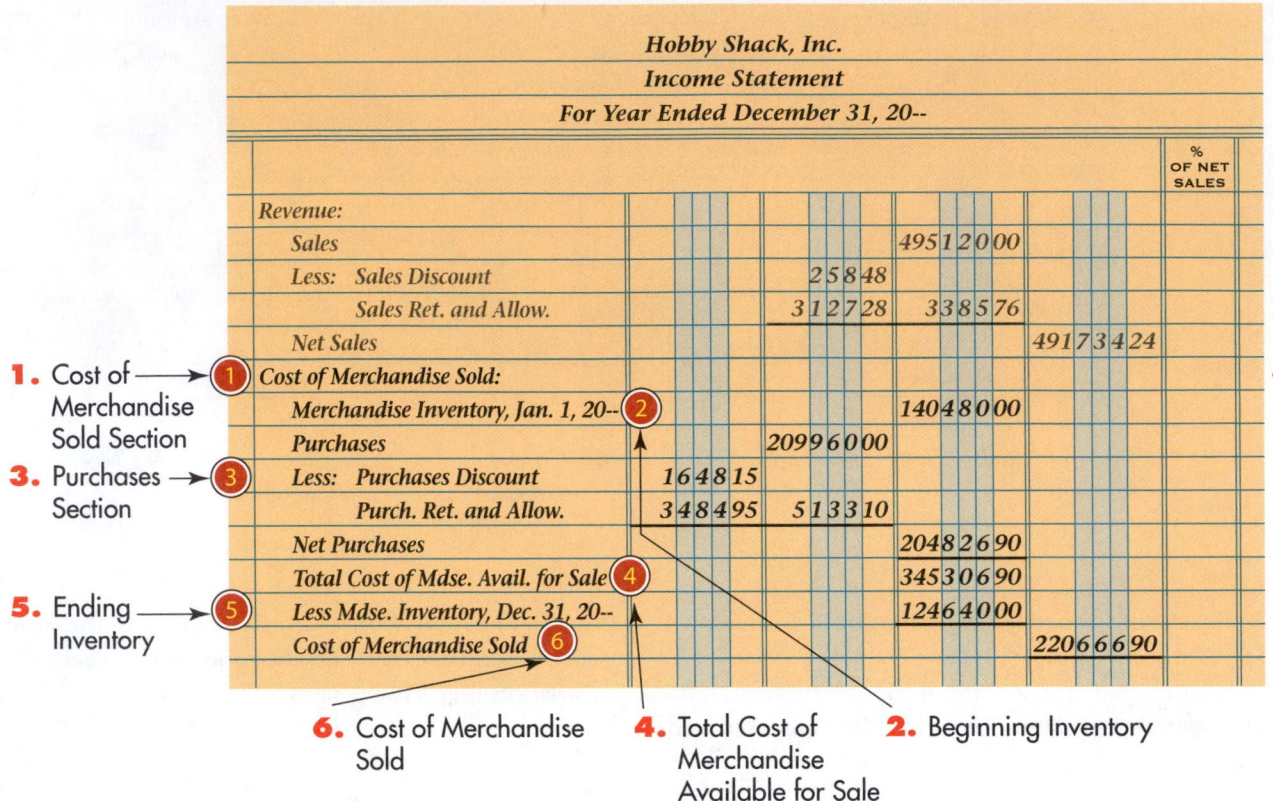

Hobby Shack, Inc.
Income Statement
For Year Ended December 31, 20--

				% OF NET SALES
Revenue:				
Sales			495 120 00	
Less: Sales Discount		25 8 48		
Sales Ret. and Allow.		3 127 28	3 385 76	
Net Sales				491 734 24
1. Cost of Merchandise Sold: **①**				
Merchandise Inventory, Jan. 1, 20-- **②**			140 480 00	
Purchases		209 960 00		
3. Less: Purchases Discount **③**	1 648 15			
Purch. Ret. and Allow.	3 484 95	5 133 10		
Net Purchases			204 826 90	
Total Cost of Mdse. Avail. for Sale **④**			345 306 90	
5. Less Mdse. Inventory, Dec. 31, 20-- **⑤**			124 640 00	
Cost of Merchandise Sold **⑥**				220 666 90

1. Cost of Merchandise Sold Section

3. Purchases Section

5. Ending Inventory

6. Cost of Merchandise Sold

4. Total Cost of Merchandise Available for Sale

2. Beginning Inventory

The original price of all merchandise sold during a fiscal period is called the **cost of merchandise sold**. [CON-CEPT: Historical Cost] Cost of merchandise sold is also known as *cost of goods sold* or *cost of sales*.

STEPS  PREPARING THE COST OF MERCHANDISE SOLD SECTION OF AN INCOME STATEMENT

① Write the name of this section, *Cost of Merchandise Sold:*, at the extreme left of the wide column.

② Write the beginning inventory found in the Trial Balance Debit column of the work sheet.
  a. Indent about one centimeter on the next line and write *Merchandise Inventory, Jan. 1, 20--*.
  b. Write the beginning merchandise inventory balance, $140,480.00, in the third amount column.

③ Prepare the Purchases section.
  a. Indent about one centimeter on the next line and write *Purchases*. Enter the purchases amount, $209,960.00, in the second amount column.
  b. Write *Less:* on the next line, indented about one centimeter, followed by *Purchases Discount* and *Purchases Returns and Allowances* on the next line. It is permissible to abbreviate long titles when necessary.
  c. Write the balances of the purchases discount account, $1,648.15, and purchases returns and allowances account, $3,484.95, in the first amount column.
  d. Add purchases discounts, $1,648.15, and purchases returns and allowances, $3,484.95, and write the amount, $5,133.10, in the second amount column.
  e. Write *Net Purchases* on the next line, indented about one centimeter.
  f. Subtract the total of the contra accounts, $5,133.10, from purchases, $209,960.00, to calculate net purchases, $204,826.90. Write this amount in the third amount column.

4 Calculate the total cost of merchandise available for sale.
  a. Indent about one centimeter on the next line, and write *Total Cost of Merchandise Available for Sale*.
  b. Add the beginning merchandise inventory balance, *$140,480.00*, and net purchases, *$204,826.90*, to calculate the total cost of merchandise available for sale, *$345,306.90*. Write this amount in the third amount column.

5 Write the ending inventory found in the Balance Sheet Debit column of the work sheet.
  a. Indent about one centimeter on the next line, and write *Less Merchandise Inventory, Dec. 31, 20--*.
  b. Write the ending merchandise inventory balance, *$124,640.00*, found in the Balance Sheet Debit column of the work sheet, in the third amount column.

6 Calculate the cost of merchandise sold.
  a. Indent about one centimeter on the next line, and write *Cost of Merchandise Sold*.
  b. Subtract the ending merchandise inventory balance, *$124,640.00*, from the total cost of merchandise available for sale, *$345,306.90*, to calculate the cost of merchandise sold, *$220,666.90*. Write the amount in the fourth amount column.

Most calculated amounts reported on a financial statement have a related description. Net sales and net purchases are two examples. However, the totals of the sales contra accounts, $3,385.76, and the purchases contra accounts, $5,133.10, are not described. Instead, the reader of the financial statement is expected to understand the amount by its physical position on the statement. Each amount is immediately to the right of an amount column ruled with a single line.

The single ruled line indicates that the column is being totaled. The amount adjacent to the column is the sum of that column.

					% OF NET SALES
Hobby Shack, Inc.					
Income Statement					
For Year Ended December 31, 20--					
Revenue:					
Sales			495 1 2 0 00		
Less: Sales Discount	2 5 8 48				
Sales Ret. and Allow.	3 1 2 7 28	3 3 8 5 76			
Net Sales				491 7 3 4 24	

Total of adjacent column

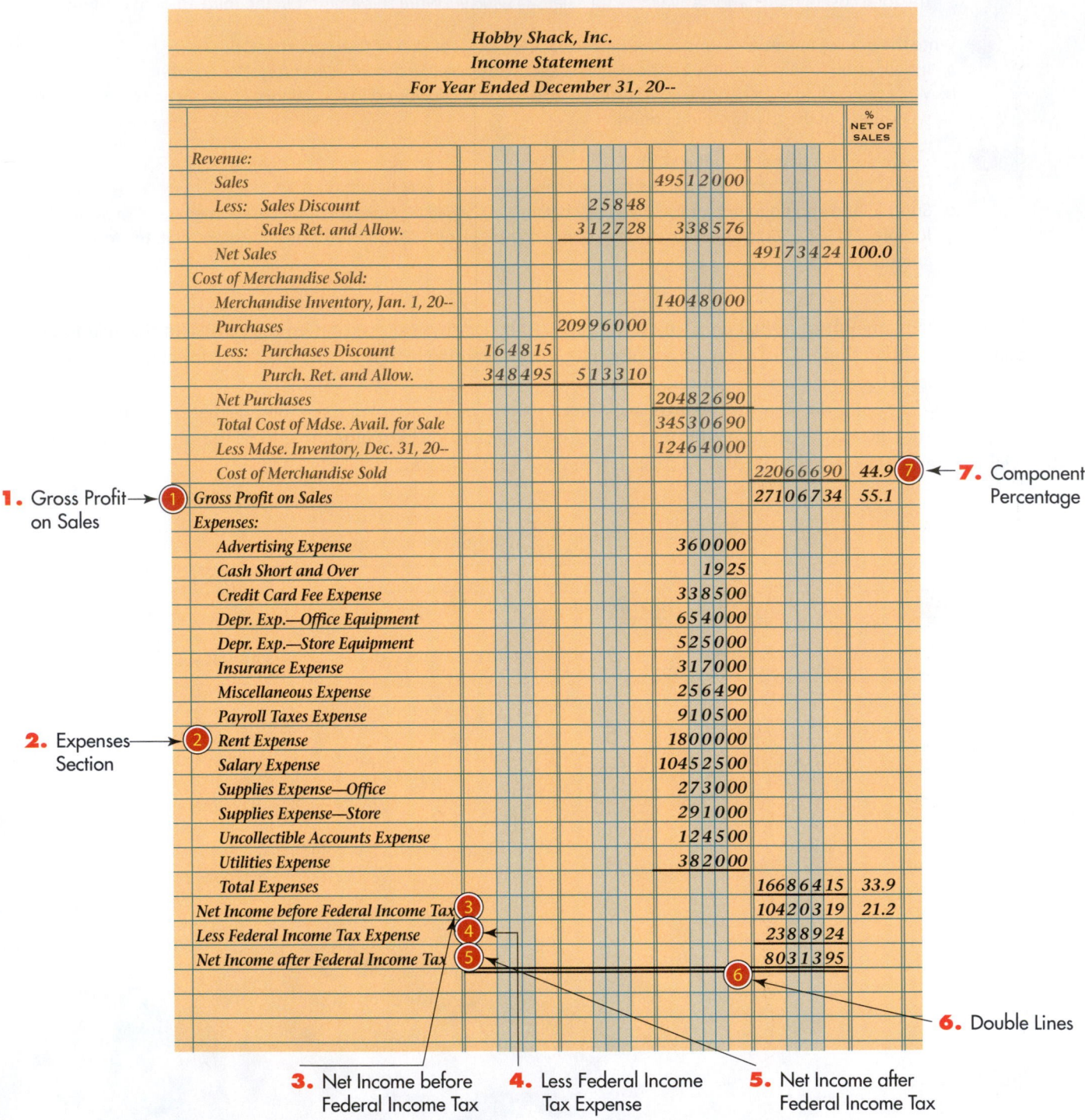

Hobby Shack, Inc.
Income Statement
For Year Ended December 31, 20--

					% NET OF SALES
Revenue:					
Sales			4951 20 00		
Less: Sales Discount		2 5 8 48			
Sales Ret. and Allow.		3 1 2 7 28	3 3 8 5 76		
Net Sales				4917 34 24	100.0
Cost of Merchandise Sold:					
Merchandise Inventory, Jan. 1, 20--			1404 80 00		
Purchases		2099 60 00			
Less: Purchases Discount	1 6 4 8 15				
Purch. Ret. and Allow.	3 4 8 4 95	5 1 3 3 10			
Net Purchases			2048 26 90		
Total Cost of Mdse. Avail. for Sale			3453 06 90		
Less Mdse. Inventory, Dec. 31, 20--			1246 40 00		
Cost of Merchandise Sold				2206 66 90	44.9
Gross Profit on Sales				2710 67 34	55.1
Expenses:					
Advertising Expense			36 0 0 00		
Cash Short and Over			1 9 25		
Credit Card Fee Expense			33 8 5 00		
Depr. Exp.—Office Equipment			65 4 0 00		
Depr. Exp.—Store Equipment			52 5 0 00		
Insurance Expense			31 7 0 00		
Miscellaneous Expense			25 6 4 90		
Payroll Taxes Expense			91 0 5 00		
Rent Expense			180 0 0 00		
Salary Expense			1045 2 5 00		
Supplies Expense—Office			27 3 0 00		
Supplies Expense—Store			29 1 0 00		
Uncollectible Accounts Expense			12 4 5 00		
Utilities Expense			38 2 0 00		
Total Expenses				1668 64 15	33.9
Net Income before Federal Income Tax				1042 03 19	21.2
Less Federal Income Tax Expense				238 89 24	
Net Income after Federal Income Tax				803 13 95	

1. Gross Profit on Sales

2. Expenses Section

3. Net Income before Federal Income Tax

4. Less Federal Income Tax Expense

5. Net Income after Federal Income Tax

6. Double Lines

7. Component Percentage

The revenue remaining after cost of merchandise sold has been deducted is called **gross profit on sales**. Management uses gross profit on sales as a measure for how effectively the business is performing in its primary functions of buying and selling merchandise. Calculating a ratio between gross profit on sales and net sales enables management to compare its performance to prior fiscal periods. The percentage relationship between one financial statement item and the total that includes that item is known as a *component percentage*. Hobby Shack calculates a component percentage for most calculated amounts reported in the fourth column of the income statement.

1 Calculate the gross profit on sales.
  a. Write *Gross Profit on Sales* on the next line at the extreme left of the wide column.
  b. Write the gross profit on sales amount, *$271,067.34*, in the second amount column. (Total revenue, *$491,734.24*, less cost of merchandise sold, *$220,666.90*, equals gross profit on sales, *$271,067.34*.)

2 Prepare the expenses section. Use the information from the Income Statement Debit column of the work sheet.
  a. Write the name of this section, *Expenses:*, at the extreme left of the wide column.
  b. On the next line, indented about one centimeter, list the expense account titles, one per line, in the order in which they appear on the work sheet.
  c. Write the amount of each expense account balance in the third amount column.
  d. Indent about one centimeter, and write Total Expenses on the next line in the wide column below the last expense account title.
  e. Total the individual expense amounts and write the total, *$166,864.15*, in the fourth amount column on the total line.

3 Calculate the net income before federal income tax.
  a. Write *Net Income before Federal Income Tax* on the next line at the extreme left of the wide column.
  b. Write the amount, *$104,203.19*, in the fourth amount column. (Gross profit on sales, *$271,067.34*, less total expenses, *$166,864.15*, equals net income before federal income tax, *$104,203.19*.)

4 Write *Less Federal Income Tax Expense* on the next line at the extreme left of the wide column. Write the amount, *$23,889.24*, on the same line in the fourth amount column.

5 Calculate net income after federal income tax.
  a. Write *Net Income after Federal Income Tax* on the next line at the extreme left of the wide column.
  b. Write the amount, *$80,313.95*, in the fourth amount column. (Net income before federal income tax, *$104,203.19*, less federal income tax expense, *$23,889.24*, equals net income after federal income tax, *$80,313.95*.)
  c. Verify accuracy by comparing the amount of net income after federal income tax calculated on the income statement, *$80,313.95*, with the amount on the work sheet, *$80,313.95*. The two amounts must be the same.

6 Rule double lines across the four amount columns to show that the income statement has been verified as correct.

7 Calculate a component percentage for each amount in the fourth amount column through the Net Income before Federal Income Tax. Divide the amount of each component by the amount of net sales. Round each component percentage to the nearest 0.1%. Write the component percentage in the % of Net Sales column.

Income Statement Component	Amount	÷	Net Sales	=	Component Percentage
Cost of Merchandise Sold	$220,666.90	÷	$491,734.24	=	44.9%
Gross Profit on Sales	$271,067.34	÷	$491,734.24	=	55.1%
Total Expenses	$166,864.15	÷	$491,734.24	=	33.9%
Net Income before Federal Income Tax	$104,203.19	÷	$491,734.24	=	21.2%

End of Lesson
REVIEW

1. What is the major difference between the income statement for a merchandising business and a service business?
2. How is the cost of merchandise sold calculated?
3. How can the amount of net income calculated on the income statement be verified?

TERMS REVIEW

net sales

cost of merchandise sold

gross profit on sales

WORK TOGETHER 15-1

Preparing an income statement for a merchandising business

The work sheet for Interstate Tires, Inc., for the year ended December 31 of the current year is given in the *Working Papers*. Your instructor will guide you through the following examples.

1. Prepare an income statement.
2. Calculate and record on the income statement the following component percentages: (a) cost of merchandise sold, (b) gross profit on sales, (c) total expenses, and (d) net income before federal income tax. Round percentage calculations to the nearest 0.1%. Save your work to complete Work Together 15-2.

ON YOUR OWN 15-1

Preparing an income statement for a merchandising business

Osborn Corporation's work sheet for the year ended December 31 of the current year is given in the *Working Papers*. Work this problem independently.

1. Prepare an income statement.
2. Calculate and record on the income statement the following component percentages: (a) cost of merchandise sold, (b) gross profit on sales, (c) total expenses, and (d) net income before federal income tax. Round percentage calculations to the nearest 0.1%. Save your work to complete On Your Own 15-2.

Analyzing an Income Statement

USING COMPONENT PERCENTAGES

A percentage relationship between one financial statement item and the total that includes that item is known as a *component percentage*. For Hobby Shack, a merchandising business, every sales dollar reported on the income statement includes four components: (1) cost of merchandise sold, (2) gross profit on sales, (3) total expenses, and (4) net income before income tax. To help make decisions about future operations, Hobby Shack analyzes relationships between these four income statement components and sales. Hobby Shack calculates a component percentage for each of the four components. The relationship between each component and sales is shown in a separate column on the income statement.

Acceptable Component Percentages

	Acceptable Industry Standards	Hobby Shack Component Percentages
Sales	100%	100%
Cost of merchandise sold	not more than 46.0%	44.9%
Gross profit on sales	not less than 54.0%	55.1%
Total expenses	not more than 35.0%	33.9%
Net income before federal income tax	not less than 19.0%	21.2%

For a component percentage to be useful, a business must know acceptable percentages. This information is determined by making comparisons with prior fiscal periods as well as with industry standards published by industry organizations. Based on these sources, Hobby Shack determines acceptable component percentages for the current fiscal period. Each percentage represents the amount of each sales dollar that is considered acceptable. For example, Hobby Shack determines that the cost of merchandise sold should be no more than 46.0%, or 46 cents, of each sales dollar.

FOR YOUR INFORMATION

FYI

Unacceptable component percentages serve as a warning that management action is necessary. Calculating and reporting component percentages is an example of how accounting information can help management planning and decision making. Effective managers rely on the information provided from accounting records.

Hobby Shack compares four of its component percentages to its acceptable component percentages. The four component percentages are for cost of merchandise sold, gross profit on sales, total expenses, and net income before federal income tax.

Cost of Merchandise Sold Component Percentage

The cost of merchandise sold is a major cost and must be kept as low as possible. Analysis of Hobby Shack's component percentages shows that the cost of merchandise sold is 44.9% of sales.

The component percentage for cost of merchandise sold, *44.9%*, is less than the maximum acceptable percentage, *46.0%*. Therefore, Hobby Shack's component percentage for cost of merchandise sold is considered acceptable.

Gross Profit on Sales Component Percentage

Gross profit must be large enough to cover total expenses and the desired amount of net income. Acceptable industry standards show that at least 54 cents, or 54.0%, of each sales dollar should result in gross profit. Hobby Shack's component percentage for gross profit on sales is 55.1%.

The component percentage for gross profit on sales, *55.1%*, is not less than the minimum acceptable percentage, *54.0%*. Therefore, Hobby Shack's component percentage for gross profit on sales is considered acceptable.

Total Expenses Component Percentage

Total expenses must be less than gross profit on sales to provide a desirable net income. Acceptable industry standards show that no more than 35 cents, or 35.0%, of each sales dollar should be devoted to total expenses. Hobby Shack's component percentage for total expenses is 33.9%.

The component percentage for total expenses, *33.9%*, is not more than the maximum acceptable percentage, *35.0%*. Therefore, Hobby Shack's component percentage for total expenses is considered acceptable.

Net Income before Federal Income Tax Component Percentage

The component percentage for net income before federal income tax shows the progress being made by a business. Acceptable industry standards show that at least 19 cents, or 19.0%, of each sales dollar should result in net income. Hobby Shack's component percentage for net income is 21.25%.

The component percentage for net income, *21.2%*, is not less than the minimum acceptable percentage, *19.0%*. Therefore, Hobby Shack's component percentage for net income is considered acceptable.

REMEMBER

The cost of merchandise sold and total expenses reduce owner's equity. For this reason, a business wants actual component percentages of these financial statement totals to be less than the acceptable component percentage. A business wants the gross profit on sales and net income before federal income tax to be as high as possible. Thus, a business wants the actual component percentage for these financial statement totals to be higher than the acceptable component percentages.

Cloth Circuit						% OF NET SALES
Income Statement						
For Year Ended December 31, 20--						
Revenue:						
Sales				848 18 4 10		
Cost of Merchandise Sold					485 76 3 95	58.0
Gross Profit on Sales					351 95 6 98	42.0
Expenses:						
Advertising Expense				32 55 0 00		
Credit Card Fee Expense				5 11 8 20		
Utilities Expense				5 18 4 00		
Total Expenses					393 72 6 94	47.0
Net Loss before Federal Income Tax					(41 76 9 96)	(5.0)
Plus Federal Income Tax Benefit					6 26 5 49	
Net Loss after Federal Income Tax					(35 50 4 47)	

When a business's total expenses are greater than the gross profit on sales, the difference is known as a *net loss*. Cloth Circuit's total expenses, $393,726.94, less gross profit on sales, $351,956.98, equals net loss before federal income taxes, $41,769.96. The net loss before federal income taxes, $41,769.96, is written in parentheses in the fourth amount column on the line with the words *Net Loss before Federal Income Taxes*. An amount written in parentheses on a financial statement indicates a negative amount.

Cloth Circuit's managers can compare its component percentages to acceptable component percentages. The component percentage for cost of merchandise sold, *58.0%*, is less than Cloth Circuit's maximum acceptable component percentage, *60.0%*. The component percentage for gross profit on sales, *42.0%*, is greater than the minimum acceptable component percentage, *40.0%*. These component percentages indicate that management is doing a good job controlling the cost of merchandise inventory.

The component percentage for total expenses, *47.0%*, is more than the maximum acceptable component percentage, *37.0%*. Because a net loss occurred, the component percentage for net income before federal income tax, *(5.0%)*, means that Cloth Circuit lost 5.0 cents on each sales dollar. These component percentages indicate that management is not effective in controlling its expenses.

To return to profitability, management must take action to reduce its expenses. Advertising and salary expense are the two largest expenses that management could quickly control. Rent expense, although one of the three largest expenses, is more difficult to control in the short term since most lease agreements are signed for a year or more.

FOR YOUR INFORMATION

FYI

A corporation having a net loss before federal income taxes can file for a tax refund from the federal government. To qualify for this benefit, the corporation must have paid at least an equal amount of federal income taxes in the previous three years. Cloth Circuit calculates its tax refund using the same tax schedule Hobby Shack used to calculate its federal income tax expense. Cloth Circuit's tax benefit, $6,265.49, is shown as a positive amount, thus reducing the amount of the net loss to $35,504.47.

ACTIONS TO CORRECT UNACCEPTABLE COMPONENT PERCENTAGES

The goal of any business is to earn an acceptable net income. When component percentages are not acceptable, regardless of whether a net income or net loss occurred, management action is necessary.

Unacceptable Component Percentage for Gross Profit on Sales

The component percentage for gross profit on sales is directly related to sales revenue and cost of merchandise sold. An unacceptable component percentage for gross profit on sales requires one of three actions: (1) increase sales revenue, (2) decrease cost of merchandise sold, or (3) increase sales revenue and also decrease cost of merchandise sold.

Increasing sales revenue while keeping the cost of merchandise sold the same will increase gross profit on sales. To increase sales revenue, management may consider increasing the markup on merchandise purchased for sale. However, a business must be cautious on the amount of the markup increase. If the increase in markup is too large, a decrease in sales revenue could occur for two reasons: (1) the sales price is beyond what customers are willing to pay or (2) the sales price is higher than what competing businesses charge for the same merchandise.

Decreasing the cost of merchandise sold while keeping the sales revenue the same will also increase gross profit on sales. To decrease cost of merchandise sold, management should review purchasing practices. For example, would purchasing merchandise in larger quantities or from other vendors result in a lower cost?

Combining a small increase in sales revenue and a small decrease in the cost of merchandise sold may also result in an acceptable component percentage for gross profit on sales.

Unacceptable Component Percentage for Total Expenses

Each expense account balance must be reviewed to determine if major increases have occurred. This review should include comparisons with prior fiscal periods as well as with industry standards. Actions must then be taken to reduce any expenses for which major increases have occurred or that are beyond industry standards.

Unacceptable Component Percentage for Net Income before Federal Income Tax

If the component percentages for cost of merchandise sold, gross profit on sales, and total expenses are brought within acceptable ranges, net income before federal income tax will also be acceptable.

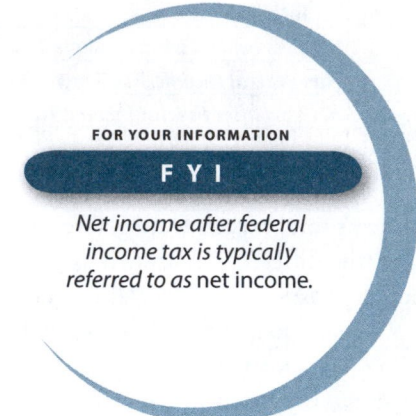

FOR YOUR INFORMATION

F Y I

Net income after federal income tax is typically referred to as net income.

DIGITAL VISION/GETTY IMAGES

Individual amounts reported on an income statement have little meaning without being compared to another amount. Suppose a company has net income before federal income taxes of $1,000,000.00. Is the company successful? Only by calculating the net income before federal income taxes component percentage could this question begin to be answered.

Comparisons between other financial items can also provide valuable information about the financial performance of a business. A comparison between two items of financial information is called a **financial ratio**. Most financial ratios include at least one amount reported on the financial statements.

Earnings per Share

Net Income after Federal Income Tax	÷	Number of Shares Outstanding	=	Earnings per Share
$80,313.95	÷	2,500	=	$32.13

The amount of net income after federal income tax belonging to a single share of stock is called **earnings per share**. The ratio is calculated by dividing net income after federal income taxes by the number of shares outstanding.

Earnings per share is one of the most widely recognized measures of a corporation's financial performance. The financial ratio is often referred to as *EPS*. Unlike component percentages, earnings per share cannot be compared to industry standards. Instead, earnings per share is compared to (1) prior year's earnings per share or (2) the market price of the stock.

Price-Earnings Ratio

Market Price per Share	÷	Earnings per Share	=	Price-Earnings Ratio
$345.00	÷	$32.13	=	10.7

The relationship between the market value per share and earnings per share of a stock is called the **price-earnings ratio**. The ratio is calculated as the market price per share divided by the earnings per share as determined by the stock markets. The ratio is often referred to as the *P-E ratio*.

The price-earnings ratio provides investors with information concerning the price of the stock relative to the earnings. Low price-earnings ratios are typically associated with slow growth companies, such as public utilities. Companies expected to have dynamic growth in future earnings typically have a high price-earnings ratio.

Online sources of financial information highlight the earnings per share and price-earnings ratio over several years. Investors can analyze the trends in the earnings per share to project future earnings of the company. Then, using historical price-earnings ratios, investors can predict future market prices of the company's stock.

DIGITAL VISION/GETTY IMAGES

FOR YOUR INFORMATION

FYI

Some financial ratios are unique to companies in a particular industry. For example, a critical financial ratio for the airline industry is revenue per passenger mile, calculated as sales divided by total passenger miles. Managers of airline companies rely on this ratio to measure how effectively the airline is pricing its tickets.

End of Lesson REVIEW

WORK TOGETHER 15-2

Analyzing an income statement

Use the income statement for Interstate Tires, Inc., from Work Together 15-1. A form for completing this problem is given in the *Working Papers*. Your instructor will guide you through the following examples.

1. Interstate Tires determines that no more than 53 cents, or 53.0%, of each sales dollar should be devoted to cost of merchandise sold. Compare the actual component percentage for cost of merchandise sold to the acceptable percentage. Indicate if the actual component percentage is acceptable or unacceptable. If it is unacceptable, suggest an action that corrects it.

2. Acceptable auto parts industry standards show that at least 47 cents, or 47.0%, of each sales dollar should result in gross profit. For Interstate Tires, compare the actual component percentage for gross profit on sales to the acceptable percentage. Indicate if the actual component percentage is acceptable or unacceptable. If it is unacceptable, suggest an action that corrects it.

3. Interstate Tires currently has 110,000 of shares outstanding with a market price of $13.75 per share. Calculate the earnings per share and price-earnings ratio.

ON YOUR OWN 15-2

Analyzing an income statement

Use the income statement for Osborn Corporation from On Your Own 15-1. A form for completing this problem is given in the *Working Papers*. Work this problem independently.

1. Acceptable game industry standards show that no more than 30 cents, or 30.0%, of each sales dollar should be devoted to total expenses. For Osborn Corporation, compare the actual component percentage for total expenses to the acceptable percentage. Indicate if the actual component percentage is acceptable or unacceptable. If it is unacceptable, suggest an action that corrects it.

2. Acceptable game industry standards show that at least 15 cents, or 15.0%, of each sales dollar should result in net income before federal income tax. For Osborn Corporation, compare the actual component percentage for net income before federal income tax to the acceptable percentage. Indicate if the actual component percentage is acceptable or unacceptable. If it is unacceptable, suggest an action that corrects it.

3. Osborn Corporation currently has 8,000 shares outstanding with a market price of $104.50 per share. Calculate the earnings per share and price-earnings ratio.

CAPITAL STOCK SECTION OF THE STATEMENT OF STOCKHOLDERS' EQUITY

2. Words *Capital Stock* and Par Value   **1.** Heading

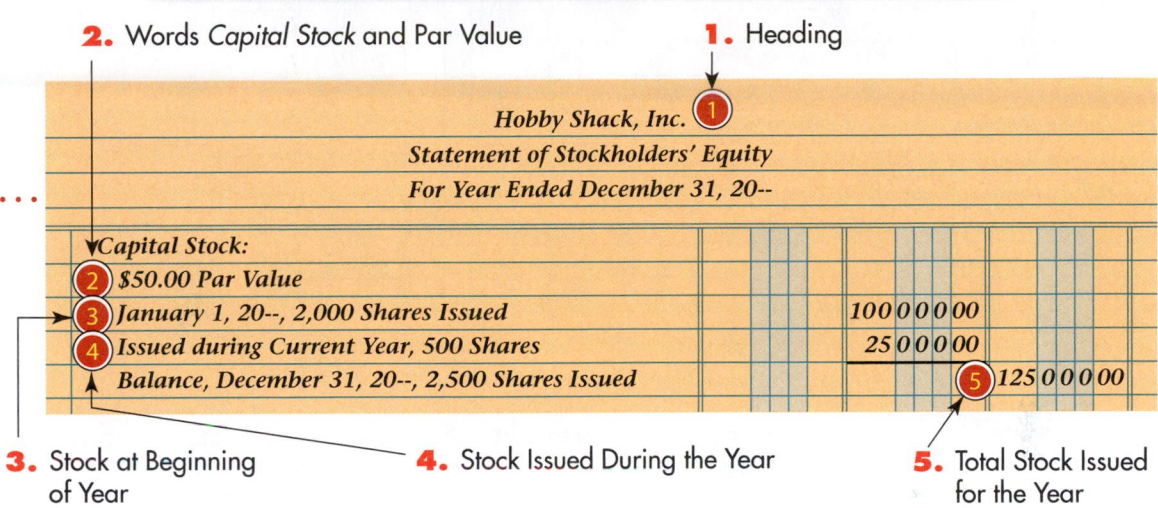

3. Stock at Beginning of Year

4. Stock Issued During the Year

5. Total Stock Issued for the Year

A financial statement that shows changes in a corporation's ownership for a fiscal period is called a **statement of stockholders' equity**. A statement of stockholders' equity contains two major sections: (1) capital stock and (2) retained earnings.

The amount of capital stock issued as of the beginning of the year is the beginning balance of the capital stock account. Any additional stock transactions recorded in the general ledger during the fiscal year would be added to calculate the amount of stock issued during the fiscal year. Thus, the amounts in the capital stock section of the statement of stockholders' equity are obtained from the general ledger account, Capital Stock.

Each share of stock issued by a corporation has a monetary value. A value assigned to a share of stock and printed on the stock certificate is called **par value**.

STEPS PREPARING THE CAPITAL STOCK SECTION OF A STATEMENT OF STOCKHOLDERS' EQUITY

1 Write the heading: company name, *Hobby Shack, Inc.*; statement name, *Statement of Stockholders' Equity*; and fiscal period, *For Year Ended December 31, 20--*, in the statement heading.

2 Write the heading *Capital Stock:* and on the next line write the par value of the stock, *$50.00 Par Value*, indented about 1 centimeter.

3 Write the number of shares, *2,000*, and dollar amount, *$100,000.00*, of stock issued as of the beginning of the year.

4 Write the number of shares, *500*, and dollar amount, *$25,000.00*, of stock issued during the year.

5 Calculate the total dollar amount of stock issued as of the end of the year, *$125,000.00*, by adding the dollar amount of beginning stock, *$100,000.00*, and the dollar amount of shares issued during the year, *$25,000.00*.

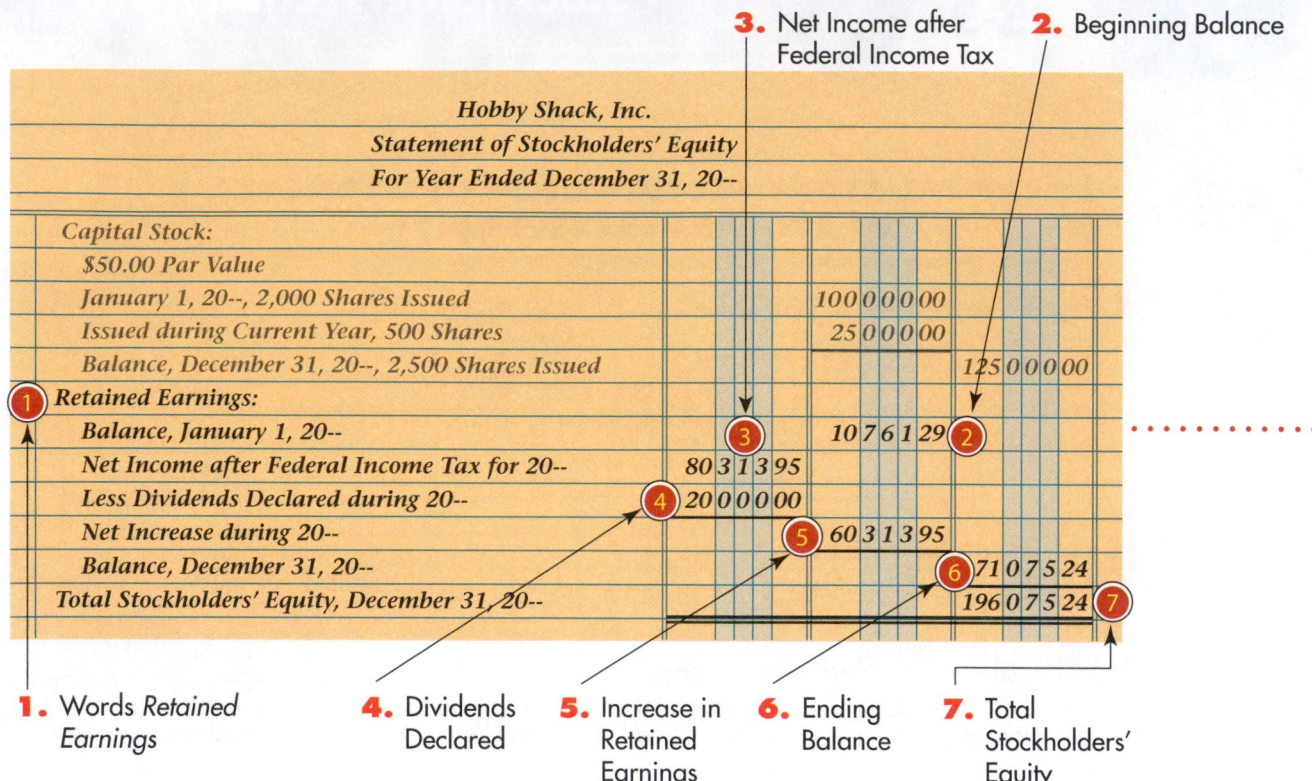

3. Net Income after Federal Income Tax   **2.** Beginning Balance

Hobby Shack, Inc.
Statement of Stockholders' Equity
For Year Ended December 31, 20--

Capital Stock:			
$50.00 Par Value			
January 1, 20--, 2,000 Shares Issued		100 000 00	
Issued during Current Year, 500 Shares		25 000 00	
Balance, December 31, 20--, 2,500 Shares Issued			125 000 00
① Retained Earnings:			
Balance, January 1, 20--	③	10 761 29 ②	
Net Income after Federal Income Tax for 20--	80 313 95		
Less Dividends Declared during 20--	④ 20 000 00		
Net Increase during 20--		⑤ 60 313 95	
Balance, December 31, 20--			71 075 24 ⑥
Total Stockholders' Equity, December 31, 20--			196 075 24 ⑦

1. Words *Retained Earnings*

4. Dividends Declared

5. Increase in Retained Earnings

6. Ending Balance

7. Total Stockholders' Equity

Net income increases a corporation's total capital. Some income may be retained by a corporation for business expansion. Some income may be distributed as dividends to provide stockholders with a return on their investments. During the year, Hobby Shack's board of directors declared $20,000.00 in dividends.

Amounts used to prepare the statement of stockholders' equity are obtained from the income statement and balance sheet columns of the work sheet shown in Chapter 14.

STEPS — **PREPARING THE RETAINED EARNINGS SECTION OF A STATEMENT OF STOCKHOLDERS' EQUITY**

① Write the heading *Retained Earnings*.

② Write the beginning balance of Retained Earnings, $10,761.29, from the Balance Sheet Credit column, indented about 1 centimeter.

③ Write the net income after federal income tax, $80,313.95, from the Income Statement Debit column.

④ Write the amount of dividends, $20,000.00, from the Balance Sheet Debit column.

⑤ Subtract dividends, $20,000.00, from net income after federal income tax, $80,313.95, to calculate the increase in retained earnings, $60,313.95.

⑥ Add the beginning balance of retained earnings, $10,761.29, and the increase in retained earnings, $60,313.95, to calculate the ending balance of retained earnings, $71,075.24.

⑦ Add the ending amounts of capital stock, $125,000.00, and retained earnings, $71,075.24, to calculate the total amount of stockholders' equity, $196,075.24.

End of Lesson REVIEW

AUDIT YOUR UNDERSTANDING

1. What financial information does a statement of stockholders' equity report?
2. What are the two major sections of a statement of stockholders' equity?
3. Where is the information found to prepare the capital stock section of a statement of stockholders' equity?
4. Where is the beginning balance of retained earnings found?
5. How does a corporation distribute a portion of income to stockholders?
6. Where is the amount of dividends found?

TERMS REVIEW

statement of stockholders' equity

par value

WORK TOGETHER 15-3

Preparing a statement of stockholders' equity

Use the work sheet and income statement for Interstate Tires, Inc., from Work Together 15-2. A form for the statement of stockholders' equity is given in the *Working Papers*. Your instructor will guide you through the following example.

1. Prepare a statement of stockholders' equity for the current year. As of January 1, Interstate Tires, Inc., had issued 100,000 shares of capital stock with a par value of $1.00 per share. During the fiscal year, the corporation issued 10,000 additional shares of capital stock. Save your work to complete Work Together 15-4.

ON YOUR OWN 15-3

Preparing a statement of stockholders' equity

Use the work sheet and income statement for Osborn Corporation from On Your Own 15-2. A form for the statement of stockholders' equity is given in the *Working Papers*. Work this problem independently.

1. Prepare a statement of stockholders' equity for the current year. As of January 1, Osborn Corporation had issued 7,500 shares of capital stock with a par value of $25.00 per share. During the fiscal year, the corporation issued 500 additional shares of stock. Save your work to complete On Your Own 15-4.

Preparing a Balance Sheet

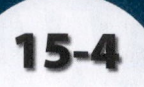

········· BALANCE SHEET INFORMATION ON A WORK SHEET ·········

Hobby Shack, Inc.
Work Sheet
For Year Ended December 31, 20--

	ACCOUNT TITLE	TRIAL BALANCE DEBIT	TRIAL BALANCE CREDIT	ADJUSTMENTS DEBIT	ADJUSTMENTS CREDIT	INCOME STATEMENT DEBIT	INCOME STATEMENT CREDIT	BALANCE SHEET DEBIT	BALANCE SHEET CREDIT	
1	Cash	2908028						2908028		1
2	Petty Cash	30000						30000		2
3	Accounts Receivable	1469840						1469840		3
4	Allow. for Uncoll. Accts.		12752		(e) 124500				137252	4
5	Merchandise Inventory	14048000			(d)1584000			12464000		5
6	Supplies—Office	348000			(a) 273000			75000		6
7	Supplies—Store	394400			(b) 291000			103400		7
8	Prepaid Insurance	580000			(c) 317000			263000		8
9	Office Equipment	3586450						3586450		9
10	Acc. Depr.—Office Equipment		649700		(f) 654000				1303700	10
11	Store Equipment	4084950						4084950		11
12	Acc. Depr.—Store Equipment		506900		(g) 525000				1031900	12
13	Accounts Payable		1158303						1158303	13
14	Federal Income Tax Payable				(h) 588924				588924	14
15	Employee Income Tax Payable		75700						75700	15
16	Social Security Tax Payable		145138						145138	16
17	Medicare Tax Payable		39942						39942	17
18	Sales Tax Payable		255670						255670	18
19	Unemployment Tax Payable—Federal		3460						3460	19
20	Unemployment Tax Payable—State		23355						23355	20
21	Health Insurance Premiums Payable		100800						100800	21
22	U.S. Savings Bonds Payable		6000						6000	22
23	United Way Donations Payable		7000						7000	23
24	Dividends Payable		500000						500000	24

A corporation's balance sheet reports assets, liabilities, and stockholders' equity on a specific date. [CONCEPT: Accounting Period Cycle] Some management decisions can best be made after owners have analyzed the balance sheet. For example, balance sheet information would enable management to determine whether the corporation should incur additional liabilities to acquire additional plant assets.

The information used to prepare a balance sheet is obtained from two sources: (1) the Balance Sheet columns of a work sheet and (2) the owners' equity statement.

Procedures for preparing Hobby Shack's balance sheet are similar to those used by TechKnow in Part 1. A balance sheet may be prepared in account form or report form. As described in Chapter 7, TechKnow uses the account form. Hobby Shack uses the report form.

2. Begin Assets Section

1. Heading

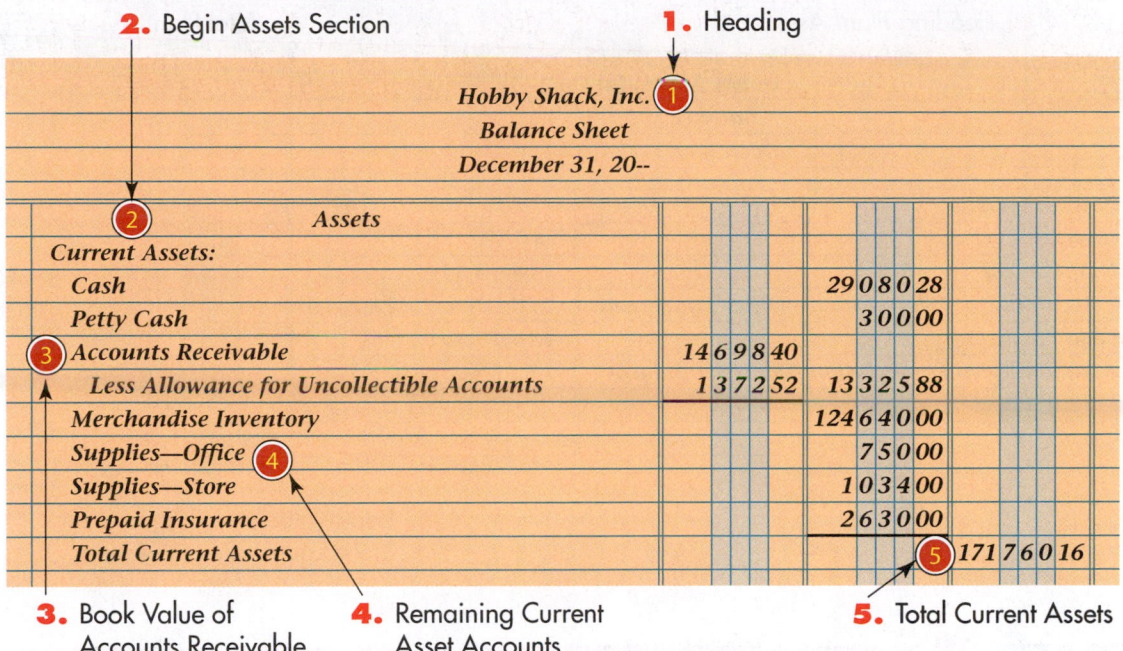

Hobby Shack, Inc. ①
Balance Sheet
December 31, 20--

	Assets				
Current Assets:					
Cash				29 0 8 0 28	
Petty Cash				3 0 0 00	
Accounts Receivable	14 6 9 8 40				
Less Allowance for Uncollectible Accounts	1 3 7 2 52		13 3 2 5 88		
Merchandise Inventory			124 6 4 0 00		
Supplies—Office			7 5 0 00		
Supplies—Store			1 0 3 4 00		
Prepaid Insurance			2 6 3 0 00		
Total Current Assets				171 7 6 0 16	

3. Book Value of
Accounts Receivable

4. Remaining Current
Asset Accounts

5. Total Current Assets

Hobby Shack classifies its assets as current assets and plant assets. A business owning both current and plant assets usually lists them under separate headings on a balance sheet. Some of Hobby Shack's asset accounts have related contra accounts that reduce the related account on the balance sheet. The difference between an asset's account balance and its related contra account balance is known as *book value*. An asset's book value is reported on a balance sheet by listing three amounts: (1) the balance of the asset account, (2) the balance of the asset's contra account, and (3) the book value.

STEPS 〉 **PREPARING THE CURRENT ASSETS SECTION OF A BALANCE SHEET**

① Write the balance sheet heading on three lines.

② Begin preparing the assets section of the balance sheet. Use information from the work sheet.
 a. Write the section title, *Assets*, on the first line in the middle of the wide column.
 b. Write the section title, *Current Assets:*, on the next line at the extreme left of the wide column.
 c. Beginning on the next line, indented about one centimeter, write the *Cash* and *Petty Cash* account titles in the order in which they appear on the work sheet.
 d. Write the balance of each asset account in the second column.

③ Calculate the book value of accounts receivable.
 a. Write *Accounts Receivable* on the next line, indented about one centimeter.
 b. Write the total amount of accounts receivable, $14,698.40, in the first amount column.
 c. Write *Less Allowance for Uncollectible Accounts* on the next line, indented about two centimeters.
 d. Write the amount of the allowance for uncollectible accounts, $1,372.52, in the first amount column.
 e. Subtract the allowance for uncollectible accounts, $1,372.52, from the total amount of accounts receivable, $14,698.40, to calculate the book value of accounts receivable, $13,325.88. Write the amount in the second amount column on the same line.

④ Write the remaining current asset account titles and amounts.

⑤ Calculate total current assets.
 a. Write *Total Current Assets* on the next line, indented about one centimeter.
 b. Add the amounts in the second amount column and write the total, $171,760.16, in the third amount column.

1. Heading *Plant Assets*   **4.** Total Plant Assets

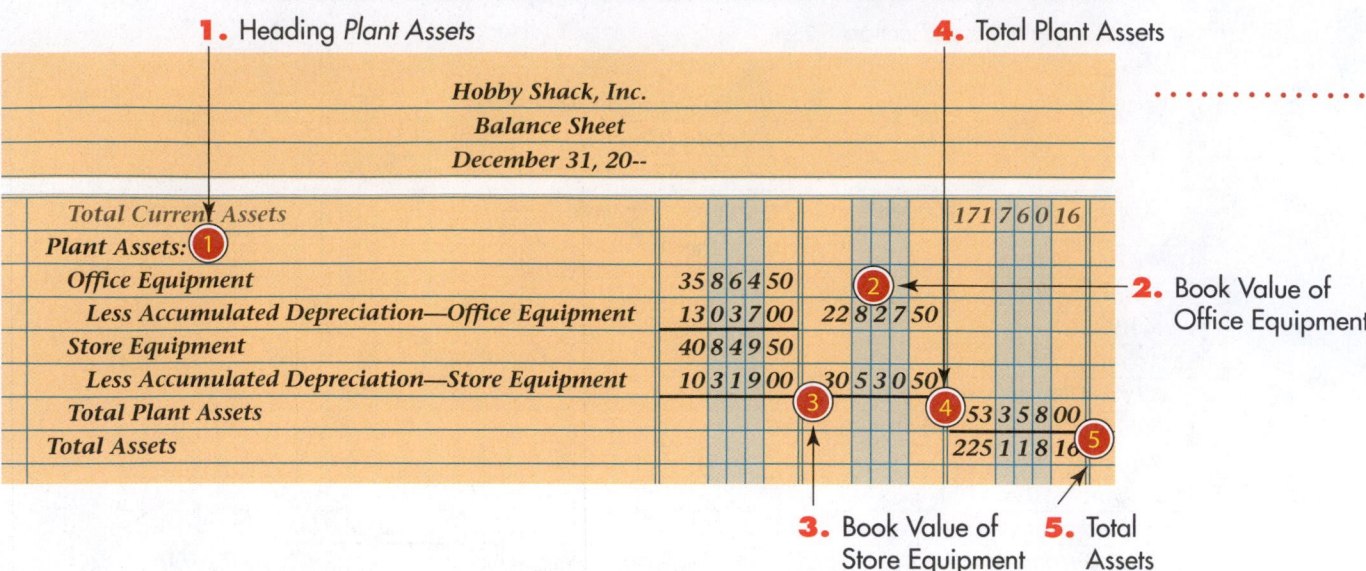

Hobby Shack, Inc.
Balance Sheet
December 31, 20--

Total Current Assets				171 760 16
Plant Assets: ①				
Office Equipment	35 864 50			
Less Accumulated Depreciation—Office Equipment	13 037 00	22 827 50 ②		
Store Equipment	40 849 50			
Less Accumulated Depreciation—Store Equipment	10 319 00	30 530 50		
Total Plant Assets		③	53 358 00 ④	
Total Assets				225 118 16 ⑤

2. Book Value of Office Equipment

3. Book Value of Store Equipment   **5.** Total Assets

S T E P S **PREPARING THE PLANT ASSETS SECTION OF A BALANCE SHEET**

① Write the heading *Plant Assets* on the next line at the extreme left of the wide column.

② Calculate the book value of office equipment using information from the work sheet.
   a. Write *Office Equipment* on the next line, indented about one centimeter.
   b. Write the total amount of office equipment, $35,864.50, in the first amount column.
   c. Write *Less Accumulated Depreciation—Office Equipment* on the next line, indented about two centimeters.
   d. Write the amount of the accumulated depreciation—office equipment, $13,037.00, in the first amount column.
   e. Subtract the accumulated depreciation—office equipment, $13,037.00, from the total amount of office equipment, $35,864.50, to calculate the book value of office equipment, $22,827.50. Write the amount in the second amount column on the same line.

③ Use the same procedure to calculate the book value of store equipment.

④ Calculate total plant assets.
   a. Write *Total Plant Assets* on the next line, indented about one centimeter.
   b. Add the amounts in the second amount column and write the total, $53,358.00, in the third amount column.

⑤ Calculate total assets.
   a. Write *Total Assets* on the next line at the extreme left of the wide column.
   b. Add the current and plant asset totals and write the amount, $225,118.16, on the same line in the third amount column.

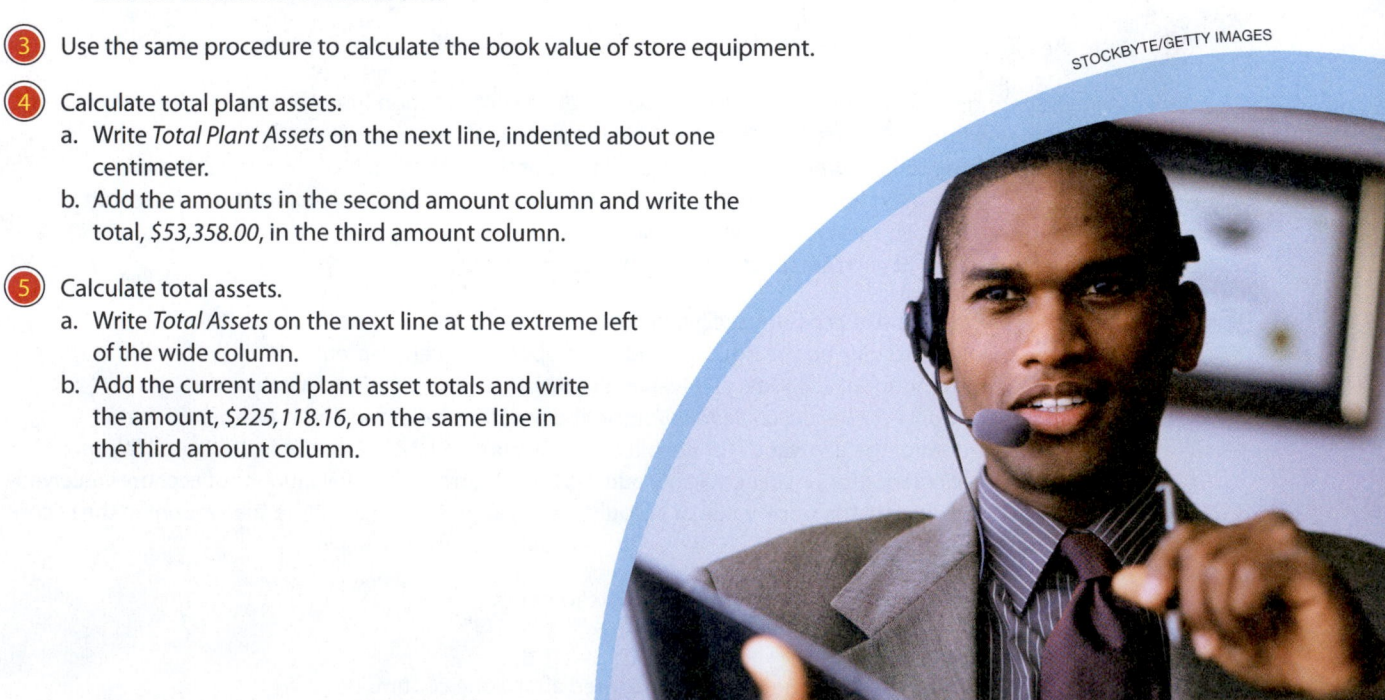

1. Heading *Liabilities*

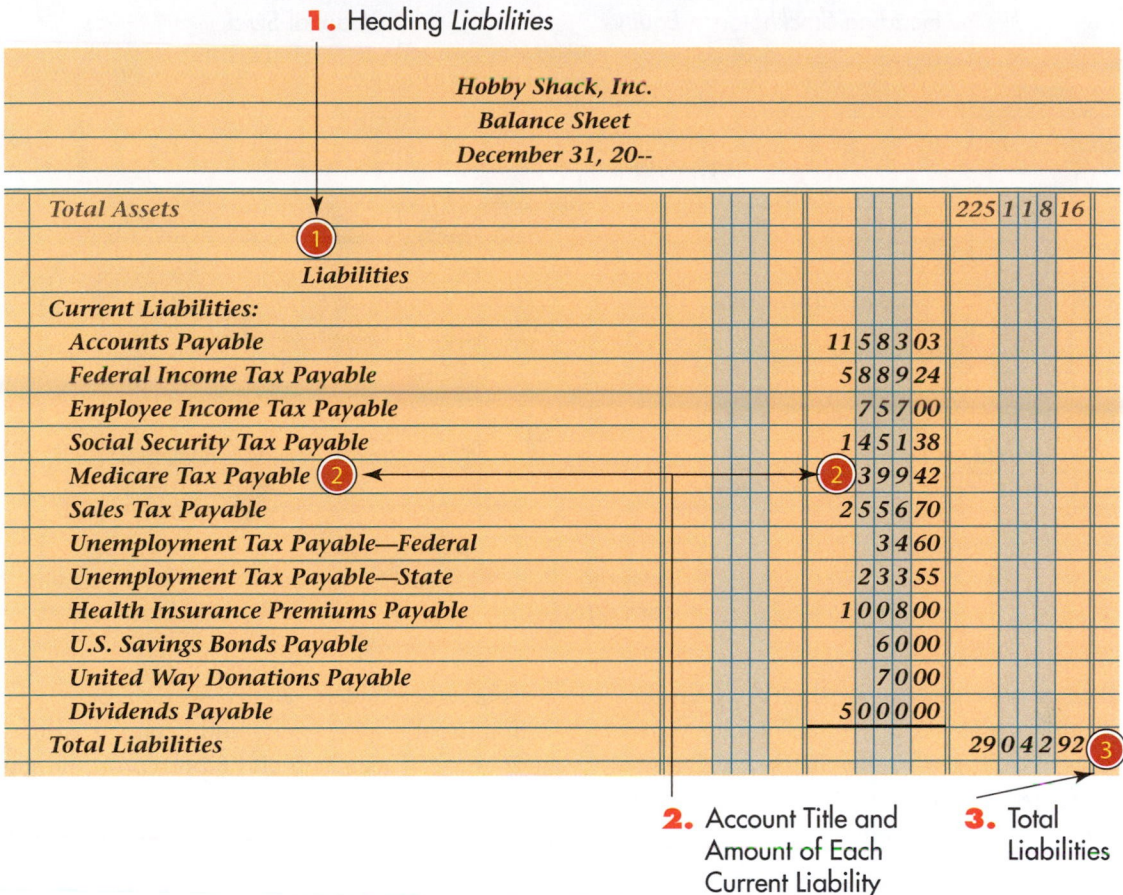

Hobby Shack, Inc.										
Balance Sheet										
December 31, 20--										
Total Assets								225	1 1 8	16
Liabilities										
Current Liabilities:										
Accounts Payable					11 5 8 3	03				
Federal Income Tax Payable					5 8 8 9	24				
Employee Income Tax Payable					7 5 7	00				
Social Security Tax Payable					1 4 5 1	38				
Medicare Tax Payable					3 9 9	42				
Sales Tax Payable					2 5 5 6	70				
Unemployment Tax Payable—Federal					3 4	60				
Unemployment Tax Payable—State					2 3 3	55				
Health Insurance Premiums Payable					1 0 0 8	00				
U.S. Savings Bonds Payable					6 0	00				
United Way Donations Payable					7 0	00				
Dividends Payable					5 0 0 0	00				
Total Liabilities								29 0 4 2	92	

2. Account Title and Amount of Each Current Liability

3. Total Liabilities

Liabilities are classified according to the length of time until they are due. Liabilities due within a short time, usually within a year, are called **current liabilities**.

Liabilities owed for more than a year are called **long-term liabilities**. An example of a long-term liability is Mortgage Payable. On December 31 of the current year, Hobby Shack does not have any long-term liabilities.

To prepare the liabilities section of the balance sheet, use information from the work sheet.

STEPS PREPARING THE LIABILITIES SECTION OF A BALANCE SHEET

1 Write the section title, *Liabilities*, on the next line in the middle of the wide column.

2 Write the title *Current Liabilities:* on the next line at the extreme left of the wide column.
   a. Beginning on the next line, indented about one centimeter, write the liability account titles in the order in which they appear on the work sheet.
   b. Write the balance of each liability account in the second amount column.

3 Calculate total liabilities.
   a. Write *Total Liabilities* on the next line below the last liability account title at the extreme left of the wide column.
   b. Write the total liabilities, *$29,042.92*, on the same line in the third amount column.

FOR YOUR INFORMATION

FYI

A company having both current liabilities and long-term liabilities would include headings and totals for each category. The process is similar to preparing the assets section of a balance sheet.

1. Heading *Stockholders' Equity*   **2.** Capital Stock

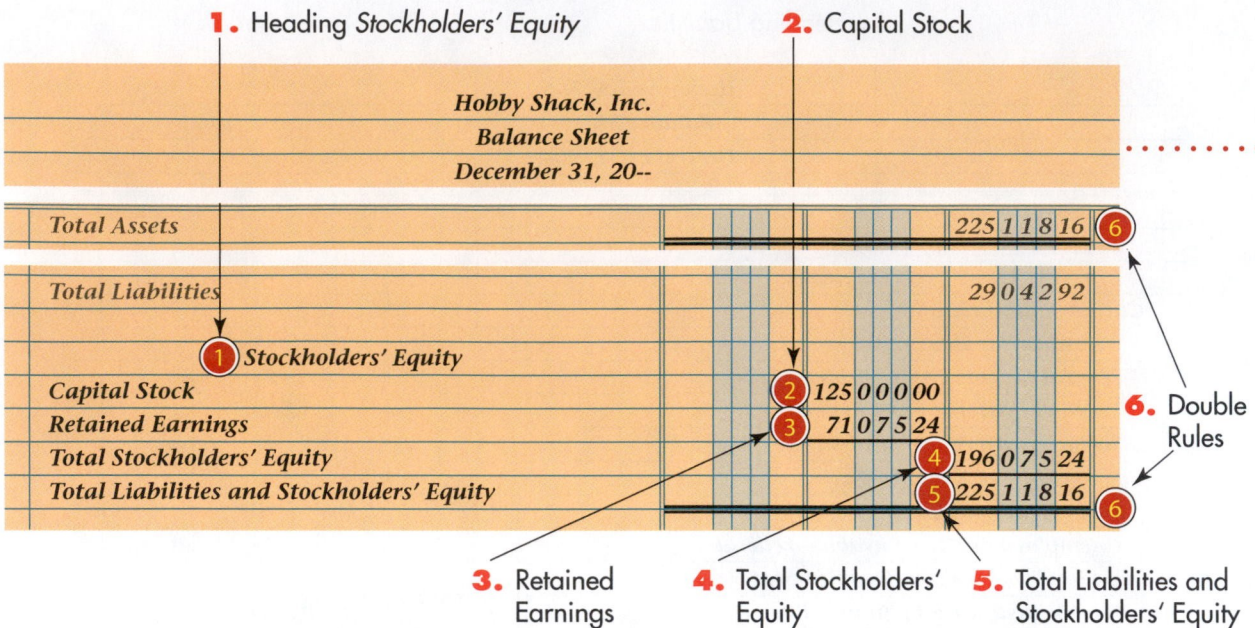

3. Retained Earnings   **4.** Total Stockholders' Equity   **5.** Total Liabilities and Stockholders' Equity

A major difference between balance sheets of a corporation and a proprietorship is the owners' equity section. The owners' equity section of Hobby Shack's balance sheet is labeled *Stockholders' Equity*. Some corporations use the same label, *Owners' Equity*, as proprietorships. Either label is acceptable.

The stockholders' equity section contains the total amounts of capital stock and retained earnings. These amounts are calculated and reported on the statement of stockholders' equity.

Hobby Shack's completed balance sheet is shown on the following page.

STEPS

PREPARING THE STOCKHOLDERS' EQUITY SECTION OF A BALANCE SHEET

① Write the heading *Stockholders' Equity* on the next line centered in the wide column.

② Write the title and amount of *Capital Stock*, $125,000.00, calculated on the statement of stockholders' equity.

③ Write the title and amount of *Retained Earnings*, $71,075.24, calculated on the statement of stockholders' equity.

④ Add the amount of capital stock, $125,000.00, and retained earnings, $71,075.24, to calculate the total of stockholders' equity, $196,075.24.

⑤ Add the amount of total liabilities, $29,042.92, and total stockholders' equity, $196,075.24, to calculate the total of liabilities and stockholders' equity, $225,118.16. Verify accuracy by comparing the total amount of assets and the total amount of liabilities and stockholders' equity. These two amounts must be the same.

⑥ Draw double rules across the three columns at the end of the Assets section and the Stockholders' Equity section to show that assets equal liabilities plus owners' equity.

REMEMBER

Total assets must equal the total of liabilities and stockholders' equity. If these totals are not equal, identify the errors before preparing adjusting and closing entries.

Hobby Shack, Inc.

Balance Sheet

December 31, 20--

Assets				
Current Assets:				
Cash			2 9 0 8 0 28	
Petty Cash			3 0 0 00	
Accounts Receivable	1 4 6 9 8 40			
Less Allowance for Uncollectible Accounts	1 3 7 2 52	1 3 3 2 5 88		
Merchandise Inventory			12 4 6 4 0 00	
Supplies—Office			7 5 0 00	
Supplies—Store			1 0 3 4 00	
Prepaid Insurance			2 6 3 0 00	
Total Current Assets				171 7 6 0 16
Plant Assets:				
Office Equipment	3 5 8 6 4 50			
Less Accumulated Depreciation—Office Equipment	13 0 3 7 00	2 2 8 2 7 50		
Store Equipment	40 8 4 9 50			
Less Accumulated Depreciation—Store Equipment	10 3 1 9 00	30 5 3 0 50		
Total Plant Assets				5 3 3 5 8 00
Total Assets				225 1 1 8 16
Liabilities				
Current Liabilities:				
Accounts Payable			1 1 5 8 3 03	
Federal Income Tax Payable			5 8 8 9 24	
Employee Income Tax Payable			7 5 7 00	
Social Security Tax Payable			1 4 5 1 38	
Medicare Tax Payable			3 9 9 42	
Sales Tax Payable			2 5 5 6 70	
Unemployment Tax Payable—Federal			3 4 60	
Unemployment Tax Payable—State			2 3 3 55	
Health Insurance Premiums Payable			1 0 0 8 00	
U.S. Savings Bonds Payable			6 0 00	
United Way Donations Payable			7 0 00	
Dividends Payable			5 0 0 0 00	
Total Liabilities				29 0 4 2 92
Stockholders' Equity				
Capital Stock			125 0 0 0 00	
Retained Earnings			7 1 0 7 5 24	
Total Stockholders' Equity				196 0 7 5 24
Total Liabilities and Stockholders' Equity				225 1 1 8 16

A report prepared to give details about an item on a principal financial statement is called a **supporting schedule**. A supporting schedule is sometimes referred to as a *supplementary report* or an *exhibit*.

Hobby Shack prepares two supporting schedules to accompany the balance sheet. The supporting schedules are a schedule of accounts payable and a schedule of accounts receivable. A balance sheet shows only the accounts payable total amount. The account balance for each vendor is not shown. When detailed information is needed, a supporting schedule of accounts payable is prepared, showing the balance for each vendor. A balance sheet also shows only the accounts receivable total amount. When information about the account balance for each customer is needed, a supporting schedule of accounts receivable is prepared. Hobby Shack's supporting schedules on December 31 are similar to the supporting schedules for November 30 shown in Chapter 11.

BUSINESS STRUCTURES

Who Owns the Corporation?

A share of stock is a unit of ownership in a corporation. Stock may be purchased by individuals, investment companies, pension funds, institutions, banks, and other companies. Publicly traded stocks are bought and sold on stock exchanges throughout the world. Ownership of a corporation's stock entitles the owner to distributions of earnings if there are dividends declared. Many stock owners, however, buy stock with the expectation that the stock will increase in value and they can then sell the stock at a profit.

Stock ownership also entitles the owner to vote at stockholders' meetings, where important issues regarding the corporation may be decided. The membership of the board of directors of the corporation is also determined at stockholders' meetings. Sometimes individuals or other stock owners will attempt to gain a majority holding of a company's stock in order to take control of the company.

Sometimes investors determine which corporation's stock they will purchase based on political or social issues. For example, one investor might buy stocks only of companies that have good reputations on environmental issues. Others might buy stocks only of companies that have good policies regarding racial or gender discrimination.

Critical Thinking

1. If you were buying stock as an investment for your retirement years, would you be more concerned with the future resale value of the stock or its dividends? Would the answer be different for 18-year-olds and 60-year-olds?

2. What are some other kinds of social issues that might be important considerations for some people in purchasing corporate stock?

PHOTO: PHOTODISC/GETTY IMAGES

End of Lesson REVIEW

AUDIT YOUR UNDERSTANDING

1. How does Hobby Shack classify its assets?
2. What three items are listed on the balance sheet for an account having a related contra asset account?
3. What is an example of a long-term liability?
4. Where are the amounts obtained for the stockholders' equity section of the balance sheet?
5. What are two supporting schedules that might accompany a balance sheet?

TERMS REVIEW

current liabilities

long-term liabilities

supporting schedule

WORK TOGETHER 15-4

Preparing a balance sheet for a corporation

Use Interstate Tires' work sheet and statement of stockholders' equity from Work Together 15-3. A form for the balance sheet is given in the *Working Papers*. Your instructor will guide you through the following examples.

1. Prepare a balance sheet for the current year.

ON YOUR OWN 15-4

Preparing a balance sheet for a corporation

Use Osborn Corporation's work sheet and statement of stockholders' equity from On Your Own 15-3. A form for the balance sheet is given in the *Working Papers*. Work this problem independently.

1. Prepare a balance sheet for the current year.

After completing this chapter, you can:

1. Define accounting terms related to financial statements for a merchandising business organized as a corporation.

2. Identify accounting concepts and practices related to financial statements for a merchandising business organized as a corporation.

3. Prepare an income statement for a merchandising business organized as a corporation.

4. Analyze an income statement using component percentages and financial ratios.

5. Prepare a statement of stockholders' equity for a merchandising business organized as a corporation.

6. Prepare a balance sheet for a merchandising business organized as a corporation.

EXPLORE ACCOUNTING

Alternative Fiscal Years

Most small companies use a fiscal year that is the same as the calendar year, January 1 to December 31. However, there may be several reasons why a different fiscal period would be beneficial. If the calendar year end comes in the middle of a high sales period, a fiscal year ending at this time can be more difficult. All employees are extremely busy with sales and shipping. Because of this activity, accurately identifying sales, inventory, and accounts receivable is more difficult. If the calendar year end comes just before the high sales period begins, an analysis of the company's financial condition will not be as favorable. The company may have borrowed money to buy a high level of inventory, so the company has higher debt and high inventory levels. Therefore, some companies choose to use a natural business year as the fiscal year, as discussed in Chapter 6.

FanciFoods is a corporation that makes and sells decorative cakes, cookies, and candies. Approximately 90% of its sales are made between November 1 and February 15 because of the three holidays of Thanksgiving, Christmas, and Valentine's Day. The company spends six months—May to November—preparing for its heavy sales period. The company has selected April 1 to March 31 as its fiscal year. By March 31, inventory is low, most accounts receivable have been collected, and the company has not yet replaced inventory to begin preparing for the next season. Thus, this is an ideal time to end the fiscal period. Inventory is easier to count, the level of accounts receivable is lower, and more employees are available to help with the closing activities.

Research: What other types of companies may find it beneficial to use a fiscal year different from the calendar year? What would be the ideal fiscal period for these companies? You may wish to find a local business that has a fiscal period different from the calendar year. If so, determine the reasons for selecting the fiscal period it now uses.

PHOTO: PHOTOGRAPHER'S CHOICE/GETTY IMAGES

15-1 APPLICATION PROBLEM

Preparing an income statement for a merchandising business

A work sheet for Historic Doors, Inc., for the year ended December 31 of the current year is given in the *Working Papers*.

Instructions:

1. Prepare an income statement.

2. Calculate and record on the income statement the following component percentages: (a) cost of merchandise sold, (b) gross profit on sales, (c) total expenses, and (d) net income before federal income tax. Round percentage calculations to the nearest 0.1%.

15-2 APPLICATION PROBLEM

Analyzing component percentages and financial ratios

The income statement for Custom Jewelry, Inc., and a form for completing this problem are given in the *Working Papers*. The managers of Custom Jewelry have established the following target component percentages:

Cost of Merchandise Sold	35.0%
Gross Profit on Sales	65.0%
Expenses	40.0%
Net Income before Federal Income Tax	25.0%

Instructions:

1. Compare the actual component percentages to the target percentage. Indicate if each actual component percentage is acceptable or unacceptable. If a percentage is unacceptable, suggest a possible action to correct the unacceptable component percentage.

2. Custom Jewelry has 110,000 shares of stock outstanding on December 31. The company's market price is $13.75 per share. Calculate the earnings per share and price-earnings ratio.

15-3 APPLICATION PROBLEM

Preparing a statement of stockholders' equity

A form for completing this problem is given in the *Working Papers*.

Instructions:

1. Prepare a statement of stockholders' equity for Classic Interiors, Inc., for the fiscal year ended on December 31 of the current year. Use the following additional information.

Capital stock outstanding on January 1	50,000 shares
Capital stock issued during the year	10,000 shares
Capital stock par value	$5.00
Retained earnings, January 1	$59,485.50
Dividends declared during year	$66,000.00
Net income after federal income tax	$110,635.34

Go Beyond the Book
For more information go to
www.C21accounting.com

15-4   APPLICATION PROBLEM

Preparing a balance sheet for a corporation

Henderson Corporation's partial work sheet for the year ended December 31 of the current year is given in the *Working Papers*. A form for completing this problem is also given in the *Working Papers*. The December 31 balance in retained earnings reported on the statement of stockholders' equity is $97,294.85.

Instructions:

1. Prepare a balance sheet in report form.

15-5   MASTERY PROBLEM   Peachtree *by Sage*   QB *Quick Books*

Preparing financial statements

The work sheet for Lighting Center, Inc., for the year ended December 31 of the current year and forms for completing this problem are given in the *Working Papers*.

Instructions:

1. Prepare an income statement. Calculate and record the following component percentages: (a) cost of merchandise sold, (b) gross profit on sales, (c) total expenses, and (d) net income or loss before federal income tax. Round percentage calculations to the nearest 0.1%.
2. Prepare a statement of stockholders' equity. The company had 90,000 shares of $1.00 par value stock outstanding on January 1. The company issued an additional 10,000 shares during the year.
3. Prepare a balance sheet in report form.
4. Calculate the earnings per share and price-earnings ratio. The current market price of the stock is $28.50.

15-6   CHALLENGE PROBLEM

Analyzing component percentages and financial ratios

Instructions:

1. Obtain the financial statements of two corporations in similar industries. Calculate the income statement component percentages, earnings per share, and price-earnings ratio of each corporation. The current market price of each stock can be obtained from a newspaper or online. *Note: Annual reports may be available in your classroom, school library, or public library. They can also be found online.*
2. Contrast the component percentages of the companies. Identify which company you believe is performing better.

A long written report should contain numerous headings. A heading enables the reader to focus on the primary idea of the next section. An outline is a special document that lists only the headings of a report. By reviewing an outline before and after reading a report, the reader can gain a better understanding of the relationship among the topics being presented.

Each chapter of this textbook is similar to a long report. Headings are used to separate and emphasize major concepts.

Instructions: Prepare an outline of this chapter.

CASE FOR CRITICAL THINKING

Christy Burch and Myung Lim, business managers, compared their current income statement with the income statement of a year ago. They noted that sales were 12.0% higher than a year ago. They also noted that the total expenses were 20.0% higher than a year ago. What type of analysis should be done to determine whether the increase in expenses is justified?

GRAPHING WORKSHOP

Evaluating Department Sales

Collinsville Home Center made a strategic decision in 2002 to carry a line of home appliances. The following graph depicts sales for the company's three departments for the recent eight-year period. Analyze the graph to answer the following questions.

1. Describe the sales growth in the Appliances department.

2. State the approximate total company sales for 2007.

3. Describe the performance of the Lumber Department.

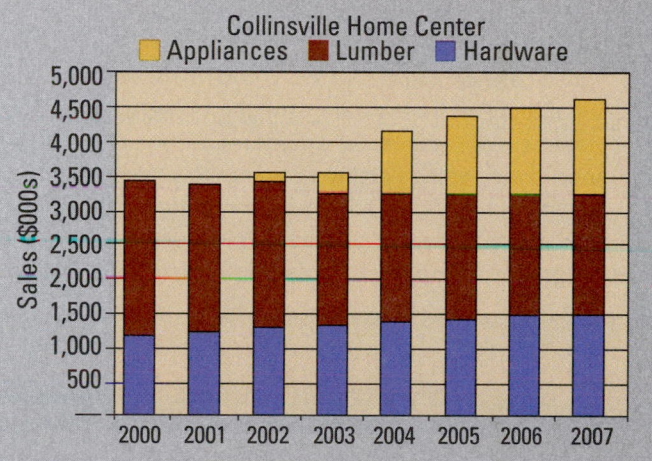

ANALYZING BEST BUY'S FINANCIAL STATEMENTS

Gross profit on sales is the amount of revenue remaining after the cost of merchandise has been deducted. Best Buy's gross profit on sales, labeled simply as "gross profit" on its income statement, has increased dramatically over the past three fiscal periods, a very favorable trend. But sales have also increased, making it difficult to determine how effectively Best Buy has been controlling its cost of merchandise sold.

The component percentage for gross profit on sales is also referred to as the *gross margin* or *gross profit rate*.

Instructions

1. Use Best Buy's Financial Highlights on page B-2 in Appendix B to identify the gross profit rate for 2005–2007.

2. Is the trend in the gross profit rate favorable or unfavorable?

3. Demonstrate how amounts on Best Buy's Consolidated Statement of Earnings, on page B-6, were used to calculate the gross profit rate for 2007.

Accounting
SOFTWARE

FINANCIAL STATEMENTS

Component percentages are an essential tool for understanding financial statements. Peachtree includes component percentages on many, but not all, of its financial statements.

What if a manager requests that you add the component percentages to a report? Peachtree provides you with an easy method for accomplishing this task. With the report displayed on the screen, you can instruct Peachtree to export the financial statement to an electronic spreadsheet file.

This feature provides you with two important benefits. First, formulas can be entered to quickly and accurately calculate the component percentages. Second, the financial statement printed from the electronic spreadsheet will have a more professional appearance than might have been available otherwise.

PEACHTREE MASTERY PROBLEM 15-5
1. Open (Restore) file 15-5MP.ptb.
2. Print an income statement. Calculate the component percentages for (a) cost of merchandise sold, (b) gross profit on sales, (c) total expenses, and (d) net income or loss before federal income tax. Round percentage calculations to the nearest 0.1%.
3. Print a balance sheet.
4. Substitute Peachtree's statement of retained earnings for the statement of stockholders' equity. Peachtree's Statement of Retained Earnings does not show the beginning Capital Stock balance of $100,000. Add that balance to the Ending Retained Earnings Balance so that Peachtree's statement agrees with the manually-prepared statement that would have been completed in the Working Papers.
5. As an optional activity, use the Help feature to learn how to export the income statement to an electronic spreadsheet. Then use formulas to calculate additional component percentages. Format the spreadsheet.

FINANCIAL STATEMENTS

QuickBooks is a very useful software program for recording transactions and producing reports and financial statements. It is not as helpful when it comes to trying to look into the future and answer questions, such as "How much will the net income be if the revenues increase by 25% and expenses only increase 10%?"

This type of question is better answered by electronic spreadsheet software. Thus, in order to answer the question, the current accounting data would have to be exported into the electronic spreadsheet program. QuickBooks has a function that allows data to be transferred to an electronic spreadsheet program.

In addition to answering "what if" questions such as that above, exporting data into a spreadsheet also makes it possible to change a report's appearance or contents without affecting your QuickBooks data.

QUICKBOOKS MASTERY PROBLEM 15-5
1. Open the Lighting Center Inc. file.
2. Print the Profit & Loss Standard report, using January 1 and December 31 for the dates.
3. Add component percentages calculated as a percentage of income to the report. Change the report subtitle to "For Year Ended December 31." Print the report.
4. To create a year-end balance sheet in QuickBooks, it is necessary to make a closing entry to close the equity account Dividends to retained earnings. Print a Trial Balance report to use as the basis for journalizing the closing transaction.
5. Use the Make General Journal Entries window to journalize the closing entry, using December 31 for the date.
6. Print a Journal report and a Balance Sheet Standard report, using December 31 for the dates.
7. As an optional activity, use the Help feature to learn how to export the income statement to an electronic spreadsheet. Then use formulas to calculate additional component percentages. Format the spreadsheet.

FORMATTING FINANCIAL STATEMENTS

Indenting section and account titles on a financial statement helps the reader identify the major sections of the statement. For example, having all the expenses indented under the Expense title clearly identifies these accounts as expenses.

The traditional method for indenting on an electronic spreadsheet was to have a series of thin columns on the left of the template. Each column allowed for one indentation. Modern electronic spreadsheets have tools that allow you to increase and decrease the indentation of text within a cell. Using these tools eliminates the need for many thin columns and allows you to easily change the level of indentation.

EXCEL APPLICATION PROBLEM 15-1

Open the F15-1 Excel data file. Follow the step-by-step instructions in the Instructions work sheet to calculate component percentages and indent text within cells for a better appearance.

EXCEL APPLICATION PROBLEM 15-3

Open the F15-3 Excel data file. Follow the step-by-step instructions in the Instructions work sheet to complete the statement of stockholders' equity.

FINANCIAL STATEMENTS

Sometimes it is not enough to simply display or print a financial statement. It might be desirable to paste a copy of the income statement or balance sheet in a memo or report. There could be an advantage in copying and pasting a financial statement in a spreadsheet where different assumptions could be tried to see how the business could be improved. For example, you might change the cost of purchases and see what effect the change has on net income.

Automated Accounting has a Copy function in the report window that allows you to copy the displayed financial statement in either a word processing or a spreadsheet format. When the report is displayed, click the Copy button. You then must choose either a word processing or a spreadsheet format. The report is saved on the operating system's Clipboard. You can then open an existing word processing document or start a new one, click the Paste tool on the toolbar or select Edit Paste, and the report is copied into a word processing document.

To make columns align, it is necessary to reformat the entire report in a monotype font, such as Courier New, so that each character occupies the same amount of space. A similar process is used to copy a report to a spreadsheet.

Optional Automated Accounting Problem

Open file F15-CP.AA8. Display the problem instructions and complete the problem.

CHAPTER 16

Recording Adjusting and Closing Entries for a Corporation

OBJECTIVES

After studying Chapter 16, you will be able to:

1. Identify accounting concepts and practices related to adjusting and closing entries for a merchandising business organized as a corporation.

2. Record adjusting entries.

3. Record closing entries for income statement accounts.

4. Record closing entry for dividends.

5. Prepare a post-closing trial balance.

STOCKBYTE/GETTY IMAGES

Point Your Browser
www.C21accounting.com

478

Apple

Apple Spreads Its Wings

Recent world history would be incomplete without a reference to three computers—Apple II, Macintosh, and iMac—that pushed computer technology beyond the standard of their day.

The Apple II was the first personal computer to gain wide distribution and put the Apple Computer company on the technology map. The Macintosh introduced the graphical interface and mouse technologies we now take for granted. The iMac merged digital audio and video into traditional computer technology to enable stunning editing of video and audio files.

Although Apple's foundation is in computers, the company has spread its wings into related technology markets. The widely successful iPod is the driving force in the popular digital music player market. iTunes was the first Internet site to offer legal, digital copies of music files. Together, iPod and iTunes have revolutionized how people access and play music.

Apple has clearly demonstrated that it can be a player in any market that requires the innovative application of computer technology.

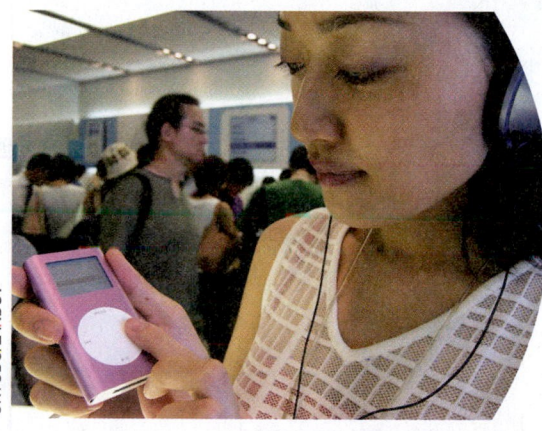

©KYODO/LANDOV

DIGITAL_VISION/GETTY IMAGES

Critical Thinking

1. Identify other companies that have extended their product lines beyond their original market.

2. Identify at least five expenses Apple incurs to support its iTunes business.

Source: www.apple.com, www.apple-history.com

INTERNET ACTIVITY

EDGAR—Part 2

Go to the homepage for EDGAR (www.sec.gov/edgar.shtml). Click on "Search for Company Filings," and then click on "Latest Filings."

Instructions

1. Look at the most recent filing (top of the list) and record the company name and the date and time the filing was accepted.

2. Click the "Back" button to return to "Search the EDGAR Database" page. Again, click on "Latest Filings." Scroll down the list to find the company filing you recorded in instruction 1. Count and record the number of additional filings that are listed.

LESSON **16-1**

Recording Adjusting Entries

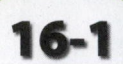

ADJUSTING ENTRIES RECORDED FROM A WORK SHEET

		1	2	3	4	
	ACCOUNT TITLE	TRIAL BALANCE		ADJUSTMENTS		
		DEBIT	CREDIT	DEBIT	CREDIT	
1	Cash	29080 28				1
2	Petty Cash	300 00				2
3	Accounts Receivable	14698 40				3
4	Allow. for Uncoll. Accts.		127 52		(e) 1245 00	4
5	Merchandise Inventory	140480 00			(d) 15840 00	5
6	Supplies—Office	3480 00			(a) 2730 00	6
7	Supplies—Store	3944 00			(b) 2910 00	7
8	Prepaid Insurance	5800 00			(c) 3170 00	8
28	Income Summary			(d) 15840 00		28
45	Supplies Expense—Office			(a) 2730 00		45
46	Supplies Expense—Store			(b) 2910 00		46
47	Uncollectible Accounts Expense			(e) 1245 00		47
48	Utilities Expense	3820 00				48
49	Federal Income Tax Expense	18000 00		(h) 5889 24		49

3. Identify the first adjustment.

2. Date **1.** Heading **4.** Account Debited **5.** Debit **7.** Credit

GENERAL JOURNAL PAGE 15

	DATE		ACCOUNT TITLE	DOC. NO.	POST. REF.	DEBIT	CREDIT	
1			(1) Adjusting Entries					1
2	20-- Dec.	31	Uncollectible Accounts Expense (4)			(5) 1245 00		2
3			Allowance for Uncoll. Accounts (6)				1245 00 (7)	3
4		31	Income Summary			15840 00		4
5			Merchandise Inventory				15840 00	5
6		31	Supplies Expense—Office			2730 00		6
7			Supplies—Office				2730 00	7
16		31	Federal Income Tax Expense			5889 24		16
17			Federal Income Tax Payable				5889 24	17
18								18

6. Account Credited

General ledger account balances are changed only by posting journal entries. Two types of journal entries change general ledger account balances at the end of a fiscal period: (1) Adjusting entries bring general ledger account balances up to date. (2) Closing entries prepare temporary accounts for the next fiscal period. [CONCEPT: Matching Expenses with Revenue] Adjusting entries recorded in a work sheet are journalized in a general journal. Hobby Shack begins the adjusting entries on a new general journal page. The adjusting entries are entered in the Debit and Credit columns of the general journal.

 S T E P S · **RECORDING ADJUSTING ENTRIES IN A GENERAL JOURNAL**

1. Write the heading, *Adjusting Entries,* in the middle of the general journal's Account Title column. This heading explains all of the adjusting entries that follow. Therefore, indicating a source document is unnecessary. The first adjusting entry is recorded on the first two lines below the heading.

2. For the first adjusting entry in the work sheet Adjustments columns, write the date, *Dec. 31, 20--,* in the Date column.

3. Scan down the Adjustments column of the work sheet to identify the first adjustment, *(e),* to *Allowance for Uncollectible Accounts.* Identify the debit and credit parts of this entry.

4. Write the title of the account debited in the Account Title column.

5. Write the debit adjustment amount in the Debit column.

6. Write the title of the account credited in the Account Title column, indented about 1 centimeter.

7. Write the credit adjustment amount in the Credit column.

8. Continue down the Adjustments columns, repeating Steps 4 through 7 for each of the additional adjustments.

R E M E M B E R

Remember to start a new general journal page for adjusting entries.

CHARACTER COUNTS

Insider Trading

Ben Levine works in the research unit of a large chemical company. His group has recently discovered a new chemical process that will revolutionize how household cleaning products are manufactured. The discovery should have a significant positive impact on his company's profitability and its stock price.

Ben purchases shares of his company every month through a payroll deduction program. He is considering using a large portion of his savings to buy additional shares of the company. Since you are the ethics officer of the company, he has asked your opinion on his proposed stock purchase.

Instructions

Access the *Code of Business Conduct* of Dow at www.dow.com. Using this code of conduct as a guide, provide Ben with guidance on his proposed stock purchase. Can Ben continue his monthly purchases?

GENERAL JOURNAL   PAGE 15

	DATE		ACCOUNT TITLE	DOC. NO.	POST. REF.	DEBIT	CREDIT	
1			*Adjusting Entries*					1
2	20-- Dec.	31	*Uncollectible Accounts Expense*			1 2 4 5 00		2
3			*Allowance for Uncoll. Accounts*				1 2 4 5 00	3

Hobby Shack estimated that $1,245.00 of the current fiscal year's sales on account will eventually be uncollectible. The amount is added to the existing balance in Allowance for Uncollectible Accounts, $127.52. The adjusted balance of Allowance for Uncollectible Accounts, $1,372.52, is the amount of the current accounts receivable that Hobby Shack expects to become uncollectible.

The effect of posting the adjusting entry (e) for Uncollectible Accounts is shown in the T accounts. The debit to Uncollectible Accounts Expense recognizes this as an expense for the fiscal period.

Allowance for Uncollectible Accounts

Bal.	127.52
Adj. (e)	1,245.00
(New Bal.	*1,372.52)*

Uncollectible Accounts Expense

Adj. (e)	1,245.00

ADJUSTING ENTRY FOR MERCHANDISE INVENTORY

GENERAL JOURNAL   PAGE 15

	DATE		ACCOUNT TITLE	DOC. NO.	POST. REF.	DEBIT	CREDIT	
4		31	*Income Summary*			15 8 4 0 00		4
5			*Merchandise Inventory*				15 8 4 0 00	5

The merchandise inventory account has a January 1 debit balance of $140,480.00. The inventory was counted at the end of the fiscal period and determined to cost $124,640.00. Adjustment *(d)* for $15,840.00 reduces the cost of inventory, $140,480.00, to $124,640.00. The effect of posting the adjusting entry for merchandise inventory is shown in the T accounts.

Merchandise Inventory

Bal.	140,480.00	Adj. (d)	15,840.00
(New Bal.	*124,640.00)*		

Income Summary

Adj. (d)	15,840.00

ADJUSTING ENTRY FOR SUPPLIES—OFFICE

GENERAL JOURNAL

PAGE 15

	DATE	ACCOUNT TITLE	DOC. NO.	POST. REF.	DEBIT	CREDIT	
6	31	Supplies Expense—Office			2730 00		6
7		Supplies—Office				2730 00	7

Hobby Shack counted $750.00 of office supplies on hand at the end of the fiscal period. The balance of Supplies—Office in the trial balance, $3,480.00, is the cost of office supplies on hand at the beginning of the year plus the office supplies purchased during the year. Adjustment (a) for $2,730.00 reduces the balance in Supplies—Office from $3,480.00 to $750.00.

The effect of posting the adjusting entry for office supplies is shown in the T accounts. The debit to Supplies Expense—Office recognizes the amount of supplies used during the period as an expense.

Supplies—Office

Bal.	3,480.00	Adj. (a)	2,730.00
(New Bal.	750.00)		

Supplies Expense—Office

Adj. (a)	2,730.00

ADJUSTING ENTRY FOR SUPPLIES—STORE

GENERAL JOURNAL

PAGE 15

	DATE	ACCOUNT TITLE	DOC. NO.	POST. REF.	DEBIT	CREDIT	
8	31	Supplies Expense—Store			2910 00		8
9		Supplies—Store				2910 00	9

Hobby Shack also counted $1,034.00 of store supplies on hand at the end of the fiscal period. Adjustment (b) for $2,910.00 reduces the balance in Supplies—Store, $3,944.00, to the current cost of store supplies on hand, $1,034.00. The effect of posting the adjusting entry for store supplies inventory is shown in the T accounts. The debit to Supplies Expense—Store recognizes the amount of supplies used during the period as an expense.

Supplies—Store

Bal.	3,944.00	Adj. (b)	2,910.00
(New Bal.	1,034.00)		

Supplies Expense—Store

Adj. (b)	2,910.00

GENERAL JOURNAL
PAGE 15

	DATE	ACCOUNT TITLE	DOC. NO.	POST. REF.	DEBIT	CREDIT	
10	31	Insurance Expense			3 1 7 0 00		10
11		Prepaid Insurance				3 1 7 0 00	11

During the fiscal period, Hobby Shack paid $5,800.00 for future insurance coverage. At the end of the fiscal year, Hobby Shack determined that the value of prepaid insurance on December 31 is $2,630.00. Adjustment *(c)* reduces Prepaid Insurance by $3,170.00, the value of insurance used during the year.

The effect of posting the adjusting entry for Prepaid Insurance is shown in the T accounts. The debit to Insurance Expense recognizes the amount of insurance used during the fiscal period as an expense.

Prepaid Insurance

Bal.	5,800.00	Adj. (c)	3,170.00
(New Bal.	2,630.00)		

Insurance Expense

Adj. (c)	3,170.00

ADJUSTING ENTRY FOR DEPRECIATION— OFFICE EQUIPMENT

GENERAL JOURNAL
PAGE 15

	DATE	ACCOUNT TITLE	DOC. NO.	POST. REF.	DEBIT	CREDIT	
12	31	Depreciation Exp.—Office Equip.			6 5 4 0 00		12
13		Accum. Depr.—Office Equip.				6 5 4 0 00	13

Hobby Shack estimated its depreciation of office equipment during the fiscal year to be $6,540.00. Adjustment *(f)* increases Accum. Depr.—Office Equip. by $6,540.00, resulting in a new balance of $13,037.00.

The effect of posting the adjusting entry for office equipment depreciation is shown in the T accounts. The debit to Depreciation Exp.—Office Equip. recognizes the depreciation as an expense for the fiscal period.

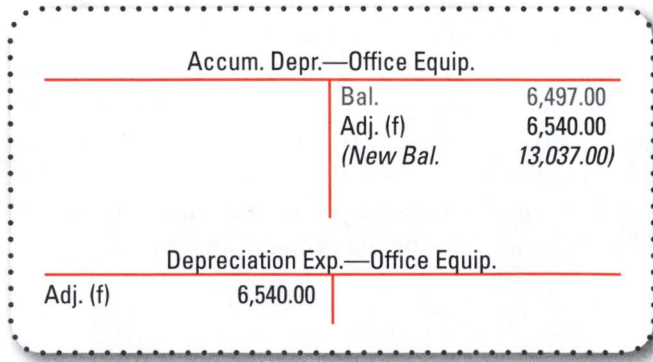

Accum. Depr.—Office Equip.

		Bal.	6,497.00
		Adj. (f)	6,540.00
		(New Bal.	13,037.00)

Depreciation Exp.—Office Equip.

Adj. (f)	6,540.00

	DATE	ACCOUNT TITLE	DOC. NO.	POST. REF.	DEBIT	CREDIT	
14	31	Depreciation Exp.—Store Equip.			5 25 0 00		14
15		Accum. Depr.—Store Equip.				5 25 0 00	15

GENERAL JOURNAL — PAGE 15

Hobby Shack estimated its depreciation of store equipment during the fiscal year to be $5,250.00. Adjustment *(g)* increases Accum. Depr.—Store Equip. by $5,250.00, resulting in a new balance of $10,319.00.

The effect of posting the adjusting entry for store equipment depreciation is shown in the T accounts. The debit to Depreciation Exp.—Store Equip. recognizes the depreciation as an expense for the fiscal period.

Accum. Depr.—Store Equip.

Bal.	5,069.00
Adj. (g)	5,250.00
(New Bal.	10,319.00)

Depreciation Exp.—Store Equip.

Adj. (g)	5,250.00

ADJUSTING ENTRY FOR FEDERAL INCOME TAXES

	DATE	ACCOUNT TITLE	DOC. NO.	POST. REF.	DEBIT	CREDIT	
16	31	Federal Income Tax Expense			5 88 9 24		16
17		Federal Income Tax Payable				5 88 9 24	17

GENERAL JOURNAL — PAGE 15

Hobby Shack made four quarterly estimated payments of $4,500.00. The actual federal income tax expense, $23,889.24, was calculated based on the company's net income before federal income tax. Hobby Shack must make an extra payment of $5,889.24 to pay its tax liability. Adjustment *(h)* increases Federal Income Tax Expense by $5,889.24, resulting in a new balance of $23,889.24. The adjustment also creates the $5,889.24 tax liability.

The effect of posting the adjusting entry for federal income tax is shown in the T accounts.

Federal Income Tax Payable

Adj. (h)	5,889.24
(New Bal.	5,889.24)

Federal Income Tax Expense

Bal.	18,000.00
Adj. (h)	5,889.24
(New Bal.	23,889.24)

End of Lesson REVIEW

1. When adjusting entries are journalized, why is no source document recorded?
2. What adjusting entry is recorded for a merchandising business that is not recorded for a service business?
3. What balance sheet account is increased from a zero balance after adjusting entries are journalized and posted?

WORK TOGETHER 16-1

Journalizing adjusting entries

The work sheet for Discount Books, Inc., is given in the *Working Papers*. Your instructor will guide you through the following example.

1. Record the appropriate adjusting entries on page 18 of a general journal provided in the *Working Papers*. Use December 31 of the current year as the date. Save your work to complete Work Together 16-2.

ON YOUR OWN 16-1

Journalizing adjusting entries

The work sheet for Sturgis Supply, Inc., is given in the *Working Papers*. Work this problem independently.

1. Record the appropriate adjusting entries on page 24 of a general journal provided in the *Working Papers*. Use December 31 of the current year as the date. Save your work to complete On Your Own 16-2.

Closing entries for a corporation are made from information in a work sheet. Closing entries for revenue and expense accounts are similar to those for proprietorships. A corporation's closing entries to close net income and temporary equity accounts are also similar to those for a proprietorship. However, these closing entries affect different accounts. A corporation records four closing entries:

1. A closing entry for income statement accounts with credit balances (revenue and contra cost accounts)

2. A closing entry for income statement accounts with debit balances (cost, contra revenue, and expense accounts)
3. A closing entry to record net income or net loss in the retained earnings account and close the income summary account
4. A closing entry for the dividends account

THE INCOME SUMMARY ACCOUNT

At the end of a fiscal period, the temporary accounts are closed to prepare the general ledger for the next fiscal period. [CONCEPT: Matching Expenses with Revenue] To close a temporary account, an amount equal to its balance is recorded on the side opposite the balance.

Amounts needed for the closing entries are obtained from the Income Statement and Balance Sheet columns of the work sheet and from the statement of stockholders' equity. Closing entries are recorded in the general journal.

Chapter 8 discusses the difference between permanent accounts and temporary accounts. Permanent accounts, also referred to as *real accounts*, include the asset and liability accounts as well as the owners' capital accounts. The ending account balances of permanent accounts for one fiscal period are the beginning account balances for the

next fiscal period. Temporary accounts, also referred to as *nominal accounts*, include the revenue, cost, expense, and dividend accounts.

Another temporary account is used to summarize the closing entries for revenue, cost, and expenses. The account is titled Income Summary because it is used to summarize information about net income. Income Summary is used only at the end of a fiscal period to help prepare other accounts for a new fiscal period.

The income summary account is unique because it does not have a normal balance side. The balance of this account is determined by the amounts posted to the account at the end of a fiscal period. When revenue is greater than total expenses, resulting in a net income, the income summary account has a credit balance, as shown in the T account.

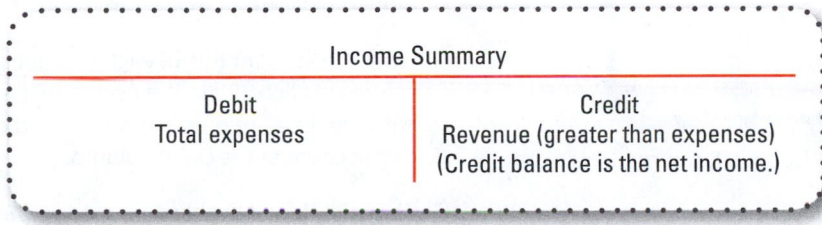

Income Summary	
Debit	Credit
Total expenses	Revenue (greater than expenses)
	(Credit balance is the net income.)

REMEMBER

The income summary account is used only at the end of the fiscal period to help prepare other accounts for a new fiscal period.

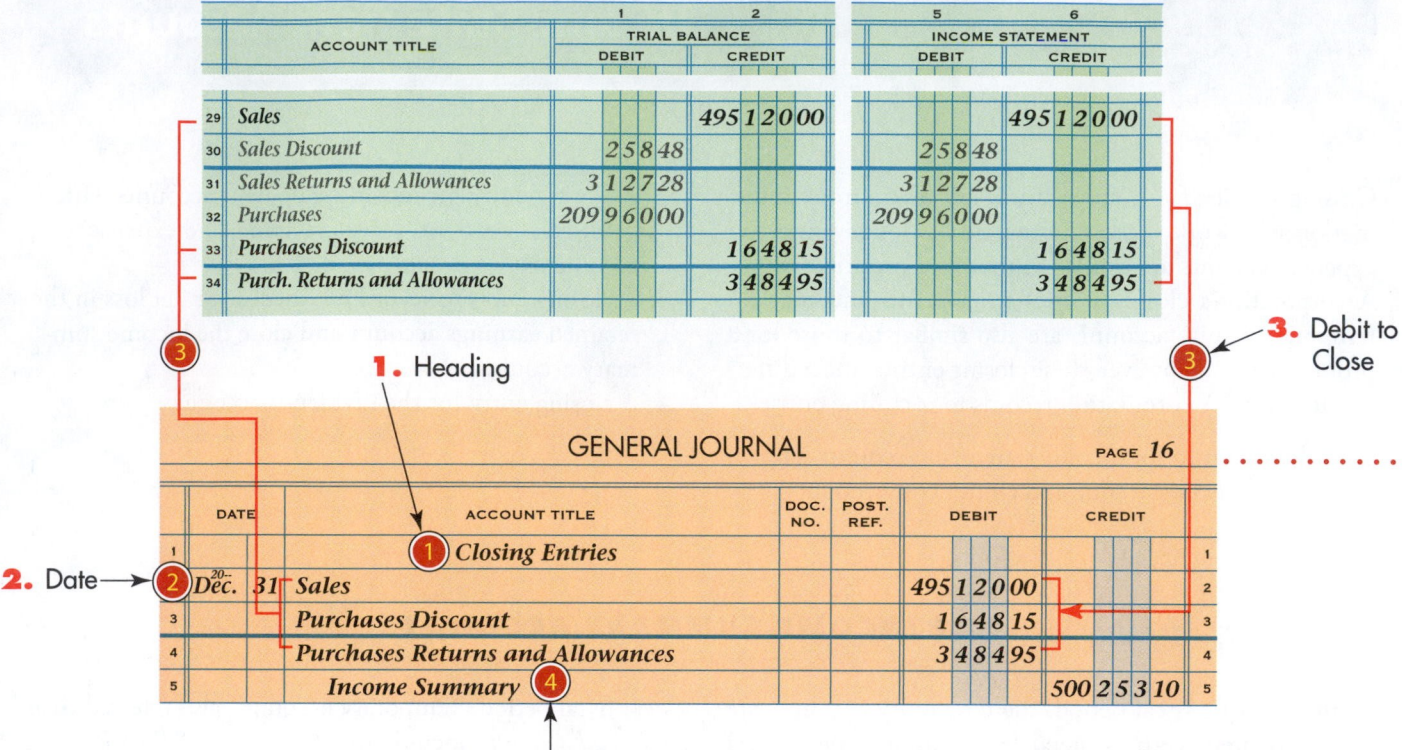

1. Heading

2. Date →

3. Debit to Close

4. Credit to Income Summary

Hobby Shack's work sheet has three income statement accounts with credit balances. One account, Sales, is a revenue account. The other two accounts, Purchases Discount and Purchases Returns and Allowances, are contra cost accounts. Each account has a normal credit balance that must be reduced to zero to prepare the account for the next fiscal period. [CONCEPT: Matching Expenses with Revenue]

To reduce each balance to zero, each account is debited for the amount of the balance. The impact of the closing entry on the sales account is shown in the T account.

Sales			
Closing	495,120.00	Bal. *(New Bal. zero)*	495,120.00

Income Summary is credited for $500,253.10, the total of the three debits in this closing entry.

Income Summary			
Adj. (mdse. inv.)	15,840.00	Closing *(credit accounts)*	500,253.10

The balance in Income Summary will be adjusted by other closing entries.

CLOSING INCOME STATEMENT ACCOUNTS WITH CREDIT BALANCES

1 Write the heading, *Closing Entries,* in the middle of the general journal's Account Title column on a new page. This heading explains all of the closing entries that follow. Therefore, indicating a source document is unnecessary. The first closing entry is recorded on the first four lines below the heading.

2 Write the date, *Dec. 31, 20--,* in the Date column.

3 Write the account title of each revenue and contra cost account in the Account Title column. Write the balance of each revenue and contra cost account in the Debit column.

4 Write the title of the account credited, *Income Summary,* in the Account Title column, indented about 1 centimeter. Write the amount, *$500,253.10,* in the Credit column.

CLOSING ENTRY FOR INCOME STATEMENT ACCOUNTS WITH DEBIT BALANCES

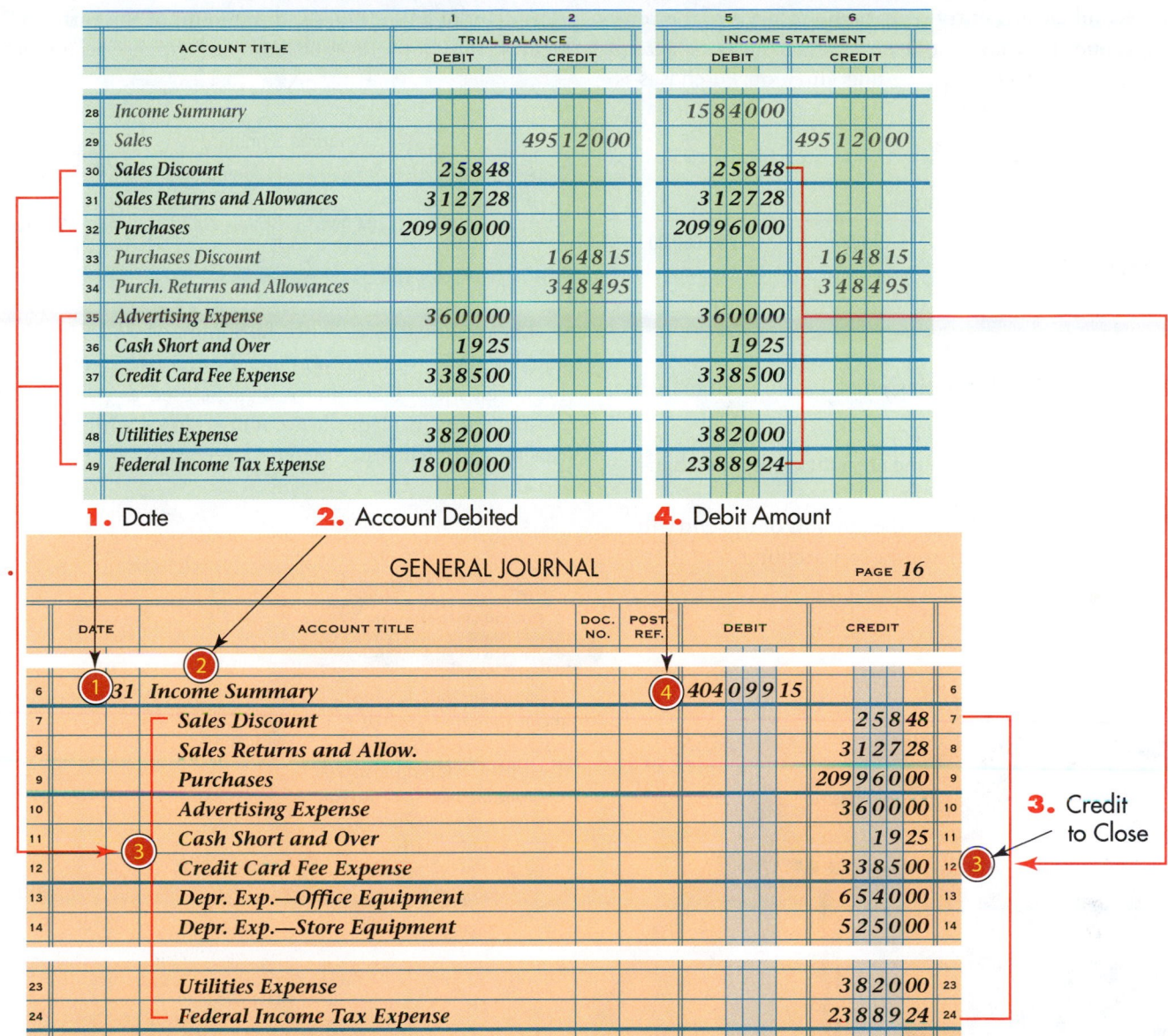

	ACCOUNT TITLE	1 TRIAL BALANCE DEBIT	2 TRIAL BALANCE CREDIT	5 INCOME STATEMENT DEBIT	6 INCOME STATEMENT CREDIT
28	Income Summary			15 84 00 0	
29	Sales		495 12 0 00		495 12 0 00
30	Sales Discount	2 58 48		2 58 48	
31	Sales Returns and Allowances	3 1 27 28		3 1 27 28	
32	Purchases	209 9 60 00		209 9 60 00	
33	Purchases Discount		1 6 48 15		1 6 48 15
34	Purch. Returns and Allowances		3 4 84 95		3 4 84 95
35	Advertising Expense	3 6 00 00		3 6 00 00	
36	Cash Short and Over	1 9 25		1 9 25	
37	Credit Card Fee Expense	3 3 85 00		3 3 85 00	
48	Utilities Expense	3 8 20 00		3 8 20 00	
49	Federal Income Tax Expense	18 0 00 00		23 8 89 24	

1. Date **2.** Account Debited **4.** Debit Amount

GENERAL JOURNAL

PAGE 16

	DATE	ACCOUNT TITLE	DOC. NO.	POST. REF.	DEBIT	CREDIT	
6	31	Income Summary			404 0 99 15		6
7		Sales Discount				2 58 48	7
8		Sales Returns and Allow.				3 1 27 28	8
9		Purchases				209 9 60 00	9
10		Advertising Expense				3 6 00 00	10
11		Cash Short and Over				1 9 25	11
12		Credit Card Fee Expense				3 3 85 00	12
13		Depr. Exp.—Office Equipment				6 5 40 00	13
14		Depr. Exp.—Store Equipment				5 2 50 00	14
23		Utilities Expense				3 8 20 00	23
24		Federal Income Tax Expense				23 8 89 24	24

3. Credit to Close

Hobby Shack's work sheet has many income statement accounts with debit balances—contra revenue accounts, Purchases, and the expense accounts. These debit balances must be reduced to zero to prepare the accounts for the next fiscal period. [CONCEPT: Matching Expenses with Revenue] To reduce the balances to zero, the accounts are credited for the amount of their balances. Income Summary is debited for the total amount.

STEPS CLOSING INCOME STATEMENT ACCOUNTS WITH DEBIT BALANCES

1. Write the date, *31*, in the Date column.

2. Write the title of the account debited, *Income Summary*, in the Account Title column. The debit to *Income Summary* is not entered in the amount column until all contra revenue, cost, and expense balances have been journalized and the total amount calculated.

3. Write the account title of each contra revenue, cost, and expense account in the Account Title column, each indented about 1 centimeter. Write the balance of each cost and expense account in the Credit column.

4. Add the credit amounts for this entry. Write the total of the credited accounts, *$404,099.15*, in the Debit column on the same line as the account title *Income Summary*.

The second closing entry reduces the balance of the contra revenue, Purchases, and expense accounts to a zero balance. The effect of the closing entry on Purchases is shown in the T account.

Purchases			
Bal.	209,960.00	Closing	209,960.00
(New Bal. zero)			

After recording this closing entry, Income Summary has three amounts:

1. A debit of $15,840.00, the amount of the merchandise inventory adjustment
2. A credit of $500,253.10, the amount of the entry to close the revenue and contra cost accounts

3. A debit of $404,099.15, the amount of the entry to close the contra revenue, cost, and expense accounts

Income Summary			
Adj. (mdse. inv.)	15,840.00	Closing (credit amounts)	500,253.10
Closing (debit accounts)	404,099.15	*(New Bal.*	*80,313.95)*

The credit balance of Income Summary, *$80,313.95*, is equal to the net income amount shown on the work sheet. However, Income Summary is not closed as part of this closing entry. Instead, the account is closed with the third closing entry when net income is recorded.

FSTOP/GETTY IMAGES

CLOSING ENTRY TO RECORD NET INCOME

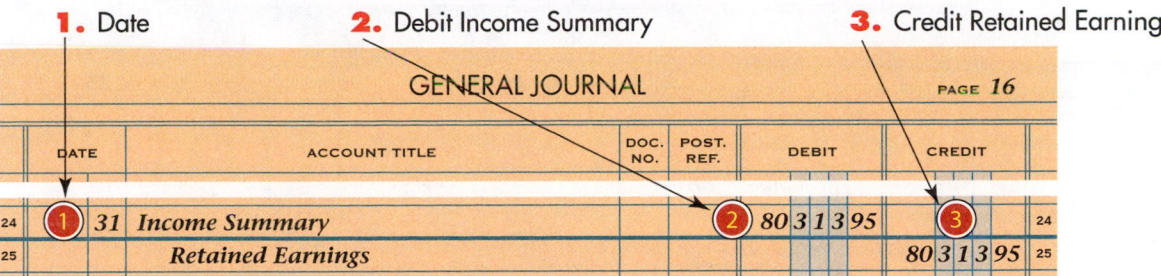

1. Date **2.** Debit Income Summary **3.** Credit Retained Earnings

After closing entries for the income statement accounts are posted, Income Summary has a credit balance of $80,313.95. This credit balance equals the net income calculated on the work sheet.

A corporation's net income should be recorded in the retained earnings account at the end of the fiscal year. After the closing entry is posted, Income Summary has a zero balance.

The new balance in retained earnings, $91,075.24, does not yet equal the amount reported on the statement of stockholders' equity. The fourth closing entry is required to adjust Retained Earnings to the correct amount.

Income Summary

Adj. (mdse. inv.)	15,840.00	Closing (credit	
Closing (debit		accounts)	500,253.10
accounts)	404,099.15		
Closing (retained			
earnings)	80,313.95	*(New Bal. zero)*	

Retained Earnings

		Bal.	10,761.29
		Closing (Income	
		Summary)	80,313.95
		(New Bal.	*91,075.24)*

CLOSING ENTRY FOR DIVIDENDS

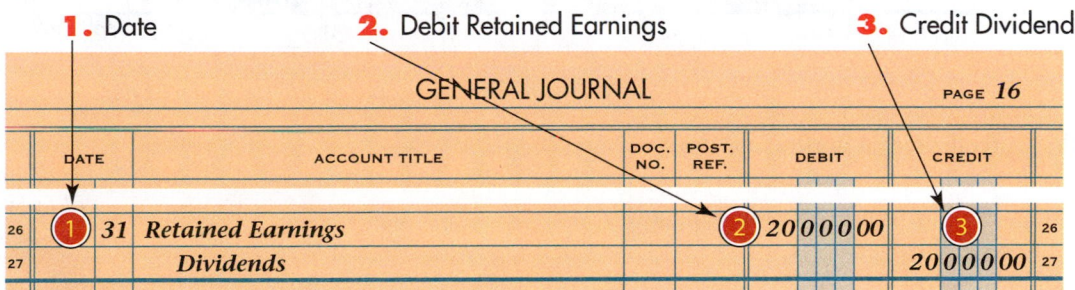

1. Date **2.** Debit Retained Earnings **3.** Credit Dividends

Because dividends decrease the earnings retained by a corporation, the dividends account is closed to Retained Earnings. After the closing entry for the dividends account is posted, Dividends has a zero balance. The amount of the dividends, $20,000.00, has reduced the balance of Retained Earnings. The new balance in Retained Earnings, $71,075.24, now equals the amount reported on the statement of stockholders' equity. Therefore, the retained earnings account is now up to date.

Retained Earnings

		Bal.	10,761.29
Closing		Closing (Income	
(dividends)	20,000.00	Summary)	80,313.95
		(New Bal.	*71,075.24)*

Dividends

Bal.	20,000.00	Closing	
		(dividends)	20,000.00
(New Bal. zero)			

GENERAL JOURNAL

PAGE 16

	DATE		ACCOUNT TITLE	DOC. NO.	POST. REF.	DEBIT	CREDIT	
1			*Closing Entries*					1
2	Dec.²⁰⁻⁻	31	Sales			495 120 00		2
3			Purchases Discount			1 648 15		3
4			Purchases Ret. and Allow.			3 484 95		4
5			Income Summary				500 253 10	5
6		31	Income Summary			404 099 15		6
7			Sales Discount				258 48	7
8			Sales Returns and Allow.				3 127 28	8
9			Purchases				209 960 00	9
10			Advertising Expense				3 600 00	10
11			Cash Short and Over				19 25	11
12			Credit Card Fee Expense				3 385 00	12
13			Depr. Exp.—Office Equipment				6 540 00	13
14			Depr. Exp.—Store Equipment				5 250 00	14
15			Insurance Expense				3 170 00	15
16			Miscellaneous Expense				2 564 90	16
17			Payroll Taxes Expense				9 105 00	17
18			Rent Expense				18 000 00	18
19			Salary Expense				104 525 00	19
20			Supplies Expense—Office				2 730 00	20
21			Supplies Expense—Store				2 910 00	21
22			Uncollectible Accounts Expense				1 245 00	22
23			Utilities Expense				3 820 00	23
24			Federal Income Tax Expense				23 889 24	24
25		31	Income Summary			80 313 95		25
26			Retained Earnings				80 313 95	26
27		31	Retained Earnings			20 000 00		27
28			Dividends				20 000 00	28

Hobby Shack's general journal appears as shown above, after all closing entries have been recorded.

The next step would be to post the adjusting and closing entries to the general ledger.

FSTOP/GETTY IMAGES

FOR YOUR INFORMATION

FYI

If a corporation has a net loss, Income Summary has a debit balance. Retained Earnings would then be debited and Income Summary credited for the net loss amount.

Recording Adjusting and Closing Entries for a Corporation

End of Lesson
REVIEW

1. Where is the information obtained for journalizing closing entries for revenue, cost, and expenses?
2. What is the name of the temporary account that is used to summarize the closing entries for revenue, cost, and expenses?

WORK TOGETHER 16-2

Journalizing closing entries

Use the work sheet of Discount Books, Inc., from Work Together 16-1. A general journal is given in the *Working Papers*. Your instructor will guide you through the following example.

1. Record the following closing entries on page 19 of the general journal.
   a. Close the income statement accounts with credit balances.
   b. Close the income statement accounts with debit balances.
   c. Close Income Summary.
   d. Close the dividend account.

ON YOUR OWN 16-2

Journalizing closing entries

Use the work sheet of Sturgis Supply, Inc., from On Your Own 16-1. A general journal is given in the *Working Papers*. Work this problem independently.

1. Record the following closing entries on page 25 of the general journal.
   a. Close the income statement accounts with credit balances.
   b. Close the income statement accounts with debit balances.
   c. Close Income Summary.
   d. Close the dividend account.

COMPLETED GENERAL LEDGER AFTER ADJUSTING AND CLOSING ENTRIES ARE POSTED

ACCOUNT Cash   ACCOUNT NO. 1110

DATE		ITEM	POST. REF.	DEBIT	CREDIT	BALANCE DEBIT	BALANCE CREDIT
20-- Dec.	31	Balance	✓			29 080 28	

ACCOUNT Petty Cash   ACCOUNT NO. 1120

DATE		ITEM	POST. REF.	DEBIT	CREDIT	BALANCE DEBIT	BALANCE CREDIT
20-- Dec.	31	Balance	✓			300 00	

ACCOUNT Accounts Receivable   ACCOUNT NO. 1130

DATE		ITEM	POST. REF.	DEBIT	CREDIT	BALANCE DEBIT	BALANCE CREDIT
20-- Dec.	31	Balance	✓			14 698 40	

ACCOUNT Allow. for Uncoll. Acc.   ACCOUNT NO. 1135

DATE		ITEM	POST. REF.	DEBIT	CREDIT	BALANCE DEBIT	BALANCE CREDIT
20-- Dec.	31	Balance	✓				127 52
	31		G15		1 245 00		1 372 52

ACCOUNT Merchandise Inventory   ACCOUNT NO. 1140

DATE		ITEM	POST. REF.	DEBIT	CREDIT	BALANCE DEBIT	BALANCE CREDIT
20-- Dec.	31	Balance	✓			140 480 00	
	31		G15		15 840 00	124 640 00	

ACCOUNT Supplies—Office   ACCOUNT NO. 1145

DATE		ITEM	POST. REF.	DEBIT	CREDIT	BALANCE DEBIT	BALANCE CREDIT
20-- Dec.	31	Balance	✓			3 480 00	
	31		G15		2 730 00	750 00	

ACCOUNT Supplies—Store   ACCOUNT NO. 1150

DATE		ITEM	POST. REF.	DEBIT	CREDIT	BALANCE DEBIT	BALANCE CREDIT
20-- Dec.	31	Balance	✓			3 944 00	
	31		G15		2 910 00	1 034 00	

ACCOUNT Prepaid Insurance   ACCOUNT NO. 1160

DATE		ITEM	POST. REF.	DEBIT	CREDIT	BALANCE DEBIT	BALANCE CREDIT
20-- Dec.	31	Balance	✓			5 800 00	
	31		G15		3 170 00	2 630 00	

ACCOUNT Office Equipment   ACCOUNT NO. 1205

DATE		ITEM	POST. REF.	DEBIT	CREDIT	BALANCE DEBIT	BALANCE CREDIT
20-- Dec.	31	Balance	✓			35 864 50	

ACCOUNT Acc. Depr.— Office Equipment   ACCOUNT NO. 1210

DATE		ITEM	POST. REF.	DEBIT	CREDIT	BALANCE DEBIT	BALANCE CREDIT
20-- Dec.	31	Balance	✓				6 497 00
	31		G15		6 540 00		13 037 00

ACCOUNT Store Equipment   ACCOUNT NO. 1215

DATE		ITEM	POST. REF.	DEBIT	CREDIT	BALANCE DEBIT	BALANCE CREDIT
20-- Dec.	31	Balance	✓			40 849 50	

ACCOUNT Acc. Depr.— Store Equipment   ACCOUNT NO. 1220

DATE		ITEM	POST. REF.	DEBIT	CREDIT	BALANCE DEBIT	BALANCE CREDIT
20-- Dec.	31	Balance	✓				5 069 00
	31		G15		5 250 00		10 319 00

ACCOUNT Accounts Payable   ACCOUNT NO. 2110

DATE		ITEM	POST. REF.	DEBIT	CREDIT	BALANCE DEBIT	BALANCE CREDIT
20-- Dec.	31	Balance	✓				11 583 03

ACCOUNT Federal Income Tax Payable   ACCOUNT NO. 2120

DATE		ITEM	POST. REF.	DEBIT	CREDIT	BALANCE DEBIT	BALANCE CREDIT
20-- Dec.	31	Balance	G15		5 889 24		5 889 24

ACCOUNT Employee Income Tax Payable   ACCOUNT NO. 2130

DATE		ITEM	POST. REF.	DEBIT	CREDIT	BALANCE DEBIT	BALANCE CREDIT
20-- Dec.	31	Balance	✓				757 00

ACCOUNT Social Security Tax Payable   ACCOUNT NO. 2135

DATE		ITEM	POST. REF.	DEBIT	CREDIT	BALANCE DEBIT	BALANCE CREDIT
20-- Dec.	31	Balance	✓				1 451 38

ACCOUNT Medicare Tax Payable   ACCOUNT NO. 2140

DATE		ITEM	POST. REF.	DEBIT	CREDIT	BALANCE DEBIT	BALANCE CREDIT
20-- Dec.	31	Balance	✓				399 42

ACCOUNT Sales Tax Payable   ACCOUNT NO. 2145

DATE		ITEM	POST. REF.	DEBIT	CREDIT	BALANCE DEBIT	BALANCE CREDIT
20-- Dec.	31	Balance	✓				2 555 70

ACCOUNT Unemployment Tax Payable—Federal   ACCOUNT NO. 2150

DATE		ITEM	POST. REF.	DEBIT	CREDIT	BALANCE DEBIT	BALANCE CREDIT
20-- Dec.	31	Balance	✓				34 60

ACCOUNT Unemployment Tax Payable—State   ACCOUNT NO. 2155

DATE		ITEM	POST. REF.	DEBIT	CREDIT	BALANCE DEBIT	BALANCE CREDIT
20-- Dec.	31	Balance	✓				233 55

ACCOUNT Health Insurance Premiums Payable   ACCOUNT NO. 2160

DATE		ITEM	POST. REF.	DEBIT	CREDIT	BALANCE DEBIT	BALANCE CREDIT
20-- Dec.	31	Balance	✓				1 008 00

ACCOUNT U.S. Savings Bonds Payable   ACCOUNT NO. 2165

DATE		ITEM	POST. REF.	DEBIT	CREDIT	BALANCE DEBIT	BALANCE CREDIT
20-- Dec.	31	Balance	✓				60 00

ACCOUNT United Way Donations Payable   ACCOUNT NO. 2170

DATE		ITEM	POST. REF.	DEBIT	CREDIT	BALANCE DEBIT	BALANCE CREDIT
20-- Dec.	31	Balance	✓				70 00

ACCOUNT Dividends Payable   ACCOUNT NO. 2180

DATE		ITEM	POST. REF.	DEBIT	CREDIT	BALANCE DEBIT	BALANCE CREDIT
20-- Dec.	31	Balance	✓				5 000 00

Hobby Shack's completed general ledger after adjusting and closing entries are posted is shown above and on the following page.

Balance sheet accounts (asset, liability, and capital accounts) have up-to-date balances to begin the new fiscal period.

Income statement accounts (revenue, cost, and expense accounts) have zero balances to begin the new fiscal period. [CONCEPT: Matching Expenses with Revenue]

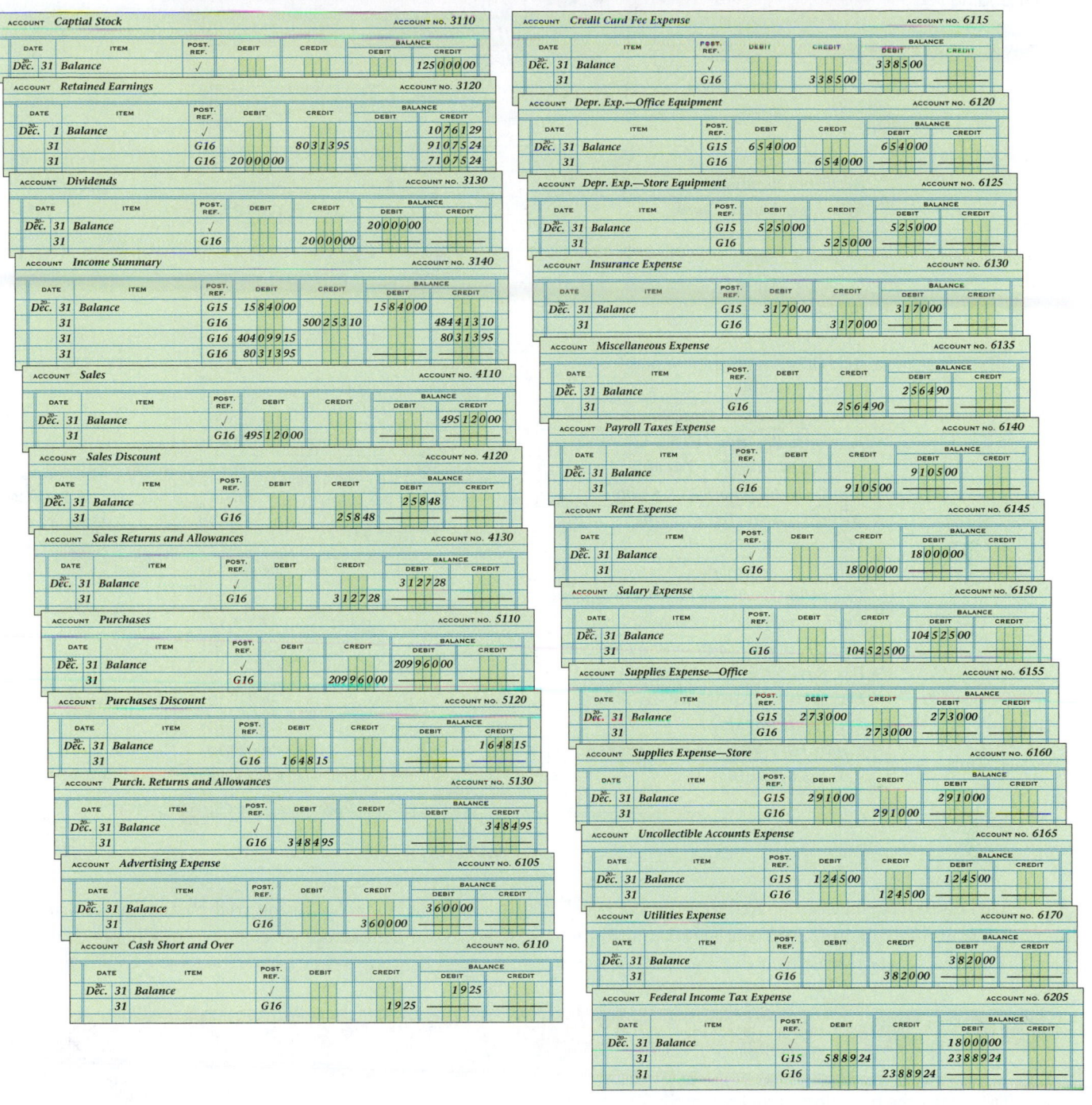

ACCOUNT **Captial Stock** — ACCOUNT NO. 3110

DATE	ITEM	POST. REF.	DEBIT	CREDIT	BALANCE DEBIT	BALANCE CREDIT
20-- Dec. 31	Balance	✓				125 000 00

ACCOUNT **Retained Earnings** — ACCOUNT NO. 3120

DATE	ITEM	POST. REF.	DEBIT	CREDIT	BALANCE DEBIT	BALANCE CREDIT
20-- Dec. 1	Balance	✓				10 761 29
31		G16		80 313 95		91 075 24
31		G16	20 000 00			71 075 24

ACCOUNT **Dividends** — ACCOUNT NO. 3130

DATE	ITEM	POST. REF.	DEBIT	CREDIT	BALANCE DEBIT	BALANCE CREDIT
20-- Dec. 31	Balance	✓			20 000 00	
31		G16		20 000 00		

ACCOUNT **Income Summary** — ACCOUNT NO. 3140

DATE	ITEM	POST. REF.	DEBIT	CREDIT	BALANCE DEBIT	BALANCE CREDIT
20-- Dec. 31	Balance	G15	15 840 00		15 840 00	
31		G16		500 253 10		484 413 10
31		G16	404 099 15			80 313 95
31		G16	80 313 95			

ACCOUNT **Sales** — ACCOUNT NO. 4110

DATE	ITEM	POST. REF.	DEBIT	CREDIT	BALANCE DEBIT	BALANCE CREDIT
20-- Dec. 31	Balance	✓				495 120 00
31		G16	495 120 00			

ACCOUNT **Sales Discount** — ACCOUNT NO. 4120

DATE	ITEM	POST. REF.	DEBIT	CREDIT	BALANCE DEBIT	BALANCE CREDIT
20-- Dec. 31	Balance	✓			2 584 8	
31		G16		2 584 8		

ACCOUNT **Sales Returns and Allowances** — ACCOUNT NO. 4130

DATE	ITEM	POST. REF.	DEBIT	CREDIT	BALANCE DEBIT	BALANCE CREDIT
20-- Dec. 31	Balance	✓			3 127 28	
31		G16		3 127 28		

ACCOUNT **Purchases** — ACCOUNT NO. 5110

DATE	ITEM	POST. REF.	DEBIT	CREDIT	BALANCE DEBIT	BALANCE CREDIT
20-- Dec. 31	Balance	✓			209 960 00	
31		G16		209 960 00		

ACCOUNT **Purchases Discount** — ACCOUNT NO. 5120

DATE	ITEM	POST. REF.	DEBIT	CREDIT	BALANCE DEBIT	BALANCE CREDIT
20-- Dec. 31	Balance	✓				1 648 15
31		G16	1 648 15			

ACCOUNT **Purch. Returns and Allowances** — ACCOUNT NO. 5130

DATE	ITEM	POST. REF.	DEBIT	CREDIT	BALANCE DEBIT	BALANCE CREDIT
20-- Dec. 31	Balance	✓				3 484 95
31		G16	3 484 95			

ACCOUNT **Advertising Expense** — ACCOUNT NO. 6105

DATE	ITEM	POST. REF.	DEBIT	CREDIT	BALANCE DEBIT	BALANCE CREDIT
20-- Dec. 31	Balance	✓			3 600 00	
31		G16		3 600 00		

ACCOUNT **Cash Short and Over** — ACCOUNT NO. 6110

DATE	ITEM	POST. REF.	DEBIT	CREDIT	BALANCE DEBIT	BALANCE CREDIT
20-- Dec. 31	Balance	✓			19 25	
31		G16		19 25		

ACCOUNT **Credit Card Fee Expense** — ACCOUNT NO. 6115

DATE	ITEM	POST. REF.	DEBIT	CREDIT	BALANCE DEBIT	BALANCE CREDIT
20-- Dec. 31	Balance	✓			3 385 00	
31		G16		3 385 00		

ACCOUNT **Depr. Exp.—Office Equipment** — ACCOUNT NO. 6120

DATE	ITEM	POST. REF.	DEBIT	CREDIT	BALANCE DEBIT	BALANCE CREDIT
20-- Dec. 31	Balance	G15	6 540 00		6 540 00	
31		G16		6 540 00		

ACCOUNT **Depr. Exp.—Store Equipment** — ACCOUNT NO. 6125

DATE	ITEM	POST. REF.	DEBIT	CREDIT	BALANCE DEBIT	BALANCE CREDIT
20-- Dec. 31	Balance	G15	5 250 00		5 250 00	
31		G16		5 250 00		

ACCOUNT **Insurance Expense** — ACCOUNT NO. 6130

DATE	ITEM	POST. REF.	DEBIT	CREDIT	BALANCE DEBIT	BALANCE CREDIT
20-- Dec. 31	Balance	G15	3 170 00		3 170 00	
31		G16		3 170 00		

ACCOUNT **Miscellaneous Expense** — ACCOUNT NO. 6135

DATE	ITEM	POST. REF.	DEBIT	CREDIT	BALANCE DEBIT	BALANCE CREDIT
20-- Dec. 31	Balance	✓			2 564 90	
31		G16		2 564 90		

ACCOUNT **Payroll Taxes Expense** — ACCOUNT NO. 6140

DATE	ITEM	POST. REF.	DEBIT	CREDIT	BALANCE DEBIT	BALANCE CREDIT
20-- Dec. 31	Balance	✓			9 105 00	
31		G16		9 105 00		

ACCOUNT **Rent Expense** — ACCOUNT NO. 6145

DATE	ITEM	POST. REF.	DEBIT	CREDIT	BALANCE DEBIT	BALANCE CREDIT
20-- Dec. 31	Balance	✓			18 000 00	
31		G16		18 000 00		

ACCOUNT **Salary Expense** — ACCOUNT NO. 6150

DATE	ITEM	POST. REF.	DEBIT	CREDIT	BALANCE DEBIT	BALANCE CREDIT
20-- Dec. 31	Balance	✓			104 525 00	
31		G16		104 525 00		

ACCOUNT **Supplies Expense—Office** — ACCOUNT NO. 6155

DATE	ITEM	POST. REF.	DEBIT	CREDIT	BALANCE DEBIT	BALANCE CREDIT
20-- Dec. 31	Balance	G15	2 730 00		2 730 00	
31		G16		2 730 00		

ACCOUNT **Supplies Expense—Store** — ACCOUNT NO. 6160

DATE	ITEM	POST. REF.	DEBIT	CREDIT	BALANCE DEBIT	BALANCE CREDIT
20-- Dec. 31	Balance	G15	2 910 00		2 910 00	
31		G16		2 910 00		

ACCOUNT **Uncollectible Accounts Expense** — ACCOUNT NO. 6165

DATE	ITEM	POST. REF.	DEBIT	CREDIT	BALANCE DEBIT	BALANCE CREDIT
20-- Dec. 31	Balance	G15	1 245 00		1 245 00	
31		G16		1 245 00		

ACCOUNT **Utilities Expense** — ACCOUNT NO. 6170

DATE	ITEM	POST. REF.	DEBIT	CREDIT	BALANCE DEBIT	BALANCE CREDIT
20-- Dec. 31	Balance	✓			3 820 00	
31		G16		3 820 00		

ACCOUNT **Federal Income Tax Expense** — ACCOUNT NO. 6205

DATE	ITEM	POST. REF.	DEBIT	CREDIT	BALANCE DEBIT	BALANCE CREDIT
20-- Dec. 31	Balance	✓			18 000 00	
31		G15	5 889 24		23 889 24	
31		G16		23 889 24		

1. Heading

2. Accounts That Have Balances

3. Balances of Asset Accounts

4. Balances of Contra Asset, Liability and Capital Accounts

5. Word *Totals*

6. Totals

7. Double Lines

Hobby Shack, Inc.
Post-Closing Trial Balance
December 31, 20--

ACCOUNT TITLE	DEBIT	CREDIT
Cash	29 0 8 0 28	
Petty Cash	3 0 0 00	
Accounts Receivable	14 6 9 8 40	
Allow. for Uncoll. Accts.		1 3 7 2 52
Merchandise Inventory	124 6 4 0 00	
Supplies—Office	7 5 0 00	
Supplies—Store	1 0 3 4 00	
Prepaid Insurance	2 6 3 0 00	
Office Equipment	35 8 6 4 50	
Acc. Depr.—Office Equipment		13 0 3 7 00
Store Equipment	40 8 4 9 50	
Acc. Depr.—Store Equipment		10 3 1 9 00
Accounts Payable		11 5 8 3 03
Federal Income Tax Payable		5 8 8 9 24
Employee Income Tax Payable		7 5 7 00
Social Security Tax Payable		1 4 5 1 38
Medicare Tax Payable		3 9 9 42
Sales Tax Payable		2 5 5 6 70
Unemployment Tax Payable—Federal		3 4 60
Unemployment Tax Payable—State		2 3 3 55
Health Insurance Premiums Payable		1 0 0 8 00
U.S. Savings Bonds Payable		6 0 00
United Way Donations Payable		7 0 00
Dividends Payable		5 0 0 00
Capital Stock		125 0 0 0 00
Retained Earnings		71 0 7 5 24
Totals	249 8 4 6 68	249 8 4 6 68

A post-closing trial balance is prepared to prove the equality of debits and credits in the general ledger and to prepare the general ledger for the next fiscal period. Account balances on the post-closing trial balance agree with the balances on the balance sheet shown in Chapter 15.

STEPS — PREPARING A POST-CLOSING TRIAL BALANCE

1 Write the post-closing trial balance heading on three lines.

2 List all general ledger accounts that have balances in the Account Title column.

3 Write the balance of each asset account in the Debit column. Write the balance of each contra account in the Credit column.

4 Write the balance of each liability and capital account in the Credit column.

5 Write the word *Totals* on the next line below the last account title.

6 Total the columns and write the totals, *$249,846.68*, on the Totals line.

7 Verify equality. Rule double lines below both column totals.

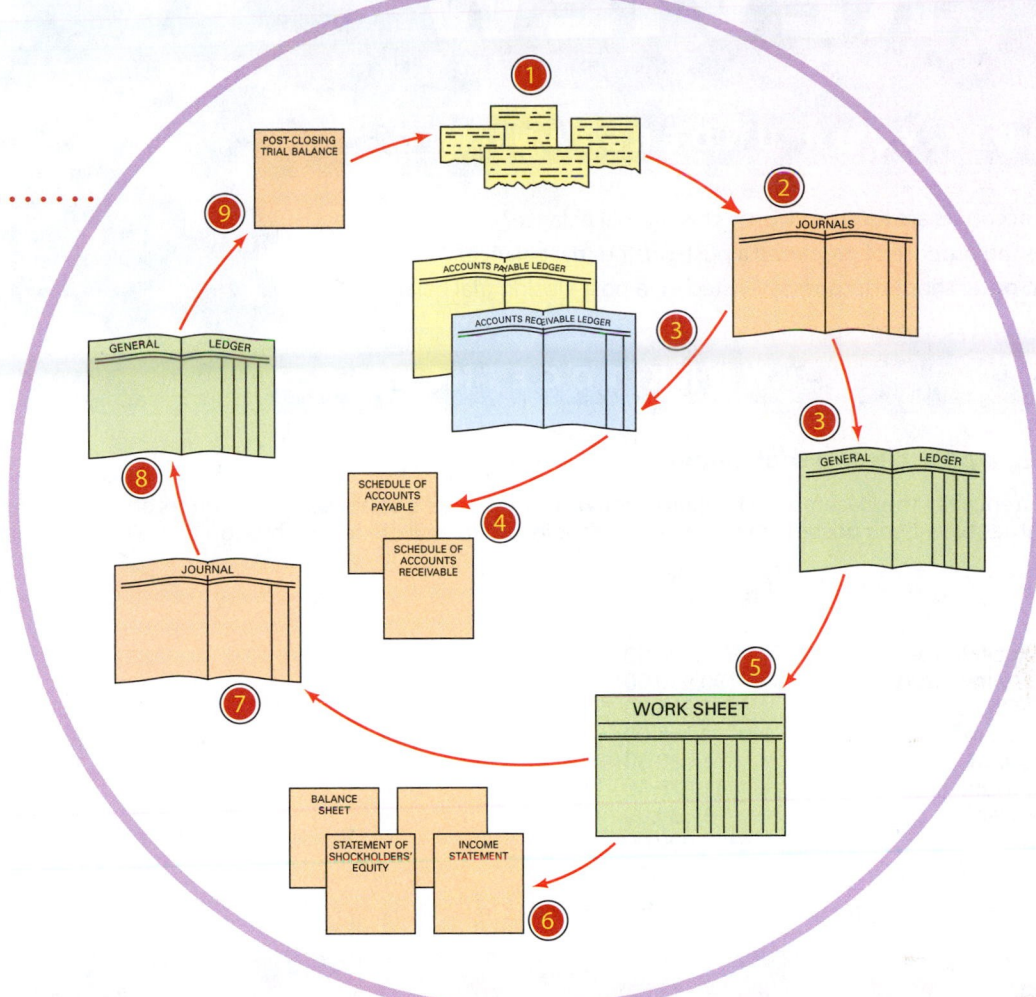

Service and merchandising businesses use a similar accounting cycle. The accounting cycles are also similar for a proprietorship and a corporation. Variations occur when subsidiary ledgers are used. Variations also occur in preparing financial statements.

STEPS ACCOUNTING CYCLE FOR A MERCHANDISING BUSINESS

1. Source documents are checked for accuracy, and transactions are analyzed into debit and credit parts.

2. Transactions, from information on source documents, are recorded in journals.

3. Journal entries are posted to the accounts payable ledger, the accounts receivable ledger, and the general ledger.

4. Schedules of accounts payable and accounts receivable are prepared from the subsidiary ledgers.

5. A work sheet, including a trial balance, is prepared from the general ledger.

6. Financial statements are prepared from the work sheet.

7. Adjusting and closing entries are journalized from the work sheet.

8. Adjusting and closing entries are posted to the general ledger.

9. A post-closing trial balance of the general ledger is prepared.

End of Lesson REVIEW

1. Which accounts are listed on a post-closing trial balance?
2. What is the purpose of preparing a post-closing trial balance?
3. In what order should accounts be listed on a post-closing trial balance?

WORK TOGETHER 16-3

Preparing a post-closing trial balance

For the current year, the December 31 balances for Visual Art Center's balance sheet accounts after adjusting and closing entries have been posted are given below. Your instructor will guide you through the following example.

Account	Balance
Cash	$ 21,810.20
Petty Cash	350.00
Accounts Receivable	8,398.80
Merchandise Inventory	190,980.00
Supplies—Office	1,314.00
Supplies—Store	2,268.00
Prepaid Insurance	1,980.00
Accounts Payable	11,676.50
Sales Tax Payable	1,584.00
Capital Stock	100,000.00
Retained Earnings	113,840.50

1. Prepare a post-closing trial balance on the form provided in the *Working Papers*.

ON YOUR OWN 16-3

Preparing a post-closing trial balance

For the current year, the December 31 balances for Welding Supply's balance sheet accounts after adjusting and closing entries have been posted are given below. Work this problem independently.

Account	Balance
Cash	$ 26,485.00
Petty Cash	500.00
Accounts Receivable	15,487.00
Allow. for Uncoll. Accts.	1,457.00
Merchandise Inventory	134,152.00
Supplies	741.00
Prepaid Insurance	1,000.00
Equipment	25,487.00
Acc. Dep.—Equipment	12,450.00
Accounts Payable	13,154.00
Federal Income Tax Payable	2,489.00
Sales Tax Payable	1,548.00
Dividends Payable	5,000.00
Capital Stock	50,000.00
Retained Earnings	117,754.00

1. Prepare a post-closing trial balance on the form provided in the *Working Papers*.

EXPLORE ACCOUNTING

Freight Charges

When a business purchases merchandise from a vendor, ordinarily a third-party freight company is used to deliver the merchandise from the seller (vendor) to the buyer (purchasing business). As part of the terms of sale, the buyer and seller must agree on who is responsible for the freight charges. Those terms will be listed on the seller's sales invoice as either FOB shipping point or FOB destination. *FOB* is an abbreviation for the phrase "Free on Board." *FOB shipping point* means that the buyer is responsible for the freight charges. *FOB destination* means that the seller is responsible for the freight charges. *Shipping point* is the location where the freight company receives the merchandise from the seller. *Destination* refers to the receiving point of the buyer.

The accounting entries for freight charges can be complicated when one business is responsible for the freight charges according to the terms of sale, but the other business pays the freight company. For example, terms of sale may be FOB shipping point, meaning that the buyer is responsible for the freight charges. However, the freight company may require payment in advance. Therefore, the seller pays the freight company for the freight charges.

Four different situations may occur:

1. FOB shipping point, seller pays freight company

2. FOB shipping point, buyer pays freight company

3. FOB destination, seller pays freight company

4. FOB destination, buyer pays freight company

Research: Investigate this issue by reviewing collegiate Principles of Accounting or Intermediate Accounting textbooks. Also, you might interview a merchandising business manager to determine how the business accounts for freight charges. After completing your research, write a report on the issue of freight charges that would clearly explain the correct accounting procedures to a new accounting department employee.

16-1 APPLICATION PROBLEM

Journalizing adjusting entries

A partial work sheet for Cellar Books, Inc., for the year ended December 31 is given in the *Working Papers*.

Instructions:

1. Record the appropriate adjusting entries on page 22 of the general journal provided in the *Working Papers*. Use December 31 of the current year as the date.

16-2 APPLICATION PROBLEM

Journalizing closing entries

Use the partial work sheet for Cellar Books, Inc., given in Problem 16-1.

Instructions:

Prepare the following closing entries on page 23 of the general journal provided in the *Working Papers*.

1. Close the income statement accounts with credit balances.
2. Close the income statement accounts with debit balances.
3. Close Income Summary.
4. Close the dividend account.

16-3 APPLICATION PROBLEM

Preparing a post-closing trial balance

For the current year, the December 31 balances for the balance sheet accounts of Cellar Books, Inc., after adjusting and closing entries have been posted are given below.

Account	Balance	Account	Balance
Cash	$ 16,485.00	Federal Income Tax Payable	$ 3,660.23
Petty Cash	400.00	Employee Income Tax Payable	1,248.20
Accounts Receivable	41,483.15	Social Security Tax Payable	903.96
Allow. for Uncoll. Accts.	2,406.15	Medicare Tax Payable	211.41
Merchandise Inventory	246,598.05	Sales Tax Payable	2,458.25
Supplies—Office	329.62	Unemployment Tax Payable—Federal	28.00
Supplies—Store	326.81	Unemployment Tax Payable—State	189.00
Prepaid Insurance	2,000.00	Health Insurance Premiums Payable	400.00
Office Equipment	38,458.25	U.S. Savings Bonds Payable	25.00
Acc. Dep.—Office Equipment	23,960.00	United Way Donations Payable	40.00
Store Equipment	41,478.50	Dividends Payable	3,000.00
Acc. Dep.—Store Equipment	31,100.00	Capital Stock	60,000.00
Accounts Payable	19,948.80	Retained Earnings	237,980.38

Instructions:

1. Prepare a post-closing trial balance on the form provided in the *Working Papers*.

Go Beyond the Book
For more information go to
www.C21accounting.com

Recording Adjusting and Closing Entries for a Corporation

16-4 APPLICATION PROBLEM

AUTOMATED ACCOUNTING | **Peachtree** by Sage | **QB** Quick Books

Journalizing and posting adjusting and closing entries; preparing a post-closing trial balance

Use the partial work sheet of Wilson Paint, Inc., for the year ended December 31 of the current year, on page 502. The general ledger accounts and their balances as well as forms for completing this problem are in the *Working Papers*.

Instructions:

1. Journalize the adjusting entries using page 22 of a general journal.
2. Post the adjusting entries.
3. Journalize the closing entries using page 23 of a general journal.
4. Post the closing entries.
5. Prepare a post-closing trial balance.

16-5 MASTERY PROBLEM

AUTOMATED ACCOUNTING | **Peachtree** by Sage | **QB** Quick Books

Journalizing and posting adjusting and closing entries; preparing a post-closing trial balance

Use the partial work sheet of Northern Lights for the year ended December 31 of the current year, on page 503. The general ledger accounts and their balances as well as forms for completing this problem are in the *Working Papers*.

Instructions:

1. Journalize the adjusting entries using page 18 of a general journal.
2. Post the adjusting entries.
3. Journalize the closing entries using page 19 of a general journal.
4. Post the closing entries.
5. Prepare a post-closing trial balance.

	ACCOUNT TITLE	TRIAL BALANCE DEBIT	TRIAL BALANCE CREDIT	ADJUSTMENTS DEBIT	ADJUSTMENTS CREDIT	INCOME STATEMENT DEBIT	INCOME STATEMENT CREDIT
1	Cash	15 4 8 2 00					
2	Petty Cash	5 0 0 00					
3	Accounts Receivable	42 1 5 8 80					
4	Allow. for Uncoll. Accts.		6 8 4 20		(e) 3 5 6 0 00		
5	Merchandise Inventory	274 5 3 5 33			(d) 1 4 8 3 60		
6	Supplies—Office	6 1 5 8 84			(a) 5 8 4 7 10		
7	Supplies—Store	5 5 4 8 55			(b) 4 9 1 8 50		
8	Prepaid Insurance	8 0 0 0 00			(c) 7 2 0 0 00		
9	Office Equipment	22 1 5 8 66					
10	Acc. Depr.—Office Equipment		4 8 4 8 00		(f) 3 5 8 0 00		
11	Store Equipment	34 1 5 8 11					
12	Acc. Depr.—Store Equipment		12 4 8 0 00		(g) 6 1 4 0 00		
13	Accounts Payable		15 4 8 7 99				
14	Federal Income Tax Payable				(h) 1 3 5 6 14		
15	Employee Income Tax Payable		1 1 2 5 58				
16	Social Security Tax Payable		9 0 3 96				
17	Medicare Tax Payable		2 1 1 41				
18	Sales Tax Payable		2 3 4 5 99				
19	Unemployment Tax Pay.—Federal		2 5 60				
20	Unemployment Tax Pay.—State		1 7 2 80				
21	Health Insurance Premiums Payable		3 5 0 00				
22	U.S. Savings Bonds Payable		5 0 00				
23	United Way Donations Payable		6 0 00				
24	Dividends Payable		5 0 0 0 00				
25	Capital Stock		125 0 0 0 00				
26	Retained Earnings		136 8 4 3 68				
27	Dividends	20 0 0 0 00					
28	Income Summary			(d) 1 4 8 3 60			1 4 8 3 60
29	Sales		724 1 8 3 99				724 1 8 3 99
30	Sales Discount	1 6 9 4 48				1 6 9 4 48	
31	Sales Returns and Allowances	4 1 8 9 64				4 1 8 9 64	
32	Purchases	331 8 0 5 18				331 8 0 5 18	
33	Purchases Discount		3 4 1 8 47				3 4 1 8 47
34	Purch. Returns and Allowances		4 6 8 4 69				4 6 8 4 69
35	Advertising Expense	14 5 1 8 00				14 5 1 8 00	
36	Cash Short and Over		4 60			4 60	
37	Credit Card Fee Expense	12 1 8 0 00				12 1 8 0 00	
38	Depr. Exp.—Office Equipment			(f) 3 5 8 0 00		3 5 8 0 00	
39	Depr. Exp.—Store Equipment			(g) 6 1 4 0 00		6 1 4 0 00	
40	Insurance Expense			(c) 7 2 0 0 00		7 2 0 0 00	
41	Miscellaneous Expense	6 4 8 1 00				6 4 8 1 00	
42	Payroll Taxes Expense	14 1 8 4 60				14 1 8 4 60	
43	Rent Expense	20 1 5 0 00				20 1 5 0 00	
44	Salary Expense	168 4 8 3 60				168 4 8 3 60	
45	Supplies Expense—Office			(a) 5 8 4 7 10		5 8 4 7 10	
46	Supplies Expense—Store			(b) 4 9 1 8 50		4 9 1 8 50	
47	Uncollectible Accounts Expense			(e) 3 5 6 0 00		3 5 6 0 00	
48	Utilities Expense	5 4 8 4 97				5 4 8 4 97	
49	Federal Income Tax Expense	30 0 0 0 00		(h) 1 3 5 6 14		31 3 5 6 14	
50		1037 8 7 6 36	1037 8 7 6 36	34 0 8 5 34	34 0 8 5 34	641 7 7 7 81	733 7 7 0 75
51	Net Income after Federal Income Tax					91 9 9 2 94	
52						733 7 7 0 75	733 7 7 0 75

Recording Adjusting and Closing Entries for a Corporation

Partial Work Sheet for Mastery Problem 16-5 (Northern Lights)

	ACCOUNT TITLE	TRIAL BALANCE DEBIT	TRIAL BALANCE CREDIT	ADJUSTMENTS DEBIT	ADJUSTMENTS CREDIT	INCOME STATEMENT DEBIT	INCOME STATEMENT CREDIT
1	Cash	5 124 12					
2	Petty Cash	25 000					
3	Accounts Receivable	14 843 30					
4	Allow. for Uncoll. Accts.		1 24 55		(e) 2 120 00		
5	Merchandise Inventory	154 318 22			(d) 3 488 14		
6	Supplies—Office	3 415 58			(a) 3 148 66		
7	Supplies—Store	6 184 56			(b) 5 348 84		
8	Prepaid Insurance	7 000 00			(c) 6 000 00		
9	Office Equipment	21 482 66					
10	Acc. Depr.—Office Equipment		6 480 00		(f) 3 580 00		
11	Store Equipment	40 481 66					
12	Acc. Depr.—Store Equipment		18 480 00		(g) 6 140 00		
13	Accounts Payable		8 418 36				
14	Federal Income Tax Payable				(h) 965 64		
15	Employee Income Tax Payable		4 58 00				
16	Social Security Tax Payable		5 28 24				
17	Medicare Tax Payable		1 23 54				
18	Sales Tax Payable		1 415 30				
19	Unemployment Tax Pay.—Federal		4 00				
20	Unemployment Tax Pay.—State		27 00				
21	Health Insurance Premiums Payable		2 50 00				
22	U.S. Savings Bonds Payable		40 00				
23	United Way Donations Payable		60 00				
24	Dividends Payable		4 000 00				
25	Capital Stock		80 000 00				
26	Retained Earnings		89 761 21				
27	Dividends	16 000 00					
28	Income Summary			(d) 3 488 14		3 488 14	
29	Sales		514 815 35				514 815 35
30	Sales Discount	2 154 94				2 154 94	
31	Sales Returns and Allowances	6 184 74				6 184 74	
32	Purchases	301 548 60				301 548 60	
33	Purchases Discount		2 154 65				2 154 65
34	Purch. Returns and Allowances		2 889 41				2 889 41
35	Advertising Expense	2 491 95				2 491 95	
36	Cash Short and Over	5 25				5 25	
37	Credit Card Fee Expense	8 154 62				8 154 62	
38	Depr. Exp.—Office Equipment			(f) 3 580 00		3 580 00	
39	Depr. Exp.—Store Equipment			(g) 6 140 00		6 140 00	
40	Insurance Expense			(c) 6 000 00		6 000 00	
41	Miscellaneous Expense	4 100 0				4 100 0	
42	Payroll Taxes Expense	14 184 60				14 184 60	
43	Rent Expense	15 400 00				15 400 00	
44	Salary Expense	102 240 30				102 240 30	
45	Supplies Expense—Office			(a) 3 148 66		3 148 66	
46	Supplies Expense—Store			(b) 5 348 84		5 348 84	
47	Uncollectible Accounts Expense			(e) 2 120 00		2 120 00	
48	Utilities Expense	4 154 51				4 154 51	
49	Federal Income Tax Expense	4 000 00		(h) 965 64		4 965 64	
50		730 029 61	730 029 61	30 791 28	30 791 28	491 720 79	519 859 41
51	Net Income after Federal Income Tax					28 138 62	
52						519 859 41	519 859 41

CHALLENGE PROBLEM

Inventory auditing challenges

For most businesses, merchandise inventory is a major portion of the business's assets. Therefore, reporting an accurate amount on the financial statements is important to accurate financial reporting. Whether a member of the business's accounting staff or an outside auditor audits the merchandise inventory of the business, determining an accurate count of the merchandise inventory is very important. Different types of merchandise present different kinds of challenges for the auditor.

a. *Actual count, common costs:* A sports store has 50 tennis rackets, all the same model. The rackets should be counted and multiplied times the cost per racket to determine the inventory value.

b. *Actual count, unique costs:* An automobile dealer has 60 new automobiles. Since each automobile probably has a unique and significant cost, the cost of each automobile should be totaled to determine the inventory value.

c. *Sampling:* A hardware store has many machine bolts. Since the value of each is low and there are many items, a small quantity may be counted or weighed. Then estimate the total cost based on the sample size or weight.

d. *Measuring/calculating:* An oil company stores crude oil in large tanks. The depth of the oil in the tank can be measured with a measuring rod; then the circumference of the tank can be measured. The total volume of crude oil can be calculated, then divided by the volume of one barrel of crude oil to determine the total barrels. This number can then be multiplied by the cost per barrel of crude oil.

Instructions:
How would you determine the value of the following inventory items? Record your answers in the *Working Papers*.

1. Grain in a grain elevator
2. Lumber in a lumber yard
3. Diamond rings in a jewelry store
4. Nails in a home improvement store

APPLIED COMMUNICATION

Public speakers are judged by the ability of the audience to remember important points of their presentation. Effective public speakers use a variety of techniques to encourage the audience to listen to their message.

Instructions: Contact an instructor in your school or a local businessperson you have heard speak at school or community functions. Ask the person to describe the techniques used to help the audience listen and remember the message. Write a short report summarizing these techniques. Be prepared to present your report orally in class.

CASE FOR CRITICAL THINKING

Antwan Jones, a new accounting clerk, has just experienced his first closing of a fiscal period. He questions why the adjustments on the work sheet have to be recorded in a general journal. Antwan maintains that the adjustments can simply be posted from the work sheet. As the senior accounting clerk, how would you respond to his statement?

Thinking Skills: Knowing how to learn

Concept: One way to learn new concepts is to build on knowledge already acquired. For example, you might learn how to create your own filing system after using a filing system created by someone else.

Application: Describe how the financial statements and adjusting and closing entries for a corporation differ from those of a proprietorship. Could a proprietorship prepare a statement of stockholders' equity?

AUDITING FOR ERRORS

Editing an Accounting Policies Manual

The Sarbanes-Oxley Act requires publicly traded corporations to document and test their accounting systems. The documentation for Mateen Supply Corporation contains the following section on the preparation of closing entries. Identify the errors in this section of Mateen's accounting systems documentation.

Closing Entries

After the worksheet has been completed and verified, journal entries are recorded to close temporary accounts. Three entries are recorded:

1. Sales and contra purchases accounts are debited for their year-end balances. The total of the accounts is credited to Income Summary.

2. Purchasing and expense accounts are credited for their year-balances. The total of the accounts is debited to Income Summary.

3. If the company had a net income, record a debit to Income Summary for the difference of the closing entries recorded in steps 1 and 2. If the company had a net loss, record a credit to Income Summary for this difference. In either case, record the same amount to Retained Earnings to balance the entry.

ANALYZING BEST BUY'S FINANCIAL STATEMENTS

Generally accepted accounting principles require several forms of earnings per share to be reported. Earnings per share from the normal operations of the business is presented first. The effect on earnings per share from unusual, nonrecurring events is added or deducted. The net of these items is the earnings per share that is typically reported in the financial news.

Instructions: Use Best Buy's Consolidated Statements of Earnings on page B-6 in Appendix B to answer the following questions.

1. What is the label given to the net earnings per share amount, and what are its components?

2. What earnings per share amount would be reported in the financial news for the most recent fiscal year?

Accounting
SOFTWARE

GROUPING FINANCIAL STATEMENT REPORTS

Peachtree has a feature that allows you to create and print a group of reports. Creating a group is as easy as selecting each report and giving the group a name. The group appears in the report menu along with the other reports you have become accustomed to printing.

PEACHTREE APPLICATION PROBLEM 16-4
1. Open (Restore) file 16-4AP.ptb.
2. Journalize and post the adjusting entries.
3. Print the income statement, and compare the amounts with the work sheet.
4. Journalize and post the closing entries.
5. Print the December 31 general journal, the general ledger, and the post-closing trial balance.

PEACHTREE MASTERY PROBLEM 16-5
1. Open (Restore) file 16-5MP.ptb.
2. Journalize and post the adjusting entries.
3. Print the income statement, and compare the amounts with the work sheet.
4. Journalize and post the closing entries.
5. Print the general ledger and post-closing trial balance.

GROUPING FINANCIAL STATEMENT REPORTS

One way QuickBooks supports efficiency is by allowing common tasks to be completed quickly. QuickBooks can be programmed to memorize the format of any financial statement and also to group financial statements together. When it is time to prepare financial statements, the user can print the entire group with a minimum of commands.

QUICKBOOKS APPLICATION PROBLEM 16-4
1. Open the Wilson Paint Inc. file.
2. Journalize the adjusting entries using the Make General Journal Entries window.
3. Print a Profit & Loss Standard report using January 1 and December 31 for the dates.
4. To create a year-end balance sheet in QuickBooks, it is necessary to make a closing entry to close the equity account Dividends to Retained Earnings. Print a Trial Balance report to use for the closing transaction.
5. Use the General Journal Entries window to journalize the closing entry dated December 31.
6. Print a Journal report, a Balance Sheet Standard report, and a Trial Balance report.
7. As an optional activity, group the financial statement reports and print them. Then, record the closing entries and print a post-closing trial balance.

QUICKBOOKS MASTERY PROBLEM 16-5
1. Open the Northern Lights file.
2. Journalize the adjusting entries using the Make General Journal Entries window.
3. Print a Profit & Loss Standard report using January 1 and December 31 for the dates.
4. Journalize the closing entry for Dividends using the Make General Journal Entries window.
5. Print a Journal report, a Balance Sheet Standards report, and a Trial Balance report. The trial balance will show only balance sheet accounts so you will need to edit the Report Title field to read "Post-Closing Trial Balance." Edit the Subtitle field to read "As of December 31."

FORMATTING GRIDLINES ON REPORTS

What do a football field and journal paper have in common? Each has many lines to help provide structure to its activity. Lines on the football field guide players where to run and mark the end zones. Journal paper lines guide accountants where to write account information and related amounts. These lines also help readers accurately locate information on a journal.

Spreadsheets also display row and column lines, called *gridlines*, to provide you with this structure as you enter text and numbers in a template. Unfortunately, these lines do not automatically appear on printed output.

Lines can be added to an electronic spreadsheet using two methods. A single command will print all gridlines. This quick solution may be overwhelming as the lines surrounding every cell will be printed. In contrast, the Borders tool allows you to insert a variety of line styles exactly where you want them—you decide what lines will provide readers with the structure they need.

EXCEL APPLICATION PROBLEM 16-3

Open the F16-3 Excel data file. Follow the step-by-step instructions in the Instructions work sheet. Use the Borders tool to insert horizontal and vertical lines to provide structure to the trial balance.

ADJUSTING ENTRIES, CLOSING ENTRIES, AND POST-CLOSING TRIAL BALANCE

Adjusting Entries

At the end of a fiscal period, many accounts need to be adjusted to recognize changes and expenses of the fiscal period. Adjusting entries are recorded in the general journal. The reference used for adjusting entries is *Adj.Ent*. After all adjusting entries have been entered and posted, the file should be saved with the letters *BC* in the filename. *BC* stands for *Before Closing*. Once closing entries are posted, it is very difficult to correct any errors that may have been made during the fiscal period. Therefore, having a file saved before the closing entries ensures that a before-closing file exists if corrections are necessary.

Closing Entries

In an automated accounting system, closing entries are generated and posted by the software. *Automated Accounting* automatically prepares all closing entries with the Generate Closing Journal Entries option from the Options menu. Once generated, the journal entries should be examined for accuracy and then posted.

Post-Closing Trial Balance

After closing entries are journalized and posted, a general ledger trial balance report is selected from the Reports menu. Because the closing entries have been posted, this trial balance is a post-closing trial balance.

AUTOMATED ACCOUNTING APPLICATION PROBLEM 16-4

Open file F16-4.AA8. Display the problem instructions and complete the problem.

AUTOMATED ACCOUNTING MASTERY PROBLEM 16-5

Open file F16-5.AA8. Display the problem instructions and complete the problem.

An Accounting Cycle for a Corporation: End-of-Fiscal-Period Work

The ledgers used in Reinforcement Activity 2—Part A are needed to complete Reinforcement Activity 2—Part B. Reinforcement Activity 2—Part B includes those accounting activities needed to complete the accounting cycle of Medical Services Company (MSC).

END-OF-FISCAL-PERIOD WORK

INSTRUCTIONS:

12. Prepare a trial balance on a work sheet. Use December 31 of the current year as the date.

13. Complete the work sheet using the following adjustment information:

    a. Office supplies inventory $ 476.60
    b. Store supplies inventory   817.00
    c. Merchandise inventory   33,278.01
    d. Uncollectible accounts are 2.0% of credit sales of $65,000.00
    e. Value of prepaid insurance $ 500.00
    f. Estimate of office equipment depreciation   3,520.00
    g. Estimate of store equipment depreciation   2,240.00

14. Using the tax table shown in Chapter 14, calculate federal income tax expense and record the income tax adjustment on the work sheet.

15. Prepare an income statement. Figure and record the following component percentages of net sales: (a) cost of merchandise sold, (b) gross profit on sales, (c) total expenses, and (d) net income or loss before federal income tax. Round percentage calculations to the nearest 0.1%.

16. Prepare a statement of stockholders' equity. The company had 9,500 shares of $1.00 par value stock outstanding on January 1. The company issued an additional 500 shares during the year.

17. Prepare a balance sheet in report form.

18. Calculate the earnings per share and price-earnings ratio. The current market price of the stock is $87.50.

19. Use page 13 of a general journal. Journalize and post the adjusting entries.

20. Use page 14 of a general journal. Journalize and post the closing entries.

21. Prepare a post-closing trial balance.

This simulation covers the realistic transactions completed by Unique Global Imports. The business sells imported goods, including fabrics, clothing, furniture, and decorative accessories.

Transactions are recorded in special journals similar to the ones used by Hobby Shack, Inc., in this accounting cycle. The activities included in the accounting cycle for Unique Global Imports are listed below.

This real-life business simulation comes with source documents. It is available in manual and automated versions. The automated version is used with *Automated Accounting* software.

The following activities are included in the Unique Global Imports simulation:

1. Recording transactions in special journals from source documents.

2. Posting items to be posted individually to a general ledger and subsidiary ledgers.

3. Recording a payroll in a payroll register. Updating the employee earnings records. Recording payroll journal entries.

4. Posting column totals to a general ledger.

5. Preparing schedules of accounts receivable and accounts payable from subsidiary ledgers.

6. Preparing a trial balance on a work sheet.

7. Planning adjustments and completing a work sheet.

8. Preparing financial statements.

9. Journalizing and posting adjusting entries.

10. Journalizing and posting closing entries.

11. Preparing a post-closing trial balance.

12. Preparing a post-closing trial balance.

13. Completing Think Like an Accountant Financial Analysis.

PART 3

Accounting for a Merchandising Business Organized as a Corporation—Adjustments and Valuation

THE BUSINESS— RESTAURANT SUPPLY CO.

Restaurant Supply Co., the business described in Part 3, is a retail merchandising business organized as a corporation. The business purchases and sells a wide variety of cooking and restaurant supplies and equipment. Restaurant Supply purchases its merchandise directly from the manufacturers and distributors. Restaurant Supply rents the building in which the business is located.

PHOTOS: IMAGEMORE, PHOTODISC, STOCKBYTE (ALL GETTY IMAGES)

CHAPTER 17

CHAPTER 18

CHAPTER 19

RESTAURANT SUPPLY CO. CHART OF ACCOUNTS

GENERAL LEDGER

Balance Sheet Accounts

(1000) ASSETS

1100	Current Assets
1105	Cash
1110	Petty Cash
1115	Notes Receivable
1120	Interest Receivable
1125	Accounts Receivable
1130	Allowance for Uncollectible Accounts
1135	Merchandise Inventory
1140	Supplies
1145	Prepaid Insurance
1200	Plant Assets
1205	Office Equipment
1210	Accumulated Depreciation—Office Equipment
1215	Store Equipment
1220	Accumulated Depreciation—Store Equipment

(2000) LIABILITIES

2100	Current Liabilities
2105	Notes Payable
2110	Interest Payable
2115	Accounts Payable
2120	Employee Income Tax Payable
2125	Federal Income Tax Payable
2130	Social Security Tax Payable
2135	Medicare Tax Payable
2140	Sales Tax Payable
2145	Unemployment Tax Payable—Federal
2150	Unemployment Tax Payable—State
2155	Health Insurance Premiums Payable
2160	Dividends Payable

(3000) STOCKHOLDERS' EQUITY

3105	Capital Stock
3110	Retained Earnings
3115	Dividends
3120	Income Summary

Income Statement Accounts

(4000) OPERATING REVENUE

4105	Sales
4110	Sales Discount
4115	Sales Returns and Allowances

(5000) COST OF MERCHANDISE

5105	Purchases
5110	Purchases Discount
5115	Purchases Returns and Allowances

(6000) OPERATING EXPENSES

6105	Advertising Expense
6110	Cash Short and Over
6115	Credit Card Fee Expense
6120	Depreciation Expense—Office Equipment
6125	Depreciation Expense—Store Equipment
6130	Insurance Expense
6135	Miscellaneous Expense
6140	Payroll Taxes Expense
6145	Rent Expense
6150	Repair Expense
6155	Salary Expense
6160	Supplies Expense
6165	Uncollectible Accounts Expense
6170	Utilities Expense

(7000) OTHER REVENUE

7105	Gain on Plant Assets
7110	Interest Income

(8000) OTHER EXPENSES

8105	Interest Expense
8110	Loss on Plant Assets

(9000) INCOME TAX EXPENSE

9105	Federal Income Tax Expense

The chart of accounts for Restaurant Supply Co. is illustrated here for ready reference as you study Part 3 of this textbook.

CHAPTER 20

CHAPTER 21

CHAPTER 22

IMAGEMORE/GETTY IMAGES

CHAPTER 17

Accounting for Uncollectible Accounts Receivable

OBJECTIVES

After studying Chapter 17, you will be able to:

1. Define accounting terms related to uncollectible accounts.

2. Identify accounting concepts and practices related to uncollectible accounts.

3. Calculate, journalize, and post estimated uncollectible accounts expense.

4. Journalize and post entries related to writing off and collecting uncollectible accounts receivable.

KEY TERMS

- writing off an account

Point Your Browser
www.C21accounting.com

Performance Food Group

Dining Out with Performance Food Group

You can't drive down the road and find a restaurant by its name. But chances are you have eaten recently at a restaurant that purchased its food from Performance Food Group (PFG). The company is one of the leading food distributors in the United States.

PFG purchases food products from manufacturers and produces its own line of ready-to-eat products. The company delivers these products to more than 47,000 customers that include restaurants, schools, cafeterias, healthcare facilities, and grocery stores. To provide superior service, PFG sells to some customers on account.

Unfortunately, the food service business can be challenging, even for entrepreneurs with experience in the industry. As a result, some of PFG's customers cannot pay their accounts. PFG is unable to collect approximately 0.1% of its sales, or approximately $5.5 million per year.

Critical Thinking

1. Using the information provided, estimate PFG's annual sales.

2. What account is used to record the period estimate of future uncollectible accounts? What is the classification of this account?

Source: www.pfgc.com

INTERNET ACTIVITY

EDGAR—Part 3

Go to the homepage for EDGAR (www.sec.gov/edgar/searchedgar/webusers.htm). Click on "Companies & Other Filers." Search the EDGAR database for the most recent 10K report from Dell, Inc. (Enter "Dell Inc" for company name, click on "Find Companies," and then scroll down and click on "10-K" in the first column.) The 10-K form is very similar to and contains much of the same information as the annual report.

Instructions

1. Find the balance sheet and record the net amount of Accounts Receivable.

2. Find the "Notes" to the financial statements and record the amount of "gross accounts receivable" and the amount of "allowance for doubtful accounts."

Uncollectible Accounts

A business sells on account to encourage sales. Customers can buy merchandise even though they will not have the cash needed to pay the account until days or months later.

A business that sells on account expects full payment within the terms of sale. Before selling to a customer on account, management should perform a thorough credit check on a customer.

A credit customer's financial condition may decline over time. Business customers may experience increased competition or a catastrophic event, such as a weather disaster. Individual customers may lose their employment. Regardless of the reason, creditworthy customers may later be unable to pay their accounts. Accounts receivable that cannot be collected are known as *uncollectible accounts*.

THE BUSINESS—RESTAURANT SUPPLY CO.

Miguel Lopez, Keisha Tomkins, and Joseph Weisbaum worked as chefs at restaurants in a trendy part of the city. They all had dreams of owning their own businesses, but they tired of the long hours involved in restaurant operations. Since they had experience using cooking tools and equipment, they explored the restaurant supply business and decided to form a corporation to sell to restaurants. Because of widespread consumer interest in cooking, they also make cash and credit card sales to individual customers. They sell on account to restaurants and catering operations.

The chart of accounts on page 511 is similar to that of the corporation in Part 2. However, Restaurant Supply has two new sections in the chart of accounts: Other Revenue and Other Expenses. The accounts in these sections are income statement accounts that are used for interest they pay on loans or earn on extended credit terms for customers. They also have accounts for recording gains and losses on plant assets they sell, trade, or discard.

CHARACTER COUNTS

Lifelong Learning

When you are ill, you expect your doctor to know the latest methods and medicines to restore your health. Businesses should expect nothing less from their accountants. Therefore, accountants must constantly improve their knowledge and skills to provide their clients, employees, and the public with the highest level of professional service.

The code of conduct for every major accounting organization includes some reference to lifelong learning. Many organizations require their members to complete a specified number of continuing education credits annually. For example, most certified public accountants must complete 40 hours of continuing education every year. This education may be in the form of self-study courses, college courses, seminars, or conferences.

Instructions

Access the code of conduct from the American Institute of Certified Public Accountants (AICPA), the Institute of Internal Auditors (IIA), the Institute of Management Accountants (IMA), and the Association of Certified Fraud Examiners (ACFE). Identify what each code states about lifelong learning.

PHOTO: DIGITAL VISION/GETTY IMAGES

Allowing customers to buy now and pay later is an effective method for increasing sales. Unfortunately, some customers may later become unable or unwilling to pay their account. These uncollectible accounts must be recorded as an expense.

The allowance method of recording losses from uncollectible accounts attempts to match the expense of uncollectible accounts in the same fiscal year the related sales are recorded. At the end of the fiscal year, the business does not know which specific accounts will become uncollectible. Therefore, an estimate of the uncollectible accounts is recorded to the contra asset account Allowance for Uncollectible Accounts and the expense account Uncollectible Accounts Expense. [CONCEPT: Matching Expenses with Revenue]

Restaurant Supply estimates uncollectible accounts expense by calculating a percentage of total sales on account. A review of Restaurant Supply's previous experience in collecting sales on account shows that actual uncollectible accounts expense has been about 1.0% of total sales on account. The company's total sales on account for the year is $1,287,330.00. Thus, Restaurant Supply estimates that $12,873.30 of the current fiscal period's sales on account will eventually be uncollectible.

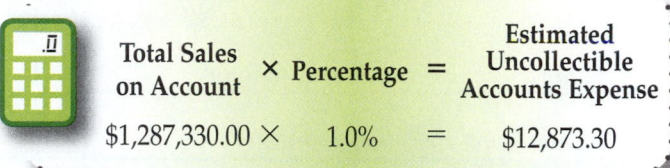

Total Sales on Account	×	Percentage	=	Estimated Uncollectible Accounts Expense
$1,287,330.00	×	1.0%	=	$12,873.30

FOR YOUR INFORMATION

F Y I

A credit check might involve an analysis of the customer's financial statements, a review of reports from national credit agencies, and interviews with other businesses that sell to the customer on account.

BUSINESS STRUCTURES

Dissolving a Corporation

Because the corporation is the most complex form of business, dissolution involves many legal procedures. Thus, the board of directors should seek the legal advice of an attorney.

In some states, the Secretary of State may take action to dissolve a corporation if one or more of the three following conditions exists: (1) The corporation is 60 days late in paying franchise taxes. (2) The corporation does not file its annual report within 60 days of the due date. (3) The corporation does not have a registered agent or office for 60 days or more.

Judicial proceedings may be brought against a corporation if the corporation acts beyond the powers it has been granted or engages in illegal activity. These proceedings may force the corporation to give up its charter.

Once a corporation is dissolved, the liquidation process can begin. Noncash assets usually are sold, and the proceeds are used to pay creditors. The procedure for selling noncash assets is similar to that for proprietorships. However, because a corporation's earnings are taxable, the gains and losses on the sales of noncash assets are subject to taxation. Therefore, additional tax reports for the corporation must be filed.

Critical Thinking

What do you think are some circumstances that might lead a corporation to dissolve voluntarily?

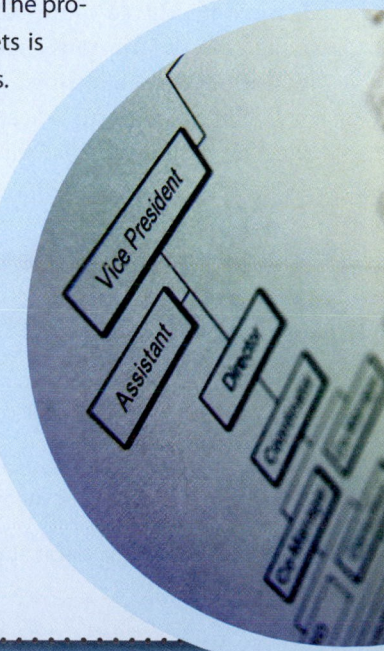

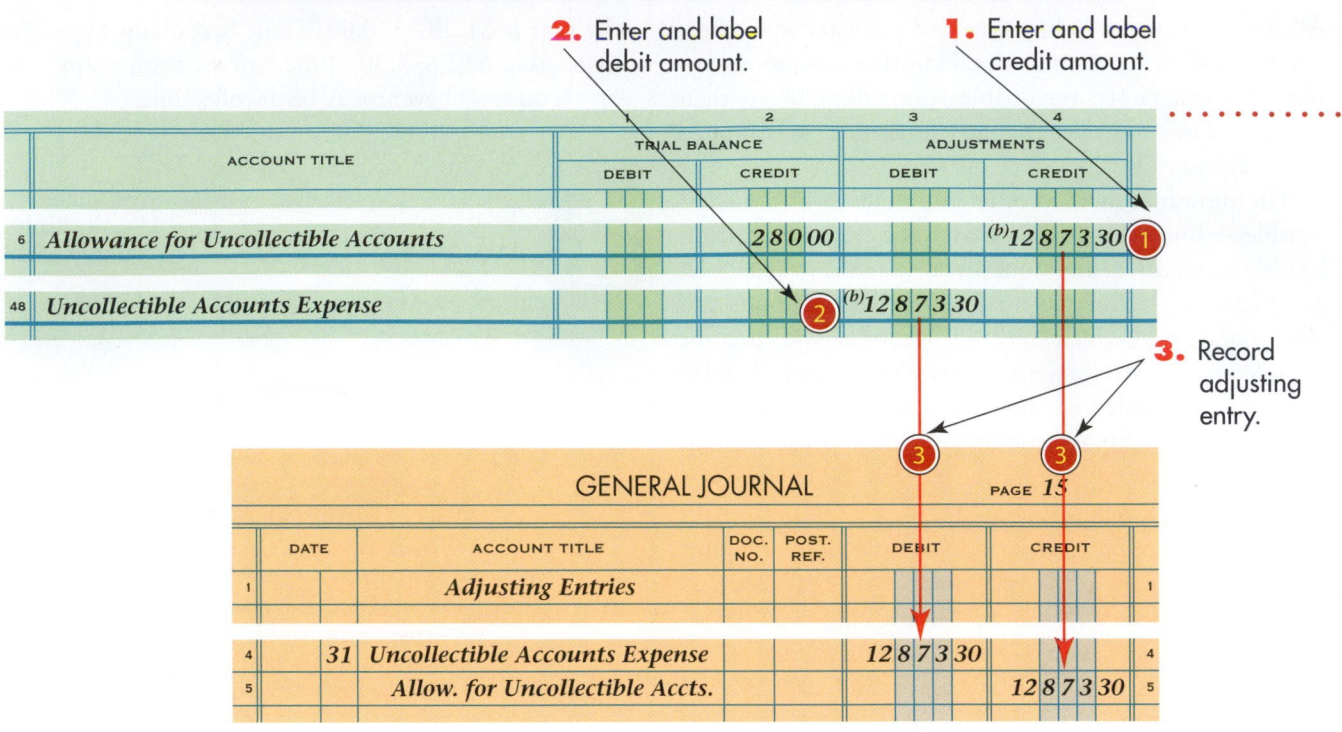

The percentage of total sales on account method of estimating uncollectible accounts expense assumes that a portion of every sale on account dollar will become uncollectible. Restaurant Supply has estimated that 1% of its $1,287,330.00 sales on account, or $12,873.30, will eventually become uncollectible.

At the end of a fiscal period, an adjustment for uncollectible accounts expense is planned on a work sheet. The Allowance for Uncollectible Accounts balance in the Trial Balance Credit column, $280.00, is the allowance estimate from the previous fiscal period that has not yet been identified as uncollectible.

When the allowance account has a previous credit balance, the amount of the adjustment is added to the previous balance. This new balance of the allowance account is the estimated amount of accounts receivable that will eventually become uncollectible.

Uncollectible Accounts Expense	
Dec. 31 Adj. 12,873.30	

Allowance for Uncollectible Accounts	
	Bal. 280.00
	Dec. 31 Adj. 12,873.30
	(New Bal. 13,153.30)

STEPS

ANALYZING AND JOURNALIZING AN ADJUSTMENT FOR UNCOLLECTIBLE ACCOUNTS EXPENSE

(1) Enter the estimated uncollectible amount, *$12,873.30*, in the Adjustments Credit column on the *Allowance for Uncollectible Accounts* line of the work sheet. Label the adjustment *(b)* with a small letter in parentheses.

(2) Enter the same amount, *$12,873.30*, in the Adjustments Debit column on the *Uncollectible Accounts Expense* line of the work sheet. Label the adjustment using the same letter, *(b)*.

(3) Use the debit and credit amounts on the work sheet to record an adjusting entry in a general journal.

POSTING AN ADJUSTING ENTRY FOR UNCOLLECTIBLE ACCOUNTS EXPENSE

GENERAL JOURNAL — PAGE 15

	DATE		ACCOUNT TITLE	DOC. NO.	POST. REF.	DEBIT	CREDIT	
1			*Adjusting Entries*					1
4		*31*	*Uncollectible Accounts Expense*		*6165*	*12,873.30*		4
5			*Allow. for Uncollectible Accts.*		*1130*		*12,873.30*	5

ACCOUNT *Accounts Receivable* — ACCOUNT NO. *1125*

DATE		ITEM	POST. REF.	DEBIT	CREDIT	BALANCE DEBIT	BALANCE CREDIT
Dec.	*31*		*S49*	*84,451.25*		*142,624.50*	
	31		*CR54*		*64,284.20*	*78,340.30*	

1. Debit

2. Credit

ACCOUNT *Allowance for Uncollectible Accounts* — ACCOUNT NO. *1130*

DATE		ITEM	POST. REF.	DEBIT	CREDIT	BALANCE DEBIT	BALANCE CREDIT
Dec.	*22*		*G14*	*810.00*			*280.00*
	31		*G15*		*12,873.30*		*13,153.30*

ACCOUNT *Uncollectible Accounts Expense* — ACCOUNT NO. *6165*

DATE		ITEM	POST. REF.	DEBIT	CREDIT	BALANCE DEBIT	BALANCE CREDIT
20-- *Dec.*	*31*		*G15*	*12,873.30*		*12,873.30*	

The adjustment for uncollectible accounts expense planned on the work sheet is recorded as an adjusting entry in the general journal. The adjusting entry is then posted to the general ledger.

The adjusting entry affects two of the three accounts related to accounts receivable. After the adjustment, Allowance for Uncollectible Accounts has a credit balance of $13,153.30. The balance of this contra account is an estimate of outstanding accounts receivable that will become uncollectible during the next fiscal period.

The debit balance of Uncollectible Accounts Expense, $12,873.30, is the estimated uncollectible accounts resulting from sales on account during the current fiscal year.

The adjusting entry does not affect the balance of Accounts Receivable. Accounts Receivable has a debit balance of $78,340.30 before and after the adjusting entry is posted. The book value of accounts receivable on December 31, $65,187.00, is an estimate of the amount of the December 31 balance of accounts receivable Restaurant Supply expects to collect during the next fiscal year.

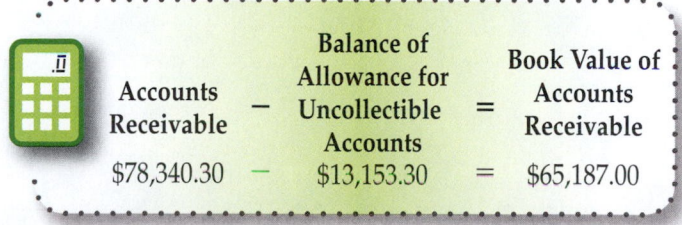

Accounts Receivable	–	Balance of Allowance for Uncollectible Accounts	=	Book Value of Accounts Receivable
$78,340.30	–	$13,153.30	=	$65,187.00

End of Lesson REVIEW

1. How are uncollectible accounts recorded?
2. Explain why an adjustment for uncollectible accounts is an application of the *Matching Expenses with Revenue* concept.
3. How is the account Accounts Receivable affected by the estimate of uncollectible accounts?

WORK TOGETHER 17-1

Estimating and journalizing entries for uncollectible accounts expense

A general journal, work sheet, and selected general ledger accounts for Velson Company are given in the *Working Papers*. Your instructor will guide you through the following examples.

1. Velson Company estimates uncollectible accounts expense as 0.3% of its total sales on account. During the current year, Velson had credit sales of $2,152,000.00. The balance in Allowance for Uncollectible Accounts before adjustment is an $853.00 credit. Record the December 31 uncollectible accounts expense adjustment on a work sheet. Label the adjustment *(e)*.
2. Journalize the adjusting entry on page 13 of a general journal.
3. Post the adjusting entry to the general ledger.

ON YOUR OWN 17-1

Estimating and journalizing entries for uncollectible accounts expense

A general journal, work sheet, and selected general ledger accounts for McCaffery Industries are given in the *Working Papers*. Work this problem independently.

1. McCaffery Industries estimates uncollectible accounts expense as 0.4% of its total sales on account. During the current year, McCaffery had credit sales of $1,548,050.00. The balance in Allowance for Uncollectible Accounts before adjustment is a $216.00 credit. Record the December 31 uncollectible accounts expense adjustment on a work sheet. Label the adjustment *(e)*.
2. Journalize the adjusting entry on page 26 of a general journal.
3. Post the adjusting entry to the general ledger.

JOURNALIZING WRITING OFF AN UNCOLLECTIBLE ACCOUNT RECEIVABLE

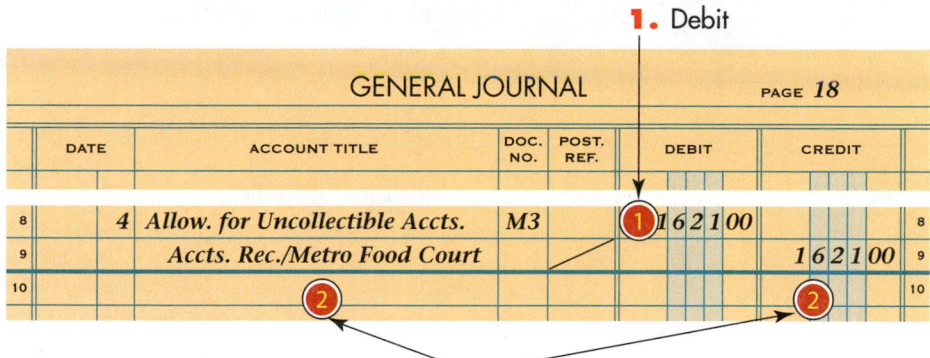

1. Debit

2. Credit and Customer's Name

When a customer account is determined to be uncollectible, a journal entry is made to cancel the uncollectible account. This entry cancels the uncollectible amount from the general ledger account Accounts Receivable as well as the customer account in the accounts receivable subsidiary ledger. Canceling the balance of a customer account because the customer does not pay is called **writing off an account**.

After months of unsuccessful collection efforts, Restaurant Supply decides that the past-due account of Metro Food Court is uncollectible.

> *January 4. Wrote off Metro Food Court's past-due account as uncollectible, $1,621.00. Memorandum No. 3.*

Because the account of Metro Food Court has been determined to be uncollectible, the $1,621.00 is now an actual uncollectible amount. Therefore, the amount of the uncollectible account is deducted from the allowance account.

Accounts Receivable is credited to reduce the balance due from customers. Metro Food Court's account is also credited to cancel the debit balance of the account. Metro Food Court's account is written off.

The book value of accounts receivable is the same both before and after writing off an uncollectible account. This is true because the same amount is deducted from both the accounts receivable and the allowance accounts.

GENERAL LEDGER
Allowance for Uncollectible Accounts

| Jan. 4 | 1,621.00 | Bal. | 13,153.30 |
| | | *(New Bal.* | *11,532.30)* |

Accounts Receivable

| Bal. | 78,340.30 | Jan. 4 | 1,621.00 |
| *(New Bal.* | *76,719.30)* | | |

ACCOUNTS RECEIVABLE LEDGER
Metro Food Court

| Bal. | 1,621.00 | Jan. 4 | 1,621.00 |
| *(New Bal.* | *zero)* | | |

	Before Account Written Off	After Account Written Off
Accounts Receivable	$ 78,340.30	$76,719.30
Allowance for Uncollectible Accounts	–13,153.30	–11,532.30
Book Value	$ 65,187.00	$ 65,187.00

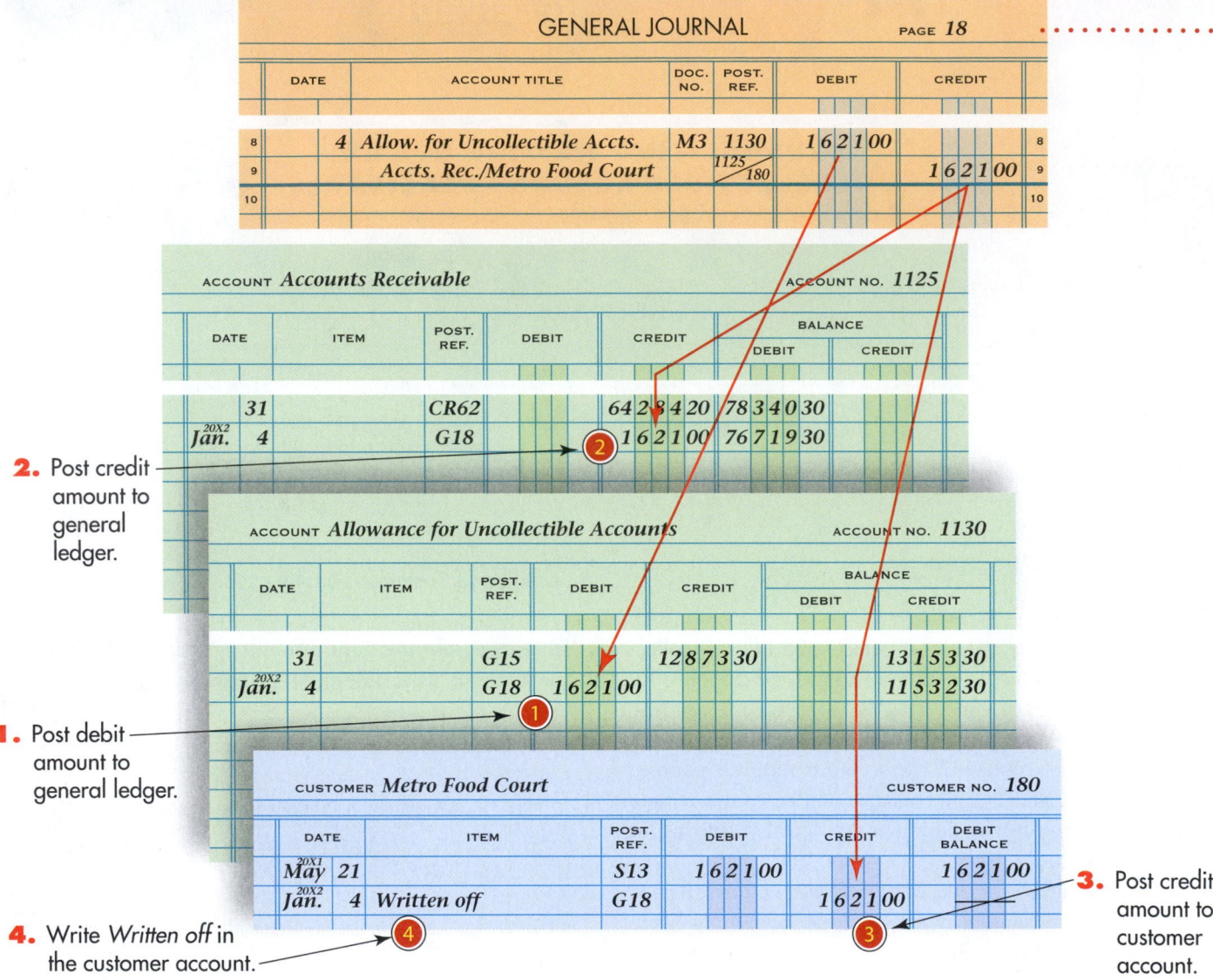

2. Post credit amount to general ledger.

1. Post debit amount to general ledger.

4. Write *Written off* in the customer account.

3. Post credit amount to customer account.

The journal entry to write off an uncollectible account affects the two general ledger accounts Accounts Receivable and Allowance for Uncollectible Accounts, and the customer account. The words *Written off* are written in the Item column of the customer account to show the full credit history for the customer.

STEPS · POSTING AN ENTRY TO WRITE OFF AN UNCOLLECTIBLE ACCOUNT RECEIVABLE

① Post the debit, *$1,621.00*, to *Allowance for Uncollectible Accounts* in the general ledger.

② Post the credit, *$1,621.00*, to *Accounts Receivable* in the general ledger.

③ Post the credit, *$1,621.00*, to the customer account, *Metro Food Court*, in the accounts receivable ledger.

④ Write the words *Written off* in the Item column of the customer account.

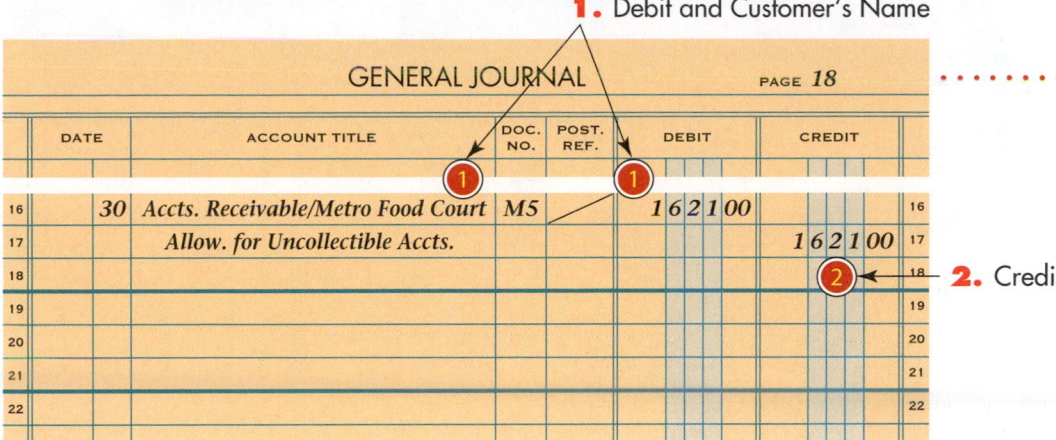

1. Debit and Customer's Name

2. Credit

A business writes off a specific account receivable after determining that the account probably will not be collected. Occasionally, after an account has been written off, the customer pays the delinquent account. Several accounts must be changed to recognize payment of a written-off account receivable.

> **January 30. Received cash in full payment of Metro Food Court's account, previously written off as uncollectible, $1,621.00. Memorandum No. 5 and Receipt No. 12.**

GENERAL LEDGER
Accounts Receivable

Bal.	78,340.30	Jan. 4	1,621.00
Jan. 30	1,621.00		
(New Bal.	78,340.30)		

Allowance for Uncollectible Accounts

Jan. 4	1,621.00	Bal.	13,153.30
		Jan. 30	1,621.00
		(New Bal.	13,153.30)

ACCOUNTS RECEIVABLE LEDGER
Metro Food Court

Bal.	1,621.00	Jan. 4	1,621.00
Jan. 30	1,621.00		
(New Bal.	1,621.00)		

Several accounts must be changed to show that Metro Food Court did pay its account. The accounts also should be changed to show a complete credit history of Metro Food Court's dealings with Restaurant Supply Co.

Two journal entries are recorded for the collection of a written-off account receivable: (1) a general journal entry to reopen the customer account and (2) a cash receipts journal entry to record the cash received on account.

To show an accurate credit history, Metro Food Court's account is reopened. Accounts Receivable is debited for $1,621.00 to replace the amount previously written off in the general ledger account. Allowance for Uncollectible Accounts is credited for $1,621.00 to replace the amount that was removed when Metro Food Court's account was previously written off. Also, Metro Food Court's account in the accounts receivable ledger is debited for $1,621.00. This entry to reopen the account is the exact reverse of the entry to write off Metro Food Court's account.

STEPS — REOPENING AN ACCOUNT PREVIOUSLY WRITTEN OFF

1. Enter a debit, *$1,621.00*, to *Accounts Receivable*. Place a diagonal line after the account title and enter the customer's name, *Metro Food Court*. Place a diagonal line in the Post. Ref. column.

2. Enter a credit, *$1,621.00*, to *Allowance for Uncollectible Accounts*.

	DATE	ACCOUNT TITLE	DOC. NO.	POST. REF.	GENERAL DEBIT	GENERAL CREDIT	ACCOUNTS RECEIVABLE CREDIT	SALES CREDIT	SALES TAX PAYABLE CREDIT	SALES DISCOUNT DEBIT	CASH DEBIT	
					1	2	3	4	5	6	7	
21	30	Metro Food Court	R12				1 6 2 1 00				1 6 2 1 00	21
22												22

CASH RECEIPTS JOURNAL   PAGE 54

After the entry to reopen Metro Food Court's account is recorded, an entry is made to record the cash received on Metro Food Court's account.

January 30. Received cash in full payment of Metro Food Court's account, previously written off as uncollectible, $1,621.00. Memorandum No. 5 and Receipt No. 12.

The entry in the cash receipts journal is the same as for any other collection of accounts receivable.

GENERAL LEDGER
Cash

Jan. 30	1,621.00		

Accounts Receivable

Bal.	78,340.30	Jan. 4	1,621.00
Jan. 30	1,621.00	Jan. 30	1,621.00

ACCOUNTS RECEIVABLE LEDGER
Metro Food Court

Bal.	1,621.00	Jan. 4	1,621.00
Jan. 30	1,621.00	Jan. 30	1,621.00
		(New Bal.	zero)

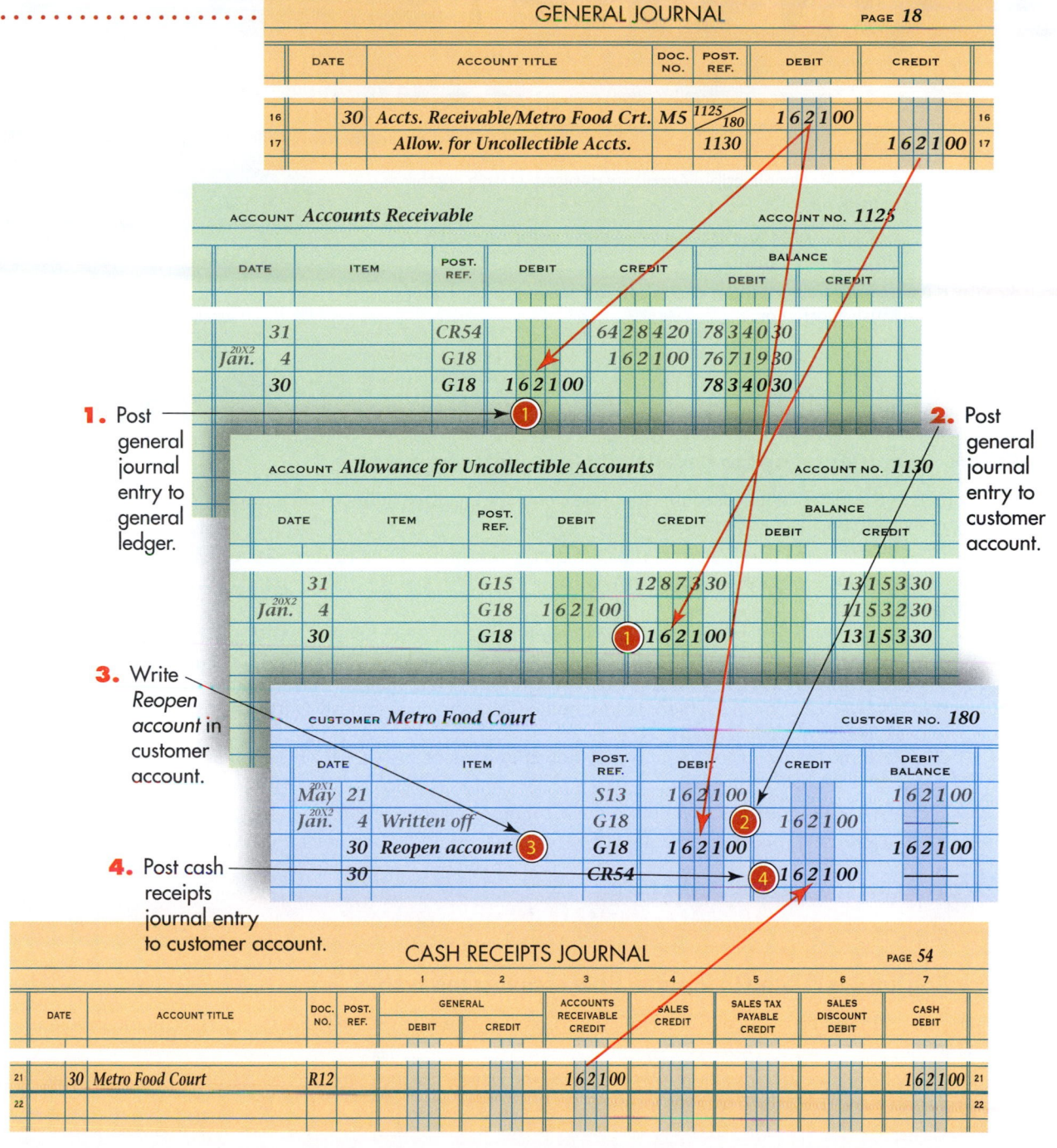

1. Post general journal entry to general ledger.

2. Post general journal entry to customer account.

3. Write *Reopen account* in customer account.

4. Post cash receipts journal entry to customer account.

STEPS

POSTING ENTRIES FOR COLLECTING A WRITTEN-OFF ACCOUNT RECEIVABLE

1. Post the general journal entry to the general ledger.

2. Post the debit portion of the general journal entry to the customer account.

3. Write the words *Reopen account* in the Item column of the customer account.

4. Post the cash receipts journal entry to the customer account.

End of Lesson REVIEW

AUDIT YOUR UNDERSTANDING

1. Why is Allowance for Uncollectible Accounts debited when a customer account is written off?
2. Does the book value of accounts receivable differ before and after writing off an account? Explain.
3. Why is a customer account reopened when the account is paid after being previously written off?

TERM REVIEW

writing off an account

WORK TOGETHER 17-2

Recording entries related to uncollectible accounts receivable

The journals and selected ledger accounts for Cross Company are given in the *Working Papers*. Your instructor will guide you through the following examples.

1. Journalize the following transactions completed during November of the current year. Use page 15 of a general journal and page 24 of a cash receipts journal.

Transactions:

Nov. 2. Wrote off Davidson Corp.'s past-due account as uncollectible, $849.00. M245.
3. Wrote off JGF Industries' past-due account as uncollectible, $2,488.00. M247.
4. Wrote off Sansing Co.'s past-due account as uncollectible, $609.00. M251.
14. Received cash in full payment of Lynchburg Co.'s account, previously written off as uncollectible, $1,548.00. M258 and R415.
29. Received cash in full payment of JGF Industries' account, previously written off as uncollectible, $2,488.00. M261 and R429.

2. Post each entry to the customer accounts in the accounts receivable ledger.
3. Post general journal entries to the general ledger.

ON YOUR OWN 17-2

Recording entries related to uncollectible accounts receivable

The journals and selected ledger accounts for Potera Company are given in the *Working Papers*. Work this problem independently.

1. Journalize the following transactions completed during October of the current year. Use page 11 of a general journal and page 15 of a cash receipts journal.

Transactions:

Oct. 5. Wrote off Angela White's past-due account as uncollectible, $159.00. M45.
8. Wrote off Peter Ewing's past-due account as uncollectible, $612.00. M47.
12. Received cash in full payment of Mike Novak's account, previously written off as uncollectible, $853.00. M51 and R313.
16. Wrote off Tim Haley's past-due account as uncollectible, $238.00. M58.
23. Received cash in full payment of Peter Ewing's account, previously written off as uncollectible, $612.00. M61 and R345.

2. Post each entry to the customer accounts in the accounts receivable ledger.
3. Post general journal entries to the general ledger.

After completing this chapter, you can:

1. Define accounting terms related to uncollectible accounts.

2. Identify accounting concepts and practices related to uncollectible accounts.

3. Calculate, journalize, and post estimated uncollectible accounts expense.

4. Journalize and post entries related to writing off and collecting uncollectible accounts receivable.

EXPLORE ACCOUNTING

Accounting Estimates Use Interesting Assumptions

Accountants use many accounting estimates to adjust the historical cost of certain transactions to better reflect the company's financial condition.

One of the most interesting accounting estimates concerns a payroll-related expense known as post-retirement benefits other than pensions. Some companies offer their employees free services, such as health care, during their retirement. For many years, companies have expensed these costs when the services were actually provided and paid for in cash. Accounting rules recently changed to require that these costs be recognized as an expense over the employee's years of work. The promise of free health care during retirement is part of the total benefits that the company provides an employee in exchange for the employee's services.

For example, Watanabe Industries has promised free health care to its retired employees and their family members under 21 years of age. Carmen Suarez is expected to work for Watanabe Industries for 30 years. Health care costs for Carmen, her husband, and any future children during her retirement are currently estimated to be $30,000. Rather than expense the $30,000 when the bills are paid during Carmen's retirement, the new accounting rule requires that the $30,000 be expensed over Carmen's 30 years of service. Therefore, $1,000 will be expensed each year.

To estimate the projected benefit, assumptions must be made regarding the following items: (1) percentage annual growth rate in health care costs, (2) life expectancy, (3) retirement age, (4) number of children, and (5) interest costs. Management's assumptions can dramatically affect accounting estimates. Companies that prepare public financial statements have independent auditors examine the assumptions used to compute accounting estimates to assure that these assumptions are reasonable.

Research: Research the annual growth rate of health care costs. Do you believe this growth rate will continue? Identify factors that might cause further increases or decreases in growth rate.

17-1 APPLICATION PROBLEM

Estimating and journalizing entries for uncollectible accounts expense

A general journal, partial work sheet, and selected general ledger accounts for Kellogg, Inc., are given in the *Working Papers*.

Instructions:

1. Kellogg, Inc., estimates uncollectible accounts expense as 1.0% of its total sales on account. During the current year, Kellogg had credit sales of $3,426,000.00. The balance in Allowance for Uncollectible Accounts before adjustment is a $534.00 credit. Record the uncollectible accounts expense adjustment on a work sheet. Label the adjustment *(e)*.
2. Journalize the adjusting entry on page 25 of a general journal.
3. Post the adjusting entry to the general ledger.

17-2 APPLICATION PROBLEM

Recording entries related to uncollectible accounts receivable

The journals and selected ledger accounts for Waldron Company are given in the *Working Papers*.

Instructions:

1. The following transactions related to accounts receivable occurred during September of the current year. Journalize the transactions using page 14 of a general journal and page 19 of a cash receipts journal.

Transactions:

Sept. 5. Wrote off Jackson Company's past-due account as uncollectible, $124.00. M234.
    7. Received cash in full payment of Davis Industries' account, previously written off as uncollectible, $185.00. M235 and R339.
    14. Wrote off Lancing, Inc.'s past-due account as uncollectible, $215.00. M238.
    19. Wrote off Sanders Mfg.'s past-due account as uncollectible, $842.00. M243.
    27. Received cash in full payment of Jackson Company's account, previously written off as uncollectible, $124.00. M251 and R362.

2. Post each entry to the customer accounts in the accounts receivable ledger.
3. Post each entry in the general journal to the general ledger.

Go Beyond the Book
For more information go to
www.C21accounting.com

Accounting for Uncollectible Accounts Receivable

17-3 APPLICATION PROBLEM

Recording entries related to uncollectible accounts receivable

The journals and selected ledger accounts for Weatherly Co. are given in the *Working Papers*.

Instructions:

1. The following transactions related to accounts receivable occurred during February of the current year. Journalize the transactions using page 4 of a general journal and page 2 of a cash receipts journal.

Transactions:

Feb. 3. Received a $1,458.00 check from Bearden Co. in full payment of its account. The account was written off in the previous month based on a newspaper story that indicated the company was about to close. M24 and R134.

7. Monique Pearce, controller of Hampton Industries, just called, stating that the company had serious cash flow problems and would not be able to pay its $2,584.00 account balance. M25.

10. Received a letter from Rankin Co.'s legal counsel, stating that the company was in the process of filing bankruptcy. The letter gave little hope that Weatherly would collect Rankin's $948.00 account. M28.

12. Received a check from Camden Enterprises in full payment of its $1,784.00 account. The account was written off in January after months of efforts to collect the account. M31 and R142.

21. A letter from Wilmont Co.'s receiving department supervisor, Daymon Lewis, stated that Wilmont refuses to pay for a prior year shipment of product for $548.00. The supervisor contends that the products were spoiled on arrival and were discarded. M34.

27. Received a letter and check in the mail from Monique Pearce of Hampton Industries. Two weeks ago the company was purchased by another company and therefore has access to cash to pay its debt. M35 and R159.

2. Post each entry to the customer accounts in the accounts receivable ledger.

3. Post each entry in the general journal to the general ledger.

17-4 MASTERY PROBLEM

Recording entries for uncollectible accounts

Selected accounts receivable and general ledger accounts for Sing Industries are given in the *Working Papers*. The following transactions relating to uncollectible accounts receivable occurred during the final quarter of the current fiscal year.

Instructions:

1. Journalize the following transactions completed during October using page 20 of a general journal. Post the transactions to the customer accounts and general ledger accounts.

Transactions:

Oct. 8. Wrote off Keller Corporation's past-due account as uncollectible, $648.25. M243.

19. Wrote off Gason Company's past-due account as uncollectible, $948.00. M252.

2. Journalize the following transactions completed during November using page 22 of a general journal and page 24 of a cash receipts journal. Prove the cash receipts journal. Post the transactions and the total of the Accounts Receivable Credit column to the customer accounts and general ledger accounts.

Transactions:

Nov. 9. Wrote off Baker Co.'s past-due account as uncollectible, $815.00. M267.

18. Received cash in full payment of Keller Corporation's account, previously written off as uncollectible, $648.25. M274 and R453.

23. Received cash in full payment of Pearson Industries' account, previously written off as uncollectible, $251.80. M281 and R476.

3. Journalize the following transactions for December. Use page 24 of a general journal and page 26 of a cash receipts journal. Prove the cash receipts journal. Post the transactions and the total of the Accounts Receivable Credit column to the customer accounts and general ledger accounts.

Transactions:

Dec. 4. Wrote off Franklin, Inc.'s past-due account as uncollectible, $1,458.00. M291.
   10. Received cash in full payment of Baker Corp.'s account, previously written off as uncollectible, $815.00. M293 and R489.
   29. Received cash in full payment of Gason Company's account, previously written off as uncollectible, $948.00. M297 and R502.

4. Journalize the December 31 adjusting entry for estimated uncollectible accounts expense for the year. Use page 26 of the general journal. Uncollectible accounts expense is estimated as 0.5% of total sales on account. Total sales on account for the year were $1,654,800.00. Post the transaction to the general ledger accounts.

17-5 | CHALLENGE PROBLEM

Recording entries for uncollectible accounts

Information from the accounting records of Rosedale Company concerning uncollectible accounts during the past five years follows (presented in thousands of dollars).

	20X1	20X2	20X3	20X4	20X5
Sales on account	$575	$700	$850	$1,050	$1,200
Ending Accounts Receivable	50	60	80	90	100
Uncollectible Accounts Expense	8	8	15	15	15
Ending Allowance for Uncollectible Accounts	5	1	4	3	1
Accounts written off	10	13	14	18	19
Accounts collected after being written off	1	1	2	2	2

Yu-lan Cheng, the controller of the company, has asked you to evaluate the prior annual adjustments to Allowance for Uncollectible Accounts. If the company expects to have sales of $1,400,000.00 next year, what amount would you suggest be expensed to Uncollectible Accounts Expense? Support your answer.

APPLIED COMMUNICATION

For many years, the accounting staff at St. Charles Furniture has written off uncollectible accounts receivable by debiting Uncollectible Accounts Expense and crediting Accounts Receivable. Despite relatively constant sales and collections on account, the annual amount of Uncollectible Accounts Expense has fluctuated between $5,000.00 and $90,000.00 during the past six years. Management admits that the amount of accounts written off depends largely on the time the managers have devoted to evaluating accounts receivable for possible collection problems.

Instructions: Prepare a memorandum to Tomas Gonzalez, president of St. Charles Furniture, explaining the correct way to account for uncollectible accounts receivable. The memorandum should persuade him to implement a change from the current accounting procedure.

CASE FOR CRITICAL THINKING

Some businesses have a policy of accepting only cash sales. Depending on economic conditions or the time of year, many potential customers may not be able to pay with currency, check, or debit card. Businesses with cash-only policies will lose those potential sales. As has been discussed in previous chapters, other businesses encourage more sales by selling on account to customers with approved credit. The key decision is defining what is approved credit. Employees responsible for meeting the sales goals of a business might choose one set of standards for approving credit. Employees responsible for maintaining merchandise inventory and filling orders might choose a different set of standards for approving credit. What role, if any, do you believe that accounting employees should play in setting a company's standards for approving credit? What contributions can accounting employees make to discussions about credit standards?

Predicting Uncollectible Accounts

Each year Hitesh Nizami, the controller for Southern Electronics, evaluates the percentage to be used to estimate uncollectible accounts expense. The company adopted a more liberal credit policy, resulting in a significant but acceptable increase in the accounts that were actually written off.

1. In what year did the company implement its new credit policy?

2. What percentage would you recommend Hitesh use to calculate the 2005 adjustment for allowance for uncollectible accounts? Justify your answer.

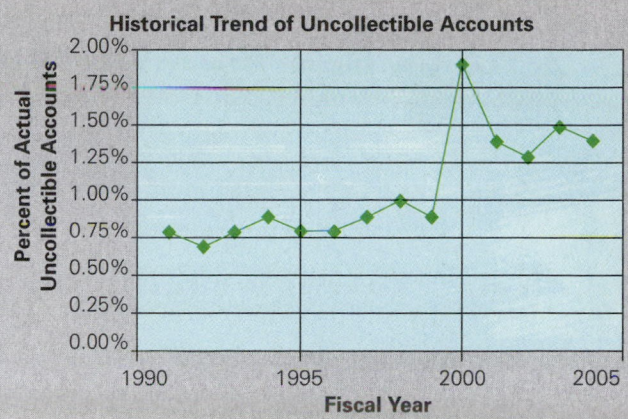

Historical Trend of Uncollectible Accounts

ANALYZING BEST BUY'S FINANCIAL STATEMENTS

A standard set of financial ratios has been developed to help individuals understand financial statements. Not every ratio, however, can be applied to every company. Best Buy customers must pay for their purchases with cash or a credit card. Thus, Best Buy does not have any trade accounts receivable. The small amount of accounts receivable reported on Best Buy's Consolidated Balance Sheets results from miscellaneous transactions.

For companies that do have trade accounts receivable, the accounts receivable turnover ratio measures how quickly a company is collecting its trade accounts receivable (A/R). The ratio is calculated as shown below:

$$\text{Accounts Receivable Turnover} = \frac{\text{Sales}}{(\text{Beginning balance of A/R} + \text{Ending balance of A/R}) \div 2}$$

Dividing the sum of the beginning and ending accounts receivable by 2 approximates the average accounts receivable for the fiscal year.

The accounts receivable turnover for Hershey Foods Corporation, based on its 2006 fiscal year financial statements, is calculated below (www.hersheys.com):

$$\text{A/R Turnover} = \frac{\$4,944,230,000}{(\$507,119,000 + \$522,673,000) \div 2} = 9.60 \text{ times}$$

Dividing 365 by the turnover ratio yields a financial ratio known as the *number of days' sales in receivables*. Hershey Foods' number of days' sales in receivables is 38.0 days. Thus, the average account is collected in approximately 38 days.

Instructions

1. What is the amount of accounts receivable for Best Buy reported on its fiscal year 2006 and 2007 financial statements on Appendix B page B-5?

2. Calculate the accounts receivable turnover and number of days' sales in receivables for the Procter & Gamble Company. The company reported $4,185 and $5,725 million of accounts receivable on June 30, 2005 and 2006, respectively, and sales of $68,222 million for fiscal year 2006. (www.pg.com)

Accounting
SOFTWARE

UNCOLLECTIBLE ACCOUNTS RECEIVABLE

Any transaction with a customer, whether it's a sale or cash receipt, results in transactions being posted to both the general ledger and the accounts receivable ledger. Writing off a customer's account is no different. Not only is the transaction posted to the general ledger, but the outstanding invoice in the customer's account must also be written off as uncollectible.

How does a business determine if an account is uncollectible? The process often begins with preparing an aging of accounts receivable report, which is a list of outstanding invoices. This report classifies outstanding invoices by the time each is overdue, such as 1 to 30 days overdue, 30 to 60 days overdue, 60 to 90 days overdue, and over 90 days overdue.

PEACHTREE APPLICATION PROBLEM 17-2

1. Open (Restore) file 17-2AP.ptb.
2. Use the Receipts task to write off the customer accounts.
3. To record payment of previously written-off amounts, go to the menu and select Tasks, Sales Invoicing, and the appropriate account. Remember to post when you have completed the transaction. Complete all the transactions.
4. Print the sales journal, cash receipts journal, and the customer ledger.
5. Print the accounts receivable and allowance for uncollectible accounts from the general ledger.

PEACHTREE APPLICATION PROBLEM 17-3

1. Open (Restore) file 17-3AP.ptb.
2. Journalize the entries related to accounts receivable using the sales journal and cash receipts journal.
3. Print the sales journal, cash receipts journal, and customer ledger.
4. Print the accounts receivable and allowance for uncollectible accounts in the general ledger.

UNCOLLECTIBLE ACCOUNTS RECEIVABLE

There are no special systems in QuickBooks software for handling the recording of uncollectible accounts. The transactions for recording uncollectible accounts are recorded in journals just as in a manual accounting system.

QuickBooks does, however, have some additional features that make the tracking of uncollectible accounts more efficient. One of these features is the ability to print out a report that lists the accounts receivables according to how old they are. This report is sometimes called an *Aging Schedule of Accounts Receivable*. This schedule can usually be set up to list if an account is current, 1 to 30 days overdue, 30 to 60 days overdue, 60 to 90 days overdue, 90 to 120 days overdue, and over 120 days overdue.

QUICKBOOKS APPLICATION PROBLEM 17-2

1. Open the Waldron Company file.
2. Journalize the transactions; use the Create Credit Memos/Refunds window to write off customer invoices.
3. Use the Make General Journal Entries window to record the reinstatement of previously written-off invoices and receipts from customers in payment.
4. Print a Journal report using September 1 and September 30 as the dates.
5. Print a Customer Balance Detail report using January 1 and September 30 for the dates.

QUICKBOOKS APPLICATION PROBLEM 17-3

1. Open the Weatherly Company file.
2. Journalize the transactions related to accounts receivable; use the Create Credit Memos/Refunds window to write off customer invoices.
3. Use the Make General Journal Entries window to record the reinstatement of previously written-off invoices and to record receipts from customers in payment of the invoices.
4. Print a Journal report using February 1 and February 28 as the dates.
5. Print a Customer Balance Detail report.

FORMATTING THE DISPLAY OF RATIOS

The relationship of two amounts can provide managers with useful information for making business decisions. For example, the ratio of accounts written off to sales on account provides important information about the actual rate of uncollectible accounts receivable.

Most accountants believe that only the first three digits of a ratio are meaningful for making business decisions. Suppose you learned that your credit manager had been able to reduce the ratio of accounts written off to sales on account to 1.23%. Would you think differently about the credit manager's performance if you knew that the ratio was actually 1.234567%?

Electronic spreadsheets make it easy for you to modify the format of a cell to display any number of decimal places. Displaying amounts with proper formatting makes printed schedules more useful.

EXCEL CHALLENGE PROBLEM 17-5

Open the F17-5OPT Excel data file. Follow the step-by-step instructions in the Instructions worksheet. Use the Format Cells feature to display ratios with the proper number of decimal places.

UNCOLLECTIBLE ACCOUNTS RECEIVABLE

There are no special systems in the Automated Accounting software for handling the recording of uncollectible accounts. Instead, transactions for uncollectible accounts are recorded in journals, just as in a manual accounting system. There are four kinds of entries described in this chapter that can be recorded using the Automated Accounting software:

1. *Adjusting Entry for Uncollectible Accounts:* This entry is recorded in the general journal with a debit to Uncollectible Accounts Expense and a credit to Allowance for Uncollectible Accounts.
2. *Writing Off an Account Receivable:* This entry is also recorded in the general journal. The entry includes a debit to Allowance for Uncollectible Accounts and a credit to Accounts Receivable and the customer's account. When the general ledger account number for Accounts Receivable is keyed in the Account Title field, a drop-down list for selecting the individual customer's account will appear. A separate entry for the Customer account is not recorded.
3. *Collecting a Previously Written-Off Account Receivable:* This transaction requires two entries: (a) an entry in the general journal to re-open the account and (b) an entry in the cash receipts journal to record the receipt of cash.

AUTOMATED ACCOUNTING APPLICATION PROBLEM 17-2

Open file F17-2.AA8. Display the problem instructions and complete the problem.

AUTOMATED ACCOUNTING MASTERY PROBLEM 17-4

Open file F17-4.AA8. Display the problem instructions and complete the problem.

CHAPTER 18

Accounting for Plant Assets and Depreciation

OBJECTIVES

After studying Chapter 18, you will be able to:

1. Define accounting terms related to plant assets, depreciation, and property tax expense.

2. Identify accounting concepts and practices related to accounting for plant assets, depreciation, and property tax expense.

3. Record the buying of a plant asset and the paying of property tax.

4. Calculate depreciation expense and book value using the straight-line method of depreciation.

5. Prepare plant asset records and journalize annual depreciation expense.

6. Record entries related to disposing of plant assets.

7. Calculate depreciation expense using the double declining-balance method of depreciation.

KEY TERMS

- real property
- personal property
- assessed value
- plant asset record
- gain on plant assets
- loss on plant assets
- declining-balance method of depreciation

Point Your Browser
www.C21accounting.com

Carnival Cruise Lines

Carnival Invests in Fun

Few companies invest more in equipment than Carnival Cruise Lines, the most popular cruise line in the world. Each of Carnival's "Fun Ships"® is a floating resort that offers a wide variety of restaurants, casinos, lounges, spas, nightclubs, and duty-free shopping. Ports of call allow passengers the opportunity to explore port cities in the Caribbean, Alaska, Mexico, and Canada, just to name a few.

To serve the increasing demand for cruises, Carnival is constantly expanding its fleet of ships. At up to $500 million per ship, the cost of the cruise ships is one of Carnival's most significant expenses. Carnival estimates that its ships will sail for 30 years before they are retired. Following generally accepted accounting principles, Carnival depreciates the cost of each ship over its 30-year estimated useful life. Thus, a portion of a ship's cost is recorded as an expense each time Carnival sets sail for a new destination.

©ANDY NEWMAN/EPA/LANDOV

Critical Thinking

1. A properly maintained ship can easily last more than 30 years. Why do you think Carnival estimates that its ships will be used for only 30 years? (Hint: What is the estimated life of your car?)

2. Suppose Carnival installs a teen club in a ship that was added to the fleet 10 years ago. How should the cost of this enhancement be accounted for?

Source: www.carnival.com

DIGITAL VISION/GETTY IMAGES

INTERNET ACTIVITY

Notes to the Financial Statements— Depreciation Methods

Go to the homepage for Carnival Cruise Lines (www.carnival.com) and Royal Caribbean Cruise Lines (www.royalcaribbean.com). Search for the latest annual report for each company. The annual report is usually found under the heading "About Us" or "Investor Relations." In the annual report, usually after the financial statements, you will find the notes to the financial statements. Using these notes (probably Note #1 or #2), look for the information about depreciating their ships.

Instructions

1. For each company, state the method of depreciation used to depreciate the ships.

2. For each company, state the number of years used in estimating the "useful life" of the ships.

Assets that will be used for a number of years in the operation of a business are known as *plant assets*. A business may have several types of plant assets, including equipment, buildings, and land. Businesses often subdivide plant assets into more focused categories and create an account for each category. For example, a company may divide its equipment into office, store, warehouse, and transportation equipment.

Restaurant Supply Co. owns its equipment but rents the building and the land where the business is located. Therefore, Restaurant Supply has only accounts for equipment. To provide more detailed financial information, Restaurant Supply records its equipment in two different equipment accounts—Office Equipment and Store Equipment. [CONCEPT: Adequate Disclosure]

Most plant assets are useful for only a limited period of time. Over time, most equipment wears out and can no longer perform its functions. Other equipment, such as computers, becomes technologically outdated. Regardless of the reason, the cost of a plant asset should be depreciated over its useful life. Each plant asset account should

have a related accumulated depreciation account—a contra asset account—to accumulate the annual depreciation expense of the plant assets in the account.

IMAGE SOURCE/GETTY IMAGES

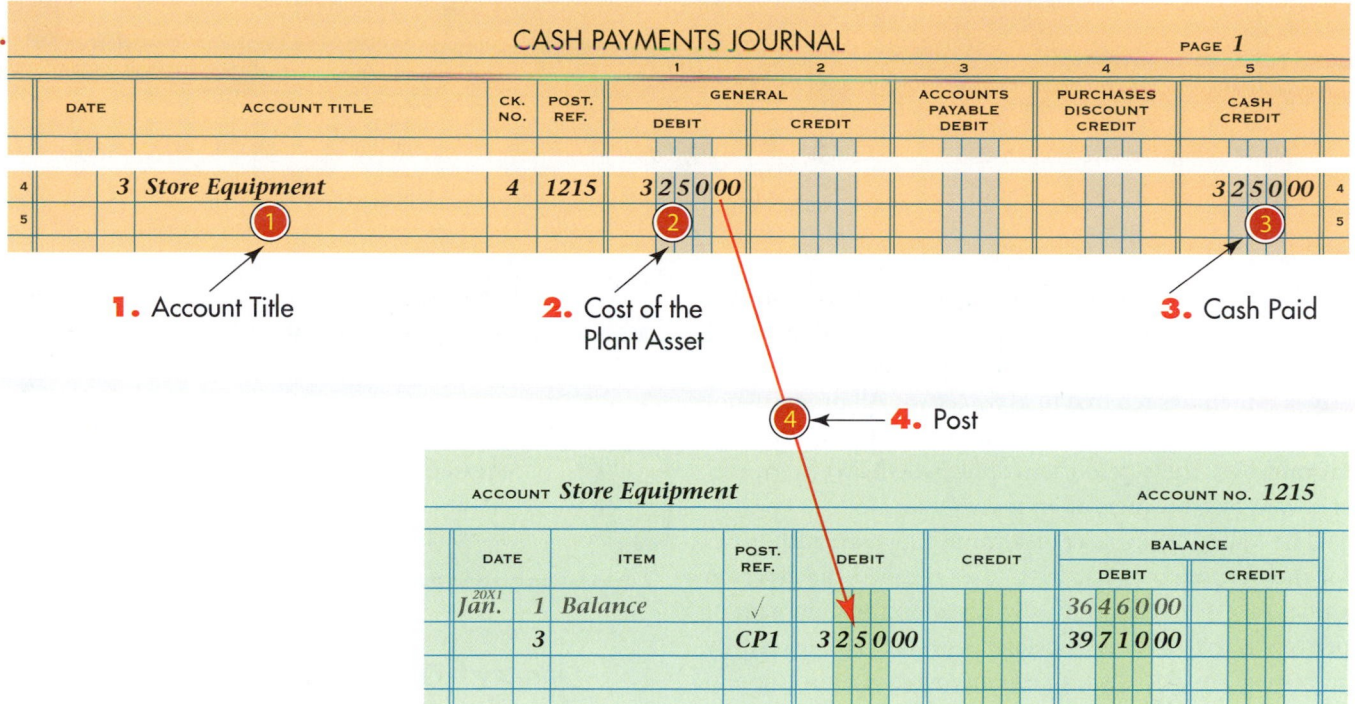

CASH PAYMENTS JOURNAL PAGE 1

DATE	ACCOUNT TITLE	CK. NO.	POST. REF.	GENERAL DEBIT	GENERAL CREDIT	ACCOUNTS PAYABLE DEBIT	PURCHASES DISCOUNT CREDIT	CASH CREDIT	
3	Store Equipment	4	1215	3 2 5 0 00				3 2 5 0 00	4
									5

1. Account Title

2. Cost of the Plant Asset

3. Cash Paid

4. Post

ACCOUNT *Store Equipment*   ACCOUNT NO. *1215*

DATE	ITEM	POST. REF.	DEBIT	CREDIT	BALANCE DEBIT	BALANCE CREDIT
Jan.^{20X1} 1	Balance	✓			36 4 6 0 00	
3		CP1	3 2 5 0 00		39 7 1 0 00	

Procedures for recording the buying of a plant asset are similar to procedures for recording the buying of current assets such as supplies. The amount paid for a plant asset is debited to a plant asset account with a title such as Store Equipment. [CONCEPT: Historical Cost]

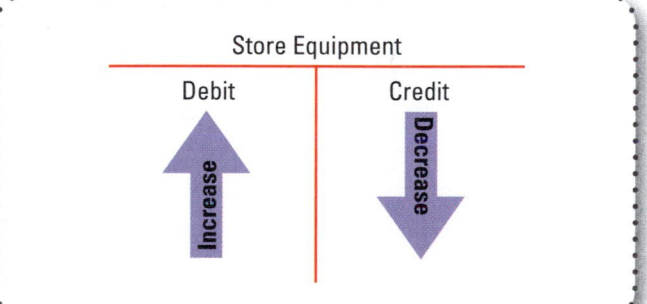

Store Equipment

Debit	Credit
Increase ↑	Decrease ↓

January 3, 20X1. Paid cash for a display case, $3,250.00. Check No. 4.

The entry in the General Debit column of the cash payments journal is posted individually to the account named in the Account Title column.

Store Equipment	
3,250.00	

Cash	
	3,250.00

STEPS — JOURNALIZING AND POSTING THE BUYING OF A PLANT ASSET

1. Write the plant asset account, *Store Equipment*, in the Account Title column of the cash payments journal.

2. Enter the cost of the plant asset, $3,250.00, in the General Debit column.

3. Enter the same amount, $3,250.00, in the Cash Credit column.

4. Post the entry in the general debit column to the general ledger.

FOR YOUR INFORMATION

FYI

Because of its permanent nature, land is generally not subject to depreciation. Buildings, after years of use, eventually become unusable. A building may be torn down and a new building constructed on the same land. However, since land can be used indefinitely, it is considered permanent and is not depreciated.

			CASH PAYMENTS JOURNAL								PAGE 3	
						1	2	3	4	5		
	DATE		ACCOUNT TITLE	CK. NO.	POST. REF.	GENERAL		ACCOUNTS PAYABLE DEBIT	PURCHASES DISCOUNT CREDIT	CASH CREDIT		
						DEBIT	CREDIT					
1	20-- Feb.	1	Property Tax Expense	69		720 00				720 00		1
2												2

For tax purposes, state and federal governments define two kinds of property—real and personal. Land and anything attached to the land is called **real property**. Real property is sometimes referred to as *real estate*. All property not classified as real property is called **personal property**. For tax purposes, these definitions apply whether the property is owned by a business or an individual.

The value of an asset determined by tax authorities for the purpose of calculating taxes is called the **assessed value**. Assessed value is usually based on the judgment of persons referred to as assessors. Assessors are elected by citizens or are specially trained employees of a governmental unit.

Most governmental units with taxing power have a tax based on the value of real property. The real property tax is used on buildings and land. Some governmental units also tax personal property such as cars, boats, trailers, and airplanes.

A governmental taxing unit determines a tax rate to use in calculating taxes. The tax rate is multiplied by an asset's assessed value, not the value recorded on a business's records.

Classic Parts, Inc., owns real property that has been assessed for a total of $60,000.00. The city tax rate is 1.2%.

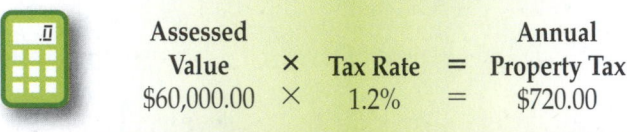

Assessed Value		Tax Rate		Annual Property Tax
$60,000.00	×	1.2%	=	$720.00

February 1. Classic Parts, Inc., paid cash for property tax, $720.00. Check No. 69.

Payment of property taxes is necessary if a firm is to continue in business. Therefore, Classic Parts, Inc., classifies property tax as an operating expense.

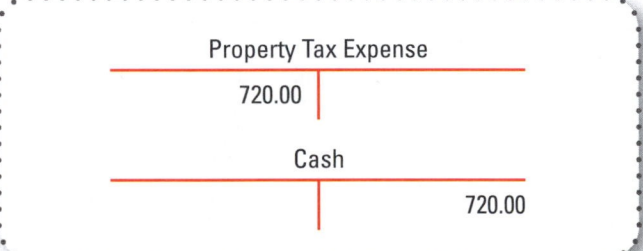

Property Tax Expense	
720.00	

Cash	
	720.00

FOR YOUR INFORMATION

FYI

The assessed value of an asset may not be the same as the value on the business's or individual's records. The assessed value is assigned to an asset for tax purposes only. Often the assessed value is only a part of the true value of the asset.

Accounting for Plant Assets and Depreciation

End of Lesson
REVIEW

TERMS REVIEW

real property

personal property

assessed value

AUDIT YOUR UNDERSTANDING

1. What accounts are affected, and how, when cash is paid for office equipment?
2. What items are included in real property?
3. Who determines the assessed value of plant assets?

WORK TOGETHER 18-1

Journalizing buying plant assets and paying property tax

The cash payments journal and selected general ledger accounts for Singh Paint Store are given in the *Working Papers*. Your instructor will guide you through the following examples.

1. Journalize the following transactions completed during the current year. Use page 1 of a cash payments journal. The abbreviation for a check is C.

Transactions:
- Jan. 3. Paid cash for a paint mixer, $500.00. C142.
- 5. Paid cash for an office chair, $400.00. C145.
- Feb. 26. Paid property taxes on real property with an assessed value of $80,000.00. The tax rate in the city where the property is located is 3.0% of assessed value. C182.
- July 2. Paid cash for a filing cabinet, $260.00. C216.

2. Post the general columns of the cash payments journal.

ON YOUR OWN 18-1

Journalizing buying plant assets and paying property tax

The cash payments journal and selected general ledger accounts for Herrera Tile Center are given in the *Working Papers*. Work this problem independently.

1. Journalize the following transactions completed during the current year. Use page 1 of a cash payments journal. The abbreviation for a check is C.

Transactions:
- Jan. 2. Paid cash for a computer printer, $1,800.00. C215.
- 5. Paid cash for a tile cutter, $520.00. C216.
- Feb. 24. Paid property taxes on real property with an assessed value of $72,000.00. The tax rate in the city where the property is located is 2.5% of assessed value. C232.
- Mar. 13. Paid cash for a dolly, $325.00. C283.

2. Post the general columns of the cash payments journal.

Calculating Depreciation Expense

STRAIGHT-LINE DEPRECIATION

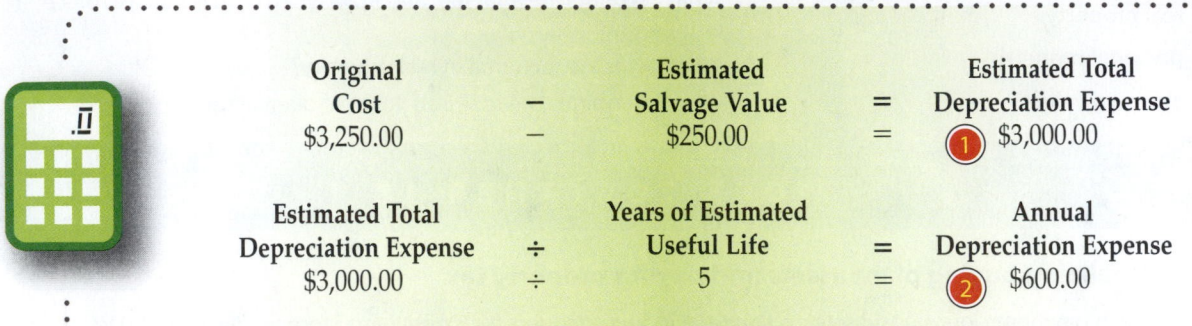

Original Cost	–	Estimated Salvage Value	=	Estimated Total Depreciation Expense
$3,250.00	–	$250.00	=	① $3,000.00

Estimated Total Depreciation Expense	÷	Years of Estimated Useful Life	=	Annual Depreciation Expense
$3,000.00	÷	5	=	② $600.00

Plant assets are expected to be used in the business for many years. Generally accepted accounting principles require that the cost of a plant asset be expensed over the plant asset's useful life. [CONCEPT: Matching Expenses with Revenues] The annual expense is recorded in Depreciation Expense and the contra asset account Accumulated Depreciation.

Several methods for calculating depreciation expense are available. The easiest and most widely used method is known as the *straight-line method of depreciation*. The method requires the business to know the cost of the plant asset and to estimate two amounts:

1. The amount the business expects to receive when a plant asset is removed from use, known as the *estimated salvage value*.
2. The number of years a plant asset is expected to be used, known as the *estimated useful life*.

The straight-line method of depreciation charges an equal amount of depreciation expense in each full year in which the asset is used.

On January 3, 20X1, Restaurant Supply bought a lighted display case for $3,250.00 with an estimated salvage value of $250.00 and an estimated useful life of 5 years.

FOR YOUR INFORMATION

FYI

The estimated useful life should be based on prior experience with similar assets and on available guidelines. Trade associations frequently publish guidelines for specialized plant assets. The Internal Revenue Service also publishes depreciation guidelines for plant assets.

 STEPS **CALCULATING ANNUAL DEPRECIATION EXPENSE**

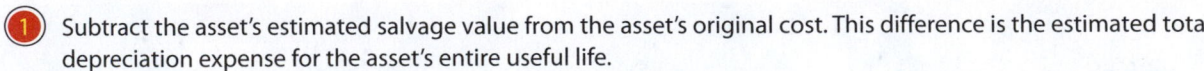

① Subtract the asset's estimated salvage value from the asset's original cost. This difference is the estimated total depreciation expense for the asset's entire useful life.

② Divide the estimated total depreciation expense by the years of estimated useful life. The result is the annual depreciation expense.

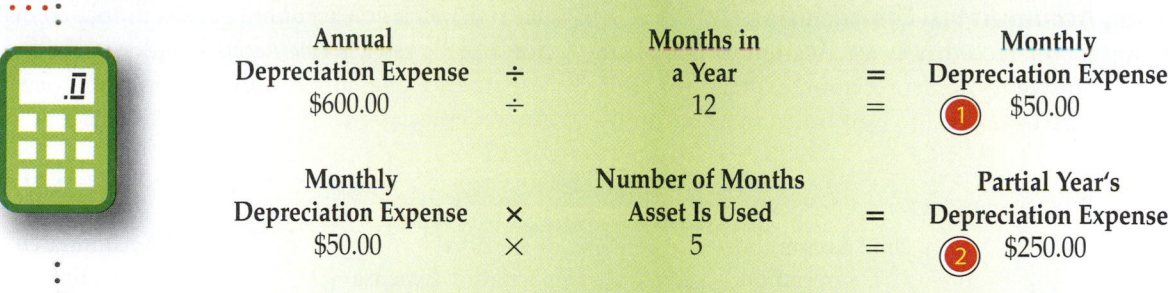

Annual Depreciation Expense $600.00	÷	Months in a Year 12	=	Monthly Depreciation Expense ① $50.00
Monthly Depreciation Expense $50.00	×	Number of Months Asset Is Used 5	=	Partial Year's Depreciation Expense ② $250.00

A month is the smallest unit of time used to calculate depreciation. A plant asset may be placed in service at a date other than the first day of a fiscal period. In such cases, a business may elect to calculate depreciation expense to the nearest first of a month. A partial year's depreciation may also be recorded in the year the plant asset is sold or disposed of.

Restaurant Supply bought a point-of-sale terminal on August 2, 20X1. The annual straight-line depreciation expense is $600.00. The depreciation expense is $250.00 for the remaining 5 months of the year in which Restaurant Supply used the computer.

 **STEPS** CALCULATING PARTIAL YEAR'S DEPRECIATION EXPENSE

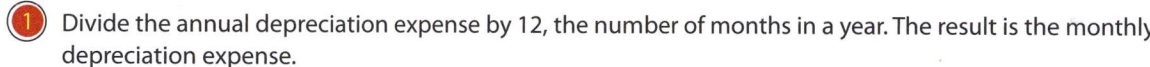 ① Divide the annual depreciation expense by 12, the number of months in a year. The result is the monthly depreciation expense.

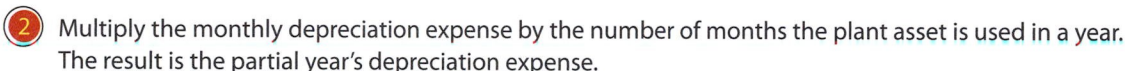 ② Multiply the monthly depreciation expense by the number of months the plant asset is used in a year. The result is the partial year's depreciation expense.

The five years' depreciation expense is illustrated below. In the first year, a partial year's depreciation is recorded: August 1, 20X1 to December 31, 20X1—five months. If the asset had been purchased August 16 or later, only four months' depreciation would be expensed because the date would be closer to September 1 than August 1. In the next four years, a full year's depreciation, $600.00, would be expensed each year. In 20X6, the original five-year useful life ends July 31, so seven months' depreciation would be recorded.

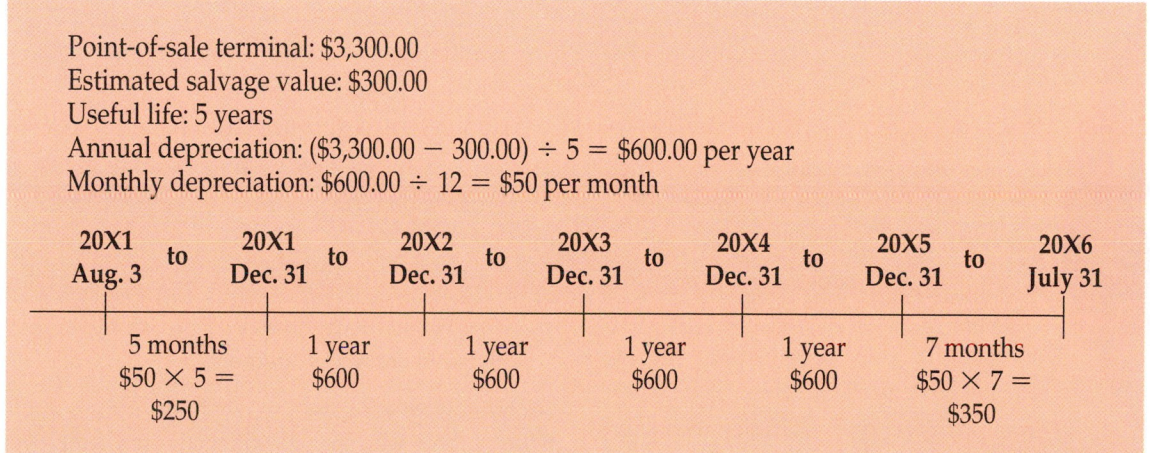

Point-of-sale terminal: $3,300.00
Estimated salvage value: $300.00
Useful life: 5 years
Annual depreciation: ($3,300.00 − 300.00) ÷ 5 = $600.00 per year
Monthly depreciation: $600.00 ÷ 12 = $50 per month

20X1 Aug. 3	to	20X1 Dec. 31	to	20X2 Dec. 31	to	20X3 Dec. 31	to	20X4 Dec. 31	to	20X5 Dec. 31	to	20X6 July 31
5 months $50 × 5 = $250		1 year $600		1 year $600		1 year $600		1 year $600		7 months $50 × 7 = $350		

Plant assets may continue to be used after their estimated useful lives have ended; however, no additional depreciation is recorded.

Calculating Accumulated Depreciation

Depreciation is not recorded as a reduction of the plant asset account. Instead, the depreciation expense for each year of a plant asset's useful life is recorded in an accumulated depreciation account. The accumulated depreciation for a plant asset is calculated by adding the depreciation expense for the current year to the prior year's accumulated depreciation.

20X2 Accumulated Depreciation	+	20X3 Depreciation Expense	=	20X3 Accumulated Depreciation
$1,200.00	+	$600.00	=	$1,800.00

Calculating Book Value

The original cost of a plant asset minus accumulated depreciation is known as the *book value of a plant asset*. The book value is calculated by subtracting the accumulated depreciation from the original cost of the plant asset. The ending book value is the beginning book value for the next year.

Original Cost	−	Accumulated Depreciation	=	Ending Book Value
$3,250.00	−	$1,800.00	=	$1,450.00

The book value can also be calculated by subtracting the year's depreciation from that year's beginning book value. Either method of calculating a book value is acceptable because both methods calculate the same amount.

CULTURAL DIVERSITY

Valuing Diversity in the Workplace

Employees in the U.S. have diverse cultural backgrounds. This diversity reflects the cultural differences in society. All employees bring their cultural backgrounds and values with them to the workplace.

Cultural differences do not exist only between people from different countries. They may arise with anyone in the workplace perceived to be different from the norm. Consider the differences in employees who are younger or older than average, who are physically challenged, or who speak English as a second language.

Enlightened companies will encourage "valuing diversity" in the workplace. This means valuing the cultural backgrounds of each individual. It means respecting each person for what he or she can contribute to the goals of the organization.

Critical Thinking

1. What would be the result if culturally different employees could not work together?

2. What do you think should be the consequence for an employee who cannot work with other employees of different cultural backgrounds?

PHOTO: DIGITAL VISION/GETTY IMAGES

End of Lesson REVIEW

1. Which accounting concept is being applied when depreciation expense is recorded for plant assets?
2. What three amounts are used to calculate a plant asset's annual depreciation expense using the straight-line method of depreciation?

WORK TOGETHER 18-2

Calculating depreciation

Depreciation tables for Fairbrother, Inc., are given in the *Working Papers*. Your instructor will guide you through the following example.

1. Fairbrother, Inc., bought the following assets during 20X1. Complete a depreciation table for each asset using the straight-line depreciation method. If the asset was not bought at the beginning of 20X1, calculate the depreciation expense for the part of 20X1 in which the company owned the asset. Save your work to complete Work Together 18-3.

Transactions:

Jan. 3. Bought a computer monitor costing $560.00; estimated salvage value, $60.00; estimated useful life, 5 years.

Oct. 19. Bought a notebook computer, $2,750.00; estimated salvage value, $350.00; estimated useful life, 4 years.

ON YOUR OWN 18-2

Calculating depreciation

Depreciation tables for Wrench Co. are given in the *Working Papers*. Work this problem independently.

1. Wrench Co. bought the following assets during 20X1. Complete a depreciation table for each asset using the straight-line depreciation method. If the asset was not bought at the beginning of 20X1, calculate the depreciation expense for the part of 20X1 in which the company owned the asset. Save your work to complete On Your Own 18-3.

Transactions:

Jan. 6. Bought a sound system costing $5,600.00; estimated salvage value, $400.00; estimated useful life, 8 years.

May 22. Bought a shredder, $1,250.00; estimated salvage value, $50.00; estimated useful life, 5 years.

PREPARING PLANT ASSET RECORDS

PLANT ASSET RECORD No. _62_			General Ledger Account No. _____ 1215	
Description _____ *Display Case*			General Ledger Account _____ *Store Equipment*	
Date Bought _____ *January 3, 20X1*	Serial Number _____ D2679-26		Original Cost _____ $3,250.00	①
Estimated Useful Life _____ *5 years*	Estimated Salvage Value _____ $250.00		Depreciation Method _____ *Straight-line*	
Disposed of: _____ Discarded _____		Sold _____	Traded _____	②
Date _____		Disposal Amount _____		

YEAR	ANNUAL DEPRECIATION EXPENSE	ACCUMULATED DEPRECIATION	ENDING BOOK VALUE	
20X1	$600.00	$ 600.00	$2650.00	③
20X2	600.00	1,200.00	2,050.00	
20X3	600.00	1,800.00	1,450.00	
20X4	600.00	2,400.00	850.00	
20X5	600.00	3,000.00	250.00	

Continue record on back of card

A separate record is kept for each plant asset. An accounting form on which a business records information about each plant asset is called a **plant asset record**.

Plant asset records may vary in arrangement for different businesses, but most records contain similar information. Restaurant Supply's plant asset record has three sections. Section 1 is prepared when a plant asset is bought. Section 2 provides space for recording the disposition of the plant asset. When the asset is disposed of, this information will be filled in. Section 3 provides space for recording annual depreciation expense and the changing book value of the asset each year it is used.

At the end of each fiscal period, Restaurant Supply brings each plant asset record up to date by recording three amounts: (1) annual depreciation expense, (2) accumulated depreciation, and (3) ending book value.

The amount recorded in the Annual Depreciation Expense column is the amount calculated for each year. These amounts may be different if the asset is bought or sold at a time other than near the fiscal year beginning or end.

Accumulated depreciation for the first year is the annual depreciation expense for the first year. In later years, accu-

mulated depreciation is the depreciation expense that has accumulated over all prior years added to that year's annual depreciation expense.

The ending book value is the original cost less that year's accumulated depreciation.

STEPS — **PREPARING A PLANT ASSET RECORD**

① Write the information in Section 1 when the plant asset is purchased.

② Do not write in Section 2 until the asset is disposed of.

③ Each year the asset is owned, record the year's annual depreciation expense in Section 3. Calculate and record accumulated depreciation and ending book value.

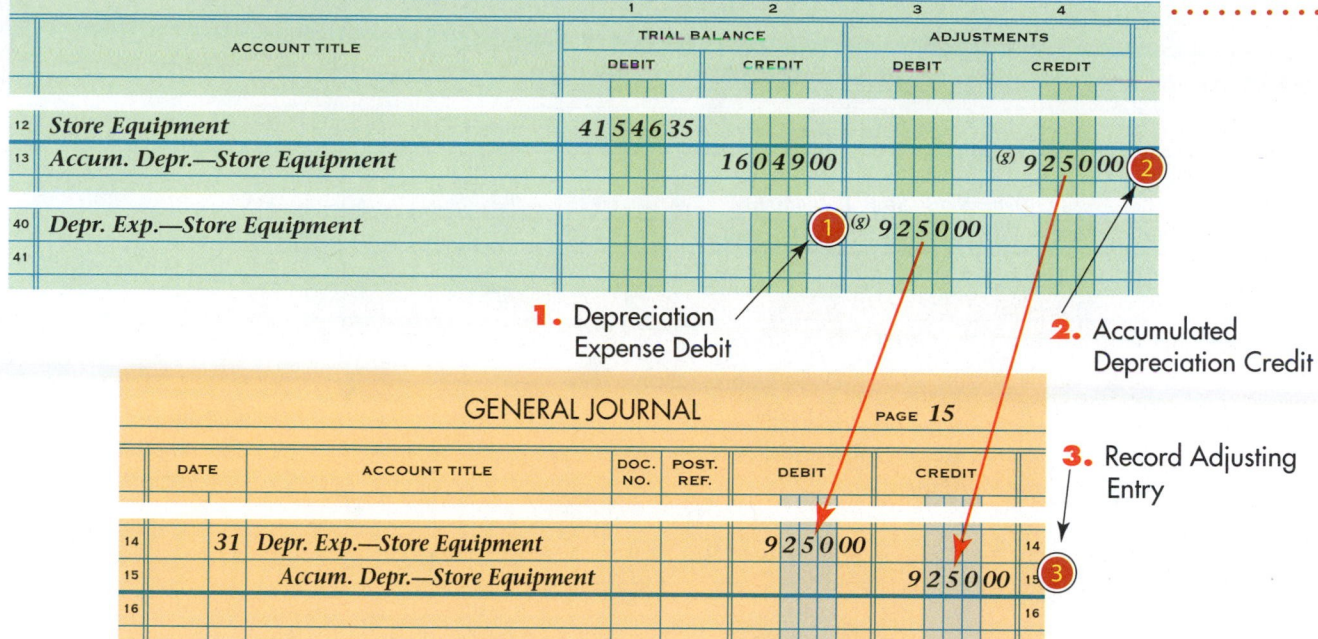

1. Depreciation Expense Debit

2. Accumulated Depreciation Credit

3. Record Adjusting Entry

At the end of the fiscal year, Restaurant Supply calculates the depreciation expense for each plant asset. The depreciation expense for each asset is recorded on its plant asset record. Next, the total depreciation expense is calculated for all plant assets recorded in the same plant asset account.

Restaurant Supply determined that total depreciation expense for store equipment is $9,250.00. An adjustment is planned in the Adjustments columns of the work sheet. Using this information, an adjusting entry is then recorded in a general journal.

It is important to retain original cost information for plant assets. Rather than credit the plant asset account, depreciation is recorded to the contra asset account Accumulated Depreciation.

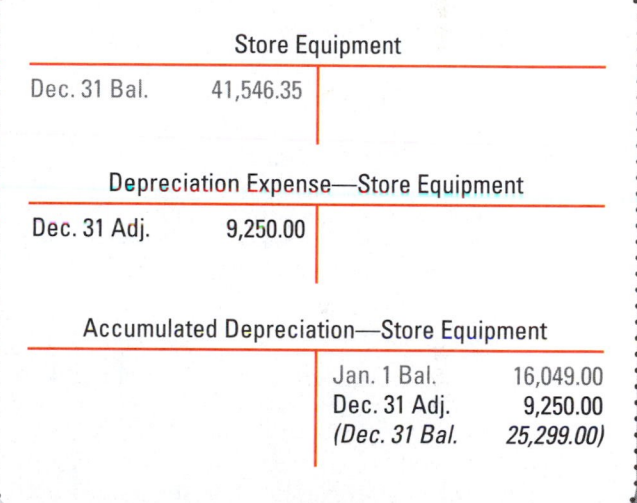

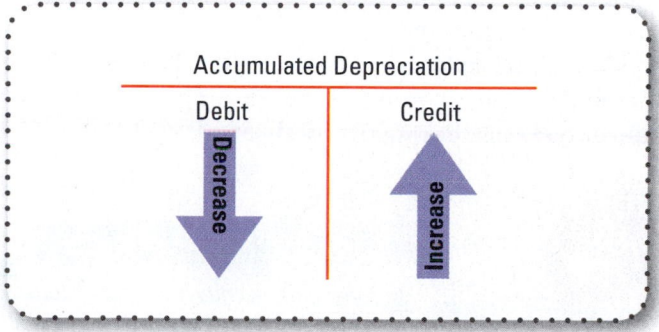

At any time, the book value of plant assets can be calculated by subtracting Accumulated Depreciation from the plant asset account.

STEPS — ANALYZING AND JOURNALIZING ANNUAL DEPRECIATION EXPENSE

1. Write the total annual depreciation expense, *$9,250.00*, in the Adjustments Debit column on the *Depreciation Expense—Store Equipment* line of the work sheet. Label the adjustment *(g)*, with a small letter in parentheses.

2. Write the same amount, *$9,250.00*, in the Adjustments Credit column on the *Accumulated Depreciation—Store Equipment* line of the work sheet. Label the adjustment using the same letter, *(g)*.

3. Use the debit and credit accounts on the work sheet to record an adjusting entry in a general journal.

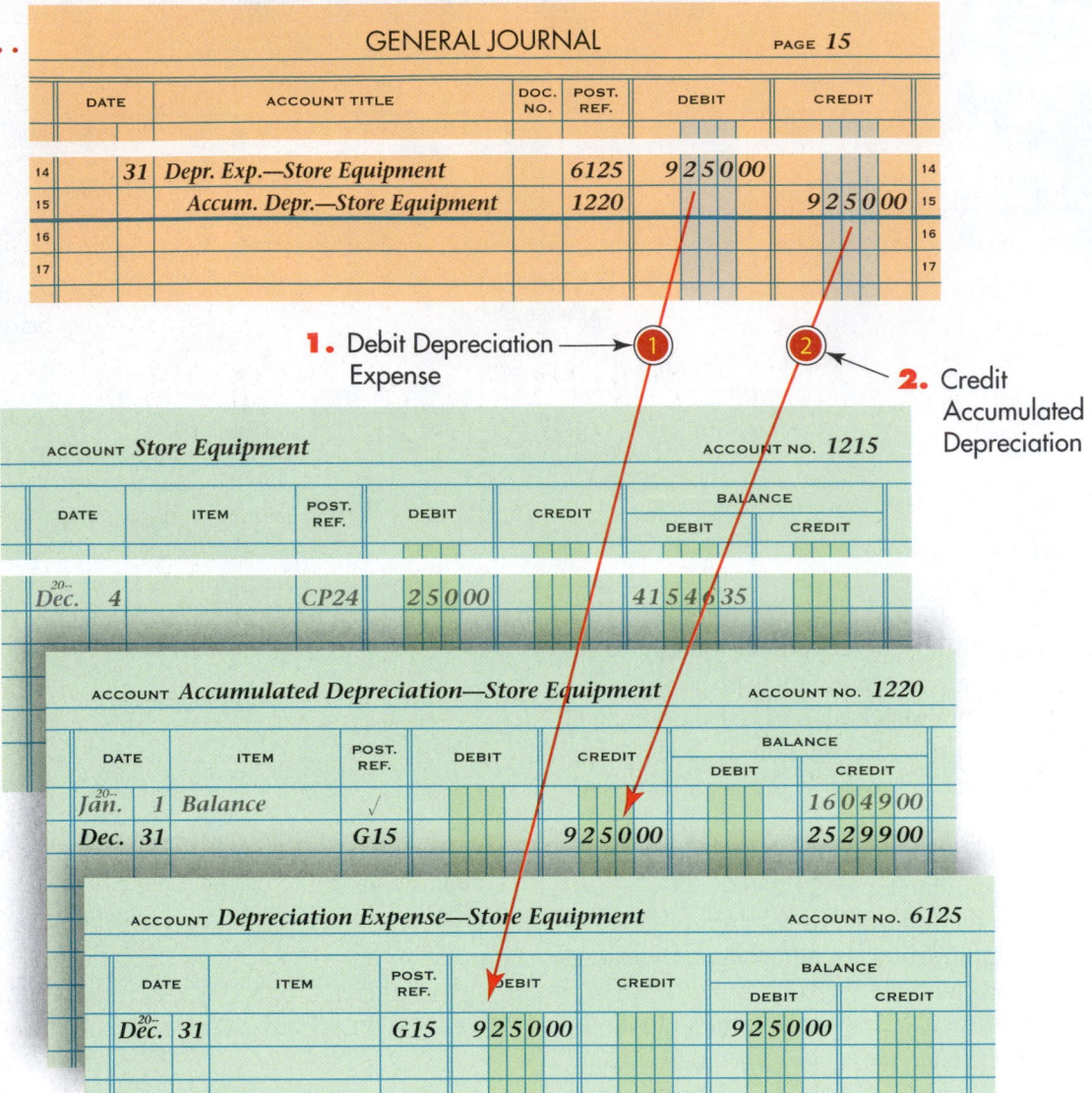

1. Debit Depreciation Expense ① ② **2.** Credit Accumulated Depreciation

The adjustment for depreciation expense planned on the work sheet is recorded as an adjusting entry in the general journal. The adjusting entry is then posted to the general ledger.

After posting, Store Equipment has a debit balance showing the original cost of all store equipment. The con-

tra account Accumulated Depreciation—Store Equipment has a credit balance showing the accumulated depreciation recorded to date.

The debit balance of Depreciation Expense—Store Equipment is the portion of the cost of plant assets allocated to expense during the fiscal period.

STEPS ◉ POSTING AN ADJUSTING ENTRY FOR DEPRECIATION EXPENSE

① Post the debit, $9,250.00, to Depreciation Expense—Store Equipment.

② Post the credit, $9,250.00, to Accumulated Depreciation—Store Equipment.

REMEMBER

An adjusting entry is made to record the depreciation expense for each category of plant assets. Restaurant Supply also records an adjusting entry for Depreciation Expense—Office Equipment and Accumulated Depreciation—Office Equipment.

TERM REVIEW

plant asset record

1. What method is used to record accumulated depreciation while also retaining original cost information for plant assets?
2. How does an adjusting entry for depreciation expense change the balance of the asset account?

WORK TOGETHER 18-3

Journalizing depreciation

Use the depreciation tables from Work Together 18-2. Additional forms are given in the *Working Papers*. Your instructor will guide you through the following examples.

1. Complete each plant asset record for the years 20X1 through 20X3. Use the following additional information.

Description	General Ledger Account	Date Bought	Plant Asset No.	Serial No.
Computer Monitor	1215-Store Equipment	Jan. 3	241	51-4882
Notebook Computer	1205-Office Equipment	Oct. 19	242	GY1281

2. On December 31, Fairbrother, Inc., determined that total depreciation expense for office equipment was $4,230.00. Plan the work sheet adjustment and label the adjustment (f). Record the adjusting entry on page 20 of a general journal and post the entry to the general ledger. Save your work to complete Work Together 18-4.

ON YOUR OWN 18-3

Journalizing depreciation

Use the depreciation tables from On Your Own 18-2. Additional forms are given in the *Working Papers*. Work this problem independently.

1. Complete each plant asset record from the years 20X1 through 20X3. Use the following additional information:

Description	General Ledger Account	Date Bought	Plant Asset No.	Serial No.
Sound System	1215-Store Equipment	Jan. 6	353	12488BF2
Shredder	1205-Office Equipment	May 22	354	34-432-2

2. On December 31, Wrench Co. determined that total depreciation expense for store equipment was $9,880.00. Plan the work sheet adjustment and label the adjustment (g). Record the adjusting entry on page 18 of a general journal and post the entry to the general ledger. Save your work to complete On Your Own 18-4.

Disposing of Plant Assets

SALE OF A PLANT ASSET FOR BOOK VALUE

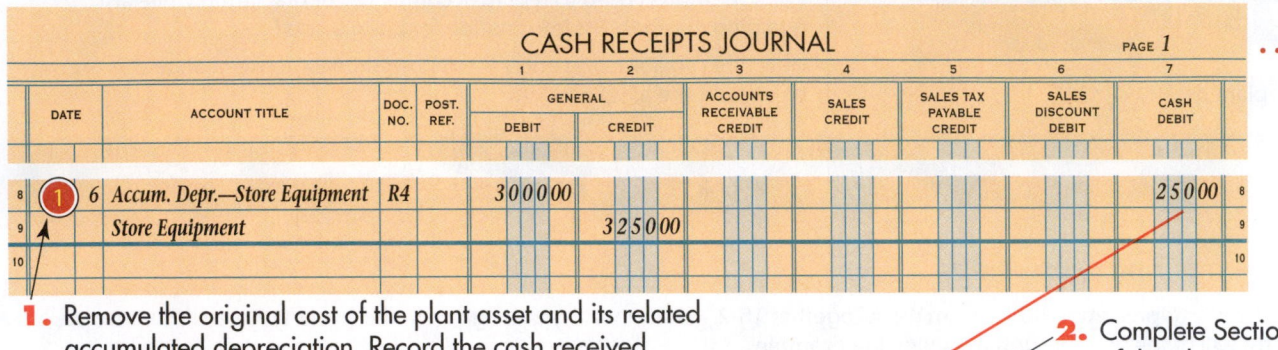

						1	2	3	4	5	6	7	
						GENERAL		ACCOUNTS RECEIVABLE CREDIT	SALES CREDIT	SALES TAX PAYABLE CREDIT	SALES DISCOUNT DEBIT	CASH DEBIT	
	DATE	ACCOUNT TITLE	DOC. NO.	POST. REF.		DEBIT	CREDIT						
8	6	Accum. Depr.—Store Equipment	R4			3 0 0 0 00						2 5 0 00	8
9		Store Equipment					3 2 5 0 00						9
10													10

CASH RECEIPTS JOURNAL   PAGE 1

1. Remove the original cost of the plant asset and its related accumulated depreciation. Record the cash received.

Disposed of: Discarded _____   Sold ___✓___   Traded _____

Date _____ **January 6, 20X6** _____   Disposal Amount _____ **$250.00** _____

2. Complete Section 2 of the plant asset record.

When a plant asset is no longer useful to a business, the asset may be disposed of. The old plant asset may be sold, traded for a new asset, or discarded.

When a plant asset is disposed of, a journal entry is recorded that achieves the following:

1. Removes the original cost of the plant asset and its related accumulated depreciation.
2. Recognizes any cash or other asset received for the old plant asset.
3. Recognizes any gain or loss on the disposal.

Cash received		$250.00
Less: Book value of asset sold:		
Cost	$3,250.00	
Accum. Depr.	3,000.00	250.00
Gain (loss) on sale of plant asset		$ 0.00

The amount of gain or loss, if any, is calculated by subtracting the book value from the cash received. The display case was sold for its book value. Therefore, no gain or loss exists.

January 6, 20X6. Received cash from sale of display case, $250.00: original cost, $3,250.00; total accumulated depreciation through December 31, 20X5, $3,000.00. Receipt No. 4.

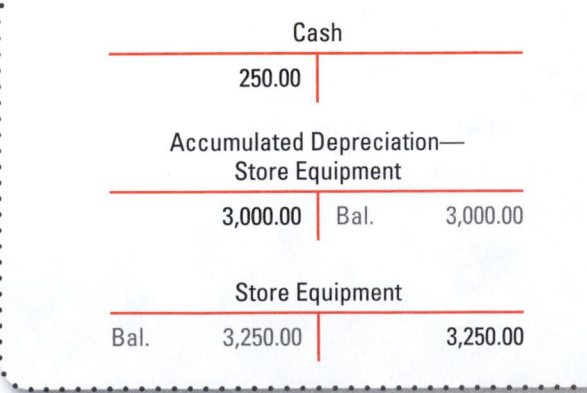

STEPS   **RECORDING SALE OF A PLANT ASSET FOR BOOK VALUE**

1. Record an entry in the cash receipts journal to remove the original cost, *$3,250.00*, from *Store Equipment* and *$3,000.00* from *Accumulated Depreciation—Store Equipment*. Record the cash received from the sale, *$250.00*, as a debit to *Cash*.

2. Check the type of disposal, *Sold*, and write the date, *January 6, 20X6*, and disposal amount, *$250.00*, in Section 2 of the plant asset record.

RECORDING A PLANT ASSET'S DEPRECIATION EXPENSE FOR A PARTIAL YEAR

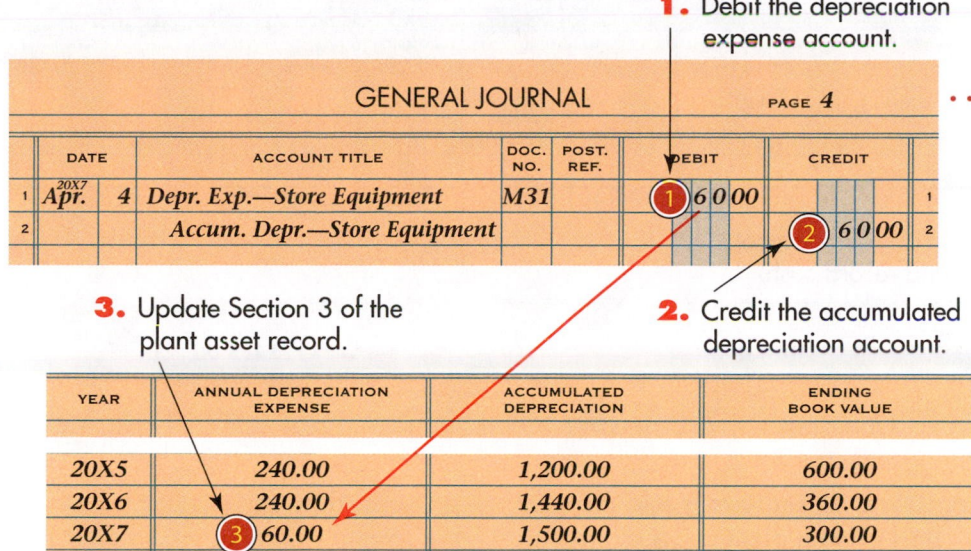

1. Debit the depreciation expense account.

GENERAL JOURNAL   PAGE **4**

	DATE		ACCOUNT TITLE	DOC. NO.	POST. REF.	DEBIT	CREDIT	
1	20X7 Apr.	4	Depr. Exp.—Store Equipment	M31		① 6 0 00		1
2			Accum. Depr.—Store Equipment				② 6 0 00	2

2. Credit the accumulated depreciation account.

3. Update Section 3 of the plant asset record.

YEAR	ANNUAL DEPRECIATION EXPENSE	ACCUMULATED DEPRECIATION	ENDING BOOK VALUE
20X5	240.00	1,200.00	600.00
20X6	240.00	1,440.00	360.00
20X7	③ 60.00	1,500.00	300.00

A plant asset may be sold at any time during the asset's useful life. When a plant asset is sold, its depreciation from the beginning of the current fiscal year to the date of disposal must be recorded.

On April 4, 20X7, Restaurant Supply intends to sell a safe that was bought on January 12, 20X1, for $1,800.00. Annual depreciation expense for the safe is $240.00. Depreciation recorded through December 31, 20X6, is $1,440.00.

The method to calculate a partial year's depreciation is the same as calculating depreciation when an asset is purchased during the fiscal year. The monthly depreciation expense is multiplied by the number of months the asset is used during the current fiscal year. Depreciation is calculated for each month prior to the month the plant asset is sold. Thus, Restaurant Supply will depreciate the safe for three months, January through March.

April 4, 20X7. Recorded a partial year's depreciation on a safe to be sold, $60.00. Memorandum No. 31.

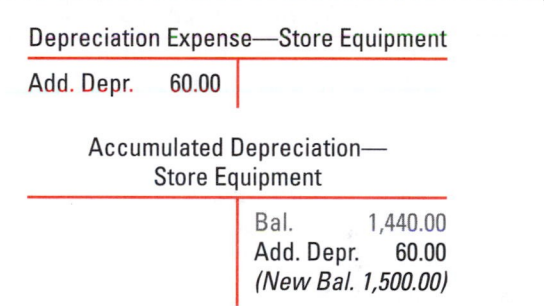

Depreciation Expense—Store Equipment

| Add. Depr. | 60.00 | |

Accumulated Depreciation—Store Equipment

	Bal.	1,440.00
	Add. Depr.	60.00
	(New Bal. 1,500.00)	

The depreciation is also recorded on the plant asset record for the safe.

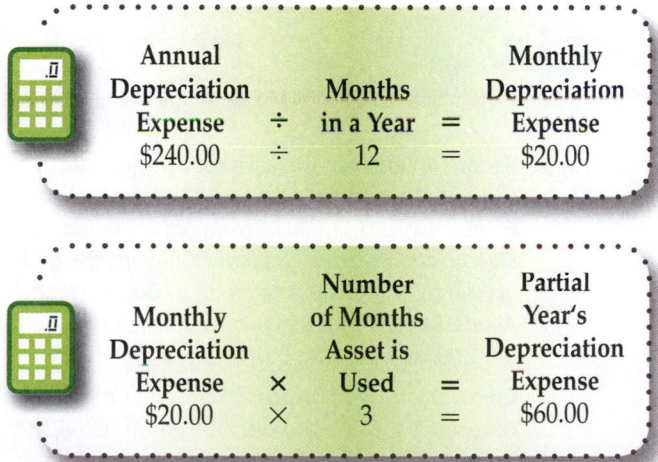

Annual Depreciation Expense	÷	Months in a Year	=	Monthly Depreciation Expense
$240.00	÷	12	=	$20.00

Monthly Depreciation Expense	×	Number of Months Asset is Used	=	Partial Year's Depreciation Expense
$20.00	×	3	=	$60.00

STEPS   **RECORDING A PARTIAL YEAR'S DEPRECIATION**

① Record a debit, *$60.00*, to *Depreciation Expense—Store Equipment* in the general journal.

② Record a credit, *$60.00*, to *Accumulated Depreciation—Store Equipment* in the general journal.

③ Record the depreciation expense in Section 3 of the plant asset record for the safe. Calculate and record accumulated depreciation and ending book value.

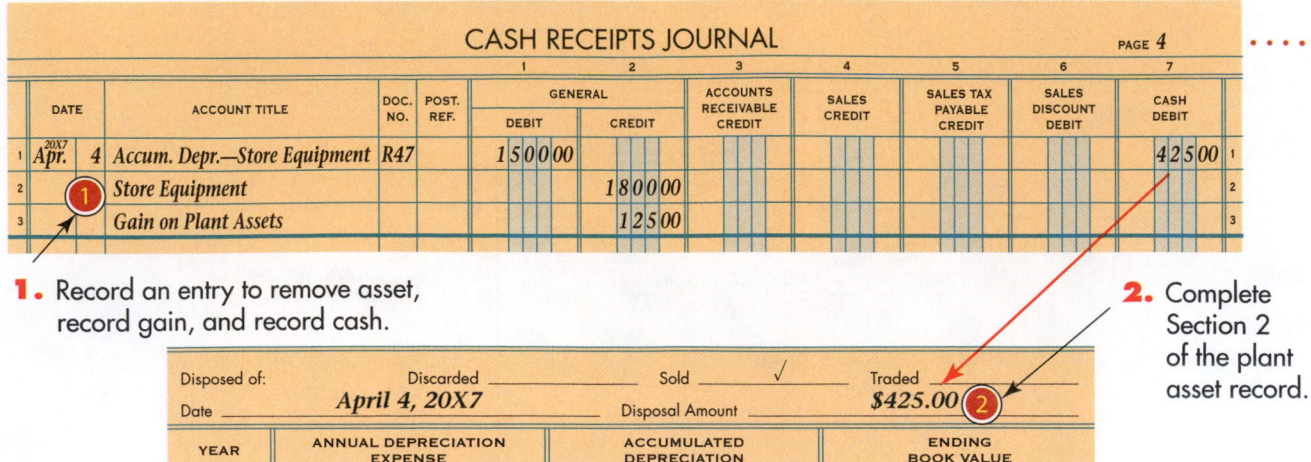

1. Record an entry to remove asset, record gain, and record cash.

2. Complete Section 2 of the plant asset record.

Revenue that results when a plant asset is sold for more than book value is called **gain on plant assets**. Restaurant Supply is selling a safe for $425.00. After the partial year's depreciation is recorded, a journal entry is made to record the sale of the safe.

> *April 4, 20X7. Received cash from sale of safe, $425.00: original cost, $1,800.00; accumulated depreciation through April 4, 20X7, $1,500.00. Receipt No. 47.*

The gain or loss on the sale of a plant asset is the book value subtracted from cash received.

Cash received		$425.00
Less: Book value of asset sold:		
Cost	$1,800.00	
Accum. Depr.	1,500.00	300.00
Gain (loss) on sale of plant asset		$125.00

The gain realized on the disposal of a plant asset is credited to a revenue account titled Gain on Plant Assets.

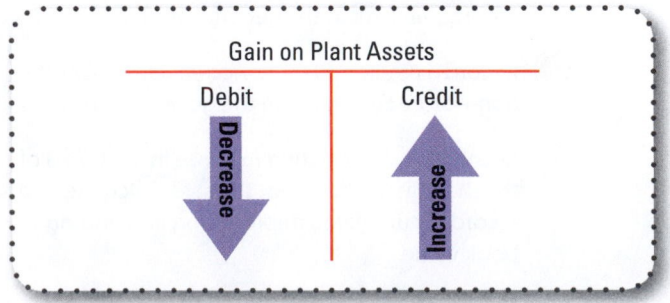

A gain from the sale of plant assets is not an operating revenue. Therefore, Gain on Plant Assets is listed in a classification titled "Other Revenue" in the chart of accounts.

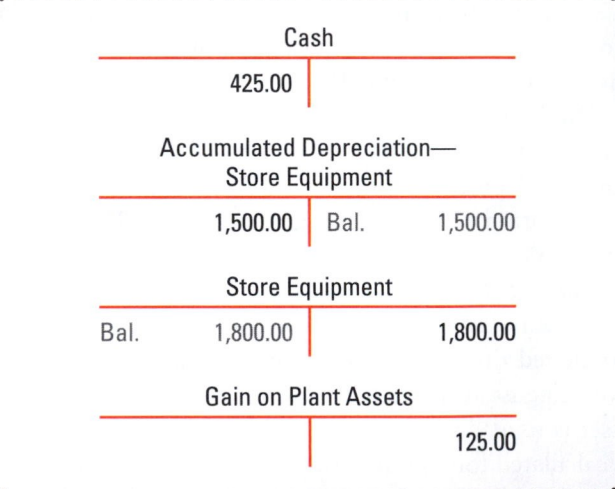

RECORDING SALE OF A PLANT ASSET FOR MORE THAN BOOK VALUE

S T E P S

1. Record an entry in the cash receipts journal to remove the original cost, *$1,800.00*, from *Store Equipment* and *$1,500.00* from *Accumulated Depreciation—Store Equipment*. Record the gain on the sale, *$125.00*, as a credit to *Gain on Plant Assets*. Record the cash received from the sale, *$425.00*, as a debit to *Cash*.

2. Check the type of disposal, *Sold*, and write the date, *April 4, 20X7*, and disposal amount, *$425.00*, in Section 2 of the plant asset record for the safe.

	DATE	ACCOUNT TITLE	DOC. NO.	POST. REF.	GENERAL		ACCOUNTS RECEIVABLE CREDIT	SALES CREDIT	SALES TAX PAYABLE CREDIT	SALES DISCOUNT DEBIT	CASH DEBIT	
					DEBIT	CREDIT						
1	20X7 Oct. 6	Accum. Depr.—Office Equipment	R281		1 5 0 0 00						1 5 0 00	1
2		Loss on Plant Assets			2 5 0 00							2
3		Office Equipment				1 9 0 0 00						3

1. Record an entry to dispose of the asset, record a loss on plant assets, and record cash.

2. Complete Section 2 of the plant asset record.

Disposed of:		Discarded _____	Sold ____✓____	Traded _____	
Date	October 6, 20X7		Disposal Amount _____	$150.00	2

The loss that results when a plant asset is sold for less than book value is called **loss on plant assets**. Restaurant Supply sold a computer after three years of use. After the partial year's depreciation is recorded, a journal entry is made to record the sale of the computer.

October 6, 20X7. Received cash from sale of a computer, $150.00: original cost, $1,900.00; total accumulated depreciation through October 1, 20X7, $1,500.00. Receipt No. 281.

The gain or loss on the sale of a plant asset is the book value subtracted from cash received.

Cash received		$ 150.00
Less: Book value of asset sold:		
Cost	$1,900.00	
Accum. Depr.	1,500.00	400.00
Gain (loss) on sale of plant asset		$(250.00)

The loss realized on the disposal of a plant asset is debited to an other expense account titled Loss on Plant Assets.

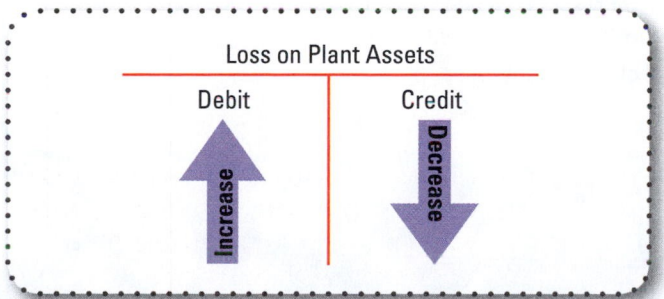

A loss from the sale of plant assets is not an operating expense. Therefore, Loss on Plant Assets is listed in a classification titled "Other Expenses" in the chart of accounts.

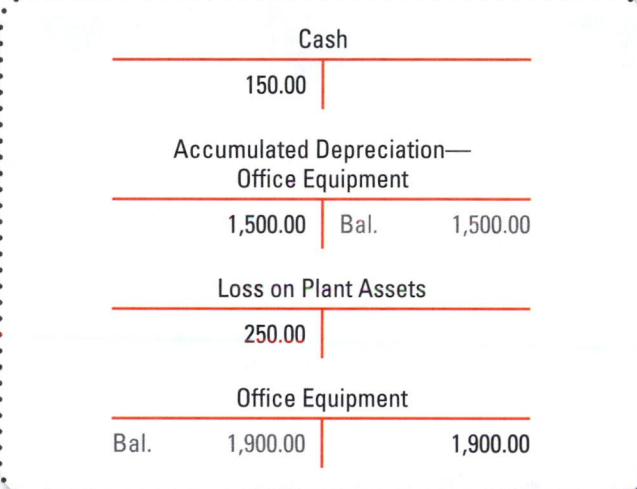

STEPS — RECORDING SALE OF A PLANT ASSET FOR LESS THAN BOOK VALUE

1. Record an entry in the cash receipts journal to remove the original cost, *$1,900.00*, from *Office Equipment* and *$1,500.00* from *Accumulated Depreciation—Office Equipment*. Record the loss on the sale, *$250.00*, as a debit to *Loss on Plant Assets*. Record the cash received from the sale, *$150.00*, as a debit to *Cash*.

2. Check the type of disposal, *Sold*, and write the date, *Oct. 6, 20X7*, and disposal amount, *$150.00*, in Section 2 of the plant asset record for the computer.

End of Lesson REVIEW

1. What is recorded on plant asset records for plant assets that have been disposed of?
2. When an asset is disposed of after the beginning of the fiscal year, what entry may need to be recorded before an entry is made for the discarding of a plant asset?
3. What is the formula to calculate the gain or loss on the sale of a plant asset?
4. In what account classification is Loss on Plant Assets listed?

TERMS REVIEW

gain on plant assets

loss on plant assets

WORK TOGETHER 18-4

Recording the disposal of plant assets

Use the plant asset records from Work Together 18-3. Your instructor will guide you through the following examples.

1. For each of the following transactions completed in 20X4, journalize an entry for additional depreciation, if needed. Use page 11 of a general journal given in the *Working Papers*. Source documents are abbreviated as follows: memorandum, M; receipt, R.

Transactions:
    Jan. 6. Received cash for sale of a computer monitor, plant asset No. 241, $290.00. R4.
    Jul. 12. Received cash for sale of a notebook computer, plant asset No. 242, $800.00. M67 and R203.

2. Use page 1 of a cash receipts journal to record the disposal of each plant asset.

3. Make appropriate notations in the plant asset records.

ON YOUR OWN 18-4

Recording the disposal of plant assets

Use the plant asset records from On Your Own 18-3. Work this problem independently.

1. For each of the following transactions completed in 20X4, journalize an entry for additional depreciation, if needed. Use page 10 of a general journal given in the *Working Papers*. Source documents are abbreviated as follows: memorandum, M; receipt, R.

Transactions:
    Jan. 2. Received cash for sale of a sound system, plant asset No. 353, $4,000.00. R11.
    Oct. 3. Received cash for sale of a shredder, plant asset No. 354, $325.00. M82 and R255.

2. Use page 8 of a cash receipts journal to record the disposal of each plant asset.

3. Make appropriate notations in the plant asset records.

Declining-Balance Method of Depreciation

CALCULATING DEPRECIATION USING THE DOUBLE DECLINING-BALANCE METHOD

Plant Asset: Truck
Depreciation Method: Double Declining-Balance

Original Cost: $25,000.00
Estimated Salvage Value: $2,500.00
Estimated Useful Life: 5 years

Year	Beginning Book Value	Declining-Balance Rate ①	Annual Depreciation	Ending Book Value
1	$25,000.00	40%	② $10,000.00	③ $15,000.00
2	④ 15,000.00	40%	6,000.00	9,000.00

4. Transfer the book value to the following year.

1. Calculate rate.

2. Determine the annual depreciation expense.

3. Determine the ending book value.

The straight-line method charges an equal amount of depreciation expense each year. However, many plant assets depreciate more in the early years of useful life than in later years. For example, a truck's value will decrease more in the first year than in later years. Therefore, charging more depreciation expense in the early years may be more accurate than charging the same amount each year. [CONCEPT: Matching Expenses with Revenue]

Multiplying the book value by a constant depreciation rate at the end of each fiscal period is called the ==declining-balance method of depreciation==.

The declining-balance depreciation rate is a multiple of the straight-line rate. Many businesses use a declining-balance rate that is two times the straight-line rate. This method of depreciation is referred to as the *double declining-balance method*.

STEPS CALCULATING DEPRECIATION USING THE DOUBLE DECLINING-BALANCE METHOD

① Calculate the double declining-balance rate. An example of a plant asset with a five-year life is shown.

Estimated Depreciation Expense	÷	Years of Estimated Useful Life	=	Straight-line Rate of Depreciation
100%	÷	5	=	20%

Straight-line Rate of Depreciation	×		=	Double Declining-balance Rate
20%	×	2	=	40%

② Multiply the double declining-balance rate by the beginning book value to determine the annual depreciation expense for a given year ($25,000.00 × 40% = $10,000.00).

③ Subtract the annual depreciation expense from the beginning book value to determine the ending book value ($25,000.00 − $10,000.00 = $15,000.00).

④ Transfer the ending book value to the beginning book value for the following year. Calculating the depreciation expense in the last year of an asset's life is described on the next page.

Plant Asset: Truck
Depreciation Method: Double Declining-Balance

Original Cost: $25,000.00
Estimated Salvage Value: $2,500.00
Estimated Useful Life: 5 years

Year	Beginning Book Value	Declining-Balance Rate	Annual Depreciation	Ending Book Value
1	$25,000.00	40%	$10,000.00	$15,000.00
2	15,000.00	40%	6,000.00	9,000.00
3	9,000.00	40%	3,600.00	5,400.00
4	5,400.00	40%	2,160.00	3,240.00
5	3,240.00	———	740.00	2,500.00
Total Depreciation			$22,500.00	

1. Transfer the book value.

2. Determine the last year's depreciation.

3. Verify the ending book value.

Although the depreciation rate is the same each year, the annual depreciation expense declines from one year to the next.

A plant asset is never depreciated below its estimated salvage value. Therefore, in the last year, only enough depreciation expense is recorded to reduce the book value of the plant asset to its salvage value.

Sometimes in the last year of a plant asset's useful life, the formula for the double declining-balance method of depreciation results in an ending book value greater than the estimated salvage value. In other words, the depreciation formula does not create enough accumulated depreciation to reduce the book value down to what is a relatively small estimated salvage value.

When this situation exists, most companies that use the declining-balance method of depreciation switch to the straight-line method sometime during the life of the plant asset. To determine when to switch to the straight-line method of depreciation, each year a company compares the annual depreciation expense calculated using the straight-line method to the annual depreciation expense calculated using the declining-balance method. If the annual depreciation expense using the straight-line method is greater than the annual depreciation expense using the declining-balance method, the company should use the straight-line method.

STEPS **CALCULATING THE LAST YEAR'S DEPRECIATION EXPENSE**

① Transfer the ending book value from Year 4 to the beginning book value of Year 5.

② Subtract the salvage value of the plant asset from the beginning book value to determine the depreciation expense for the last year of useful life ($3,240.00 − $2,500.00 = $740.00).

③ Verify that the ending book value is equal to the salvage value.

REMEMBER

Unlike the straight-line method, the declining-balance method does not use the estimated salvage value to calculate depreciation. The estimated salvage value is used only to limit the last year's depreciation expense.

Plant Asset: Computer
Depreciation Method: Comparison of Two Methods

Original Cost: $4,000.00
Estimated Salvage Value: $500.00
Estimated Useful Life: 5 years

Year	Straight-Line Method			Double Declining-Balance Method		
	Beginning Book Value	Annual Depreciation	Ending Book Value	Beginning Book Value	Annual Depreciation	Ending Book Value
1	$4,000.00	$700.00	$3,300.00	$4,000.00	$1,600.00	$2,400.00
2	3,300.00	700.00	2,600.00	2,400.00	960.00	1,440.00
3	2,600.00	700.00	1,900.00	1,440.00	576.00	864.00
4	1,900.00	700.00	1,200.00	864.00	345.60	518.40
5	1,200.00	700.00	500.00	518.40	18.40	500.00
Total Depreci- ation	——	$3,500.00	——	——	$3,500.00	——

Regardless of the depreciation method used, the total depreciation expense over the useful life of a plant asset is the same. The accounts used in the journal entries to record depreciation expense and the sale of plant assets are also the same.

Each depreciation method is acceptable according to generally accepted accounting principles. The straight-line method is easy to calculate. The same amount of depreciation expense is recorded for each year of estimated useful life.

The double declining-balance method is slightly more complicated. This method records a greater depreciation expense in the early years than the straight-line method. The declining-balance method is referred to as an *accelerated depreciation method*. The method accelerates the recording of depreciation in the early years of the asset's useful life.

BUSINESS STRUCTURES

Piercing the Corporate Veil

A major advantage of a corporation is the limited liability for its owners. This protection from liability is sometimes referred to as a *corporate veil*, or shield. It protects the personal assets of stockholders from creditors' claims.

To benefit from the corporate veil, however, stockholders must keep corporate affairs completely separate from their personal affairs. If this separation is maintained, only the corporation's assets are available for payment of creditors' claims. If the owners do not maintain this separation and, for example, pay personal bills with corporate funds, the corporate protection may be lost.

A court "pierces the corporate veil" when it imposes personal liability for corporate debts on shareholders active in the management of a corporation. For example, owners might pay themselves excessive salaries or other benefits.

If this type of abuse occurs and creditors are not being paid, the court will pierce the corporate veil and hold owners active in management personally liable to creditors.

Critical Thinking

Why would courts consider paying personal expenses from corporate funds to be a reason for piercing the corporate veil?

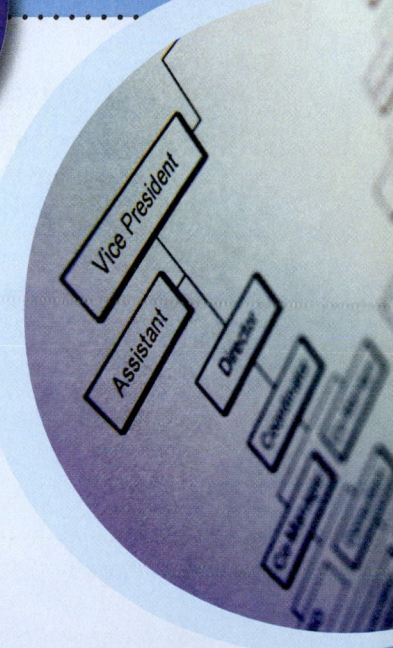

End of Lesson
REVIEW

AUDIT YOUR UNDERSTANDING

1. When calculating depreciation expense using the declining-balance method, what number stays constant each fiscal period?
2. What is the declining-balance method that uses twice the straight-line rate?
3. What change occurs in the annual depreciation expense calculated using the declining-balance method?
4. An asset is never depreciated below what amount?

TERM REVIEW

declining-balance
method of depreciation

WORK TOGETHER 18-5

Calculating depreciation using the double declining-balance depreciation method

Depreciation tables for Clearwater Clothiers are given in the *Working Papers*. Your instructor will guide you through the following example.

1. Complete a depreciation table for each of the following plant assets purchased during the current year. Use the double declining-balance depreciation method. Round amounts to the nearest cent.

Date	Description	Original Cost	Estimated Salvage Value	Estimated Useful Life
Jan. 4	Truck	$22,000.00	$2,200.00	4 years
Jan. 6	Cash Register	$1,200.00	$100.00	5 years
Jan. 7	Clothing Rack	$500.00	$50.00	8 years

ON YOUR OWN 18-5

Calculating depreciation using the double declining-balance depreciation method

Depreciation tables for Teton Skis are given in the *Working Papers*. Work this problem independently.

1. Complete a depreciation table for each of the following plant assets purchased during the current year. Use the double declining-balance depreciation method. Round amounts to the nearest cent.

Date	Description	Original Cost	Estimated Salvage Value	Estimated Useful Life
Jan. 2	Ski Rack	$1,200.00	$100.00	5 years
Jan. 4	Delivery Truck	$25,000.00	$2,000.00	3 years
Jan. 6	Filing Cabinet	$600.00	$50.00	4 years

SUMMARY

After completing this chapter, you can:

1. Define accounting terms related to plant assets, depreciation, and property tax expense.

2. Identify accounting concepts and practices related to accounting for plant assets, depreciation, and property tax expense.

3. Record the buying of a plant asset and the paying of property tax.

4. Calculate depreciation expense and book value using the straight-line method of depreciation.

5. Prepare plant asset records and journalize annual depreciation expense.

6. Record entries related to disposing of plant assets.

7. Calculate depreciation expense using the double declining-balance method of depreciation.

EXPLORE ACCOUNTING

Accounting for Leases

Leasing has become a popular alternative to purchasing a new car. The customer, called the *lessee*, has use of the car during the lease period. At the end of the lease term, the car dealer, called the *lessor*, may give the lessee the option to purchase the car.

The accounting for a lease and the buying of an asset on account are very different. Normally, a leased asset is not recorded on the balance sheet as a plant asset, and the future lease payments are not recorded as a liability. Lease payments are charged to Rent Expense when paid. In contrast, an asset bought on account is recorded on the balance sheet as a plant asset and the total payments are recorded as a liability. Each month, Depreciation Expense is charged and the interest expense is recorded on the monthly note payment. In addition, the liability account is debited; the cash and accumulated depreciation accounts are credited. Thus, the decision to lease or buy plant assets can have a dramatic impact on the financial statements of a company.

Accountants often apply the concept of substance over form when accounting for economic transactions. *Substance* refers to the underlying nature of the transaction. *Form* considers only the appearance of the transaction. FASB (Financial Accounting Standards Board) Statement No. 13, Accounting for Leases, provides accountants with guidelines for evaluating lease agreements. If one of four criteria is met, the lease is recorded as if the asset were purchased, referred to as a *capital lease*.

Research: Investigate the terms of leases offered by a local car dealership and an apartment complex. Identify factors, such as lease term and maintenance, that differ between the two leases. Disregarding the rules of FASB Statement No. 13, would you consider the substance of either lease to be a purchase of the asset?

APPLICATION PROBLEM

Journalizing buying plant assets and paying property tax

The cash payments journal and selected general ledger accounts for Umeki Food Source are given in the *Working Papers*.

Instructions:

1. Journalize the following transactions completed during the current year. The abbreviation for a check is C.

Transactions:

Jan. 4. Paid cash for office desk, $700.00. C334.
    5. Paid cash for a freezer, $4,200.00. C337.
Feb. 24. Paid property taxes on real property with an assessed value of $240,000.00. The tax rate in the city where the property is located is 1.4% of assessed value. C411.
May 12. Paid cash for shopping carts, $1,250.00. C534.

2. Post the general columns of the cash payments journal.

18-2 | APPLICATION PROBLEM

Calculating straight-line depreciation

Planter Stores depreciates plant assets using the straight-line depreciation method. If the asset was not bought at the beginning of 20X1, calculate the depreciation expense for the part of 20X1 during which the company owned the asset.

Instructions:

1. Prepare a depreciation table for each of the following plant assets bought by Planter Stores during 20X1. Depreciation tables are given in the *Working Papers*. Save your work to complete Application Problem 18-3.

Transactions:

Jan. 4. Bought a cooler costing $1,400.00; estimated salvage value, $350.00; estimated useful life, 7 years; plant asset No. 311; serial number, 47367BX34.
Mar. 30. Bought an office chair, $500.00; estimated salvage value, $50.00; estimated useful life, 5 years; plant asset No. 312; serial number, 1727X6B3.
Aug. 2. Bought a sale sign, $350.00; estimated salvage value, $50.00; estimated useful life, 5 years; plant asset no. 313; serial number, BC762761.

18-3 | APPLICATION PROBLEM

Preparing plant asset records

Instructions:

1. Using the depreciation tables prepared in Application Problem 18-2, prepare a plant asset record for each plant asset. Plant asset records are given in the *Working Papers*. Record the depreciation and book values for 20X1–20X4. Save the plant asset records for use in Application Problem 18-5.

Go Beyond the Book
For more information go to
www.C21accounting.com

APPLICATION PROBLEM Peachtree by Sage   QB Quick Books

Journalizing annual depreciation expense

Instructions:

1. On December 31, Ester Engineering, Inc., determined that total depreciation expense for office equipment was $4,320.00. Plan the work sheet adjustment and label the adjustment *(f)*. Record the adjusting entry on page 14 of a general journal and post the transaction to the general ledger. Forms are given in the *Working Papers*.

18-5 ## APPLICATION PROBLEM

Recording the disposal of plant assets

During 20X5, Planter Stores had the following transactions involving the sale of plant assets. Use the plant asset records completed in Application Problem 18-3. Journals are given in the *Working Papers*.

Transactions:

Jan. 6. Received cash for sale of an office chair, plant asset No. 312, $250.00. R4.
Mar. 29. Received cash for sale of a sale sign, plant asset No. 313, $130.00. M3 and R53.
July 8. Received cash for sale of a cooler, plant asset No. 311, $300.00. M34 and R125.

Instructions:

1. For each plant asset disposed of in 20X5, journalize an entry for additional depreciation, if needed. Use page 3 of a general journal. Source documents are abbreviated as follows: check, C; memorandum, M; receipt, R.
2. Use page 3 of a cash receipts journal to record the disposal of each plant asset.
3. Make appropriate notations in the plant asset records.

18-6 ## APPLICATION PROBLEM Microsoft Office

Calculating depreciation using the double declining-balance depreciation method

Instructions:

1. Depreciation tables are given in the *Working Papers*. Complete a depreciation table for each of the following plant assets purchased during the current year. Use the double declining-balance depreciation method. Round amounts to the nearest cent.

Date	Description	Original Cost	Estimated Salvage Value	Estimated Useful Life
Jan. 3	Display Case	$1,600.00	$200.00	8 years
Jan. 5	Truck	$30,000.00	$2,500.00	4 years
Jan. 8	Mixer	$2,400.00	$300.00	5 years

18-7 ## MASTERY PROBLEM AUTOMATED ACCOUNTING

Recording transactions for plant assets

Hillside Resort records plant assets in two accounts: Room Furnishings, Account No. 1205, and Equipment, Account No. 1215. Room furnishings are depreciated using the double declining-balance method. Equipment is depreciated using the straight-line method. Forms are given in the *Working Papers*.

Instructions:

1. Record the following transactions completed during 20X1 on page 1 of a cash payments journal.

Transactions:

Jan. 5. Bought a dining table: cost, $2,200.00; estimated salvage value, $200.00; estimated useful life, 5 years; plant asset No. 892; serial number, 903452. C435.

Feb. 26. Paid property taxes on plant assets assessed at $1,600,000.00. The tax rate is 0.8%. C534.

Apr. 5. Bought an air purifier for the office: cost, $1,300.00; estimated salvage value, $100.00; estimated useful life, 6 years; plant asset No. 893; serial number, BE35CC. C577.

2. Complete Section 1 of a plant asset record for each new plant asset.
3. Prepare a depreciation table for each new plant asset.
4. Complete Section 3 of the plant asset records for 20X1–20X4.
5. Record the following transactions completed during 20X5. Use page 2 of a cash receipts journal and page 18 of a general journal.

Transactions:

Jan. 6. Received cash for sale of a dining table, plant asset No. 892, $300.00. R4.

Jul. 2. Received cash for sale of an air purifier, plant asset No. 893, $200.00. M31 and R77.

Dec. 31. Recorded the adjusting entry for depreciation expense—room furnishings. Total 20X5 depreciation expense of room furnishings was $38,520.00.

6. Complete the plant asset records for each plant asset sold during 20X5.

18-8 CHALLENGE PROBLEM

Calculating a partial year's depreciation using the double declining-balance method

Yann Landscaping uses the double declining-balance depreciation method for its equipment. Because many purchases are made during the year, Yann must calculate a partial year's depreciation in the first year. Yann uses the same method to calculate a partial year's depreciation as was described for Restaurant Supply in this chapter. The annual depreciation expense is divided by 12 to calculate a monthly depreciation. The monthly depreciation is then multiplied by the number of months the plant asset was owned during the year. For subsequent years, the annual depreciation is calculated using the normal method—book value multiplied by the depreciation rate.

Instructions:

1. Depreciation tables are given in the *Working Papers*. Prepare depreciation tables for the following assets purchased in 20X1. Round to the nearest cent.

Transactions:

Apr. 2. Bought a lift, $3,600.00; estimated salvage value, $250.00; estimated useful life, 5 years.

July 24. Purchased a lawnmower, $5,400.00; estimated salvage value, $300.00; estimated useful life, 4 years.

APPLIED COMMUNICATION

Public accountants often work with persons who do not understand the concept of depreciation. Although these individuals realize that equipment wears out and loses its value over time, they do not understand why depreciation is shown as an expense on the income statement.

Keyondra Lynch owns a business that manages several apartment buildings. The business had a net loss of $25,000.00 last year, largely because of $300,000.00 in building depreciation expense. The business also generated over $200,000.00 in cash. Ms. Lynch is confused by the financial statements and asks, "Did I make any money or not?"

Instructions: Write a letter to Ms. Lynch, explaining the concept of depreciation. Explain how her business can both "lose money" (incur expenses) yet have a positive cash flow (pay no cash for certain expenses).

Miguel Quintanilla, owner of a business, does not record depreciation expense for the business's plant assets. Mr. Quintanilla says that he does not make actual cash payments for depreciation. Therefore, he records an expense for the use of plant assets only when cash is paid for a plant asset. Do you agree with Mr. Quintanilla's method? Explain.

AUDITING FOR ERRORS

Jaudon Industries recently purchased two new plant assets. Danielle Hess, accounting clerk, has prepared the following depreciation schedule for the assets.

Plant Asset: Copier Machine
Depreciation Method: Straight-line

Original Cost: $6,000.00
Estimated Salvage Value: $1,000.00
Estimated Useful Life: 5 years

Year	Beginning Book Value	Annual Depreciation	Accumulated Depreciation	Ending Book Value
20X1	$6,000.00	$1,200.00	$1,200.00	$4,800.00
20X2	$4,800.00	$1,200.00	$2,400.00	$3,600.00
20X3	$3,600.00	$1,200.00	$3,600.00	$2,400.00
20X4	$2,400.00	$1,200.00	$4,800.00	$1,200.00
20X5	$1,200.00	$1,200.00	$6,000.00	$0.00

Plant Asset: Computer System
Depreciation Method: Declining-balance

Original Cost: $8,000.00
Estimated Salvage Value: $1,000.00
Estimated Useful Life: 5 years

Year	Beginning Book Value	Annual Depreciation	Accumulated Depreciation	Ending Book Value
20X1	$8,000.00	$2,800.00	$2,800.00	$5,200.00
20X2	$5,200.00	$2,080.00	$4,880.00	$3,120.00
20X3	$3,120.00	$1,248.00	$6,128.00	$1,872.00
20X4	$1,872.00	$748.80	$6,876.80	$1,123.20
20X5	$1,123.20	$449.28	$7,326.08	$673.92

Instructions: Determine the accuracy of each depreciation schedule. Identify any corrections that Danielle should make.

ANALYZING BEST BUY'S FINANCIAL STATEMENTS

Merchandising businesses often rent buildings from companies that specialize in building management. Any modifications made to the building become the property of the building owner at the end of the lease. These fixed assets are known as *leasehold improvements*.

Instructions

1. Review Best Buy's annual report in Appendix B of this text. Referring to Note 1 beginning on page B-9, what method of depreciation does Best Buy use to depreciate property and equipment?
2. How does Best Buy determine the useful life of leasehold improvements?

Accounting
SOFTWARE

PLANT ASSETS AND DEPRECIATION

In information technology terms, the ability of users to perform a specific task is known as *functionality*. Most software companies offer their product with the basic functionality, such as recording journal entries, sales, and cash disbursements, that is needed by all businesses. Additional functionality, such as payroll, fixed assets, credit card processing, and e-commerce, can be purchased separately if needed.

A company with only a few fixed assets may find it easier and more economical to keep their fixed asset records on an electronic spreadsheet. The amount of depreciation expense to be recorded would be calculated by the spreadsheet and recorded in the accounting system using a journal entry.

PEACHTREE APPLICATION PROBLEM 18-1
1. Open (Restore) file 18-1AP.ptb.
2. Journalize and post the transactions related to acquiring plant assets and paying property taxes. Use the Write Checks task; you do not need to change accounting periods.
3. Print the office equipment and store equipment general ledger accounts from Period 1 through Period 5.
4. Print the Property Tax account for February.

PEACHTREE APPLICATION PROBLEM 18-4
1. Open (Restore) file 18-4AP.ptb.
2. Record entries related to depreciation expense. Record and post $4,320 as the adjusting entry in the general journal for the total depreciation expense for office equipment.
3. Print the December 31 general journal, the general ledger's Office Equipment and Accumulated Depreciation-Office Equipment accounts, and the general ledger's Depreciation Expense—Office Equipment account.

PLANT ASSETS AND DEPRECIATION

The information about plant assets is used to prepare depreciation schedules and to prepare the adjusting entries for depreciation. In QuickBooks, when a new plant asset is acquired, a new plant asset record must be established. The information to be recorded includes the name of the asset, the seller's name, the date acquired, the amount, the serial number of the asset (if available), and the title of the account that will be debited. When the asset is sold or retired, the plant asset record must be updated to show the asset disposal. Information recorded at this time includes: the date of sale or disposal; the amount of cash received for the asset; and other information if the asset was traded for a new asset. QuickBooks requires you to calculate the amount of depreciation for each plant asset and to enter all depreciation entries into the general journal.

QUICKBOOKS APPLICATION PROBLEM 18-1
1. Open the Umeki Food Source file if it is not already open.
2. Use the Write Checks window to record entries, creating an item for each new asset purchased in the Fixed Asset Item List option. Record all transactions related to acquiring plant assets, preparing fixed plant asset records, and paying property taxes.
3. Print a Journal report using January 1 and May 31 as the dates.
4. Print a Fixed Asset Listing report.

QUICKBOOKS APPLICATION PROBLEM 18-4
1. Open the Ester Engineering Inc file.
2. Journalize the depreciation expense in the Make General Journal Entries window. Print a Journal report using December 31 for the dates.

CALCULATING DEPRECIATION EXPENSE

The many calculations required by a depreciation schedule make this task a perfect application for an electronic spreadsheet. Armed with your understanding of how depreciation is calculated, you would begin by creating the formulas for the first year. Those formulas could be copied down the columns to quickly complete the schedule. You also need a good understanding of how formulas are copied. By default, formula cell references are *relative references*, meaning that the column and row of a cell reference change when the formula is copied. In contrast, the column and row of *absolute references* do not change when copied.

When creating the formulas for annual depreciation expense using the straight-line method, you will need to reference the cells containing the original cost, salvage value, and useful life. These cell references are the same whether calculating depreciation for year 1 or year 5. Therefore, identifying these cells as absolute references will enable you to copy the year 1 formula for each year on the schedule.

EXCEL APPLICATION PROBLEM 18-2
Open the F18-2 Excel data file. Follow the step-by-step instructions in the Instructions worksheet. Use absolute references to create the formulas for annual depreciation expense.

EXCEL APPLICATION PROBLEM 18-3
Open the F18-3 Excel data file. Follow the step-by-step instructions in the Instructions worksheet.

EXCEL APPLICATION PROBLEM 18-6
Open the F18-6 Excel data file. Follow the step-by-step instructions in the Instructions worksheet.

PLANT ASSETS AND DEPRECIATION

In order for the accounting system to prepare depreciation schedules, complete information must be entered for each plant asset.
1. Click the Accounts toolbar button.
2. Click the Plant Assets tab.
3. To add a new asset:
    a. Enter the asset number.
    b. Complete the data fields in the text boxes—asset name, date acquired, useful life, original cost, and salvage value.
    c. Enter the appropriate accumulated depreciation and depreciation expense account numbers.
    d. Select the desired depreciation method from the drop-down list.
    e. Click Add Asset.
4. To change or delete data for an existing plant asset:
    a. Select the asset by clicking the text box containing the data you wish to change.
    b. Enter the correct data and click the Change Asset button, or click the Delete button to remove the asset from the database.

Generating and Posting Depreciation Adjusting Entries
At the end of the fiscal period (month or year), the computerized accounting system will generate the adjusting entries from the information in the plant asset records. To generate and post the adjusting entries:
1. Choose Depreciation Adjusting Entries from the Options menu.
2. Click Yes to generate the depreciation adjusting entries.
3. Click the Post button. The general journal will appear, containing the posted journal entry. Verify the accuracy of the entry and click the Close button.

AUTOMATED ACCOUNTING APPLICATION PROBLEM 18-2
Open file F18-2.AA8. Display the problem instructions and complete the problem.

AUTOMATED ACCOUNTING MASTERY PROBLEM 18-7
Open file F18-7.AA8. Display the problem instructions and complete the problem.

STOCKBYTE/GETTY IMAGES

CHAPTER 19

Accounting for Inventory

CHAPTER 19

OBJECTIVES

After studying Chapter 19, you will be able to:

1. Define accounting terms related to inventory.

2. Identify accounting concepts and practices related to inventory.

3. Prepare a stock record.

4. Determine the cost of merchandise inventory using the fifo, lifo, and weighted-average inventory costing methods.

5. Estimate the cost of merchandise inventory using the gross profit method of estimating inventory.

KEY TERMS

- periodic inventory
- perpetual inventory
- inventory record
- stock record
- stock ledger
- first-in, first-out inventory costing method
- last-in, first-out inventory costing method
- weighted-average inventory costing method
- gross profit method of estimating inventory

Point Your Browser
www.C21accounting.com

Fender Guitars

Fender Guitars Are Everywhere

When you enter a music store searching for that perfect guitar, you expect to be able to choose from an extensive variety of guitars. You want a style and color that reflects your personality, an awesome sound, and a great price. Equally important, you want a brand name that is respected by musicians worldwide.

Beginning with its legendary Telecaster®, Fender has produced renowned electric guitars for more than 50 years. The company now offers a wide variety of electric basses and amplifiers.

Have you ever wondered how small music stores can afford to have such an extensive selection of guitars and amplifiers? The money required to maintain this level of inventory is beyond the financial resources of the typical music store.

To solve this problem, Fender has established relationships with various floor-planning companies that provide reasonable financing to Fender dealers. The dealers can purchase product beyond their financial resources, and pay for the product as it is sold. The floor-plan methodology enables Fender's dealers to provide their customers with a full range of product from which to select. In addition, the inventory can be very easily replenished.

Critical Thinking

1. Manufacturers in other industries, including automobiles, motorcycles, and appliances, often floor-plan inventory for their distributors. What do these industries have in common with musical instruments?

2. How does the floor-plan method benefit customers who do not live in large metropolitan areas?

Source: www.fender.com

INTERNET ACTIVITY

Notes to the Financial Statements—Inventory Costing Methods

Go to the homepage for Wal-Mart (www.walmart.com) and Target Corporation (www.target.com). Search for the latest annual report for each company. The annual report is usually found under the heading "About Us" or "Investor Relations." In the annual report, usually after the financial statements, you will find the notes to the financial statements. Using these notes (probably Note #1 or #2), look for the information about inventory.

Instructions

1. For each company, state which note contains the information about inventory.

2. For each company, find the method(s) used to calculate the cost of inventory (fifo, lifo, or weighted average.)

©AFP/GETTY IMAGES

DIGITAL VISION/GETTY IMAGES

Determining the Quantity of Merchandise Inventory

WHY MERCHANDISE INVENTORY IS IMPORTANT

Merchandise inventory on hand is typically the largest asset of a merchandising business. Successful businesses must have merchandise available for sale that customers want. A business therefore needs controls that assist managers in maintaining a merchandise inventory of sufficient quantity, variety, and price.

The cost of merchandise inventory is reported on both the balance sheet and the income statement. An accurate cost of merchandise inventory is required to correctly report current assets and retained earnings on the balance sheet. The accuracy of the inventory cost will also assure that gross profit and net income are reported correctly on the income statement. [CONCEPT: Adequate Disclosure]

SMALL BUSINESS
SPOTLIGHT

Every state has a Small Business Development Center (SBDC) office, which provides a wide range of consulting services and seminars. Funded by state and federal governments, SBDCs are directed by the Small Business Administration and state university personnel.

CHARACTER COUNTS

Hotlines

The accounting scandals of the early 21st century led the U.S. Congress to pass legislation designed to protect investors by improving the accuracy and reliability of financial reporting. The bill, known as the Sarbanes-Oxley Act of 2002 (SOX), contains a section that requires management to make a written statement about the effectiveness of its internal control system. External auditors must test the internal control system to ensure that management's conclusions are appropriate.

In an effective internal control system, employees and other stakeholders must be able to communicate possible ethics violations. A phone number that allows an individual to provide confidential information regarding possible ethics violations is called a *hotline*. An effective hotline must ensure an individual that:

1. Management takes hotline calls seriously.

2. The information provided will be maintained on an anonymous or confidential basis.

3. No retaliation or harassment will be tolerated.

Instructions
Dow's EthicsLine is available to Dow employees to report possible violations of its *Code of Business Conduct* (www.dow.com). Describe how EthicsLine is designed to meet the three criteria presented above.

To determine the most efficient quantity of inventory, a business makes frequent analysis of purchases, sales, and inventory records. Many businesses fail because too much or too little merchandise inventory is kept on hand. A business that stocks merchandise that does not satisfy the demand of its customers is also likely to fail.

A merchandise inventory that is larger than needed may decrease the net income of a business for several reasons.

1. Excess inventory requires that a business spend money for expensive store and warehouse space.
2. Excess inventory uses capital that could be invested in other assets to earn a profit for the business.
3. Excess inventory requires that a business spend money for expenses, such as taxes and insurance premiums, which increase with the cost of the merchandise inventory.
4. Excess inventory may become obsolete and unsalable.

Merchandise inventory that is smaller than needed may also decrease the net income of a business for several reasons.

1. Sales may be lost to competitors if items wanted by customers are not on hand.
2. Sales may be lost to competitors if there is an insufficient variety of merchandise to satisfy customers.
3. When a business frequently orders small quantities of an item, the price paid is often more per unit than when merchandise is ordered in large quantities.

The quantity of items in inventory at the end of a fiscal period must be determined in order to calculate the cost of merchandise sold.

Two principal methods are used to determine the quantity of each item of merchandise on hand.

1. A merchandise inventory determined by counting, weighing, or measuring items of merchandise on hand is called a **periodic inventory**. A periodic inventory is also referred to as a *physical inventory*.
2. A merchandise inventory determined by keeping a continuous record of increases, decreases, and balance on hand is called a **perpetual inventory**. A perpetual inventory is also referred to as a *book inventory*.

Because controlling the quantity of merchandise inventory is so important to a business's success, many methods of keeping inventory records are used. Today, most companies use computers to keep track of the inventory on hand.

Keeping track of merchandise inventory also involves knowing the ideal quantity for each kind of merchandise in inventory. To ensure having the appropriate quantity, companies frequently establish an ideal minimum quantity and an ideal reorder quantity. When the minimum quantity is reached, new merchandise is ordered.

Minimum quantity levels must be established with consideration for how long it may take to receive new inventory. Otherwise, merchandise may not be available when a customer wants to buy it. Those who order new merchandise must also be aware of the ideal quantities to order to get the best prices and trade discounts.

BLEND IMAGES/GETTY IMAGES

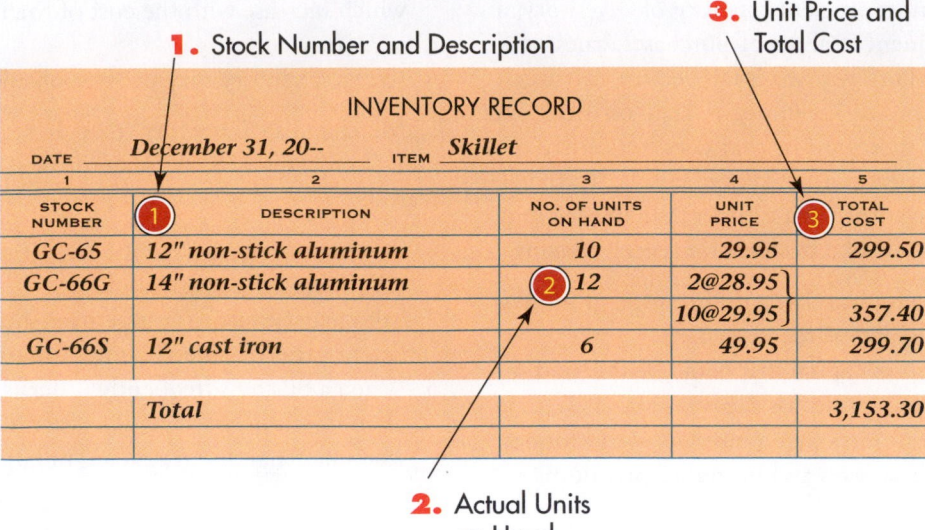

1. Stock Number and Description

3. Unit Price and Total Cost

2. Actual Units on Hand

Counting, weighing, or measuring merchandise on hand for a periodic inventory is commonly referred to as "taking an inventory." Employees count each item of inventory and record the quantities on special forms. To assure an accurate and complete count, a business will typically be closed during the periodic inventory.

Businesses frequently establish their fiscal period to end when inventory is at a minimum because it takes less time to count a smaller inventory. For example, a department store may take an inventory at the end of December. The amount of merchandise on hand is smaller because of holiday sales. Few purchases of additional merchandise are made in December after the holiday sales. All of these activities make the merchandise inventory smaller at the end of December.

A form used during a periodic inventory to record information about each item of merchandise on hand is called an **inventory record**. The inventory record has space to record the stock number, description, number of units on hand, unit price, and total cost of each item.

Columns 1–3 are completed when the business is taking an inventory. Columns 4–5 are completed after the taking of inventory. The methods used to determine the unit prices are discussed later in this chapter.

FOR YOUR INFORMATION

F Y I

Taking an inventory is an involved and expensive task. An efficient inventory count requires extensive management planning and employee training. Some businesses hire independent companies that specialize in taking inventories to assist in planning for and counting the inventory.

S T E P S   ●   **PREPARING AN INVENTORY RECORD**

① Write the stock number and description before the periodic inventory begins.

② Write the actual count in the No. of Units on Hand column.

③ Write the unit price and calculate the total cost after the physical inventory is completed. These columns are usually completed by the accounting department.

STOCK RECORD

Description **Skillet, 14" cast iron**   Stock No. **GC-66**

Reorder **20**   Minimum **10**   Location **Rack C-24**

INCREASES			DECREASES			BALANCE
DATE	PURCHASE INVOICE NO.	QUANTITY	DATE	SALES INVOICE NO.	QUANTITY	QUANTITY
			Oct. 10		5	9
Nov. 2	968 ①	20				29
			Nov. 12	1726	4	25
			Nov. 29	1792	2	23
			Dec. 6	1841 ②	3	20 ③

1. Purchase Information   **2.** Sales Information   **3.** New Balance on Hand

Some businesses keep inventory records that show continuously the quantity on hand for each kind of merchandise. A form used to show the kind of merchandise, quantity received, quantity sold, and balance on hand is called a **stock record**. A separate stock record is prepared for each kind of merchandise on hand. A file of stock records for all merchandise on hand is called a **stock ledger**.

A perpetual inventory system provides day-to-day information about the quantity of merchandise on hand. The minimum balance allowed before a reorder must be placed is also shown on each stock record. The minimum balance is the quantity that will typically last until the ordered merchandise can be received from the vendors. When the quantity falls below the minimum, additional merchandise is ordered in the quantity shown on the reorder line of the stock record. A stock record shows the quantity but usually not the cost of the merchandise.

Purchase information is recorded in the Increases columns when additional merchandise is received. Sales information is recorded in the Decreases columns when merchandise is sold. The new balance on hand is recorded after each purchase and sale.

When a perpetual inventory is kept, errors may be made in recording or calculating amounts. Also, some stock records may be incorrect because merchandise is taken from stock and not recorded on stock records. A business should take a periodic inventory at least once a fiscal period. The perpetual records are corrected to reflect the actual quantity on hand as determined by the periodic inventory.

•••••••••••••••• **PERPETUAL INVENTORY USING A COMPUTER** ••••••••••••••••

Many merchandising businesses use a computer to keep perpetual inventory records. The point-of-sale terminals at the customer check-out counters are connected to the computer. The terminals read the Universal Product Codes (UPC) marked on products.

The stock ledger is stored in the computer. When a UPC is read at the terminal, the product description and the sales price are retrieved from the stock ledger and displayed on the terminal. The computer reduces the units on hand to reflect the item sold. The computer may also periodically check the quantities in the stock ledger and print a list of items that need to be reordered.

End of Lesson REVIEW

AUDIT YOUR UNDERSTANDING

1. Why do successful businesses need an effective inventory system?
2. Identify four reasons why a merchandise inventory that is larger than needed may decrease the net income of a business.
3. When are periodic inventories normally taken?
4. How do inventory levels affect the period a business selects for its fiscal year? Why?
5. How is the accuracy of a perpetual inventory checked?

TERMS REVIEW

periodic inventory

perpetual inventory

inventory record

stock record

stock ledger

WORK TOGETHER 19-1

Preparing a stock record

A stock record for Sound Station is given in the *Working Papers*. Your instructor will guide you through the following example.

1. Enter the following transactions on the stock record of Stock No. W-394, 16-gauge speaker wire. Source documents are abbreviated as follows: purchase invoice, P; sales invoice, S.

Transactions:

Oct. 3. Sold 250 feet of W-394 speaker wire. S2543.

    27. Purchased 750 feet of W-394 speaker wire. P1542.

    29. Sold 300 feet of W-394 speaker wire. S2654.

Dec. 4. Sold 170 feet of W-394 speaker wire. S2801.

ON YOUR OWN 19-1

Preparing a stock record

A stock record for Frames-R-Us is given in the *Working Papers*. Work this problem independently.

1. Enter the following transactions on the stock record of Stock No. M-253, an 8″ × 10″ white metal frame. Source documents are abbreviated as follows: purchase invoice, P; sales invoice, S.

Transactions:

Nov. 4. Sold 10 M-253 picture frames. S590.

    16. Sold 25 M-253 picture frames. S624.

    22. Received 50 M-253 picture frames. P223.

Dec. 9. Sold 15 M-253 picture frames. S645.

Determining the Cost of Merchandise Inventory

FIRST-IN, FIRST-OUT INVENTORY COSTING METHOD

3. Units Needed to Equal the Total Units on Hand

4. Unit Price Times Fifo Units

Purchase Dates	Units Purchased	Unit Price	Total Cost	FIFO Units on Hand	FIFO Cost
January 1, beginning inventory	10	$18.80	$188.00		
February 16, purchases	6	19.60	117.60		
April 17, purchases	14	20.40	285.60		
September 5, purchases	12	21.40	256.80	③ 10	$214.00 ④
November 22, purchases	8	21.50	172.00	② 8	172.00
Totals	50		$1,020.00	① 18	$386.00 ⑤

2. Units from the Most Recent Purchase

1. Total Units on Hand

5. Total Fifo Cost

After the quantities of merchandise on hand are counted, purchase invoices are used to find merchandise unit prices. The total costs are then calculated using the quantities and unit prices recorded on the inventory records. Most businesses use one of three inventory costing methods: (1) first-in, first-out, (2) last-in, first-out, or (3) weighted-average.

Restaurant Supply uses the most recent invoices for purchases to determine the unit price of an item in inventory. The earliest invoices for purchases, therefore, are used to determine the cost of merchandise sold. Using the price of merchandise purchased first to calculate the cost of merchandise sold first is called the **first-in, first-out inventory costing method**. The first-in, first-out method is frequently abbreviated as *fifo*.

On December 31, a periodic inventory of 12-inch aluminum skillets, Model No. GS-67, showed 18 units on hand. Using the fifo method, the 18 units would show a total cost of $386.00.

STEPS — COSTING INVENTORY USING THE FIFO METHOD

① Enter the total number of units on hand, *18*.

② From the most recent purchase, November 22, enter the number of units purchased, *8*. In some cases, the number of units of the most recent purchase will be greater than or equal to the total number of units on hand. In such a case, enter the total number of units on hand and do not complete Step 3 below.

③ From the next most recent purchase, September 5, enter the number of units, *10*, needed for the fifo units to equal the total number on hand, 18. Continue with the next invoices as needed.

④ Multiply the unit price of each appropriate purchase by the fifo units on hand to determine the fifo cost.

⑤ Add the individual fifo costs to determine the fifo cost of the total number of units in ending inventory.

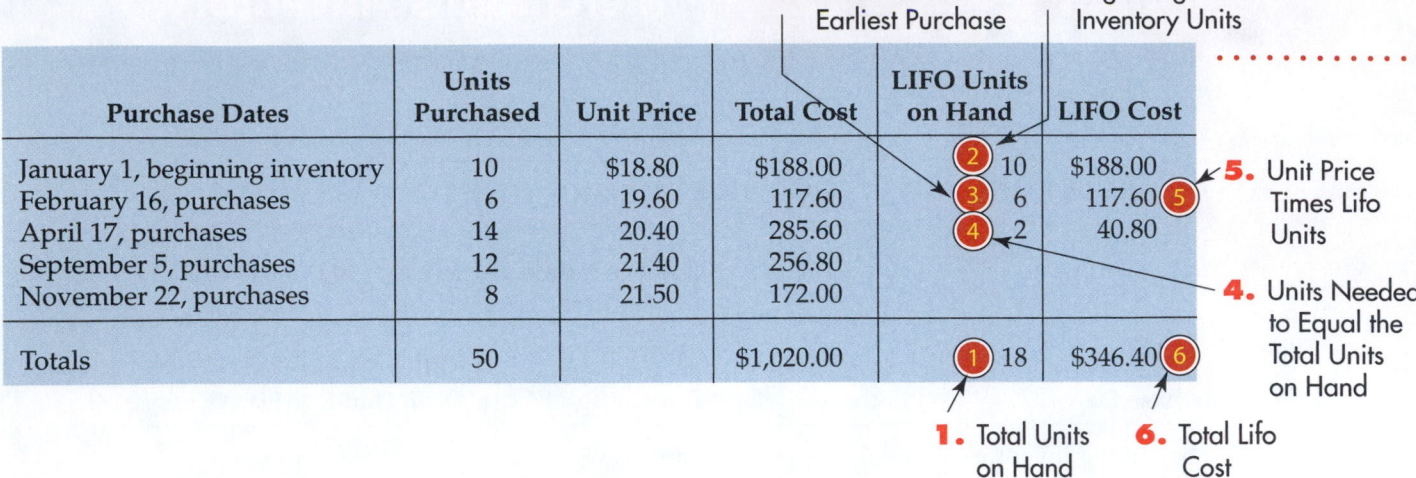

3. Units from the Earliest Purchase **2.** Beginning Inventory Units

Purchase Dates	Units Purchased	Unit Price	Total Cost	LIFO Units on Hand		LIFO Cost	
January 1, beginning inventory	10	$18.80	$188.00	②	10	$188.00	
February 16, purchases	6	19.60	117.60	③	6	117.60	⑤
April 17, purchases	14	20.40	285.60	④	2	40.80	
September 5, purchases	12	21.40	256.80				
November 22, purchases	8	21.50	172.00				
Totals	50		$1,020.00	①	18	$346.40	⑥

5. Unit Price Times Lifo Units

4. Units Needed to Equal the Total Units on Hand

1. Total Units on Hand   **6.** Total Lifo Cost

Using the price of merchandise purchased last to calculate the cost of merchandise sold first is called the ==last-in, first-out inventory costing method==. The last-in, first-out method is frequently abbreviated as *lifo*. This method is based on the idea that the most recent costs of merchandise should be charged against current revenue. [CONCEPT: Matching Expenses with Revenue]

Using the lifo method, each item on the inventory records is recorded at the earliest prices paid for the merchandise.

The earliest prices for the 18 skillets would consist of the 10 units in the January 1 beginning inventory. The next earliest purchase, February 16, of 6 units is then used to cost 6 units in ending inventory. The remaining 2 units in ending inventory are costed using the next earliest purchase, April 17. On the inventory record, the 18 units would show a total cost of $346.40.

STEPS   **COSTING INVENTORY USING THE LIFO METHOD**

① Enter the total number of units on hand, *18*.

② Enter the number of units in beginning inventory, *10*. In some cases, the number of units of beginning inventory will be greater than or equal to the total number of units on hand. In such a case, enter the total number of units on hand and do not complete Steps 3 and 4 below.

③ From the earliest purchase, February 16, enter the number of units purchased, *6*.

④ From the next earliest purchase, April 17, enter the number of units, *2*, needed for the lifo units to equal the total number of units on hand, *18*.

⑤ Multiply the unit price of the beginning inventory by the lifo units on hand to determine the lifo cost for beginning inventory. Repeat this process for each appropriate purchase.

⑥ Add the lifo cost for the beginning inventory and each appropriate purchase to determine the lifo cost of the total number of units in ending inventory.

REMEMBER

In the lifo method, the latest purchases are assumed to be sold first (first-out). Therefore, ending inventory consists of the units purchased the earliest, and the earliest purchase invoice costs are used to value the ending inventory.

| Purchases | | | Total |
Date	Units	Unit Price	Cost
January 1, beginning inventory	10	$18.80	$188.00
February 16, purchases	6	19.60	117.60
April 17, purchases	14	20.40	285.60
September 5, purchases	12	21.40	256.80
November 22, purchases	8	21.50	172.00
Totals	50		$1,020.00

1. Total Cost of Inventory Available

Total of Beginning Inventory and Purchases	÷	Total Units	=	Weighted-Average Price per Unit
$1,020.00	÷	50	=	$20.40

2. Weighted-Average Price per Unit

Units in Ending Inventory	×	Weighted-Average Price per Unit	=	Cost of Ending Inventory
18	×	$20.40	=	$367.20

3. Cost of Ending Inventory

Using the average cost of beginning inventory plus merchandise purchased during a fiscal period to calculate the cost of merchandise sold is called the **weighted-average inventory costing method**. The average unit price of the total inventory available is calculated. This average unit price is used to calculate both ending inventory and cost of merchandise sold. The average cost of merchandise is then charged against current revenue. [CONCEPT: Matching Expenses with Revenue]

Using the weighted-average method, the inventory is costed at the average price per unit of the beginning inventory plus the cost of all purchases during the fiscal year. On the inventory record, the 18 units would show a total cost of $367.20.

STEPS — COSTING INVENTORY USING THE WEIGHTED-AVERAGE METHOD

1. Calculate the total cost of beginning inventory and each purchase, *$1,020.00*, by multiplying the units by each unit price.

2. Calculate the weighted-average price per unit, *$20.40*, by dividing the total cost, *$1,020.00*, by the number of units available, *50*.

3. Calculate the cost of ending inventory, *$367.20*, by multiplying the weighted-average price per unit, *$20.40*, by the units in ending inventory, *18*.

FOR YOUR INFORMATION

FYI

A business usually determines the order in which products are sold, based on the type of inventory. A grocery store, for example, must sell its earliest purchases first. A hardware store, however, could sell its most recent purchases first. The inventory costing method used to calculate the cost of merchandise sold should not, however, be determined by the order in which items are sold. A business should choose the inventory costing method that provides its managers with the best accounting information.

CALCULATING THE COST OF MERCHANDISE SOLD

The cost of ending inventory determined using any of the three inventory costing methods can be used to calculate the cost of merchandise sold. The cost of ending inventory is subtracted from the total cost of units available for sale. Although the formula is the same, under each inven-tory costing method the amount determined will be dif-ferent. Restaurant Supply uses the fifo method. Therefore, the fifo cost of $386.00 is subtracted from the total cost of merchandise available for sale, $1,020.00, to calculate the cost of merchandise sold of $634.00.

| Cost of Merchandise Available for Sale $1,020.00 | − | Fifo Cost of Ending Inventory $386.00 | = | Cost of Merchandise Sold $634.00 |

COMPARISON OF INVENTORY METHODS

	Fifo	Lifo	Weighted Average
Cost of Merchandise Sold:			
Merchandise Inventory, Jan. 1	$ 188.00	$ 188.00	$ 188.00
Net Purchases	832.00	832.00	832.00
Merchandise Available for Sale	$ 1,020.00	$ 1,020.00	$ 1,020.00
Less Ending Inventory, Dec. 31	386.00	346.40	367.20
Cost of Merchandise Sold	$ 634.00	$ 673.60	$ 652.80
In a period of rising prices:			
Relative Cost of Ending Inventory	highest	lowest	intermediate
Relative Cost of Merchandise Sold	lowest	highest	intermediate

In a period of rising prices, the fifo method gives the high-est possible ending inventory cost and the lowest cost of merchandise sold. The lifo method gives the lowest pos-sible ending inventory cost and the highest cost of mer-chandise sold. The weighted-average method gives ending inventory cost and cost of merchandise sold between fifo and lifo. As the cost of merchandise sold increases, gross profit and net income decrease. Thus, net income is high-est under the fifo method, lowest under the lifo method, and intermediate under the weighted-average method.

In a period of declining prices, the results for the fifo and lifo methods are reversed.

All three inventory costing methods are acceptable accounting practices. A business should select one method and use that same method continuously for each fiscal period. If a business changed inventory costing methods, part of the difference in gross profit and net income would be caused by the change in methods. To provide financial statements that can be analyzed and compared with state-ments of other fiscal periods, the same inventory costing method should be used each fiscal period. [CONCEPT: Consistent Reporting]

End of Lesson
REVIEW

TERMS REVIEW

first-in, first-out inventory
costing method

last-in, first-out inventory
costing method

weighted-average
inventory costing method

AUDIT YOUR UNDERSTANDING

1. When the fifo method is used, how is the cost of each kind of ending merchandise inventory determined?
2. On what idea is the lifo method based?
3. In a period of rising prices, which inventory costing method gives the highest cost of merchandise sold?
4. Why should a business select one inventory costing method and use that same method continuously for each fiscal period?

WORK TOGETHER 19-2

Determining the cost of inventory using the fifo, lifo, and weighted-average inventory costing methods

Inventory costing information for Riverville Electronics is given in the *Working Papers*. Your instructor will guide you through the following example.

1. Calculate the cost of ending inventory using the fifo, lifo, and weighted-average methods. There are 16 units in ending inventory.

ON YOUR OWN 19-2

Determining the cost of inventory using the fifo, lifo, and weighted-average inventory costing methods

Inventory costing information for Venture Plumbing is given in the *Working Papers*. Work this problem independently.

1. Calculate the cost of ending inventory using the fifo, lifo, and weighted-average methods. There are 24 units in ending inventory.

GROSS PROFIT METHOD OF ESTIMATING INVENTORY

STEP 1: Beginning inventory, January 1 . . . . $ 142,536.20
    Plus   net purchases for January 1 to January 31. . . . .   + 42,452.80
    Equals cost of merchandise available for sale . . . . $ 184,989.00

STEP 2: Net sales for January 1 to January 31. . . . . $ 99,340.00
    Times previous year's gross profit percentage . . . .   × 40.00%
    Equals estimated gross profit on operations . . . . $ 39,736.00

STEP 3: Net sales for January 1 to January 31. . . . . $ 99,340.00
    Less   estimated gross profit on operations . . . .   − 39,736.00
    Equals estimated cost of merchandise sold . . . . $ 59,604.00

STEP 4: Cost of merchandise available for sale . . . . $ 184,989.00
    Less   estimated cost of merchandise sold . . . .   − 59,604.00
    Equals estimated ending merchandise inventory. . . . . $ 125,385.00

Restaurant Supply Co.
Income Statement
For Month Ended January 31, 20--

		% of Net Sales
Operating Revenue:		
Net Sales	$ 99,340.00	100.0
Cost of Merchandise Sold:		
Beginning Inventory, January 1 . . . . . $142,536.20		
Net Purchases 42,452.80		
Merchandise Available for Sale $184,989.00		
Less Est. Ending Inv., January 31 . . . . 125,385.00		
Cost of Merchandise Sold	59,604.00	60.0
Gross Profit on Operations	$ 39,736.00	40.0
Operating Expenses	30,298.70	30.5
Net Income	$ 9,437.30	9.5

Estimating inventory by using the previous year's percentage of gross profit on operations is called the **gross profit method of estimating inventory**. The gross profit method is often used to estimate the cost of the ending inventory reported on monthly financial statements. The gross profit method is a less expensive method of calculating inventory costs than taking a periodic inventory or maintaining a perpetual inventory system.

Four values are needed to perform the four-step process. Actual net sales and net purchases amounts are obtained from the general ledger. The beginning inventory amount is obtained from the prior period's financial statements. The gross profit percentage is estimated by management based on the previous year's actual percentage, adjusted for any significant changes in economic conditions.

When the gross profit method of estimating inventory is used for months other than the first month of the fiscal period, the process is the same as that just illustrated. Net sales and purchases amounts are obtained from the general ledger. For the sales account, the previous month's ending balance is subtracted from the current month's ending balance to calculate the amount of sales for just the current month. The same process is used for the purchases account. The beginning inventory for the month is the same as the ending inventory from the previous month. Note that both the beginning and ending inventory amounts will be based on estimated amounts.

FINANCIAL LITERACY

Synopsis of Investments

There is much pressure on individuals to save for retirement. Where do you start? If you have money available to put away for retirement, where should you invest it to get the best return? There are many investment options available to today's workers.

One kind of fund is called an Individual Retirement Account (IRA). There are several forms of IRAs. A deductible IRA means that the investor does not have to pay tax on the money deposited or on the interest earned on the account until it is withdrawn at retirement. A non-deductible IRA means that the investor does pay tax on the money deposited but does not pay tax on the interest earned on the account until it is withdrawn at retirement. A Roth IRA is one where the person pays tax on the amount deposited but never has to pay tax on the interest earned on the account.

A certificate of deposit (CD) is an investment product offered by banks. Interest is paid on the CD on a specific date in the future. The term of the CD can range from 30 days to more than five years. If you want to share directly in the success of a corporation, you may purchase shares of stock in that company. Each share of stock represents an ownership interest. Your investment can reward you either in the form of dividends or by an increase in the value of your shares of stock. Another investment is to purchase the bond of a company or government entity, which is similar to a loan that pays periodic interest. The repayment of the principal amount occurs at a specified date in the future.

If you want to invest in stocks and bonds but don't want to deal directly with each company, you can invest in a mutual fund, which means you buy shares in an entity designed to collect the investments from many investors. In turn, these funds are invested in the stocks and bonds of many companies by fund managers.

Activities

1. Contact a financial planner. Ask his or her advice on how much is needed to start investing and what types of investments are appropriate for someone your age. Prepare a written summary of your findings.

2. Pick two publicly traded companies in the same industry. Track each company's stock price daily for two weeks. Summarize your findings in a chart or graph.

PHOTO: PHOTODISC/GETTY IMAGES

End of Lesson
REVIEW

AUDIT YOUR UNDERSTANDING

1. When neither a perpetual system is maintained nor a periodic inventory is taken, how can an ending merchandise inventory be determined that is accurate enough for a monthly income statement?

2. What amounts are needed to estimate ending merchandise inventory?

3. What amount is used for beginning inventory for a month that is not the first month of a fiscal period?

TERM REVIEW

gross profit method of estimating inventory

WORK TOGETHER 19-3

Estimating ending inventory using the gross profit method

A form for making estimated inventory calculations and a form for completing an income statement are given in the *Working Papers*. Your instructor will guide you through the following examples.

1. Use the following information obtained from the records and management of Evans Company to estimate the cost of the ending inventory on June 30.

Estimated beginning inventory, June 1	$154,800.00
Actual net purchases for June	$ 47,800.00
Actual net sales for June	$245,000.00
Estimated gross profit percentage	45.0%
Actual operating expenses for June	$ 76,930.00

2. Prepare an income statement for the month ended June 30 of the current year.

ON YOUR OWN 19-3

Estimating ending inventory using the gross profit method

A form for making estimated inventory calculations and a form for completing an income statement are given in the *Working Papers*. Work this problem independently.

1. Use the following information obtained from the records and management of Luke Enterprises to estimate the cost of the ending inventory on April 30.

Estimated beginning inventory, April 1	$24,500.00
Actual net purchases for April	$12,100.00
Actual net sales for April	$56,000.00
Estimated gross profit percentage	55.0%
Actual operating expenses for April	$17,920.00

2. Prepare an income statement for the month ended April 30 of the current year.

After completing this chapter, you can:

1. Define accounting terms related to inventory.

2. Identify accounting concepts and practices related to inventory.

3. Prepare a stock record.

4. Determine the cost of merchandise inventory using the fifo, lifo, and weighted-average inventory costing methods.

5. Estimate the cost of merchandise inventory using the gross profit method of estimating inventory.

EXPLORE ACCOUNTING

Costing a CD Can Make Your Head Spin

Determining the cost of an item of inventory, often referred to as *costing* an item, is a relatively easy task for a merchandising business. However, costing can be a complex task for the company that manufactures the item.

Consider the challenge of a music company costing a music CD. Stardust Music has signed a new group, SeaMist, to its first contract. Included in the cost of the CD is all the labor required to produce the CD. Stardust Music will pay SeaMist $1.50 for every CD sold. Studio artists, however, were paid a fixed fee totaling $30,000.

If Stardust Music sells 100,000 CDs, its labor cost will be $180,000, or $1.80 per CD—$150,000 to SeaMist and $30,000 to the studio artists. If the CD is an unexpected smash hit, selling 300,000 CDs, Stardust's labor cost will be $480,000, or $1.60 per CD—$450,000 to SeaMist and $30,000 for the studio artists.

The artist cost, $1.50 per CD, is referred to as a *variable cost*. The total artist cost varies, depending on the number of units sold. The studio artist cost of $30,000 is referred to as a *fixed cost* because the total studio artist cost is fixed (constant), regardless of the number of units sold.

When preparing the first monthly financial statement after the release of SeaMist's CD, Stardust's accountants must assign a labor cost to SeaMist's CD. What amount should be used? $1.80? $1.60? Another amount?

Accountants must make good sales estimates and constantly reevaluate these estimates to calculate the most accurate cost information possible. Accountants must constantly communicate with the sales staff to update sales projections.

Required: Calculate the total and unit labor costs for SeaMist's second CD using the following assumptions: (1) SeaMist receives $1.75 per CD. (2) Studio artists cost $60,000. (3) A famous guest artist used on one track receives $30,000 plus $0.10 for every CD sold. Prepare estimates for 400,000; 500,000; and 600,000 unit sales.

PHOTO: PHOTOGRAPHER'S CHOICE/GETTY IMAGES

19-1 APPLICATION PROBLEM

Preparing a stock record

A stock record for Mountain Pool & Spa is given in the *Working Papers*.

Instructions:
Enter the following transactions on the stock record of a 450-gallon spa, model no. HT-450. The units cost $1,299.00 and are sold for $2,599.00. Source documents are abbreviated as follows: purchase invoice, P; sales invoice, S.

Transactions:
- Feb. 4. Sold 1 model no. HT-450 spa to Jan Ellis, n/30. S2433.
- 28. Sold 2 model no. HT-450 spas to Lake County Hospital, 2/10, n/30. S2478.
- Mar. 10. Received 5 units of model no. HT-450 spas from SunSpa Manufacturing, 2/10, n/30. P789.
- 24. Sold 1 model no. HT-450 spa to John Pierce, n/30. S2502.

19-2 APPLICATION PROBLEM   AUTOMATED ACCOUNTING   Microsoft Office

Determining the cost of inventory using the fifo, lifo, and weighted-average inventory costing methods

Forms for costing inventory for Orlando Supply are given in the *Working Papers*. There are 172 units in ending inventory.

Purchase Date	Quantity	Unit Price
January 1, beginning inventory	90	$2.00
March 13, purchases	78	2.10
June 8, purchases	80	2.25
September 16, purchases	84	2.30
December 22, purchases	88	2.40

Instructions:
Calculate the cost of ending inventory using the fifo, lifo, and weighted-average methods.

Go Beyond the Book
For more information go to
www.C21accounting.com

19-3 APPLICATION PROBLEM

Estimating ending inventory using the gross profit method

Use the following information obtained from the records and management of Fultz Industries. A form for making inventory calculations and a form for completing an income statement are given in the *Working Papers*.

Instructions:

1. Estimate the cost of the ending inventory on March 31.

Estimated beginning inventory, March 1	$ 98,700.00
Actual net purchases for March	$ 45,800.00
Actual net sales for March	$186,000.00
Estimated gross profit percentage	58.0%
Actual operating expenses for March	$ 80,352.00

2. Prepare an income statement for the month ended March 31 of the current year.

19-4 MASTERY PROBLEM

Determining the cost of inventory using the fifo, lifo, and weighted-average inventory costing methods

Fratisi Company began the year with 8 units of its model P-234 electronic switch in beginning inventory. Each unit sells for $9.95. The following transactions involving model P-234 occurred during the year. Forms are given in the *Working Papers*. Source documents are abbreviated as follows: purchase invoice, P; sales invoice, S.

Transactions:

    Jan. 6. Purchased 20 units from Master Electronics for $5.12 per unit, 2/10, n/30. P154.
    Apr. 5. Sold 22 units to Evan Construction, n/30. S1998.
         14. Purchased 20 units from Master Electronics for $5.18 per unit, 2/10, n/30. P223.
    Jul. 28. Sold 25 units to Pette Hardware, n/30. S2245.
    Aug. 3. Purchased 20 units from Master Electronics for $5.23 per unit, 2/10, n/30. P298.
    Dec. 2. Sold 15 units to Century Homebuilders, n/30. S2848.
         12. Purchased 20 units from Master Electronics for $5.27 per unit, 2/10, n/30. P332.

Instructions:

1. Enter the transactions on the stock record and determine the number of units in ending inventory.

2. Calculate the cost of ending inventory using the fifo, lifo, and weighted-average methods.

3. Which of the inventory costing methods resulted in the highest cost of merchandise sold? Merchandise available for sale is the total cost of beginning inventory plus all purchases during the year.

CHALLENGE PROBLEM

Determining the cost of merchandise inventory destroyed in a fire

A fire completely destroyed the warehouse of Murphy Electronics Company on the night of May 12 of the current year. The accounting records of the company and $1,890.00 of merchandise inventory were salvaged. The company does not maintain a perpetual inventory system. The insurance company therefore has requested an estimate of the merchandise inventory destroyed in the fire. Forms are given in the *Working Papers*. The following income statement is for the previous fiscal year.

Murphy Electronics Company Income Statement For Year Ended April 30, 20--		
Operating Revenue:		
Net Sales		$645,217.90
Cost of Merchandise Sold:		
Beginning Inventory, May 1 (prior year).	$ 33,298.45	
Net Purchases	322,564.03	
Merchandise Available for Sale	$355,862.48	
Less Ending Inv., April 30	34,543.98	
Cost of Merchandise Sold		321,318.50
Gross Profit on Operations		$323,899.40
Operating Expenses		284,535.22
Net Income		$ 39,364.18

The following additional financial information is obtained from the current year's accounting records.

Net purchases, May 1 to May 12	$ 6,754.03
Net sales, May 1 to May 12	22,432.87
Operating expenses, May 1 to May 12	9,875.40

Instructions:

1. Calculate the prior year's gross profit on operations as a percentage of net sales. Round the percentage calculation to the nearest 0.1 percent.

2. Use the percentage calculated in Instruction 1 and the current year's financial information to calculate an estimate of the total merchandise inventory as of May 12.

3. To calculate the cost of the inventory destroyed in the fire, subtract the cost of the merchandise inventory that was not destroyed from the estimate of the total merchandise inventory as of May 12.

4. Prepare an income statement for the period May 1 through May 12.

The insurance company maintains that it is liable for paying only the book value of the inventory destroyed by fire. Murphy Electronics Company maintains that the insurance company should pay the replacement cost of the destroyed inventory.

Instructions:

5. What is meant by the book value and the replacement value of the inventory?

6. Murphy Electronics Company uses the fifo inventory costing method. How does using fifo affect the difference between the book value and the replacement value of the destroyed inventory?

7. What should determine which value the insurance company uses?

APPLIED COMMUNICATION

Arrange with your instructor to call the manager of a local merchandising company. Ask the manager questions concerning how the company maintains a count and cost of its merchandise inventory. Suggested questions include:

1. Does the company maintain a perpetual inventory system?
2. How often does the company take an inventory?
3. Who counts the inventory during a periodic inventory?
4. What method is used to cost the ending inventory?
5. If a perpetual inventory is used, how closely do the year-end quantities match the periodic counts?

CASES FOR CRITICAL THINKING

Case 1

Ballston Company uses the fifo method of costing its merchandise inventory. The manager is considering a change to the lifo method. Costs have increased steadily over the past three years. What effect will the change have on the following items? (1) The amount of net income on the income statement. (2) The amount of income taxes to be paid. (3) The quantity of each item of merchandise that must be kept in stock. Why?

Case 2

The Pet Center stocks many kinds of merchandise. The store has always taken a periodic inventory at the end of a fiscal year. The store has not kept a perpetual inventory because of the cost. However, the manager wants a reasonably accurate cost of merchandise inventory at the end of each month. The manager needs the amount to prepare monthly income statements and to help in making decisions about the business. What would you recommend?

SCANS WORKPLACE COMPETENCY

Personal Quality: Sociability

Concept: Sociability involves understanding, friendliness, adaptability, empathy, and politeness in new and on-going group settings. It includes asserting oneself in familiar and unfamiliar social situations, relating well to others, responding appropriately as a situation might require, and taking an interest in what others say and do.

Application: Consider each element in the concept of sociability. Rate yourself on each element. List ways you could improve. Discuss whether there are workplace situations that require greater or lesser degrees of sociability.

DIGITAL VISION/GETTY IMAGES

Employees responsible for purchasing inventory can be tempted to accept bribes from unscrupulous vendors. In exchange for the bribe, the employee favors the vendor in future purchasing decisions. This fraud is known as a *kickback*. Because the bribe is not recorded in the accounting records, it can be difficult to detect.

Marcus Salazar suspects one of his purchasing agents may be involved in a kickback scheme. To gather support for his suspicion, he has created graphs that depict the quantity and price paid for purchases of each inventory item from each vendor. An increase in the number of units purchased from a vendor, together with an increase in price, is a red flag of a kickback, since the vendor must raise the price to pay for the kickback.

The graphs for model AX-43 motors are shown below.

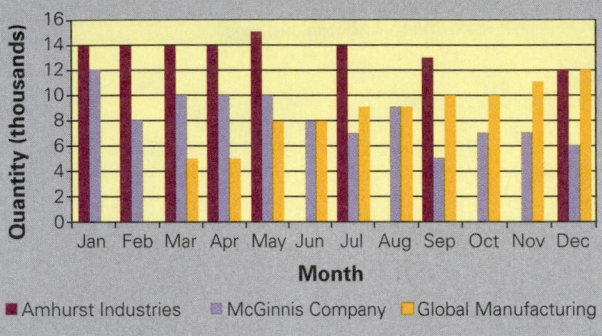

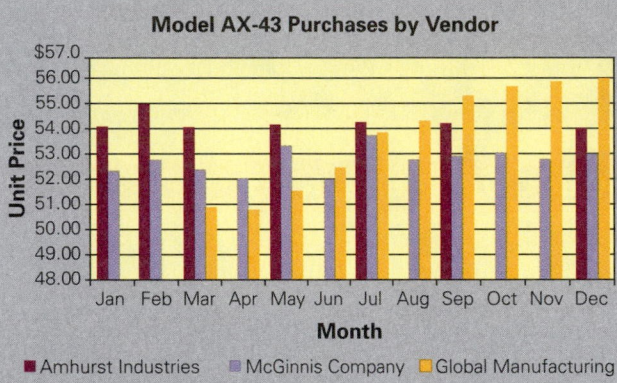

The first graph shows the monthly purchase quantity (in thousands) for each vendor. The second graph shows the unit price charged by vendor.

Assist Marcus in interpreting this data by answering the following questions.

1. From which vendor did the number of units purchased tend to increase over time?

2. How did the unit prices change for the vendor with increasing purchases? Support your answer.

3. Could there be a valid explanation why the buyer might purchase more from a vendor despite an increase in the unit price?

The managers at Best Buy need to constantly monitor the amount of inventory available for sale. Having too little inventory can cause the company to miss sales if the product is out of stock. Holding too much inventory increases its operating expenses. A financial ratio that evaluates the amount of inventory available for sale is known as the *inventory turnover ratio*. The ratio is calculated as follows:

$$\text{Inventory Turnover} = \frac{\text{Cost of Goods Sold}}{(\text{Beginning Inventory} + \text{Ending Inventory}) \div 2}$$

Dividing the sum of the beginning and ending inventory by 2 approximates the average inventory for the fiscal year. The inventory turnover for Wendy's International, based on its 2006 fiscal year financial statements, is calculated below:

$$\text{Inventory Turnover} = \frac{\$1,352,312,000}{(\$30,252,000 + \$29,798,000) \div 2} = 45$$

Dividing 365 by the turnover ratio yields a financial ratio known as *days' sales in inventory*. Wendy's number of days' sales in inventory is 8.1 days. Thus, the average item remains in its inventory for approximately 8 days (www.wendys.com).

Instructions

1. Using the financial information in Appendix B of this text, calculate Best Buy's inventory turnover ratio and number of days' sales in inventory for 2007.

2. Why would the inventory turnover ratios for Best Buy and Wendy's differ?

Accounting
SOFTWARE

MERCHANDISE INVENTORY

Generally accepted accounting principles require that a business use a recognized method for determining the cost of merchandise inventory. The FIFO, LIFO, and weighted-average methods are all recognized methods. Two variations of each method are also acceptable.

In this chapter, the cost of the units in ending inventory was determined at the end of a fiscal period. This method of applying FIFO, LIFO, and weighted-average is known as a *periodic method*—the calculation is made only at the end of a period. The *perpetual method* results in the cost of inventory sold being determined every time an item is sold. Thus, the perpetual variation keeps a continual count of the number and cost of the units in inventory.

Periodic and perpetual methods of FIFO, LIFO, and weighted-average inventories result in different values for ending inventory and the cost of goods sold. For this reason, generally accepted accounting principles require the consistent use of an inventory method. Peachtree uses the perpetual FIFO method of costing inventory and produces an Item Costing report to account for how every purchase and sale affects the value of inventory items.

PEACHTREE MASTERY PROBLEM 19-4
1. Open (Restore) file 19-4MP.ptb.
2. Journalize and post the transactions for the purchase and sale of inventory.
3. Print the purchase journal from January 6 to December 12.
4. Print the sales journal from April 5 to December 2.
5. Print the Item Costing report from January 1 to December 31.

MERCHANDISE INVENTORY

In QuickBooks, an inventory record is created for each item in inventory. The inventory record can include the item number, description, unit of measure, reorder point, quantity on hand, preferred vendor, cost, and selling price. When you purchase more of an item or sell it, the inventory record is automatically updated.

As discussed in this chapter, inventory can be accounted for on a periodic or perpetual basis. Also, inventory can be assigned a value based on a FIFO, LIFO, or weighted-average costing method. QuickBooks uses the perpetual basis and the weighted-average costing method.

In an automated accounting system, inventory reports can be produced anytime. These reports can be customized to contain all the information that is needed at the time. If the quantity of an item drops below the reorder point, QuickBooks will remind the user that it is time to reorder that inventory item.

QUICKBOOKS MASTERY PROBLEM 19-4
1. Open the Fratisi Company file.
2. Record the purchase of inventory by choosing the Enter Bills option from the Vendors menu.
3. Select Create Invoices from the Customers menu to record merchandise sales on account.
4. Choose Inventory from the Reports menu and Select Inventory Valuation Detail. Use January 1 and December 31 for the dates and print the report.

CALCULATING MERCHANDISE INVENTORY

"If the number of units in beginning inventory is less than the units on hand, enter the units in beginning inventory. Otherwise, enter the number of units on hand." This statement illustrates one of the decisions you must make in costing merchandise inventory using the LIFO method. Electronic spreadsheets can help you make these decisions. Through the use of its IF function, the electronic spreadsheet can compare two numbers and enter one of two values in the cell.

The syntax of the IF function is =IF(logical_test, true_value, false_value). Suppose there are 10 units (cell C17) in beginning inventory and 18 units (cell F22) on hand. The IF function to calculate the units from the beginning inventory would be:

=IF(C17< F22, C17, F22)

This function would calculate the value 10—it is true that C17 is less than F22, thus the true_value, 10 in cell C17, is calculated by the IF function.

Creating IF functions for a LIFO or FIFO template requires a full understanding of the logic of each inventory costing method. The logical tests for other purchases can become rather complex.

EXCEL APPLICATION PROBLEM 19-2

Open the F19-2 Excel data file. Follow the step-by-step instructions in the Instructions worksheet.

EXCEL APPLICATION PROBLEM 19-3

Open the F19-3 Excel data file. Follow the step-by-step instructions in the Instructions worksheet.

EXCEL MASTERY PROBLEM 19-4

Open the F19-4 Excel data file. Follow the step-by-step instructions in the Instructions worksheet.

AUTOMATED MERCHANDISE INVENTORY

A computerized inventory system provides better access to accurate information about the inventory. Managers need information about which items are selling, the number of items currently in inventory, and when to reorder an item.

All inventory transactions are recorded in the Other Activities Inventory window. These transactions include sales, purchases ordered, purchases received, and sales and purchases returns.

To enter inventory transactions:

1. Click the Other toolbar button.
2. Click the appropriate tab and enter the information about the purchase order, purchase invoice, or sales invoice; then click OK.
   a. Click Purch. Order if you are ordering items.
   b. Click Purch. Invoice if you are entering the receipt of merchandise purchased from a purchase invoice.
   c. Click Sales Invoice if you are entering the sale of merchandise from a sales invoice.

AUTOMATED ACCOUNTING APPLICATION PROBLEM 19-2

Open file F19-2.AA8. Display the problem instructions and complete the problem.

AUTOMATED ACCOUNTING MASTERY PROBLEM 19-4

Open file F19-4.AA8. Display the problem instructions and complete the problem.

PHOTODISC/GETTY IMAGES

CHAPTER 20

Accounting for Notes and Interest

Point Your Browser
www.C21accounting.com

Bank of America

Achieving Dreams with the Bank of America

Your first home. A new car. Opening your own business. Sending a child to college.

Many of the dreams we share require that we borrow money. That's how Bank of America helps people achieve their dreams. Through a national network of more than 16,000 ATMs and 5,700 branches, Bank of America is there to ensure that individuals, companies, and even government agencies have access to financial resources and services.

Bank of America is in the business of loaning money to its customers. In return, Bank of America expects the borrower to periodically pay interest on the loan until the loan matures. Interest income for a bank is equivalent to inventory sales of a retail company.

©QILAI SHEN/EPA/LANDOV

The timing of when interest is earned and recorded in the accounts is a significant issue for any bank. Interest income is earned each day a loan is outstanding, regardless of when the borrower pays the interest. As a result, banks must record the interest income earned, but not yet collected, in order for its financial statements to be in accordance with generally accepted accounting principles.

Critical Thinking

1. Banks make loans to individuals, companies, and many other groups, including cities. Why would a city need to borrow money?

2. If you borrow money, how is the interest rate usually stated?

Source: www.bankofamerica.com

INTERNET ACTIVITY

Federal Reserve

Go to the homepage for the Federal Reserve System (www.federalreserve.gov). The Federal Reserve's duties fall into four broad categories.

Instructions

1. List the four broad categories of duties of the Federal Reserve.

2. The United States is divided into 12 Federal Reserve districts. Find the district in which your school is located. List the district number and the headquarter city.

Promissory Notes

Cash is the primary medium of exchange for business transactions. [CONCEPT: Unit of Measurement] Cash is used to purchase merchandise and to pay salaries and other expenses. In turn, businesses receive cash when they sell their products or services and collect payment. The cash received can be used to purchase more merchandise and continue to pay salaries and other expenses. Thus, the business cycle continues.

Sometimes a business receives more cash from sales than is needed to pay for purchases and expenses. A business may deposit the extra cash in a bank for a short period. At other times, the receipt of cash from sales does not occur at the same time and in amounts sufficient to pay for needed purchases and expenses. When this occurs, a business needs to borrow additional cash or make arrangements with its vendors to delay payment for a period of time. Generally, when a bank or other business lends money to another business, the loan agreement is made in writing.

RUBBERBALL PRODUCTIONS/GETTY IMAGES

CHARACTER COUNTS

Only Full-Time Workers Receive Benefits

At the Backyard Gourmet, most employees work less than 30 hours per week. However, only employees who work a minimum of 30 hours per week are eligible for the company's health insurance plan. Thus, only the company's managers and officers are covered by health insurance. Lashonda Ethridge, a CPA and member of the American Institute of Certified Public Accountants, has just been hired as the company's chief financial officer. Having just learned of the company's hiring practices, she is considering resigning her position.

Instructions

Assume that Backyard Gourmet does not have a code of conduct. Use the ethical model to evaluate the company's hiring practices. Do you have any recommendations for Lashonda?

PHOTO: RISER/GETTY IMAGES

JOSÉ

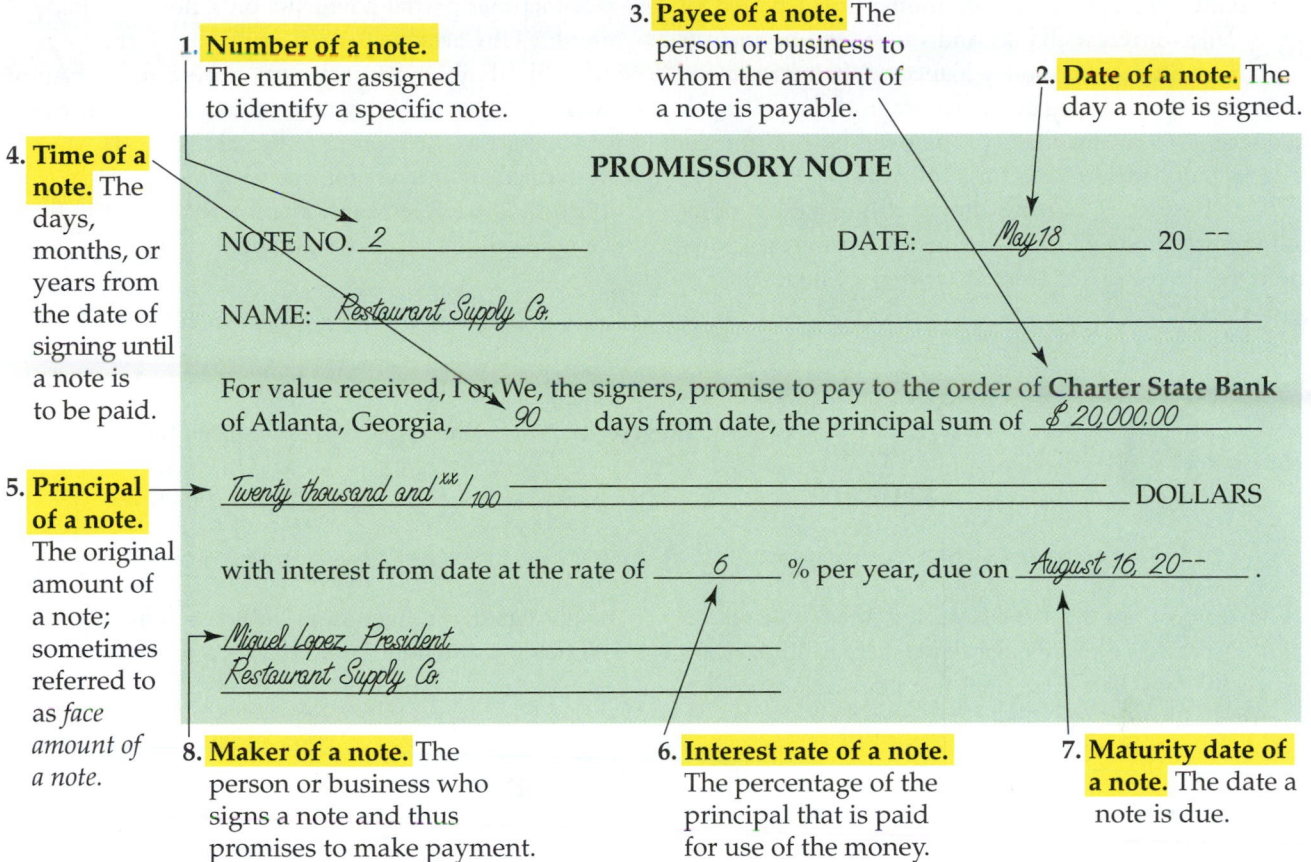

1. Number of a note. The number assigned to identify a specific note.

3. Payee of a note. The person or business to whom the amount of a note is payable.

2. Date of a note. The day a note is signed.

4. Time of a note. The days, months, or years from the date of signing until a note is to be paid.

5. Principal of a note. The original amount of a note; sometimes referred to as *face amount of a note.*

8. Maker of a note. The person or business who signs a note and thus promises to make payment.

6. Interest rate of a note. The percentage of the principal that is paid for use of the money.

7. Maturity date of a note. The date a note is due.

PROMISSORY NOTE

NOTE NO. *2*   DATE: *May 18*   20 *--*

NAME: *Restaurant Supply Co.*

For value received, I or We, the signers, promise to pay to the order of **Charter State Bank** of Atlanta, Georgia, *90* days from date, the principal sum of *$ 20,000.00*

Twenty thousand and *xx* / *100* _____ DOLLARS

with interest from date at the rate of *6* % per year, due on *August 16, 20--* .

Miguel Lopez, President
Restaurant Supply Co.

A written and signed promise to pay a sum of money at a specified time is called a **promissory note**. A person or organization to whom a liability is owed is called a **creditor**. Promissory notes signed by a business and given to a creditor are called **notes payable**. A note payable is frequently referred to as a *note*.

Promissory notes are used when money is borrowed for a period of time from a bank or other lending agency. Sometimes a business requests a note from a customer who wants credit beyond the usual time given for sales on account. Notes have an advantage over oral promises and accounts receivable or payable. Notes can be useful in a court of law as written evidence of a debt.

PHOTODISC/GETTY IMAGES

An amount paid for the use of money for a period of time is called **interest**. Banks and other lending institutions charge interest on money loaned to their customers. The interest rate is stated as a percentage of the principal. Interest at 10% means that 10 cents will be paid for the use of each dollar borrowed for a full year.

When businesses borrow money from banks, other lending institutions, or other businesses, promissory notes should be prepared to provide written evidence of the transaction.

Sometimes partial payments on a note are made each month. This arrangement is particularly true when an individual buys a car and signs a note for the amount owed. Each monthly payment includes part of the principal and part of the interest to be paid.

To calculate interest for one year, the principal is multiplied by the interest rate. The interest on a $20,000.00, 6% note for one year is $1,200.00.

	Principal	×	Interest Rate	×	Time in Years	=	Interest for One Year
	$20,000.00	×	6%	×	1	=	$1,200.00

The time of a note issued for less than one year is typically stated as a number of days, such as 30 days, 60 days, or 90 days. The time used in calculating interest is usually stated as a fraction of 360 days. The interest on a $20,000.00, 6% note for 90 days is $300.00.

	Principal	×	Interest Rate	×	Time as Fraction of Year	=	Interest for Fraction of Year
	$20,000.00	×	6%	×	$\frac{90}{360}$	=	$300.00

The amount that is due on the maturity date of a note is called the **maturity value**. A 90-day note with a principal of $20,000.00 and interest rate of 6% will have a maturity value of $20,300.00.

	Principal	+	Interest	=	Maturity Value
	$20,000.00	+	$300.00	=	$20,300.00

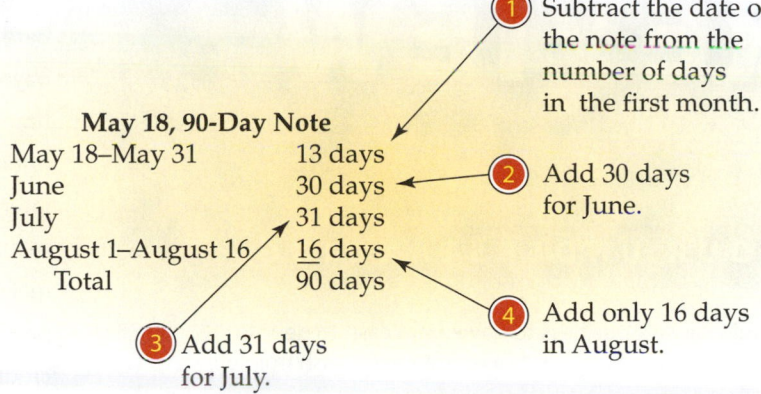

May 18, 90-Day Note

May 18–May 31	13 days
June	30 days
July	31 days
August 1–August 16	16 days
Total	90 days

① Subtract the date of the note from the number of days in the first month.

② Add 30 days for June.

③ Add 31 days for July.

④ Add only 16 days in August.

The time between the date a note is signed and the date a note is due is typically expressed in days. The maturity date is calculated by counting the exact number of days.

The date on which the note is written is not counted, but the maturity date is counted. For example, a 90-day note dated May 18 is due on August 16.

STEPS — CALCULATING THE MATURITY DATE OF A NOTE

① Calculate the number of days remaining in May, *13*, by subtracting the date of the note, *18*, from the number of days in May, *31*.

② Calculate the number of days remaining in the term of the note, *77*, by subtracting the number of days in the previous month, *13*, from the term of the note, *90*. Because *77* is greater than the number of days in June, *30*, add all of the days in June.

③ Calculate the number of days remaining in the term of the note, *47*, by subtracting the number of days in the previous months, *43 (13 + 30)*, from the term of the note, *90*. Because *43* is greater than the number of days in July, *31*, add all of the days in July.

④ Calculate the number of days remaining in the term of the note, *16*, by subtracting the number of days in the previous months, *74 (13 + 30 + 31)*, from the term of the note, *90*. Because *16* is less than the number of days in August, *31*, add only 16 days in August.

GLOWIMAGES/GETTY IMAGES

FOR YOUR INFORMATION

F Y I

Agencies of the federal government generally use a 365-day year when calculating interest. Consumer interest is also generally calculated on a 365-day year. However, many banks use a 360-day year when calculating interest. Therefore, the interest calculations in this textbook use a 360-day year.

FOR YOUR INFORMATION

F Y I

An interest rate can be entered on a calculator or electronic spreadsheet by using either the Percent key (%) or the decimal equivalent of the interest rate. For example, 12% could be keyed as 0.12.

End of Lesson
REVIEW

AUDIT YOUR UNDERSTANDING

1. What conditions would cause a business to have extra cash to deposit in a bank, yet at another time of year need to borrow extra cash from a bank?

2. What is the advantage of a promissory note over an account receivable?

3. What does interest at 10% mean?

4. How is interest calculated for a fraction of a year?

WORK TOGETHER 20-1

Calculating interest, maturity dates, and maturity values for promissory notes

Write the answers to the following problem in the *Working Papers*. Your instructor will guide you through the following example.

1. For each of the following promissory notes, calculate (a) the interest on the note, (b) the maturity date of the note, and (c) the maturity value of the note. Save your work to complete Work Together 20-2.

Date	Principal	Interest Rate	Time
March 3	$6,000.00	6%	90 days
March 18	$2,000.00	9%	60 days

ON YOUR OWN 20-1

Calculating interest, maturity dates, and maturity values for promissory notes

Write the answers to the following problem in the *Working Papers*. Work this problem independently.

1. For each of the following promissory notes, calculate (a) the interest on the note, (b) the maturity date of the note, and (c) the maturity value of the note. Save your work to complete On Your Own 20-2.

Date	Principal	Interest Rate	Time
June 8	$20,000.00	8%	180 days
June 12	$10,000.00	6%	90 days

SIGNING A NOTE PAYABLE

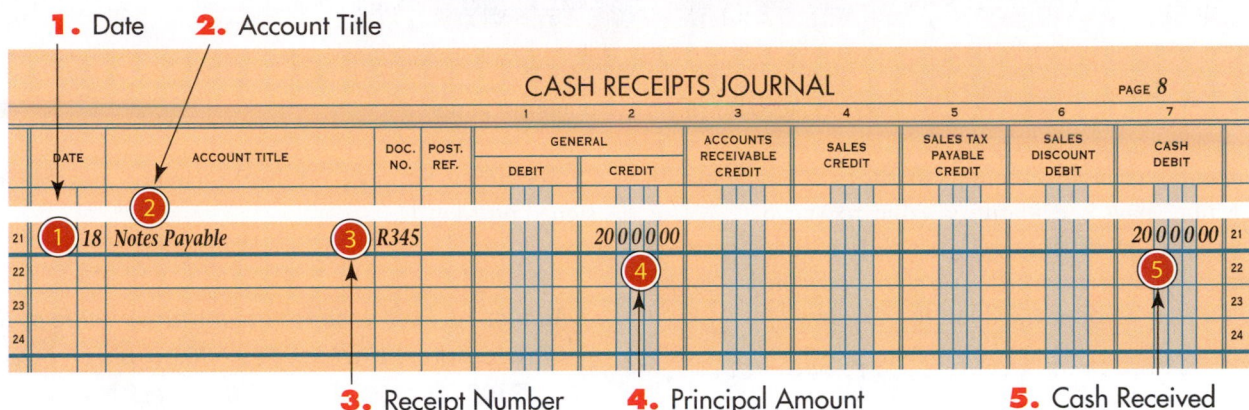

1. Date **2.** Account Title

3. Receipt Number **4.** Principal Amount **5.** Cash Received

Liabilities due within a short time, usually within a year, are called **current liabilities**. Because notes payable generally are paid within one year, they are classified as current liabilities.

When a business signs a note payable, the principal or face amount of the note is credited to a liability account titled Notes Payable.

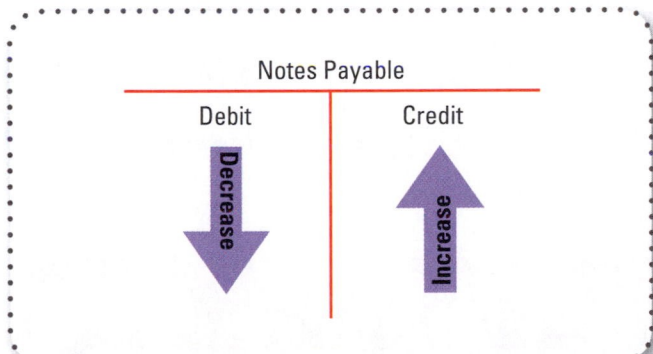

Restaurant Supply arranges to borrow money from its bank. A note payable is signed with the bank as evidence of the debt. The bank issues a check or deposits the principal amount of the note in Restaurant Supply's checking account.

> *May 18. Signed a 90-day, 6% note, $20,000.00. Receipt No. 345.*

The bank retains the original of the note until Restaurant Supply pays the maturity value. A receipt is prepared

to show the receipt of the principal amount of the note. [CONCEPT: Objective Evidence]

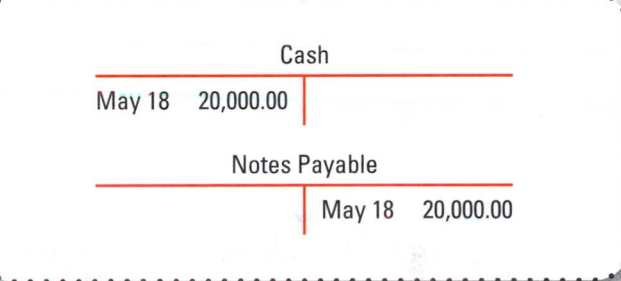

No entry is made for interest until a later date when the interest is paid.

STEPS **JOURNALIZING THE RECEIPT OF CASH FROM A NOTE PAYABLE**

1. Write the date, *18*, in the Date column of the cash receipts journal.

2. Write the account title, *Notes Payable*, in the Account Title column.

3. Write the receipt number, *R345*, in the Doc. No. column.

4. Write the principal amount, *$20,000.00*, in the General Credit column.

5. Write the same amount, *$20,000.00*, in the Cash Debit column.

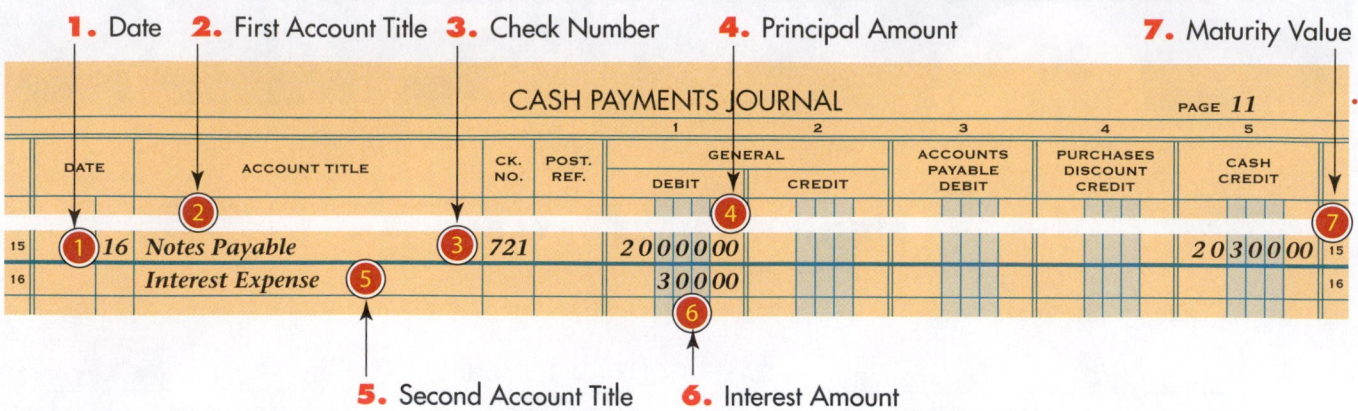

1. Date **2.** First Account Title **3.** Check Number **4.** Principal Amount **7.** Maturity Value

5. Second Account Title **6.** Interest Amount

When a note payable reaches its maturity date, the maker of the note pays the maturity value to the payee. The interest accrued on money borrowed is called **interest expense**. The interest accrued on a note payable is debited to an expense account titled Interest Expense.

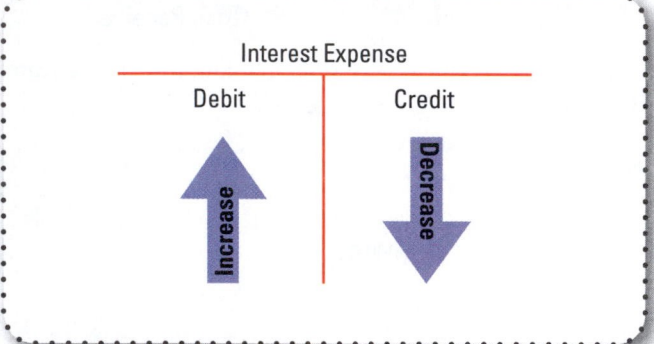

Interest expense is a financial expense rather than an expense of the business's normal operations. Therefore, Interest Expense is listed in a classification titled *Other Expenses* in a chart of accounts.

Restaurant Supply paid the 90-day note payable it had signed on May 18.

August 16. Paid cash for the maturity value of the May 18 note: principal, $20,000.00, plus interest, $300.00; total, $20,300.00. Check No. 721.

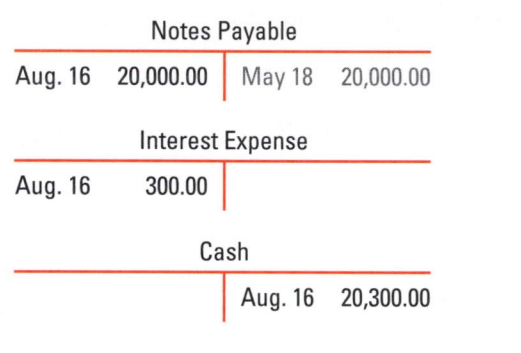

STEPS JOURNALIZING A CASH PAYMENT FOR THE MATURITY VALUE OF A NOTE PAYABLE

1. Write the date, *16*, in the Date column of the cash payments journal.

2. Write the account title, *Notes Payable*, in the Account Title column.

3. Write the check number, *721*, in the Ck. No. column.

4. Write the note's principal amount, *$20,000.00*, in the General Debit column.

5. Write the account title, *Interest Expense*, in the Account Title column on the next line.

6. Write the interest expense amount, *$300.00*, in the General Debit column.

7. Write the amount of cash paid, *$20,300.00*, in the Cash Credit column on the first line of the entry.

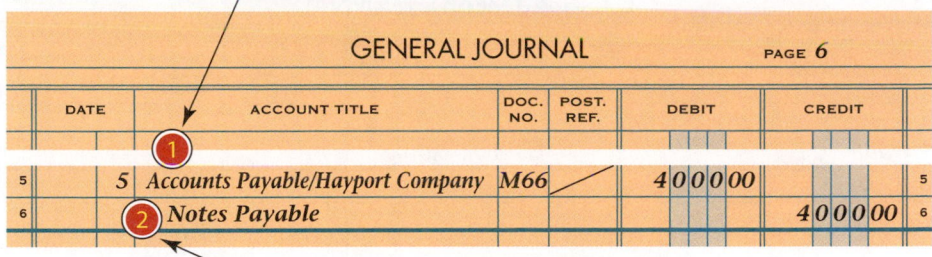

1. Debit to Accounts Payable

		DATE	ACCOUNT TITLE	DOC. NO.	POST. REF.	DEBIT	CREDIT	
5		5	Accounts Payable/Hayport Company	M66		4 0 0 0 00		5
6			Notes Payable				4 0 0 0 00	6

GENERAL JOURNAL   PAGE **6**

2. Credit to Notes Payable

A business may ask for an extension of time if it is unable to pay an account when due. The vendor may ask the business to sign a note payable. The note payable does not pay the amount owed to the vendor. However, the form of the liability is changed from an account payable to a note payable. When this entry is posted, the balance of the accounts payable account for Hayport Company will be zero. One liability, Accounts Payable, is replaced by another liability, Notes Payable.

June 5. Restaurant Supply signed a 90-day, 12% note to Hayport Company for an extension of time on its account payable, $4,000.00. Memorandum No. 66.

GENERAL LEDGER
Accounts Payable

June 5	4,000.00	Bal.	4,000.00

Notes Payable

		June 5	4,000.00

ACCOUNTS PAYABLE LEDGER
Hayport Company

June 5	4,000.00	Bal.	4,000.00

STEPS **JOURNALIZING SIGNING A NOTE PAYABLE FOR AN EXTENSION OF TIME**

1. Record a debit, $4,000.00, to *Accounts Payable/Hayport Company* in the general journal.

2. Record a credit, $4,000.00, to *Notes Payable.*

FOR YOUR INFORMATION

F Y I

There are advantages to accepting a note from a customer for an extension of time. In addition to serving as legal evidence of the debt, accepting a note may avoid having an account become uncollectible if additional time is all the customer needs in order to pay the account eventually. The business accepting the note will also earn interest on the overdue account, usually at a relatively high interest rate. Also, in some industries, these notes can be sold for cash if that cash is needed to meet operating expenses.

REMEMBER

When a note payable is signed for an extension of time on account, both the general ledger account, Accounts Payable, and the subsidiary ledger account are changed to a note payable. Therefore, both accounts must be debited to remove the amount from the accounts.

		CASH PAYMENTS JOURNAL									PAGE 11	
					1	2	3	4	5			
DATE		ACCOUNT TITLE	CK. NO.	POST. REF.	GENERAL		ACCOUNTS PAYABLE DEBIT	PURCHASES DISCOUNT CREDIT	CASH CREDIT			
					DEBIT	CREDIT						
3	3	Notes Payable	722		4 0 0 0 00				4 1 2 0 00			3
4		Interest Expense			1 2 0 00							4
5												5
6												6
7												7

The entry to record the cash payment at the maturity date of a note payable is the same regardless of the reason the note was signed.

September 3. Paid cash for the maturity value of the note payable to Hayport Company: principal, $4,000.00, plus interest, $120.00; total, $4,120.00. Check No. 722.

Notes Payable			
Sept. 3	4,000.00	Jan. 5	4,000.00

Interest Expense		
Sept. 3	120.00	

Cash		
		Sept. 3	4,120.00

CULTURAL DIVERSITY

Ancient China

By approximately 1000 c/b/, the Chinese had developed one of the most sophisticated accounting systems in the world. The Chao Dynasty ruled China from 1122 to 256 c/b/ During this time, the dynasty oversaw territorial expansion and a Golden Age in literature and philosophy. The famous philosopher Confucius lived during this dynasty. Confucius was said to have been a government recordkeeper.

During the Chao Dynasty, the Chinese used a system of currency and had a central bank. The Office of the Superintendent of Records furnished compilations of receipts and payments. It also kept maps and records of production tools used. Many of the accounting and record keeping tasks that affect businesses and governments today can be traced back to systems established in ancient China.

Critical Thinking

1. Early civilizations did not have currency. How do you think people would buy and sell goods and services without currency?

2. If you owned a store, what kinds of records would you want to keep about your sales?

End of Lesson REVIEW

TERMS REVIEW

current liabilities

interest expense

AUDIT YOUR UNDERSTANDING

1. Why are notes payable generally classified as current liabilities?
2. What accounts are affected, and how, when a business signs a note payable for an extension of time on an account payable?

WORK TOGETHER 20-2

Journalizing notes payable transactions

The journals for Landings, Inc., are provided in the *Working Papers*. Your instructor will guide you through the following examples.

1. Using the current year, journalize the following transactions. Use page 3 of a general journal and page 5 of a cash receipts journal. Source documents are abbreviated as follows: check, C; receipt, R; memorandum, M.

Transactions:

Mar. 3. Signed a 90-day, 6% note, for $6,000.00 with First National Bank. R279.
18. Signed a 60-day, 9% note with DryCreek Company for an extension of time on this account payable, $2,000.00. M288.

2. Journalize the following transactions on page 9 of a cash payments journal. Use the maturity dates and maturity values calculated in Work Together 20-1.

Transactions:

Paid cash for the maturity value of the $2,000.00 note. C255.
Paid cash for the maturity value of the $6,000.00 note. C263.

ON YOUR OWN 20-2

Journalizing notes payable transactions

The journals for Modisto Corporation are provided in the *Working Papers*. Work this problem independently.

1. Using the current year, journalize the following transactions. Use page 10 of a general journal and page 20 of a cash receipts journal. Source documents are abbreviated as follows: check, C; receipt, R; memorandum, M.

Transactions:

June 8. Signed a 180-day, 8% note, for $20,000.00 with First National Bank. R361.
12. Signed a 90-day, 6% note with Best Company for an extension of time on this account payable, $10,000.00. M165.

2. Journalize the following transactions on page 17 of a cash payments journal. Use the maturity dates and maturity values calculated in On Your Own 20-1.

Transactions:

Paid cash for the maturity value of the $10,000.00 note. C601.
Paid cash for the maturity value of the $20,000.00 note. C882.

ACCEPTING A NOTE RECEIVABLE FROM A CUSTOMER

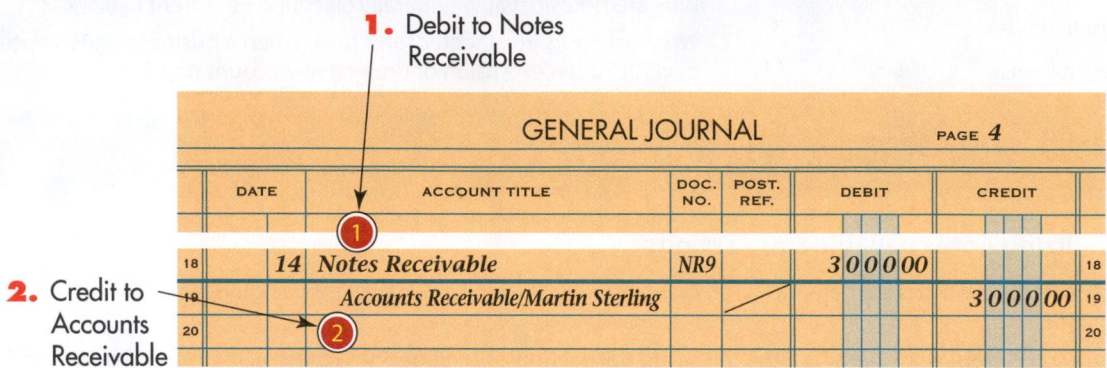

1. Debit to Notes Receivable

2. Credit to Accounts Receivable

	DATE		ACCOUNT TITLE	DOC. NO.	POST. REF.	DEBIT	CREDIT	
18	14	①	Notes Receivable	NR9		3 0 0 0 00		18
19			Accounts Receivable/Martin Sterling				3 0 0 0 00	19
20		②						20

GENERAL JOURNAL PAGE **4**

Promissory notes that a business accepts from customers are called **notes receivable**. Notes receivable are usually paid within one year. Therefore, they are classified as current assets.

A customer who is unable to pay an account on the due date may request additional time. The business should require the customer to sign a note. A note does not pay the amount the customer owes. However, the form of the asset is changed from an account receivable to a note receivable. The promissory note is a written confirmation of the amount owed, which provides the business with evidence of the debt in case legal action is required to collect.

When a customer signs a note, the principal amount of the note is debited to an asset account titled Notes Receivable. One asset, Accounts Receivable, is replaced by another asset, Notes Receivable.

GENERAL LEDGER
Notes Receivable

Apr. 14	3,000.00	

Accounts Receivable

Bal.	3,000.00	Apr. 14	3,000.00

ACCOUNTS RECEIVABLE LEDGER
Martin Sterling

Bal.	3,000.00	Apr. 14	3,000.00

When this entry is posted, the balance of the accounts receivable account for Mr. Sterling is zero.

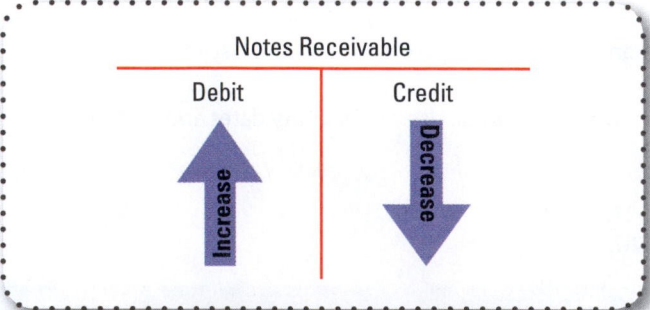

Notes Receivable

Debit	Credit
Increase	Decrease

April 14. Accepted a 90-day, 8% note from Martin Sterling for an extension of time on his account, $3,000.00. Note Receivable No. 9.

STEPS

JOURNALIZING ACCEPTING A NOTE FOR AN EXTENSION OF TIME ON AN ACCOUNT RECEIVABLE

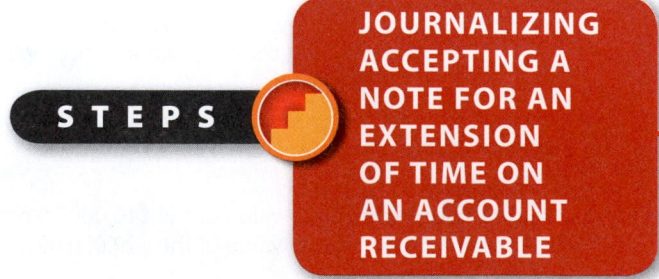

① Record a debit to *Notes Receivable* for the amount of the note, *$3,000.00,* in the general journal.

② Record a credit to *Accounts Receivable/Martin Sterling* for the same amount, *$3,000.00.*

COLLECTING PRINCIPAL AND INTEREST ON A NOTE RECEIVABLE

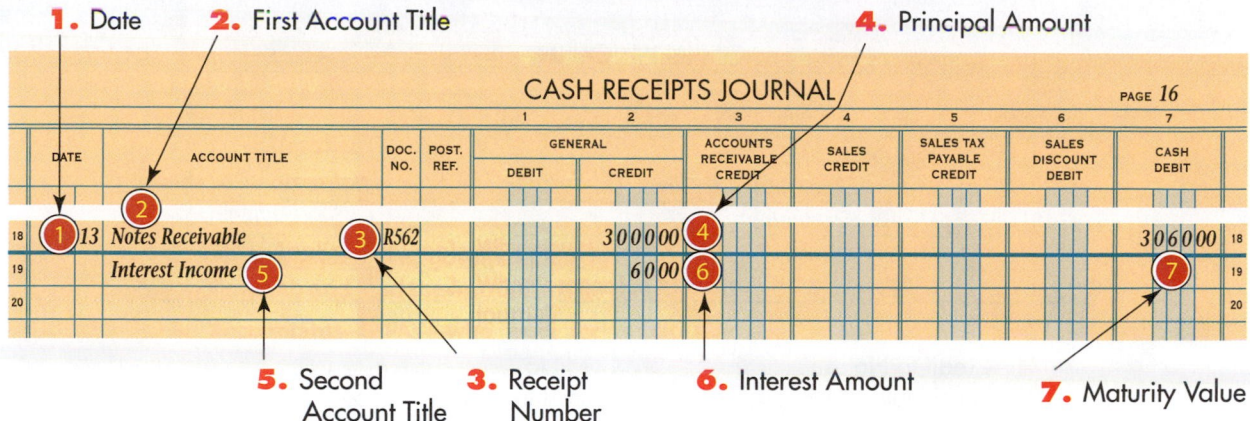

1. Date   **2.** First Account Title   **4.** Principal Amount

5. Second Account Title   **3.** Receipt Number   **6.** Interest Amount   **7.** Maturity Value

When a note receivable reaches its maturity date, the payee receives the maturity value from the maker. The interest earned on money loaned is called **interest income**. The interest earned on a note receivable is credited to a revenue account titled Interest Income.

Interest income is investment revenue rather than revenue from normal operations. Therefore, Interest Income is listed in a classification titled *Other Revenue* in a chart of accounts.

Restaurant Supply received cash for the principal and interest of the note signed by Mr. Sterling on April 14.

> **July 13. Received cash for the maturity value of Note Receivable No. 9, a 90-day, 8% note: principal, $3,000.00, plus interest, $60.00; total, $3,060.00. Receipt No. 562.**

Interest Income	
Debit	Credit
Decrease ↓	Increase ↑

Cash	
July 13 3,060.00	

Notes Receivable	
Apr. 14 3,000.00	July 13 3,000.00

Interest Income	
	July 13 60.00

Interest income is calculated using the same method as that used for notes payable. The principal is multiplied by the interest rate and the fraction of the year ($3,000.00 $\times$ 8% $\times$ 90/360) to calculate interest income, $60.00.

After the entry is recorded, the original of Note Receivable No. 9 is marked *Paid*. The original is given to Mr. Sterling and a copy is kept by Restaurant Supply.

STEPS — JOURNALIZING CASH RECEIVED FOR MATURITY VALUE OF A NOTE RECEIVABLE

1. Write the date, *13*, in the Date column of the cash receipts journal.
2. Write the account title, *Notes Receivable*, in the Account Title column.
3. Write the receipt number, *R562*, in the Doc. No. column.
4. Write the principal amount, *$3,000.00*, in the General Credit column.
5. On the next line, write the account title, *Interest Income*, in the Account Title column.
6. Calculate and write the interest income amount, *$60.00*, in the General Credit column.
7. Write the maturity value, *$3,060.00*, in the Cash Debit column on the first line of the entry.

1. Debit to Accounts Receivable

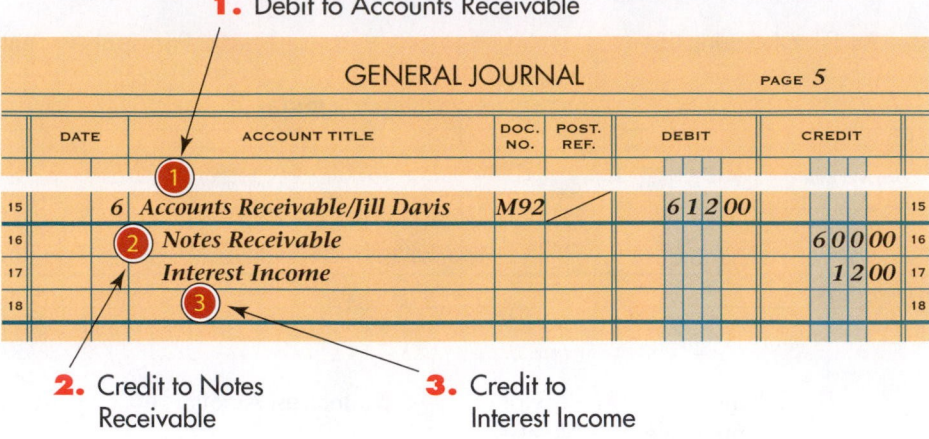

2. Credit to Notes Receivable

3. Credit to Interest Income

A note that is not paid when due is called a **dishonored note**. The balance of the notes receivable account should show only the total amount of notes that probably will be collected. The amount of a dishonored note receivable should be removed from the notes receivable account.

The amount of the note plus interest income earned on the note is still owed by the customer. Therefore, the total amount owed should be debited to the accounts receivable account in the general ledger. The amount owed should also be debited to the customer account in the accounts receivable ledger. This information may be important if the customer requests credit in the future or if collection is achieved later.

May 6. Jill Davis dishonored Note Receivable No. 12, a 90-day, 8% note, maturity value due today: principal, $600.00; interest, $12.00; total, $612.00. Memorandum No. 92.

The interest income on the note has been earned as of the maturity date even though the note has not been paid. Jill Davis owes the principal amount of the note plus the interest earned. Therefore, the maturity value, *$612.00*, is debited to Accounts Receivable and to Jill Davis's account

in the accounts receivable ledger. One asset, Notes Receivable, is replaced by another asset, Accounts Receivable.

GENERAL LEDGER
Accounts Receivable

May 6	612.00		

Notes Receivable

Feb. 5	600.00	May 6	600.00

Interest Income

		May 6	12.00

ACCOUNTS RECEIVABLE LEDGER
Jill Davis

May 6	612.00		

Restaurant Supply does not write off Ms. Davis's account when the note is dishonored. The company continues to try to collect the account.

Later, Restaurant Supply may decide that the account cannot be collected. At that time, the balance of the account will be written off as an uncollectible account. Allowance for Uncollectible Accounts will be debited, and Accounts Receivable and Jill Davis's account will be credited.

STEPS **JOURNALIZING A DISHONORED NOTE RECEIVABLE**

1. Record a debit to *Accounts Receivable/Jill Davis* for the total maturity value of the note, *$612.00*, in the general journal.

2. Record a credit to *Notes Receivable* for the principal amount of the dishonored note, *$600.00*.

3. Record a credit to *Interest Income* for the interest earned on the note, *$12.00*.

Missie T. Talbot, Law Firm Office Manager

Missie T. Talbot first became interested in accounting when she elected to take her first accounting course as a high school junior. She had always enjoyed working with numbers.

During the first accounting class, she learned how to write checks properly, open a bank account, and balance a checking account—skills she believes every high school student should learn. Realizing that she enjoyed accounting, Missie elected to take a second year of high school accounting. She recalls, "We were able to set up our own company, record all the cash receipts, write checks, and perform the accounting procedures involved with running a business. I found the task a rewarding experience."

After graduation, she enrolled in accounting and data processing courses in college. Her accounting knowledge enabled her to become a bookkeeper for a forestry equipment manufacturer. She was later promoted to office manager while still performing her bookkeeping responsibilities. A family move led her to become an accounts payable clerk for a contact lens manufacturer and distributor. In that position, she prepared sales tax returns for over six states and many local taxing authorities, along with monthly, quarterly, and year-end closings.

Missie says, "During this time, my husband and I were approached by a corporation in Dallas to open and operate a dry cleaner. After considerable discussion and relying on my bookkeeping knowledge, we decided to go for it." Organized in 1992 as a sole proprietorship, the business was a grand success because all garments were cleaned for the same low price. Within two years, they opened another location in their hometown.

Successful businesses often catch the attention of investors. When Missie and her husband sold their business to investors, she became the office manager and paraprofessional for T. E. Lott & Company, PA, a regional accounting firm. There she prepared the monthly financial statements, quarterly payroll tax returns, sales tax reports, and payroll checks for its clients.

Missie is now the firm administrator for the law firm of Gholson, Hicks and Nichols, PA. She is responsible for the financial management of the firm and supervises its 16 staff members. She believes that "without the basics of accounting that I received in high school, I know that I would not be here in this law firm today."

Missie credits her high school math teacher, Mrs. Mythle Hodges, for encouraging her to stick with math and accounting. "I do regret never completing my college degree—but it's never too late!"

Salary Range: The median annual earnings of office support supervisors and managers were $41,030 in 2004. The middle 50 percent earned between $31,860 and $53,110, according to the *Occupational Outlook Handbook*. (Bureau of Labor Statistics, U.S. Department of Labor, *Occupational Outlook Handbook, 2006–07 Edition*, Secretaries and Administrative, on the Internet at www.bls.gov/oco/ocos127.htm.)

Qualifications: An office manager must possess a wide variety of skills, including communication, technology, and organizational skills. Accounting courses in high school and college are highly desirable.

Occupational Outlook: As the economy becomes more service oriented, more job opportunities will become available in the offices of small service businesses.

End of Lesson
REVIEW

1. When a business asks a customer to sign a note receivable for an extension of time on the customer's account receivable, how do the amount and form of the business asset change?

2. In which chart of accounts classification is Interest Income listed?

3. What accounts are affected, and how, when a customer dishonors a note receivable?

4. Why is interest income recorded at the time a note is dishonored even though cash has not been received?

TERMS REVIEW

notes receivable

interest income

dishonored note

WORK TOGETHER 20-3

Journalizing notes receivable transactions

The journals for Cruz Corporation are provided in the *Working Papers*. Your instructor will guide you through the following example.

1. Using the current year, journalize the following transactions. Use page 2 of a general journal and page 3 of a cash receipts journal. Source documents are abbreviated as follows: note receivable, NR; receipt, R; memorandum, M.

Transactions:

Feb. 2. Accepted a 90-day, 8% note from Paul Gary for an extension of time on his account, $1,800.00. NR17.

18. Received cash for the maturity value of NR14, a 60-day, 9% note for $500.00. R67.

27. Kirk Adams dishonored NR9, a 90-day, 9% note, for $400.00. M25.

ON YOUR OWN 20-3

Journalizing notes receivable transactions

The journals for Reality, Inc., are provided in the *Working Papers*. Work this problem independently.

1. Using the current year, journalize the following transactions. Use page 3 of a general journal and page 5 of a cash receipts journal. Source documents are abbreviated as follows: note receivable, NR; receipt, R; memorandum, M.

Transactions:

Mar. 4. Accepted a 90-day, 10% note from Kim Pratt for an extension of time on her account, $2,500.00. NR24.

18. Received cash for the maturity value of NR18, a 60-day, 12% note for $1,500.00. R68.

26. T. J. Cross dishonored NR15, a 90-day, 10% note, for $1,800.00. M21.

After completing this chapter, you can:

1. Define accounting terms related to notes and interest.

2. Identify accounting concepts and practices related to notes and interest.

3. Calculate interest and maturity dates for notes.

4. Analyze and record transactions for notes payable.

5. Analyze and record transactions for notes receivable.

EXPLORE ACCOUNTING

Low Interest or Cash Back?

"For a limited time, receive 1.9% financing or $2,000 cash back on your new car!" We often hear car dealers offer customers incentives of below-market financing or a cash refund. Each option provides the customer with a monetary value. The below-market financing spreads this value—a reduced monthly payment—over a period of time. The cash refund is received when the car is purchased.

Should the customer's choice have an impact on the way the sales transaction is recorded by the car dealer? Hammond Motors has two cars with sticker prices of $18,000.00. Pedro Diaz purchased one car, paying $3,000.00 down and financing the remaining $15,000.00 over 4 years at the 1.9% interest rate. Tatsu Hamazaki purchased the other car, paying only $1,000.00 down and using her $2,000.00 cash back option to reduce her 12% note to $15,000.00. Using this information, it appears that Hammond Auto sold Pedro's car for $18,000.00 and Tatsu's car for $16,000.00. It also appears that both customers are responsible for $15,000.00 notes receivable.

However, accountants believe that, regardless of which sales incentive is offered, the value of the incentive should be deducted from the sales price. Accounting rules require that the recorded amount of below-market loans be reduced by the value of the incentive. This process, known as *imputing interest*, adjusts the note receivable to an amount that will yield a market rate of interest over the life of the note. Using the imputing interest rules, the below-market financing provided Pedro Diaz with a $2,000.00 benefit. Thus, Hammond Auto must record a $2,000.00 credit to Discount on Notes Receivable. The credit to Sales for Pedro's car, therefore, is only $15,000.00.

Instructions: Identify a below-market financing or cash refund currently being offered by an auto dealer. If you were purchasing the car, which offer would you accept? Without knowing the accounting rules for imputing interest, how could you make an informed decision?

20-1 APPLICATION PROBLEM

Calculating interest, maturity dates, and maturity values for promissory notes

Information regarding Shinoda, Inc., is provided in the *Working Papers*.

Instructions:

1. For each of the following promissory notes, calculate (a) the interest on the note, (b) the maturity date of the note, and (c) the maturity value of the note. Save your work to complete Application Problem 20-2.

Date	Principal	Interest Rate	Time
April 6	$10,000.00	12%	180 days
April 12	$600.00	9%	60 days
April 15	$5,000.00	10%	90 days
April 23	$3,000.00	14%	60 days

20-2 APPLICATION PROBLEM

Journalizing notes payable transactions

The journals for Webster Company are provided in the *Working Papers*.

Instructions:

1. Using the current year, journalize each of the following transactions using page 4 of a general journal and page 6 of a cash receipts journal. Source documents are abbreviated as follows: receipt, R; memorandum, M.

Transactions:
    Apr. 6. Signed a 180-day, 12% note for $10,000.00 with First American Bank. R127.
          12. Signed a 60-day, 9% note with Milligan Company for an extension of time on this account payable, $600.00. M32.
          15. Signed a 90-day, 10% note for $5,000.00 with First National Bank. R142.
          23. Signed a 60-day, 14% note with Yeatman Industries for an extension of time on this account payable, $3,000.00. M42.

2. Journalize the following transactions on page 9 of a cash payments journal. Use the maturity dates and maturity values calculated in Application Problem 20-1. The abbreviation for a check is C.

Transactions:
    Paid cash for the maturity value of the $600.00 note dated April 12. C310.
    Paid cash for the maturity value of the $3,000.00 note dated April 23. C318.
    Paid cash for the maturity value of the $5,000.00 note dated April 15. C456.
    Paid cash for the maturity value of the $10,000.00 note dated April 6. C645.

(Go Beyond the Book)
For more information go to
www.C21accounting.com

20-3 APPLICATION PROBLEM

Journalizing notes receivable transactions

The journals for Compression Services are provided in the *Working Papers*.

Instructions:

1. Using the current year, journalize the following transactions. Use page 14 of a general journal and page 10 of a cash receipts journal. Source documents are abbreviated as follows: notes receivable, NR; receipt, R; memorandum, M.

Transactions:

Jul. 5. Accepted a 90-day, 12% note from Peter Lamb for an extension of time on his account, $3,000.00. NR25.

11. Received cash for the maturity value of NR20, a 60-day, 9% note for $800.00. R321.

15. Accepted a 90-day, 10% note from Pam Sellers for an extension of time on her account, $2,400.00. NR26.

21. Josh Kemp dishonored NR16, a 90-day, 12% note, for $3,500.00. M62.

22. Received cash for the maturity value of NR17, a 90-day, 10% note for $1,000.00. R339.

27. Phil Pellum dishonored NR18, a 90-day, 15% note, for $2,500.00. M63.

20-4 APPLICATION PROBLEM

Journalizing notes receivable transactions

Savath Rajady, the credit manager of Jenkin Company, encourages customers of past-due accounts to sign notes receivable. Mr. Rajady informs customers that future sales on account will be accepted only if the customers sign a note and subsequently pay the note with interest. Using this strategy, most of Jenkin's customers agree to sign notes. Jenkin Company requires all customers to sign 90-day, 18% notes.

Instructions:

1. Journalize the following transactions completed by Jenkin Company during the current year. The journals are provided in the *Working Papers*. Use page 18 of a general journal and page 11 of a cash receipts journal. Source documents are abbreviated as follows: notes receivable, NR; receipt, R; memorandum, M.

Transactions:

Nov. 3. Savath Rajady visited the offices of AutoCare Industries. AutoCare's president agreed to sign a note for $3,000.00. NR63.

14. Received a check for $2,090.00 from Teltor Company. The payment covers a $2,000.00 note, number 52. R245.

28. A $4,000.00, 18%, 90-day note receivable from Sanford Company was due today, but no check has been received. Savath Rajady attempted to call the company but discovered that its phone has been disconnected. M69.

MASTERY PROBLEM

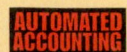  

Journalizing notes payable and notes receivable transactions

The following transactions related to notes payable and notes receivable were completed by Amory Company during March of the current year. Journals are provided in the *Working Papers*.

Transactions:

Jul. 2. Signed a 90-day, 10% note for $5,000.00 with Commercial National Bank. R51.

7. Accepted a 90-day, 10% note from Nan Abert for an extension of time on her account, $1,500.00. NR9.

9. Received cash for the maturity value of NR4, a 60-day, 9% note for $1,600.00. R62.

12. Accepted a 90-day, 10% note from Tom Burns for an extension of time on his account, $400.00. NR10.

17. Received cash for the maturity value of NR5, a 60-day, 9% note for $800.00. R65.

23. Signed a 180-day, 8% note for $8,000.00 with American National Bank. R74.

24. Gibson Co. dishonored NR2, a 90-day, 12% note, for $3,000.00. M43.

28. Received cash for the maturity value of NR3, a 90-day, 12% note for $4,500.00. R79.

29. Signed a 60-day, 12% note with Daily Supply for an extension of time on this account payable, $2,500.00. M44.

Instructions:

1. Journalize each transaction, using page 7 of a general journal and page 6 of a cash receipts journal. Source documents are abbreviated as follows: check, C; receipt, R; memorandum, M; note receivable, NR.

2. Determine the maturity date and maturity value of each note signed by Amory Company.

3. Journalize the following transactions on page 9 of a cash payments journal. Use the maturity dates and maturity values calculated in previous steps.

Transactions:

Paid cash for the maturity value of the $2,500.00 note dated July 29. C417.

Paid cash for the maturity value of the $5,000.00 note dated July 2. C610.

Paid cash for the maturity value of the $8,000.00 note dated July 23. C821.

20-6 CHALLENGE PROBLEM

Recording notes receivable stated in months

On June 18, James Whiley signed a $10,000.00 note payable with National Bank of Cressville. At his request, the bank drafted the note for a 3-month term, payable on September 18, with 15% interest. Mr. Whiley proudly stated, "Since my company began in 1972, we have never had to borrow money for more than 90 days." The loan officer, believing that Mr. Whiley did not fully understand the terms of the note, explained that the company would be responsible for interest for the number of days between June 18 and September 18. That number, he continued, would be slightly more than 90 days.

Instructions:

1. Use the forms given in the *Working Papers*. Determine the maturity value of the note on September 18. Use the actual number of days from June 18 in your calculation.

2. Mr. Whiley expected to pay only 90 days of interest on the note. Determine the maturity value of the note assuming interest is charged for only 90 days.

3. Assume the bank allows Mr. Whiley to pay only the interest amount calculated in Instruction 2, even though the money will be borrowed for more than 90 days. Determine the actual interest rate of the note.

4. Should the bank allow Mr. Whiley to pay for only 90 days' interest?

As an accountant for Hasler Corporation, you have been asked to assist the president in making a presentation to the board of directors. The president wants to report the 4-year growth in sales of four major products. The following table presents product sales (in thousands of dollars) from 20X1 to 20X4.

	20X1	20X2	20X3	20X4
Lumber	$253	$316	$324	$315
Hardware	166	182	169	175
Carpet	153	176	189	201
Housewares	122	112	114	103

Instructions: Prepare a graph displaying the data presented in the table. Determine what type of graph (pie, line, bar, stacked-bar) best communicates the sales trend of each product. If available, use the graph or chart feature of a spreadsheet program to create the graph.

TayVon Johnson, a new accounting department employee, questions the practice of recording interest income when a note is dishonored. Instead, he believes that the interest earned on the note should be recorded only if and when the account is subsequently paid. Is this alternative method acceptable? Why or why not?

Every week Sandie Oswalt, Vice-President, compares the certificate of deposit (CD) rates for her bank, National Bank, to three local competing banks. Sandie uses the information to decide when and by how much to raise or lower National Bank's CD rates.

Use the graph to answer the following questions. Support your answers.

1. Is the National Bank competitive with short-term (90 day or less) CDs?
2. Is the National Bank competitive with long-term (1 year or more) CDs?
3. Which bank has the least variation in its CD rates?

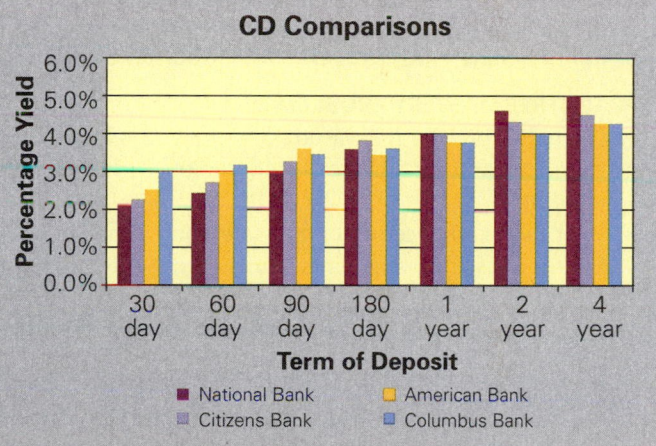

Just as no two individuals are exactly the same, no two companies are exactly the same. Management decisions, such as the ownership of property and equipment, the types and amounts of inventory, and customer credit policies, all cause the economic events of each company to be different.

The summary of these economic events is reflected in financial statements. Financial statements should enable the reader to learn the important financial information of the company. Thus, just as each company is different, each company's financial statements are different.

Many companies have large levels of long-term debt and, as a result, report interest expense on their income statements. Compared with other companies, Best Buy has a relatively low level of long-term debt and incurs a small amount of interest expense.

Instructions: Refer to Best Buy's financial statements on pages B-5 and B-7 in Appendix B of this textbook.

1. What are Best Buy's long-term liabilities and debt as a percent of total liabilities and shareholders' equity for fiscal year 2007?
2. What was the amount of cash paid for interest expense in fiscal year 2007 as reported on the Consolidated Statements of Cash Flows?

Accounting
SOFTWARE

NOTES PAYABLE AND RECEIVABLE

Peachtree keeps records of every purchase on account from each vendor. At any time, a business can see a listing of the outstanding invoices owed to a vendor. When the business pays the account, the payment is applied against specific outstanding invoices in the vendor's account. This method of maintaining an accounts payable ledger is known as an *open item system*.

When a business pays an outstanding invoice with a note payable, the outstanding invoice in the vendor's account should be marked as paid. Therefore, Peachtree has you record the signing of a note payable using the same window you would use if the business paid the invoice with a check.

Similarly, the receipt of cash from the signing of a note payable is recorded in a window normally used to record the receipt of cash from sales or the collection of accounts receivable. Changes in the default general ledger accounts are necessary to ensure the transaction is journalized properly.

PEACHTREE APPLICATION PROBLEM 20-2

1. Open (Restore) file 20-2AP.ptb.
2. Journalize and post each of the transactions covering the signing of notes payable and the payment of cash for a notes payable.
3. Print the April 6 to April 15 cash receipts journal.
4. Print the April 12 to April 23 purchase journal.
5. Print the June 11 to October 3 cash disbursements journal.

PEACHTREE MASTERY PROBLEM 20-5

1. Open (Restore) file 20-5MP.ptb.
2. Journalize and post the transactions in the cash disbursements journal related to notes payable and notes receivable.
3. Print July's cash receipts journal, sales journal, and purchase journal.
4. Print the cash disbursements journal from September 27 to January 19.

NOTES PAYABLE AND RECEIVABLE

Using an accounting software package to record notes payable and notes receivable is very similar to recording these transactions in a manual accounting system.

The entry to record signing a note payable in exchange for cash or other assets is entered in the Make Deposits window. The entry to record signing a note payable for an extension of time on an account is entered in the Enter Bills window. The entry to record the payment of a note payable is entered in the Write Checks window.

Notes receivable are handled in a similar manner. The entry to record accepting a note receivable from a customer for an extension of time is entered in the Receive Payments window. The entry to record the receipt of cash from a note receivable is entered in the Make Deposits window.

While QuickBooks does not calculate maturity dates or maturity values, it does have a calculator feature available. To open the calculator, click in the amount field and either press = or enter a number followed by +, −, *, /, or =. A paper tape, much like the paper tape in a calculator, will appear, and your calculations will appear on the tape. To enter the calculation result in the field, press Enter or Tab, or click anywhere outside the lines of the tape.

QUICKBOOKS APPLICATION PROBLEM 20-2

1. Open the Webster Company file.
2. To record a note payable for cash, use the Make Deposits option from the Banking menu. To record a note payable to extend payment terms, choose the Enter Bills option from the Vendors menu. Record the signing of a note payable and the payment of cash for a note payable.
3. Print a Journal report using April 1 and October 31 for the dates.

QUICKBOOKS MASTERY PROBLEM 20-5

1. Open the Amory Company file.
2. Journalize the notes payable and notes receivable transactions for July.
3. Journalize the transactions for later months for notes paid at maturity using the Write Checks window to record the transactions.
4. Print a Journal report using July 1 and January 31 of the following year for the dates.

CALCULATING DATES FOR NOTES

Mitchell Nelson was born on the 33,131st day of the 20th century. Why would Mitchell or anyone else care about this number? Electronic spreadsheets use sequential numbers, beginning with January 1, 1900, to perform date calculations. A variety of date and time functions allows you to determine dates, such as the age of a person or the due date of a note payable.

Open a blank worksheet and enter Mitchell's birthday of 9/15/1990 in cell A1. The spreadsheet displays the date but stores the 33,131 in the cell. Let's assume today's date is January 1, 2009. How old is Mitchell on that date? To find out, enter 1/01/2009 in cell A2; then enter the following formula in cell A3: =(A2 − A1)/365. Subtracting Mitchell's birthday from today's value calculates his age in days; dividing this number by 365 completes the calculation of his age in years. The age displayed is 18.30959. Mitchell is 18 years old.

When does a 135-day note signed on 6/17/2010 mature? Enter the date in cell B1 and enter the formula +B1+135 in cell B2. The spreadsheet recognizes you are working with dates and automatically formats the new cell as a date—10/30/2010. But the number that is stored in the cell is actually 40,481.

Not sure you believe it? Format the four cells using a number or currency format and see it for yourself.

EXCEL APPLICATION PROBLEM 20-1

Open the F20-1 Excel data file. Follow the step-by-step instructions in the Instructions worksheet.

CALCULATING NOTES AND INTEREST

The Planning Tools in *Automated Accounting* perform specific types of interest and loan calculations.

The Notes and Interest Planner is used to calculate maturity date, amount of interest, and the maturity value of the note. A business can use the planner to calculate the total amount to be received or paid (maturity value) of its notes receivable or notes payable. The planner may also be used to determine the exact due date of a note when the term is stated as a number of days or months. To use the Notes and Interest Planner:

1. Click the Tools toolbar button.
2. Click the Notes and Interest tab.
3. In the Time Basis box, select the time basis to be used by clicking on the appropriate option button. (This textbook uses a 360-day year.)
4. Enter the data and press the Tab key to move among the text boxes. The calculated results for Maturity Date of Note, Amount of Interest, and Maturity Value will appear at the bottom of the Planning dialog box.
5. Click on the Report button to produce a schedule of the results. Once displayed, the report may be printed or copied to the clipboard for pasting into a spreadsheet or word processor.
6. Click the Close button to exit the report and return to the planner.
7. Click the Close button or press ESC to exit the planner.

AUTOMATED ACCOUNTING APPLICATION PROBLEM 20-1

Open file F20-14.AA8. Display the problem instructions and complete the problem.

AUTOMATED ACCOUNTING MASTERY PROBLEM 20-5

Open file F20-5.AA8. Display the problem instructions and complete the problem.

OPTIONAL ACTIVITY

On your own, explore the other planning tools. For example, you could use the Savings Planner to calculate the monthly deposit required to save enough to buy a car in the future.

An Accounting Cycle for a Corporation: Journalizing and Posting Transactions

Reinforcement Activity 3 reinforces learning from Parts 2 and 3. Activities cover a complete accounting cycle for a merchandising business organized as a corporation. Reinforcement Activity 3 is a single problem divided into two parts. Part A includes learning from Part 2 and Chapters 17 through 20 of Part 3. Part B includes learning from Chapters 21 and 22.

The accounting work of a single merchandising business for the last month of a yearly fiscal period is used in this reinforcement activity. The records kept and reports prepared, however, illustrate the application of accounting concepts for all merchandising businesses.

SPARKLE, INC.

Sparkle, Inc., a merchandising business, is organized as a corporation. The business sells a complete line of cleaning and maintenance supplies, mostly to business customers. Sparkle is located within an industrial park and is open for business Monday through Saturday. A monthly rent is paid for the building. Sparkle sells to some businesses on account and accepts cash or credit cards from small business owners.

CHART OF ACCOUNTS

Sparkle uses the chart of accounts shown on the next page.

JOURNALS AND LEDGERS

The journals, ledgers, and forms used by Sparkle are listed below. Models of these items are shown in the textbook chapters indicated.

Journals and Ledgers	Chapter
Purchases journal	9
Cash payments journal	9
General journal	9
Sales journal	10
Cash receipts journal	10
Accounts payable ledger	11
Accounts receivable ledger	11
General ledger	11
Plant asset record	18

CHART OF ACCOUNTS
GENERAL LEDGER

Balance Sheet Accounts

(1000) ASSETS

1100 Current Assets

1105 Cash

1110 Petty Cash

1115 Notes Receivable

1120 Interest Receivable

1125 Accounts Receivable

1130 Allowance for Uncollectible Accounts

1135 Merchandise Inventory

1140 Supplies

1145 Prepaid Insurance

1200 Plant Assets

1205 Office Equipment

1210 Accumulated Depreciation—Office Equipment

1215 Warehouse Equipment

1220 Accumulated Depreciation—Warehouse Equipment

(2000) LIABILITIES

2100 Current Liabilities

2105 Notes Payable

2110 Interest Payable

2115 Accounts Payable

2120 Federal Income Tax Payable

2125 Employee Income Tax Payable

2130 Social Security Tax Payable

2135 Medicare Tax Payable

2140 Sales Tax Payable

2145 Unemployment Tax Payable—Federal

2150 Unemployment Tax Payable—State

2155 Health Insurance Premiums Payable

2160 Dividends Payable

(3000) OWNER'S EQUITY

3105 Capital Stock

3110 Retained Earnings

3115 Dividends

3120 Income Summary

Income Statement Accounts

(4000) OPERATING REVENUE

4105 Sales

4110 Sales Discount

4115 Sales Returns and Allowances

(5000) COST OF MERCHANDISE

5105 Purchases

5110 Purchases Discount

5115 Purchases Returns and Allowances

(6000) OPERATING EXPENSES

6105 Advertising Expense

6110 Cash Short and Over

6115 Credit Card Fee Expense

6120 Depreciation Expense—Office Equipment

6125 Depreciation Expense—Warehouse Equipment

6130 Insurance Expense

6135 Miscellaneous Expense

6140 Payroll Taxes Expense

6145 Rent Expense

6150 Repairs Expense

6155 Salary Expense

6160 Supplies Expense

6165 Uncollectible Accounts Expense

6170 Utilities Expense

(7000) OTHER REVENUE

7105 Gain on Plant Assets

7110 Interest Income

(8000) OTHER EXPENSES

8105 Interest Expense

8110 Loss on Plant Assets

(9000) INCOME TAX EXPENSE

9105 Federal Income Tax Expense

SUBSIDIARY LEDGERS

Accounts Receivable Ledger

110 Baker & Associates

120 Felton Industries

130 Hilldale School

140 Horton Company

150 Nelson Co.

160 Ruocco Plastics

Accounts Payable Ledger

210 Buntin Supply Company

220 Draper Company

230 Glenson Company

240 Hinsdale Supply Co.

250 SHF Corp.

260 Walbash Manufacturing

RECORDING TRANSACTIONS

The December 1, 20X4, account balances for the general and subsidiary ledgers are given in the *Working Papers*.

Instructions:

1. Journalize the following transactions completed during December, 20X4. Use page 12 of a sales journal, page 12 of a purchases journal, page 12 of a general journal, page 12 of a cash receipts journal, and page 23 of a cash payments journal. Sparkle offers sales terms of 2/10, n/30. The sales tax rate is 6%. Source documents are abbreviated as follows: check, C; memorandum, M; purchase invoice, P; receipt, R; sales invoice, S; terminal summary, TS; debit memorandum, DM; credit memorandum, CM; NR, note receivable; NP, note payable.

Dec. 1. Paid cash for rent, $1,750.00. C578.
   2. Received cash on account from Ruocco Plastics, covering S637 for $3,250.00. R671.
   3. Paid cash on account to Walbash Manufacturing, covering P324 for $620.00, less 2% discount. C579.
   3. Paid cash for the maturity value of NP31, a 180-day, 9% note for $10,000.00 to First American Bank. C580.
   5. Bought a printer/scanner for the office: cost, $1,200.00; estimated salvage value, $200.00; estimated useful life, 3 years; plant asset No. 998; serial number, MNT-9343. C581. Open a plant asset record for this office equipment. Sparkle Inc. uses the straight-line method of depreciation. C581.
   5. Sold merchandise on account to Horton Company, $500.00, plus sales tax. S657.
   6. Recorded cash and credit card sales, $5,430.00, plus sales tax, $325.80; total, $5,755.80. TS49.
   6. Bought supplies on account from Draper Company, $362.40. M45.
   Posting. Post the items that are to be posted individually. Always post the journals in this order: sales journal, purchases journal, general journal, cash receipts journal, and cash payments journal.
   7. Accepted a 90-day, 10% note from Nelson Co. for an extension of time on its account, $3,600.00. NR34.
   8. Purchased merchandise on account from Glenson Company, $4,518.00. P332.
   9. Sold merchandise on account to Ruocco Plastics, $480.00, plus sales tax. S658.
   9. Wrote off Felton Industries' past-due account as uncollectible, $2,460.00. M46.
   10. Paid cash for supplies, $223.00. C582.
   12. Received cash on account from Horton Company, covering S657 for $530.00, less 2% discount. R672.
   12. Purchased merchandise on account from Hinsdale Supply Co., $6,812.00. P333.
   13. Recorded cash and credit card sales, $5,987.00, plus sales tax, $359.22; total, $6,346.22. TS50.
   Posting. Post the items that are to be posted individually.
   14. Received cash for sale of a hand truck, plant asset No. 432, $1,400.00. M47 and R673.
   14. Returned merchandise purchased from Glenson Company on P332, $198.00. DM34.
   15. Paid cash liability for employee income tax, $324.00; social security tax, $742.00; and Medicare tax, $162.35. C583.
   15. Paid cash for semimonthly payroll, $2,256.27 (total payroll, $2,820.00, less deductions: employee income tax, $158.00; social security tax, $174.84; Medicare tax, $40.89; health insurance, $190.00). C584.
   15. Recorded employer payroll taxes, $250.45, for the semimonthly pay period ended December 15. Taxes owed are: social security tax, $174.84; Medicare tax, $40.89; federal unemployment tax, $4.48; and state unemployment tax, $30.24. M48.
   16. Purchased merchandise on account from Buntin Supply Company, $4,833.00. P334.
   17. Paid cash for electric bill, $346.20. C585.
   17. Paid cash on account to Glenson Company, covering P332 for $4,518.00, less 2% discount. C586.
   18. Received cash in full payment of Baker & Associates' account, previously written off as uncollectible, $948.00. M49 and R674.
   19. Paid cash for miscellaneous expense, $72.00. C587.
   20. Sold merchandise on account to Hilldale School, $1,560.00. Hilldale School is exempt from sales tax. S659.
   20. Recorded cash and credit card sales, $3,554.00, plus sales tax, $213.24; total, $3,767.24. TS51.
   Posting. Post the items that are to be posted individually.
   21. Paid cash for merchandise, $357.00. C588.
   22. Granted credit to Ruocco Plastics for merchandise returned, $120.00; plus sales tax, $7.20; $127.20 total. CM15.
   23. Paid cash on account to Hinsdale Supply Co., covering P333 for $6,812.00. C589.
   26. Received cash for the maturity value of NR32, a 90-day, 12% note for $5,800.00. R675.
   27. Recorded cash and credit card sales, $2,337.00, plus sales tax, $140.22; total, $2,477.22. TS52.
   Posting. Post the items that are to be posted individually.
   28. Sold merchandise on account to Horton Company, $2,500.00, plus sales tax. S660.

28. Purchased merchandise on account from Draper Company, $6,148.00. P335.

28. Signed a 90-day, 10% note, for $6,000.00 with Commercial National Bank. NP33 and R676.

28. Received cash for sale of a computer printer, plant asset No. 667, $150.00. M50 and R677. Update the plant asset record and record the sale.

29. Paid $500.00 on the outstanding balance of the SHF Corp. account. C590.

30. Ruocco Plastics dishonored NR33, a 60-day, 12% note, for $3,000.00. M51.

30. Recorded credit card fee expense, $418.00. M52.

31. Paid cash to replenish the petty cash fund, $84.96: supplies, $12.50; advertising, $50.00; miscellaneous, $22.37; cash short, $.09. C591.

31. Paid cash for semimonthly payroll, $2,206.86 (total payroll, $2,760.00, less deductions: employee income tax, $152.00; social security tax, $171.12; Medicare tax, $40.02; health insurance, $190.00. C592.

31. Recorded employer payroll taxes, $242.14, for the semimonthly pay period ended December 31. Taxes owed are: social security tax, $171.12: Medicare tax, $40.02; federal unemployment tax, $4.00; and state unemployment tax, $27.00. M53.

31. Recorded cash and credit card sales, $465.00, plus sales tax, $27.90; total, $492.90. TS53.

Posting. Post the items that are to be posted individually.

2. Prove and rule the sales journal. Post the totals of the special columns.

3. Total and rule the purchases journal. Post the total.

4. Prove the equality of debits and credits for the cash receipts and cash payments journals.

5. Prove cash. The balance on the next unused check stub is $8,100.70.

6. Rule the cash receipts journal. Post the totals of the special columns.

7. Rule the cash payments journal. Post the totals of the special columns.

8. Prepare a schedule of accounts receivable and a schedule of accounts payable. Prove the accuracy of the subsidiary ledgers by comparing the schedule totals with the balances of the controlling accounts in the general ledger. If the totals are not the same, find and correct the errors.

The ledgers used in Reinforcement Activity 3—Part A are needed to complete Reinforcement Activity 3—Part B.

TETRA IMAGES/GETTY IMAGES

CHAPTER 21

Accounting for Accrued Revenue and Expenses

OBJECTIVES

After studying Chapter 21, you will be able to:

1. Define accounting terms related to accrued revenue and accrued expenses.

2. Identify accounting concepts and practices related to accrued revenue and accrued expenses.

3. Record adjusting, closing, and reversing entries for accrued revenue.

4. Record adjusting, closing, and reversing entries for accrued expenses.

KEY TERMS

- accrued revenue
- intellectual property
- accrued interest income
- reversing entry
- accrued expenses
- accrued interest expense

Point Your Browser
www.C21accounting.com

USA Today

Deferred Revenue at *USA Today*

You've probably heard someone use the phrase "timing is everything." This phrase has a special meaning to the accountants at *USA Today*, a division of Gannett Co., Inc.

USA Today collects fees for advertising before the advertisements appear. Customers pay subscriptions for paper delivery or online editions as much as a year in advance. Receiving these fees does not, however, mean that *USA Today* can record the amounts as current revenue. In accordance with generally accepted accounting principles, advertising fees are recorded as revenue when the advertising is printed or placed on a web site. In the same manner, subscription fees are recorded as revenue when purchased newspapers are delivered.

When preparing financial statements, accountants at *USA Today* must analyze the money collected from advertising and subscriptions to determine what amount should be recorded as revenue.

©JAY CARRIER/BLOOMBERG NEWS/LANDOV

Critical Thinking

1. Suppose you purchase a $150.00 annual subscription to *USA Today* on November 1. How much should *USA Today* recognize as revenue on its December financial statements?

2. Would your answer to question 1 differ if the customer selected online delivery of *USA Today*?

Source: http://library.corporate-ir.net/library/84/846/84662/items/233865/06AnnualReport.pdf

INTERNET ACTIVITY

Mission Statements

Go to the homepage for Ben and Jerry's Ice Cream (www.benandjerrys.com). Search for Ben and Jerry's Mission Statement.

Instructions

1. List Ben and Jerry's Mission Statement in full.

2. Expand your search by reading about Ben and Jerry's commitment to the environment. List one interesting fact that you find.

ACCOUNTING FOR INTEREST AT THE FISCAL YEAR END

Generally accepted accounting principles (GAAP) require that revenue and expenses be recorded in the accounting period in which revenue is earned and expenses are incurred. [CONCEPT: Matching Expenses with Revenue] Some revenues, however, are earned each day but are usually recorded only when cash is actually received. For example, interest is earned for each day a note receivable is held.

However, the interest may not be received until the maturity date of the note. Likewise, some expenses may be incurred before they are actually paid. A note payable incurs interest expense each day the note is outstanding. However, the interest generally is not paid until the note's

maturity date. At the end of the fiscal period, adjusting entries are recorded for these revenues and expenses.

Revenue earned in one fiscal period but not received until a later fiscal period is called **accrued revenue**. At the end of a fiscal period, accrued revenue is recorded by an adjusting entry. [CONCEPT: Realization of Revenue] The adjusting entry for accrued revenue increases a revenue account. The adjusting entry also increases a receivable account. The income statement will then report all revenue earned for the period, even though some of the revenue has not yet been received. The balance sheet will report all the assets, including the accrued revenue receivable. [CONCEPT: Adequate Disclosure]

CHARACTER COUNTS

Guarding Intellectual Property

Is it ethical to download free music from the Internet? This hotly debated issue provides interesting insight into our society and individuals' ability to make ethical decisions. Have you heard people attempt to justify copying music? "It doesn't cost the artists anything." "They're so rich anyway." "I can't afford to purchase the music I like." "If it's on the Internet, I can download it."

Any product that is protected by patents, trademarks, and copyrights is called **intellectual property**. Music, videos, and computer software

are examples of intellectual property. Regardless of how individuals attempt to justify downloading free music from the Internet, there is no escaping the fact that these downloads are illegal.

Businesses recognize that the unauthorized copying of computer software is also illegal. Many companies address this issue in their code of conduct.

Instructions

Do an Internet search to access "Everyday Values," the code of conduct for Harley-Davidson, Inc. What guidance does Harley-Davidson provide its employees about copying software for both business and personal use?

Source: http://investor.harley-davidson.com/downloads/CG_CodeConduct.pdf.

PHOTO: BLEND IMAGES/GETTY IMAGES

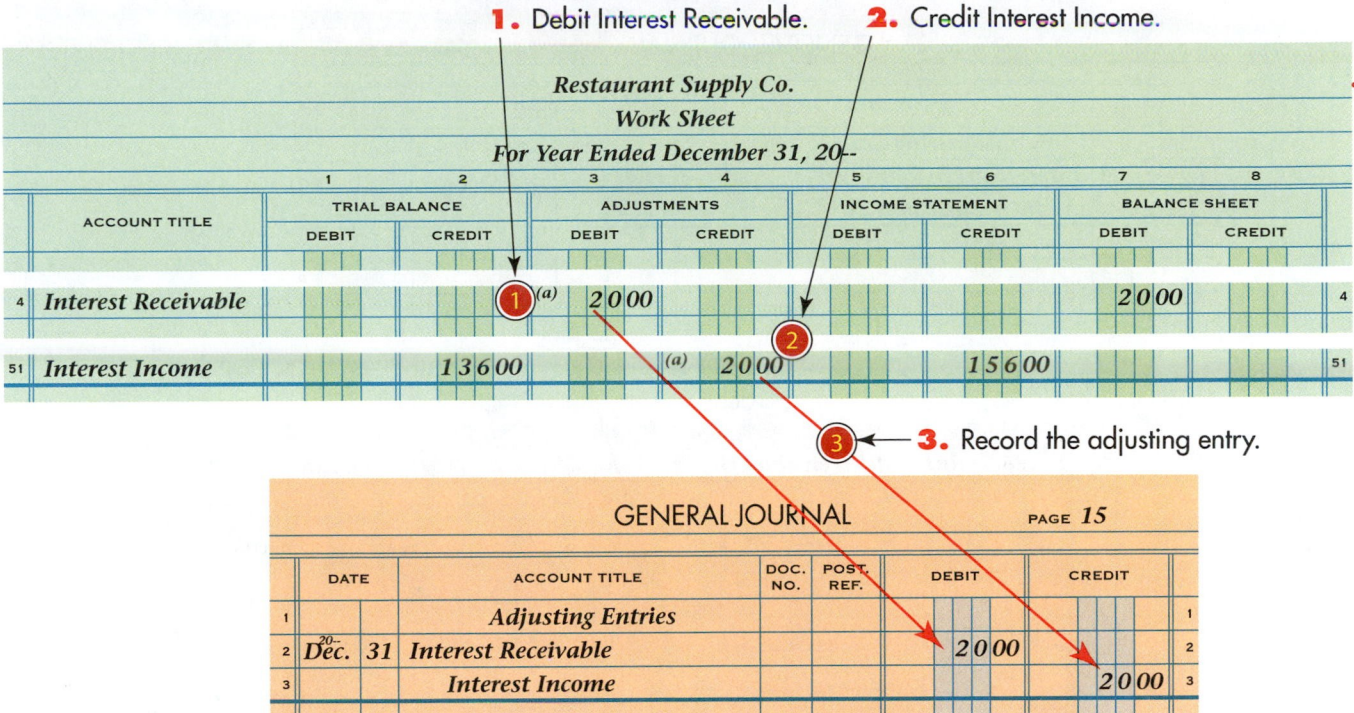

1. Debit Interest Receivable. **2.** Credit Interest Income.

Restaurant Supply Co.
Work Sheet
For Year Ended December 31, 20--

		1	2	3	4	5	6	7	8
	ACCOUNT TITLE	TRIAL BALANCE		ADJUSTMENTS		INCOME STATEMENT		BALANCE SHEET	
		DEBIT	CREDIT	DEBIT	CREDIT	DEBIT	CREDIT	DEBIT	CREDIT
4	Interest Receivable			① (a) 20 00				20 00		4
51	Interest Income	136 00			② (a) 20 00		156 00			51

3. Record the adjusting entry.

GENERAL JOURNAL   PAGE 15

	DATE	ACCOUNT TITLE	DOC. NO.	POST. REF.	DEBIT	CREDIT	
1		*Adjusting Entries*					1
2	Dec. 31	Interest Receivable			20 00		2
3		Interest Income				20 00	3

At the end of each fiscal period, Restaurant Supply examines the notes receivable on hand. The amount of interest income earned but not yet collected is calculated. Interest earned but not yet received is called **accrued interest income**. On December 31, Restaurant Supply has one note receivable on hand, a 90-day, 6%, $2,000.00 note dated November 1. An adjusting entry must be made to record the amount of interest earned to date on this note.

The time period from November 1 through December 31 is 60 days. Therefore, the interest earned on the note is calculated for 60/360 of a year.

Interest Receivable is debited for $20.00 to show the interest income that has accrued at the end of the fiscal period. This revenue will not be collected until the next fiscal period.

The credit of $20.00 is added to the previous balance in Interest Income. The new account balance, $156.00, is the total amount of interest income earned during the fiscal period.

Principal	×	Interest Rate	×	Time as Fraction of Year	=	Accrued Interest Income
$2,000.00	×	6%	×	$\frac{60}{360}$	=	$20.00

Interest Receivable	
Dec. 31 Adj. 20.00	

Interest Income	
	Dec. 31 Bal. 136.00
	Dec. 31 Adj. 20.00
	(New Bal. 156.00)

STEPS ── **RECORDING AN ADJUSTMENT FOR ACCRUED INTEREST INCOME**

① Write the accrued interest income amount, *$20.00*, in the Adjustments Debit column on the Interest Receivable line of the work sheet. Label the adjustment with a small letter *a* in parentheses, *(a)*.

② Write the same amount, *$20.00*, in the Adjustments Credit column on the Interest Income line of the work sheet. Label the adjustment using the same letter, *(a)*.

③ Use the debit and credit amounts on the work sheet to record an adjusting entry in the general journal.

POSTING AN ADJUSTING ENTRY FOR ACCRUED INTEREST INCOME

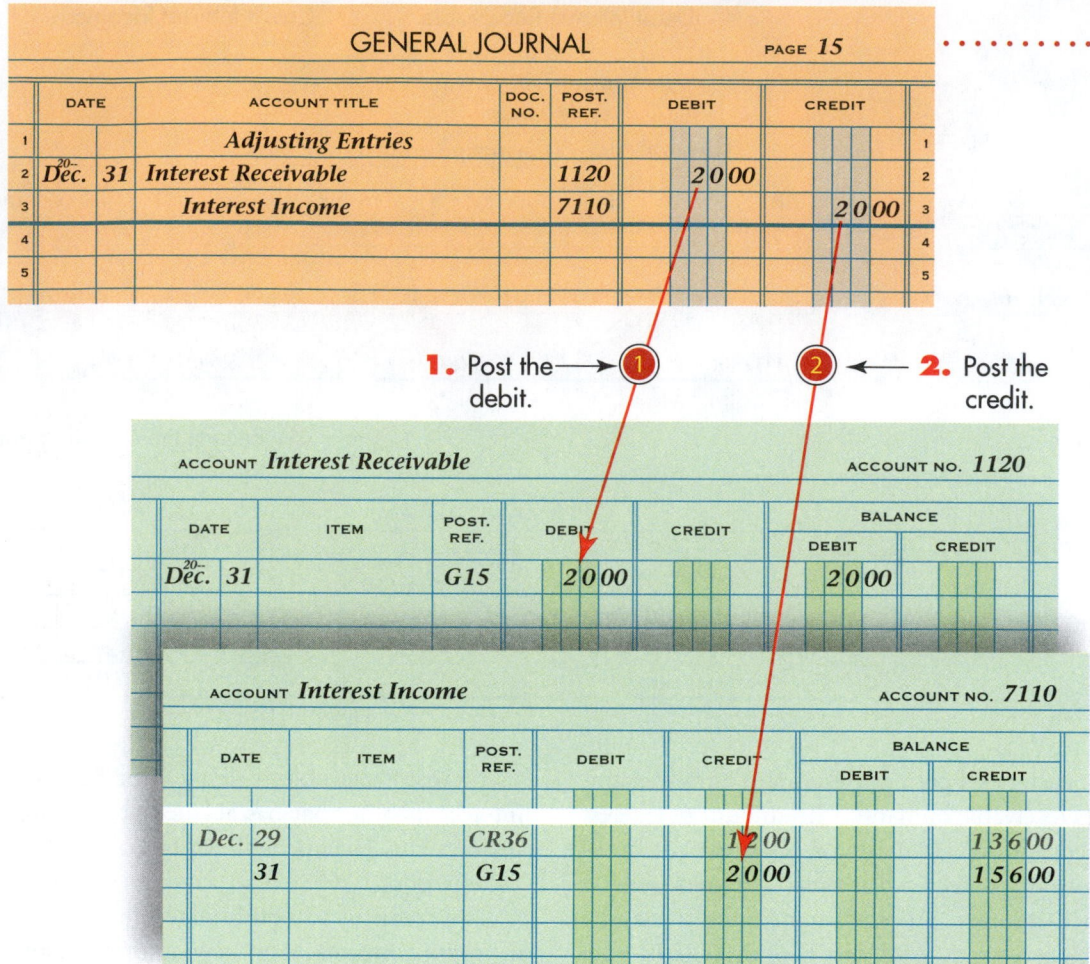

GENERAL JOURNAL   PAGE 15

	DATE	ACCOUNT TITLE	DOC. NO.	POST. REF.	DEBIT	CREDIT	
1		*Adjusting Entries*					1
2	20-- Dec. 31	*Interest Receivable*		1120	20 00		2
3		*Interest Income*		7110		20 00	3
4							4
5							5

1. Post the debit. ①   ② **2.** Post the credit.

ACCOUNT *Interest Receivable*   ACCOUNT NO. *1120*

DATE	ITEM	POST. REF.	DEBIT	CREDIT	BALANCE DEBIT	BALANCE CREDIT
20-- Dec. 31		G15	20 00		20 00	

ACCOUNT *Interest Income*   ACCOUNT NO. *7110*

DATE	ITEM	POST. REF.	DEBIT	CREDIT	BALANCE DEBIT	BALANCE CREDIT
Dec. 29		CR36		1 2 00		1 3 6 00
31		G15		2 0 00		1 5 6 00

The adjustment for accrued interest income planned on a work sheet is recorded as an adjusting entry in a general journal. The adjusting entry is then posted to the general ledger.

After posting, the interest receivable account has a debit balance of $20.00 and will appear on the balance sheet as a current asset. This debit balance is the accrued interest income earned but not yet collected at the end of the year. The interest income account has a credit balance of $156.00 and will appear on the income statement as other revenue. This amount is the total interest income for the year.

STEPS 〔icon〕 **POSTING AN ADJUSTING ENTRY FOR ACCRUED INTEREST INCOME**

① Post the debit, *$20.00*, to *Interest Receivable.*

② Post the credit, *$20.00*, to *Interest Income.*

REMEMBER

The interest receivable account appears in the Current Assets section of the balance sheet. The interest income account appears in the Other Revenue section of the income statement.

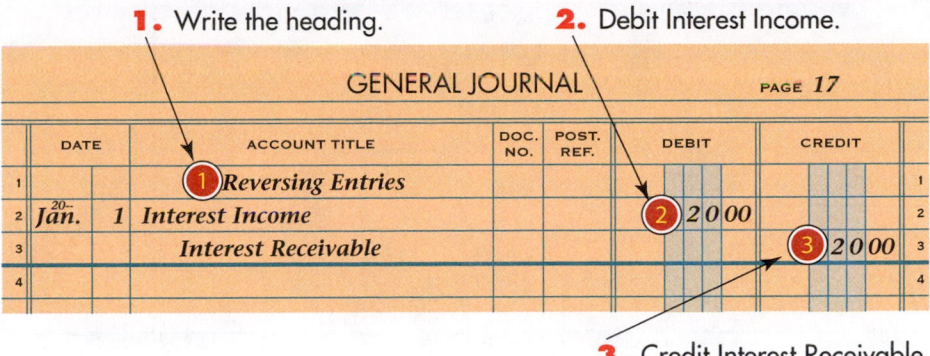

1. Write the heading. **2.** Debit Interest Income.

3. Credit Interest Receivable.

On December 31, Interest Income is closed as part of the regular closing entry for income statement accounts with credit balances. Interest Income is debited for $156.00 to reduce the account balance to zero.

Adjusting entries for accrued revenues have an effect on transactions that will be recorded in the following fiscal period. On the maturity date of the outstanding 90-day note receivable, Restaurant Supply will receive interest of $30.00.

However, an adjusting entry was made to record the amount of interest earned last year, $20.00. Thus, $20.00 of the $30.00 total interest income has already been recorded as revenue. The remaining $10.00 of the $30.00 total interest will be earned during the current fiscal period.

It is inconvenient to determine how much, if any, of cash received from notes receivable relates to interest accrued during the prior fiscal period. To avoid this inconvenience, an entry is made at the beginning of the new fiscal period to reverse the adjusting entry. An entry made at the beginning of one fiscal period to reverse an adjusting entry made in the previous fiscal period is called a **reversing entry**.

Interest Income

Dec. 31 Closing	156.00	Dec. 31 Bal.	136.00
Jan. 1 Rev.	20.00	Dec. 31 Adj.	20.00
(New Bal.	20.00)		

Interest Receivable

Dec. 31 Adj.	20.00	Jan. 1 Rev.	20.00
(New Bal. zero)			

The reversing entry is the opposite of the adjusting entry. The entry creates a debit balance of $20.00 in Interest Income. A debit balance is the opposite of the normal balance of Interest Income. When the full amount of interest is received, the $30.00 will be credited to Interest Income, resulting in a $10.00 credit balance ($30.00 credit − $20.00 debit), the amount of interest earned in the new year.

The reversing entry reduced the balance in Interest Receivable to zero. When the interest is received, no entry will be made to Interest Receivable. Instead, the total amount of interest received will be credited to Interest Income.

STEPS   **REVERSING AN ADJUSTING ENTRY FOR ACCRUED INTEREST INCOME**

1 Write the heading, *Reversing Entries*, in the middle of the general journal's Account Title column. This heading explains all the reversing entries that follow. Therefore, indicating a source document is unnecessary.

2 Record a debit, *$20.00*, to *Interest Income*.

3 Record a credit, *$20.00*, to *Interest Receivable*.

COLLECTING A NOTE RECEIVABLE ISSUED IN A PREVIOUS FISCAL PERIOD

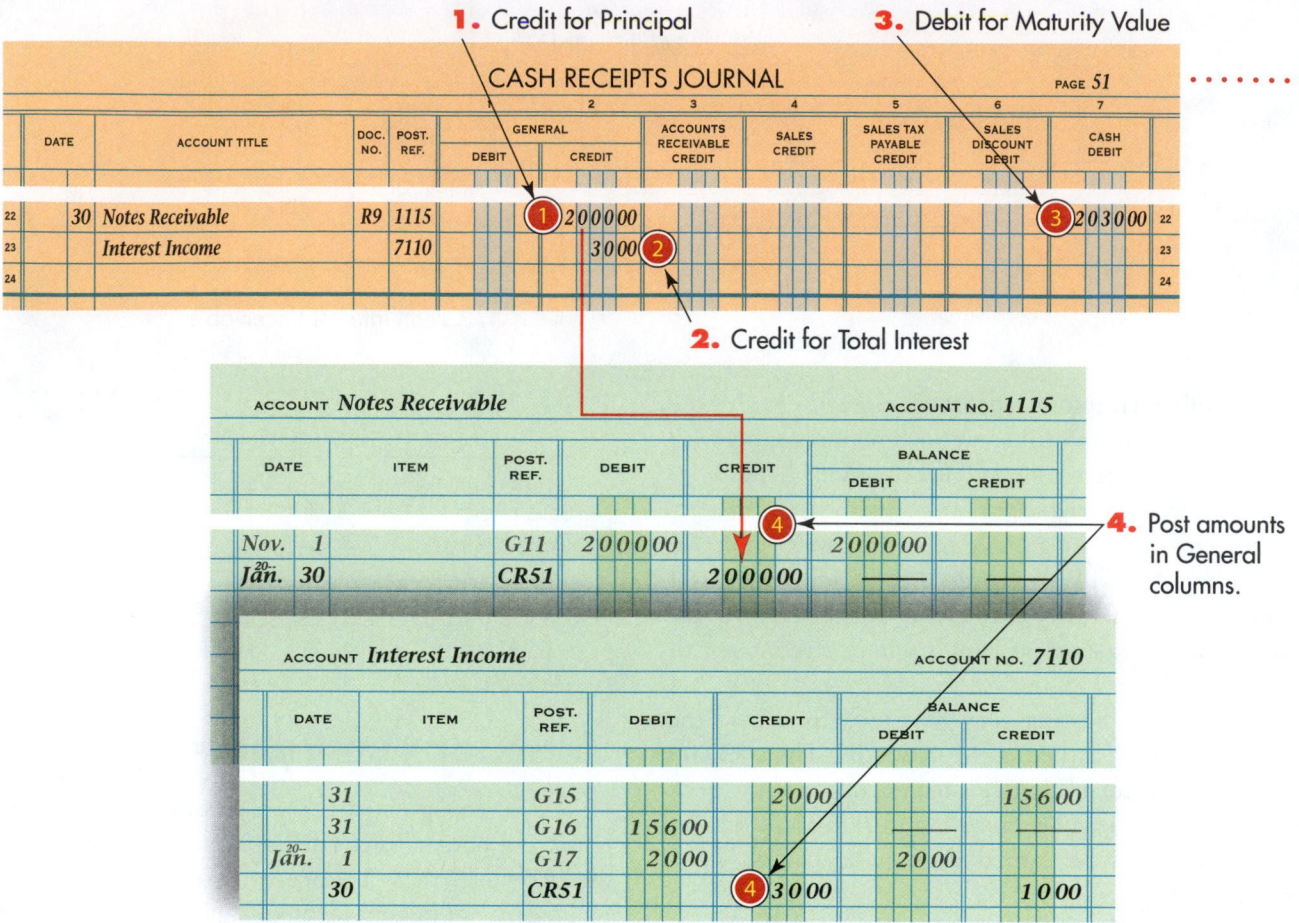

1. Credit for Principal

3. Debit for Maturity Value

2. Credit for Total Interest

4. Post amounts in General columns.

On January 30, Restaurant Supply received the maturity value of the only note receivable on hand on December 31, the end of the previous fiscal year.

January 30. Received cash for the maturity value of a 90-day, 6% note: principal, $2,000.00, plus interest, $30.00; total, $2,030.00. Receipt No. 9.

Cash		
Jan. 30 Rec'd	2,030.00	

Notes Receivable			
Nov. 1	2,000.00	Jan. 30 Rec'd	2,000.00

Interest Income			
Dec. 31 Closing	156.00	Dec. 31 Bal.	136.00
Jan. 1 Rev.	20.00	Dec. 31 Adj.	20.00
		Jan. 30 Rec'd	30.00
		(New Bal.	10.00)

The total interest, $30.00, was earned during two fiscal periods—$20.00 during the previous fiscal period and $10.00 during the current fiscal period. The reversing entry created a $20.00 debit balance in Interest Income. After the $30.00 credit is posted, Interest Income has a credit balance of $10.00, the amount of interest earned during the current fiscal period.

STEPS

COLLECTING A NOTE RECEIVABLE ISSUED IN A PREVIOUS FISCAL PERIOD

1 Record a credit to *Notes Receivable* in the General Credit column of the cash receipts journal for the principal of the note, *$2,000.00*.

2 Record a credit to *Interest Income* in the General Credit column for the total interest, *$30.00*.

3 Record a debit in the Cash Debit column for the maturity value of the note, *$2,030.00*.

4 Post the amounts in the General columns.

End of Lesson REVIEW

TERMS REVIEW

accrued revenue

intellectual property

accrued interest income

reversing entry

AUDIT YOUR UNDERSTANDING

1. Which accounting concept is being applied when an adjusting entry is made at the end of the fiscal period to record accrued revenue?
2. Why does a business use reversing entries as part of its procedures for accounting for accrued interest income?

WORK TOGETHER 21-1

Journalizing and posting entries for accrued revenue

The accounting forms for the following problem are in the *Working Papers*. Your instructor will guide you through the following examples.

On December 31 of the current year, Marris Corporation has one note receivable outstanding, a 120-day, 12%, $4,000.00 note dated November 16.

1. Plan the adjustment on a work sheet. Label the adjustment (a).
2. Journalize and post the adjusting entry for accrued interest income on December 31. Use page 14 of a general journal.
3. Journalize and post the closing entry for interest income using page 14 of a general journal.
4. Journalize and post the January 1 reversing entry for accrued interest income on page 15 of a general journal.
5. Journalize the receipt of cash for the maturity value of the note on March 16, Receipt No. 32. Use page 16 of a cash receipts journal. Post the amounts in the General columns.

ON YOUR OWN 21-1

Journalizing and posting entries for accrued revenue

The accounting forms for the following problem are in the *Working Papers*. Work this problem independently.

On December 31 of the current year, ExMark, Inc., has one note receivable outstanding, a 90-day, 10%, $6,000.00 note dated December 1.

1. Plan the adjustment on a work sheet. Label the adjustment (a).
2. Journalize and post the adjusting entry for accrued interest income on December 31. Use page 14 of a general journal.
3. Journalize and post the closing entry for interest income using page 14 of a general journal.
4. Journalize and post the January 1 reversing entry for accrued interest income on page 15 of a general journal.
5. Journalize the receipt of cash for the maturity value of the note on March 1, Receipt No. 65. Use page 19 of a cash receipts journal. Post the amounts in the General columns.

Accrued Expenses

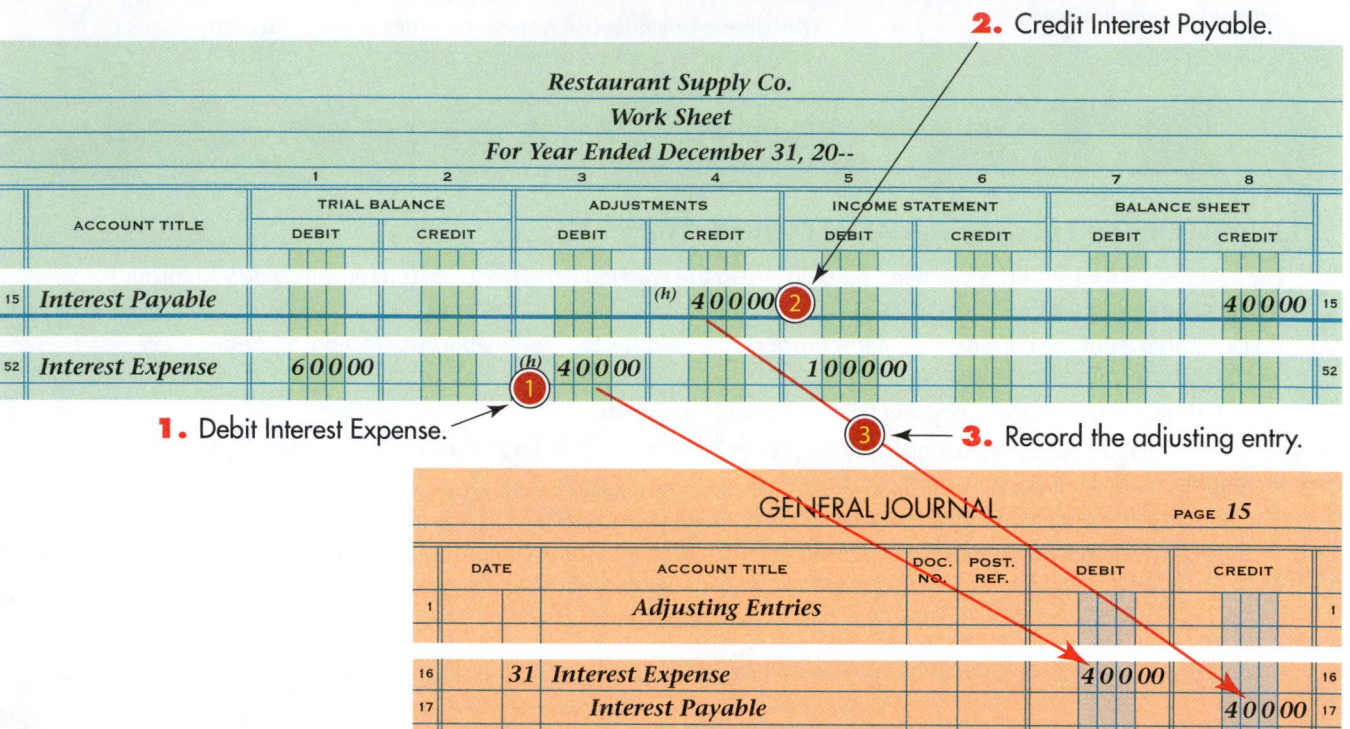

ANALYZING AN ADJUSTMENT FOR ACCRUED INTEREST EXPENSE

2. Credit Interest Payable.

1. Debit Interest Expense.

3. Record the adjusting entry.

Expenses incurred in one fiscal period but not paid until a later fiscal period are called **accrued expenses**. At the end of a fiscal period, accrued expense is recorded by an adjusting entry. [CONCEPT: Matching Expenses with Revenue] The adjusting entry increases an expense account. The adjusting entry also increases a payable account.

Interest incurred but not yet paid is called **accrued interest expense**. On December 31, Restaurant Supply has one note payable outstanding, a 180-day, 12%, $10,000.00 note dated September 2. Restaurant Supply owes $400.00 interest for the 120 days from September 2 through December 31.

Principal	×	Interest Rate	×	Time as Fraction of Year	=	Accrued Interest Expense
$10,000.00	×	12%	×	$\frac{120}{360}$	=	$400.00

Interest Expense	
Dec. 31 Bal.	600.00
Dec. 31 Adj.	400.00
(New Bal.	1,000.00)

Interest Payable	
	Dec. 31 Adj. 400.00

Interest Expense is debited for $400.00 to show the increase in the balance of this other expense account. The new balance of Interest Expense, $1,000.00, is the total amount of interest expense incurred during the fiscal period.

The credit to Interest Payable creates a $400.00 account balance that represents the interest owed on December 31 that will be paid in the next fiscal period.

POSTING AN ADJUSTING ENTRY FOR ACCRUED INTEREST EXPENSE

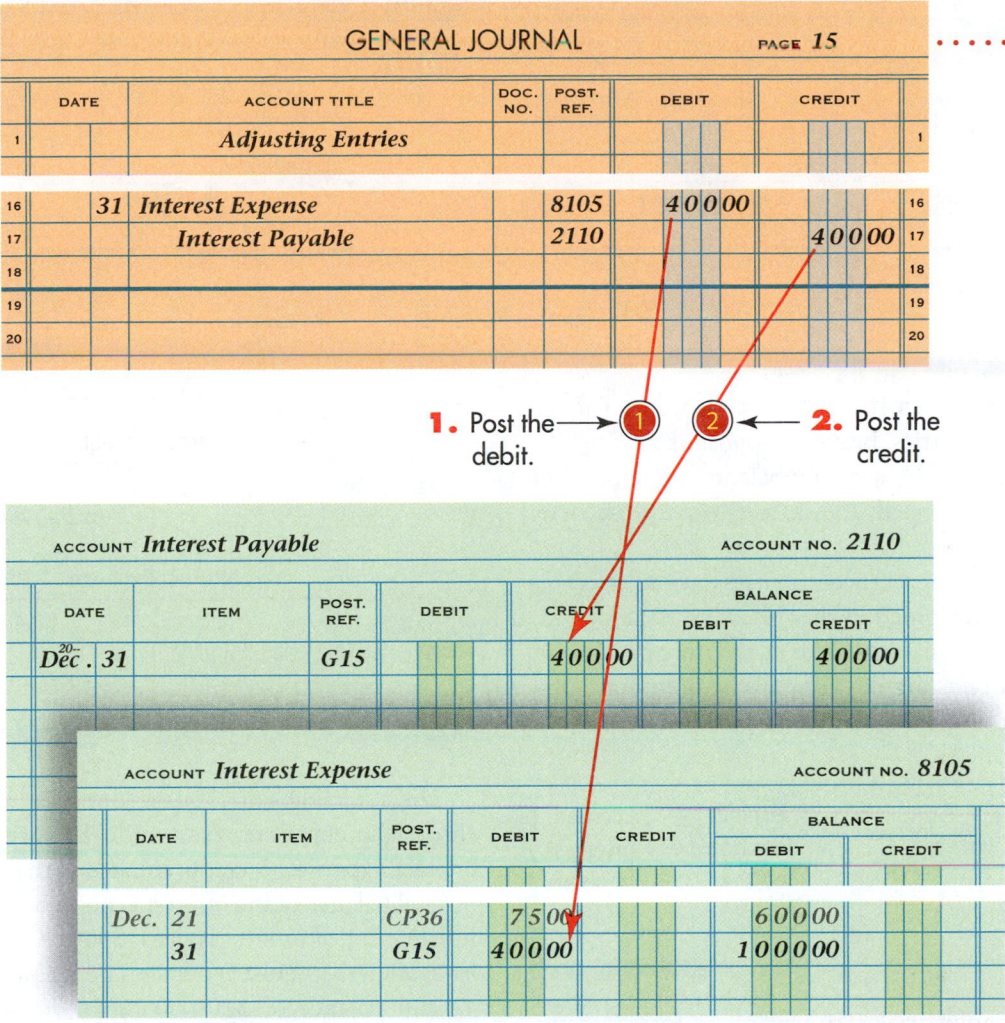

1. Post the debit. ① ② **2.** Post the credit.

The adjustment for accrued interest expense planned on a work sheet is recorded as an adjusting entry in a general journal. The adjusting entry is then posted to the general ledger.

After posting, the interest payable account has a credit balance of $400.00 and will appear on the December 31 balance sheet as a current liability. This credit balance is the accrued interest expense incurred but not yet paid at the end of the year.

The interest expense account has a debit balance of $1,000.00 and will appear on the income statement for the year ended December 31 as an other expense. This amount is the total interest expense for the year.

POSTING AN ADJUSTING ENTRY FOR ACCRUED INTEREST EXPENSE

① Post the debit, *$400.00*, to *Interest Expense*.

② Post the credit, *$400.00*, to *Interest Payable*.

REMEMBER

The adjusting entry for accrued interest expense affects both the income statement and the balance sheet. The income statement will report all expenses for the period even though some of the expenses have not yet been paid. The balance sheet will report all liabilities, including the accrued expenses payable. (CONCEPT: Adequate Disclosure)

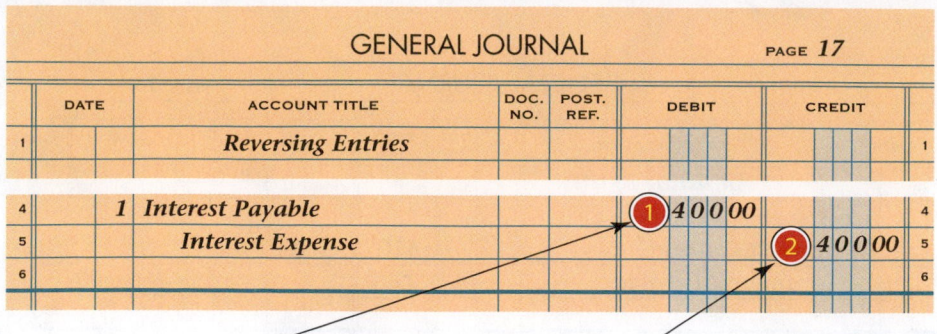

		GENERAL JOURNAL				PAGE 17
	DATE	ACCOUNT TITLE	DOC. NO.	POST. REF.	DEBIT	CREDIT
1		*Reversing Entries*				
4	1	Interest Payable			① 4 0 0 00	
5		Interest Expense				② 4 0 0 00
6						

1. Debit Interest Payable. **2.** Credit Interest Expense.

On December 31, Interest Expense is closed as part of the regular closing entries. Interest Expense is credited for $1,000.00 to reduce the account balance to zero. After the closing entry is posted, the interest expense account is closed.

Adjusting entries for accrued expenses have an effect on transactions to be recorded in the following fiscal period. For example, on the maturity date of the note payable on March 1, Restaurant Supply will pay the note's maturity value, including interest of $600.00.

Interest Payable			
Jan. 1 Rev.	400.00	Dec. 31 Adj. *(New Bal. zero)*	400.00

Interest Expense			
Dec. 31 Bal.	600.00	Dec. 31 Closing	1,000.00
Dec. 31 Adj.	400.00	Jan. 1 Rev. *(New Bal.*	400.00 *400.00)*

Principal	×	Interest Rate	×	Time as Fraction of Year	=	Accrued Interest Expense
$10,000.00	×	12%	×	$\frac{120}{360}$	=	$400.00

However, an adjusting entry was made to record the amount of accrued interest expense last year, $400.00. Thus, $400.00 of the $600.00 total interest expense was incurred and recorded in the previous year. The remaining $200.00 was incurred during the current year.

Determining how much of the cash paid is for accrued interest expense and how much applies to the current year is an inconvenience. To avoid this inconvenience, a reversing entry is made at the beginning of the new fiscal period.

The reversing entry is the opposite of the adjusting entry. The entry creates a credit balance of $400.00 in Interest Expense. A credit balance is the opposite of the normal balance of the interest expense account. When the full amount of interest is paid, $600.00, this amount will be debited to Interest Expense. The account will then have a debit balance of $200.00 ($600.00 debit – $400.00 credit), the amount of interest expense incurred in the new year.

The reversing entry to Interest Payable reduces that account to a zero balance. Thus, when the interest is paid, no debit entry will be required to recognize payment of the balance of Interest Payable. The total amount of interest paid will be debited to Interest Expense.

STEPS REVERSING AN ADJUSTING ENTRY FOR ACCRUED INTEREST EXPENSE

① Record a debit, *$400.00*, to *Interest Payable* in the general journal.

② Record a credit, *$400.00*, to *Interest Expense*.

PAYING A NOTE PAYABLE SIGNED IN A PREVIOUS FISCAL PERIOD

1. Debit for Principal

CASH PAYMENTS JOURNAL
PAGE 55

		DATE	ACCOUNT TITLE	CK. NO.	POST. REF.	GENERAL DEBIT (1)	GENERAL CREDIT (2)	ACCOUNTS PAYABLE DEBIT (3)	PURCHASES DISCOUNT CREDIT (4)	CASH CREDIT (5)	
21	1		Notes Payable	916	2105	1 000 000 ①				1 060 000	21
22			Interest Expense		8105	600 00 ②					22

2. Debit for Total Interest   **3.** Credit for Maturity Value

ACCOUNT Notes Payable   ACCOUNT NO. 2105

DATE	ITEM	POST. REF.	DEBIT	CREDIT	BALANCE DEBIT	BALANCE CREDIT
Sept. 2		CR28		10 000 00		10 000 00
20-- Mar. 1		CP55	10 000 00 ④		—	—

4. Post amounts in General columns.

ACCOUNT Interest Expense   ACCOUNT NO. 8105

DATE	ITEM	POST. REF.	DEBIT	CREDIT	BALANCE DEBIT	BALANCE CREDIT
31		G15	400 00		1 000 00	
31		G16		1 000 00	—	
20-- Jan. 1		G17		400 00		400 00
Mar. 1		CP55	600 00 ④		200 00	

March 1. Paid cash for the maturity value of the September 2 note: principal, $10,000.00, plus interest, $600.00; total, $10,600.00. Check No. 916.

The total interest, $600.00, was incurred during two fiscal periods—$400.00 during the previous fiscal period and $200.00 during the current fiscal period. The reversing entry created a $400.00 credit balance in Interest Expense. After the $600.00 debit is recorded, Interest Expense has a debit balance of $200.00, the amount of interest expense incurred during the current fiscal period.

Notes Payable

Mar. 1 Paid	10,000.00	Sept. 2	10,000.00

Interest Expense

Dec. 31 Bal.	600.00	Dec. 31 Closing	1,000.00
Dec. 31 Adj.	400.00	Jan. 1 Rev.	400.00
Mar. 1 Paid	600.00		
(New Bal.	200.00)		

Cash

		Mar. 1 Paid	10,600.00

STEPS

PAYING A NOTE PAYABLE SIGNED IN A PREVIOUS FISCAL PERIOD

① Record a debit to *Notes Payable* in the General Debit column for the principal of the note, $10,000.00.

② Record a debit to *Interest Expense* in the General Debit column for the total interest, $600.00.

③ Record a credit to *Cash* in the Cash Credit column for the maturity value of the note, $10,600.00.

④ Post the amounts in the General columns.

If Restaurant Supply did not use a reversing entry for accrued interest expense, $400.00 of the interest would be reported twice. The $400.00 amount is recorded once as an adjusting entry to Interest Expense in the previous fiscal period. The amount is recorded a second time as part of the $600.00 debit to Interest Expense in the current fiscal period when the note is paid.

The double charge might be avoided if accounting personnel are careful to divide the interest amount when the note is paid. The part of the interest chargeable to the previous fiscal period, $400.00, would be recorded as a debit in Interest Payable. The part chargeable to the current fiscal period, $200.00, is recorded as a debit in Interest Expense.

Restaurant Supply prefers to use reversing entries. Restaurant Supply's accounting personnel do not have to remember to check an entry each time a note is paid to determine if interest should be divided. Restaurant Supply, like other companies that use reversing entries, records a reversing entry whenever an adjusting entry creates a balance in an asset or liability account that initially had a zero balance.

PHOTOGRAPHER'S CHOICE RF/GETTY IMAGES

BUSINESS STRUCTURES

Selling a Corporation's Stock

Many small corporations are owned by a few individuals, the original investors who founded the corporation. Sometimes these corporations require greater investments in order to expand to meet the needs of the marketplace or to achieve greater success. One way for a corporation to expand is to make a public offering of its stock. When a corporation issues new stock and the public buys it, the corporation receives the additional investment, minus any commissions, legal fees, and other costs of issuing stock. New offerings of stock are usually sold by investment bankers who have expertise in new stock offerings.

A public corporation which already has stock issued that is owned by the general public can also issue additional shares of stock to the public to attract funds for expansion, new product offerings, research, and many other purposes.

New stock offerings are sold in what is called *primary markets* and usually require the services of an investment banker.

A corporation's existing stock is sold by another means. Stock that has already been issued and sold may be sold again by whoever owns it. This is generally done through a stockbroker who buys and sells stock in a stock market. In the United States, the two national stock exchanges are the New York Stock Exchange (www.nyse.com) and the American Stock Exchange (www.amex.com). There are also regional stock exchanges in several large cities, such as Chicago and Philadelphia. In addition, Nasdaq (www.nasdaq.com) is a network of brokers who trade securities.

Critical Thinking

1. Do you think that issuing new stock is a guaranteed method of acquiring new funds? Why or why not?

2. Select a major corporation and study its stock listings in the newspaper or on the Internet for several days or weeks. What trends do you notice?

PHOTO: PHOTODISC/GETTY IMAGES

AUDIT YOUR UNDERSTANDING

TERMS REVIEW

accrued expenses

accrued interest expense

1. Why should accrued expenses be recorded by an adjusting entry before financial statements are prepared at the end of a fiscal period?
2. What accounts are affected, and how, by the reversing entry for accrued interest expense?

WORK TOGETHER 21-2

Journalizing and posting entries for accrued expenses

The accounting forms for this problem are in the *Working Papers*. Your instructor will guide you through the following examples.

On December 31 of the current year, Powers Corporation has one note payable outstanding, a 90-day, 12%, $2,000.00 note dated December 1.

1. Plan the adjustment on a work sheet. Label the adjustment *(h)*.
2. Journalize and post the adjusting entry for accrued interest expense on December 31. Use page 14 of a general journal.
3. Journalize and post the closing entry for interest expense on page 14 of a general journal.
4. Journalize and post the January 1 reversing entry for accrued interest expense on page 15 of a general journal.
5. Journalize the payment of cash for the maturity value of the note on March 1, Check No. 543. Use page 25 of a cash payments journal. Post the amounts in the General columns.

ON YOUR OWN 21-2

Journalizing and posting entries for accrued expenses

The accounting forms for this problem are in the *Working Papers*. Work this problem independently.

On December 31 of the current year, Latham Industries has one note payable outstanding, a 180-day, 9%, $5,000.00 note dated October 17.

1. Plan the adjustment on a work sheet. Label the adjustment *(h)*.
2. Journalize and post the adjusting entry for accrued interest expense on December 31. Use page 14 of a general journal.
3. Journalize and post the closing entry for interest expense using page 14 of a general journal.
4. Journalize and post the January 1 reversing entry for accrued interest expense on page 15 of a general journal.
5. Journalize the payment of cash for the maturity value of the note on April 15, Check No. 668. Use page 30 of a cash payments journal. Post the amounts in the General columns.

After completing this chapter, you can:

1. Define accounting terms related to accrued revenue and accrued expenses.

2. Identify accounting concepts and practices related to accrued revenue and accrued expenses.

3. Record adjusting, closing, and reversing entries for accrued revenue.

4. Record adjusting, closing, and reversing entries for accrued expenses.

Go Beyond the Book
For more information go to
www.C21accounting.com

EXPLORE ACCOUNTING

Annual Reports—Financial Information and More

Corporations publish annual reports to communicate the results of operations to interested parties, such as stockholders, creditors, and government agencies. The typical annual report is a colorful, soft-cover brochure printed on glossy paper and 40 to 60 pages in length. Most companies post a copy of this report on their web site. The reports are grouped in two sections:

1. *Management's Analysis and Discussion.* This section provides management with an opportunity to promote the corporation. Through the use of pictures, graphs, and narrative, management can highlight the achievements of the past fiscal year and present its plans. Some corporations report on how the volunteer work of their employees is having a positive impact in their communities. Discussions of environmental and recycling programs could demonstrate how the corporation is socially responsible.

   The ultimate objective of any corporation is to increase the market price of its stock, thereby raising stockholders' investment. By "putting its best foot forward" in this section, management can increase the demand for the corporation's products and stock, thus increasing the stock's price.

2. *Financial Statements.* The financial statements section contains several items in addition to basic financial statements. Most of the additional items are required by GAAP or the Securities and Exchange Commission. As a result, these items are similar among corporations.

   a. *Notes to the Financial Statements.* The notes contain additional, detailed information about items presented on the financial statements. For example, the note related to long-term debt would include the projected loan repayments for the next five years.

   b. *Auditor's Report.* The report of the independent auditor states that a public accounting firm has tested the financial statements for accuracy and fair presentation. The report gives the reader confidence to use the financial statements to make business decisions.

   c. *Financial Analysis.* Summary financial information, such as total assets, net income, and common financial ratios, are presented for several years.

Instructions: Access an annual report using a library or the Internet and prepare a detailed outline of its contents. Summarize the major topics in management's analysis and discussion. Did management do a good job of "putting its best foot forward?" Would you recommend that a friend purchase the corporation's stock? Support your answers.

21-1 APPLICATION PROBLEM

Journalizing and posting entries for accrued revenue

The accounting forms for this problem are in the *Working Papers*.
On December 31 of the current year, Velma Parts Company has one note receivable outstanding, a 120-day, 10%, $8,100.00 note dated November 6.

Instructions:
1. Plan the adjustment on a work sheet. Label the adjustment *(a)*.
2. Journalize and post the adjusting entry for accrued interest income on December 31. Use page 14 of a general journal.
3. Journalize and post the closing entry for interest income using page 14 of a general journal.
4. Journalize and post the January 1 reversing entry for accrued interest income on page 15 of a general journal.
5. Journalize the receipt of cash for the maturity value of the note on March 6, Receipt No. 457. Use page 8 of a cash receipts journal. Post the amounts in the General columns of the cash receipts journal.

21-2 APPLICATION PROBLEM

Journalizing and posting entries for accrued expenses

The accounting forms for this problem are in the *Working Papers*.
On December 31 of the current year, Delmar Plumbing Supply has one note payable outstanding, a 180-day, 10%, $12,000.00 note dated December 1.

Instructions:
1. Plan the adjustment on a work sheet. Label the adjustment *(h)*.
2. Journalize and post the adjusting entry for accrued interest expense on December 31. Use page 14 of a general journal.
3. Journalize and post the closing entry for interest expense using page 14 of a general journal.
4. Journalize and post the January 1 reversing entry for accrued interest expense on page 15 of a general journal.
5. Journalize the payment of cash for the maturity value of the note on May 30, Check No. 756. Use page 27 of a cash payments journal. Post the amounts in the General columns of the cash payments journal.

21-3 APPLICATION PROBLEM

Journalizing and posting entries for accrued expenses

The accounting forms for this problem are in the *Working Papers*.
On October 14 of the current year, Patti's Dress Shop signed a $10,000.00 note with National Bank of Columbus. The note term is 180 days at 12% interest.

Instructions:
1. Plan the adjustment on a work sheet for the fiscal year ended December 31. Label the adjustment *(h)*.
2. Journalize and post the transactions to accrue, close, and reverse interest-related accounts at the fiscal year-end. Use page 16 of a general journal for December 31 transactions and page 17 for the January 1 transactions.
3. Journalize the payment of cash for the maturity value of the note paid on April 12 with Check No. 377. Use page 23 of a cash payments journal. Post the amounts in the General columns of the cash payments journal.

MASTERY PROBLEM

Journalizing and posting entries for accrued interest revenue and expense

The accounting forms for Youngblood, Inc., are given in the *Working Papers*. The balances are recorded as of December 31 of the current year before adjusting entries. Youngblood, Inc., completed the following transactions related to notes receivable and notes payable during the current year and the following year. The first two transactions have already been journalized and posted. One note receivable and one note payable are the only notes on hand at the end of the fiscal period. Source documents are abbreviated as follows: receipt, R; check, C; note receivable, NR.

Transactions:
20X1
Nov. 11. Accepted a 90-day, 12% note from Centre Plaza for an extension of time on their account, $900.00. NR10.
Dec. 6. Signed a 120-day, 8% note, $7,200.00 with First American Bank. R336.
20X2
Feb. 9. Received cash for the maturity value of NR10. R336.
Apr. 5. Paid cash for the maturity value of the First American Bank note. C612.

Instructions:

1. Plan the adjustments on a work sheet. Label the interest income adjustment *(a)* and the interest expense adjustment *(h)*.

2. Journalize and post the adjusting entries for accrued interest income and accrued interest expense on December 31. Use page 15 of a general journal.

3. Journalize and post the closing entries for interest income and interest expense. Continue to use page 15 of a general journal.

4. Journalize and post the reversing entries for accrued interest income and accrued interest expense. Use page 16 of a general journal.

5. Journalize the receipt of cash for the maturity value of NR10. Use page 16 of a cash receipts journal. Post the amounts in the General columns of the cash receipts journal.

6. Journalize the cash payment for the maturity value of the note payable. Use page 28 of a cash payments journal. Post the amounts in the General columns of the cash payments journal.

CHALLENGE PROBLEM

Journalizing and posting entries for accrued interest revenue and expenses

The accounting forms for Blackwell Corporation are given in the *Working Papers*. The balances are recorded as of December 31 of the current year before adjusting entries. Blackwell Corporation completed the following transactions related to notes receivable and notes payable during the current year and the following year. The first two transactions have already been journalized and posted. These notes are the only notes outstanding on December 31, 20X1, the fiscal year-end.

Transactions:
20X1
Dec. 8. Margaret Snider signed a 90-day, 18% note for an extension of time on her account, $900.00. NR56.
15. Signed a 180-day, 12% note with American National Bank, $10,000.00. R416.
20X2
Mar. 8. Margaret Snider dishonored NR56, maturity value due today. M98.
12. Paid off the American National Bank note ahead of the maturity date. American National charges interest only for the number of days the note is outstanding, with no early payment penalty. C645.

Instructions:

1. Plan the adjustments on a work sheet. Label the interest income adjustment *(a)* and the interest expense adjustment *(h)*.
2. Journalize and post the transactions to accrue, close, and reverse interest-related accounts at the fiscal year-end. Use page 16 of a general journal for December 31 transactions and page 17 for January 1 transactions.
3. Journalize the 20X2 transactions using page 18 of a general journal and page 15 of a cash payments journal. Post the Credit column of the general journal and the amounts in the General columns of the cash payments journal.

APPLIED COMMUNICATION

Employers often screen prospective employees for written communication skills. As an applicant, you may be asked to write a short essay. Therefore, it is important for you to practice preparing documents that clearly communicate a message, demonstrate proper usage of grammar rules, and project a professional image.

Instructions: Write a one-page memo to Gerard Spikes, Controller of Jenkins Company, that gives your opinion on one of the following questions: (1) Why is a basic knowledge of accounting important for all employees of a company, even for those not directly involved in accounting? (2) Why should the company help its employees to continue their formal education by paying for one technical or college course each year?

CASE FOR CRITICAL THINKING

At the end of each fiscal period, Kimura Corporation prepares adjusting entries to record accrued interest expense. However, the company does not record reversing entries for the accrued interest expense. At the end of the current fiscal year, Kimura had a $3,000.00, 90-day, 10% note payable outstanding, signed November 1. Kimura made the following journal entries related to the note.

Signed Note Nov. 1		
Cash....................	$3,000.00	
Notes Payable		$3,000.00
Adj. Entry Dec. 31		
Interest Expense	50.00	
Interest Payable.....		50.00

Closing Entry Dec. 31		
Income Summary	50.00	
Interest Expense		50.00
Paid Note Jan. 30		
Notes Payable	3,000.00	
Interest Payable........	50.00	
Interest Expense	25.00	
Cash...................		3,075.00

Isabel Lugo, an accounting supervisor, says that generally accepted accounting principles require that reversing entries be used in conjunction with adjusting entries for accrued expenses. Thus, Ms. Lugo says Kimura must begin using reversing entries for all accrued expenses. Is she correct? Do the procedures Kimura has been using result in incorrect financial statements? Explain.

ANALYZING BEST BUY'S FINANCIAL STATEMENTS

Reward Zone, Best Buy's customer loyalty program, awards discount certificates to members, based on their purchases. The value of the discount certificate must be recorded as an accrued liability until the customer redeems the certificate. Use the Sales Incentives section in the Notes to Consolidated Financial Statements on page B-16 in Best Buy's annual report in Appendix B.

Instructions

1. What account title is used to record discount certificates on the Consolidated Balance Sheets on page B-5?
2. What impact would the recorded debit have on the income statement when a discount certificate is issued?

Accounting
SOFTWARE

ACCRUED REVENUE AND EXPENSES

One of the most valuable assets of any business is its financial information. The actions that ensure that a business can quickly restore its access to and use its financial data is referred to as a *disaster recovery plan*. Creating a backup copy of financial data is one of the most common components of a disaster recovery plan. Peachtree has a menu option for creating a backup copy. Backup copies should be stored on a removable storage device and, preferably, stored at a remote location. Of course, after transactions are recorded in the restored backup copy, a new backup copy needs to be made.

PEACHTREE MASTERY PROBLEM 21-4
1. Open (Restore) file 21-4MP.ptb.
2. Journalize and post the adjusting entries for accrued interest income and accrued expense on December 31.
3. Journalize and post the closing entries for interest income and interest expense.
4. Journalize the post the reversing entries for accrued interest income and accrued interest expense.
5. Journalize and post the receipt of cash for the maturity value of NR10.
6. Journalize the cash payment for the maturity value of the note payable.
7. Print the December 31 to January 1 general journal, the February 9 cash receipts journal, the April 5 cash disbursements journal, and the general ledger from December 1 to April 30.

PEACHTREE CHALLENGE PROBLEM 21-5
1. Open (Restore) file 21-5CP.ptb.
2. Journalize and post the adjusting, closing, and reversing entries for interest-related accounts.
3. Journalize and post the 2006 transactions.
4. Print the general journal, the cash receipts journal, the cash disbursements journal, and the general ledger.

ACCRUED REVENUE AND EXPENSES

QuickBooks

When using accounting software, critical financial information about the company is stored in an electronic file. QuickBooks allows the user to make a backup copy of the company's data. If there is a problem with the original file, the backup copy can be used. Any transactions recorded since the last backup was made will be lost. Therefore, if any entries are recorded, a backup copy should be made at the end of the day.

It is important to store the backup file on something other than the computer on which the original file is stored. It is also preferable to keep the removable storage device at a remote location.

QUICKBOOKS MASTERY PROBLEM 21-4
1. Open the Youngblood Inc file if it is not already open.
2. Journalize the reversing entries for accrued interest income and accrued interest expense as of January 1, 20X2.
3. Use the Make Deposits window to record the receipt of payment from Centre Plaza.
4. Print a journal report.

QUICKBOOKS CHALLENGE PROBLEM 21-5
1. Open the Blackwell Corporation file if it is not already open.
2. Journalize the adjusting entries for accrued interest income and expense as of December 31, 20X1.
3. Journalize the reversing entries for interest income and expense as of January 1, 20X2.
4. Calculate the maturity value of NR56. Record the dishonored note using the Make General Journal Entries window.
5. Calculate the maturity value of the note from First National Bank as of March 12, 20X2, and record the payment.
6. Print the Journal report using December 31, 20X1 and March 31, 20X2 as the dates.

Annual reports of many public companies contain summary financial information for 10 years. This information provides investors with a rich history of the company's operating results and financial strength.

Absorbing 10 years of financial information can be overwhelming if that information is presented in a table. Charts provide a better approach of reporting this information. Line graphs are particularly adept at indicating trends.

Electronic spreadsheets provide a variety of tools to modify the chart's appearance. From adding titles to changing the scale of an axis, you can enhance the chart to ensure that the story of the financial information is clearly communicated.

EXCEL MASTERY PROBLEM 21-4

Open the F21-4 Excel data file. Follow the step-by-step instructions in the Instructions work sheet.

OPTIONAL SPREADSHEET ACTIVITY

Open the F21-OPT Excel data file. Follow the step-by-step instructions in the Instructions work sheet. This problem is not related to a specific problem in the textbook; however, it is related to the Explore Accounting feature in this chapter.

ENTRIES FOR ACCRUED REVENUE AND EXPENSES

To complete the accounting cycle, adjusting entries are entered and verified for accuracy. The financial statements are generated and then closing entries are generated and posted by the software. On the first day of the next fiscal period, some adjusting entries for accrued revenue and expense items affecting the next fiscal period are reversed by recording reversing entries.

Closing entries are made to close all temporary accounts at the end of the accounting period. *Automated Accounting* automatically prepares and posts closing entries.

To generate closing entries:
1. Choose Generate Closing Journal Entries from the Options menu.
2. Click Yes to generate the closing entries.
3. The general journal will appear, containing the journal entries.
4. Check the entries for accuracy, then click the Post button.
5. To display a post-closing trial balance report:
    a. Click on the Reports toolbar button, or choose the Reports Selection menu item from the Reports menu.
    b. Select the Ledger Reports option button from the Report Selection dialog box.
    c. Choose Trial Balance report.

Revenue and expense items that affect two fiscal periods are adjusted at the end of a fiscal period and then reversed at the beginning of the next fiscal period. Reversing entries are recorded in the general journal the same way as adjusting entries. Use *Rev.Ent.* as the reference.

AUTOMATED ACCOUNTING MASTERY PROBLEM 21-4

Open file F21-4.AA8. Display the problem instructions and complete the problem.

STOCKBYTE/GETTY IMAGES

CHAPTER 22

End-of-Fiscal-Period Work for a Corporation

OBJECTIVES

After studying Chapter 22, you will be able to:

1. Define accounting terms related to financial statements for a merchandising business organized as a corporation.

2. Identify accounting concepts and practices related to financial statements and end-of-fiscal-period entries for a merchandising business organized as a corporation.

3. Plan end-of-fiscal-period adjustments for a merchandising business organized as a corporation.

4. Calculate federal income tax, plan an adjustment for federal income tax expense, and complete a work sheet.

5. Prepare and analyze an income statement for a merchandising business organized as a corporation.

6. Prepare a statement of stockholders' equity for a merchandising business organized as a corporation.

7. Prepare and analyze a balance sheet for a merchandising business organized as a corporation.

8. Record adjusting, closing, and reversing entries for a merchandising business organized as a corporation.

KEY TERMS

- long-term liabilities
- working capital
- current ratio

Point Your Browser
www.C21accounting.com

Chico's

Store Efficiency Fuels Chico's Growth

Chico's FAS, Inc., is a specialty retailer of private-label, sophisticated, casual-to-dressy clothing. The company focuses on women who are 35 years old and up, with moderate to higher incomes. This focus has enabled the company to achieve dramatic growth since opening its first store in 1983. With sales of $1,646,482,000 in fiscal year 2006, the company now operates over 920 stores under its Chico's and White House | Black Market brands.

Chico's sales growth has also been achieved by improving the efficiency of each store. Similar to other retail businesses, Chico's tracks the change in its total sales per store. This financial ratio, often referred to as same-store sales, is calculated by dividing the change in sales by the prior period's sales. Chico's achieved same-store sales growth of 2.1% in its fiscal year 2006.

©JEFFERY ALLAN SALTER/CORBIS SABA

Chico's takes this analysis a step further by measuring its sales per square foot. Average net sales per selling square foot grew from below $700 in fiscal year 1999 to over $950 per square foot in fiscal year 2006.

Critical Thinking

1. Suggest three steps a clothing retailer can take to increase its sales per square foot.

2. What measure could Chico's managers use to evaluate the efficiency of its store employees?

Source: www.chicos.com

INTERNET ACTIVITY

Fiscal Year End

Go to the homepage for Home Depot(www.homedepot.com) and Lowe's (www.lowes.com).

Instructions

1. List the last day of the fiscal period for each company.

2. Are the dates similar for both companies? Why might these two companies have a similar year end?

· · · · · · · · · · · · · (**PREPARING FINANCIAL STATEMENTS**) · · · · · · · · · · · · · ·

The preparation of financial statements begins with the work sheet. Account titles and balances are entered on the work sheet. Any adjustments to account balances are entered in the Adjustments columns. Restaurant Supply records adjustments affecting several accounts, including notes receivable, notes payable, allowance for uncollectible accounts, merchandise inventory, supplies, and depreciation. Since Restaurant Supply is a corporation, an adjustment is also planned for federal income tax expense.

The completed work sheet is used to prepare the financial statements. The income statement is prepared from amounts in the Income Statement columns of the work sheet. Restaurant Supply uses ratios to analyze its performance relative to industry standards and prior year's performance.

The amount of net income, selected balance sheet accounts, and other accounting information is used to prepare the statement of stockholders' equity. Summary amounts on this statement and account balances in the work sheet's Balance Sheet columns are used to prepare a balance sheet. Restaurant Supply uses ratios to evaluate its financial strength relative to expected measures.

In preparation for recording transactions during the next period, adjusting entries are journalized to record the work sheet adjustments in the accounts. After recording closing and reversing entries, the accounts are ready to record transactions for the next fiscal period. Businesses use work sheets to plan adjustments and provide information needed to prepare financial statements. Restaurant Supply may prepare a work sheet at any time financial statements are needed. However, Restaurant Supply always prepares a work sheet and financial statements at the end of a fiscal year. [CONCEPT: Accounting Period Cycle]

CHARACTER COUNTS

The Newspaper Test

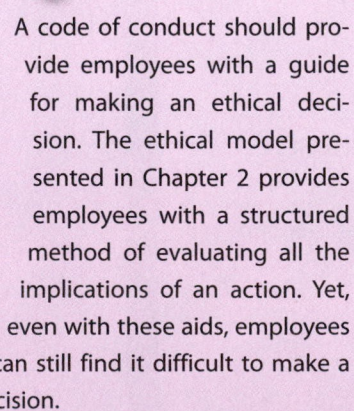

A code of conduct should provide employees with a guide for making an ethical decision. The ethical model presented in Chapter 2 provides employees with a structured method of evaluating all the implications of an action. Yet, even with these aids, employees can still find it difficult to make a decision.

Some companies provide their employees with a simple set of questions.

The most popular question is: "Would I be comfortable if my actions were reported in the newspaper?" If employees are uncomfortable with their actions becoming public knowledge, chances are their actions are unethical. At the very least, the employees should realize that they should consult their company's ethics officer and legal department.

Instructions

Use the Internet to access the code of conduct for Lockheed Martin, the Coca-Cola Company, and Shell Oil Company. Prepare a list of questions that could help you determine if an action is ethical.

Entering a Trial Balance on a Work Sheet

To prepare a work sheet, a trial balance is first entered in the Trial Balance columns. All general ledger accounts are listed in the same order as they appear in the general ledger. Trial Balance columns are totaled to prove equality of debits and credits.

Planning Adjustments on a Work Sheet

Some general ledger accounts need to be brought up to date before financial statements are prepared. Accounts are brought up to date by planning and entering adjustments on a work sheet. Two methods are used to determine the amount of each adjustment.

For some accounts, the calculated estimate of the account is also the amount used in the work sheet adjustment. These adjustments include:

1. Interest Income
2. Uncollectible Accounts Expense
3. Depreciation Expense—Office Equipment
4. Depreciation Expense—Store Equipment
5. Interest Expense

Other accounts require the end-of-period balance to be estimated. The current balance is typically subtracted from the estimated end-of-period account balance to determine the amount of the adjustment. Thus, the work sheet adjustment brings the account balance up to date. These adjustments include:

1. Merchandise Inventory
2. Supplies
3. Prepaid Insurance
4. Federal Income Tax Expense

Examples of both types of adjustments are shown on the following page. Adjustments generally are made in the order that accounts are listed on a work sheet.

DIGITAL VISION/GETTY IMAGES

1. Debit Interest Receivable

	ACCOUNT TITLE	TRIAL BALANCE		ADJUSTMENTS	
		DEBIT	CREDIT	DEBIT	CREDIT
4	*Interest Receivable*			① (a) 20 00	
51	*Interest Income*		1 36 00		(a) 20 00 ②

2. Credit Interest Income

Interest income earned during the current fiscal period but not yet received needs to be recorded. Two accounts are used for the adjustment for accrued interest income: Interest Receivable and Interest Income. An analysis of Restaurant Supply's adjustment for accrued interest income is described in Chapter 21. The estimate of accrued interest income is the amount used in the work sheet adjustment.

STEPS **PLANNING A WORK SHEET ADJUSTMENT FOR INTEREST INCOME**

① Enter the accrued interest income amount, $20.00, in the Adjustments Debit column on the *Interest Receivable* line of the work sheet. Label the adjustment (a).

② Enter the same amount, $20.00, in the Adjustments Credit column on the *Interest Income* line. Label the adjustment (a).

SUPPLIES ADJUSTMENT

1. Credit Supplies

	ACCOUNT TITLE	TRIAL BALANCE		ADJUSTMENTS	
		DEBIT	CREDIT	DEBIT	CREDIT
8	*Supplies*	8 745 25			① (d) 7 837 00
47	*Supplies Expense*			② (d) 7 837 00	

2. Debit Supplies Expense

The balance of Supplies in the trial balance, $8,745.25, is the cost of supplies on hand at the beginning of the year plus the supplies purchased during the year. The supplies on hand on December 31 are counted and determined to be $908.25. To bring the account up to date, the balance of Supplies needs to be decreased by $7,837.00 ($8,745.25 − $908.25), the cost of supplies used during the year. Supplies Expense is debited, and Supplies is credited for the amount of the decrease.

STEPS **PLANNING A WORK SHEET ADJUSTMENT FOR SUPPLIES**

① Enter the amount of supplies used, $7,837.00, in the adjustments credit column on the *Supplies* line of the work sheet. Label the adjustment (d).

② Enter the same amount, $7,837.00, in the Adjustments Debit column on the *Supplies Expense* line of the work sheet. Label the adjustment (d).

2. Credit Federal Income Tax Payable

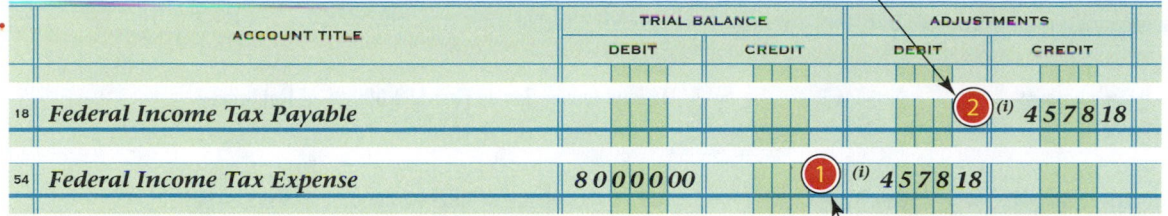

	ACCOUNT TITLE	TRIAL BALANCE		ADJUSTMENTS	
		DEBIT	CREDIT	DEBIT	CREDIT
18	Federal Income Tax Payable				(i) 4 5 7 8 18 ②
54	Federal Income Tax Expense	8 0 0 0 0 00		① (i) 4 5 7 8 18	

1. Debit Federal Income Tax Expense

Detailed instructions for preparing the federal income tax adjustment were presented in Chapter 14. The first step is to calculate the corporation's net income before federal income tax. This procedure can be summarized in four steps:

1. Complete all adjustments other than federal income taxes.
2. Extend all the accounts except Federal Income Tax Expense to the Income Statement or Balance Sheet columns.
3. Calculate temporary totals of the Income Statement accounts in the Income Statement columns.
4. The difference between the two Income Statement columns, excluding the estimated federal income taxes, is the net income or loss before income taxes.

The amount of federal income tax is calculated using tax rates provided by the Internal Revenue Service. The tax rate varies, depending on the amount of net income earned. Restaurant Supply's net income before income tax expense is $259,815.85. The tax rates are given in the table on the next page.

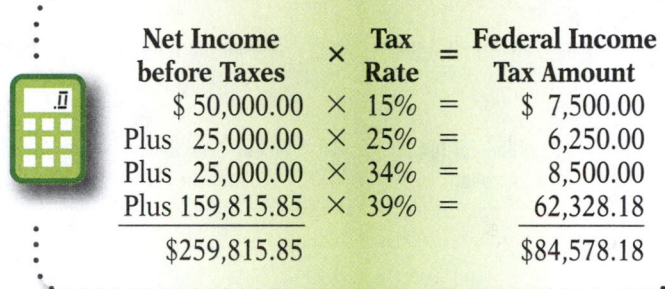

Net Income before Taxes	×	Tax Rate	=	Federal Income Tax Amount
$ 50,000.00	×	15%	=	$ 7,500.00
Plus 25,000.00	×	25%	=	6,250.00
Plus 25,000.00	×	34%	=	8,500.00
Plus 159,815.85	×	39%	=	62,328.18
$259,815.85				$84,578.18

The estimated tax payments already made are subtracted from the total federal income tax expense to calculate the adjustment for federal income tax expense.

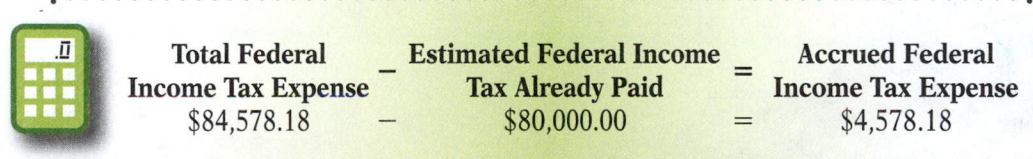

Total Federal Income Tax Expense	−	Estimated Federal Income Tax Already Paid	=	Accrued Federal Income Tax Expense
$84,578.18	−	$80,000.00	=	$4,578.18

STEPS — PLANNING A WORK SHEET ADJUSTMENT FOR FEDERAL INCOME TAX EXPENSE

① Enter the federal income tax expense adjustment amount, *$4,578.18,* in the Adjustments Debit column on the *Federal Income Tax Expense* line of the work sheet. Label the adjustment *(i)*.

② Enter the same amount, *$4,578.18,* in the Adjustments Credit column on the *Federal Income Tax Payable* line of the work sheet. Label the adjustment *(i)*.

15% of net income before taxes, zero to $50,000.00 (15% tax on the *first* $50,000.00 of net income)
Plus 25% of net income before taxes, $50,000.00 to $75,000.00 (25% tax on the *next* $25,000.00 of net income)
Plus 34% of net income before taxes, $75,000.00 to $100,000.00 (34% tax on the *next* $25,000.00 of net income)
Plus 39% of net income before taxes, $100,000.00 to $335,000.00 (39% tax on the *next* $225,000.00 of net income)
Plus 34% of net income before taxes over $335,000.00 (34% tax on net income *above* $335,000.00)

Step 1:

First Net Income Amount	×	**First Tax Rate**	=	**Federal Income Tax on First $50,000.00 of Net Income**
$50,000.00	×	15%	=	$7,500.00

Step 2:

Second Net Income Amount	×	**Second Tax Rate**	=	**Federal Income Tax on Next $25,000.00 of Net Income**
$25,000.00	×	25%	=	$6,250.00

Step 3:

Third Net Income Amount	×	**Third Tax Rate**	=	**Federal Income Tax on Next $25,000.00 of Net Income**
$25,000.00	×	34%	=	$8,500.00

Step 4:

Total Net Income	−	**Lowest Dollar Amount of Fourth Tax Range**	=	**Amount of Net Income to Which Fourth Tax Rate Is Applied**
$259,815.85	−	$100,000.00	=	$159,815.85

Step 5:

Fourth Net Income Amount	×	**Fourth Tax Rate**	=	**Federal Income Tax on Next $159,815.85 of Net Income**
$159,815.85	×	39%	=	$62,328.18

Step 6:

First Federal Tax Amount	+	**Second Federal Tax Amount**	+	**Third Federal Tax Amount**	+	**Fourth Federal Tax Amount**	=	**Total Federal Tax Amount**
$7,500.00	+	$6,250.00	+	$8,500.00	+	$62,328.18	=	$84,578.18

1. Total the income statement and balance sheet columns.

ACCOUNT TITLE	TRIAL BALANCE DEBIT	TRIAL BALANCE CREDIT	ADJUSTMENTS DEBIT	ADJUSTMENTS CREDIT	INCOME STATEMENT DEBIT	INCOME STATEMENT CREDIT	BALANCE SHEET DEBIT	BALANCE SHEET CREDIT	
14 Notes Payable		1000000						1000000	14
15 Interest Payable				(h) 40000				40000	15
16 Accounts Payable		2495035						2495035	16
17 Employee Income Tax Payable		204900						204900	17
18 Federal Income Tax Payable				(i) 457818				457818	18
52 Interest Expense	60000		(h) 40000		100000				52
53 Loss on Plant Assets	140000				140000				53
54 Federal Income Tax Expense	8000000		(i) 457818		8457818				54
55	22645 22 37	22645 22 37	5819848	5819848	19570093 3	21322 47 00	34627452	17103685	55
56 Net Income after Federal Income Tax					17523767			17523767	56
57					2132247 00	2132247 00	34627452	34627452	57

2. Calculate and enter the net income after federal income tax.

5. Draw double lines.   **4.** Calculate the column totals.   **3.** Extend the net income amount.

After the adjustment for federal income tax expense has been recorded, the work sheet is ready to be completed. Income Statement column totals are used to calculate net income after federal income tax. Restaurant Supply's completed work sheet is shown on the following two pages.

STEPS — **COMPLETING A WORK SHEET**

1 Total the Income Statement and Balance Sheet columns.

2 Write the words *Net Income after Federal Income Tax* on line 56 of the work sheet. Calculate and enter the net income after federal income tax, *$175,237.67*, in the Income Statement Debit column on this new line of the work sheet.

Total of Income Statement Credit column	$ 2,132,247.00
Less Total of Income Statement Debit column	−1,957,009.33
Equals Net Income after Federal Income Tax	$ 175,237.67

3 Extend the net income after federal income tax amount, *$175,237.67*, to the Balance Sheet Credit column.

4 Total the four Income Statement and Balance Sheet columns. Determine that the totals of each pair of columns are in balance.

5 Rule double lines across the Income Statement and Balance Sheet columns to show that the totals have been verified as correct.

Preparing a Work Sheet for a Corporation

COMPLETED WORK SHEET

Restaurant Supply Co.
Work Sheet
For Year Ended December 31, 20--

ACCOUNT TITLE	TRIAL BALANCE DEBIT	TRIAL BALANCE CREDIT	ADJUSTMENTS DEBIT	ADJUSTMENTS CREDIT	INCOME STATEMENT DEBIT	INCOME STATEMENT CREDIT	BALANCE SHEET DEBIT	BALANCE SHEET CREDIT
1 Cash	1120310						1120310	
2 Petty Cash	25000						25000	
3 Notes Receivable	200000						200000	
4 Interest Receivable			(a) 2000				2000	
5 Accounts Receivable	7834030						7834030	
6 Allowance for Uncollectible Accts.		28000		(b) 1287330				1315330
7 Merchandise Inventory	14253620		(c) 529000				14782620	
8 Supplies	874525			(d) 783700			90825	
9 Prepaid Insurance	1380000			(e) 1160000			220000	
10 Office Equipment	3198032						3198032	
11 Accum. Depr.—Office Equipment		1876000		(f) 635000				2511000
12 Store Equipment	4154635						4154635	
13 Accum. Depr.—Store Equipment		1604900		(g) 925000				2529900
14 Notes Payable		1000000						1000000
15 Interest Payable				(h) 40000				40000
16 Accounts Payable		2495035						2495035
17 Employee Income Tax Payable		204900						204900
18 Federal Income Tax Payable				(i) 457818				457818
19 Social Security Tax Payable		176776						176776
20 Medicare Tax Payable		42724						42724
21 Sales Tax Payable		498000						498000
22 Unemployment Tax Payable—Federal		3800						3800
23 Unemployment Tax Payable—State		24400						24400
24 Health Insurance Premiums Payable		56000						56000
25 Dividends Payable		750000						750000
26 Capital Stock		15000000						15000000
27 Retained Earnings		3498002						3498002
28 Dividends	3000000						3000000	
29 Income Summary				(c) 529000		529000		
30 Sales		210989430				210989430		
31 Sales Discount	695820				695820			

#	Account Title	Trial Balance Debit	Trial Balance Credit	Adjustments Debit	Adjustments Credit	Income Statement Debit	Income Statement Credit	Balance Sheet Debit	Balance Sheet Credit
32	Sales Returns and Allowances	2405940				2405940			
33	Purchases	121232150				121232150			
34	Purchases Discount		1109420				1109420		
35	Purchases Returns and Allowances		514250				514250		
36	Advertising Expense	2432225				2432225			
37	Cash Short and Over	1423				1423			
38	Credit Card Fee Expense	1534244				1534244			
39	Depr. Expense—Office Equipment			(f) 635000		635000			
40	Depr. Expense—Store Equipment			(g) 925000		925000			
41	Insurance Expense			(e) 1160000		1160000			
42	Miscellaneous Expense	3002443				3002443			
43	Payroll Taxes Expense	2931005				2931005			
44	Rent Expense	6000000				6000000			
45	Repair Expense	454313				454313			
46	Salary Expense	39384428				39384428			
47	Supplies Expense			(d) 783700		783700			
48	Uncollectible Accounts Expense			(b) 1287330		1287330			
49	Utilities Expense	2138094				2138094			
50	Gain on Plant Assets		67000				67000		
51	Interest Income		13600		(a) 2000		15600		
52	Interest Expense	60000		(h) 40000		100000			
53	Loss on Plant Assets	140000				140000			
54	Federal Income Tax Expense	8000000		(i) 457818		8457818			
55		226452237	226452237	5819848	5819848	195700933	213224700	34627452	17103685
56	Net Income after Federal Income Tax					17523767			17523767
57						213224700	213224700	34627452	34627452

End of Lesson
REVIEW

1. Describe the two methods used to determine the amount of an adjustment on a work sheet.
2. Summarize the four steps to calculate net income before federal income taxes.

WORK TOGETHER 22-1

Preparing a work sheet for a corporation

Webster Corporation's work sheet is given in the *Working Papers*. Your instructor will guide you through the following example.

1. For the current year ended December 31, record the adjustments on the work sheet using the following information. Do not total the Adjustments columns.

Accrued interest income	$ 275.00
Uncollectible accounts expense estimated as 1.5% of sales on account.	
Sales on account for year, $490,000.00.	
Merchandise inventory	90,116.30
Supplies inventory	252.08
Value of prepaid insurance	3,071.60
Annual depreciation expense—office equipment	2,800.00
Annual depreciation expense—store equipment	1,700.60
Accrued interest expense	555.16

2. Using the tax table shown in this chapter, calculate federal income tax expense and record the income tax adjustment on the work sheet. Complete the work sheet. Save your work to complete Work Together 22-2.

ON YOUR OWN 22-1

Preparing a work sheet for a corporation

Osborn Corporation's work sheet is given in the *Working Papers*. Work this problem independently.

1. For the current year ended December 31, record the adjustments on the work sheet using the following information. Do not total the Adjustments columns.

Accrued interest income	$ 160.00
Uncollectible accounts expense estimated as 0.8% of sales on account.	
Sales on account for year, $914,000.00.	
Merchandise inventory	197,992.26
Supplies inventory	802.50
Value of prepaid insurance	1,200.00
Annual depreciation expense—office equipment	6,440.00
Annual depreciation expense—store equipment	8,250.00
Accrued interest expense	300.00

2. Using the tax table shown in this chapter, calculate federal income tax expense and record the income tax adjustment on the work sheet. Complete the work sheet. Save your work to complete On Your Own 22-2.

INCOME STATEMENT

					% OF NET SALES
Restaurant Supply Co.					
Income Statement					
For Year Ended December 31, 20--					
Operating Revenue:					
Sales			2109 89 4 30		
Less: Sales Discount		6 95 8 20			
Sales Returns and Allowances		24 05 9 40	31 01 7 60		
Net Sales				2078 87 6 70	100.0
Cost of Merchandise Sold:					
Merchandise Inventory, Jan. 1, 20--			142 53 6 20		
Purchases		1212 32 1 50			
Less: Purchases Discount	11 09 4 20				
Purchases Returns and Allow.	5 14 2 50	16 23 6 70			
Net Purchases			1196 08 4 80		
Total Cost of Mdse. Avail. for Sale			1338 62 1 00		
Less Mdse. Inventory, Dec. 31, 20--			147 82 6 20		
Cost of Merchandise Sold				1190 79 4 80	57.3
Gross Profit on Operations				888 08 1 90	42.7
Operating Expenses:					
Advertising Expense			24 32 2 25		
Cash Short and Over			1 4 23		
Credit Card Fee Expense			1 53 4 2 44		
Depr. Expense—Office Equipment			6 35 0 00		
Depr. Expense—Store Equipment			9 25 0 00		
Insurance Expense			11 60 0 00		
Miscellaneous Expense			30 02 4 43		
Payroll Taxes Expense			29 31 0 05		
Rent Expense			60 00 0 00		
Repair Expense			4 54 3 13		
Salary Expense			393 84 4 28		
Supplies Expense			7 83 7 00		
Uncollectible Accounts Expense			12 87 3 30		
Utilities Expense			21 38 0 94		
Total Operating Expenses				626 69 2 05	30.1
Income from Operations				261 38 9 85	12.6
Other Revenue:					
Gain on Plant Assets		6 7 0 00			
Interest Income		1 5 6 00			
Total Other Income			8 2 6 00		
Other Expenses:					
Interest Expense		1 00 0 00			
Loss on Plant Assets		1 40 0 00			
Total Other Expenses			2 40 0 00		
Net Deduction				1 57 4 00	0.1
Net Income before Federal Income Tax				259 81 5 85	12.5
Less Federal Income Tax Expense				84 57 8 18	
Net Income after Federal Income Tax				175 23 7 67	

An income statement reports the financial progress of a business during a fiscal period. [CONCEPT: Accounting Period Cycle] Revenue, cost of merchandise sold, gross profit on operations, operating expenses, and net income or net loss are reported on an income statement. [CONCEPT: Adequate Disclosure] To help make decisions about current and future operations, Restaurant Supply also analyzes relationships between revenue and expense items. Based on this analysis, Restaurant Supply reports component percentages for all major income statement items.

Restaurant Supply's income statement is very similar to Hobby Shack's income statement, shown in Part 2. Both companies report net sales, net purchases, gross profit on operations, and income from operations. However, Restaurant Supply has two additional types of accounts that are reported on the income statement: (1) gains and losses from the sale of plant assets and (2) accruals for interest receivable and payable. These accounts are reported after income from operations.

STEPS   NEW ELEMENTS IN THE INCOME STATEMENT FOR RESTAURANT SUPPLY

1 Income from operations, $261,389.85, is the income earned only from normal business activities. Restaurant Supply's normal business activities are selling kitchen equipment and supplies. Revenue from the sales of plant assets, $670.00, and interest earned on notes receivable, $156.00, are not normal operating activities. Therefore, these accounts are reported after income from operations in a section labeled *Other Revenue*.

2 The interest expense on notes payable, $1,000.00, and the loss from the sales of plant assets, $1,400.00, are not normal operating activities. Therefore, these accounts are reported after income from operations in a section labeled *Other Expenses*.

3 The difference between other revenue and other expenses, $1,574.00, is reported as a net addition or net deduction. The difference is added to or deducted from income from operations to determine the net income before federal income tax.

GLOBAL PERSPECTIVE

International Quality Standards

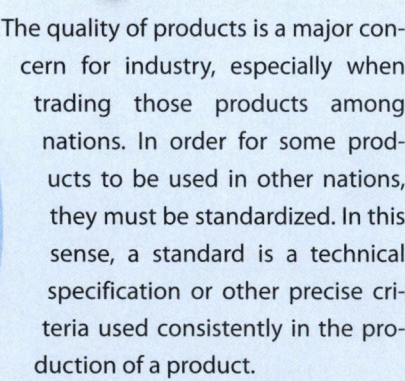

The quality of products is a major concern for industry, especially when trading those products among nations. In order for some products to be used in other nations, they must be standardized. In this sense, a standard is a technical specification or other precise criteria used consistently in the production of a product.

Companies who intend to sell their products globally must produce them in compliance with the standards set for the industry. International standard-

ization has been established for many fields, including information processing and communications, textiles, packaging, energy production, shipbuilding, and banking and financial services. Standardization will continue to grow in importance for all sectors of business activity.

Critical Thinking

1. How would your company benefit from international quality standards if it were buying the same product from different vendors in different countries?

2. Could meeting international quality standards give a company a competitive advantage?

PHOTO: STOCKBYTE/GETTY IMAGES

Income Statement Items	Acceptable Component Percentages	Actual Component Percentages
Net sales	100.0%	100.0%
Cost of merchandise sold	not more than 58.0%	57.3%
Gross profit on operations	not less than 42.0%	42.7%
Total operating expenses	not more than 35.0%	30.1%
Income from operations	not less than 7.0%	12.6%
Net deduction	not more than 0.1%	0.1%
Net income before federal income tax	not less than 6.9%	12.5%

For a business to determine whether it is progressing satisfactorily, results of operations are compared with industry standards and/or previous fiscal periods. By analyzing revenues, costs, and expenses, management can gain information that it can use to improve future operations.

The percentage relationship between one financial statement item and the total that includes that item is known as a *component percentage*. Restaurant Supply prepares component percentages for six major items on its income statement, as shown in the illustration. Restaurant Supply uses net sales as the base for calculating component percentages.

The amount of each item on the income statement is divided by the amount of net sales. Thus, each component percentage shows the percentage that item is of net sales. For example, the cost of merchandise sold component percentage indicates that Restaurant Supply spent 57.3 cents out of each $1.00 of sales for the merchandise sold.

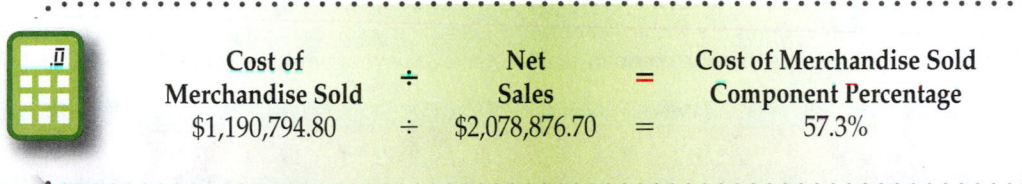

Cost of Merchandise Sold	÷	Net Sales	=	Cost of Merchandise Sold Component Percentage
$1,190,794.80	÷	$2,078,876.70	=	57.3%

Acceptable Component Percentages

Based on comparisons with industry standards as well as previous accounting periods, Restaurant Supply has determined acceptable component percentages for each major item of cost and expense on its income statement.

If the component percentage of any cost or expense item for a fiscal period exceeds the acceptable percentage, that cost or expense is reviewed further to determine the reason. After determining the reason why a cost or expense exceeded the acceptable percentage, ways are sought to bring the expense within acceptable limits.

FOR YOUR INFORMATION

FYI

Component percentages are not calculated for federal income tax expense and net income after federal income tax. Corporations do not have much control over the amount of federal income taxes to be paid. Thus, the net income before federal income tax is the best measure the corporation has to assess its profitability.

End of Lesson
REVIEW

1. Why are other revenue and other expenses reported separately from sales, cost of merchandise sold, and operating expenses on the income statement?
2. What information is shown by component percentages on an income statement?

WORK TOGETHER 22-2

Preparing an income statement for a corporation

The completed work sheet for Webster Corporation and a blank income statement form are given in the *Working Papers*. Your instructor will guide you through the following examples.

1. Prepare an income statement for the current year. Calculate and record the following component percentages: (a) cost of merchandise sold; (b) gross profit on operations; (c) total operating expenses; (d) income from operations; (e) net addition or deduction resulting from other revenue and expenses; and (f) net income before federal income tax. Round percentage calculations to the nearest 0.1%.
2. The acceptable component percentages are given in the *Working Papers*. Analyze the income statement by determining if component percentages are within acceptable levels. If any component percentage is not within an acceptable level, suggest steps that the company should take. Save your work to complete Work Together 22-3.

ON YOUR OWN 22-2

Preparing an income statement for a corporation

The completed work sheet you prepared for Osborn Corporation and a blank income statement form are given in the *Working Papers*. Work this problem independently.

1. Prepare an income statement for the current year. Calculate and record the following component percentages: (a) cost of merchandise sold; (b) gross profit on operations; (c) total operating expenses; (d) income from operations; (e) net addition or deduction resulting from other revenue and expenses; and (f) net income before federal income tax. Round percentage calculations to the nearest 0.1%.
2. The acceptable component percentages are given in the *Working Papers*. Analyze the income statement by determining if component percentages are within acceptable levels. If any component percentage is not within an acceptable level, suggest steps that the company should take. Save your work to complete On Your Own 22-3.

············ **STATEMENT OF STOCKHOLDERS' EQUITY** ···············

1. Write Heading

2. Prepare Capital Stock Section

3. Prepare Retained Earnings Section

① **Restaurant Supply Co.**
Statement of Stockholders' Equity
For Year Ended December 31, 20--

② **Capital Stock**			
$1.00 Per Share			
January 1, 20--, 15,000 Shares Issued		15 0 0 0 00	
Issued during Current Year, None		0 00	
Balance, December 31, 20--, 15,000 Shares Issued			15 0 0 0 00
③ Retained Earnings:			
Balance, January 1, 20--		34 9 8 0 02	
Net Income after Federal Income Tax for 20--	175 2 3 7 67		
Less Dividends Declared during 20--	30 0 0 0 00		
Net Increase during 20--		145 2 3 7 67	
Balance, December 31, 20--			180 2 1 7 69
Total Stockholders' Equity, December 31, 20--			195 2 1 7 69

The statement of stockholders' equity shows changes in a corporation's ownership for a fiscal period. A statement of stockholders' equity contains two major sections: (1) capital stock and (2) retained earnings.

The capital stock section reports the amount of capital stock issued at the start of the year and any shares issued during the year. Information about the par value and the number of shares is also presented.

The lower section of the statement reports the changes in retained earnings. Net income after federal income taxes increases retained earnings. In contrast, dividends reduce retained earnings. The net difference of these amounts is added to beginning retained earnings to calculate the balance at the fiscal year end.

Detailed instructions for preparing the statement of stockholders' equity were presented in Chapter 15 and are summarized below.

S T E P S PREPARING A STATEMENT OF STOCKHOLDERS' EQUITY

① Write the heading: company name, *Restaurant Supply Co.*; statement name, *Statement of Stockholders' Equity*; and fiscal period, *For Year Ended December 31, 20--*, in the statement heading.

② Use information in the accounting records and account balances on the work sheet to prepare the capital stock section of the statement.

③ Use account balances on the work sheet and the amount of net income after federal income tax reported on the income statement to prepare the retained earnings section of the statement.

Restaurant Supply Co.

Balance Sheet

December 31, 20--

Assets				
Current Assets:				
Cash			11 203 10	
Petty Cash			2 500 00	
Notes Receivable			2 000 00	
Interest Receivable			20 00	
Accounts Receivable	78 340 30			
Less Allowance for Uncollectible Accounts	13 153 30	65 187 00		
Merchandise Inventory		147 826 20		
Supplies		908 25		
Prepaid Insurance		2 200 00		
Total Current Assets			229 594 55	
Plant Assets:				
Office Equipment	31 980 32			
Less Accumulated Depreciation—Office Equipment	25 110 00	6 870 32		
Store Equipment	41 546 35			
Less Accumulated Depreciation—Store Equipment	25 299 00	16 247 35		
Total Plant Assets			23 117 67	
Total Assets			252 712 22	
Liabilities				
Current Liabilities:				
Notes Payable		10 000 00		
Interest Payable		400 00		
Accounts Payable		24 950 35		
Employee Income Tax Payable		2 049 00		
Federal Income Tax Payable		4 578 18		
Social Security Tax Payable		1 767 76		
Medicare Tax Payable		427 24		
Sales Tax Payable		4 980 00		
Unemployment Tax Payable—Federal		38 00		
Unemployment Tax Payable—State		244 00		
Health Insurance Premiums Payable		560 00		
Dividends Payable		7 500 00		
Total Liabilities			57 494 53	
Stockholders' Equity				
Capital Stock		15 000 00		
Retained Earnings		180 217 69		
Total Stockholders' Equity			195 217 69	
Total Liabilities and Stockholders' Equity			252 712 22	

A corporation's balance sheet reports assets, liabilities, and stockholders' equity on a specific date. [CONCEPT: Accounting Period Cycle] A balance sheet is prepared from information found in the Balance Sheet columns of the work sheet and on the statement of stockholders' equity.

Detailed procedures for preparing a balance sheet were presented in Chapter 15. These procedures are summarized below by the three primary account classifications.

Assets

Restaurant Supply classifies its assets as current assets and plant assets. Cash and other assets expected to be exchanged for cash or consumed within a year are known as *current assets*. Assets that will be used for a number of years in the operation of a business are known as *plant assets*. A business owning both current and plant assets usually lists them under separate headings on a balance sheet.

Some of Restaurant Supply's asset accounts have related contra accounts that reduce the related account on the balance sheet. The difference between an asset's account balance and its related contra account balance is known as *book value*. An asset's book value is reported on a balance sheet by listing three amounts: (1) the balance of the asset account, (2) the balance of the asset's contra account, and (3) book value.

Liabilities

Liabilities are classified according to the length of time until they are due. Liabilities due within a short time, usually within a year, are known as *current liabilities*. All of Restaurant Supply's liabilities are current liabilities because they come due within a year.

Liabilities owed for more than a year are called **long-term liabilities**. An example of a long-term liability is Mortgage Payable. On December 31 of the current year, Restaurant Supply does not have any long-term liabilities.

Stockholders' Equity

The stockholders' equity section contains the total amounts of capital stock and retained earnings. These amounts are calculated and reported on the statement of stockholders' equity, as well as on the balance sheet.

PHOTOALTO/GETTY IMAGES

FOR YOUR INFORMATION

F Y I

A company having both current liabilities and long-term liabilities would include headings and totals for each category. The process is similar to preparing the asset section of a balance sheet.

To continue operating successfully, a business must have adequate financial resources to buy additional merchandise, pay employee salaries, and pay for other operating expenses. Financial strength analysis measures the level of financial resources. The balance sheet is the primary source of data to determine the financial strength of a business.

Restaurant Supply analyzes its financial strength to assist the company in planning for future periods and to ensure that adequate resources are available to operate the business. Creditors and investors also use financial strength analysis to determine if the company is a good credit and investment risk. Before a creditor sells merchandise to a company on account, the creditor must believe that the company will later pay for the merchandise. A company that is considered to be a poor credit risk is usually a bad investment for an investor.

Working Capital

The amount of total current assets less total current liabilities is called **working capital**. The amount is stated in dollars. Working capital is a measure of the financial resources available for the daily operations of the business. Restaurant Supply's working capital is calculated as shown below.

Working capital should not be confused with cash. Restaurant Supply does not have $172,100.02 of excess cash. However, Restaurant Supply does have $172,100.02 of financial resources that are available for use in daily operations at the beginning of the next fiscal year.

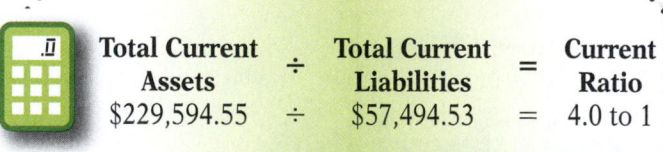

	Total Current Assets	−	Total Current Liabilities	=	Working Capital
	$229,594.55	−	$57,494.53	=	$172,100.02

Current Ratio

Although working capital is a useful measure, working capital does not permit a business to compare itself to its industry or to provide a convenient relative measurement from year to year.

A more useful measure results from comparing the amount of total current assets to total current liabilities. A comparison between two numbers showing how many times one number exceeds the other is known as a *ratio*. A ratio that shows the numeric relationship of current assets to current liabilities is called the **current ratio**. The current ratio is a measure of a company's ability to pay its current liabilities when due. Creditors use the ratio to determine if merchandise should be sold to a company on account. Restaurant Supply's current ratio is calculated as shown.

Restaurant Supply's current ratio is stated as 4.0 to 1, which means that total current assets are 4.0 times total current liabilities.

Based on previous experience, industry guidelines, and the need to maintain sufficient merchandise inventory, Restaurant Supply considers a current ratio between 3.0 to 1 and 4.5 to 1 to be acceptable. On December 31 of the current year, Restaurant Supply's current ratio, 4.0 to 1, is acceptable. This year's current ratio indicates a favorable condition of financial strength.

	Total Current Assets	÷	Total Current Liabilities	=	Current Ratio
	$229,594.55	÷	$57,494.53	=	4.0 to 1

End of Lesson
REVIEW

TERMS REVIEW

long-term liabilities

working capital

current ratio

AUDIT YOUR UNDERSTANDING

1. What is an example of a long-term liability?
2. What is working capital?
3. Why is the current ratio a useful measure of financial strength?

WORK TOGETHER 22-3

Preparing a statement of stockholders' equity and balance sheet for a corporation

Use the work sheet and income statement for Webster Corporation from Work Together 22-2. Forms are given in the *Working Papers*. Your instructor will guide you through the following example.

1. Prepare a statement of stockholders' equity for the current year. As of January 1, Webster Corporation had issued 9,000 shares of capital stock with a par value of $10.00 per share. During the fiscal year, the corporation issued 1,000 additional shares of capital stock.
2. Prepare a balance sheet for the current year.
3. Calculate Webster Corporation's (a) working capital and (b) current ratio.
4. Determine if these items are within acceptable levels. The corporation considers working capital in excess of $150,000.00 and a current ratio between 2.0 to 1 and 3.0 to 1 to be acceptable indications of financial strength. Save your work to complete Work Together 22-4.

ON YOUR OWN 22-3

Preparing a statement of stockholders' equity and balance sheet for a corporation

Use the work sheet and income statement for Osborn Corporation from On Your Own 22-2. Forms are given in the *Working Papers*. Work this problem independently.

1. Prepare a statement of stockholders' equity for the current year. As of January 1, Osborn Corporation had issued 45,000 shares of capital stock with a par value of $1.00 per share. During the fiscal year, the corporation issued 5,000 additional shares of stock.
2. Prepare a balance sheet for the current year.
3. Calculate Osborn Corporation's (a) working capital and (b) current ratio.
4. Determine if these items are within acceptable levels. The corporation considers working capital in excess of $100,000.00 and a current ratio between 5.0 to 1 and 6.0 to 1 to be acceptable indications of financial strength. Save your work to complete On Your Own 22-4.

Adjusting, Closing, and Reversing Entries for a Corporation

.... **ADJUSTING ENTRIES** ....

	DATE	ACCOUNT TITLE	DOC. NO.	POST. REF.	DEBIT	CREDIT	
1		*Adjusting Entries*					1
2	Dec. 31	**Interest Receivable**			20 00		2
3		**Interest Income**				20 00	3
4	31	**Uncollectible Accounts Expense**			12 873 30		4
5		**Allowance for Uncoll. Accts.**				12 873 30	5
6	31	**Merchandise Inventory**			5 290 00		6
7		**Income Summary**				5 290 00	7
8	31	**Supplies Expense**			7 837 00		8
9		**Supplies**				7 837 00	9
10	31	**Insurance Expense**			11 600 00		10
11		**Prepaid Insurance**				11 600 00	11
12	31	**Depreciation Exp.—Office Equip.**			6 350 00		12
13		**Accum. Depr.—Office Equip.**				6 350 00	13
14	31	**Depreciation Exp.—Store Equip.**			9 250 00		14
15		**Accum. Depr.—Store Equip.**				9 250 00	15
16	31	**Interest Expense**			40 00		16
17		**Interest Payable**				40 00	17
18	31	**Federal Income Tax Expense**			4 578 18		18
19		**Federal Income Tax Payable**				4 578 18	19
20							20

GENERAL JOURNAL — PAGE 15

After financial statements are prepared, adjusting and closing entries are journalized and posted. A post-closing trial balance is then prepared to prove the equality of debits and credits in the general ledger after adjusting and closing entries have been posted. The steps for preparing a post-closing trial balance are the same as discussed in Chapter 16. Finally, reversing entries are journalized and posted.

A corporation's adjusting entries are made from the Adjustments columns of a work sheet. To assure that each work sheet adjustment is journalized, record the entries in the order of the letters assigned to each adjustment on the work sheet.

Restaurant Supply's work sheet is shown in Lesson 22-1.

Closing entries for a corporation are made from information in a work sheet. A corporation records four closing entries:

1. Closing entry for income statement accounts with credit balances (revenue and contra cost accounts).
2. Closing entry for income statement accounts with debit balances (cost, contra revenue, and expense accounts).
3. Closing entry to record net income or net loss in the retained earnings account and close the income summary account.
4. Closing entry for the dividends account.

CLOSING ENTRY FOR ACCOUNTS WITH CREDIT BALANCES

1. Enter the balance of every Income Statement credit account in the debit column.

	DATE		ACCOUNT TITLE	DOC. NO.	POST. REF.	DEBIT	CREDIT	
1			*Closing Entries*					1
2	20-- Dec.	31	Sales			2109894 30		2
3			Purchases Discount		①	110 94 20		3
4			Purchases Returns and Allow.			5142 50		4
5			Gain on Plant Assets			670 00		5
6			Interest Income			156 00		6
7			Income Summary				2126957 00	7
8							②	8
9								9

GENERAL JOURNAL PAGE 16

2. Enter the total of debit entries as a credit to Income Summary.

The income statement credit balance accounts consist of the revenue (Sales, Gain on Plant Assets, and Interest Income) and the contra cost accounts (Purchases Discount and Purchases Returns and Allowances). Information needed for closing income statement credit balance accounts is obtained from the work sheet. Closing entries are recorded on a new page of the general journal.

STEPS — JOURNALIZING A CLOSING ENTRY FOR ACCOUNTS WITH CREDIT BALANCES

① Except for *Income Summary*, enter the balance of every account found in the Income Statement credit column of the work sheet as a debit entry in a general journal.

② Enter the total of the debit entries, $2,126,957.00, as a credit to *Income Summary*.

3. Enter the total as a debit to Income Summary.

1. Enter Income Summary.

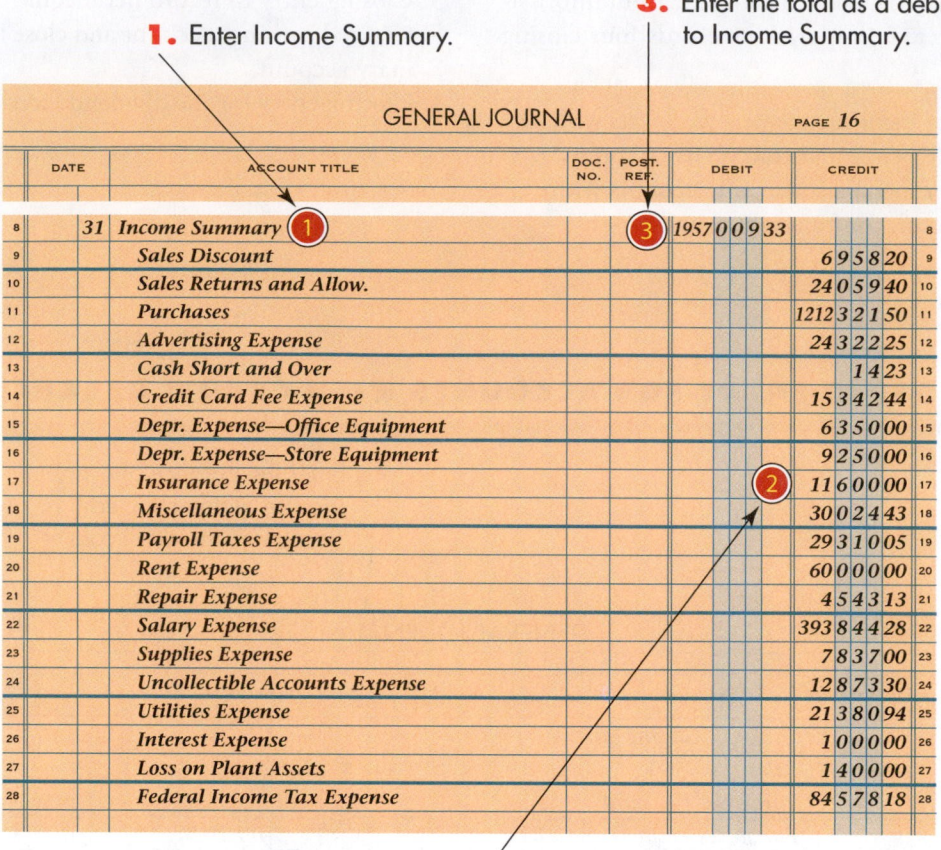

	DATE	ACCOUNT TITLE	DOC. NO.	POST. REF.	DEBIT	CREDIT	
8	31	Income Summary ①		③	1957009 33		8
9		Sales Discount				6958 20	9
10		Sales Returns and Allow.				24059 40	10
11		Purchases				1212321 50	11
12		Advertising Expense				24322 25	12
13		Cash Short and Over				14 23	13
14		Credit Card Fee Expense				15342 44	14
15		Depr. Expense—Office Equipment				6350 00	15
16		Depr. Expense—Store Equipment				9250 00	16
17		Insurance Expense		②		11600 00	17
18		Miscellaneous Expense				30024 43	18
19		Payroll Taxes Expense				29310 05	19
20		Rent Expense				60000 00	20
21		Repair Expense				4543 13	21
22		Salary Expense				393844 28	22
23		Supplies Expense				7837 00	23
24		Uncollectible Accounts Expense				12873 30	24
25		Utilities Expense				21380 94	25
26		Interest Expense				1000 00	26
27		Loss on Plant Assets				1400 00	27
28		Federal Income Tax Expense				84578 18	28

GENERAL JOURNAL   PAGE *16*

2. Enter the balance of every Income Statement debit account in the credit column.

The income statement debit balance accounts consist of the contra revenue accounts (Sales Discount and Sales Returns and Allowances), the cost (Purchases), and all expense accounts. Information needed for closing income statement debit balance accounts is obtained from the work sheet's Income Statement Debit column.

Because Cash Short and Over has a debit balance in this fiscal period, the account balance amount is closed to Income Summary with the debit balance accounts.

S T E P S **JOURNALIZING A CLOSING ENTRY FOR ACCOUNTS WITH DEBIT BALANCES**

① Enter the account title *Income Summary*.

② Enter the balance of every account found in the Income Statement debit column of the work sheet as a credit entry in a general journal.

③ Enter the total of the credit entries, $1,957,009.33, as a debit to *Income Summary*.

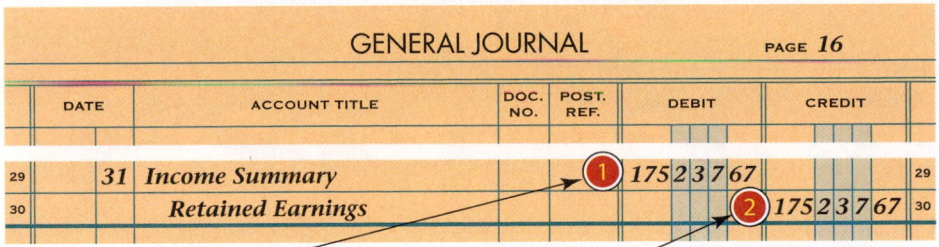

1. Debit Income Summary.   **2.** Credit Retained Earnings.

After closing entries for the income statement accounts are posted, Income Summary has a credit balance of $175,237.67. This credit balance equals the net income calculated on the work sheet.

As reported on the statement of stockholders' equity, the net income of a corporation increases retained earnings. Closing the balance of Income Summary actually increases the Retained Earnings account by the amount

of net income. After the closing entry is posted, Income Summary has a zero balance.

A corporation having a net loss will have a debit balance in Income Summary. Retained Earnings would then be debited and Income Summary credited for the net loss amount. The entry would reduce the balance of Retained Earnings.

STEPS   JOURNALIZING A CLOSING ENTRY FOR NET INCOME TO RETAINED EARNINGS

① Record a debit to *Income Summary* for the amount of net income, $175,237.67.

② Record a credit to *Retained Earnings* for the same amount, $175,237.67.

CLOSING ENTRY FOR DIVIDENDS

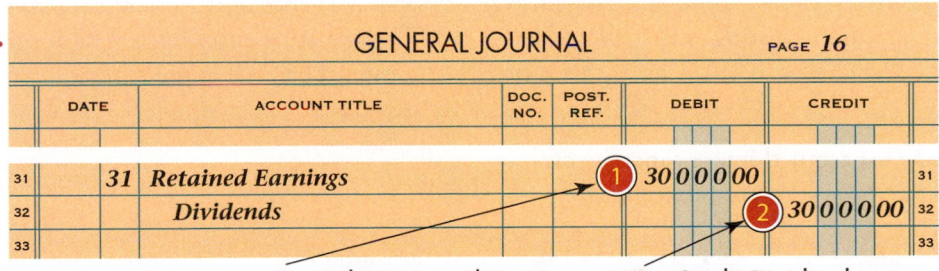

1. Debit Retained Earnings.   **2.** Credit Dividends.

Dividends reduce the earnings retained by a corporation, as reported on the Statement of Stockholders' Equity. The

closing entry reduces the balance in the Retained Earnings account by the amount of the dividends.

STEPS   JOURNALIZING A CLOSING ENTRY FOR DIVIDENDS

① Record a debit to *Retained Earnings* for the amount of dividends, $30,000.00.

② Record a credit to *Dividends* for the same amount, $30,000.00.

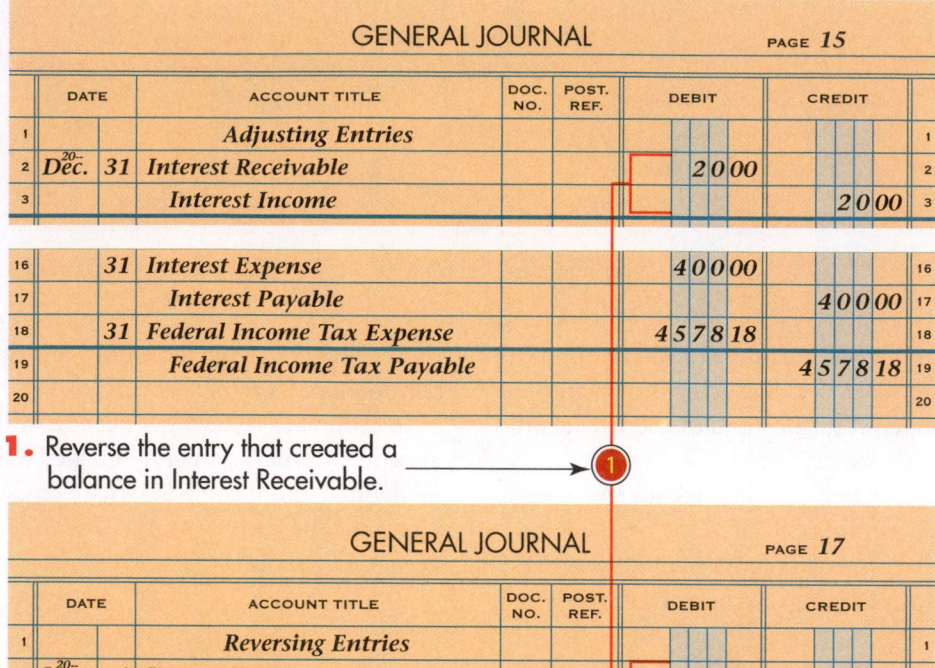

GENERAL JOURNAL   PAGE **15**

	DATE	ACCOUNT TITLE	DOC. NO.	POST. REF.	DEBIT	CREDIT	
1		*Adjusting Entries*					1
2	20-- Dec. 31	Interest Receivable			20 00		2
3		Interest Income				20 00	3
16	31	Interest Expense			400 00		16
17		Interest Payable				400 00	17
18	31	Federal Income Tax Expense			4 578 18		18
19		Federal Income Tax Payable				4 578 18	19
20							20

1. Reverse the entry that created a balance in Interest Receivable. ——→ ①

GENERAL JOURNAL   PAGE **17**

	DATE	ACCOUNT TITLE	DOC. NO.	POST. REF.	DEBIT	CREDIT	
1		*Reversing Entries*					1
2	20-- Jan. 1	Interest Income			20 00		2
3		Interest Receivable				20 00	3
4	1	Interest Payable		②	400 00		4
5		Interest Expense				400 00	5
6	1	Federal Income Tax Payable		③	4 578 18		6
7		Federal Income Tax Expense				4 578 18	7

2. Reverse the entry that created a balance in Interest Payable.

3. Reverse the entry that created a balance in Federal Income Tax Payable.

If an adjusting entry creates a balance in an asset or liability account, the adjusting entry should be reversed. A review of Restaurant Supply's adjusting entries shows that three adjusting entries created a balance in an asset or liability account.

1. The adjusting entry for accrued interest income created a balance in the interest receivable account.

2. The adjusting entry for accrued interest expense created a balance in the interest payable account.

3. The adjusting entry for federal income tax expense created a balance in the federal income tax payable account.

STEPS **JOURNALIZING REVERSING ENTRIES**

① Reverse the entry that created a balance in *Interest Receivable*.

② Reverse the entry that created a balance in *Interest Payable*.

③ Reverse the entry that created a balance in *Federal Income Tax Payable*.

REMEMBER

A post-closing trial balance is prepared to prove the equality of debits and credits in the general ledger after adjusting and closing entries have been posted, but before reversing entries are posted.

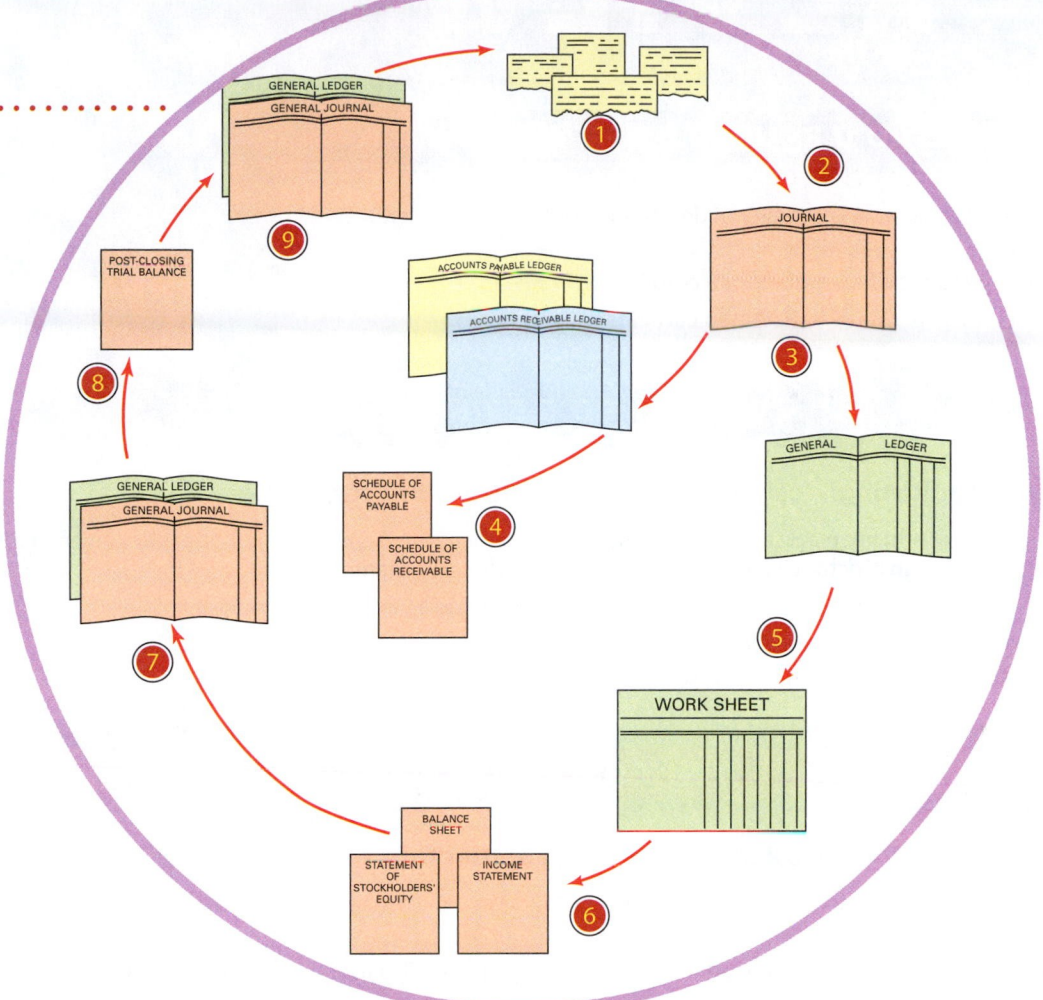

The accounting cycles are similar for merchandising businesses, regardless of how the businesses are organized.

Variations occur in preparing financial statements. Variations also occur when reversing entries are recorded.

STEPS — ACCOUNTING CYCLE FOR A MERCHANDISING BUSINESS ORGANIZED AS A CORPORATION

1. Source documents are checked for accuracy, and transactions are analyzed into debit and credit parts.

2. Transactions, from information on source documents, are recorded in journals.

3. Journal entries are posted to the accounts payable, accounts receivable, and general ledgers.

4. Schedules of accounts payable and accounts receivable are prepared from the subsidiary ledgers.

5. A work sheet, including a trial balance and an adjustment for federal income tax expense, is prepared from the general ledger.

6. Financial statements are prepared from the work sheet.

7. Adjusting and closing entries are journalized from the work sheet and posted to the general ledger.

8. A post-closing trial balance of the general ledger is prepared.

9. Reversing entries are journalized and posted to the general ledger.

End of Lesson
REVIEW

AUDIT YOUR UNDERSTANDING

1. What is used to prove the equality of debits and credits in the general ledger?
2. What are the four closing entries for a corporation?
3. What accounts are closed to Retained Earnings?

WORK TOGETHER 22-4

Journalizing adjusting, closing, and reversing entries for a corporation

Use the work sheet and financial statements from Work Together 22-3. General journal pages are given in the *Working Papers*. Your instructor will guide you through the following examples.

1. For the current year, journalize the adjusting entries using page 15 of a general journal.
2. For the current year, journalize the closing entries using page 16 of a general journal.
3. For the following year, journalize the reversing entries using page 17 of a general journal.

ON YOUR OWN 22-4

Journalizing adjusting, closing, and reversing entries for a corporation

Use the work sheet and financial statements from On Your Own 22-3. General journal pages are given in the *Working Papers*. Work this problem independently.

1. For the current year, journalize the adjusting entries using page 18 of a general journal.
2. For the current year, journalize the closing entries using page 19 of a general journal.
3. For the following year, journalize the reversing entries using page 20 of a general journal.

After completing this chapter, you can:

1. Define accounting terms related to financial statements for a merchandising business organized as a corporation.

2. Identify accounting concepts and practices related to financial statements and end-of-fiscal-period entries for a merchandising business organized as a corporation.

3. Plan end-of-fiscal-period adjustments for a merchandising business organized as a corporation.

4. Calculate federal income tax, plan an adjustment for federal income tax expense, and complete a work sheet.

5. Prepare and analyze an income statement for a merchandising business organized as a corporation.

6. Prepare a statement of stockholders' equity for a merchandising business organized as a corporation.

7. Prepare and analyze a balance sheet for a merchandising business organized as a corporation.

8. Record adjusting, closing, and reversing entries for a merchandising business organized as a corporation.

EXPLORE ACCOUNTING

Audits Provide Stockholders with Positive Assurance

Stockholders want assurance that the financial statements of their corporation accurately present its financial condition and results of operations. To provide this assurance, corporations hire independent public accountants to audit the financial statements. These accountants, referred to as *auditors*, provide a written opinion that informs stockholders whether the financial statements can be relied upon for making informed business decisions.

Auditors examine documents, journals, ledgers, and other accounting records to collect evidence that supports five declarations, or assertions, about each amount in the financial statements. Each assertion addresses a unique quality about the amount in the financial statements. These assertions are summarized as follows.

1. *Existence or Occurrence.* All assets and liabilities actually exist, and all income statement transactions actually occurred during the period.

2. *Completeness.* All assets and liabilities that exist have been reported, and all revenue and expense events have been recorded.

3. *Rights and Obligations.* All assets and liabilities are those of the corporation and not of its owners or another corporation.

4. *Valuation or Allocation.* Transactions are reported using amounts that correctly reflect the value of the item or event.

5. *Presentation and Disclosure.* Accounts are properly classified, described, and disclosed in conformity with generally accepted accounting principles.

Instructions: Create a table that shows how the five financial statement assertions relate to any one particular amount reported on the financial statements.

APPLICATION PROBLEM

Preparing a work sheet for a corporation

Donovan Lumber Corporation's work sheet is given in the *Working Papers*.

Instructions:

1. For the current year ended December 31, record the adjustments on the work sheet using the following information. Do not total the Adjustments columns. Save your work to complete Application Problem 22-2.

Adjustment Information, December 31

Accrued interest income	$ 315.00
Uncollectible accounts expense estimated as 1.0% of sales on account.	
Sales on account for year, $685,000.00.	
Merchandise inventory	81,284.50
Supplies inventory	1,847.50
Value of prepaid insurance	4,180.00
Annual depreciation expense—office equipment	3,128.00
Annual depreciation expense—store equipment	3,389.00
Accrued interest expense	300.00

2. Using the tax table shown in this chapter, calculate federal income tax expense and record the income tax adjustment on the work sheet. Complete the work sheet. Save your work to complete Application Problem 22-2.

APPLICATION PROBLEM

Preparing an income statement for a corporation

Use the work sheet from Application Problem 22-1 and the financial analysis form provided in the *Working Papers* to complete this problem. Save your work to complete Application Problem 22-3.

Instructions:

1. Prepare an income statement for Donovan Lumber Corporation for the fiscal year ending December 31 of the current year.

2. Calculate and record the following component percentages: (a) cost of merchandise sold; (b) gross profit on operations; (c) total operating expenses; (d) income from operations; (e) net addition or deduction from other revenue and expenses; and (f) net income before federal income tax. Round percentage calculations to the nearest 0.1%.

3. Analyze the corporation's income statement by determining if component percentages are within acceptable levels. If any component percentage is not within an acceptable level, suggest steps that the company should take. The corporation considers the following component percentages acceptable.

Cost of merchandise sold	Not more than 70.0%
Gross profit on operations	Not less than 30.0%
Total operating expenses	Not more than 25.0%
Income from operations	Not less than 5.0%
Net deduction from other revenue and expenses	Not more than 0.1%
Net income before federal income tax	Not less than 4.9%

Go Beyond the Book
For more information go to
www.C21accounting.com

22-3 APPLICATION PROBLEM · Office

Preparing a statement of stockholders' equity and balance sheet for a corporation

Use the work sheet and income statement from Application Problems 22-1 and 22-2 to complete this problem. Save your work to complete Application Problem 22-4.

Instructions:

1. Prepare a statement of stockholders' equity for Donovan Lumber Corporation for the fiscal year ended on December 31 of the current year. Use the following additional information.

January 1 balance of capital stock account (8,000 shares issued for $5.00 per share)	$40,000.00
Shares issued during the year	2,000 shares

2. Prepare a balance sheet for Donovan Lumber Corporation as of December 31 of the current year.

3. Calculate the corporation's (a) working capital and (b) current ratio.

4. Determine if these items are within acceptable levels. The corporation considers the following levels acceptable. Save your work to complete Application Problem 22-4.

Working capital	Not less than $100,000.00
Current ratio	Between 3.0 to 1 and 3.5 to 1

22-4 APPLICATION PROBLEM

Journalizing adjusting, closing, and reversing entries for a corporation

Use the work sheet and financial statements from Application Problem 22-3 to complete this problem.

Instructions:

1. For the current year, journalize the adjusting entries using page 15 of a general journal.
2. For the current year, journalize the closing entries using page 16 of a general journal.
3. For the following year, journalize the reversing entries using page 17 of a general journal.

22-5 MASTERY PROBLEM · AUTOMATED ACCOUNTING · Peachtree by Sage · QB Quick Books

Preparing a work sheet, financial statements, and end-of-fiscal-period entries for a corporation

Accounting forms are given in the *Working Papers*. Benford Corporation completed the following transactions during December of the current year and January of the next year.

Instructions:

1. Prepare Benford Corporation's work sheet for the current year ended December 31. Record the adjustments on the work sheet using the following information.

Adjustment Information, December 31

Accrued interest income	$ 80.00
Uncollectible accounts expense estimated as 0.6% of sales on account.	
Sales on account for year, $945,000.00.	
Merchandise inventory	283,028.08
Supplies inventory	998.99
Value of prepaid insurance	2,000.00
Annual depreciation expense—office equipment	5,480.00
Annual depreciation expense—store equipment	5,060.00
Accrued interest expense	312.50

Federal income tax is calculated using the tax table presented in this chapter.

2. Prepare an income statement. Calculate and record the following component percentages: (a) cost of merchandise sold; (b) gross profit on operations; (c) total operating expenses; (d) income from operations; (e) net addition or deduction from other revenue and expenses; and (f) net income before federal income tax. Round percentage calculations to the nearest 0.1%.

3. Analyze the corporation's income statement by determining if component percentages are within acceptable levels. If any component percentage is not within an acceptable level, suggest steps that the company should take. The corporation considers the following component percentages acceptable.

Cost of merchandise sold	Not more than 70.0%
Gross profit on operations	Not less than 30.0%
Total operating expenses	Not more than 25.0%
Income from operations	Not less than 5.0%
Net deduction from other revenue and expenses	Not more than 0.1%
Net income before federal income tax	Not less than 4.9%

4. Prepare a statement of stockholders' equity. Use the following additional information.

January 1 balance of capital stock account	$140,000.00
(14,000 shares issued for $10.00 per share)	
Shares issued during the year	1,000 shares

5. Prepare a balance sheet.

6. Calculate the corporation's (a) working capital and (b) current ratio. Determine if these items are within acceptable levels. The corporation considers the following levels acceptable.

Working capital	Not less than $150,000.00
Current ratio	Between 3.0 to 1 and 4.0 to 1

7. Journalize the adjusting entries using page 15 of a general journal.

8. Journalize the closing entries using page 16 of a general journal.

9. Journalize the reversing entries using page 17 of a general journal.

22-6   CHALLENGE PROBLEM

Analyzing financial strength

Instructions:

1. Obtain the financial statements of two corporations from two different industries. Calculate the amount of working capital and the current ratio of each corporation.

2. Discuss the usefulness of each measure of financial strength between the companies in each industry and among the different industries.

3. The current ratio is often considered to be acceptable within a specified range. Investigate why a current ratio being too high might be undesirable.

You have learned a wide variety of facts and concepts about accounting for service and merchandising businesses and for proprietorships, corporations, and the business world. Regardless of your future educational and career goals, this knowledge will provide you with a sound foundation to become a productive member of society.

Instructions: Prepare an essay to discuss how your knowledge of accounting will be useful to you in the future. How will accounting help you to complete your education, obtain a job, start a business, make personal investment decisions, and be successful in other facets of your life?

CASE FOR CRITICAL THINKING

The president of Reyes Company asked the accounting department to provide information to help management improve the company's net income. Accountant Pemlata Rathi suggests that an income statement showing all the revenue and expense amounts should provide all the information needed to analyze the company's results of operations. Do you agree? If not, what additional information do you recommend?

GRAPHING WORKSHOP

Stock prices are often presented in a high-low-close graph. The vertical line represents the range—the high and low price—in which the stock traded during the fiscal year. The following graph shows that Burnett Company's stock reached a high of $40 per share some time during 20X1. However, during the year the stock fell to as low as $30 per share. The small tab within each line shows the market price on the last day of the fiscal year—the close price.

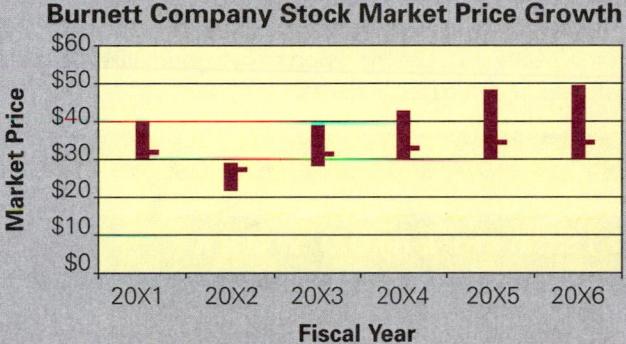

In its annual report, the president of Burnett Company made the following statement:

  "In 20X2, we implemented a strategic plan to reverse the decline in the market price of the company's stock. The installation of a new information system has increased sales and reduced the costs of purchasing materials and services. As evidenced by the steady increase in the stock price, stockholders who retained their investment in the company have been rewarded with significant appreciation in the value of their investments."

Instructions: Evaluate the president's statement. Does the information in the high-low-close graph support the president's analysis?

ANALYZING BEST BUY'S FINANCIAL STATEMENTS

A statement of shareholders' equity reports changes in each of the capital accounts. The amount of stock issued and repurchased is reported as changes in the common stock account. The company's operations for the year are reflected as changes in the retained earnings account.

Instructions

1. Use Best Buy's Consolidated Statements of Changes in Shareholders' Equity on page B-8 in Appendix B of this textbook to identify the changes in the retained earnings account for fiscal years 2005–2007.

2. Describe the change, if any, in the amount of dividends per share for the fiscal years 2005–2007.

Accounting SOFTWARE

END-OF-FISCAL-PERIOD WORK FOR A CORPORATION

It is common practice for businesses to set limits on the amount of unpaid sales on account to each customer. Businesses have learned these credit limits help limit bad debt expenses. A method or process that achieves a desired result for many businesses is referred to as a *best practice*. In your accounting education, you have learned many best practices, such as the use of work sheets, special journals, and sales discounts.

Peachtree uses best practices for maintaining customer information and selling to customers. First, you can establish default options for all customers, including credit terms, credit limits, shipment methods, and finance charges. When a new customer is entered into Peachtree, the customer is initially assigned the default options. You can then change any of the options for that customer. For example, if your business offers most customers 2/10, n/30 credit terms, these terms would be entered in the default options. If you wanted to offer a particular customer different terms, those new terms would be entered into that customer's information.

Peachtree Mastery Problem 22-5
1. Open (Restore) file 22-5MP.ptb.
2. Print a Profit & Loss Standard report using January 1 and December 31 as the dates.
3. View a Trial Balance report for December 31. Use the report to help journalize the closing entry for Dividends.
4. Print a Balance Sheet Standard report dated December 31.

END-OF-FISCAL-PERIOD WORK FOR A CORPORATION

QuickBooks allows the user to customize lists, forms, and financial statements to meet the needs of each company. When creating lists, such as customers, vendors, employees, and inventory items, extra fields can be added. For example, a Sales Region field can be added to the customer list. This field can then be used to sort sales by region of the country.

Invoices, credit memos, sales receipts, statements, and other forms can be customized in several ways. Columns can be added, the format can be changed, columns can appear on the form when entering data but be hidden on the printed form, text can be automatically added to a form, or the style, color, and size of the font can be changed.

Reports can be modified in several ways. An income statement, for example, can be designed to show revenue month by month or week by week for the entire accounting period. Financial statements can show amounts for the previous period along with amounts for the current period.

QUICKBOOKS MASTERY PROBLEM 22-5
1. Open the Benford Corporation file if it is not already open.
2. Journalize and post the adjusting entries.
3. Print an income statement.
4. Print a statement of retained earnings.
5. Print a balance sheet.
6. Journalize and post the closing entries.
7. Print the December 31 to January 1 (of the following year) general journal.

CHARTS AND GRAPHS

Large work sheets can be difficult to print. Using default print settings, the template for this chapter prints, section by section, over six pages. You would have to tape the pages together to create a document that you could review. Obviously, such a method of printing a large work sheet is unacceptable in business today.

Electronic spreadsheets provide you with numerous tools to modify how a document is printed. One of the most powerful tools is called *scaling*. If you have ever used a copy machine to reduce a document to a certain percentage of its normal size, you have scaled a document.

The level of scaling can be entered as a percentage, or the electronic spreadsheet can determine the required scaling for you. By instructing the computer to print the document by a certain number of pages wide and pages tall, the computer automatically determines the required level of scaling.

EXCEL APPLICATION PROBLEM 22-1

Open the F22-1 Excel data file. Follow the step-by-step instructions in the Instructions work sheet. Scale the template to print one page wide and two pages tall.

EXCEL APPLICATION PROBLEM 22-3

Open the F22-1 Excel data file. Follow the step-by-step instructions in the Instructions work sheet.

END-OF-FISCAL-PERIOD WORK FOR A CORPORATION

Adjusting entries must be planned and then entered into the software. The first step is to display or print a trial balance and use the data on that report to plan the adjusting entries. The adjusting entries are then journalized in the general journal and posted. The same reference, such as *Adj.Ent.*, should be used for each adjusting entry.

Financial statements are generated by the software by clicking the Reports toolbar button and then selecting the desired reports. The reports may be displayed, printed, or copied in word processing or spreadsheet format for pasting into another document or spreadsheet. Financial statements should be generated before closing entries are recorded and posted.

Closing entries can be generated automatically by the software. Click Options on the menu and select Generate Closing Entries. The closing entries are then displayed in the general journal and should be checked and then posted. Note that it is important to save a copy of the file before closing entries (use *BC* in the filename) so that the file can be opened in case corrections are needed. Another version of the file should be saved after closing entries (use *AC* in the filename).

After closing entries are posted, reversing entries are recorded in the general journal. The same reference, such as *Rev.Ent.*, should be used for each reversing entry.

AUTOMATING MASTERY PROBLEM 22-5

Open file F22-5.AA8. Display the problem instructions and complete the problem.

An Accounting Cycle for a Corporation: End-of-Fiscal-Period Work

The general ledger used in Reinforcement Activity 3—Part A is needed to complete Reinforcement Activity 3—Part B.

END-OF-FISCAL-PERIOD WORK

INSTRUCTIONS:

9. Record the 20X4 depreciation on the plant asset record of plant asset no. 998.

10. Prepare a trial balance as of December 31, 20X4, on a work sheet.

11. Complete the work sheet using the following adjustment information:

   a. Outstanding notes receivable consist of NR34, a 90-day, 10% note accepted from Nelson Co. on December 7, 20X4, for an extension of time on its account, $3,600.00.

   b. Uncollectible accounts expense is estimated as 4.0% of sales on account. Sales on account for the year, $90,000.

   c. Merchandise inventory $80,491.95

   d. Supplies inventory $425.05

   e. Value of prepaid insurance $600.00

   f. Estimate of office equipment depreciation $6,520.00

   g. Estimate of warehouse equipment depreciation $4,210.00

   h. Outstanding notes payable consist of (1) NP32, a 90-day, 12% note for $10,000.00 signed on November 16, 20X4, and (2) NP33, a 90-day, 10% note for $6,000.00 signed on December 28, 20X4.

12. Calculate federal income tax expense and record the adjustment on the work sheet.

13. Prepare an income statement. Calculate and record the following component percentages: (a) cost of merchandise sold; (b) gross profit on operations; (c) total operating expenses; (d) income from operations; (e) net addition or deduction from other revenue and expenses; and (f) net income before federal income tax. Round percentage calculations to the nearest 0.1%.

14. Analyze the corporation's income statement by determining if component percentages are within acceptable levels. If any component percentage is not within an acceptable level, suggest steps that the company should take. The corporation considers the following component percentages acceptable:

   Cost of merchandise sold: Not more than 62.0%
   Income from operations: Not less than 10.0%
   Gross profit on operations: Not less than 38.0%
   Net deduction from other revenue and expenses: Not more than 0.5%
   Total operating expenses: Not more than 28.0%
   Net income before federal income tax: Not less than 9.5%

15. Calculate the earnings per share and price-earnings ratio. Current market price is $225.00.

16. Prepare a statement of stockholders' equity. The company had 3,000 shares of $10.00 par-value stock outstanding on January 1. The company did not issue any additional shares during the year.

17. Prepare a balance sheet in report form.

18. Journalize and post the adjusting entries. Use page 13 of a general journal.

19. Journalize and post the closing entries. Use page 14 of a general journal.

20. Prepare a post-closing trial balance.

21. Journalize and post the reversing entries. Use page 15 of a general journal.

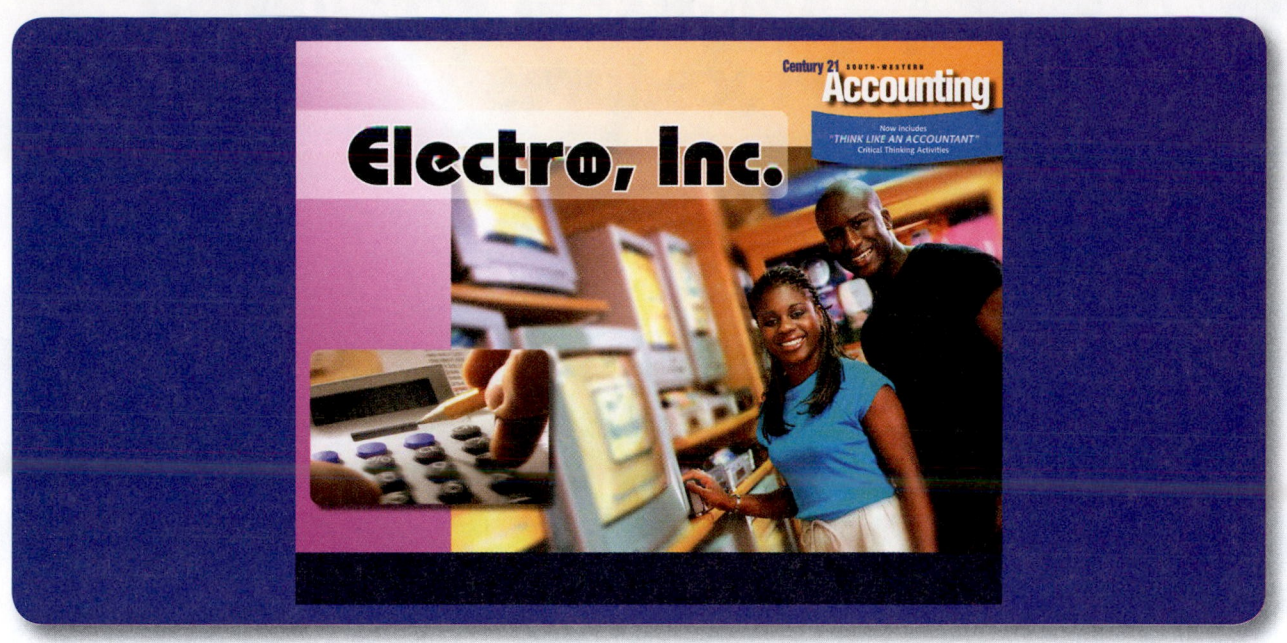

Electro, Inc., is a merchandising business organized as a corporation. The company specializes in selling electronic items, including computers and audio and video systems and accessories. This simulation includes the realistic transactions completed by Electro, Inc., in the month of December, including end-of-fiscal-year activities.

Source documents are provided for transactions that are recorded in special journals and a general journal, similar to the ones used by Restaurant Supply Co. in Part 3.

This real-life business simulation is available in manual and automated versions. The automated version is used with Automated Accounting software.

The following activities are included in the Electro, Inc. simulation:

1 Recording transactions in special journals from source documents.

2 Posting items to be posted individually to a general ledger and subsidiary ledger.

3 Posting column totals to a general ledger.

4 Preparing schedules of accounts receivable and accounts payable from subsidiary ledgers.

5 Preparing a trial balance on a work sheet.

6 Planning adjustments and completing a work sheet.

7 Preparing financial statements.

8 Journalizing and posting adjusting entries.

9 Journalizing and posting closing entries.

10 Preparing a post-closing trial balance.

11 Journalizing and posting reversing entries.

12 Think Like an Accountant Financial Analysis Activity

PART 4

Additional Accounting Procedures

THE BUSINESS—GIFTPAK COMPANY

GiftPak Company is the business that will be used in Chapters 23 and 24 in Part 4 to illustrate the chapter concepts. The company is a partnership that sells gift baskets with both national and international sales. The company also sells merchandise on the Internet through its web site. GiftPak rents the building that it uses for its operations.

PHOTO: IMAGE SOURCE/GETTY IMAGES

CHAPTER 23

GIFTPAK COMPANY CHART OF ACCOUNTS

GENERAL LEDGER

Balance Sheet Accounts

(1000) ASSETS

1100   Current Assets
1110   Cash
1120   Petty Cash
1130   Accounts Receivable
1135   Allowance for Uncollectible
       Accounts
1137   Time Drafts Receivable
1140   Merchandise Inventory
1150   Supplies
1160   Prepaid Insurance
1200   Plant Assets
1210   Office Equipment
1215   Accumulated Depreciation—
       Office Equipment

(2000) LIABILITIES

2100   Current Liabilities
2110   Accounts Payable

(3000) OWNERS' EQUITY

3110   Sawyer Hess, Capital
3120   Sawyer Hess, Drawing
3130   Kendra Sullivan, Capital
3140   Kendra Sullivan, Drawing
3150   Income Summary

Income Statement Accounts

(4000) OPERATING REVENUE

4110   Sales
4115   Sales Returns and Allowances
4120   Sales Discount

(5000) COST OF MERCHANDISE

5110   Purchases

5115   Purchases Returns and
       Allowances
5120   Purchases Discount

(6000) OPERATING EXPENSES

6110   Advertising Expense
6120   Credit Card Fee Expense
6130   Depreciation Expense—
       Office Equipment
6135   Insurance Expense
6140   Miscellaneous Expense
6150   Rent Expense
6160   Supplies Expense
6170   Uncollectible Accounts Expense

The chart of accounts for GiftPak Company is illustrated above for ready reference as you study Part 4 of this textbook.

PHOTO: STOCKBYTE/GETTY IMAGES

CHAPTER 24

CHAPTER 23

Accounting for Partnerships

OBJECTIVES

After studying Chapter 23, you will be able to:

1. Define accounting terms related to forming, dissolving, and distributing the earnings of a partnership.

2. Identify accounting concepts and practices related to forming, dissolving, and distributing the earnings of a partnership.

3. Journalize entries related to forming, dissolving, and distributing the earnings of a partnership.

4. Calculate the distribution of partnership earnings.

5. Prepare a distribution of net income statement for a business organized as a partnership.

6. Prepare an owners' equity statement for a business organized as a partnership.

KEY TERMS

- partnership
- partner
- partnership agreement
- distribution of net income statement
- owners' equity statement
- liquidation of a partnership
- realization
- limited liability partnership (LLP)

Point Your Browser
www.C21accounting.com

Cold Stone Creamery®

Today's Business World—Cold Stone Creamery®

Do you love ice cream? Donald and Susan Sutherland's passion for ice cream led them to open Cold Stone Creamery® in Tempe, Arizona, in 1988. The Sutherlands make their ice cream daily, using only the finest ingredients. But what makes Cold Stone Creamery® unique is how the ice cream is prepared. As customers watch, their desired mix-ins are blended with the ice cream on a frozen granite stone and served in a fresh-baked waffle cone.

The success of Cold Stone Creamery® motivated the Sutherlands to begin franchising their concept in 1995. With nearly 1,400 franchise stores in operation in 2007 and many more in development, Cold Stone Creamery® was ranked #12 in Entrepreneur Magazine's 2007 100 Fastest Growing Franchises (Entrepreneur.com).

In exchange for an initial investment, Cold Store Creamery® franchisees receive step-by-step guidance in choosing a site, negotiating the lease, transforming the store, and, most important, learning how to create the best ice cream creations at the Cold Store Creamery® Ice Cream University.

©LON C. DIEHL/PHOTOEDIT

Critical Thinking

1. What other kinds of support and training might be provided to a franchisee?

2. If you were going to start a business with someone else, how would you choose your partner?

Source: www.coldstonecreamery.com

INTERNET ACTIVITY

Partnership Agreements

Search the Internet for information about partnership agreements.

Instructions

1. List the purpose of a partnership agreement.

2. List at least four items that should be included in a partnership agreement.

PARTNERSHIPS

TechKnow Consulting, the business described in Part 1, is a proprietorship, a small business owned by one person. Hobby Shack, Inc., and Restaurant Supply Co., the businesses described in Parts 2 and 3, are organized as corporations. Businesses that require the skills and capital of more than one person, but that do not wish to be organized as a corporation, may choose another form of business. A business in which two or more persons combine their assets and skills is called a **partnership**. Each member of a partnership is called a **partner**. As in other forms of own-

ership, reports and financial records of the business are kept separate from the personal records of the partners. [CONCEPT: Business Entity]

A partnership prepares four financial statements. It prepares an income statement and a balance sheet similar to those used by a proprietorship or corporation. It also prepares two additional financial statements. One statement reports the distribution of net income or net loss for each partner. The other statement reports the changes in owners' equity for the fiscal period.

THE BUSINESS—GIFTPAK COMPANY

Sawyer Hess and Kendra Sullivan own a partnership called GiftPak Company. The business purchases gourmet foods and novelty gifts and packages these items into gift boxes and baskets. The company accepts orders through its web site and has customers in other countries.

The partners do all the work in the company; there are no employees. Partners are not employees, and the money that partners receive from a partnership is not considered salaries. Therefore, GiftPak Company does not need accounts for recording salaries and payroll taxes.

CHARACTER COUNTS

Setting the Tone at the Top

A certain company's code of conduct prohibits employees from accepting gifts, favors, or entertainment that would influence their sound business decisions. Despite the rule, the company president is known to accept lavish gifts from suppliers. Do you think the employees will be motivated to adhere to the code of conduct?

The employees at the top of a company—managers, officers, and directors—must provide leadership in making ethical decisions. Among the many ways companies can "set the tone at the top" is to have a special code of conduct for members of the board of directors.

Instructions

Access the *Code of Conduct for Kellogg Company Directors* at http://investor.kelloggs.com. Determine whether directors can own stock in companies that do business with Kellogg Company.

PHOTO: BLEND IMAGES/GETTY IMAGES

PARTNERSHIP AGREEMENT

THIS CONTRACT is made and entered into this thirty-first day of December, 20--, by and between Sawyer Hess and Kendra Sullivan, of Glendive, MT.

WITNESSETH: That the said parties have this date formed a partnership to engage in and conduct a business under the following stipulations which are a part of this contract. The partnership will begin operation January 1, 20--.

FIRST: The business shall be conducted under the name of GiftPak Company, located initially at 234 North River Avenue, Glendive, MT 59330.

SECOND: The investment of each partner is: Sawyer Hess: Cash of $15,000. Kendra Sullivan: Cash of $10,000 and office equipment with a value of $5,000; total investment, $15,000.

THIRD: Both partners are to (a) participate in all general policy-making decisions, (b) devote full time and attention to the partnership business, and (c) engage in no other business enterprise without the written consent of the other partner. Mr. Hess is to be general manager of the business's operations.

FOURTH: Neither partner is to become a surety or bonding agent for anyone without the written consent of the other partner.

FIFTH: The partners will share equally in all profits and losses of the partnership.

SIXTH: No partner is to withdraw assets without the other partner's written consent.

SEVENTH: All partnership transactions are to be recorded in accordance with standard and generally accepted accounting procedures and concepts. The partnership records are to be open at all times for inspection by either partner.

EIGHTH: In case of either partner's death or legal disability, the equity of the partners is to be determined as of the time of the death or disability of the one partner. The continuing partner is to have first option to buy the deceased/disabled partner's equity at recorded book value.

NINTH: This partnership agreement is to continue indefinitely unless (a) terminated by death of one partner, (b) terminated by either partner giving the other partner written notice at least ninety (90) days prior to the termination date, or (c) terminated by written mutual agreement signed by both partners.

TENTH: At the termination of this partnership agreement, the partnership's assets, after all liabilities are paid, will be distributed according to the balance in partners' capital accounts.

IN WITNESS WHEREOF, the parties to this contract have set their hands and seals on the date and year written.

Signed: *Sawyer Hess*   (Seal) Date   December 31, 20--

Signed: *Kendra Sullivan*   (Seal) Date   December 31, 20--

A written agreement setting forth the conditions under which a partnership is to operate is called a **partnership agreement**. Legally, a partnership agreement may be either written or oral. However, a written agreement may limit misunderstandings in the future; therefore, a partnership agreement should be in writing. It should include the name of the business and the partners, the investments of each partner, the duties and responsibilities of each partner, how profits and losses are to be divided, what happens if a partner dies, how the partnership is to be dissolved, and the duration of the agreement.

INITIAL INVESTMENTS BY OWNERS

1. Write the date.
2. Write the account titles.
3. Write the receipt numbers.
4. Write the debit and credit amounts.
5. Write the debit to Cash.

CASH RECEIPTS JOURNAL   PAGE *1*

	DATE	ACCOUNT TITLE	DOC. NO.	POST. REF.	GENERAL DEBIT	GENERAL CREDIT	ACCOUNTS RECEIVABLE CREDIT	SALES CREDIT	SALES DISCOUNT DEBIT	CASH DEBIT	
1	*Jan.* 20-- 1	*Sawyer Hess, Capital*	R1			15000 00				15000 00	1
2	1	*Office Equipment*	R2		5000 00					10000 00	2
3		*Kendra Sullivan, Capital*				15000 00					3
4											4

GiftPak's partnership agreement calls for Sawyer Hess to contribute cash and for Kendra Sullivan to contribute cash and office equipment to the new partnership. A separate journal entry is made for each partner's initial investment.

January 1. Received cash from partner, Sawyer Hess, as an initial investment, $15,000.00. Receipt No. 1.

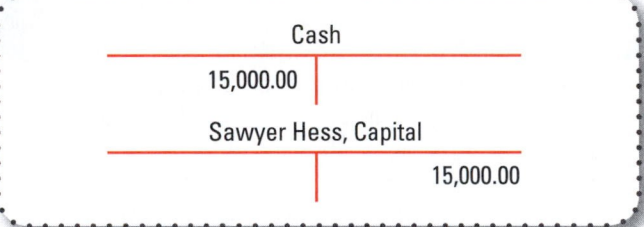

The asset account, Cash, increases by a debit, $15,000.00. The owner's capital account, Sawyer Hess, Capital, increases by a credit, $15,000.00.

January 1. Received cash, $10,000.00, and office equipment valued at $5,000.00, from partner, Kendra Sullivan, as an initial investment. Receipt No. 2.

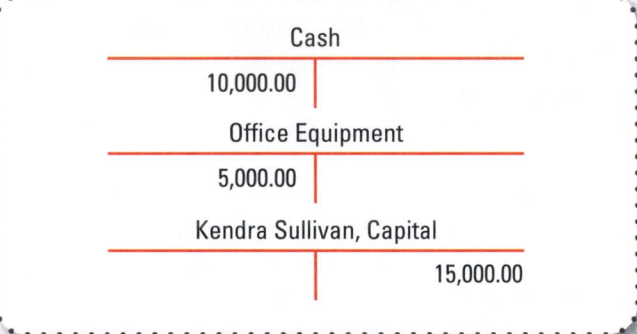

The asset account, Cash, increases by a debit, $10,000.00. The asset account, Office Equipment, increases by a debit, $5,000.00. The owner's capital account, Kendra Sullivan, Capital, increases by a credit, $15,000.00.

STEPS   JOURNALIZING RECEIPT OF PARTNERS' INITIAL INVESTMENTS

① Write the date, *20--, Jan. 1*, in the Date column.

② Write the account titles in the Account Title column. For Sawyer Hess's investment, write the account to be credited, *Sawyer Hess, Capital*. For Kendra Sullivan's investment, write the account to be debited, *Office Equipment*. Also write the account to be credited, *Kendra Sullivan, Capital*.

③ Write the receipt numbers, *R1* and *R2*, in the Doc. No. column.

④ Write the amounts in the General Debit and Credit columns. The only credit amount for Sawyer Hess is $15,000 for the cash investment. For Kendra Sullivan's investment, the debit amount is $5,000.00 for the office equipment. The credit amount for Kendra Sullivan is $15,000.00 for the total investment.

⑤ Write the debits to *Cash, $15,000.00* and *$10,000.00*, in the Cash Debit column.

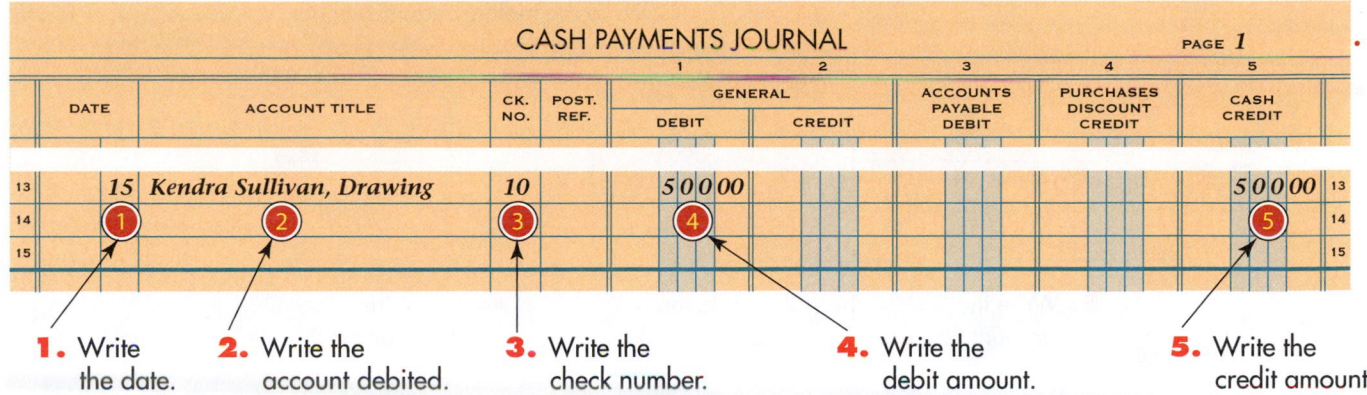

CASH PAYMENTS JOURNAL   PAGE 1

	DATE	ACCOUNT TITLE	CK. NO.	POST. REF.	GENERAL DEBIT	GENERAL CREDIT	ACCOUNTS PAYABLE DEBIT	PURCHASES DISCOUNT CREDIT	CASH CREDIT	
13	15	Kendra Sullivan, Drawing	10		500 00				500 00	13
14	①	②	③		④				⑤	14
15										15

1. Write the date. **2.** Write the account debited. **3.** Write the check number. **4.** Write the debit amount. **5.** Write the credit amount.

During a fiscal period, partners may take assets out of the partnership in anticipation of the net income for the period. As in a proprietorship, assets taken out of a business for the personal use of an owner are known as *withdrawals*. The two assets generally taken out of a merchandising business are cash and merchandise. The partnership agreement may limit the amount of assets that may be withdrawn.

Withdrawals reduce the amount of a business's capital. The account titles of the partners' drawing accounts are Sawyer Hess, Drawing and Kendra Sullivan, Drawing. Since capital accounts have credit balances, partners' drawing accounts have normal debit balances. Therefore, the drawing accounts increase by a debit and decrease by a credit, as shown in the T accounts.

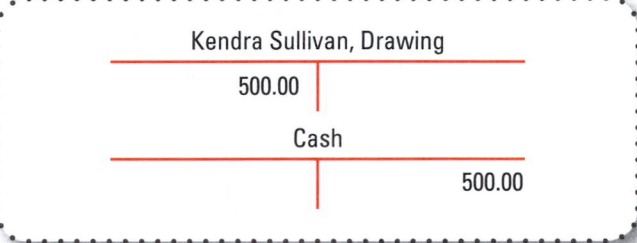

The owner's drawing account, Kendra Sullivan, Drawing, has a normal debit balance because withdrawals decrease owner's equity. Therefore, increases in withdrawals are recorded by a debit, $500.00. The asset account, Cash, decreases by a credit, $500.00.

Withdrawals could be recorded as debits directly to the partners' capital accounts. However, withdrawals are normally recorded in separate accounts so that the total amounts are easily determined for each accounting period.

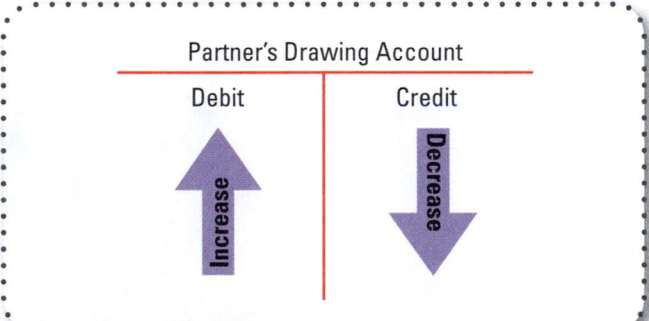

January 15. Kendra Sullivan, partner, withdrew cash for personal use, $500.00. Check No. 10.

STEPS · **JOURNALIZING WITHDRAWALS OF CASH BY PARTNERS**

① Write the date, *15*, in the Date column.

② Write the title of the account debited, *Kendra Sullivan, Drawing*, in the Account Title column.

③ Write the check number, *10*, in the Ck. No. column.

④ Write the debit amount, *$500.00*, in the General Debit column.

⑤ Write the credit amount, *$500.00*, in the Cash Credit column.

WITHDRAWAL OF MERCHANDISE BY PARTNER

1. Write the date.

3. Write the memorandum number.

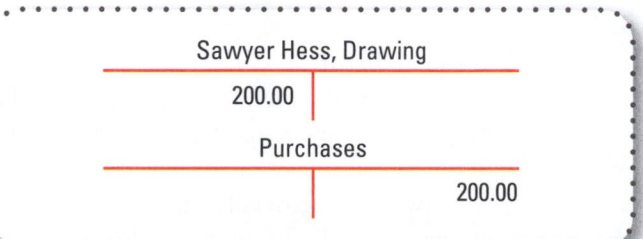

GENERAL JOURNAL   PAGE *1*

DATE	ACCOUNT TITLE	DOC. NO.	POST. REF.	DEBIT	CREDIT	
20-- Jan. 15	*Sawyer Hess, Drawing*	M1		2 0 0 00		1
	Purchases				2 0 0 00	2
						3

5. Write the account title.

2. Write the account title.

4. Write the debit amount.

6. Write the credit amount.

A partner usually withdraws cash for personal use. However, a partner may also withdraw merchandise for personal use. This merchandise withdrawal increases the account balance of Sawyer Hess, Drawing and decreases the purchases account balance.

> *January 15. Sawyer Hess, partner, withdrew merchandise for personal use, $200.00. Memorandum No. 1.*

Sawyer Hess, Drawing	
200.00	

Purchases	
	200.00

Sawyer Hess's drawing account increases by a debit, $200.00. The cost account, Purchases, decreases by a credit, $200.00. This transaction is recorded in the general journal.

STEPS   JOURNALIZING WITHDRAWALS OF MERCHANDISE BY PARTNERS

1 Write the date, *20--, Jan. 15*, in the Date column.

2 Write the account title, *Sawyer Hess, Drawing*, in the Account Title column.

3 Write the memorandum number, *M1*, in the Doc. No. column.

4 Write the debit amount, *$200.00*, in the Debit column on the same line as the account title.

5 On the next line, indented about one centimeter, write the account title, *Purchases*, in the Account Title column.

6 Write the credit amount, *$200.00*, in the Credit column on the same line as the account title.

AUDIT YOUR UNDERSTANDING

TERMS REVIEW

partnership

partner

partnership agreement

1. What two financial statements prepared by a partnership are similar to those prepared by a proprietorship?
2. List at least three items that should be included in a partnership agreement.
3. What accounts are debited and credited when a partner withdraws cash from the partnership?

WORK TOGETHER 23-1

Journalizing partners' investments and withdrawals

Cash receipts, cash payments, and general journals are given in the *Working Papers*. Your instructor will guide you through the following examples.

B and B Diving completed the following transactions during March of the current year.

Transactions:

Mar. 1. Received cash of $22,000.00 and office supplies valued at $3,000.00 from partner, Robert Billings, as an initial investment. Receipt No. 1.
  1. Received cash from partner, Susan Billings, as an initial investment, $25,000.00. Receipt No. 2.
  30. Susan Billings, partner, withdrew cash for personal use, $600.00. Check No. 23.
  30. Robert Billings, partner, withdrew merchandise for personal use, $600.00. Memorandum No. 4.

1. Use page 1 of a cash receipts journal. Journalize the investments on March 1.

2. Use page 1 of a cash payments journal and page 3 of a general journal. Journalize the withdrawals on March 30.

ON YOUR OWN 23-1

Journalizing partners' investments and withdrawals

Cash receipts, cash payments, and general journals are given in the *Working Papers*. Work this problem independently.

Northern Lights completed the following transactions during September of the current year.

Transactions:

Sept. 1. Received cash of $45,000.00 and inventory valued at $5,000.00 from partner, Loane Le, as an initial investment. Receipt No. 1.
  1. Received cash from partner, Wheatonia Makebu, as an initial investment, $30,000.00 Receipt No. 2.
  30. Loane Le, partner, withdrew cash for personal use, $1,000.00. Check No. 65.
  30. Wheatonia Makebu, partner, withdrew merchandise for personal use, $1,500.00. Memorandum No. 6.

1. Use page 1 of a cash receipts journal. Journalize the investments on September 1.

2. Use page 1 of a cash payments journal and page 9 of a general journal. Journalize the withdrawals on September 30.

······ **DISTRIBUTION OF NET INCOME STATEMENT** ······

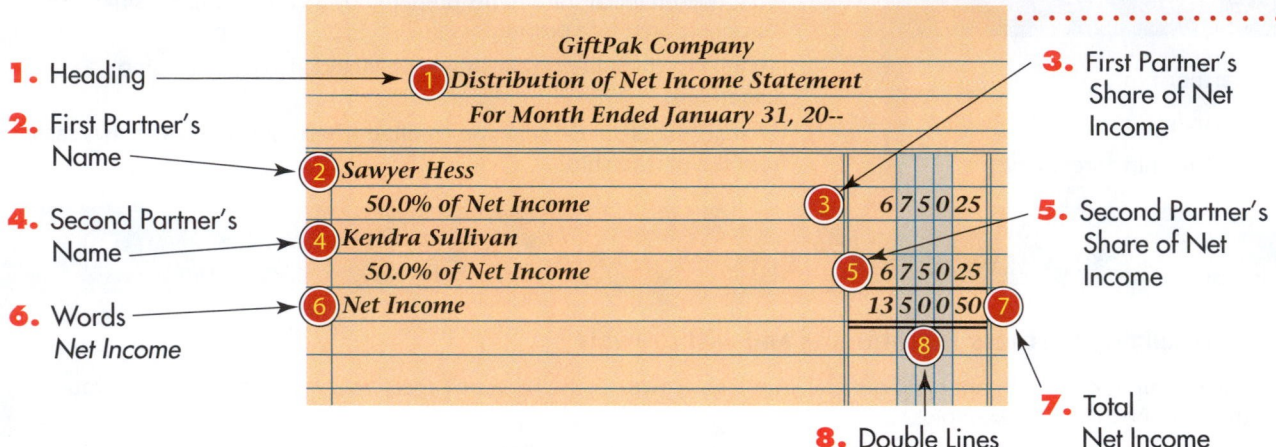

1. Heading

2. First Partner's Name

4. Second Partner's Name

6. Words
   Net Income

3. First Partner's Share of Net Income

5. Second Partner's Share of Net Income

7. Total Net Income

8. Double Lines

A partnership's net income or net loss may be divided in any way agreed upon by the partners in their partnership agreement. Sawyer Hess and Kendra Sullivan, partners in GiftPak Company, agreed to share net income or net loss equally.

A partnership's distribution of net income or net loss is usually shown on a separate financial statement. A partnership financial statement showing net income or loss distribution to partners is called a **distribution of net income statement**.

The income statement for a partnership is prepared in the same way as an income statement for a proprietorship, described in Chapter 7. GiftPak Company's income statement shows a net income of $13,500.50 for the month ended January 31. This net income is used to prepare the distribution of net income statement.

STEPS **PREPARING A DISTRIBUTION OF NET INCOME STATEMENT**

1. Write the heading of the distribution of net income statement on three lines.

2. Write one partner's name, *Sawyer Hess*, on the first line at the extreme left.

3. Indent about one centimeter on the next line, and write Sawyer Hess's share of net income as a percentage, *50.0% of Net Income*. Write Mr. Hess's share of net income, *$6,750.25* (50.0% × $13,500.50), in the amount column on the same line.

4. Write the other partner's name, *Kendra Sullivan*, on the next line.

5. Indent about one centimeter on the next line, and write Kendra Sullivan's share of net income as a percentage, *50.0% of Net Income*. Write Ms. Sullivan's share of net income, *$6,750.25* (50.0% × $13,500.50), in the amount column on the same line.

6. Write *Net Income* on the next line at the extreme left of the wide column.

7. Add the distribution of net income and write the total amount, *$13,500.50*, in the amount column. Verify accuracy by comparing the total amount, *$13,500.50*, with the net income reported on the income statement, *$13,500.50*. The two amounts must be the same.

8. Rule double lines across the amount column to show that the distribution of net income statement has been verified as correct.

Custom Cabinets		
Distribution of Net Income Statement		
For Year Ended December 31, 20--		
Beth Castillo		
60.0% of Net Income	38 5 2 0 00	
Jana Kenyon		
40.0% of Net Income	25 6 8 0 00	
Net Income	64 2 0 0 00	

Regardless of how earnings are shared, the steps in preparing a distribution of net income statement are the same. The only difference is the description of how the earnings are to be shared by the partners.

Beth Castillo and Jana Kenyon are partners in a business. Because Ms. Castillo spends more time in the business than Ms. Kenyon, the partners agree to share net income or loss unequally. Ms. Castillo gets 60.0% of net income or loss. Ms. Kenyon gets 40.0% of net income or loss. With a net income of $64,200.00, Ms. Castillo receives 60.0%, or $38,520.00. Ms. Kenyon receives 40.0%, or $25,680.00.

CULTURAL DIVERSITY

Business Culture and Accountancy in Russia

The changeover of Russia's economy from socialism to free enterprise has strongly influenced Russian business culture. Employees, who for generations have depended on the government to fulfill their needs, now have the opportunity to get ahead individually. Russian business culture—the way Russians do business—is changing gradually. An example of this change can be seen in the accounting profession.

In the emerging Russian market economy, the person performing the role of accountant is called an "economist." These employees have a degree in "economics" and years of experience. Employees performing the role of "bookkeeper" have lower status and lower pay. The chief bookkeeper, however, has a prominent position because of his or her responsibility for the accuracy of financial statements.

The accounting profession in Russia is devising a regulatory framework based upon similar frameworks in existing market economies. Regulations are being written that include precise definitions for accounting terms. Regulations on the qualifications of auditors also are being developed.

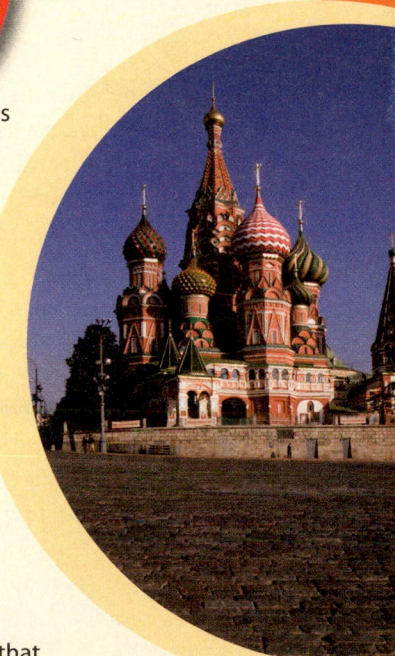

Critical Thinking

1. What are the advantages if the accounting standards in Russia are similar to those in the rest of the world?

2. What factors might require that some accounting standards differ from those in other countries?

ACCOUNT *Sawyer Hess, Capital*					ACCOUNT NO. *3110*	
DATE	ITEM	POST. REF.	DEBIT	CREDIT	BALANCE DEBIT	BALANCE CREDIT
20-- Jan. 1		CR1		15 00 0 00		15 00 0 00

ACCOUNT *Sawyer Hess, Drawing*					ACCOUNT NO. *3120*	
DATE	ITEM	POST. REF.	DEBIT	CREDIT	BALANCE DEBIT	BALANCE CREDIT
20-- Jan. 15		G1	2 0 0 00		2 0 0 00	

ACCOUNT *Kendra Sullivan, Capital*					ACCOUNT NO. *3130*	
DATE	ITEM	POST. REF.	DEBIT	CREDIT	BALANCE DEBIT	BALANCE CREDIT
20-- Jan. 1		CR1		15 00 0 00		15 00 0 00

ACCOUNT *Kendra Sullivan, Drawing*					ACCOUNT NO. *3140*	
DATE	ITEM	POST. REF.	DEBIT	CREDIT	BALANCE DEBIT	BALANCE CREDIT
20-- Jan. 15		CP1	5 0 0 00		5 0 0 00	

The amount of net income earned is important to business owners. Owners are also interested in changes that occur in owners' equity during a fiscal period. A financial statement that summarizes the changes in owners' equity during a fiscal period is called an ==owners' equity statement==. Business owners can review an owners' equity statement to determine if owners' equity is increasing or decreasing and what is causing the change. Three factors can change owners' equity: (1) additional investments, (2) withdrawals, and (3) net income or net loss.

An owners' equity statement shows information about changes in each partner's capital during a fiscal period. Information needed to prepare an owners' equity state-ment is obtained from the distribution of net income statement, shown on page 680, and the general ledger capital and drawing accounts shown above. The distribution of net income statement shows each partner's share of net income or net loss. Three kinds of information are obtained from each partner's capital and drawing account:

(1) beginning capital amount,
(2) any additional investments made during the fiscal period, and
(3) each partner's withdrawal of assets during the fiscal period.

1. Heading

2. First Partner's Name

3. First Partner's Ending Capital

4. Second Partner's Name

5. Second Partner's Ending Capital

6. Total Owners' Equity

7. Double Lines

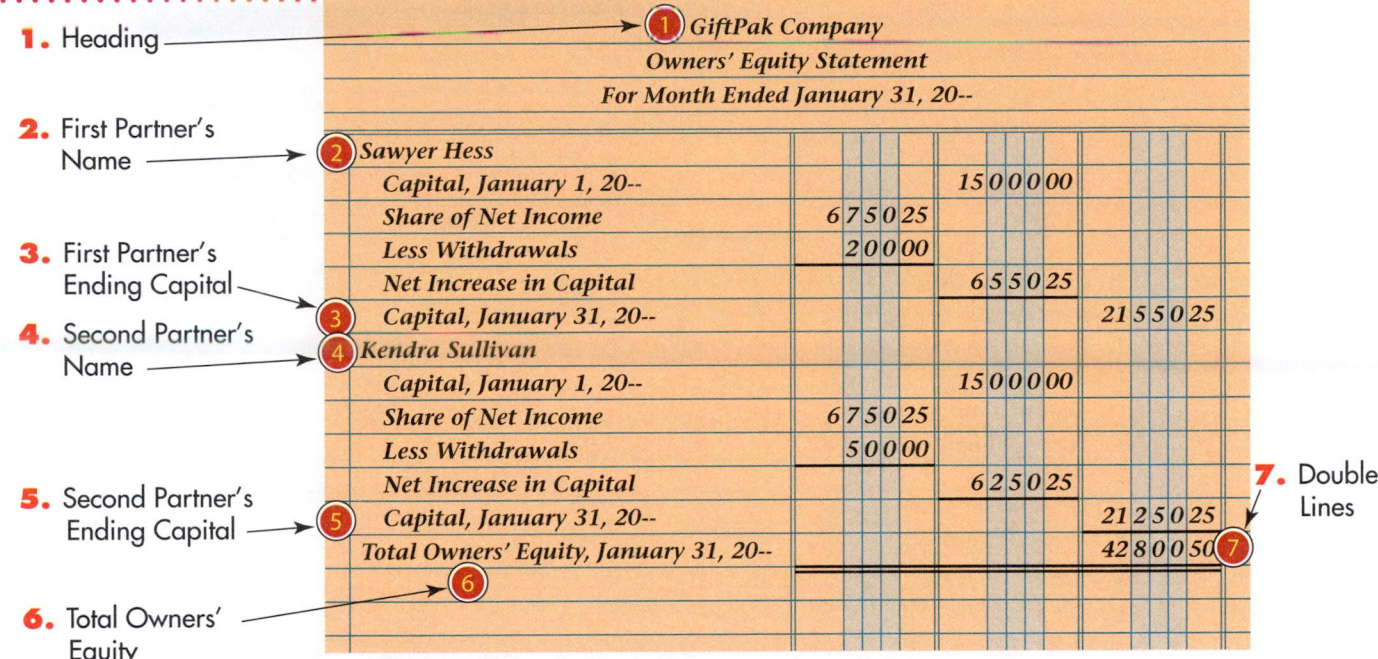

GiftPak Company			
Owners' Equity Statement			
For Month Ended January 31, 20--			
Sawyer Hess			
Capital, January 1, 20--		15 0 0 0 00	
Share of Net Income	6 7 5 0 25		
Less Withdrawals	2 0 0 00		
Net Increase in Capital		6 5 5 0 25	
Capital, January 31, 20--			21 5 5 0 25
Kendra Sullivan			
Capital, January 1, 20--		15 0 0 0 00	
Share of Net Income	6 7 5 0 25		
Less Withdrawals	5 0 0 00		
Net Increase in Capital		6 2 5 0 25	
Capital, January 31, 20--			21 2 5 0 25
Total Owners' Equity, January 31, 20--			42 8 0 0 50

Neither Sawyer Hess nor Kendra Sullivan invested any additional capital during the month ended January 31 after the initial investments on January 1. Both partners withdrew either cash or merchandise during the month.

Some businesses include the owners' equity statement information as part of the balance sheet. An example of this method of reporting changes in owner's equity is shown in Chapter 7.

STEPS **PREPARING AN OWNERS' EQUITY STATEMENT**

① Write the heading of the owners' equity statement on three lines.

② Write the name *Sawyer Hess* on the first line at the extreme left.

③ Calculate the net increase in capital and ending capital amount for Sawyer Hess.
  a. Indent about one centimeter on the next line, and write *Capital, January 1, 20--*. Write the amount $15,000.00 in the second amount column. (This amount is obtained from the capital account.)
  b. Indent about one centimeter on the next line, and write *Share of Net Income*. Write the amount $6,750.25 in the first amount column. (This amount is obtained from the distribution of net income statement.)
  c. Indent about one centimeter on the next line, and write *Less Withdrawals*. Write the amount $200.00 in the first amount column. (This amount is obtained from the drawing account.)
  d. Indent about one centimeter on the next line, and write *Net Increase in Capital*. Write the amount $6,550.25 in the second amount column. ($6,750.25 − $200.00 = $6,550.25)
  e. Indent about one centimeter on the next line, and write *Capital, January 31, 20--*. Write the amount $21,550.25 in the third amount column. ($15,000.00 + $6,550.25 = $21,550.25)

④ Write the name *Kendra Sullivan* on the next line at the extreme left of the wide column.

⑤ Calculate the net increase in capital and ending capital amount for Kendra Sullivan. Follow Step 3.

⑥ Write *Total Owners' Equity, January 31, 20--* on the next line at the extreme left of the wide column. Write the amount $42,800.50 in the third amount column.

⑦ Rule double lines across the three amount columns to show that the totals have been verified as correct.

Cloth Circuit Owners' Equity Statement For Year Ended December 31, 20--			
Mark Gavin			
Capital, January 1, 20--	125 20 0 00		
Plus Additional Investment	12 00 0 00		
Total		137 20 0 00	
Share of Net Loss	2 84 0 00		
Plus Withdrawals	17 76 0 00		
Net Decrease in Capital		20 60 0 00	
Capital, December 31, 20--			116 60 0 00
Judy Oliver			
Capital, January 1, 20--	123 40 0 00		
Plus Additional Investment	12 00 0 00		
Total		135 40 0 00	
Share of Net Loss	2 84 0 00		
Plus Withdrawals	18 12 0 00		
Net Decrease in Capital		20 96 0 00	
Capital, December 31, 20--			114 44 0 00
Total Owners' Equity, December 31, 20--			231 04 0 00

On December 31, the capital accounts of Mark Gavin and Judy Oliver showed additional investments of $12,000.00 each. Also, the income statement for their company, Cloth Circuit, showed a net loss of $5,680.00. The partners agreed to share net income or net loss equally. The owners' equity statement above shows the net loss as a deduction from the owners' capital.

BALANCE SHEET FOR A PARTNERSHIP

GiftPak Company Balance Sheet January 31, 20--		
Total Liabilities		10 27 6 11
Owners' Equity		
Sawyer Hess, Capital	21 55 0 25	
Kendra Sullivan, Capital	21 25 0 25	
Total Owners' Equity		42 80 0 50
Total Liabilities and Owners' Equity		53 07 6 61

The asset and liability sections of a balance sheet for a partnership are prepared in the same way as the asset and liability sections of a balance sheet for a proprietorship. The only section that is different is the equity section. The equity section lists the capital account for each partner. The balances of these two accounts are added together and listed as Total Owners' Equity. Total Liabilities and Total Owners' Equity are added together to determine Total Liabilities and Owners' Equity.

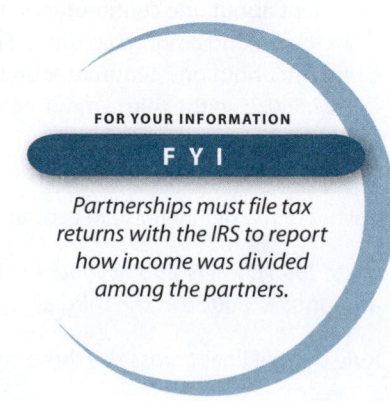

FOR YOUR INFORMATION

FYI

Partnerships must file tax returns with the IRS to report how income was divided among the partners.

End of Lesson REVIEW

TERMS REVIEW

distribution of net income statement

owners' equity statement

1. What information used to prepare an owners' equity statement is obtained from the distribution of net income statement?
2. What information used to prepare an owners' equity statement is obtained from the partners' capital and drawing accounts?
3. What is the procedure for calculating an owner's end-of-year capital?

WORK TOGETHER 23-2

Preparing distribution of net income and owners' equity statements

B and B Diving is a partnership owned by Susan and Robert Billings. Information from B and B's worksheet and income statement is given below. Forms for completing these problems are given in the *Working Papers*. Your instructor will guide you through the following examples.

Net Income for the month ended March 31	$29,600.00
Robert Billings, Capital March 1 balance	25,000.00
Susan Billings, Capital March 1 balance	25,000.00
Robert Billings, Drawing March 31 balance	600.00
Susan Billings, Drawing March 31 balance	600.00

1. Prepare a distribution of net income statement for B and B Diving. Net income or loss is to be shared equally.
2. Using the balances of the general ledger capital and drawing accounts from the work sheet, prepare an owners' equity statement for B and B Diving. No additional investments were made.

ON YOUR OWN 23-2

Preparing distribution of net income and owners' equity statements

Northern Lights is a partnership owned by Loane Le and Wheatonia Makebu. Information from Northern Lights' worksheet and income statement is given below. Forms for completing these problems are given in the *Working Papers*. Work this problem independently.

Net Income for the month ended September 30	$58,800.00
Leone Le, Capital September 1 balance	35,000.00
Wheatonia Makebu, Capital September 1 balance	28,000.00
Leone Le, Drawing September 30 balance	4,500.00
Wheatonia Makebu, Drawing September 30 balance	2,600.00

1. Prepare a distribution of net income statement for Northern Lights. Net income or loss is to be distributed 60% to Mr. Le and 40% to Ms. Makebu.
2. Using the balances of the general ledger capital and drawing accounts from the work sheet, prepare an owners' equity statement for Northern Lights. No additional investments were made.

Dissolving a Partnership

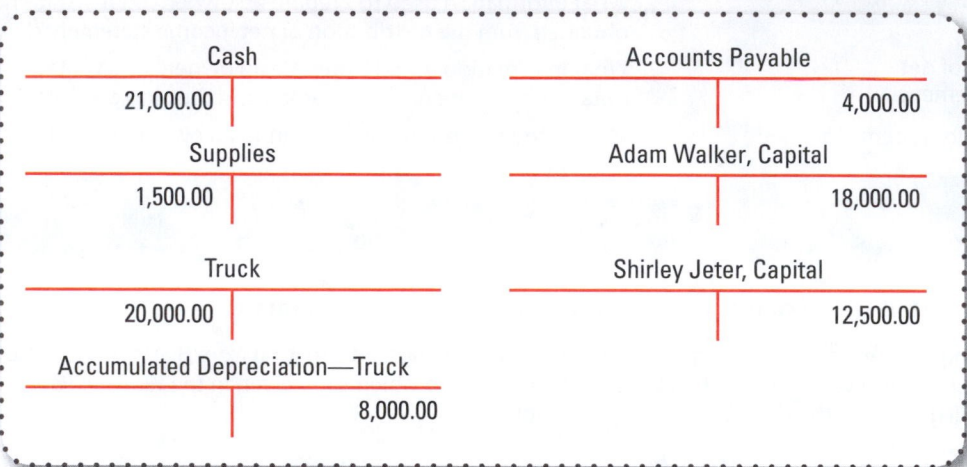

Cash		Accounts Payable	
21,000.00			4,000.00
Supplies		**Adam Walker, Capital**	
1,500.00			18,000.00
Truck		**Shirley Jeter, Capital**	
20,000.00			12,500.00
Accumulated Depreciation—Truck			
		8,000.00	

If a partnership goes out of business, its assets are distributed to the creditors and partners. The process of paying a partnership's liabilities and distributing remaining assets to the partners is called **liquidation of a partnership**.

Cash received from the sale of assets during liquidation of a partnership is called **realization**. Typically, when a partnership is liquidated, the noncash assets are sold, and the available cash is used to pay the creditors. Any remaining cash is distributed to the partners according to each partner's total equity.

On July 31, Adam Walker and Shirley Jeter liquidated their partnership. At that time, financial statements were prepared and adjusting and closing entries were journalized and posted. After the end-of-fiscal-period work was completed, the partnership had account balances as shown in the T accounts above.

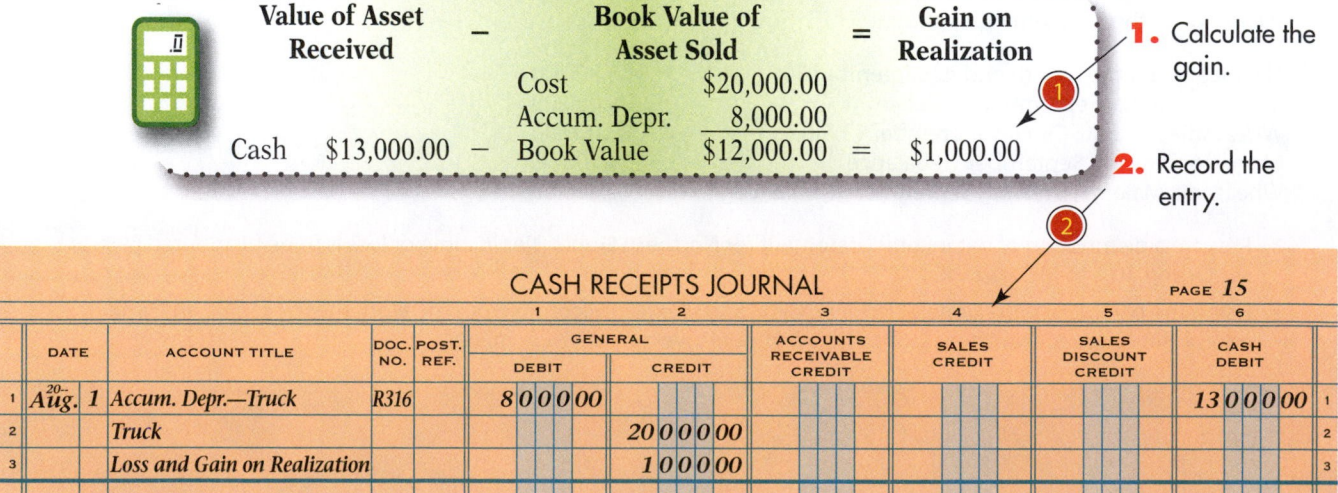

	Value of Asset Received	–	Book Value of Asset Sold	=	Gain on Realization
			Cost $20,000.00		
			Accum. Depr. 8,000.00		
Cash	$13,000.00	–	Book Value $12,000.00	=	$1,000.00

1. Calculate the gain.

2. Record the entry.

CASH RECEIPTS JOURNAL   PAGE 15

				GENERAL		ACCOUNTS RECEIVABLE CREDIT	SALES CREDIT	SALES DISCOUNT CREDIT	CASH DEBIT	
	DATE	ACCOUNT TITLE	DOC. NO.	POST. REF.	DEBIT	CREDIT				
1	20-- Aug. 1	Accum. Depr.—Truck	R316		8 0 0 0 00					13 0 0 0 00	1
2		Truck				20 0 0 0 00					2
3		Loss and Gain on Realization				1 0 0 0 00					3

Noncash assets might be sold for more than the recorded book value. When this happens, the amount received in excess of the book value is recorded as a gain on realization. The gain is recorded as a credit in an account titled Loss and Gain on Realization.

August 1, 20--. Received cash from sale of truck, $13,000.00: original cost, $20,000.00; total accumulated depreciation recorded to date, $8,000.00. Receipt No. 316.

The partnership's gain on the sale of the truck is calculated as shown.

STEPS — **RECOGNIZING A GAIN ON REALIZATION**

① Calculate the gain on the sale of the asset, *$1,000.00* ($13,000.00 cash received − $12,000.00 book value of asset).

② Record the entry in the cash receipts journal, as shown on the previous page.

LOSS ON REALIZATION

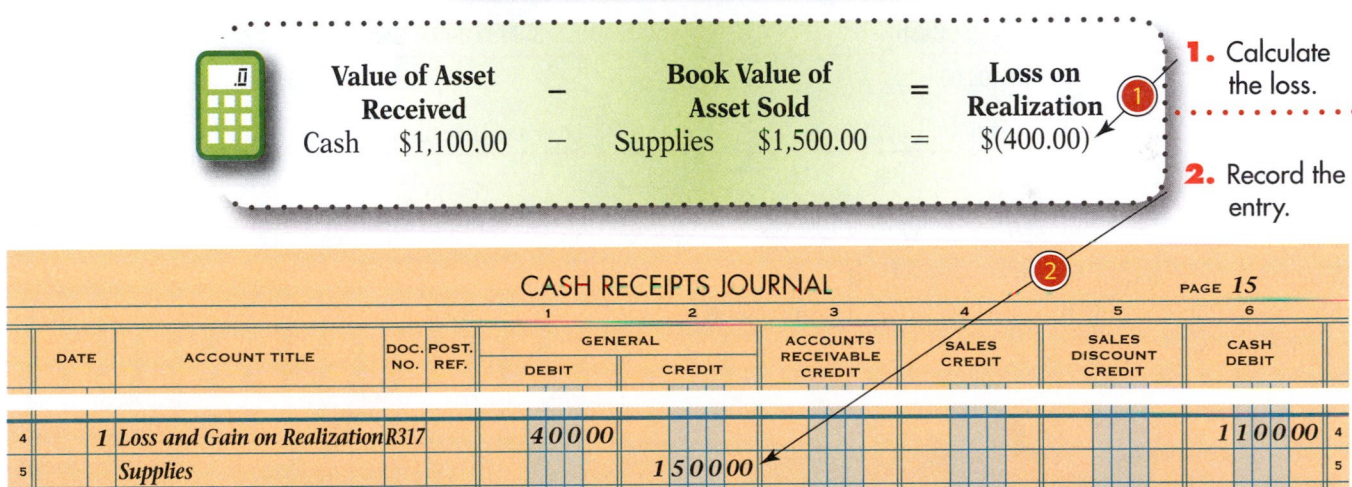

	Value of Asset Received	−	Book Value of Asset Sold	=	Loss on Realization
	Cash $1,100.00	−	Supplies $1,500.00	=	$(400.00)

1. Calculate the loss.

2. Record the entry.

CASH RECEIPTS JOURNAL — PAGE 15

	DATE	ACCOUNT TITLE	DOC. NO.	POST. REF.	GENERAL DEBIT	GENERAL CREDIT	ACCOUNTS RECEIVABLE CREDIT	SALES CREDIT	SALES DISCOUNT CREDIT	CASH DEBIT	
4	1	Loss and Gain on Realization	R317		400 00					1 100 00	4
5		Supplies				1 500 00					5

Sometimes during liquidation, the sale of an asset brings in less cash than the recorded book value.

August 1. Received cash from sale of supplies, $1,100.00; balance of supplies account, $1,500.00. Receipt No. 317.

The journal entry to record this transaction is shown. After both liquidation entries have been journalized, the credit balance of Loss and Gain on Realization, $600.00, is the amount received in excess of the value of the truck and supplies combined.

STEPS — **RECOGNIZING A LOSS ON REALIZATION**

① Calculate the loss on the sale of the asset, *$400.00* ($1,500.00 book value of supplies − $1,100.00 cash received).

② Record the entry in the cash receipts journal.

FOR YOUR INFORMATION

FYI

A partnership usually tries to sell the business before it begins the process of liquidation.

					GENERAL		ACCOUNTS PAYABLE DEBIT	PURCHASES DISCOUNT CREDIT	CASH CREDIT
	DATE	ACCOUNT TITLE	CK. NO.	POST. REF.	DEBIT	CREDIT			
1	Aug. 4	✓	422				4 000 00		4 000 00

CASH PAYMENTS JOURNAL — PAGE 15

The partnership's available cash is used to pay creditors. The entry is recorded in the cash payments journal as shown.

August 4, 20--. Paid cash to all creditors for the amounts owed, $4,000.00. Check No. 422.

ACCOUNT BALANCES AFTER LIQUIDATION OF NONCASH ASSETS AND PAYMENT OF LIABILITIES

Cash	
Bal. 31,100.00	

Shirley Jeter, Capital	
	Bal. 12,500.00

Adam Walker, Capital	
	Bal. 18,000.00

Loss and Gain on Realization	
	Bal. 600.00

When this transaction has been journalized and posted, the partnership has only four general ledger accounts with balances as shown.

BUSINESS STRUCTURES

Limited Liability Partnerships

A partnership that combines the advantages of the partnership and the corporation, while avoiding their disadvantages, is called a **limited liability partnership (LLP)**. At least two members, or partners, are necessary to form an LLP. The primary advantage of the LLP is that it does not pay separate income tax. LLP partners allocate profits and losses among themselves, according to the partnership agreement.

All members in the LLP have "limited" liability for the debts of the business. This means that none of the personal assets of the members are subject to the claims of business creditors.

The LLP follows partnership rules for dissolution. If one member drops out, all others must formally agree to continue the business.

Many major accounting firms have changed to the LLP form of business organization in an effort to limit the costs associated with malpractice liability.

Critical Thinking

What other professions might organize as LLPs to limit the costs associated with malpractice liability?

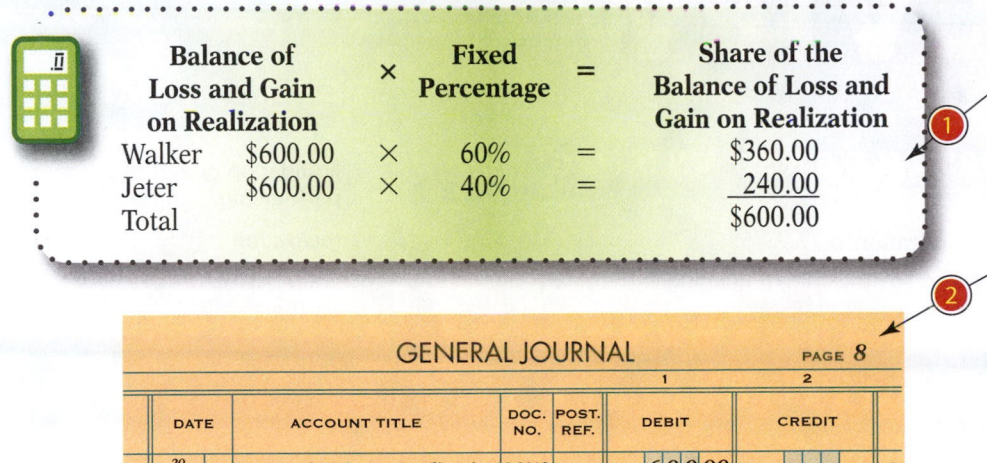

Balance of Loss and Gain on Realization	×	Fixed Percentage	=	Share of the Balance of Loss and Gain on Realization
Walker $600.00	×	60%	=	$360.00
Jeter $600.00	×	40%	=	240.00
Total				$600.00

1. Calculate each partner's share of gain or loss.

2. Record entry to distribute gain or loss.

GENERAL JOURNAL   PAGE 8

	DATE	ACCOUNT TITLE	DOC. NO.	POST. REF.	DEBIT	CREDIT	
1	Aug. 6	Loss and Gain on Realization	M412		600 00		1
2		Adam Walker, Capital				360 00	2
3		Shirley Jeter, Capital				240 00	3

When all creditors have been paid, the balance of Loss and Gain on Realization is distributed to the partners. A credit balance indicates a gain on realization. A debit balance indicates a loss. The distribution is based on the method of distributing net income or net loss as stated in the partnership agreement. The percentages for the Walker and Jeter partnership are Adam Walker, 60%, and Shirley Jeter, 40%. The distribution of the balance of Loss and Gain on Realization is calculated as shown.

August 6, 20--. Recorded distribution of gain on realization: to Adam Walker, $360.00; to Shirley Jeter, $240.00. Memorandum No. 412.

If a loss on realization is distributed to the partners, Loss and Gain on Realization is credited to close the account. Each partner's capital account is debited for the partner's share of the loss on realization.

DISTRIBUTING REMAINING CASH TO PARTNERS

CASH PAYMENTS JOURNAL   PAGE 15

	DATE	ACCOUNT TITLE	CK. NO.	POST. REF.	GENERAL DEBIT	GENERAL CREDIT	ACCOUNTS PAYABLE DEBIT	PURCHASES DISCOUNT CREDIT	CASH CREDIT	
2	6	Adam Walker, Capital	423		18 360 00				31 100 00	2
3		Shirley Jeter, Capital	424		12 740 00					3

Any remaining cash is distributed to the partners. The cash is distributed according to each partner's capital account balance, regardless of the method used to distribute net income or net loss.

August 6. Recorded final distribution of remaining cash to partners: to Adam Walker, $18,360.00; to Shirley Jeter, $12,740.00. Check Nos. 423 and 424.

After this journal entry is journalized (as shown) and posted, all of the partnership's general ledger accounts will have zero balances. The partnership is liquidated.

End of Lesson
REVIEW

TERMS REVIEW

liquidation of a partnership

realization

limited liability partnership (LLP)

AUDIT YOUR UNDERSTANDING

1. What is meant by the term "realization"?
2. What accounts are debited when distributing remaining cash to partners during liquidation?

WORK TOGETHER 23-3

Liquidation of a partnership

Jason Edson and Peggy Karam agreed to liquidate their partnership on April 30 of the current year. On that date, after financial statements were prepared and closing entries were posted, the general ledger accounts had the balances shown in the *Working Papers*.

A cash receipts journal, page 6, a cash payments journal, page 8, and a general journal, page 4, are provided in the *Working Papers*. Your instructor will guide you through the following examples.

Transactions:

May 1. Received cash from sale of office equipment, $6,000.00. R86.
  1. Received cash from sale of supplies, $950.00. R87.
  3. Received cash from sale of truck, $7,500.00. R88.
  5. Paid cash to all creditors for amounts owed. C116.
  6. Distributed loss or gain to Jason Edson, 60%; to Peggy Karam, 40%. M21.
  6. Distributed remaining cash to partners. C117 and C118.

1. Journalize the transactions.

ON YOUR OWN 23-3

Liquidation of a partnership

Daska Madura and Lawrence Neary agreed to liquidate their partnership on May 31 of the current year. On that date, after financial statements were prepared and closing entries were posted, the general ledger accounts had the balances shown in the *Working Papers*.

A cash receipts journal, page 8, a cash payments journal, page 10, and a general journal, page 5, are provided in the *Working Papers*. Work this problem independently.

Transactions:

June 1. Received cash from sale of office equipment, $800.00. R96.
  1. Received cash from sale of supplies. $1,600.00. R97.
  3. Received cash from sale of truck, $5,400.00. R98.
  5. Paid cash to all creditors for amounts owed. C125.
  6. Distributed loss or gain to Daska Madura, 60%; to Lawrence Neary, 40%. M29.
  6. Distributed remaining cash to partners. C126 and C127.

1. Journalize the transactions.

After completing this chapter, you can:

1. *Define accounting terms related to forming, dissolving, and distributing the earnings of a partnership.*

2. *Identify accounting concepts and practices related to forming, dissolving, and distributing the earnings of a partnership.*

3. *Journalize entries related to forming, dissolving, and distributing the earnings of a partnership.*

4. *Calculate the distribution of partnership earnings.*

5. *Prepare a distribution of net income statement for a business organized as a partnership.*

6. *Prepare an owners' equity statement for a business organized as a partnership.*

EXPLORE ACCOUNTING

Business Forms

Properly designed business forms can accomplish several important purposes for a company. Business forms may (1) initiate action, (2) exercise control, (3) provide essential accounting information, and (4) provide information to multiple users. Consider how a sales invoice accomplishes these purposes.

1. *Initiate action.* The major action initiated in a sales invoice is the collection of the amount owed by a customer for merchandise received. Information needed to accomplish this action is the customer's name and address; stock number, description, quantity, unit price, and total amounts owed for items purchased; the seller's name and address; date of the invoice; and terms of sale, such as 2/10, n/30.

2. *Exercise control.* The seller needs to insure that all merchandise shipped is properly invoiced to the customer and that the information on the invoice is correct. A seller's invoices should be sequentially numbered to insure that all invoices are accounted for. The invoice date and terms permit the seller to file the invoice by the due date so that the company can follow up if payment is not received.

   The sales clerk's initials show who made the sale so that person can be consulted if there are any questions. If the merchandise is delivered in person, the customer's signature confirms the delivery. If the merchandise is delivered by a freight company, the freight company normally requires a signature to verify delivery.

3. *Provide essential accounting information.* To account for the merchandise sold, the accounting department needs the description, unit price, and total amounts of merchandise; name, address, and customer number; and invoice date and terms of sale.

4. *Provide information to multiple users.* Several individuals or departments need some or all of the information on a business form. A company may color-code multiple copies of its sales invoice. For example, the first copy (white) goes to the customer. The second copy (yellow) goes to the seller's shipping department. The third copy (salmon) goes to the seller's accounts receivable department. Although different businesses may use different colors, the use of color-coding insures that the appropriate copy goes to the correct user.

Required: With your instructor's permission, visit a local business and request a copy of one of its business forms. Identify the items on the form that achieve important purposes for the company.

23-1 APPLICATION PROBLEM

Journalizing partners' investments and withdrawals

Cash receipts, cash payments, and general journals are given in the *Working Papers*.
Kopy King completed the following transactions during April of the current year.

Transactions:

Apr. 1. Received cash of $2,000.00 and equipment valued at $33,000.00 from partner, Wilhelm Mellberg, as an investment. Receipt No. 1.
1. Received cash from partner, Julie Jenson, as an initial investment, $30,000.00. Receipt No. 2.
30. Julie Jenson, partner, withdrew cash for personal use, $3,600.00. Check No. 66.
30. Wilhelm Mellberg, partner, withdrew merchandise for personal use, $4,800.00. Memorandum No. 10.

Instructions:

1. Use page 1 of a cash receipts journal. Journalize the investments on April 1.

2. Use page 5 of a cash payments journal and page 12 of a general journal. Journalize the withdrawals on April 30.

23-2 APPLICATION PROBLEM

Preparing distribution of net income and owners' equity statements (net income)

Janet Kelly and Paul Sharp are partners in a merchandising business, Kelly Appliances. Forms for completing this problem are given in the *Working Papers*. The following information was taken from the records on December 31 of the current year.

Partner	Balance of Capital Account January 1	Balance of Drawing Account	Distribution of Net Income
Kelly	$159,000.00	$17,550.00	60.0%
Sharp	$142,600.00	$18,800.00	40.0%

Instructions:

1. On December 31, the partnership had a net income of $83,260.00. Prepare a distribution of net income statement for the partnership.

2. Prepare an owners' equity statement for Kelly Appliances. No additional investments were made.

(**Go Beyond the Book**
For more information go to
www.C21accounting.com)

APPLICATION PROBLEM

Preparing an owners' equity statement (net loss)

Judy Fulton and Lee Terry are partners in a merchandising business, Elegant Cosmetics. Forms for completing this problem are given in the *Working Papers*. The following information was taken from the records on December 31 of the current year.

Partner	Balance of Capital Account January 1	Balance of Drawing Account	Distribution of Net Loss
Fulton	$124,300.00	$13,950.00	$3,750.00
Terry	$118,000.00	$14,900.00	$3,750.00

Instructions:

1. Prepare an owners' equity statement for Elegant Cosmetics. Additional investments made during the year: Judy Fulton, $12,000.00; Lee Terry, $10,000.00.

23-4

APPLICATION PROBLEM   AUTOMATED ACCOUNTING

Liquidating a partnership

Donald Winn and Judy Reed agreed to liquidate their partnership on July 30 of the current year. On that date, after financial statements were prepared and closing entries were posted, the general ledger accounts had the following balances.

Cash	$ 5,000.00
Supplies	500.00
Office Equipment	10,000.00
Accumulated Depreciation—Office Equipment	5,500.00
Truck	17,000.00
Accumulated Depreciation—Truck	12,200.00
Accounts Payable	500.00
Donald Winn, Capital	7,300.00
Judy Reed, Capital	7,000.00

The following transactions occurred during July of the current year.

Transactions:

July 1. Received cash from sale of office equipment, $4,000.00. R114.
 1. Received cash from sale of supplies, $200.00. R115.
 3. Received cash from sale of truck, $5,000.00. R116.
 5. Paid cash to all creditors for amounts owed. C156.
 6. Distributed balance of Loss and Gain on Realization to Donald Winn, 65%; to Judy Reed, 35%. M34.
 6. Distributed remaining cash to partners. C157 and C158.

Instructions:

1. Journalize the transactions. Use page 13 of a cash receipts journal, page 13 of a cash payments journal, and page 7 of a general journal.

MASTERY PROBLEM

Recording partners' investments and withdrawals, preparing financial statements, and liquidating a partnership

Darren and Karen Greenlund are partners in a business called GreenGarden. Journals and forms for completing this problem are given in the *Working Papers*. GreenGarden completed the following transactions during July of the current year.

Transactions:

July 15. Received cash from partner, Darren Greenlund, as an investment, $10,000.00. Receipt No. 87.
    15. Received cash of $3,000.00 and equipment valued at $8,000.00 from partner, Karen Greenlund, as an investment. Receipt No. 88.
    31. Karen Greenlund, partner, withdrew merchandise for personal use, $1,000.00. Memorandum No. 61.
    31. Darren Greenlund, partner, withdrew cash for personal use, $800.00. Check No. 321.

Instructions:

1. Use page 13 of a cash receipts journal. Journalize the investments on July 15.

2. Use page 19 of a cash payments journal and page 23 of a general journal. Journalize the withdrawals on July 31.

Information from GreenGarden's worksheet and income statement for the month ended July 31 is given below.

Net Income for the month ended July 31	$14,600.00
Darren Greenlund, Capital July 1 balance	32,310.00
Karen Greenlund, Capital July 1 balance	28,880.00

Instructions:

3. Prepare a distribution of net income statement for Green Garden. Net income or loss is to be distributed equally to the partners.

4. Using the balances of the general ledger capital accounts, prepare an owners' equity statement for GreenGarden. The investments made on July 15 are the only additional investments made by the partners this month. The withdrawals made on July 31 are the only withdrawals made by the partners this month.

The Greenlunds decided to liquidate GreenGarden and retire on July 31. On that date, after financial statements were prepared and closing entries were posted, the general ledger accounts had the following balances.

Cash	$90,490.00
Merchandise Inventory	2,000.00
Equipment	15,000.00
Accumulated Depreciation—Equipment	10,000.00
Accounts Payable	2,500.00
Darren Greenlund, Capital	48,810.00
Karen Greenlund, Capital	46,180.00

The following transactions occurred on July 31 of the current year.

Transactions:

a. Received cash from the sale of merchandise inventory, $1,800.00. R89.

b. Received cash from the sale of equipment, $7,000.00. R90.

c. Paid cash to all creditors for amounts owed. C322.

d. Distributed balance of Loss and Gain on Realization to the partners on an equal basis. M62.

e. Distributed remaining cash to partners. C323 and C324.

Instructions:

5. Journalize the transactions. Continue on the next available line of the journals used in instructions 1 and 2.

23-6   CHALLENGE PROBLEM

Preparing a distribution of net income statement and owners' equity statement (unequal distribution of net loss; additional investment)

Kaye Skousen and Timothy Tripp are partners in a merchandising business, Jewelry Joint. Forms for completing this problem are given in the *Working Papers*. The following information was taken from the records on December 31 of the current year.

Partner	Balance of Capital Account January 1	Balance of Drawing Account	Distribution of Net Loss
Skousen	$125,294.00	$18,000.00	65.0%
Tripp	$101,961.00	$16,300.00	35.0%

Instructions:

1. On December 31, the partnership had a net loss of $32,340.00. Prepare a distribution of net income statement for the partnership.

2. Prepare an owners' equity statement for Jewelry Joint. Additional investments made during the year: Kaye Skousen, $11,000.00; Timothy Tripp, $9,500.00.

PHOTODISC/GETTY IMAGES

APPLIED COMMUNICATION

Since reports are valuable communication tools used to make decisions, they must be clearly written.

Instructions: Research the advantages and disadvantages of three types of business ownership: proprietorship, partnership, and corporation. Write a clear, concise report on your findings.

CASE FOR CRITICAL THINKING

Rena Jacques and George Nadler are partners in a paint and decorating store. The store operates on a yearly fiscal period. At the end of each year, an accountant is hired to prepare financial statements. At the end of each month during the year, Ms. Jacques prepares a work sheet. The work sheet is prepared to determine if the business made or lost money that month. The accountant suggests that monthly financial statements also be prepared. Ms. Jacques believes, however, that the monthly work sheet is sufficient to determine how the business is doing. Do you agree with Ms. Jacques or the accountant? Why?

SCANS WORKPLACE COMPETENCY

Systems Competency: Monitors and Corrects Performance

Concept: A workplace consists of many different systems, from the human resources system to the computer network to the order fulfillment system. Every employee needs to understand the system in which he or she works. Managers of a system need to distinguish trends, predict impacts on systems operations, diagnose deviations in systems' performance, and correct malfunctions in a system.

Application: Your company has just introduced a new product with predictions that it will be enormously popular and increase sales 50% after a large advertising campaign. List the systems that could be affected by a sudden large increase in demand for the company's products. Suggest ways this increased demand can be handled.

Wendy Winger and Leo Zenisek are partners in Old World Bakery. The following information was taken from the records on December 31 of the current year.

Partner	Balance of Capital Account January 1	Balance of Drawing Account	Distribution of Net Income
Winger	$15,000.00	$2,300.00	40.0%
Zenisek	$12,000.00	$1,100.00	60.0%

On December 31, the partnership had a net income of $14,500.00. No additional investments were made.

The following statements were prepared using the information above. Audit the statements. Prepare a list that describes any errors you discover and how they should be corrected.

Old World Bakery
Distribution of Net Income Statement
December 31, 20--

Wendy Winger	
40.0% of Net Income	7 2 5 0 00
Leo Zenisek	
60.0% of Net Income	7 2 5 0 00
Net Income	14 5 0 0 00

Old World Bakery
Owners' Equity Statement
For Year Ended December 31, 20--

Wendy Winger		
Capital Balance, January 1, 20--		51 0 0 0 00
Share of Net Income	7 2 5 0 00	
Less Withdrawals	2 3 0 0 00	
Increase in Capital		4 9 5 0 00
Capital, December 31, 20--		46 0 5 0 00
Leo Zenisek		
Capital Balance, January 1, 20--		12 0 0 0 00
Share of Net Income	7 2 5 0 00	
Less Withdrawals	1 1 0 0 00	
Increase in Capital		8 3 5 0 00
Capital, December 31, 20--		20 3 5 0 00
Total Owners' Equity, December 31, 20--		66 4 0 0 00

ANALYZING BEST BUY'S FINANCIAL STATEMENTS

Look at the equity section of Best Buy's consolidated balance sheets on Appendix B page B-5 in this textbook.

Instructions: How would this section be different if Best Buy were a partnership owned by two partners instead of a corporation?

Accounting
SOFTWARE

MEMORIZED JOURNAL ENTRIES

Peachtree strives to make entering journal entries as efficient as possible. For many transactions, such as a credit sale, you don't even have to enter a debit or credit--Peachtree assigns the appropriate account titles based on previously entered customer default options.

In contrast, some journal entries, such as accruals, must be entered using a general journal. These transactions require that you identify each debit and credit account. Over time, you might wonder if there is a way that you can eliminate the need to enter these accounts.

Peachtree's memorized transaction feature is the solution. Imagine entering the debit and credit accounts (but no amounts) of a general journal entry you record frequently. You can save this transaction as a memorized transaction. Then, when entering a general journal entry, you can select the appropriate entry from a list of memorized journal entries. With the accounts titles automatically identified, you only have to enter the amounts to save the entry.

The more often a journal entry is recorded, the more efficient you will be by creating a memorized journal entry. Of equal importance, the chance of entering an incorrect account title is reduced because you do not enter this information each time an entry is recorded.

OPTIONAL PEACHTREE ACTIVITY
Identify five general journal entries that could be entered as memorized journal entries.

MEMORIZED JOURNAL ENTRIES

Much of the work of a computerized accounting system is focused on recording transactions. Some of these transactions are repeated, possibly several times a day. The QuickBooks "memorize a transaction" function allows the user to enter a transaction one time and then memorize it for later use.

When a memorized transaction is created, it can be set up to be automatically entered into the system on a set schedule. The user can also call up a memorized transaction to enter it into the system. A reminder can also be set up to prompt the user to enter a recurring transaction.

Reminders are another QuickBooks feature designed to increase efficiency and accuracy. QuickBooks can be programmed to remind the user to send out invoices, pay the payroll, print checks, make deposits, and perform other functions.

A good example of the use of reminders and memorized transactions could be applied to the adjusting entry for supplies. The entry could be memorized, with the amounts omitted since the amount will change each period. A reminder can be set to prompt the user to enter the adjusting entry at the end of each fiscal period. Once reminded, the user can recall the memorized adjusting entry and insert the amount of supplies used that period.

OPTIONAL QUICKBOOKS ACTIVITY
Identify five general journal entries that could be entered as memorized journal entries.

MERGING AND CENTERING TITLES

Throughout this textbook you have used Excel templates in which document titles were centered over several columns. For example, the corporation's name and statement title are usually centered over the statement.

The Merge and Center tool allows you to combine a group of adjacent cells into a single cell. Any text to be displayed in the combined cell should be entered in the upper left cell of the range.

Once the cells are merged, you can do anything you would do to any other cell: change the font size or color, right or left justify, or add a border. Selecting the Merge and Center tool again returns the cells to their original condition.

EXCEL APPLICATION PROBLEM 23-2

Open the F23-2 Excel data file. Follow the step-by-step instructions in the Instructions work sheet. Merge and center each financial statement heading.

CUSTOMIZING THE AUTOMATED ACCOUNTING SYSTEM

Many of the functions of the accounting cycle are performed automatically by the Automated Accounting system after journal entries are recorded and posted. Journal entry, ledger reports, financial statement, payroll, plant asset, and closing entries are generated automatically. The options that determine the nature of these reports and entries are determined by the settings in the Company Info. Window, which is accessed from the Custom toolbar button.

Company Name: The name of the company is entered in the Company name text box. The company name is displayed and printed as part of the heading for each report.

Problem Name: The problem name entered in this textbox is printed at the top of every report along with the user name. The problem name also appears in the title bar of the Automated Accounting main window.

Departments: The Departments drop-down list allows you to select from three options: None, 2, or 3 to set the number of departments in the business. In this course, none of the problems involve a departmentalized business, so None is selected.

Business Organization: The type of business organization selected determines the format and nature of financial statements. If Partnership Equal Distribution is selected, the automatic closing entries will distribute net income equally between the partners' capital accounts. If Partnership Unequal Distribution is selected, the closing entries to close Income Summary and distribute net income to the partners' capital accounts must be journalized and posted.

Features: Turning on the various features enables the use of plant assets, payroll, inventory, and/or budgeting systems. Employee deductions for the Payroll system can be entered under Voluntary Deductions.

Type of Business: The type of business selected determines the format of the income statement.

Income Statement: The Report by Month and Year option will show both the current month and the current year on the income statement. There must be enough data available to make this option meaningful. The problems in this textbook use the Report by Fiscal Period.

Accounting System: The Standard option is selected for all the problems in this textbook. The Voucher option is an alternative to an accounts payable system.

Computer Checks: If Accounts Payable Checks is turned on, checks will be created each time a cash payment that involves a vendor is entered. If the Payroll Checks option is turned on, paychecks will be created each time a payroll transaction is entered for an employee.

AUTOMATED ACCOUNTING APPLICATION PROBLEM 23-1

Open file F23-1.AA8. Display the problem instructions and complete the problem.

AUTOMATED ACCOUNTING APPLICATION PROBLEM 23-4

Open file F23-4.AA8. Display the problem instructions and complete the problem.

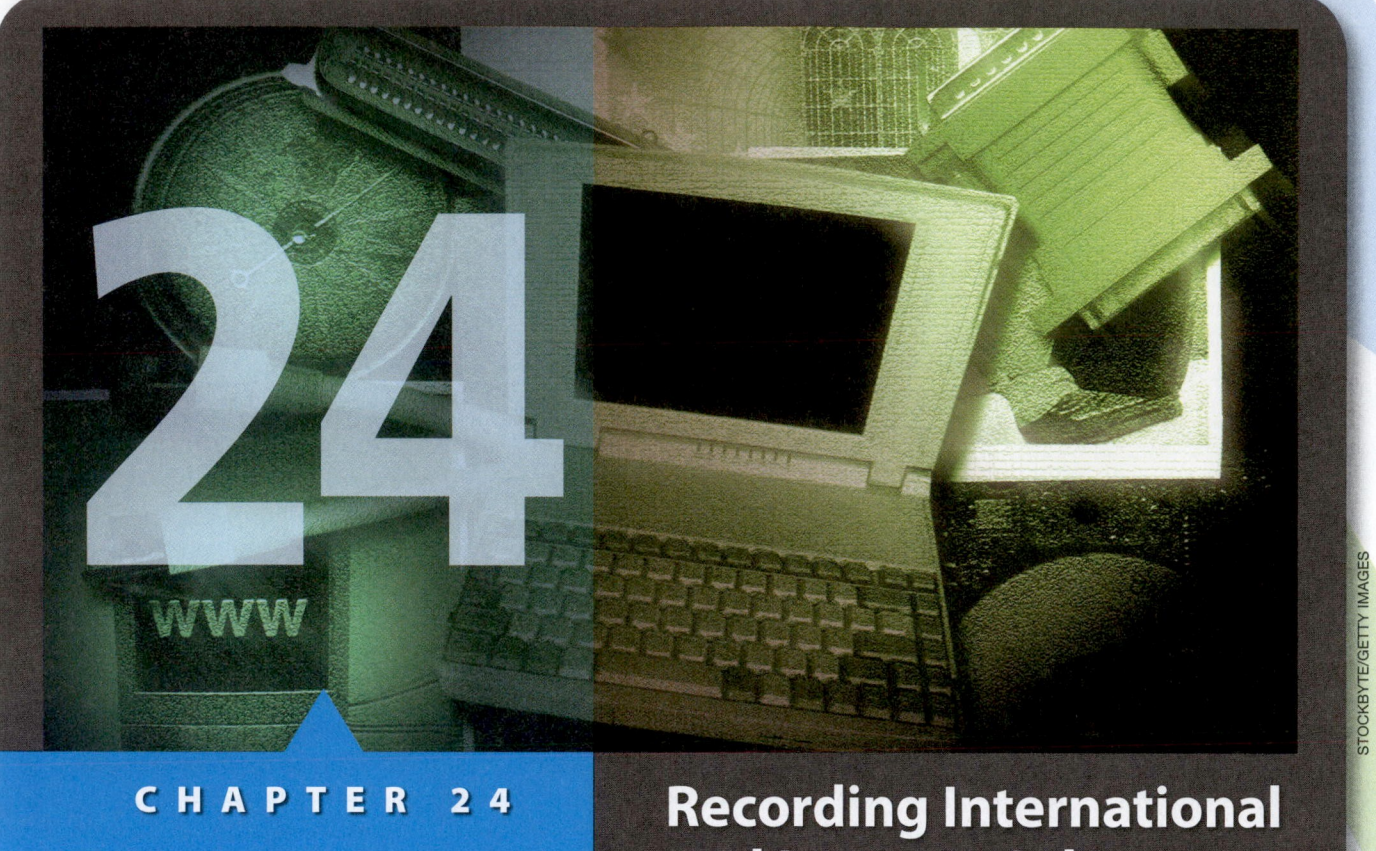

STOCKBYTE/GETTY IMAGES

CHAPTER 24

Recording International and Internet Sales

OBJECTIVES

After studying Chapter 24, you will be able to:

1. Define accounting terms related to international sales.

2. Identify accounting concepts and practices related to international and Internet sales.

3. Record transactions for international sales.

4. Record transactions for Internet sales.

KEY TERMS

- exports
- imports
- contract of sale
- letter of credit
- bill of lading
- commercial invoice
- draft
- sight draft
- time draft
- trade acceptance

Point Your Browser
www.C21accounting.com

Honeywell

Honeywell Around the World

"You can't see most of our products, but you can count on them." This is a quote from the Honeywell web site. Sometimes the products we don't think about or can't see are some of the most important products for our safety and comfort.

Honeywell manufactures collision avoidance and traffic control systems for the aerospace industry. They also make wing-ice and wind-shear sensors and landing systems. Most of us will never see these products, but we rely on them to help get us safely to our destination. Honeywell also makes controls to keep airport facilities efficient, safe, and comfortable. Again, most of us will never see these products, but we count on them to keep us comfortable as we travel.

Honeywell has manufacturing facilities and affiliates around the world, including the Asia Pacific region, Europe, the Middle East, Africa, Latin America, Brazil, and Mexico. It is estimated that Honeywell employs nearly 62,000 people outside North America.

©BLOOMBERG NEWS/LANDOV

Critical Thinking

1. Name at least two challenges Honeywell faces because of its world-wide operations.
2. Name at least two benefits Honeywell has because of its world-wide operations.

Source: www.honeywell.com

INTERNET ACTIVITY

Foreign Exchange Rates

There are several Internet sites designed to help you convert foreign currency. Perform an Internet search for the phrase "foreign currency." Find a site that converts currency.

Instructions

1. Pick the currency of a foreign country. List the exchange rate for that currency.
2. If you gave the exchange organization 100 U.S. dollars, how much foreign currency would you receive?

INTERNATIONAL SALES

Sales in the international market have become a major source of revenue for both small and large businesses. Improved technology has helped support international trade. It is no longer necessary to talk to your vendor or customer via telephone. E-mail, fax, and the Internet have made it possible to do business without as much concern about time zones and business hours around the world.

Goods or services shipped out of a seller's home country to a foreign country are called **exports**. Goods or services bought from a foreign country and brought into a buyer's home country are called **imports**.

Businesses may be able to import materials or services that are not available or are less expensive than within their own country. Thus, many companies have entered into the export and import markets to maintain their competitiveness and provide the products and services to meet customer demand.

GiftPak Company imports merchandise such as Swiss chocolate and Chinese tea from a variety of countries. GiftPak also exports its gift boxes and baskets to customers around the world. Selling merchandise to individuals or other businesses within one's own country, generally referred to as *domestic sales*, is much simpler than international sales.

CHARACTER COUNTS

Become an Ethics Officer

While researching the ethics activities in this textbook, you have reviewed the codes of conduct for several companies. You have seen references to individuals with titles such as ethics officer, governance manager, or compliance officer. These individuals are charged with ensuring that the company has an effective ethics policy, educating employees on the code of conduct, and resolving ethical issues reported by employees.

Have you considered a career in business ethics? Beyond earning a college education, you would need to constantly increase your knowledge of business ethics and corporate governance. One resource of information available to ethics officers is the Ethics Resource Center (ERC), a nonprofit organization devoted to helping individuals and organizations act with integrity. The ERC provides a wide range of resources to help ethics officers. The ERC is also involved in ethics education for students.

Instructions

Access the Ethics Resource Center at www.ethics.org. Prepare a list of the various resources available to ethics officers. How does the ERC help provide ethics education to students?

PHOTO: PHOTODISC/GETTY IMAGES

INTERNATIONAL SALES COMPARED WITH DOMESTIC SALES

Most domestic sales are sold for cash or on account after reviewing and approving a customer's credit. Because all transactions in the United States are covered by the same universal commercial laws and the same accounting standards, many transactions are based on trust. A customer with approved credit orders merchandise. The merchandise is shipped, and an invoice is sent by the vendor. After receiving the merchandise and invoice, the customer pays the vendor.

However, because of the increased complexities of international sales, several issues must be considered. The lack of uniform commercial laws among countries makes settlement of disputes more difficult. Greater distances and sometimes more complex transportation methods increase the time to complete the transaction. Because it may be difficult to determine a customer's financial condition and to take legal action if a customer does not pay, the risk of uncollected amounts is increased. Unstable political conditions in some countries may affect the ability to receive payments from those countries. Therefore, most businesses dealing in exports and/or imports follow a general process in international trade that ensures that the vendor receives payment for merchandise sold and the customer receives the merchandise ordered.

PROCESSING AN INTERNATIONAL SALE

A document that details all the terms agreed to by seller and buyer for a sales transaction is called a **contract of sale**. The contract includes a description and quantity of merchandise, price, point of delivery, packing and marking instructions, shipping information, insurance provisions, and method of payment.

GiftPak Company, located in Glendive, Montana, contracts to sell merchandise to Santiago Company in Mexico City, Mexico. The contract price is $5,000.00 in U.S. dollars, and merchandise is to be delivered to Mexico City. The Santiago Company is to pay transportation charges.

A letter issued by a bank guaranteeing that a named individual or business will be paid a specified amount provided stated conditions are met is called a **letter of credit**. The contract of sale between GiftPak and Santiago specified a letter of credit as the method of payment.

Santiago prepared an application with its bank, Banco Nacional de México, to issue a letter of credit. Banco Nacional de México approved Santiago's application and issued the letter of credit. Banco Nacional de México forwarded the letter of credit to GiftPak's bank, First Bank in Glendive.

First Bank delivered the letter of credit to GiftPak. GiftPak reviewed the letter of credit to ensure that the provisions in the letter agreed with the contract of sale. GiftPak then shipped the merchandise.

PHOTODISC/GETTY IMAGES

FOR YOUR INFORMATION

F Y I

The International Chamber of Commerce publishes "Incoterms" to attempt to coordinate international sales. This set of international rules interprets common sales terms used in foreign trade that are adopted by most international trade associations.

In order for GiftPak to collect payment, three documents specified in the letter of credit must be submitted to First Bank: (1) a bill of lading, (2) a commercial invoice, and (3) a draft.

A receipt signed by the authorized agent of a transportation company for merchandise received that also serves as a contract for the delivery of the merchandise is called a **bill of lading**. The transportation company sends the bill of lading to GiftPak when the merchandise is shipped. GiftPak then prepares the other two documents. A statement prepared by the seller of merchandise addressed to the buyer showing a detailed listing and description of merchandise sold, including prices and terms, is called a **commercial invoice**. A written, signed, and dated order from one party ordering another party, usually a bank, to pay money to a third party is called a **draft**. A draft is sometimes referred to as a *bill of exchange*. A draft payable on sight when the holder presents it for payment is called a **sight draft**.

First Bank examines the documents submitted by Gift-Pak to ensure that all terms of sale are in compliance with the letter of credit. First Bank then forwards the documents to Santiago's bank, Banco Nacional de México. Banco Nacional de México examines the documents to ensure they are in compliance with the terms and conditions of the letter of credit. When Banco Nacional de México determines that all documents are in compliance, it deducts the amount of the sight draft from Santiago's account and sends that amount, $5,000.00, to GiftPak's bank, First Bank.

Banco Nacional de México then forwards the documents to Santiago Company. By presenting the bill of lading and letter of credit to the transportation company, Santiago can receive the merchandise.

FOR YOUR INFORMATION

FYI

The United States federal government does not collect a sales tax. However, many countries of the world, including most of the major industrial powers, do collect what is referred to as a value added tax, or VAT. *A value added tax is basically a national sales tax.*

BLEND IMAGES/GETTY IMAGES

Foreign Currency

As our world becomes smaller and global trade increases, U.S. businesses become more involved in transactions with foreign businesses. These transactions can be stated in terms of U.S. dollars or in the currency of the other country. If the transaction involves foreign currency, a U.S. business must convert the foreign currency into U.S. dollars before the transaction can be recorded. [CONCEPT: Unit of Measurement]

The value of foreign currency may change daily. In the United States, the exchange rate is the value of foreign currency in relation to the U.S. dollar. Banks, online services, and many daily newspapers list current exchange rates.

The exchange rate is stated in terms of one unit of foreign currency. Using Argentina as an example, assume that one Argentine peso is worth 0.33820 U.S. dollar (or about 34 U.S. cents). This rate would be used when exchanging Argentine pesos for U.S. dollars.

A conversion formula can be used to find out how many foreign currency units can be purchased with one U.S. dollar. The formula is:

÷ exchange rate = foreign currency per U.S. dollar
1 dollar ÷ 0.33820 = 2.9568 pesos per dollar

To convert an amount in Argentine pesos to U.S. dollars, divide the amount of pesos by the number of pesos per dollar as shown.

350 Argentine pesos ÷ 2.9568 pesos per U.S. dollar = $118.37 US

Instructions

1. Current exchange rates change constantly. Do an Internet search and report the current exchange rate for the Argentine peso.

2. If the exchange rate for one Japanese yen is .0085143 U.S. dollar, what U.S. dollar amount would be recorded for a receipt of 5,200 Japanese yen?

3. If the exchange rate for one European euro is 1.08944 U.S. dollars, what amount would be recorded for a receipt of 197 euros?

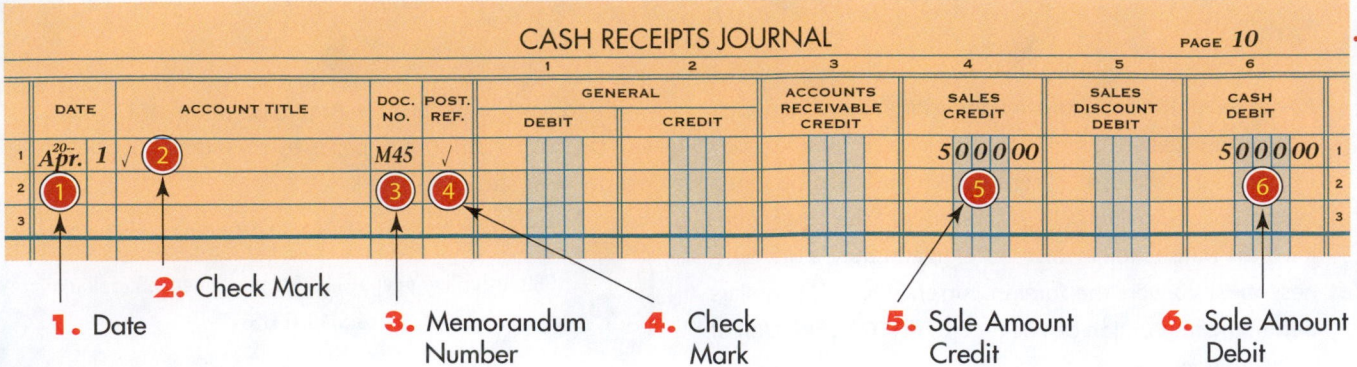

CASH RECEIPTS JOURNAL   PAGE 10

	DATE	ACCOUNT TITLE	DOC. NO.	POST. REF.	GENERAL DEBIT	GENERAL CREDIT	ACCOUNTS RECEIVABLE CREDIT	SALES CREDIT	SALES DISCOUNT DEBIT	CASH DEBIT	
1	20-- Apr. 1	✓ ②	M45	✓				5 0 0 0 00		5 0 0 0 00	1
2	①		③ ④					⑤		⑥	2
3											3

2. Check Mark

1. Date   **3.** Memorandum Number   **4.** Check Mark   **5.** Sale Amount Credit   **6.** Sale Amount Debit

After receiving payment from Banco Nacional de México, First Bank deposits the payment for the sale in GiftPak's account and sends GiftPak a deposit slip for the amount deposited. After receiving the deposit slip from First Bank, GiftPak prepares a memorandum as a source document for the cash received. The sale is then recorded as a cash sale.

Sales taxes are normally paid only on sales to the final consumer. GiftPak's sale is to Santiago Company, a merchandising company. Therefore, sales tax is not collected.

The sales and collection process GiftPak followed assured GiftPak of receiving payment for its sale and Santiago Company of receiving the merchandise it ordered.

April 1. Recorded international cash sale, $5,000.00. Memorandum 45.

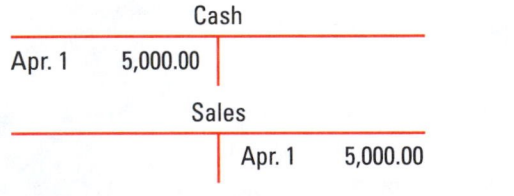

Cash	
Apr. 1 5,000.00	

Sales	
	Apr. 1 5,000.00

FOR YOUR INFORMATION

F Y I

Visitors to foreign countries with a value added tax (VAT) typically are required to pay the VAT. However, if items purchased exceed a specified amount, a refund of a portion of the VAT can be requested.

S T E P S   **RECORDING AN ENTRY FOR AN INTERNATIONAL SALE**

① Write the date, *20--, Apr. 1*, in the Date column.

② Place a check mark in the Account Title column to indicate that no account title needs to be entered.

③ Write the source document number, *M45*, in the Doc. No. column.

④ Place a check mark in the Post. Ref. column to indicate that the amounts on this line are not posted individually.

⑤ Write the sale amount, *$5,000.00*, in the Sales Credit column.

⑥ Write the sale amount, *$5,000.00*, in the Cash Debit column.

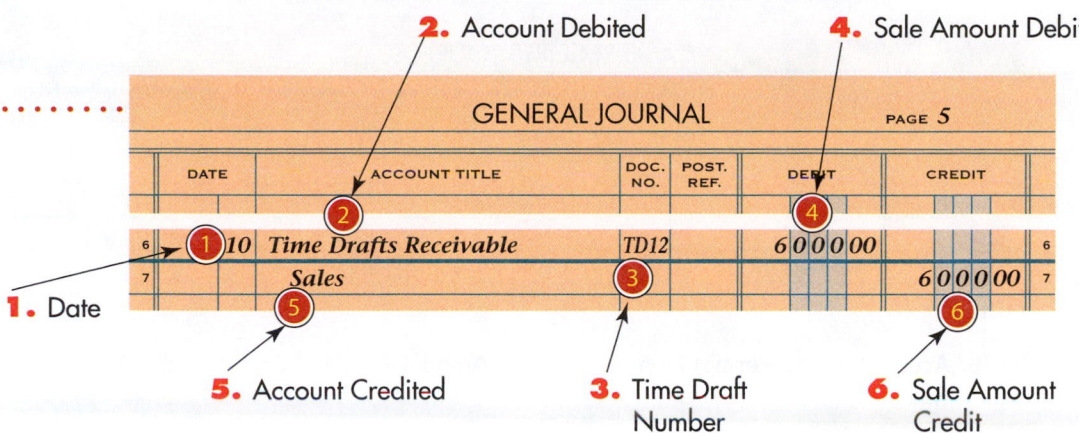

2. Account Debited

4. Sale Amount Debit

1. Date

5. Account Credited

3. Time Draft Number

6. Sale Amount Credit

GiftPak Company sold $6,000.00 of merchandise to Simov Co., located in Istanbul, Turkey. The contract of sale with Simov was similar to the contract with Santiago Company, with one exception. GiftPak agreed to delay receipt of payment 60 days. A draft that is payable at a fixed or determinable future time after it is accepted is called a **time draft**.

The sales process with Simov is the same as with Santiago, except GiftPak submits with the documentation a time draft due 60 days from the date the draft is accepted. On May 10, all documentation for the Simov sale is verified to be correct by the seller's and buyer's banks, and GiftPak's time draft is accepted.

After verifying the documentation, Simov's bank, Bank of Istanbul, returns the accepted time draft to GiftPak and forwards the other documents to Simov Co. Simov can receive the merchandise by presenting the bill of lading and letter of credit to the transportation company.

May 10. Received a 60-day time draft from Simov Co. for an international sale, $6,000.00. Time Draft No. 12.

STEPS  **JOURNALIZING A TIME DRAFT**

① Write the date, *10*, in the Date column.

② Write *Time Drafts Receivable* in the Account Title column.

③ Write *TD* and the time draft number, *12*, in the Doc. No. column.

④ Write the sale amount, *$6,000.00*, in the Debit column.

⑤ On the next line, indent and write *Sales* in the Account Title column.

⑥ Write the sale amount, *$6,000.00*, in the Credit column.

FOR YOUR INFORMATION

FYI

The minimum value added tax (VAT) in the European Community is 15%; however, there is no additional local sales tax. The Philippines has a 10% VAT that applies to the sale, barter, or exchange of goods, properties, or services. Thailand applies a 7% VAT to selected beverages.

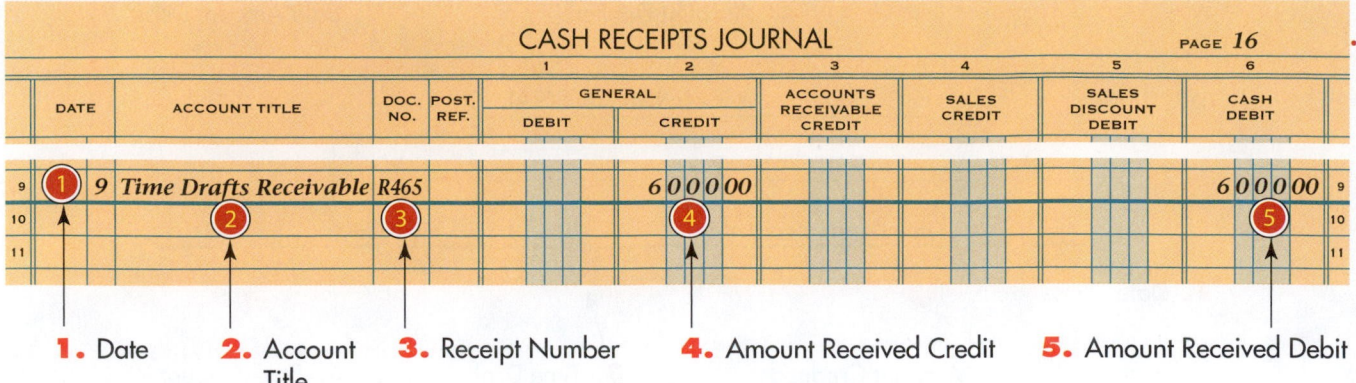

1. Date **2.** Account Title **3.** Receipt Number **4.** Amount Received Credit **5.** Amount Received Debit

When Simov's time draft is due and presented to its bank, Bank of Istanbul, the bank pays the draft. The payment process is the same as the payment of Santiago Company's sight draft.

July 9. Received cash for the value of Time Draft No. 12, $6,000.00. Receipt No. 465.

Cash	
July 9	6,000.00	

Time Drafts Receivable	
May 10	6,000.00	July 9	6,000.00

The process used by GiftPak Company for international sales relies upon letters of credit from banks to assure receipt of payment for those sales. Occasionally, GiftPak grants an extension of time for payment to long-time international customers by submitting a time draft.

Trade Acceptances

A form signed by a buyer at the time of a sale of merchandise in which the buyer promises to pay the seller a specified sum of money, usually at a stated time in the future, is called a ==trade acceptance==.

A trade acceptance is similar to a draft except a draft is generally paid by a bank and a trade acceptance is paid by the buyer. A seller generally has much more assurance of receiving payment from a bank than from a buyer. Because of the many complexities, few businesses use trade acceptances in international sales. Some businesses, however, use trade acceptances for domestic sales to very reliable customers.

STEPS  JOURNALIZING CASH RECEIVED FROM A TIME DRAFT

1. Write the date, *9*, in the Date column.

2. Write *Time Drafts Receivable* in the account title column.

3. Write the source document number, *R465*, in the Doc. No. column.

4. Write the amount received, *$6,000.00*, in the General Credit column.

5. Write the same amount, *$6,000.00*, in the Cash Debit column.

REMEMBER

A sight draft and a time draft are similar. Both methods of international sales require the buyer's bank to guarantee the cash payment for the sale. The primary difference between a sight draft and a time draft is the timing of the payment. Cash payment of a time draft is delayed for a period of time after the delivery of the goods to the buyer.

exports

imports

contract of sale

letter of credit

bill of lading

commercial invoice

draft

sight draft

time draft

trade acceptance

AUDIT YOUR UNDERSTANDING

1. What are some of the issues that must be considered before making international sales?
2. What two purposes does a bill of lading serve?
3. How does a sight draft differ from a time draft?
4. Why do many companies dealing in international sales rely upon letters of credit from banks?
5. How does a trade acceptance differ from a draft?

WORK TOGETHER 24-1

Journalizing international sales transactions

The cash receipts and general journals for Marlon Exports, Ltd. are given in the *Working Papers*. Your instructor will guide you through the following examples.

1. Using the current year, journalize the following international sales on page 9 of a cash receipts journal and page 5 of a general journal. Sales tax is not charged on these sales. Source documents are abbreviated as follows: memorandum, M; time draft, TD; receipt, R.

Transactions

May 1. Recorded an international cash sale, $14,000.00. M323.
　　5. Received a 30-day time draft from Ying Shen for an international sale, $18,000.00. TD32.
　　9. Received cash for the value of Time Draft No. 10, $21,000.00. R221.

2. Prove and rule the cash receipts journal.

ON YOUR OWN 24-1

Journalizing international sales transactions

The cash receipts and general journals for Hakim Handicrafts are given in the *Working Papers*. Work this problem independently.

1. Using the current year, journalize the following international sales on page 17 of a cash receipts journal and page 9 of a general journal. Sales tax is not charged on these sales. Source documents are abbreviated as follows: memorandum, M; time draft, TD; receipt, R.

Transactions

Sep. 3. Recorded an international cash sale, $9,400.00. M256.
　　5. Received a 45-day time draft from Ledah Patel for an international sale, $7,800.00. TD81.
　　6. Received cash for the value of Time Draft No. 73, $13,500.00. R211.

2. Prove and rule the cash receipts journal.

INTERNET SALES

More and more companies are turning to the Internet as an additional way of selling goods and services. Internet shopping provides customers the opportunity to browse the products offered by a company, compare competitors' products, and do so at a time and place convenient to the customer.

Selling goods over the Internet, however, also presents some challenges to the seller. The web site developed must be easy to navigate and safe to use. Customers must feel that the web site uses up-to-date security procedures to protect credit card information as it is being transmitted. The selling company must also be able to accept credit card sales, which means it must contract with a bank to offer this service or with a company that will offer this service to businesses for a fee.

GiftPak has prepared a web site that will accept credit card orders and transmit the sales information for immediate shipping and billing. An order confirmation is also immediately sent to the buyer, containing information about the order and expected shipping date.

Internet sales at GiftPak must be completed with a credit card. At the end of each day, GiftPak will be able to print out a terminal summary similar to the terminal summary discussed in Chapter 10. The terminal summary is used as the source document for recording online sales.

PHOTOGRAPHER'S CHOICE RF/GETTY IMAGES

FOR YOUR INFORMATION

FYI

Credit card companies are taking measures to protect online shoppers. Some companies offer a safe-shopping option, which allows the credit card holder to instantly obtain a temporary credit card account number good only for one purchase.

FOR YOUR INFORMATION

FYI

Companies such as PayPal offer services to online customers and sellers. For customers, these companies offer sites that use the most modern methods to safeguard credit card information as it is transmitted online. For sellers, these companies offer the availability of credit card sales with less cost and red tape.

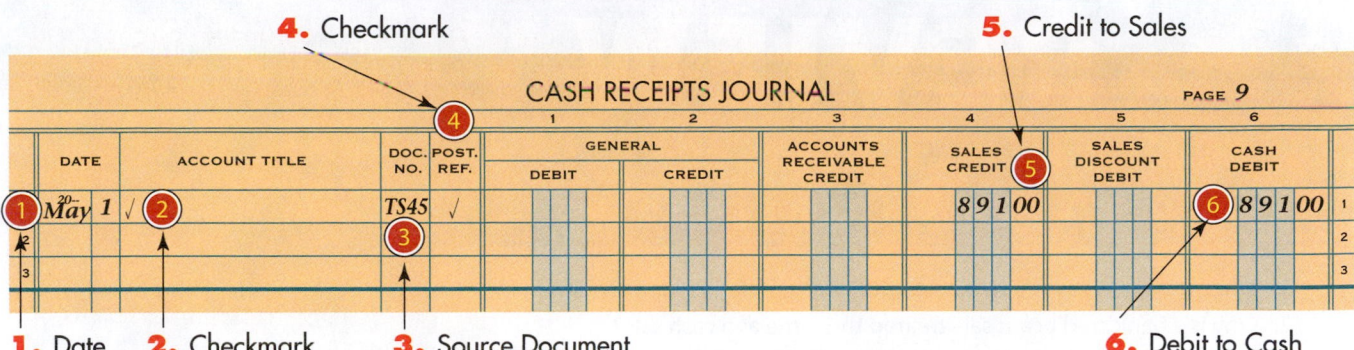

4. Checkmark **5.** Credit to Sales

1. Date **2.** Checkmark **3.** Source Document **6.** Debit to Cash

> *May 1. Recorded Internet credit card sales,*
> *$891.00. Terminal Summary 45.*

GiftPak Company processes its credit card sales at the end of each day. At the same time, the information is electronically transmitted to First Bank, with whom GiftPak has contracted to process its credit card sales. This information is transferred to the Federal Reserve Bank and processed in a manner similar to checks. Therefore, GiftPak considers these sales to be cash sales.

The asset account Cash has a normal debit balance and is debited for the amount of the credit card sales, $891.00. The sales account has a normal credit balance. Therefore, Sales is credited for the amount of the sales, $891.00.

Cash	
May 1 891.00	

Sales	
	May 1 891.00

FOR YOUR INFORMATION

F Y I

In order to process bank credit cards such as Visa and MasterCard, a business must set up a merchant account with a bank. The business pays a fee to the bank for processing credit card sales.

STEPS   RECORDING AN ENTRY FOR AN INTERNET SALE

1 Write the date, *20--, May 1*, in the Date column.

2 Place a check mark in the Account Title column to indicate that no account title needs to be entered.

3 Write the source document number, *TS45*, in the Doc. No. column.

4 Place a check mark in the Post. Ref. column to indicate that the amounts on this line are not posted individually.

5 Write the sale amount, *$891.00*, in the Sales Credit column.

6 Write the sale amount, *$891.00*, in the Cash Debit column.

End of Lesson REVIEW

AUDIT YOUR UNDERSTANDING

1. What are two reasons why a customer might prefer online shopping?
2. Why is a bank credit card sale treated the same as a cash sale?

WORK TOGETHER 24-2

Journalizing Internet sales transactions

The cash receipts journal for Teddy Bears Galore is given in the *Working Papers*. Your instructor will guide you through the following examples.

1. Using the current year, journalize the following Internet sales on page 5 of a cash receipts journal.

Transactions

Mar. 5. Recorded Internet credit card sales, $2,432.00. Terminal Summary 331.
 12. Recorded Internet credit card sales, $3,010.00. Terminal Summary 332.
 19. Recorded Internet credit card sales, $1,550.00. Terminal Summary 333.

ON YOUR OWN 24-2

Journalizing Internet sales transactions

The cash receipts journal for Labels World is given in the *Working Papers*. Work this problem independently.

1. Using the current year, journalize the following Internet sales on page 9 of a cash receipts journal.

Transactions

May 7. Recorded Internet credit card sales, $352.00. Terminal Summary 44.
 12. Recorded Internet credit card sales, $187.00. Terminal Summary 45.
 20. Recorded Internet credit card sales, $319.00. Terminal Summary 46.

After completing this chapter, you can:

1. Define accounting terms related to international sales.

2. Identify accounting concepts and practices related to international and Internet sales.

3. Record transactions for international sales.

4. Record transactions for Internet sales.

EXPLORE ACCOUNTING

How Credit Card Systems Work

To promote sales, Chimes Music Store accepts major credit cards, such as Visa, MasterCard, American Express, and Discover. To process these sales, Chimes Music contracted with a processing center to install and maintain its credit card system.

When a customer presents Chimes with a credit card, the card is scanned and the amount of purchase is entered in a credit card reader. The reader uses phone lines to contact the processing center. If the processing center determines that the customer has an adequate amount of unused credit, the transaction is approved and a sales receipt is printed. At the same time, the transaction is added to daily totals maintained by the processing center. After the customer signs the credit card receipt, both the customer and business keep a copy.

At the end of the day, Chimes enters a command to instruct the system to close its account. The credit card reader prints a summary receipt that lists the total number and amount of sales by credit card company. The process-ing center notifies each credit card company of its daily total. The credit card companies then make electronic funds transfers to Chimes Music's bank account. This process often requires several days to complete.

Both the processing center and the credit card companies charge Chimes with a fee for processing credit card sales. These charges are accumulated, and a monthly fee is charged directly to Chimes Music's bank account.

Research: Credit card processing companies can use different equipment and procedures to process credit card sales. Ask a local retailer to describe its credit card processing system. Prepare a report that describes the equipment and procedures used as well as the fees charged. Contrast the system you observed with Chimes Music's system. Which system is better? How could the system you researched be improved?

24-1 APPLICATION PROBLEM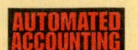

Journalizing international sales transactions

The cash receipts and general journals for Parker Exports, Ltd. are given in the *Working Papers*.

Instructions:

1. Journalize the following international sales completed by Parker Exports, Ltd. during June of the current year. Use page 10 of a cash receipts journal and page 6 of a general journal. Sales tax is not charged on these sales. Source documents are abbreviated as follows: memorandum, M; time draft, TD; receipt, R.

Transactions:

June 1. Recorded an international cash sale, $12,000.00. M82.
    5. Received a 30-day time draft from Bella Lamas for an international sale, $13,000.00. TD32.
    9. Received cash for the value of Time Draft No. 24, $16,000.00. R116.
   12. Received a 60-day time draft from Pablo Fuentes for an international sale, $8,000.00. TD33.
   19. Received cash for the value of Time Draft No. 21, $22,000.00. R117.
   21. Recorded an international cash sale, $17,500.00. M83.
   25. Received a 30-day time draft from Rodrigo Soto for an international sale, $24,000.00. TD34.

2. Prove and rule the cash receipts journal.

24-2 APPLICATION PROBLEM

Journalizing Internet sales transactions

The cash receipts journal for Sports Memorabilia is given in the *Working Papers*.

Instructions:

1. Journalize the following Internet sales completed by Sports Memorabilia during August of the current year. Use page 15 of a cash receipts journal. Source documents are abbreviated as follows: Terminal Summary, TS.

Transactions:

Aug. 6. Recorded Internet credit card sales, $909.00. TS116.
   13. Recorded Internet credit card sales, $1,480.00. TS117.
   20. Recorded Internet credit card sales, $1,147.00. TS118.
   27. Recorded Internet credit card sales, $2,843.00. TS119.

2. Total and rule the cash receipts journal.

Go Beyond the Book
For more information go to
www.C21accounting.com

MASTERY PROBLEM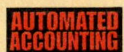

Recording international and Internet sales

Argo Corporation has both international and Internet sales.

Instructions:

1. Journalize the following transactions affecting sales and cash receipts completed during February of the current year. Use page 2 of a general journal and a cash receipts journal. Source documents are abbreviated as follows: memorandum, M; receipt, R; time draft, TD; terminal summary, TS.

Transactions:

Feb. 5. Received a 30-day time draft from Akeo Doi for an international sale, $5,000.00. TD10.
   8. Recorded Internet credit card sales, $12,300.00. TS23.
   12. Recorded an international cash sale, $10,500.00. M8.
   14. Received cash for the value of Time Draft No. 4, $23,000.00. R35.
   18. Recorded Internet credit card sales, $18,400.00. TS24.
   21. Received cash for the value of Time Draft No. 7, $8,000.00. R37.
   24. Recorded an international cash sale, $13,500.00. M12.
   27. Recorded Internet credit card sales, $9,200.00. TS25.
   28. Received a 30-day time draft from Sachi Nozaki for international sale of merchandise, $6,000.00. TD11.

2. Prove and rule the cash receipts journal.

CHALLENGE PROBLEM

Recording international sales and converting foreign currency

International sales can be stated in terms of U.S. dollars or in the foreign currency. The transaction statements below are stated in terms of the foreign currency of the customer.

Instructions:

1. Journalize the following transactions affecting sales. Use the foreign currency exchange rates given in the table below to translate the amount of the sales into U.S. dollars. Use page 11 of a cash receipts journal. Source documents are abbreviated as follows: memorandum, M.

Transactions:

June 1. Recorded international cash sale, 7,026 Chinese yuan. M46.
   8. Recorded international cash sale, 13,782 Mexican pesos. M49.
   14. Recorded international cash sale, 1,364 New Zealand dollars. M55.
   19. Recorded international cash sale, 354 European euros. M57.
   28. Recorded international cash sale, 3,174,060 Zimbabwe dollars. M68.

Currency	1 U.S. Dollar Equals...
Chinese Yuan	8.26650 Yuan
European Euro	.78796 Euro
Mexican Peso	11.48500 Pesos
New Zealand Dollar	1.43616 New Zealand Dollars
Zimbabwe Dollar	5,290.10 Zimbabwe Dollars

2. Prove and rule the cash receipts journal.

Internet sites must be easy to use and provide the customer with the information needed to make buying decisions.

Instructions: Investigate the web sites of two businesses. Write a report stating which site you feel is more customer friendly. Be sure to support your opinion with facts and examples.

CASE FOR CRITICAL THINKING

Julie Lindstrom is the bookkeeper for a small company that imports handcrafted items from foreign countries. Most of its suppliers are individuals who sell handmade crafts. All purchases are stated in the currency of the supplier's country but paid in U.S. dollars. When Julie pays the suppliers for their goods, she must look up the exchange rate in effect at the time and convert the foreign currency into U.S. dollars.

Most of the suppliers are not knowledgeable about the current exchange rates. Julie calculates the amount of U.S. dollars owed to each supplier, but she then rounds down to the lower whole dollar. She reasons that this saves time for both parties by eliminating "cents" from all transactions. Is this the correct procedure? What would you say to Julie about her policy?

GRAPHING WORKSHOP

Data regarding unit sales of Import/Export World are given in the table below.

Instructions: For each year, create a pie graph showing the amount of unit sales in each country.

	China	Italy	Bolivia	Germany	Total Sales
Year 1	10,000	5,000	8,000	15,000	38,000
Year 2	25,000	4,000	10,000	18,000	57,000

ANALYZING BEST BUY'S FINANCIAL STATEMENTS

When a company does business in a foreign country, it often deals in the currency of that country. When financial statements are prepared, the company must convert these amounts to U.S. dollars. Note 1 to Best Buy's financial statements on Appendix pages B-9 through B-20 explains how many different financial statement items are presented.

Instructions

1. When Best Buy translates foreign currency into U.S. dollars, what rate is used when listing the amounts for assets and liabilities?

2. When Best Buy translates its results of operations and cash flows into U.S. dollars, what rate is used?

Accounting SOFTWARE

PEACHTREE REMINDERS AND ALERTS

Today's computerized accounting systems are designed to do more than organize transactions and prepare financial statements. These systems also provide features to help you get organized.

Imagine starting your computer each morning and receiving a list of items that require your attention. You might begin by looking at your "to-do" list, notes you create for yourself to remind you of tasks to be performed. Then, examine your list of "events," such as the time and location of a meeting, the deadline for a report, or a desired date to contact a potential customer. As you enter a new event, Peachtree asks you identify the number of days before the event will be listed. For example, your event list might include a meeting scheduled for tomorrow while also listing an important report due in one week.

PEACHTREE MASTERY PROBLEM 24-3

1. Open (Restore) file 24-3MP.ptb.
2. Journalize the international sales involving a time draft using the Make General Journal Entries window.
3. Use the Enter Sales Receipts window to journalize Internet sales.
4. Use the Enter Sales Receipts window to journalize international sales.
5. Use the Make Deposits window to journalize the receipt of time draft payments.
6. Print a Journal report using February 1 and February 28 for the dates.

QUICKBOOKS PORTABLE FILES

A previous chapter discussed the importance of making a backup copy of accounting data stored electronically. Backup files contain all of the financial data for the company and can be quite large.

If you need to email or transport the financial data to a different location, it is not reasonable to use the backup file because of its size. A better solution is provided by QuickBooks. A portable file is a compact version of company's file and is small enough to be sent via email or saved to a portable media device.

If the person receiving the portable file is only looking at the data and will not be changing any data, no special considerations need to be made. However, if that person will be changing the data, no additional changes should be made to the main company files. When the portable file with changes is received by the company, it is not possible to merge the portable file back into the company files. Instead, the new, changed portable file will be used in place of the old company file.

QUICKBOOKS MASTERY PROBLEM 24-3

1. Open the Argo Corporation file.
2. Journalize the transactions affecting sales and cash receipts completed during February in the appropriate journal.
3. Print the general journal and cash receipts journal.

OPTIONAL QUICKBOOKS ACTIVITY

If directed by your instructor, make a portable file from your solution to Mastery Problem 24-3 and email it to your instructor.

FORMATS FOR CURRENCY

As a student of accounting, you have become accustomed to writing amounts in dollars and cents. On a spreadsheet, monetary amounts are almost always presented using a number, currency, or accounting format with two decimal places.

In today's global economy, accountants need to create workbooks that can accurately translate U.S. dollars to any of the world's many currencies. For example, one U.S. dollar may equal 8.2665 Chinese Yuan or 0.78796 European Euro.

Electronic spreadsheets allow you to display amounts to 30 or more decimal places. Although it is unlikely you will ever need that level of accuracy, it demonstrates the flexibility of today's electronic spreadsheets.

EXCEL CHALLENGE PROBLEM 24-4
Open the F24-4 Excel data file. Follow the step-by-step instructions in the Instructions work sheet. Modify the decimal places of the foreign currency amounts.

AUTOMATED ACCOUNTING TOOLS

Automated Accounting has several tools available to help perform certain tasks when using the system. You have already learned about the Planning Tools which perform various savings, loan, and interest calculations. Two other useful tools are the Calculator and the Find tool.

Calculator
Click the Calc. button on the toolbar to open the on-screen Calculator. A help menu is available for the Calculator by clicking Help at the top of the calculator. The results of a calculation can be pasted into the text box in which the cursor is located.

The Find Tool
When a journal is displayed, the Find tool from the Edit menu can be used to locate any previously entered transaction. You may enter the date, reference, amount, or any other data from the transaction in the Find What text box and click OK. If a matching transaction is found, it will be displayed in the journal where it can be checked, changed, or deleted. If you select Find Next in the Edit menu, you will locate the next occurrence of the search criteria.

AUTOMATED ACCOUNTING APPLICATION PROBLEM 24-1
Open file F24-1.AA8. Display the problem instructions and complete the problem.

AUTOMATED ACCOUNTING MASTERY PROBLEM 24-3
Open file F24-3.AA8. Display the problem instructions and complete the problem.

STATEMENT OF CASH FLOWS

CASH FLOW ANALYSIS

Financial statements provide managers, investors, and other individuals with financial information about the operating efficiency and financial condition of a business. The income statement, balance sheet, and statement of stockholders' equity are prepared using accounting records of a business. On the income statement, revenues are recorded when the revenue is earned, regardless of when the cash is received. Expenses are recorded when incurred, regardless of when the cash is paid. The accounting method that records revenues when they are earned and expenses when they are incurred is called the *accrual basis of accounting*.

Accrual-based financial statements report useful information. Some individuals, however, may need more information about why cash is received and how cash is spent in a business. The cash receipts and cash payments of a company are called *cash flows*. A financial statement that reports the cash flows of a business for a fiscal period is called a *statement of cash flows*. The statement reports the source of all cash receipts and the reason for all cash payments during a fiscal period.

The statement of cash flows is divided into three sections: cash flows from operating activities, cash flows from investing activities, and cash flows from financing activities.

CASH FLOWS FROM OPERATING ACTIVITIES

The cash receipts and payments necessary to operate a business on a day-to-day basis are called *operating activities*.

Cash inflows and outflows from operating activities are listed below.

Operating Activities	
Cash Inflows	**Cash Outflows**
Cash sales of merchandise	Cash paid for salaries
Cash sales of services	Cash paid for merchandise
Cash received on account	Cash paid on account
Interest income	Cash paid for supplies
	Cash paid for utilities
	Cash paid for interest

CASH FLOWS FROM INVESTING ACTIVITIES

Cash receipts and cash payments involving the sale or purchase of assets used to earn revenue over a period of time are called *investing activities*. Cash inflows and outflows from investing activities are listed below.

Investing Activities	
Cash Inflows	**Cash Outflows**
Sale of property/building	Purchase of property/building
Sale of investments	Cash paid for investment
Sale of machinery/equipment	Purchase of machinery/equipment

CASH FLOWS FROM FINANCING ACTIVITIES

Cash receipts and payments involving debt or equity transactions are called *financing activities*. Cash inflows and outflows from financing activities are listed below.

Financing Activities	
Cash Inflows	**Cash Outflows**
Issuing stock	Payment of cash dividends
Long-term loans	Repayment of loan principal
Issuing bonds	Retirement of bond principal

PREPARING THE OPERATING ACTIVITIES SECTION OF A STATEMENT OF CASH FLOWS

The first item listed in the operating activities section is the net income for the period. Since this amount is calculated using the accrual basis of accounting, several adjustments must be made to adjust the net income to actual cash flow from operating activities.

Adjusting Net Income for Depreciation

Depreciation expense is recorded on the income statement and reduces net income. However, depreciation expense is a non-cash expense, because cash is not paid out for depreciation. Therefore, even though it is an expense, it is not an outflow of cash. Since it has already been subtracted to determine net income, it has to be added back in when adjusting net income to cash flow. Sanibel Sports recorded $1,500.00 of depreciation expense for 20X2. The adjustment to add back in the amount of depreciation expense is the first adjustment listed on the statement of cash flows for Sanibel Sports on page A-5.

Adjusting Net Income for Changes in Current Assets

Increases and decreases in current assets affect cash flows and require adjustments. The balance in accounts receivable for Sanibel Sports on December 31, 20X1, was $78,550.00. On December 31, 20X2, the balance was $64,270.00. The accounts receivable account balance decreased by $14,280.00 during the year. A decrease in accounts receivable means that the sales amount reported on the income statement was less than the cash received on account. The $14,280.00 decrease in accounts receivable represents additional cash that has been received and is added to net income to determine cash flow on Sanibel Sports' statement of cash flows.

The balance in the supplies account for Sanibel Sports on December 31, 20X1, was $6,702.00. On December 31, 20X2, the balance was $7,377.00. The supplies account balance increased by $675.00 during the year. An increase in supplies means that Sanibel Sports bought more supplies than it used during the period. The amount of supplies used is listed on the income statement as an expense and reduces net income. The $675.00 increase in supplies represents additional cash that was used and is deducted from net income to determine cash flow on Sanibel Sports' statement of cash flows.

In a similar manner, all decreases in current assets will be added to net income as an adjustment. All increases in current assets will be deducted from net income as an adjustment.

Effect of Changes in Current Assets on Cash Flows	
Increases in current assets ———→	Deducted from net income
Decreases in current assets ———→	Added to net income

Adjusting Net Income for Changes in Current Liabilities

Increases and decreases in current liabilities also affect cash flows and require adjustments. The balance in accounts payable for Sanibel Sports on December 31, 20X1, was $79,290.00. On December 31, 20X2, the balance was $63,400.00. The accounts payable account balance decreased by $15,890.00 during the year. A decrease in accounts payable means that the cash flow for purchases on account was more than the amount of purchases reported on the income statement. The $15,890.00 decrease in accounts payable represents additional cash that has been paid out and is deducted from net income to determine cash flow on Sanibel Sports' statement of cash flows.

The balance in the salaries payable account for Sanibel Sports on December 31, 20X1, was $12,500.00. On December 31, 20X2, the balance was $20,900.00. The salaries payable account balance increased by $8,400.00 during the year. An increase in salaries payable means that not all of the salaries earned during the year were paid. The amount of salaries earned is listed on the income statement and reduces net income. The $8,400.00 increase in salaries payable represents a cash savings and is added to net income to determine cash flow on Sanibel Sports' statement of cash flows.

In a similar manner, all decreases in current liabilities will be deducted from net income as an adjustment. All increases in current liabilities will be added to net income as an adjustment.

Effect of Changes in Current Liabilities on Cash Flows	
Increases in current liabilities ———→	Added to net income
Decreases in current liabilities ———→	Deducted from net income

When all adjustments are recorded, the total adjustment to net income, $7,615.00, is calculated and entered on the statement of cash flows. Finally, net cash flows from operating activities, $69,965.00, are calculated and recorded.

PREPARING THE INVESTING ACTIVITIES SECTION OF A STATEMENT OF CASH FLOWS

The second section of the statement of cash flows reports the cash effect of investing activities. Cash flows resulting from a company's investing activities are identified by analyzing the changes in long-term asset accounts.

The balance in the equipment account for Sanibel Sports on December 31, 20X1, was $45,000.00. On December 31, 20X2, the balance was $95,000.00. The $50,000.00 increase represents the cost of new equipment purchased for cash. This amount is shown as an outflow of cash on Sanibel Sports' statement of cash flows.

The balance in the land account for Sanibel Sports on December 31, 20X1, was $35,500.00. On December 31, 20X2, the balance was $25,200.00. The $10,300.00 decrease represents land sold by Sanibel during this period.

Further investigation reveals that Sanibel sold the land for $10,300.00 during 20X2. The sale of land is an inflow of cash of $10,300.00. This amount is shown as an inflow of cash on Sanibel Sports' statement of cash flows.

When the changes in all long-term asset accounts have been analyzed and cash flows listed, the net cash flows from investing activities ($39,700.00), is calculated and recorded.

PREPARING THE FINANCING ACTIVITIES SECTION OF A STATEMENT OF CASH FLOWS

The third section of the statement of cash flows reports the cash effect of financing activities. Cash flows resulting from a company's financial activities are identified by analyzing the changes in long-term debt and stockholders' equity accounts. The balance in the loans payable account for Sanibel Sports on December 31, 20X1, was zero. On December 31, 20X2, the balance was $12,500.00. The $12,500.00 increase represents the proceeds from a loan Sanibel Sports received. This amount is shown as an inflow of cash on Sanibel Sports' statement of cash flows.

The balance in the retained earnings account for Sanibel Sports on December 31, 20X1, was $73,670.00. On December 31, 20X2, the balance was $128,020.00.

The change in this account is caused by two items. The retained earnings account increases by the amount of net income for a period and decreases by the amount of dividends paid during a period. The beginning balance of $73,670.00, plus the net income of $62,350.00, would give a balance of $136,020.00. Any difference between that amount and the actual ending balance in retained earnings is caused by dividends. Therefore, the amount of dividends declared by Sanibel Sports this period equals $8,000.00. Since this was a cash dividend, this amount is shown as an outflow of cash on Sanibel Sports' statement of cash flows.

Retained Earnings, beginning balance	$ 73,670.00
Plus net income	62,350.00
Equals	$136,020.00
Minus current balance of Retained Earnings	128,020.00
Equals dividend paid	$ 8,000.00

When all the changes in long-term debt and stockholder equity accounts have been analyzed and cash flows listed, the net cash flows from financing activities, $4,500.00, is calculated and recorded.

Sanibel Sports
Statement of Cash Flows
For Year Ended December 31, 20X2

Cash Flows from Operating Activities:			
Net Income		62 3 5 0 00	
Adjustments to Net Income:			
Depreciation Expense	1 5 0 0 00		
Changes in current assets and liabilities:			
Decrease in accounts receivable	14 2 8 0 00		
Increase in supplies	(6 7 5 00)		
Decrease in accounts payable	(15 8 9 0 00)		
Increase in salaries payable	8 4 0 0 00		
Total adjustments to net income		7 6 1 5 00	
Net cash flows from operating activities			69 9 6 5 00
Cash Flows from Investing Activities:			
Purchased equipment		(50 0 0 0 00)	
Sold land		10 3 0 0 00	
Net cash flows from investing activities			(39 7 0 0 00)
Cash Flows from Financing Activities:			
Proceeds from loan payable		12 5 0 0 00	
Dividend payment		(8 0 0 0 00)	
Net cash flows from financing activities			4 5 0 0 00
Net Change in Cash			34 7 6 5 00
Cash Balance, Beginning of Period			62 7 5 0 00
Cash Balance, End of Period			97 5 1 5 00

COMPLETING THE STATEMENT OF CASH FLOWS

The sum of the operating, investing, and financing activities sections of the statement of cash flows are added in order to calculate the net increase or decrease in cash. If all cash transactions have been accounted for, the change in cash plus the beginning cash balance should equal the ending cash balance reported on the balance sheet.

Sanibel Sports' increase in cash, $34,765.00, is added to the beginning cash balance, $62,750.00, to calculate the ending cash balance, $97,515.00. The ending cash balance equals the cash balance reported on Sanibel Sports' balance sheet. Thus, the statement of cash flows has been prepared accurately.

The following information was taken from the financial records of Bonita Body Shop for the year ending December 31, 20X2:

| Net Income | $15,495.00 |
| Depreciation Expense | 2,300.00 |

Account Title	Balance Dec. 31, 20X1	Balance Dec. 31, 20X2
Cash	$70,700.00	$51,795.00
Accounts Receivable	10,500.00	12,300.00
Prepaid Insurance	7,000.00	6,000.00
Accounts Payable	13,000.00	15,500.00
Interest Payable	1,400.00	0.00
Equipment	18,000.00	22,000.00
Loans Payable	40,000.00	10,000.00
Retained Earnings	42,000.00	54,495.00

Additional information: Equipment was purchased for $4,000.00 cash.
All dividends were paid in cash.

Statement paper is provided in the *Working Papers.*

Instructions:

1. Complete a statement of cash flows for the year ending December 31, 20X2, for Bonita Body Shop.

The following information was taken from the financial records of Terrace Yard Care for the year ending December 31, 20X2:

| Net Income | $3,500.00 |
| Depreciation Expense | 2,000.00 |

Account Title	Balance Dec. 31, 20X1	Balance Dec. 31, 20X2
Cash	$13,300.00	$15,000.00
Accounts Receivable	20,500.00	25,900.00
Supplies	700.00	400.00
Accounts Payable	18,600.00	16,600.00
Salaries Payable	0.00	800.00
Equipment	4,000.00	5,500.00
Land	8,000.00	6,000.00
Loans Payable	0.00	3,000.00
Retained Earnings	11,200.00	13,700.00

Additional information: Equipment was purchased for $1,500.00 cash.
Land was sold for $2,000.00 cash.
All dividends were paid in cash.

Statement paper is provided in the *Working Papers.*

Instructions:

1. Complete a statement of cash flows for the year ending December 31, 20X2, for Terrace Yard Care.

A WORLD OF OPPORTUNITY

Fiscal 2007 Annual Report

BEST BUY™

Item 6. Selected Financial Data.

The following table presents our selected financial data. The table should be read in conjunction with Item 7, *Management's Discussion and Analysis of Financial Condition and Results of Operations*, and Item 8, *Financial Statements and Supplementary Data*, of this Annual Report on Form 10-K. Certain prior-year amounts have been reclassified to conform to the current-year presentation. In fiscal 2004, we sold our interest in Musicland. All fiscal years presented reflect the classification of Musicland's financial results as discontinued operations.

Five-Year Financial Highlights

$ in millions, except per share amounts

Fiscal Year	2007[1]	2006[2]	2005[3]	2004	2003
Consolidated Statements of Earnings Data					
Revenue	$35,934	$30,848	$27,433	$24,548	$20,943
Operating income	1,999	1,644	1,442	1,304	1,010
Earnings from continuing operations	1,377	1,140	934	800	622
Loss from discontinued operations, net of tax	—	—	—	(29)	(441)
Gain (loss) on disposal of discontinued operations, net of tax	—	—	50	(66)	—
Cumulative effect of change in accounting principles, net of tax[4]	—	—	—	—	(82)
Net earnings	1,377	1,140	984	705	99
Per Share Data[5]					
Continuing operations	$ 2.79	$ 2.27	$ 1.86	$ 1.61	$ 1.27
Discontinued operations	—	—	—	(0.06)	(0.89)
Gain (loss) on disposal of discontinued operations	—	—	0.10	(0.13)	—
Cumulative effect of accounting changes	—	—	—	—	(0.16)
Net earnings	2.79	2.27	1.96	1.42	0.20
Cash dividends declared and paid	0.36	0.31	0.28	0.27	—
Common stock price:					
High	59.50	56.00	41.47	41.80	35.83
Low	43.51	31.93	29.25	17.03	11.33
Operating Statistics					
Comparable store sales gain[6]	5.0%	4.9%	4.3%	7.1%	2.4%
Gross profit rate	24.4%	25.0%	23.7%	23.9%	23.6%
Selling, general and administrative expenses rate	18.8%	19.7%	18.4%	18.6%	18.8%
Operating income rate	5.6%	5.3%	5.3%	5.3%	4.8%
Year-End Data					
Current ratio[7][8]	1.4	1.3	1.4	1.3	1.3
Total assets[7]	$13,570	$11,864	$10,294	$ 8,652	$ 7,694
Debt, including current portion[7]	650	596	600	850	834
Total shareholders' equity	6,201	5,257	4,449	3,422	2,730
Number of stores					
Domestic	868	774	694	631	567
International	304	167	144	127	112
Total	1,172	941	838	758	679
Retail square footage (000s)					
Domestic	33,959	30,826	28,465	26,640	24,432
International	7,926	3,564	3,139	2,800	2,375
Total	41,885	34,390	31,604	29,440	26,807

[1] Fiscal 2007 included 53 weeks. All other periods presented included 52 weeks.

[2] In the first quarter of fiscal 2006, we early-adopted the fair value recognition provisions of Statement of Financial Accounting Standards ("SFAS") No. 123 (revised 2004), *Share-Based Payment* ("123(R)"), requiring us to recognize expense related to the fair value of our stock-based compensation awards. We elected the modified prospective transition method as permitted by SFAS No. 123(R) and, accordingly, financial results for years prior to fiscal 2006 have not been restated. Stock-based compensation expense in fiscal 2007 and 2006 was $121 ($82 net of tax) and $132 ($87 net of tax), respectively. Stock-based compensation expense recognized in our financial results for years prior to fiscal 2006 was not significant.

Footnotes continue on next page.

$ in millions, except per share amounts

(footnotes continued)

(3) During the fourth quarter of fiscal 2005, following a review of our lease accounting practices, we recorded a cumulative charge of $36 pre-tax ($23 net of tax) to correct our accounting for certain operating lease matters. Additionally, during the same quarter, we established a sales return liability which reduced gross profit by $15 pre-tax ($10 net of tax). Further, in fiscal 2005 we recognized a $50 tax benefit related to the reversal of valuation allowances on deferred tax assets as a result of the favorable resolution of outstanding tax matters with the Internal Revenue Service regarding the disposition of our interest in Musicland. The tax benefit was classified as discontinued operations.

(4) Effective on March 3, 2002, we adopted SFAS No. 142, *Goodwill and Other Intangible Assets*. During fiscal 2003, we completed the required goodwill impairment testing and recognized an after-tax, noncash impairment charge of $40 that was reflected in our fiscal 2003 financial results as a cumulative effect of a change in accounting principle. Also effective on March 3, 2002, we changed our method of accounting for vendor allowances in accordance with Emerging Issues Task Force ("EITF") Issue No. 02-16, *Accounting by a Reseller for Cash Consideration Received from a Vendor*. The change resulted in an after-tax, noncash charge of $42 that also was reflected in our fiscal 2003 financial results as a cumulative effect of a change in accounting principle.

(5) Earnings per share is presented on a diluted basis and reflects three-for-two stock splits effected in August 2005 and May 2002.

(6) Comprised of revenue at stores and Web sites operating for at least 14 full months, as well as remodeled and expanded locations. Relocated stores are excluded from the comparable store sales calculation until at least 14 full months after reopening. Acquired stores are included in the comparable store sales calculation beginning with the first full quarter following the first anniversary of the date of acquisition. The calculation of the comparable store sales percentage gain excludes the effect of fluctuations in foreign currency exchange rates. All comparable store sales percentage calculations reflect an equal number of weeks. The method of calculating comparable store sales varies across the retail industry. As a result, our method of calculating comparable store sales may not be the same as other retailers' methods.

During fiscal 2004, we refined our methodology for calculating our comparable store sales percentage gain to reflect the impact of non-point-of-sale (non-POS) revenue transactions. We refined our comparable store sales calculation in light of changes in our business. Previously, our comparable store sales calculation was based on store POS revenue. The comparable store sales percentage gains for fiscal 2007, 2006, 2005 and 2004 have been computed using the refined methodology. The comparable store sales percentage gain for fiscal 2003 has not been computed using the refined methodology. Refining the methodology for calculating our comparable store sales percentage gain did not impact previously reported revenue, net earnings or cash flows.

(7) Includes both continuing and discontinued operations.

(8) The current ratio is calculated by dividing total current assets by total current liabilities.

Item 8. Financial Statements and Supplementary Data.

Management's Report on the Financial Statements

Our management is responsible for the preparation, integrity and objectivity of the accompanying consolidated financial statements and the related financial information. The financial statements have been prepared in conformity with accounting principles generally accepted in the United States of America and necessarily include certain amounts that are based on estimates and informed judgments. Our management also prepared the related financial information included in this Annual Report on Form 10-K and is responsible for its accuracy and consistency with the financial statements.

The consolidated financial statements have been audited by Deloitte & Touche LLP for the years ended March 3, 2007, and February 25, 2006, and by Ernst & Young LLP for the year ended February 26, 2005, independent registered public accounting firms who conducted their audits in accordance with the standards of the Public Company Accounting Oversight Board (United States). The independent registered public accounting firms' responsibility is to express an opinion as to the fairness with which such financial statements present our financial position, results of operations and cash flows in accordance with accounting principles generally accepted in the United States.

Management's Report on Internal Control Over Financial Reporting

Our management is responsible for establishing and maintaining adequate internal control over financial reporting as defined in Rule 13a-15(f) under the Securities Exchange Act of 1934. Our internal control over financial reporting is designed under the supervision of our principal executive officer and principal financial officer, and effected by our Board of Directors, management and other personnel, to provide reasonable assurance regarding the reliability of financial reporting and the preparation of financial statements for external purposes in accordance with accounting principles generally accepted in the United States and include those policies and procedures that:

(1) Pertain to the maintenance of records that in reasonable detail accurately and fairly reflect our transactions and the dispositions of our assets;

(2) Provide reasonable assurance that our transactions are recorded as necessary to permit preparation of financial statements in accordance with accounting principles generally accepted in the United States, and that our receipts and expenditures are being made only in accordance with authorizations of our management and Board of Directors; and

(3) Provide reasonable assurance regarding prevention or timely detection of unauthorized acquisition, use or disposition of our assets that could have a material effect on our financial statements.

Because of its inherent limitations, internal control over financial reporting may not prevent or detect misstatements. Therefore, even those systems determined to be effective can provide only reasonable assurance with respect to financial statement preparation and presentation.

Under the supervision and with the participation of our management, including our principal executive officer and principal financial officer, we assessed the effectiveness of our internal control over financial reporting as of March 3, 2007, using the criteria set forth by the Committee of Sponsoring Organizations of the Treadway Commission ("COSO") in *Internal Control — Integrated Framework*. Based on its assessment, management has concluded that our internal control over financial reporting was effective as of March 3, 2007. During its assessment, management did not identify any material weaknesses in our internal control over financial reporting. Management has excluded from its assessment the internal control over financial reporting at Pacific Sales Kitchen and Bath Centers, which was acquired on March 7, 2006, and whose financial statements reflect total assets and total revenues constituting 3% and 1%, respectively, of the consolidated financial statement amounts as of and for the year ended March 3, 2007. Management has also excluded from its assessment the internal control over financial reporting at Jiangsu Five Star Appliance Co., in which a 75% interest was acquired on June 8, 2006, and whose financial statements reflect total assets and total revenues constituting 5% and 2%, respectively, of the consolidated financial statement amounts as of and for the year ended March 3, 2007. Deloitte & Touche LLP, the independent registered public accounting firm that audited our consolidated financial statements for the year ended March 3, 2007, included in Item 8, *Financial Statements and Supplementary Data,* of this Annual Report on Form 10-K, has issued an unqualified attestation report on management's assessment of internal control over financial reporting.

Bradbury H. Anderson
Vice Chairman and Chief Executive Officer
(Principal Executive Officer)

Darren R. Jackson
Executive Vice President — Finance
and Chief Financial Officer
(Principal Financial Officer)

Consolidated Balance Sheets

$ in millions, except per share amounts

	March 3, 2007	February 25, 2006
Assets		
Current Assets		
Cash and cash equivalents	$ 1,205	$ 748
Short-term investments	2,588	3,041
Receivables	548	449
Merchandise inventories	4,028	3,338
Other current assets	712	409
Total current assets	9,081	7,985
Property and Equipment		
Land and buildings	705	580
Leasehold improvements	1,540	1,325
Fixtures and equipment	2,627	2,898
Property under capital lease	32	33
	4,904	4,836
Less accumulated depreciation	1,966	2,124
Net property and equipment	2,938	2,712
Goodwill	919	557
Tradenames	81	44
Long-Term Investments	318	218
Other Assets	233	348
Total Assets	$ 13,570	$11,864
Liabilities and Shareholders' Equity		
Current Liabilities		
Accounts payable	$ 3,934	$ 3,234
Unredeemed gift card liabilities	496	469
Accrued compensation and related expenses	332	354
Accrued liabilities	990	878
Accrued income taxes	489	703
Short-term debt	41	—
Current portion of long-term debt	19	418
Total current liabilities	6,301	6,056
Long-Term Liabilities	443	373
Long-Term Debt	590	178
Minority Interests	35	—
Shareholders' Equity		
Preferred stock, $1.00 par value: Authorized — 400,000 shares; Issued and outstanding — none	—	—
Common stock, $.10 par value: Authorized — 1 billion shares; Issued and outstanding — 480,655,000 and 485,098,000 shares, respectively	48	49
Additional paid-in capital	430	643
Retained earnings	5,507	4,304
Accumulated other comprehensive income	216	261
Total shareholders' equity	6,201	5,257
Total Liabilities and Shareholders' Equity	$ 13,570	$11,864

See Notes to Consolidated Financial Statements.

Consolidated Statements of Earnings

$ in millions, except per share amounts

Fiscal Years Ended	March 3, 2007	February 25, 2006	February 26, 2005
Revenue	$35,934	$30,848	$27,433
Cost of goods sold	27,165	23,122	20,938
Gross profit	8,769	7,726	6,495
Selling, general and administrative expenses	6,770	6,082	5,053
Operating income	1,999	1,644	1,442
Net interest income	111	77	1
Gain on investments	20	—	—
Earnings from continuing operations before income tax expense	2,130	1,721	1,443
Income tax expense	752	581	509
Minority interest in earnings	1	—	—
Earnings from continuing operations	1,377	1,140	934
Gain on disposal of discontinued operations (Note 2), net of tax	—	—	50
Net earnings	$ 1,377	$ 1,140	$ 984
Basic earnings per share:			
Continuing operations	$ 2.86	$ 2.33	$ 1.91
Gain on disposal of discontinued operations	—	—	0.10
Basic earnings per share	$ 2.86	$ 2.33	$ 2.01
Diluted earnings per share:			
Continuing operations	$ 2.79	$ 2.27	$ 1.86
Gain on disposal of discontinued operations	—	—	0.10
Diluted earnings per share	$ 2.79	$ 2.27	$ 1.96
Basic weighted-average common shares outstanding (in millions)	482.1	490.3	488.9
Diluted weighted-average common shares outstanding (in millions)	496.2	504.8	505.0

See Notes to Consolidated Financial Statements.

Consolidated Statements of Cash Flows

$ in millions

Fiscal Years Ended	March 3, 2007	February 25, 2006	February 26, 2005
Operating Activities			
Net earnings	$ 1,377	$ 1,140	$ 984
Gain from disposal of discontinued operations, net of tax	—	—	(50)
Earnings from continuing operations	1,377	1,140	934
Adjustments to reconcile earnings from continuing operations to total cash provided by operating activities from continuing operations:			
Depreciation	509	456	459
Asset impairment charges	32	4	22
Stock-based compensation	121	132	(1)
Deferred income taxes	82	(151)	(28)
Excess tax benefits from stock-based compensation	(50)	(55)	—
Other, net	(11)	(3)	24
Changes in operating assets and liabilities, net of acquired assets and liabilities:			
Receivables	(70)	(43)	(30)
Merchandise inventories	(550)	(457)	(240)
Other assets	(47)	(11)	(50)
Accounts payable	320	385	347
Other liabilities	185	165	243
Accrued income taxes	(136)	178	301
Total cash provided by operating activities from continuing operations	1,762	1,740	1,981
Investing Activities			
Additions to property and equipment, net of $75 and $117 non-cash capital expenditures in fiscal 2006 and 2005, respectively	(733)	(648)	(502)
Purchases of available-for-sale securities	(4,541)	(4,319)	(8,517)
Sales of available-for-sale securities	4,886	4,187	7,730
Acquisitions of businesses, net of cash acquired	(421)	—	—
Proceeds from disposition of investments	24	—	—
Change in restricted assets	—	(20)	(140)
Other, net	5	46	7
Total cash used in investing activities from continuing operations	(780)	(754)	(1,422)
Financing Activities			
Repurchase of common stock	(599)	(772)	(200)
Issuance of common stock under employee stock purchase plan and for the exercise of stock options	217	292	256
Dividends paid	(174)	(151)	(137)
Repayments of debt	(84)	(69)	(371)
Proceeds from issuance of debt	96	36	—
Excess tax benefits from stock-based compensation	50	55	—
Other, net	(19)	(10)	(7)
Total cash used in financing activities from continuing operations	(513)	(619)	(459)
Effect of Exchange Rate Changes on Cash	(12)	27	9
Increase in Cash and Cash Equivalents	457	394	109
Cash and Cash Equivalents at Beginning of Year	748	354	245
Cash and Cash Equivalents at End of Year	$ 1,205	$ 748	$ 354
Supplemental Disclosure of Cash Flow Information			
Income taxes paid	$ 804	$ 547	$ 241
Interest paid	14	16	35

See Notes to Consolidated Financial Statements.

PART II

Consolidated Statements of Changes in Shareholders' Equity

$ and shares in millions

	Common Shares	Common Stock	Additional Paid-In Capital	Retained Earnings	Accumulated Other Comprehensive Income	Total
Balances at February 28, 2004	**487**	**$ 49**	**$ 819**	**$ 2,468**	**$ 86**	**$ 3,422**
Net earnings	—	—	—	984	—	984
Other comprehensive income, net of tax:						
Foreign currency translation adjustments	—	—	—	—	59	59
Other	—	—	—	—	4	4
Total comprehensive income						1,047
Stock options exercised	10	1	219	—	—	220
Tax benefit from stock options exercised and employee stock purchase plan	—	—	60	—	—	60
Issuance of common stock under employee stock purchase plan	2	—	36	—	—	36
Vesting of restricted stock awards	—	—	1	—	—	1
Common stock dividends, $0.28 per share	—	—	—	(137)	—	(137)
Repurchase of common stock	(6)	(1)	(199)	—	—	(200)
Balances at February 26, 2005	**493**	**49**	**936**	**3,315**	**149**	**4,449**
Net earnings	—	—	—	1,140	—	1,140
Other comprehensive income, net of tax:						
Foreign currency translation adjustments	—	—	—	—	101	101
Other	—	—	—	—	11	11
Total comprehensive income						1,252
Stock options exercised	9	1	256	—	—	257
Tax benefit from stock options exercised and employee stock purchase plan	—	—	55	—	—	55
Issuance of common stock under employee stock purchase plan	1	—	35	—	—	35
Stock-based compensation	—	—	132	—	—	132
Common stock dividends, $0.31 per share	—	—	—	(151)	—	(151)
Repurchase of common stock	(18)	(1)	(771)	—	—	(772)
Balances at February 25, 2006	**485**	**49**	**643**	**4,304**	**261**	**5,257**
Net earnings	—	—	—	1,377	—	1,377
Other comprehensive loss, net of tax:						
Foreign currency translation adjustments	—	—	—	—	(33)	(33)
Other	—	—	—	—	(12)	(12)
Total comprehensive income						1,332
Stock options exercised	7	1	167	—	—	168
Tax benefit from stock options exercised and employee stock purchase plan	—	—	47	—	—	47
Issuance of common stock under employee stock purchase plan	1	—	49	—	—	49
Stock-based compensation	—	—	121	—	—	121
Common stock dividends, $0.36 per share	—	—	—	(174)	—	(174)
Repurchase of common stock	(12)	(2)	(597)	—	—	(599)
Balances at March 3, 2007	**481**	**$ 48**	**$ 430**	**$ 5,507**	**$ 216**	**$ 6,201**

See Notes to Consolidated Financial Statements.

Notes to Consolidated Financial Statements

$ in millions, except per share amounts

1. Summary of Significant Accounting Policies

Description of Business

Best Buy Co., Inc. is a specialty retailer of consumer electronics, home-office products, entertainment software, appliances and related services, with fiscal 2007 revenue from continuing operations of $35.9 billion.

We operate two reportable segments: Domestic and International. The Domestic segment is comprised of all U.S. store and online operations of Best Buy, Geek Squad, Magnolia Audio Video and Pacific Sales Kitchen and Bath Centers, Inc. ("Pacific Sales"). We acquired Pacific Sales on March 7, 2006. U.S. Best Buy stores offer a wide variety of consumer electronics, home-office products, entertainment software, appliances and related services through 822 stores at the end of fiscal 2007. Geek Squad provides residential and commercial computer repair, support and installation services in all U.S. Best Buy stores and at 12 stand-alone stores at the end of fiscal 2007. Magnolia Audio Video stores offer high-end audio and video products and related services through 20 stores at the end of fiscal 2007. Pacific Sales stores offer high-end home-improvement products, appliances and related services through 14 stores at the end of fiscal 2007.

The International segment is comprised of all Canada store and online operations, including Best Buy, Future Shop and Geek Squad, as well as all China store and online operations, including Best Buy, Geek Squad and Jiangsu Five Star Appliance Co., Ltd. ("Five Star"). We acquired a 75% interest in Five Star on June 8, 2006. We opened our first China Best Buy store in Shanghai on December 28, 2006. The International segment offers products and services similar to those offered by the Domestic segment. However, Canada Best Buy stores do not carry appliances. Further, Five Star stores and our China Best Buy store do not carry entertainment software. At the end of fiscal 2007, the International segment operated 121 Future Shop stores and 47 Best Buy stores in Canada, and 135 Five Star stores and one Best Buy store in China.

In support of our retail store operations, we also maintain Web sites for each of our brands (BestBuy.com, BestBuyCanada.ca, BestBuy.com.cn, Five-Star.cn, FutureShop.ca, GeekSquad.com, GeekSquad.ca, MagnoliaAV.com and PacificSales.com).

In fiscal 2004, we sold our interest in Musicland Stores Corporation ("Musicland"). The transaction resulted in the transfer of all of Musicland's assets other than a distribution center in Franklin, Indiana, and selected nonoperating assets. In fiscal 2005, we reversed previously recorded valuation allowances on deferred tax assets related to the disposition of our interest in Musicland and recognized a tax benefit. As described in Note 2, *Discontinued Operations*, we have classified Musicland's financial results as discontinued operations for all periods presented. These Notes to Consolidated Financial Statements, except where otherwise indicated, relate to continuing operations only.

Basis of Presentation

The consolidated financial statements include the accounts of Best Buy Co., Inc. and its subsidiaries. Investments in unconsolidated entities over which we exercise significant influence but do not have control are accounted for using the equity method. Our share of the net earnings or loss was not significant for any period presented. We have eliminated all intercompany accounts and transactions.

Effective June 8, 2006, we acquired a 75% interest in Five Star. Consistent with China's statutory requirements, Five Star's fiscal year ends on December 31. Therefore, we have elected to consolidate Five Star's financial results on a two-month lag. There were no significant intervening events which would have materially affected our consolidated financial statements had they been recorded during the fiscal year. See Note 3, *Acquisitions*, for further details regarding this transaction.

Reclassifications

To maintain consistency and comparability, certain amounts from previously reported consolidated financial statements have been reclassified to conform to the current-year presentation:

- We reclassified selected balances from receivables to cash and cash equivalents in our February 25, 2006, consolidated balance sheet.

- During the third quarter of fiscal 2007, we made a one-time election to adopt the alternative transition method described in Financial Accounting Standards Board ("FASB") Staff Position ("FSP") No. FAS 123(R)-3, *Transition Election Related to*

$ in millions, except per share amounts

Accounting for the Tax Effects of Share-Based Payment Awards. This election resulted in the reclassification of excess tax benefits from operating activities to financing activities, as presented in the statement of cash flows. See *Stock-Based Compensation* below, for further details.

These reclassifications had no effect on previously reported operating income, net earnings or shareholders' equity.

Change in Accounting Principle

During the fourth quarter of fiscal 2007, we elected to change our accounting principle to recognize the purchase and sale of investments in marketable debt and equity securities on the trade date. Prior to the fourth quarter of fiscal 2007, we recognized these transactions in our consolidated financial statements on the settlement date. We concluded that use of the trade date was preferable to the settlement date as trade date reflects the risks and rewards of investment ownership on a more timely basis. In addition, this method more closely aligns with the standard methodology utilized by our new investment custodian to account for investment transactions. In accordance with Statement of Financial Accounting Standards ("SFAS") No. 154, *Accounting Changes and Error Corrections,* this change in accounting principle has been applied retrospectively to our consolidated financial statements for all prior periods. This change in accounting principle had no effect on previously reported operating income, net earnings, shareholders' equity or cash flows. The effect on the consolidated balance sheets for each applicable quarter was as follows in fiscal 2007 and 2006 (unaudited):

	2007		2006	
	3rd Quarter	2nd Quarter	4th Quarter	1st Quarter
Cash and cash equivalents				
As reported	$1,202	$1,104	$ 748	$ 458
As adjusted	1,208	1,104	748	458
Short-term investments				
As reported	1,513	1,564	3,051	2,148
As adjusted	1,802	1,534	3,041	2,101
Receivables				
As reported	1,112	483	439	350
As adjusted	1,115	513	449	413
Accrued liabilities				
As reported	1,315	958	878	741
As adjusted	1,613	958	878	757

This change in accounting principle had no effect on any quarter of fiscal 2007 or 2006 other than those in the table above.

Use of Estimates in the Preparation of Financial Statements

The preparation of financial statements in conformity with accounting principles generally accepted in the United States ("GAAP") requires us to make estimates and assumptions. These estimates and assumptions affect the reported amounts in the consolidated balance sheets and statements of earnings, as well as the disclosure of contingent liabilities. Future results could be materially affected if actual results differ from these estimates and assumptions.

Fiscal Year

Our fiscal year ends on the Saturday nearest the end of February. Fiscal 2007 included 53 weeks and fiscal 2006 and 2005 each included 52 weeks.

Cash and Cash Equivalents

Cash primarily consists of cash on hand and bank deposits. Cash equivalents primarily consist of money market accounts and other highly liquid investments with an original maturity of three months or less when purchased. We carry these investments at cost, which approximates market value. The amounts of cash equivalents at March 3, 2007, and February 25, 2006, were $695 and $350, respectively, and the weighted-average interest rates were 4.8% and 3.3%, respectively.

Outstanding checks in excess of funds on deposit ("book overdrafts") totaled $183 and $230 at March 3, 2007, and February 25, 2006, respectively, and are reflected as current liabilities in our consolidated balance sheets.

Merchandise Inventories

Merchandise inventories are recorded at the lower of average cost or market. In-bound freight-related costs from our vendors are included as part of the net cost of merchandise inventories. Also included in the cost of inventory are certain vendor allowances that are not a reimbursement of specific, incremental and identifiable costs to promote a vendor's products. Other costs associated with acquiring, storing and transporting

$ in millions, except per share amounts

merchandise inventories to our retail stores are expensed as incurred and included in cost of goods sold.

Our inventory loss reserve represents anticipated physical inventory losses (e.g., theft) that have occurred since the last physical inventory date. Independent physical inventory counts are taken on a regular basis to ensure that the inventory reported in our consolidated financial statements is properly stated. During the interim period between physical inventory counts, we reserve for anticipated physical inventory losses on a location-by-location basis.

Our markdown reserve represents the excess of the carrying value, typically average cost, over the amount we expect to realize from the ultimate sale or other disposal of the inventory. Markdowns establish a new cost basis for our inventory. Subsequent changes in facts or circumstances do not result in the reversal of previously recorded markdowns or an increase in that newly established cost basis.

Restricted Assets

Restricted cash and investments in debt securities totaled $382 and $178, at March 3, 2007, and February 25, 2006, respectively, and are included in other current assets. Such balances are pledged as collateral or restricted to use for vendor payables, general liability insurance, workers' compensation insurance and warranty programs. The increase in restricted cash and investments in debt securities compared with February 25, 2006, was due primarily to restricted cash assumed in connection with the acquisition of Five Star. Five Star's restricted cash represents bank deposits pledged as security for certain vendor payables.

Property and Equipment

Property and equipment are recorded at cost. We compute depreciation using the straight-line method over the estimated useful lives of the assets. Leasehold improvements are depreciated over the shorter of their estimated useful lives or the period from the date the assets are placed in service to the end of the initial lease term. Leasehold improvements made significantly after the initial lease term are depreciated over the shorter of their estimated useful lives or the remaining lease term, including renewal periods, if reasonably assured. Accelerated depreciation methods are generally used for income tax purposes.

When property is fully depreciated, retired or otherwise disposed of, the cost and accumulated depreciation are removed from the accounts and any resulting gain or loss is reflected in the consolidated statement of earnings.

Repairs and maintenance costs are charged directly to expense as incurred. Major renewals or replacements that substantially extend the useful life of an asset are capitalized and depreciated.

Costs associated with the acquisition or development of software for internal use are capitalized and amortized over the expected useful life of the software, from three to seven years. A subsequent addition, modification or upgrade to internal-use software is capitalized only to the extent that it enables the software to perform a task it previously did not perform. Capitalized software is included in fixtures and equipment. Software maintenance and training costs are expensed in the period incurred.

Property under capital lease is comprised of buildings and equipment used in our retail operations and corporate support functions. The related depreciation for capital lease assets is included in depreciation expense. Accumulated depreciation for property under capital lease was $6 and $5 at March 3, 2007, and February 25, 2006, respectively.

Estimated useful lives by major asset category are as follows:

Asset	Life (in years)
Buildings	30–40
Leasehold improvements	3–25
Fixtures and equipment	3–20
Property under capital lease	3–20

During the fourth quarter of fiscal 2007, we removed from our fixed asset balances $621 of fully depreciated assets that were no longer in service. This asset adjustment was based primarily on an analysis of our fixed asset records and certain other validation procedures and had no net impact to our fiscal 2007 consolidated balance sheet, statement of earnings or statement of cash flows.

Impairment of Long-Lived Assets and Costs Associated With Exit Activities

We account for the impairment or disposal of long-lived assets in accordance with SFAS No. 144, *Accounting for the Impairment or Disposal of Long-Lived Assets*, which requires long-lived assets, such as property and equipment, to be evaluated for impairment whenever events or changes in circumstances indicate the carrying value of an asset may not be recoverable. Factors considered important that could result in an impairment review include, but are not limited to, significant underperformance relative to historical or planned operating results, significant changes in the manner of use of the assets or significant changes in our business strategies. An impairment loss is recognized when the estimated undiscounted cash flows expected to result from the use of the asset plus net proceeds expected from disposition of the asset (if any) are less than the carrying value of the asset. When an impairment loss is recognized, the carrying amount of the asset is reduced to its estimated fair value based on quoted market prices or other valuation techniques.

The present value of costs associated with location closings, primarily future lease costs (net of expected sublease income), are charged to earnings when a location is vacated.

Pre-tax asset impairment charges recorded in selling, general and administrative expenses ("SG&A") by segment were as follows in fiscal 2007, 2006 and 2005:

	2007	2006	2005
Domestic	$26	$ 4	$22
International	6	—	—
Total	$32	$ 4	$22

The impairment charges in fiscal 2007 and 2006 related to technology and store assets that were taken out of service due to changes in our business. The impairment charges in fiscal 2005 related to technology assets that were taken out of service due to changes in our business and charges associated with the disposal of corporate facilities that had been vacated.

Leases

We conduct the majority of our retail and distribution operations from leased locations. The leases require payment of real estate taxes, insurance and common area maintenance, in addition to rent. The terms of our lease agreements generally range from 10 to 20 years. Most of the leases contain renewal options and escalation clauses, and certain store leases require contingent rents based on factors such as specified percentages of revenue or the consumer price index. Other leases contain covenants related to the maintenance of financial ratios.

For leases that contain predetermined fixed escalations of the minimum rent, we recognize the related rent expense on a straight-line basis from the date we take possession of the property to the end of the initial lease term. We record any difference between the straight-line rent amounts and amounts payable under the leases as part of deferred rent, in accrued liabilities or long-term liabilities, as appropriate.

Cash or lease incentives ("tenant allowances") received upon entering into certain store leases are recognized on a straight-line basis as a reduction to rent from the date we take possession of the property through the end of the initial lease term. We record the unamortized portion of tenant allowances as a part of deferred rent, in accrued liabilities or long-term liabilities, as appropriate.

At March 3, 2007, and February 25, 2006, deferred rent included in accrued liabilities in our consolidated balance sheets was $18 and $16, respectively, and deferred rent included in long-term liabilities in our consolidated balance sheets was $237 and $211, respectively.

Prior to fiscal 2007, we capitalized straight-line rent amounts during the major construction phase of leased properties. Beginning in the first quarter of fiscal 2007, we adopted on a prospective basis, FSP No. FAS 13-1, *Accounting for Rental Costs Incurred During a Construction Period.* FSP No. FAS 13-1 requires companies to expense rent payments for building or ground leases incurred during the construction period. The adoption of FSP No. FAS 13-1 did not have a significant effect on our operating income or net earnings. Straight-line rent is expensed as incurred subsequent to the major construction phase, including the period prior to the store opening.

Transaction costs associated with the sale and leaseback of properties and any related gain or loss are recognized on a straight-line basis over the initial period of the lease agreements. We do not have any retained or contingent interests in the properties nor do we provide any guarantees in connection with the sale and leaseback of properties, other than a corporate-level guarantee of lease payments.

We also lease certain equipment under noncancelable operating and capital leases. Assets acquired under capital leases are depreciated over the shorter of the useful life of the asset or the lease term, including renewal periods, if reasonably assured.

Goodwill and Intangible Assets

Goodwill

Goodwill is the excess of the purchase price over the fair value of identifiable net assets acquired in business combinations accounted for under the purchase method. We do not amortize goodwill but test it for impairment annually, or when indications of potential impairment exist, utilizing a fair value approach at the reporting unit level. A reporting unit is the operating segment, or a business unit one level below that operating segment, for which discrete financial information is prepared and regularly reviewed by segment management.

Tradenames

We have an indefinite-lived intangible asset related to our Pacific Sales tradename which is included in the Domestic segment. We also have indefinite-lived intangible assets related to our Future Shop and Five Star tradenames which are included in the International segment.

We determine fair values utilizing widely accepted valuation techniques, including discounted cash flows and market multiple analyses. During the fourth quarter of fiscal 2007, we completed our annual impairment testing of our goodwill and tradenames, using the valuation techniques as described above, and determined there was no impairment.

The changes in the carrying amount of goodwill and tradenames by segment for continuing operations were as follows in fiscal 2007, 2006 and 2005:

	Goodwill			Tradenames		
	Domestic	International	Total	Domestic	International	Total
Balances at February 28, 2004	$ 3	$474	$477	$ —	$37	$ 37
Changes in foreign currency exchange rates	—	36	36	—	3	3
Balances at February 26, 2005	3	510	513	—	40	40
Changes in foreign currency exchange rates	—	40	40	—	4	4
Changes resulting from acquisitions	3	1	4	—	—	—
Balances at February 25, 2006	6	551	557	—	44	44
Changes resulting from acquisitions	369	27	396	17	21	38
Changes resulting from tax adjustment[1]	—	(21)	(21)	—	—	—
Changes in foreign currency exchange rates	—	(13)	(13)	—	(1)	(1)
Balances at March 3, 2007	$375	$544	$919	$17	$64	$ 81

[1] Adjustment related to the resolution of certain tax matters associated with our acquisition of Future Shop.

Lease Rights

Lease rights represent costs incurred to acquire the lease of a specific commercial property. Lease rights are recorded at cost and are amortized to rent expense over the remaining lease term, including renewal periods, if reasonably assured. Amortization periods range up to 16 years, beginning with the date we take possession of the property.

The gross cost and accumulated amortization of lease rights were $32 and $13 at March 3, 2007; and $29 and $10 at February 25, 2006. Lease rights amortization was $4, $3 and $4 in fiscal 2007, 2006 and 2005, respectively. Current lease rights amortization is expected to be approximately $3 for each of the next five fiscal years.

Investments

Short-term and long-term investments are comprised of municipal and United States government debt securities as well as auction-rate securities and variable rate-demand notes. In accordance with SFAS No. 115, *Accounting for Certain Investments in Debt and Equity Securities*, and based on our ability to market and sell these instruments, we classify auction-rate securities, variable-rate demand notes and other investments in debt securities as available-for-sale and carry them at amortized cost, which approximates fair value. Auction-rate securities and variable-rate demand notes are similar to short-term debt instruments because their interest rates are reset periodically. Investments in these securities can be sold for cash on the auction date. We classify auction-rate securities and variable-rate demand notes as short-term or long-term investments based on the reset dates.

$ in millions, except per share amounts

In accordance with our investment policy, we place our investments with issuers who have high-quality credit and limit the amount of investment exposure to any one issuer. We seek to preserve principal and minimize exposure to interest-rate fluctuations by limiting default risk, market risk and reinvestment risk.

We also hold investments in marketable equity securities and classify them as available-for-sale. Investments in marketable equity securities are included in other assets in our consolidated balance sheets. Investments in marketable equity securities are reported at fair value, based on quoted market prices when available. All unrealized holding gains or losses are reflected net of tax in accumulated other comprehensive income in shareholders' equity.

We review the key characteristics of our debt and marketable equity securities portfolio and their classification in accordance with GAAP on an annual basis, or when indications of potential impairment exist. If a decline in the fair value of a security is deemed by management to be other than temporary, the cost basis of the investment is written down to fair value, and the amount of the write-down is included in the determination of net earnings.

Insurance

We are self-insured for certain losses related to health, workers' compensation and general liability claims, although we obtain third-party insurance coverage to limit our exposure to these claims. A portion of these self-insured losses is managed through a wholly-owned insurance captive. We estimate our self-insured liabilities using a number of factors including historical claims experience, an estimate of incurred but not reported claims, demographic factors, severity factors and valuations provided by independent third-party actuaries. Our self-insurance liabilities included in the consolidated balance sheets were as follows:

	March 3, 2007	Feb. 25, 2006
Accrued liabilities	$51	$83
Long-term liabilities	44	—
Total	$95	$83

Inventory Financing

We have inventory financing facilities through which certain suppliers receive payments from a designated finance company on invoices we owe them. Amounts due under the facilities are collateralized by a security interest in certain merchandise inventories. The amounts extended bear interest, if we exceed certain terms, at rates specified in the agreements. We impute interest based on our borrowing rate where there is an average balance outstanding. Imputed interest is not significant. Certain agreements have provisions that entitle the lenders to a portion of the cash discounts provided by the suppliers.

At March 3, 2007, and February 25, 2006, $39 and $59, respectively, were outstanding and included in accrued liabilities on our consolidated balance sheets; and $196 and $177, respectively, were available for use under these inventory financing facilities.

Borrowings and payments on our inventory financing facilities were classified as financing activities in our consolidated statements of cash flows in other, net.

Income Taxes

We account for income taxes under the liability method. Under this method, deferred tax assets and liabilities are recognized for the estimated future tax consequences attributable to differences between the financial statement carrying amounts of existing assets and liabilities and their respective tax bases, and operating loss and tax credit carryforwards. Deferred tax assets and liabilities are measured using enacted income tax rates in effect for the year in which those temporary differences are expected to be recovered or settled. The effect on deferred tax assets and liabilities of a change in income tax rates is recognized in our consolidated statement of earnings in the period that includes the enactment date. A valuation allowance is recorded to reduce the carrying amounts of deferred tax assets if it is more likely than not that such assets will not be realized.

In determining our provision for income taxes, we use an annual effective income tax rate based on annual income, permanent differences between book and tax income, and statutory income tax rates. The effective income tax rate also reflects our assessment of the ultimate outcome of tax audits. We adjust our annual effective income tax rate as additional information on outcomes or events becomes available. Discrete events such as audit settlements or changes in tax laws are recognized in the period in which they occur.

Our income tax returns, like those of most companies, are periodically audited by domestic and foreign tax authorities. These audits include questions regarding our tax filing positions, including the timing and amount of deductions and the allocation of income among various tax jurisdictions. At any one time, multiple tax years are subject to audit by the various tax authorities. In evaluating the exposures associated with our various tax filing positions, we record reserves for probable exposures. A number of years may elapse before a particular matter, for which we have established a reserve, is audited and fully resolved or clarified. We adjust our tax contingencies reserve and income tax provision in the period in which actual results of a settlement with tax authorities differs from our established reserve, the statute of limitations expires for the relevant taxing authority to examine the tax position or when more information becomes available. We include our tax contingencies reserve, including accrued penalties and interest, in accrued income taxes on our consolidated balance sheets and in income tax expense in our consolidated statements of earnings.

In July 2006, the FASB issued FASB Interpretation ("FIN") No. 48, *Accounting for Uncertainty in Income Taxes, an Interpretation of FASB Statement No. 109.* In May 2007, the FASB issued FSP FIN No. 48-1, *Definition of "Settlement" in FASB Interpretation No.48.* We will adopt FIN No. 48 and FSP FIN No. 48-1 beginning in the first quarter of fiscal 2008. See *New Accounting Standards* below for further details.

Long-Term Liabilities

The major components of long-term liabilities at March 3, 2007, and February 25, 2006, included long-term rent-related liabilities, deferred compensation plan liabilities, self-insurance reserves and advances received under vendor alliance programs.

Foreign Currency

Foreign currency denominated assets and liabilities are translated into U.S. dollars using the exchange rates in effect at our consolidated balance sheet date. Results of operations and cash flows are translated using the average exchange rates throughout the period. The effect of exchange rate fluctuations on translation of assets and liabilities is included as a component of shareholders' equity in accumulated other comprehensive income. Gains and losses from foreign currency transactions, which are included in SG&A, have not been significant.

Revenue Recognition

We recognize revenue when the sales price is fixed or determinable, collectibility is reasonably assured and the customer takes possession of the merchandise, or in the case of services, at the time the service is provided. Amounts billed to customers for shipping and handling are included in revenue. Revenue is reported net of estimated sales returns and excludes sales taxes.

We estimate our sales returns reserve based on historical return rates. We initially established our sales returns reserve in the fourth quarter of fiscal 2005. Our sales returns reserve was $104 and $78, at March 3, 2007, and February 25, 2006, respectively.

We sell extended service contracts on behalf of an unrelated third party. In jurisdictions where we are not deemed to be the obligor on the contract, commissions are recognized in revenue at the time of sale. In jurisdictions where we are deemed to be the obligor on the contract, commissions are recognized in revenue ratably over the term of the service contract. Commissions represented 2.2%, 2.5% and 2.6% of revenues in fiscal 2007, 2006 and 2005, respectively.

For revenue transactions that involve multiple deliverables, we defer the revenue associated with any undelivered elements. The amount of revenue deferred in connection with the undelivered elements is determined using the relative fair value of each element, which is generally based on each element's relative retail price. See additional information regarding our customer loyalty program in *Sales Incentives* below.

Gift Cards

We sell gift cards to our customers in our retail stores, through our Web sites, and through selected third parties. We do not charge administrative fees on unused gift cards and our gift cards do not have an expiration date. We recognize income from gift cards when: (i) the gift card is redeemed by the customer; or (ii) the likelihood of the gift card being redeemed by the customer is remote ("gift card breakage") and we determine that we do not have a legal obligation to remit the value of unredeemed gift cards to the relevant jurisdictions. We determine our gift card breakage rate based upon historical redemption patterns. Based on our historical information, the likelihood of a gift card remaining unredeemed can be determined 24 months after the gift card is issued. At that time, we recognize breakage income for those cards for which the likelihood of redemption is deemed remote and we do not have a legal obligation to remit the value of such unredeemed gift cards to the relevant jurisdictions. Gift card breakage income is included in revenue in our consolidated statements of earnings.

We began recognizing gift card breakage income during the third quarter of fiscal 2006. Gift card breakage income was as follows in fiscal 2007, 2006 and 2005:

	2007[1]	2006[1]	2005
Gift card breakage income	$ 46	$ 43	$ —

[1] Due to the resolution of certain legal matters associated with gift card liabilities, we recognized $19 and $27 of gift card breakage income in fiscal 2007 and 2006, respectively, that related to prior fiscal years.

Sales Incentives

We frequently offer sales incentives that entitle our customers to receive a reduction in the price of a product or service. Sales incentives include discounts, coupons and other offers that entitle a customer to receive a reduction in the price of a product or service by submitting a claim for a refund or rebate. For sales incentives issued to a customer in conjunction with a sale of merchandise or services, for which we are the obligor, the reduction in revenue is recognized at the time of sale, based on the retail value of the incentive expected to be redeemed.

Customer Loyalty Program

We have a customer loyalty program which allows members to earn points for each qualifying purchase. Points earned enable members to receive a certificate that may be redeemed on future purchases at U.S. Best Buy stores. There are two ways that members may participate and earn loyalty points.

First, we have a customer loyalty card where members earn points for each purchase completed at U.S. Best Buy stores or through our BestBuy.com Web site. We account for our customer loyalty program in accordance with Emerging Issues Task Force ("EITF") Issue No. 00-22, *Accounting for "Points" and Certain Other Time-Based or Volume-Based Sales Incentive Offers, and Offers for Free Products or Services to Be Delivered in the Future*. The retail value of points earned by our customer loyalty members is included in accrued liabilities and recorded as a reduction of revenue at the time the points are earned, based on the percentage of points that are projected to be redeemed. Prior to October 2006, we charged a loyalty program membership fee which was initially deferred and then recognized in revenue ratably over the membership period. Beginning in October 2006, we no longer charge a membership fee for our customer loyalty program.

Second, we have a co-branded credit card agreement with a third-party bank (the "Bank") for the issuance of a customer loyalty credit card bearing the Best Buy brand. Cardholders earn points for qualifying purchases, including purchases made at Best Buy. Points earned enable cardholders to receive certificates that may be redeemed on future purchases at U.S. Best Buy stores. The Bank is the sole owner of the accounts issued under the program and absorbs losses associated with non-payment by the cardholders and fraudulent usage of the accounts. We are responsible for redeeming the points earned by the cardholders. The Bank pays fees to us based on the number of credit card accounts activated and card usage, and reimburses us for certain costs associated with the program. In accordance with EITF No. 00-21, *Revenue Arrangements with Multiple Deliverables*, we defer revenue received from cardholder account activations and recognize revenue on a straight-line basis over the remaining term of the agreement. Card usage fees are recognized in revenue as actual credit card usage occurs.

$ in millions, except per share amounts

Cost of Goods Sold and Selling, General and Administrative Expenses

The following table illustrates the primary costs classified in each major expense category:

Cost of Goods Sold	SG&A

• Total cost of products sold including:
  —Freight expenses associated with moving merchandise inventories from our vendors to our distribution centers;
  —Vendor allowances that are not a reimbursement of specific, incremental and identifiable costs to promote a vendor's products; and
  —Cash discounts on payments to vendors;
• Cost of services provided including;
  —Payroll and benefits costs for services employees; and
  —Cost of replacement parts and related freight expenses;
• Physical inventory losses;
• Markdowns;
• Customer shipping and handling expenses;
• Costs associated with operating our distribution network, including payroll and benefit costs, occupancy costs, and depreciation;
• Freight expenses associated with moving merchandise inventories from our distribution centers to our retail stores; and
• Promotional financing costs.
	• Payroll and benefit costs for retail and corporate employees;
	• Occupancy costs of retail, services and corporate facilities;
	• Depreciation related to retail, services and corporate assets;
	• Advertising;
	• Vendor allowances that are a reimbursement of specific, incremental and identifiable costs to promote a vendor's products;
	• Charitable contributions;
	• Outside service fees;
	• Long-lived asset impairment charges; and
	• Other administrative costs, such as credit card service fees, supplies, and travel and lodging.

Vendor Allowances

We receive vendor allowances for various programs, primarily volume incentives and reimbursements for specific costs such as markdowns, margin protection, advertising and sales incentives. Vendor allowances provided as reimbursement of specific, incremental and identifiable costs incurred to promote a vendor's products are included as an expense reduction when the cost is incurred. All other vendor allowances, including vendor allowances received in excess of our cost to promote a vendor's product, are initially deferred and recorded as a reduction of merchandise inventories. The deferred amounts are then included as a reduction of cost of goods sold when the related product is sold.

Vendor allowances included in revenue for reimbursement of vendor-provided sales incentives and in SG&A for reimbursement of specific, incremental and identifiable SG&A costs to promote a vendor's products were as follows in fiscal 2007, 2006 and 2005:

	2007	2006	2005
Revenue	$ 29	$141	$ 85
SG&A	$158	$138	$140

Advertising Costs

Advertising costs, which are included in SG&A, are expensed the first time the advertisement runs. Advertising costs consist primarily of print and television advertisements as well as promotional events. Net advertising expenses were $692, $644 and $597 in fiscal 2007, 2006 and 2005, respectively. Allowances received from vendors for advertising of $140, $123 and $115, in fiscal 2007, 2006 and 2005, respectively, were classified as reductions of advertising expenses.

Pre-Opening Costs

Non-capital expenditures associated with opening new stores are expensed as incurred.

Stock-Based Compensation

SFAS No. 123(R)

At the beginning of fiscal 2006, we early-adopted the fair value recognition provisions of SFAS No. 123 (revised 2004), *Share-Based Payment* (123(R)), requiring us to recognize expense related to the fair value of our stock-

PART II

based compensation awards. We elected the modified prospective transition method as permitted by SFAS No. 123(R). Under this transition method, stock-based compensation expense in fiscal 2007 and 2006 includes: (i) compensation expense for all stock-based compensation awards granted prior to, but not yet vested as of February 26, 2005, based on the grant date fair value estimated in accordance with the original provisions of SFAS No. 123, *Accounting for Stock-Based Compensation*; and (ii) compensation expense for all stock-based compensation awards granted subsequent to February 26, 2005, based on the grant-date fair value estimated in accordance with the provisions of SFAS No. 123(R). We recognize compensation expense on a straight-line basis over the requisite service period of the award (or to an employee's eligible retirement date, if earlier). Total stock-based compensation expense included in our consolidated statement of earnings in fiscal 2007 and 2006 was $121 ($82, net of tax) and $132 ($87, net of tax), respectively. In accordance with the modified prospective transition method of SFAS No. 123(R), financial results for prior periods have not been restated.

APB Opinion No. 25

Prior to fiscal 2006, we applied Accounting Principles Board ("APB") Opinion No. 25, *Accounting for Stock Issued to Employees*, and related Interpretations in accounting for stock-based compensation awards. Prior to fiscal 2006, no stock-based compensation expense was recognized in our consolidated statements of earnings for non-qualified stock options ("stock options"), as the exercise price was equal to the market price of our stock on the date of grant. In addition, we did not recognize any stock-based compensation expense for our employee stock purchase plan ("ESPP"), as it was intended to be a plan that qualifies under Section 423 of the Internal Revenue Code of 1986, as amended. However, we did recognize stock-based compensation expense for share awards.

We recognized compensation expense for time-based share awards on a straight-line basis over the vesting period (or to an employee's eligible retirement date, if earlier) based on the fair value of the award on the grant date. We recognized compensation expense for market-based share awards based on the current stock price, the number of

shares expected to ultimately vest and the vesting period. Outside valuation advisors assisted us in determining the number of shares ultimately expected to vest. We recognized compensation expense for performance-based awards on a straight-line basis over the requisite service period (or to an employee's eligible retirement date, if earlier) based on management's estimate of the likelihood of achieving company or personal performance goals. If an award recipient's relationship with us is terminated, all shares still subject to restrictions are forfeited and returned to the plan.

Stock-based compensation income recognized in fiscal 2005 on a pre-tax basis was $1. The fiscal 2005 income reflects a change in vesting assumptions based on our total shareholder return relative to the performance of the Standard & Poor's 500 Index ("S&P 500") and an increase in our expected forfeiture rate.

Transition

In November 2005, the FASB issued FSP No. FAS 123(R)-3, *Transition Election Related to Accounting for Tax Effects of Share-Based Payment Awards*. During the third quarter of fiscal 2007, we elected to adopt the alternative transition method provided in FSP No. FAS 123(R)-3 to calculate the tax effects of stock-based compensation. The alternative transition method includes simplified methods to determine the beginning balance of the additional paid-in capital ("APIC") pool related to the tax effects of stock-based compensation, and to determine the subsequent impact on the APIC pool and the statement of cash flows of the tax effects of stock-based awards that were fully vested and outstanding upon the adoption of SFAS No. 123(R).

In accordance with SFAS No. 154, *Accounting Changes and Error Corrections*, this change in accounting principle has been applied retrospectively to our fiscal 2006 consolidated statement of cash flows. The effect on the consolidated statement of cash flows was a decrease in operating activities with an offsetting increase in financing activities of $22 in fiscal 2006. The adoption of FSP No. FAS 123(R)-3 did not have an impact on our operating income, net earnings or shareholders' equity.

$ in millions, except per share amounts

The table below illustrates the effect on net earnings and earnings per share as if we had applied the fair value recognition provisions of SFAS No. 123 to stock-based compensation in fiscal 2005:

Net earnings, as reported	$ 984
Add: Stock-based compensation income included in reported net earnings, net of tax[1]	(1)
Deduct: Stock-based compensation expense determined under fair value method for all awards, net of tax[2]	(60)
Net earnings, pro forma	$ 923
Earnings per share:	
Basic — as reported	$2.01
Basic — pro forma	$1.89
Diluted — as reported	$1.96
Diluted — pro forma	$1.87

[1] Amount represents the stock-based compensation costs, net of tax, recognized under APB Opinion No. 25.

[2] In the fourth quarter of fiscal 2005, we increased our expected participant stock option forfeiture rate as a result of transferring to a third-party provider certain corporate employees, and the departure of certain senior executives. This higher level of expected stock option forfeitures reduced our fiscal 2005 pro forma stock-based compensation expense. Fiscal 2005 pro forma stock-based compensation expense may not be indicative of future stock-based compensation expense.

The weighted-average fair value of stock options granted during fiscal 2005 used in computing pro forma compensation expense was $14.18 per share. The fair value of each stock option was estimated on the date of grant using the Black-Scholes option-pricing model with the following assumptions in fiscal 2005:

Risk-free interest rate[1]	3.4%
Expected dividend yield	0.9%
Expected stock price volatility[2]	40%
Expected life of stock options[3]	5.5 years

[1] Based on the five-year U.S. Treasury constant maturity interest rate whose term is consistent with the expected life of our stock options.

[2] We used an outside valuation advisor to assist us in projecting the expected stock price volatility. We considered both historical data and observable market prices of similar equity instruments.

[3] We estimated the expected life of stock options based upon historical experience.

New Accounting Standards

In July 2006, the FASB issued FIN No. 48, *Accounting for Uncertainty in Income Taxes, an Interpretation of FASB Statement No. 109.* FIN No. 48 provides guidance regarding the recognition, measurement, presentation and disclosure in the financial statements of tax positions taken or expected to be taken on a tax return, including the decision whether to file or not to file in a particular jurisdiction. FIN No. 48 is effective for fiscal years beginning after December 15, 2006. We will adopt FIN No. 48 beginning in the first quarter of fiscal 2008. The cumulative effect of applying the provisions of FIN No. 48 upon initial adoption will be reported as an adjustment to retained earnings as of the beginning of fiscal 2008. We are evaluating the impact, if any, the adoption of FIN No. 48 will have on our operating income, net earnings or retained earnings.

In May 2007, the FASB issued FSP FIN No. 48-1, *Definition of "Settlement" in FASB Interpretation No. 48.* FSP FIN No. 48-1 provides guidance on how a company should determine whether a tax position is effectively settled for the purpose of recognizing previously unrecognized tax benefits. FSP FIN No. 48-1 is effective upon initial adoption of FIN No. 48, which we will adopt in the first quarter of fiscal 2008, as indicated above.

In September 2006, the U.S. Securities and Exchange Commission ("SEC") issued Staff Accounting Bulletin ("SAB") No. 108, *Considering the Effects of Prior Year Misstatements when Quantifying Misstatements in Current Year Financial Statements*, which provides interpretive guidance on the consideration of the effects of prior-year misstatements in quantifying current-year misstatements for the purpose of a materiality assessment. SAB No. 108 is effective for fiscal years ending after November 15, 2006.

$ in millions, except per share amounts

We adopted SAB No. 108 in the fourth quarter of fiscal 2007. The cumulative effect of initially applying the provisions of SAB No. 108, may be reported as a cumulative adjustment to retained earnings at the beginning of the year of adoption. The adoption of SAB No. 108 had no impact on our net earnings or financial position.

In September 2006, the FASB issued SFAS No. 157, *Fair Value Measurements*. SFAS No. 157 defines fair value, establishes a framework for measuring fair value in generally accepted accounting principles and expands disclosures about fair value measurements. SFAS No. 157 applies under other accounting pronouncements that require or permit fair value measurements, the FASB having previously concluded in those accounting pronouncements that fair value is the relevant measurement attribute. Accordingly, SFAS No. 157 does not require any new fair value measurements. SFAS No. 157 is effective for fiscal years beginning after December 15, 2007. We plan to adopt SFAS No. 157 beginning in the first quarter of fiscal 2009. We are evaluating the impact, if any, the adoption of SFAS No. 157 will have on our operating income or net earnings.

In February 2007, the FASB issued SFAS No. 159, *The Fair Value Option for Financial Assets and Financial Liabilities*. SFAS No. 159 permits companies to choose to measure many financial instruments and certain other items at fair value. The objective is to improve financial reporting by providing companies with the opportunity to mitigate volatility in reported earnings caused by measuring related assets and liabilities differently without having to apply complex hedge accounting provisions. SFAS No. 159 is effective for fiscal years beginning after November 15, 2007. Companies are not allowed to adopt SFAS No. 159 on a retrospective basis unless they choose early adoption. We plan to adopt SFAS No. 159 at the beginning of fiscal 2009. We are evaluating the impact, if any, the adoption of SFAS No. 159 will have on our operating income or net earnings.

2. Discontinued Operations

In fiscal 2004, we sold our interest in Musicland. The buyer assumed all of Musicland's liabilities, including approximately $500 in lease obligations and paid no cash consideration, in exchange for all of the capital stock of Musicland. The transaction also resulted in the transfer of all of Musicland's assets, other than a distribution center in Franklin, Indiana, and selected nonoperating assets.

On March 25, 2005, we received notification from the Internal Revenue Service ("IRS") of a favorable resolution of outstanding tax matters regarding the disposition of our interest in Musicland. Based on the agreement with the IRS, we reversed previously recorded valuation allowances on deferred tax assets related to the disposition of our interest in Musicland and recognized a $50 tax benefit in fiscal 2005.

In accordance with SFAS No. 144, Musicland's financial results are reported separately as discontinued operations for all periods presented. No assets or liabilities of Musicland were included in our consolidated balance sheets at March 3, 2007, or February 25, 2006.

3. Acquisitions

Pacific Sales Kitchen and Bath Centers, Inc.

On March 7, 2006, we acquired all of the common stock of Pacific Sales for $411, or $408, net of cash acquired, including transaction costs. We acquired Pacific Sales, a high-end home-improvement and appliance retailer, to enhance our ability to grow with an affluent customer base and premium brands using a proven and successful showroom format. Utilizing the existing store format, we expect to expand the number of stores in order to capitalize on the expanding high-end segment of the U.S. appliance market. The acquisition was accounted for using the purchase method in accordance with SFAS No. 141, *Business Combinations*. Accordingly, we recorded the net assets at their estimated fair values, and included operating results in our Domestic segment from the date of acquisition. We allocated the purchase price on a preliminary basis using information then available. The allocation of the purchase price to the assets and liabilities acquired was finalized in the fourth quarter of fiscal 2007. There were no significant adjustments to the preliminary purchase price allocation. All goodwill is deductible for tax purposes.

USING A CALCULATOR AND COMPUTER KEYPAD

KINDS OF CALCULATORS

Many different models of calculators, both desktop and handheld, are available. All calculators have their own features and particular placement of operating keys. Therefore, it is necessary to refer to the operator's manual for specific instructions and locations of the operating keys for the calculator being used. A typical keyboard of a desktop calculator is shown in the illustration.

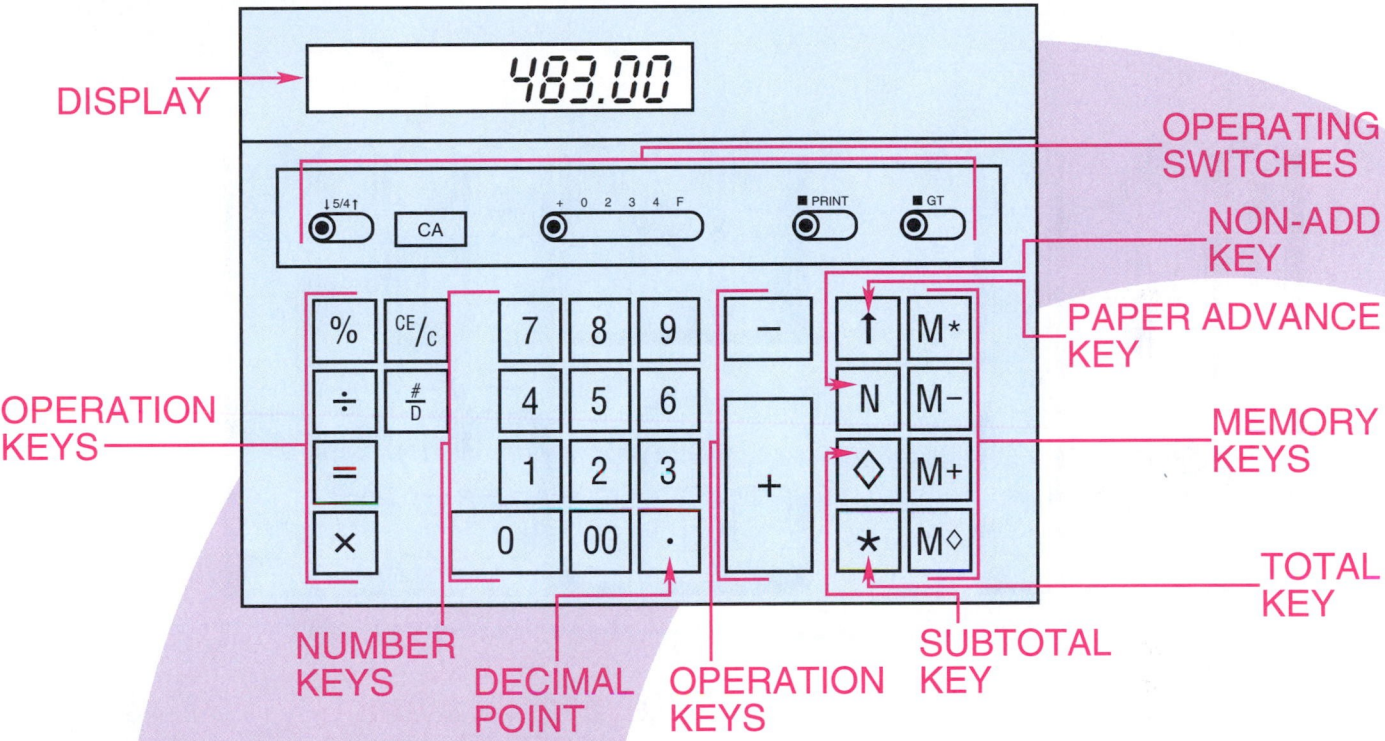

DISPLAY

OPERATING SWITCHES

NON-ADD KEY

PAPER ADVANCE KEY

OPERATION KEYS

MEMORY KEYS

TOTAL KEY

NUMBER KEYS

DECIMAL POINT

OPERATION KEYS

SUBTOTAL KEY

DESKTOP CALCULATOR SETTINGS

Several operating switches on a desktop calculator must be engaged before the calculator will produce the desired results.

The *decimal selector* sets the appropriate decimal places necessary for the numbers that will be entered. For example, if the decimal selector is set at 2, both the numbers entered and the answer will have two decimal places. If the decimal selector is set at F, the calculator automatically sets the decimal places. The F setting allows the answer to be unrounded and carried out to the maximum number of decimal places possible.

The *decimal rounding selector* rounds the answers. The down arrow position will drop any digits beyond the last digit desired. The up arrow position will drop any digits beyond the last digit desired and round the last digit up. In the 5/4 position, the calculator rounds the last desired digit up only when the following digit is 5 or greater. If the following digit is less than 5, the last desired digit remains unchanged.

The *GT* or *grand total switch* in the on position accumulates totals.

The computer has a keypad on the right side of the keyboard, called the *numeric keypad*. Even though several styles of keyboards are found, there are two basic layouts for the numeric keypad. The standard layout and enhanced layout are shown in the illustration. On the standard keyboard, the directional arrow keys are found on the number keys. To use the numbers, press the key called *Num Lock*. (This key is found above the "7" key.) When the Num Lock is turned on, numbers are entered when the keys on the keypad are pressed. When the Num Lock is off, the arrow, Home, Page Up, Page Down, End, Insert, and Delete keys can be used.

The enhanced keyboards have the arrow keys and the other directional keys mentioned above to the left of the numeric keypad. When using the keypad on an enhanced keyboard, Num Lock can remain on.

The asterisk (*) performs a different function on the computer than the calculator. The asterisk on the calculator is used for the total while the computer uses it for multiplication.

Another difference is the division key. The computer key is the forward slash key (/). The calculator key uses the division key (÷).

Standard Keyboard Layout

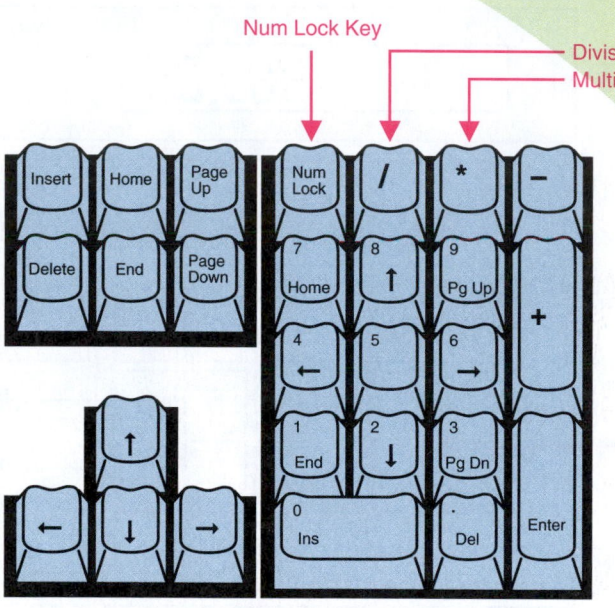

Enhanced Keyboard Layout

Striking the numbers 0 to 9 on a calculator or numeric keypad without looking at the keyboard is called the *touch system*. Using the touch system develops both speed and accuracy.

The 4, 5, and 6 keys are called the *home row*. If the right hand is used for the keyboard, the index finger is placed on the 4 key, the middle finger on the 5 key, and the ring finger on the 6 key. If the left hand is used, the ring finger is placed on the 4 key, the middle finger on the 5 key, and the index finger on the 6 key.

Place the fingers on the home row keys. Curve the fingers and keep the wrist straight. These keys may feel slightly concaved or the 5 key may have a raised dot. The differences in the home row allow the operator to recognize the home row by touch rather than by sight.

Maintain the position of the fingers on the home row. The finger used to strike the 4 key will also strike the 7 key and the 1 key. Stretch the finger up to reach the 7; then stretch the finger down to reach the 1 key. Visualize the position of these keys.

Again, place the fingers on the home row. Stretch the finger that strikes the 5 key up to reach the 8 key, then down to reach the 2 key. Likewise, stretch the finger that strikes the 6 key up to strike the 9 and down to strike the 3 key. This same finger will stretch down again to hit the decimal point.

If the right hand is used, the thumb will be used to strike the 0 and 00 keys and the little finger to strike the addition key. If the left hand is used, the little finger will be used to strike the 0 and 00 keys and the thumb to strike the addition key.

HANDHELD CALCULATORS

Handheld calculators are slightly different from desktop calculators, not only in their size and features but also in their operation. Refer to the operator's manual for specific instructions for the calculator being used.

On a handheld calculator, the numeric keys are usually very close together. In addition, the keys do not respond to touch as easily as on a desktop calculator. Therefore, the touch system is usually not used on a handheld calculator.

PERFORMING MATHEMATICAL OPERATIONS ON DESKTOP CALCULATORS

Mathematical operations can be performed on a calculator both quickly and efficiently. The basic operations of addition, subtraction, multiplication, and division are used frequently on a calculator.

Addition

Each number to be added is called an *addend*. The answer to an addition problem is called the *sum*.

Addition is performed by entering an addend and striking the addition key (+). All numbers are entered on a calculator in the exact order they are given. To enter the number 4,455.65, strike the 4, 4, 5, 5, decimal, 6, and 5 keys in that order, and then strike the addition key. Commas are not entered. Continue in this manner until all addends have been entered. To obtain the sum, strike the total key on the calculator.

Subtraction

The top number or first number of a subtraction problem is called the *minuend*. The number to be subtracted from the minuend is called the *subtrahend*. The answer to a subtraction problem is called the *difference*.

Subtraction is performed by first entering the minuend and striking the addition key (+). The subtrahend is then entered, followed by the minus key (−), followed by the total key.

Multiplication

The number to be multiplied is called the *multiplicand*. The number of times the multiplicand will be multiplied is called the *multiplier*. The answer to a multiplication problem is called the *product*.

Multiplication is performed by entering the multiplicand and striking the multiplication key (×). The multiplier is then entered, followed by the equals key (=). The calculator will automatically multiply and give the product.

Division

The number to be divided is called the *dividend*. The number the dividend will be divided by is called the *divisor*. The answer to a division problem is called the *quotient*.

Division is performed by entering the dividend and striking the division key (÷). The divisor is then entered, followed by the equals key (=). The calculator will automatically divide and give the quotient.

Correcting Errors

If an error is made while using a calculator, several methods of correction may be used. If an incorrect number has been entered and the addition key or equals key has not yet been struck, strike the clear entry (CE) key one time. This key will clear only the last number that was entered. However, if the clear entry key is depressed more than one time, the entire problem will be cleared on some calculators. If an incorrect number has been entered and the addition key has been struck, strike the minus key one time only. This will automatically subtract the last number added, thus removing it from the total.

PERFORMING MATHEMATICAL OPERATIONS ON COMPUTERS AND HANDHELD CALCULATORS

On a computer keypad or a handheld calculator, addition is performed in much the same way as on a desktop calculator. However, after the + key is depressed, the display usually shows the accumulated total. Therefore, the total key is not found. Some computer programs will not calculate the total until Enter is pressed.

Subtraction is performed differently on many computer keypads and handheld calculators. The minuend is usually entered, followed by the minus (−) key. Then the subtrahend is entered. Pressing either the + key or the = key will display the difference. Some computer programs will not calculate the difference until Enter is pressed.

Multiplication and division are performed the same way on a computer keypad and handheld calculator as on a desktop calculator. Keep in mind that computers use the * for multiplication and / for division.

SAFETY CONCERNS

Whenever electrical equipment such as a calculator or computer is being operated in a classroom or office, several safety rules apply. These rules protect the operator of the equipment, other persons in the environment, and the equipment itself.

1. Do not unplug equipment by pulling on the electrical cord. Instead, grasp the plug at the outlet and remove it.
2. Do not stretch electrical cords across an aisle where someone might trip over them.
3. Avoid food and beverages near the equipment where a spill might result in an electrical short.
4. Do not attempt to remove the cover of a calculator, computer, or keyboard for any reason while the power is turned on.
5. Do not attempt to repair equipment while it is plugged in.
6. Always turn the power off or unplug equipment when finished using it.

CALCULATION DRILLS

Instructions for Desktop Calculators
Complete each drill using the touch method. Set the decimal selector at the setting indicated in each drill. Compare the answer on the calculator to the answer in the book. If the two are the same, progress to the next problem. It is not necessary to enter 00 in the cents column if the decimal selector is set at 0-F. However, digits other than zeros in the cents column must be entered preceded by a decimal point.

Instructions for Computer Keypads
Complete each drill using the touch method. There is no decimal selector on computer keypads. Set the number of decimal places as directed in the instructions for the computer program. In spreadsheets, for example, use the formatting options to set the number of decimal places. When the drill indicates "F" for floating, leave the computer application in its default format. Compare the answer on the computer monitor to the answer in the book. If the two are the same, progress to the next problem. It is not necessary to enter 00 in the cents column. However, digits other than zeros in the cents column must be entered, preceded by a decimal point.

DRILL C-1 Performing addition using the home row keys
Decimal Selector—2

4.00	44.00	444.00	4,444.00	44,444.00
5.00	55.00	555.00	5,555.00	55,555.00
6.00	66.00	666.00	6,666.00	66,666.00
5.00	45.00	455.00	4,455.00	44,556.00
4.00	46.00	466.00	4,466.00	44,565.00
5.00	54.00	544.00	5,544.00	55,446.00
6.00	56.00	566.00	5,566.00	55,664.00
5.00	65.00	655.00	6,655.00	66,554.00
4.00	64.00	644.00	6,644.00	66,555.00
5.00	66.00	654.00	6,545.00	65,465.00
49.00	561.00	5,649.00	56,540.00	565,470.00

DRILL C-2 Performing addition using the 0, 1, 4, and 7 keys
Decimal Selector—2

4.00	11.00	444.00	4,440.00	44,000.00
7.00	44.00	777.00	7,770.00	77,000.00
4.00	74.00	111.00	1,110.00	11,000.00
1.00	71.00	741.00	4,400.00	41,000.00
4.00	70.00	740.00	1,100.00	71,000.00
7.00	10.00	101.00	4,007.00	10,000.00
4.00	14.00	140.00	7,001.00	10,100.00
1.00	17.00	701.00	1,007.00	40,100.00
4.00	40.00	700.00	1,004.00	70,100.00
7.00	77.00	407.00	7,700.00	74,100.00
43.00	428.00	4,862.00	39,539.00	448,400.00

DRILL C-3 Performing addition using the 2, 5, and 8 keys
Decimal Selector—2

5.00	58.00	588.00	8,888.00	88,855.00
8.00	52.00	522.00	5,555.00	88,822.00
5.00	85.00	888.00	2,222.00	88,852.00
2.00	52.00	222.00	8,525.00	88,222.00
5.00	25.00	258.00	2,585.00	85,258.00
8.00	58.00	852.00	8,258.00	22,255.00
5.00	82.00	225.00	8,585.00	22,288.00
2.00	28.00	885.00	5,258.00	22,258.00
5.00	88.00	882.00	2,852.00	22,888.00
8.00	22.00	228.00	2,288.00	25,852.00
53.00	550.00	5,550.00	55,016.00	555,550.00

DRILL C-4   Performing addition using the 3, 6, 9, and decimal point keys
Decimal Selector—2

6.00	66.66	666.66	6,666.99	66,699.33
9.00	99.99	999.99	9,999.66	99,966.66
6.00	33.33	333.33	3,333.99	33,366.33
3.00	33.66	666.99	3,366.99	36,963.36
6.36	33.99	999.66	6,699.33	69,636.36
3.36	99.66	333.66	9,966.33	33,333.66
9.36	99.33	696.36	9,636.69	66,666.99
9.63	33.36	369.63	3,696.36	99,999.33
6.33	33.69	336.69	6,963.99	96,369.63
9.93	69.63	963.36	6,699.33	36,963.36
68.97	603.30	6,366.33	67,029.66	639,965.01

DRILL C-5   Performing subtraction using all number keys
Decimal Selector—F

456.73	789.01	741.00	852.55	987.98
−123.21	−456.00	−258.10	−369.88	−102.55
333.52	333.01	482.90	482.67	885.43

DRILL C-6   Performing multiplication using all number keys
Decimal Selector—F

654.05	975.01	487.10	123.56	803.75
× 12.66	× 27.19	× 30.21	× 50.09	× 1.45
8,280.273	26,510.5219	14,715.291	6,189.1204	1,165.4375

DRILL C-7   Performing division using all number keys
Decimal Selector—F

900.56	÷	450.28	=	2.
500.25	÷	100.05	=	5.
135.66	÷	6.65	=	20.4
269.155	÷	105.55	=	2.550023685*
985.66	÷	22.66	=	43.49779346*

Number of decimal places may vary, due to machine capacity.

RECYCLING PROBLEMS

RECYCLING PROBLEM 1-1

Determining how transactions change an accounting equation

Brian Frizza is a personal trainer and operates a business called FitnessPro. FitnessPro uses the accounts shown in the following accounting equation. Use the form given in the *Recycling Problem Working Papers* to complete this problem.

| Trans. No. | Assets | | | | = | Liabilities | + | Owner's Equity |
	Cash	+	Accts. Rec.— Dean Mills	+	Supplies	+	Prepaid Insurance	=	Accts. Pay.— Topline	+	Brian Frizza, Capital
Beg. Bal. 1.	2,200 −120		—0—		1,100		200		200		3,300 −120 (expense)
New Bal. 2.	2,080		—0—		1,100		200		200		3,180

Transactions:

1. Paid cash for telephone bill, $120.00.
2. Received cash from owner as an investment, $400.00.
3. Paid cash for rent, $600.00.
4. Received cash from sales, $425.00.
5. Bought supplies on account from Topline, $310.00.
6. Sold services on account to Dean Mills, $500.00.
7. Paid cash for supplies, $250.00.
8. Paid cash for advertising, $700.00.
9. Received cash on account from Dean Mills, $400.00.
10. Paid cash on account to Topline, $200.00.
11. Paid cash for insurance, $225.00.
12. Received cash from sales, $675.00.
13. Paid cash to owner for personal use, $1,000.00.

Instructions:

For each transaction, complete the following. Transaction 1 is given as an example.

1. Analyze the transaction to determine which accounts in the accounting equation are affected.
2. Write the amount in the appropriate columns, using a plus (+) if the account increases or a minus (−) if the account decreases.
3. For transactions that change owner's equity, write in parentheses a description of the transaction to the right of the amount.
4. Calculate the new balance for each account in the accounting equation.
5. Before going on to the next transaction, determine that the accounting equation is still in balance.

Analyzing transactions into debit and credit parts

Luke Harris owns a business called Colato Copies. Colato Copies uses the following accounts.

Cash
Accounts Receivable—Flowerama
Accounts Receivable—Seaside Inn
Supplies
Prepaid Insurance
Accounts Payable—Pacific Paper
Accounts Payable—Raffi Supplies
Luke Harris, Capital

Luke Harris, Drawing
Sales
Advertising Expense
Miscellaneous Expense
Rent Expense
Repair Expense
Utilities Expense

Instructions:

Use the forms given in the *Recycling Problem Working Papers*.

1. Prepare a T account for each account.

2. Analyze each transaction into its debit and credit parts. Write the debit and credit amounts in the proper T accounts to show how each transaction changes account balances. Write the date of the transaction in parentheses before each amount.

Transactions:

July 1. Received cash from owner as an investment, $4,500.00.

    2. Paid cash for rent, $520.00.

    4. Paid cash for supplies, $300.00.

    4. Received cash from sales, $400.00.

    5. Paid cash for insurance, $200.00.

    8. Sold services on account to Flowerama, $450.00.

    9. Bought supplies on account from Raffi Supplies, $700.00.

  10. Paid cash for rent, $120.00.

  11. Received cash from owner as an investment, $2,300.00.

  11. Received cash from sales, $800.00.

  12. Bought supplies on account from Pacific Paper, $300.00.

  13. Received cash on account from Flowerama, $250.00.

  15. Paid cash for miscellaneous expense, $40.00.

  16. Paid cash on account to Raffi Supplies, $350.00.

  22. Paid cash for electric bill (utilities expense), $70.00.

  23. Paid cash for advertising, $160.00.

  25. Sold services on account to Seaside Inn, $640.00.

  26. Paid cash to owner for personal use, $1,200.00.

  30. Received cash on account from Seaside Inn, $300.00.

Journalizing transactions and proving and ruling a journal

Adeline Stein owns a service business called Stein Express, which uses the following accounts:

Cash	Accts. Pay.—Rim Supply	Sales	Repair Expense
Supplies	Accts. Pay.— Parks Co.	Advertising Expense	Utilities Expense
Prepaid Insurance	Adeline Stein, Capital	Miscellaneous Expense	
Accts. Rec.—M. Bien	Adeline Stein, Drawing	Rent Expense	

Transactions:

Aug. 1. Received cash from owner as an investment, $8,750.00. R1.
2. Paid cash for supplies, $500.00. C1.
3. Paid cash for rent, $300.00. C2.
4. Bought supplies on account from Rim Supply, $1,200.00. M1.
5. Paid cash for electric bill, $250.00. C3.
8. Paid cash on account to Rim Supply, $700.00. C4.
8. Received cash from sales, $425.00. T8.
8. Sold services on account to M. Bien, $125.00. S1.
9. Paid cash for insurance, $1,900.00. C5.
10. Paid cash for miscellaneous expense, $27.00. C6.
10. Received cash from sales, $297.00. T10.
11. Paid cash for supplies, $770.00. C7.
11. Received cash from sales, $493.00. T11.
12. Received cash from sales, $294.00. T12.
15. Paid cash to owner for personal use, $125.00. C8.
15. Received cash from sales, $275.00. T15.
16. Paid cash for repairs, $88.00. C9.
17. Received cash on account from M. Bien, $125.00. R2.
17. Bought supplies on account from Parks Co., $345.00. M2.
17. Received cash from sales, $200.00. T17.
18. Received cash from sales, $600.00. T18.
19. Received cash from sales, $175.00. T19.
22. Bought supplies on account from Parks Co., $80.00. M3.
22. Received cash from sales, $450.00. T22.
23. Paid cash for telephone bill, $50.00. C10.
23. Sold services on account to M. Bien, $425.00. S2.
24. Paid cash for advertising, $80.00. C11.
24. Received cash from sales, $250.00. T24.
25. Received cash from sales, $325.00. T25.
26. Paid cash for supplies, $45.00. C12.
26. Received cash from sales, $310.00. T26.
29. Received cash on account from M. Bien, $425.00. R3.
30. Paid cash to owner for personal use, $150.00. C13.
31. Received cash from sales, $450.00. T31.

Instructions:

1. Use page 1 of the journal given in the *Recycling Problem Working Papers*. Journalize the transactions for August 1 through August 19 of the current year. Source documents are abbreviated as follows: check, C; memorandum, M; receipt, R; sales invoice, S; calculator tape, T.
2. Prove and rule page 1 of the journal. Carry the column totals forward to page 2 of the journal.
3. Use page 2 of the journal to journalize the transactions for the remainder of August.
4. Prove page 2 of the journal.
5. Prove cash. The beginning cash balance on August 1 is zero. The balance on the next unused check stub is $8,859.00.
6. Rule page 2 of the journal.

Journalizing transactions and posting to a general ledger

Janet Porter owns a service business called Porter's Parties. Porter's Parties' general ledger accounts are given in the *Recycling Problem Working Papers*.

Transactions:

Aug. 1. Received cash from owner as an investment, $4,500.00. R1.

3. Paid cash for supplies, $300.00. C1.

5. Sold services on account to Nicholas Calendo, $650.00. S1.

6. Received cash from sales, $630.00. T6.

9. Paid cash for electric bill, $130.00. C2.

11. Paid cash for rent, $530.00. C3.

13. Bought supplies on account from Jordan Supplies, $800.00. M1.

13. Received cash from sales, $650.00. T13.

16. Paid cash for miscellaneous expense, $55.00. C4.

18. Paid cash on account to Jordan Supplies, $500.00. C5.

20. Paid cash for supplies, $105.00. C6.

20. Received cash on account from Nicholas Calendo, $350.00. R2.

25. Paid cash for advertising, $250.00. C7.

27. Paid cash for supplies, $75.00. C8.

27. Received cash from sales, $1,200.00. T27.

30. Paid cash to owner for personal use, $800.00. C9.

31. Received cash from sales, $780.00. T31.

Instructions:

1. Open an account for Utilities Expense. Use the 3-digit numbering system described in the chapter.

2. Journalize the transactions completed during August of the current year. Use page 1 of a journal. Source documents are abbreviated as follows: check, C; memorandum, M; receipt, R; sales invoice, S; calculator tape, T.

3. Prove the journal.

4. Prove cash. The beginning cash balance on August 1 is zero. The balance on the next unused check stub is $5,365.00.

5. Rule the journal.

6. Post from the journal to the general ledger.

Reconciling a bank statement; journalizing a bank service charge, a dishonored check, and petty cash transactions

Tao Vang owns a business called Fast Print. Selected general ledger accounts are given below. Forms are given in the *Recycling Problem Working Papers*.

110 Cash	140 Prepaid Insurance	535 Repair Expense
115 Petty Cash	320 Tao Vang, Drawing	540 Supplies Expense
120 Accts. Rec.—Corner Cafe	520 Miscellaneous Expense	550 Utilities Expense
130 Supplies	530 Rent Expense	

Instructions:

1. Journalize the following transactions completed during May of the current year. Use page 12 of a journal. Source documents are abbreviated as follows: check, C; memorandum, M.

Transactions:

May 21. Paid cash to establish a petty cash fund, $150.00. C51.

24. Paid cash for supplies, $72.00. C52.

26. Paid cash for repairs, $85.00. C53.

27. Received notice from the bank of a dishonored check from Corner Cafe, $70.00, plus $25.00 fee; total, $95.00. M22.

28. Paid cash for miscellaneous expense, $42.00. C54.

31. Paid cash to owner for personal use, $200.00. C55.

31. Paid cash to replenish the petty cash fund, $105.00: supplies, $85.00; miscellaneous expense, $20.00. C56.

2. On May 31 of the current year, Fast Print received a bank statement dated May 30. Prepare a bank statement reconciliation. Use May 31 of the current year as the date. The following information is obtained from the May 30 bank statement and from the records of the business.

Bank statement balance	$1,586.00
Bank service charge	25.00
Outstanding deposit, May 31	285.00
Outstanding checks, Nos. 55 and 56	
Checkbook balance on Check Stub No. 57	$1,591.00

3. Continue using the journal and journalize the following transaction.

Transaction:

May 31. Received bank statement showing May bank service charge, $25.00. M23.

RECYCLING PROBLEM 6-1

Completing a work sheet

On February 28 of the current year, Hibbing Hair Care has the following general ledger accounts and balances. The business uses a monthly fiscal period.

Account Balances

Account Titles	Debit	Credit
Cash	$2,609.00	
Petty Cash	300.00	
Accounts Receivable—Robert Perpich	581.00	
Supplies	895.00	
Prepaid Insurance	1,200.00	
Accounts Payable—Ely Supplies		$ 450.00
Jens Miller-Smith, Capital		4,550.00
Jens Miller-Smith, Drawing	300.00	
Income Summary		
Sales		3,100.00
Advertising Expense	425.00	
Insurance Expense		
Miscellaneous Expense	250.00	
Rent Expense	1,100.00	
Supplies Expense		
Utilities Expense	440.00	

Instructions:

1. Prepare the heading and trial balance on the work sheet given in the *Recycling Problem Working Papers*. Total and rule the Trial Balance columns.

2. Analyze the following adjustment information into debit and credit parts. Record the adjustments on the work sheet.

Adjustment Information, February 28

Supplies inventory	$ 450.00
Value of prepaid insurance	1,000.00

3. Total and rule the Adjustments columns.

4. Extend the up-to-date balances to the Balance Sheet or Income Statement columns.

5. Rule a single line across the Income Statement and Balance Sheet columns. Total each column. Calculate and record the net income or net loss. Label the amount in the Account Title column.

6. Total and rule the Income Statement and Balance Sheet columns.

RECYCLING PROBLEM 7-1

Preparing financial statements

The following information is obtained from the work sheet of SuperClean for the month ended August 31 of the current year. Forms are given in the *Recycling Problem Working Papers*.

	ACCOUNT TITLE	INCOME STATEMENT DEBIT	INCOME STATEMENT CREDIT	BALANCE SHEET DEBIT	BALANCE SHEET CREDIT	
1	Cash			5 6 3 2 00		1
2	Accounts Receivable—D. Dawson			1 7 5 00		2
3	Accounts Receivable—K. Keene			3 1 5 00		3
4	Supplies			4 6 7 00		4
5	Prepaid Insurance			9 0 0 00		5
6	Accounts Payable—DV Supply				5 9 3 00	6
7	Accounts Payable—Supply Warehouse				7 0 0 00	7
8	Michelle Delist, Capital				5 0 3 1 00	8
9	Michelle Delist, Drawing			1 5 0 0 00		9
10	Income Summary					10
11	Sales		5 8 8 1 00			11
12	Advertising Expense	6 2 5 00				12
13	Insurance Expense	1 5 0 00				13
14	Miscellaneous Expense	1 4 5 00				14
15	Supplies Expense	9 2 5 00				15
16	Utilities Expense	1 3 7 1 00				16
17		3 2 1 6 00	5 8 8 1 00	8 9 8 9 00	6 3 2 4 00	17
18	Net Income	2 6 6 5 00			2 6 6 5 00	18
19		5 8 8 1 00	5 8 8 1 00	8 9 8 9 00	8 9 8 9 00	19
20						20

Instructions:

1. Prepare an income statement for the month ended August 31 of the current year.

2. Calculate and record the component percentages for total expenses and net income. Round percentage calculations to the nearest 0.1%.

3. Prepare a balance sheet for August 31 of the current year.

Journalizing adjusting and closing entries

The following information is obtained from the partial work sheet of SuperClean for the month ended August 31 of the current year.

	3	4	5	6	7	8	
	ADJUSTMENTS		INCOME STATEMENT		BALANCE SHEET		
ACCOUNT TITLE	DEBIT	CREDIT	DEBIT	CREDIT	DEBIT	CREDIT	
1 Cash					5 6 3 2 00		1
2 Accounts Receivable—D. Dawson					1 7 5 00		2
3 Accounts Receivable—K. Keene					3 1 5 00		3
4 Supplies		(a) 9 2 5 00			4 6 7 00		4
5 Prepaid Insurance		(b) 1 5 0 00			9 0 0 00		5
6 Accounts Payable—DV Supply						5 9 3 00	6
7 Accounts Payable—Supply Warehouse						7 0 0 00	7
8 Michelle Delist, Capital						5 0 3 1 00	8
9 Michelle Delist, Drawing					1 5 0 0 00		9
10 Income Summary							10
11 Sales				5 8 8 1 00			11
12 Advertising Expense			6 2 5 00				12
13 Insurance Expense	(b) 1 5 0 00		1 5 0 00				13
14 Miscellaneous Expense			1 4 5 00				14
15 Supplies Expense	(a) 9 2 5 00		9 2 5 00				15
16 Utilities Expense			1 3 7 1 00				16
17	1 0 7 5 00	1 0 7 5 00	3 2 1 6 00	5 8 8 1 00	8 9 8 9 00	6 3 2 4 00	17
18 Net Income			2 6 6 5 00			2 6 6 5 00	18
19			5 8 8 1 00	5 8 8 1 00	8 9 8 9 00	8 9 8 9 00	19
20							20

Instructions:

1. Use page 16 of the journal given in the *Recycling Problem Working Papers*. Journalize the adjusting entries.
2. Continue to use page 16 of the journal. Journalize the closing entries.

Journalizing purchases, cash payments, and other transactions

Backwoods, Inc., is a sporting goods store organized as a corporation.

Instructions:

1. Using the journals given in the *Recycling Problem Working Papers*, journalize the following transactions completed during August of the current year. Use page 9 of a purchases journal, page 15 of a cash payments journal, and page 12 of a general journal. Source documents are abbreviated as follows: check, C; memorandum, M; purchase invoice, P; debit memorandum, DM.

Transactions:

Aug. 1. Paid cash to Keller Realty for rent, $1,000.00. C772.

2. Paid cash to LWAP Radio for advertising, $720.00. C773.

3. Bought office supplies on account from Johnson Office Supply, $420.00. M62.

4. Paid cash on account to Arrowhead Supply, $4,210.00, covering P436. No cash discount was offered. C774.

6. Paid cash to City Utilities for electric bill, $420.00. C775.

7. Paid cash on account to Johnson Office Supply covering M62, less 2% discount. C776.

9. Paid cash to Mark's Discount Stores for store supplies, $224.00. C777.

9. Purchased merchandise on account from Peterson Sports, $3,560.00. P445.

11. Purchased merchandise for cash from Atlas Sports Co., $3,480.00, less a 60% trade discount. C778.

13. Returned merchandise to Peterson Sports from P445, $233.00. DM19.

13. Purchased merchandise for cash from Duck Crafts, $495.00. C779.

15. Returned merchandise to Evans Sports Corporation from P438, $112.00. DM20.

15. Paid cash on account to Peterson Sports covering P445 after a purchase return, DM19, less 2% discount. C780.

20. Purchased merchandise for cash from Atlas Sports Co., $156.00. C781.

21. Paid cash on account to Evans Sports Corporation, $1,950.00. No cash discount was offered. C782.

22. Purchased merchandise on account from Camo Clothing, $8,100, less a 50% trade discount. P446.

23. Bought store supplies on account from Mancil Marketing, $120.00. M63.

24. Paid cash to Velmar Company for store supplies, $245.00. C783.

29. Purchased merchandise for cash from Paintball Central, $1,154.00. C784.

2. Total the amount columns of cash payments journal page 15. Prove the equality of debits and credits and rule the cash payments journal to carry the totals forward.

3. Record the totals brought forward from cash payments journal page 15 to line 1 of page 16 of the cash payments journal.

4. Journalize the following transactions.

Transactions:

Aug. 31. Paid cash on account to Camo Clothing covering P446, less 2% cash discount. C785.

31. Paid cash to replenish the petty cash fund, $127.80: supplies—office, $25.66; supplies—store, $48.25; miscellaneous, $54.33; and cash over, $0.44. C786.

5. Total and rule page 9 of the purchases journal.

6. Total the amount columns of cash payments journal page 16. Prove the equality of debits and credits of cash payments journal page 16.

7. Rule page 16 of the cash payments journal.

· (**RECYCLING PROBLEM 10-1**) ·

Journalizing sales and cash receipts transactions; proving and ruling journals

Burge Supply sells lumber, brick, and other construction materials.

Sales journal page 22, cash receipts journal page 23, and general journal page 17 are given in the *Recycling Problem Working Papers*. Balances brought forward are provided on line 1 of the sales and cash receipts journals.

Instructions:

1. Journalize the following transactions completed during the remainder of November in the appropriate journal. Sales tax rate is 6%. Source documents are abbreviated as follows: receipt, R; sales invoice, S; terminal summary, TS.

Transactions:

Nov. 25. Received cash on account from Davis Construction, $1,379.84, covering S845 for $1,408.00, less 2% cash discount, $28.16. R334.

26. Recorded cash and credit card sales, $4,844.00, plus sales tax, $290.64; total, $5,134.64. TS38.

28. Sold merchandise on account to Margaret Sienna, $664.00, plus sales tax, $39.84; total, $703.84. S889.

28. Received cash on account from Ventura Fencing, $2,849.00, covering S861. R335.

29. Granted credit to Davis Construction for merchandise returned, $1,820.00, plus sales tax, $109.20; total, $1,929.20. CM43.

30. Sold merchandise on account to State University, $2,118.00. State University is exempt from sales tax. S890.

30. Recorded cash and credit card sales, $839.00, plus sales tax, $50.34; total, $889.34. TS39.

2. Total and prove the equality of debits and credits for the sales journal.

3. Rule the sales journal.

4. Total and prove the equality of debits and credits for the cash receipts journal.

5. Prove cash. The November 1 cash account balance in the general ledger was $8,483.31. The November 31 cash credit total in the cash payments journal was $42,194.33. On November 31 the balance on the next unused check stub was $16,626.70.

6. Rule the cash receipts journal.

RECYCLING PROBLEM 11-1

Posting to general and subsidiary ledgers

The journals and ledgers for Custom Boots are given in the *Recycling Problem Working Papers*.

Instructions:

1. Post the separate items in the following journals to the general and subsidiary ledgers. Use the current year.
   a. Sales journal.
   b. Purchases journal.
   c. General journal.
   d. Cash receipts journal.
   e. Cash payments journal.

2. Prove and rule the sales journal. Post the totals of the special amount columns.

3. Total and rule the purchases journal. Post the total.

4. Prove and rule the cash receipts journal. Post the totals of the special amount columns.

5. Prove and rule the cash payments journal. Post the totals of the special amount columns.

6. Prepare a schedule of accounts payable and a schedule of accounts receivable. Compare the totals of the schedules with the balances of the controlling accounts, Accounts Payable and Accounts Receivable, in the general ledger. If the totals are not the same, find and correct the errors.

RECYCLING PROBLEM 12-1

Preparing a semimonthly payroll

The following information is for the semimonthly pay period July 16–31 of the current year. Forms are given in the *Recycling Problem Working Papers*.

	EMPL. NO.	EMPLOYEE'S NAME	MARITAL STATUS	NO. OF ALLOWANCES	EARNINGS REGULAR	EARNINGS OVERTIME	DEDUCTIONS HEALTH INSURANCE
1	5	Abrams, Thomas	S	1	892 00		35 00
2	6	Carroll, John	M	2	880 00	90 00	60 00
3	1	Harris, Jonathan	S	1	924 00		35 00
4	4	Kennard, Mary	S	1	1056 00	72 00	35 00
5	2	Locke, Anna	M	2	994 00		60 00
6	7	Rayford, Stan	M	2	812 00		60 00
7	3	Suell, Nicole	M	3	860 00		80 00
8							
9							
10							
11							
12							

SEMIMONTHLY PERIOD ENDED *July 31, 20--*

Instructions:

1. Prepare a payroll register. The date of payment is July 31. Use the income tax withholding tables shown in Chapter 12 to find the income tax withholding for each employee. Calculate social security and Medicare tax withholdings using 6.2% and 1.45% tax rates, respectively. None of the employee-accumulated earnings has exceeded the social security tax base.

2. Prepare a check for the total amount of the net pay. Make the check payable to Payroll Account 982-561-4732 and sign your name as the manager of Sanford Company. The beginning check stub balance is $11,530.50.

3. Prepare payroll checks for Thomas Abrams, Check No. 558, and Anna Locke, Check No. 562. Sign your name as the manager of Sanford Company. Record the two payroll check numbers in the payroll register.

· (**RECYCLING PROBLEM 13-1**) ·

Journalizing payroll transactions

Wooden Cycles completed payroll transactions during the period January 1 to March 31 of the current year. Payroll tax rates are as follows: social security, 6.2%; Medicare, 1.45%; federal unemployment, 0.8%; state unemployment, 5.4%. No total earnings have exceeded the tax base for calculating unemployment taxes. Wooden Cycles is a monthly schedule depositor for payroll taxes.

Instructions:

1. Journalize the following transactions on page 14 of the cash payments journal and page 10 of the general journal given in the *Recycling Problem Working Papers*. Source documents are abbreviated as follows: check, C, and memorandum, M.

Transactions:

Jan. 31. Paid cash for monthly payroll. Gross wages, $5,920.00; withholdings: employee income tax, $360.00; calculate social security and Medicare taxes. C555.

31. Recorded employer payroll taxes expense for the January payroll. M24.

Feb. 15. Paid cash for the January liability for employee income tax, social security tax, and Medicare tax. C575.

28. Paid cash for monthly payroll. Gross wages, $6,058.00; withholdings: employee income tax, $372.00; calculate social security and Medicare taxes. C601.

28. Recorded employer payroll taxes expense for the February payroll. M28.

Mar. 15. Paid cash for the February liability for employee income tax, social security tax, and Medicare tax. C624.

31. Paid cash for monthly payroll. Gross wages, $6,120.00; withholdings: employee income tax, $394.00; calculate social security and Medicare taxes. C658.

31. Recorded employer payroll taxes expense for the March payroll. M35.

Apr. 15. Paid cash for the March liability for employee income tax, social security tax, and Medicare tax. C699.

15. Paid cash for federal unemployment tax liability for quarter ended March 31. C700.

15. Paid cash for state unemployment tax liability for quarter ended March 31. C701.

2. Prove and rule the cash payments journal.

Preparing an 8-column work sheet for a merchandising business

The trial balance for Audio Source, Inc., as of December 31 of the current year is recorded on a work sheet in the *Recycling Problem Working Papers*. Audio Source completed the following transactions during December of the current year and January of the next year.

Transactions:

Dec. 15. The board of directors declared a dividend of $0.375 per share; capital stock issued is 20,000 shares. M114.

Jan. 15. Paid cash for dividend declared December 15. C924.

Instructions:

1. Use page 12 of a general journal. Journalize the dividend declared on December 15.

2. Use page 18 of a cash payments journal. Journalize payment of the dividend on January 15.

3. Analyze the following adjustment information collected on December 31 and record the adjustments on the work sheet. Label each adjustment using labels *(a)* through *(g)*.
   a. Uncollectible accounts are 0.4% of credit sales of $620,000.00.
   b. Merchandise inventory $270,461.36
   c. Office supplies inventory   1,081.34
   d. Store supplies inventory   1,585.90
   e. Value of prepaid insurance   160.00
   f. Estimate of office equipment depreciation   6,140.00
   g. Estimate of store equipment depreciation   5,520.00

4. Using the federal income tax table shown in Chapter 14, calculate federal income tax expense and record the income tax adjustment on the work sheet. Label the adjustment *(h)*.

5. Complete the work sheet.

Preparing financial statements

The completed work sheet for Hawkins Parts, Inc., for the year ended December 31 of the current year and forms for completing this problem are given in the *Recycling Problem Working Papers*.

Instructions:

1. Prepare an income statement. Calculate and record the following component percentages: (a) cost of merchandise sold, (b) gross profit on sales, (c) total expenses, and (d) net income or loss before federal income tax. Round percentage calculations to the nearest 0.1%.

2. Prepare a statement of stockholders' equity. The company had 30,000 shares of $1.00 par value stock outstanding on January 1. The company issued an additional 2,000 shares during the year.

3. Prepare a balance sheet in report form.

4. Calculate the earnings per share and price-earnings ratio. The current market price of the stock is $89.00.

Journalizing and posting adjusting and closing entries; preparing a post-closing trial balance

Use the following partial work sheet of Southern Fixtures, Inc., for the year ended December 31 of the current year. The general ledger accounts and their balances as well as forms for completing this problem are in the *Recycling Problem Working Papers*.

Southern Fixtures, Inc.

Work Sheet

For Year Ended December 31, 20--

	ACCOUNT TITLE	ADJUSTMENTS DEBIT	ADJUSTMENTS CREDIT	INCOME STATEMENT DEBIT	INCOME STATEMENT CREDIT
4	Allow. for Uncoll. Accts.		(a) 2 2 1 5 00		
5	Merchandise Inventory	(b) 4 8 1 9 00			
6	Supplies—Office		(c) 6 1 0 6 00		
7	Supplies—Store		(d) 3 1 5 4 00		
8	Prepaid Insurance		(e) 9 6 0 0 00		
9	Office Equipment				
10	Acc. Depr.—Office Equipment		(f) 4 4 2 0 00		
11	Store Equipment				
12	Acc. Depr.—Store Equipment		(g) 4 9 5 0 00		
13	Accounts Payable				
14	Federal Income Tax Payable		(h) 6 4 2 9 62		
28	Income Summary		(b) 4 8 1 9 00		4 8 1 9 00
38	Depr. Exp.—Office Equipment	(f) 4 4 2 0 00		4 4 2 0 00	
39	Depr. Exp.—Store Equipment	(g) 4 9 5 0 00		4 9 5 0 00	
40	Insurance Expense	(e) 9 6 0 0 00		9 6 0 0 00	
41	Miscellaneous Expense			13 1 8 4 80	
42	Payroll Taxes Expense			18 7 8 5 24	
43	Rent Expense			12 8 0 0 00	
44	Salary Expense			151 5 8 4 73	
45	Supplies Expense—Office	(c) 6 1 0 6 00		6 1 0 6 00	
46	Supplies Expense—Store	(d) 3 1 5 4 00		3 1 5 4 00	
47	Uncollectible Accounts Expense	(a) 2 2 1 5 00		2 2 1 5 00	
48	Utilities Expense			3 2 9 4 47	
49	Federal Income Tax Expense	(h) 6 4 2 9 62		46 4 2 9 62	
50		41 6 9 3 62	41 6 9 3 62	641 8 7 4 48	757 4 4 3 89
51	Net Income after Federal Income Tax			115 5 6 9 41	
52				757 4 4 3 89	757 4 4 3 89

Instructions:

1. Journalize the adjusting entries using page 18 of a general journal.
2. Post the adjusting entries.
3. Journalize the closing entries using page 19 of a general journal.
4. Post the closing entries.
5. Prepare a post-closing trial balance.

Recording entries for uncollectible accounts

The accounts receivable and general ledger accounts for Fincher Industries are given in the *Recycling Problem Working Papers*. The following transactions relating to uncollectible accounts receivable occurred during the final quarter of the current fiscal year.

Instructions:

1. Journalize the following transactions completed during October using page 10 of a general journal. Post the transactions to the customer accounts and general ledger accounts.

Transactions:

Oct. 6. Wrote off Chittenden Corporation's past-due account as uncollectible, $284.75. M216.

   19. Wrote off Foster Corporation's past-due account as uncollectible, $574.10. M221.

2. Journalize the following transactions completed during November using page 11 of a general journal and page 11 of a cash receipts journal. Prove the cash receipts journal. Post the transactions to the customer accounts and general ledger accounts.

Transactions:

Nov. 5. Wrote off Agnew Company's past-due account as uncollectible, $804.24. M236.

   12. Received cash in full payment of Chittenden Corporation's account, previously written off as uncollectible, $284.75. M241 and R616.

   17. Received cash in full payment of Dionne, Inc.'s account, previously written off as uncollectible, $468.30. M243 and R627.

3. Journalize the following transactions completed during December using page 12 of a general journal and page 12 of a cash receipts journal. Prove the cash receipts journal. Post the transactions to the customer accounts and general ledger accounts.

Transactions:

Dec. 4. Wrote off Grant Company's past-due account as uncollectible, $705.18. M257.

   10. Received cash in full payment of Agnew Company's account, previously written off as uncollectible, $804.24. M259 and R702.

   21. Received cash in full payment of Foster Corporation's account, previously written off as uncollectible, $574.10. M265 and R729.

4. Journalize the December 31 adjusting entry for estimated uncollectible accounts expense for the year. Use page 13 of the general journal. Uncollectible accounts expense is estimated as 1.2% of total sales on account. Total sales on account for the year were $987,660.00. Post the transaction to the general ledger accounts.

Recording transactions for plant assets

Diamond Clothing records plant assets in two accounts: Store Equipment, Account No. 1215, and Office Equipment, Account No. 1205. Store equipment is depreciated using the straight-line method. Office equipment is depreciated using the double declining-balance method. Journals and plant asset records are given in the *Recycling Problem Working Papers*.

Instructions:

1. Record the following transactions completed during 20X1 on page 1 of a cash payments journal.

Transactions:

Jan. 3. Bought a color printer for the office: cost, $900.00; estimated salvage value, $100.00; estimated useful life, 4 years; plant asset No. 642; serial number, ZE532N34. C168.

Feb. 26. Paid property taxes on plant assets assessed at $620,000.00. The tax rate is 1.4%. C216.

Apr. 3. Purchased a store display: cost, $3,000.00; estimated salvage value, $500.00; estimated useful life, 5 years; plant asset No. 643; serial number, 754NFE. C275.

2. Complete Section 1 of a plant asset record for each new plant asset.

3. Prepare a depreciation table for each new plant asset.

4. Complete Section 3 of the plant asset records for 20X1–20X4.

5. Record the following transactions completed during 20X5. Use page 2 of a cash receipts journal and page 2 of a general journal.

Transactions:

Jan. 3. Received cash for sale of a color printer, plant asset No. 642, $60.00. R7.

June 29. Received cash for sale of a store display, plant asset No. 643, $950.00. M69 and R171.

Dec. 31. Recorded the adjusting entry for depreciation expense—store equipment. Total 20X5 depreciation expense of store equipment was $17,765.00.

6. Complete the plant asset records for each plant asset sold during 20X5.

· (**RECYCLING PROBLEM 19-1**) ·

Determining the cost of inventory using the fifo, lifo, and weighted-average inventory costing methods

Mayfair Industries made the following purchases of a part during the fiscal year. There are 32 units in ending inventory. Forms for costing inventory are given in the *Recycling Problem Working Papers*.

Purchase Date	Quantity	Unit Price
January 1, beginning inventory	3	$12.30
January 3, purchases	20	13.00
March 29, purchases	20	13.20
August 15, purchases	15	13.25
November 13, purchases	15	13.45

Instructions:

1. Calculate the cost of ending inventory using the fifo, lifo, and weighted-average methods.

2. Which of the inventory costing methods resulted in the highest cost of merchandise sold?

· (**RECYCLING PROBLEM 20-1**) ·

Journalizing notes payable and notes receivable transactions

The following transactions related to notes payable and notes receivable were completed by Wolverton Company during April of the current year. Journals are provided in the *Recycling Problem Working Papers*.

Transactions:

Apr. 5. Signed a 90-day, 10% note, for $30,000.00 with First National Bank. R34.

9. Accepted a 90-day, 15% note from Phillip Majure for an extension of time on his account, $650.00. NR18.

12. Received cash for the maturity value of a 60-day, 18% note for $900.00. R67.

16. Accepted a 60-day, 14% note from Avery Harris for an extension of time on her account, $2,450.00. NR19.

19. Received cash for the maturity value of a 60-day, 18% note for $500.00. R74.

20. Signed a 90-day, 15% note with Rossman Supply for an extension of time on this account payable, $2,500.00. M49.

22. Patrick Isamen dishonored his 90-day, 15% note, for $3,000.00. M53.

27. Signed a 120-day, 12% note for $20,000.00 with First Commerce Bank. R84.

29. Received cash for the maturity value of a 90-day, 18% note for $1,800.00. R89.

Instructions:

1. Journalize each transaction using page 3 of a general journal and page 6 of a cash receipts journal. Source documents are abbreviated as follows: check, C; receipt, R; memorandum, M; note receivable, NR.

2. Determine the maturity date and maturity value of each note signed by Wolverton Company.

3. Journalize the following transactions on page 10 of a cash payments journal. Use the maturity dates and maturity values calculated in Instruction 2.

Transactions:

Paid cash for the maturity value of the $30,000.00 note dated April 5. C452.
Paid cash for the maturity value of the $2,500.00 note dated April 20. C489.
Paid cash for the maturity value of the $20,000.00 note dated April 27. C672.

· **RECYCLING PROBLEM 21-1** ·

Journalizing and posting entries for accrued interest revenue and expense

The accounting forms for Farrell Company are given in the *Recycling Problem Working Papers*. The balances are recorded as of December 31 of the current year before adjusting entries.

Farrell Company completed the following transactions related to notes receivable and notes payable during the current year and the following one year. The first two transactions have already been journalized and posted. One note receivable and one note payable are the only notes on hand at the end of the fiscal period. Source documents are abbreviated as follows: receipt, R; check, C; note receivable, NR.

Transactions:

20X1

Nov. 9. Accepted a 90-day, 18% note from Kayla Nelson for an extension of time on her account, $800.00. NR18.

Dec. 14. Signed a 120-day, 12% note, $4,800.00 with First National Bank. R364.

20X2

Feb. 7. Received cash for the maturity value of NR18. R132.

Apr. 13. Paid cash for the maturity value of the First National Bank note. C342.

Instructions:

1. Plan the adjustments on a work sheet. Use (a) for accrued interest income and (h) for accrued interest expense.

2. Journalize and post the adjusting entries for accrued interest income and accrued interest expense on December 31. Use page 15 of a general journal.

3. Journalize and post the closing entries for interest income and interest expense. Continue to use page 15 of a general journal.

4. Journalize and post the reversing entries for accrued interest income and accrued interest expense. Use page 16 of a general journal.

5. Journalize the receipt of cash for the maturity value of NR18. Use page 13 of a cash receipts journal. Post the amounts in the General columns of the cash receipts journal.

6. Journalize the cash payment for the maturity value of the note payable. Use page 18 of a cash payments journal. Post the amounts in the General columns of the cash payments journal.

Preparing financial statements and end-of-fiscal-period entries for a corporation

Accounting forms are given in the *Recycling Problem Working Papers*. Applewhite Corporation completed the following transactions during December of the current year and January of the next year.

Instructions:

1. Prepare Applewhite Corporation's work sheet for the current year ended December 31. Record the adjustments on the work sheet using the following information.

Adjustment Information, December 31

Accrued interest income	$ 64.00
Uncollectible accounts expense estimated as 0.6% of sales on account.	
Sales on account for year, $554,000.00.	
Merchandise inventory	$229,406.46
Supplies inventory	573.52
Value of prepaid insurance	1,200.00
Annual depreciation expense—office equipment	4,850.00
Annual depreciation expense—store equipment	3,480.00
Accrued interest expense	250.00

Federal income tax is calculated using the tax table presented in Chapter 22.

2. Prepare an income statement. Calculate and record the following component percentages: (a) cost of merchandise sold; (b) gross profit on operations; (c) total operating expenses; (d) income from operations; (e) net addition or deduction resulting from other revenue and expenses; and (f) net income before federal income tax. Round percentage calculations to the nearest 0.1%.

3. Analyze the corporation's income statement by determining if component percentages are within acceptable levels. If any component percentage is not within an acceptable level, suggest steps that the company should take. The corporation considers the following component percentages acceptable.

Cost of merchandise sold	Not more than 68.0%
Gross profit on operations	Not less than 32.0%
Total operating expenses	Not more than 25.0%
Income from operations	Not less than 7.0%
Net deduction from other revenue and expenses	Not more than 0.5%
Net income before federal income tax	Not less than 6.5%

4. Prepare a statement of stockholders' equity. Use the following additional information.

January 1 balance of capital stock account	$100,000.00
(10,000 shares issued for $10.00 per share)	
Shares issued during the year	2,000 shares

5. Prepare a balance sheet.

6. Calculate the corporation's (a) working capital and (b) current ratio. Determine if these items are within acceptable levels. The corporation considers the following levels acceptable.

Working capital	Not less than $250,000.00
Current ratio	Between 4.0 to 1 and 6.0 to 1

7. Journalize the adjusting entries using page 15 of a general journal.

8. Journalize the closing entries using page 16 of a general journal.

9. Journalize the reversing entries using page 17 of a general journal.

Recording partners' investments and withdrawals, preparing financial statements, and liquidating a partnership

Ashwin Akabu and Chen Wong are partners in a business called Total Toys. Journals and forms for completing this problem are given in the *Recycling Problem Working Papers*.

Total Toys completed the following transactions during June of the current year.

Transactions:

June 15. Received cash from partner, Ashwin Akabu, as an investment, $15,000.00. Receipt No. 128.

15. Received cash of $7,000 and supplies valued at $5,000.00 from partner, Chen Wong, as an investment. Receipt No. 129.

30. Ashwin Akabu, partner, withdrew merchandise for personal use, $900.00. Memorandum No. 74.

30. Chen Wong, partner, withdrew cash for personal use, $1,200. Check No. 141.

Instructions:

1. Use page 11 of a cash receipts journal. Journalize the investments on June 15.

2. Use page 17 of a cash payments journal and page 21 of a general journal. Journalize the withdrawals on June 30.

Information from Total Toys' worksheet and income statement for the month ended June 30 is given below.

Net Income for the month ended June 30	$ 7,200.00
Ashwin Akabu, Capital June 1 balance	31,770.00
Chen Wong, Capital June 1 balance	25,441.00

Instructions:

3. Prepare a distribution of net income statement for Total Toys. Net income or loss is to be distributed equally to the partners.

4. Using the balances of the general ledger capital accounts, prepare an owners' equity statement for Total Toys. The investments made on June 15 are the only additional investments made by the partners this month. The withdrawals made on June 30 are the only withdrawals made by the partners this month.

Total Toys was liquidated on June 30. On that date, after financial statements were prepared and closing entries were posted, the general ledger accounts had the following balances.

Cash	$87,061.00
Merchandise Inventory	1,000.00
Equipment	7,500.00
Accumulated Depreciation—Equipment	5,000.00
Accounts Payable	1,250.00
Ashwin Akabu, Capital	49,470.00
Chen Wong, Capital	39,841.00

The following transactions occurred on June 30 of the current year.

Transactions:

a. Received cash from the sale of merchandise inventory, $900.00. R130.

b. Received cash from the sale of equipment, $3,500.00. R131.

c. Paid cash to all creditors for amounts owed. C142.

d. Distributed balance of Loss and Gain on Realization to the partners on an equal basis. M75.

e. Distributed remaining cash to partners. C143 and C144.

Instructions:

5. Journalize the transactions. Continue on the next available line of the journals used in instructions 1 and 2.

Recording international and Internet sales

Pacific Trade Inc. sells folk art domestically and internationally. The company has Internet sales as well. Journals and forms for completing this problem are given in the *Recycling Problem Working Papers*.

Instructions:

1. Journalize the following transactions affecting sales and cash receipts completed during November of the current year. Use page 23 of a general journal and a cash receipts journal. Source documents are abbreviated as follows: memorandum, M; receipt, R; time draft, TD; and terminal summary, TS.

Transactions:

Nov. 4. Received a 30-day time draft from Hong Kong Importers for an international sale, $2,200.00. TD72.

7. Recorded Internet credit card sales, $8,450.00. TS330.

12. Recorded international cash sale, $11,800.00. M65.

14. Recorded Internet credit card sales, $5,670.00. TS331.

15. Received cash for the value of Time Draft No. 68, $3,000.00. R103.

18. Received cash for the value of Time Draft No. 71, $5,900.00. R110.

21. Recorded Internet cash sale, $16,400. TS332.

24. Recorded international cash sale, $7,500.00. M76.

28. Recorded Internet cash sale, $3,300.00. TS333.

30. Received a 30-day time draft from Australian Arts for international sale of merchandise, $16,040.00. TD73.

2. Prove and rule the cash receipts journal.

ANSWERS TO AUDIT YOUR UNDERSTANDING

Chapter 1, Page 9

1. Planning, recording, analyzing, and interpreting financial information.
2. Answers will vary but should involve businesses that perform activities for a fee.
3. A business owned by one person.
4. Assets = Liabilities + Owner's Equity.

Chapter 1, Page 13

1. The right side must be increased.
2. If one account is increased, another account on the same side of the equation must be decreased by the same amount.
3. Buying items or services and paying for them at a future date.

Chapter 1, Page 17

1. Increased.
2. Increased
3. Decreased.

Chapter 2, Page 31

1. ASSETS = LIABILITIES + OWNER'S EQUITY
2. (1) Account balances increase on the normal balance side of an account. (2) Account balances decrease on the side opposite the normal balance side of an account.

Chapter 2, Page 37

1. (1) Which accounts are affected? (2) How is each account classified? (3) How is each classification changed? (4) How is each amount entered in the accounts?
2. Supplies and Cash.

Chapter 2, Page 44

1. Cash and Sales.
2. Accounts Receivable and Sales.
3. Owner's drawing account and Cash.
4. Credit, because revenue increases owner's equity.
5. Debit, because expenses decrease owner's equity.

Chapter 3, Page 62

1. By date.
2. Source documents are one way to verify the accuracy of a specific journal entry.
3. Date, debit, credit, and source document.

Chapter 3, Page 66

1. General Debit and Cash Credit.
2. General Debit and General Credit.
3. General Debit and Cash Credit.

Chapter 3, Page 72

1. Cash Debit and Sales Credit.
2. General Debit and Sales Credit.
3. General Debit and Cash Credit.
4. Cash Debit and General Credit.
5. General Debit and Cash Credit.

Chapter 3, Page 78

1. (1) Add each of the amount columns. (2) Add the debit column totals, and then add the credit column totals. (3) Verify that the total debits and total credits are equal.
2. Cash on hand at the beginning of the month, plus total cash received, less total cash paid.
3. (1) Rule a single line across all amount columns directly below the last entry to indicate that the columns are to be added. (2) On the next line, write the date in the Date column. (3) Write the word *Totals* in the Account Title column. (4) Write each column total below the single line. (5) Rule double lines below the column totals across all amount columns. The double lines mean that the totals have been verified as correct.

Chapter 4, Page 95

1. The first digit indicates in which general ledger division the account is located. The second and third digits indicate the location of the account within that division.
2. (1) Write the account title in the heading. (2) Write the account number in the heading.

Chapter 4, Page 99

1. (1) Write the date in the Date column of the account. (2) Write the journal page number in the Post. Ref. column of the account. (3) Write the amount in the Debit or Credit column. (4) Calculate and write the new account balance in the Balance Debit or Balance Credit column. (5) Write the account number in the Post. Ref. column of the journal.
2. No. Each separate amount in the General Debit and General Credit columns of a journal is posted to the account written in the Account Title column.

Chapter 4, Page 104

1. Special amount columns.
2. Whenever the debits in an account exceed the credits.
3. Whenever the credits in an account exceed the debits.

Chapter 4, Page 109

1. A journal entry made to correct an error in the ledger.
2. When a transaction has been improperly journalized and posted to the ledger.
3. To show the increase in this expense account.
4. To show the decrease in this expense account.

Chapter 5, Page 123

1. Blank endorsement, special endorsement, and restrictive endorsement.
2. (1) Write the amount of the check after the dollar sign at the top of the stub. (2) Write the date of the check on the Date line. (3) Write to whom the check is to be paid on the To line. (4) Record the purpose of the check on the For line. (5) Write the amount of the check after the words *Amt. This Check*. (6) Calculate the new checking balance and record it in the amount column on the last line of the stub.
3. (1) Write the date. (2) Write to whom the check is to be paid following the words *Pay to the order of*. (3) Write the amount in figures following the dollar sign. (4) Write the amount in words on the line with the word *Dollars*. (5) Write the purpose of the check on the line labeled For. (6) Sign the check.

Chapter 5, Page 128

1. (1) A service charge may not have been recorded in the depositor's business records. (2) Outstanding deposits may be recorded in the depositor's records but not on a bank statement. (3) Outstanding checks may be recorded in the depositor's records but not on a bank statement. (4) A depositor may have made a math or recording error.
2. An outstanding check.

Chapter 5, Page 133

1. (1) The check appears to be altered. (2) The signature on the check does not match the signature on the signature card. (3) The amounts written in figures and in words do not agree. (4) The check is postdated. (5) The person who wrote the check has stopped payment on it. (6) The account of the person who wrote the check has insufficient funds to pay the check.
2. Cash.
3. Cash.

Chapter 5, Page 137

1. For making small cash payments.
2. The check issued to replenish petty cash is a credit to Cash and does not affect Petty Cash.

Chapter 6, Page 155

1. Name of the business, name of report, and date of report.
2. All general ledger accounts are listed in the Trial Balance columns of a work sheet, even if some accounts do not have balances.

Chapter 6, Page 161

1. An expense should be reported in the same fiscal period that it is used to produce revenue.
2. (1) What is the balance of the account? (2) What should the balance be for this account? (3) What must be done to correct the account balance? (4) What adjustment is made?

Chapter 6, Page 166

1. Asset, liability, and owner's equity accounts.
2. Revenue and expense accounts.
3. Balance Sheet Credit column.
4. Balance Sheet Debit column.

Chapter 6, Page 170

1. Subtract the smaller total from the larger total to find the difference.
2. The difference between two column totals can be divided evenly by 9.
3. A slide.

Chapter 7, Page 186

1. Heading, revenue, expenses, and net income or net loss.
2. Total Expenses *divided by* Total Sales *equals* Total Expenses Component Percentage.
3. Net Income *divided by* Total Sales *equals* Net Income Component Percentage.

Chapter 7, Page 192

1. Heading, assets, liabilities, and owner's equity.
2. Capital Account Balance *plus* Net Income *minus* Drawing Account Balance *equals* Current Capital.

Chapter 8, Page 205

1. To update general ledger accounts at the end of a fiscal period.
2. Adjustments column of the work sheet.
3. Supplies Expense and Insurance Expense.

Chapter 8, Page 212

1. Beginning balances.
2. Changes in the owner's capital for a single fiscal period.
3. (1) An entry to close income statement accounts with credit balances. (2) An entry to close income statement accounts with debit balances. (3) An entry to record net income or net loss and close the income summary account. (4) An entry to close the owner's drawing account.

Chapter 8, Page 219

1. To assure a reader that a balance has not been omitted.
2. Only those with balances (permanent accounts).
3. Because they are closed and have zero balances.

Chapter 9, Page 241

1. Purchases of merchandise on account.
2. Frequently occurring transactions.
3. Because the same two accounts are always affected by purchase on account transactions.
4. Time is saved because using special amount columns eliminates writing an account title in the Account Title column.

Chapter 9, Page 247

1. To encourage early payment.
2. Cash payment transactions that do not occur often.
3. A business purchases merchandise to sell but buys supplies for use in the business. Supplies are not intended for sale.
4. Two ten means 2% of the invoice amount may be deducted if the invoice is paid within 10 days of the invoice date. Net thirty means that the total invoice amount must be paid within 30 days.

Chapter 9, Page 253

1. The titles of the accounts for which the petty cash fund was used.
2. The balance is usually a debit because the petty cash fund is more likely to be short than over.
3. (1) Rule a single line across all amount columns. (2) Write the date in the Date column. (3) Write *Totals* in the Account Title column. (4) Write each column total below the single line. (5) Rule a double line across all amount columns.

Chapter 9, Page 258

1. General journal.
2. To note that the invoice is for store supplies and not for purchases, ensuring that no mistake is made.
3. Because the single credit amount is posted to two accounts.
4. After each general journal entry is recorded.
5. A business can track the amount of purchases returns and allowances in a fiscal period if a separate account is used.
6. A purchases return is credit allowed for the purchase price of returned merchandise. A purchases allowance is credit allowed for part of the purchase price of merchandise that is not returned.
7. When the customer wants to record the transaction immediately, without waiting for written confirmation from the vendor.

Chapter 10, Page 275

1. A merchandising business sells merchandise; a service business sells services.
2. As a percentage of sales.
3. The amount of sales tax collected is a business liability until paid to the government.
4. Accounts Receivable.

Chapter 10, Page 284

1. The POS system produces a receipt that contains detailed information about the sale, including the merchandise's description and price. The cash register receipt does not include such detailed information.
2. A batch report can be detailed, showing each credit card sale, or it can provide a summary of the number and total of sales by credit card type.
3. The funds are transferred among the banks issuing the credit cards.

Chapter 10, Page 287

1. A sales return is credit allowed a customer for the sales price of returned merchandise; a sales allowance is credit allowed a customer for part of the sales price of merchandise that is not returned.
2. Credit memorandum.
3. Sales Returns and Allowances and Sales Tax Payable are debited; Accounts Receivable is credited.
4. To provide better information to quickly identify if the amount of sales returns and allowances is greater than expected.

Chapter 11, Page 306

1. A controlling account summarizes all accounts in a subsidiary ledger. The balance of a controlling account equals the total of all account balances in its related subsidiary ledger.
2. Accounts Payable Debit column.

Chapter 11, Page 314

1. Customer accounts listed in the Accounts Receivable Debit column.
2. Accounts Receivable Credit column.
3. All customer accounts that have balances.

Chapter 11, Page 319

1. Amounts in the Debit and Credit columns.
2. (1) Write the date in the Date column of the account. (2) Write the journal page number in the Post. Ref. column of the account. (3) Write the amount in the Debit or Credit column of the account. (4) Calculate and write the new account balance in the Balance Debit or Balance Credit column of the account. (5) Write the general ledger account number in the Post. Ref. column of the journal.

Chapter 11, Page 326

1. Each special amount column.

2. (1) Sales journal, (2) purchases journal, (3) general journal, (4) cash receipts journal, (5) cash payments journal.

Chapter 11, Page 329

1. Memorandum.

2. It does not affect the general ledger accounts.

3. Only a reference to the subsidiary ledger account is entered in the Post. Ref. column of the general journal.

Chapter 12, Page 344

1. The total amount earned by all employees for a pay period.

2. $3^1/_2$ hours.

3. Overtime hours $\times$ the overtime rate.

4. $506 (40 $\times$ $11.00 + 4 $\times$ $16.50).

Chapter 12, Page 350

1. Form W-4, Employee's Withholding Allowance Certificate.

2. Employee marital status and number of withholding allowances.

3. Both the employee and the employer.

Chapter 12, Page 355

1. The payroll register summarizes the payroll for one pay period and shows total earnings, payroll withholdings, and net pay of all employees.

2. By subtracting total deductions from total earnings.

3. Because a business must send a quarterly report to federal and state governments showing employee taxable earnings and taxes withheld from employee earnings.

Chapter 12, Page 358

1. To help protect and control payroll payments.

2. The payroll register.

3. Individual checks are not written and do not have to be distributed.

Chapter 13, Page 372

1. Salary Expense.

2. Employee Income Tax Payable.

3. Social Security Tax Payable.

4. Medicare Tax Payable.

Chapter 13, Page 377

1. Social security: 6.2% of earnings up to a maximum of $87,000.00 in each calendar year; Medicare: 1.45% of total employee earnings; federal unemployment: 0.8% on the first $7,000.00 earned by each employee; state unemployment: 5.4% on the first $7,000.00 earned by each employee.

2. The first $7,000.00.

Chapter 13, Page 382

1. By January 31.

2. Federal income tax, social security tax, and Medicare tax.

Chapter 13, Page 389

1. By the 15th day of the following month.

2. For paying payroll taxes and for paying federal unemployment tax.

Chapter 14, Page 408

1. Stockholders' Equity.

2. One account called Capital Stock.

3. Retained Earnings.

4. The board of directors declares a dividend.

Chapter 14, Page 414

1. Supplies—Office and Supplies Expense—Office.

2. Prepaid Insurance and Insurance Expense.

Chapter 14, Page 418

1. In the same order they appear in the general ledger.

2. Merchandise Inventory and Income Summary.

3. Debit Income Summary and credit Merchandise Inventory.

4. The Income Summary account is used to adjust the Merchandise Inventory account at the end of a fiscal period.

Chapter 14, Page 422

1. The loss is considered a regular expense of doing business. Revenue was earned when the sale was made. Failing to collect an account does not cancel the sale.

2. At the end of the fiscal period.

3. (1) Report a balance sheet amount for Accounts Receivable that reflects the amount the business expects to collect in the future. (2) Recognize the expense of uncollectible accounts in the same period in which the related revenue is recorded.

4. It reduces its related asset account, Accounts Receivable.

5. The difference between the balance of Accounts Receivable and its contra account, Allowance for Uncollectible Accounts.

Chapter 14, Page 426

1. Current assets and plant assets.

2. Original cost; estimated salvage value; estimated useful life.

Chapter 14, Page 436

1. Income Statement Debit or Credit column.

2. Balance Sheet Debit.

3. Trial balance amounts after adjustments are extended to the Adjusted Trial Balance columns, and the Adjusted Trial Balance columns are proved before extending amounts to the Income Statement and Balance Sheet columns.

Chapter 15, Page 454

1. The cost of merchandise sold section
2. Beginning merchandise inventory, *plus* purchases, *equals* total cost of merchandise available for sale, *less* ending merchandise inventory, *equals* cost of merchandise sold.
3. By comparing the amount calculated on the income statement with the amount on the work sheet.

Chapter 15, Page 460

1. (1) Cost of merchandise sold, (2) gross profit on sales, (3) total expenses, and (4) net income.
2. By making comparisons with prior fiscal periods as well as with industry standards that are published by industry organizations.
3. Net loss.

Chapter 15, Page 463

1. The changes in a corporation's ownership for a fiscal period.
2. Capital stock and retained earnings.
3. In the Capital Stock general ledger account.
4. In the Balance Sheet Credit column of a work sheet.
5. As a dividend.
6. In the Balance Sheet Debit column of a work sheet.

Chapter 15, Page 471

1. Current and plant assets.
2. (1) The balance of the asset account, (2) the balance of the asset's contra account, and (3) book value.
3. Mortgage payable.
4. From the statement of stockholders' equity.
5. Schedule of accounts payable and schedule of accounts receivable.

Chapter 16, Page 486

1. Because the heading *Adjusting Entries* is recorded in the Account Title column to explain all of the adjusting entries that follow.
2. Adjusting entry for merchandising inventory.
3. Federal Income Tax Payable.

Chapter 16, Page 493

1. Income Statement and Balance Sheet columns of the work sheet and the distribution of net income statement.
2. Income Summary.

Chapter 16, Page 498

1. General ledger accounts with balances.
2. To prove the equality of debits and credits in the general ledger.
3. In the same order as they appear in the general ledger.

Chapter 17, Page 518

1. To the contra asset account Allowance for Uncollectible Accounts and the expense account Uncollectible Accounts Expense.
2. The allowance method of recording losses from uncollectible accounts attempts to match the expense of uncollectible accounts in the same fiscal year the related sales are recorded.
3. The account is not affected.

Chapter 17, Page 524

1. The balance of the customer account is an *actual* uncollectible amount and no longer an *estimate* of an uncollectible amount.
2. The book value is the same because the same amount is deducted from the accounts receivable and the allowance accounts.
3. To show an accurate credit history.

Chapter 18, Page 537

1. Office Equipment is debited; Cash is credited.
2. Land and anything attached to the land.
3. Tax authorities referred to as assessors.

Chapter 18, Page 541

1. Matching Expenses with Revenues.
2. Original cost; estimated salvage value; estimated useful life.

Chapter 18, Page 545

1. Depreciation is credited to the contra asset account, Accumulated Depreciation, rather than crediting the asset account.
2. The balance of the asset account is not changed.

Chapter 18, Page 550

1. Disposal date, disposal method, and disposal amount.
2. Partial year's depreciation.
3. Cash received less the book value of the asset sold.
4. Other Expenses.

Chapter 18, Page 554

1. Depreciation rate.
2. Double declining-balance method.
3. It declines.
4. Its estimated salvage value.

Chapter 19, Page 568

1. Successful businesses must have merchandise available for sale that customers want. A business needs controls that assist managers in maintaining a merchandise inventory of sufficient quantity, variety, and price.

2. (1) Excess inventory requires that a business spend money for expensive store and warehouse space. (2) Excess inventory uses capital that could be invested in other assets to earn a profit for the business. (3) Excess inventory requires that a business spend money for expenses, such as taxes and insurance premiums, that increase with the cost of the merchandise inventory. (4) Excess inventory may become obsolete and unsalable.

3. At the end of a fiscal period.

4. A business frequently establishes its fiscal period to end when inventory normally is at a minimum because it takes less time to count a smaller inventory.

5. A customary practice is to take a periodic inventory at least once a fiscal period. The periodic inventory is then compared with the perpetual inventory records.

Chapter 19, Page 573

1. The most recent invoices for purchases are used in recording prices for each item on the inventory record.

2. The most recent costs of merchandise should be charged against current revenue.

3. Lifo.

4. Using the same inventory costing method for all fiscal periods provides financial statements that can be compared with other fiscal period statements. If a business changes inventory cost methods, part of the difference in gross profit and net income may be caused by the change in methods.

Chapter 19, Page 576

1. By using the gross profit method of estimating inventory.

2. Actual net sales and net purchases amounts; the beginning inventory amount; and the gross profit percentage.

3. The beginning inventory for the month is the same as the ending inventory from the previous month.

Chapter 20, Page 592

1. Sometimes a business receives more cash from sales than is needed to pay for purchases and expenses. When this occurs, a business may deposit the extra cash in a bank or other financial institution for a short period. At other times, the receipt of cash from sales does not occur at the same time and in sufficient amounts to pay for needed purchases and expenses. When this occurs, a business needs to borrow additional cash or make arrangements with its vendors to delay payment for a period of time.

2. A note can be useful in a court of law as written evidence of a debt.

3. Ten cents will be paid for the use of each dollar borrowed for a full year.

4. Multiply the principal times the interest rate times the time stated as a fraction of a year.

Chapter 20, Page 597

1. Because notes payable generally are paid within one year.

2. Accounts Payable and the vendor are debited. Notes Payable is credited.

Chapter 20, Page 602

1. A note receivable does not pay the amount the customer owes. Therefore, the amount of the asset does not change at the time the note is signed. The form of the asset does change from an account receivable to a note receivable. However, the asset will remain classified as a current asset.

2. Other Revenue.

3. Accounts Receivable and the customer account are each debited for the principal of the note and the interest. Notes Receivable is credited for the principal of the note. Interest Income is credited for the interest.

4. Because the interest has been earned.

Chapter 21, Page 621

1. Realization of Revenue.

2. To avoid the inconvenience of determining how much, if any, of each cash receipt is for interest income earned and accrued during the previous year and how much is earned in the current year.

Chapter 21, Page 627

1. So that the income statement will report all expenses for the period even though some of the expenses have not yet been paid. Also, so that the balance sheet will report all liabilities, including the accrued expenses payable.

2. Interest Payable is debited; Interest Expense is credited.

Chapter 22, Page 644

1. (1) For some accounts, the calculated estimate of the account is also the amount used in the work sheet adjustment. (2) Other accounts have a current balance when the work sheet adjustment is planned. The current balance is typically subtracted from the estimated account balance to determine the amount of the adjustment.

2. (1) Complete all adjustments other than federal income tax. (2) Extend all the accounts except Federal Income Tax Expense to the Income Statement or Balance Sheet columns. (3) Calculate temporary totals of the Income Statement accounts. (4) The difference of the Income Statement columns, excluding the estimated federal income taxes, is the net income or loss before income taxes.

Chapter 22, Page 648

1. Sales, cost of merchandise sold, and operating expenses are used to determine income from operations. Other revenue and other expenses, such as interest income, interest expense, and gains or losses on plant assets, are not normal business activities. Therefore, they are not included in calculating income from operations and are reported separately.

2. Each component percentage shows the percentage that each item is of net sales.

Chapter 22, Page 653

1. Mortgage payable.

2. The amount of total current assets less total current liabilities.

3. The current ratio permits a business to compare itself to its industry and to provide a convenient relative measure from year to year.

Chapter 22, Page 660

1. Post-closing trial balance.
2. (1) Closing entry for income statement accounts with credit balances (revenue and contra cost accounts). (2) Closing entry for income statement accounts with debit balances (cost, contra revenue, and expense accounts). (3) Closing entry to record net income or net loss in the retained earnings account and close the income summary account. (4) Closing entry for the dividends account.
3. Income Summary and Dividends.

Chapter 23, Page 679

1. Income statement and balance sheet.
2. A partnership agreement should include: the name of the business and the partners, the investments of each partner, the duties and responsibilities of each partner, how profits and losses are to be divided, what happens if a partner dies, how the partnership is to be dissolved, and the duration of the agreement.
3. The partner's drawing account increases by a debit; Cash decreases by a credit.

Chapter 23, Page 685

1. Each partner's share of net income or net loss.
2. (1) Beginning capital amount, (2) any additional investments made during the fiscal period, and (3) each partner's withdrawal of assets during the fiscal period.
3. Compute Ending Capital as follows: (1) Share of Net Income *less* Withdrawals *equals* Net Increase in Capital. (2) Beginning Capital *plus* Net Increase in Capital *equals* Ending Capital.

Chapter 23, Page 690

1. Cash received from the sale of assets during liquidation of a partnership.
2. Each partner's capital account.

Chapter 24, Page 709

1. (1) The lack of uniform commercial laws among countries makes settlement of disputes more difficult. (2) Greater distances and sometimes more complex transportation methods increase the time to complete the transaction. (3) Because it may be difficult to determine a customer's financial condition and to take legal action if a customer does not pay, the risk of uncollected amounts is increased. (4) Unstable political conditions in some countries may affect the ability to receive payments from those countries.
2. The bill of lading serves as a receipt for merchandise received and as a contract for the delivery of the merchandise.
3. A sight draft is payable when the holder presents it for payment. A time draft is payable at a fixed or determinable future time after it is accepted.
4. To assure receipt of payment for those sales.
5. A draft is generally paid by a bank and a trade acceptance is paid by the buyer. A seller generally has much more assurance of receiving payment from a bank than from a buyer.

Chapter 24, Page 712

1. To browse and compare the products offered by companies, and to do so at a convenient time and place.
2. Credit card sales information is processed in a manner similar to checks. Therefore, these sales are considered cash sales.

GLOSSARY

Account a record summarizing all the information pertaining to a single item in the accounting equation. (p. 10)

Account balance the amount in an account. (p. 10)

Account number the number assigned to an account. (p. 92)

Account title the name given to an account. (p. 10)

Accounting planning, recording, analyzing, and interpreting financial information. (p. 6)

Accounting cycle the series of accounting activities included in recording financial information for a fiscal period. (p. 217)

Accounting equation an equation showing the relationship among assets, liabilities, and owner's equity. (p. 8)

Accounting period *see* fiscal period

Accounting records organized summaries of a business's financial activities. (p. 6)

Accounting system a planned process for providing financial information that will be useful to management. (p. 6)

Accounts payable ledger a subsidiary ledger containing only accounts for vendors from whom items are purchased or bought on account. (p. 298)

Accounts receivable ledger a subsidiary ledger containing only accounts for charge customers. (p. 298)

Accrued expenses expenses incurred in one fiscal period but not paid until a later fiscal period. (p. 622)

Accrued interest expense interest incurred but not yet paid. (p. 622)

Accrued interest income interest earned but not yet received. (p. 617)

Accrued revenue revenue earned in one fiscal period but not received until a later fiscal period. (p. 616)

Accumulated depreciation the total amount of depreciation expense that has been recorded since the purchase of a plant asset. (p. 424)

Adjusting entries journal entries recorded to update general ledger accounts at the end of a fiscal period. (p. 202)

Adjustments changes recorded on a work sheet to update general ledger accounts at the end of a fiscal period. (p. 157)

Allowance method of recording losses from uncollectible accounts crediting the estimated value of uncollectible accounts to a contra account. (p. 419)

Assessed value the value of an asset determined by tax authorities for the purpose of calculating taxes. (p. 536)

Asset anything of value that is owned. (p. 8)

Bad debts *see* uncollectible accounts

Balance sheet a financial statement that reports assets, liabilities, and owner's equity on a specific date. (p. 162)

Bank statement a report of deposits, withdrawals, and bank balances sent to a depositor by a bank. (p. 124)

Batch report a report of credit card sales produced by a point-of-sale terminal. (p. 278)

Batching out the process of preparing a batch report of credit card sales from a point-of-sale terminal. (p. 278)

Bill of exchange *see* draft

Bill of lading a receipt signed by the authorized agent of a transportation company for merchandise received that also serves as a contract for the delivery of the merchandise. (p. 704)

Blank endorsement an endorsement consisting only of the endorser's signature. (p. 120)

Board of directors a group of persons elected by the stockholders to manage a corporation. (p. 406)

Book inventory *see* perpetual inventory

Book value the difference between an asset's account balance and its related contra account balance. (p. 419)

Book value of a plant asset the original cost of a plant asset minus accumulated depreciation. (p. 424)

Book value of accounts receivable the difference between the balance of Accounts Receivable and its contra account, Allowance for Uncollectible Accounts. (p. 419)

Business ethics the use of ethics in making business decisions. (p. 8)

Capital the account used to summarize the owner's equity in a business. (p. 10)

Capital stock total shares of ownership in a corporation. (p. 234)

Cash discount a deduction from the invoice amount, allowed by a vendor to encourage early payment. (p. 242)

Cash over a petty cash on hand amount that is more than a recorded amount. (p. 248)

Cash payments journal a special journal used to record only cash payment transactions. (p. 242)

Cash receipts journal a special journal used to record only cash receipt transactions. (p. 278)

Cash sale a sale in which cash is received for the total amount of the sale at the time of the transaction. (p. 276)

Cash short a petty cash on hand amount that is less than a recorded amount. (p. 248)

Charge sale *see* sale on account

Chart of accounts a list of accounts used by a business. (p. 32)

Check a business form ordering a bank to pay cash from a bank account. (p. 58)

Checking account a bank account from which payments can be ordered by a depositor. (p. 119)

Closing entries journal entries used to prepare temporary accounts for a new fiscal period. (p. 206)

Code of conduct a statement that guides the ethical behavior of a company and its employees. (p. 118)

Commercial invoice a statement prepared by the seller of merchandise addressed to the buyer, showing a detailed listing and description of merchandise sold, including prices and terms. (p. 704)

Component percentage the percentage relationship between one financial statement item and the total that includes that item. (p. 184)

Contra account an account that reduces a related account on a financial statement. (p. 245)

Contract of sale a document that details all the terms agreed to by seller and buyer for a sales transaction. (p. 703)

Controlling account an account in a general ledger that summarizes all accounts in a subsidiary ledger. (p. 298)

Corporation an organization with the legal rights of a person and which may be owned by many persons. (p. 234)

Correcting entry a journal entry made to correct an error in the ledger. (p. 108)

Cost of goods sold *see* cost of merchandise sold

Cost of merchandise the price a business pays for goods it purchases to sell. (p. 236)

Cost of merchandise sold the total original price of all merchandise sold during a fiscal period. (p. 450)

Credit an amount recorded on the right side of a T account. (p. 29)

Credit card sale a sale in which a credit card is used for the total amount of the sale at the time of the transaction. (p. 276)

Credit memorandum a form prepared by the vendor showing the amount deducted for returns and allowances. (p. 285)

Creditor a person or organization to whom a liability is owed. (p. 589)

Current assets cash and other assets expected to be exchanged for cash or consumed within a year. (p. 423)

Current liabilities liabilities due within a short time, usually within a year. (p. 467)

Current ratio a ratio that shows the numeric relationship of current assets to current liabilities. (p. 652)

Customer a person or business to whom merchandise or services are sold. (p. 270)

Date of a note the day a note is signed. (p. 589)

Debit an amount recorded on the left side of a T account. (p. 29)

Debit card a bank card that automatically deducts the amount of the purchase from the checking account of the cardholder. (p. 132)

Debit memorandum a form prepared by the customer showing the price deduction taken by the customer for returns and allowances. (p. 256)

Declaring a dividend action by a board of directors to distribute corporate earnings to stockholders. (p. 406)

Declining-balance method of depreciation multiplying the book value by a constant depreciation rate at the end of each fiscal period. (p. 551)

Depreciation expense the portion of a plant asset's cost that is transferred to an expense account in each fiscal period during a plant asset's useful life. (p. 423)

Dishonored check a check that a bank refuses to pay. (p. 129)

Dishonored note a note that is not paid when due. (p. 600)

Distribution of net income statement a partnership financial statement showing net income or loss distribution to partners. (p. 680)

Dividends earnings distributed to stockholders. (p. 405)

Double-entry accounting the recording of debit and credit parts of a transaction. (p. 57)

Doubtful accounts *see* uncollectible accounts

Draft a written, signed, and dated order from one party ordering another party, usually a bank, to pay money to a third party. (p. 704)

Earnings per share the amount of net income after federal income tax belonging to a single share of stock. (p. 459)

Electronic funds transfer a computerized cash payments system that transfers funds without the use of checks, currency, or other paper documents. (p. 131)

Employee earnings record a business form used to record details affecting payments made to an employee. (p. 353)

Endorsement a signature or stamp on the back of a check transferring ownership. (p. 120)

Endorsement in full *see* special endorsement

Entry information for each transaction recorded in a journal. (p. 57)

Equities financial rights to the assets of a business. (p. 8)

Estimated salvage value the amount an owner expects to receive when a plant asset is removed from use. (p. 423)

Ethics the principles of right and wrong that guide an individual in making decisions. (p. 8)

Exhibit *see* supporting schedule

Expense a decrease in owner's equity resulting from the operation of a business. (p. 15)

Exports goods or services shipped out of a seller's home country to a foreign country. (p. 702)

Face amount *see* principal of a note

Federal unemployment tax a federal tax used for state and federal administrative expenses of the unemployment program. (p. 375)

Fifo *see* first-in, first-out inventory costing method

File maintenance the procedure for arranging accounts in a general ledger, assigning account numbers, and keeping records current. (p. 93)

Financial ratio a comparison between two items of financial information. (p. 459)

Financial statements financial reports that summarize the financial conditions and operations of a business. (p. 6)

First-in, first-out inventory costing method using the price of merchandise purchased first to calculate the cost of merchandise sold first. (p. 569)

Fiscal period the length of time for which a business summarizes and reports financial information. (p. 152)

G

Gain on plant assets revenue that results when a plant asset is sold for more than book value. (p. 548)

General amount column a journal amount column that is not headed with an account title. (p. 57)

General ledger a ledger that contains all accounts needed to prepare financial statements. (p. 92)

Gross earnings *see* total earnings

Gross pay *see* total earnings

Gross profit method of estimating inventory estimating inventory by using the previous year's percentage of gross profit on operations. (p. 574)

Gross profit on sales the revenue remaining after cost of merchandise sold has been deducted. (p. 452)

I

Imports goods or services bought from a foreign country and brought into a buyer's home country. (p. 702)

Income statement a financial statement showing the revenue and expenses for a fiscal period. (p. 163)

Intellectual property any product that is protected by patents, trademarks, and copyrights. (p. 616)

Interest an amount paid for the use of money for a period of time. (p. 590)

Interest expense the interest accrued on money borrowed. (p. 594)

Interest income the interest earned on money loaned. (p. 599)

Interest rate of a note the percentage of the principal that is paid for use of the money. (p. 589)

Inventory *see* merchandise inventory

Inventory record a form used during a periodic inventory to record information about each item of merchandise on hand. (p. 566)

Invoice a form describing the goods or services sold, the quantity, and the price. (p. 58)

J

Journal a form for recording transactions in chronological order. (p. 56)

Journalizing recording transactions in a journal. (p. 56)

L

Last-in, first-out inventory costing method using the price of merchandise purchased last to calculate the cost of merchandise sold first. (p. 570)

Ledger a group of accounts. (p. 92)

Letter of credit a letter issued by a bank guaranteeing that a named individual or business will be paid a specified amount, provided stated conditions are met. (p. 703)

Liability an amount owed by a business. (p. 8)

Lifo *see* last-in, first-out inventory costing method

Limited liability partnership (LLP) a partnership that combines the advantages of the partnership and the corporation, while avoiding their disadvantages. (p. 688)

Liquidation of a partnership the process of paying a partnership's liabilities and distributing remaining assets to the partners. (p. 686)

List price the retail price listed in a catalog or on an Internet site. (p. 244)

Long-term liabilities liabilities owed for more than a year. (p. 467)

Lookback period the 12-month period that ends on June 30th of the prior year. (p. 383)

Loss on plant assets the loss that results when a plant asset is sold for less than book value. (p. 549)

M

Maker of a note the person or business who signs a note and thus promises to make payment. (p. 589)

Markup the amount added to the cost of merchandise to establish the selling price. (p. 236)

Maturity date of a note the date a note is due. (p. 589)

Maturity value the amount that is due on the maturity date of a note. (p. 590)

Medicare tax a federal tax paid for hospital insurance. (p. 349)

Memorandum a form on which a brief message is written describing a transaction. (p. 59)

Merchandise goods that a merchandising business purchases to sell. (p. 234)

Merchandise inventory the amount of goods on hand for sale to customers. (p. 415)

Merchandising business a business that purchases and sells goods. (p. 234)

N

Net income the difference between total revenue and total expenses when total revenue is greater. (p. 164)

Net loss the difference between total revenue and total expenses when total expenses are greater. (p. 165)

Net pay the total earnings paid to an employee after payroll taxes and other deductions. (p. 352)

Net sales total sales less sales discount and sales returns and allowances. (p. 449)

Nominal account *see* temporary accounts

Normal balance the side of the account that is increased. (p. 29)

Note *see* notes payable

Notes payable promissory notes signed by a business and given to a creditor. (p. 589)

Notes receivable promissory notes that a business accepts from customers. (p. 598)

Number of a note the number assigned to identify a specific note. (p. 589)

O

Opening an account writing an account title and number on the heading of an account. (p. 94)

Owner's equity the amount remaining after the value of all liabilities is subtracted from the value of all assets. (p. 8)

Owners' equity statement a financial statement that summarizes the changes in owners' equity during a fiscal period. (p. 682)

P

Par value a value assigned to a share of stock and printed on the stock certificate. (p. 461)

Partner each member of a partnership. (p. 674)

Partnership a business in which two or more persons combine their assets and skills. (p. 674)

Partnership agreement a written agreement setting forth the conditions under which a partnership is to operate. (p. 675)

Pay period the period covered by a salary payment. (p. 340)

Payee of a note the person or business to whom the amount of a note is payable. (p. 589)

Payroll the total amount earned by all employees for a pay period. (p. 340)

Payroll register a business form used to record payroll information. (p. 351)

Payroll taxes taxes based on the payroll of a business. (p. 345)

Periodic inventory a merchandise inventory determined by counting, weighing, or measuring items of merchandise on hand. (p. 565)

Permanent accounts accounts used to accumulate information from one fiscal period to the next. (p. 206)

Perpetual inventory a merchandise inventory determined by keeping a continuous record of increases, decreases, and balance on hand. (p. 565)

Personal property all property not classified as real property. (p. 536)

Petty cash an amount of cash kept on hand and used for making small payments. (p. 134)

Petty cash slip a form showing proof of a petty cash payment. (p. 135)

Physical inventory *see* periodic inventory

Plant asset record an accounting form on which a business records information about each plant asset. (p. 542)

Plant assets assets that will be used for a number of years in the operation of a business. (p. 423)

Point-of-sale (POS) terminal a computer used to collect, store, and report all the information of a sales transaction. (p. 276)

Post-closing trial balance a trial balance prepared after the closing entries are posted. (p. 216)

Postdated check a check with a future date on it. (p. 121)

Posting transferring information from a journal entry to a ledger account. (p. 96)

Price-earnings ratio the relationship between the market value per share and earnings per share of a stock. (p. 459)

Principal of a note the original amount of a note; sometimes referred to as face amount of a note. (p. 589)

Promissory note a written and signed promise to pay a sum of money at a specified time. (p. 589)

Proprietorship a business owned by one person. (p. 6)

Proving cash determining that the amount of cash agrees with the accounting records. (p. 76)

Purchase invoice an invoice used as a source document for recording a purchase on account transaction. (p. 238)

Purchase on account a transaction in which the merchandise purchased is to be paid for later. (p. 236)

Purchases allowance credit allowed for part of the purchase price of merchandise that is not returned, resulting in a decrease in the customer's accounts payable. (p. 256)

Purchases discount a cash discount on purchases taken by a customer. (p. 242)

Purchases journal a special journal used to record only purchases of merchandise on account. (p. 237)

Purchases return credit allowed for the purchase price of returned merchandise, resulting in a decrease in the customer's accounts payable. (p. 256)

R

Real accounts *see* permanent accounts

Real estate *see* real property

Real property land and anything attached to the land. (p. 536)

Realization cash received from the sale of assets during liquidation of a partnership. (p. 686)

Receipt

Receipt a business form giving written acknowledgement for cash received. (p. 59)

Residual value *see* estimated salvage value

Restrictive endorsement an endorsement restricting further transfer of a check's ownership. (p. 120)

Retail merchandising business a merchandising business that sells to those who use or consume the goods. (p. 234)

Retained earnings an amount earned by a corporation and not yet distributed to stockholders. (p. 405)

Revenue an increase in owner's equity resulting from the operation of a business. (p. 14)

Reversing entry an entry made at the beginning of one fiscal period to reverse an adjusting entry made in the previous fiscal period. (p. 619)

S

Salary the money paid for employee services. (p. 340)

Sale on account a sale for which cash will be received at a later date. (p. 14)

Sales allowance credit allowed a customer for part of the sales price of merchandise that is not returned, resulting in a decrease in the vendor's accounts receivable. (p. 285)

Sales discount a cash discount on sales. (p. 278)

Sales invoice an invoice used as a source document for recording a sale on account. (p. 58)

Sales journal a special journal used to record only sales of merchandise on account. (p. 272)

Sales return credit allowed a customer for the sales price of returned merchandise, resulting in a decrease in the vendor's accounts receivable. (p. 285)

Sales slip *see* sales invoice

Sales tax a tax on a sale of merchandise or services. (p. 270)

Salvage value *see* estimated salvage value

Schedule of accounts payable a listing of vendor accounts, account balances, and total amount due all vendors. (p. 305)

Schedule of accounts receivable a listing of customer accounts, account balances, and total amount due from all customers. (p. 313)

Scrap value *see* estimated salvage value

Service business a business that performs an activity for a fee. (p. 6)

Share of stock each unit of ownership in a corporation. (p. 234)

Sight draft a draft payable on sight when the holder presents it for payment. (p. 704)

Social security tax a federal tax paid for old-age, survivors, and disability insurance. (p. 349)

Sole proprietorship *see* proprietorship

Source document a business paper from which information is obtained for a journal entry. (p. 57)

Special amount column a journal amount column headed with an account title. (p. 57)

Special endorsement an endorsement indicating a new owner of a check. (p. 120)

Special journal a journal used to record only one kind of transaction. (p. 235)

Stakeholders any persons or groups who will be affected by an action.(p. 181)

State unemployment tax a state tax used to pay benefits to unemployed workers. (p. 375)

Statement of stockholders' equity a financial statement that shows changes in a corporation's ownership for a fiscal period. (p. 461)

Stock ledger a file of stock records for all merchandise on hand. (p. 567)

Stock record a form used to show the kind of merchandise, quantity received, quantity sold, and balance on hand. (p. 567)

Stockholder an owner of one or more shares of a corporation. (p. 234)

Straight-line method of depreciation charging an equal amount of depreciation expense for a plant asset in each year of useful life. (p. 424)

Subsidiary ledger a ledger that is summarized in a single general ledger account. (p. 298)

Supplementary report *see* supporting schedule

Supporting schedule a report prepared to give details about an item on a principal financial statement. (p. 470)

T account an accounting device used to analyze transactions. (p. 29)

Tax base the maximum amount of earnings on which a tax is calculated. (p. 349)

Temporary accounts accounts used to accumulate information until it is transferred to the owner's capital account. (p. 206)

Terminal summary the report that summarizes the cash and credit card sales of a point-of-sale terminal. (p. 276)

Terms of sale an agreement between a buyer and a seller about payment for merchandise. (p. 238)

Time draft a draft that is payable at a fixed or determinable future time after it is accepted. (p. 707)

Time of a note the days, months, or years from the date of signing until a note is to be paid. (p. 589)

Total earnings the total pay due for a pay period before deductions. (p. 343)

Trade acceptance a form signed by a buyer at the time of a sale of merchandise in which the buyer promises to pay the seller a specified sum of money, usually at a stated time in the future. (p. 708)

Trade discount a reduction in the list price granted to customers. (p. 244)

Transaction a business activity that changes assets, liabilities, or owner's equity. (p. 10)

Trial balance a proof of the equality of debits and credits in a general ledger. (p. 154)

Uncollectible accounts accounts receivable that cannot be collected. (p. 419)

Vendor a business from which merchandise is purchased or supplies or other assets are bought. (p. 236)

Weighted-average inventory costing method using the average cost of beginning inventory plus merchandise purchased during a fiscal period to calculate the cost of merchandise sold. (p. 571)

Wholesale merchandising business a business that buys and resells merchandise to retail merchandising businesses. (p. 234)

Withdrawals assets taken out of a business for the owner's personal use. (p. 16)

Withholding allowance a deduction from total earnings for each person legally supported by a taxpayer, including the employee. (p. 346)

Work sheet a columnar accounting form used to summarize the general ledger information needed to prepare financial statements. (p. 153)

Working capital the amount of total current assets less total current liabilities. (p. 652)

Writing off an account canceling the balance of a customer account because the customer does not pay. (p. 519)